VISUAL QUICKPRO GUIDE

AFTER EFFECTS 6.5

FOR WINDOWS AND MACINTOSH

Antony Bolante

Peachpit Press

Visual QuickPro Guide

After Effects 6.5 for Windows and Macintosh

Antony Bolante

Peachpit Press
1249 Eighth Street
Berkeley, CA 94710
510/524-2178
800/283-9444
510/524-2221 (fax)
Find us on the World Wide Web at: http://www.peachpit.com
To report errors, please send a note to errata@peachpit.com
Peachpit Press is a division of Pearson Education

Editor: Rebecca Gulick
Copy Editor: Tiffany Taylor
Proofreader: Whitney Walker
Production Coordinator: Myrna Vladic
Graphics Contributor: Ako Nakamura
Compositors: Jerry Ballew, Kelli Kamel
Indexer: James Minkin
Cover Design: The Visual Group
Cover Production: George Mattingly/GMD

ISBN 0-321-19957-x

9 8 7 6 5 4 3 2 1

Printed and bound in the United States of America

Dedication

To my family.

Thanks To

Everyone involved in creating the earlier editions of this book; I hope this one does you proud.

All the good people at Peachpit Press, especially Rebecca Gulick, Tiffany Taylor, Whitney Walker, Myrna Vladic, Jerry Ballew, and James Minkin.

The clever folks at Adobe Systems.

Ako Nakamura, for her help on the screen-shots and the tips on Japanese language.

The nice folks at Stardust Coffee and Video.

Family and friends who've let me share their beautiful photos and faces (and everyone else to whom I've made some sly reference).

Friends who've supported me in countless other ways during a challenging transition—including new friends.

My family, as always.

Table of Contents

Chapter 1 After Effects: The Big Picture 1

The QuickPro Series . . . 2
Adobe's Dynamic Media Suite . . . 2
Minimum Requirements . . . 2
Suggested System Features . . . 3
Professional System Additions . . . 4
New Features . . . 5
After Effects Standard and Professional . . . 7
Mac vs. Windows . . . 8
Work Flow Overview . . . 9
Interface Overview . . . 10
Using Tabbed Windows and Palettes . . . 16

Chapter 2 Importing Footage into a Project 19

Creating and Saving Projects . . . 20
Opening and Closing Projects . . . 22
Choosing a Time Display . . . 24
Choosing the Bit-Depth Mode . . . 27
Importing Files . . . 29
Setting Still-Image Durations . . . 34
Importing Still Image Sequences . . . 37
Importing Files with Alpha Channels . . . 40
Photoshop and Illustrator Files . . . 45
Importing a Layered File as a Single Footage Item . . . 46
Importing a Layered File as a Composition . . . 48
Importing Premiere Pro and After Effects Projects . . . 50
Motion Footage . . . 56
Setting the Frame Rate . . . 57
Looping Footage . . . 59
Removing Film 3:2 Pulldown and 24Pa Pulldown . . 60
Pixel Aspect Ratios . . . 65
Setting the EPS Options . . . 68
Reapplying the Interpret Footage Command . . . 69
Using Interpretation Rules . . . 70

Chapter 3 **Managing Footage** 71
Displaying Information in the Project Window . . 72
Finding Items in a Project 75
Sorting Footage in the Project Window 77
Using Labels 80
Organizing Footage in Folders 82
Renaming and Removing Items 84
Proxies and Placeholders 87
Proxies in the Project Window 90
Viewing Footage 92
Opening Footage in the Original Application . . . 94
The Footage Window 96
Cueing Motion Footage 97
Magnification and Safe Zones 98
Video-Safe Zones and Grids 100
Rulers and Guides 104
Snapshots 108
Channels 110
Viewing Transparency 111
Correcting for Pixel Aspect Ratios 112

Chapter 4 **Compositions** 115
Creating Compositions 116
Choosing Composition Settings 118
Selecting Composition Presets 119
Advanced Composition Settings 129
Background Color 133
The Composition and Timeline Windows 134
Setting the Time 137
Adding Footage to a Composition 140
Adding Layers Using Insert and Overlay 142
Creating Solid Layers 145
Creating Adjustment Layers 149
Nesting Compositions 151

Chapter 5 **Layer Basics** 153
Selecting Layers 154
Stacking Order 156
Naming Layers 158
Layer Numbers and Labels 160
Switching Video and Audio On and Off 161
Locking a Layer 164
Basic Layer Switches 165
Shy Layers 167
Continuously Rasterizing a Layer 168
Quality Setting Switches 170

Chapter 6 Layer Editing 171

Viewing Layers in the Timeline and Layer Windows . . . 172
The Time Graph . . . 174
Navigating the Time Graph . . . 176
The Layer Window . . . 178
Trimming Layers . . . 181
Moving Layers in Time . . . 184
The In/Out Panel . . . 185
Performing a Slip Edit . . . 188
Sequencing and Overlapping Layers . . . 189
Removing a Range of Frames . . . 192
Duplicating Layers . . . 194
Splitting Layers . . . 195
Changing a Layer's Speed . . . 197
Using Markers . . . 199

Chapter 7 Properties and Keyframes 205

Layer Property Types . . . 206
Viewing Properties . . . 207
Setting Global vs. Animated Property Values . . . 208
Viewing Spatial Controls in the Comp Window . . . 209
Transform Properties . . . 211
Specifying Property Values . . . 220
Alternative Controls for Setting Properties . . . 223
Nudging Layer Properties . . . 224
Audio Properties . . . 225
Viewing an Audio Waveform . . . 226
Using the Audio Palette . . . 228
Animating Layer Properties with Keyframes . . . 231
Moving Keyframes . . . 238
Copying Values and Keyframes . . . 239
Using Animation Presets . . . 242

Chapter 8 Playback, Previews, and RAM 245

Rendering and RAM . . . 246
Previewing to a Video Device . . . 249
Setting the Region of Interest . . . 251
Using the Time Controls . . . 252
Using the Live Update Option . . . 254
Specifying a Fast Preview Option . . . 255
Using Adaptive Resolution . . . 257
Using OpenGL . . . 258
Suppressing Window Updates . . . 261
Scrubbing Audio . . . 262

Comparing Preview Options 263
Setting the Work Area 264
Previewing Audio Only 266
Previewing Wireframes 271
Rendering RAM Previews 273
Saving RAM Previews 279
Managing RAM 281

Chapter 9 Mask Essentials 285

Viewing Masks in the Layer and Comp windows 286
Viewing Masks in the Layer Outline 287
Hiding and Showing Mask Paths 288
Targeting Masks 289
Comparing Mask Creation Methods 290
Comparing Closed and Open Paths 291
Understanding Mask Anatomy 292
Creating Simple Mask Shapes 294
Building a Standard Mask with the Pen 295
How Mighty Is Your Pen? 298
Creating a RotoBezier Mask 302
Converting Masks 304
Changing the Shape of a Mask 305
Selecting Masks and Points 306
Moving and Deleting Control Points 309
Adding and Deleting Control Points with the Pen Tool 311
Converting Control Points in a Standard Mask 313
Adjusting RotoBezier Mask Tension 316
Opening and Closing Paths 318
Scaling and Rotating Masks 319
Using Masks from Photoshop and Illustrator . . . 321
Setting Custom Mask Colors 322
Locking and Hiding Masks 324
Moving Masks Relative to the Layer Image . . . 326
Adjusting Other Mask Properties 329
Inverting a Mask 332
Mask Modes 333

Chapter 10 Effects Fundamentals 335

Effect Categories 336
Using the Effects & Presets Palette 337
Applying Effects 342
Viewing Effect Property Controls 344
Using the Effect Controls Window 345

Removing and Resetting Effects 347
Disabling Effects Temporarily 349
Adjusting Effects in the
Effect Controls Window 351
Setting Color in the Effect Controls Window . . . 352
Setting Values in the Effect Controls Window . . . 354
Setting the Angle in the
Effect Controls Window 355
Setting an Effect Point 356
Saving and Applying Effect Presets 358
Copying and Pasting Effects 362
Applying Multiple Effects 363
Applying Effects to an Adjustment Layer 364
Understanding Compound Effects 366
Using Compound Effects 367
Animating Effects 370

Chapter 11 Effects in Action 373

3D Channel Effects 374
Adjust Effects 374
Using the Levels Effect 375
Audio Effects 379
Using the Stereo Mixer Effect 380
Blur and Sharpen Effects 384
Using the Compound Blur Effect 385
Channel Effects 387
Using the Blend Effect 388
Distort Effects 390
Using the Displacement Map Effect 391
Image Control Effects 394
Using the Grow Bounds Effect 395
Keying Effects 397
Matte Tools Effects 397
Noise & Grain Effects 398
Perspective Effects 399
Using Bevel Alpha 400
Render Effects 401
Using the Audio Waveform Effect 402
Simulation Effects 405
Stylize Effects 405
Using Texturize 406
Text Effects 408
Time Effects 408
Using the Echo Effect 409
Transition Effects 411
Using the Gradient Wipe Effect 412

Video Effects 414
Using Broadcast Colors 415

Chapter 12 Creating and Animating Text 417
Creating Type 418
Editing Type 426
Using the Character and Paragraph Palettes . . . 430
Formatting Characters 433
Setting Options for Chinese,
Japanese, and Korean Text 448
Blending Characters 450
Making Text Follow a Path 451
Formatting Paragraph Text 453
Animating Text 458
Animating Source Text 459
Using Text Animation Presets 461
Understanding Animator Groups 463
Animating Type with Animator Groups 465
Creating Animator Groups 468
Choosing Animator Group Properties 470
Choosing a Range Selector 472
Specifying a Range 473
Understanding Range Selector Options 475
Using Multiple Selectors and Selector Modes . . . 477
Specifying Wiggly Selector Options 478

Chapter 13 Painting on a Layer 479
Using the Paint and Brush Tips palettes 480
Specifying Paint Stroke Options 481
Painting with the Brush Tool 485
Erasing Strokes 488
Using Brush Tips 491
Customizing Brush Tips 496
Using Brush Dynamics 498
Adjusting Strokes 499
Animating Strokes 502
Cloning 507
Using the Clone Stamp Tool 511
Overlaying the Clone Source 513
Saving Clone Stamp Settings 514

Chapter 14 More Layer Techniques 515
Using Frame Blending 516
Using Motion Blur 518
Understanding Time Remapping 520

Work Flow Overview

Any project, it can be argued, begins at the same point: the end. Setting your output goal determines the choices you make to achieve it. Whether your animation is destined for film, videotape, DVD, CD-ROM, or the Web, familiarize yourself with the specifications of your output goal, such as frame size, frame rate, and file format. Only when you've determined the output goal can you make intelligent choices about source material and setting up a project.

That established, the typical workflow might resemble the outline that follows. However, every aspect of After Effects is tightly integrated and interdependent. Between import and output, the steps of the project won't necessarily proceed in a simple linear fashion:

Import—After Effects coordinates a wide range of source materials, including digital video, audio, bitmapped still images, path-based graphics and text, and even 3D and film transfer formats. However, it doesn't furnish you with a way to directly acquire these assets—you'll need a video and audio capture device, a digital still camera, a scanner, or other software packages to do that. This is not to say that After Effects doesn't generate its own graphic and sound elements; it does.

Arranging layers in time—Although it's not designed for long-form nonlinear editing, After Effects ably arranges shorter sequences for compositing and effects work. You can instantly access and rearrange layers, and use the same file repeatedly without copying or altering it.

Arranging layers in space—After Effects' ability to layer, combine, and composite images earned it its reputation as the Photoshop of dynamic media. Moreover, these capabilities extend into the 3D realm.

Adding effects—Or does "the Photoshop of dynamic media" refer to After Effects' ability to add visual effects to motion footage? After Effects offers many effects to combine, enhance, transform, and distort layers of both video and audio. An entire industry has grown up around developing and accelerating effects for After Effects.

Animating attributes—One of After Effects' greatest strengths is its ability to change the attributes of layers over time. You can give layers motion, make layers appear and fade, or intensify and diminish an effect.

Previewing—You can play back your animation at any time to evaluate its appearance and timing and then change it accordingly. After Effects maximizes your computer's playback capabilities by utilizing RAM to render frames, dynamically adjusting resolution, allowing you to specify a region of interest, and taking advantage of OpenGL.

Adding complexity—Some projects require more complex structures than others. You may need to group layers as a single element or circumvent the program's default rendering hierarchy to achieve a certain effect. Or, you may need to restructure your project to make it more efficient and allow it to render faster. With features like parenting and expressions, you have the power to create complex animations with relatively little effort.

Output—When you're satisfied with your composition, you can output the result in a number of file formats, depending on the presentation media (which, of course, you planned for from the start).

Interface Overview

Before you begin exploring the program's terrain, let's take in a panoramic view.

Primary windows

Most of your work will be concentrated in three windows: the Project window, the Composition window, and the Timeline window (**Figure 1.3**).

The **Project window** lists references to audio and visual files, or footage, that you plan to use in your animation. It also lists compositions, which describe how you want to use the footage, including its arrangement in time, motion, and effects.

The **Composition window** represents the layers of a composition spatially. The visible area of the Composition window corresponds to the frame of the output animation and displays the composition's current frame. You can open more than one Composition window; doing so is particularly useful when you want to compare the image in a composition to a corresponding frame in a nested composition, or view a 3D composition from different angles. It's common to call compositions *comps* and a Composition window a *Comp window*, for short.

The **Timeline window** represents the composition as a graph in which time is measured horizontally. When a footage item is added to the composition, it becomes a layer. The horizontal arrangement of layers indicates their place in the time of the composition; their vertical arrangement indicates their stacking order. You access and manipulate layer properties from the Timeline window.

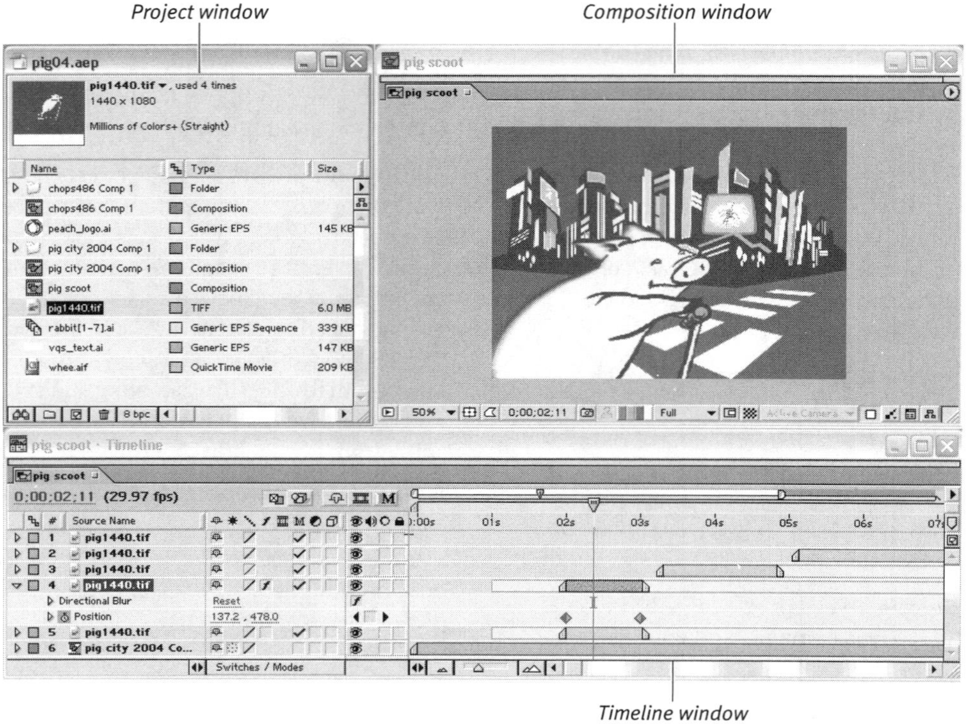

Project window

Composition window

Timeline window

Figure 1.3 Your work takes place primarily in the Project, Composition, and Timeline windows.

✔ Tips

- You can control the brightness and color of UI elements by choosing Edit > Preferences > User Interface Colors (Windows) or After Effects > Preferences > User Interface Colors (Mac).
- In previous versions of After Effects, the Timeline window was known as the Time Layout window. *Timeline* is more consistent with other Adobe programs.
- Looking for scroll bars in the Composition window? They've been eliminated. Instead, use the Hand tool to view different areas of a zoomed-in composition's image. With the Comp window selected, press the Spacebar to toggle to the Hand tool.

Secondary windows

If the Timeline and Composition windows are the parent windows of a composition, the Layer and Effect Controls windows are their children. Similarly, the Footage window is ancillary to the Project window (**Figure 1.4**).

The **Footage window** allows you to view the source footage listed in the Project window before it becomes an editable layer in a composition.

The **Layer window** allows you to view each layer in a composition individually, outside the context of the Composition or Timeline window. For example, it can be the most convenient place to manipulate a layer's mask shape. When you paint on a layer, you do so in the Layer window.

The **Effect Controls window** provides separate, roomier, and often more convenient effect controls than those available in the Timeline window.

✔ Tips

- The Window menu contains options for you to quickly arrange the workspace. For example, selecting Cascade automatically arranges the windows into a cascading pattern, whereas Tile resizes and distributes the windows evenly over the screen, like tiles.
- You can save the current arrangement of windows by choosing Window > Workspace > Save Workspace.
- When you're compositing in 3D, it's common to have more than one view of the same composition open at once. Using multiple comp views is discussed in detail in Chapter 4, "Compositions," and Chapter 16, "3D Layers."

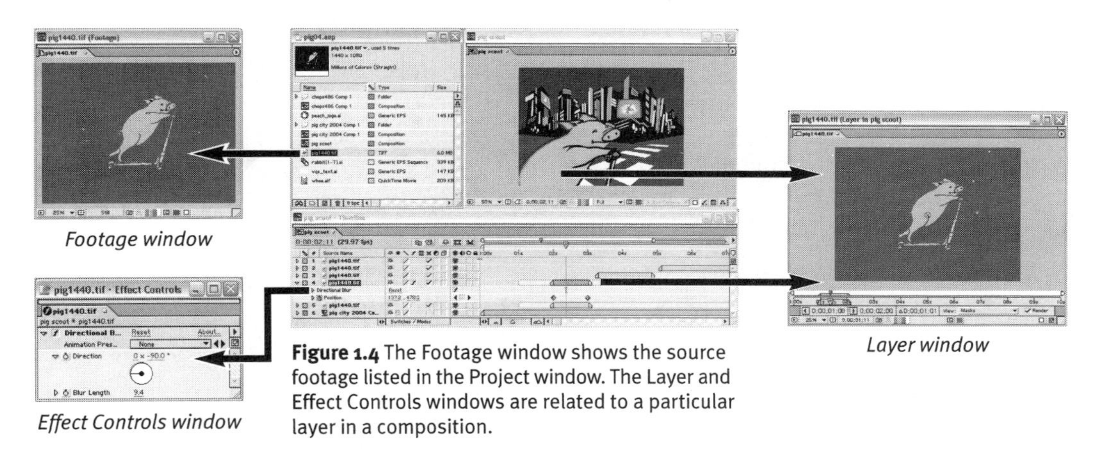

Figure 1.4 The Footage window shows the source footage listed in the Project window. The Layer and Effect Controls windows are related to a particular layer in a composition.

Other windows

At the bottom of the Window menu are two windows that are each in a class of their own.

The **Render Queue window** allows you to control and monitor the rendering process (**Figure 1.5**).

The **Render View window** lets you see your project's elements in the form of a flowchart, which can make it easier to understand the structure and hierarchies of your project—particularly a complex one (**Figure 1.6**).

Palettes

An assortment of palettes provides additional controls. Palettes float, or appear in front of other windows, so you won't lose track of them.

The **Tools palette**, as its name implies, contains an assortment of tools that change the function of the mouse pointer. Each tool allows you to perform specialized tasks (**Figure 1.7**).

As in other programs, a small triangle in the corner of a tool button indicates that related tools are hidden. Press and hold the button to reveal and select a hidden tool.

The **Info palette** displays all kinds of information about the current task, from the cursor's current position in a composition to the In and Out points of a layer (**Figure 1.8**).

The **Time Controls palette** contains controls for playing back and previewing the composition. When you set a composition's current time, the time is also set in all windows related to that composition (**Figure 1.9**).

The **Audio palette** allows you to monitor and control audio levels (**Figure 1.10**).

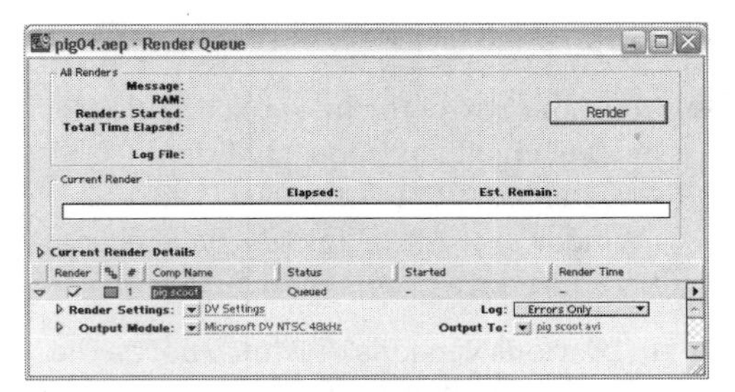

Figure 1.5 The Render Queue window lets you control and monitor the rendering process.

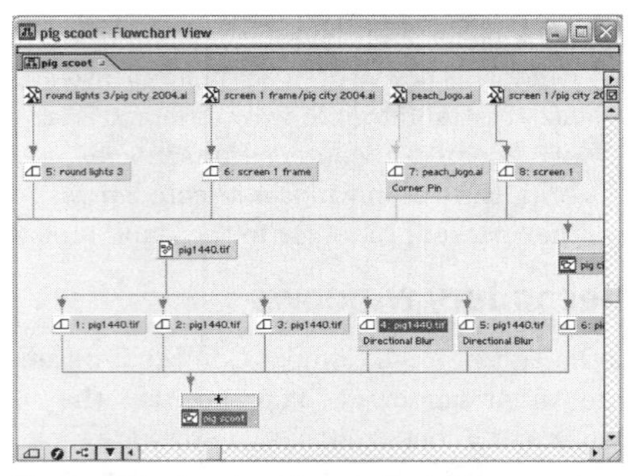

Figure 1.6 The Flowchart View window helps you analyze the hierarchical structure of a complex project.

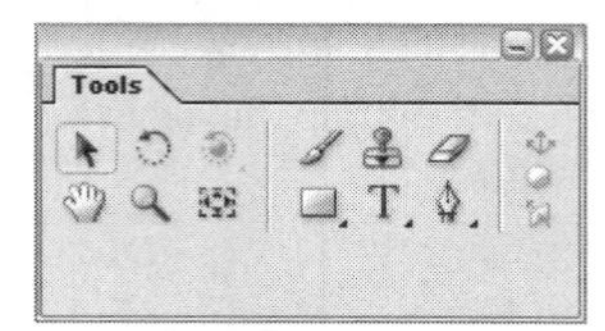

Figure 1.7 The Tools palette contains tools for working with layers and windows.

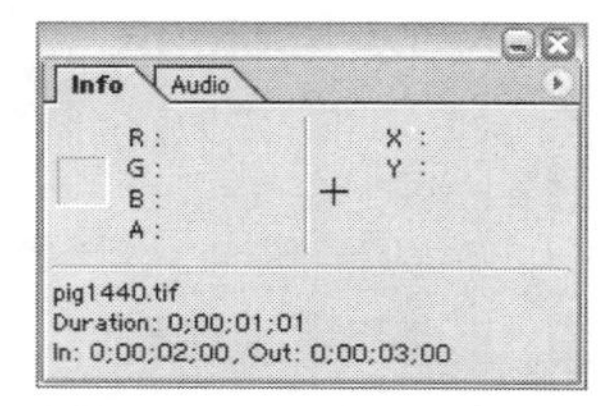

Figure 1.8 The Info palette displays information such as the current position of the cursor in a composition and the In and Out points of a layer.

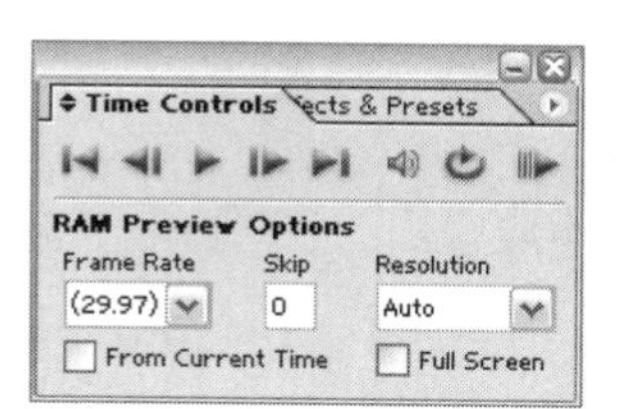

Figure 1.9 The Time Controls palette contains controls to play back and preview the composition.

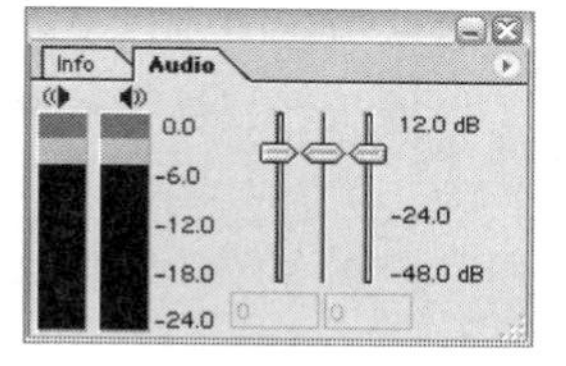

Figure 1.10 The Audio palette allows you to monitor and control audio levels.

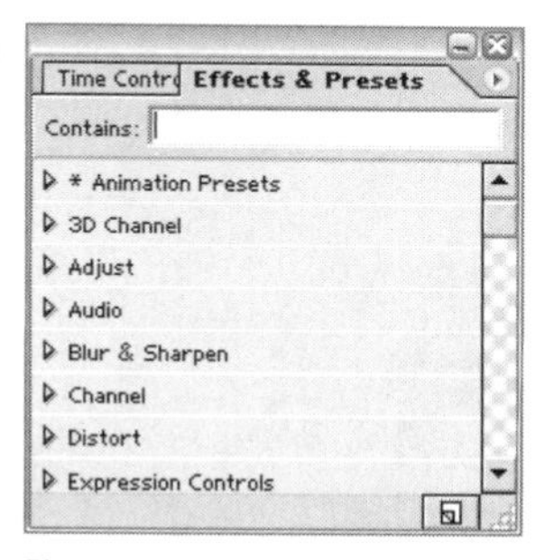

Figure 1.11 The Effects & Presets palette makes it easy to find effects and save custom presets for animation.

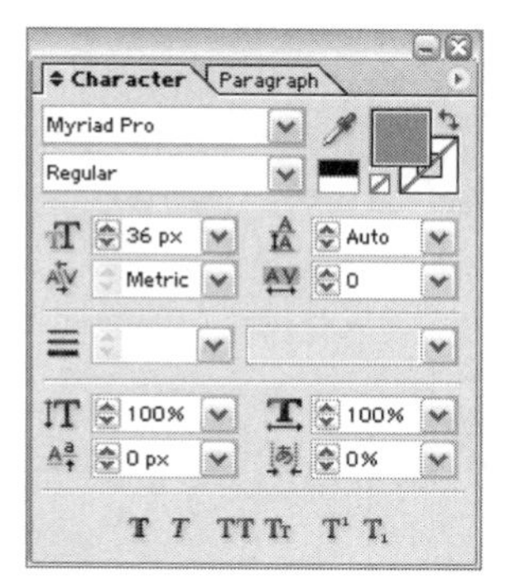

Figure 1.12 The full-featured Character palette lets you control the characteristics of text you create in After Effects.

The **Effects & Presets palette** provides a convenient way to view and apply effects. You can reorganize the list, create and view favorites, and find a particular effect in the list or on your hard drive (**Figure 1.11**).

The **Character palette** provides convenient text controls to support After Effects' direct text creation feature. It includes all the controls you'd expect—font, size, fill and stroke, kerning, leading, and the like. It also includes a few you might not expect—baseline shift, vertical and horizontal scaling, superscript and subscript, and a feature to aid in laying out characters in vertically oriented languages like Chinese, Japanese, and Korean (**Figure 1.12**).

The **Paragraph palette** lets you control blocks of text as you would in a word-processing or layout program. You can specify justification, alignment, indents, and the spacing before and after paragraphs (**Figure 1.13**).

continues on next page

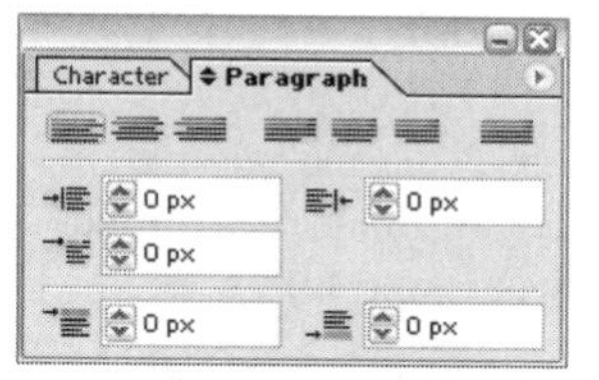

Figure 1.13 You can control blocks of text using the Paragraph palette, which lets you adjust things like alignment, justification, and indentation.

The **Paint palette** gives you full control over the characteristics of paint, such as color, opacity, and flow. You can also specify which channel you want to paint onto, and whether to apply a mode to each stroke (**Figure 1.14**).

The **Brush Tips palette** not only provides a menu of preset brushes, but also lets you create brushes and specify their characteristics, such as diameter, angle, roundness, hardness, and so on (**Figure 1.15**).

Secondary palettes

These palettes are listed separately only because you'll probably use them less frequently than the others. You can open the previously listed nine palettes by using keyboard shortcuts; but to open these palettes, you'll have to choose them from the Windows pull-down menu.

The **Motion Sketch palette** allows you to set motion keyframes by dragging the mouse (or by using a pen stroke on a graphics tablet) (**Figure 1.16**).

The **Smart Mask Interpolation palette** (Professional only) helps you animate mask shapes more precisely (**Figure 1.17**).

The **Smoother palette** helps you smooth changes in keyframe values automatically, to create more gradual changes in an animation (**Figure 1.18**).

The **Wiggler palette** (Professional only) generates random deviations in keyframed values automatically (**Figure 1.19**).

The **Align and Distribute palette** works like Illustrator's palette and helps you arrange layers (**Figure 1.20**).

The **Tracker Controls palette** (Professional only), an advanced feature, helps you generate keyframes by detecting and following a moving object in a shot. You can use this

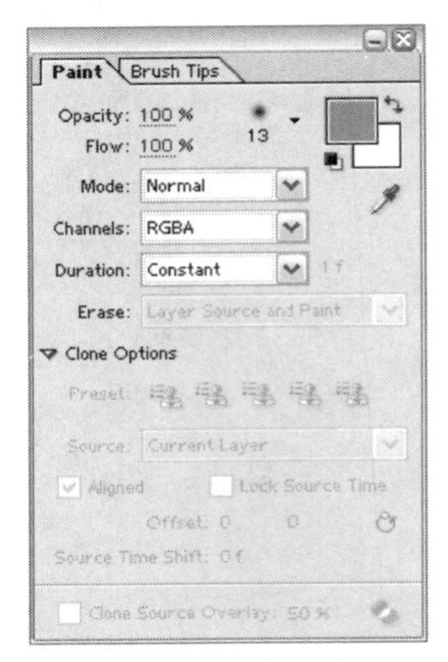

Figure 1.14 The Paint palette gives you control over After Effects' painting and cloning features...

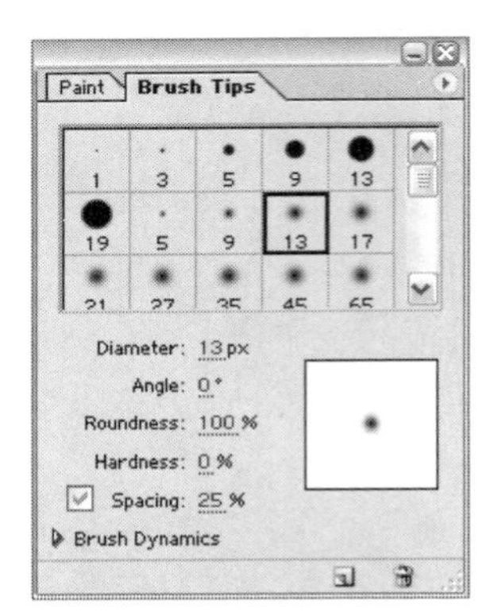

Figure 1.15 ...while its companion, the Brush Tips palette, lets you select the characteristics of the brush you employ.

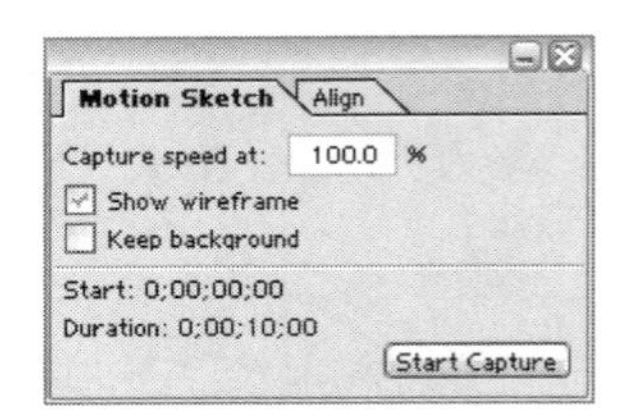

Figure 1.16 The Motion Sketch palette allows you to set motion keyframes by dragging your mouse.

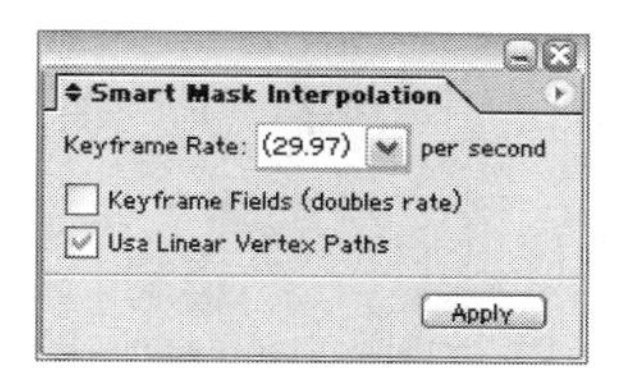

Figure 1.17 The Smart Mask Interpolation palette (Professional only) provides a greater degree of control when you're animating mask shapes.

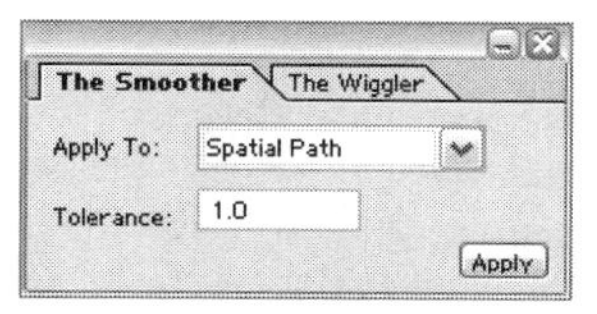

Figure 1.18 The Smoother palette helps you smooth changes in keyframe values.

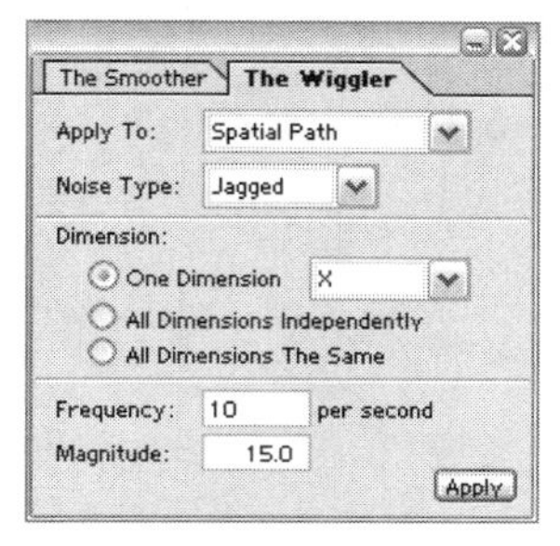

Figure 1.19 You can generate random deviations in keyframed values automatically using the Wiggler palette (Professional only).

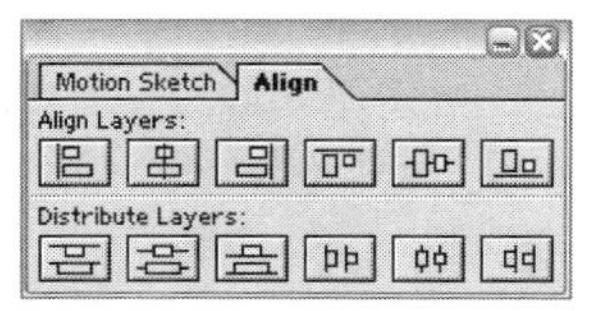

Figure 1.20 The Align palette helps you arrange layers.

information to make an effect track an object or to stabilize a scene shot with shaky camera work (**Figure 1.21**).

✔ Tips

- The Tools palette's Auto Open Palettes option automatically opens the palettes related to the selected tool. This way, selecting the Brush tool also opens the Paint and Brush Tips palettes.
- Prior to After Effects 6, tools were contained in a floating window, not a palette. The new Tools palette has all the advantages of other palettes: You can dock them and group them as tabbed palettes in a single window.
- If you've moved palettes, you can quickly return them to their default positions by selecting Window > Reset Palette Locations.

Figure 1.21 Using the Tracker Controls palette (Professional only), you can generate keyframes to follow a moving object automatically or, conversely, to stabilize a shaky image.

Using Tabbed Windows and Palettes

Like other Adobe programs, After Effects uses tabbed windows. By default, similar windows can be grouped in a single window. When you do this, tabs let you select the window you want to use without closing the other windows.

By default, the Comp, Footage, and Layer windows open in a single grouped window as tabbed items. An icon on the left side of the tab indicates the type of window in the group of windows (**Figure 1.22**). The Timeline window can contain tabs for several compositions (**Figure 1.23**). Similarly, the Effect Controls window can contain tabs for several layers in different compositions (**Figure 1.24**). To view the window you want, click the tab. You can also *tear off* a tab, or drag it away from the group to view it in a separate window.

Because only one Project window can be open at a time, you can't group the Project window with another window.

To set a default for tabbed or untabbed windows:

1. Choose Edit > Preferences > General (Windows) or After Effects > Preferences > General (Mac) (**Figure 1.25**).

   The General panel of the Preferences dialog box appears.

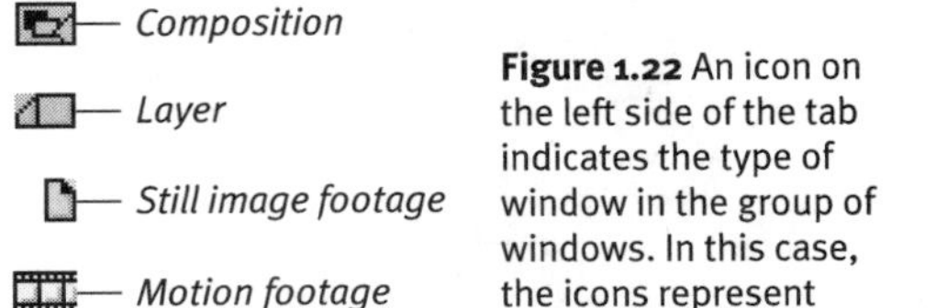

Figure 1.22 An icon on the left side of the tab indicates the type of window in the group of windows. In this case, the icons represent Composition, Layer, and Footage windows.

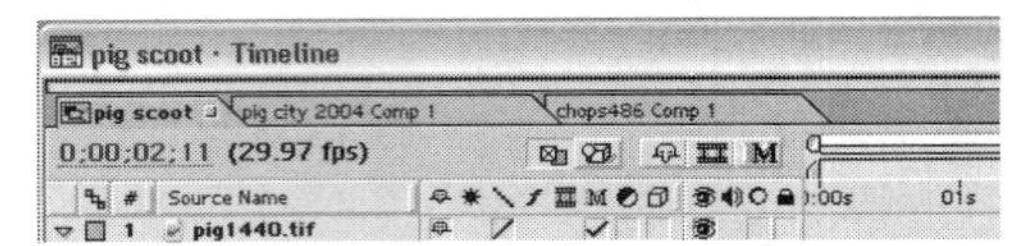

Figure 1.23 Using tabs, the Timeline window can contain Timeline windows for several compositions.

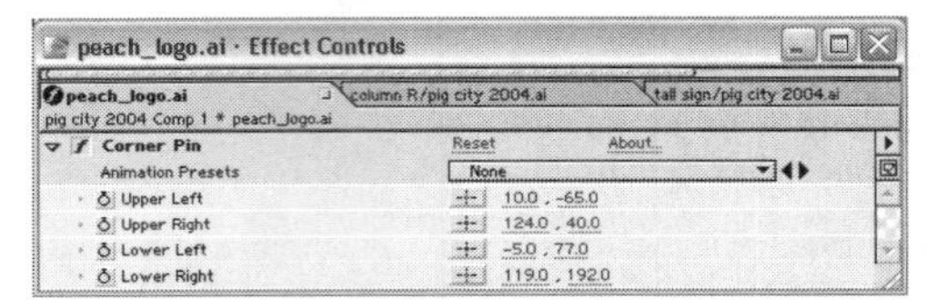

Figure 1.24 The Effect Controls window can contain the Effect Controls windows for several layers.

Figure 1.25 Choose Edit > Preferences > General (Windows) or After Effects > Preferences > General (Mac).

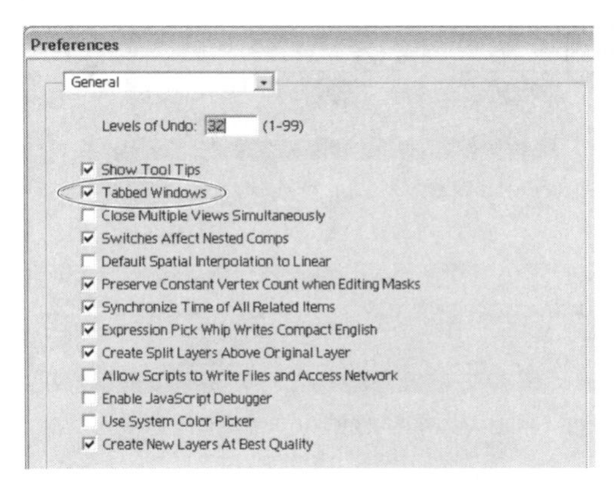

Figure 1.26 To use grouped windows by default, select Tabbed Windows.

Figure 1.27 Dragging a tab to another window group...

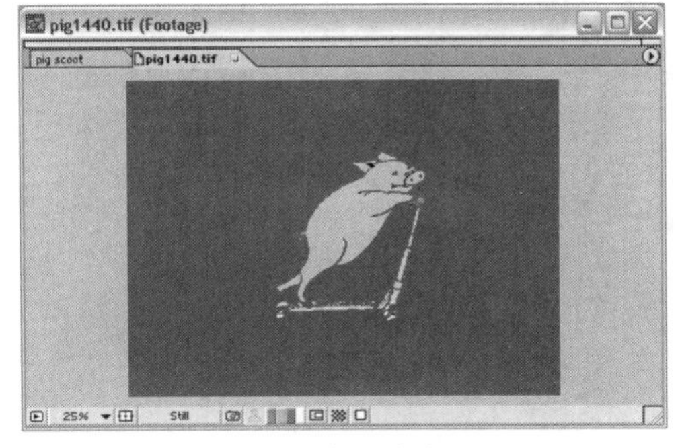

Figure 1.28 ...moves it to that window.

2. In the Preferences dialog box, *do one of the following:*
   - ▲ To use grouped windows by default, select Tabbed Windows (**Figure 1.26**).
   - ▲ To use ungrouped, untabbed windows by default, deselect Tabbed Windows.
3. Click OK to close the dialog box.

   From now on, your window preference will be used. Windows that are already open don't reflect a change.

✔ Tips

- Palettes can always be grouped in tabbed palettes, regardless of how you set the Tabbed Windows preference.
- You can dock palettes—that is, attach a palette or palette group to another—by dragging one palette's tab to the bottom of another palette and releasing the mouse button when a horizontal gray line appears between the two.
- Double-clicking a palette's tab cycles through different views: a default view, a view showing the hidden options, and a view showing the palette's tab only.

To organize grouped and tabbed windows:

In a tabbed window, *do any of the following:*

- ◆ To make a window appear in front of the group, click its tab.
- ◆ To move a window to another group window, drag its tab to that group (**Figures 1.27** and **1.28**).

continues on next page

- To separate a window from its group, drag the tab out of the group.
- To rearrange tabs, drag a tab to a new location relative to the other tabs (**Figures 1.29** and **1.30**).
- To view tabs that extend beyond the edge of the window group, drag the slider below the tabs (**Figure 1.31**).
- To close a tabbed window, click the window to bring it to the front, and then click the close box (**Figure 1.32**).
- To close the window group and all its included tabbed windows, click the close box for the window (not the individual tab).

There are a few timesaving keyboard shortcuts that are particularly handy to keep in mind (**Table 1.1**).

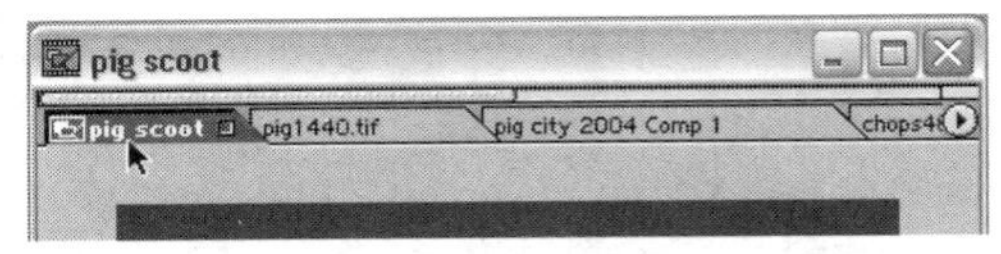

Figure 1.29 Drag a tab left or right...

Figure 1.30 ...to change its arrangement.

Figure 1.31 To view tabs that extend beyond the window, drag the slider below the tabs.

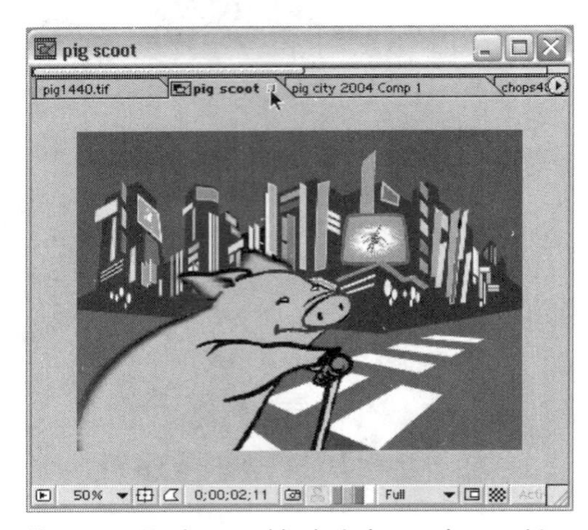

Figure 1.32 To close a tabbed window, make sure it's active and click its close box.

Table 1.1

Shortcuts	
To do this	Press this shortcut
Display/hide palettes	Tab
Close active tab/window	Cmd-W (Mac) or Ctrl-W (Windows)
Close active window (all tabs)	Shift-Cmd-W (Mac) or Shift-Ctrl-W (Windows)
Close all windows except Project	Cmd-Opt-W (Mac) or Ctrl-Alt-W (Windows)

Importing Footage into a Project

2

Think of an After Effects project as a musical score. Just as a score refers to instruments and indicates how they should be played, your project lists the files you want to use and how you want to use them. When you've finished creating your project, you can output an animation as a movie file or an image sequence. The important thing to remember is that the project contains only *references* to the source files, not the files themselves. The project contains neither the sources nor the end result, any more than a sheet of music contains a tuba or a recording of the concert. For this reason, a project file takes up little drive space.

Source files, on the other hand, consume considerably more storage. You need both the project and the source files to preview or output your animation, just as a composer needs the orchestra to hear a work-in-progress or, ultimately, to perform it in concert. Nonlinear editing systems (such as Adobe Premiere Pro and Apple Final Cut Pro) also work by referring to source files. Thus, if you're familiar with those programs, you have a head start on the concept of using file references in a project.

In this chapter, you'll learn how to create a project and import various types of footage. The chapter covers the specifics of importing still images, motion footage, and audio. It even shows you how to import other projects (and their file references) into your current project.

Don't be intimidated by the length or depth of the chapter. Importing different types of footage into your project is a simple and straightforward process. As you go through the chapter, take just what you need. As you begin to incorporate a wider range of formats in your work, revisit sections to learn the idiosyncrasies of those particular formats. To revisit the musical metaphor, if a project is like a score, start by composing for an ensemble, and then build up to an orchestra.

Creating and Saving Projects

Creating a project is especially simple in After Effects, which doesn't prompt you to select project settings. Although there are a few project settings, you can change their default values at any time (as explained later in this chapter). As you'll see in the next chapter, most settings you specify are associated with compositions within the project.

Saving projects is also easier than ever. To more easily track changes to your work, you can instruct After Effects to save each successive version of a project using an incremental naming scheme.

To create a new project:

Do one of the following:

- Launch After Effects.
- If you've just closed another After Effects project, choose File > New > New Project (**Figure 2.1**).

The Project window appears (**Figure 2.2**).

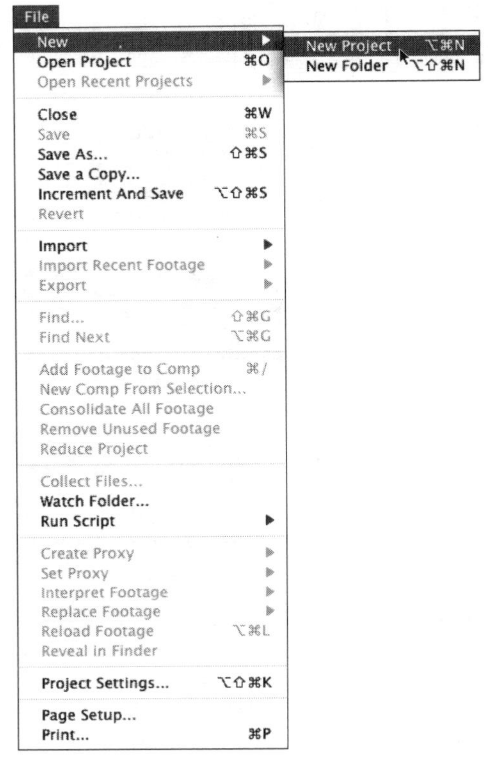

Figure 2.1 Choose File > New > New Project.

Figure 2.2 A new, untitled Project window appears.

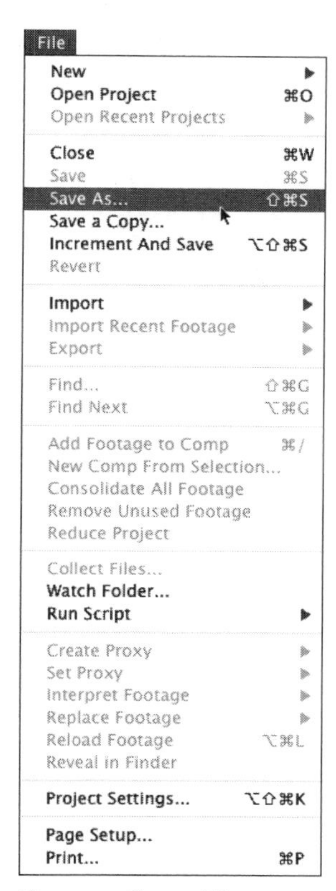

Figure 2.3 Choose File > Save As.

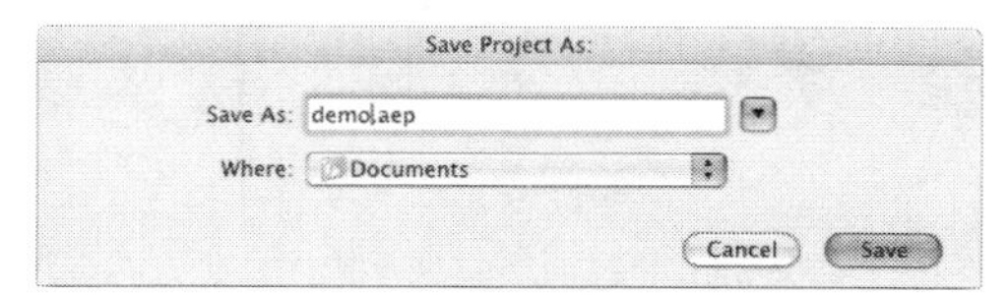

Figure 2.4 Specify a name and location for your project.

To save a project for the first time or using a new name or location:

1. Choose File > Save As (**Figure 2.3**).

   A Save Project As dialog box appears.

2. In the Save Project As dialog box, type a name for the project and choose a location (**Figure 2.4**).

3. Click Save.

To save a project using the same name and location:

◆ After the project has been saved the first time, Choose File > Save, or press Command-S (Macintosh) or Ctrl-S (Windows).

To save using incremental project names automatically:

◆ After the project has been saved, choose File > Increment and Save, or press Command-Opt-Shift-S (Mac) or Ctrl-Alt-Shift-S (Windows).

  After Effects saves a copy of the project, appending a number to the filename that increases incrementally with each successive Increment and Save command.

✔ Tips

- As with any computer program, save often and keep backups of your project files. Doing so is especially important with After Effects because it doesn't offer an Autosave feature.

- As you might expect, the File menu also includes Save, Copy, and Revert to Last Saved commands.

Opening and Closing Projects

In After Effects, you may have only one project open at a time. Closing the Project window or opening another project closes the current project.

As you learned in this chapter's introduction, an After Effects project contains footage items that refer to files on your system. When you reopen a project, After Effects must locate the source files to which each footage item refers. If After Effects can't locate a source file, the project considers it missing (**Figure 2.5**). (In Premiere Pro and other nonlinear editing programs, missing footage is called *offline*.) The names of missing footage items appear in italics (**Figure 2.6**), and a placeholder consisting of colored bars temporarily replaces the source footage. You can continue working with the project, or you can locate the source footage. For more about missing source footage, see Chapter 3, "Managing Footage."

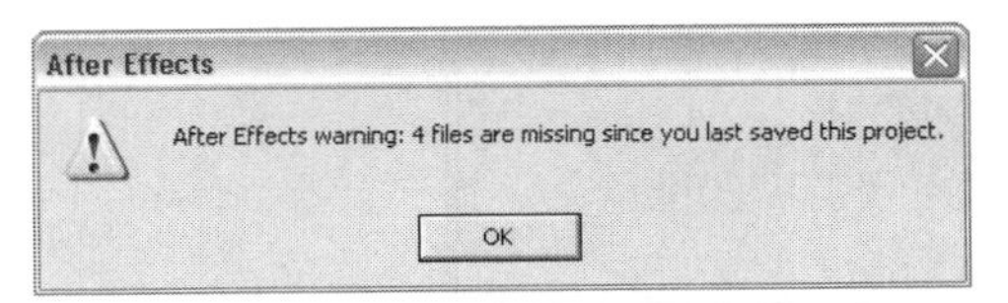

Figure 2.5 After Effects alerts you if it can't locate source files.

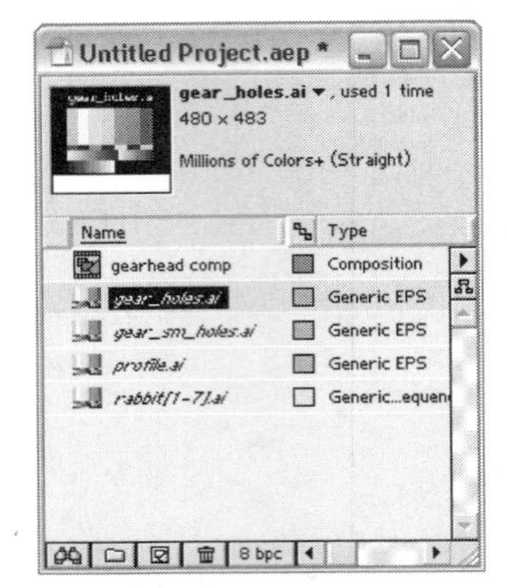

Figure 2.6 The names of missing footage items appear in italics, and the source footage is temporarily replaced by a color bar placeholder.

To close a project:

Do one of the following:

- Select the Project window and choose File > Close.
- Press Command-W (Mac) or Ctrl-W (Windows).
- Click the close box on the Project window.

To open a project:

1. In After Effects, choose File > Open Project, or press Command-O (Mac) or Ctrl-O (Windows) (**Figure 2.7**).

   An Open dialog box appears.

   If you already have a project open, After Effects prompts you to save the existing project (**Figure 2.8**). Click Save to save the open project before closing it.

2. In the Open dialog box, locate an After Effects project and click Open (**Figure 2.9**).

✔ Tips

- When you're opening a project, press Shift to prevent all but the Project window from opening.
- With After Effects running, press Shift-Command-Opt-P (Mac) or Shift-Ctrl-Alt-P (Windows) to open the most recently opened project (think *p* for *previous project*).

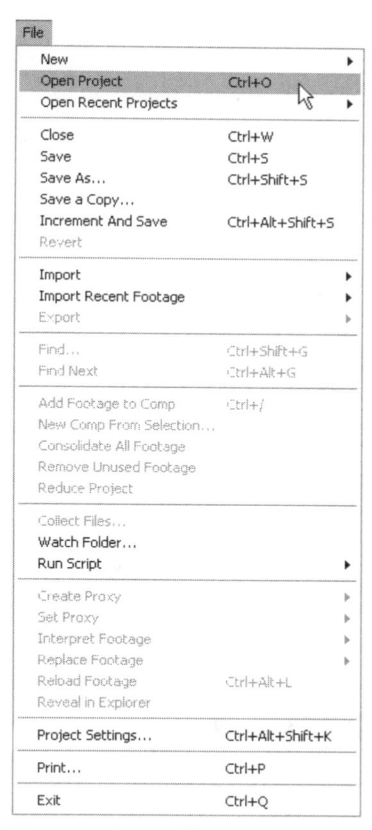

Figure 2.7 Choose File > Open Project to open an existing project while After Effects is running.

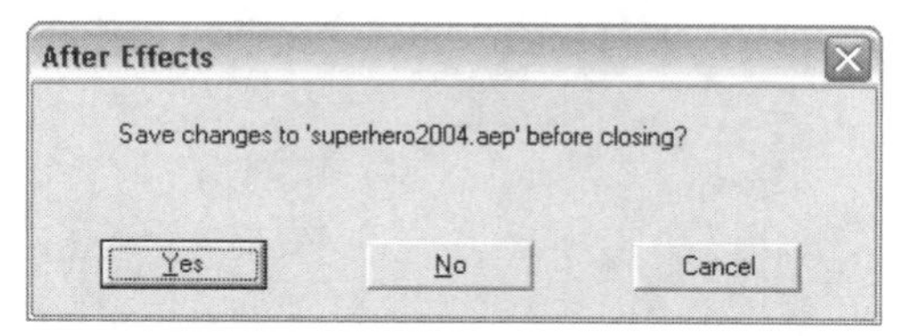

Figure 2.8 Because you may have only one project open at a time, After Effects prompts you to save an open project before opening another one.

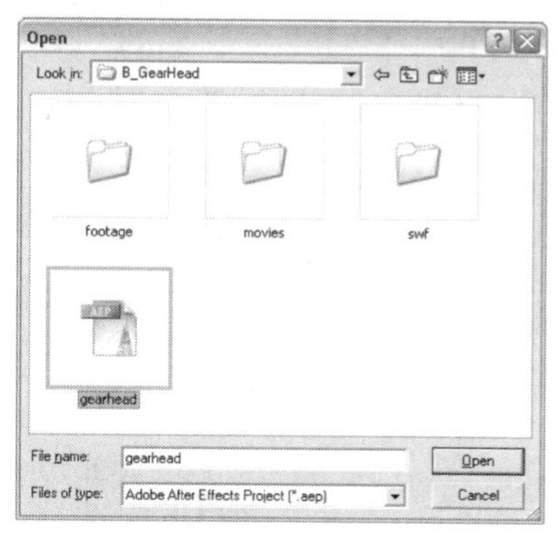

Figure 2.9 In the Open dialog box, locate an After Effects project and click Open.

Choosing a Time Display

When you begin a project, you may want to pay a quick visit to the Project Settings dialog box, which includes options for setting the style in which the time will be displayed in your compositions.

The display style won't affect the frame rate of your compositions, only the way time is counted and displayed. This means you can change the display style whenever you want without adversely affecting the project (or its compositions).

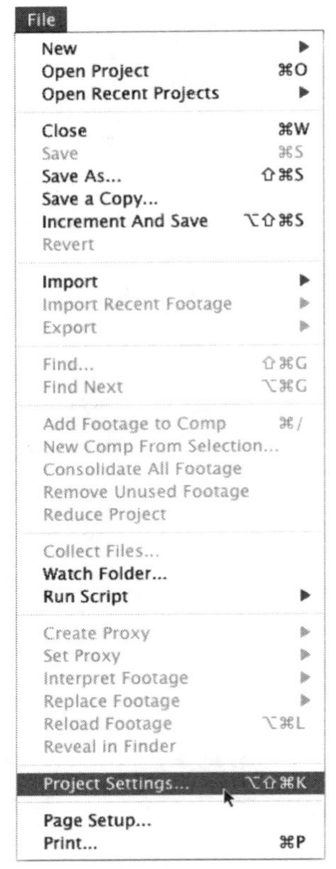

Figure 2.10 Choose File > Project Settings.

To set the project display style:

1. Choose File > Project Settings (**Figure 2.10**).

   The Project Settings dialog box appears (**Figure 2.11**).

2. In the Project Settings dialog box, set the display style by selecting the radio button next to the appropriate option:

   Timecode Base—After Effects uses timecode to number frames (displayed as hours, minutes, seconds, and frames).

   Frames—Frames are numbered sequentially, without regard to time.

   Feet + Frames—Frame numbers are based on 16mm or 35mm motion picture film (both of which are displayed at 24 frames per second, or *fps*).

3. If necessary, choose additional options for the Timecode Base or Feet + Frames display options (explained in the following sections), and then click OK to close the dialog box.

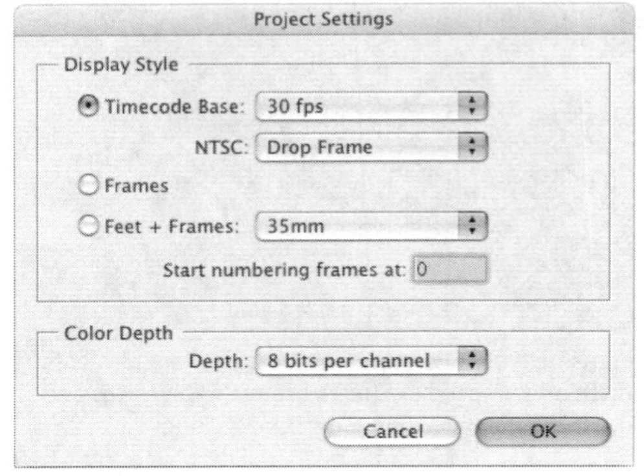

Figure 2.11 In the Project Settings dialog box, set the display style.

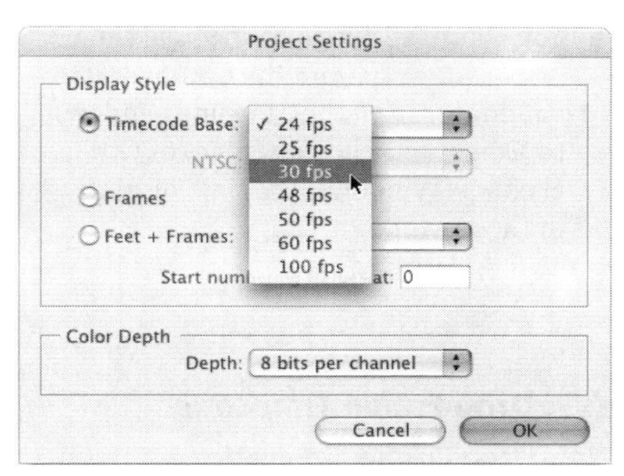

Figure 2.12 Choose a timebase from the pull-down menu.

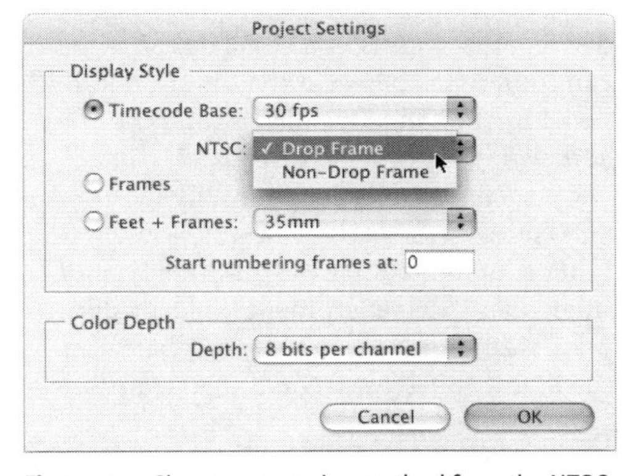

Figure 2.13 Choose a counting method from the NTSC pull-down menu.

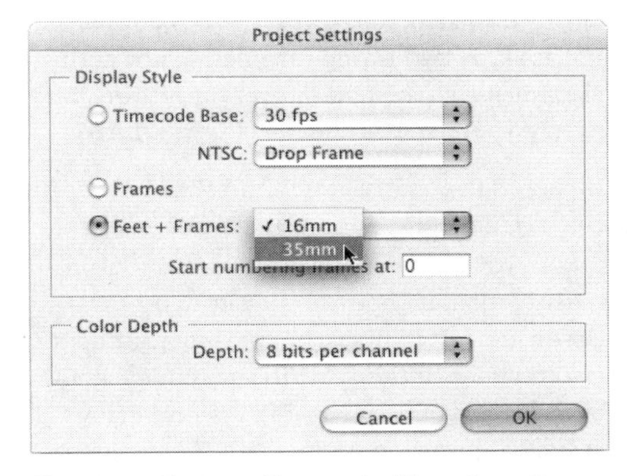

Figure 2.14 Choose a film standard from the pull-down menu.

To select Timecode Base display options:

1. If you chose Timecode Base as the time display in the Project Settings dialog box, choose a timebase from the pull-down menu (**Figure 2.12**).

   For standard video projects, choose 30 fps.

2. *Choose one of the following* counting methods from the NTSC pull-down menu (**Figure 2.13**):

   Drop Frame—Uses NTSC drop-frame timecode to count frames. Most master tapes and DV camera–recorded video use drop-frame timecode.

   Non-Drop Frame—Employs NTSC non-drop frame timecode to count frames.

   For a detailed explanation of drop-frame and non-drop frame timecode, see the sidebar "Counting Time," later in this chapter.

3. Click OK to close the Project Settings dialog box.

To select Feet + Frames time display options:

1. If you chose Feet + Frames as the display style in the Project Settings dialog box, *choose one* of two film standards from the pull-down menu (**Figure 2.14**):

   16mm—Runs at 24 frames per second and 40 frames per foot

   35mm—Runs at 24 frames per second and 16 frames per foot

2. If you want, in the Start Numbering Frames At field, enter a frame number at which you want the project to begin.

3. Click OK to close the Project Settings dialog box.

continues on next page

✔ Tips

- The time display you select in the Project Settings dialog box will also be reflected in the settings for compositions you create within the project. See "Choosing Composition Settings," in Chapter 4.
- You'll also be able to change the time display directly from the Composition window or from the Timeline window by Command-clicking (Mac) or Ctrl-clicking (Windows) the time display in those windows.

Counting Time: Non-Drop Frame vs. Drop Frame Timecode

Timecode refers to a method of counting video frames that was developed by the Society of Motion Picture and Television Engineers, (SMPTE). Timecode is counted in hours, minutes, seconds, and frames. It extends to just under 24 hours: 23:59:59:29.

Because the true frame rate of NTSC video is always 29.97 fps, measuring time accurately in hours, minutes, seconds, and frames can get complicated. (In fact, 29.97 is only a commonly used approximation—but that's another story.) To simplify matters, SMPTE timecode rounds off the decimal and counts at an even 30 fps. However, it can use one of two counting schemes: non-drop frame or drop-frame timecode.

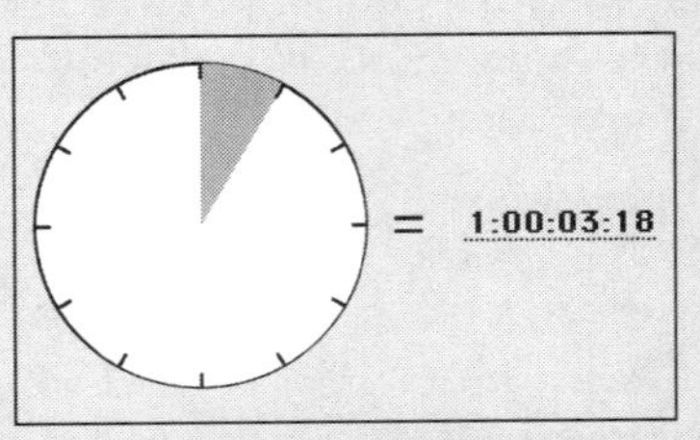

Figure 2.15 For every hour of real time that elapses, non-drop frame timecode counts an additional 3 seconds and 18 frames.

0;00;59;29

0;01;00;02

Figure 2.16 To accurately reflect elapsed time, DF timecode skips two frame numbers at the end of every minute except every tenth minute.

Non-Drop Frame Timecode

Even though the true frame rate of NTSC video is 29.97 fps, non-drop frame (NDF) timecode counts 30 fps. Over time, this discrepancy results in a small but significant difference between the duration indicated by the timecode display and the actual elapsed time (**Figure 2.15**). Nevertheless, NDF is easy to understand and calculate, so camera originals and other source tapes usually use this type of timecode. Video equipment typically displays NDF timecode with colons between the hours, minutes, seconds, and frames.

Drop-Frame Timecode

To compensate for the discrepancy caused by the 30-fps counting scheme, SMPTE developed drop-frame (DF) timecode. Drop-frame timecode also counts 30 fps, but it skips two frame numbers—not actual frames—at the end of every minute except every tenth minute (**Figure 2.16**).

If you do the math, you'll find that DF timecode displays durations that closely match the actual elapsed time. For this reason, master tapes usually employ DF timecode. (Of course, the missing numbers also make it difficult to do timecode calculations manually.) After Effects and other video equipment display drop-frame timecode semicolons between hours, minutes, seconds, and frames.

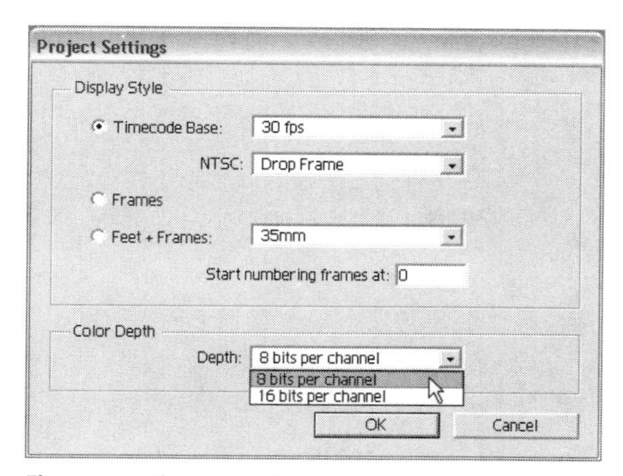

Figure 2.17 The Project Settings dialog box contains controls to set the color bit depth.

Choosing the Bit-Depth Mode

If you're using After Effects Professional, you can also set the bit-depth mode from the Project Settings dialog box. However, you'll probably find it more convenient to toggle the bit-depth mode using the button in the Project window.

The fact that After Effects Pro provides 16 bit-per-channel (bpc) support means that your images not only can have higher color fidelity from the start, but also will retain that quality even after repeated color processing (for example, from transfer modes and effects).

To set the project color bit depth:

1. Choose File > Project Settings.

   The Project Settings dialog box appears (**Figure 2.17**).

2. In the Color Depth section of the Project Settings dialog box, select the color depth of your project from the Depth pull-down menu:

   8 bits per channel—Imports and processes images that use 8 bits to describe the R, G, B, and alpha channels, or 32-bit RGB

   16 bits per channel—Imports and processes images that use 16 bits to describe the R, G, B, and alpha channels, or 64-bit RGB

3. Click OK to close the Project Settings dialog box.

To toggle the project bit depth from the Project window:

- In the Project window, Option-click (Mac) or Alt-click (Windows) the Bit Depth button to toggle between 8 bpc and 16 bpc (**Figures 2.18** and **2.19**).

✔ Tips

- You can also press Shift-Command-Opt-K (Mac) or Shift-Ctrl-Alt-K (Windows) to open the Project Settings dialog box.
- Processing color in 16 bpc is twice as demanding as processing it in 8 bpc—that is, doing so requires twice the RAM and processing time. To save time, you may want to work in 8 bpc initially, and then switch to 16 bpc when you're ready for critical color processing.

Figure 2.18 The Project window includes a button you can click to toggle between 8 bits per channel...

Figure 2.19 ...and 16 bpc processing—provided you have After Effects Pro, which supports 16 bpc.

Importing Files

After Effects allows you to import a wide variety of still images, motion footage, and audio, as well as projects from After Effects and Premiere Pro. The procedures for importing footage are essentially variations on a theme, so you should get the hang of them quickly.

Although you may be tempted to speed through some sections in this part of the chapter, make sure you understand how the methods differ for each file type. Depending on the file, you may need to invoke the Interpret Footage command, which contains special handling options such as how to set the duration of stills or the frame rate of motion footage. The Interpret Footage command also allows you to properly handle other aspects of footage, such as the alpha channel, field order, and pixel aspect ratio. If you're already familiar with these concepts, go directly to the numbered tasks; if not, check out the sidebars in this chapter for some technical grounding.

You'll find that you can often use several methods to import footage: menu bar, keyboard shortcuts, or context menu. You can even drag and drop from the desktop. Once you know your options, you can choose the method that best fits your needs or preferences.

The maximum resolution for import and export is 30,000 × 30,000 pixels. However, the PICT format is still limited to 4,000 × 4,000 pixels; BMP to 16,000 × 30,000; and PXR to 30,000 × 16,000 pixels.

As you've already learned, After Effects Professional allows you to import images with 16 bpc—an indispensable capability if you're doing high-end work.

Of course, the maximum image size and bit depth are limited by the amount of RAM available to After Effects (see the sidebar "Wham, Bam—Thank You, RAM").

After Effects supports an extensive and growing list of file formats, depending on your platform. Photoshop and other third-party plug-ins can also expand the possibilities.

Wham, Bam—Thank You, RAM

Here's the formula for calculating how much RAM an image requires:

Width in pixels × height in pixels × 4 bytes = RAM needed to display image

So, the largest file allowed would require 3.35 GB RAM (30,000 × 30,000 × 4 bytes)—ouch!

A tall image used as an end credit roll for video output provides a less extreme example, as you can see:

720 × 30,000 × 4 bytes = 82.4 MB RAM

To import a file or files:

1. *Do one of the following:*
   - ▲ Choose File > Import > File to import one item.
   - ▲ Choose File > Import > Multiple Files to import several items (**Figure 2.20**).

   The Import File or Import Multiple Files dialog box appears (**Figure 2.21**).

2. To expand or reduce the list of files, choose an option for Enable (**Figure 2.22**):

   All Files—Enables all files in the list, including files of an unrecognized file type.

   All Acceptable Files—Enables only file types supported by After Effects.

   All Footage Files—Enables only files that can be imported as footage items, and excludes otherwise acceptable file types (such as After Effects or Premiere Pro project files).

   AAF, AE Project, and so on—Enables only files of the same file type you select.

   Enabled files can be selected for import, whereas other files are unavailable and appear grayed-out.

Figure 2.20 Choose File > Import > File or > Multiple Files.

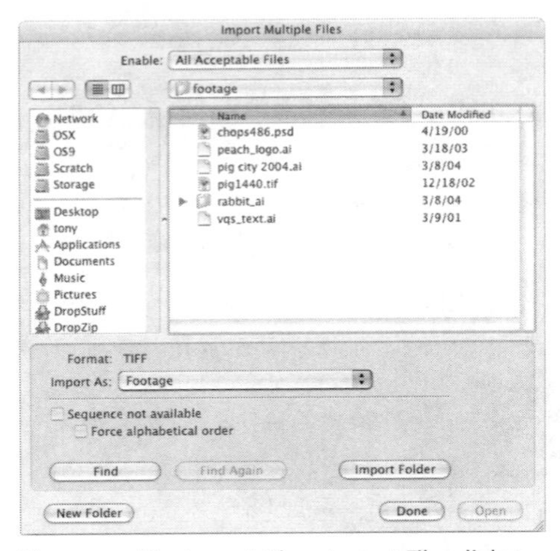

Figure 2.21 The Import File or Import Files dialog box appears.

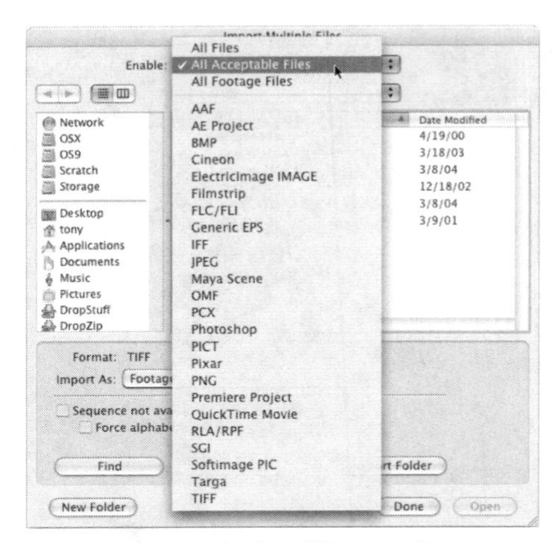

Figure 2.22 To sift the list of files, specify an option in the Enable pull-down menu.

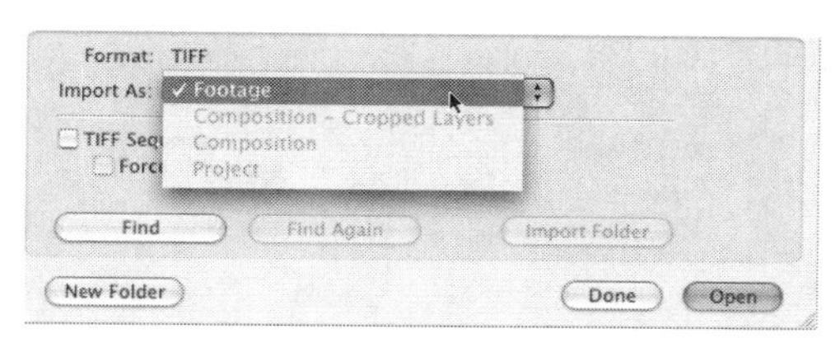

Figure 2.23 Choose Footage from the Import As pull-down menu.

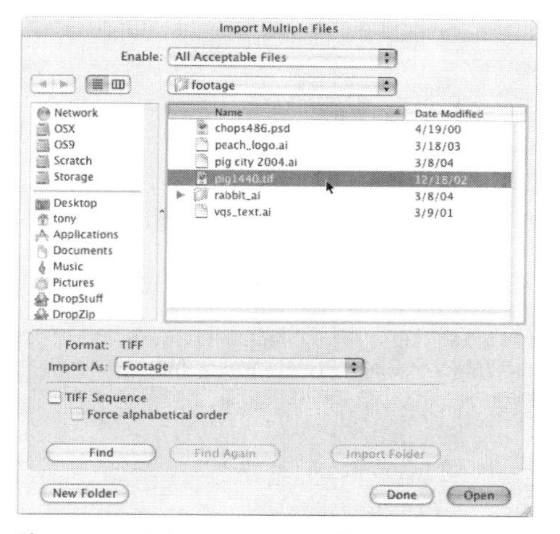

Figure 2.24 Select one or more files.

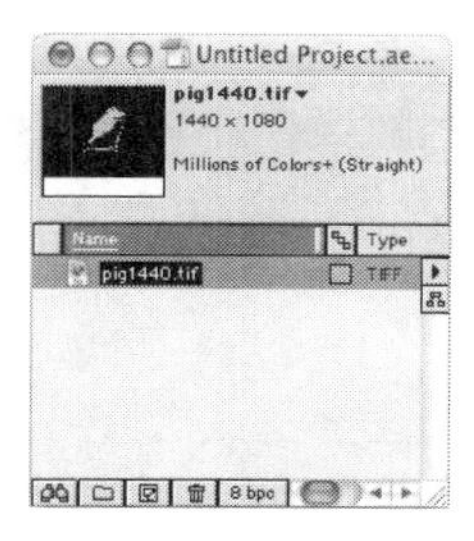

Figure 2.25 Imported items appear in the Project window as footage files.

3. In the Import File or Import Multiple Files dialog box, choose Footage from the Import As pull-down menu (**Figure 2.23**).

   To import files as compositions or to import projects, see the corresponding sections later in this chapter.

4. In the Import File or Import Multiple Files dialog box, select the file you want to import, and then click Open.

   To select a range of files in the same folder, click the file at the beginning of the range to select it, Shift-click the end of the range, and then click Open.

   To select multiple noncontiguous files in the same folder, Command-click (Mac) or Control-click (Windows) multiple files, and then click Open (**Figure 2.24**).

5. If prompted, specify other options for each file you import (such as its alpha channel type, or how to import a layered file). The options for particular file types are discussed later in this chapter.

6. If you chose to import multiple files in step 1, repeat the subsequent steps until you've imported all the files you want to use; and then click Done to close the Import Multiple Files dialog box.

   The file(s) appear as item(s) in the Project window (**Figure 2.25**).

✔ Tip

- You can also double-click in an empty area of the Project window to open an Import File dialog box.

To set the default for importing by dragging:

1. Choose Edit > Preferences > Import (Windows) or After Effects > Preferences > Import (Mac) (**Figure 2.26**).

   The Import panel of the Preferences dialog box appears.

2. *Choose one of the following* options from the Default Drag Import As pull-down menu (**Figure 2.27**):

   Footage—Files dragged from the desktop appear as footage items in the Project window.

   Composition—Files dragged from the desktop appear as compositions in the Project window.

3. Click OK to close the Preferences dialog box.

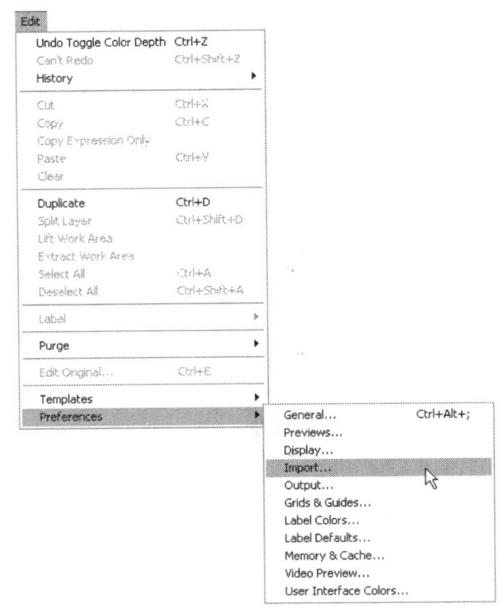

Figure 2.26 Choose After Effects > Preferences > Import (Mac) or Edit > Preferences > Import (Windows).

To import multiple files by dragging:

1. From the desktop (Mac) or Explorer (Windows), select the files you want to import.

2. Drag the selected files to the After Effects Project window (**Figure 2.28**).

3. If prompted, specify options for each file imported. These options are explained for each file type later in this chapter.

   The files appear in the Project window as either footage items or compositions, depending on the Import preference you set (see the previous task, "To set the default for importing by dragging"). To import a sequence of still images as a single item, see "To import a still-image sequence," later in this chapter.

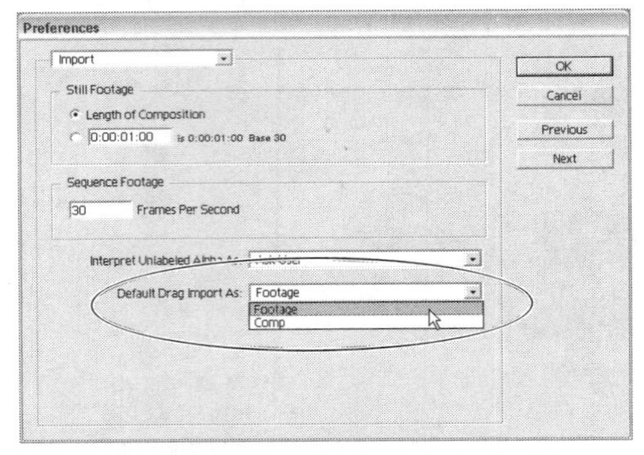

Figure 2.27 Choose an option from the Default Drag Import As pull-down menu.

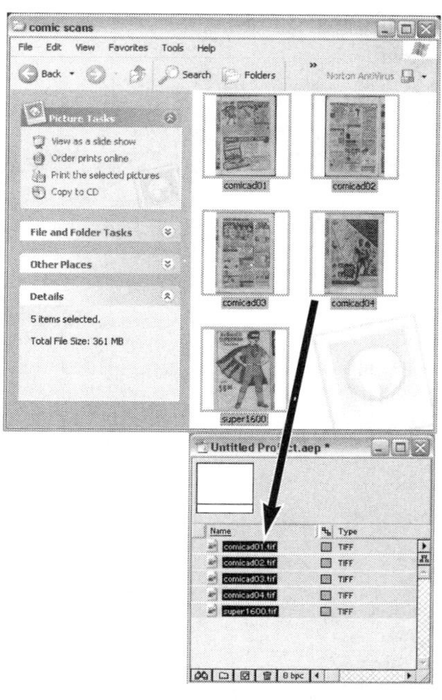

Figure 2.28 You can import files by dragging and dropping them directly into the Project window.

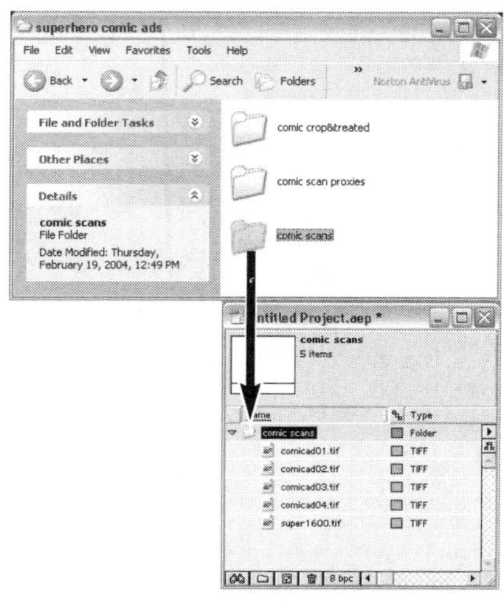

Figure 2.29 You can also import files by holding down Option (Mac) or Alt (Windows) as you drag an entire folder directly to the Project window.

To import a folder by dragging:

1. Hold down the Option key (Mac) or Alt key (Windows) to drag a folder from the desktop directly to the After Effects Project window (**Figure 2.29**).
2. If prompted, specify options for each file imported. These options are explained for each file type later in this chapter.

   The folder appears in the Project window. Click the triangle next to the folder icon to view the contents of the folder. See Chapter 3, "Managing Footage," for more about viewing and managing footage items in the Project window.

✔ Tip

- If you don't hold down Option (Mac) or Alt (Windows) as you drag a folder from the desktop to the Project window, the files in the folder will be imported as a sequence rather than as individual files. See "To import a still-image file sequence by dragging," later in this chapter.

Setting Still-Image Durations

When you import a still image as a footage file and make it a layer in a composition, you can set its duration to any length. By default, the duration of a still image matches the duration of the composition. However, you can also manually set the default duration for still images. Doing so comes in handy when you plan to use several stills for the same duration, such as a series of title cards for a credit sequence. Of course, you can always change the duration (or trim) of the layer later. See Chapter 4, "Compositions," for more about adding footage to a composition as layers; see Chapter 6, "Layer Editing," for more about editing layers.

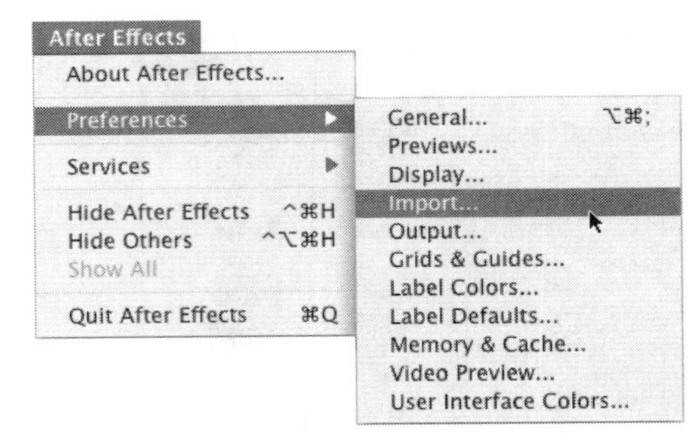

Figure 2.30 Choose After Effects > Preferences > Import (Mac) or Edit > Preferences > Import (Windows).

To change the default duration of still images:

1. Choose After Effects > Preferences > Import (Mac) or Edit > Preferences > Import (Windows) (**Figure 2.30**).

   The Import panel of the Preferences dialog box appears (**Figure 2.31**).

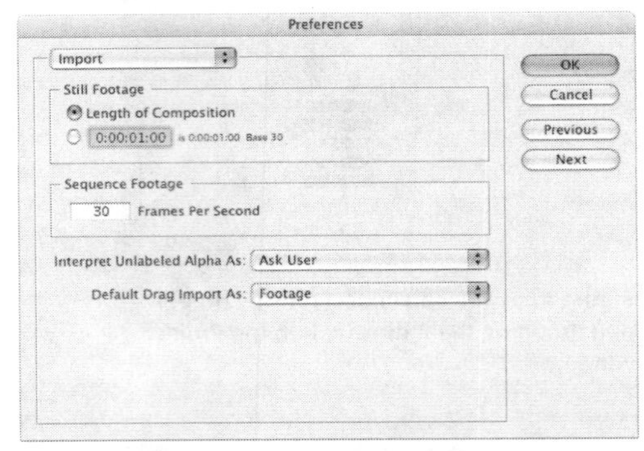

Figure 2.31 The Import panel of the Preferences dialog box appears.

2. In the Still Footage section of the Preferences dialog box, *do one of the following* (**Figure 2.32**):

   ▲ Select Length of Composition to make the still images' duration the same as that of the composition you're adding them to.

   ▲ Select the radio button next to the Time field and enter a default duration for imported still images.

3. Click OK to set the changes and exit the Preferences dialog box.

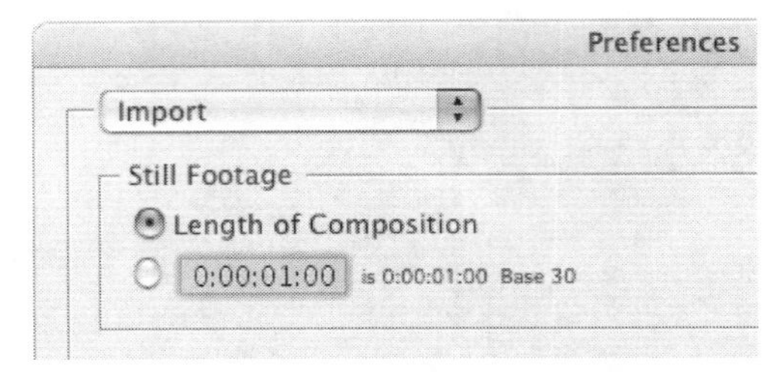

Figure 2.32 Set the default duration of still images to the duration of the composition, or enter a custom duration.

Preparing Still Images for Import

Which sounds faster and more efficient: altering a single image file or making the same adjustment to 900 identical files? If you prepare a still image beforehand, you spare After Effects from having to process every frame in which the image appears in a composition.

To avoid adding time to previews and renders, do the following before you import a still image into After Effects:

- Set the pixel dimensions to the size at which the image will be used in After Effects. This means that if you plan to scale up the image (as in a zoom-in effect), you should set its pixel dimensions to be proportionally greater. (For example, if you plan to scale the image to 200 percent, its pixel dimensions should be at least twice the size of the output frame.) If you don't do this, the image will appear more and more pixelated as you scale it up.
- Set the pixel dimensions of the still image to even numbers if the composition uses even-numbered pixel dimensions and to odd numbers if the composition uses odd-numbered pixel dimensions. (Most standard screen sizes use even pixel resolutions.) This makes it easier to position the image without causing it to be resampled and appear to soften.
- Crop the areas of the image that won't be visible in the After Effects composition.
- Create an alpha channel to define transparent areas in the image. (See "Importing Files with Alpha Channels," later in this chapter.)
- Make any other image adjustments, such as color corrections or touch-ups.
- Use a deinterlace filter on areas that show field artifacts if you're using a still image grabbed from interlaced video. Field artifacts often appear in areas of the image where the subject is moving. (See the sidebar "Working the Fields," later in this chapter).
- Take into consideration the pixel aspect ratio of your final output. Most images generated on your computer (in Photoshop, for example) use a square-pixel aspect ratio, whereas some output resolutions (such as D1 or DV) are based on a nonsquare-pixel aspect ratio. (See "Pixel Aspect Ratios," later in this chapter.)
- Use the proper file-naming conventions for your platform. Save the still image in a format that After Effects supports. Even after you import a still image, After Effects allows you to edit the file using the original application (Photoshop, for example). The After Effects footage file reflects any changes you make to the original file. (See Chapter 3 for more about the Edit Original command.)

continues on next page

Preparing Still Images for Import *(continued)*

For broadcast video output, you should also consider doing the following:

- Make sure color saturation doesn't exceed National Television Standards Committee (NTSC) safe color limitations.
- Make sure luminance values don't exceed NTSC limits for "legal" black-and-white levels. For more about NTSC limits, see the sidebar "Illegal and Dangerous" in Chapter 11, "Standard Effects in Action."
- Avoid thin horizontal lines in both images and text (including serifs), because interlaced video makes 1-pixel lines appear to flicker. To get around the problem, increase the thickness of the lines or apply a blur. For more about interlaced video, see the sidebar "Working the Fields," later in this chapter.
- Take television's 4:3 image aspect ratio into consideration, as well as title and action safe zones. For more about safe zones, see the sidebar "Better Safe Than Sorry" in Chapter 3.

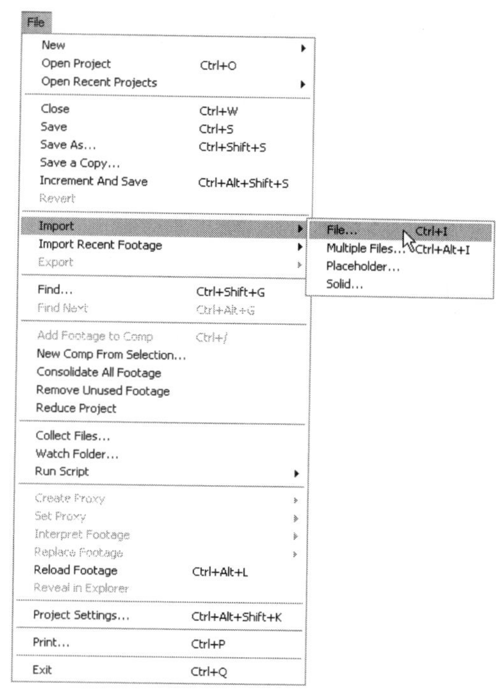

Figure 2.33 In After Effects, choose File > Import > File.

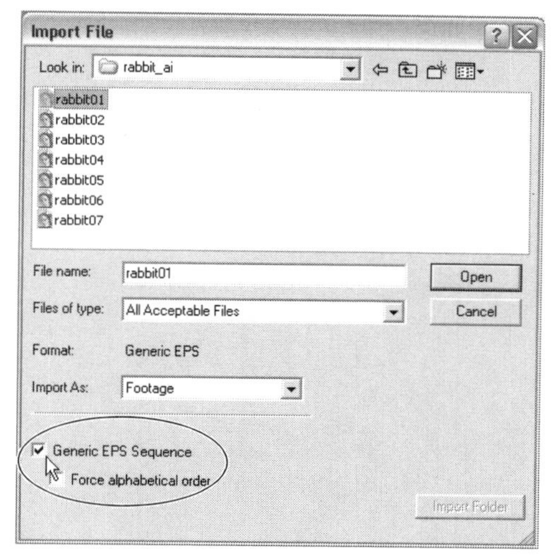

Figure 2.34 In the Import dialog box, select the first image in the sequence, and select the Sequence option.

Importing Still Image Sequences

Many programs (including After Effects) can export motion footage not as a single movie file, but as a series of still images, or a *still-image sequence*. You can import all or part of a still image sequence as a single motion footage item.

To import a still-image sequence:

1. Make sure all the still-image files in the sequence follow a consistent numeric or alphabetical filename pattern and are contained in the same folder.
2. In After Effects, choose File > Import > File (**Figure 2.33**).

   The Import File dialog box appears.
3. In the Import File dialog box, *do either of the following*:
   - ▲ To import the entire sequence as a single motion footage item, select the first file in the sequence.
   - ▲ To import part of the sequence as a single motion footage item, select the first file in the range, then Shift-click the last file in the range.
4. Select the box for the Sequence option (**Figure 2.34**).

   The Import File dialog box automatically indicates the file format for the Sequence check box (for example, TIFF Sequence). If you specified a limited range of sequence to import, the dialog box also displays the range next to the Sequence check box.

continues on next page

5. Click Open to import the file sequence and close the dialog box.

   The image file sequence appears as a single footage item in the Project window.

To import a still-image file sequence by dragging:

◆ Drag a folder containing a still-image sequence from the desktop directly to the After Effects Project window (**Figure 2.35**).

  The still-image file sequence contained in the folder appears in the Project window as a single footage item (**Figure 2.36**).

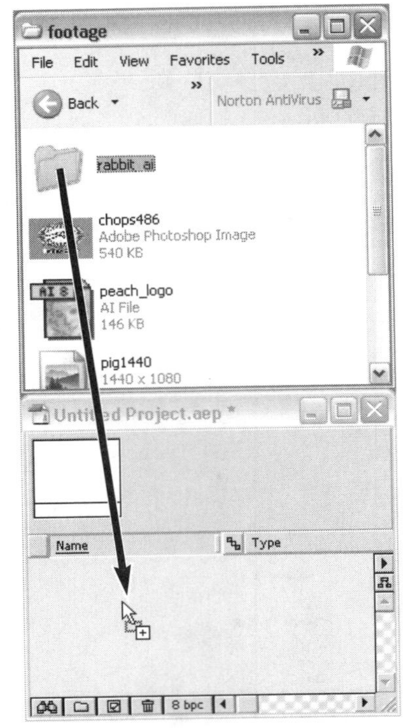

Figure 2.35 Drag a folder of sequential still-image files directly to the Project window.

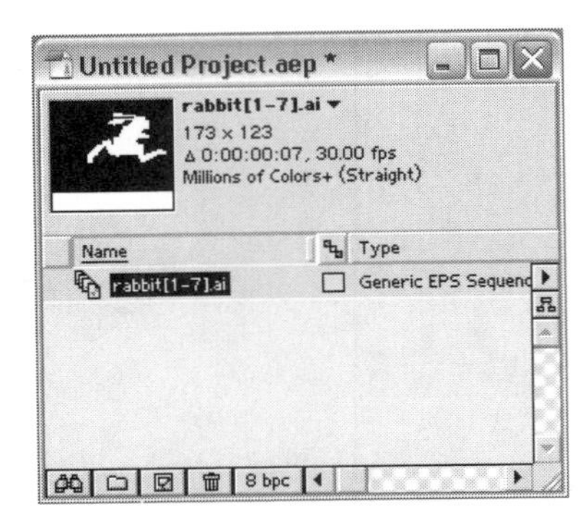

Figure 2.36 The image file sequence appears in the Project window as a single footage item.

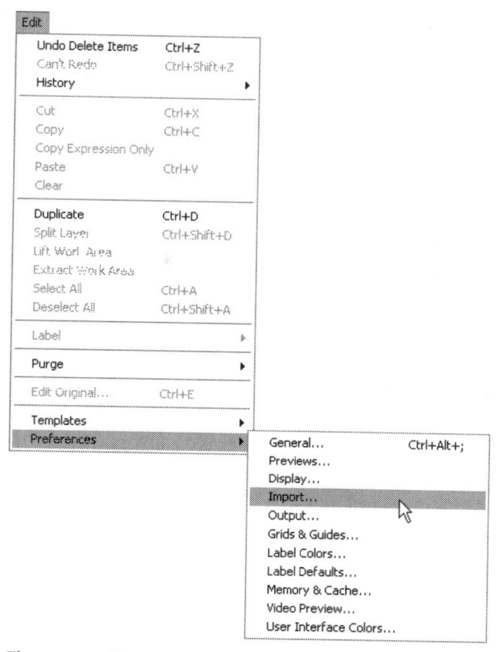

Figure 2.37 Choose After Effects > Preferences > Import (Mac) or Edit > Preferences > Import (Windows).

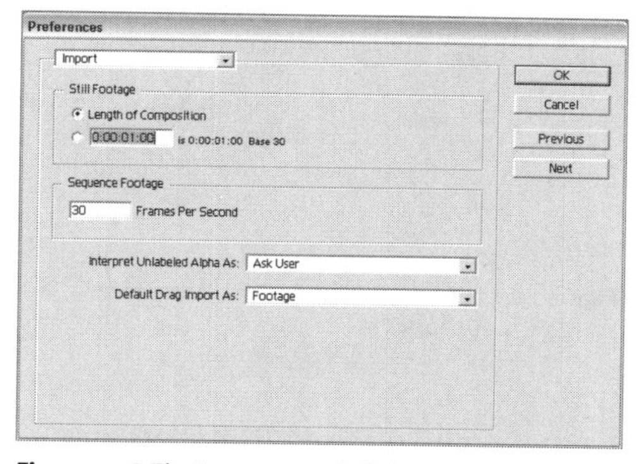

Figure 2.38 The Import panel of the Preferences dialog box appears.

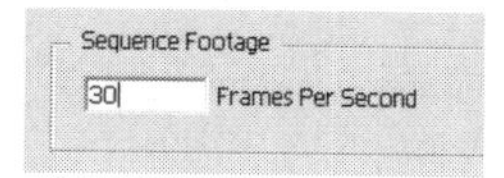

Figure 2.39 Enter a frame rate for imported still-image sequences.

To set the default frame rate for still-image sequences:

1. Choose After Effects > Preferences > Import (Mac) or Edit > Preferences > Import (Windows) (**Figure 2.37**).

   The Import panel of the Preferences dialog box appears (**Figure 2.38**).

2. In the Sequence Footage section of the Preferences dialog box, enter a frame rate (**Figure 2.39**). See Chapter 4 for more about frame rates.

3. Click OK to set the default frame rate and close the Preferences dialog box.

Importing Files with Alpha Channels

A file containing an alpha channel can be saved in two ways: as straight alpha or as premultiplied alpha. When you import a file containing an alpha channel, After Effects tries to detect a label (encoded in the file) that indicates whether the alpha is straight or premultiplied. If the alpha is unlabeled, After Effects prompts you with an Interpret Footage dialog box where you manually select how to interpret the alpha. You may ignore the alpha; interpret it as straight, premultiplied with black, or premultiplied with white; or allow After Effects to guess the type of alpha.

If you know how you want to interpret the alpha of your imported footage, you can select a default interpretation. You can also change the interpretation of a footage file after you import it.

If you interpret the alpha channel incorrectly, footage may appear with an unwanted black or white halo or fringe around the edges of objects (**Figure 2.40**). Incorrect interpretation can also cause color inaccuracies. If you need help interpreting footage containing an alpha channel, see the sidebar "Alpha Bits: Understanding Straight and Premultiplied Alpha," later in this chapter.

Figure 2.40 Misinterpreting the type of alpha results in an unwanted halo or fringe around objects. Note the dark fringe around the letters and the darkness in the transparency.

To set the default alpha interpretation:

1. Choose After Effects > Preferences > Import (Mac) or Edit > Preferences > Import (Windows).

   The Import panel of the Preferences dialog box appears (**Figure 2.41**).

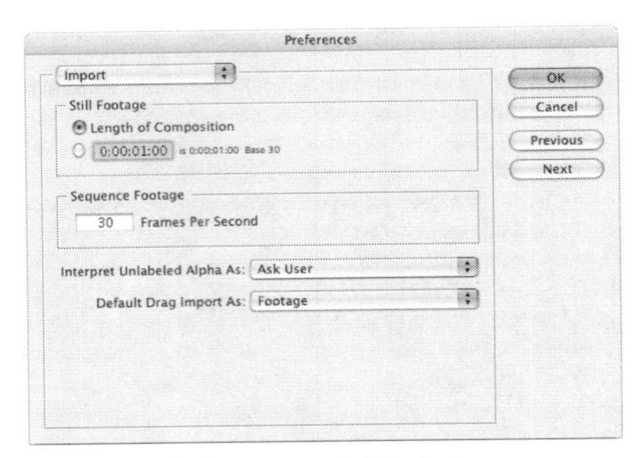

Figure 2.41 The Import panel of the Preferences dialog box appears.

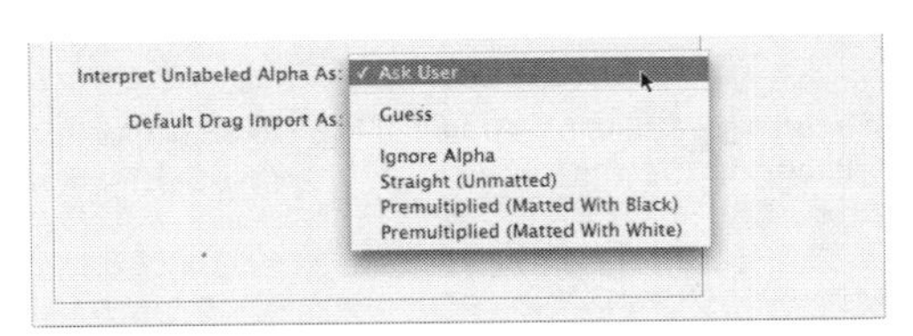

Figure 2.42 Choose a default interpretation method from the pull-down menu.

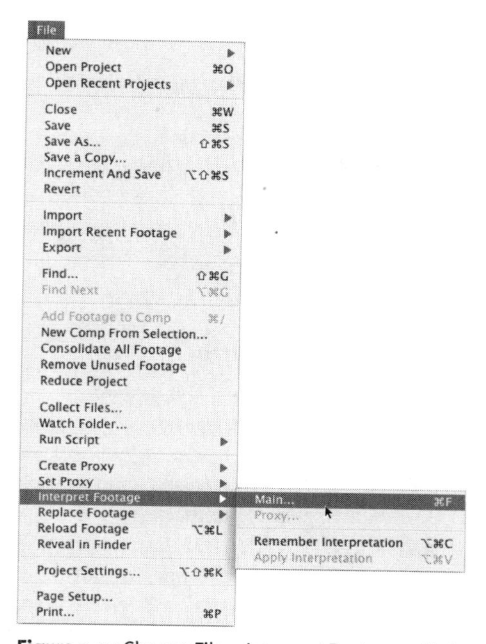

Figure 2.43 Choose File > Interpret Footage > Main.

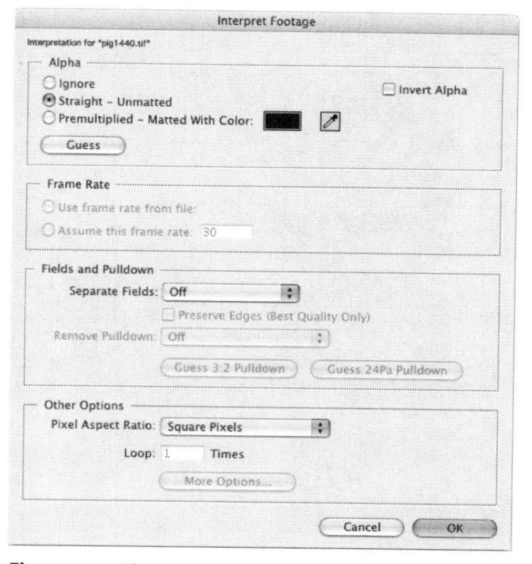

Figure 2.44 The Interpret Footage dialog box appears.

2. *Choose one of the following* default interpretation methods from the Interpret Unlabeled Alpha As pull-down menu (**Figure 2.42**):

   Ask User—You're prompted to choose an interpretation method each time you import footage with an unlabeled alpha channel.

   Guess—After Effects attempts to automatically detect the file's alpha channel type. If After Effects can't make a confident guess, it beeps at you.

   Ignore Alpha—After Effects disregards the alpha channel of imported images.

   Straight (Unmatted)—After Effects interprets the alpha channel as straight alpha. Choose this option for a single Photoshop layer with an alpha or layer mask.

   Premultiplied (Matted With Black)—After Effects interprets the alpha channel as premultiplied with black.

   Premultiplied (Matted With White)—After Effects interprets the alpha channel as premultiplied with white. Choose this option to import merged Photoshop layers that use transparency.

3. Click OK to close the Preferences dialog box.

To set the alpha channel interpretation for a file in a project:

1. In the Project window, select a file containing an alpha channel.

2. Choose File > Interpret Footage > Main (**Figure 2.43**).

   The Interpret Footage dialog box appears (**Figure 2.44**).

continues on next page

3. In the Alpha section of the Interpret Footage dialog box, choose an interpretation method (**Figure 2.45**).

   If the options are grayed out, the footage doesn't contain an alpha channel.

4. Click OK to close the Interpret Footage dialog box.

✔ Tips

- If an unexpected fringe or halo appears around the edges of a composited image, you should change the alpha interpretation.
- Internally, After Effects works in 32-bit depth (when a project is set to 8-bpc mode; see "Choosing the Bit-Depth Mode" earlier in this chapter). If a footage item's color space is less than this—as with a grayscale image—After Effects converts it to 32-bit depth when it displays. Similarly, if the footage doesn't contain an alpha channel, After Effects automatically supplies a full white alpha channel (which defines the image as fully opaque and visible).

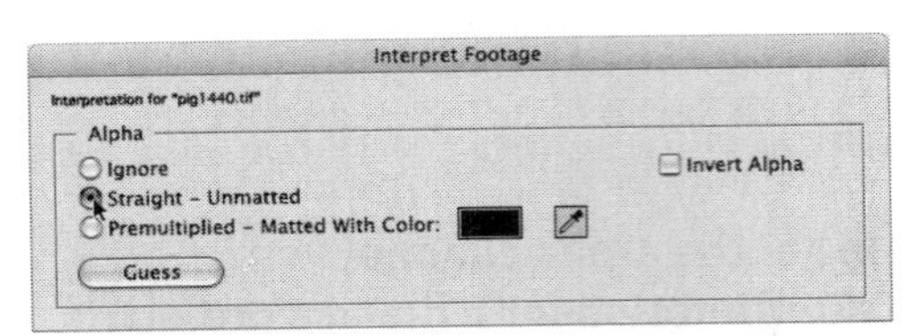

Figure 2.45 Choose an alpha channel interpretation method from the Interpret Footage dialog box.

Alpha Bits: Understanding Straight and Premultiplied Alpha

In 8-bit RGB color images, each channel—red, green, and blue—uses 8 bits (for a total of 24 bits), yielding millions of colors. A 32-bit file contains a fourth 8-bit channel, known as an *alpha channel*. Whereas the RGB channels define the visible color of each pixel in the image, the alpha channel defines the pixels' transparency. The alpha channel is usually depicted as a grayscale matte, where black defines a pixel as transparent, white as opaque, and gray as semitransparent. After Effects and other programs can use the alpha channel to make parts of an image transparent—a familiar concept to users of these programs (**Figure 2.46**).

continues on next page

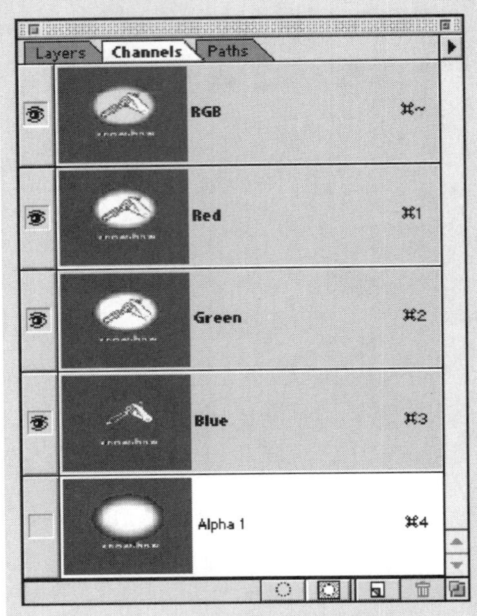

Figure 2.46 The channels of a 32-bit image, as viewed in Photoshop.

Alpha Bits: Understanding Straight and Premultiplied Alpha *(continued)*

Less widely known, however, is the fact that you can save files containing an alpha channel in two ways: as *straight alpha* or as *premultiplied alpha*. The alpha is the same in both types of files; however, the files differ in the way they factor visible channels into the transparency information.

A file saved with a *straight alpha* channel stores transparency information strictly in the alpha channel, not in any of the visible color channels. Ordinarily, you see the RGB channels combined, or multiplied, with the alpha channel. In After Effects, however, you can see the color information without the alpha channel (or an *unmultiplied* RGB image) by Shift-clicking the channel switch. Because the RGB channels don't take into account the transparency information, the color information bleeds across areas that the alpha channel defines as semitransparent. The all-or-nothing RGB channels of a straight alpha image look bad by themselves, but when they're combined with the alpha channel, transparent areas and soft edges are perfectly represented (**Figures 2.47**, **2.48**, and **2.49**). Incorrectly interpreting a straight alpha as premultiplied causes semitransparent objects to appear more opaque and brighter than they should.

continues on next page

Figure 2.47 The RGB channels of an image with a straight alpha don't factor in transparency. If you Shift-click the alpha switch , you can see how the unmultiplied color information bleeds across transparent areas.

Figure 2.48 An image with a straight alpha stores transparency information strictly in the alpha channel. You can view the alpha channel if you simply click the alpha switch.

Figure 2.49 In the final composite, the RGB and the alpha channel create smooth edges and transparencies.

Alpha Bits: Understanding Straight and Premultiplied Alpha *(continued)*

A file saved with a *premultiplied alpha* also stores transparency values in the alpha channel. However, the RGB channels take the transparency information into account as well. In semitransparent areas (including antialiased edges), the RGB channels are mixed—or *multiplied*—with the background color (usually black or white). Instead of bleeding across transparent areas, the RGB colors fade to the background color according to the amount of transparency. This is why incorrectly interpreting a premultiplied alpha as straight causes objects to appear with a black or white halo or fringe around them.

After Effects correctly interprets premultiplied alpha by "unmultiplying," or removing, the background color before it composites the image (**Figures 2.50**, **2.51**, and **2.52**).

Although it achieves great results from footage using either kind of alpha, After Effects works internally with straight alpha. Because straight alpha is native to After Effects, many consider it to be more precise—and more desirable—than premultiplied alpha.

Straight alpha is also known as *unmatted alpha*. Premultiplied alpha is also called *matted*, or *preshaped*, alpha.

Figure 2.50 In an image with premultiplied alpha, RGB colors are mixed with a background color according to the amount of transparency. Correctly interpreted, transparent areas composite smoothly.

Figure 2.51 Incorrectly interpreting the alpha as matted with white results in a dark halo, revealing how the colors are matted with black.

Figure 2.52 Incorrectly interpreting the alpha as straight has a similar effect.

Photoshop and Illustrator Files

Not surprisingly, After Effects fully embraces files generated by its Adobe siblings, Photoshop and Illustrator. After Effects not only accepts the standard single-layer file types (PCT, TIF, EPS, Filmstrip, and so on) but also supports layered Photoshop and Illustrator files.

After Effects can import Photoshop and Illustrator files as individual layers, as merged layers, or as a layered composition. After Effects preserves practically every aspect of your Photoshop work, including position, transfer modes, opacity, layer masks, clipping groups, adjustment layers, and layer effects. After Effects even preserves vector masks created in Photoshop. And, as pointed out earlier in this chapter, you can import Photoshop images saved with 16 bits per channel when you use the Professional version of After Effects.

When you import an Illustrator or EPS file, After Effects automatically converts text to paths, creates alpha channels from empty areas, and antialiases the edges of the artwork. After Effects also allows you to control how it rasterizes your artwork in order to preserve smooth edges at any scale. Just as After Effects has kept pace with the latest innovations in Photoshop, it also supports the transparency settings and transfer modes created for Illustrator.

In addition, After Effects allows you to copy a path from Illustrator or Photoshop and paste it directly as an After Effects mask. (See Chapter 9, "Mask Essentials," for more on copying paths.)

If these features don't mean much to you yet, don't worry. Their advantages will become apparent as you transfer your work seamlessly from one program to the other. The following sections cover the basics of importing Photoshop and Illustrator files. Future chapters show you how to take advantage of that footage once it's in your After Effects composition.

Importing a Layered File as a Single Footage Item

When you import a layered Photoshop or Illustrator file as a footage item, you can either import all the layers as a single merged item or import layers individually. Naturally, importing the merged file results in a footage item with the same dimensions of the source file (**Figure 2.53**).

However, when you import individual layers, you have a choice. You can import the layer at the document's dimensions so that the layer appears as it did in the context of the other layers (**Figure 2.54**). On the other hand, you can choose to use the layer's dimensions—that is, the size of the layer only, regardless of the document's size (**Figure 2.55**). (Of course, After Effects can also import all the layers assembled just as they were in Photoshop or Illustrator; you'll learn that technique in the following section.)

Figure 2.53 You can import a layered file so that the layers are merged into a single footage item that uses the source document's dimensions.

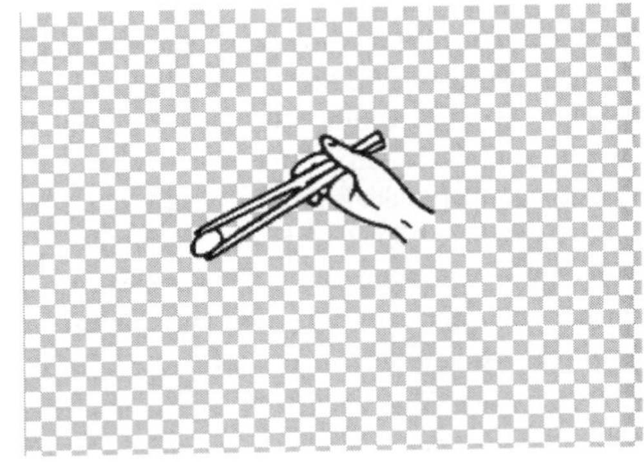

Figure 2.54 You can also import an individual layer using either the dimensions of the document (in this case, 720x486)...

Figure 2.55 ...or the minimum dimensions to contain the layer's image (this layer is 228x142).

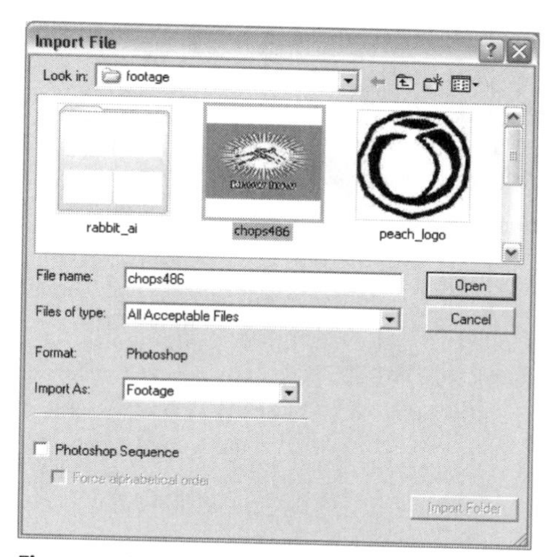

Figure 2.56 In the Import File dialog box, locate a Photoshop or Illustrator file and be sure Footage is selected in the Import As pull-down menu.

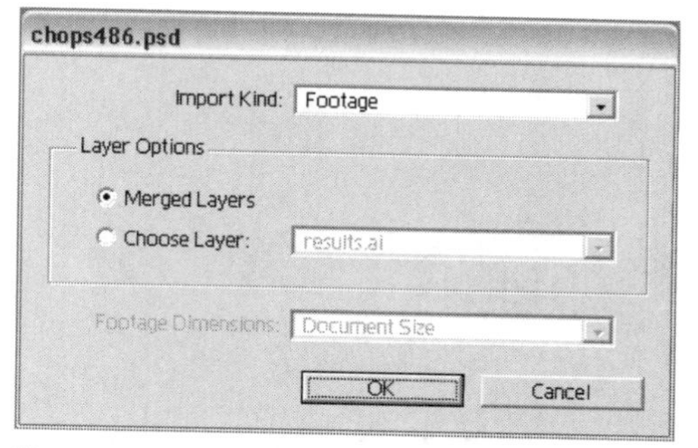

Figure 2.57 You can choose to import a single layer of a Photoshop or Illustrator file or to import merged layers.

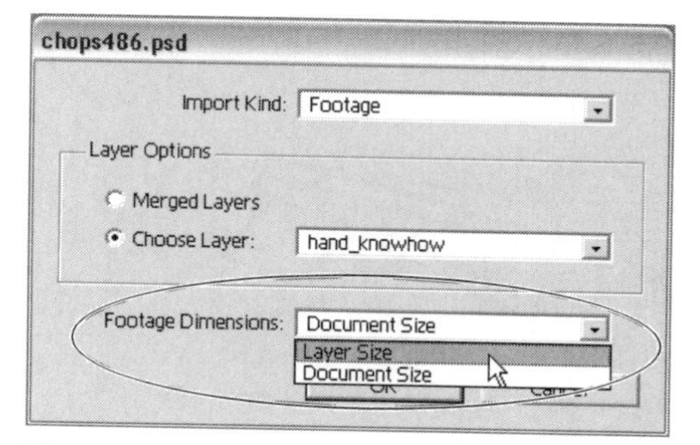

Figure 2.58 If you chose to import a single layer, specify an option in the Footage Dimensions pull-down menu.

To import a Photoshop or Illustrator file or layer as a single footage item:

1. Choose File > Import > File.
   The Import File dialog box appears.
2. In the Import File dialog box, locate and select a Photoshop or Illustrator file.
3. Make sure Footage is selected in the Import As pull-down menu, and then click Open (**Figure 2.56**).
   The Import Photoshop/Illustrator dialog box appears. The dialog box has the same name as the file you're importing.
4. In the dialog box's Import Kind pull-down menu, make sure Footage is selected.
5. In the Layer Options area of the dialog box, *do either of the following* (**Figure 2.57**):
   - ▲ Choose Merged Layers to import all layers in the file as a single footage item in After Effects.
   - ▲ Select Choose Layer. Then, in the pull-down menu, choose a layer to import.
6. If you chose a single layer in step 5, specify an option in the Footage Dimensions pull-down menu (**Figure 2.58**):
   Layer Size—Imports the layer at its native size. Choose this option when you plan to use the layer outside the context of the other layers in the file.
   Document Size—Imports the layer using the frame size of the document that contains the layer. Choose this option to maintain the layer's size and position relative to the document as a whole.

continues on next page

7. Click OK to close the dialog box.

   A footage item appears in the Project window. When you import a single layer, the name of the footage item is the name of the layer followed by the name of the Photoshop or Illustrator file. When you import merged layers, the name of the footage item is the name of the Photoshop or Illustrator file (**Figure 2.59**).

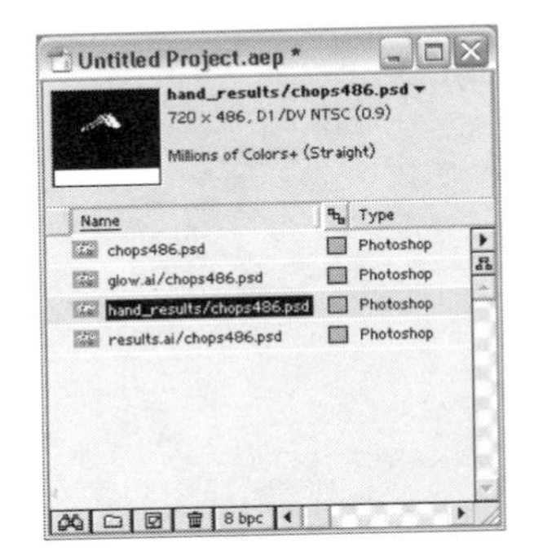

Figure 2.59 In the Project window, single and merged Photoshop or Illustrator layers are clearly named.

✔ Tips

- A single Photoshop layer with a layer mask uses straight alpha.
- When you import a layered Photoshop file as a merged layer, transparent areas of all layers are merged into a single alpha channel premultiplied with white.
- Empty areas of Illustrator artwork are converted into straight alpha.
- Although After Effects can import Illustrator files in the CMYK color space, you should convert them to RGB first.

Importing a Layered File as a Composition

One of After Effects' greatest strengths is its ability to import a layered Photoshop or Illustrator file as a ready-made composition—which, as you'll recall from chapter 1, consists of footage items arranged in time and space. After Effects not only imports all the layers as footage items, but also arranges the layers in a composition of the same dimensions. In essence, the composition replicates the layered file—suddenly transported into the world of After Effects (**Figure 2.60**).

As when you import layers separately (see "Importing a Layered File as a Single Footage Item," earlier in this chapter), you can choose whether the imported footage items (conveniently located in their own folder) use their native dimensions or share the new comp's dimensions (**Figures 2.61** and **2.62**).

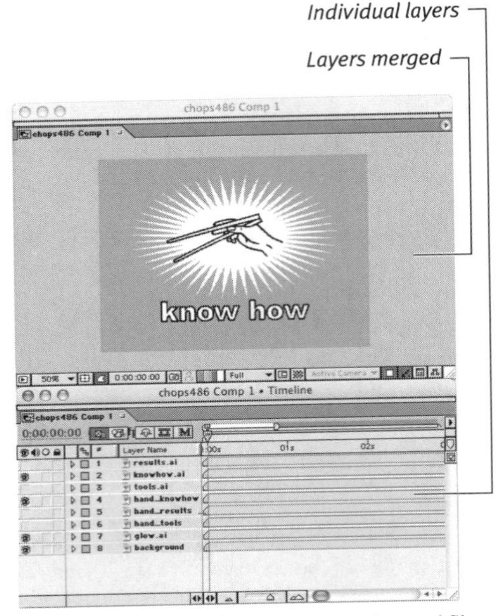

Figure 2.60 After Effects can convert a layered file into a composition containing the same layers. This way, you can manipulate each layer individually in After Effects.

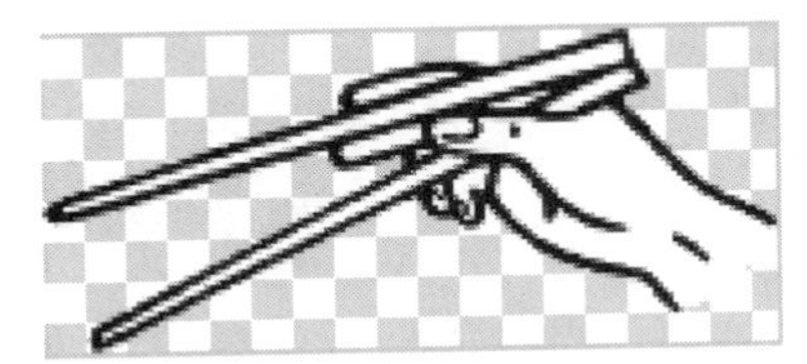

Figure 2.61 When you choose Composition-Cropped Layers, the imported footage includes the image only—in this case, the footage's dimensions are 314x125.

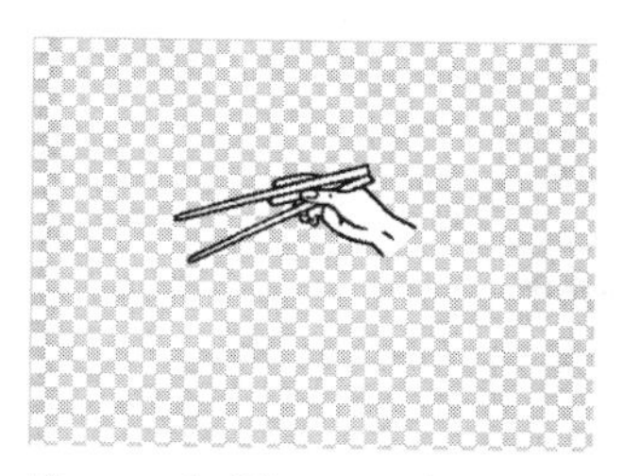

Figure 2.62 When you choose Composition, each layer uses the source document's dimensions, which of course, match those of the imported composition. In this example, the source file's and comp's dimensions are 720x846.

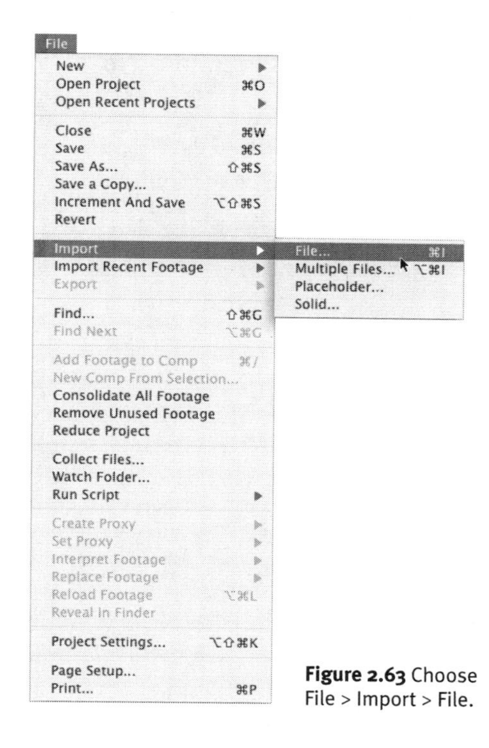

Figure 2.63 Choose File > Import > File.

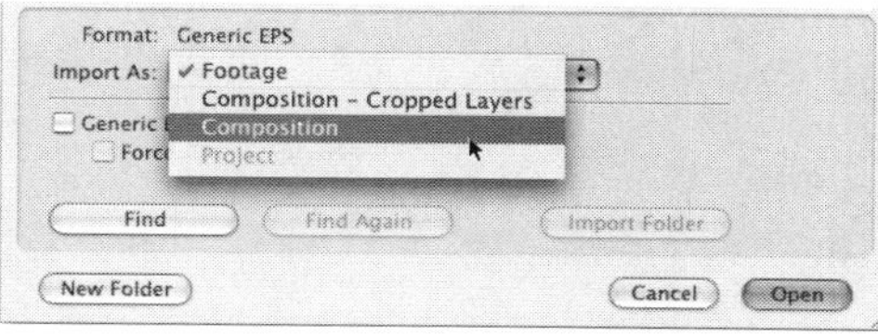

Figure 2.64 In the Import As pull-down menu of the Import File dialog box, choose the appropriate option.

To import an Adobe Photoshop or Illustrator file as a composition:

1. Choose File > Import > File (**Figure 2.63**).

   The Import File dialog box appears.

2. In the Import File dialog box, select an Adobe Photoshop or Illustrator file.

3. In the Import As pull-down menu of the Import File dialog box, *choose either of the following* (**Figure 2.64**):

   Composition - Cropped Layers—Imports each source layer at its native size

   Composition—Imports each source layer at the document's size

4. Click Import.

   In the Project window, the imported Photoshop or Illustrator file appears both as a composition and as a folder containing the individual layers imported as separate footage items (**Figure 2.65**).

✔ Tip

- After Effects imports Photoshop clipping groups as nested compositions within the main composition of the Photoshop file. After Effects automatically applies the Preserve Underlying Transparency option to each layer in the clipping group.

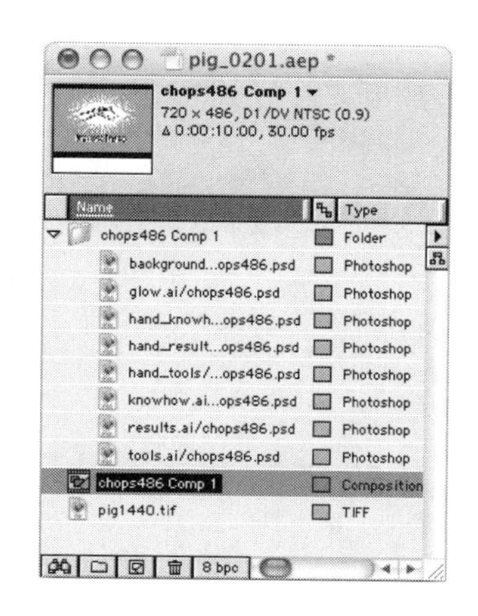

Figure 2.65 The Photoshop file appears both as a composition and as a folder containing individual layers.

Importing Premiere Pro and After Effects Projects

Because After Effects can import projects from Premiere Pro, it's now simple to move work from Adobe's nonlinear editor for treatment in the company's advanced animation/compositing/effects program (and vice versa).

Each sequence in the Premiere Pro project appears in After Effects as a composition (in which each clip is a layer) and a folder of clips. In the composition, After Effects preserves the clip order, duration, and In and Out points, as well as marker and transition locations (**Figures 2.66** and **2.67**). Because Premiere Pro includes many After Effects filters, any effects shared by the two programs will also be transferred from Premiere Pro into After Effects—including their keyframes.

You'll learn more about compositions in Chapter 4, "Compositions"; more about keyframes in Chapter 7, "Properties and Keyframes"; and more about effects in Chapter 10, "Effects Fundamentals." For the moment, suffice it to say that you can easily integrate Premiere Pro's advantages in nonlinear editing with After Effects' superior compositing and effects features.

Similarly, you can import an After Effects project into your current project—a capability that makes it possible to combine work, create complex sequences as different "modules," and repeat complex effects. All the elements of an imported After Effects project are contained in a folder in the current project.

To import an Adobe Premiere Pro project:

1. Choose File > Import > File.
   The Import File dialog box appears.
2. Select a Premiere Pro project file (**Figure 2.68**).

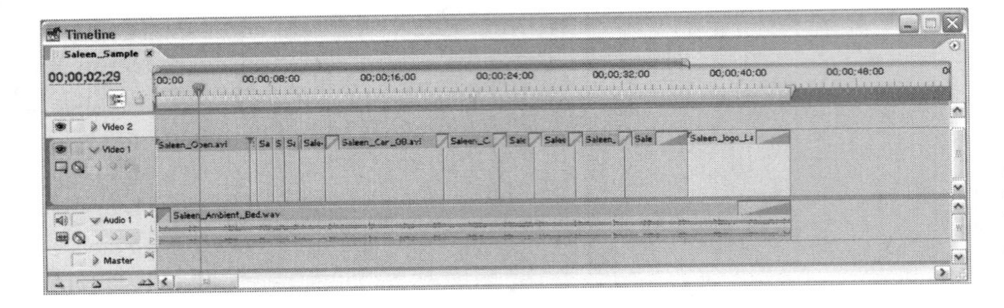

Figure 2.66 When you compare the Timeline window of a Premiere project (top)...

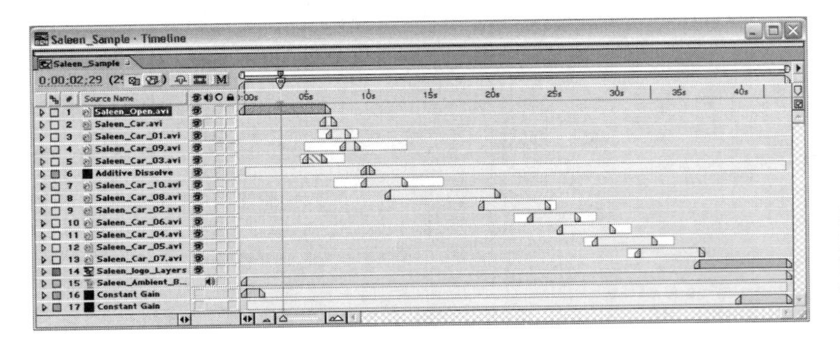

Figure 2.67 ...you can see how clips translate into layers in the Timeline window of After Effects (bottom).

After Effects recognizes the file type automatically and selects Composition from the Import As pull-down menu.

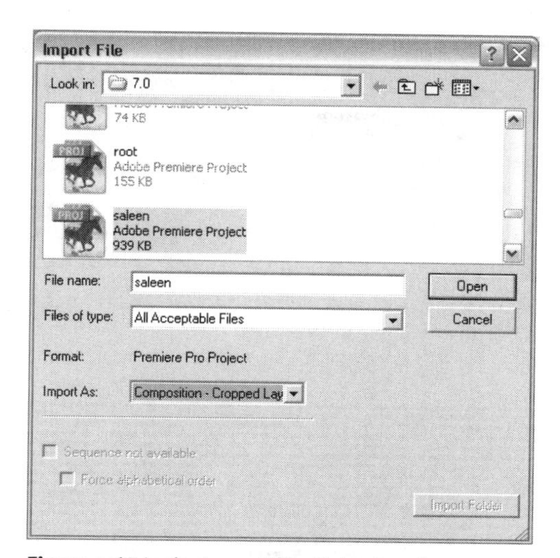

Figure 2.68 In the Import File dialog box, locate a Premiere Pro project and click Open.

3. Click Open.

   An Import Project dialog box appears.

4. In the Import Project dialog box, select the Premiere Pro sequences you want to import as compositions (**Figure 2.69**).

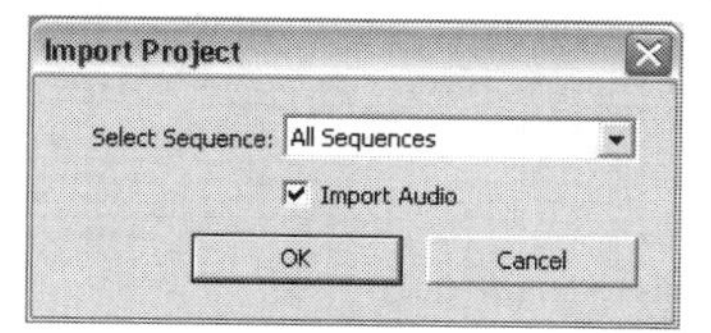

Figure 2.69 Specify the Premiere Pro sequences you want to import as compositions in After Effects, and select whether you want to include audio.

5. To import the audio clips in the selected sequences as audio footage items, select Import Audio. Leave the option unselected to omit the audio.

   The Premiere Pro project appears in the Project window as a composition. Clips appear as footage items, and bins appear as folders (**Figure 2.70**). An After Effects project appears in the Project window as a folder containing compositions and footage items.

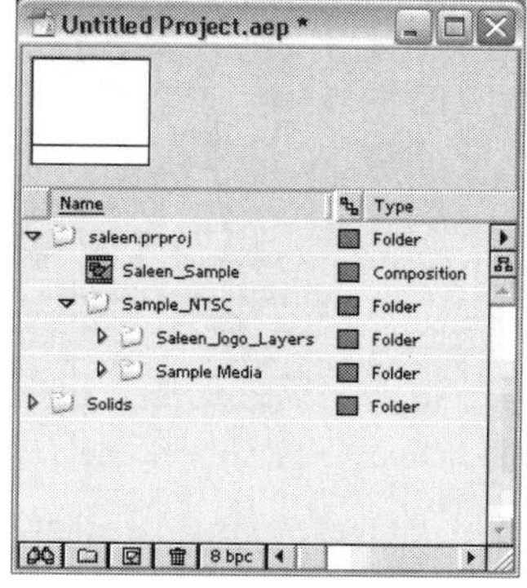

Figure 2.70 An imported Premiere Pro sequence appears in the Project window as a composition. Clips appear as footage items, and bins appear as folders.

✔ Tips

- You can also use a *program link*—which, as its name implies, is simply a link to the program that created it—to embed any movie exported from After Effects. For more about embedding program links, see Chapter 18, "Output."
- Like After Effects projects, Premiere Pro projects only refer to source files; they don't contain them. These source files must be available on a local storage device in order to be played back. If a file is unavailable, you can use a placeholder or proxy to substitute temporarily for the source file. For more about placeholders and proxies, see Chapter 3, "Managing Footage."
- To use a complex effect from another project, import the project and replace the source footage. Doing so will retain the effect you created before, but with different footage. See Chapter 3 for more about replacing footage.

Working with Interlaced Video and Field Order

Video designed exclusively for computer monitors uses a progressive scan; full-frame, full-motion video for television is interlaced.

In a *progressive scan,* the horizontal lines of each frame are displayed (progressively) from the top of the frame to the bottom, in a single pass (**Figure 2.71**).

Figure 2.71 In a progressive scan, the complete image is drawn in a single pass.

Interlaced video divides each frame of video into two fields. Each field includes every other horizontal line (*scan line*) in the frame. One field is displayed first, drawn as alternating lines from the top of the image to the bottom (**Figure 2.72**). Starting from the top again, the alternate field is displayed, filling in the gaps to complete the frame (**Figure 2.73**).

Figure 2.72 Interlaced video presents a single field that includes every other line of the image...

The field that contains the topmost scan line is called *field 1,* the *odd field,* or the *upper field.* The other field is known as *field 2,* the *even field,* or the *lower field.* Your video equipment and the settings you choose determine which field is the *dominant* field—that is, the one displayed first.

When you import interlaced video, After Effects must correctly interpret the field order to play back the video accurately. If the fields are presented in the wrong order, movement appears staggered.

Figure 2.73 ...and then interlaces the opposite field to create the full frame.

Figure 2.74 Select a footage item that uses interlaced video fields.

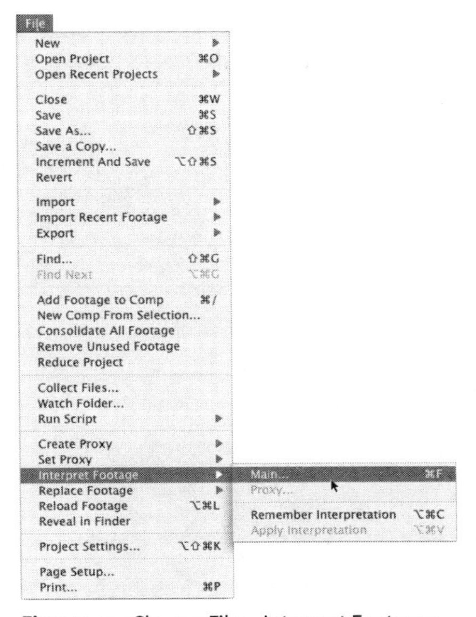

Figure 2.75 Choose File > Interpret Footage > Main.

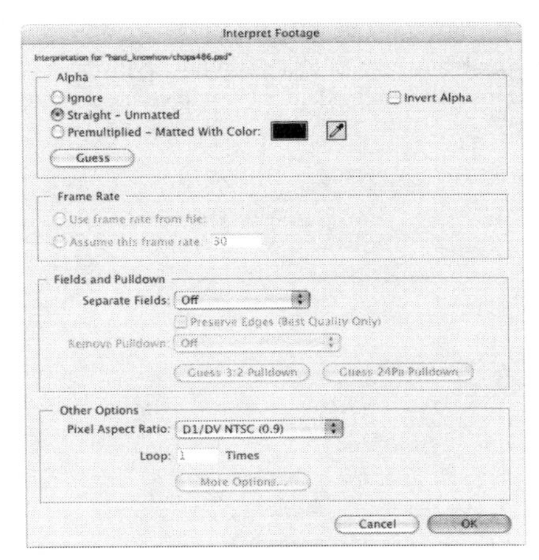

Figure 2.76 The Interpret Footage dialog box opens.

To interpret fields in video footage:

1. In the Project window, select an interlaced video or field-rendered footage item (**Figure 2.74**).
2. Choose File > Interpret Footage > Main (**Figure 2.75**), or press Command-F (Mac) or Ctrl-F (Windows).

   The Interpret Footage dialog box opens (**Figure 2.76**).
3. In the Fields and Pull-Down section of the Interpret Footage dialog box, *select one of the following* options from the Separate Fields pull-down menu (**Figure 2.77**):

   Off—After Effects won't separate fields. Use this option for footage that doesn't contain interlaced video fields.

   Upper Field First—The fields of upper-field dominant source files will be separated correctly.

   Lower Field First—The fields of lower-field dominant source files will be separated correctly.
4. Click OK to close the Interpret Footage dialog box.

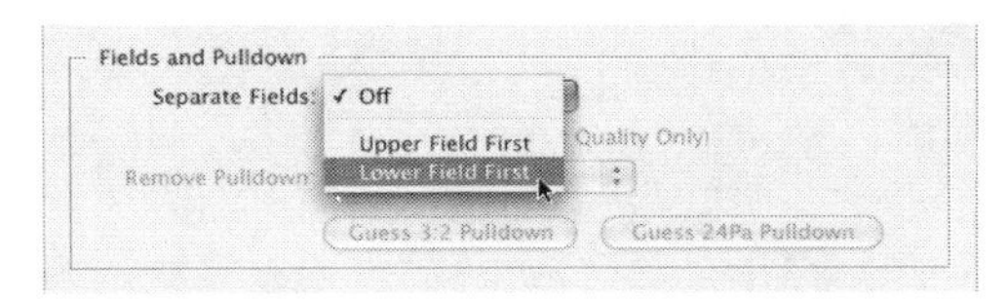

Figure 2.77 Choose the correct field dominance from the pull-down menu.

To determine field order manually:

1. In the Project window, select an interlaced video or field-rendered footage item.
2. Choose File > Interpret Footage > Main, or press Command-F (Mac) or Ctrl-F (Windows).

   The Interpret Footage dialog box appears.
3. In the Fields and Pulldown section of the Interpret Footage dialog box, select Upper Field First.
4. Click OK to close the Interpret Footage dialog box.
5. In the Project window, Option-double-click (Mac) or Alt-double-click (Windows) the footage item.

   The footage item opens in a Footage window, where its resolution appears lower because only one field is visible and it's been doubled to complete the frame. Despite the lower resolution, this display allows you to examine one field at a time and determine the field order.
6. In the Time Controls window, use the Frame Advance button or press Page Down on an extended keyboard to play the footage one field at a time (**Figure 2.78**).

Reversing Field Order

Occasionally, you may need to use After Effects to reverse the field order of an interlaced footage item. For example, you may need to export the footage to equipment that only understands the opposite field order. *To do this:*

1. Import the footage but don't separate the fields using the Interpret Footage command.
2. Center the footage in a composition of the same size, but then move it down 1 pixel.
3. When you render the composition at 29.97 fps with no field rendering, the field dominance is reversed.

For more about moving layers in compositions, see Chapter 7; for more about rendering a composition, see Chapter 18.

Figure 2.78 Clicking the Frame Advance button steps through one field (albeit doubled) at a time. You may also press Page Down on your keyboard.

Figure 2.79 As you step through each field of video, check to see that motion continues consistently forward. The second hand moved forward in this field...

Figure 2.80 ...and forward again in the next field...

Figure 2.81 ...but moves back in the following field. This means the fields are presented out of order.

7. Examine moving objects in the image as you step through the footage. After advancing the footage five fields or more, *make one of the following determinations*:

   ▲ If the objects consistently move in one direction, the field dominance is interpreted correctly.

   ▲ If the objects seem to stutter backward, the field dominance is interpreted incorrectly (**Figures 2.79**, **2.80**, and **2.81**). You should interpret the footage using the opposite field dominance setting in the Interpret Footage command.

Table 2.1

Field Order Cheat Sheet

Device	Field Dominance
AVID MCXpress Mac	Upper
AVID MCXpress 2.5 & later Windows NT	Lower
AVID MCXpress 2.2 & earlier Windows NT	Upper
AVID Media Composer, Symphony	Lower
AVID Media Composer 6.x & 7.x Windows NT	Upper
AVID Media Composer 8.x Windows NT	Lower
AVID all PAL systems	Upper
DDR (various manufacturers)	Lower
Discreet Logic Edit*	Lower
DV (miniDV, DVCam, DVCpro)	Lower
Media 100	Upper
Media 100 Finish	Lower
Radius Video Visio·	Upper
Scitex Sphere	Lower
Truevision Targa (all cards)	Lower

Motion Footage

Motion footage sources include video digitized from analog video sources (such as Hi8 or Betacam SP), digital video (such as DV transferred via FireWire, or Digital Betacam via SDI), and film (scanned as Cineon files or transferred to video using 3:2 pulldown).

The process of importing motion footage varies little from the process of importing other types of files. But, as you've already learned, After Effects must interpret different formats according to their attributes and your requirements. In the following sections, you'll learn about the Interpret Footage command that's used to correctly identify motion footage's frame rate, field order, 3:2 pulldown, and pixel aspect ratio. The Interpret Footage command also enables you to automatically loop footage and set the display quality of EPS footage files. You can even learn to edit After Effects' internal settings.

✔ Tips

- You import audio-only files into an After Effects project just as you would any other file. Video footage that has audio can be imported as a single footage item.
- Some programs label a file with the field order when they render. After Effects recognizes the label and automatically applies the appropriate field order interpretation. You can override the interpretation by using the Interpretation Rules file, as explained later in this chapter.
- If your final output is destined for computer display only (not video display), or if it will be displayed at less than full screen size, you should deinterlace the video before you import it. Doing so spares you from separating fields in After Effects and from processing unnecessary information.

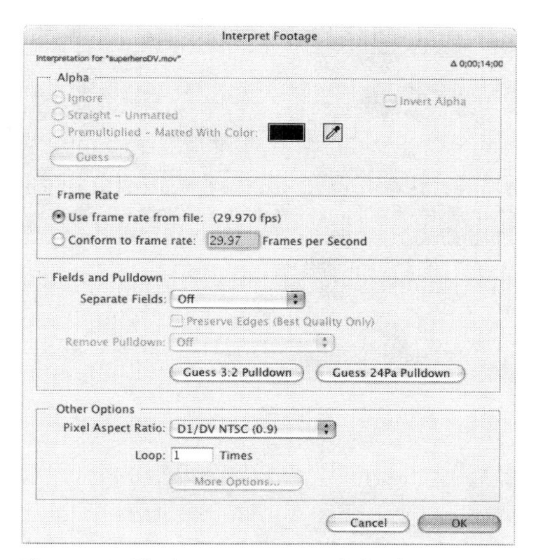

Figure 2.82 The Interpret Footage dialog box contains controls to set the frame rate of footage.

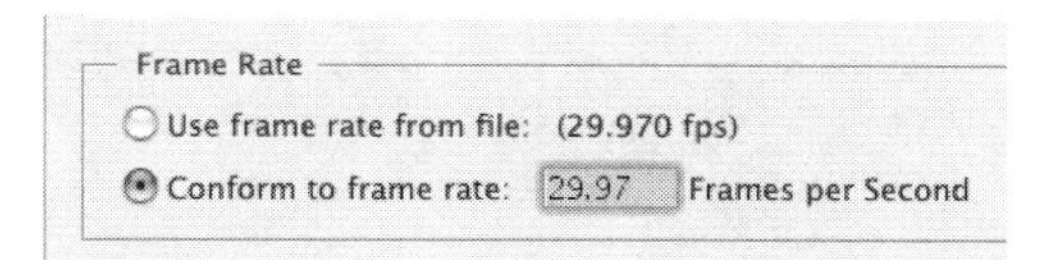

Figure 2.83 You can set movie footage to conform to a different frame rate. Note the dialog box uses the term *conform* when referring to motion footage.

Setting the Frame Rate

Generally, you use the footage's native frame rate, which also matches the frame rate of the composition. Sometimes, however, you'll want to specify a frame rate for a footage item manually.

Because features like time stretch (see Chapter 6, "Layer Editing") and time remapping (see Chapter 14, "More Layer Techniques") provide finer control over a layer's playback speed, it's more common to set the frame rate for image sequences than for movie files.

For example, some animations are designed to play back at 10 fps. If you interpreted such a sequence to match a 30-fps composition, 30 frames would play back in one second—three times as fast as they were intended to play. Manually specifying a 10-fps frame rate for a still-image sequence of 30 frames would result in a duration of three seconds when played in a 30-fps composition.

Conversely, many programs can't render interlaced video frames. Sometimes animators choose to render 60 fps, which can be interpreted at a higher frame rate and interlaced at output.

To set the frame rate for footage:

1. In the Project window, select a footage item.
2. Choose File > Interpret Footage > Main, or press Command-F (Mac) or Ctrl-F (Windows).

   The Interpret Footage dialog box appears (**Figure 2.82**).
3. For motion footage, *choose one of the following* options in the Frame Rate section of the Interpret Footage dialog box (**Figure 2.83**):

continues on next page

Use frame rate from file—Uses the native frame rate of the footage item

Conform to frame rate—Lets you enter a custom frame rate for the footage

Using a frame rate that differs from the original changes the playback speed of the movie.

4. For image sequences, enter a frame rate next to "Assume this frame rate" in the Frame Rate section of the Interpret Footage dialog box (**Figure 2.84**).
5. Click OK to close the Interpret Footage dialog box.

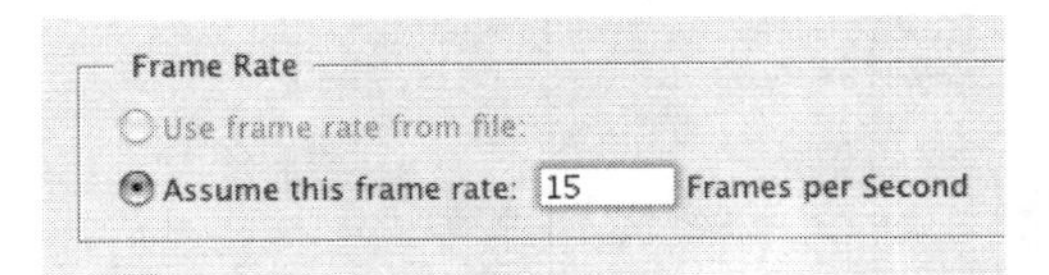

Figure 2.84 More often, you use the control to set the frame rate of still-image sequences. Note that the dialog box says "Assume this frame rate" when interpreting still-image sequences.

✔ Tip

- To interpret 60-fps animation sequences for output as interlaced fields, enter `59.94` in the "Assume this frame rate" field and use the footage item in a full-frame, 29.97-fps composition. Make sure to field-render the output. See Chapter 17, "Complex Projects," for more about rendering compositions.

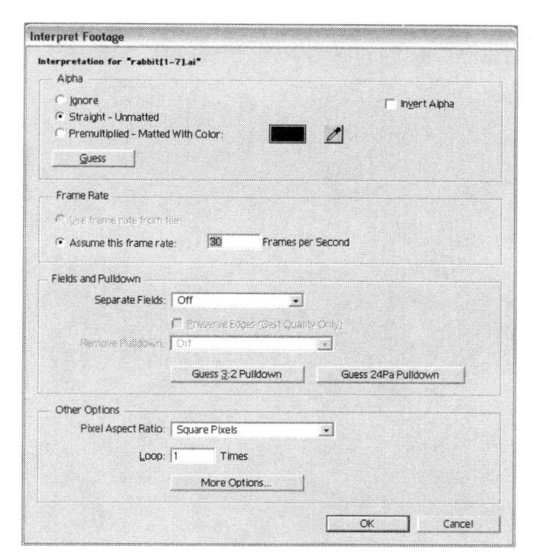

Figure 2.85 The Interpret Footage dialog box contains controls that allow you to loop a footage item (without repeating it in the composition).

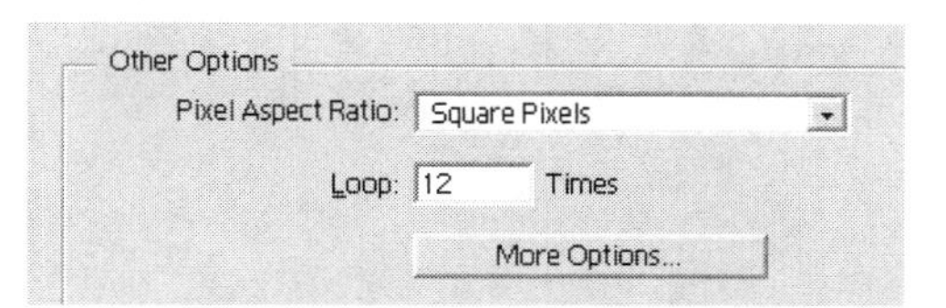

Figure 2.86 Enter the number of times you want the footage item to loop.

Looping Footage

Often, you need footage to loop continuously. Rather than add a footage item to a composition multiple times, you can set the footage item to loop using the Interpret Footage dialog box.

To loop footage:

1. In the Project window, select a footage item you want to loop.
2. Choose File > Interpret Footage > Main, or press Command-F (Mac) or Ctrl-F (Windows).

   The Interpret Footage dialog box appears (**Figure 2.85**).
3. In the Other Options section of the Interpret Footage dialog box, enter the number of times you want the footage to loop (**Figure 2.86**).

   You may only enter integers for complete cycles, not decimals for partial cycles. When you add the footage item to a composition as a layer, its duration reflects the Loop setting.

✔ Tip

- The Loop setting loops the content of the footage, not the movement of a layer—it's useful for turning an animation of two steps into a long walk, for example. You can't use this setting to repeat animated properties. For that, you'll need to use keyframes (Chapter 7) or expressions (Chapter 17).

Removing Film 3:2 Pulldown and 24Pa Pulldown

Film transferred to video presents special challenges in post-production. One of the most common issues arises from the difference in frame rates: Film plays at 24 fps (full frames); NTSC video plays at about 29.97 fps (interlaced fields). When film is transferred to video, a process called *3:2 pulldown* compensates for the difference in frame rates. In this process, one second of video plays back one second of film footage. (See the sidebar "The Lowdown on Pulldown: 3:2 Pulldown," later in this chapter.)

However, if your final output is destined for film, you should remove 3:2 pulldown from video footage to ensure that your After Effects work will synchronize frames accurately at film's 24 fps. By reducing the number of frames you have to process from 30 fps to 24 fps, you also decrease your work and the time required for rendering.

Similarly, footage shot in the 24P (24 fps progressive scan) format undergoes a pulldown process. As the sidebar "Pulldown for 24P Video" explains in detail, 24P footage is pulled down using either a normal or advanced method. Just as you would remove 3:2 pulldown from video transferred from film, you should remove 24Pa pulldown in order to restore footage to 24 progressive frames for effects work.

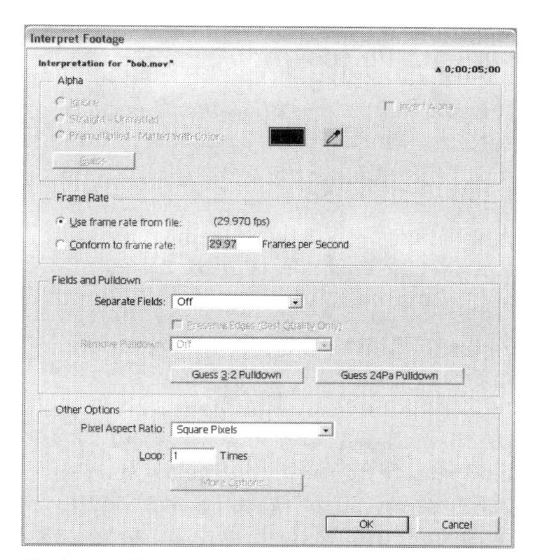

Figure 2.87 The Interpret Footage dialog box contains controls that allow you to remove 3:2 pulldown from a footage item.

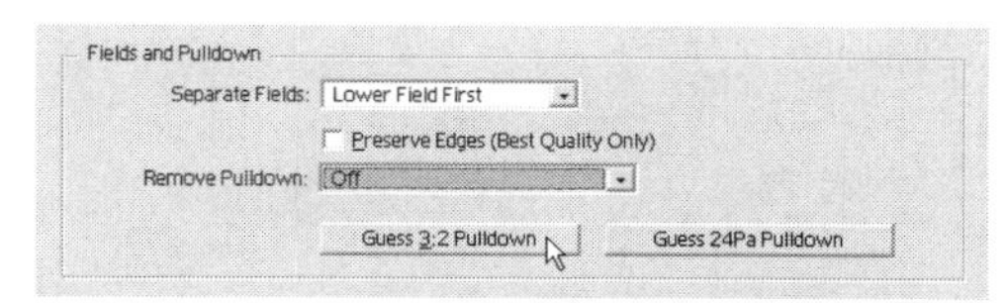

Figure 2.88 Click Guess 3:2 Pulldown to have After Effects determine the pulldown.

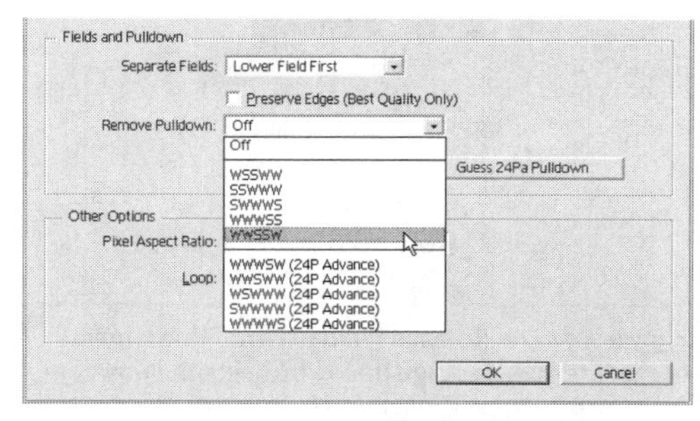

Figure 2.89 If you know the pulldown phase, select it in the Remove Pulldown pull-down menu.

To remove 3:2 or 24Pa pulldown:

1. In the Project window, select the footage item transferred from film using 3:2 pulldown or from progressive-scan video using 24Pa pulldown.
2. Choose File > Interpret Footage > Main, or press Command-F (Mac) or Ctrl-F (Windows).

   The Interpret Footage dialog box appears (**Figure 2.87**).
3. In the Fields and Pulldown section of the Interpret Footage dialog box, select the appropriate field dominance (Upper or Lower), as described previously.
4. In the Fields and Pulldown section of the Interpret Footage dialog box, *do one of the following:*
   - ▲ Click Guess 3:2 Pulldown if you want After Effects to determine automatically the correct phase in which to remove 3:2 pulldown (**Figure 2.88**).
   - ▲ Click Guess 24Pa Pulldown if you want After Effects to determine automatically the correct phase in which to remove 24Pa pulldown.
   - ▲ If you know the phase of the pulldown method, choose the correct phase from the Remove Pulldown pull-down menu (**Figure 2.89**).

The Lowdown on Pulldown: 3:2 Pulldown

In 3:2 pulldown, frames of film are transferred to fields of video in a 3:2 pattern—that is, one frame of film is transferred to three fields of video, and the next frame of film is transferred to two fields of video. As this 3:2 pattern repeats, every four frames of film get distributed across five frames of video in a consistent pattern of whole frames and split-field frames.

In *whole frames*, both video fields are drawn from the same film frame. In *split-field frames*, each video field is drawn from two different film frames. The pattern of whole frames and split frames in the first five frames of video determines the *phase* (**Figure 2.90**). There are five possible phase patterns, which are distinguished by the relative position of the two adjacent split-field (S) frames. When you remove pulldown, After Effects can detect the phase, or you can select it manually (**Figure 2.91**).

"Hold on," you say, "this process translates 24 fps to 60 fields per second. That's 30 fps, not 29.97 fps." You're right! Before the frames are distributed using the 3:2 scheme, the film is slowed down by .1 percent to compensate for the difference between 29.97 fps and 30 fps (go ahead and do the math). Remember this when you do your audio post!

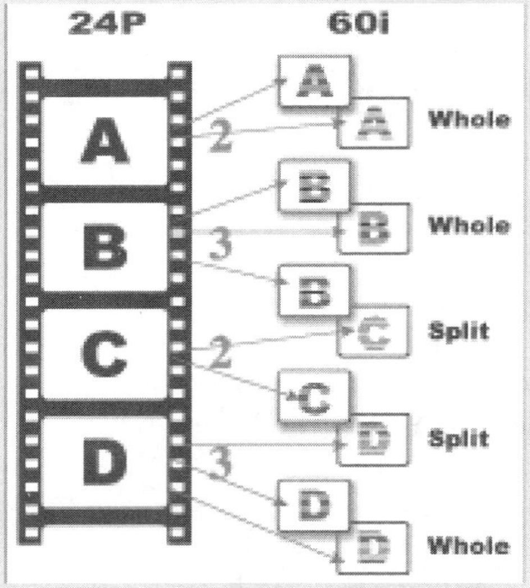

Figure 2.90 Each film frame is transferred to either three or two fields of video. This results in a five-frame pattern, or *phase*, of whole frames and split-field frames of video. The phase pictured here is described as WWSSW.

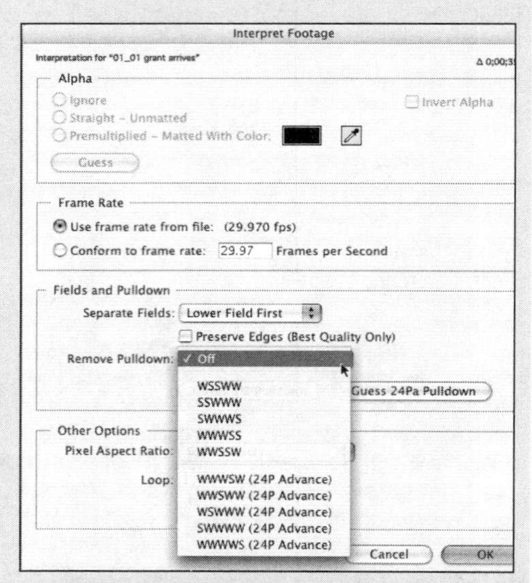

Figure 2.91 The Remove Pulldown pull-down menu in the Interpret Footage dialog box lists the possible phases, or patterns, of whole frames (W) and split-field frames (S).

Pulldown for 24P Video

Nowadays, video is no longer restricted to the timeworn NTSC and PAL standards for image size and frame rate. To facilitate video-to-film transfers (or at least to achieve a film look), some video cameras can shoot in 24P—that is, at 24 progressive frames per second. (For more about progressive and interlaced video, see the sidebar "Working the Fields," earlier in this chapter.) Once only available in expensive high-end equipment, 24P has recently found its way into much more affordable "prosumer" level cameras, such as Panasonic's DVX100 (aka DVX100P; the *P* stands for Panasonic, not *progressive* or *PAL*).

But although a camera like the DVX100 can shoot 24P, it stores the video on tape using the familiar 60 interlaced fields per second, or 60i. It does so using either of two pulldown schemes, known as *standard* and *advanced.*

Standard pulldown uses the same method as film pulldown, distributing 24P to 60i using a 3:2 cadence (explained in the sidebar "The Lowdown on Pulldown," earlier in this chapter). The downside to this method becomes apparent when it's time to convert 60i back to 24P. As you can see in **Figure 2.92**, three out of every four progressive frames—A, B, and D in the diagram—are reconstructed from two fields in the same frame, or whole frames. The C frame, on the other hand, must consist of fields from different frames, or split frames. As a result, these frames must be processed differently than the others. Unlike the whole frames, the split frames must be decompressed to retrieve the proper fields—which, as you can see, must be reversed to match the field order of the other frames. And because fields extracted from the two split frames differ more than fields taken from whole frames, they're compressed less efficiently when they're combined into a new progressive frame. In short, not all the frames are restored to 24P unscathed.

continues on next page

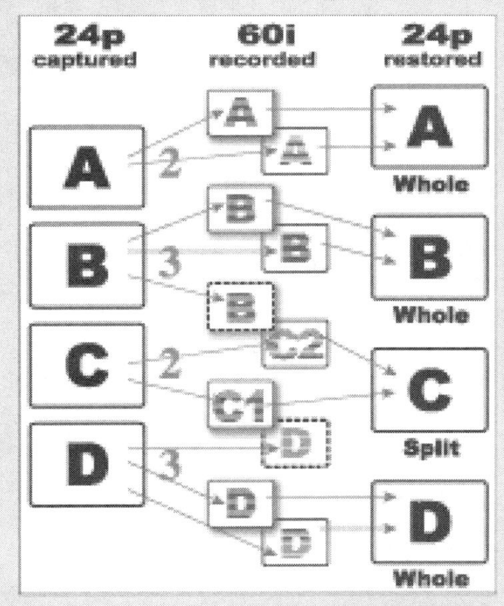

Figure 2.92 Using standard pulldown, certain frames must be reconstructed out of fields from different frames, which requires more processing. In the figure, you can see that the restored frame C must be created from field 2 of one frame and field 1 from the subsequent frame.

Pulldown for 24P Video *(continued)*

Advanced pulldown, often referred to as 24Pa, uses a 2:3:3:2 cadence. As you can see in **Figure 2.93**, this pattern permits every 24P frame to be restored from whole 60i frames. This process not only converts all frames using a consistent method, but also averts problems associated with processing fields from two split frames.

But you may ask, "Why introduce pulldown at all?" When you use a camera like the DVX100, pulldown permits you to shoot DV at 24P and capture and edit in a DV-native application. You gain this advantage regardless of which pulldown mode you select. Generally speaking, shooting with standard pulldown helps achieve a film look on video. To make the smoothest video-to-film transfer, select advanced pulldown when you shoot. Naturally, you should remove advanced pulldown for effects work (particularly compositing and rotoscoping) in After Effects.

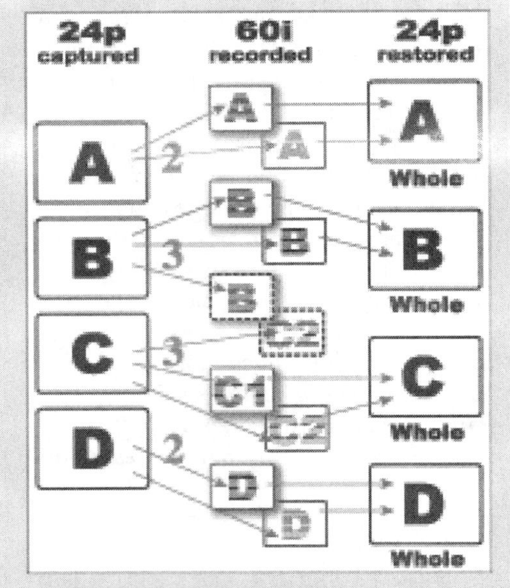

Figure 2.93 With advanced pulldown, all of the frames are restored to 24p using the same clean method.

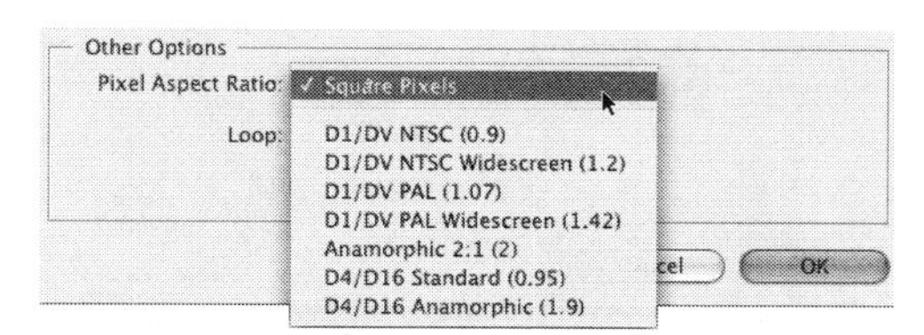

Figure 2.94 In the Interpret Footage dialog box, choose the appropriate pixel aspect ratio. Most computer monitors use square pixels to represent an image with a 4:3 aspect ratio.

Pixel Aspect Ratios

Generally, computer systems display images using square pixels (a 1:1 pixel aspect ratio, or 1.0 PAR). However, many formats, including common standards like D1 and DV, use nonsquare pixels to represent images. If you display nonsquare pixels on a square-pixel monitor, the image will appear distorted. Luckily, After Effects can compensate for the difference between standards so you can use both in the same composition and output them without distortion.

After Effects automatically interprets D1 (720×486) and DV (720×480) footage to compensate correctly for their pixel aspect ratios. Nevertheless, you should check to see that your footage is interpreted correctly, and you should understand how to set the PAR for other standards. You can even manually customize how the program automatically interprets footage (see "To set interpretation rules," later in this chapter).

To interpret the pixel aspect ratio:

1. In the Project window, select a footage item.
2. Choose File > Interpret Footage > Main, or press Command-F (Mac) or Ctrl-F (Windows).

   The Interpret Footage dialog box appears.
3. In the Other Options section of the Interpret Footage dialog box, choose the appropriate Pixel Aspect Ratio setting for your footage (**Figure 2.94**):

   Square Pixels—1.0 PAR. Use for footage with a frame size of 640×480 or 648×486 and a 4:3 image aspect ratio.

   D1/DV NTSC—.9 PAR. Use for footage with a frame size of 720×486 (D1) or 720×480 (DV) and a 4:3 image aspect ratio.

continues on next page

D1/DV NTSC Widescreen—1.2 PAR. Use for footage with a frame size of 720×486 (D1) or 720×480 (DV) to achieve a 16:9 image aspect ratio in standard definition.

D1/DV PAL—1.0666 PAR. Use for footage with a 720×576 (PAL) frame size and a 4:3 image aspect ratio.

D1/DV PAL Widescreen—1.422 PAR. Use for footage with a 720×576 (PAL) frame size and a 16:9 image aspect ratio in standard definition.

Anamorphic 2:1—2.0 PAR. Use for footage shot with a 2:1 anamorphic film lens.

D4/D16 Standard—.9481481 PAR. Use for footage with a 1440×1024 or 2880×2048 image size and a 4:3 image aspect ratio.

D4/D16 Anamorphic—1.8962962 PAR. Use for footage with a 1440×1024 or 2880×2048 image size and an 8:3 image aspect ratio.

✔ Tips

- If you import a square-pixel image that uses a frame size common to D1 (720×486) or DV (720×480), After Effects will automatically (and incorrectly) interpret that image as using nonsquare pixels. This is because After Effects' default interpretation rules are set to assume images that use these dimensions use a PAR of .9 (see "Using Interpretation Rules," later in this chapter). Use the Interpret Footage dialog box to change the pixel aspect ratio setting.
- To preview compositions that use nonsquare pixel aspect ratios without distortion, you can choose Pixel Aspect Correction from the Composition window's pull-down menu. See Chapter 4 for more.

PAR Excellence: Pixel Aspect Ratios

Image aspect ratio refers to the dimensions of the video frame, expressed as a ratio between the width and the height (horizontal and vertical aspects) of the image. Although most video uses a 4:3 aspect ratio, a more filmlike 16:9 aspect ratio is gradually becoming common.

Pixel aspect ratio (PAR) refers to the dimensions of each pixel used to create the image frame. Although some formats share the same image aspect ratio, they use different pixel aspect ratios (**Figures 2.95** and **2.96**). Images appear distorted when the PAR of the footage doesn't match the PAR of the display. Footage in professional video's D1 looks distorted when displayed on a typical computer monitor, which displays square pixels (**Figure 2.97**). Conversely, a 640x480 square-pixel image appears distorted when viewed or output at D1 resolution.

By using After Effects' Interpret Footage command, you can compensate for differences among formats, so that they display properly in the composition and in the final output.

When you create square-pixel footage for D1 or DV output, using the following image sizes allows you to create the image without distortion:

Format for Output	Create Image At	Interpret As
D1	720x540	NTSC D1 720x486
DV	720x534	NTSC DV 720x480

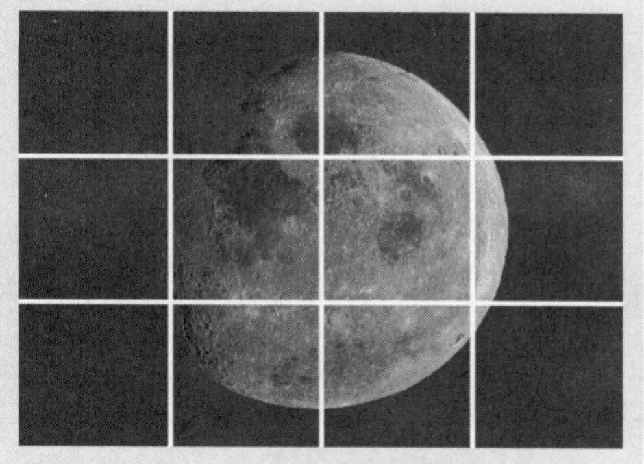

Figure 2.95 Most computer monitors use square pixels to represent an image with a 4:3 aspect ratio.

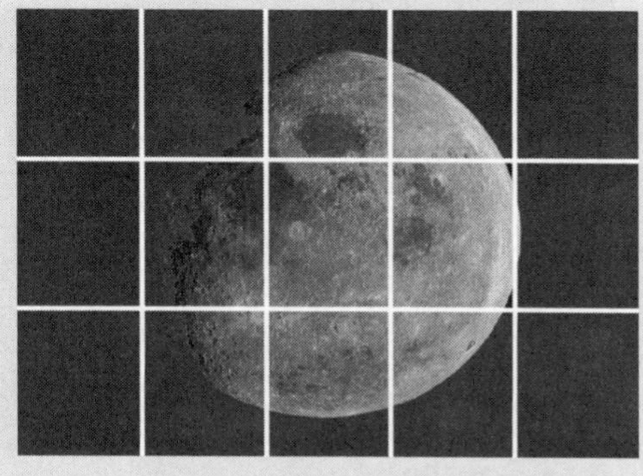

Figure 2.96 Some television standards, such as D1 and DV, use nonsquare pixels to achieve a 4:3 aspect ratio.

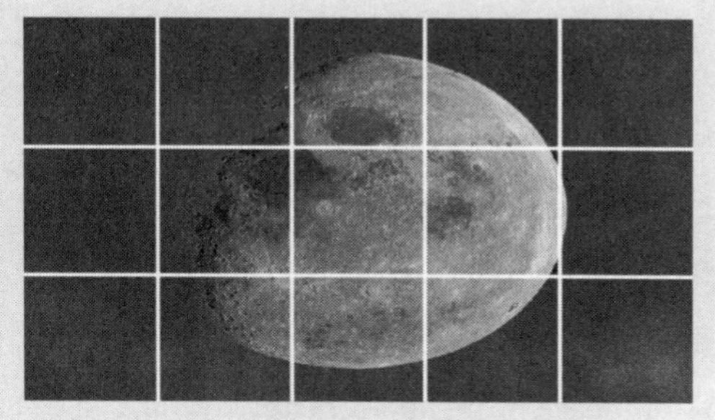

Figure 2.97 If you don't compensate for the difference between the PAR of the image and the PAR of the display, the image will appear distorted.

Setting the EPS Options

As long as you're getting familiar with the Interpret Footage dialog box, there's one more option to explore—and that's, well, Options. The Options button gives you access to an EPS Options dialog box that allows you to control the rasterization method used for EPS images. You can choose between a fast but lower-quality method and a slower but more accurate method. To learn more about rasterization, see the "Rasterization" sidebar in Chapter 5, "Layer Basics."

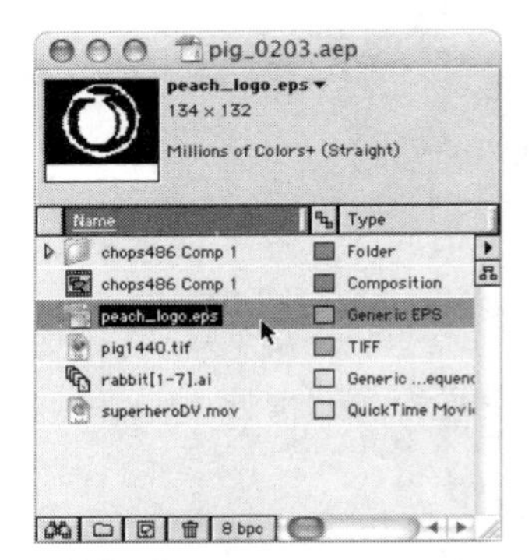

Figure 2.98 In the Project window, select an EPS footage item.

To set the EPS options:

1. In the Project window, select an EPS footage item (**Figure 2.98**).
2. Choose File > Interpret Footage > Main, or press Command-F (Mac) or Ctrl-F (Windows).

   The Interpret Footage dialog box appears.
3. In the Interpret Footage dialog box, click the More Options button (**Figure 2.99**).

   The EPS Options dialog box appears.
4. In the EPS Options dialog box, *choose either of the following options* (**Figure 2.100**):

   Faster—After Effects will rasterize the footage more quickly but won't be able to represent smooth edges and color gradients as accurately.

   More Accurate—With this slower method, you're less likely to have rough or hard edges on objects and color banding in gradients.
5. Click OK to close the dialog box.

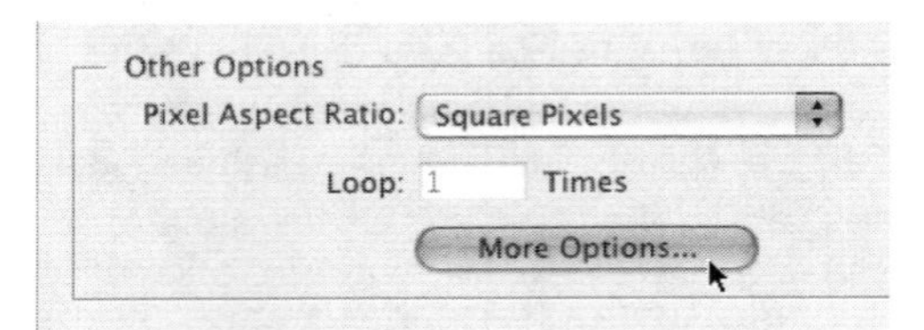

Figure 2.99 In the Interpret Footage dialog box, click More Options to access options for rasterizing EPS files.

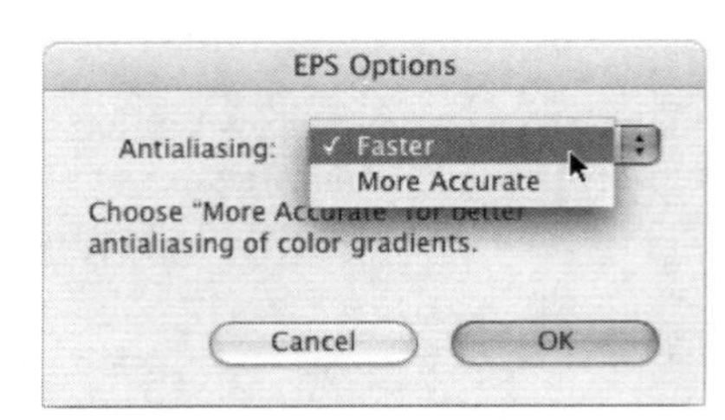

Figure 2.100 In the EPS Options dialog box, choose an option from the pull-down menu.

✔ Tip

- To learn more about rasterization, see the sidebar "Rasterization," in Chapter 5.

Figure 2.101 Choose File > Interpret Footage > Remember Interpretation to copy interpretation settings from a clip.

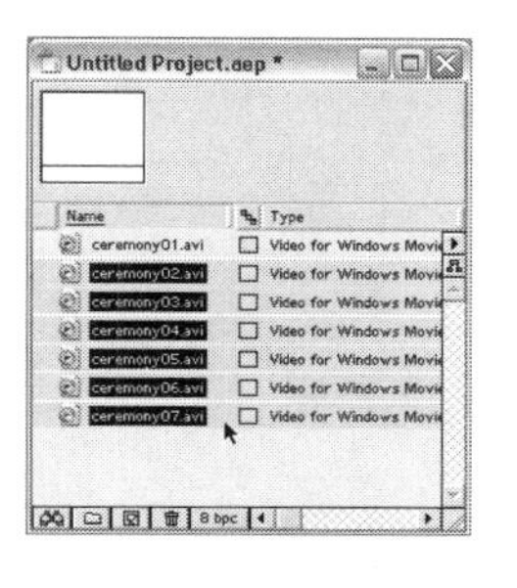

Figure 2.102 Select other clips to which you want to apply the same interpretation settings.

Figure 2.103 Select File > Interpret Footage > Apply Interpretation to paste the interpretation settings to the selected footage items.

Reapplying the Interpret Footage Command

In this chapter, you've learned how to use the Interpret Footage dialog box to help After Effects properly interpret alpha channels, field order, 3:2 pulldown, frame rate, looping, pixel aspect ratio, and EPS options. Chances are, you'll use the same settings on several items within a project. Fortunately, After Effects allows you to copy and paste these settings so you don't need to revisit the Interpret Footage dialog box repeatedly.

To reapply the Interpret Footage command to other footage items:

1. In the Project window, select a footage item that uses interpretation settings you want to apply to other items.
2. Choose File > Interpret Footage > Remember Interpretation (**Figure 2.101**).
3. In the Project window, select one or more footage items to which you want to apply the interpretation settings (**Figure 2.102**).
4. Choose File > Interpret Footage > Apply Interpretation (**Figure 2.103**).

   The interpretation settings are applied to the selected footage items.

Using Interpretation Rules

You can customize the "rules" After Effects uses to interpret footage automatically.

To set interpretation rules:

1. Locate the `Interpretation Rules.txt` file in the After Effects folder.
2. Open `Interpretation Rules.txt` in a text-editing program (such as SimpleText).
3. Change, add, or delete entries that dictate how After Effects interprets footage items.

   The text file contains instructions on how to format the entries.

✔ Tip

- The keyboard shortcuts for the interpretation settings are reminiscent of standard Copy and Paste commands: Command-Opt-C (Mac) or Ctrl-Alt-C (Windows) to remember, or copy, the interpretation; Command-Opt-V (Mac) or Ctrl-Alt-V (Windows) to apply, or paste, the interpretation to another item.

3

Managing Footage

As you saw in the previous chapter, the Project window is basically a list of all your footage and compositions. The more complex the project, the lengthier and more unwieldy this list becomes. As the receptacle of this essential information, the Project window can resemble either a cluttered junk drawer or a neat filing cabinet, a cardboard box filled with books or the Library of Congress. In this chapter, you'll learn how to use the Project window to organize and sort the items contained in your project. You'll also learn about other aspects of asset management—such as how to replace missing footage, and how to use placeholders and proxies to temporarily stand in for footage items. As always, taking a little time to prepare will save you a lot of time in the long run.

This chapter also introduces you to the Footage window, which lets you not only see your footage but really scrutinize it. Most of the controls in the Footage window are also found in the Composition and Layer windows, which means that learning these controls now will go a long way toward providing the grounding you need later.

The Footage window also includes editing buttons; however, an in-depth explanation of those features will wait for Chapter 4, "Compositions," where you'll learn how to add footage as layers in a composition.

Displaying Information in the Project Window

The Project window (**Figure 3.1**) furnishes you with several ways to manage your footage and compositions. Icons that resemble those used on the desktop (Mac) or Explorer (Windows) provide an easy means of distinguishing between footage types (**Figure 3.2**). You can also view more detailed information about items in the Project window, organize items into folders, and sort items according to categories. Depending on your needs, you can rearrange, resize, hide, or reveal the categories. You can even create a custom category and custom color labels. And if you still need help locating an item, you can find it using the Project window's Find button. There's also a button that lets you access a flowchart view of your project—but that explanation will wait for later when it will make more sense (see Chapter 17, "Complex Projects").

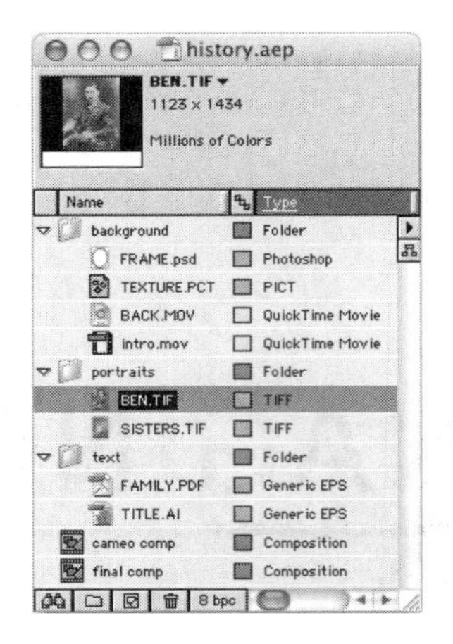

Figure 3.1 The Project window doesn't simply list items; it helps you identify, sort, and organize them.

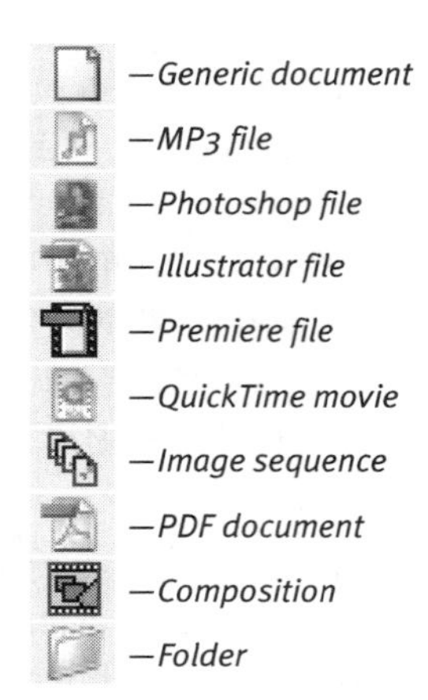

Figure 3.2 Icons identify the types of items in the Project window.

To display information about a footage item or composition:

- In the Project window, click a footage item to select it.

  At the top of the Project window, a thumbnail image of the footage item appears. Next to the thumbnail image, the name of the footage item appears, as well as information about the footage itself, such as frame size, color depth, codec, and so on (**Figure 3.3**).

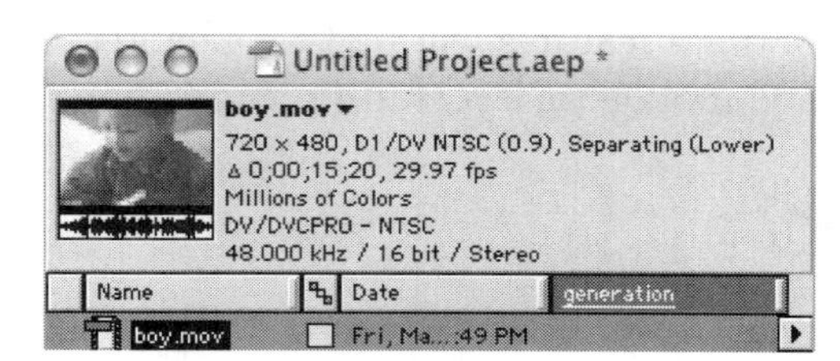

Figure 3.3 When you select an item in the Project window, information about the selected item appears at the top of the window.

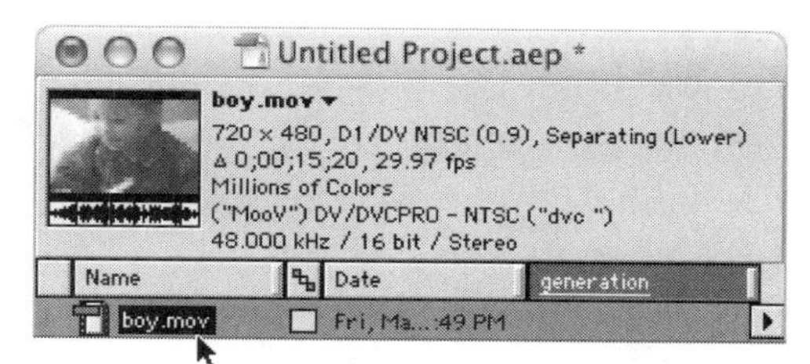

Figure 3.4 When you Option-click (Mac) or Alt-click (Windows) an item in the Project window, the file-type extension also appears.

To display the file-type extension of the footage item:

- In the Project window, Option-click (Mac) or Alt-click (Windows) a footage item.

  At the top of the Project window, underneath the other information about the footage item, the item's file-type extension appears in parentheses (**Figure 3.4**).

✔ Tips

- You can select the next footage item listed in the Project window by pressing the down arrow, or you can choose the previous item by pressing the up arrow.
- You can select all footage items that use the same label by choosing Edit > Label > Select Label Group.

To show or hide the thumbnail image of an item in the Project window:

1. Choose After Effects > Preferences > Display (Mac) or Edit > Preferences > Display (Windows) (**Figure 3.5**).

   The Display panel of the Preferences dialog box appears.

2. In the Display panel of the Preferences dialog box, *do one of the following:*

   ▲ Click Disable Thumbnails in Project Window to prevent thumbnail images from being displayed there (**Figure 3.6**).

   ▲ Unselect Disable Thumbnails in Project Window to display thumbnail images in the Project window.

3. Click OK to close the dialog box.

   Whether a thumbnail image displays in the Project window depends on the selection you made (**Figure 3.7**).

✔ Tip

■ Why would anyone want to turn off those cool thumbnail pictures? The same reason swimmers shave off their eyebrows: to go just a little bit faster. It takes time to draw those images, and the larger the source file, the longer it takes. Suppressing the display of thumbnails shaves precious moments off your processing time.

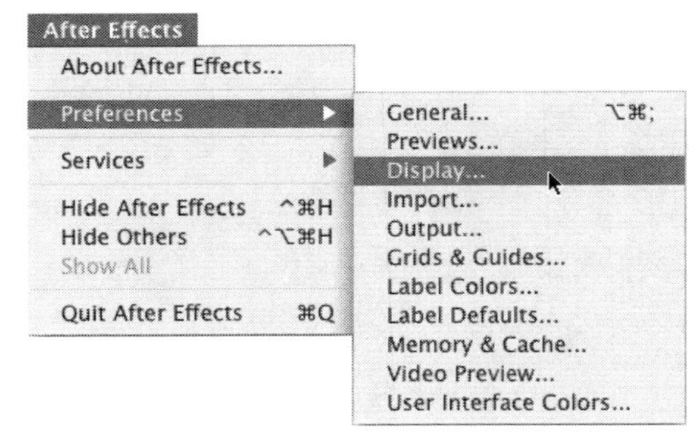

Figure 3.5 Choose After Effects > Preferences > Display (Mac) or Edit > Preferences > Display (Windows).

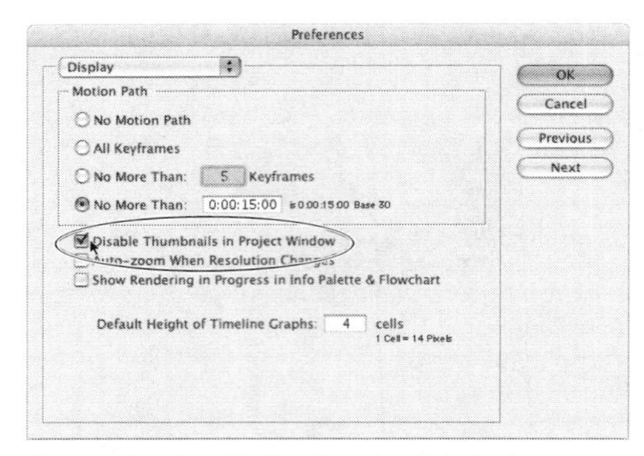

Figure 3.6 Select Disable Thumbnails in Project Window to prevent thumbnail images from being displayed in the Project window.

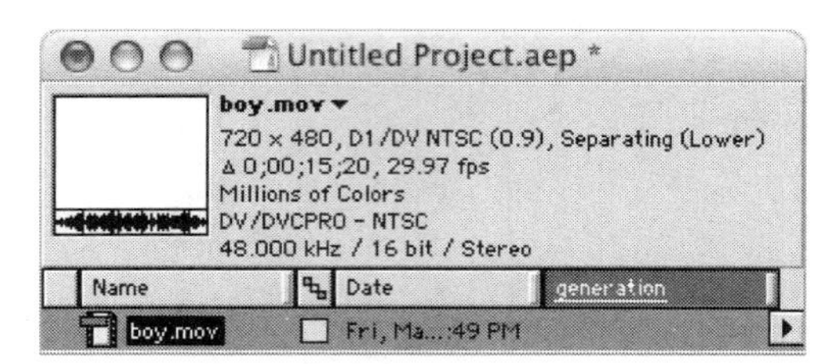

Figure 3.7 When you choose to disable thumbnails, no image displays in the Project window when you select an item.

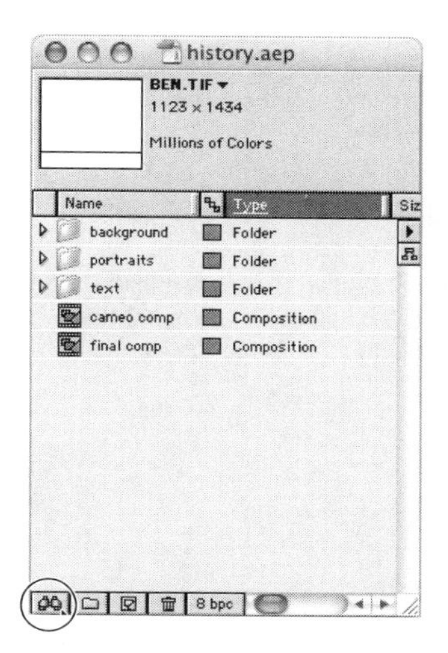

Figure 3.8 In the Project window, click the Find button.

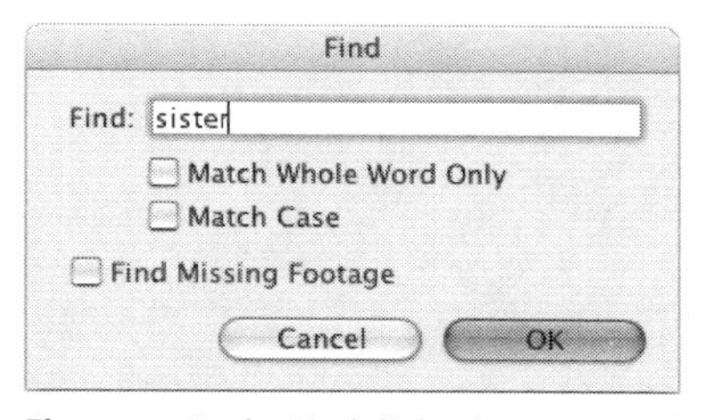

Figure 3.9 In the Find dialog box, enter all or part of the name of the item you're looking for, and select the options you want.

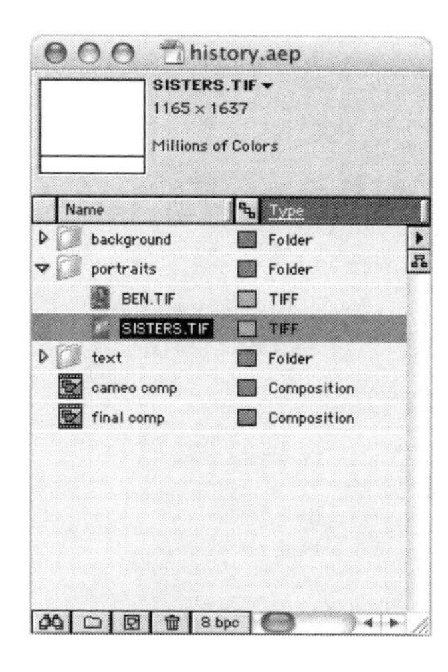

Figure 3.10 The first item that matches the criteria you specified appears selected in the Project window.

Finding Items in a Project

The Project window includes a handy Find button to help you unearth items from your project that you've lost track of. Use it, and you'll never need to search through folders again.

To find an item in the Project window:

1. In the Project window, click the Find button (**Figure 3.8**).

   A Find dialog box appears.

2. Enter all or part of the name of the item you're looking for in the Find field (**Figure 3.9**).

   You can modify the search parameters by choosing the options described in the next step.

3. In the Find dialog box, select the options you want to use to modify your search:

   Match Whole Word Only—If you select this option, After Effects will only locate items that match the entire word you entered in the Find field.

   Match Case—If you select this option, After Effects will look for items that include the Find field's content, taking letter case into account. For example, a search for *Background* (with an uppercase *B)* won't locate the item called *background* (with a lowercase *b*).

   Find Missing Footage—With this option selected, After Effects will find missing footage—that is, items that have lost their reference to a source file.

4. Click OK to search for the item.

   The first item that matches the criteria you specified appears selected in the Project window (**Figure 3.10**).

To find the next item that matches the most recent Find criteria:

- Option-click (Mac) or Alt-click (Windows) the Find button.

  The next item that matches the most recent Find criteria appears selected in the Project window. When After Effects has searched to the end of the project, a dialog box prompts you to continue the search from the beginning of the project or to cancel the search (**Figure 3.11**).

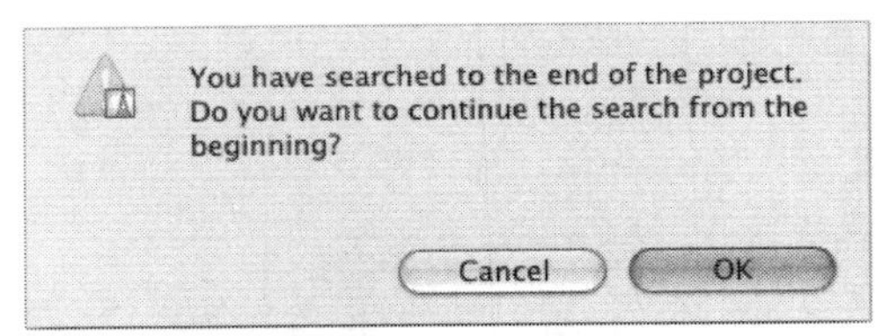

Figure 3.11 When After Effects has searched to the end of the project, a dialog box prompts you to continue the search from the beginning of the project or cancel the search.

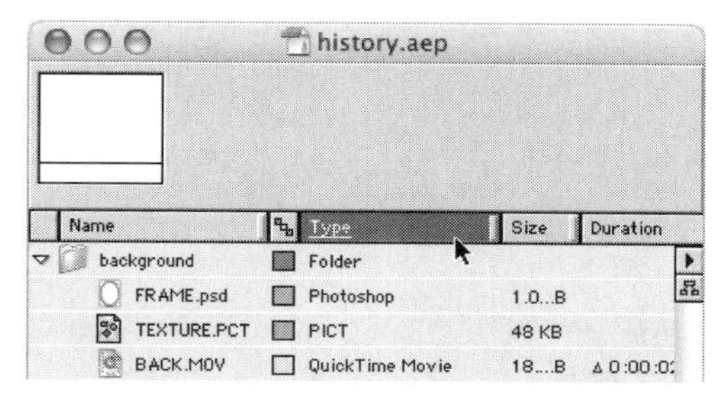

Figure 3.12 Click a heading panel to sort the items according to the information under the heading.

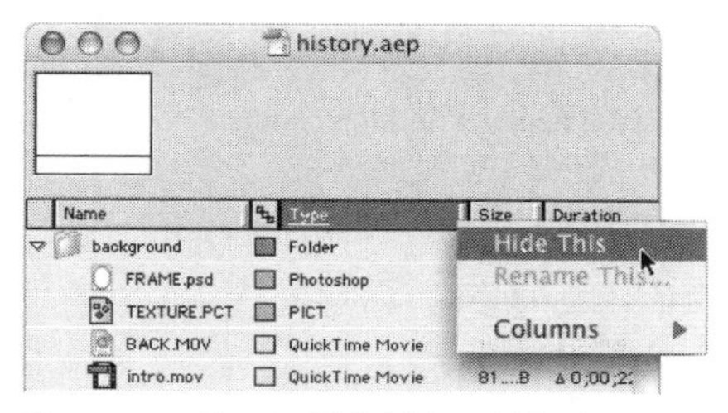

Figure 3.13 Choose Hide This to hide the selected heading panel.

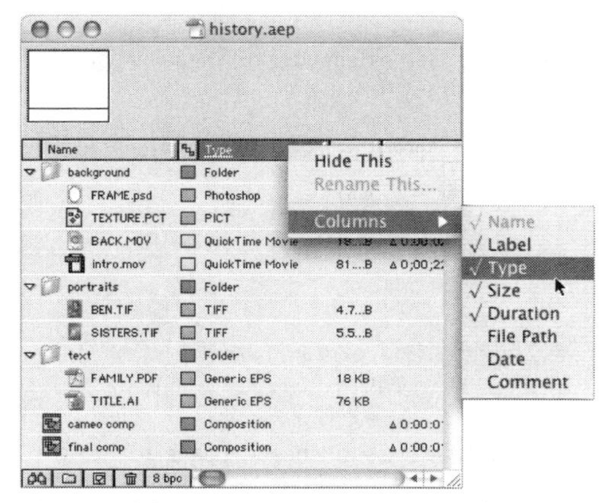

Figure 3.14 If you unselect a heading name (in this case, the Type column)...

Sorting Footage in the Project Window

By default, items in the Project window are sorted by name, but you can sort the list by an assortment of other criteria, such as file type, size, duration, and so on. You can hide the column headings you don't want to use and rearrange their order. You can even assign a custom heading.

To sort footage items in the Project window:

◆ In the Project window, click a heading panel to sort the footage items according to the name, label, type, size, duration, file path, date, or comment (**Figure 3.12**).

To hide or display a heading panel in the Project window:

1. In the Project window, Ctrl-click (Mac) or right-click (Windows) a heading panel.

   A contextual menu appears.

2. In the contextual menu, choose an option:

   ▲ To hide the selected heading panel, choose Hide This (**Figure 3.13**). (This choice isn't available for the Name heading panel.)

   ▲ To hide any heading panel, choose Columns > and a heading panel name to unselect it (**Figure 3.14**).

   ▲ To show a hidden heading panel, choose Columns > and a heading panel name to select it.

continues on next page

Depending on your choice, you can hide or display heading panels and the columns beneath them (**Figure 3.15**).

To resize or reorder headings in the Project window:

1. If necessary, resize the Project window and make sure it displays the headings you want to resize or rearrange.
2. In the Project window, *do either of the following:*
   - ▲ Drag the right edge of a heading panel to change the width of the heading and its column (**Figure 3.16**).
   - ▲ Drag the heading panel to the right or left to change the relative position of the heading columns (**Figures 3.17** and **3.18**).

To give the Comment heading panel a custom name:

1. If the Comment heading panel isn't visible, make it visible using the techniques described earlier.
2. In the Project window, Ctrl-click (Mac) or right-click (Windows) the Comment heading panel.

   A contextual menu appears.

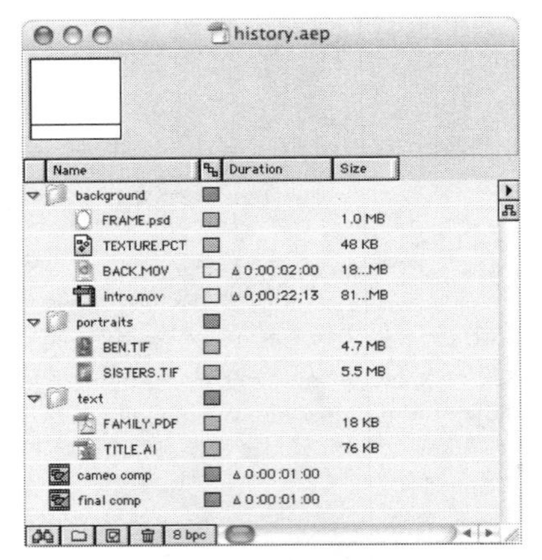

Figure 3.15 ...the heading and the column beneath it are hidden from view.

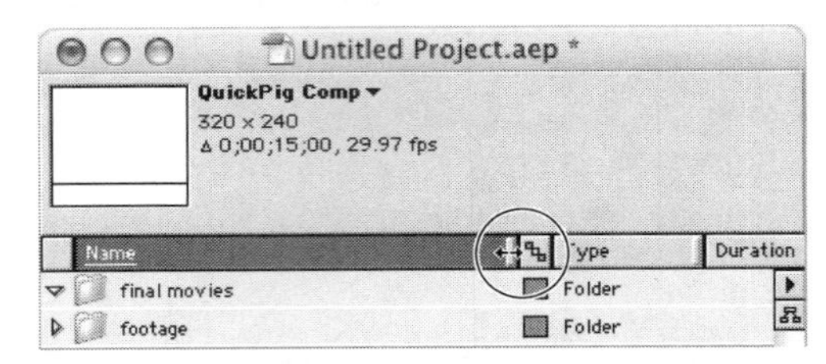

Figure 3.16 Drag the right edge of a heading panel to resize the width of the column.

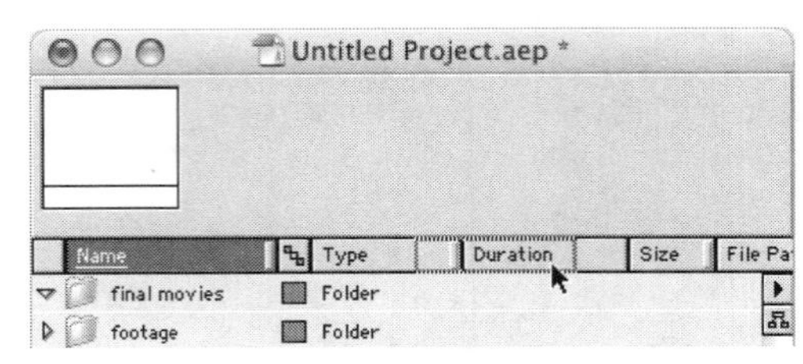

Figure 3.17 Drag the entire heading panel to the right or left...

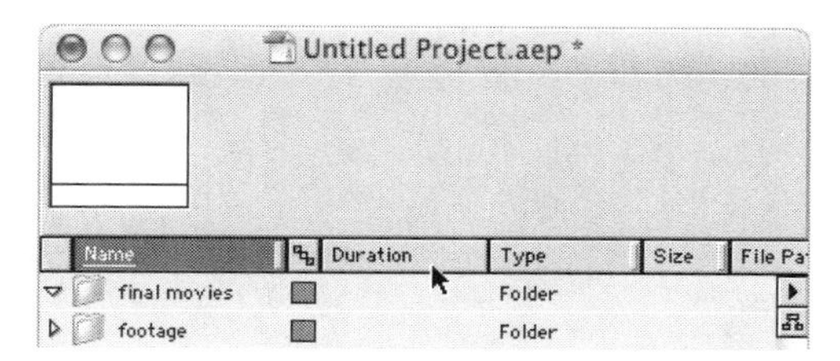

Figure 3.18 ...to change its relative position in the Project window.

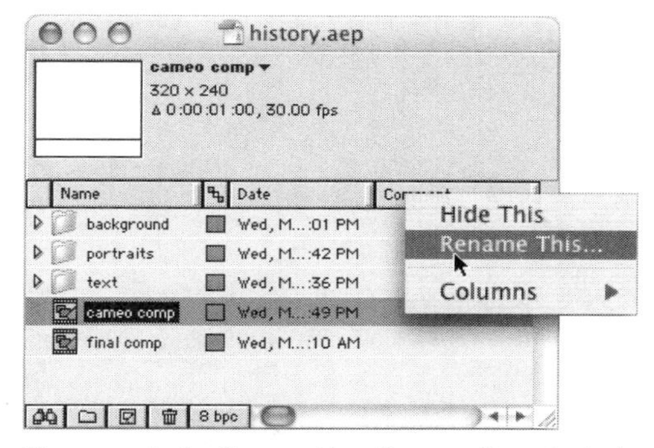

Figure 3.19 In the Comment heading panel's contextual menu, choose Rename This to give the heading a custom name.

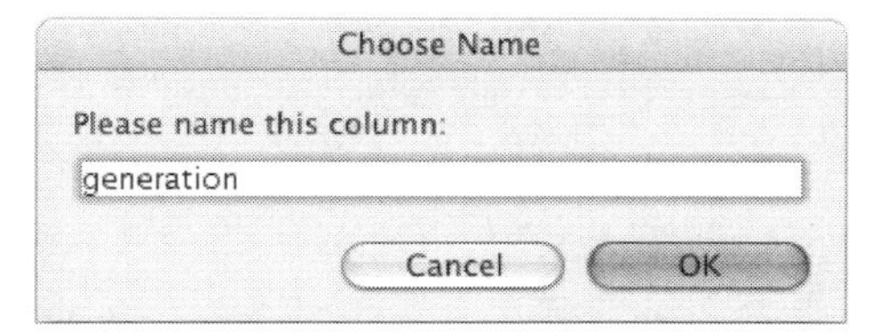

Figure 3.20. In the Choose Name dialog box, enter a custom name.

3. In the contextual menu, choose Rename This (**Figure 3.19**).

   The Choose Name dialog box appears.

4. In the Choose Name dialog box, enter a custom name (**Figure 3.20**).

5. Click OK to close the dialog box.

   The custom heading panel appears with the name you specified (**Figure 3.21**).

To enter information under the Comment or Custom heading:

1. If the Comment or Custom heading panel of the Project window isn't visible, make it visible using the techniques described above.

2. In the same row as an item in the Project window, click below the Comment or Custom heading.

   A text field and cursor appear.

3. Enter a comment for the corresponding footage item, and press Return (Mac) or Enter (Windows) (**Figure 3.22**).

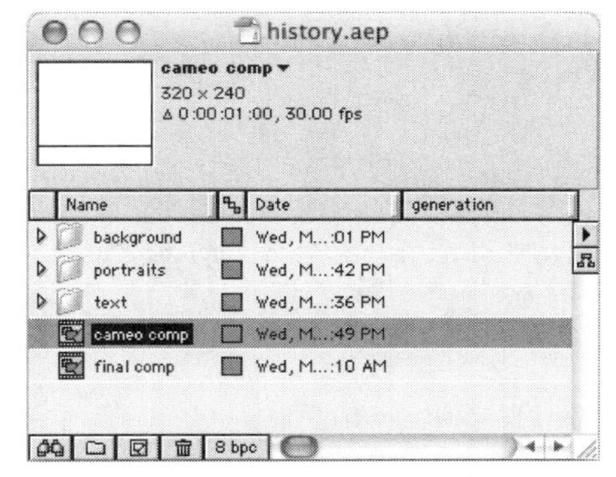

Figure 3.21 The Comment field uses the name you specify.

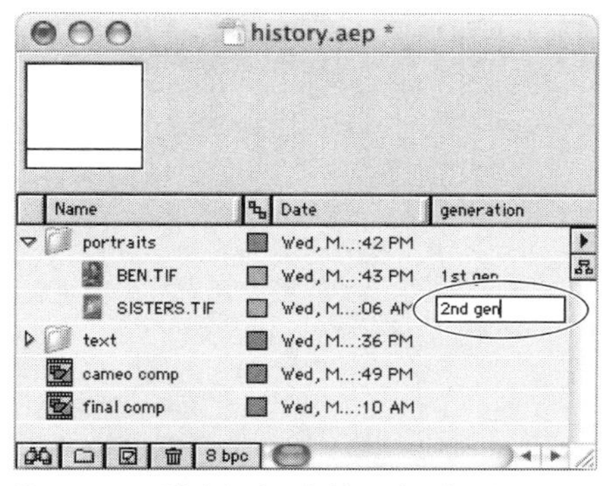

Figure 3.22 Click in the field under the Comment (or Custom) heading to enter information.

Using Labels

Color-coded labels can also help you identify and organize items in the Project window. By default, certain file types use a particular label color. However, you can also give individual items the label of your choice. The following sections deal with labels for items in the Project window. (Like items in the Project window, layers in the Timeline window also use the default label colors, or you can give individual layers the labels of your choice. For more about layers, see Chapter 5, "Layer Basics.")

To change the default label colors:

1. Choose After Effects > Preferences > Label Defaults (Mac) or Edit > Preferences > Label Defaults (Windows) (**Figure 3.23**).

   The Label panel of the Preferences dialog box appears (**Figure 3.24**).

Figure 3.23 Choose After Effects > Preferences > Label Defaults (Mac) or Edit > Preferences > Label Defaults (Windows).

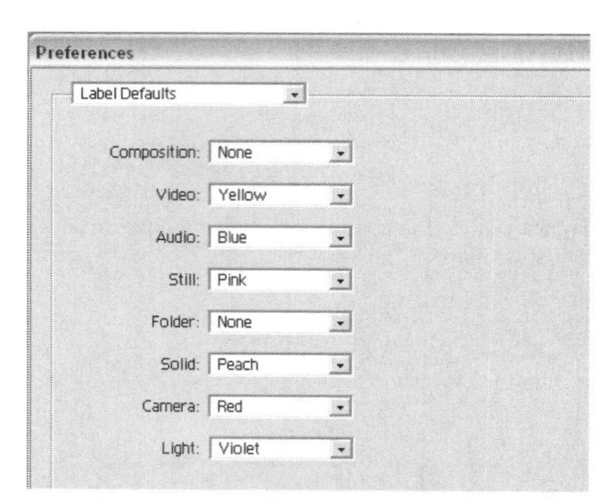

Figure 3.24 The Label panel of the Preferences dialog box allows you to choose label options.

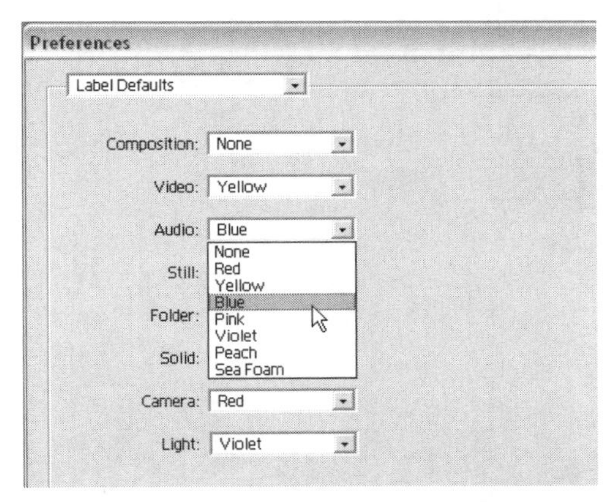

Figure 3.25 For each type of footage, choose a default color from the pull-down menu.

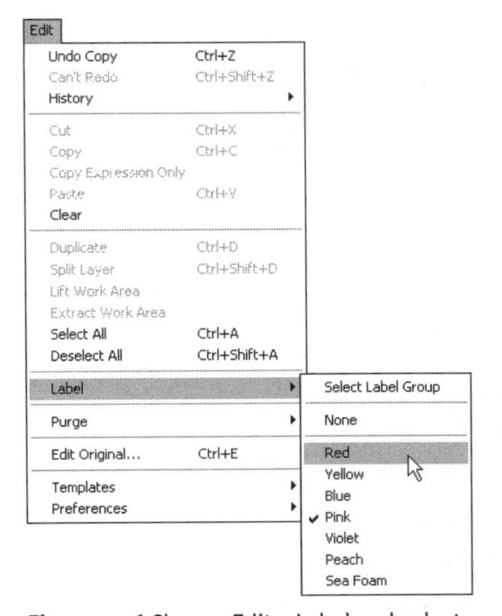

Figure 3.26 Choose Edit > Label and select a color for the selected item or layer.

2. In the Label Defaults section of the Preferences dialog box, choose a color from the pull-down menu for each type of footage (**Figure 3.25**).

   Items in the Project window and layers in the Timeline window use the color label you specified for each file type. However, if you specified a custom label color for an item or a layer, it will retain that custom color, despite changes to the default file label colors.

To change the label color for an item or layer:

1. Select an item in the Project window or select a layer in the Timeline window.
2. Choose Edit > Label > and select a label color from the list (**Figure 3.26**).

   The selected item or layer uses the color you specified.

✔ Tip

- By choosing Edit > Preferences > Label Colors, you can use the color picker or eyedropper to assign each label any color you want. And you can name the color you pick—so instead of plain "red" and "green" labels, you can have "crimson" and "clover."

Organizing Footage in Folders

As you learned in Chapter 2, "Importing Footage into a Project," footage can be imported into the Project window as items contained in a folder. Of course, you can also create your own folders to organize items in the project. Folders look and work much like they do on your operating system (particularly on the Mac's desktop). However, unlike on the desktop or explorer (or in some programs) the folder can't open in its own window.

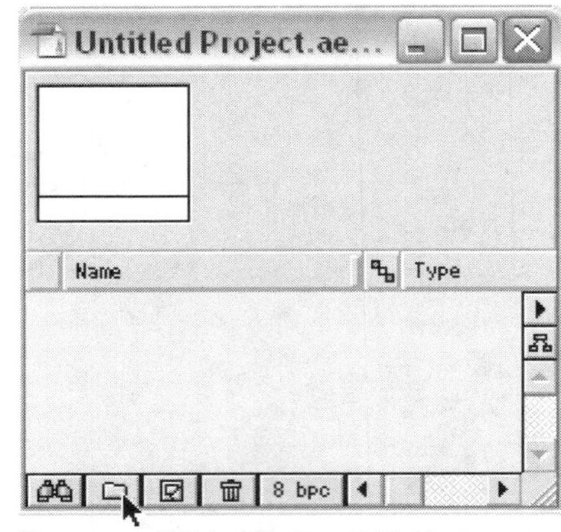

Figure 3.27 Clicking the New Folder button at the bottom of the Project window is the easiest way to create a new folder.

To create a folder in the Project window:

1. In the Project window, *do one of the following:*
   - ▲ Choose File > New > New Folder.
   - ▲ Click the folder icon at the bottom of a project window (**Figure 3.27**).

   An untitled folder appears in the Project window.
2. Press Return (Mac) or Enter (Windows) to highlight the name of the folder (**Figure 3.28**).
3. Type a name for the custom heading (**Figure 3.29**).
4. Press Return (Mac) or Enter (Windows) to apply the name to the folder.

   The folder is sorted with other items according to the currently selected column heading.

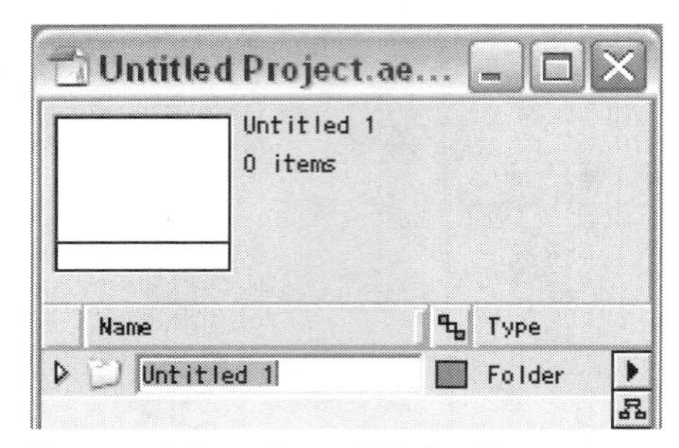

Figure 3.28 Press Return (Mac) or Enter (Windows) to highlight the name of the new folder...

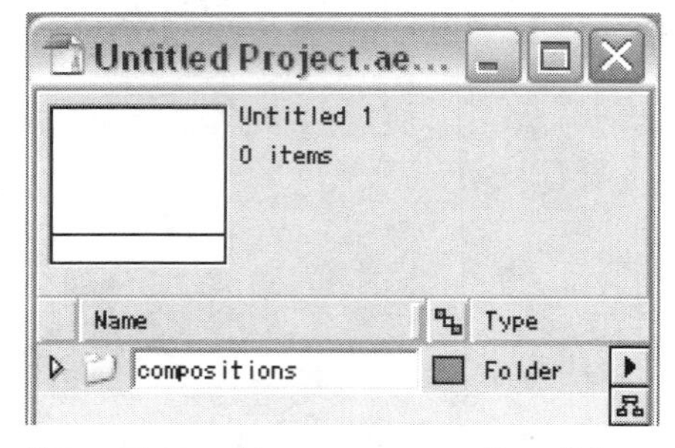

Figure 3.29 ...and type a new name. Press Return (Mac) or Enter (Windows) to apply the name.

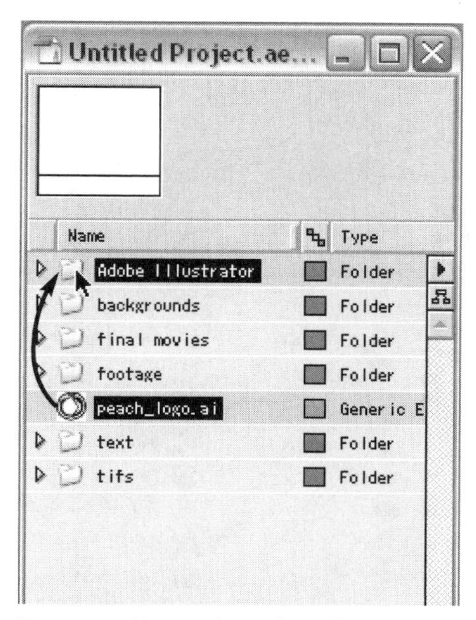

Figure 3.30. You can drag selected items directly into a folder.

To organize footage items in folders:

In the Project window, *do one of the following:*

- To move items into a folder, select and drag items into a folder (**Figure 3.30**).
- To move items out of a folder, select and drag items from a folder to the gray area at the top of the Project window (**Figure 3.31**).

To toggle a folder open and closed:

In the Project window, *do one of the following:*

- Click the triangle next to the folder.
- Double-click the folder.

  When a folder opens, the triangle spins clockwise, and the items contained in the folder appear indented beneath the folder (**Figure 3.32**). When a folder closes, the triangle spins counterclockwise, and the contents of the folder are concealed. You can't open a folder in a separate window.

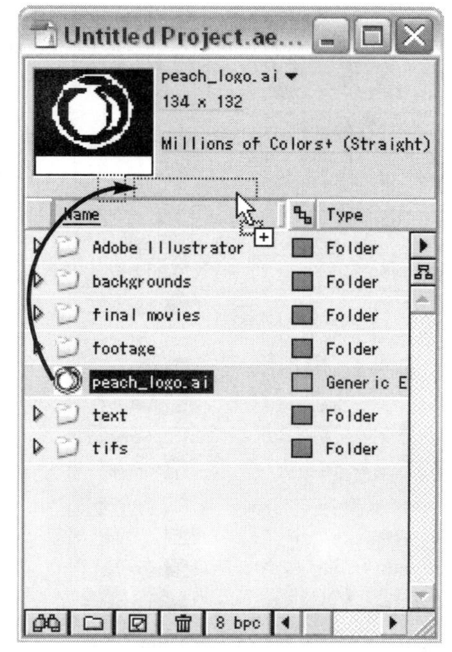

Figure 3.31 To move items out of a folder, drag them from the folder to the top of the Project window.

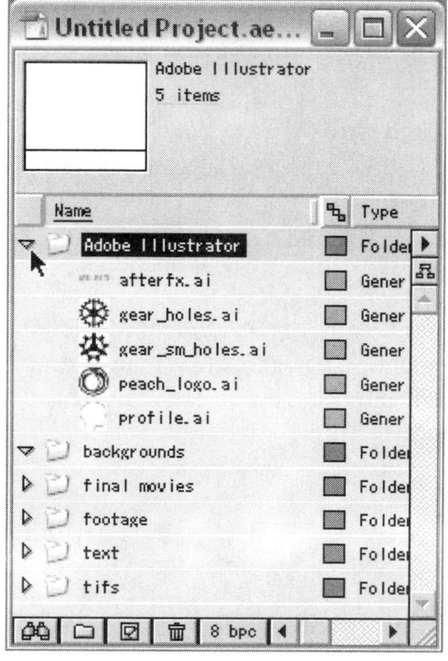

Figure 3.32 Double-click a folder to reveal the items it contains.

Renaming and Removing Items

You can't rename a footage item in the Project window or even give it a temporary alias (as you can in Adobe Premiere Pro, for example). Don't worry: You can rename it when it becomes a layer in a composition. (In later chapters, you'll see how this naming scheme allows you to give unique names to each layer while still tracing their lineage back to a single footage file.) You can, of course, name folders and compositions in the Project window.

Just as important as organizing the elements you need is disposing of the elements you don't need. You can remove individual items, or have After Effects automatically discard the items that haven't been used in a composition.

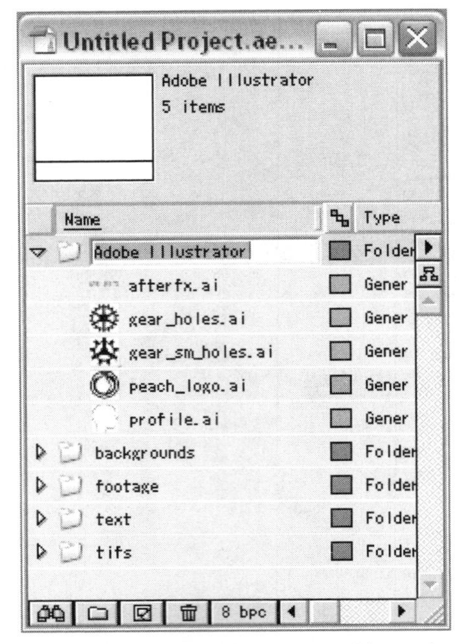

Figure 3.33 Select a folder or composition and press Return (Mac) or Enter (Windows) to highlight its name...

To rename folders or compositions in the Project window:

1. In the Project window, select a folder or composition.
2. Press Return (Mac) or Enter (Windows).
   The name of the item appears highlighted (**Figure 3.33**).
3. Enter a name for the folder or composition (**Figure 3.34**).
4. Press Return (Mac) or Enter (Windows).
   The new name of the item is no longer highlighted and becomes the current name.

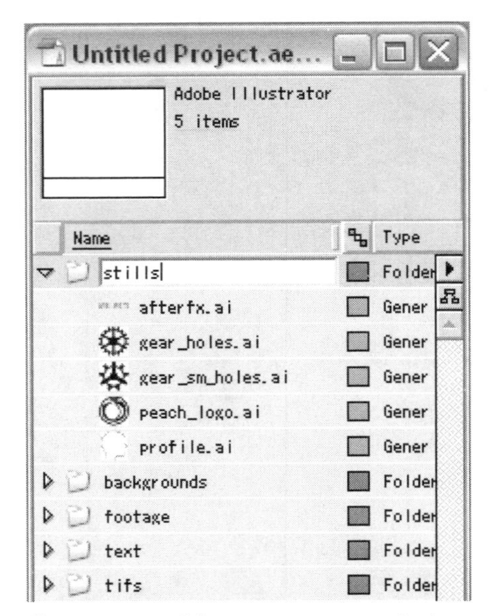

Figure 3.34 ...and then type a new name in the text box. Press Return (Mac) or Enter (Windows) again to apply the new name.

Figure 3.35 Click the Trash button at the bottom of the Project window to delete selected items.

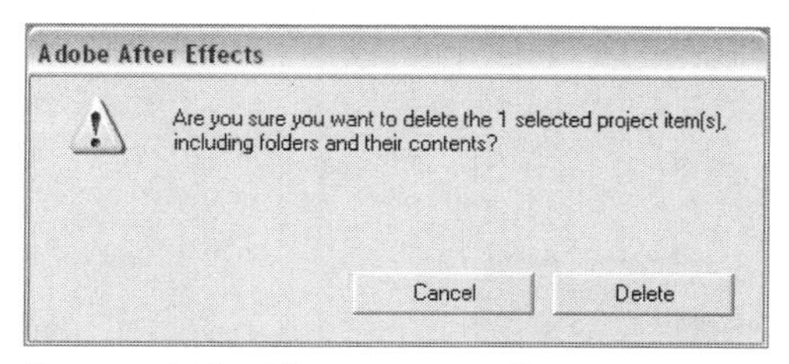

Figure 3.36 After Effects warns you if you attempt to delete an item that is in use.

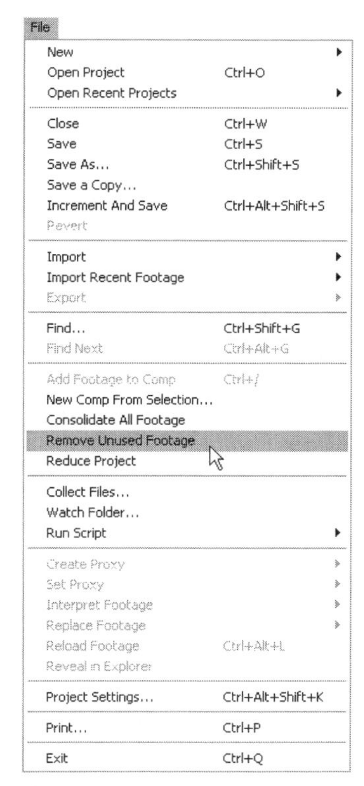

Figure 3.37 Choose File > Remove Unused Footage to remove items that aren't used in a composition.

To remove items from the project:

1. In the Project window, select one or more items.
2. *Do one of the following:*
   - ▲ Press Delete.
   - ▲ Click the Trash button at the bottom of the Project window (**Figure 3.35**).
   - ▲ Drag the items to the Trash button at the bottom of the Project window.

   If any of the items are compositions or are being used in a composition, After Effects asks you to confirm that you want to delete the items (**Figure 3.36**).
3. If After Effects prompts you to confirm your choice, click Delete to remove the footage from the project or Cancel to cancel the command and retain the footage in the project.

   The footage is removed from the project and all compositions in the project.

To remove unused footage from the project:

- ◆ Choose File > Remove Unused Footage (**Figure 3.37**).

  All footage items that aren't currently used in a composition are removed from the project.

To remove duplicate footage from the project:

◆ Choose File > Consolidate All Footage (**Figure 3.38**).

All duplicate footage items are removed from the project.

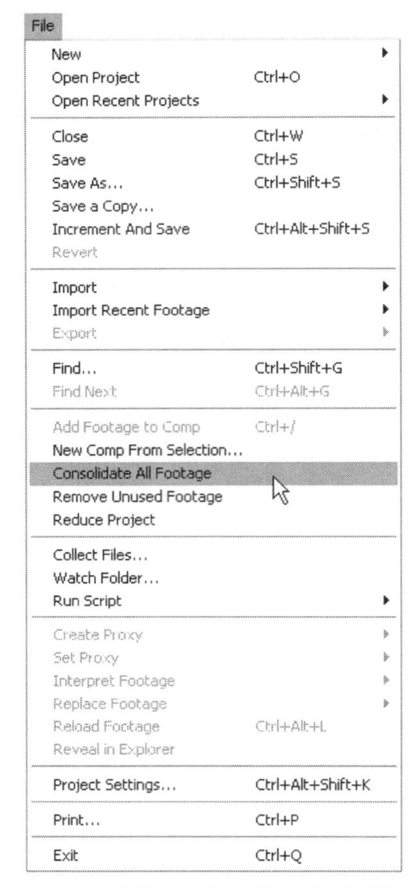

Figure 3.38 Choose File > Consolidate All Footage to remove duplicate items from the Project window.

✔ Tips

- As you'll see in Chapter 4, you can create layer solids that appear as footage items in the Project window. In the Project window, you can rename solids as you would a folder or composition.
- Although you may not be ready to remove unused and duplicate footage from the Project window yet, it's a good idea to do some housekeeping as your project nears completion. After all, if the project were a prizewinning recipe, would you list ingredients you never used?
- After Effects includes a Collect Files command that you can use to copy all of a project's requisite files into a single location, along with a report describing everything you'll need to render the project (such as fonts and effects). The Collect Files command is especially useful when you want to archive a project or move it to a different workstation.

Cueing Motion Footage

Motion footage appears in the Footage, Composition, and Layer windows with a time ruler, current time marker, and current time display. You can use the controls to view a specific frame or to play back the footage without sound.

To view a frame of motion footage by dragging:

- ◆ In the Footage window, drag the Current time marker to the frame you want to view (**Figure 3.61**).

  The Footage window displays the image at the current frame and the frame number.

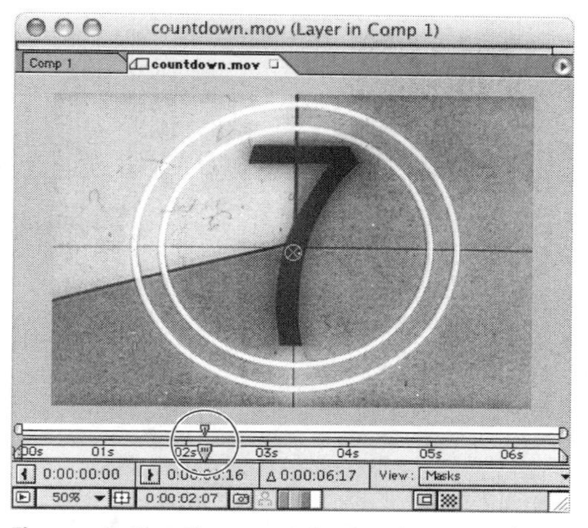

Figure 3.61 Drag the current time marker to cue the footage to a particular frame.

To cue a frame of motion footage numerically:

1. In the Footage window, click the current time display (**Figure 3.62**).

   The Go To Time dialog box opens.

2. In the Go To Time dialog box, enter a time (**Figure 3.63**).

3. Click OK.

   The current time display and the image in the Footage window show the frame you specified.

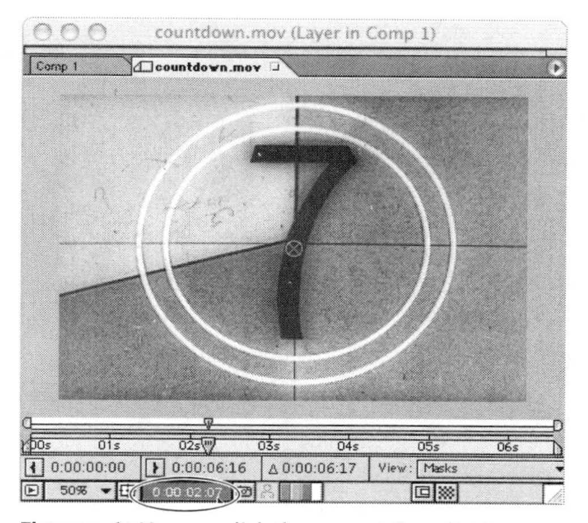

Figure 3.62 You can click the current time display...

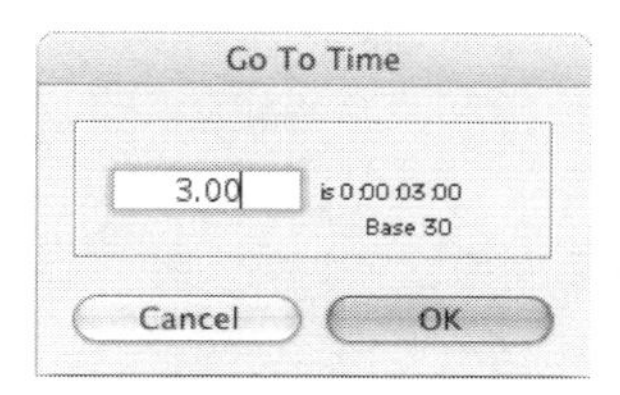

Figure 3.63 ...and enter a frame number in the Go To Time dialog box.

To play motion footage:

- ◆ Make sure the Footage, Composition, or Layer window is active. Press the spacebar to start and stop playback.

✔ Tips

- ■ The spacebar provides the easiest way to start and stop playback. The Time Controls palette provides more control (**Figure 3.64**).
- ■ In the Footage window, the time ruler shows the length of the source file; in the Composition and Layer windows, the time ruler corresponds to the length of the composition.

Figure 3.64 The Time Controls provide a complete set of playback options.

Magnification and Safe Zones

Sometimes, you'll want to magnify your footage view so that you can closely examine a detail of the image. Other times, you'll want to reduce magnification because viewing footage at 100 percent scale takes up too much screen space. After Effects lets you change the magnification ratio to suit your needs. However, keep in mind that this is for viewing purposes only: The actual scale of the footage doesn't change. You may be surprised to discover that no matter how much you magnify the image in the Footage window, scroll bars don't appear. To view different parts of a magnified image, use the Hand tool instead.

To change the magnification of the Footage or Composition window:

- In the Footage window, press and hold the Magnification Ratio pop-up menu to choose a magnification (**Figure 3.65**).

  When you release the mouse button, the Footage window uses the magnification ratio you selected (**Figure 3.66**).

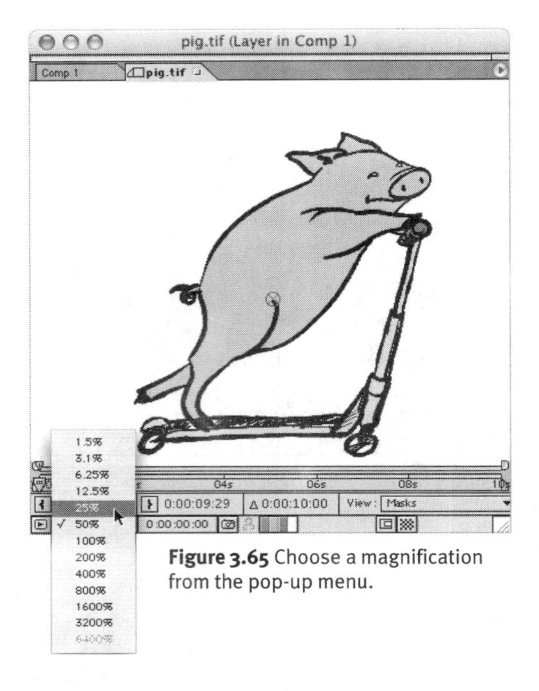

Figure 3.65 Choose a magnification from the pop-up menu.

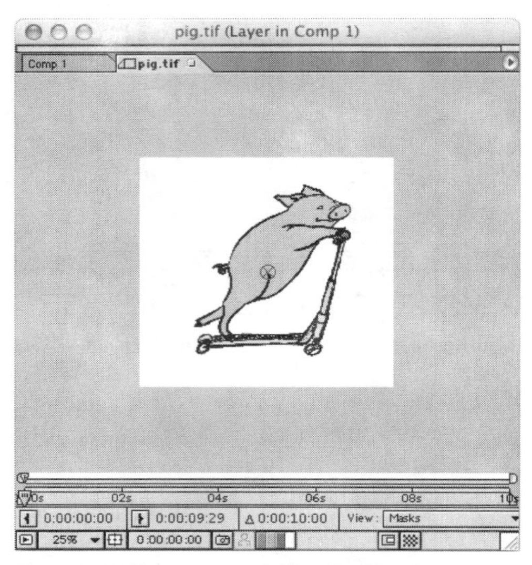

Figure 3.66 The Footage window displays the image at the magnification you specified.

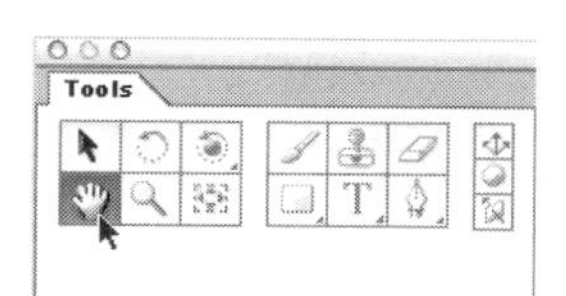

Figure 3.67 In the Tools palette, select the Hand tool...

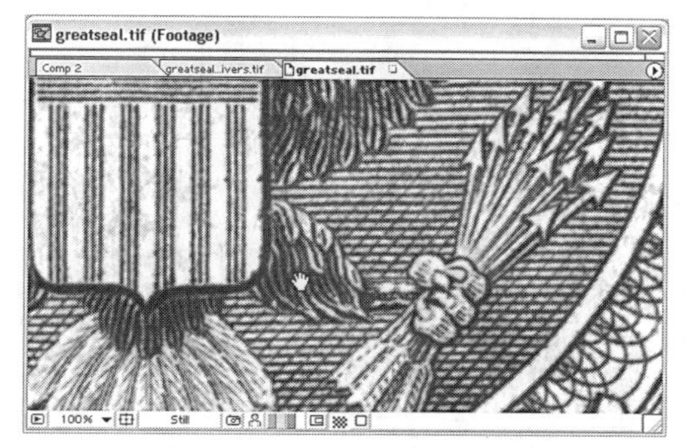

Figure 3.68 ...or position the Selection tool over the image and press the spacebar to toggle it to the Hand tool.

Figure 3.69 Drag the image with the Hand tool to move other areas into view.

To change the visible area of a magnified image in the Footage or Composition window:

1. Select the Hand tool by doing *either of the following:*
   - In the Tools palette, click the Hand tool (**Figure 3.67**).
   - With the Selection tool active (the default tool), position the mouse pointer over the image in the Footage or Composition window and press the spacebar (**Figure 3.68**).

   The mouse changes to the hand icon.
2. Drag the hand to change the visible area of the image (**Figure 3.69**).

Video-Safe Zones and Grids

You can superimpose a grid or video-safe zones over an image to better judge its placement. Obviously, these simple visual guides aren't included in the final output. In addition, because video-safe zones indicate the viewable area of standard video monitors, you should display safe zones for images that match television's 4:3 aspect ratio. For more about the safe zones, see the sidebar "Better Safe Than Sorry: Video Title- and Action-Safe Zones."

To show video-safe zones and grids:

In the Footage window, *do any of the following:*

- To view title- and action-safe zones, click the Title-Action Safe button (**Figures 3.70** and **3.71**).
- To view a proportional grid, Option-click (Mac) or Alt-click (Windows) the Title-Action Safe button (**Figure 3.72**).
- To view a standard grid, Command-click (Mac) or Ctrl-click (Windows) the Title-Action Safe button (**Figure 3.73**).

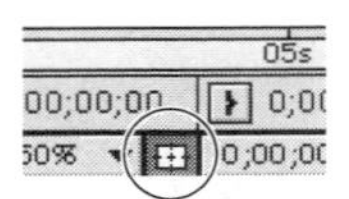

Figure 3.70 Use the Title-Action Safe button to see video-safe zones or grids.

Figure 3.71 Click the Title-Action Safe button to view video-safe zones.

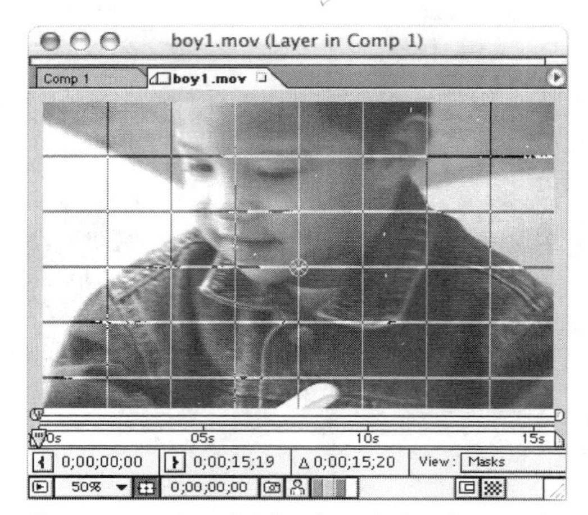

Figure 3.72 Option-click (Mac) or Alt-click (Windows) the Title-Action Safe button to view a proportional grid...

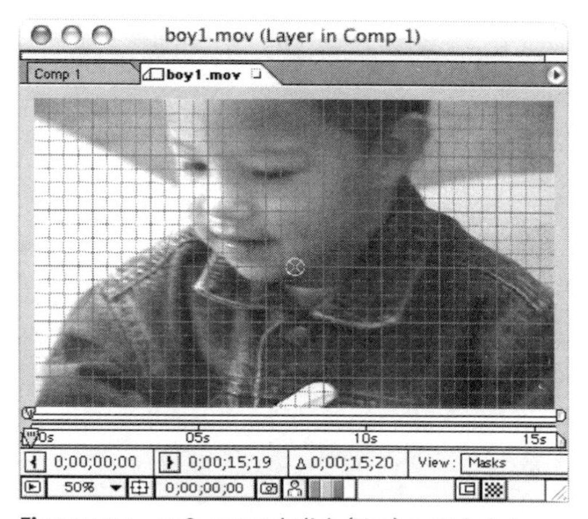

Figure 3.73 ...or Command-click (Mac) or Ctrl-click (Windows) the Title-Action Safe button to view a standard grid.

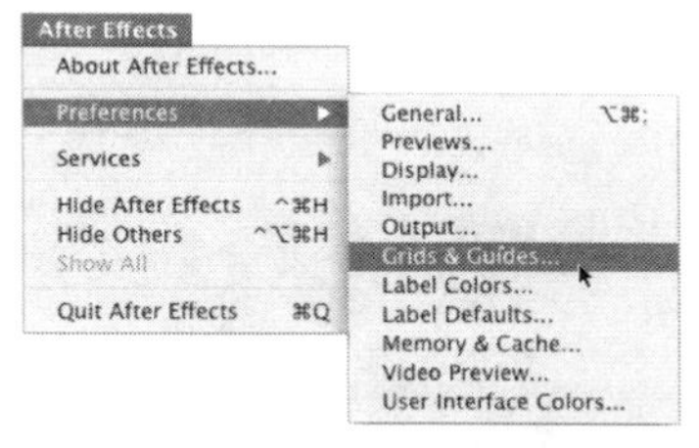

Figure 3.74 Choose After Effects > Preferences > Grids & Guides (Mac) or Edit > Preferences > Grids & Guides (Windows).

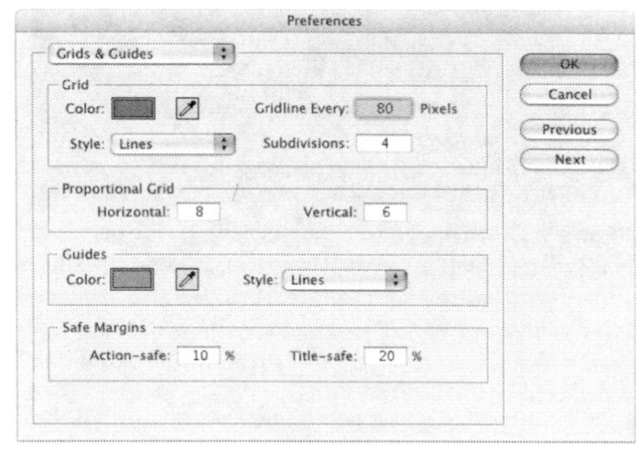

Figure 3.75 The Grids & Guides panel of the Preferences dialog box appears.

You can display any combination of zones and guides at the same time.

To set the default safe-zone areas:

1. Choose After Effects > Preferences > Grids & Guides (Mac) or Edit > Preferences > Grids & Guides (Windows) (**Figure 3.74**).

   The Grids & Guides panel of the Preferences dialog box appears (**Figure 3.75**).

2. In the Safe Margins area of the Preferences dialog box, enter a percentage value for Action-Safe Margin (10 percent is standard for video).

3. In the Safe Margins area of the Preferences dialog box, enter a percentage value for the Title-Safe Margin (20 percent is standard for video) (**Figure 3.76**).

4. Click OK to close the Preferences dialog box.

Figure 3.76 In the Safe Margins area of the Preferences dialog box, enter the default safe margins.

Better Safe than Sorry: Video Title- and Action-Safe Zones

Computer monitors display images from edge to edge. Television monitors, on the other hand, *overscan* images, or crop the outer edges. What's more, the amount of overscan differs from one television monitor to another.

Because of overscan, only the inner 90 percent of the full screen is considered *action safe*. That is, you should restrict any important onscreen actions to this area. The inner 80 percent of the image is known as *title safe*. Because you usually can't afford to lose any part of a title, you need a greater margin of error. If you're going to output your project as full-screen video, you'll need to respect the title-safe zone or suffer the consequences (**Figures 3.77** and **3.78**).

Even if you only plan to show your final movie on a computer screen, consider using the title-safe zones anyway. If you, your client, or your boss later decide to repurpose your creation for display on full-screen video, you'll be safe.

Of course, full-screen video also has a 4:3 aspect ratio (typically). In After Effects, safe-zone guides will mark the inner 80 and 90 percent of any window, even if the image doesn't match television's 4:3 aspect ratio. Because their only purpose is to indicate the overscanned areas of a standard video monitor, the safe-zone guides are relevant only in windows that correspond with television's 4:3 aspect ratio.

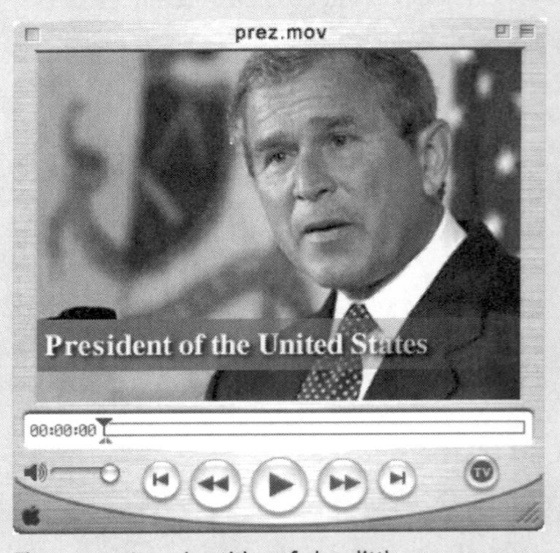

Figure 3.77 Ignoring title safe has little consequence for images displayed less than full screen or on computer monitors.

Figure 3.78 However, the same image presented as full-screen video may result in unwanted editing. In this case, the President gets a demotion to a mere "resident," without a proper election.

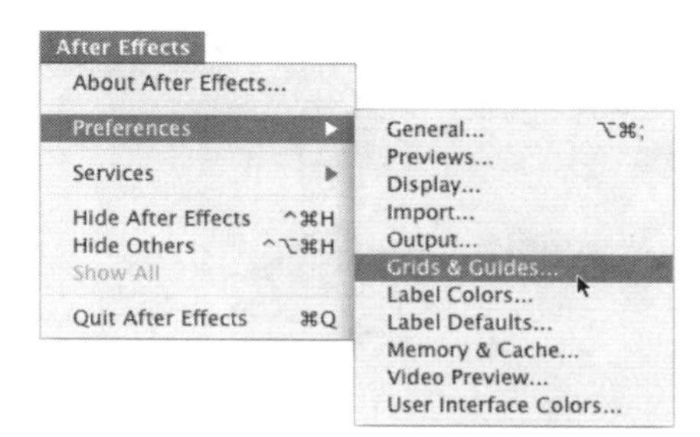

Figure 3.79 Choose After Effects > Preferences > Grids & Guides (Mac) or Edit > Preferences > Grids & Guides (Windows).

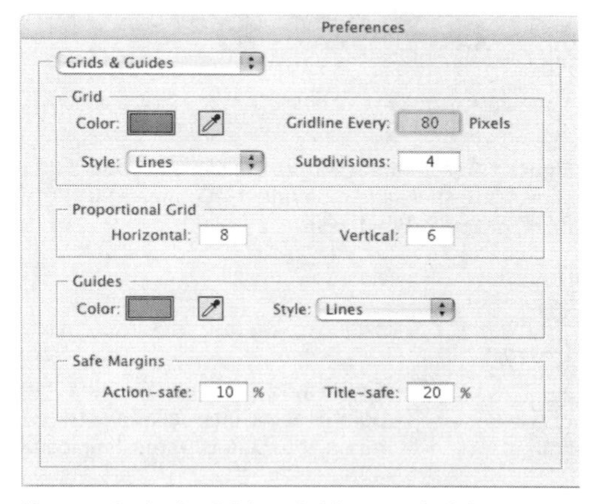

Figure 3.80 In the Grids & Guides panel of the Preferences dialog box, choose default settings.

To customize the standard grid display:

1. Choose After Effects > Preferences > Grids & Guides (Mac) or Edit > Preferences > Grids & Guides (Windows) (**Figure 3.79**).

   The Grids & Guides panel of the Preferences dialog box appears (**Figure 3.80**).

2. In the Grid section of the Preferences dialog box, *do any of the following:*

   Color—Use the color picker or eyedropper to choose a color for gridlines.

   Style—Choose whether you want the grid to appear as lines, dashed lines, or dotted lines.

   Gridline Every—Choose the spacing for the grid, in pixels.

   Subdivisions—Choose how many times to subdivide each cell of the grid.

3. In the Proportional Grid section of the Preferences dialog box, enter values to set the horizontal and vertical size of the proportional grid.

4. Click OK to close the Preferences dialog box.

Rulers and Guides

Like Adobe Photoshop and Illustrator, After Effects lets you view rulers as well as set guides to help you arrange and align images. As usual, you can change the zero point of the rulers and toggle the rulers and guides on and off.

To show or hide rulers:

With a Footage or Composition window active, *do one of the following:*

- To view rulers, choose View > Show Rulers.
- To hide rulers, choose View > Hide Rulers.
- Press Command-R (Mac) or Ctrl-R (Windows) to toggle the rulers on and off (**Figure 3.81**).

Figure 3.81 After Effects uses the same keyboard shortcut to show and hide rulers—Command-R (Mac) or Ctrl-R (Windows).

To set the zero point of rulers:

1. If the rulers aren't visible, make them visible using one of the techniques described in the previous task.
2. Position the pointer at the crosshair at the intersection of the rulers in the upper-left corner of the Footage, Composition, or Layer window.

   The pointer becomes a crosshair (**Figure 3.82**).
3. Drag the crosshair into the image area.

   Horizontal and vertical lines indicate the position of the mouse (**Figure 3.83**).
4. Release the mouse to set the zero point (**Figure 3.84**).

   The rulers use the zero point you selected.

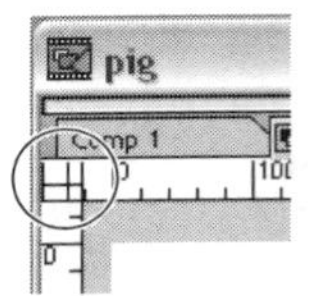

Figure 3.82 When you position the pointer at the intersection of the rulers, it becomes a crosshair icon.

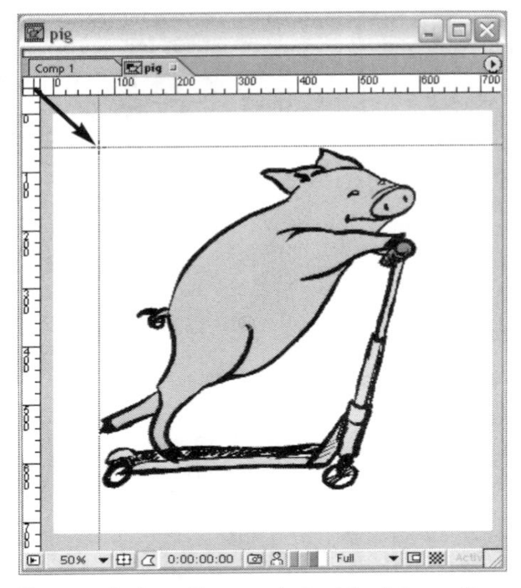

Figure 3.83 Drag the crosshair at the intersection of the rulers into the image area...

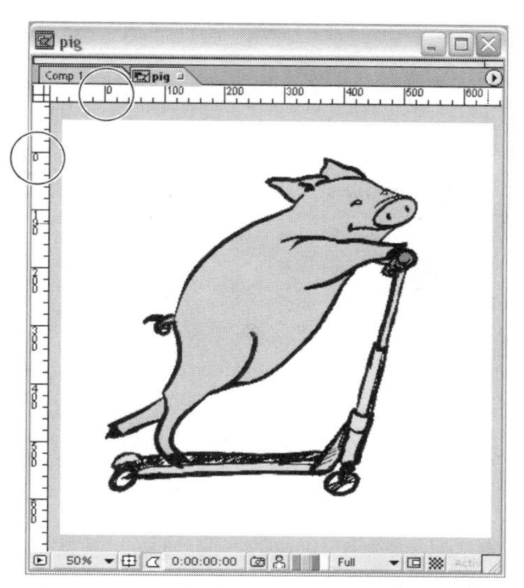

Figure 3.84 ...and release to set the zero point of the rulers.

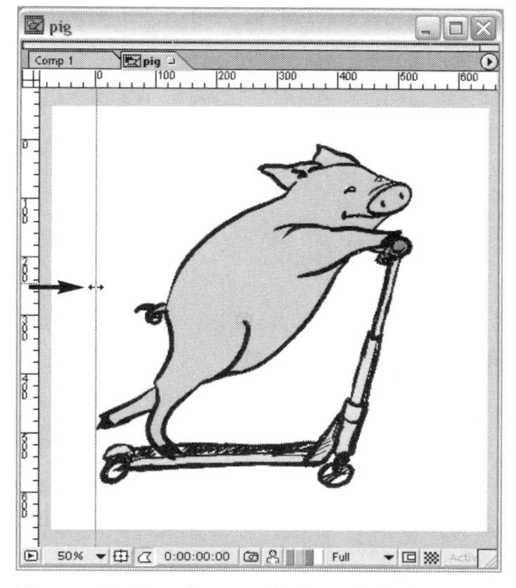

Figure 3.85 Drag from a ruler into the image area to add a guide.

To reset the zero point of the rulers:

- Double-click the crosshair at the intersection of the horizontal and vertical rulers.

  The rulers' zero point is reset to the upper-left corner of the image.

✔ Tips

- As you've probably guessed, After Effects includes a Snap to Guides feature. However, it won't do you much good in the Footage window, so that feature is covered along with the Composition window in the next chapter.
- Need to know the exact ruler coordinates of the mouse pointer? Use the Info palette.

To set guides:

1. If the rulers aren't visible, make them visible by pressing Command-R (Mac) or Ctrl-R (Windows).
2. Position the pointer inside the horizontal or vertical ruler.

   The pointer changes into a Move Guide icon ✚✚.
3. Drag into the image area (**Figure 3.85**).

   A line indicates the position of the new guide.
4. Release the mouse to set the guide.

To reposition or remove a guide:

1. Make sure the guides are visible and unlocked (see the following sections).

   You can't move a guide if guides are locked.

2. Position the pointer over a guide.

   The pointer changes into a Move Guide icon ✢.

3. *Do one of the following:*

   ▲ To reposition the guide, drag it to a new position.

   ▲ To remove the guide, drag it off the image area.

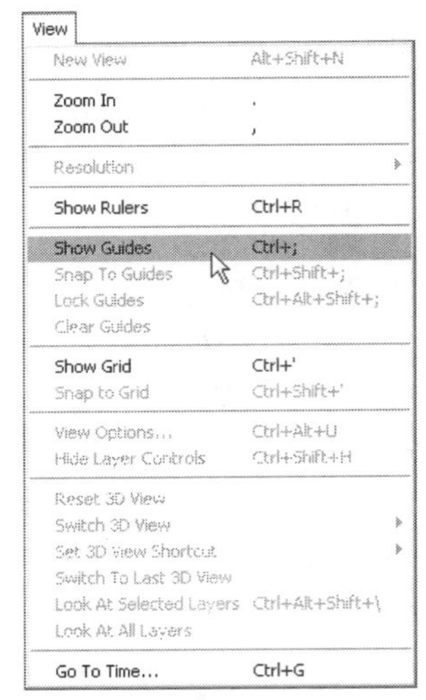

Figure 3.86 You can choose View > Show Guides or View > Hide Guides, but it's worth learning the keyboard shortcut: Command-; (Mac) or Ctrl-; (Windows). Photoshop uses the same shortcut.

To show and hide guides:

◆ To show hidden guides, choose View > Show Guides (**Figure 3.86**).

◆ To hide visible guides, choose View > Hide Guides.

◆ To toggle guides on or off, press Command-; (Mac) or Ctrl-; (Windows).

To lock and unlock guides:

◆ To lock guides, choose View > Lock Guides (**Figure 3.87**).

◆ To unlock guides, choose View > Unlock Guides.

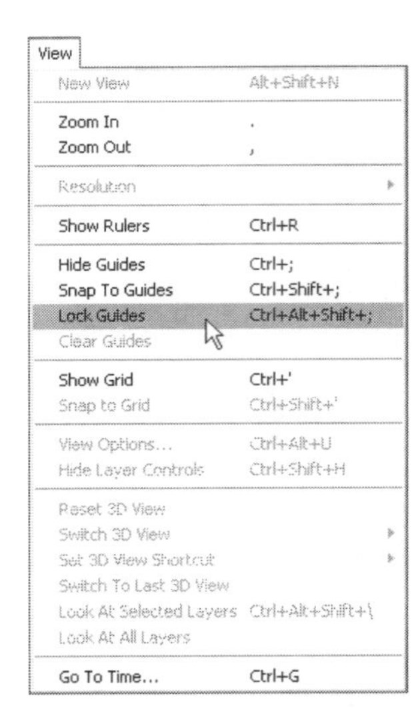

Figure 3.87 Choose View > Lock Guides to prevent guides from being moved unintentionally. To unlock the guides, Choose View > Unlock Guides.

Figure 3.88 Choose After Effects > Preferences > Grids & Guides (Mac) or Edit > Preferences > Grids & Guides (Windows).

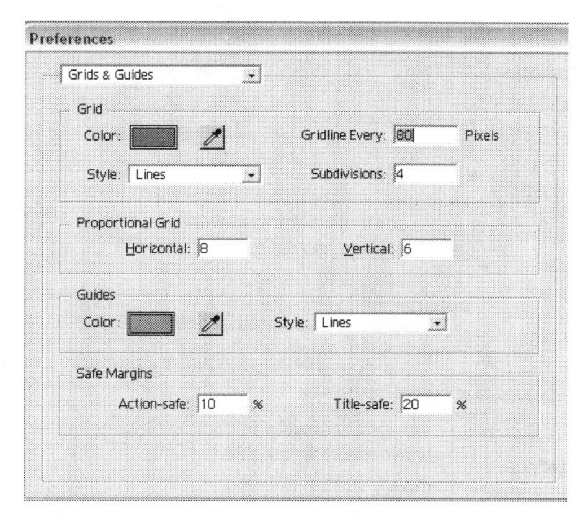

Figure 3.89 The Grids & Guides panel of the Preferences dialog box appears.

To customize the default guide options:

1. Choose After Effects > Preferences > Grids & Guides (Mac) or Edit > Preferences > Grids & Guides (Windows) (**Figure 3.88**).

   The Grids & Guides panel of the Preferences dialog box appears (**Figure 3.89**).

2. In the Guides section of the Preferences dialog box, *do any of the following* (**Figure 3.90**):

   Color—Use the color picker or eyedropper to choose a color for the guidelines.

   Style—Choose whether you want the grid to appear as lines or dashed lines.

3. Click OK to close the Preferences dialog box.

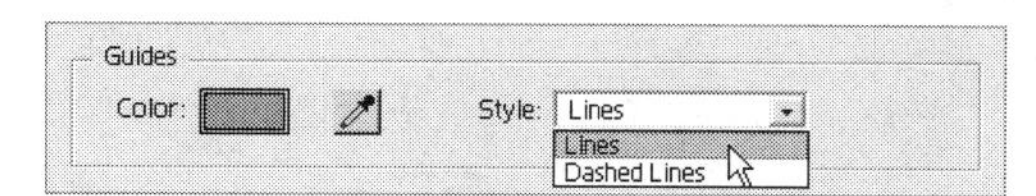

Figure 3.90 In the Guides section of the Preferences dialog box, choose a color and a line style.

Snapshots

As you work, you'll often need to closely compare different frames. In After Effects, you can take a snapshot of a frame to store for later viewing. Then, with the click of a button, you can temporarily replace the current image in a Footage, Composition, or Layer window with the snapshot image. The snapshot doesn't really replace anything; it's just used for quick reference—like holding a shirt up to yourself in a mirror to compare it with the one you're wearing. Toggling between the current frame and the snapshot makes it easier to see the differences.

Whereas previous versions of After Effects only allowed you to take a single snapshot at a time, you can now take and view as many as four separate snapshots.

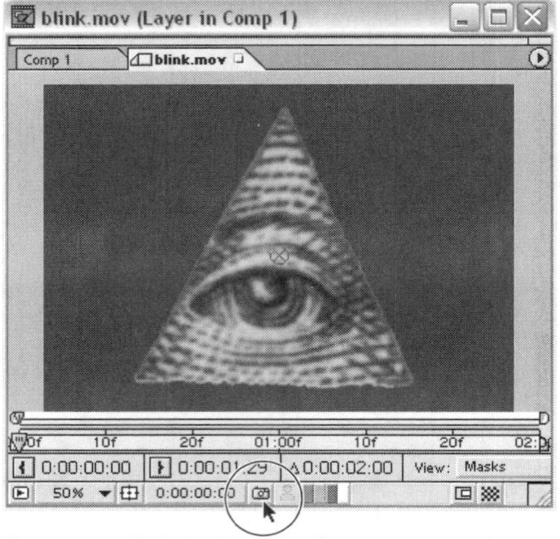

Figure 3.91 Click the Snapshot button to store the current image as a snapshot.

To take a snapshot:

1. If necessary, cue the footage to the frame you want to use as a reference snapshot.
2. Click the Snapshot button (**Figure 3.91**), or press Shift-F5.

   The current frame becomes the snapshot, and the Show Last Snapshot button becomes available (**Figure 3.92**).

Figure 3.92 The current frame becomes the snapshot, and the Show Last Snapshot button becomes available.

Figure 3.93 Press and hold the Show Last Snapshot button to replace the current image temporarily with the snapshot.

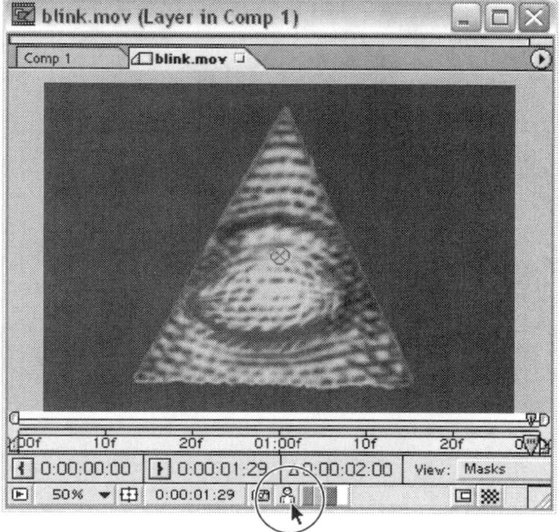

Figure 3.94 Release the Show Last Snapshot button to see the current frame again.

To view the most recent snapshot:

1. If necessary, cue the footage to the frame you want to compare to the snapshot.
2. Click and hold the Show Last Snapshot button, or press F5.

   As long as you hold down the mouse, the window displays the snapshot (**Figure 3.93**); when you release the mouse, the window displays the current frame (**Figure 3.94**).

To take and view multiple snapshots:

1. In a Footage, Layer, or Composition window, cue the footage to the frame you want to use as a reference snapshot.
2. To store as many as four separate snapshots, press Shift-F5, Shift-F6, Shift-F7, or Shift-F8—each of which stores a single snapshot.

   The frame is stored as a snapshot.
3. To view a stored snapshot, press F5, F6, F7, or F8.

   The snapshot stored using the corresponding function key is displayed in the window.

To purge a snapshot:

- Press Command-Shift (Mac) or Ctrl-Shift (Windows) and press the function key that corresponds to the snapshot you want to erase (F5, F6, F7, or F8).

  The snapshot is purged from memory.

✔ Tips

- If a window uses a different aspect ratio than that of the snapshot, the snapshot will be resized to fit into the window.
- Snapshots are stored in memory. If After Effects requires the memory that is used by a snapshot, it will discard the snapshot.

Channels

The Footage, Composition, and Layer windows allow you to view the individual red, green, blue, and alpha channels of an image. Color channels appear as grayscale images in which the degree of white corresponds to the color value. You can also view the color channel using its own color. The alpha channel appears as a grayscale image as well, where the degree of white corresponds to opacity. As you may recall from Chapter 2, you can even view the unmultiplied color channels—that is, the color channels without the alpha taken into account. For more about alpha channels, see the Chapter 2 sidebar "Alpha Bits: Understanding Straight and Premultiplied Alpha."

Figure 3.95 Click the button that corresponds to the channel you want to view. Shift-click a color channel to see the channel in color.

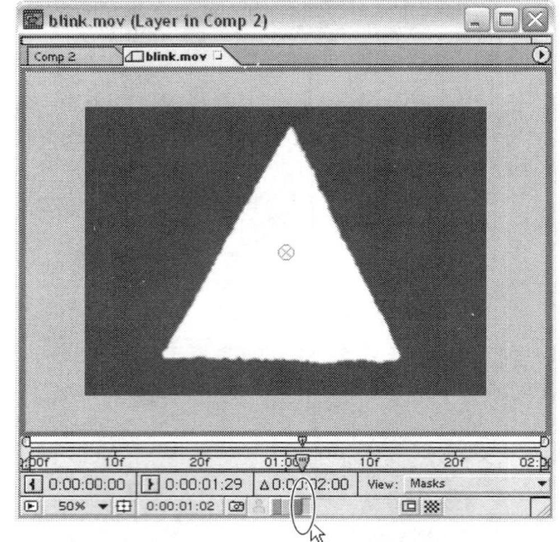

Figure 3.96 Click the Alpha Channel button to see the alpha channel.

To show individual channels:

Do any of the following:

- To show the channel depicted in grayscale, click one of the RGB channel buttons (**Figure 3.95**).
- To show the channel depicted in color, Shift-click one of the RGB channel buttons.
- To show the alpha channel as a grayscale matte, click the Alpha Channel button (**Figure 3.96**).
- To show the unmultiplied RGB channels, Option-click the Alpha Channel button.

  The selected channel button remains active until you click it again. To view all of the visible channels again, click the selected channel button.

✔ Tip

- In older versions of After Effects, you had to press and hold down the channel button. Since the release of After Effects 4, the button remains depressed when you click it; you must click it again to make it pop back up.

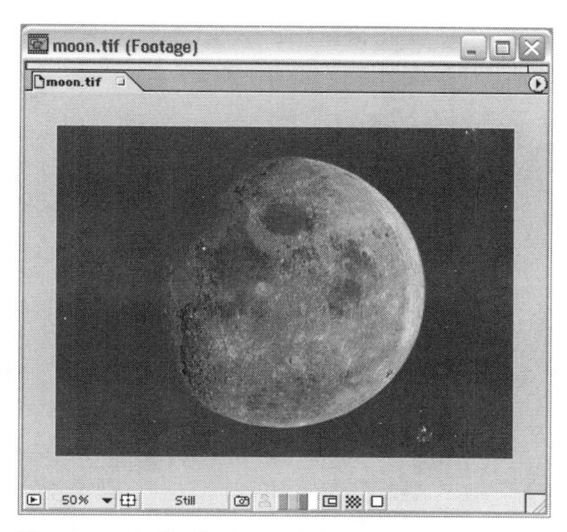

Figure 3.97 In the Footage window, transparent areas of the image appear as black.

Figure 3.98 You can also make transparent areas appear as a checkerboard pattern, or transparency grid. This also works in the Composition and Layer windows.

Figure 3.99 Click the Toggle Transparency Grid button to toggle between showing transparent areas as black (in the Footage window, or as the specified background color in the Composition window) and shown them as a checkerboard pattern.

Viewing Transparency

In Chapter 2, you learned that the footage items you import can retain almost every aspect of their source files, including transparency. In the Footage window, transparency always appears as black (**Figure 3.97**). However, if the black background isn't convenient, you can toggle the transparent areas to appear as a checkerboard pattern, or *transparency grid* (**Figure 3.98**).

Like many of the other buttons in the Footage window, the Toggle Transparency Grid button is also available in the Layer and Composition windows. However, in contrast to the Footage window, you can set the Composition window's background to any color. The next chapter revisits viewing transparency and other unique aspects of the Composition window.

To toggle the transparency grid:

- In the Footage, Composition, or Layer window, click the Toggle Transparency Grid button (**Figure 3.99**).

  When the Toggle Transparency Grid button is selected, transparent areas appear as a checkerboard pattern; when the button isn't selected, transparent areas appear black in a Footage or Layer window. In a Composition window, transparent areas appear as the color you set.

Correcting for Pixel Aspect Ratios

In Chapter 2, you learned the importance of correctly interpreting an image's pixel aspect ratio (PAR) to prevent the image from appearing distorted (if you missed the discussion, turn to the sidebar "PAR Excellence," in Chapter 2). But even properly interpreted, footage and comps that use a nonsquare PAR (such as DV or D1, with a PAR of .9) will result in an image that looks distorted on a typical computer display (PAR of 1) (**Figure 3.100**). Fortunately, After Effects can compensate for the distortion due to PAR (**Figure 3.101**). As After Effects warns you when you use the Toggle Pixel Aspect Ratio Correction button, correcting the image this way is for viewing purposes only; it doesn't affect the image's actual scale. And because correcting an image requires some processing, it will take slightly longer to render frames.

Figure 3.100 This footage uses a PAR of .9, so it appears slightly vertically squashed (or horizontally stretched) when displayed using square pixels.

Figure 3.101 You can correct the distortion in the Layer, Composition, and Footage windows.

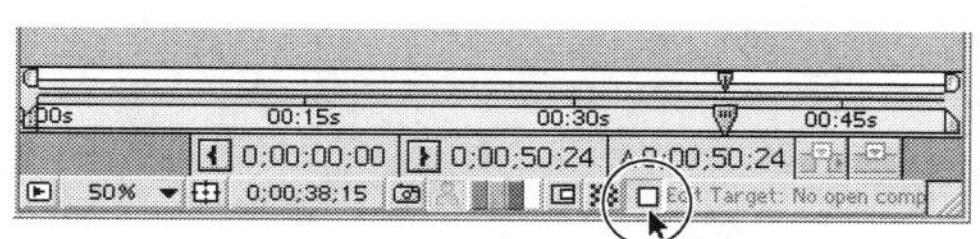

Figure 3.102 Click the Toggle Pixel Aspect Ratio Correction button.

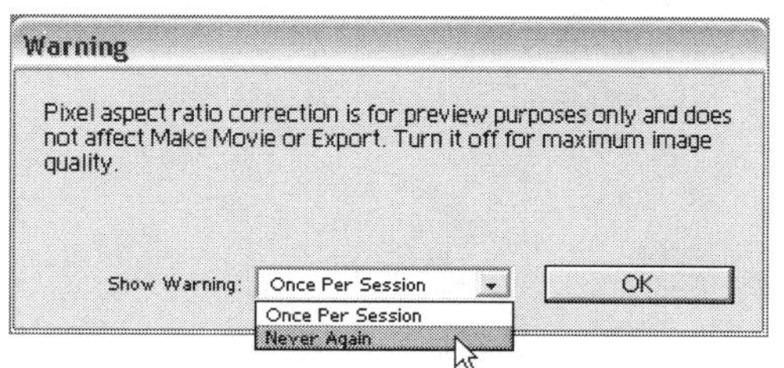

Figure 3.103 The first time you use PAR correction, After Effects reminds you how the feature works and prompts you to specify whether you want to be reminded once per session or never again.

To toggle pixel aspect correction:

1. In a Footage, Composition, or Layer window, click the Toggle Pixel Aspect Ratio Correction button ☐ to select it (**Figure 3.102**).

   If this is the first time you've used the button during this session, After Effects reminds you how PAR correction works and prompts you to specify whether you want to see the warning once per session or never again (**Figure 3.103**).

2. Select an option in the dialog box and click OK.

   If the image's PAR doesn't match your computer monitor's PAR, After Effects scales the image so that it no longer appears distorted.

✔ Tip

- This chapter hasn't covered a few buttons in the Footage window. The Region of Interest button will make more sense in the context of playback, covered in Chapter 8, "Playback, Previews, and RAM." The Footage window for motion footage also contains a number of editing controls, which are fully explained in Chapter 6, "Layer Editing."

Compositions

Without compositions, a project is nothing more than a list of footage items—a grocery list without a recipe; an ensemble without choreography; finely tuned instruments without, well, a composition. This is because *compositions* perform the essential function of describing how footage items are arranged in space and time. This chapter shows you how to create a composition and define its spatial and temporal boundaries by setting frame size, frame rate, duration, and so on.

This chapter also describes the fundamental process of layering footage in compositions (and in so doing lays the groundwork for the rest of the book, which focuses largely on how to manipulate those layers). The footage items you add to a composition become *layers,* which are manipulated in the defined space and time of the composition, as represented by Composition and Timeline windows. The following pages will give you an overview of these windows as well as the Time Controls palette. This chapter will also introduce you to the technique of nesting, using comps as layers in other comps—a concept you'll appreciate more fully as your projects grow more complex.

Creating Compositions

A composition contains layers of footage and describes how you arrange those layers in space and time. This section explains how to create a composition; the following section describes how to choose specific settings to define a composition's spatial and temporal attributes.

To create a new composition:

1. *Do one of the following:*
   - ▲ Choose Composition > New Composition (**Figure 4.1**).
   - ▲ Press Command-N (Mac) or Ctrl-N (Windows).
   - ▲ At the bottom of the Project window, click the Composition button (**Figure 4.2**).

   A Composition Settings dialog box appears (**Figure 4.3**).
2. In the Composition Settings dialog box, choose a name for the composition and specify preset or custom Composition settings (such as frame size, pixel aspect ratio, frame rate, display resolution, or duration) for the composition. (See "Choosing Composition Settings" later in this chapter for details.)

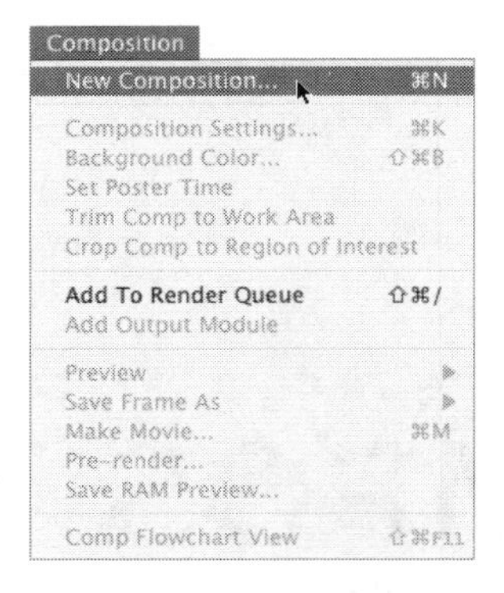

Figure 4.1 Choose Composition > New Composition, or press Command-N (Mac) or Ctrl-N (Windows)...

Figure 4.2 ...or click the Composition button at the bottom of the Project window.

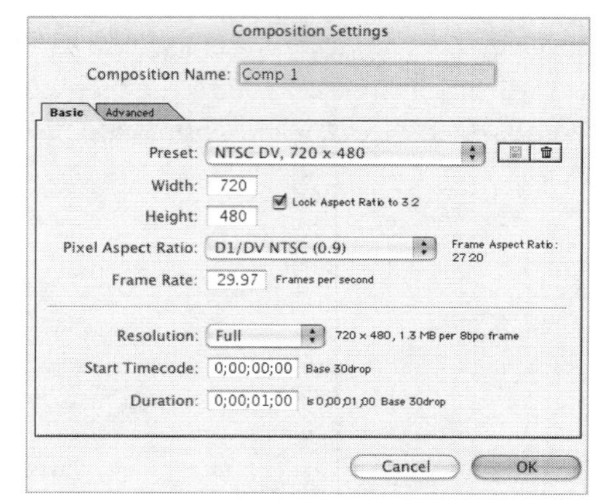

Figure 4.3 In the Composition Settings dialog box, enter the appropriate settings for the composition.

3. Click OK to close the Composition Settings dialog box.

   A new composition appears in the Project window, and related Composition and Timeline windows open (**Figure 4.4**).

✔ Tips

- It's easy to forget to name your composition or to settle for the default name, *Comp 1*. Do yourself a favor and give the composition a descriptive name. This will help you remain organized as your project becomes more complex.
- You can create a composition that contains a footage item by dragging the item's icon to the Create Composition icon in the Project window. The new composition will use the same image dimensions as the footage item it contains.

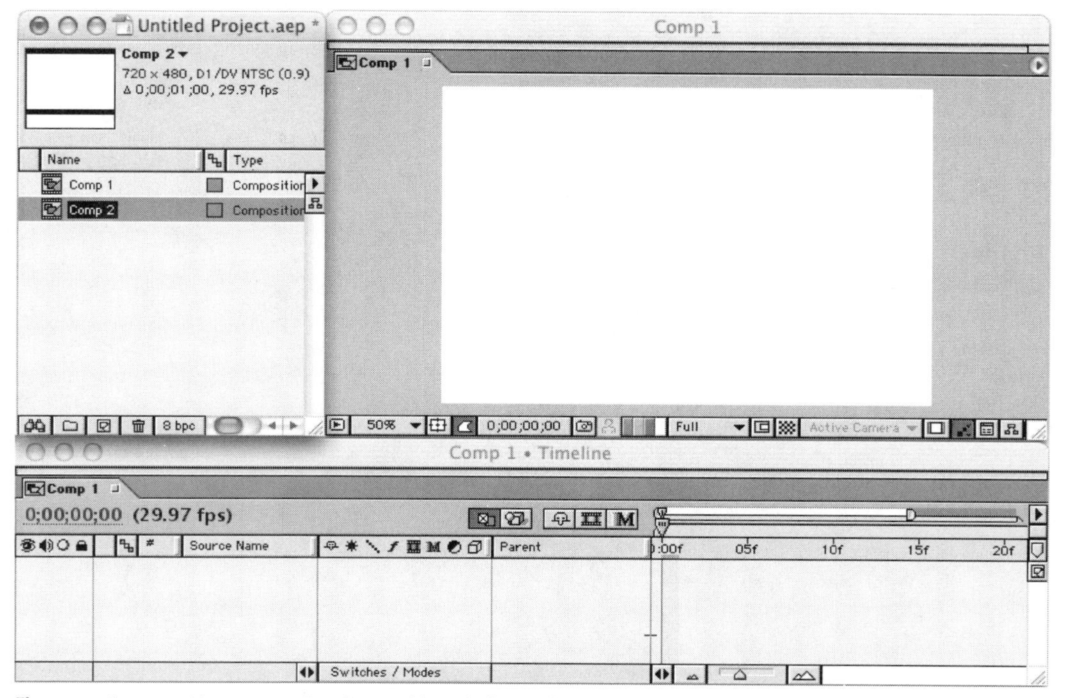

Figure 4.4 A composition appears in a Composition window and a Timeline window, and as an icon in the Project window.

Choosing Composition Settings

Because compositions describe how layers are arranged in space and time, you must define a composition's spatial attributes (such as its frame size and pixel aspect ratio) as well as its temporal aspects (such as its duration and frame rate). Composition settings allow you to specify these characteristics. You can also use the composition settings to specify the resolution or quality of the Composition window's display. You may change composition settings at any time.

A project usually contains several compositions, most of which are contained as layers (or *nested*) in a final composition. Although you can set the final composition's settings according to your output format (NTSC DV, for example), you may want to employ different settings (particularly for frame size and duration) for intermediate compositions.

✔ Tips

- You can open the Composition Settings dialog box for the current composition by selecting Command-K (Mac) or Ctrl-K (Windows).
- You can also access the Composition Settings dialog box from the Timeline window's pop-up menu; however, using the keyboard shortcut—Command-K (Mac) or Ctrl-K (Windows)—is the quickest way.

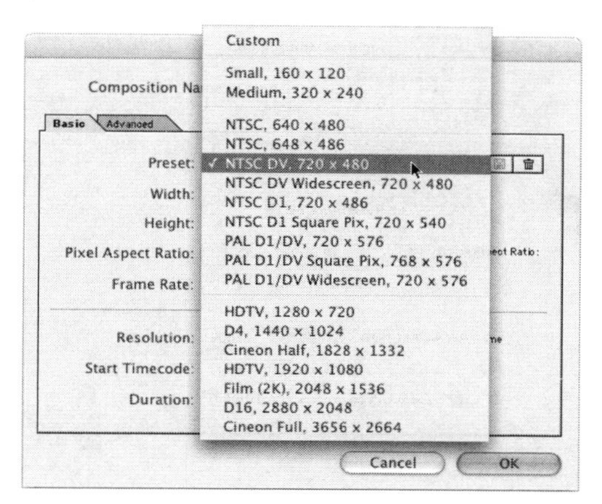

Figure 4.5 Choose an option from the Preset pull-down menu.

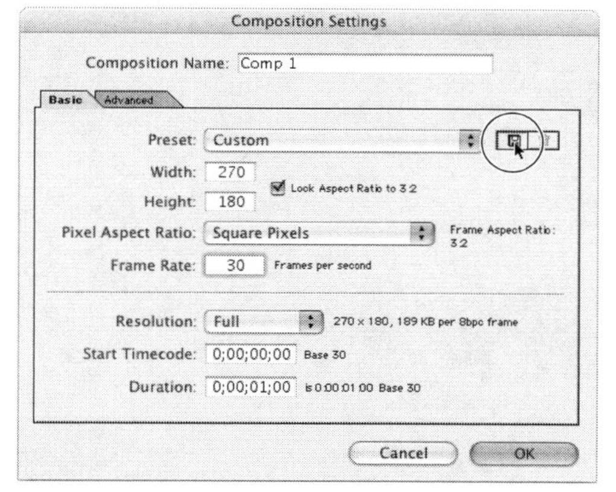

Figure 4.6 Enter the comp settings you want and click the Save button.

Selecting Composition Presets

With After Effects, you don't need to manually enter all the composition settings (frame size, pixel aspect ratio, and so on); instead, you can select the most common ones from a pull-down menu of presets. If the list doesn't include a preset for *your* most commonly used settings, you can save your custom settings to the list. You can even delete the presets you don't want.

To select a composition preset:

1. In the Composition Settings dialog box, choose an option from the Preset menu (**Figure 4.5**).

   Choose the preset that matches your needs. Presets include common settings for film, video broadcast, and multimedia projects. Individual settings are set automatically. However, you may want to enter a starting frame number and duration for the comp (see "Setting a composition's start-frame number" and "Setting a composition's duration," later in this chapter).

2. Click OK to close the Composition Settings dialog box.

   The composition appears in the Project window.

To save a composition preset:

1. In the Composition Settings dialog box, enter the settings suitable for the composition.

   See the following sections for instructions on choosing specific settings. You can choose an existing preset to use as a starting point, or you can choose Custom from the Preset pull-down menu.

2. Click the Save button (**Figure 4.6**).

   A Choose Name dialog box appears.

continues on next page

3. In the Choose Name dialog box, enter a name for your preset, and then click OK (**Figure 4.7**).

   The settings you specified are saved as a preset, and the preset's name appears in the Preset pull-down menu of the Composition Settings dialog box.

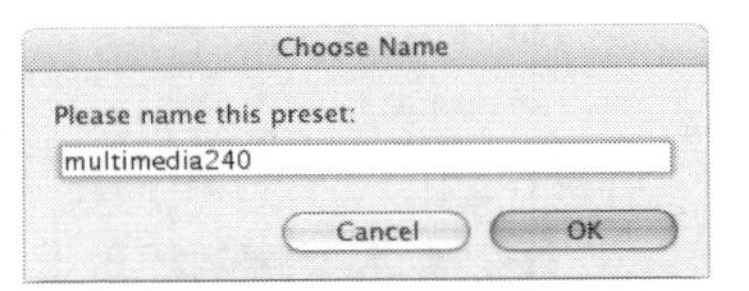

Figure 4.7 In the Choose Name dialog box, enter a name for your preset.

To delete a composition preset:

1. In the Preset pull-down menu of the Composition Settings dialog box, choose a preset.
2. Click the Delete button (**Figure 4.8**).

   A Warning dialog box prompts you to confirm whether you want to delete the preset.
3. In the Warning dialog box, click OK to delete the selected preset (**Figure 4.9**).

   The preset is deleted and no longer appears in the Preset pull-down menu.

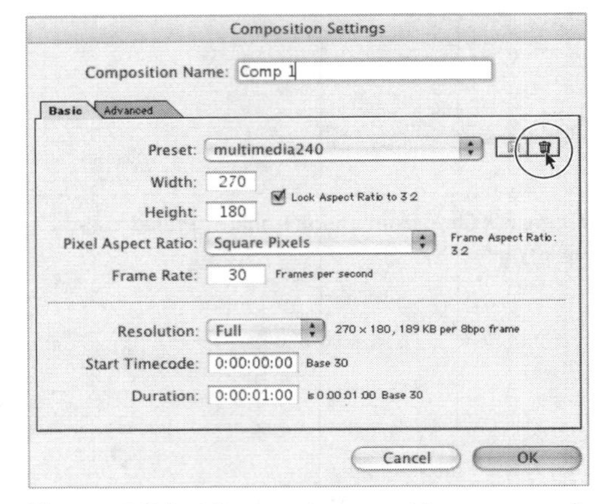

Figure 4.8 Select the preset you want to remove, and click the Delete button.

✔ Tip

- You can restore the presets that ship with After Effects by Option-clicking (Mac) or Alt-clicking (Windows) the Delete button.

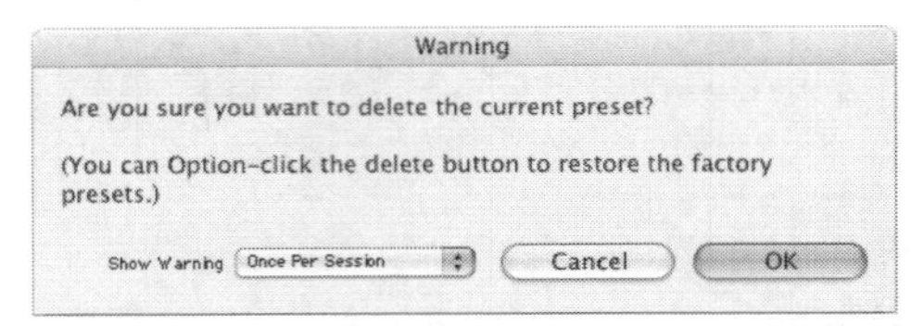

Figure 4.9 In the Warning dialog box, click OK if you're sure you want to delete the preset.

Table 4.1

Common composition presets

PRESET	FRAME SIZE	PAR	FRAME RATE	USE
NTSC	640 x 480	1	29.97	Full-screen, full-motion video, used by low-end cards
NTSC DV	720 x 480	.9	29.97	DV standard for North America
NTSC D1	720 x 486	.9	29.97	Broadcast standard for North America
HDTV	1920 x 1080	1	24	High-definition standard using 16:9 image aspect ratio
Film (2k)	2048 x 1536	1	24	Film transfers
Cineon Full	3656 x 2664	1	24	Film transferred using the Cineon file format

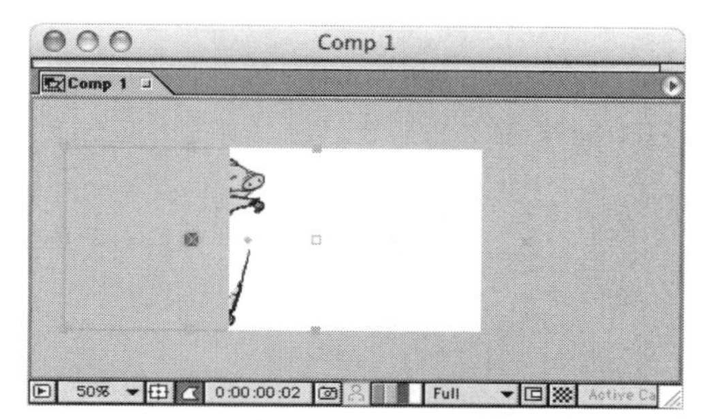

Figure 4.10 The frame size defines the dimensions of the viewable area of the composition. Over time, an element may move from the offscreen work area...

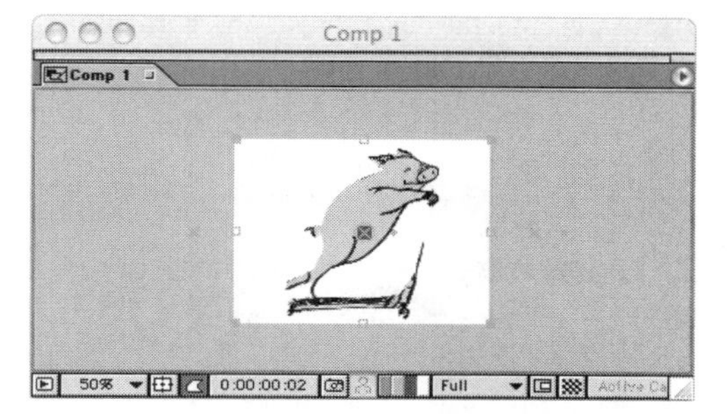

Figure 4.11 ...and into the onscreen visible frame...

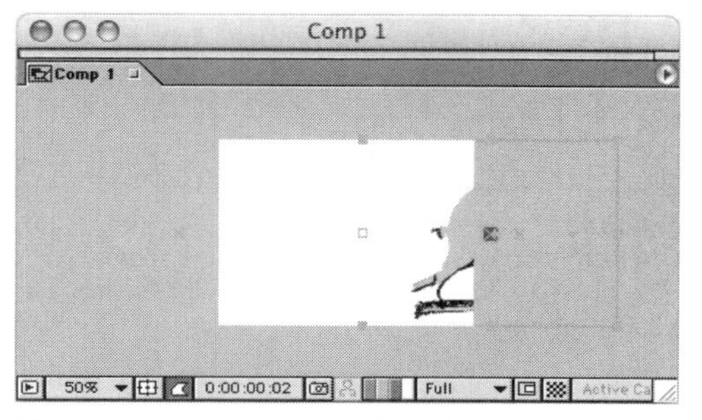

Figure 4.12 ...and vice versa. Only elements within the visible frame appear in the final output.

Choosing a frame size

The frame size determines the viewing area of the Composition window. Although you may position images in the workspace outside of this viewing area (what some call the *pasteboard*), only the elements within the visible frame will be rendered for previews and output (**Figures 4.10**, **4.11**, and **4.12**).

Often, the frame dimensions of the final output determine the frame size of a composition. However, if the composition is to be nested in another composition, the frame size may be larger or smaller than the pixel dimensions of the final output. (See "Nesting Compositions" later in this chapter, or see Chapter 17, "Complex Projects.")

The Composition Settings dialog box provides a list of preset frame sizes, or you may enter a custom frame size. The frame size you choose is centered in a workspace that's limited to the same maximum dimensions as imported image files. As with imported footage files, chances are you'll run out of available RAM before you exceed the maximum image size (up to 30,000 x 30,000 pixels, depending on the output option).

For more about the maximum frame size of images, see the sidebar "Wham, Bam—Thank You, RAM" in Chapter 2, "Importing Footage into a Project." If you change the frame size of an existing composition, the Anchor setting determines where the existing layers are placed in the new comp (see "Setting a composition's anchor," later in this chapter).

To set the frame size:

1. In the Composition Settings dialog box, *do one of the following:*
   - ▲ Enter the width and height of the frame in pixels.
   - ▲ Choose a preset frame size from the pull-down menu (**Figure 4.13**).
2. If you're changing the frame size of an existing composition, choose an anchor point from the Anchor section of the Composition Settings dialog box (visible when you select the Advanced tab).

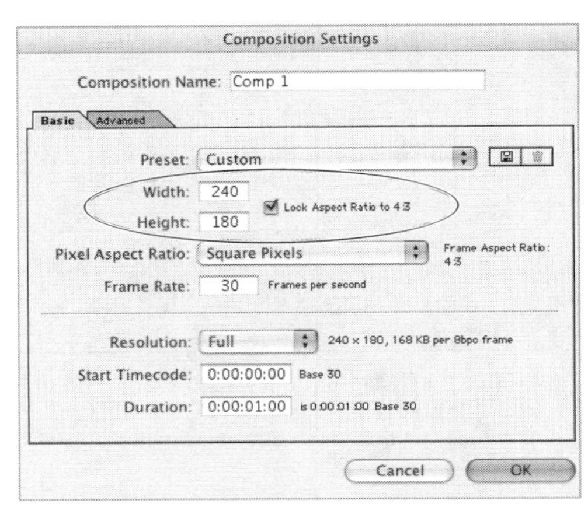

Figure 4.13 Enter the frame dimensions, or choose a preset size from the pull-down menu.

✔ Tips

- You can enter a custom frame size that uses the same image aspect ratio as a preset frame size. First, choose a preset frame size that uses the image aspect ratio you want to maintain. Then, click the "Lock Aspect Ratio to" check box and enter a custom frame size. When you enter a value for one dimension, After Effects automatically fills in the other, maintaining the same aspect ratio.
- When you go back and change a composition's frame size, you should also select an Anchor option in the Advanced tab of the Composition Settings dialog box (see "Setting a composition's anchor" later in this chapter).

Figure 4.14 Incorrectly interpreted as having nonsquare pixels, this 640 x 480 square-pixel image seems to lose its 4:3 aspect ratio in this 720 x 486 (D1/nonsquare pixels) composition.

Figure 4.15 Correctly interpreted as having square pixels, the image is automatically resized to compensate for a composition set to the D1 standard.

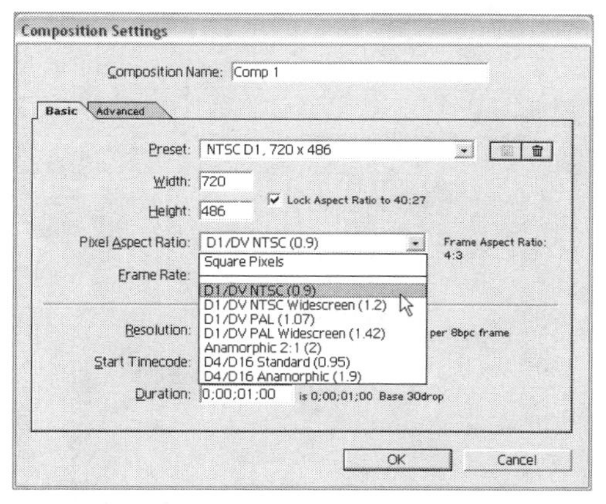

Figure 4.16 In the Pixel Aspect Ratio pull-down menu, choose the PAR that corresponds to your final output.

Pixel aspect ratio

A typical computer monitor uses square pixels to display an image. Professional video, in contrast, uses nonsquare pixels to display images. As a result, an image created on a computer can appear distorted when transferred to video, and vice versa.

One of After Effects' great advantages is that it can compensate for differences in pixel aspect ratios. In fact, when you choose a preset frame size, After Effects automatically selects the corresponding pixel aspect ratio (PAR). If you want to override this setting, or if you enter a custom frame size, you can choose the correct PAR manually.

After Effects compensates for any difference between the PAR of the composition and that of individual footage items. For example, if you add a square-pixel footage item into a D1 composition, After Effects automatically resizes the image to prevent image distortion in the final output (**Figures 4.14** and **4.15**).

For a detailed explanation of PAR, see the sidebar "PAR Excellence" in Chapter 2.

To set the pixel aspect ratio of a composition:

◆ From the Pixel Aspect Ratio pull-down menu in the Composition Settings dialog box, choose a PAR from the pull-down menu (**Figure 4.16**).

✔ Tip

■ As suggested earlier, the most common PARs are square pixel (with a PAR of 1) and D1/DV NTSC (with a PAR of .9). Square pixels correspond to formats displayed on computer monitors or consumer-level video capture cards. D1/DV NTSC corresponds to the nonsquare pixels used by professional NTSC video formats (D1 or ITU-R 601) and the DV video standards (mini DV, DVCam, and DVCPro).

Resolution

Frame size sets the actual pixel dimensions of the composition; *resolution* determines the fraction of the pixels that are displayed in the Composition window.

By lowering the resolution, you reduce not only image quality but also the amount of memory needed to render frames. Rendering speeds increase in proportion to image quality sacrificed. Typically, you work and preview your composition at a lower resolution and then render the final output at full resolution (**Figures 4.17** and **4.18**).

Figure 4.17 Typically, you work and preview a composition at a lower resolution (in this case, quarter resolution)...

Figure 4.18 ...and then switch to full resolution when you want to see the image at output quality or render the final version.

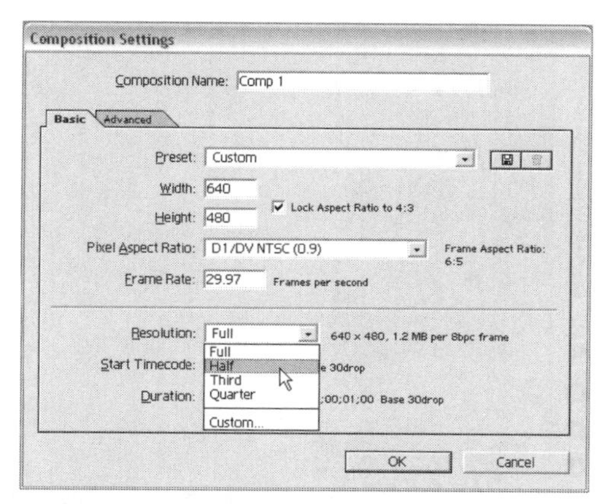

Figure 4.19 Choose a resolution from the pull-down menu.

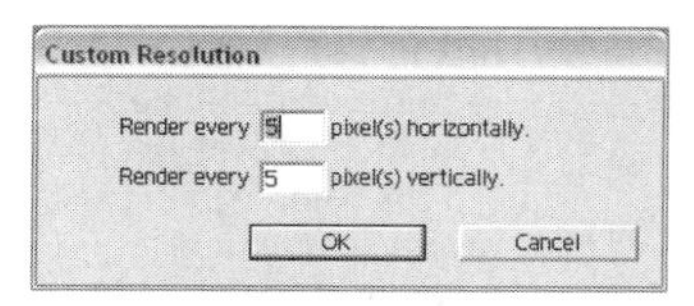

Figure 4.20 If you choose Custom from the pull-down menu, enter values to determine the resolution manually. Rendering every fifth horizontal and vertical pixel would equal one-twenty-fifth of the resolution and rendering time.

Figure 4.21 You can also change the resolution using the pull-down menu at the bottom of the Composition window.

To set a composition's resolution:

1. In the Composition Settings dialog box, choose a setting from the Resolution pull-down menu (**Figure 4.19**):

   Full—After Effects renders and displays every pixel of the composition, resulting in the highest image quality and the longest rendering time.

   Half—After Effects renders every other pixel, or one-quarter of the pixels of the full-resolution image, in one-quarter of the time.

   Third—After Effects renders every third pixel, or one-ninth of the pixels in the full-resolution image, in one-ninth of the time.

   Quarter—After Effects renders every fourth pixel, or one-sixteenth of the pixels in the full-resolution image, in one-sixteenth of the time.

   Custom—After Effects renders whatever fraction of pixels you specify.

2. If you choose Custom from the pull-down menu, enter values to determine the horizontal and vertical resolution of the image (**Figure 4.20**).

✔ Tips

- You can also change the resolution at any time by using the Resolution pull-down menu in the Composition window (**Figure 4.21**). See "The Composition Window," later in this chapter.

- You can control the quality setting of individual layers, separate from the composition as a whole. See Chapter 5, "Layer Basics," for more details.

Frame rate

The *frame rate* is the number of frames per second (fps) used by a composition. Usually, the frame rate you choose matches the frame rate of your output format.

Individual footage items have their own frame rates, which you can interpret. (See "Setting the Frame Rate" in Chapter 2.) Ideally, the footage frame rate and the composition frame rate match. If not, After Effects makes the frame rate of the footage item conform to that of the composition.

For example, if both the composition frame rate and the footage frame rate are 30 fps, the footage in a layer advances a frame whenever the composition advances a frame. However, if the footage frame rate were 10 fps and the composition frame rate were 30 fps, After Effects would distribute one second of footage (10 frames) over one second of the composition (30 frames) by displaying each frame of footage three times. In other words, the composition must advance three frames to display a new frame of the footage layer (**Figure 4.22**).

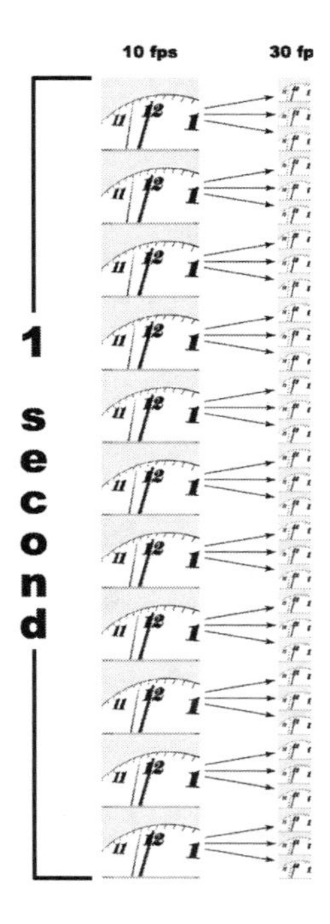

Figure 4.22 The frame rate of a footage item is conformed to the frame rate of the composition. In this case, frames of a 10-fps animation are repeated to play in a 30-fps composition to avoid an apparent change in speed.

To set the frame rate of the composition:

- From the Frame Rate pull-down menu in the Composition Settings dialog box, enter a frame rate (**Figure 4.23**).

  Usually, you'll choose a frame rate that matches the frame rate of the output format:

  - NTSC video: 29.97 fps
  - PAL video: 25 fps
  - Film: 24 fps
  - Computer presentation (often via CD-ROM or Web): 15 fps or 10 fps

  Lower frame rates help reduce file size and conform to data-rate limitations.

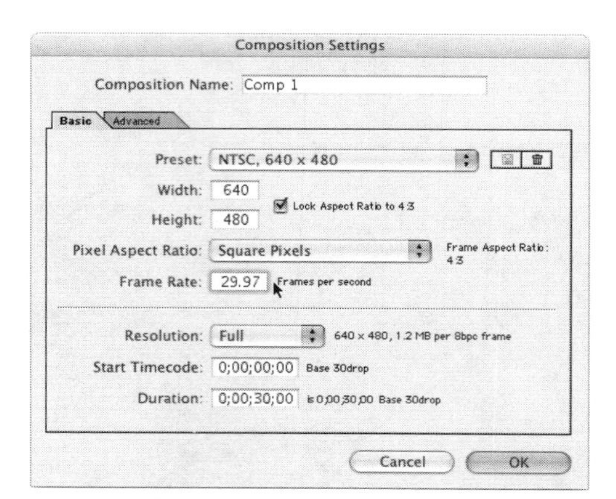

Figure 4.23 Enter the appropriate frame rate for the composition.

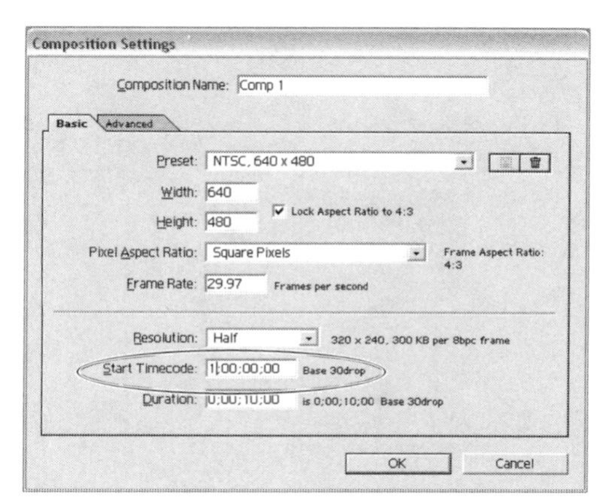

Figure 4.24 If you want to, enter a starting frame number.

✔ Tips

- Film that has been transferred to video often uses video frame rates and has undergone the process of 3:2 pulldown. For more about 3:2 pulldown, see Chapter 2.
- Use the Interpret Footage command to set the proper frame rate for a footage item; set the composition's frame rate according to your output requirements. If you're interested in changing the speed of a layer, see Chapter 6, "Layer Editing."

Setting a composition's start-frame number

When you began your project, you set its time display—that is, the method used to count your project's frames. As you may recall from Chapter 2, you can set the time display to standard video or film counting schemes (see "Choosing a Time Display" in Chapter 2). You can also set the frame number at which each composition starts. For example, you may want a composition's frame numbers to match the timecode of its source footage.

To set a composition's starting frame number:

1. In the Composition Settings dialog box, enter the starting frame number of the composition (**Figure 4.24**).

   The timebase you set for the project determines whether this number is expressed in timecode, feet and frames, or frame numbers.

2. Click OK to close the Composition Settings dialog box.

   The composition begins at the frame number you specified.

Setting a composition's duration

Duration—which sets the length of a composition—is expressed in the time display style you set in the Project Settings dialog box (timecode, frames, or feet and frames). See "Choosing Composition Settings" earlier in this chapter for more about time display options. You can change the composition's duration at any time, lengthening it to accommodate more layers or cutting it to the total duration of its layers.

To set the duration of a composition:

- From the Duration pull-down menu in the Composition Settings dialog box, enter the duration of the composition (**Figure 4.25**).

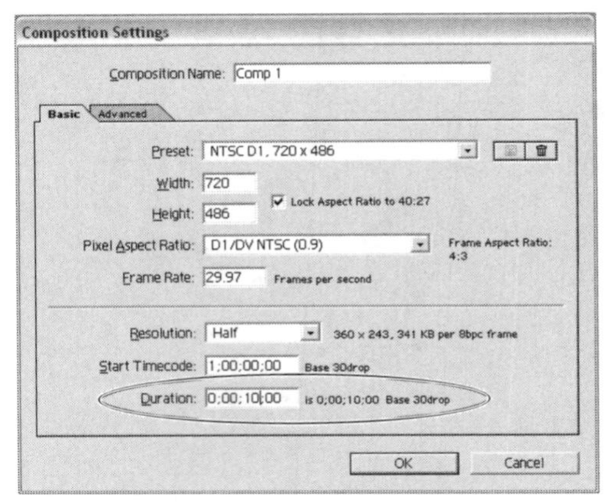

Figure 4.25 Enter the duration for the composition.

✔ Tip

- You can also quickly trim the comp's duration to the length of the work area by choosing Composition > Trim Comp to Work Area. For more about the work area, see Chapter 8, "Playback, Previews, and RAM."

Advanced Composition Settings

The Composition Settings dialog box is divided into Basic and Advanced panels. The previous sections covered the settings in the Basic panel. Clicking the Advanced tab reveals a number of additional settings, which are discussed here, although many will make more sense to you later as this book delves deeper into the program. You'll be reminded of each setting again when you encounter the task or technique to which it pertains.

Setting a composition's anchor

When you resize a composition, you use the Anchor control to determine how the composition and its layers will be placed in the new frame—that is, whether they're anchored in the center, corner, or side of the new frame.

To set the anchor of a resized composition:

1. Select a composition and press Command-K (Mac) or Ctrl-K (Windows) (**Figure 4.26**).

   The Composition Settings dialog box appears.

2. To change the frame size of the composition, enter new values in the Width and Height fields.

3. Click the Advanced tab.

   The Advanced settings panel of the Composition Settings dialog box appears.

4. In the Anchor control, click one of the nine anchor point positions (**Figure 4.27**).

5. Click OK to close the Composition Settings dialog box.

   The layers contained in the composition align to the position you specified (**Figure 4.28**).

Figure 4.26 Before the composition is resized, it looks like this.

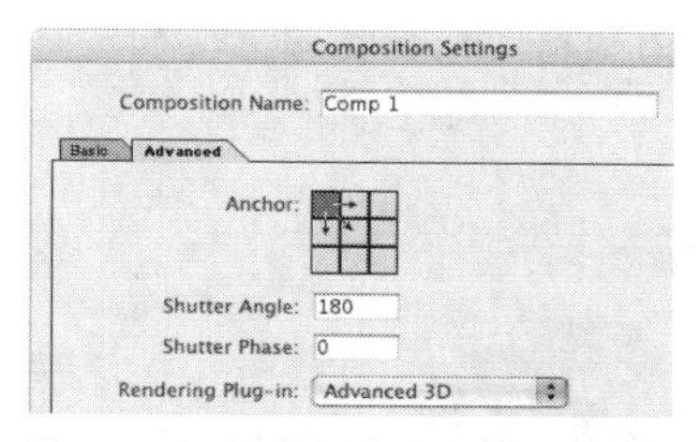

Figure 4.27 In the Advanced panel of the Composition Settings dialog box, click one of the nine anchor positions.

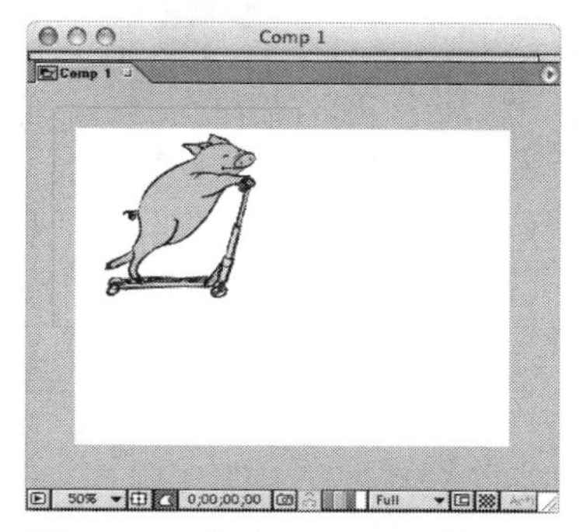

Figure 4.28 The layers are anchored to the position you specified in the resized comp.

✔ Tip

- Don't confuse the composition's anchor with a layer's anchor point, which is something else altogether. To find out about the layer Anchor Point property, see Chapter 7, "Properties and Keyframes."

Choosing a composition's shutter settings

In many ways, a composition is analogous to a camera. Just as a camera's shutter helps determine how blurry or sharp a moving object appears on film, After Effects compositions include a shutter setting that serves a similar purpose. Layers with motion blur applied to them appear blurred (when motion blur is enabled), according to the shutter settings.

As in a camera, the shutter angle and frame rate work together to simulate an exposure. Wider shutter angles result in a longer simulated exposure and blurrier motion (**Figure 4.29**); narrower shutter angles result in a shorter simulated exposure and sharper moving images (**Figure 4.30**). The optional Shutter Phase setting determines the shutter's starting position at the frame start.

Figure 4.29 Wider shutter angles result in a longer simulated exposure and blurrier motion.

Figure 4.30 Narrower shutter angles result in a shorter simulated exposure and sharper motion.

To set shutter angle and phase:

1. In the Advanced panel of the Composition Settings dialog box, enter a value for Shutter Angle (**Figure 4.31**).

   The default setting is 180 degrees.

2. To set the position of the shutter relative to the start frame, enter a value for Shutter Phase.

   You may enter an angle between 0 and 360 degrees.

3. Click OK to close the Composition Settings dialog box.

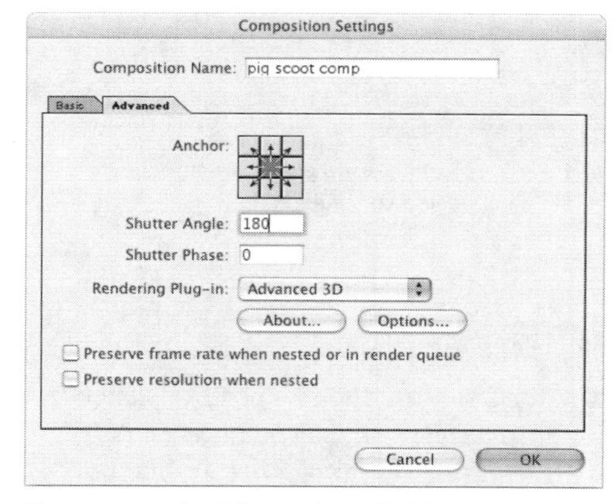

Figure 4.31 In the Advanced panel of the Composition Settings dialog box, enter a value for Shutter Angle.

✔ Tips

- If you're not sure what shutter angle to use, 180 degrees works fine. You can always change the angle when you start using and previewing motion blur. For more about motion blur, see Chapter 14, "More Layer Techniques."
- You can also set the shutter angle in the Render Queue dialog box. See Chapter 18, "Output," for more information.

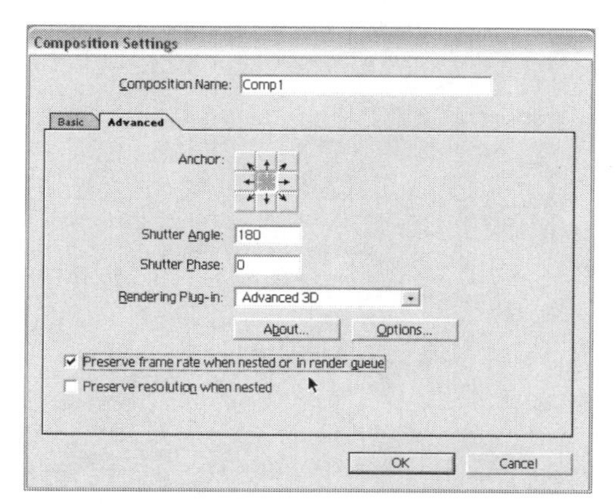

Figure 4.32 Select the nesting option(s) you want.

Nesting options

As you know by now, compositions can become layers within other compositions, a technique called *nesting*. In the composition's settings, nesting options dictate whether nested compositions retain their own frame-rate and resolution settings or assume those of the composition in which they're nested. For more about nesting compositions, see Chapter 17.

To set nesting options:

1. In the Advanced panel of the Composition Settings dialog box, *select one or both of the following* options (**Figure 4.32**):

   Preserve frame rate when nested or in render queue—Choosing this option allows nested compositions to retain their frame rates, regardless of the frame rate of the composition that contains them.

   Preserve resolution when nested—If this option is selected, nested compositions will retain their resolution settings, regardless of the resolution of the composition that contains them.

   If you select neither option, nested compositions will take on the frame rate and resolution of the composition in which they're nested.

2. Click OK to close the Composition Settings dialog box.

✔ Tips

- By preserving the frame rate of a nested composition, you can achieve results similar to those produced by the Posterize Time effect.
- The Render Queue dialog box allows you to use the current resolution settings or to reset them for all nested comps. See Chapter 18 for more about the render queue.

Rendering plug-in

In case you've forgotten, After Effects allows you to composite layers in three-dimensional space. The standard package comes with the standard 3D rendering plug-in; After Effects Pro includes an advanced 3D plug-in, which supports more sophisticated 3D features such as the intersection of 3D layers, diffuse shadows, and the like. If your computer is equipped with an After Effects–compatible OpenGL graphics card, you can designate it for 3D rendering. See Chapter 16, "3D Layers," for more about 3D layers and compositing; see Chapter 8 for more about previewing and OpenGL.

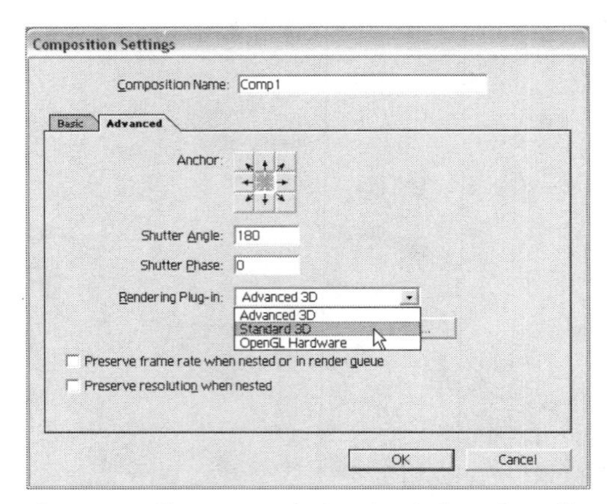

Figure 4.33 Choose a rendering plug-in from the pull-down menu.

To set the rendering plug-in:

1. In the Advanced panel of the Composition dialog box, *choose one of the following* options in the Rendering Plug-in pull-down menu (**Figure 4.33**):

   Advanced 3D—Select this option to use the advanced 3D plug-in (included with After Effects Pro).

   Standard 3D—Select this option to use the standard 3D plug-in.

   OpenGL Hardware—Select this option to use your After Effects–compatible OpenGL graphics card for 3D rendering.

2. If you chose Advanced 3D in step 1, click Options, and specify the shadow mask resolution in the Advanced 3D Options dialog box.

3. Click OK to close the Composition Settings dialog box.

   If you chose OpenGL Hardware in step 1, the Composition window displays *OpenGL* in the pasteboard area.

Background Color

The default background color of compositions is black; however, you can change the background to any color you choose. Regardless of what color you make it, the background becomes the alpha channel when you output the composition as a still-image sequence or a movie with an alpha channel. Similarly, if you use the composition as a layer in another composition, the background of the nested composition becomes transparent (**Figure 4.34**) (see "Nesting Compositions," later in this chapter). And as with the Footage window (see Chapter 3, "Managing Footage") and the Layer widow, you can also view the background as a checkerboard pattern (much like the one Photoshop uses to represent transparent areas of a layer) called a *transparency grid*.

To choose a background color for your composition:

1. Select a composition in the Project window, or activate a composition in a Composition or Timeline window.
2. Choose Composition > Background Color (**Figure 4.35**), or press Shift-Command-B (Mac) or Shift-Ctrl-B (Windows).

   A Background Color dialog box appears.

continues on next page

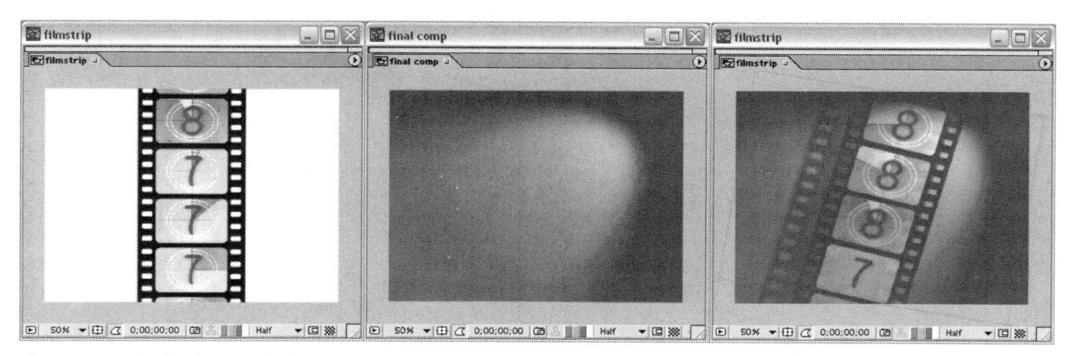

Figure 4.34 The background of a nested composition becomes transparent.

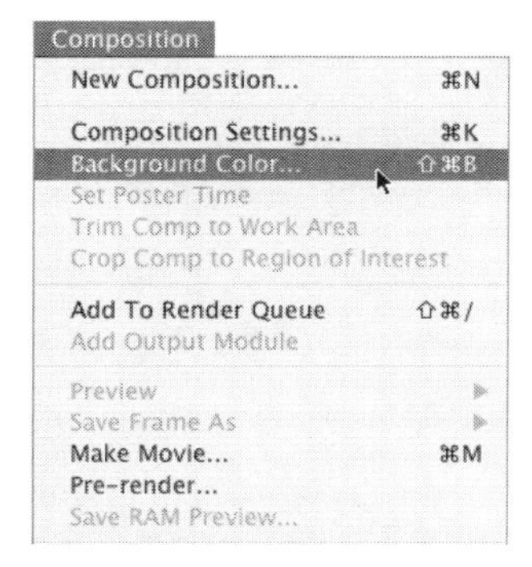

Figure 4.35 Choose Composition > Background Color.

3. In the Background Color dialog box, *do one of the following* (**Figure 4.36**):
   - ▲ Click the color swatch to open the color picker.
   - ▲ Click the eyedropper to choose a color from another window.
4. Click OK to close the Background Color dialog box.

   The selected composition uses the background color you specified.

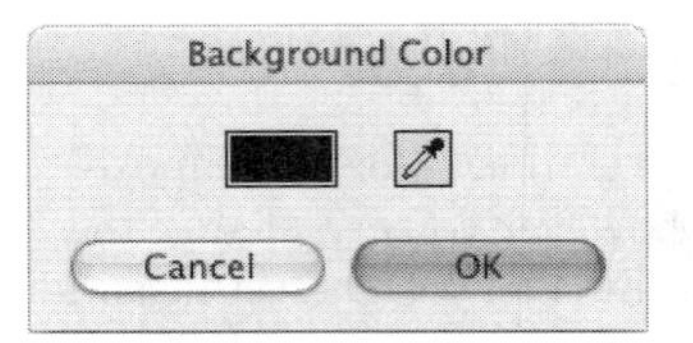

Figure 4.36 Click the eyedropper to pick a screen color, or click the swatch to open a color picker.

✔ Tip

- If you need an opaque background—in a nested composition, for example—create a solid layer as described in "To create a solid-color layer," later in this chapter.

The Composition and Timeline Windows

All of your compositions can be represented in the Composition and Timeline windows, which open automatically whenever you create or open a composition. These two windows furnish you with different ways of looking at a composition and manipulating its layers. This section will give you an overview of each window, emphasizing how they show layers along with their spatial and temporal relationships.

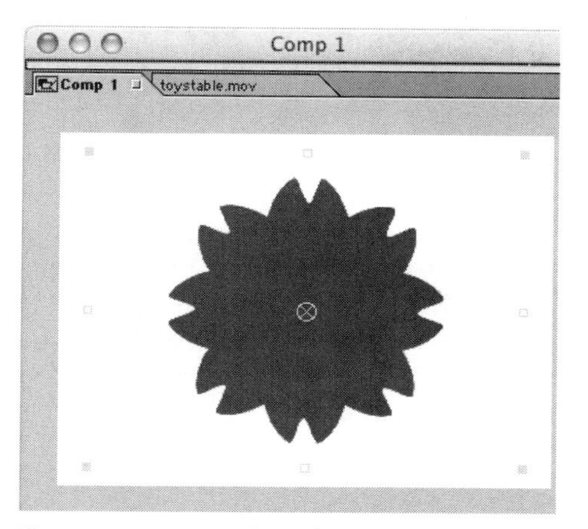

Figure 4.52 You can add text or other effects to a solid; you can mask a solid to create graphical elements (shown here); or you can use it as a solid-color background.

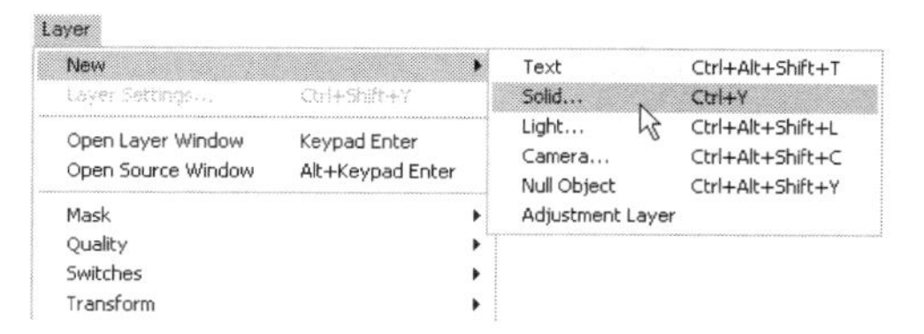

Figure 4.53 Choose Layer > New > Solid, or use the keyboard shortcut.

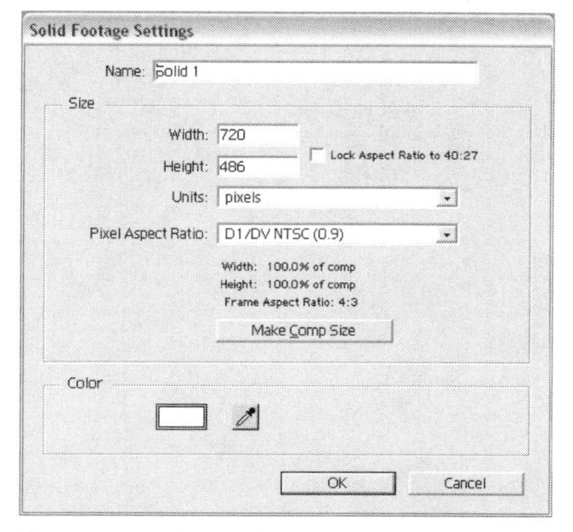

Figure 4.54 In the Solid Footage Settings dialog box, enter a name for the solid layer. Click the Make Comp Size button to make the solid the same size as the composition, or enter a custom width and height.

Creating Solid Layers

As you might expect, a *solid* layer is a layer in the size and color of your choice. You create a solid layer when you need an opaque background for a nested composition. You can also use solids with masks to create graphic elements (**Figure 4.52**). And you can even use this type of layer to create text effects within After Effects. (For more about text effects, see Chapter 10, "Effects Fundamentals"; for more about masks, see Chapter 9, "Mask Essentials.")

Creating a solid doesn't create an actual media file on your hard drive. But in other respects, a solid layer works like any other footage item: It has specified dimensions and PAR, as well as a color. (This is notable because older versions of After Effects didn't allow you to set a solid's PAR, forcing you to treat it a little differently than other footage items.) However, this doesn't mean the solid's settings are fixed; you can change its attributes at any time.

To create a solid-color layer:

1. Open the Composition window or Timeline window for the composition in which you want to add a solid layer, or make sure one is active.
2. Choose Layer > New > Solid, or press Command-Y (Mac) or Ctrl-Y (Windows) (**Figure 4.53**).

   The Solid Footage Settings dialog box appears (**Figure 4.54**).
3. Enter a name for the new solid.

   After Effects uses the solid's current color as the basis for the default name: for example, Gray Solid 1.

continues on next page

4. Set the size by *doing any of the following:*
   - ▲ To make the solid the same size as the composition, click the Make Comp Size button.
   - ▲ To enter a custom size, choose a unit of measure from the Units pull-down menu, and enter a width and height (**Figure 4.55**).
   - ▲ To maintain the aspect ratio of the current width and height, click the Lock Aspect Ratio button before you change the size.
5. Choose an option from the Pixel Aspect Ratio pull-down menu (**Figure 4.56**).

   For an explanation of PAR, see the sidebar "PAR Excellence" in Chapter 2.
6. Set the color by *doing one of the following:*
   - ▲ Click the color swatch to open the color picker and choose a color.
   - ▲ Click the eyedropper to select a color from the screen.
7. Click OK to close the Solid Footage Settings dialog box.

   The solid appears as a layer in the composition. Like any layer, the solid layer starts at the current time and uses the default duration of still images. (See "To change the default duration of still images" in Chapter 2.) In the Project window, After Effects creates a folder called Solids that contains all the solid footage items you create.

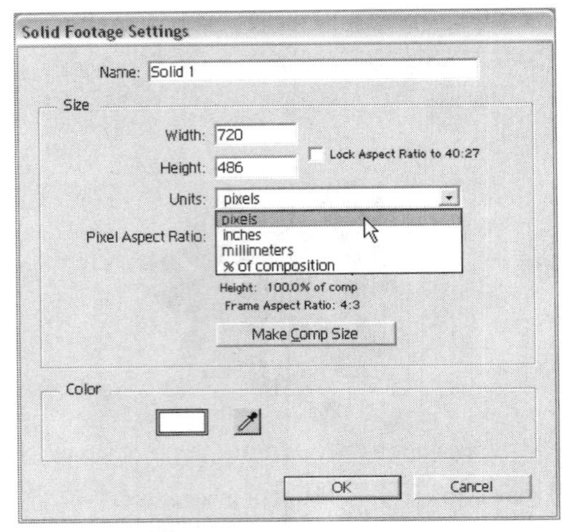

Figure 4.55 Choose a unit of measure from the pull-down menu before you enter a custom size.

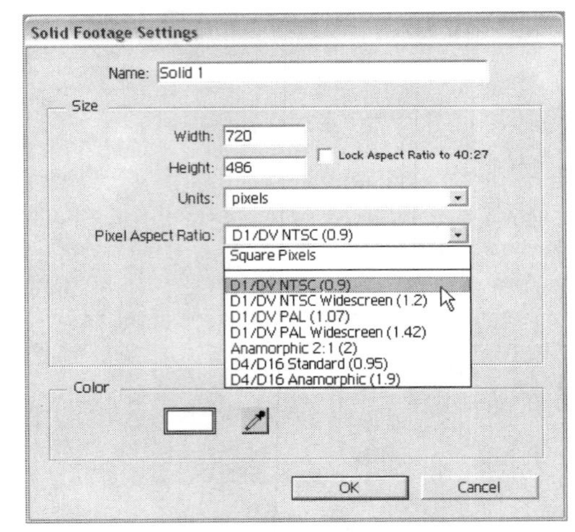

Figure 4.56 Specify an option in the Pixel Aspect Ratio pull-down menu.

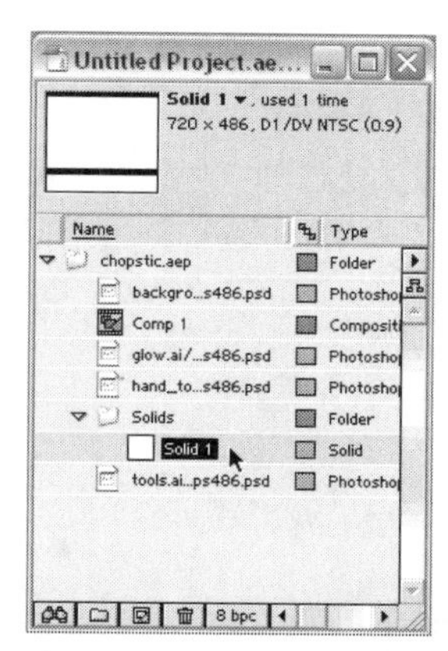

Figure 4.57 Select a solid layer in the Comp or Timeline window, or a solid footage item in the Project window (shown here).

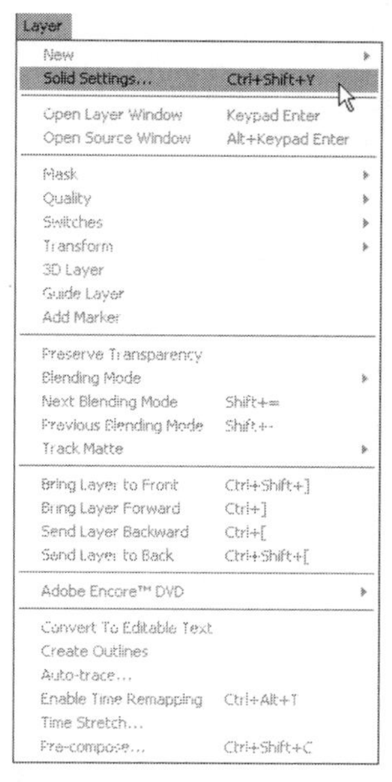

Figure 4.58 Choose Layer > Solid Settings.

To change a solid's settings:

1. *Do either of the following:*
   - ▲ In the Project window, select a solid footage item (**Figure 4.57**).
   - ▲ In the Composition or Timeline window, click a solid layer to select it.

   You may also use a variety of other methods to select a layer; for more information, see "Selecting a Layer" in Chapter 5.
2. *Do either of the following:*
   - ▲ Choose Layer > Solid Settings (**Figure 4.58**).
   - ▲ Press Shift-Command-Y (Mac) or Shift-Ctrl-Y (Windows).

   The Solid Footage Settings dialog box appears.
3. Specify any changes you want to make to the solid footage, such as its name, dimensions, PAR, or color.

continues on next page

4. If you selected the solid footage item from the Timeline or Composition window in step 1, specify whether you want the changes to affect layers already created from the solid footage item by selecting "Affect all layers that use this solid" (**Figure 4.59**).

   Leave this option unselected if you want to change only this layer and not layers already created from it.

5. Click OK.

   Depending on your choices, the changes you specified are applied to the selected solid layer, solid footage item, or both (**Figure 4.60**).

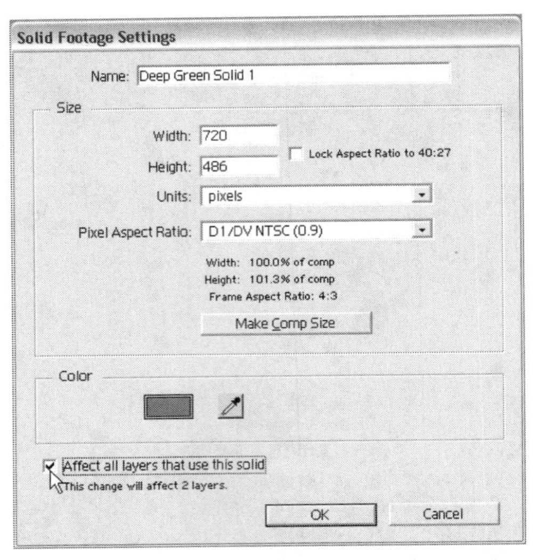

Figure 4.59 If you selected a solid footage item in the Project window, decide whether you want to select the "Affect all layers that use this solid" option.

✔ Tip

- You can continuously rasterize a solid layer. That way, its edges (particularly when you have a mask applied to it) remain crisp and smooth when you scale it up. See Chapter 5 for more about the continuous rasterize switch; see Chapter 9 for more about masks.

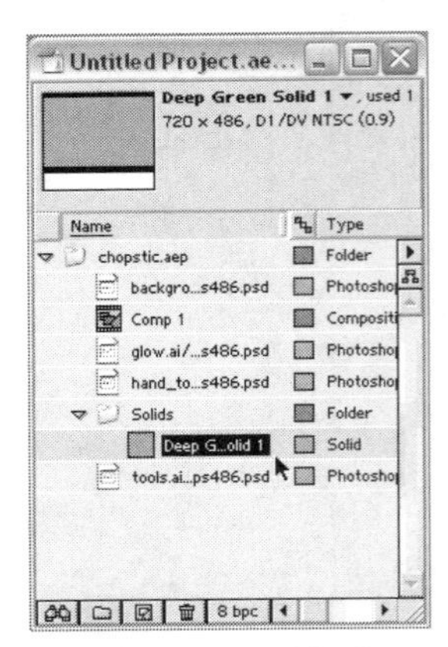

Figure 4.60 The solid reflects the changes you made. Here, you can see that the color (and hence the solid's name) has been changed.

Figure 4.61 In this example, the glowing effect is achieved by applying a radial blur to two layers. You can do this two ways...

Creating Adjustment Layers

You can also create adjustment layers within After Effects—no surprise, when you consider that After Effects can import adjustment layers from Adobe Photoshop (see Chapter 2). Whether you import them or create them in After Effects, adjustment layers work just as they do in Photoshop.

An *adjustment layer* contains effects, not footage. The effects contained in an adjustment layer are applied to all the layers below it. You save time and effort by applying effects to a single layer rather than multiple layers (**Figures 4.61**, **4.62**, and **4.63**). To cut down rendering time, hide the adjustment layer to temporarily disable its effects. You can even change an existing layer into an adjustment layer.

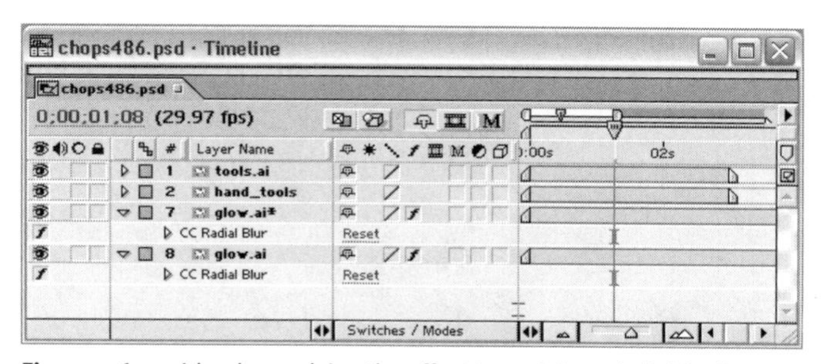

Figure 4.62 ...either by applying the effect to each layer individually...

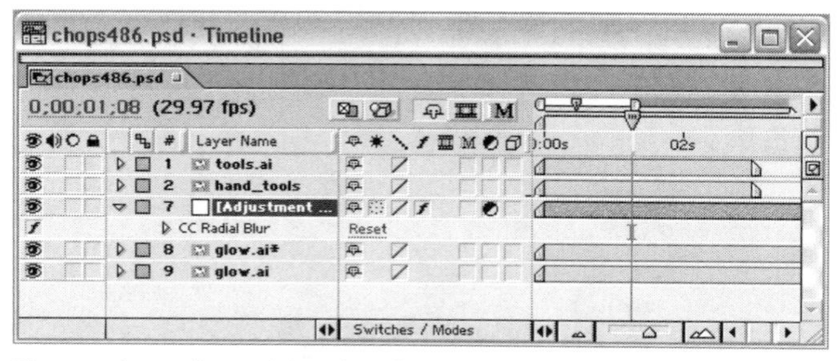

Figure 4.63 ...or by applying the effect to an adjustment layer, which affects all layers below it in the stacking order. This technique can save time and effort, and can even reduce rendering times.

To create an adjustment layer:

1. Open the Composition window or Timeline window for the composition in which you want to add an adjustment layer, or make sure one of these windows is active.
2. Choose Layer > New > Adjustment Layer (**Figure 4.64**).

   An adjustment layer appears in the composition. The adjustment layer starts at the current time and uses the default duration for still images.

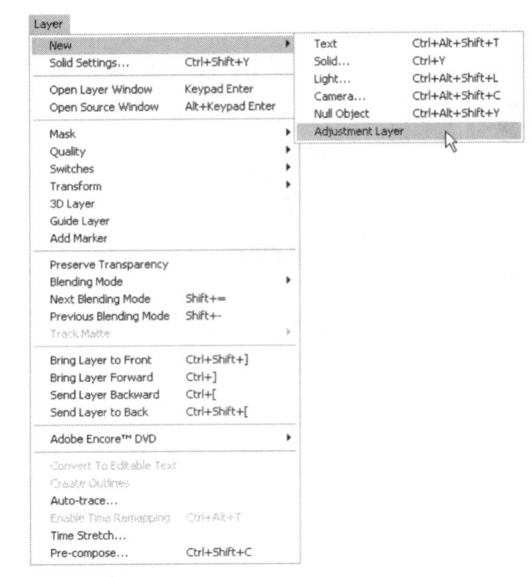

Figure 4.64 Choose Layer > New > Adjustment Layer.

✔ Tip

- You can convert an ordinary visible layer to a *guide layer*, an invisible layer you can use to position and align other layers in a composition. Because they're used in the context of setting a layer's position, guide layers are discussed in Chapter 7.

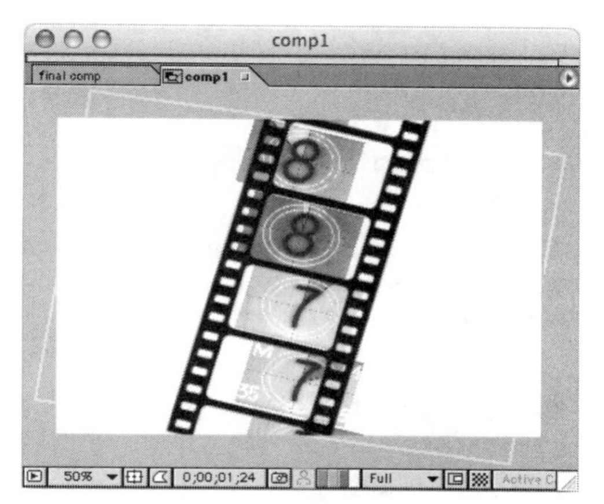

Figure 4.65 Merely rotating each layer in this composition doesn't achieve the desired effect.

Figure 4.66 Nesting the composition makes it a single layer in another composition. Rotating the nested composition easily achieves the effect.

Nesting Compositions

To achieve many effects, you must make a composition a layer in another composition—a process called *nesting*. For example, rotating each layer in the composition in **Figure 4.65** doesn't achieve the desired effect. Each layer is rotated around its own anchor point and betrays the fact that each layer is a separate element. To make the layers appear unified, it would be extremely inconvenient to adjust each layer individually.

With a nested composition, it's possible to rotate the entire composition as a single layer, as in **Figure 4.66**. As a single layer within another composition, all the elements rotate around a single anchor point. You can use nested compositions to produce complex effects, to control rendering order, or to apply effects to continuously rasterized or collapsed layers. You can always reopen the nested composition. Any changes you make to the original are reflected in the nested layer.

The following sections show you how to make one composition a layer in another. Chapter 17 revisits nested compositions in more detail.

To make a composition a layer in another composition:

1. Display the Composition window or Timeline window of the composition that will contain the nested composition.
2. Drag a composition you want to nest from the Project window to *any of the following:*
   - ▲ Composition window of the target composition
   - ▲ Timeline window of the target composition
   - ▲ Name or icon of the target composition in the Project window

   The composition becomes a layer in the target composition. The composition layer starts at the current time and has the duration of the original composition (**Figure 4.67**).

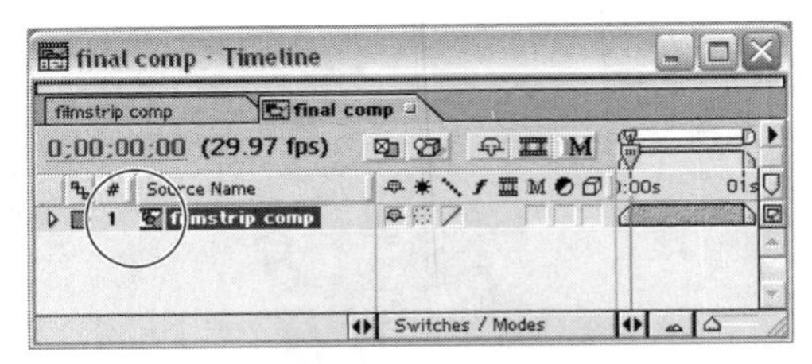

Figure 4.67 The nested composition looks and behaves much like any other layer.

To nest one composition in a new one with the same settings:

◆ Drag a composition in the Project window to the composition icon at the bottom of the Project window (**Figure 4.68**).

The composition becomes a layer in a new composition that uses the same composition settings as the nested one.

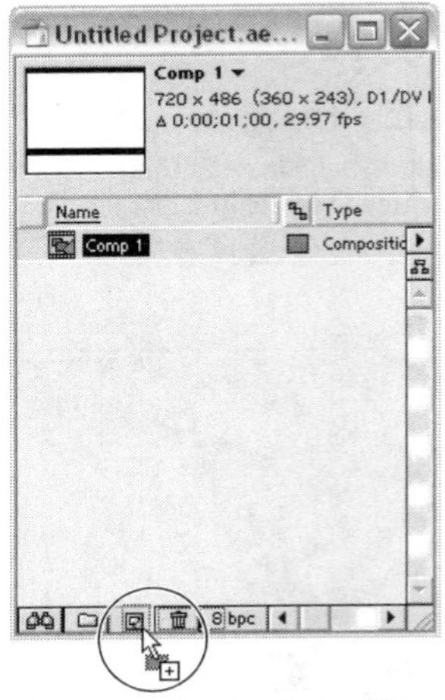

Figure 4.68 Drag a composition to the composition icon at the bottom of the Project window to nest it in a new composition with the same settings.

✔ Tips

- The default frame rate and resolution of nested compositions depend on the setting you chose in the Advanced panel of the Composition Settings dialog box. You can tell After Effects to preserve the frame rate and resolution of nested comps (see "Nesting Options" earlier in this chapter).
- After Effects' Parenting feature allows you to create even more complex relationships between layers than nesting allows. Make sure you use the best technique for the job at hand. See Chapter 17 for more about the Parenting feature.

5

Layer Basics

Previous chapters laid the groundwork for the central activity of your After Effects work: manipulating a composition's layers. Over the next several chapters, you'll gradually increase your command over layers. This chapter focuses on the bare essentials, describing how to select, name, and label layers. You'll also learn how to control layer quality and how to choose whether to include layers in previews and renders. In addition, you'll see how to simplify working with layers by concealing ones you're not using and by locking ones you don't want to disturb. In the process, you'll become a bit more familiar with your primary workspace, the Timeline window.

Selecting Layers

Naturally, you must select layers before you can adjust them. In the timeline, selected layer names are highlighted, and their duration bars (in the timeline's time ruler area) have a textured surface that distinguishes them from other layers. In the Composition window, selected layers can appear with *handles*—six small boxes that demark each layer's boundaries, and that you can use to transform the layer. However, you can specify whether you want these (or other layer controls) to appear in the Comp window. See the section "Viewing Spatial Controls in the Comp Window" in Chapter 7, "Properties and Keyframes," for more details.

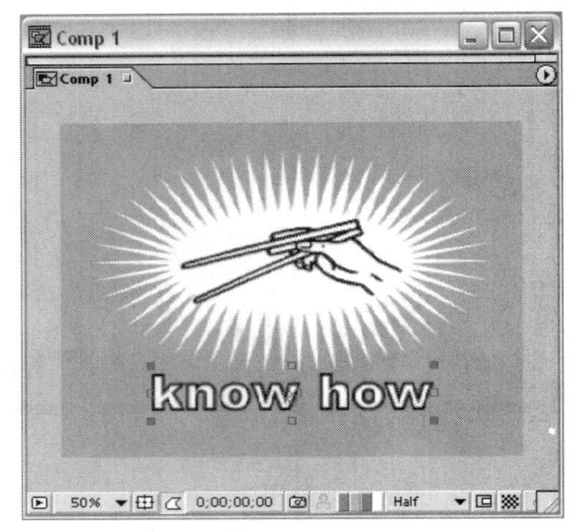

Figure 5.1 You can select a layer by directly clicking it in the Composition window. In this figure, the Comp window is set to show selected layer handles.

To select layers in the Composition window:

1. If you haven't already done so, cue the current frame of the composition so that the layer you want to select is visible in the Composition window.
2. In the Composition window, click the visible layer to select it (**Figure 5.1**).

   The selected layer's handles and anchor point appear, unless these options have been disabled (see "Viewing Spatial Controls in the Comp Window" in Chapter 7).
3. To select more than one layer, Shift-click other visible layers in the Composition window (**Figure 5.2**).

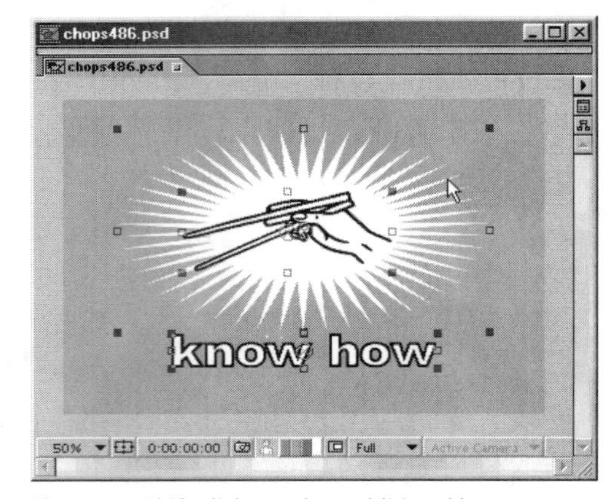

Figure 5.2 Shift-click to select additional layers.

To select layers in the Timeline window:

In the Timeline window, *do any of the following:*

◆ Click the layer name or its duration bar.

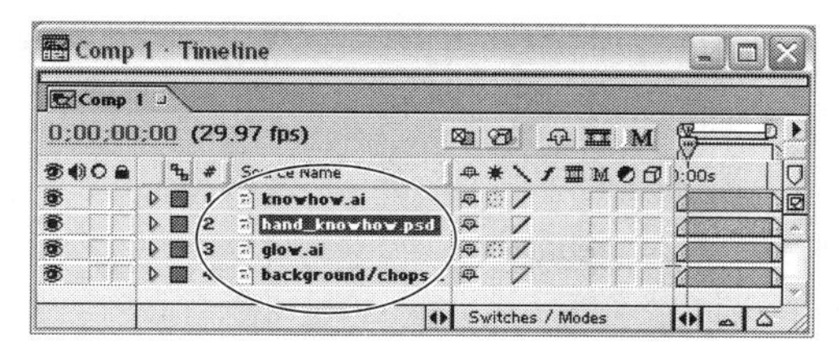

Figure 5.3 You can select layers by clicking them in the Timeline window—or simply by entering the layer's number on the numeric keypad.

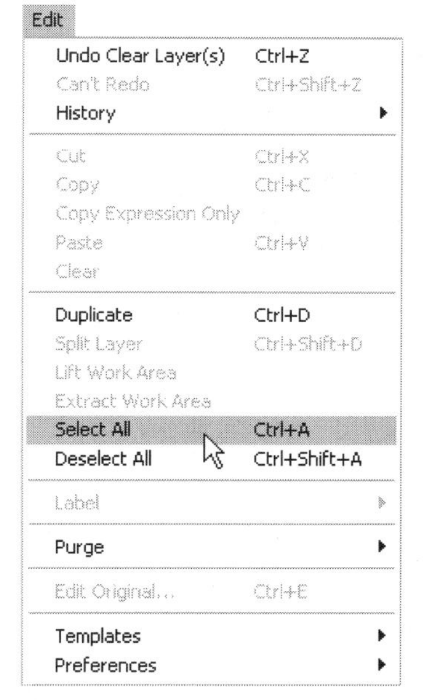

Figure 5.4 You can select all layers in the usual way—by choosing Edit > Select All (or using the keyboard shortcut).

- To select a layer by its layer number, type the layer number on the numeric keypad (not the numbers on the main keyboard) (**Figure 5.3**).
- To select a range of layers, Shift-click other layers.
- To select a range of layers, drag a marquee around several layer names. (Take care not to drag a layer to a new position in the stacking order.)

  Selected layers appear highlighted in the Timeline window.

To select all layers in a composition:

- Choose Edit > Select All, or press Command-A (Mac) or Ctrl-A (Windows) (**Figure 5.4**).

  All the layers in the composition are selected.

To deselect all layers in a composition:

Do one of the following:

- Click an empty area in the Timeline window or the Composition window.
- Choose Edit > Deselect All.

✔ Tips

- When the Timeline window is active, you can select a layer by typing its layer number. See "Layer number," later in this chapter.
- Press Command-Up Arrow (Mac) or Ctrl-Up Arrow (Windows) to select the next layer up in the stacking order. See the next section, "Stacking Order."
- Press Command-Down Arrow (Mac) or Ctrl-Down Arrow (Windows) to select the next layer down in the stacking order.

Stacking Order

As you learned in Chapter 4, "Compositions," each new layer in a composition becomes the highest layer in the Timeline window—or the highest in the *stacking order*. When layers occupy the same point in time, higher layers appear in front of lower layers when viewed in the Composition window. You can change the relative positions of the layers in the stacking order to determine which elements appear in front and which appear behind (**Figures 5.5** and **5.6**).

Figure 5.5 Layers higher in the stacking order appear in front of other layers in the Composition window (provided they're positioned at the same point in time).

Figure 5.6 When a layer is moved to a lower position in the stacking order, it appears behind the higher layers in the Composition window.

To set the In and Out points using keyboard shortcuts:

1. In the Layer window or Timeline window, set the current frame (**Figure 6.17**).
2. To set the In point of the layer, press Option-[(Mac) or Alt-[(Windows).

   The In point of the layer is set to the current frame in the composition (**Figure 6.18**).
3. To set the Out point of the layer, press Option-] (Mac) or Alt-] (Windows).

   In the Layer window and Timeline window, the edit points reflect the changes you made. Note how setting the layer's In point affects both its starting point and the layer's starting point in the composition.

To set the In and Out points by dragging:

In the time graph panel of the Timeline window, *do either of the following*:

- ◆ To set the In point, drag the In point of a layer's duration bar (the handle at the left end of the duration bar) (**Figure 6.19**).
- ◆ To set the Out point, drag the Out point of a layer's duration bar (the handle at the right end of the duration bar) (**Figure 6.20**).

  Make sure you drag the ends of the layer's duration bar, not the bar itself. Otherwise, you could change the layer's position in time rather than its In or Out point.

✔ Tips

- Pressing Shift after you begin to drag causes the In or Out point to *snap to edges*. That is, the layer's edit point will behave as though it's magnetized and align with the edit points of other layers, the current time marker, and the layer and composition markers.
- You can see the exact position of an edit point in time by looking at the Info window's time display as you drag.
- If you reach a point where you're unable to further increase a layer's duration, it means you've run out of source footage.

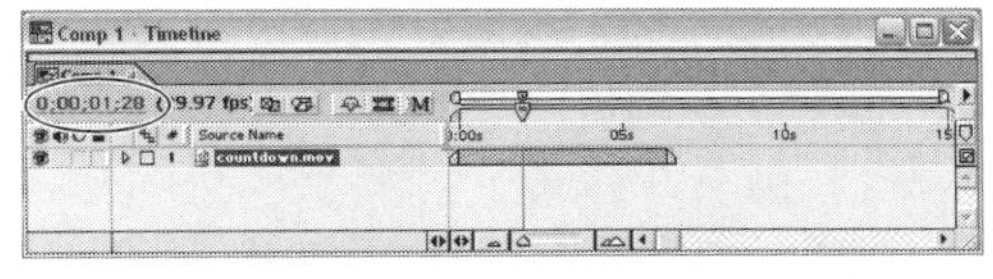

Figure 6.17 Set the current time to the frame of the layer you want to set as an edit point.

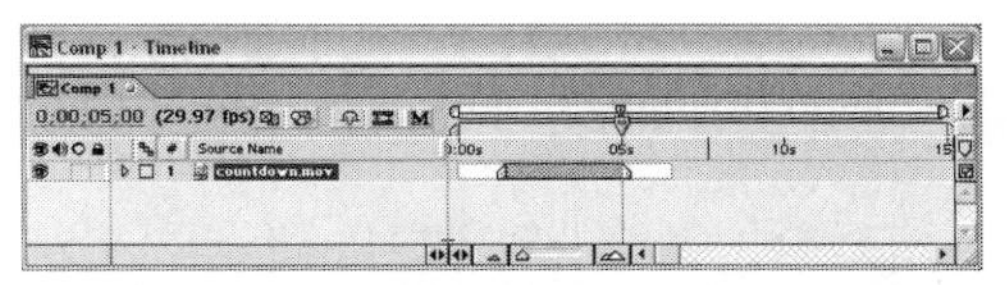

Figure 6.18 Press Option-[(Mac) or Alt-[(Windows) to set the In point of the selected layer to the current time.

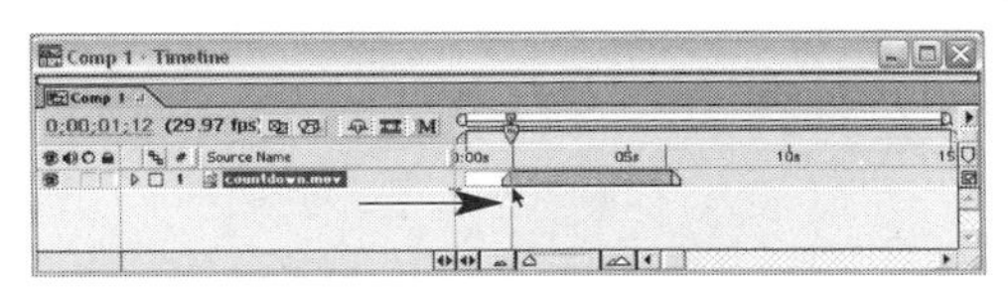

Figure 6.19 Drag the In point handle of a layer's duration bar to change both its In point and where it starts in the composition.

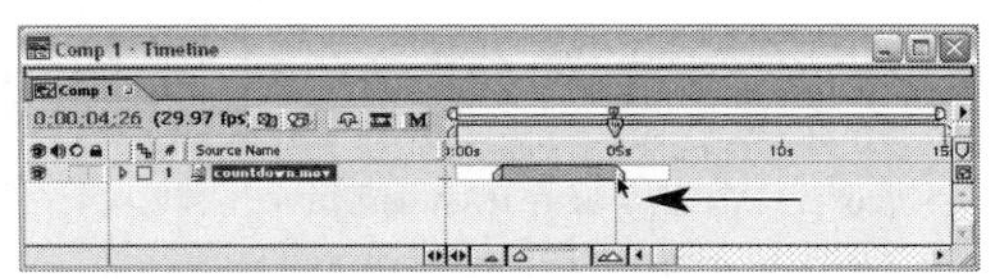

Figure 6.20 Drag the Out point handle of a layer's duration bar to change both its Out point and where it ends in the composition.

Moving Layers in Time

When you create a layer, it begins at the current time marker. After that, you can move its position in time in either by dragging the layer's duration bar or by using the controls in the In/Out panel of the Timeline window.

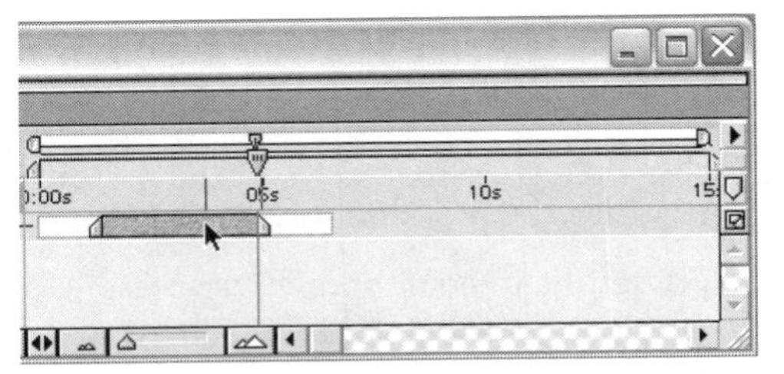

Figure 6.21 Drag a layer from the center portion of its duration bar...

To move a layer in time by dragging:

- In the time graph area of the Timeline window, drag a layer to a new position in time (**Figures 6.21** and **6.22**).
- Dragging a layer to the left causes the layer to begin earlier in the composition.
- Dragging a layer to the right causes the layer to begin later in the composition.

  Make sure you drag from the middle section of the layer's duration bar; dragging either end changes the duration of the layer.

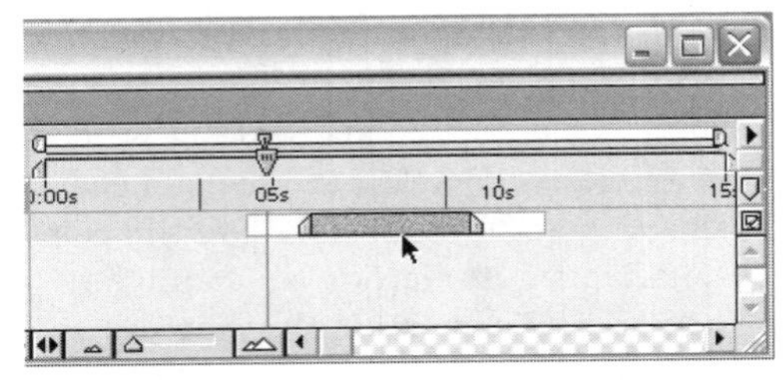

Figure 6.22 ...to shift its position in time (without changing its duration). Press Shift after you begin dragging to activate the Snap to Edges feature.

✔ Tips

- A layer's In point can occur before the beginning of the composition, just as its Out point can occur after the end of the composition. Of course, any frames beyond the beginning or end of the comp won't be included in previews or output.
- As usual, you can press Shift after you begin dragging to cause the layer to snap to edges. When you activate the Snap to Edges feature, the edges of the layer (its In and Out points) align with the edges of other layers as well as with the current time marker as you drag them near each other. The layer also snaps to layer and composition markers.
- Great keyboard shortcuts are available for trimming and moving layers. Check out the Help menu or your Quick Reference card for shortcuts not mentioned here.

The In/Out Panel

By default, one panel of the Timeline window is hidden from view. Revealing the panel gives you access to four panels: In, Out, Duration, and Stretch. You can also show these or any other panels by using a contextual menu.

The In and Out panels allow you to set the position of a layer numerically in time (in editing parlance, the program's In and Out points). You can use the Stretch panel to change the speed of the layer.

To show and hide the In/Out panel of the Timeline window:

- *Do either of the following:*
  - ▲ In the Timeline window, click the Right Optional Panel button to reveal the In/Out panel; click the button again to hide the panel (**Figures 6.23** and **6.24**).
  - ▲ Control-click (Mac) or right-click (Windows) any panel of the Timeline window, and choose the panel you want to view from the contextual menu (**Figure 6.25**).

✔ Tip

- You can show or hide the Switches/Modes panel by using the leftmost Optional Panels button.

Figure 6.23 Click the Right Optional Panel button to change the In/Out panel from hidden...

Figure 6.24 ...to visible. Click the button again to hide the panel.

To move a layer in time numerically:

1. Make sure the appropriate In or Out panel is visible (as described in the previous section).
2. To change the In point of the layer, click the In point display (**Figure 6.26**).
3. To change the Out point of the layer, click the Out point display.

   Depending on the option you selected, a Layer In Time or Layer Out Time dialog box opens.
4. In the Layer In Time or Layer Out Time dialog box, enter a time (**Figure 6.27**).
5. Click OK to close the dialog box.

   The layer moves in the timeline accordingly.

✔ Tip

- Although editing layers in After Effects is similar to editing clips in a non-linear editing program, the process isn't always identical. In many non-linear editors, changing the duration changes the Out point of a clip. In After Effects, the Duration panel changes the duration of the layer by changing its speed, not its Out point.

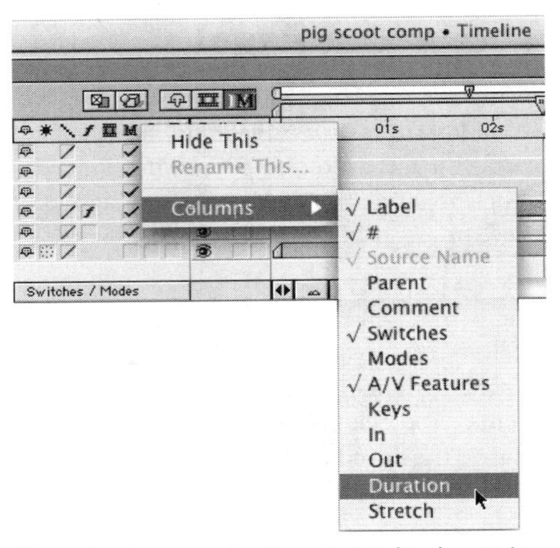

Figure 6.25 You can also Control-click (Mac) or Right-click (Windows) any panel to access a contextual menu that allows you to show or hide a panel in the Timeline window.

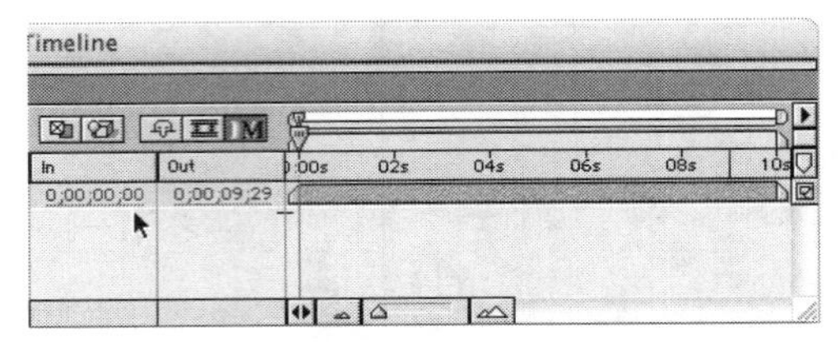

Figure 6.26 Click the In point display to move a layer to start at a new time in the composition; click the Out point display to move a layer to end at a new time.

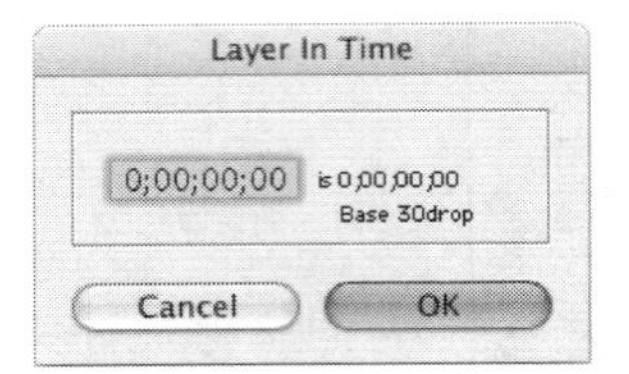

Figure 6.27 In the Layer In Time (shown here) or Layer Out Time dialog box, enter a time.

To align the In or Out point with the current time marker:

1. Set the current time of the composition where you want the layer to start or end.
2. Make sure the appropriate In or Out panel is visible (as explained in "To show or hide the In/Out Panel of the Timeline window," earlier in this chapter).
3. *Do one of the following:*
   - ▲ To align the layer's In point with the current time, Option-click (Mac) or Alt-click (Windows) the In point display (**Figure 6.28**), or press the left bracket ([) on the keyboard.
   - ▲ To align the layer's Out point with the current time, Option-click (Mac) or right-click (Windows) the Out point display, or press the right bracket (]) on the keyboard.

   Depending on your choice, the layer moves so that its In or Out point aligns with the current time (**Figure 6.29**).

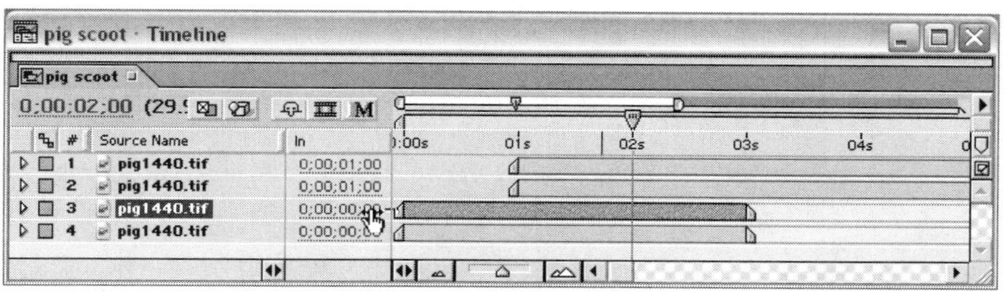

Figure 6.28 Option-click (Mac) or Alt-click (Windows) the In point display to align the beginning of the layer with the current time (shown here); use the Out point display to align the ending of the layer to the current time. Better yet, use the left bracket ([) to align the In point; use the right bracket (]) to align the Out point.

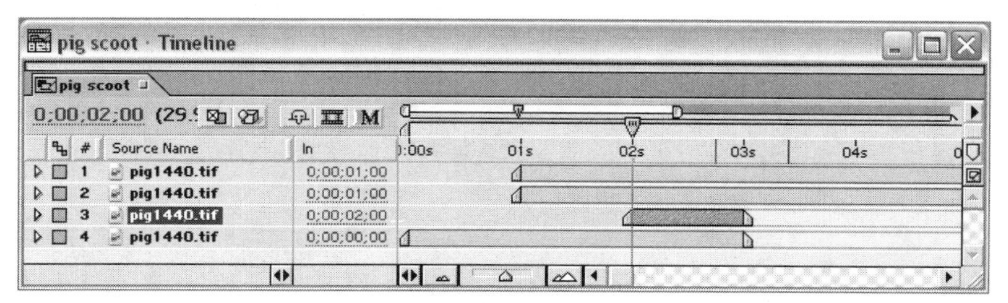

Figure 6.29 Depending on your choice, the layer moves so that its In or Out point aligns with the current time. Here, the layer moves to align its In point with the current time.

Performing a Slip Edit

After Effects includes another editing feature common to non-linear editing programs: *slip edits*.

When you're working with layers created from motion footage, you'll find that you often need to change a portion of video without altering its position or duration in the time ruler. Although you can do this by reopening the Layer window and setting new In and Out points, you must be careful to set edit points that result in the same duration. By using a slip edit, however, you can achieve the same result in a single step.

To slip a layer:

1. In the Tools palette, select the Pan Behind tool (**Figure 6.30**).

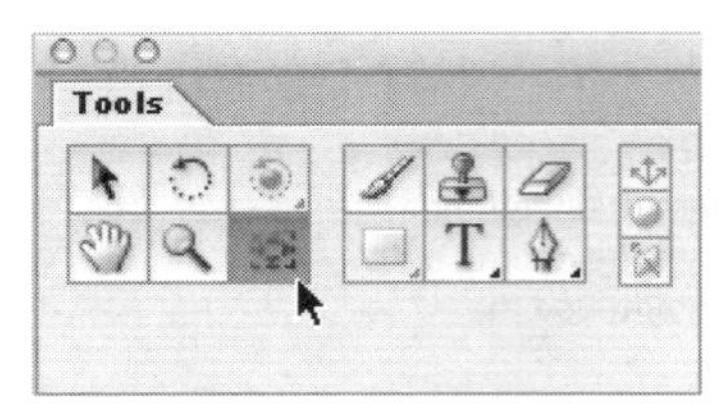

Figure 6.30 Select the Pan Behind tool.

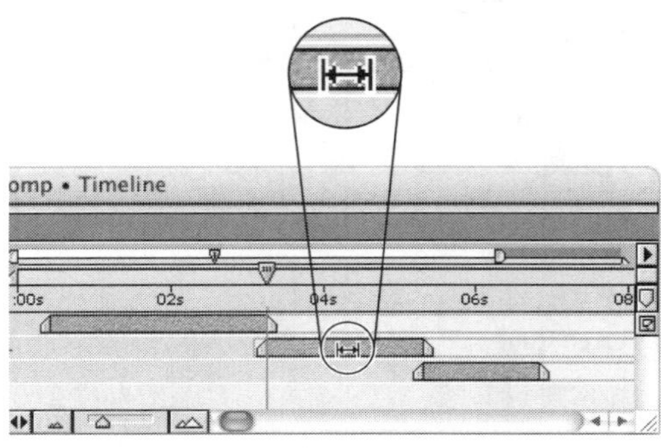

Figure 6.31 When you position the mouse over a layer created from motion footage, the mouse pointer becomes a Slip Edit tool.

2. Position the mouse over a layer created from motion footage.

   The mouse pointer becomes a Slip Edit tool (**Figure 6.31**).

3. *Do either of the following:*

   Drag left to slip the footage left, using frames that come later in the footage.

   Drag right to slip the footage right, using frames that come earlier in the footage.

   The In and Out points of the source footage change by the same amount, which means the layer maintains its duration and position in the time ruler. As you drag, you can see the "hidden" footage extending from beyond the layer's In and Out points (**Figure 6.32**).

✔ Tips

- You can also perform a slip edit by dragging the layer's "hidden" trimmed frames (you can see their outlines extending beyond the layer's In and Out handles).
- To review how to perform insert and overlay edits, see Chapter 4, "Compositing."
- Those who use non-linear editing software know that the counterpart to the slip edit is the *slide edit*. Because each layer in After Effects occupies a separate track, the program has always supported slide edits: Simply drag the layer to a new position in the time ruler.

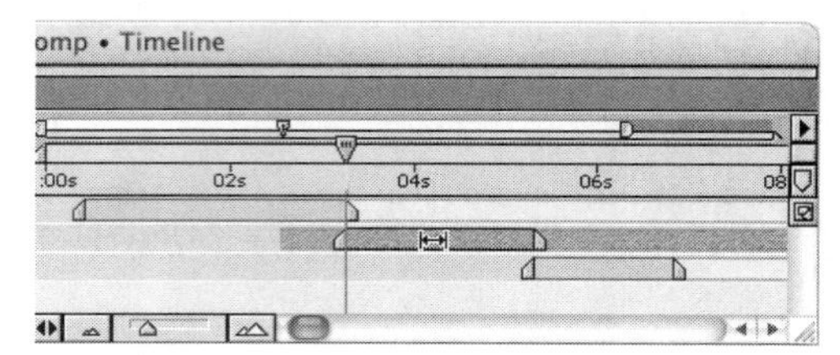

Figure 6.32 Dragging with the Slip Edit tool changes the portion of the motion footage used without changing its duration or position in the time ruler.

To lift or extract a range of frames from a composition:

1. Set the current time to the beginning of the range of frames you want to remove from a composition, and press B.

   The beginning of the work area bar is set to the current time.

2. Set the current time to the end of the range of frames you want to remove from a composition, and press N.

   The end of the work area bar is set to the current time (**Figure 6.45**).

3. *Do either of the following:*

   ▲ To lift the range of frames under the work area, choose Edit > Lift Work Area.

   ▲ To extract the range of frames under the work area, choose Edit > Extract Work Area (**Figure 6.46**).

   The range of frames under the work area is removed according to the method you selected. When frames are removed from the middle of a layer, the layer is split (**Figure 6.47**).

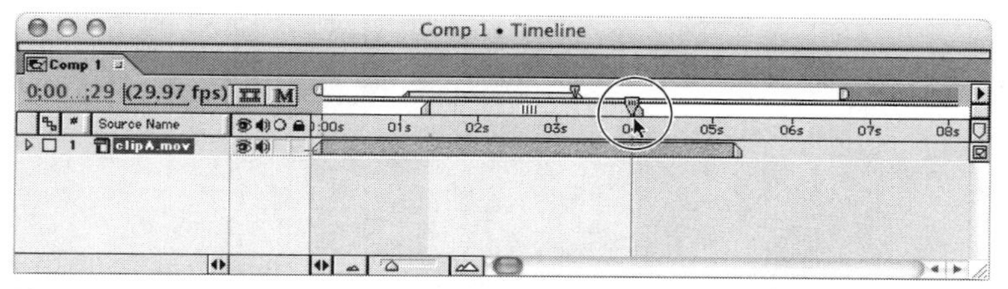

Figure 6.45 Set the work area bar over the frames of the comp you want to remove.

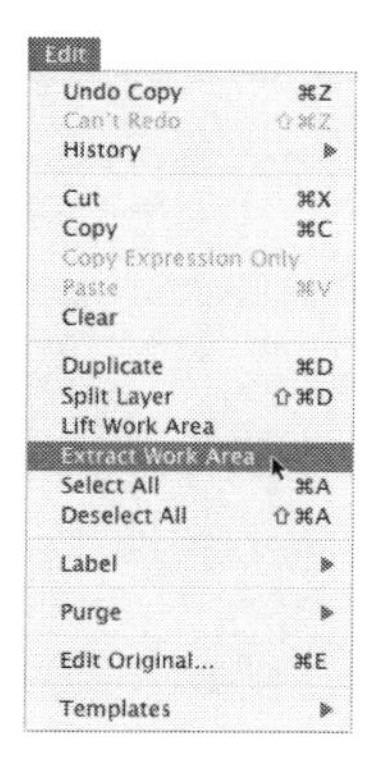

Figure 6.46 Choose Edit > Lift Work Area or Edit > Extract Work area, depending on the kind of edit you want to perform.

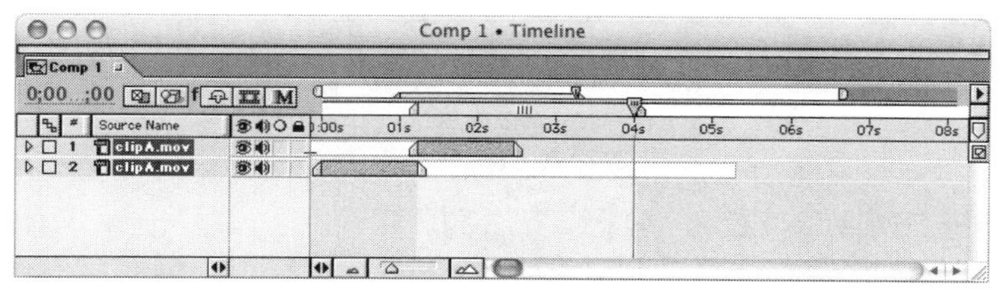

Figure 6.47 The frames you set under the work area are removed according to the type of edit you specified (here, an extract edit).

Duplicating Layers

As you learned in Chapter 4, you can add a footage item to one or more compositions as many times as you like, creating a new layer each time. However, it's often easier to duplicate a layer that's already in a composition, particularly when you want to use its edit points or other properties (such as masks, transformations, effects, and layer modes). When you create a duplicate, it appears just above the original layer in the stacking order. The duplicate uses the same name as the original, unless you specified a custom name for the original layer. When the original layer uses a custom name, duplicates have a number appended to the name; subsequent duplicates are numbered incrementally.

To duplicate a layer:

1. In the Timeline window, select a layer.
2. Choose Edit > Duplicate, or press Command-D (Mac) or Ctrl-D (Windows) (**Figure 6.48**).

   A copy of the layer appears above the original layer in the stacking order (**Figure 6.49**). The copy is selected; you may want to rename the new layer (as described in "Naming Layers," in Chapter 5).

✔ Tip

- Older versions of After Effects appended an asterisk after the name of a duplicate layer (or layers resulting from splitting a layer), and subsequent duplicates used additional asterisks. Now After Effects uses a more straightforward incremental numbering system.

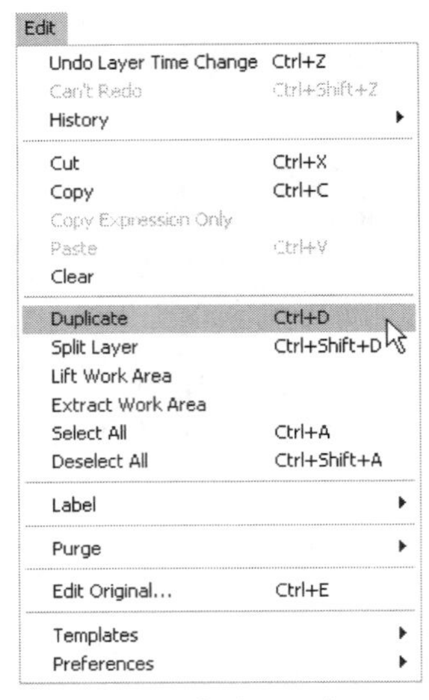

Figure 6.48 To duplicate a layer, select the layer and choose Edit > Duplicate, or press Command-D (Mac) or Ctrl-D (Windows).

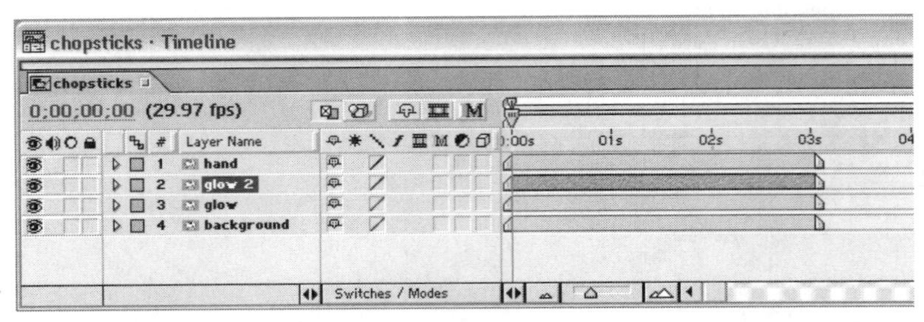

Figure 6.49 A duplicate layer appears in the composition, distinguished by a number 2 after its name.

Using Markers

Like most non-linear editing programs, After Effects enables you to mark important points in time with a visible stamp. *Markers* allow you to identify music beats visually and to synchronize visual effects with sound effects. They can also help you quickly move the current time to particular points in the composition. You can add as many as ten numbered markers to the time graph. And in individual layers, you can add any number of markers, which can include text comments to help you identify them. Because markers are for personal reference, they only appear in the time ruler and layer duration bars; they don't appear in the Composition window or in previews or renders.

In addition to text comments, layer markers can also contain Web or chapter links. These links are retained when you export to certain Web- or DVD-friendly formats. When a marker containing a link is reached during playback, a Web link automatically opens as a Web page in your browser; a chapter link cues a QuickTime movie or DVD to a specified chapter. Check the After Effects online help for more detailed information on these specialized features.

To add a composition marker by dragging:

- In the Timeline window, drag a composition time marker from the marker well to the desired point in the time graph (**Figure 6.58**).

  A marker appears in the time ruler of the Timeline window (**Figure 6.59**).

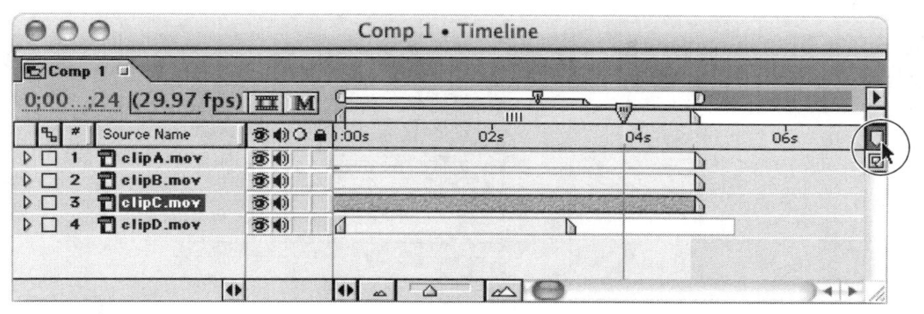

Figure 6.58 To add a composition marker, drag a marker from the marker well...

Figure 6.59 ...and drop the marker at the frame you want to mark in the time ruler. Watch the current time display of the Timeline window to help accurately place the marker.

To add a composition marker at the current time marker:

1. Move the current time marker to the frame you want to mark in the composition (**Figure 6.60**).
2. Press Shift and a number on the main keyboard (not the numeric keypad).

   A marker with the number you pressed appears in the time ruler of the Timeline window (**Figure 6.61**).

To move a composition marker:

◆ Drag a composition marker to a new position in the time ruler of the Timeline window (**Figure 6.62**).

To move the current time marker to a composition marker:

◆ Press the number of a composition marker on the main keyboard (not the numeric keypad).

The current time marker moves to the composition marker with the number you pressed.

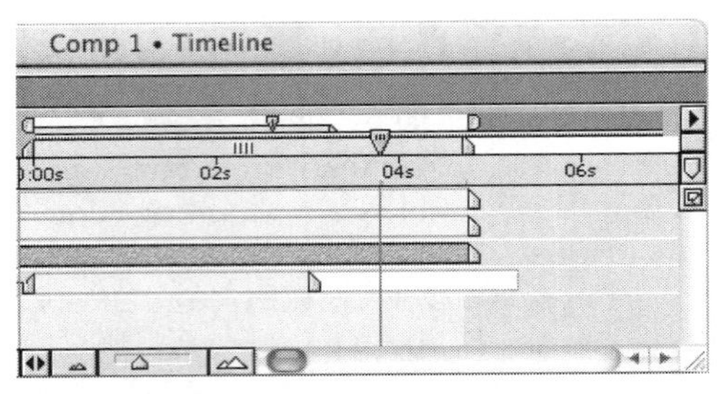

Figure 6.60 You can also place a composition marker by setting the current time...

Figure 6.61 ...and then pressing Shift and a number on the main keyboard to place the numbered marker at the current time.

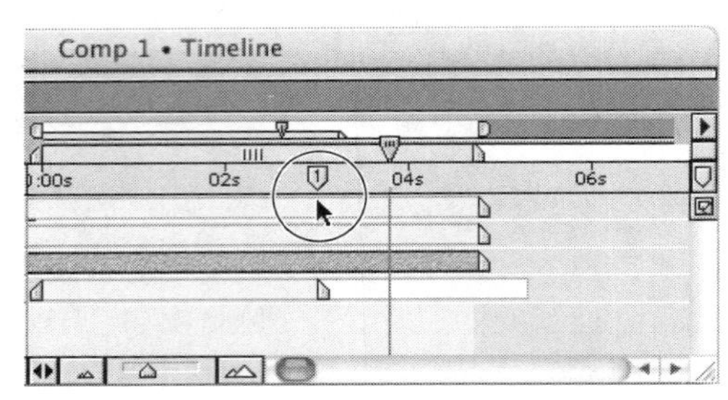

Figure 6.62 You can drag a composition marker to a new position in the time ruler.

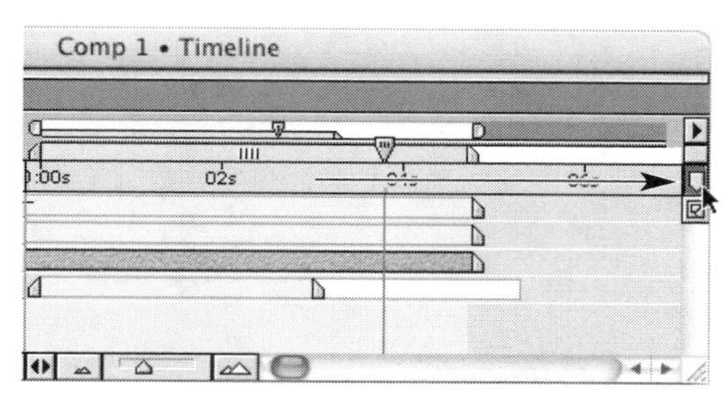

Figure 6.63 To remove a composition marker, drag it to the extreme right, until the marker well is highlighted and the marker disappears.

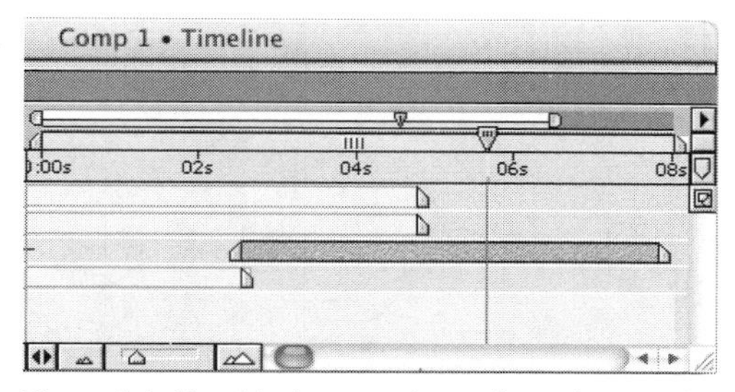

Figure 6.64 To add a layer marker, select a layer and set the current time to the frame you want to mark.

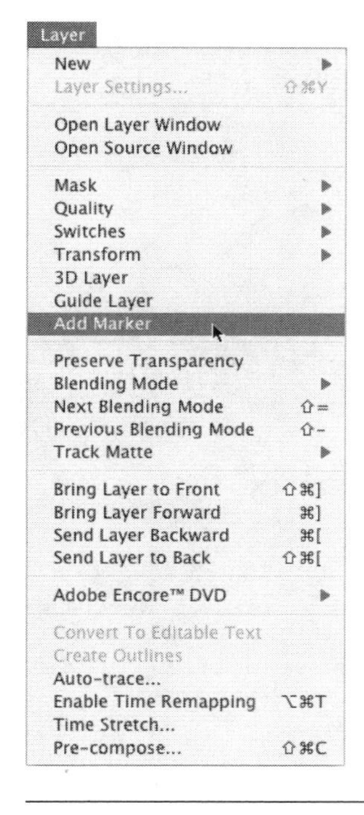

Figure 6.65 Choose Layer > Add Marker, or press the asterisk on the numeric keypad.

To remove a composition marker:

◆ Drag a composition marker to the right until the marker well is highlighted and the marker disappears from the time ruler (**Figure 6.63**).

The marker disappears from the time ruler.

To add a layer marker:

1. Select the layer to which you want to add a marker.
2. Set the current time to the frame to which you want to add a marker (**Figure 6.64**).
3. *Do one of the following:*
   - ▲ Choose Layer > Add Marker (**Figure 6.65**).
   - ▲ Press the asterisk (*) on the numeric keypad (not the main keyboard).

   A marker appears on the layer's duration bar at the current time marker (**Figure 6.66**).

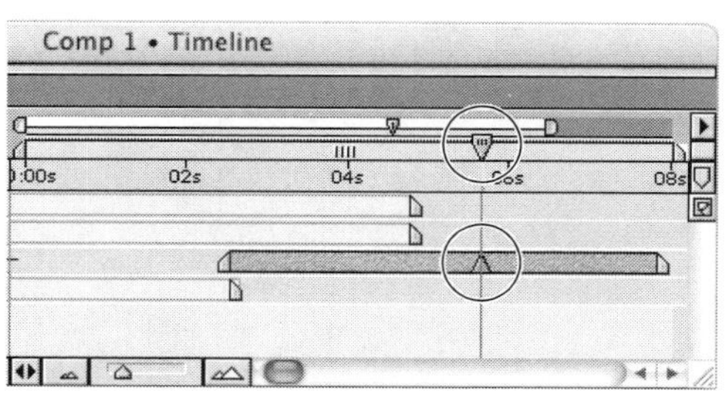

Figure 6.66 The marker appears in the duration bar of the selected layer at the current time marker.

To add a layer marker comment:

1. Double-click a layer marker in a layer's duration bar (**Figure 6.67**).

   A Marker dialog box opens. If a Layer window opens, you must have double-clicked the layer's duration bar or marker name rather than the marker itself.

2. In the Marker dialog box, enter a comment for the marker in the Comment field (**Figure 6.68**).

   You can also add chapter links or Web links if your output format supports these features.

3. Click OK to close the dialog box.

   The comment you specified appears next to the layer marker (**Figure 6.69**).

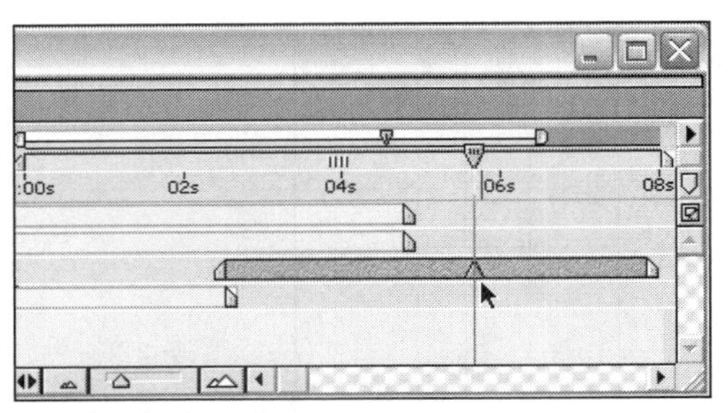

Figure 6.67 Double-click a layer marker to add a name to the marker. Make sure to double-click the marker, not the layer (or the marker name, if it already has one).

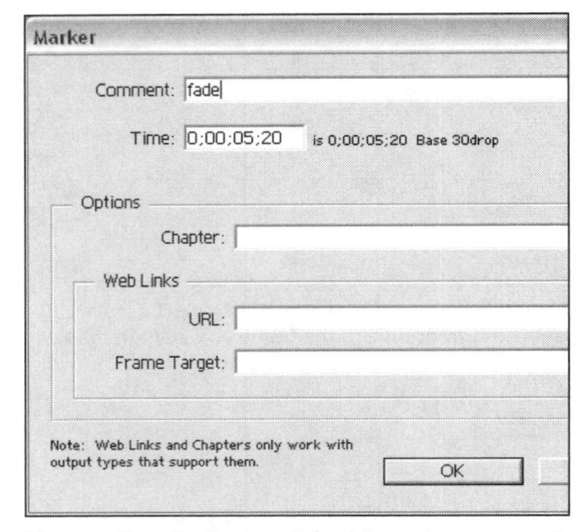

Figure 6.68 In the Marker dialog box, enter a comment for the marker.

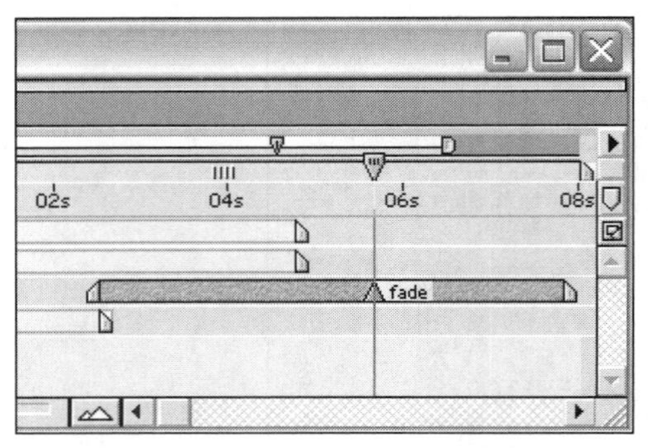

Figure 6.69 The comment you specified appears next to the marker.

Audio Properties

Although After Effects is known best for its ability to manipulate images, it also offers audio control via the Audio property, which appears last in the layer outline.

Expanding the Audio property category reveals a Levels property and an audio waveform display. The Levels property value determines the volume of the audio track, and the waveform displays a graphical representation of the audio track's left and right channels. As with other layer properties, you can set audio levels globally or animate them over time.

The following sections explain how to set audio levels for a layer using controls in the Audio palette. A more detailed explanation of playback is reserved for Chapter 8.

Viewing an Audio Waveform

You can expand the outlines of layers containing audio to reveal an audio waveform display that provides a graphical representation of the audio's left and right channels.

The waveform's shape corresponds to characteristics of the audio. For example, you can often identify the beat of the bass drum in a song by finding peaks in the waveform. The size of the waveform corresponds to the level, or volume, of the audio. Increasing the levels (by setting the Levels property or by applying an audio effect) makes the waveform taller; decreasing the levels makes the waveform shorter.

The horizontal detail of the waveform depends on your view of the time ruler. By zooming in to the time ruler to the frame level, you can view the greatest detail in the audio waveform. You can also resize the Waveform property track to increase the vertical detail of the display. Be aware, however, that doing so merely makes the waveform easier to see; it doesn't change the volume levels.

To display a layer's audio waveform:

1. Select a layer containing audio (**Figure 7.33**).
2. Press L to display the layer's Levels and Waveform properties in the layer outline.
3. Click the triangle next to the Waveform property to expand the layer outline further and to reveal the waveform display (**Figure 7.34**).

   Waveforms for the left and right channels appear in the property track. The left channel appears above the right channel.

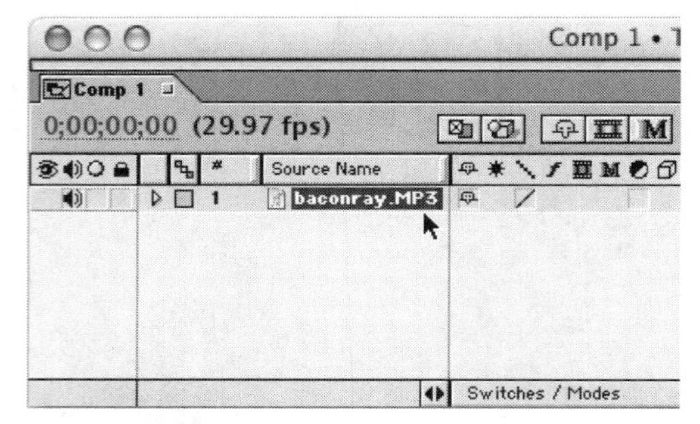

Figure 7.33 Select a layer containing audio.

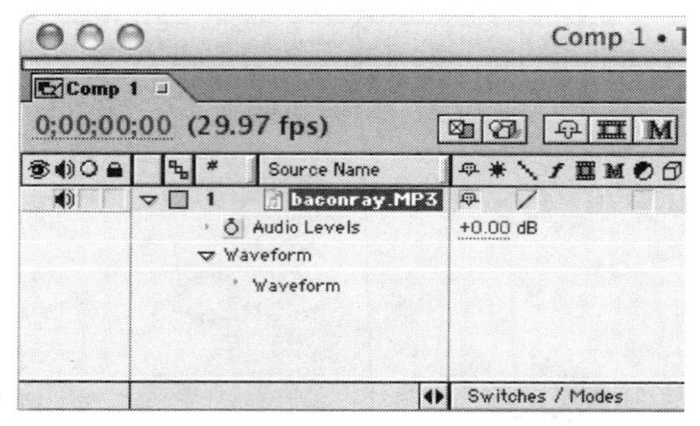

Figure 7.34 Press L to reveal the Levels property, and click the triangle next to the Waveform property to reveal waveform displays for the left and right channels.

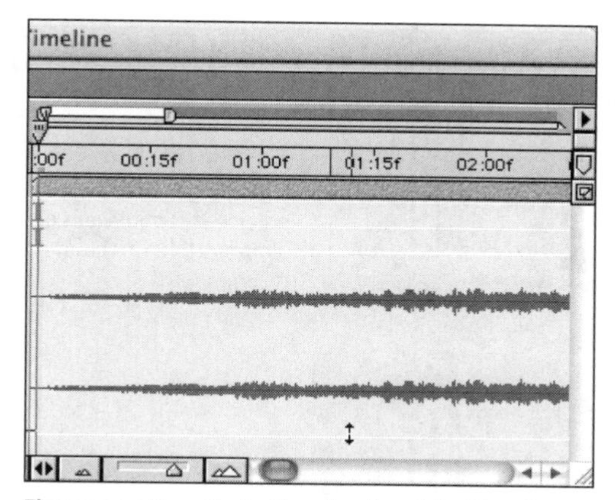

Figure 7.35 Drag the bottom border of the Waveform property track to scale the vertical aspect of the display. Doing so doesn't affect the levels.

To resize the audio Waveform property track:

1. Display the audio waveform for a layer containing audio, as described in the previous section.
2. Below the audio waveform display, drag the bottom border of the property track (**Figure 7.35**).

   Dragging down increases the size of the waveform display; dragging up decreases it. Changing the size of the waveform's property track doesn't affect audio levels, only the detail of the waveform.

✔ Tip

- For more about mono and stereo audio tracks, see the sidebar "Moving in Stereo" in Chapter 11.

Using the Audio Palette

By default, the Audio palette is grouped with the Time Controls window. You use it to monitor and control audio levels much as you would use a traditional audio mixing board (**Figure 7.36**).

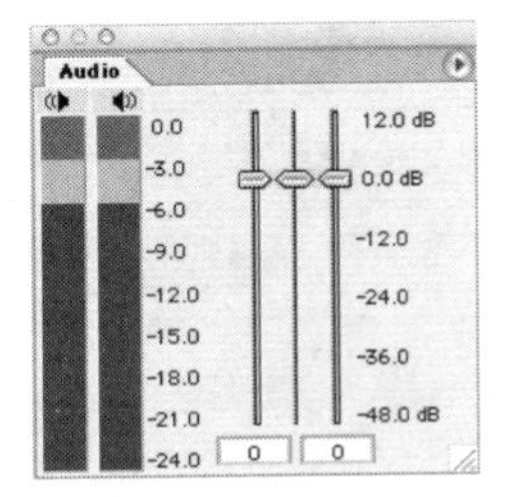

Figure 7.36 The Audio palette is reminiscent of a more traditional audio mixing board.

On the left side of the Audio palette, Volume Units (VU) meters display playback levels. On the right side of the palette, sliders control the levels for the left and right audio channels. You can set the meters to display levels as percentages or on the more traditional decibel (dB) scale. You can also set the lowest value for the slider controls.

To resize the Audio palette:

- Drag the lower-right corner of the Audio palette to increase or decrease its height.

  Increasing the height of the palette increases the precision of the meter and the slider controls (**Figure 7.37**).

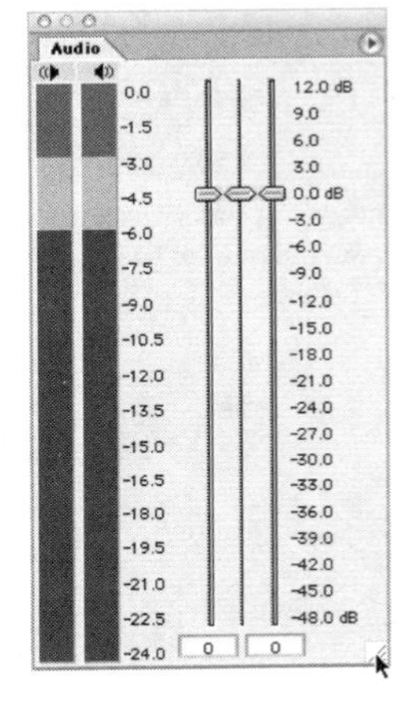

Figure 7.37 Resize the Audio palette to increase its height as well as to make its meter and controls more precise.

To set Audio palette options:

1. Click the arrow in the upper-right corner of the Audio palette, and select Options from the pop-up menu (**Figure 7.38**).

   The Audio Options dialog box appears (**Figure 7.39**).

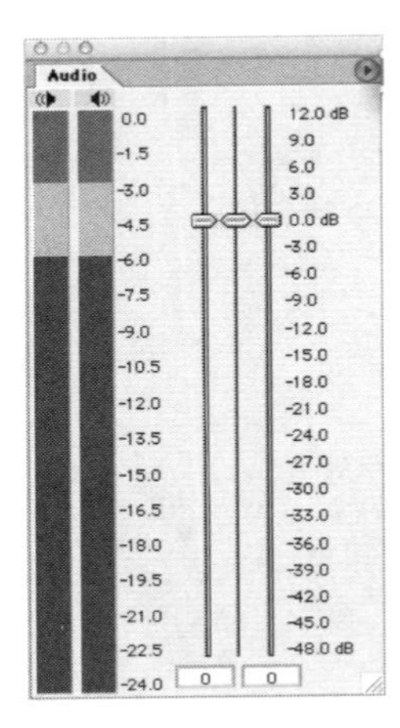

Figure 7.38 Click the arrow in the upper-right corner of the Audio palette, and select Options.

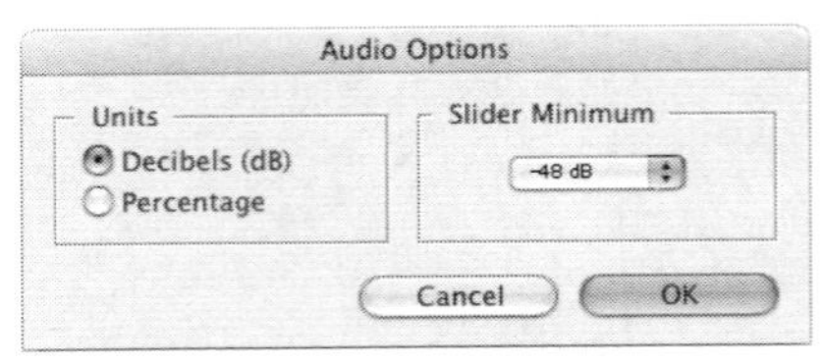

Figure 7.39 The Audio Options dialog box appears. Choose to display the audio in decibels or percentages.

2. To set the scale of the VU meter, *select one of the following:*

   Decibels (dB)—Displays levels in decibels (the standard measure of audio power, or volume)

   Percentage—Displays levels in percentages (where 100 percent is equivalent to 0 dB)

   Peak audio levels should approach but not exceed 0 dB. Otherwise, audio distortion will occur.

3. To set the minimum value of the Levels slider controls, choose an option from the Slider Minimum pull-down menu (**Figure 7.40**).

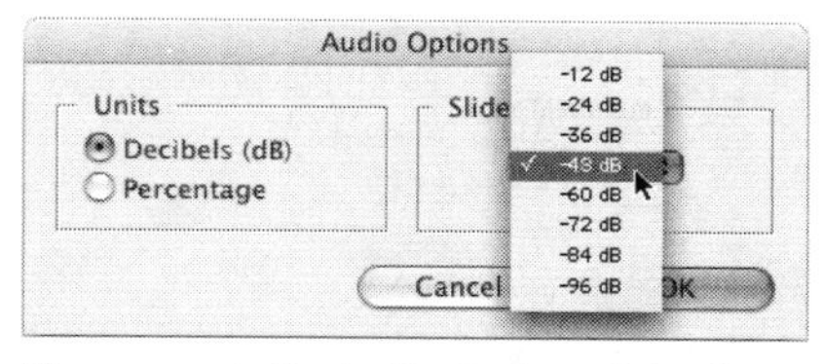

Figure 7.40 In the Audio Options dialog box, set the minimum value of the Levels slider controls.

Figure 7.41 Select a layer containing audio.

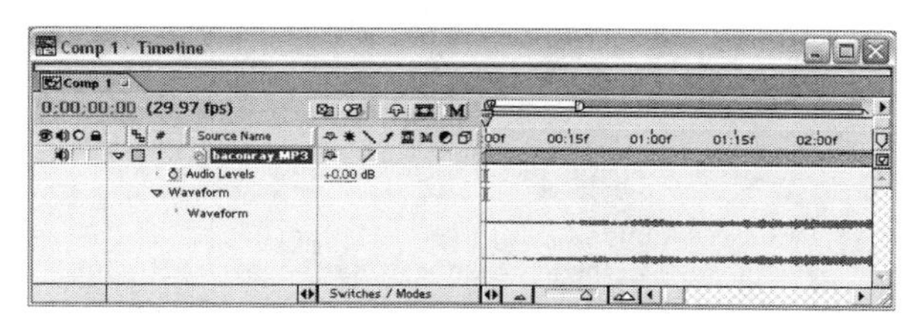

Figure 7.42 If you want, reveal the Levels property and waveform.

To set audio levels using the Audio palette:

1. Select an audio layer (**Figure 7.41**).
2. To reveal the audio Levels property, press L.

   The layer outline expands to reveal the audio Levels property.
3. To view the audio waveform, click the triangle next to the Waveform property.

   The layer outline expands to reveal the audio waveform display (**Figure 7.42**).

continues on next page

4. In the Audio palette, *do any of the following:*
   - ▲ Drag the left slider to change the left channel level, or enter a value in the box below the left slider (**Figure 7.43**).

     The center slider adjusts accordingly.
   - ▲ Drag the right slider to change the level for the right channel, or enter a value in the box below the right slider.

     The center slider adjusts accordingly.
   - ▲ Drag the center slider to change the level for both the left and right channels.

     The left and right sliders adjust accordingly.

   In the Timeline window, the layer's audio waveform reflects the changes in levels (**Figure 7.44**). If the Stopwatch icon isn't active for the layer, the audio levels are set globally. If the Stopwatch icon is active, an audio-level keyframe is created.

✔ Tips

- Although you can also set audio levels using a value graph, a more detailed discussion of that control is reserved for Chapter 14.
- The Stereo Mixer effect is one of several audio effects you can use to process audio. In addition to panning the left and right audio channels, the Stereo Mixer effect provides a useful alternative to the Levels property. See Chapter 10 for more about effects.

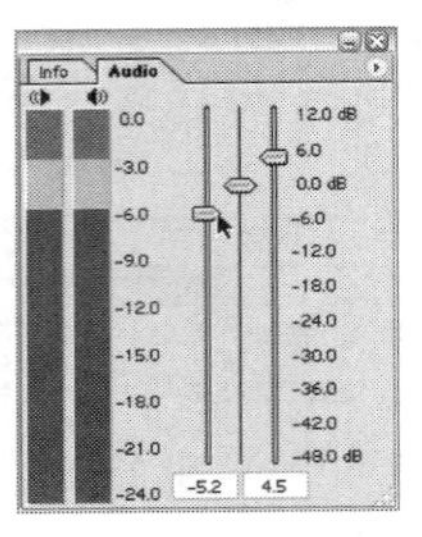

Figure 7.43 In the Audio palette, drag the left or right slider to adjust the corresponding audio channel, or drag the center slider to adjust the overall level.

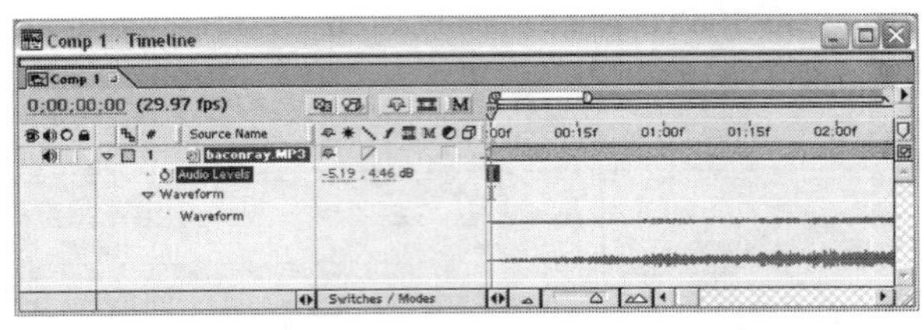

Figure 7.44 The audio waveform reflects your changes. In this example, the level of the left channel has been lowered for the entire duration of the layer. Alternatively, you can keyframe level adjustments like any other property.

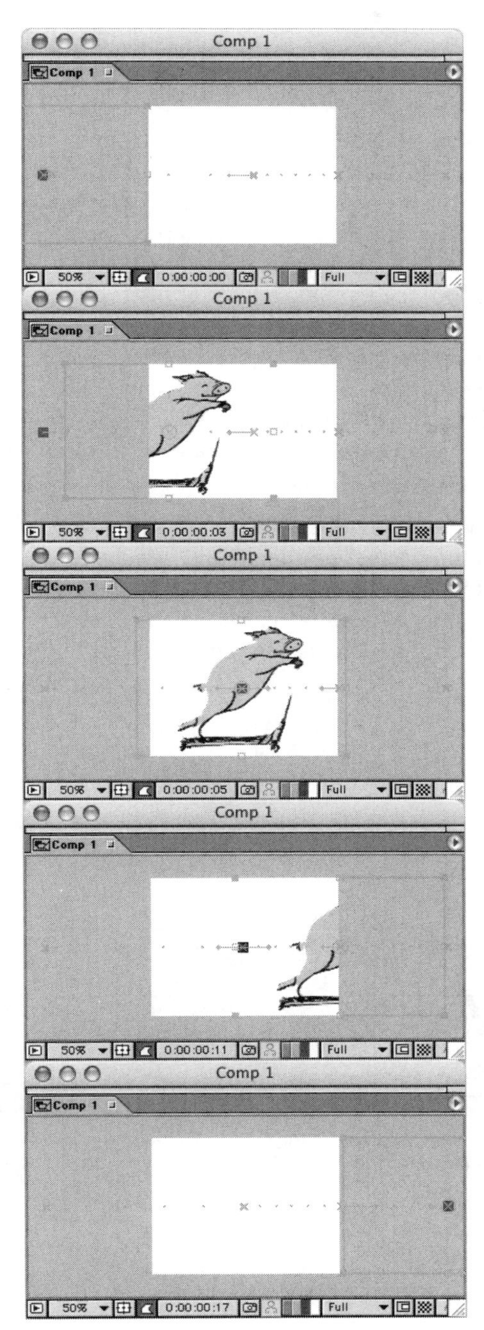

Figure 7.45 You can keyframe any property to animate it over time. In this case, After Effects calculates the position of a layer between two keyframes to create movement.

Animating Layer Properties with Keyframes

To produce animation, you change a layer's properties over time—for example, achieving motion by changing a layer's position in time. In After Effects (as with other programs), you use keyframes to define and control these changes.

A *keyframe* defines a property's value at a specific point in time. When you create at least two keyframes with different values, After Effects interpolates the value for each frame in between. In other words, After Effects calculates how to create a smooth transition from one keyframe to another—that is, how to get from point A to point B (**Figure 7.45**).

Basic keyframing

Essentially, keyframing is nothing more than repeating a two-step process: setting the current frame, and setting the property value for that frame. The specific steps are outlined in this section.

If you're new to animating with keyframes, you might want to start with one of the transform properties such as Scale. (Chapter 15 shows how to gain even greater control over your animations by manipulating the spatial and temporal interpolation method used between keyframes.)

To set keyframes for a property:

1. In the Timeline window, view the property of the layer (or layers) you want to keyframe.

   You may view the same property for more than one layer but not different properties.

continues on next page

2. Set the current time to the frame at which you want to set a keyframe.

   Although it's possible to set a keyframe beyond the duration of a layer, you won't be able to see the effects of the keyframe in the composition.

3. Click the Stopwatch icon next to the layer property you want to keyframe to activate the icon (and the keyframe process) (**Figure 7.46**).

   The Stopwatch icon appears selected. In the property tracks of the selected layers, an initial keyframe appears; in the keyframe navigator, a check appears.

4. If the property isn't set to the value you want, set the value (as explained in earlier in this chapter).

   As long as the current time is set to the keyframe, any new value is applied to the keyframe.

5. Set the current time to another frame.

Keyframes

Keyframe is a term borrowed from traditional animation. In a traditional animation studio, a senior animator might draw only the keyframes—what the character looks like at key moments in the animation. The junior animators would then draw the rest of the frames, or *in-betweens* (a process sometimes known as *tweening*). The same principle applies to After Effects animations: If you supply the keyframes for a property, the program calculates the values in-between. And you can keyframe any property, not just movement.

With After Effects, you're always the senior animator, so you should only supply the keyframes—just enough to define the animation. Setting too many keyframes defeats the purpose of this division of labor.

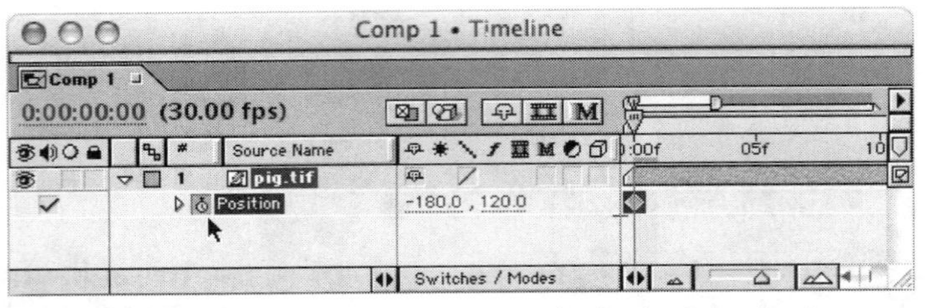

Figure 7.46 Activate the Stopwatch icon to set the first keyframe for the property at the current time marker.

6. To create additional keyframes, *do one of the following:*
   - ▲ To create a keyframe with a new value, change the value of the property.
   - ▲ In the property track of the selected layers, a new keyframe appears. In the keyframe navigator, a checkmark appears (**Figure 7.47**).
   - ▲ To create a keyframe without changing the current property value, check the box in the keyframe navigator.
   - ▲ If the new keyframe becomes the last keyframe for the property, it has the same value as the previous keyframe. Otherwise, the new keyframe's value is based on the previously interpolated value for that frame (**Figure 7.48**).
7. To create additional keyframes, repeat steps 5 and 6.

   To modify keyframe values or to change their position in time, use the methods described in the following sections.
8. To see your changes play in the Composition window, use the playback controls or create a preview (see Chapter 8).

✔ Tips

- The Motion Sketch plug-in palette provides another quick and easy way to create position keyframes: You can draw them in the Composition window.
- The Motion Tracker included in After Effects Pro helps you generate keyframes by detecting an object's movement within an image.
- People often use After Effects to pan and scale large images, emulating the motion-control camera work frequently seen in documentaries. In such cases, you create pans by animating the anchor point, not the position. This technique achieves the panning you want while keeping the anchor point in the viewing area. Because the anchor point is also used to calculate scale, you'll get more predictable results when you zoom in to and out of the image.

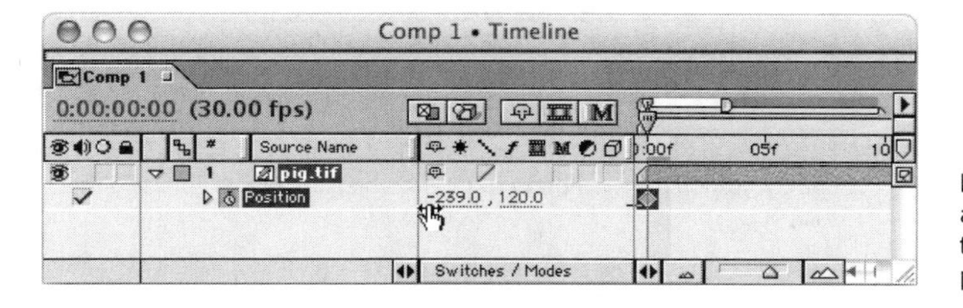

Figure 7.47 To set a keyframe with a new value, set the current time to a new frame, and change the property value.

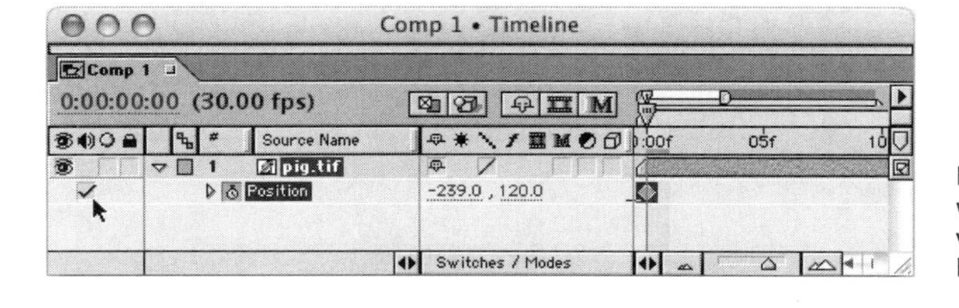

Figure 7.48 To set a keyframe without manually changing the value, check the box in the keyframe navigator.

Keyframe icons

A property's keyframes appear in its property track of the time graph. When a property heading is collapsed, the keyframes of the properties in that category appear as circles (**Figure 7.49**). When an individual property is visible, its keyframes appear as either icons or indices (**Figures 7.50** and **7.51**).

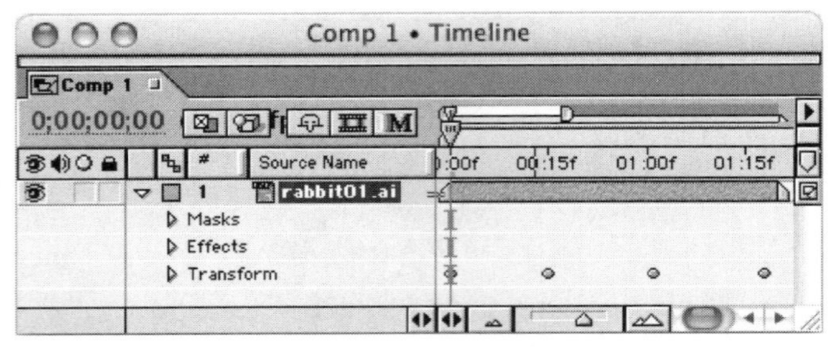

Figure 7.49 When the property heading is collapsed, keyframes appear as small dots.

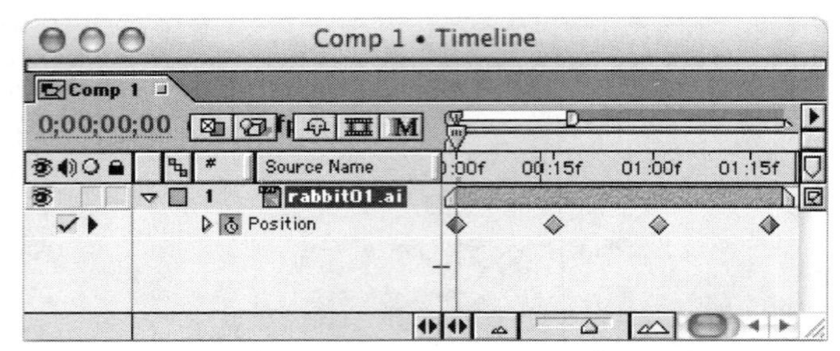

Figure 7.50 When the property track is visible, keyframes appear either as icons...

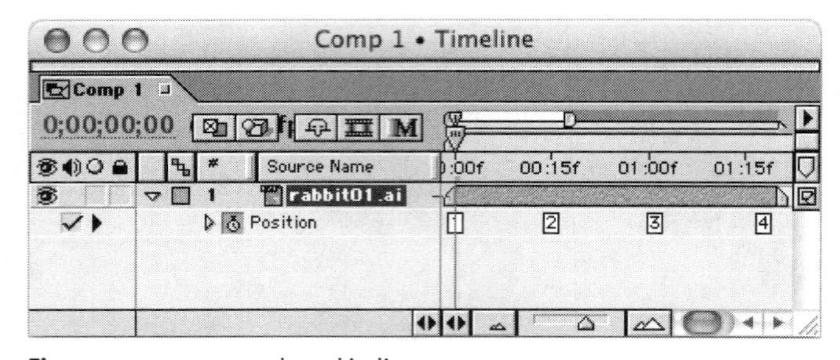

Figure 7.51 ...or as numbered indices.

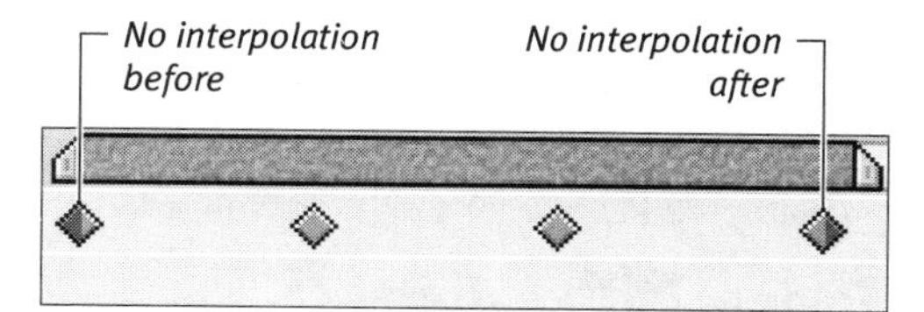

Figure 7.52 Shading indicates that the property value isn't interpolated either before or after the keyframe.

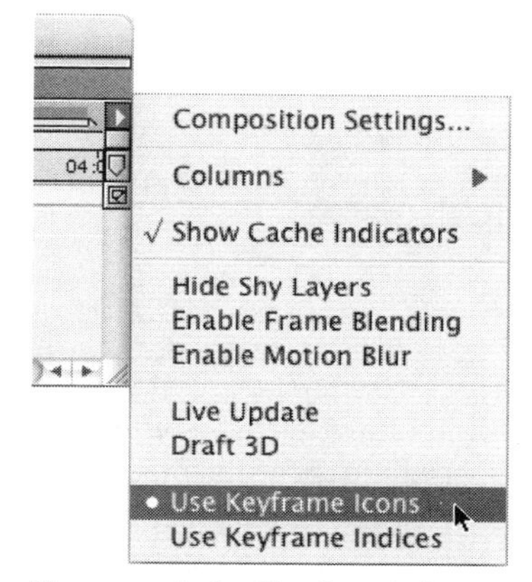

Figure 7.53 In the Timeline window menu, select whether you want to view Keyframe icons or indices.

Keyframe icons vary according to the interpolation method used by the keyframe. Regardless of method, shading indicates that the property value either before or after the keyframe hasn't been interpolated (**Figure 7.52**). This occurs for the first and last keyframes as well as for keyframes that follow hold keyframes, which are used to prevent interpolation (see Chapter 15). When viewed as indices, keyframes appear as numbered boxes, regardless of their interpolation method.

To toggle between keyframe icons and indices:

- In the Timeline window menu, *choose one of the following* options (**Figure 7.53**):
  - Use Keyframe Icons
  - Use Keyframe Indices

  The keyframes in the Timeline window reflect your choice.

✔ Tip

- Just a reminder: You can quickly view only those properties that have been keyframed by selecting layers and pressing U.

Interpolation

As you saw in the previous section, "Basic keyframing," you can create a keyframe in two ways. Once the Stopwatch icon is active, you can set the time and change the layer's property value, thereby creating a new keyframe. Alternatively, you can set the time and select the keyframe navigator's check box. Instead of using a value you actively specify, the keyframe created with the check box uses the value After Effects previously calculated for the property—typically, by interpolating the progression of values between keyframes.

Usually, you use the check box to create keyframes when you want to modify an animation—or, when no animation exists yet, to repeat a value. For example, when two keyframes don't define the animation you want, you can use the keyframe navigator's check box to create a keyframe that uses the interpolated value for that frame. Initially, the new keyframe doesn't alter the animation; it hasn't changed the property's value at that time. The new keyframe can serve as a good starting point for changing the animation, by changing the keyframe's value or interpolation method (for more about interpolation methods, see Chapter 15.

Selecting and deleting keyframes

Select keyframes when you want to move them to a different position in time, delete them, or copy and paste them to other properties or layers.

To select keyframes:

- *Do any of the following:*
  - ▲ To select a keyframe, click it in the property track.
  - ▲ To add or subtract keyframes from your selection, press Shift as you click additional keyframes (**Figure 7.54**).
  - ▲ To select multiple keyframes, drag a marquee around the keyframes in the property track (**Figure 7.55**).
  - ▲ To select all the keyframes for a property, click the name of the property in the layer outline (**Figure 7.56**).

  Selected keyframes appear highlighted.

To deselect keyframes:

- *Do either of the following:*
  - ▲ To deselect all keyframes, click in an empty area of the Timeline window.
  - ▲ To deselect certain keyframes, Shift-click an already selected keyframe.

  Deselected keyframes no longer appear highlighted.

✔ Tip

- Selecting a keyframe allows you to move it in time, delete it, or copy it. It doesn't let you edit the values of that keyframe. You can only change the value of a property at the current time marker.

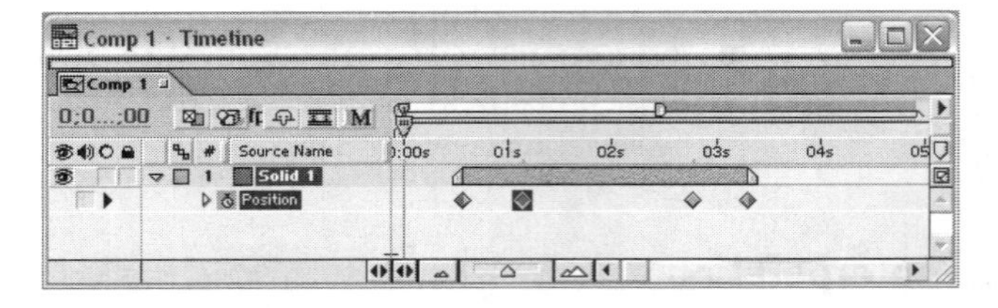

Figure 7.54 Click a keyframe to select it; Shift-click to add to your selection.

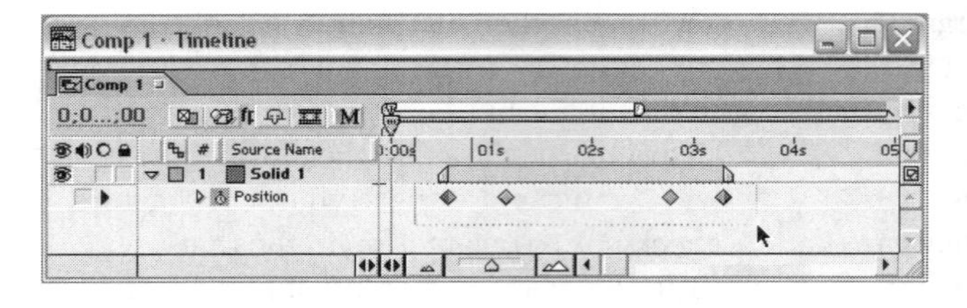

Figure 7.55 You can also select multiple keyframes by dragging a marquee around them.

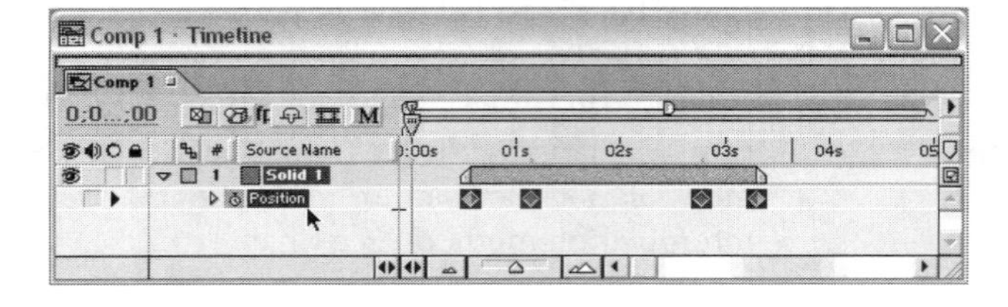

Figure 7.56 Select all the keyframes for a property by clicking the property's name in the layer outline.

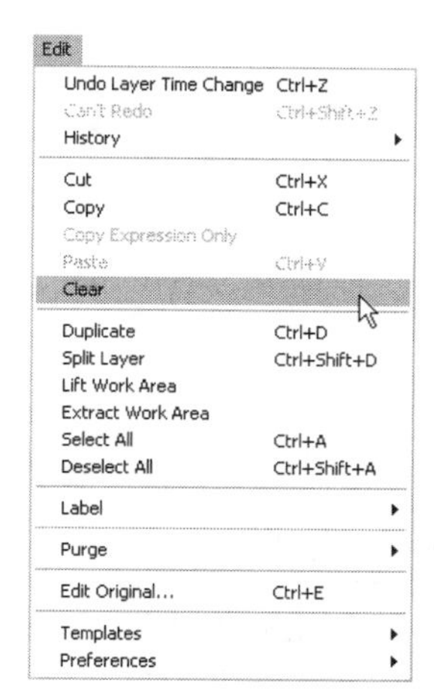

Figure 7.57 To delete selected keyframes, press Delete, uncheck the keyframe navigator, or choose Edit > Clear.

To delete keyframes:

1. Select one or more keyframes, as explained in the previous section.
2. *Do any of the following:*
   - ▲ Press Delete.
   - ▲ Choose Edit > Clear (**Figure 7.57**).
   - ▲ Uncheck the keyframe navigator box.

   The keyframe disappears, and the property's interpolated values are recalculated based on the existing keyframes.

To delete all the keyframes for a property:

- ◆ Deactivate the Stopwatch icon for the property.

  All keyframes disappear. You can't restore the keyframes by reactivating the Stopwatch (it only starts a new keyframe process).

✔ Tip

- ■ If you mistakenly remove keyframes by deselecting the Stopwatch icon, choose Edit > Undo to undo previous commands, or choose File > Revert to return to the last saved version of your project.

Moving Keyframes

You can move one or more keyframes of one or more properties to a different point in time.

To move keyframes:

1. Select one or more keyframes (explained earlier in this chapter) (**Figure 7.58**).
2. Drag the selected keyframes to a new position in the time graph (**Figure 7.59**).

   To activate the Snap to Edges feature, press Shift after you begin dragging.
3. Release the mouse when the keyframes are at the position in time you want.

✔ Tip

- Moving a layer in time also moves its keyframes, which maintain their positions relative to the layer. Trimming a layer, on the other hand, doesn't affect the keyframes. In fact, you can set a keyframe before a layer's In point or after its Out point (**Figure 7.60**).

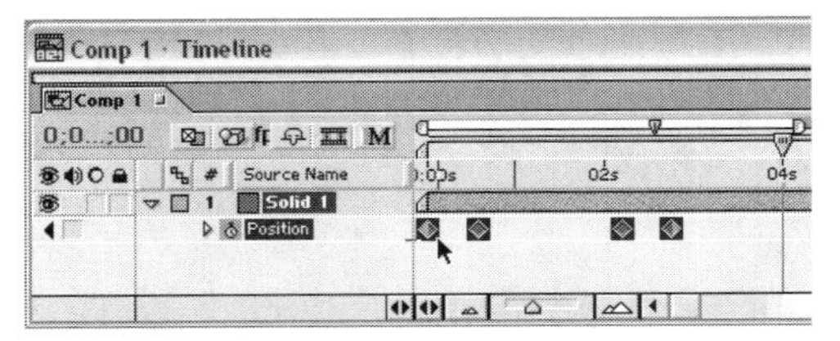

Figure 7.58 Select the keyframes you want to move...

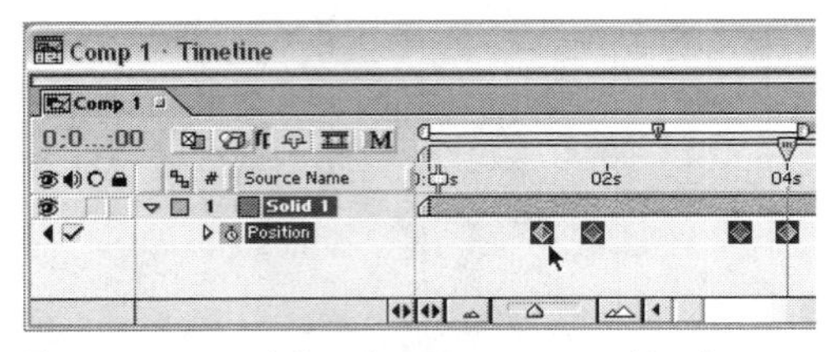

Figure 7.59 ...and drag them to a new position in the timeline. Shift-drag to activate the Snap to Edges feature.

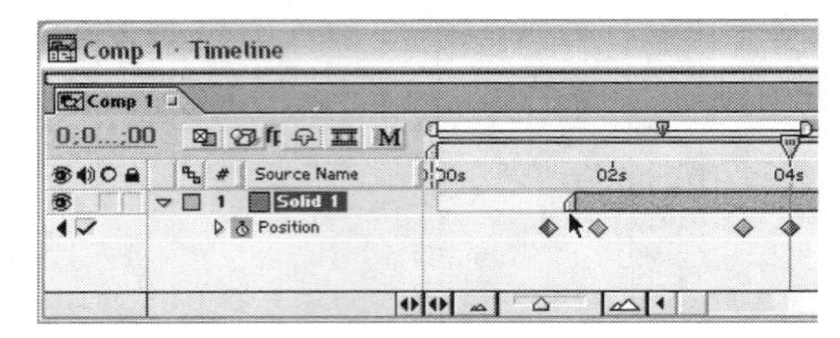

Figure 7.60 Although dragging a layer also moves its keyframes, trimming a layer doesn't trim off its keyframes, which still affect property values.

Copying Values and Keyframes

When you want to reuse values you set for a property, you can copy and paste them to a different point in time or even to different layers. Not only can you paste keyframes to the same property (such as from one position to another), you can also paste them to different properties that use the same kind of values (such as from a position to an anchor point).

Pasted keyframes appear in the property track of the destination in the order and spacing of the original, starting at the current time.

After Effects permits you to copy and paste keyframes one layer at a time. You can copy and paste keyframes of more than one property at a time, as long as you paste them into the same properties. If you want to copy and paste to different properties, however, you must do so one property at a time.

To copy and paste keyframes:

1. Select one or more keyframes (explained earlier in this chapter) (**Figure 7.61**).
2. Choose Edit > Copy, or press Command-C (Mac) or Ctrl-C (Windows) (**Figure 7.62**).
3. Set the current time to the frame where you want the pasted keyframe(s) to begin.

continues on next page

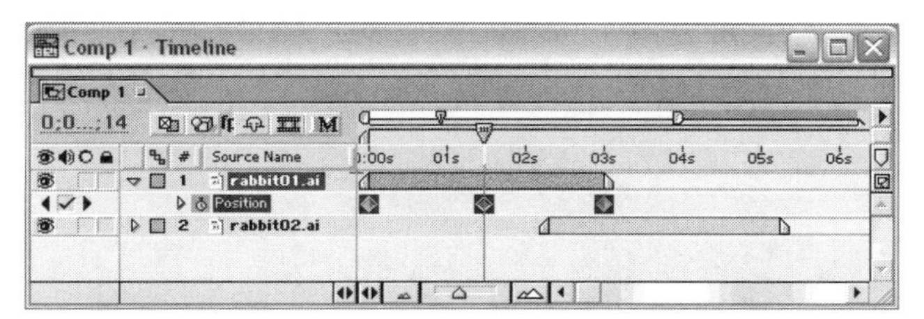

Figure 7.61 Select the keyframes you want to copy.

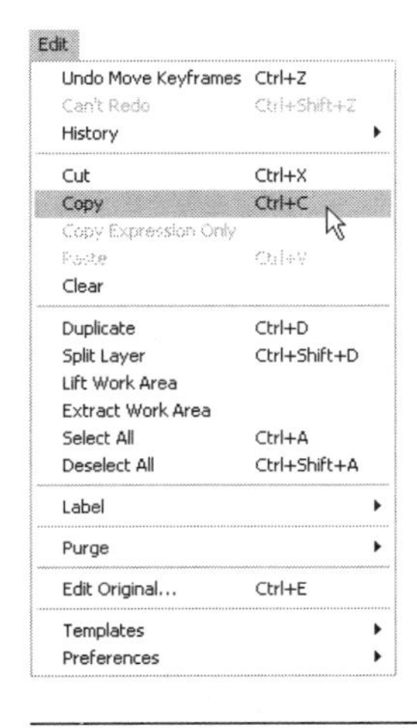

Figure 7.62 Choose Edit > Copy, or press Command-C (Mac) or Ctrl-C (Windows).

4. To select the destination, *do one of the following:*
   - ▲ To paste keyframes to the same property, select the destination layer.
   - ▲ To paste keyframes to a different property, select the destination property by clicking it in the layer outline.
5. Choose Edit > Paste, or press Command-V (Mac) or Ctrl-V (Windows) (**Figure 7.63**).

   The keyframes are pasted in the appropriate property in the destination layer (**Figure 7.64**).

✔ Tips

- You can also copy and paste a global (non-keyframed) value using the same process. Selecting the property highlights the I-beam icon in the property track rather than the keyframes.
- To reuse an animation, you can save it as an animation preset. See "Using Animation Presets," later in this chapter.
- Certain types of animations are best accomplished by using an expression instead of numerous keyframes. See Chapter 17, "Complex Projects," for more about using expressions.

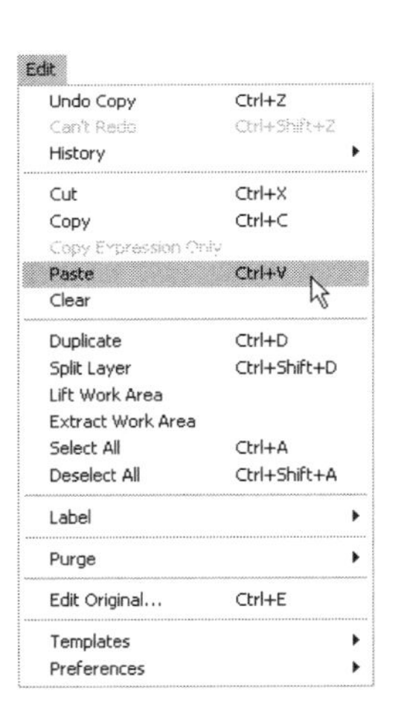

Figure 7.63 Set the current time and the destination layer or property, and choose Edit > Paste.

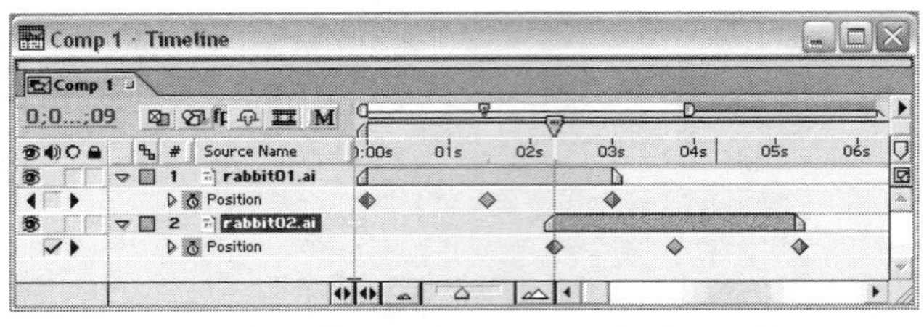

Figure 7.64 The selected keyframes appear in the destination property track, beginning at the current time.

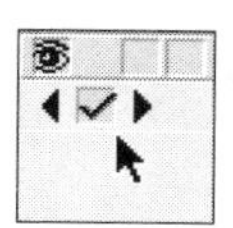

Figure 7.65 Use the keyframe navigator to cue the current time marker to the previous or next keyframe. A checkmark appears only when the current time is exactly on a keyframe.

Cueing the current time to keyframes

You can only set or change a keyframe's values at the current time marker—one reason you need a quick and convenient way to cue the time marker to keyframes. You may also want to jump to keyframes to step through your animation or to create keyframes in other layers or properties that align with existing keyframes.

To cue the current time to keyframes:

1. Make sure the property with the keyframes you want to see is visible in the layer outline.
2. In the Timeline window, *do any of the following:*
   - Shift-drag the current time marker until it snaps to a visible keyframe.
   - In the keyframe navigator for the property, click the left arrow to cue the current time to the previous keyframe.
   - In the keyframe navigator for the property, click the right arrow to cue the current time to the next keyframe (**Figure 7.65**).

Using Animation Presets

Some animations are just worth saving. Fortunately, you can save almost any animation as an *animation preset*. Presets make it easy to apply the same animation to another layer in a project or even in another project.

An animation preset contains a selected set of property keyframes in a file that uses a name you specify (with an `.ffx` filename extension). By default, it's saved in the Presets folder (inside the Adobe After Effects folder). This way, your preset will be listed in the Effects & Presets palette for easy access. You can even create a subfolder in the Presets folder, and the folder hierarchy you create will be reflected in the Effects & Presets palette. (As you might guess, the Effects & Presets palette also provides a way to find and apply effects; it's covered in more detail in Chapter 10.)

To save an animation preset:

1. Select one or more keyframes (**Figure 7.66**).

   To select all keyframes for a property, click the property's name in the layer outline. You may select keyframes for more than one property in a layer.

2. Choose Animation > Save Animation Preset (**Figure 7.67**).

   A "Save Animation Preset as" dialog box appears.

3. In the "Save Animation Preset as" dialog box, specify the name and destination for the preset (**Figure 7.68**).

   By default, the preset is saved into the Presets folder in the Adobe After Effects folder. Animation presets use the file extension `.ffx`.

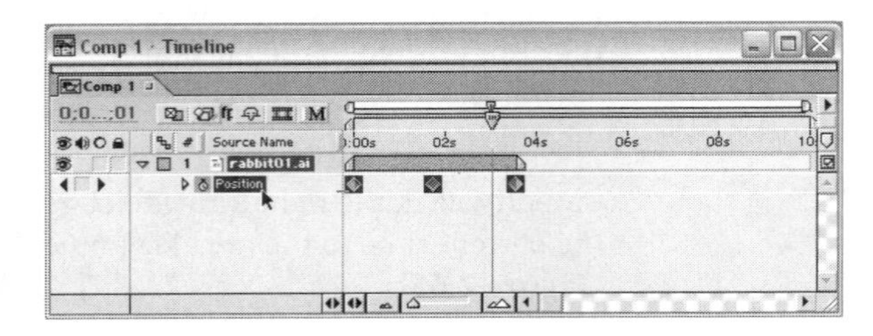

Figure 7.66 Select one or more keyframes. To select all the keyframes for a property, click the property's name.

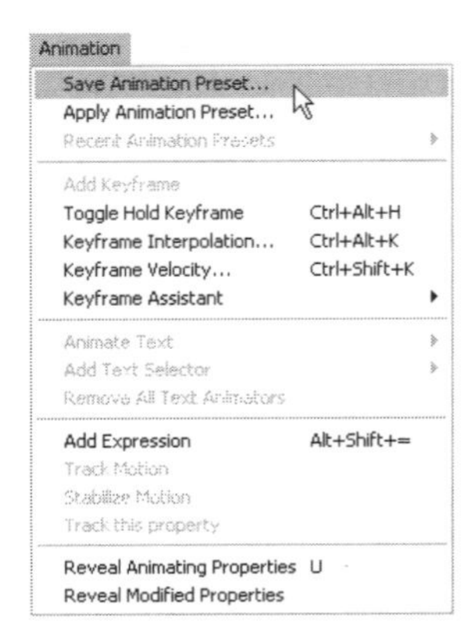

Figure 7.67 Choose Animation > Save Animation Preset.

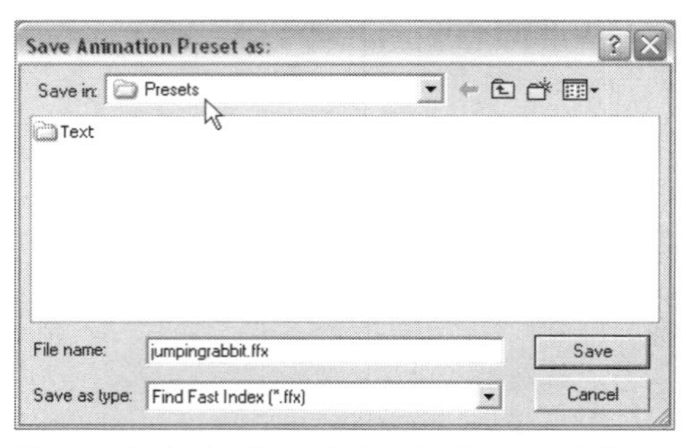

Figure 7.68 In the "Save Animation Preset as" dialog box, specify a name for the preset. You should save the file in the Presets folder (inside the Adobe After Effects folder).

To apply an animation preset:

1. Select one or more layers in a composition.
2. Set the current time at the point you want the keyframes of the animation preset to begin (**Figure 7.69**).
3. Choose Animation > Apply Animation Preset (**Figure 7.70**).

   An Open dialog box appears, with the After Effects' Presets folder open.
4. In the Open dialog box, select the preset you want to apply, and click Open (**Figure 7.71**).

   The preset animation is applied to the selected layer(s), beginning at the current time. To view the keyframes, you may need to expand the layer outline to reveal the animated properties. One way to do this is to select the layers and press U (**Figure 7.72**).

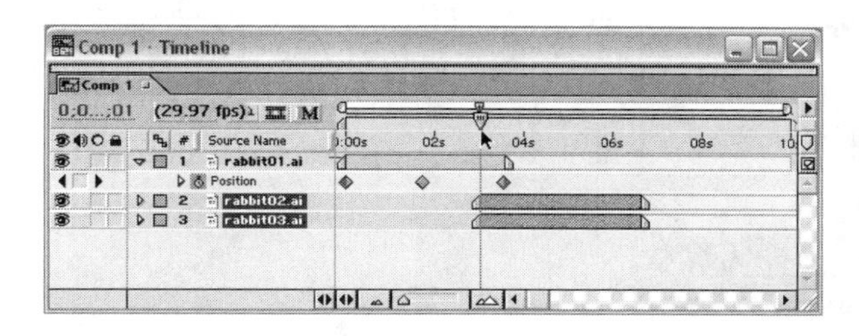

Figure 7.69 Select the layers to which you want to apply the preset animation, and set the current time to the frame at which you want the keyframes to begin.

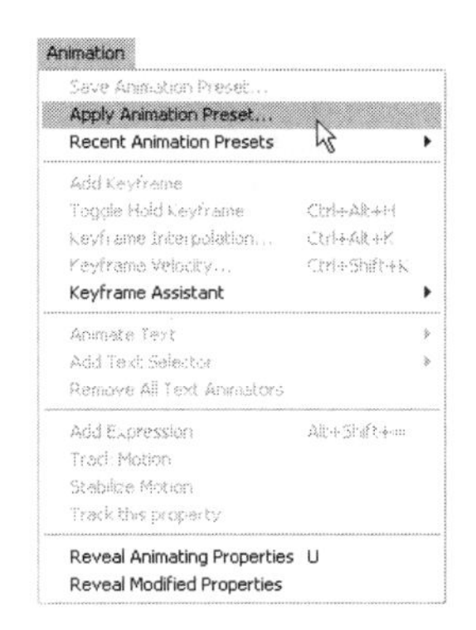

Figure 7.70 Choose Animation > Apply Preset Animation.

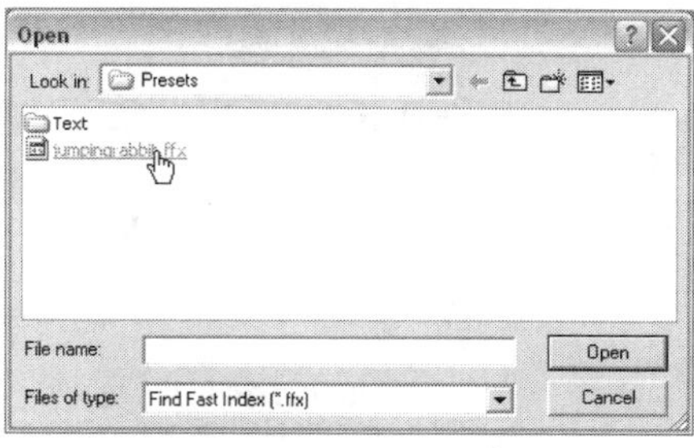

Figure 7.71 In the Open dialog box, select the preset and click Open.

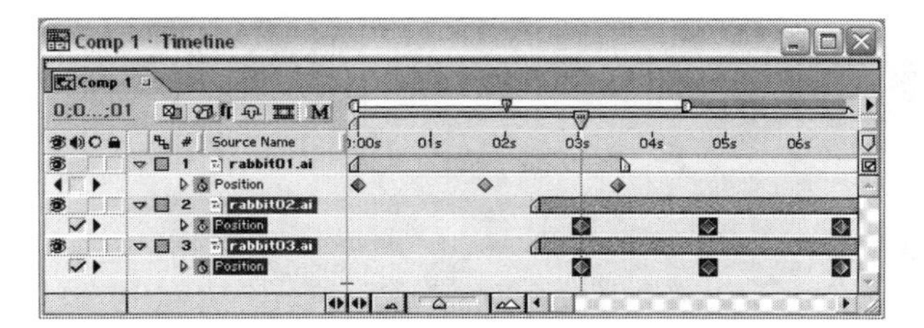

Figure 7.72 The preset animation's keyframes are applied to the selected layers, starting at the current time. To see the keyframes in the time ruler, you can select the layers and press U.

To apply an animation preset using the Effects & Presets palette:

1. Select one or more layers and set the current time to the point at which you want the keyframes to begin (**Figure 7.73**).
2. In the Effects & Presets palette, locate the preset you want from the Animation Presets folder.

   You may need to expand the Animation Presets folder or its subfolders to locate the preset. Alternatively, you can enter the name of your preset in the palette to sift the items in the palette.
3. Double-click the name of the animation preset you want to apply to the selected layers (**Figure 7.74**).

   The preset animation is applied to the selected layer(s), beginning at the current time. To view the keyframes, you may need to expand the layer outline to reveal the animated properties. One way to do this is to select the layers and press U (**Figure 7.75**).

✔ Tips

- You can apply a recently saved animation preset by choosing Animation > Recent Animation Presets and choosing a preset from the list.
- You can selectively apply certain property keyframes by expanding the preset's name in the Effect & Presets palette and double-clicking the name of the property.
- To learn how to manage items in the Effect & Presets palette, see Chapter 10.

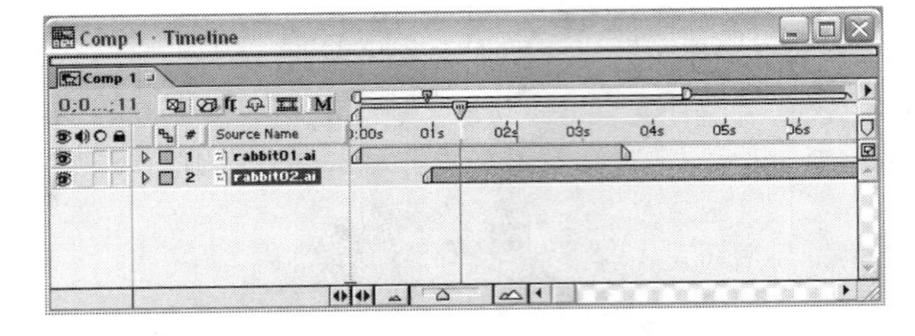

Figure 7.73 Select the layers to which you want to apply the preset animation, and set the current time to the frame at which you want the keyframes to begin.

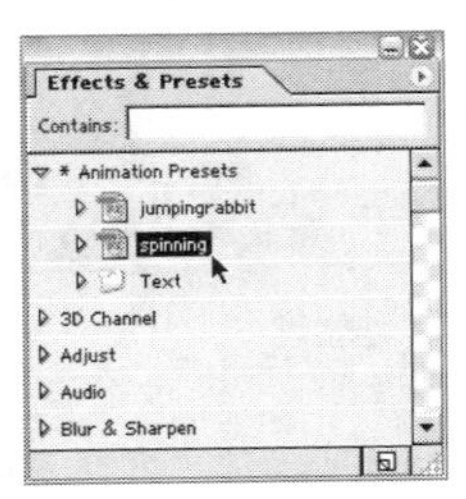

Figure 7.74 In the Effects & Presets palette, double-click the name of the preset you want to apply to the selection.

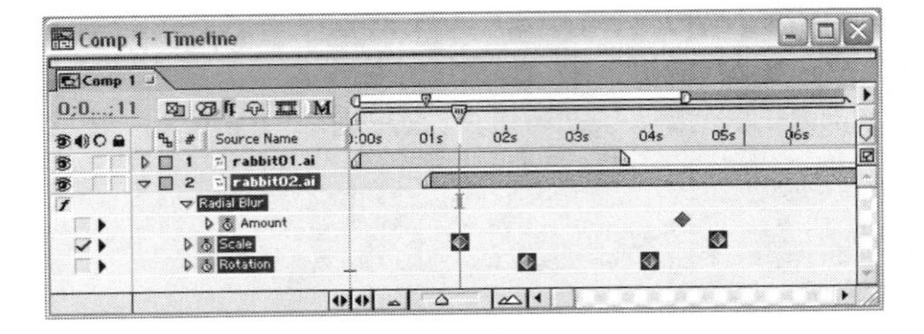

Figure 7.75 The preset animation's keyframes are applied to the selected layers, starting at the current time.

8 Playback, Previews, and RAM

You've already used some of the standard playback methods for each window in After Effects. This chapter expands your repertoire and provides a more in-depth explanation of how After Effects renders frames for viewing.

You'll focus on using the Time Controls palette, which can serve as a master playback control for any selected window. It also includes a button to render a specified range of frames (or *work area*) as a *RAM preview*. And you'll learn about other options, such as viewing your work on a video monitor, how to view changes you make to a layer interactively (using Live Update), and how to preview audio.

Whether you're using standard playback controls, rendering a RAM preview, or adjusting layers, After Effects utilizes RAM to store and more readily display frames. Consequently, the more RAM you have, the more rendered frames you can store (or *cache*) at once. After Effects makes the most of your RAM supply by retaining rendered frames as long as possible, a feature called *intelligent caching*. But you can also control the demand side of the rendering equation. Specifying RAM preview options to skip frames or reduce the resolution can lighten the rendering load—or eliminate the image altogether (along with the associated rendering delays) by previewing a bare-bones *wireframe* version of an animation. In addition, you can limit the area of the image to render by specifying a *region of interest*. After Effects can also reduce processing demands automatically, as needed, by employing *adaptive resolution*. Adaptive resolution reduces image resolution in exchange for increased rendering speed.

But rendering speed isn't necessarily attained at the expense of resolution; you can also utilize a compatible *OpenGL* graphics card. Because software-based processing usually can't match hardware dedicated to the same task, utilizing your OpenGL card's hardware-based graphics processing capabilities renders frames quickly, smoothly, and often without sacrificing resolution.

Rendering and RAM

Before proceeding to the tasks, you should familiarize yourself with how After Effects utilizes RAM. This section contrasts two basic methods used to display frames.

Cache flow

Adobe likes to describe the way After Effects uses RAM as "interactive" and "intelligent." Here's why.

Unless you specify otherwise, After Effects renders frames interactively. That is, whenever the current time is set to a previously unrendered frame, After Effects renders it and stores, or *caches*, it into RAM—which, as you're probably aware, is the memory your computer can access most quickly. So although it can take time to render a frame, once cached, the frame plays back more readily. The Timeline window indicates cached frames with a green line at the corresponding point under the time ruler (**Figure 8.1**).

When a change (such as an adjustment to a layer property) makes a rendered frame obsolete, After Effects removes the frame from the cache. However, it intelligently retains the unaffected frames. In other words, After Effects doesn't stupidly discard the entire cache when you make changes that only affect some of the frames. When the cache becomes full, the oldest frames are purged from RAM as new frames are added. You can also purge the cache yourself (as described in the task "To purge the RAM cache" later in this chapter).

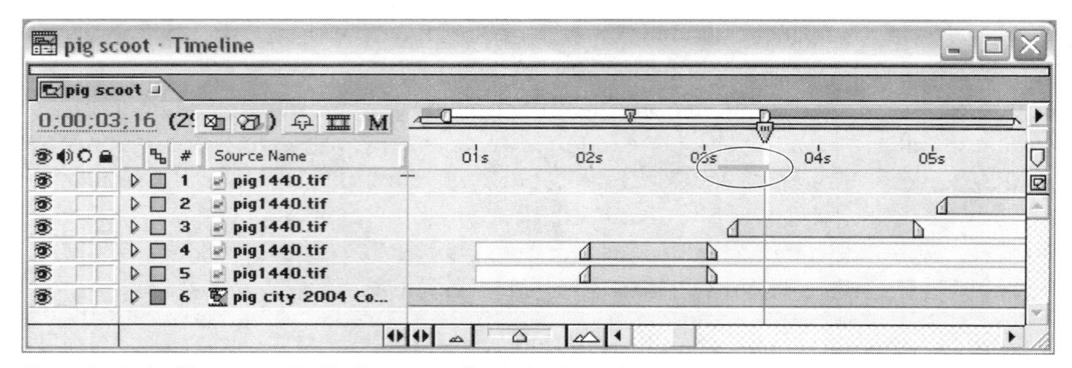

Figure 8.1 Cached frames are signified by a green line in the time ruler.

Figure 8.2 Options help you balance quality and rendering speed. The Comp window's Fast Preview button gives you access to several standard playback options...

Figure 8.3 ...whereas expanding the Time Controls palette allows you to set options for RAM previews.

Playback and previews

Although the terms *playback* and *preview* are often used interchangeably, this book uses them to refer to two rendering methods that differ in a few important respects. Standard playback caches frames at the current time—that is, sequentially when you click Play or nonsequentially as you cue the current time. A RAM preview, in contrast, loads a specified range of frames into RAM *before* playing them back.

Both the standard playback mechanism and RAM previews utilize RAM in a similar way, caching frames and retaining them intelligently (see the previous section, "Cache flow"). But whereas standard playback respects the resolution you specified for the window you're viewing, a RAM preview specifies resolution independent of the window's current setting. Each method includes different options to help you balance image quality and rendering speed. In addition to the current layer quality and comp resolution settings, standard playback abides by options you set in the Comp window's Fast Previews button (**Figure 8.2**); you set RAM preview options in the expanded Time Controls palette (**Figure 8.3**). Finally, standard playback options govern how After Effects depicts a frame while you make adjustments; or, in After Effects' parlance, during *interactions*. A RAM preview, on the other hand, only displays a range of frames at or near their full frame rate and doesn't influence the quality or speed of interactions.

continues on next page

No matter what method you use to view frames, processing demands are always related to the footage's native image size (and/or its audio quality) as well as any modifications you make to it as a layer in a composition: masks, transformations, effects, and so on. Note that because the Comp window's magnification setting (not to be confused with scaling a layer) doesn't change the number or quality of pixels to be rendered, it has little influence on rendering times.

✔ Tips

- After Effects indicates that it's busy rendering a frame (and isn't simply "hanging") by cycling the mouse pointer between black and white. In addition, the lower-right corner of the Comp window displays a small bar that indicates processing activity (provided the window is wide enough to show it).
- In the Display panel of the Preferences dialog box, you can enable an option to show rendering in progress in the Info palette and flowchart.

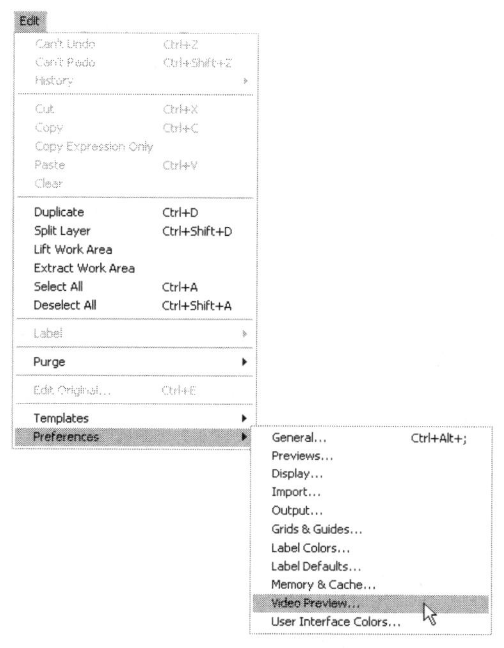

Figure 8.4 Choose Edit > Preferences > Video Preview.

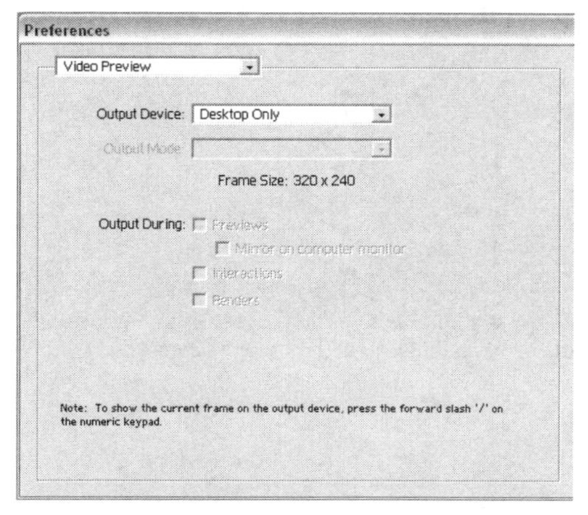

Figure 8.5 The Video Preview panel of the Preferences dialog box appears.

Previewing to a Video Device

If your system includes a video output device (such as an IEEE-1394/FireWire/iLink connection), you can view your project on a video monitor—which is crucial for evaluating images destined for video output.

Even though you can preview full-screen on your computer monitor (as explained later in this chapter), a computer monitor differs from a television monitor in several important respects. (Refer to this book's sections on interlaced video fields, pixel aspect ratio, safe zones, and NTSC video standards.)

To set video preferences:

1. Choose After Effects > Preferences > Video Preview (Mac) or Edit > Preferences > Video Preview (Windows) (**Figure 8.4**).

   The Video Preview panel of the Preferences dialog box appears (**Figure 8.5**).

continues on next page

2. In the Preferences dialog box, choose an option from the Output Device pull-down menu (**Figure 8.6**).

   Your choices will depend on your particular setup.

3. Choose an option from the Output Mode pull-down menu (**Figure 8.7**).

   Typically, you should choose an option that's equivalent to full-screen video for your output device.

4. For Output During, *choose any of the following:*

   Previews—Displays RAM previews on the NTSC monitor

   Interactions—Displays all window updates (such as while making adjustments to a layer's properties) on the NTSC monitor

   Renders—Displays rendered frames on the NTSC monitor

5. If you selected Previews in step 4, select "Mirror on computer monitor" to display previews on your computer's monitor in addition to the video device.

   To output previews to your video device only, leave this option unchecked.

6. Click OK to close the Preferences dialog box.

   Previews appear on the connected NTSC monitor according to the preferences you set.

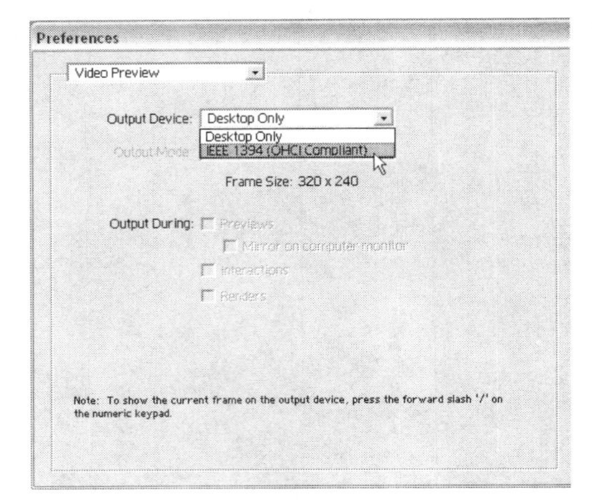

Figure 8.6 Choose an option in the Output Device pull-down menu.

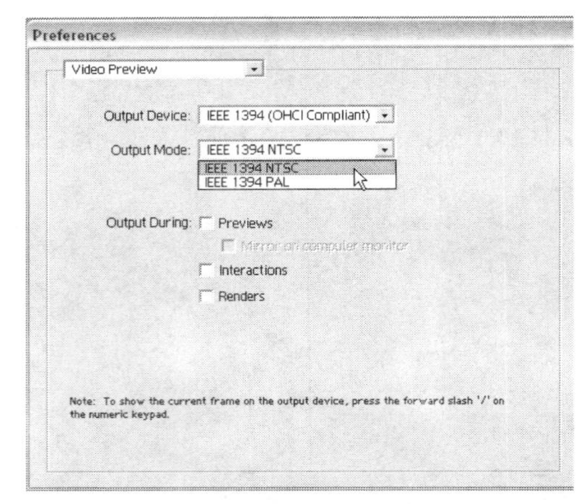

Figure 8.7 Choose an option in the Output Mode pull-down menu, and select the other options you want.

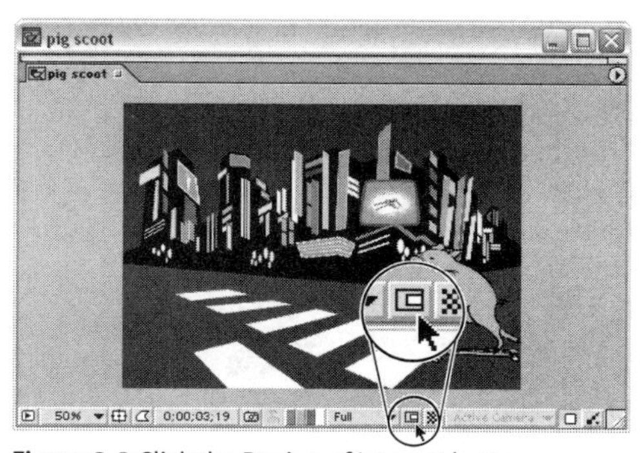

Figure 8.8 Click the Region of Interest button.

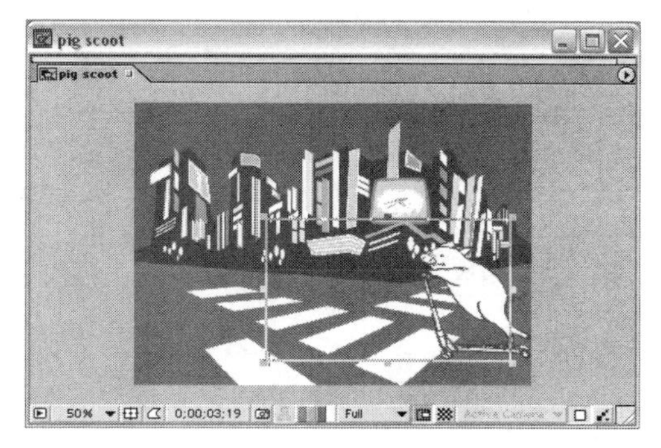

Figure 8.9 Draw a marquee in the image area to define the region of interest.

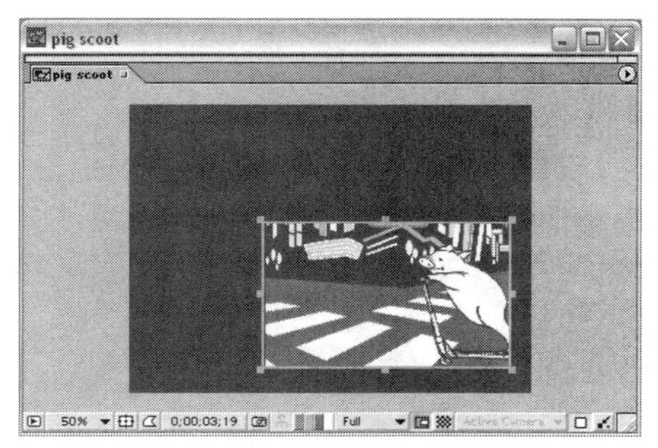

Figure 8.10 The region of interest limits the image included in playback and previews. Click the Region of Interest button to toggle between the region you specified and the full composition image.

Setting the Region of Interest

You can limit the portion of an image to be included in playback or previews by setting a *region of interest*. By restricting the image area to render, you decrease each frame's RAM requirements and increase both the rendering speed and the number of frames you can render.

To set the region of interest:

1. In a Comp, Layer, or Footage window, click the Region of Interest button (**Figure 8.8**).
2. Draw a marquee in the image area to define the region of interest (**Figure 8.9**).

   The area of the image included in playback and previews will be limited to the area within the region of interest (**Figure 8.10**).
3. To resize the region of interest, drag any of its corner handles.

To toggle between the region of interest and the full image:

◆ In the Comp, Layer, or Footage window, click the Region of Interest button.

When the button is selected, the window shows the region of interest; when the button is deselected, the window displays the full image.

✔ Tips

- To redraw the region of interest from the full image, make sure the Region of Interest button is deselected; then Option-click (Mac) or Alt-click (Windows) the Region of Interest button.
- As always, you can reduce rendering times by reducing your composition's resolution or by setting layers to Draft quality.

Using the Time Controls

Although the Footage, Layer, Composition, and Timeline windows all have their own playback controls, you can use the Time Controls palette to set the current frame in any selected window. With related windows, the current time changes in each window. For example, changing the current frame in a Layer window also changes the current time in its related Timeline and Composition windows.

You don't need to be an expert in nonlinear editing software to recognize most of the following buttons from the Time Controls palette (**Figure 8.11**); however, you may not be able to find a few of these on your home VCR:

First Frame cues the current time to the first frame in the window.

Frame Back cues the current time one frame back.

Play/Pause plays when clicked once and stops when clicked again. Playback performance depends on After Effects' ability to render the frames for viewing. During playback, the Time Controls palette displays two frame rates side by side: the frame rate your system is currently able to achieve and the frame rate you set for the composition, which is the real-time frame rate.

Frame Forward cues the current time one frame forward.

Last Frame cues the current time to the last frame in the window.

Audio lets you hear audio tracks when you preview a composition. Deselect it to suppress audio playback during previews. (Standard playback doesn't include audio.)

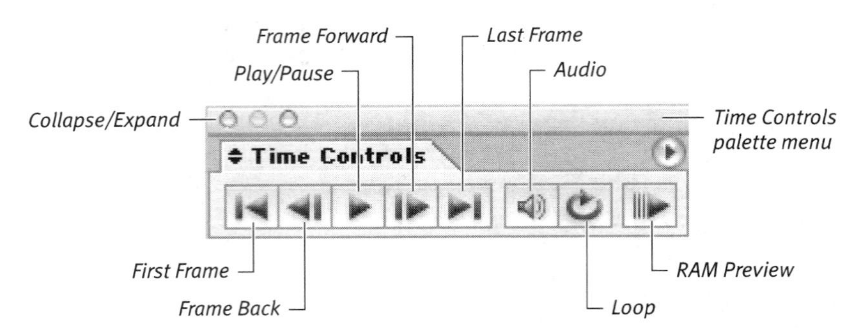

Figure 8.11 The Time Controls palette can control the playback of any selected window.

Loop comprises three states: Loop, Play Once, and Palindrome (which plays the specified area forward and backward). The frames affected by the loop setting depend on the window selected. In a Footage window, the entire duration of the footage loops. In a Layer window, the layer loops from In point to Out point. In a composition—as viewed in the Composition and Timeline windows—frames loop from the beginning to the end of the work area (see "Setting the Work Area" later in this chapter).

RAM Preview creates a RAM preview by rendering a specified range of frames, as defined by the Timeline's work area (explained later in this chapter).

The **Time Controls palette menu** opens a menu to show or hide RAM Preview and Shift-RAM Preview settings in the Time Controls palette (see the sections on RAM previews later in this chapter).

Collapse/Expand collapses the window to hide all controls, or expands it to include RAM Preview Options, or show the standard controls.

✔ Tips

- The Time Controls palette has been streamlined in After Effects 6.5. It no longer includes less-used controls better suited to an NLE: shuttle, jog, slider, or time display. Note that you can scrub the time display in the Timeline window.
- By default, the times of related windows are synchronized (for example, changing the current time of a comp is reflected in the open windows related to it, including nested comps). You can change this setting in the General panel of the Preferences dialog box. The implications of synchronizing related items is explained in Chapter 17, "Complex Projects."
- The playback performance of Footage windows doesn't benefit from the same RAM-caching mechanism as the Layer and Composition windows. Until footage becomes a layer in a composition, it depends on the movie-player software installed on your system (QuickTime or Windows Media Player).

Using the Live Update Option

There are two ways you can view a comp while you make changes to a layer property; or, in After Effects' parlance, during *interactions*. By default, the Comp window updates *after* you alter the property—after you release the mouse when dragging the layer or property value, or after you press Return (Mac) or Enter (Windows) when changing the value numerically (**Figures 8.12** and **8.13**). Alternatively, you can set the window to update *during* interactions, utilizing a feature called *Live Update*. With Live Update enabled, you can see the layer change as you adjust the property (**Figure 8.14**).

Live Update works with the current Fast Preview setting (explained in "Specifying a Fast Preview Option" later in this chapter). When the Fast Preview option is set to Wireframe, interactions are depicted using layer outlines only. With adaptive resolution enabled (either the standard option, or with OpenGL), After Effects temporarily degrades the image quality during interactions until it can process and display the layer at the specified quality and resolution (see "Using Adaptive Resolution" later in this chapter).

Naturally, you should choose the combination of settings most appropriate to the task at hand, the processing demands of the frame, and your system's processing capability.

To toggle Live Update on and off:

- In the Timeline window, click the Live Update button (**Figure 8.15**).

  When the button is selected, the image updates during interactions (while you change layer properties); when the button is deselected, the image updates after you make an adjustment (when you release the mouse button, for example).

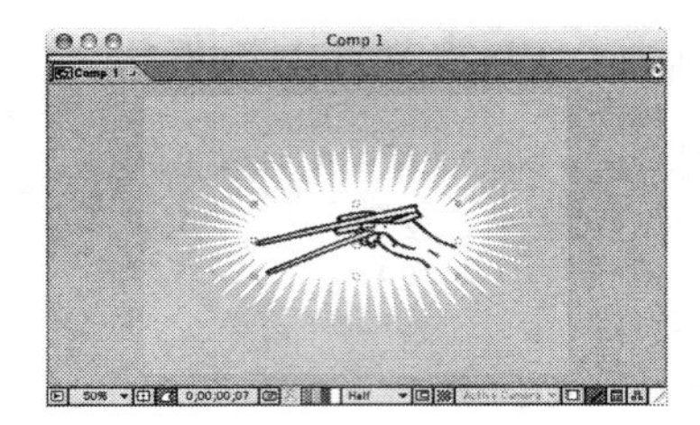

Figure 8.12 With Live Update off, the image doesn't update...

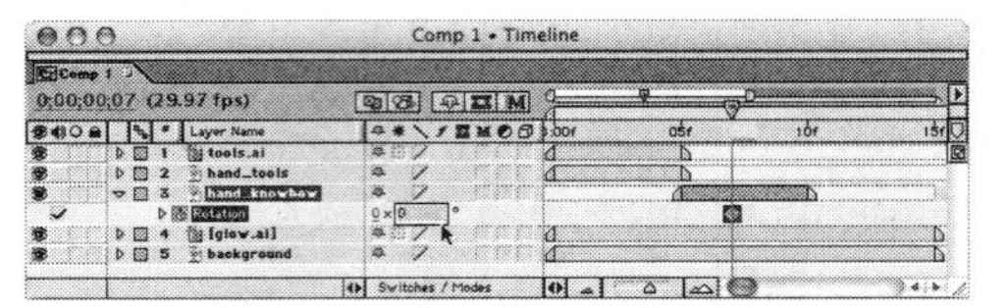

Figure 8.13 ...until you're finished with the adjustment.

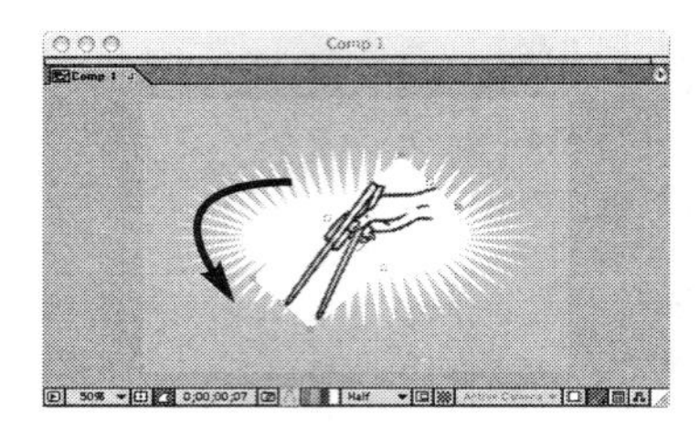

Figure 8.14 With Live Update active, the image updates interactively.

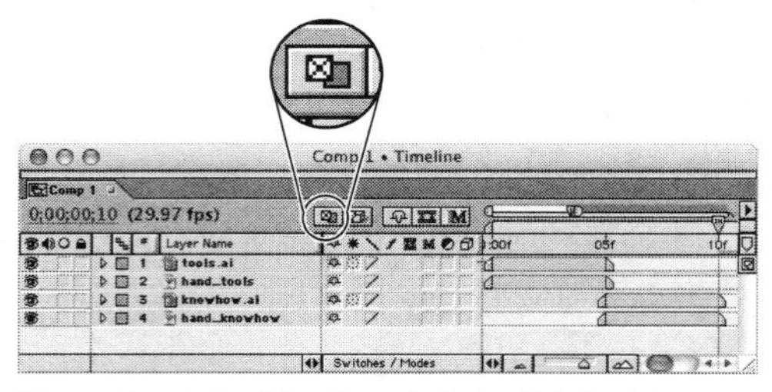

Figure 8.15 In the Timeline window, click the Live Update button.

✔ Tips

- Live Update replaces the Wireframe Interactions feature found in older versions of After Effects. Although the buttons look exactly alike, the features work differently.
- You specify whether to view interactions on an attached video monitor separately, as explained in the section "Previewing to a Video Device," earlier in this chapter.

Specifying a Fast Preview Option

As you learned in earlier chapters, the standard playback method (pressing play, or cuing the current time) is influenced by a comp's resolution as well as the quality settings of the layers it contains. (Everything else being equal, lowering quality and resolution results in shorter rendering times.) You can specify several other options to view frames as quickly as possible by using the Comp window's Fast Preview button.

This section covers how to specify the option you want to use, and summarizes each choice. Some choices (Adaptive Resolution and OpenGL options) include additional settings, which are explained fully in later sections.

To enable a Fast Preview option:

- In a Composition window, choose an option from the Fast Preview button's pull-down menu (**Figure 8.16**):

Off—Deactivates Fast Preview option; standard playback quality is governed by the comp resolution setting and layer quality settings

Wireframe—Displays layer outlines only, allowing you to quickly evaluate aspects of an animation such as movement and timing by sacrificing image content

Adaptive Resolution—Temporarily reduces the image resolution to a specified minimum setting in order to display changes to layers interactively or to maximize frame rate

OpenGL with Moving Textures—Utilizes a compatible OpenGL graphics card to process every frame requested

OpenGL with Static Textures—Utilizes a compatible OpenGL graphics card to process the image using a proxy frame

OpenGL options are available only if you have a compatible OpenGL graphics card installed in your system and you've enabled OpenGL options in the Previews panel of the Preferences dialog box.

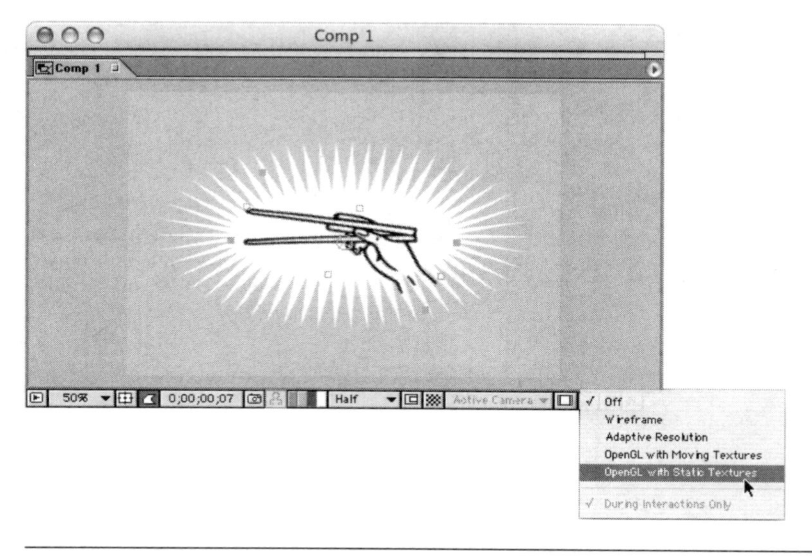

Figure 8.16 Choose an option from the Fast Preview button's pull-down menu.

To enable OpenGL during interactions only:

- In a Composition window, click the Fast Preview button and select During Interactions Only from the pull-down menu (**Figure 8.17**).

  When selected, the specified OpenGL option is used during interactions only. Leave this option unchecked to use the specified OpenGL option at all times.

✔ Tips

- A few more options are available for controlling the rendering quality of 3D layers; these are explained in Chapter 16, "3D Layers."
- The Comp window's Fast Preview button replaces the Dynamic Resolution button present in older versions of After Effects.

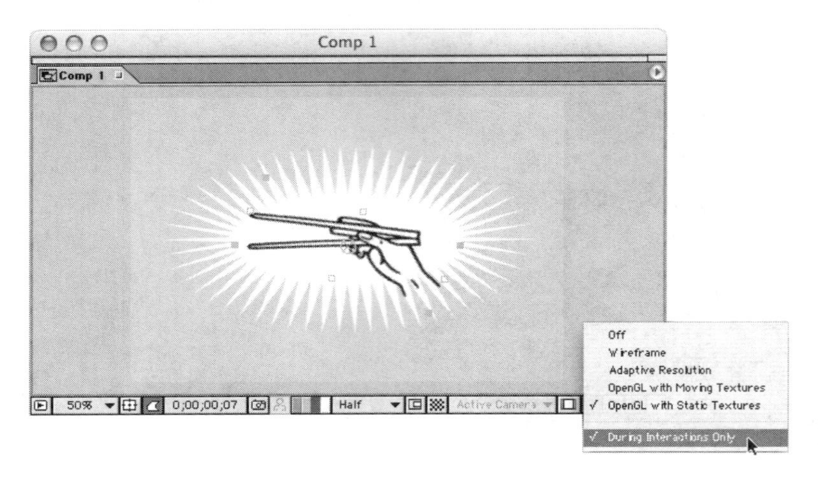

Figure 8.17 In the Fast Preview pull-down menu, select During Interactions Only.

Figure 8.18 With adaptive resolution enabled, the image degrades to keep pace with your adjustments...

Figure 8.19 ...and then assumes the comp's resolution when you stop transforming the layer.

Figure 8.20 Choose Edit > Preferences > Previews.

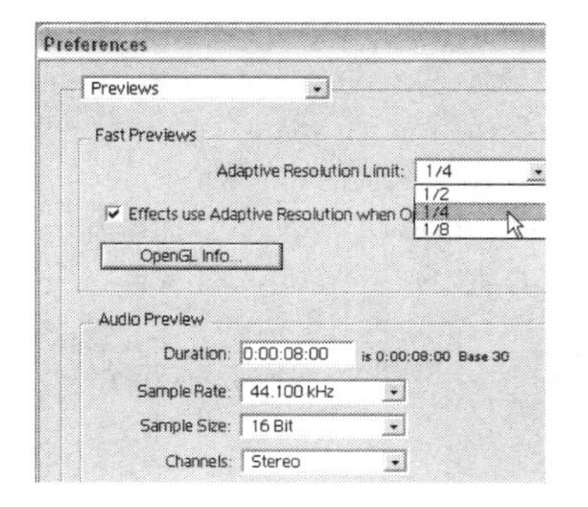

Figure 8.21 Limit the amount of degradation by choosing an option in the Adaptive Resolution Limit pull-down menu.

Using Adaptive Resolution

If your system is slow to update the Comp window's image, After Effects can reduce the image's resolution automatically—a feature called *adaptive resolution* (**Figures 8.18** and **8.19**). This way, you can get visual feedback even when your system can't keep up at the resolution you previously specified for the window. You set the maximum amount by which adaptive resolution degrades images in the Previews panel of the Preferences dialog box.

Although the adaptive resolution option is separate from the OpenGL options in the Fast Preview pull-down menu, OpenGL can also utilize adaptive resolution. However, you must enable OpenGL and its adaptive resolution setting separately (as described in the section "Using OpenGL" later in this chapter).

To set Adaptive Resolution settings:

1. Choose After Effects > Preferences > Previews (Mac) or Edit > Preferences > Previews (Windows) (**Figure 8.20**).

   The Previews panel of the Preferences dialog box appears.

2. *Select one of the following* options from the Adaptive Resolution Limit pull-down menu (**Figure 8.21**):

   1/2—After Effects temporarily displays the image at no less than one-half resolution while updating the comp preview.

   1/4—After Effects temporarily displays the image at one-quarter resolution while updating the comp preview.

   1/8—After Effects temporarily displays the image one-eighth resolution while updating the comp preview.

3. Click OK to close the Preferences dialog box.

Using OpenGL

Generally speaking, software processing can't match hardware dedicated to the same task. After Effects takes advantage of this fact by utilizing the graphics processing power of (After Effects–certified) OpenGL graphics cards.

After Effects detects whether your system has an OpenGL graphics card automatically, and if so, activates it as the default preview option.

When OpenGL is in effect, the Fast Preview button turns green. By default, OpenGL kicks in whenever you drag layers in a comp, scrub a motion-related property, or scrub a comp's current time. However, it doesn't provide a rendering boost to non–motion related effect properties. So to view effects-intensive frames, you may opt to switch to another Fast Preview method.

Overall, OpenGL provides faster, smoother screen updates than you would get otherwise, and it does so without degrading the image. But as the following task explains, you can set OpenGL to switch to adaptive resolution as you adjust effect property values (see "Using Adaptive Resolution," earlier in this chapter). This way, you can take advantage of OpenGL for most interactions, and adaptive resolution when you're adjusting effects.

You already know how to specify your OpenGL card as the Fast Preview option (see "Specifying a Fast Preview Option" earlier in this chapter). This section explains how to set several options specific to OpenGL.

OpenGL Graphics Cards

OpenGL is a technology utilized by many advanced video graphics cards that helps to enhance graphics processing, particularly for 3D objects and subtleties like shading, lights, and shadows. When a program is designed to recognize OpenGL, the increase in graphics performance can be substantial.

Usually, a high-end graphics card isn't a standard component in an average system configuration; instead, it's an often-expensive option. However, PC gamers and graphics professionals value graphics performance and are eager to upgrade to a more advanced graphics card.

Naturally, features and processing power vary from card to card. Whether your card supports features like lights and shadows in After Effects depends on the particular card.

Before you upgrade your graphics card, check Adobe's Web site to ensure it has been certified to work with After Effects. This is another quick way to see which features the card supports. And in addition to the card itself, make sure you install the latest software drivers, which should be available for download from the manufacturer's Web site.

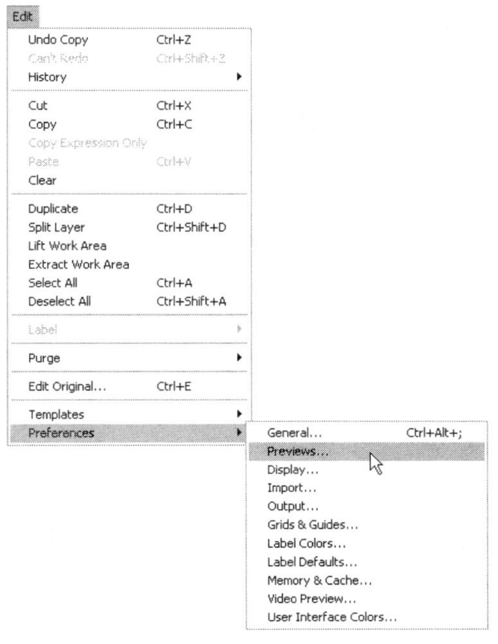

Figure 8.22 Choose After Effects > Preferences > Previews (Mac) or Edit > Preferences > Previews (Windows).

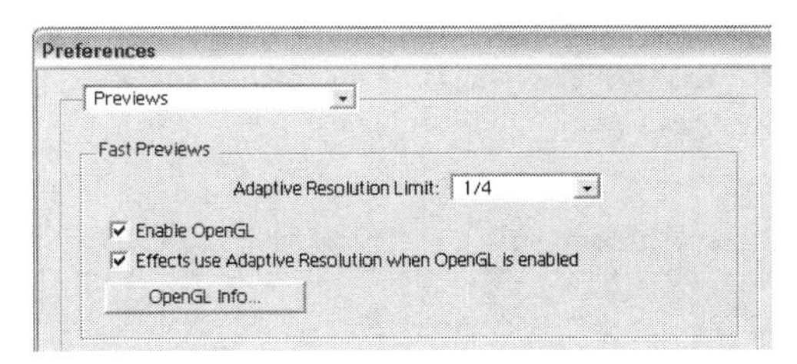

Figure 8.23 Select the OpenGL options you want.

To set OpenGL preferences:

1. Choose After Effects > Preferences > Previews (Mac) or Edit > Preferences > Previews (Windows) (**Figure 8.22**).

   The Previews panel of the Preferences dialog box appears.

2. Select the options you want (**Figure 8.23**):
   - ▲ Enable OpenGL
   - ▲ Effects use Adaptive Resolution when OpenGL is enabled

3. Click OK to close the dialog box.

To specify other OpenGL options:

1. Choose After Effects > Preferences > Previews (Mac) or Edit > Preferences > Previews (Windows).

   The Previews panel of the Preferences dialog box appears.

2. Click OpenGL Info (**Figure 8.24**).

   An OpenGL Information dialog box appears.

3. Specify the amount for Texture Memory, in MB (**Figure 8.25**).

   Adobe recommends allocating no more than 80% of the video RAM (VRAM) on your display card when using Windows; on a Mac, After Effects determines the ideal value automatically.

4. Specify an option in the Quality pull-down menu, if available (**Figure 8.26**):

   Faster—Processes more quickly, at the expense of the quality of lighting, shading, and blending, and by excluding blending modes

   More Accurate—Includes blending modes, and improves the quality of lighting, shading, and blending

5. Click OK to close the OpenGL Information dialog box, and click OK to close the Preferences dialog box.

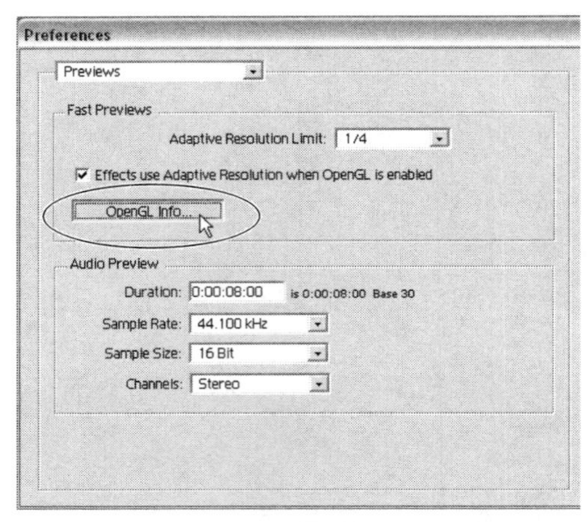

Figure 8.24 Click OpenGL Info to access more options.

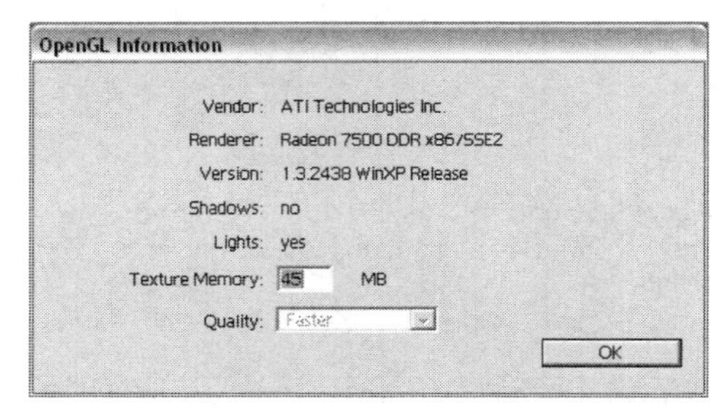

Figure 8.25 In the OpenGL Information dialog box, specify an amount for Texture Memory.

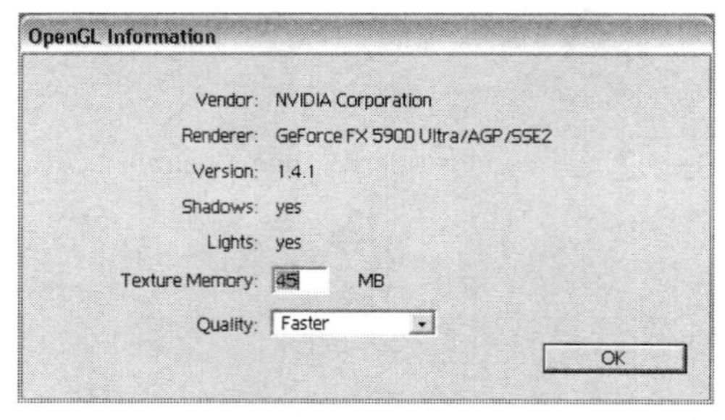

Figure 8.26 If available, choose an option from the Quality pull-down menu.

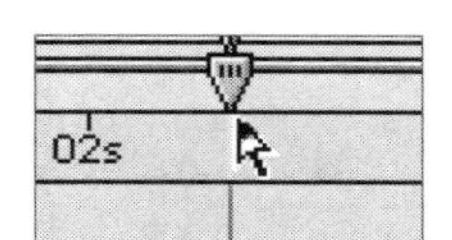

Figure 8.27 The Selection tool cycles between black and white as the program pauses to render frames.

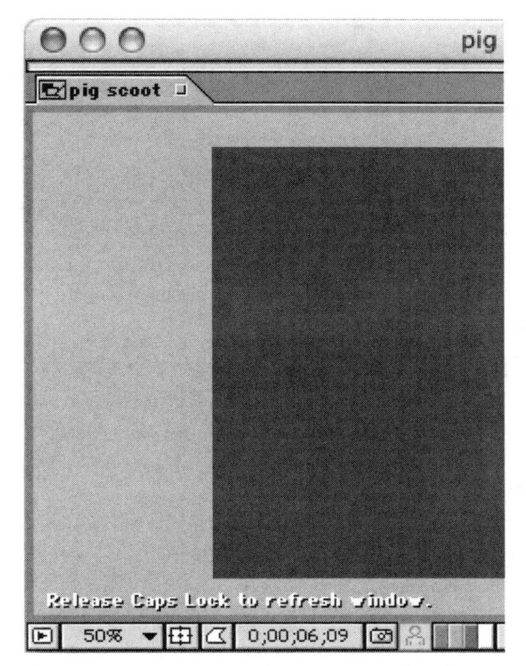

Figure 8.28 When Caps Lock is active, a red outline appears around the image in the windows that would otherwise be updated. The window also displays a friendly reminder.

Suppressing Window Updates

Once you get over the initial excitement of seeing your changes in the Composition window, you may discover that what seemed to be a blessing can also be a curse. If frames are difficult to render, it can take time to update windows. You may have already noticed how the Selection tool cycles between black and white as a particularly difficult frame renders (**Figure 8.27**). The lower-right corner of the Composition window also includes a small activity bar (provided the window is sized wide enough for you to see it). When previewing gets in the way of your progress, you can prevent the Footage, Layer, and Composition windows from updating by activating your keyboard's Caps Lock key.

When you suppress updates, windows continue to display the current frame, even after you make changes. When you alter the image in the current frame or move to a new frame, a red outline appears around the image in the windows that would otherwise be updated (**Figure 8.28**). Although window controls—anchor points, motion paths, mask outlines, and so on—continue to update, the image itself doesn't reflect your changes. When you're ready to update, or *refresh,* the affected windows, disengage Caps Lock.

To suppress window updates:

◆ Press Caps Lock to suppress window updates; press Caps Lock again to turn suppression off and refresh windows.

✔ Tip

■ If slow updates are a problem, you should consider replacing particularly demanding footage items with lower-quality proxies. See Chapter 3, "Managing Footage," for more information.

Scrubbing Audio

In After Effects, finding a particular frame based on the image is easy. Finding a particular moment based on the sound is a different matter. An audio preview plays your audio layers, but it doesn't make it easy to cue to a particular sound. When you halt an audio preview (see the next section), the current time marker goes back to the starting point—the current time marker doesn't remain at the moment you stop it. Viewing the audio waveform usually doesn't help you pinpoint a sound, either; individual sounds are difficult to discern in a waveform display (**Figure 8.29**). (See Chapter 7, "Properties and Keyframes.")

Fortunately, After Effects allows you to *scrub* the audio—that is, play it back slowly as you drag the current time marker. The term *scrubbing* refers to the back back-and-forth motion of tape over an audio head. This feature has always been taken for granted in the analog world, but it's long been considered a luxury for digital tools. (In fact, high-end equipment is still required to approximate old-fashioned tape scrubbing.)

Remember, you can always see audio levels—even while you scrub—in the Volume Units (VU) meter of the Audio palette (**Figure 8.30**).

To scrub audio:

- In the time ruler of the Timeline Layout window, Command-drag (Mac) or Ctrl-drag (Windows) the current time marker.

  The audio plays back as you drag.

✔ Tips

- To hear every syllable and beat, there's no substitute for scrubbing. Once you find the sound you're looking for, don't forget that you can mark the frame in the layer or the composition (see Chapter 6, "Layer Editing"). You can also set markers on the fly during audio previews by pressing the asterisk (*) key on the numeric keypad.
- As explained in the sidebar "Ample Samples: Audio Sample Rates," later in this chapter, audio samples occur far more frequently than video frame divisions. For precise audio editing, use a dedicated audio-editing program or NLE that allows for sample-based audio editing (like Adobe Premiere Pro or Apple Final Cut Pro). Remember, you can do all of your straightforward editing tasks in Premiere Pro and then import the entire project (see Chapter 2, "Importing Footage into a Project").

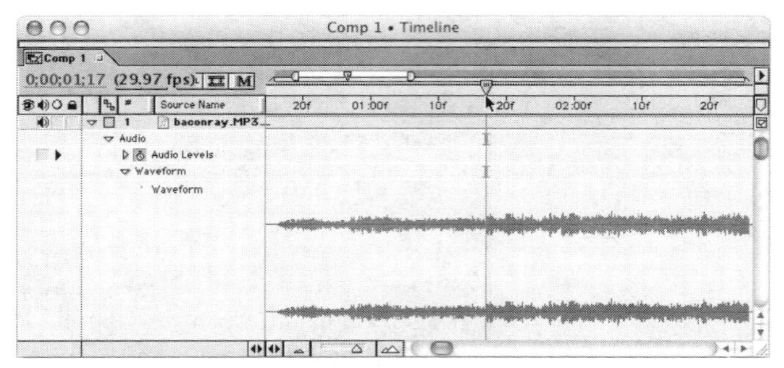

Figure 8.29 Scrubbing the audio provides an alternative (or an enhancement) to expanding the Audio Waveform property to cue the current time to a particular sound.

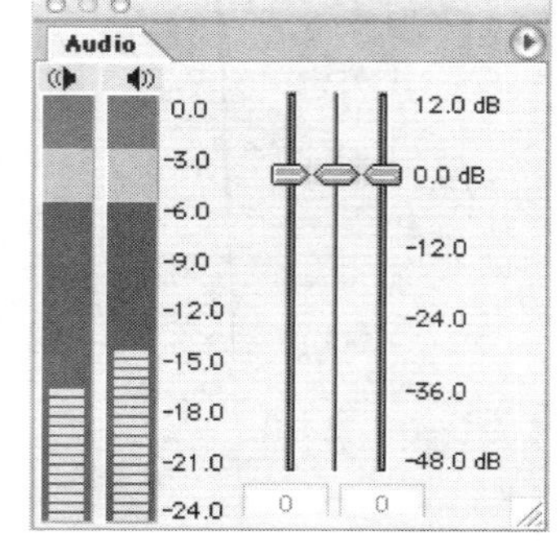

Figure 8.30 As usual, use the VU meter of the Audio palette to see audio levels as they play.

Comparing Preview Options

Until now, this chapter has focused on playback options and methods you can use to control the way the Composition window updates when you transform layer properties. The following sections discuss previewing a specified area of the composition.

You can choose from different types of preview methods. Because the complexity of the preview affects the time required to render it, choose the type best suited for your needs:

Video and audio—You can preview any combination of video and audio. Video frames require more memory and processing time than audio. You can control the relative quality of previews and thereby the relative rendering times.

Wireframe—You can preview video as *wireframes*, or outline representations, of layer images. Because they don't render the full image, wireframe previews render quickly, while accurately representing motion (changes in position, scale, and rotation).

Setting the Work Area

To preview part of a composition, you must define a range of frames with the *work area bar*, an adjustable bar located above the time ruler in the Timeline menu (**Figure 8.31**). To make it easier to identify the part of the composition that's included, the entire area under the work area bar is highlighted; it appears a little brighter than the area outside the work area.

As you learned in Chapter 6, the navigator view of the Timeline window includes a miniature version of the work area bar; however, it's for your reference only.

To set the work area by dragging:

In the Timeline window, *do any of the following:*

- Drag the left handle of the work area bar to the time you want previews to start (**Figure 8.32**).
- Drag the right handle of the work area bar to the time you want previews to end (**Figure 8.33**).
- Drag the center of the work area bar to move the work area without changing its duration (**Figure 8.34**).

  Make sure to grab the center of the bar, where vertical lines imply a textured grip. Otherwise, you'll cue the current time marker instead.

  Press Shift as you drag to snap the edges of the work area bar to the edges of layers, keyframes, markers, or the time marker.

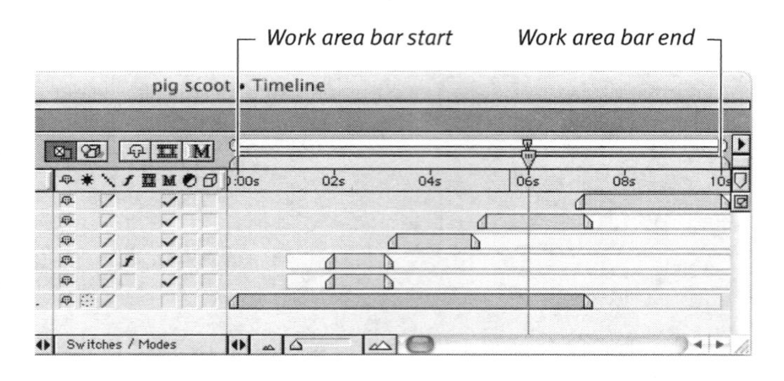

Figure 8.31 The work area bar defines the range of frames in the composition for previews.

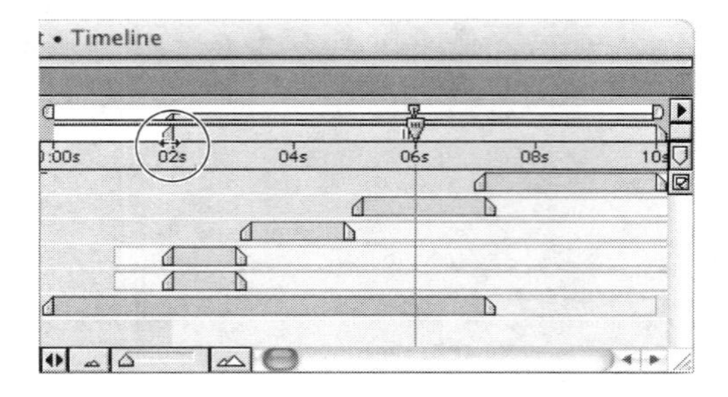

Figure 8.32 Drag the left handle of the work area bar to the time you want previews to start.

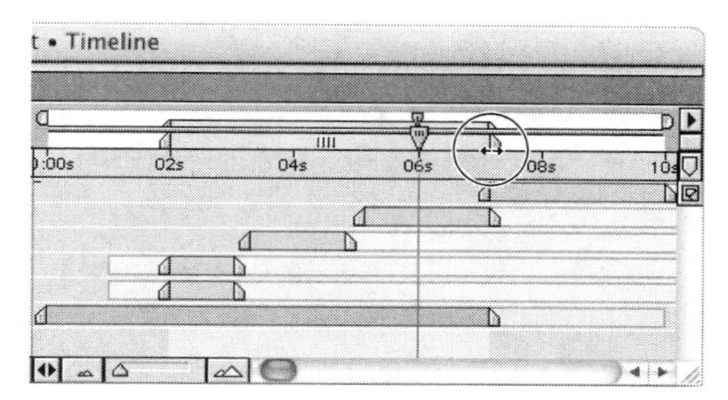

Figure 8.33 Drag the right handle of the work area bar to the time you want previews to end.

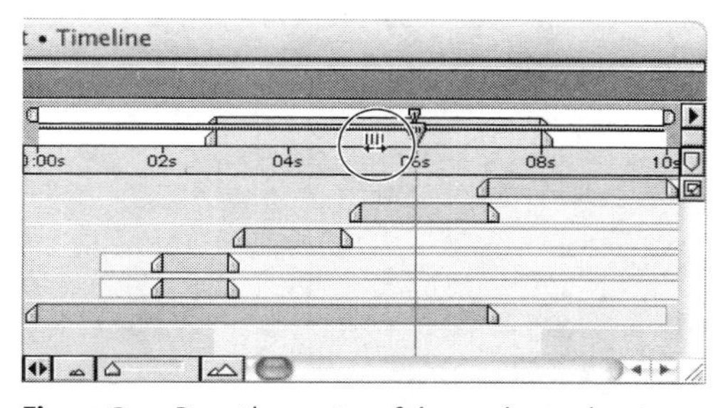

Figure 8.34 Drag the center of the work area bar to move the work area without changing its duration.

To set the work area using keyboard shortcuts:

1. In the Timeline window, set the current time to the frame at which you want the work area to begin or end.
2. *Do one of the following:*
   - ▲ Press B to set the beginning of the work area to the current time.
   - ▲ Press N to set the end of the work area to the current time.

✔ Tips

- You can't set the beginning of the work area bar after the end, or vice versa. If you can't move the end of the work area where you want, you probably have to move the other end first.
- Using an extended keyboard, you can cue the time to the beginning of the work area by pressing Shift-Home or to the end of the work area by pressing Shift-End.
- In principle, After Effects' work area bar is equivalent to the one in Premiere Pro. In practice, however, there are a few differences. For example, you can't use the same keyboard shortcuts for setting the work area (unless you create a custom shortcut in Premiere Pro).

Previewing Audio Only

If you only need to hear the audio tracks of your composition, you don't need to wait for a time-consuming video preview. With After Effects, you can also control the quality of audio previews, which affects rendering times.

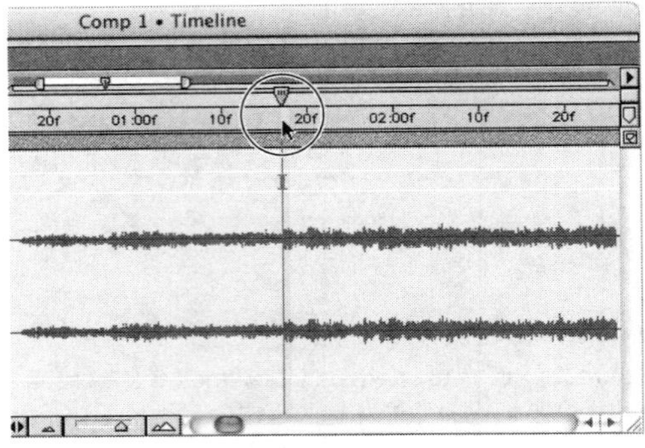

Figure 8.35 Cue the current time to the frame at which you want to begin an audio preview.

To preview audio only from the current time:

1. In the Composition or Timeline window, cue the current time to the frame at which you want to begin your audio preview (**Figure 8.35**).
2. Choose Composition > Preview > Audio Preview (Here Forward), or press the decimal point (.) on the numeric keypad (**Figure 8.36**).

   The audio starts playing from the current time and plays for the duration you set in the General Preferences (explained in the task "To set preferences for audio previews," later in this chapter).
3. Press the spacebar to stop the preview.

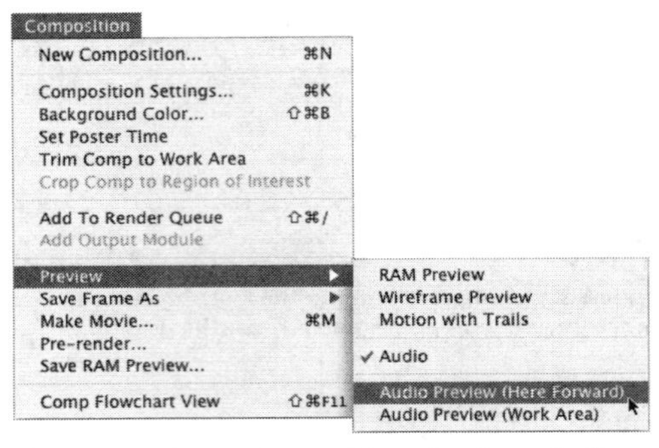

Figure 8.36 Choose Composition > Preview > Audio Preview (Here Forward).

To preview audio only under the work area:

1. Set the work area over the range of frames you want to preview (**Figure 8.37**).

   See the previous section, "Setting the Work Area."

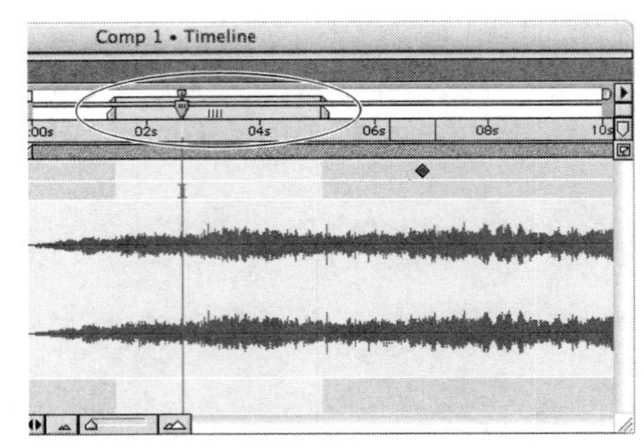

Figure 8.37 Set the work area bar over the range you want to preview.

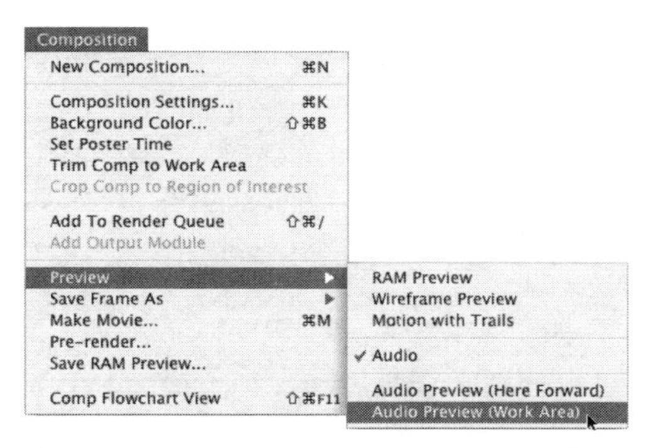

Figure 8.38 Choose Composition > Preview > Audio Preview (Work Area).

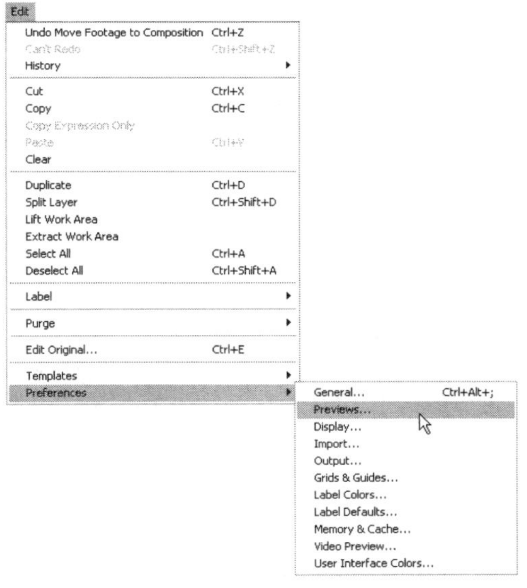

Figure 8.39 Choose After Effects > Preferences > Previews (Mac) or Edit > Preferences > Previews (Windows).

2. Choose Composition > Preview > Audio Preview (Work Area) (**Figure 8.38**).

   The audio under the work area plays.

To set preferences for audio previews:

1. Choose After Effects > Preferences > Previews (Mac) or Edit > Preferences > Previews (Windows) (**Figure 8.39**).

   The Previews panel of the Preferences dialog box appears (**Figure 8.40**).

continues on next page

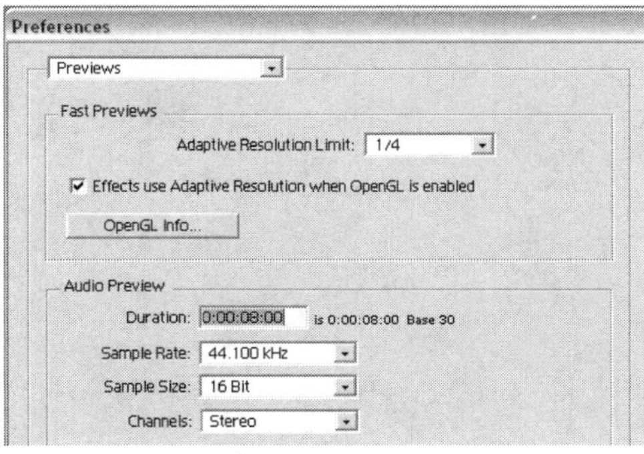

Figure 8.40 The Previews panel of the Preferences dialog box appears.

2. In the Audio Preview section of the dialog box, *specify the following settings:*
   - ▲ For Duration, enter the duration of audio previews.
   - ▲ In the Sample Rate pull-down menu, choose an audio sample rate for previews (**Figure 8.41**). (See the sidebar "Ample Samples: Audio Sample Rates.")
   - ▲ In the Sample Size pull-down menu, choose a bit depth for audio previews (**Figure 8.42**). (See the sidebar "A Bit Deeper into Bit Depth.")
   - ▲ In the Channels pull-down menu, choose to preview the audio in stereo or mono (**Figure 8.43**). (See the sidebar "Broadcast in Stereophonic Sound.")
3. Click OK to close the Preferences dialog box.

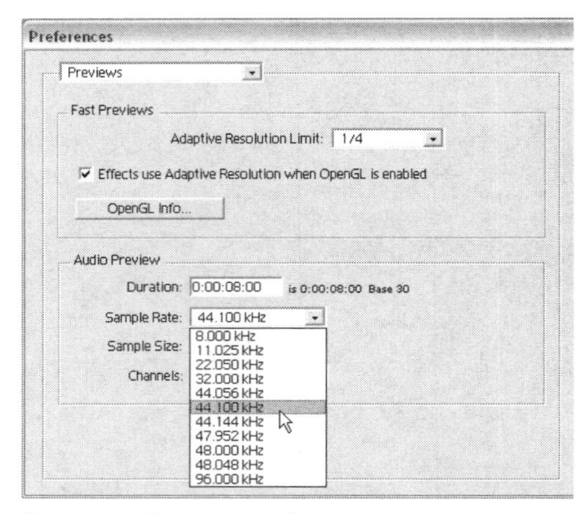

Figure 8.41 Choose an audio sample rate.

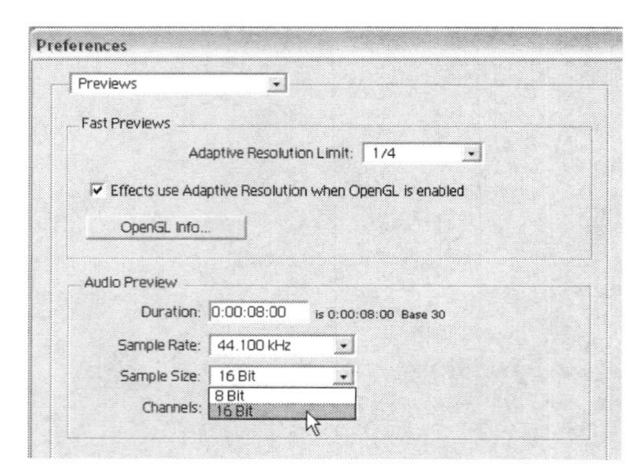

Figure 8.42 Choose an audio bit depth.

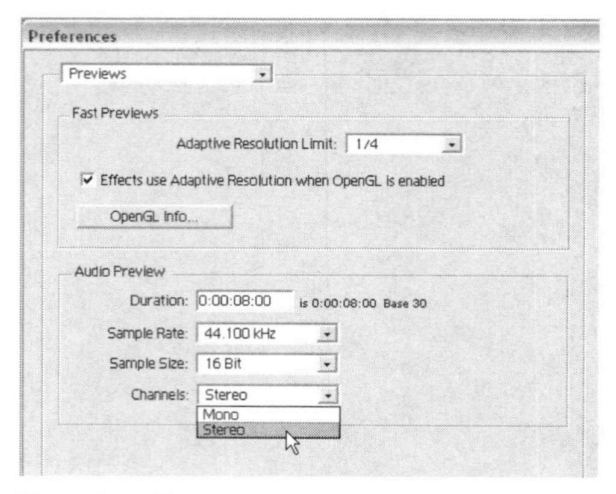

Figure 8.43 Choose mono or stereo.

Broadcast in Stereophonic Sound

For previews and renders, you can choose between stereophonic and monophonic audio. In a *stereophonic* (or simply *stereo*) recording, audio is mixed differently in the left and right channels. When the audio is played through stereo speakers (and listened to through two ears), the separate channels give the sound a sense of space. A *monophonic*, or *mono*, recording distributes the audio evenly between the two channels and plays back the same sounds through the left and right speakers.

Ample Samples: Audio Sample Rates

Analog signals are described by a continuous fluctuation of voltage. The analog signal is converted to a digital signal by being measured periodically, or *sampled*. If you think of the original audio as a curve, the digital audio would look like a connect-the-dots version of the curve. The more dots (or samples) you have, the more accurately you can reproduce the curve (**Figures 8.44** and **8.45**).

Sample rate describes the number of times audio is sampled to approximate the original sound. Sample rates are measured in samples per second, or hertz (Hz). One thousand hertz is called a kilohertz (kHz). The higher the sample rate, the more accurate the sound and the larger the file (everything else being equal).

The process of converting digital audio from one sample rate to another is called *resampling*. You can reduce the sample rate to decrease file sizes and RAM requirements—and thereby rendering speeds. Although increasing the sample rate also increases file size, it can't restore audio quality where none existed originally.

For audio previews, choose a sample rate that balances the audio quality you desire with the corresponding cost in rendering speed and RAM requirements. For rendered movies, choose the sample rate according to your output goal.

Figure 8.44 You can think of an analog audio signal as being a continuous curve.

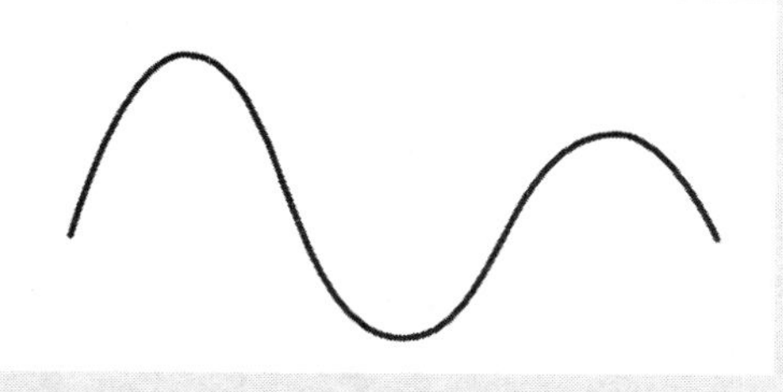

Figure 8.45 The more samples, the more accurately digital audio reproduces the original signal. Because each sample has a defined value, digital audio can be reproduced exactly.

Table 8.1

Standard Audio Sample Rates

Sample rate	Equivalent/special considerations
48 kHz	DAT or Digital Betacam; not always supported by sound or video cards
44.1 kHz	CD; best for music
32 kHz	Used by some DV cameras
22 kHz	Compromise between size and quality
11 kHz	Adequate for narration
8 kHz	Low data rates and quality; suitable for the Internet

A Bit Deeper into Bit Depth

Audio bit depth describes the number of bits used to describe each audio sample. Bit depth affects the range of sound an audio file can reproduce. This range is known as the signal-to-noise (s/n) ratio, which can be measured in decibels (dB).

Audio bit depth is often compared to image bit depth. A gradient with a higher bit depth looks smoother because it uses more steps as it transitions from one value to another (**Figures 8.46** and **8.47**). In much the same way, audio with higher bit depths has a greater range.

In After Effects, as in many other programs, you can choose a bit depth for previews and renders. Higher (or is it deeper?) bit depths produce better sound; however, they also create larger files that require more RAM and render more slowly.

Figure 8.46 Audio bit depth is comparable to image bit depth. This low-bit-depth gradient looks banded...

Figure 8.47 ...whereas this high-bit-depth gradient uses a greater range. Audio bit depth affects the range of sound.

Figure 8.48 A full preview shows everything in detail but requires both more RAM and more processing time.

Previewing Wireframes

When you want to see just the motion of an animation—changes in position, scale, and rotation—you don't have to waste precious time by rendering a full-fledged preview of the work area. Instead, use a wireframe preview for selected layers.

A *wireframe preview* represents the motion of one or more layers as an empty outline, or wireframe. A wireframe preview gives you a clear sense of motion without consuming much of your RAM or your time (**Figures 8.48** and **8.49**). To get a sense of the sweep of the layer's complete motion, the wireframe can include a trail, which leaves the previous frames visible as the preview progresses (**Figure 8.50**). Because wireframe previews don't render frames fully, no images are stored in the cache, and no green line indicator appears below the work area bar.

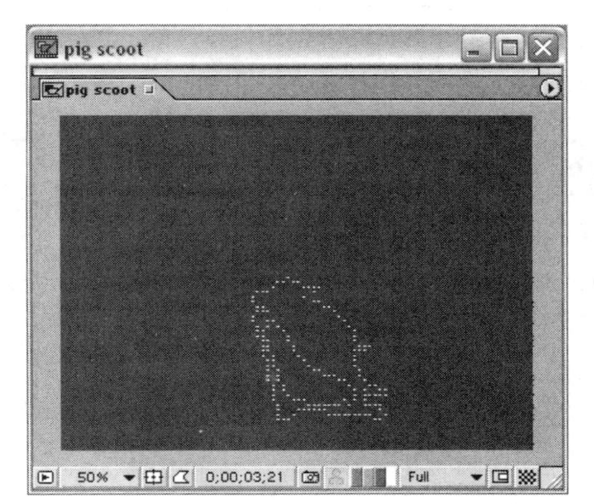

Figure 8.49 A wireframe preview represents the layer as an empty outline. It renders much faster but still shows you the motion of one or more layers.

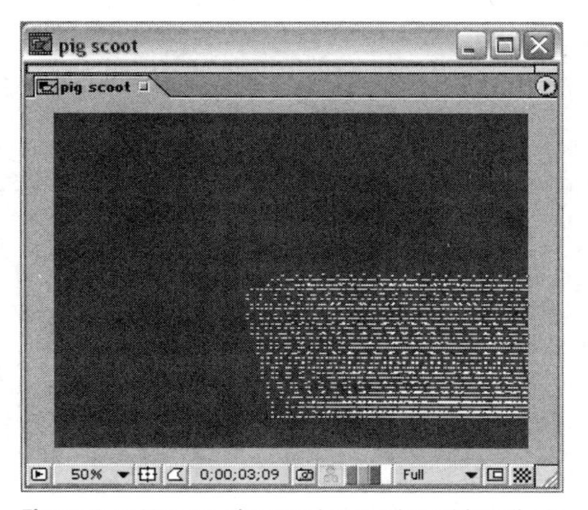

Figure 8.50 You can also preview motion with trails, in which case the wireframes at each frame remain visible as the preview progresses.

To create a wireframe preview:

1. In the Timeline window, *do one of the following:*
   - ▲ Select the layers you want to preview.
   - ▲ Deselect all layers to preview all of them.
2. Set the work area over the range of frames you want to preview (as explained in the previous section) (**Figure 8.51**).
3. *Do one of the following:*
   - ▲ Choose Composition > Preview > Wireframe Preview (**Figure 8.52**).
   - ▲ Choose Composition > Preview > Motion with Trails.
4. Press the spacebar to stop the preview.

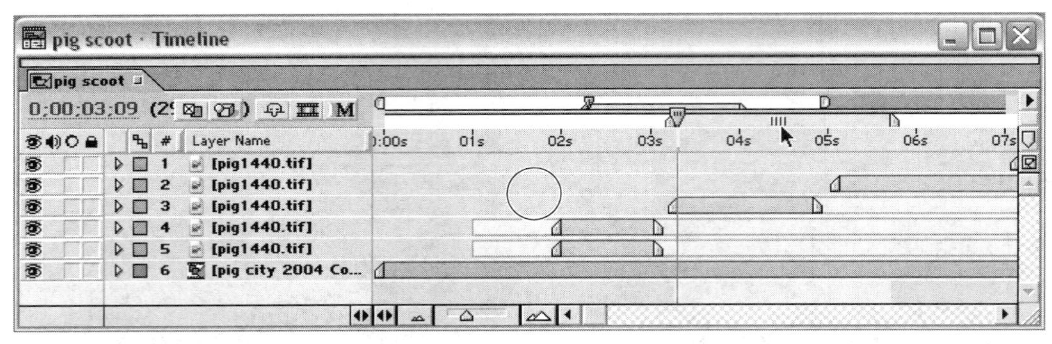

Figure 8.51 Set the work area, and select the layers you want to preview. To preview all the layers, leave them deselected.

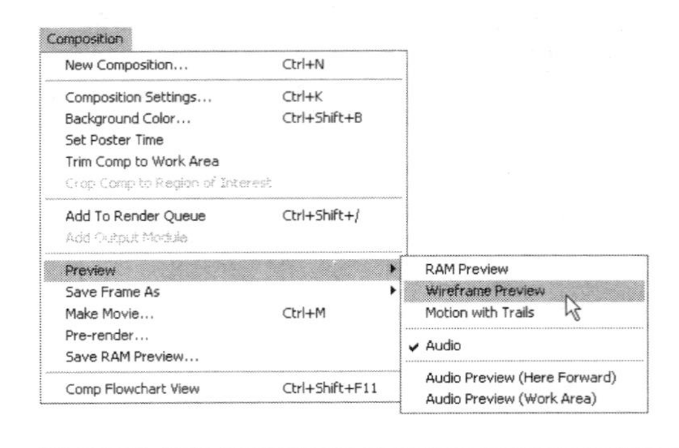

Figure 8.52 Select Composition > Preview > Wireframe Preview to view a wireframe preview, or choose Composition > Preview > Motion with Trails to view a wireframe preview with trails.

Rendering RAM Previews

To see a comp at (or near) its full frame rate, you typically render a RAM preview. In contrast to using standard playback controls, a RAM preview renders frames first and then plays them back. By default, a RAM preview renders frames in the work area only; but you can set an option to render frames beginning at the current time (similar to standard playback). RAM previews include several options to balance rendering speed with image quality and frame rate.

You can set separate options for two kinds of RAM previews: a standard RAM preview and a Shift-RAM preview. You can customize each type according to your project's demands, choosing the best RAM preview option for the task at hand. For example, you could set the standard RAM preview to render a relatively smooth, high-resolution image, and set the Shift-RAM preview to render more quickly, at the expense of smooth motion and image quality.

By default, rendering a RAM preview (including a Shift-RAM preview) renders the active window. But starting with After Effects 6.5, you can specify a particular window to preview, even if it isn't the currently active window. Doing so can streamline your workflow by freeing you from finding a particular window to preview (especially in complex projects). For example, by designating your final comp as the window to always preview, you can work in other windows and then quickly view your changes in the final comp.

Table 8.2

Keyboard Shortcuts for Playback and Preview

To do this	Press this
Start/pause	Spacebar
Frame advance	Page Down
Frame reverse	Page Up
First frame Home	Home key
Last frame End	End key
Scrub video	Option-drag (Mac) or Alt-drag (Windows) current time marker
Scrub audio	Command-drag (Mac) or Ctrl-drag (Windows) current time marker
Stop window updates	Caps Lock
Preview audio from current time	Decimal point (.) on numeric keypad
RAM preview	0 on numeric keypad
RAM preview every other frame	Shift-0 on numeric keypad
Save RAM preview	Command-0 (Mac) or Ctrl-0 (Windows) on numeric keypad
Wireframe preview	Option-0 (Mac) or Alt-0 (Windows) on numeric keypad
Wireframe preview using rectangular layer outline	Command-Option-0 (Mac) or Ctrl-Alt-0 (Windows) on numeric keypad
Show layers as background during wireframe previews	Add Shift to wireframe preview shortcut: Shift-Option-0 (Mac) or Shift-Alt-0 (Windows), using the 0 (zero) on the numeric pad

To show and hide RAM preview options:

- In the Time Controls window, click the Time Controls button and *select an option* from the pull-down menu (**Figure 8.53**):

  Show RAM Preview Options—Expands the palette to reveal the RAM preview options

  Show Shift+RAM Preview Options—Expands the palette to reveal the Shift-RAM preview options

  The Time Controls palette expands to reveal the options you selected (**Figure 8.54**). Reselect an option to hide RAM preview options.

✔ Tip

- Remember, you can repeatedly click the Time Controls palette to cycle through different views: to show the palette tab only, to add the playback controls, or to add the selected RAM or Shift-RAM preview options.

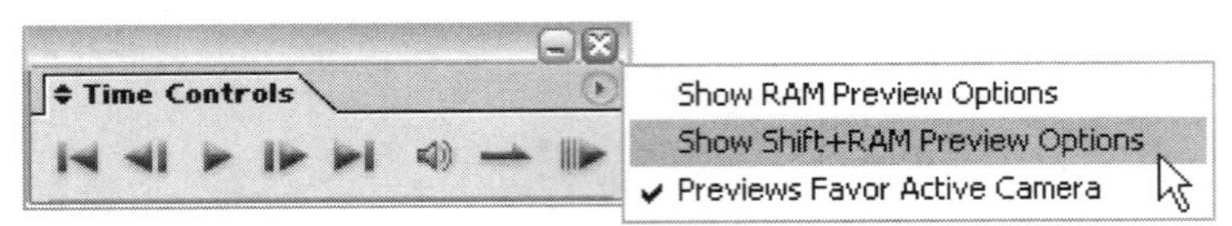

Figure 8.53 In the pull-down menu, choose the RAM preview options you want to show.

Figure 8.54 The Time Controls palette expands to reveal the options you selected.

RAMming Speed: Getting the Most Out of Your RAM and RAM Previews

In addition to using a computer with a fast processor and loads of RAM, here are some other things you can do to use RAM effectively and improve RAM playback.

Optimize Your Display

- Use a high-quality display card. Older or built-in display cards can be inadequate for animation. Try to use a display card that accelerates onscreen display. Better yet, choose an Adobe approved OpenGL graphics card, which can take over much of the processing.
- Use the latest drivers for your video display. Check with the manufacturer's Web site to make sure you're using the latest and greatest version.
- Set the color depth of your monitor to Millions of Colors (Mac) or True Color (Windows) to match After Effects' internal bit depth (24-bit plus alpha).
- Don't allow onscreen windows to overlap, especially with the Composition window. This includes system screens such as the taskbar (Windows) and dock (Mac).

Optimize Your RAM

- Reduce the number of undoable actions in General Preferences.
- Purge the image cache (as explained in the task "To purge the RAM cache" later in this chapter) to free up RAM.
- Add RAM to your system. Preferably, use interleaved RAM with matching pairs of RAM modules.

Reduce Memory Requirements for Compositions

- Set the composition to a low resolution (half, third, and so on) to achieve higher frame rates in previews.
- Match the composition's resolution and magnification factor. RAM previews work faster this way. For example, preview half-resolution compositions at 50 percent magnification.
- Use proxies when possible (see Chapter 3).
- Avoid footage items that use temporal compression (MPEG footage, for example). The frame differencing utilized by the compression scheme requires intensive processing.
- Prerender nested compositions when possible (see Chapter 17).
- Collapse transformations when possible (see Chapter 17).

To set RAM preview options:

1. In the Time Controls window, reveal either the RAM Preview or Shift-RAM Preview options, as explained in the previous task.

2. In the RAM Preview or Shift-RAM Preview Options area of the Time Controls palette, *enter the following:*

   Frame Rate—Enter the frame rate for the preview, or choose one from the pull-down menu (**Figure 8.55**).

   Lower frame rates render more quickly but at the expense of smooth motion.

   Skip—Enter the frequency with which frames are skipped and left unrendered.

   Skipping frames speeds rendering but results in choppier motion.

   Resolution—*Choose one of the following* options from the pull-down menu (**Figure 8.56**):

   Auto—Previews use the composition window's current resolution setting.

   Full—After Effects renders and displays every pixel of the composition, resulting in the highest image quality and the longest rendering time.

   Half—After Effects renders every other pixel, or one-quarter of the pixels of the full-resolution image in one-quarter of the time.

   Third—After Effects renders every third pixel, or one-ninth of the pixels in the full-resolution image in one-ninth of the time.

   Quarter—After Effects renders every fourth pixel, or one-sixteenth of the pixels in the full-resolution image in one-sixteenth of the time.

   Custom—After Effects renders whatever fraction of pixels you specify.

3. *Select either of the following* options:

   From Current Time—After Effects renders previews from the current time (instead of the frames defined by the work area).

   Full Screen—After Effects displays previews on a blank screen (with no windows visible).

Figure 8.55 Enter a frame rate used by the preview, or choose one from the pull-down menu. Also enter the frequency at which frames are skipped.

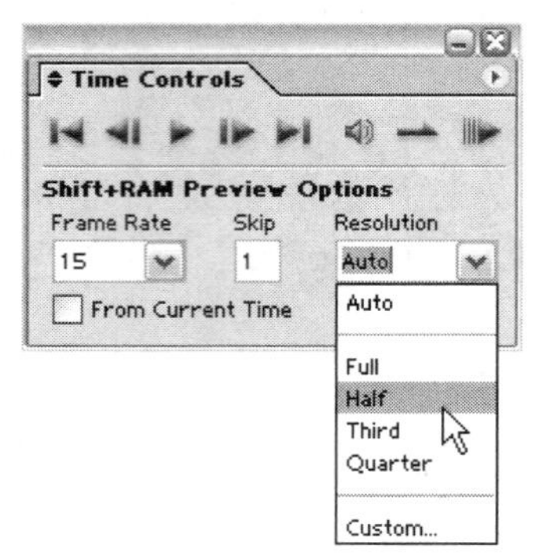

Figure 8.56 Choose an option from the Resolution pull-down menu. Select the other options you want.

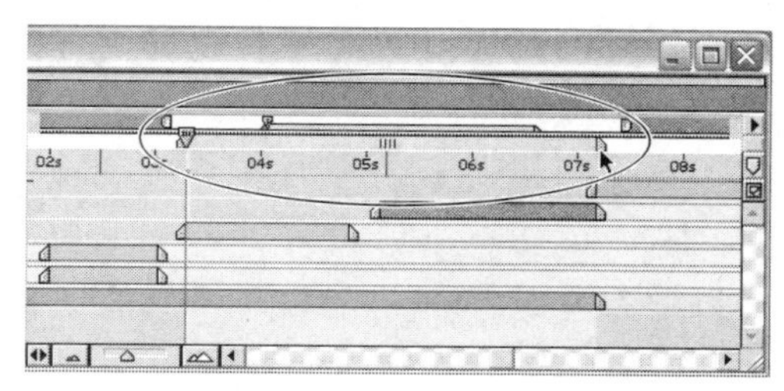

Figure 8.57 Set the work area bar over the range of frames you want to preview.

Figure 8.58 To preview audio in addition to video, click the Audio button in the Time Controls palette.

Figure 8.59 To loop the previewed frames, click the Loop button in the Time Controls palette.

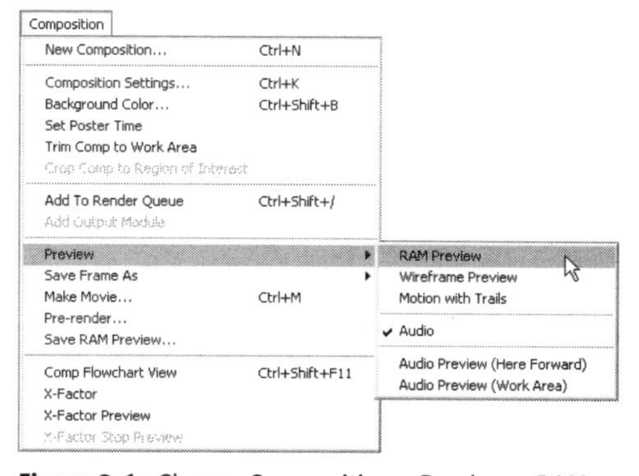

Figure 8.60 Choose Composition > Preview > RAM Preview.

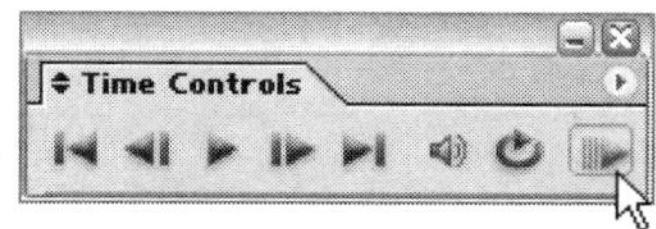

Figure 8.61 Or, click the RAM Preview button in the Time Controls palette, or press 0 in the numeric keypad.

To create a RAM preview:

1. In the Timeline window, set the work area bar to the range of frames you want to preview (**Figure 8.57**).
2. To preview audio as well as video, click the Audio button in the Time Controls palette (**Figure 8.58**).
3. To loop the previewed frames, select an option by clicking the Loop button in the Time Controls palette (**Figure 8.59**).
4. To use the standard RAM preview settings, *do any of the following:*
   - ▲ Choose Composition > Preview > RAM Preview (**Figure 8.60**).
   - ▲ Click the RAM Preview button in the Time Controls palette (**Figure 8.61**).
   - ▲ Press 0 on the numeric keypad.

continues on next page

5. To use the Shift-RAM preview settings, *do either of the following:*
   - ▲ Shift-click the RAM Preview button in the Time Controls palette.
   - ▲ Hold Shift as you press 0 on the numeric keypad.

   In the Timeline window, a green line appears over the frames that are rendered to RAM (**Figure 8.62**). When all the frames in the work area have been rendered, or when the amount of available RAM runs out, the frames play back in the Composition window.

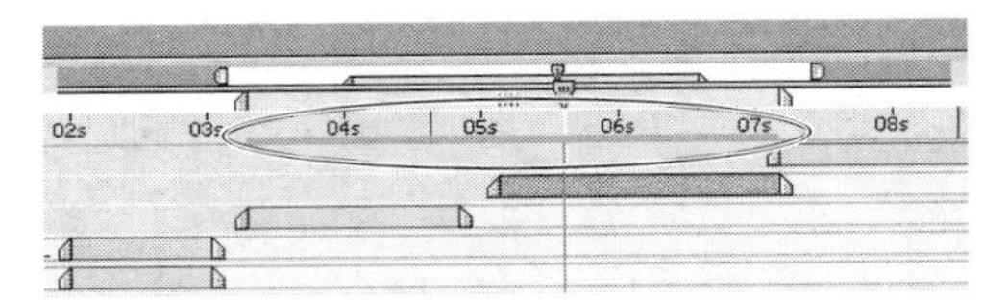

Figure 8.62 A green line appears over the frames that are rendered to RAM.

To specify a window to always preview:

◆ Click the Always Preview This View button in the window you want to designate for previews (**Figure 8.63**).

RAM Previews (including Shift-RAM previews) always render the window you specified, which becomes active for you to view.

Figure 8.63 In the lower left corner of the window you want to designate, click the Always Preview This View button.

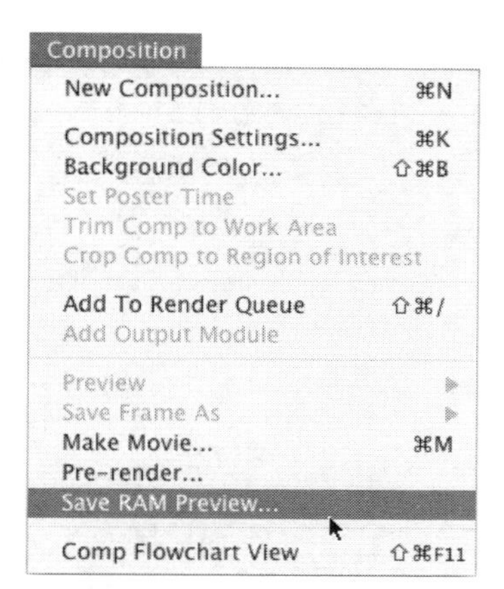

Figure 8.64 Choose Composition > Save RAM Preview.

Figure 8.65 Or, set the work area and Command-click (Mac) or Ctrl-click (Windows) the RAM Preview button.

Saving RAM Previews

After Effects not only creates RAM previews relatively quickly, it also lets you retain the ones you like as movie files. You can then use these previews as draft versions for your own reference; you can even share them with clients.

Although RAM movies can provide a more convenient way of previewing than rendering a draft movie in the traditional fashion (see Chapter 18, "Output"), they also have some limitations. RAM previews saved as movies use the same frame size and resolution as the composition (see Chapter 4, "Compositions"), but they don't use its current magnification factor. RAM movies can contain alpha channel information only if the composition's background has been set to black. (The RAM movie's alpha is premultiplied with black; see Chapter 2 for more about alpha channels.) Finally, the RAM preview movie can't contain interlaced fields.

Apart from these restrictions, the RAM preview movie settings come from a template in the Output Module. For more about the Output Module and editing templates, see Chapter 18.

To save a RAM preview as a movie file:

1. *Do one of the following:*
   - ▲ Choose Composition > Save RAM Preview (**Figure 8.64**).
   - ▲ Set the work area and Command-click (Mac) or Ctrl-click (Windows) the RAM Preview button (**Figure 8.65**) in the Time Controls palette.

   A Save As dialog box appears.

continues on next page

2. Choose a name and destination for the RAM Preview movie.
3. Click Save to close the Save As dialog box (**Figure 8.66**).

   A Render Queue window appears, and After Effects saves the RAM movie to the destination you specified (**Figure 8.67**).
4. Close the Render Queue window to continue working with your project.

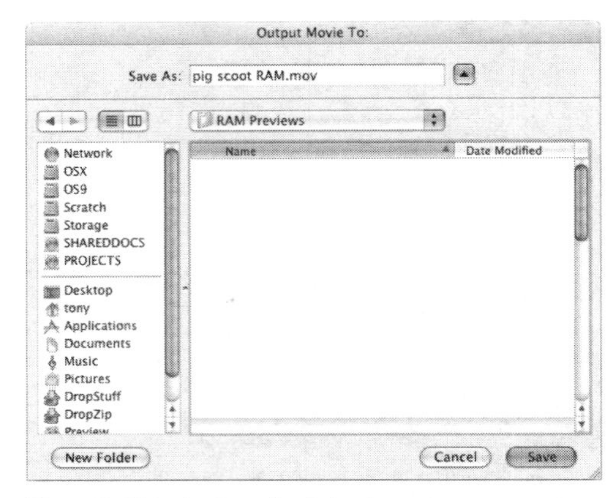

Figure 8.66 In the Save As dialog box, choose a name and destination for the RAM preview movie, and then click Save.

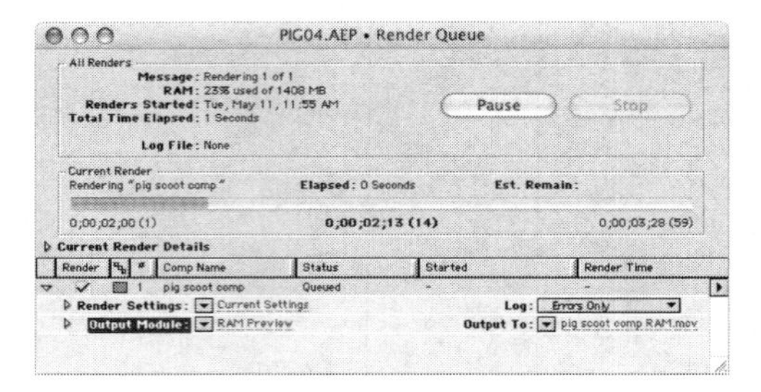

Figure 8.67 A Render Queue window appears briefly as the RAM movie is saved.

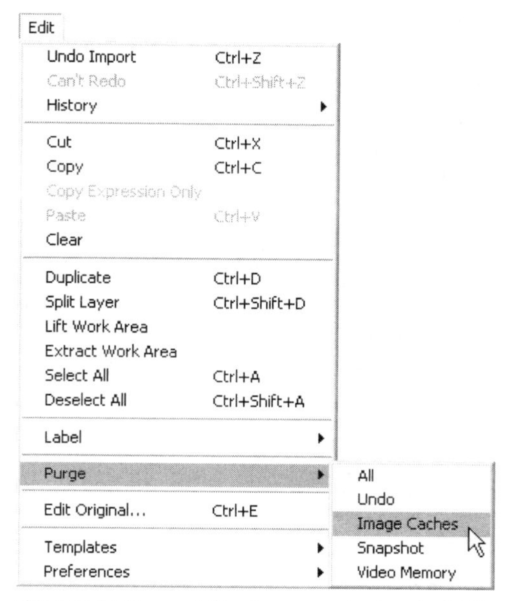

Figure 8.68 Choose Edit > Purge > and select the RAM cache you want to clear.

Managing RAM

Before you run out to add more RAM to your system, take a few moments to learn how to get the most from your existing RAM.

To purge the RAM cache:

◆ Choose Edit > Purge, and *select any of the following options* (**Figure 8.68**):

All—Clears the Undo, Image, and Snapshot caches

Undo—Clears recent actions from the cache, which prevents you from undoing any recent actions

Image Caches—Clears rendered frames from the cache

Snapshot—Clears the last snapshot from the cache, which means you won't be able to view the last snapshot in any window

Video Memory—Clears the video memory, or VRAM cache

The cached information is purged, freeing up RAM to cache new information.

To set RAM preferences:

1. Choose After Effects > Preferences > Memory & Cache (Mac) or Edit > Preferences > Memory & Cache (Windows) (**Figure 8.69**).

   The Memory & Cache panel of the Preferences dialog box appears (**Figure 8.70**).

2. For Maximum Memory Usage, enter the maximum amount of RAM to use for any purpose.

   The dialog box calculates how much RAM you allocated in terms of MB. Increase this value if you get "insufficient memory" messages. A value of 100% equals the amount of installed RAM, but virtual memory allows you to enter higher values. However, setting values greater than 200% isn't recommended.

3. In the Image Cache area of the dialog box, enter the percentage of available RAM to be allocated for storing rendered frames in the Maximum RAM Cache Size field.

   The dialog box calculates how much RAM you allocated in terms of MB. Increase the value to play more frames from RAM; decrease the value if playback becomes jerky. Use the default 60% value as a starting point; setting values greater than 90% isn't recommended.

4. Click OK to close the Preferences dialog box.

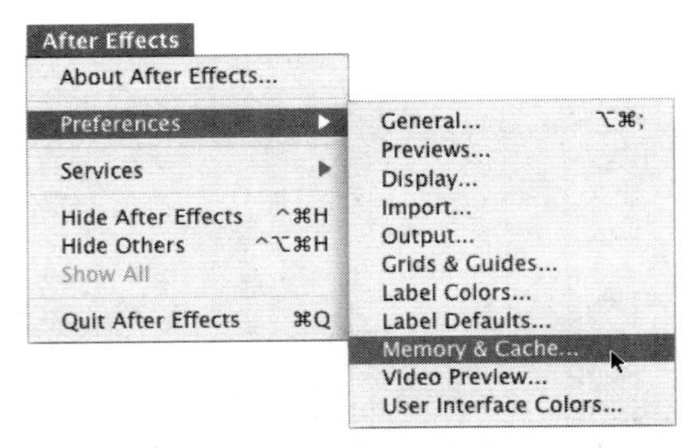

Figure 8.69 Choose After Effects > Preferences > Memory & Cache (Mac) or Edit > Preferences > Memory & Cache (Windows).

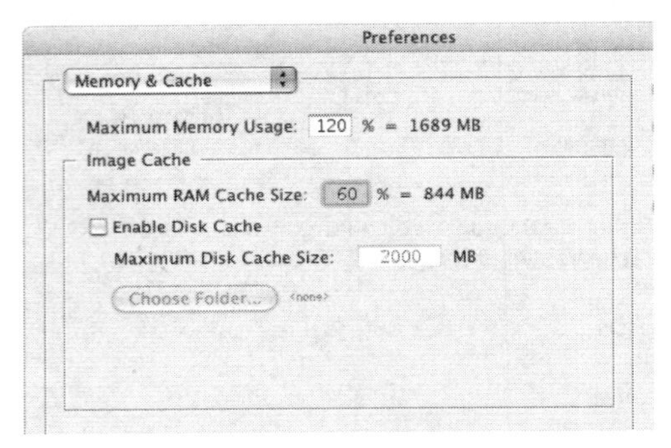

Figure 8.70 The Memory & Cache panel of the Preferences dialog box appears.

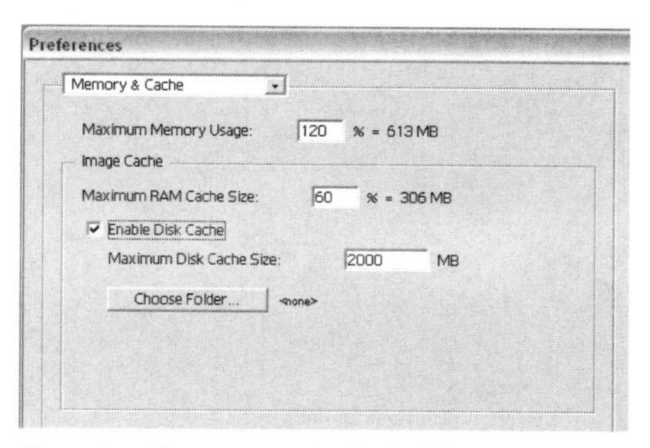

Figure 8.71 Choose an option in the Memory & Cache panel of the Preferences dialog box.

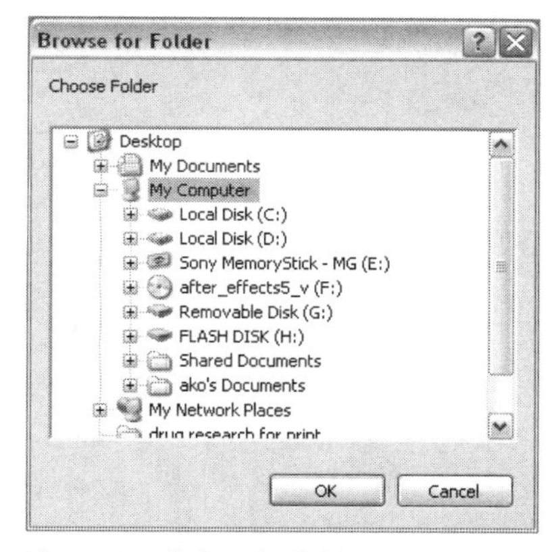

Figure 8.72 Select the folder you want to use as a cache location, and click Choose.

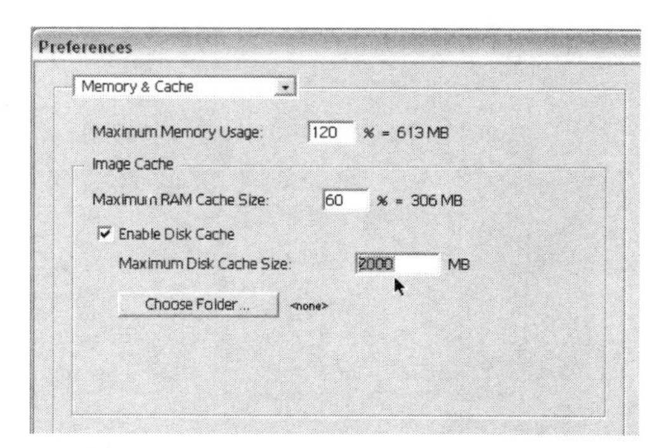

Figure 8.73 Enter the amount of disk storage you want to allocate as a disk cache for the Maximum Disc Size.

To use a disk cache:

1. Choose After Effects > Preferences > Memory & Cache (Mac) or Edit > Preferences > Memory & Cache (Windows).

   The Memory & Cache panel of the Preferences dialog box appears.

2. *Do either of the following* (**Figure 8.71**):

   ▲ If you're specifying a disk cache for the first time, select Enable Disk Cache.

   ▲ If Enable Disk Cache is already checked, click Choose Folder.

   A Choose Folder (Mac) or Browse for Folder (Windows) dialog box appears.

3. Select the folder you want to use as a cache location, and click Choose (Mac) or OK (Windows) (**Figure 8.72**).

   The Preferences dialog box displays the name of the folder you specified.

4. For Maximum Disk Cache Size, specify the amount of disk storage you want to allocate as a disk cache, in MB (**Figure 8.73**).

5. Click OK to close the dialog box.

Mask Essentials

A *mask* is a shape, or path, that you create in a layer. You can draw a mask manually with a tool, define it numerically using the Mask Shape dialog box, or copy it from Adobe Illustrator or Photoshop. A mask can be a closed shape (such as a circle) or an open path (such as a curved line). Masks are essential to compositing images and to creating a number of other effects. As the name suggests, the most common use for a mask is to mask, or preserve, parts of a layer's image while cropping out the rest. In other words, a closed mask modifies a layer's alpha channel—which, as you recall, defines the opaque and transparent areas of an image. Even if a footage item lacks an alpha channel of its own, you can define areas of transparency using masks. The image within the masked area remains visible; the area outside the mask reveals the layers below.

Whereas a closed mask defines a shape, an *open* mask creates a curve or path. By itself, an open mask can't modify a layer's transparency. However, you can use it in conjunction with other techniques to achieve a variety of effects. For example, you can use the Stroke effect to trace a mask with a color or to mask the area around the curve. Or, you can paste a mask path into the Comp window to use it as a motion path. A mask can also define a curved baseline for path text. You can apply these techniques to both open and closed masks, but you can see how an open mask is sometimes the more appropriate choice.

This chapter is devoted to creating and modifying masks; other chapters cover animating mask properties, creating motion paths from masks (and masks from motion paths), and applying effects to masks. If you're new to creating Bézier curves with the Pen tool, take a little extra time with these sections; you'll be able to apply these skills to manipulating motion paths as well. (And if you're already familiar with path editing in other programs, don't let the minor inconsistencies between programs distract you.) Try to master Bézier curves before you move on to creating masks using the RotoBezier option.

Viewing Masks in the Layer and Comp windows

You can create and work with masks not only in the Layer window but in the Composition window as well. The window you use will depend on the task at hand as well as your personal preference. A Layer window shows masks in the context of a single layer, letting you view the image outside the masked areas (**Figure 9.1**). In addition, the Layer window shows you the layer before any property changes (scale, rotation, and so on) are applied. In contrast, the Composition window shows only the masked portions of a layer and places them in the context of all the layers that are visible at the current time (**Figure 9.2**). By the time you're able to view a layer in the Comp window, Mask, Effect, Transform, and 3D properties have all been applied.

When you want to create or modify a mask in the Comp window, you must select the layer that contains the mask. Tasks throughout this chapter assume you have done so.

Figure 9.1 The Layer window shows masks in the context of the layer; it also lets you see the image outside the mask.

Figure 9.2 The Comp window shows the layer after masks and other property changes have taken effect.

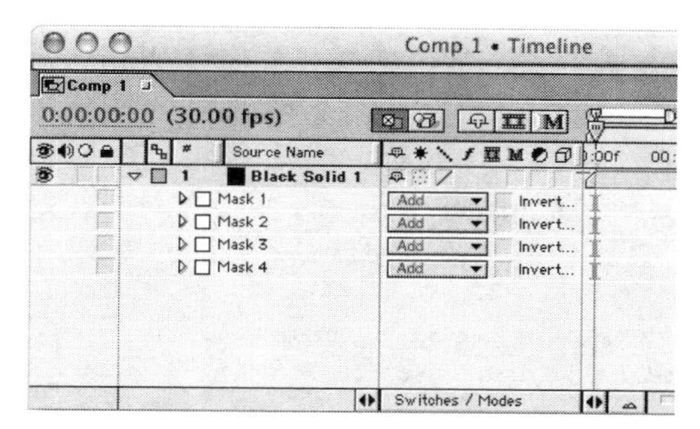

Figure 9.3 Masks appear in the layer outline in the order they were created.

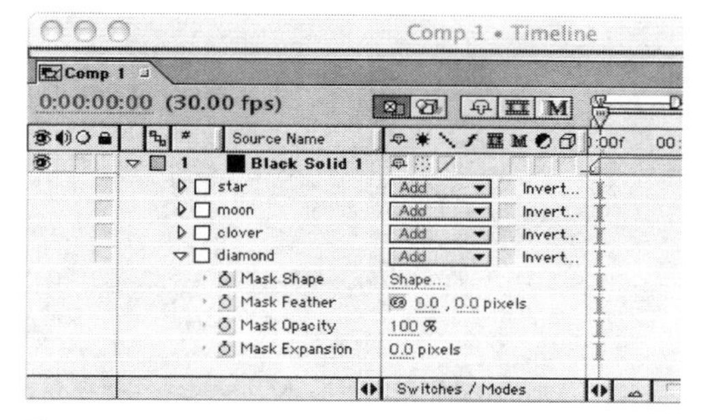

Figure 9.4 You can rename and reorder masks just like layers. Masks have several properties: Shape, Feather, Opacity, and Expansion.

Viewing Masks in the Layer Outline

Each mask you create appears in the layer outline of the Timeline window under the Mask property heading. The Target pull-down menu of the Layer window also lists the layer's masks. The most recent mask appears at the top of the stacking order (**Figure 9.3**).

In the Timeline window, you can rename and change the stacking order of masks, just as you would layers. When you expand the Mask property heading, it reveals four properties: Mask Shape, Mask Feather, Mask Opacity, and Mask Expansion (**Figure 9.4**). The following sections deal with these properties as well as other ways to control layer masks.

Hiding and Showing Mask Paths

Because the Layer and Comp windows serve several purposes, sometimes you'll want to hide the mask paths from view. When you want to work with the layer masks, you can make them visible again. Creating a new mask reveals the masks for the selected layer automatically.

To view and hide masks in the Layer window:

1. View a layer in a Layer window.
2. In the Layer window's View pull-down menu, select Masks to make mask paths visible (**Figure 9.5**).

   Selecting another option deselects the Mask option.

To view and hide masks in the Composition window:

- In the Comp window, click the View Mask button (**Figure 9.6**).

  Mask paths for selected layers can be viewed and edited in the Composition window (**Figure 9.7**). Deselect the View Masks button to hide mask paths.

Figure 9.5 In the Layer window's View pull-down menu, select Masks to make mask paths visible.

Figure 9.6 In the Comp window, select the Mask button...

Figure 9.7 ...to reveal layer masks.

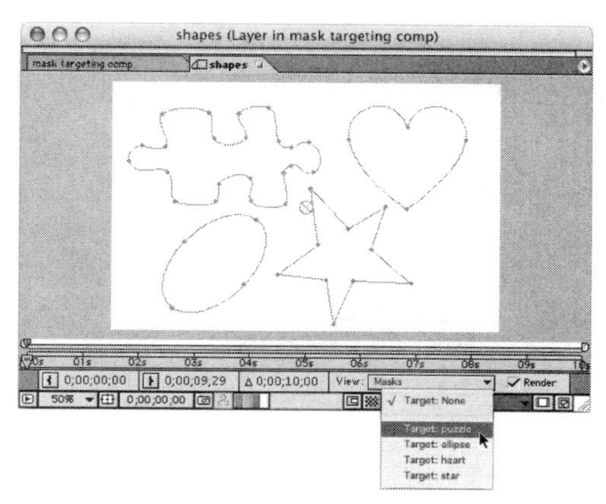

Figure 9.8 In the Target menu, choose a layer you want to select, or target, for changes.

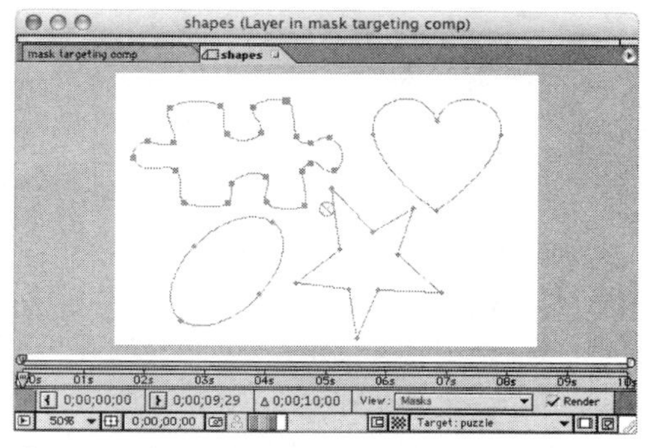

Figure 9.9 The targeted mask appears selected for you to change it. If you create a new mask shape, it replaces the targeted mask.

Targeting Masks

With After Effects, you can create as many as 127 masks for each layer. The Target pull-down menu at the bottom of the Layer window provides one way to select the mask you want to use. Note that the Target pull-down menu appears only when the layer contains one or more masks.

To choose the target mask:

1. View a layer containing one or more masks in a Layer window.
2. At the bottom of the Layer window, choose a mask from the Target pull-down menu (**Figure 9.8**):
   - ▲ Choose None to create a new mask without changing an existing mask.
   - ▲ Choose the name of an existing mask to target that mask for changes.

   The mask you choose appears selected (**Figure 9.9**).

Comparing Mask Creation Methods

The Tools palette contains several tools for creating and modifying masks (**Figure 9.10**). (These tools aren't as extensive as those found in Illustrator, but you wouldn't expect them to be—Illustrator is dedicated to such tasks.)

Rectangular Mask— Creates squares and rectangles (**Figure 9.11**)

Elliptical Mask— Creates closed elliptical and circular shapes (**Figure 9.12**)

Pen— Creates open or closed Bézier curves or RotoBezier curves (**Figure 9.13**)

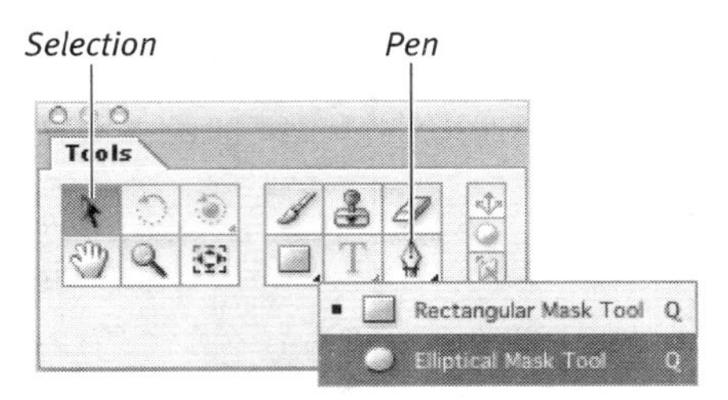

Figure 9.10 The Tools palette contains several tools to create and manipulate mask paths.

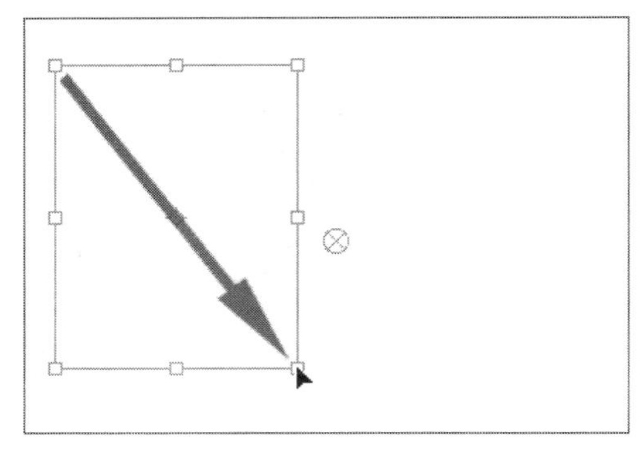

Figure 9.11 The Rectangular Mask tool creates rectangular or square mask paths.

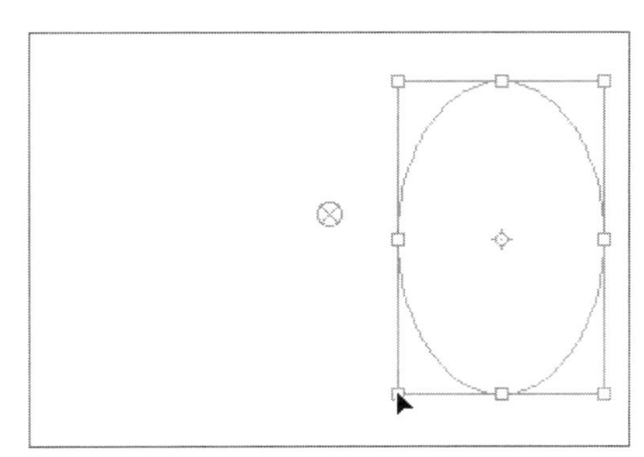

Figure 9.12 The Elliptical Mask tool creates elliptical, or circular, paths.

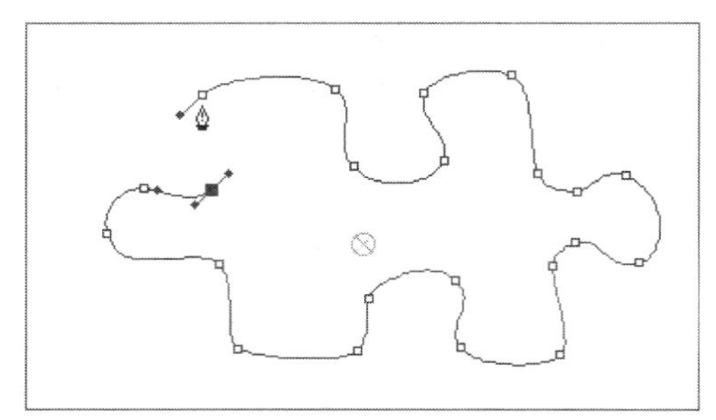

Figure 9.13 The Pen tool creates more complex paths using Bézier curves or RotoBezier curves.

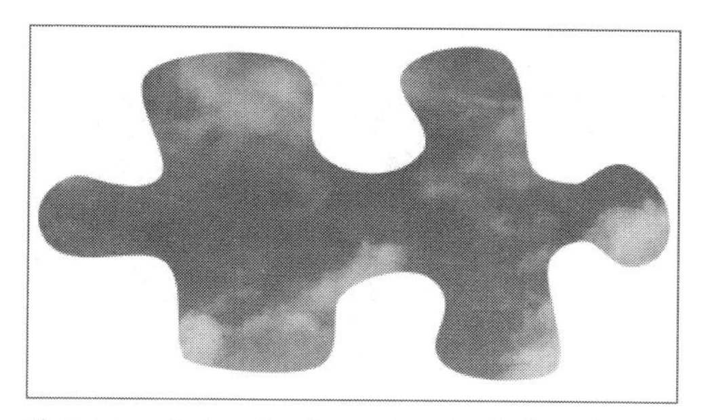

Figure 9.14 A closed path creates a typical mask, which defines the opaque areas of the layer image.

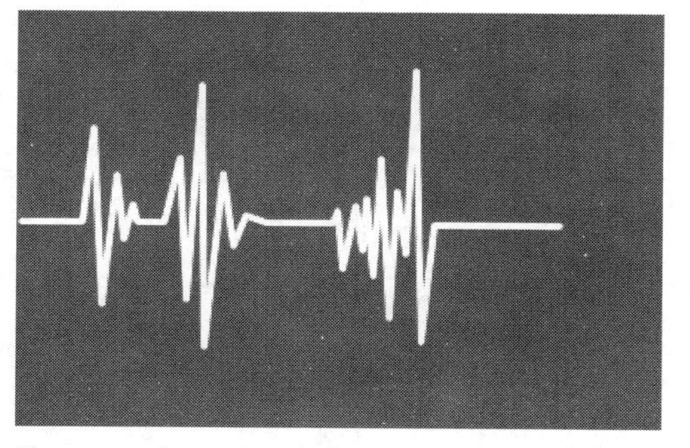

Figure 9.15 An open path doesn't create a mask per se, but it can be used for other effects, such as creating stroked lines. Open paths can also be used to create motion paths.

Comparing Closed and Open Paths

As mentioned in the introduction to this chapter, masks can be closed shapes or open paths.

Closed paths—You can draw closed paths with any of the drawing tools (**Figure 9.14**). By default, the interior of a closed mask shape defines the opaque area of a layer; the exterior defines transparency. However, you can manipulate the transparency in a number of ways (explained in later sections).

Open paths—You can create open paths with the Pen tool, or you can open a closed path by using a menu command. Open paths aren't useful as masks per se, but they can serve as the basis for path text and path-based effects (**Figure 9.15**). For example, they can be stroked to create graphical objects (such as drawn text) or pasted into a motion path.

✔ Tip

- Path text and the Stroke effect are just a couple of examples of how masks are used as part of more complex techniques. A number of effects utilize masks, including particle, distortion, and morphing effects.

Understanding Mask Anatomy

It can be useful to describe the contour of a mask as a *path*. All mask paths consist of *control points* connected by *segments*. In a straight-sided polygon, control points define the vertices; in a curved shape, however, they determine the curve of adjacent segments. You can control the curve manually by creating a standard mask that uses a *Bézier* curve (**Figure 9.16**). (Many path-based drawing programs, such as Illustrator, also employ Bézier curves.) Alternatively, you can let After Effects calculate curves automatically, creating a *RotoBezier* mask (**Figure 9.17**).

Figure 9.16 A standard mask uses Bézier curves that define curves with direction lines you set manually.

Figure 9.17 In contrast, a RotoBezier mask lacks direction lines and calculates the curves automatically.

Standard masks and Bézier curves

In a Bézier curve, you can think of a path as a line that exits one control point and enters another; the route the line takes depends on whether either point has a *direction line*. Control points define each end of a segment; direction lines define the curve of the segment.

Direction lines and handles extend from control points to define and control the curve of a path segment. The length and angle of a direction line influence the shape of a curve. (To picture this, imagine that direction lines exert a gravitational pull on the line that enters and exits a control point.) Dragging the dot, or *handle*, at the end of a direction line alters the line and thus its corresponding curve. When a point has two direction lines, the *incoming* direction line influences the preceding curve; the *outgoing* direction line influences the curve that follows.

It's helpful to categorize the following control points by how they use, or don't use, direction lines (**Figure 9.18**):

Anchor point—Click with the Pen tool to create an anchor point. Anchor points have no control handles extending from them.

Smooth point—Drag with the Pen tool to create a smooth point. Dragging extends two equal and opposite direction lines from a smooth point. Path segments connected by a smooth point result in a continuous curve.

Corner point—A corner point's direction lines operate independently. You can convert a smooth point into a corner by dragging a direction handle with the Convert Vertex tool . Path segments connected by a corner point result in a discontinuous curve, or *cusp*.

RotoBezier masks

The Pen tool's RotoBezier option lets you define a mask with curved segments without defining direction lines. Instead, you set only the control points; After Effects calculates the curved segments automatically. Without custom direction lines, you can't fully control the character of each curve; however, you can adjust each control point's *tension* to change the relative amount of curve in its adjacent segments.

Choosing a mask type

Although you can create RotoBezier masks more quickly than standard Bézier masks, they tend to require more control points. In addition, it's more difficult to create discontinuous curves (cusps), using a RotoBezier. Fortunately, you don't have to choose one method to the exclusion of the other: You can convert a RotoBezier mask to a standard mask and vice versa.

The following sections cover standard masks and Bézier curves first, then RotoBezier masks. Apart from adjusting their curves, you can edit both standard masks and RotoBezier masks in similar ways. Sections dealing with manipulating control points (such as selecting, moving, adding, and deleting them) and adjusting mask properties (such as inverting, feathering, and using mask modes) apply to both Bézier and RotoBezier masks.

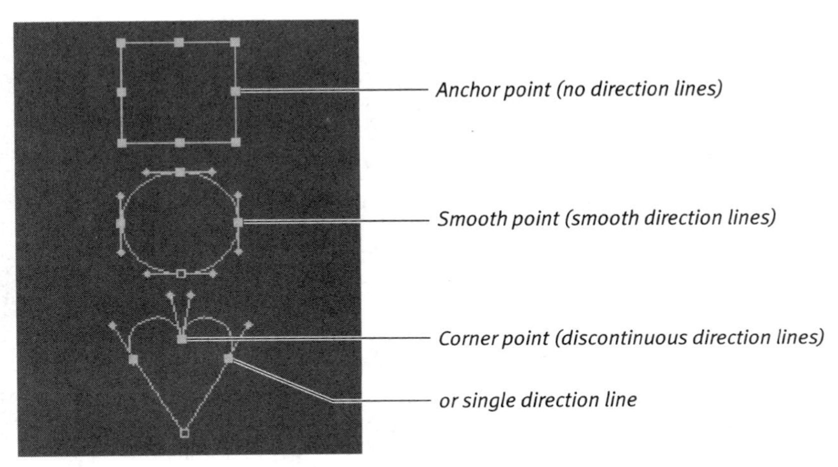

Figure 9.18 Mask paths consist of control points connected by segments.

Creating Simple Mask Shapes

You can create simple mask shapes quickly with the Rectangle and Ellipse tools. On the other hand, a simple rectangle or ellipse can serve as the starting point of a more complex shape. As you'll see in later sections, you can easily alter any mask's shape. In addition, you can effectively combine masks using mask modes.

To draw a rectangular or elliptical mask:

1. View the layer you want to mask in a Layer window, or select it in the Composition window.
2. In the Tools palette, select the Rectangular Mask tool or Elliptical Mask tool (**Figure 9.19**).
3. In the Layer or Comp window, *do any combination of the following*:
   - ▲ Drag from one corner of the mask shape to the opposite corner to create the mask (**Figure 9.20**).
   - ▲ Shift-drag to constrain the shape to equal proportions if you want to create a square or circle (**Figure 9.21**).
   - ▲ Command-drag (Mac) or Ctrl-drag (Windows) to create a mask shape that extends from the center rather than the corner (**Figure 9.22**).
   - ▲ Option-drag (Mac) or Alt-drag (Windows) to view the effects of the mask in the Composition window as you drag.
4. Release the mouse when you've finished creating the mask.

   In the Layer and Comp windows, the mask appears as a path with selected control points (as long as you set the window to display masks; see "Hiding and Showing Mask Paths," earlier in this chapter). In the Composition window, the areas of the layer outside the mask are concealed, whereas the areas inside the mask are visible.

✔ Tip

- To create a mask that fills the layer, double-click the Rectangular Mask tool or Elliptical Mask tool.

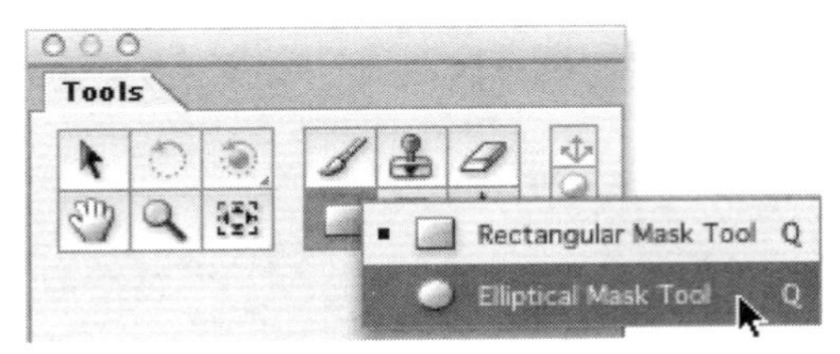

Figure 9.19 In the Tools palette, choose the Rectangular Mask or Elliptical Mask tool.

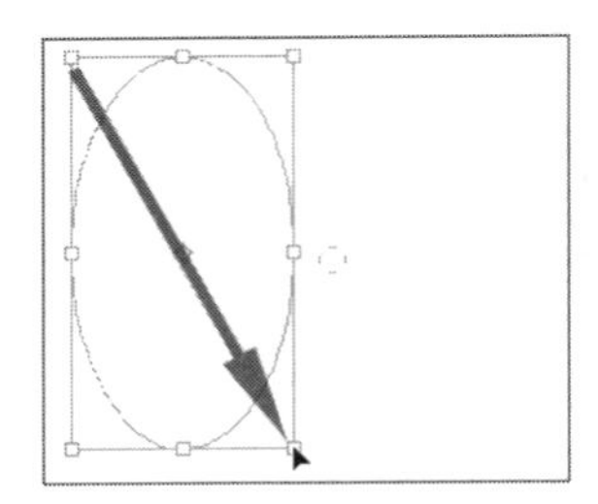

Figure 9.20 In the Layer or Comp window, drag to define the shape from one corner of the shape to its opposite corner.

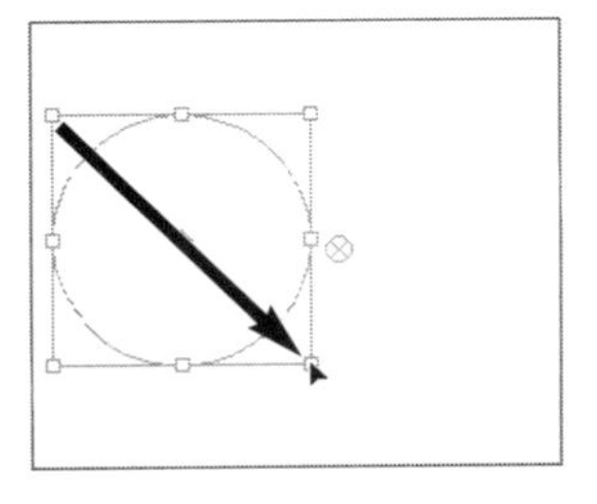

Figure 9.21 Shift-drag to constrain the shape to equal proportions so that you can create a square or circle.

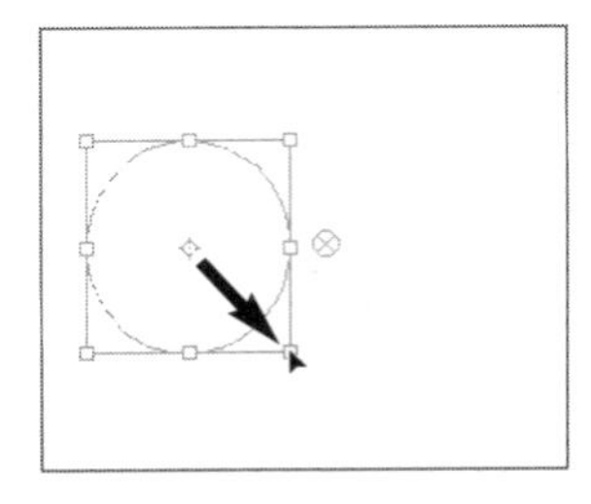

Figure 9.22 Command-drag (Mac) or Ctrl-drag (Windows) to create a mask shape that extends from the center instead of the corner.

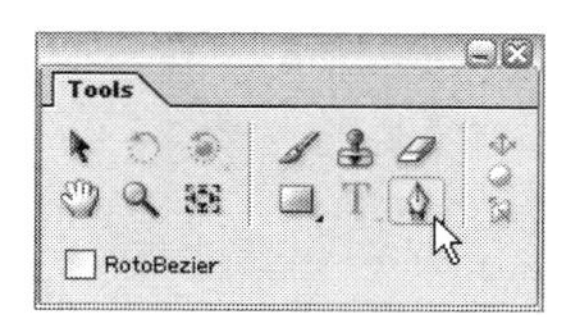

Figure 9.23 In the Tools palette, select the Pen tool.

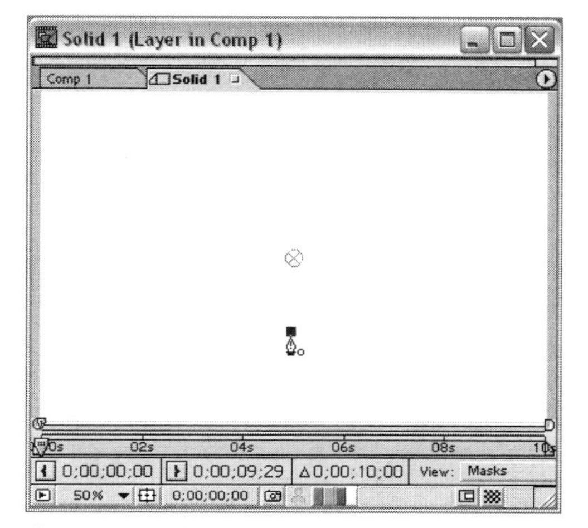

Figure 9.24 Click to create an anchor point with no direction lines.

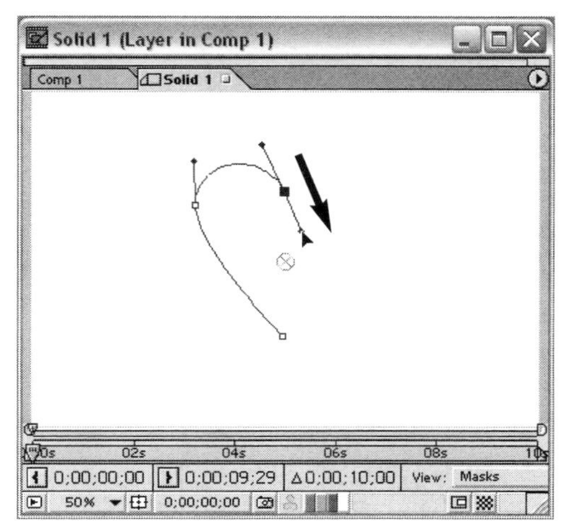

Figure 9.25 Click and drag to create a smooth point with two continuous direction lines.

Building a Standard Mask with the Pen

The following steps explain how to create a path using the Pen tool and Bézier curves. You'll probably want to start by creating simple straight segments. Then, as you become comfortable, you can try using smooth points to create curves and then corner points to create even more complex shapes. In later sections, you'll use the RotoBezier option to create curved segments without using direction lines.

To build a path:

1. *Do either of the following:*
   - ▲ Open a Layer window for the layer for which you want to create a mask.
   - ▲ Select a layer in the Composition window.
2. In the Tools palette, select the Pen tool (**Figure 9.23**).
3. In the Layer or Comp window, *do one of the following:*
   - ▲ To create an anchor point, click (**Figure 9.24**).
   - ▲ To create a smooth point, drag (**Figure 9.25**).

continues on next page

- ▲ To create a corner point, drag to create a smooth point, select one of the smooth point's direction handles, and then drag again (**Figure 9.26**).

4. Repeat step 3 to create straight and curved segments between points.

   Don't click an existing segment unless you want to add a control point to the path. Don't click an existing direction handle unless you want to convert it.

5. To leave the path open, stop clicking in the Layer window (**Figure 9.27**).

6. To close the path, *do one of the following*:

   - ▲ Double-click in the Layer window to create the final control point and connect it to the first control point.
   - ▲ Position the Pen tool over the first control point until a circle icon appears, and then click (**Figure 9.28**).
   - ▲ Choose Layer > Mask > Closed.

   If the first control point is smooth, the path will be closed with a smooth point.

   You may want to choose a new tool, such as the Selection tool.

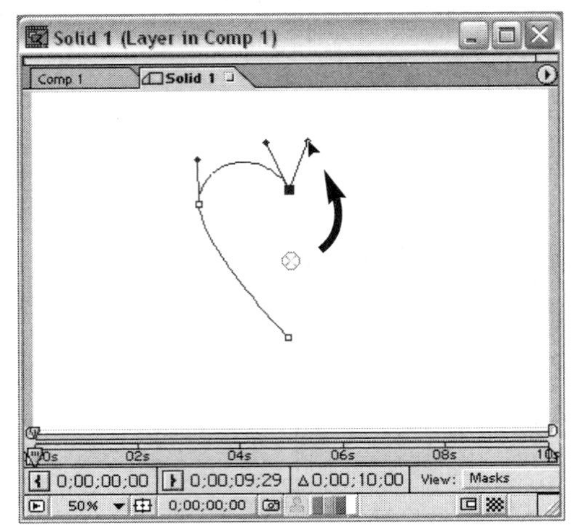

Figure 9.26 Drag a direction handle to break the relationship between the two handles, converting the point into a corner point.

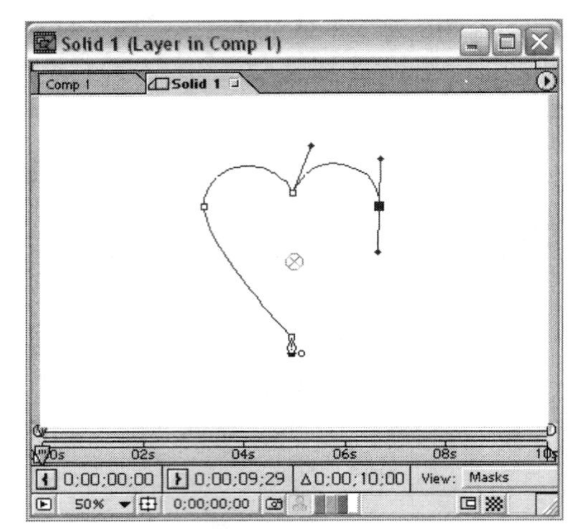

Figure 9.27 Continue clicking to create control points that define straight and curved segments. You can leave the path open, or position the tool over the first point so that a circle icon appears next to the Pen tool...

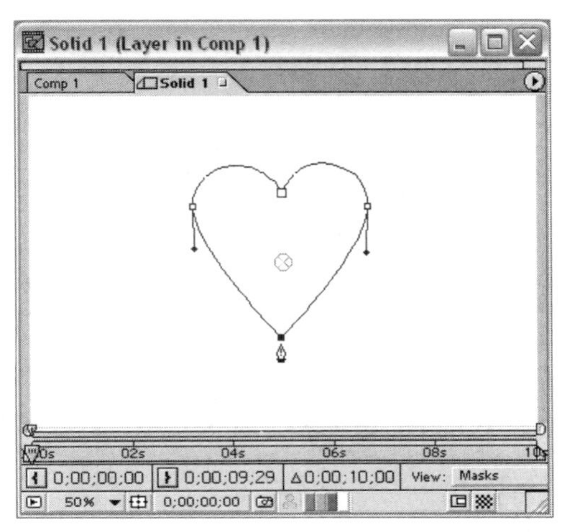

Figure 9.28 ...and click to close the path.

✔ Tips

- The Pen tool changes into the Add Vertex tool when positioned over a path; it changes into a Convert Vertex tool when positioned over a direction handle.
- When you create additional masks in the same Layer window, make sure the Target pull-down menu is set to None. Otherwise, you'll replace the target mask with the new mask.
- Bézier curves are also used to control the spatial and temporal interpolation of animations; for more on this, see Chapter 15, "Keyframe Interpolation."

Table 9.1

Keyboard Modifiers for Mask Paths

To do this	Press this
Constrain new segment to 45 degrees	Shift
Preview the next segment	Option (Mac) or Alt (Windows)
Temporarily switch to the Selection tool	Command (Mac) or Ctrl (Windows)

How Mighty Is Your Pen?

Creating Bézier curves with the Pen tool can be tricky at first. Even if you're familiar with Illustrator's Pen tool, you may have to get used to not using the Option/Alt key the same way and not having a Direct Selection tool. Test your penmanship by trying to make the following paths and mask shapes:

Anchor points only—Create and modify a polygon with straight segments only (**Figure 9.29**).

Smooth points only—Create and modify a curved shape using smooth points only (**Figure 9.30**).

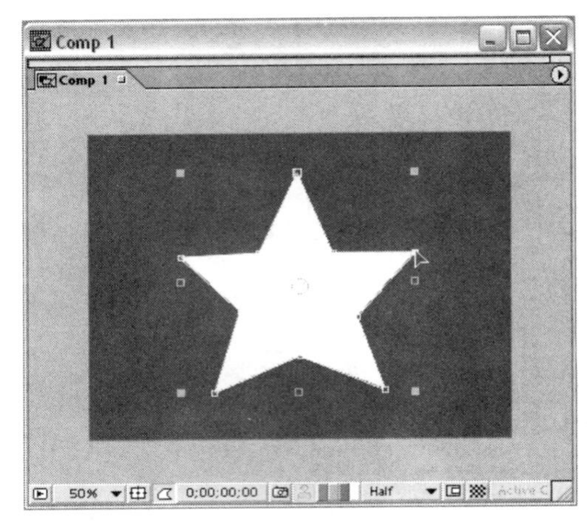

Figure 9.29 Click to create control points connected by straight segments.

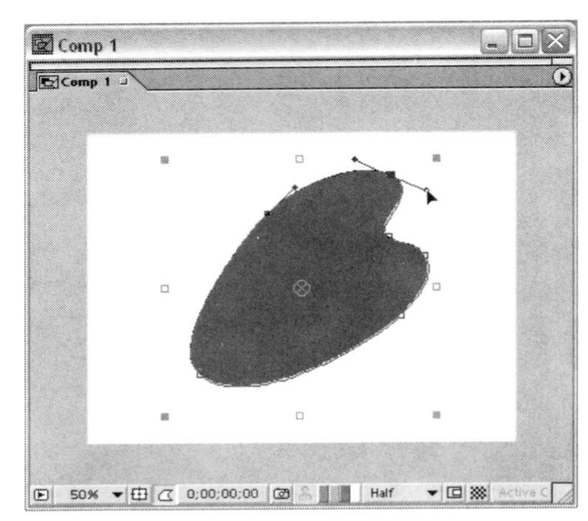

Figure 9.30 Drag to create smooth points with continuous direction lines.

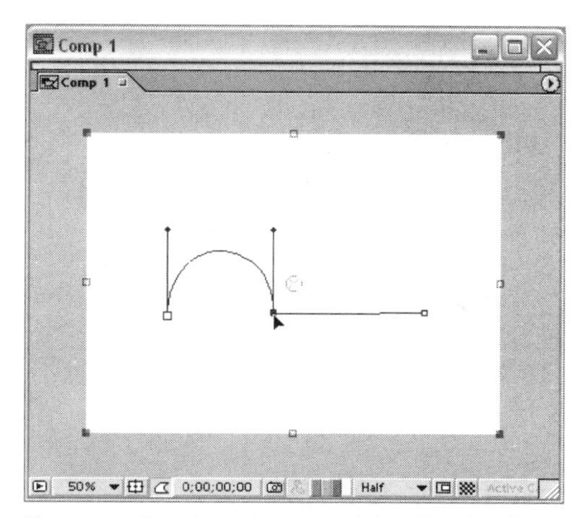

Figure 9.31 Drag incoming or outgoing direction lines back into the control point to create combinations of straight lines and curves.

Smooth and corner points—Create and modify a shape that uses straight segments followed by curved segments and vice versa (**Figure 9.31**).

Cusp points—Create and modify a shape with discontinuous curves, or cusps (**Figure 9.32**).

Trace—Follow the contours of an object in a layer's image. Try not to use more points than necessary (**Figure 9.33**).

✔ Tip

- Combining several simple masks can be faster and more effective than drawing a single complex path.

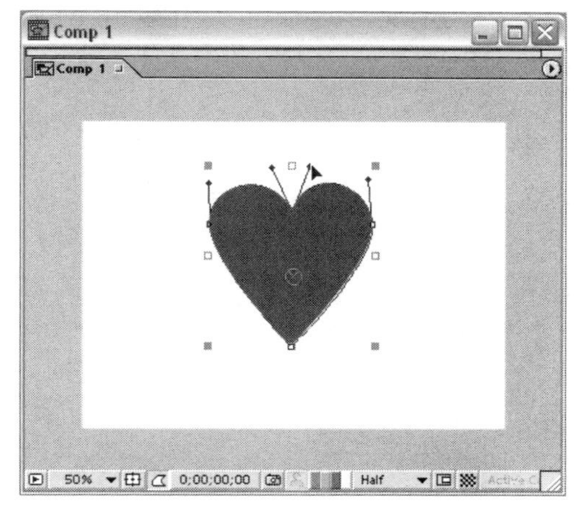

Figure 9.32 Drag direction lines to change smooth points into corner points and create discontinuous curves (sometimes called *cusps*).

Figure 9.33 Tracing an object can be the ultimate test of your penmanship.

Smooth and Shapely Curves

If your goal is to create smooth and shapely Bézier curves (rather than follow the irregular contour of an object), here are a few guidelines:

- Each direction line should be about one-third of the length of the curve it influences (**Figures 9.34** and **9.35**).
- Segments usually look best when influenced by either two direction lines or no handles. Avoid creating segments that use only one control handle (**Figures 9.36** and **9.37**).

continues on next page

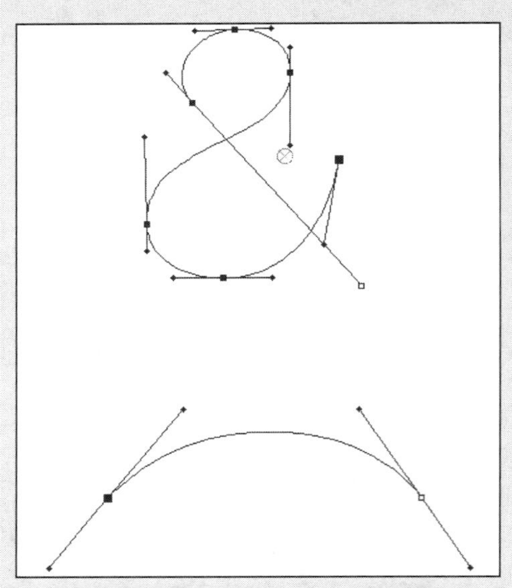

Figure 9.34 The most pleasing curves have direction handles that are about one-third the length of the curve.

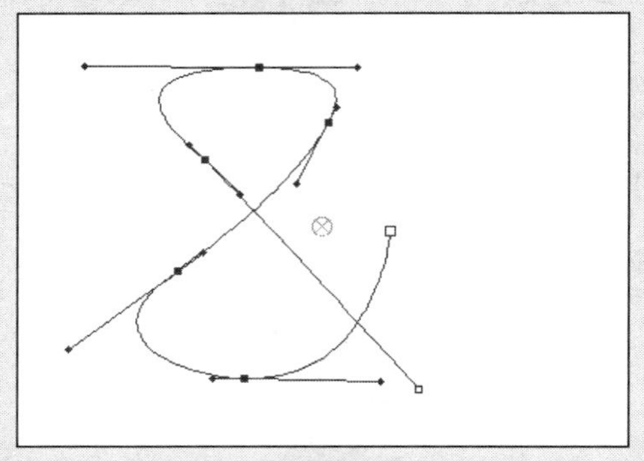

Figure 9.35 Paths that don't use the one-third rule can have an awkward gesture to the curve.

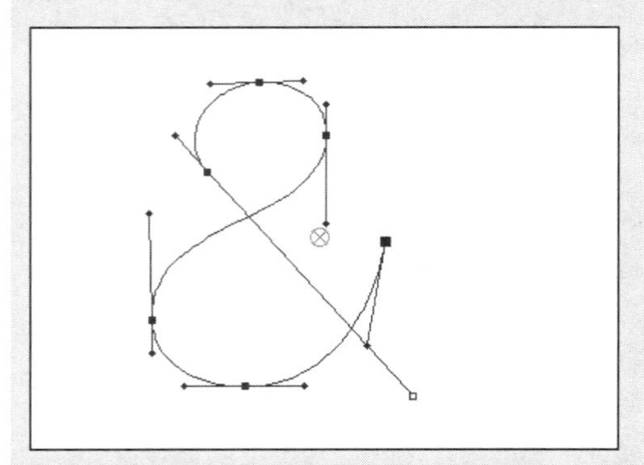

Figure 9.36 Typically, a curve should use two direction lines or none.

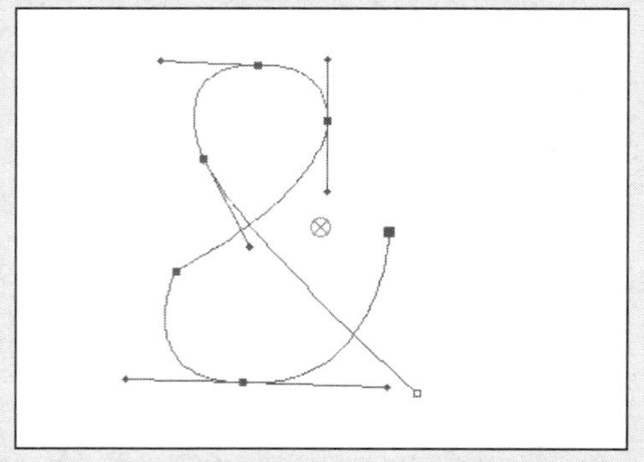

Figure 9.37 When only a single direction line influences a curve, one end flattens out, which can look awkward.

Smooth and Shapely Curves *(continued)*

- Use a minimal number of control points to achieve the curve you want. The curve will be smoother and easier to control (**Figures 9.38** and **9.39**).
- When you create a smooth point, you always extend two equal and opposite direction lines; however, you drag in the direction of the curve to follow (**Figures 9.40**, **9.41**, and **9.42**).

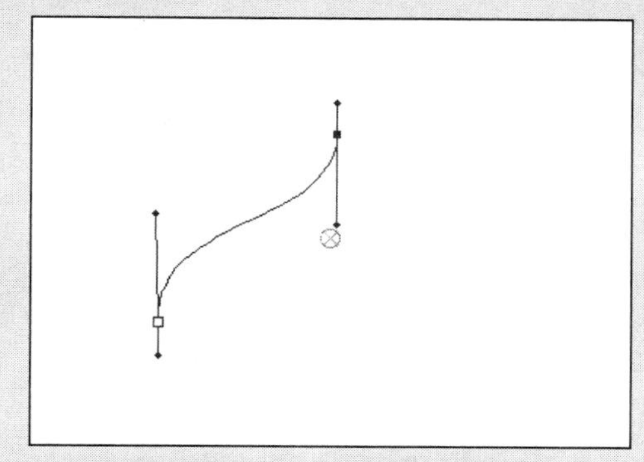

Figure 9.38 Use a minimum number of control points to create a shape.

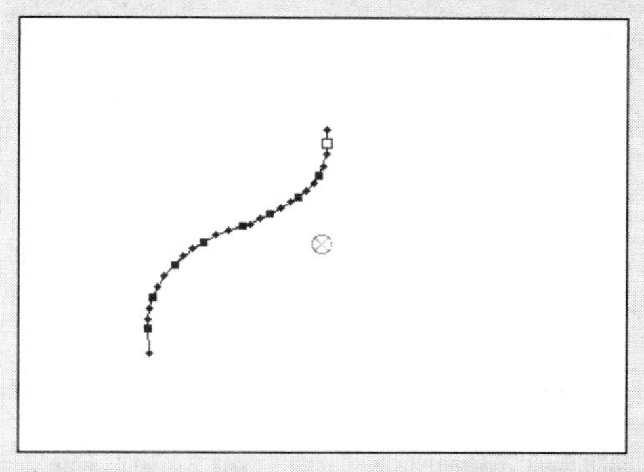

Figure 9.39 Superfluous control points can ruin the appearance of the shape.

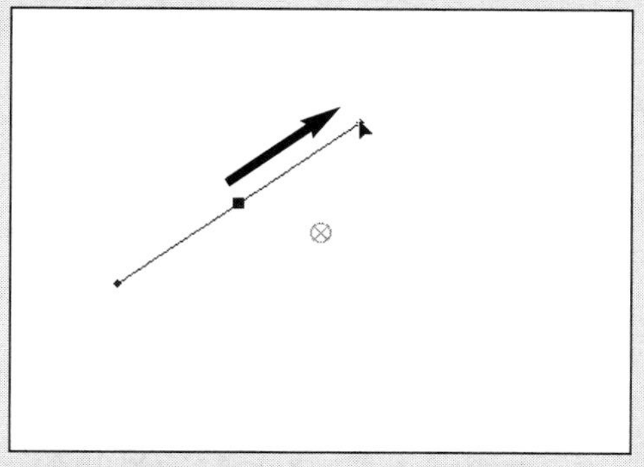

Figure 9.40 Drag the first direction handle in the direction of the curve...

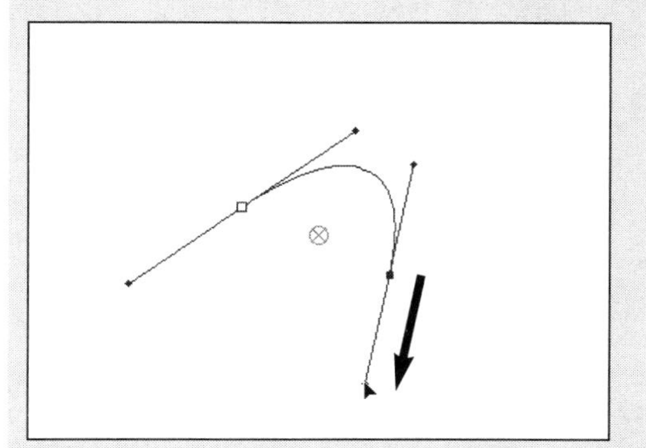

Figure 9.41 ...drag in the opposite direction to create a single and continuous curve...

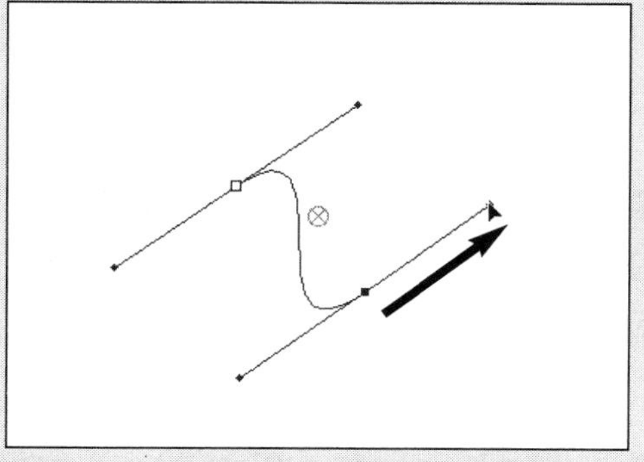

Figure 9.42 ...or in the same direction to create an S curve.

Creating a RotoBezier Mask

Even if you're a master of Bézier curves, you can often create a mask more quickly and easily using a *RotoBezier mask*. This is because the Pen tool's RotoBezier option lets you define a curved path by clicking to create control points; After Effects calculates curved segments automatically. You avoid using direction lines, which can take time to adjust properly.

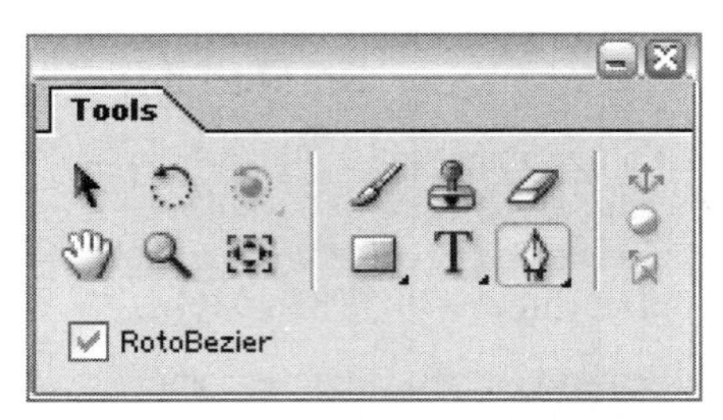

Figure 9.43 Select the Pen tool, and select the RotoBezier option.

Figure 9.44 Click to create control points. After Effects calculates the curved segments automatically.

To create a RotoBezier mask:

1. In the Tools palette, select the Pen tool.

   The RotoBezier option appears in the Tools palette.

2. In the Tools palette, select the RotoBezier option (**Figure 9.43**).

   Deselect the option to create standard masks with the Pen tool.

3. Cue the current time to the frame you want to use to create the mask, and *do either of the following*:

   ▲ Open the layer to which you want to apply a RotoBezier mask in a Layer window.

   ▲ Select a layer, and view it in the Composition window.

4. In the Layer or Composition window, click with the Pen tool to create the vertices of the mask shape.

   After Effects calculates curved segments between the control points automatically.

5. Repeat step 4 to create additional control points connected by curved segments (**Figure 9.44**).

   Don't click an existing segment unless you want to add a control point to the path.

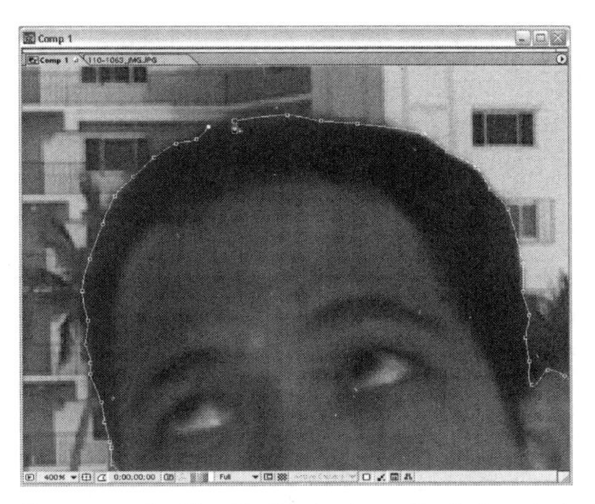

Figure 9.45 Position the Pen tool over the first control point so that a small circle appears next to the tool...

Figure 9.46 ...and click to close the shape. Otherwise, you can leave the mask open and choose another tool.

6. To close the path, *do one of the following*:
   - ▲ Double-click in the Layer window to create the final control point and connect it to the first control point (**Figure 9.45**).
   - ▲ Position the Pen tool over the first control point until a circle icon appears, and then click.
   - ▲ Choose Layer > Mask > Closed.

   The mask path closes (**Figure 9.46**).
7. To leave the path open, stop clicking in the Layer window.

   You may want to choose a new tool, such as the Selection tool.

Converting Masks

As you've seen, each type of mask has its advantages: a standard mask offers a relatively high degree of control over curved segments, whereas a RotoBezier mask is relatively easy to create. (Or, looking at it another way, creating a Bézier curve can be more time-consuming, and your control over a RotoBezier is more crude.)

You can leverage the advantages of each method—or change your mind about your initial choice—by converting one type of mask into the other. However, the conversion isn't perfect. Converting RotoBezier to Bézier curves can result in changes, because After Effects recalculates curved segments created from manually defined direction lines. And although the reverse process tends to maintain the mask's shape, a slight change may be apparent.

To convert a RotoBezier mask to a standard mask, and vice versa:

1. Select a mask by *doing any of the following*:
   - ▲ Select the mask's name in the Layer window's Target pull-down menu.
   - ▲ Click the mask's name in the Timeline window's layer outline (**Figure 9.47**).
   - ▲ Using the Selection tool, select one or more of the mask's control points in the Layer or Comp window.

   For more details, see the section "Selecting Masks and Points" later in this chapter.
2. Choose Layer > Mask > RotoBezier (**Figure 9.48**).

   Selecting the option converts a standard mask to a RotoBezier mask; deselecting the option converts a RotoBezier to a standard mask. The mask shape may change slightly.

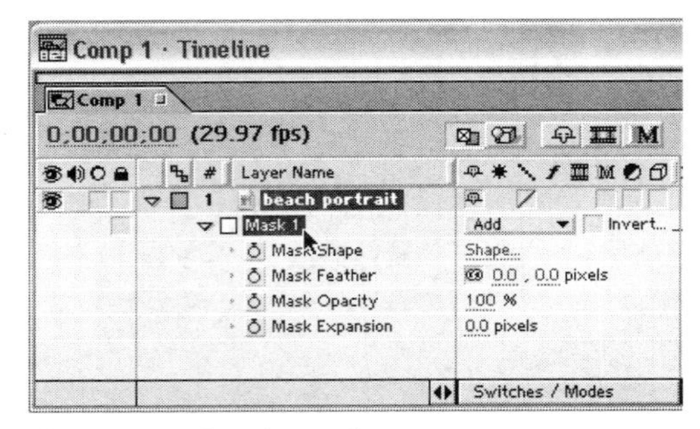

Figure 9.47 Select the mask you want to convert.

Figure 9.48 Choosing Layer > Mask > RotoBezier converts the selected mask to another type.

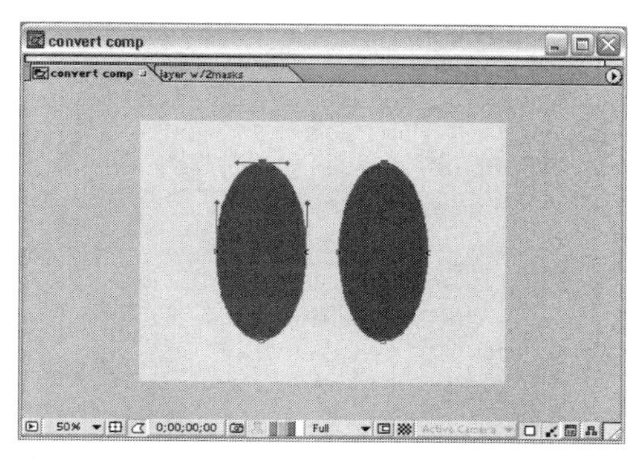

Figure 9.49 The shape on the left is a standard mask that uses Bézier curves; the identical shape on the right is a RotoBezier mask.

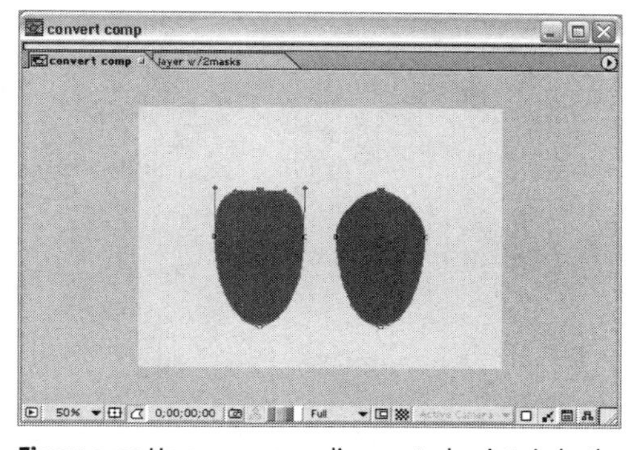

Figure 9.50 Here, corresponding control points in both masks have been moved by the same amount. Because the curves are defined differently, the masks have a slightly different shape.

Changing the Shape of a Mask

You can modify the shape of a mask at any time. The following sections explain how to move, add, and delete control points, as well as how to change the gesture of curves.

The way curves adjust to changes depends on whether you're using a standard mask with Bézier curves or a RotoBezier mask. As you learned in the section "Understanding Mask Anatomy," Bézier curves use direction lines you specify manually, whereas RotoBezier curves are calculated automatically. Each mask type's characteristic behavior continues to operate when you edit it.

For example, when you move or delete a keyframe in a standard mask, other aspects of the control points you specified—the length and angle of their direction lines—remain unchanged. RotoBezier paths, on the other hand, are recalculated when you move the point. (Therefore, if you move corresponding points on identical standard and RotoBezier masks the same distance and direction, the new mask shapes will differ slightly.) Bear this difference in mind as you do the tasks in the following sections (**Figures 9.49** and **9.50**).

Later sections cover techniques that affect the entire mask (such as using the Free Transform command), mask properties (mask feather, opacity, and expansion), and mask modes. These tasks don't vary according to the type of mask, and the results are identical.

Selecting Masks and Points

To alter all or part of a mask, you must first select its control points—usually accomplished via (what else?) the Selection tool. (Sorry, Illustrator users; you won't find a Direct Selection tool.) Select one or more control points to change the shape of a mask. Select all the points to move the mask. You can use the same methods to select masks and control points in both standard and RotoBezier masks. As usual, selected control points appear as solid dots; deselected control points appear as hollow dots.

To move, scale, or rotate the entire mask, use the transform technique described in the section "Scaling and Rotating Masks," later in this chapter.

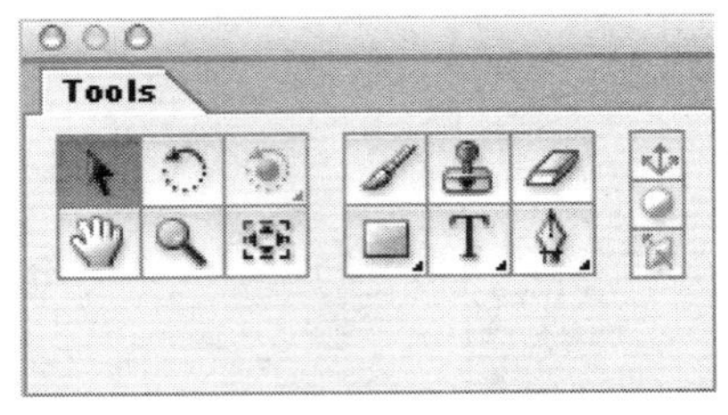

Figure 9.51 In the Tools palette, choose the Selection tool.

To select masks or points in a Layer or Comp window:

1. In the Tools palette, choose the Selection tool (if you haven't done so already) (**Figure 9.51**).
2. Make sure the Layer or Comp Window is set to show masks.

   See the sections on viewing masks earlier in this chapter.
3. To select mask points in the Comp window, select the layer containing the mask.

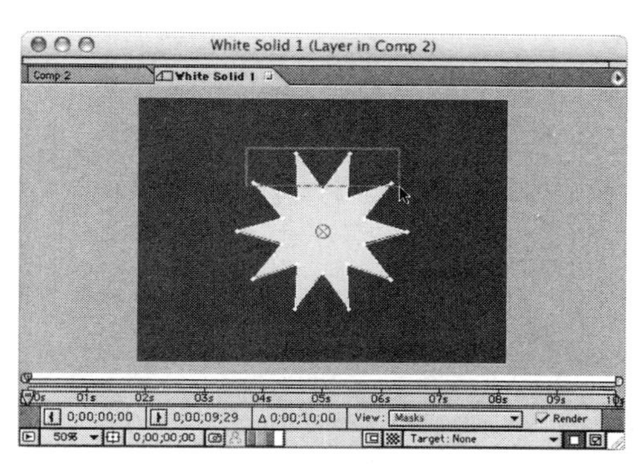

Figure 9.52 To select several control points simultaneously, you can drag a marquee around them.

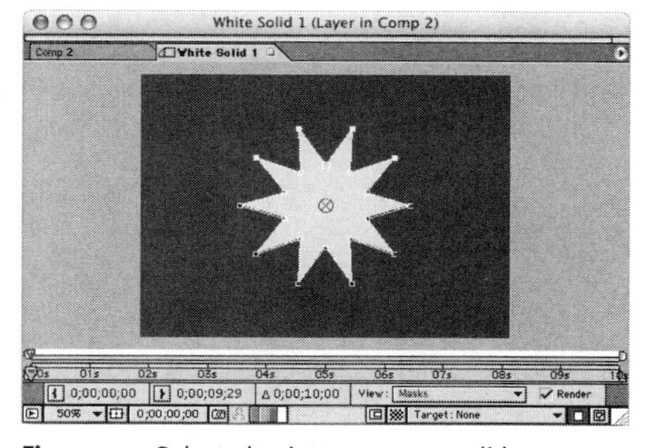

Figure 9.53 Selected points appear as solid squares; deselected points appear as hollow squares.

4. To select mask points in either the Layer window or Comp window, *do any of the following*:
   - ▲ To select a control point, click the control point on a mask.
   - ▲ To add to or subtract from your selection, press Shift as you click or drag a marquee around control points.
   - ▲ To select points at both ends of a segment, click the segment.
   - ▲ To select an entire mask with the mouse, Option-click (Mac) or Alt-click (Windows) the mask.
5. To select mask points in the Layer window only, *do any of the following*:
   - ▲ To select any or all control points, drag a marquee around the points you want to select (**Figure 9.52**).
   - ▲ To select all mask points, press Command-A (Mac) or Ctrl-A (Windows).
   - ▲ To select an entire mask by name, choose the mask from the Target pull-down menu in the Layer window.

   In the Layer or Comp window, selected control points appear solid; other control points appear as hollow outlines (**Figure 9.53**). Segments associated with the selected points also display direction lines. When no control points of a mask are selected, only the path is visible in the Layer or Comp window.

To select masks in the Timeline window:

1. In the Timeline window, select the layer that includes the mask you want to select.
2. Press M to reveal that layer's masks (**Figure 9.54**).

   The masks and the Mask Shape property appear in the expanded layer outline. If the layer doesn't contain any masks, the outline doesn't expand.
3. To select masks for the layer, *do any of the following*:
   - ▲ To select a single mask, click its name in the layer outline (**Figure 9.55**).
   - ▲ To select a range of masks, click the name of the first mask in the range and Shift-click the name of the last mask in the range (**Figure 9.56**).
   - ▲ To select multiple discontiguous masks, Command-click (Mac) or Ctrl-click (Windows) the names of the masks you want to select (**Figure 9.57**).

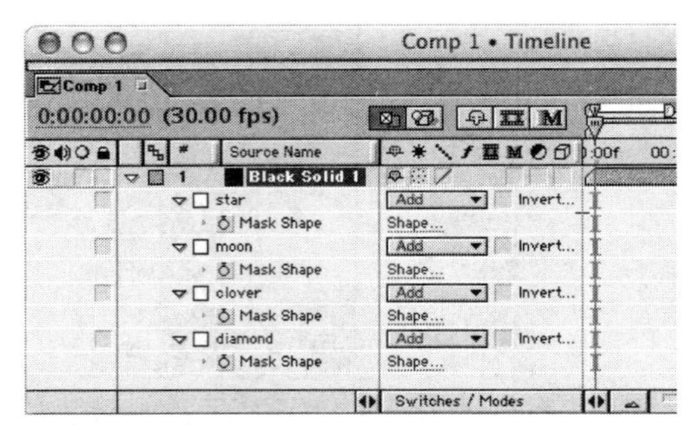

Figure 9.54 In the Timeline window, select a layer containing a mask, and press M to display its mask property in the layer outline.

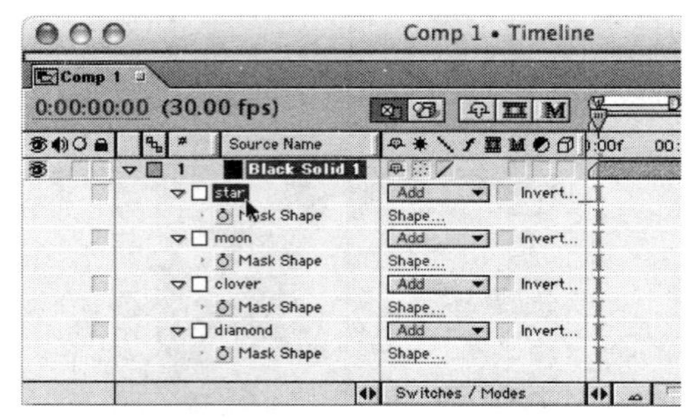

Figure 9.55 Click a mask name to select it.

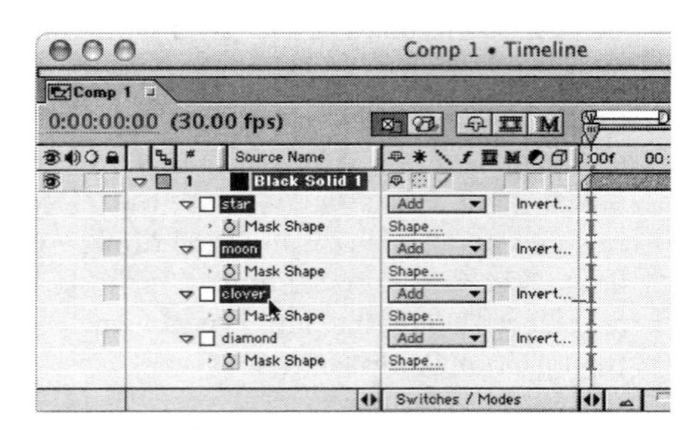

Figure 9.56 Shift-click another mask to select a range of masks...

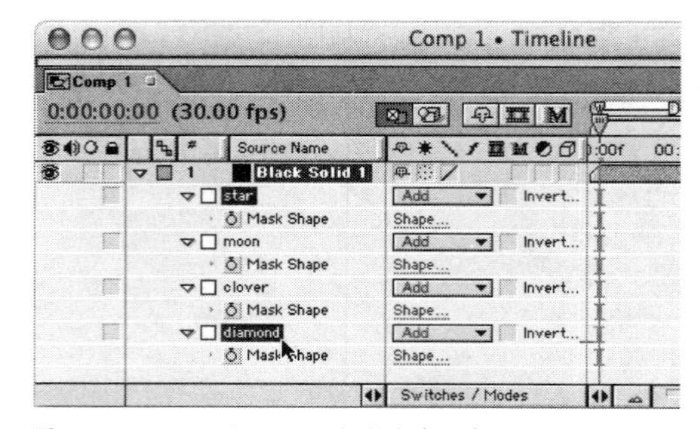

Figure 9.57 ...or Command-click (Mac) or Ctrl-click (Windows) to select several discontiguous masks.

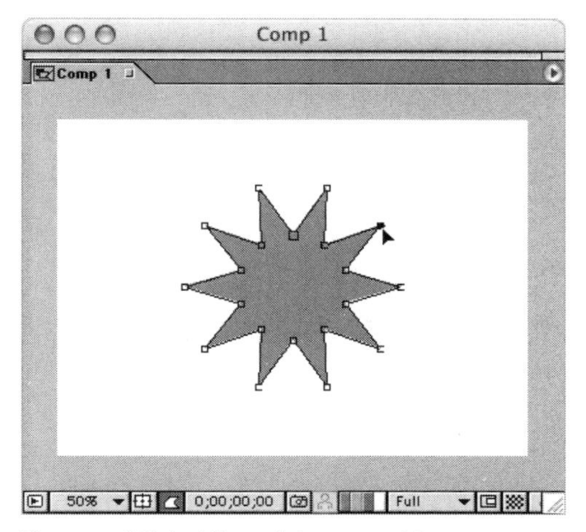

Figure 9.58 Select the points you want to move.

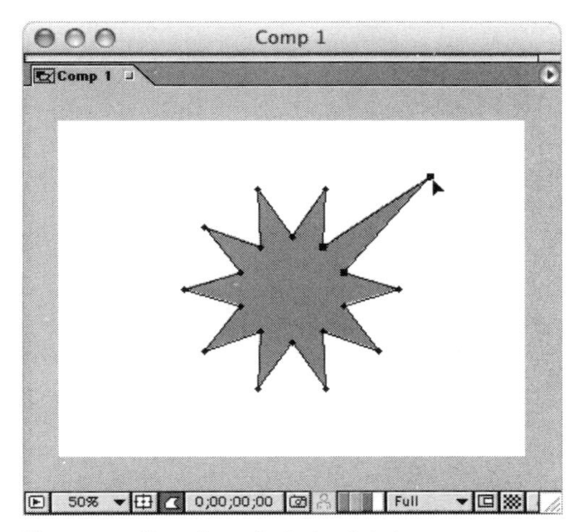

Figure 9.59 Drag the selected points to a new position, or nudge them with the arrow keys.

Moving and Deleting Control Points

You can move any combination of a mask's control points by using the mouse or by nudging them with the arrow keys. Just as when you nudge an entire layer, the precision of the arrow keys depends on the window's current magnification setting. For example, the arrow key nudges the selected points 1 pixel when the magnification is set to 100 percent; 2 pixels when set to 50 percent; and .5 pixels when set to 200 percent. (See Chapter 7, "Properties and Keyframes," for more about nudging and subpixel positioning.) You can also remove selected keyframes.

To move an entire mask (or perform other transformations), you can use the free transform technique described in the section "Scaling and Rotating Masks" later in this chapter. You can also delete points using a variation of the Pen tool (see the section "Adding and Deleting Control Points with the Pen Tool" later in this chapter).

To move a mask or its control points:

1. In the Layer window, select the points of the mask you want to move (**Figure 9.58**).
2. To move the selected points, *do any of the following*:
   - ▲ With the Selection tool, drag a selected control point (**Figure 9.59**).

   Don't drag the path segment between control points; doing so will change the curve of the segment.
   - ▲ Press the arrow keys to nudge the selected control points at the current magnification of the Layer window.
   - ▲ Hold Shift as you press an arrow key to increase the nudge distance by a factor of 10.

continues on next page

If all points are selected, the entire mask moves. Otherwise, only selected points move, and line segments reshape to accommodate their new positions.

To delete selected control points:

1. In the Layer or Comp window, select the points of the mask you want to remove.
2. *Do either of the following:*
   - ▲ Press Delete.
   - ▲ Choose Edit > Clear.

   The selected control points disappear, and the line segments reshape to connect the remaining points (**Figure 9.60**). In a Bézier curve, the direction lines of the remaining points remain unchanged; in a Roto-Bezier curve, the path is recalculated.

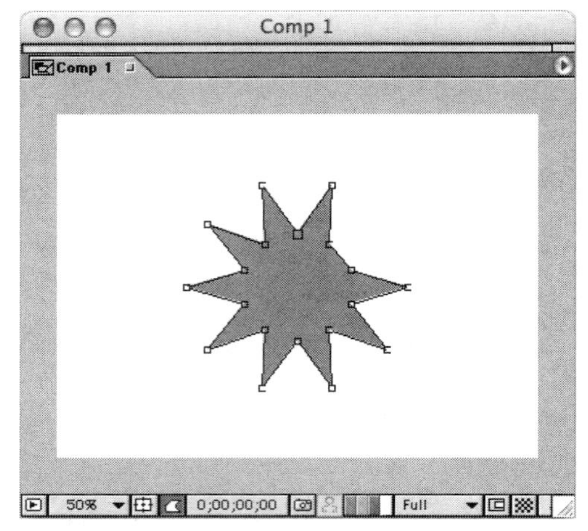

Figure 9.60 Press Delete to remove selected control points; line segments will connect the remaining points.

Figure 9.61 Clicking the Pen tool in the Tools palette reveals the Add Vertex and Delete Vertex tools.

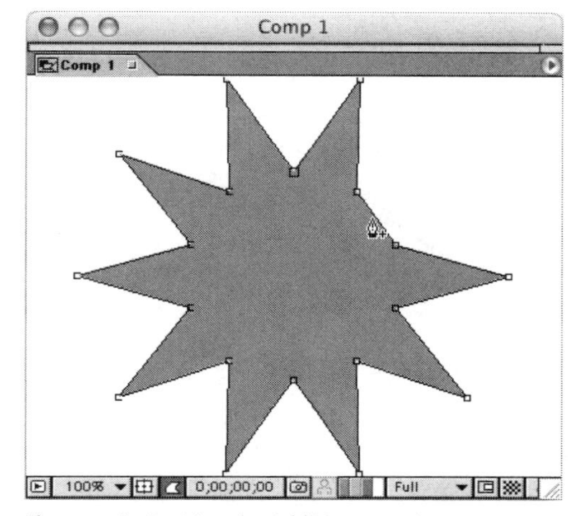

Figure 9.62 Position the Add Vertex tool over a segment...

Adding and Deleting Control Points with the Pen Tool

By default, the Tools palette displays the Pen tool. Clicking and holding the tool extends the palette to reveal additional tools: the Add Vertex tool, the Delete Vertex tool, and the Convert Vertex tool. (**Figure 9.61**). Obviously, you can use these tools to add, delete, and convert points on an existing mask path.

Note that the figures in this section use straight-sided polygons to illustrate the steps in each task. In straight-sided paths, you won't see a difference between standard masks (with all corner points) and RotoBezier masks (with the tension of all vertices set to 100 percent). When you're manipulating paths with curved segments, however, adding and deleting points yield slightly different results, depending on the type of mask you're editing. For a more detailed explanation, turn back to the sections "Understanding Mask Anatomy" and "Changing the Shape of a Mask."

To add a control point:

1. In the Tools palette, choose the Pen tool or the Add Vertex tool.
2. Position the tool on a mask path between existing control points.

   If you're using the Pen tool, it automatically becomes an Add Vertex tool when it's positioned over a segment (**Figure 9.62**). Be careful not to position the Pen tool over a control point inadvertently; it changes into a Delete Vertex tool.
3. *Do one of the following:*
   - To add a control point without changing the existing path, click on the segment.

continues on next page

A new control point appears in the mask path (**Figure 9.63**). In a standard mask, any direction lines are set to preserve the existing curve; in a RotoBezier mask, the curve is calculated automatically.

▲ To add a control point and change the curve simultaneously, click and drag the segment.

In a standard mask, dragging extends direction lines from the new point (which remains where you clicked), altering the curve of the adjacent segments (**Figure 9.64**). In a RotoBezier mask, dragging moves the new point, and the path is recalculated automatically (**Figure 9.65**).

To remove a control point:

1. In the Tools palette, choose the Delete Vertex tool.
2. Position the Delete Vertex tool over a control point (**Figure 9.66**).
3. Click an existing control point to remove it (**Figure 9.67**).

   The selected control points disappear, and the line segments reshape to connect the remaining points. In a Bézier curve, the direction lines of the remaining points remain unchanged; in a RotoBezier curve, the path is recalculated.

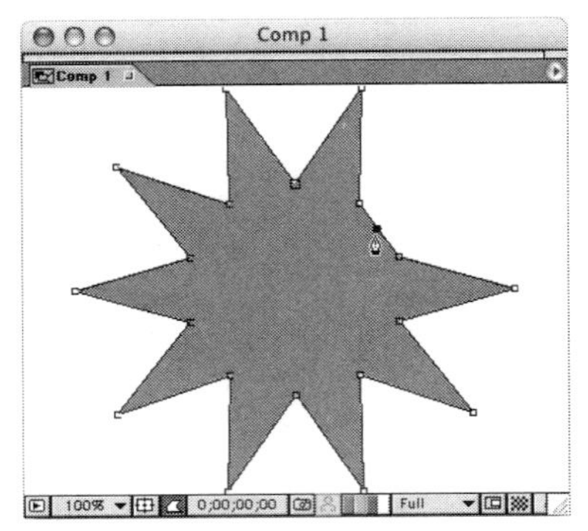

Figure 9.63 ...and click to add a control point.

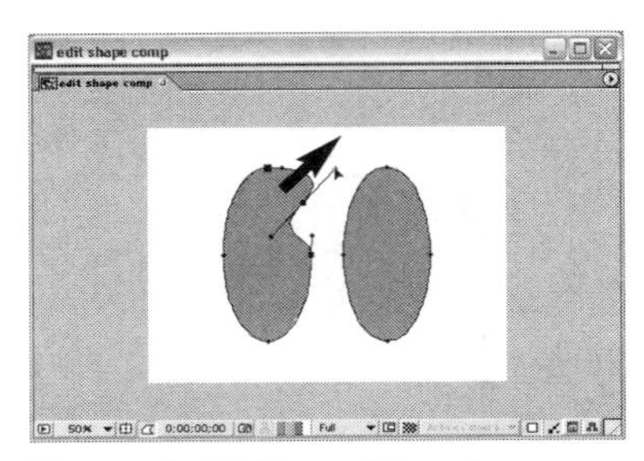

Figure 9.64 Clicking and dragging a segment in a standard path adds a smooth point and extends direction lines.

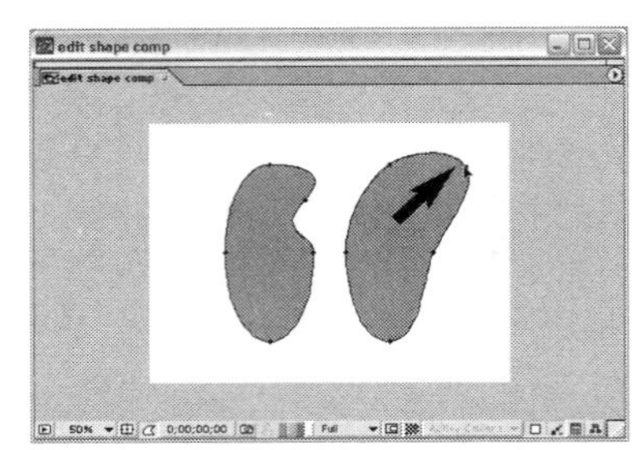

Figure 9.65 Clicking and dragging a segment in a RotoBezier path adds a control point and moves it to where you drag.

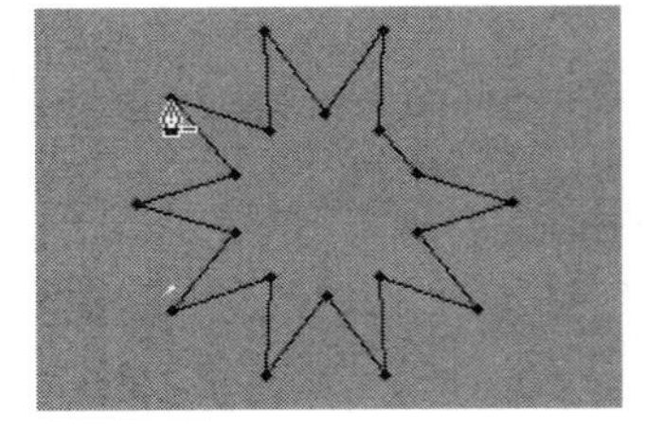

Figure 9.66 Position the Delete Vertex tool over a control point...

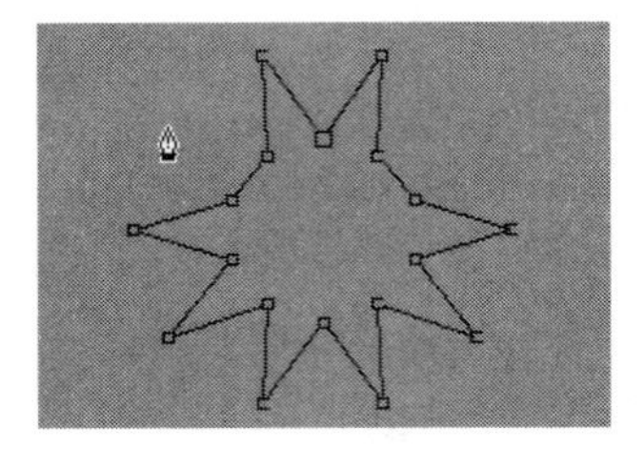

Figure 9.67 ...and click to remove the point.

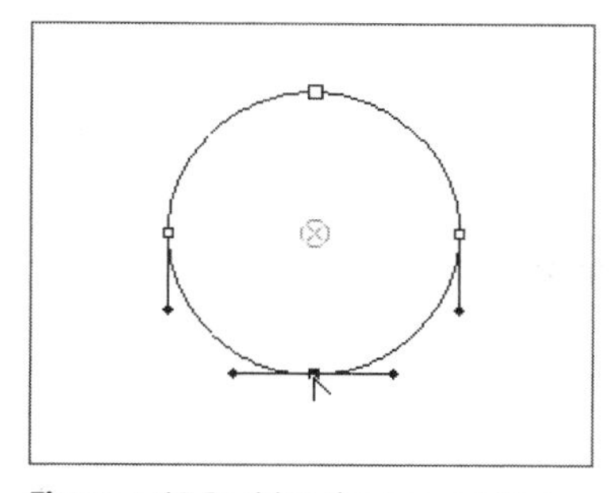

Figure 9.68 Position the Convert Vertex tool on a control point...

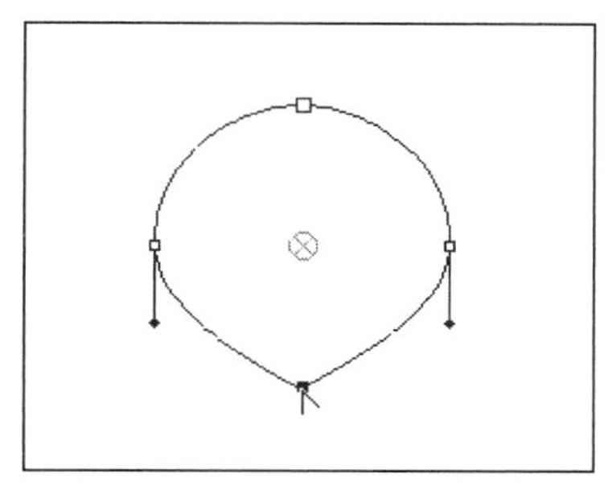

Figure 9.69 ...and click to convert a smooth point into a control point with no direction lines and vice versa.

Converting Control Points in a Standard Mask

When you create a standard mask using the Pen tool, you can create any combination of control points: anchor (with no direction lines), smooth (equal and opposite direction lines), or corner (discontinuous direction lines). You can change one type of control point into another using the Convert Vertex tool.

The Convert Vertex tool serves a similar, but more limited, purpose for RotoBezier masks. See the section "Adjusting RotoBezier Mask Tension" later in this chapter.

To convert a smooth point to an anchor point, and vice versa:

1. In the Tools palette, choose the Convert Vertex tool.
2. Click the control point (**Figure 9.68**).
   A smooth point becomes an anchor point with no direction lines; an anchor point becomes a smooth point with two equal direction lines (**Figure 9.69**).

✔ Tips

- To convert all points in a path simultaneously, select all the points before you click one with the Convert Vertex tool.
- When converting to a smooth point, you can click and drag the point to set the length and angle of the direction lines manually in a single step.

To convert a smooth point to a corner point and vice versa:

1. In the Layer or Comp window, select one or more smooth points or corner points in a mask path.

   The direction lines of selected points become visible.

2. In the Tools palette, choose the Convert Vertex tool.

3. In the mask path, position the tool on an existing direction handle.

4. Drag the direction line's handle to a new position (**Figure 9.70**).

   A smooth point converts to a corner point, and the direction line moves independently. A corner point converts to a smooth point, and both of its direction lines move together (**Figure 9.71**).

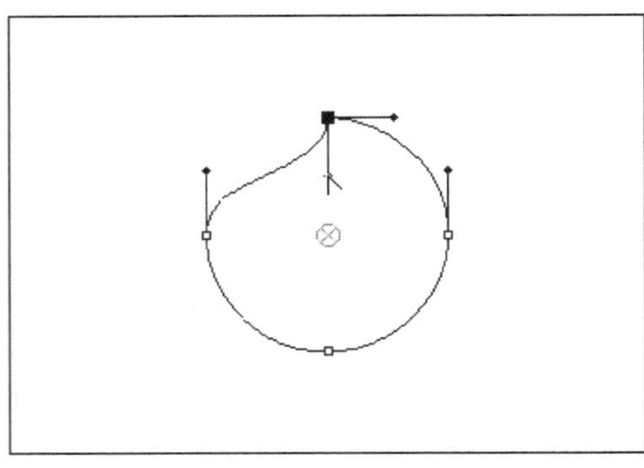

Figure 9.70 Drag a direction handle with the Convert Vertex tool to break the relationship with the opposite handle and create a corner point.

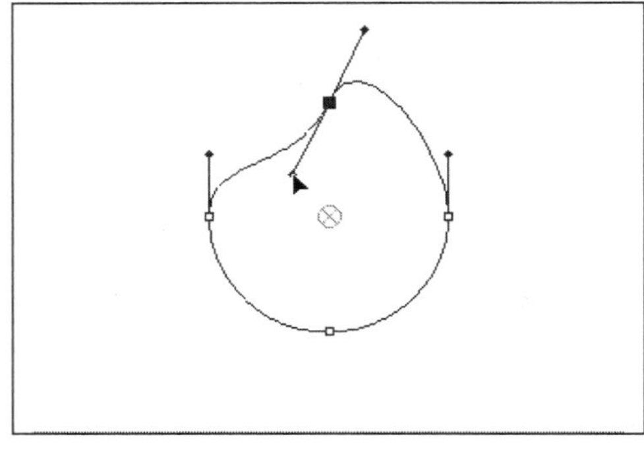

Figure 9.71 Drag a direction handle of a corner point to convert it back into a smooth point with continuous direction handles.

✔ Tips

- To remove one direction line from a corner point, drag the direction handle into the point.
- Once you have the kind of control point you want, modify it only with the Selection tool. This way, you can move the point or its direction handle without converting it.

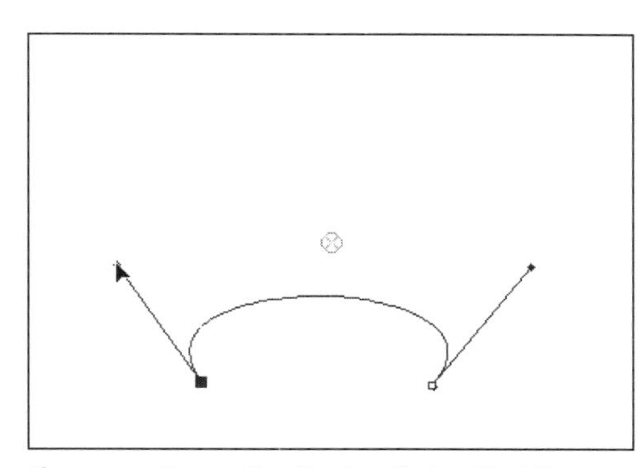

Figure 9.72 Drag a direction handle to adjust the curved segment as it exits a control point...

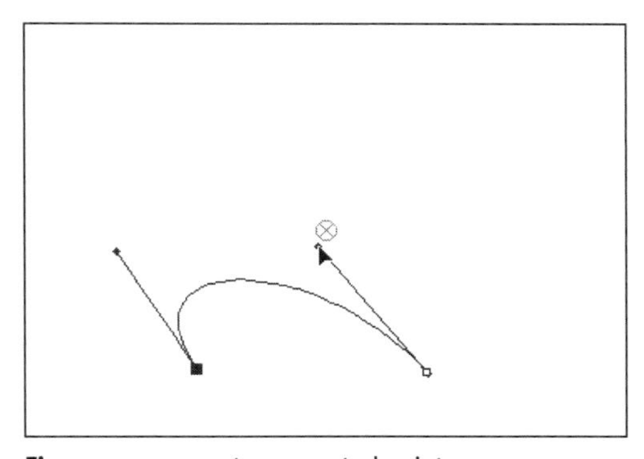

Figure 9.73 ...or enters a control point.

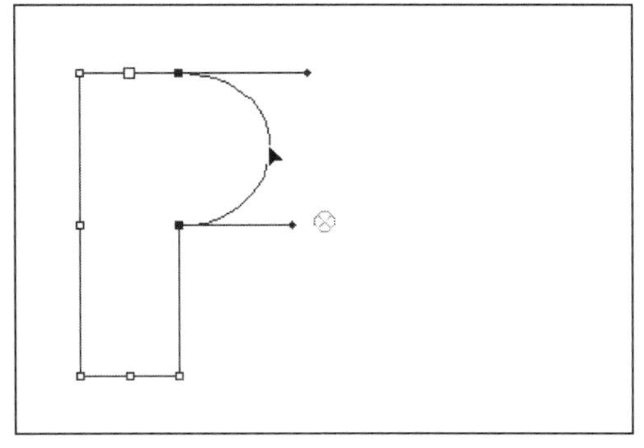

Figure 9.74 You can drag a path segment directly, but it always affects the direction lines at both ends of the curve. In this example, dragging a segment turns a rectangle into a "P" shape.

To adjust a Bézier curve:

- Using the Selection tool, *do any of the following*:
  - Drag a direction handle for a selected control point (**Figures 9.72** and **9.73**).
  - Drag a curved or straight segment.

  Be aware that this affects the direction lines at both ends of the curve. If you drag a straight segment, direction lines extend from its control points (**Figure 9.74**).

✔ Tips

- Because it modifies the direction lines at both ends of the segment simultaneously, dragging the path directly often does more harm than good. On the other hand, this technique can serve as a handy way to turn straight segments into curves.
- Press Command (Mac) or Ctrl (Windows) to switch temporarily from the currently selected Pen tool to the Selection tool and vice versa. Note that when you're editing masks, the Selection tool looks like an arrow, not the typical pointer.

Adjusting RotoBezier Mask Tension

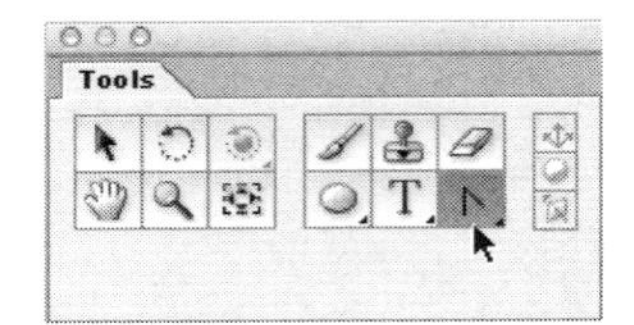

Figure 9.75 Select the Convert Vertex tool.

Naturally, you can't adjust a RotoBezier mask's curves using direction lines; RotoBezier masks don't have them. However, you can adjust the *tension* of any number of its control points to control the relative amount of curve of its adjacent segments. In other words, decreasing a point's tension relaxes the adjacent curves, making them more flat; increasing the tension increases the curve. (You might compare adjusting a RotoBezier mask's tension to adjusting a smooth point in a Bézier curve.)

As you adjust the tension, you can see the current setting in the Info palette. Increasing the tension to 100 percent creates the equivalent of a corner point in a Bézier curve; decreasing the tension makes adjacent segments less curved.

You can edit most other aspects of Bézier and RotoBezier masks using the same methods, as explained in later sections.

To adjust the tension of RotoBezier mask points:

1. To adjust multiple points at once, select them.

   See the section "Selecting Masks and Points" for more information.

2. In the Tools palette, select the Convert Vertex tool (**Figure 9.75**).

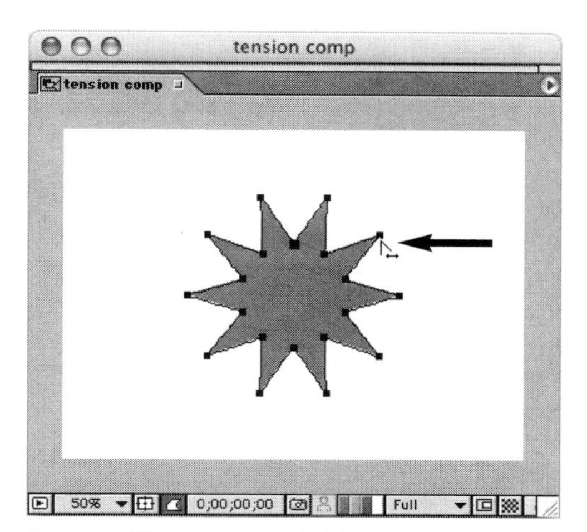

Figure 9.76 Dragging to the left increases tension at the selected points, increasing the curve of adjacent segments. Maximum tension creates a corner.

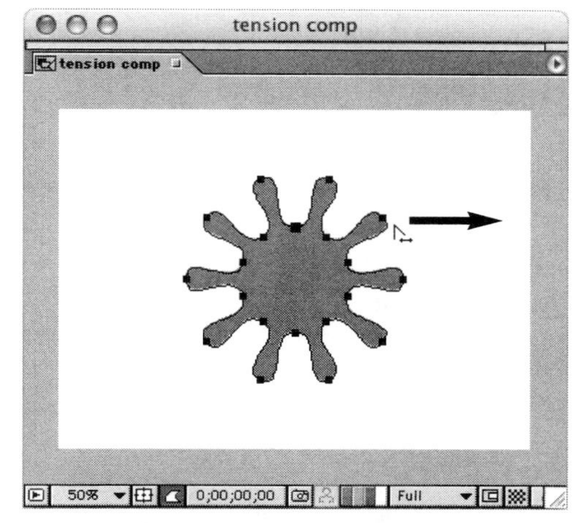

Figure 9.77 Dragging to the right decreases tension at the selected points, flattening the curve of adjacent segments.

3. Drag a control point or one of the control points you selected in step 1.

   The mouse pointer changes into the Adjust Tension icon. Dragging right decreases tension, relaxing the curve of adjacent segments; dragging left increases tension, contracting the curve (**Figures 9.76** and **9.77**).

✔ Tips

- You can convert the Pen tool to the Convert Vertex tool by pressing and holding Command (Mac) or Ctrl (Windows); press Cmd+Opt (Mac) or Ctrl+Alt (Windows) to change the Selection tool to the Convert Vertex tool.
- Option-clicking (Mac) or Alt-clicking (Windows) a control point in a Bézier curve converts it from a smooth point to a corner point and vice versa; the same shortcut changes the tension of selected RotoBezier control points from an automatically calculated value to 100 percent and vice versa. Although the result is equivalent, this action doesn't convert the mask from one type to another.

Opening and Closing Paths

You can use menu commands to close an open path or open a closed one.

To close an open path:

1. In a Layer window, choose the control points at each end of an open path (**Figure 9.78**).
2. Choose Layer > Mask > Closed (**Figure 9.79**).

   The control points are connected to close the path (**Figure 9.80**).

To open a closed path:

1. In a Layer window, choose two adjacent control points in a closed path.
2. Choose Layer > Mask > Closed.

   The Closed option becomes unselected, and the segment between the control points disappears.

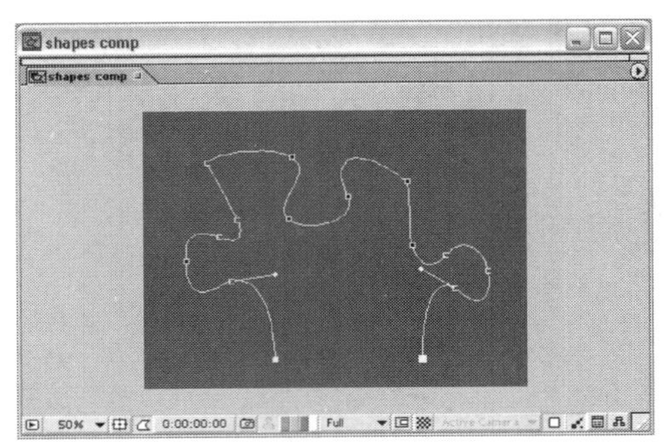

Figure 9.78 Choose the control points at each end of an open path.

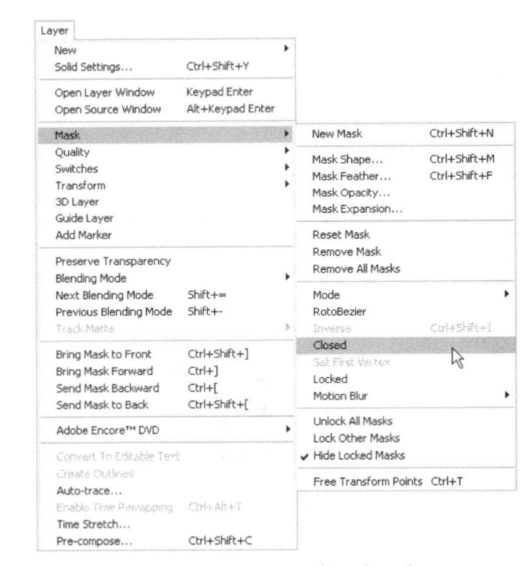

Figure 9.79 Choose Layer > Mask > Closed.

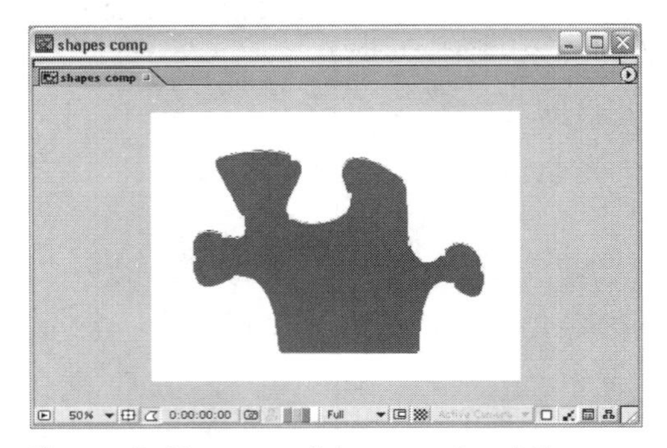

Figure 9.80 The open path becomes closed. You can use the same method to open a closed path.

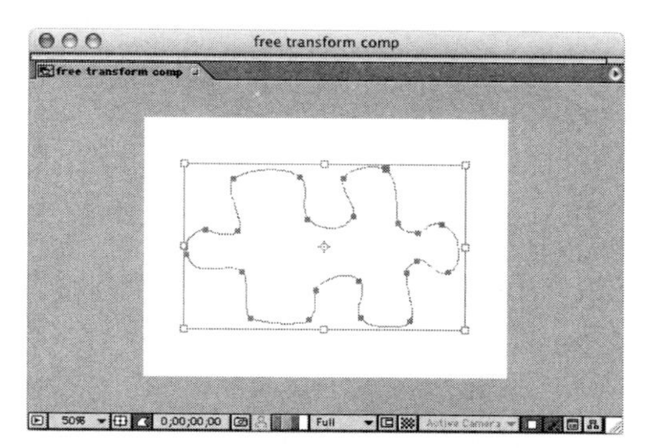

Figure 9.81 A bounding box and mask anchor point appear.

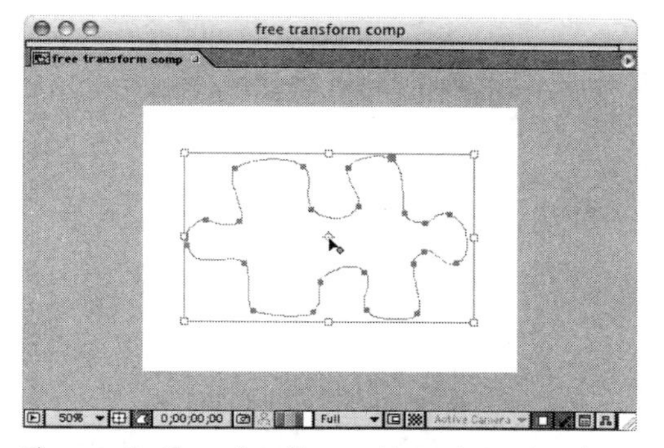

Figure 9.82 If you drag the mask's anchor point, the Selection tool becomes a Move Anchor Point icon.

Scaling and Rotating Masks

Using the Free Transform Points command, you can scale and rotate all or part of one or more masks. Masks are rotated and scaled around their own anchor points, separate from the anchor point of the layer that contains them. As the word *free* suggests, these adjustments are controlled manually, not numerically, and they can't be keyframed to animate over time. Of course, you can still keyframe the rotation and scale of the layer containing the masks.

To move, scale, or rotate all or part of a mask:

1. Open a Layer window for the layer that contains the mask you want to transform, or select the layer in the Comp window.
2. *Do one of the following:*
   - ▲ Select the mask or mask points you want to transform, and Choose Layer > Mask > Free Transform Points.
   - ▲ Double-click a mask to transform it completely.

   A bounding box and mask anchor point appear (**Figure 9.81**).
3. To reposition the anchor point for the mask's bounding box, drag the anchor.

   The selection tool turns into a Move Anchor Point icon when you position it over the anchor point (**Figure 9.82**).

continues on next page

4. *Do any of the following*:
   - ▲ To move the mask or selected points, place the cursor inside the bounding box and drag to a new position (**Figure 9.83**).
   - ▲ To scale the mask or selected points, place the cursor on one of the handles of the bounding box until it becomes a Scale icon, and then drag (**Figure 9.84**).
   - ▲ To rotate the mask or selected points, place the pointer slightly outside the bounding box until it becomes a Rotation icon, and then drag (**Figure 9.85**).
5. To exit Free Transform Points mode, double-click anywhere in the Layer or Comp window, or press Enter.

✔ Tip

- As you can see, using the Free Transform Points command to scale and rotate a mask or mask points works much the same way as transforming a layer. You'll be happy to know that all the keyboard modifications—Shift, Command/Ctrl, Option/Alt—also work the same.

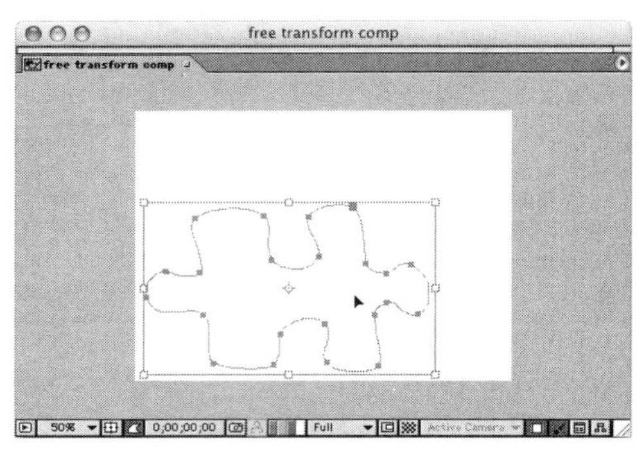

Figure 9.83 To move the mask or selected points, place the cursor inside the bounding box and drag to a new position.

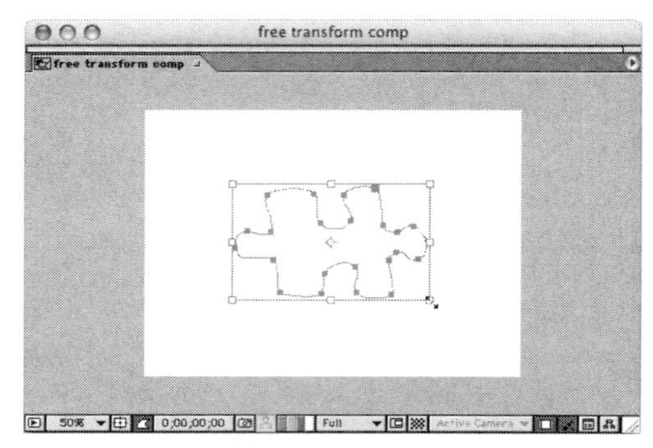

Figure 9.84 To scale the mask or selected points, place the cursor on one of the handles of the bounding box until it becomes a Scale icon, and then drag.

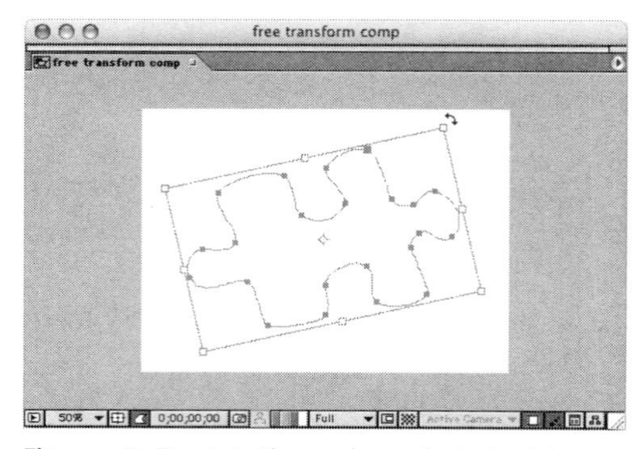

Figure 9.85 To rotate the mask or selected points, place the pointer slightly outside the bounding box until it becomes a Rotation icon, and then drag.

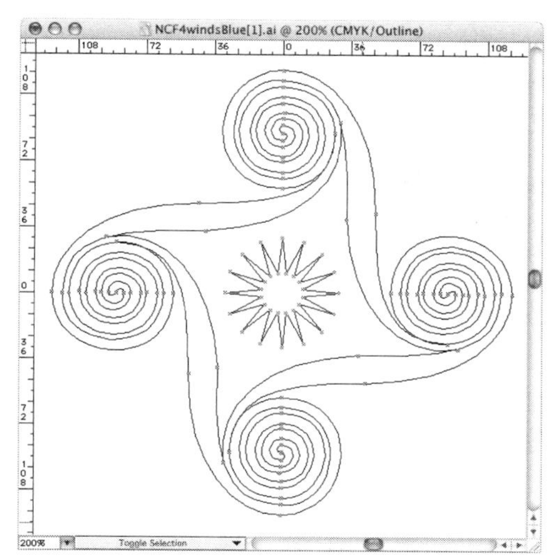

Figure 9.86 Copy a path from Photoshop or Illustrator (shown here)...

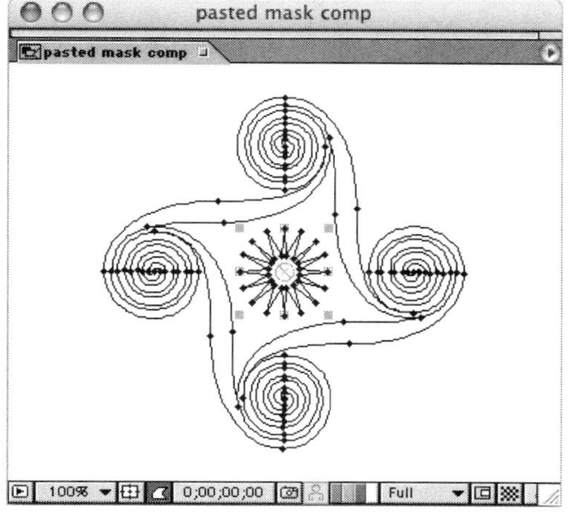

Figure 9.87 ...and paste it into After Effects as a mask.

Using Masks from Photoshop and Illustrator

You can copy paths from Adobe Photoshop or Illustrator and paste them as a layer mask in After Effects. Why not just import the file as a still image? By pasting a path as a layer mask, you can take advantage of After Effects' ability to animate its Shape, Feather, Opacity, and Expansion properties.

To use a mask from Illustrator or Photoshop:

1. In Illustrator or Photoshop, select the paths you want to copy (**Figure 9.86**).
2. Choose Edit > Copy.
3. In After Effects, view a layer in a Layer window.
4. Choose Edit > Paste.

   The mask is pasted into the Layer window (**Figure 9.87**).

✔ Tips

- If you try to paste the mask in the Composition window, it appears as a motion path, not a mask.
- In Illustrator's File & Clipboard Preferences, make sure you specify clipboard options. Otherwise, you won't be able to copy from Illustrator into After Effects.

Setting Custom Mask Colors

By default, mask paths appear yellow. To help distinguish multiple masks from one another, you can assign each a unique color. You can even have After Effects assign each subsequent mask a different color automatically.

To assign a mask color:

1. In the Timeline window, select the layer containing the mask you want to color-code.
2. Press M to reveal the masks contained by the layer.
   The masks and the Mask Shape property appear in the expanded layer outline. If the layer doesn't contain any masks, the outline doesn't expand.
3. Next to the mask name, click the color swatch (**Figure 9.88**).
   A color picker appears (**Figure 9.89**).
4. In the color picker, select a color for the mask, and then click OK.
   When selected, the mask uses the color you chose.

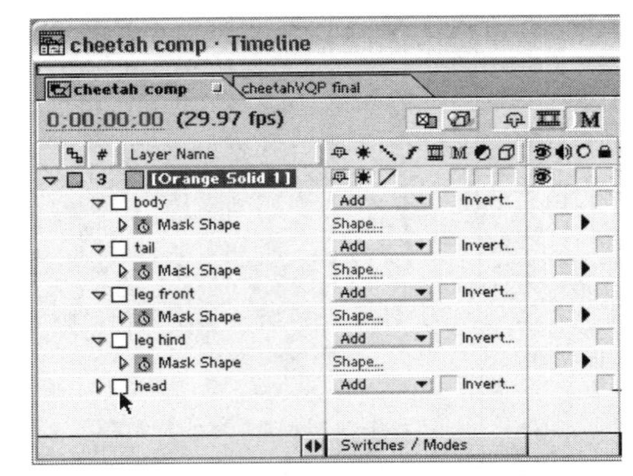

Figure 9.88 Click the color swatch next to the mask's name.

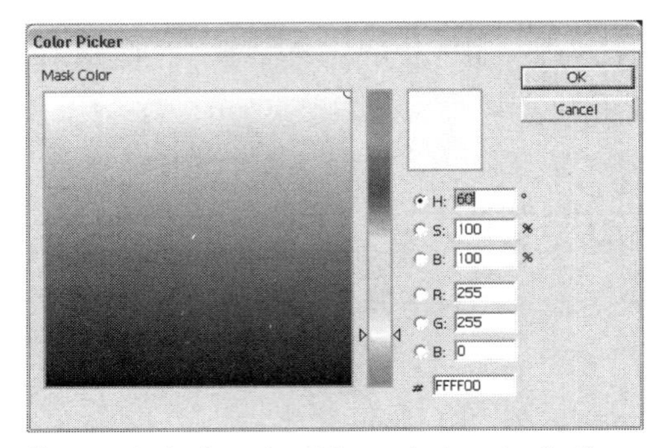

Figure 9.89 In the color picker, select a color for the mask path.

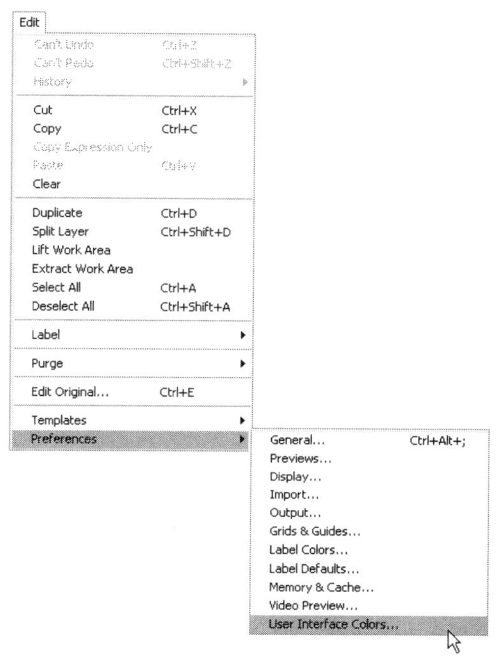

Figure 9.90 Choose After Effects > Preferences > User Interface Colors (Mac) or Edit > Preferences > User Interface Colors (Windows).

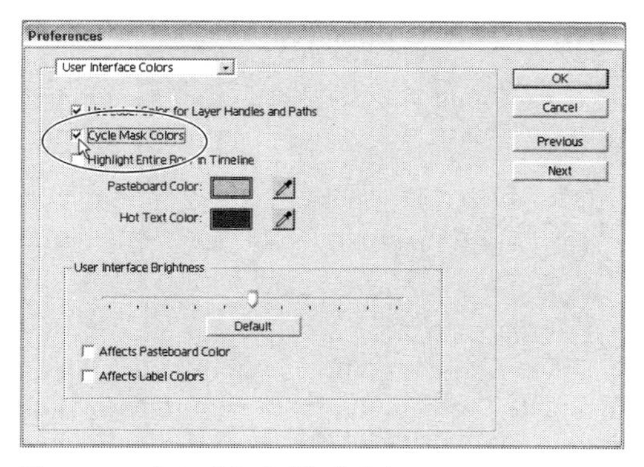

Figure 9.91 Select Cycle Mask Colors.

To cycle through mask colors automatically:

1. Choose After Effects > Preferences > User Interface Colors (Mac) or Edit > Preferences > User Interface Colors (Windows) (**Figure 9.90**).

   The User Interface Colors panel of the Preferences dialog box appears.

2. Select Cycle Mask Colors and click OK (**Figure 9.91**).

   Each successive mask uses a different color. After Effects uses eight different colors before repeating the cycle.

Locking and Hiding Masks

Because you can place several masks in the same layer, it can become difficult to isolate the one you want to modify. Fortunately, you can lock masks, both to protect them from unintentional changes and to make it easier to select an unlocked mask. In the Timeline window, a Lock icon appears next to a locked mask. If you're still having a hard time isolating the mask you wish to use, you can hide locked masks. Although hiding locked masks conceals them in the Layer window, they still function normally, and their effects can be seen in the Composition window.

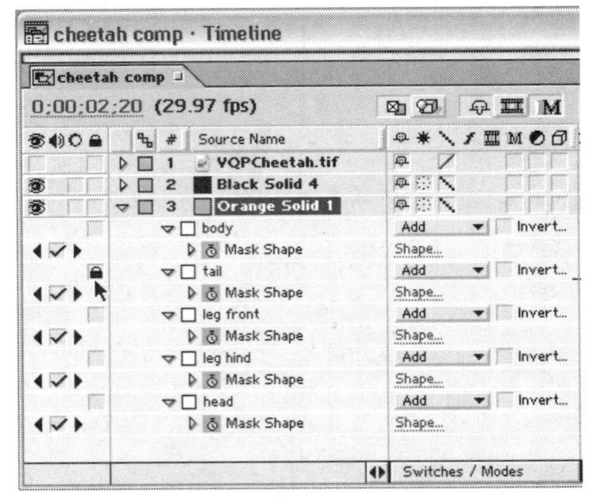

Figure 9.92 Click the box to the left of the mask's name to toggle the Lock icon on and off.

To lock masks:

1. In the Layer, Comp, or Timeline window, select the mask you want to lock.
2. *Do one of the following:*
   - ▲ In the Timeline window, click to the left of the selected mask name to make the Lock icon appear (**Figure 9.92**).
   - ▲ Choose Layer > Mask > Locked.
   - ▲ To lock the unselected masks contained in the layer, Choose Layer > Mask > Lock Other Masks (**Figure 9.93**).

   Locked masks become unselected and can't be modified until they're unlocked.

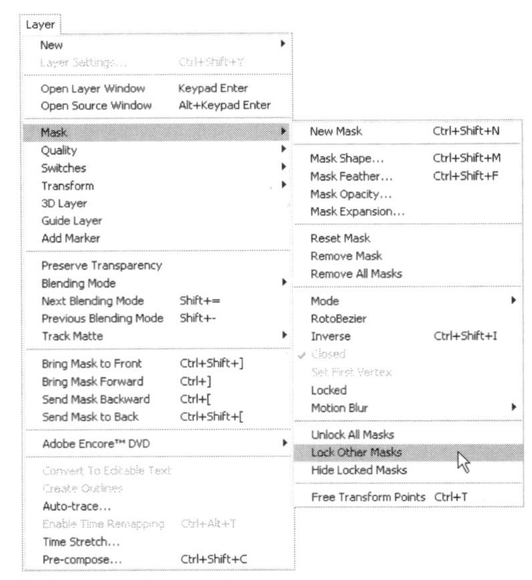

Figure 9.93 Choose Layer > Mask > Lock Other Masks to lock the unselected masks.

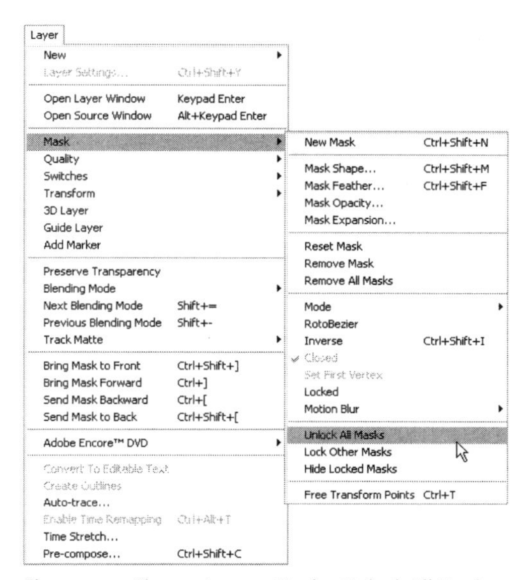

Figure 9.94 Choose Layer > Mask > Unlock All Masks to unlock all the masks contained in the selected layer.

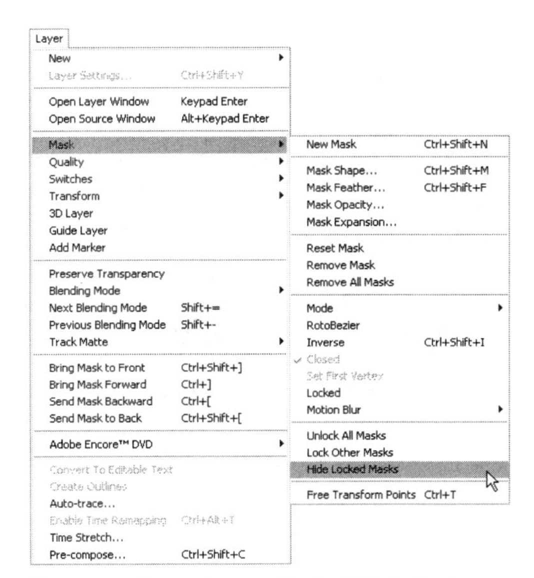

Figure 9.95 Choose Layer > Mask > Hide Locked Masks to conceal or reveal the locked masks in the Layer window.

To unlock masks:

Do any of the following:

- In the Timeline window, click the Lock icon to the left of the mask name to make the Lock icon disappear.
- To unlock all masks contained in a layer, select the layer and choose Layer > Mask > Unlock All Masks (**Figure 9.94**).

To hide and reveal locked masks in the Layer window:

1. In the Timeline window or Layer window, select the layer containing the locked masks you want to hide or show.
2. Choose Layer > Mask > Hide Locked Masks (**Figure 9.95**).

   Selecting the command hides locked masks in the selected layer's Layer window; unselecting the command reveals the locked masks. This doesn't alter the mask's effect in the composition (**Figure 9.96**).

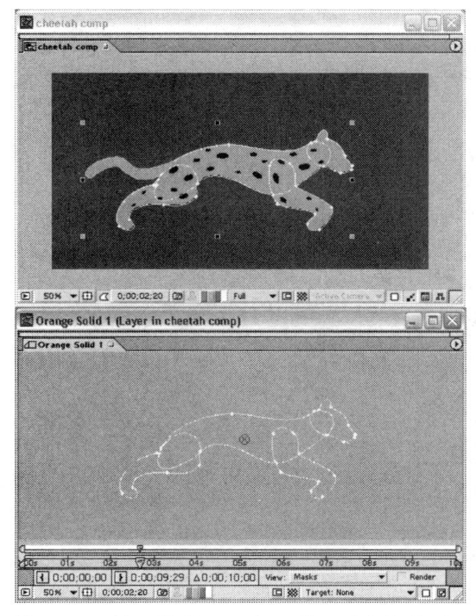

Figure 9.96 In this figure, the tail mask is locked and hidden; its path isn't visible in the layer window.

Moving Masks Relative to the Layer Image

There are two ways you can move a mask to reveal a different part of a layer: in a Layer window or in a Composition window.

When you move a mask in a Layer window, its relative position in the Composition window also changes (**Figures 9.97** and **9.98**).

This works well if you want to change both the part of the image revealed by the mask and the mask's position in the composition. The mask moves, but the layer's position remains the same. Think of an iris effect at the end of a cartoon, in which the circular mask closes in on the character for a final good-bye.

Figure 9.97 When you move a mask in a Layer or Comp window...

Figure 9.98 ...the mask's position changes in both the layer and the Comp window. The position value of the layer containing the mask doesn't change.

Alternatively, you can use the Pan Behind tool in the Composition window. Panning the layer behind the mask reveals a different part of the image without moving the mask's relative position in the composition. When you look back at the Layer window, you can see that the mask has moved. However, After Effects recalculates the layer's position to compensate for this movement, maintaining the layer's position in the composition (**Figures 9.99** and **9.100**). Imagine a scene from a pirate movie, in which a spyglass scans the horizon. The circle doesn't move, but the horizon pans through the viewfinder to reveal an island.

Figure 9.99 When you use the Pan Behind tool in the Composition window...

Figure 9.100 ...the mask changes its position in the layer while maintaining its position in the composition. After Effects recalculates the layer's position value automatically. You can see the anchor point's new position in the Comp window.

To move a mask in the Layer window:

1. Select an entire mask in the Layer window.
2. Drag one of the control points to move the entire mask to a new position.

   Make sure to drag a control point, not a path segment. The mask changes position in both the Layer window and the composition.

To pan a layer behind its mask:

1. In the Tools palette, select the Pan Behind tool (**Figure 9.101**).
2. In the Composition window, position the Pan Behind tool inside the masked area of the layer, and then drag (**Figure 9.102**).

   In the Composition window, the mouse pointer becomes the Pan Behind icon, and the layer pans behind the masked area. After Effects calculates the layer's position in the composition and the mask's placement in the Layer window.

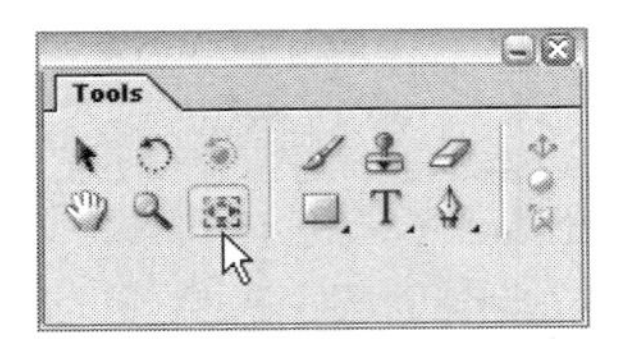

Figure 9.101 In the Tools palette, choose the Pan Behind tool.

Figure 9.102 In the Comp window, place the Pan Behind tool inside the masked area, and drag.

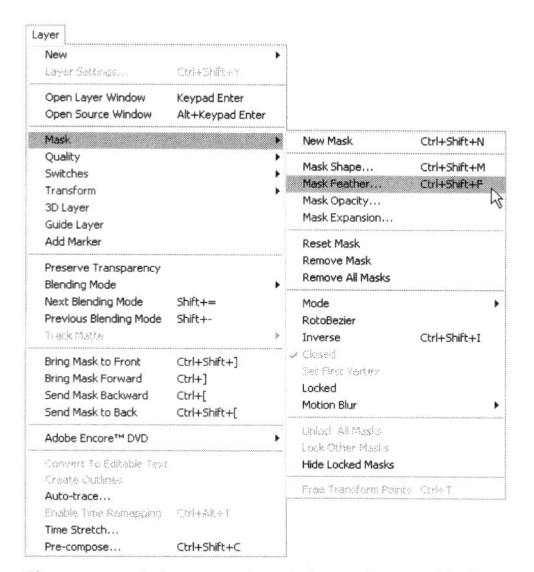

Figure 9.103 Select a mask and choose Layer > Mask > Mask Feather or its keyboard equivalent.

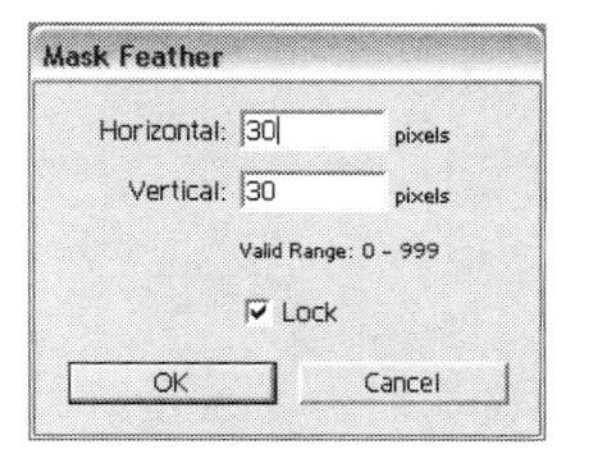

Figure 9.104 In the Mask Feather dialog box, enter a value for the horizontal and vertical mask feather.

Adjusting Other Mask Properties

In addition to Mask Shape, mask properties include Feather, Opacity, and Expansion.

Feather controls the softness of a mask's edge; the Mask Feather value determines the width of the edge's transition from opacity to transparency. The feathered width always extends equally from each side of the mask edge—that is, a Feather value of 30 extends 15 pixels both outside and inside the mask edge.

Expansion lets you expand or contract a mask's edges and is particularly useful for fine-tuning the feathered edge of a mask.

Opacity controls the mask's overall opacity—that is, how solid the masked area of the layer appears. Mask opacity works in conjunction with the layer's Opacity setting. If the layer is 100 percent opaque and a mask is 50 percent opaque, the masked area of the layer appears 50 percent opaque. Each mask's opacity also influences the net effect of mask modes, which are explained later in this chapter.

To feather the edges of a mask:

1. In the Layer, Comp, or Timeline window, select a mask.
2. *Do any of the following:*
   - ▲ Press Shift-Command-F (Mac) or Shift-Ctrl-F (Windows).
   - ▲ Choose Layer > Mask > Mask Feather (**Figure 9.103**).

   The Mask Feather dialog box appears.
3. Enter the number of pixels for the horizontal and vertical feathering (**Figure 9.104**).

   To enter equal values for horizontal and vertical feather automatically, click Lock.

continues on next page

4. Click OK to close the Mask Feather dialog box.

   The mask edges appear feathered by the value you specified (**Figure 9.105**).

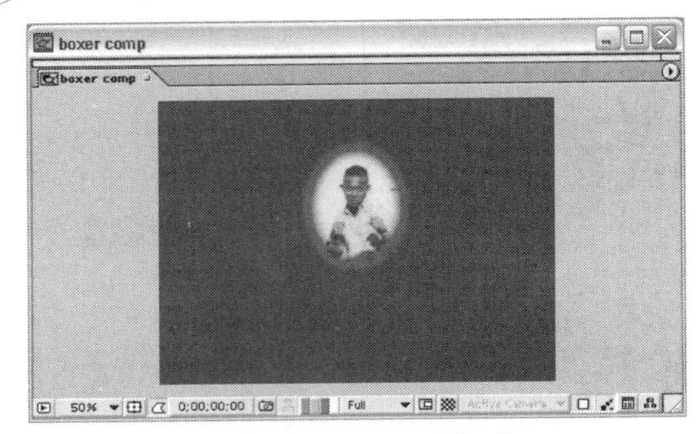

Figure 9.105 The edge of the mask feathers, or softens, by the amount you specified.

✔ Tip

- If you set the feather to extend beyond the perimeter of the layer containing the mask, the feather will appear cut off and the edges of the layer will be apparent. Make the mask or feather small enough to fit within the confines of the layer. If the layer is a solid or nested composition, you can also increase the size of the layer.

To adjust mask opacity:

1. In the Timeline window, select the layer containing the masks you want to adjust, and press MM.

   This shortcut reveals the selected layer's masks and their properties in the layer outline.

2. Adjust the Opacity value for the masks you want to adjust (**Figure 9.106**).

   The mask uses the opacity setting you specify. Each mask's opacity setting interacts with the layer's overall Opacity setting, as well as mask mode settings (**Figure 9.107**).

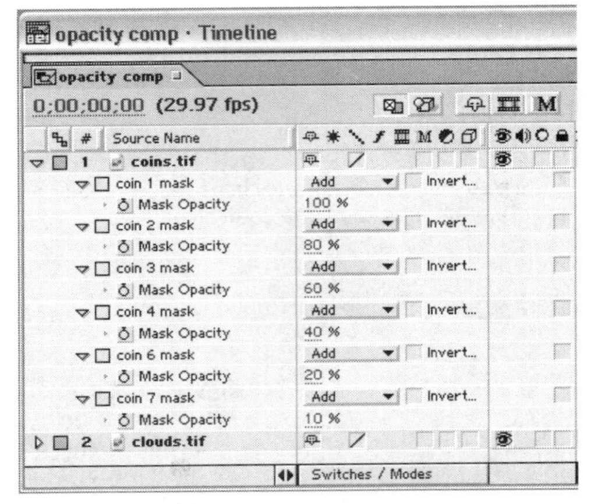

Figure 9.106 Adjust a mask's Opacity value in the layer outline.

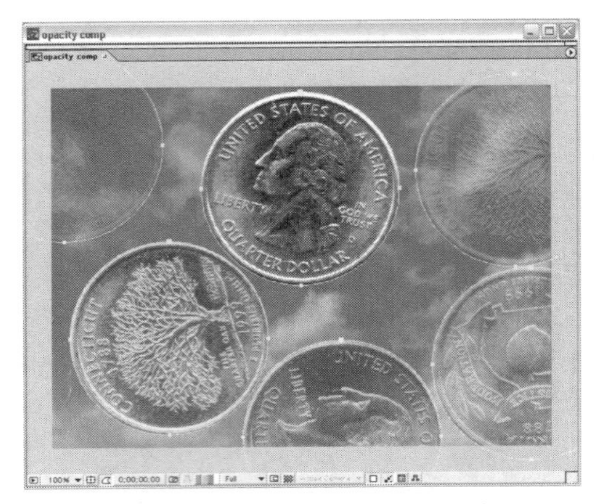

Figure 9.107 In this figure, several masks in the same layer use different opacity values.

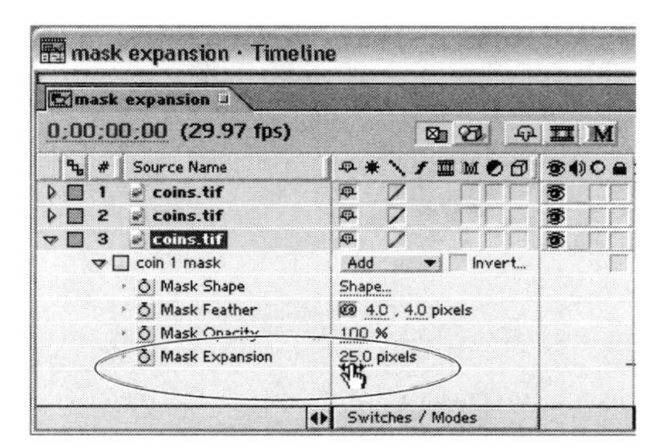

Figure 9.108 Adjust a mask's Expansion value in the layer outline.

Figure 9.109 This figure shows three masks with identical shapes and feather values. However, each mask's Expansion value is different.

To expand or contract the mask:

1. In the Timeline window, select the layer containing the masks you want to adjust, and press MM.

   This shortcut reveals the selected layer's masks and their properties in the layer outline.

2. Adjust the Expansion value for the masks you want to adjust (**Figure 9.108**).

   Positive values expand the masked area beyond its defined edges; negative values contract the masked area (**Figure 9.109**).

✔ Tip

- The Layer Mask properties—Shape, Feather, Opacity, and Expansion—work like other properties. You can adjust their values and animate them as you would other properties. For more about properties and keyframes, see Chapter 7.

Inverting a Mask

Ordinarily, the area within a closed layer mask defines the opaque parts of the layer's image; the area outside the mask is transparent, revealing the layers beneath it. However, just as you can invert a layer's alpha channel, you can invert a layer mask to reverse the opaque and transparent areas.

To invert a mask created in After Effects:

1. In the Layer, Comp, or Timeline window, select the mask you want to invert.
2. *Do one of the following:*
   - ▲ In the Timeline window, click Invert for the selected mask (**Figure 9.110**).
   - ▲ Choose Layer > Mask > Invert.
   - ▲ Press Shift-Command-I (Mac) or Shift-Ctrl-I (Windows).

   Viewed in the Composition window, the mask is inverted (**Figures 9.111** and **9.112**).

Figure 9.110 Click Invert for the mask in the layer outline of the Timeline window, or use the equivalent menu command or keyboard shortcut.

Figure 9.111 Ordinarily, the area within the mask defines the opaque parts of the layer's image.

Figure 9.112 Inverting the mask reverses the opaque and transparent areas of the layer.

Figure 9.113 Two masks at 75 percent opacity, one with the mask's mode set to None.

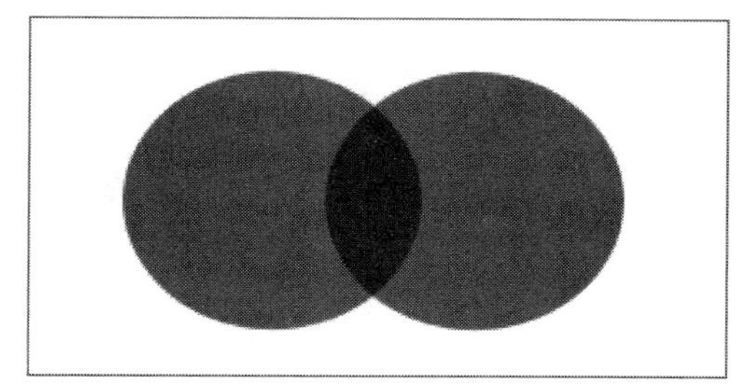

Figure 9.114 Mask mode set to Add.

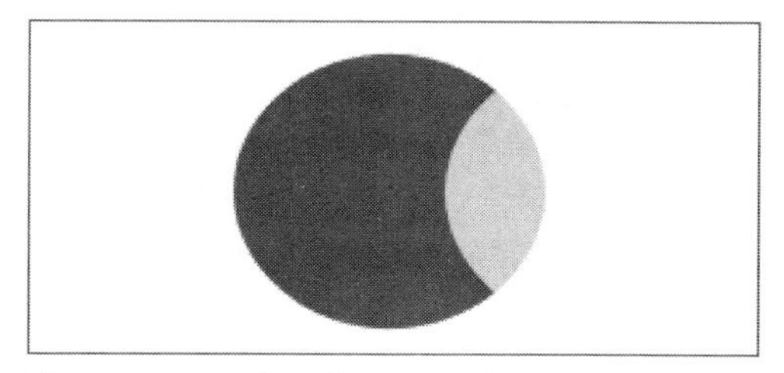

Figure 9.115 Mask mode set to Subtract.

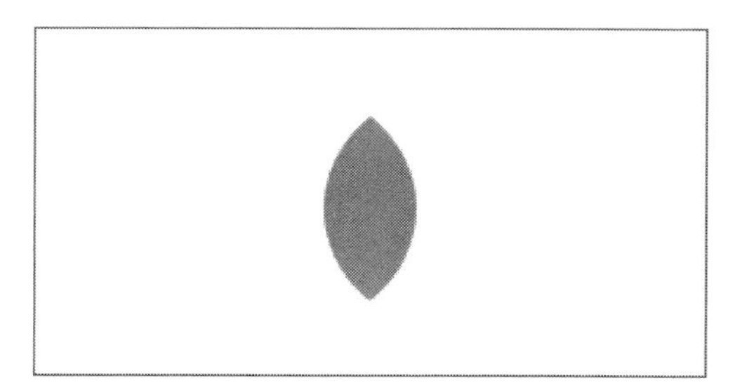

Figure 9.116 Mask mode set to Intersect.

Mask Modes

When you add multiple masks to the same layer, you can determine how the masks interact by selecting a mask *mode*. Although modes don't create compound paths (as do the Boolean functions in Illustrator), you can use them to achieve similar effects in a composition.

In the following examples, the upper mask is set to the default mode: None. See how changing the mode of the lower mask changes the way it interacts with the one above it? Both masks are set to 75 percent opacity so you can see the difference between the Add, Lighten, and Darken modes.

None eliminates the effects of the mask on the layer's alpha channel. However, you can still apply effects (such as strokes or fills) to the mask (**Figure 9.113**).

Add includes the mask with the masks above it to display all masked areas. Areas where the mask overlaps with the masks above it use their combined opacity values (**Figure 9.114**).

Subtract cuts, or subtracts, areas where the mask overlaps with the mask above it (**Figure 9.115**).

Intersect adds the mask to all the masks above it so that only the areas where the mask overlaps with higher masks display in the composition (**Figure 9.116**).

continues on next page

Lighten adds the mask to the masks above it to display all masked areas. Areas where the mask overlaps with the masks above it use the highest opacity value, not the combined values (**Figure 9.117**).

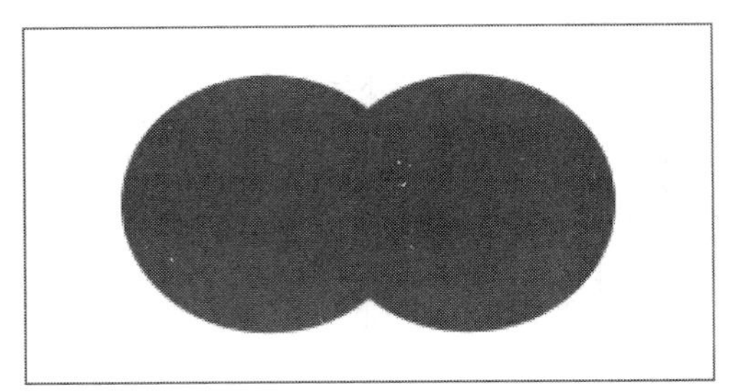

Figure 9.117 Mask mode set to Lighten.

Darken adds the mask to the masks above it to display only the areas where the masks overlap. Areas where multiple masks overlap use the highest opacity value, not the combined values (**Figure 9.118**).

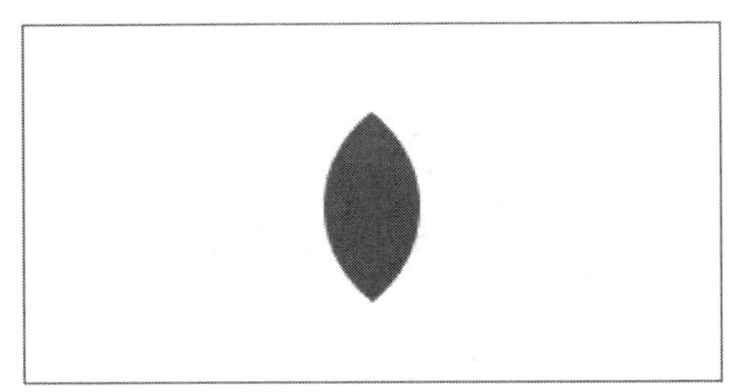

Figure 9.118 Mask mode set to Darken.

Difference adds the mask to the masks above it to display only the areas where the masks don't overlap (**Figure 9.119**).

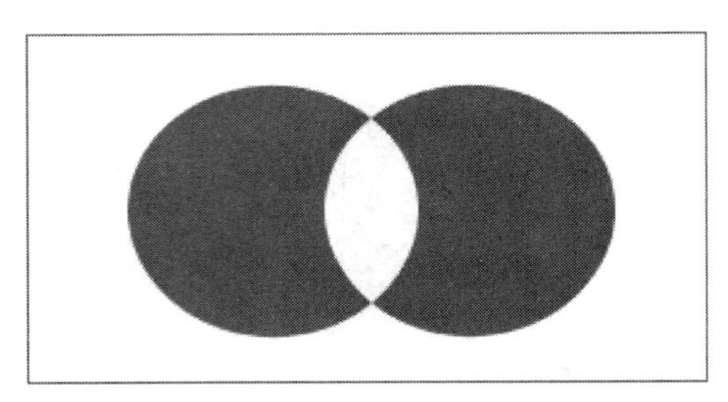

Figure 9.119 Mask mode set to Difference.

To set the mask mode:

1. Select the mask for which you want to set the mode.
2. *Do one of the following:*
   - ▲ In the Timeline window, choose a mode from the pull-down menu across from the mask (in the Switches/Modes panel) (**Figure 9.120**).
   - ▲ Choose Layer > Mask > Mode > and select a mode from the submenu.

   The mode you choose affects how the mask interacts with the masks above it in the layer outline (for that layer only).

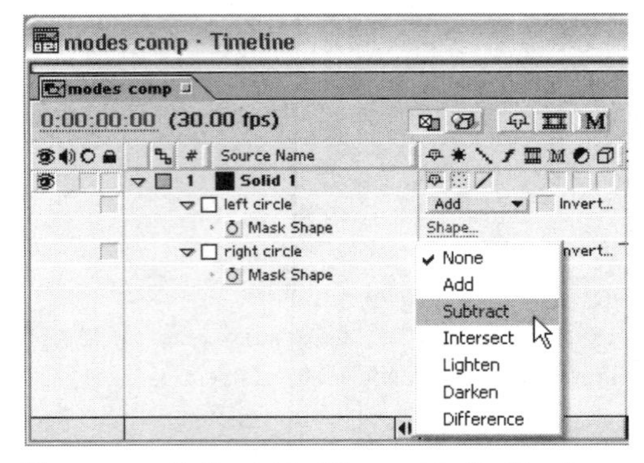

Figure 9.120 To the right of the mask in the Timeline window, choose a mask mode from the pull-down menu.

10

Effects Fundamentals

At last, you come to the long menu: Effects. As if you didn't already know, effects are used to alter the audio and visual characteristics of layers in almost countless ways. You can employ them to enhance, combine, or distort layers. You can simulate audio-visual phenomenon from light to lightning. You can make changes that are subtle or spectacular. And most important, you can animate these effects over time.

Effects are stored in the Plug-Ins folder, which is itself contained in the After Effects folder. The number and type of effects at your disposal will depend on whether you have the standard version of After Effects or After Effects Pro. You can also add to your repertoire by using effects created by third-party developers.

This is the first of two chapters covering effects. Together, they move from the general to the specific. This chapter begins with an overview of effect categories and then goes on to explain the process you use to apply effects to layers. It also describes how to use the Effect Controls window as a complement or alternative to the property controls in the layer outline. Chapter 11, "Effects in Action," lists each effect by category and highlights prime examples of Standard effects.

Effect Categories

By default, the effects in the Effects menu are organized in the following categories according to function. After Effects Pro includes a number of effects and entire effect categories not found in the Standard version. When you add third-party plug-ins, you can often choose whether the added effect appears under an existing category or one that you create specifically for it.

***Animation Presets** includes any combination of effects or other keyframed properties you save, as well as a number of built-in presets for animating text.

3D Channel (Pro only) includes effects that can use information saved in a number of 3D image file formats, allowing you to incorporate scenes created in 3D applications.

Adjust alters a layer's colors or brightness.

Audio processes audio.

Blur and Sharpen adjusts the focus of a layer's images.

Channel manipulates a layer's individual channels—red, green, blue, or alpha—and the color information derived from them.

Distort deforms or distorts a layer's image.

Expression Controls enables you to more easily manipulate property values contained in expressions—math-like statements you define to create animation (covered in Chapter 17, "Complex Projects").

Image Control alters the color values of a layer image.

Keying makes areas of an image transparent, based on color or brightness.

Matte Tools (Pro only) fine-tune keying effects to create more convincing composites.

Noise and Grain effects either add visual noise or grain—to create a pixilated or film-like texture, for example—or reduce it.

Paint lets you modify a layer using familiar paint and cloning tools, and animate individual paint strokes over time (see Chapter 13, "Painting on a Layer," for a full explanation).

Perspective simulates positioning a layer in three-dimensional space.

Render creates graphical elements.

Simulation emulates a number of real-world phenomena, such as bubbles, shattering glass, water, and particle effects.

Stylize alters an image's pixels to produce abstract, stylized effects.

Text creates text elements (for other text-creation techniques, see Chapter 12, "Creating and Animating Text").

Time alters the layer image based on its timing.

Transition refers to effects that are designed to gradually replace one image with the one preceding it.

Video prepares images for video output.

 —*Video effect*

 —*Audio effect*

 —*16 bpc effect*

 —*Effect preset*

 —*Animated property*

Figure 10.1 In the Effects & Presets palette, icons indicate the type of item listed.

Using the Effects & Presets Palette

Although you can find and apply any effect using the Effects menu, it can be more convenient to use the Effects & Presets palette. As its name implies, the Effects & Presets palette lists not only effects, but also animation presets. (In Chapter 7, "Properties and Keyframes," you learned how to save animations as a preset that can be easily applied to other layers. Animation presets also include a number of built-in text animations, as explained in Chapter 12.

The Effects & Presets palette makes it easy to find an effect based on its name. You can sort the list alphabetically, according to category, or to help you locate the effect's plug-in file on your system. You can sift the list to show effects or animation presets, and specify whether to show the effects contained in a preset.

As usual, you can click the triangle next to the item to expand it, revealing its contents in outline form. By expanding items, you can view effects contained in a category or see the components of a saved preset (when those viewing options are selected).

Icons indicate the type of item listed (**Figure 10.1**). A standard video effect's icon uses a plug-in symbol, depicting a real-world plug (the two-pronged Edison type); an audio effect adds a small speaker icon; 16 bit-per-channel effects add the number 16; presets use a file icon with the letters *FX*; and keyframed properties within an animation preset are represented by a stopwatch icon.

To find an item in the Effects & Presets palette:

- In the Effects & Presets palette, type all or part of the name of the item you want in the Contains field (**Figure 10.2**).

  As you type, the items on the list that don't match are hidden from view, leaving only matching items (**Figure 10.3**).

To show all the items in the Effects & Presets palette:

- Highlight the search criteria in the Effects & Presets palette's Contains field, and press Delete (Mac) or Backspace (Windows).

  The palette lists all items (**Figure 10.4**) according to other sorting options you specify (explained in the following tasks).

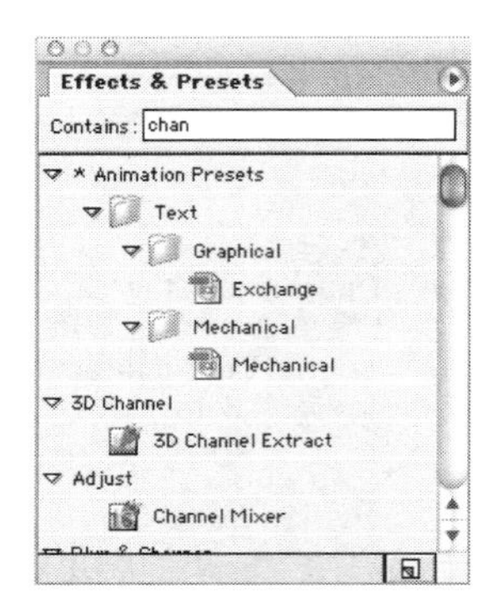

Figure 10.2 As you type the name of the item you want in the Contains field...

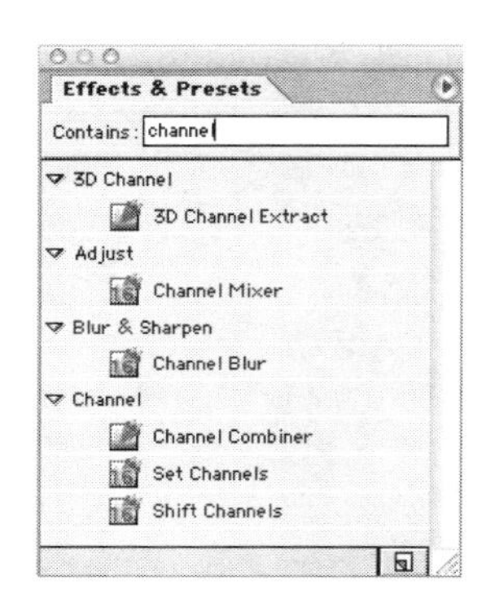

Figure 10.3 ...the list sifts to show only the matching items.

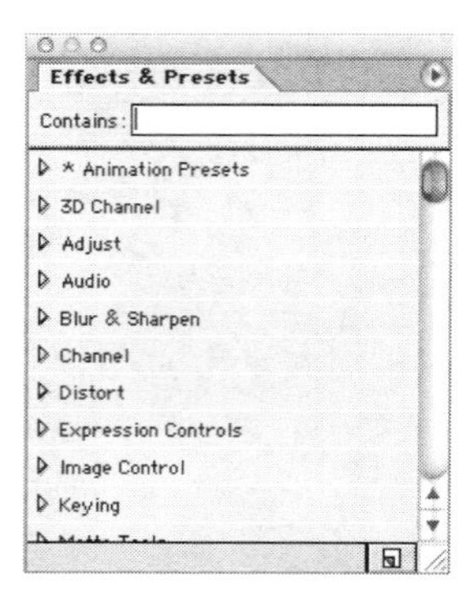

Figure 10.4 Clear the Contains field to make the palette list all items again.

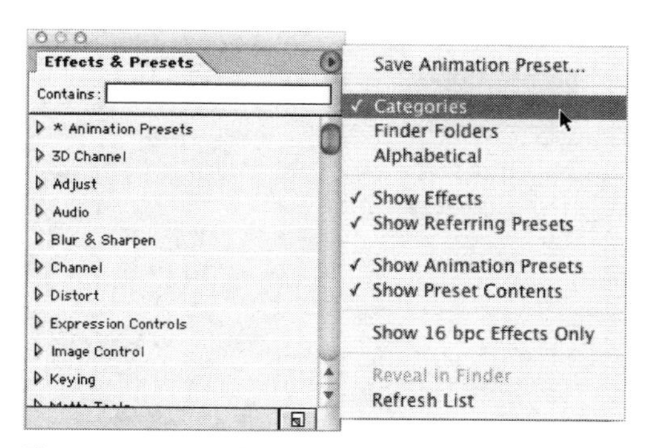

Figure 10.5 In the Effects & Presets palette's pull-down menu, choose an option to sort the list by category, finder folders, or alphabetically.

To sort the Effects & Presets palette's list:

◆ In the Effects & Presets palette's menu, select one of the following (**Figure 10.5**):

Categories—Groups items in folders according to categories determined by function (listed earlier in this chapter) (**Figure 10.6**)

Finder Folders—Groups items in pull-down folders according to how their source files are organized on your computer (**Figure 10.7**)

Alphabetical—Lists all items in alphabetical order (numbered items appear first, then items from A–Z) (**Figure 10.8**)

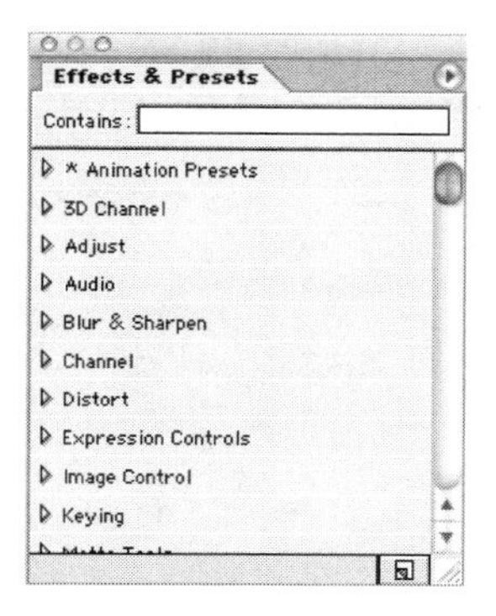

Figure 10.6 Choosing Categories sorts the items according to their general function, such as Adjust and Blur & Sharpen.

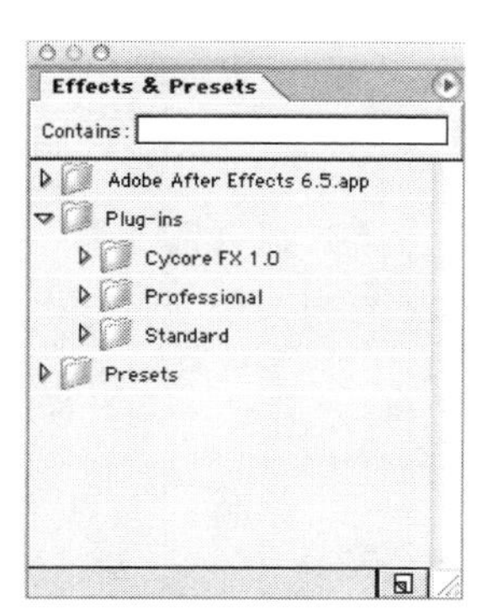

Figure 10.7 Choosing Finder Folders sorts items according to how their plug-in files are organized on your system.

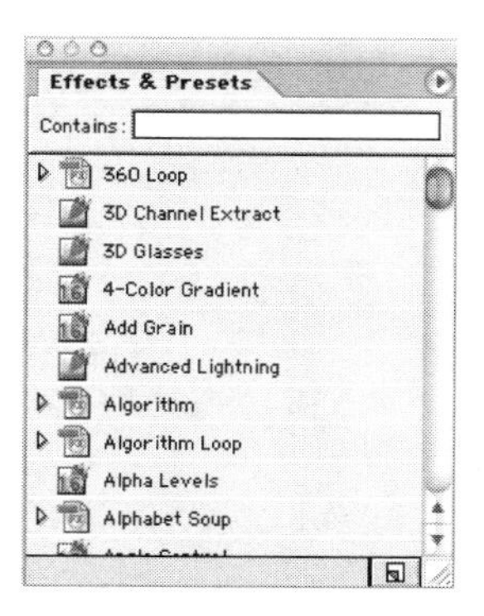

Figure 10.8 Choosing Alphabetical lists all items in alphabetical order.

To include or exclude items in the Effects & Presets palette by type:

- In the Effects & Presets palette's pull-down menu, choose the type of items you want the list to include (**Figure 10.9**):

  Show Effects—Shows effects; deselect this option to exclude effects in order to view presets only

  Show Referring Presets—Lists effects with the name of any presets that use the effect (**Figure 10.10**)

  Show Animation Presets—Shows animation and effect presets you've saved

  Show Preset Contents—Shows individual effects included in a preset, in outline form (**Figure 10.11**)

  Show 16 bpc Effects Only—Shows effects that can be applied to 16 bit-per-channel (bpc) images, and excludes other effects

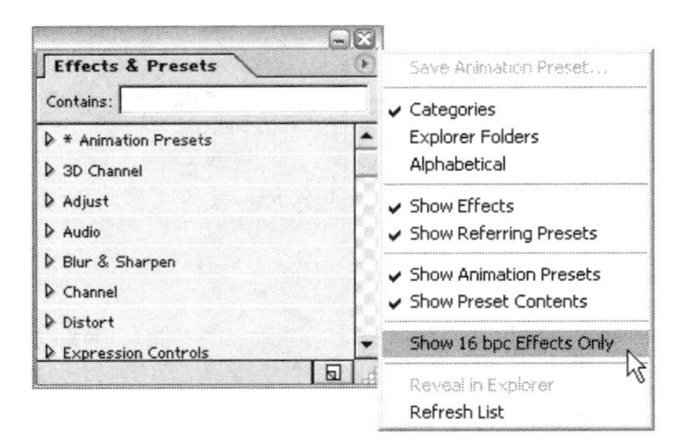

Figure 10.9 Choose the types of items you want to include in the list.

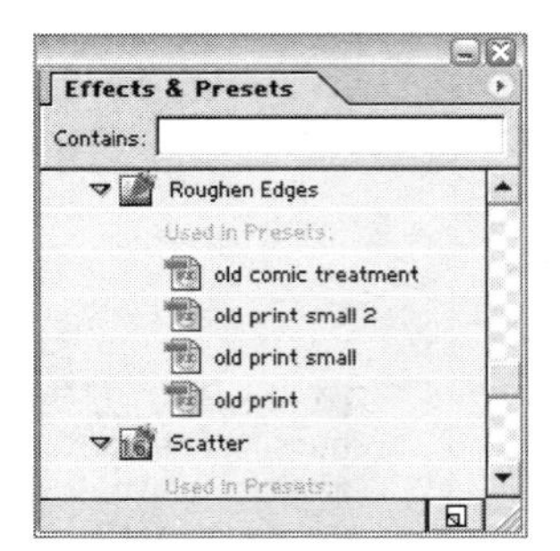

Figure 10.10 Choosing Show Referring Presets lists presets alongside the effects used by the preset.

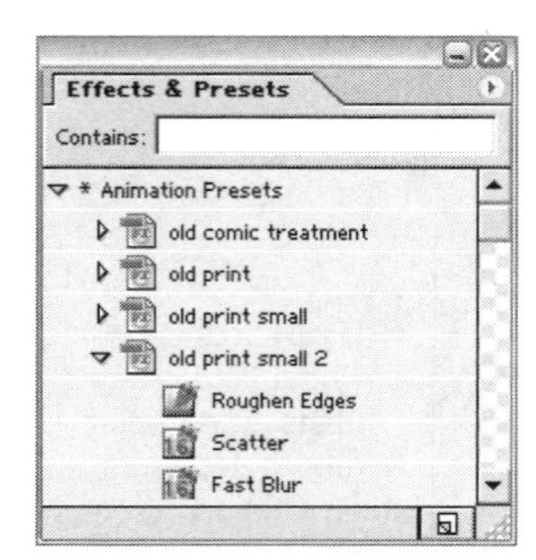

Figure 10.11 Choosing Show Preset contents lets you expand a preset to see the individual effects it contains.

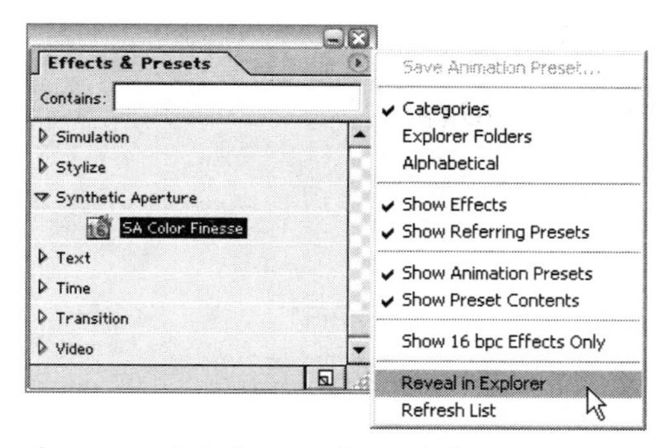

Figure 10.12 Selecting an effect and choosing Reveal in OS (Mac) or Reveal in Explorer (Windows)...

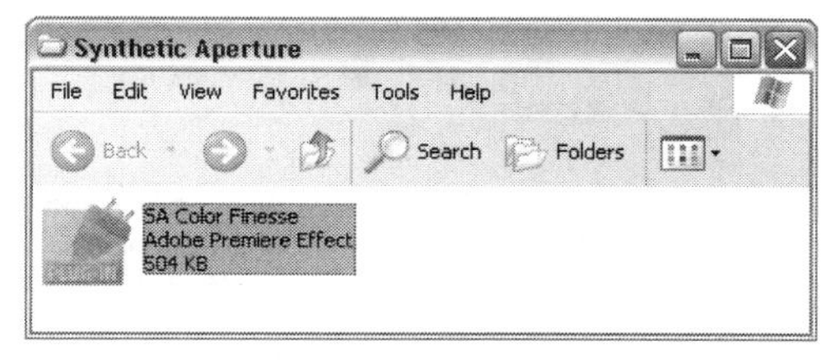

Figure 10.13 ...locates and selects the item's source plug-in file on your system.

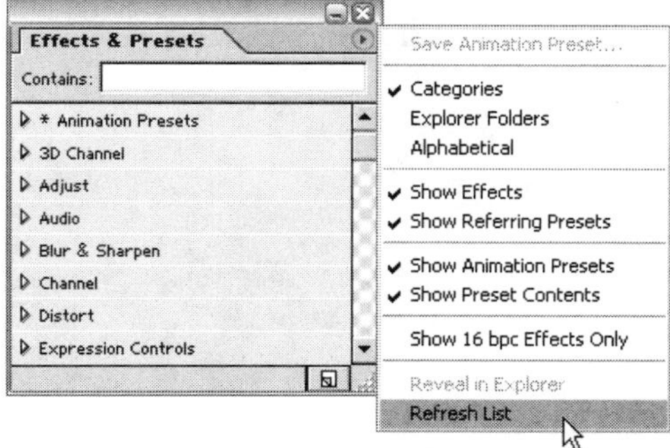

Figure 10.14 To make the Effects & Presets palette reflect any changes you made to the source files, choose Refresh List.

To reveal an item in the OS:

1. In the Effects & Presets palette, select an effect.
2. In the Effects & Presets palette's menu, choose Reveal in OS (Mac) or Reveal in Explorer (Windows) (**Figure 10.12**).

   After Effects locates the item's source file in your system, opens the item's containing folder, and selects the item (**Figure 10.13**).

To refresh the list:

◆ In the Effects & Presets palette's menu, choose Refresh List (**Figure 10.14**).

  The list reflects changes caused by adding, deleting, or moving source files on the finder level (aka the Desktop [Mac] or Explorer [Windows]).

✔ Tip

■ If you're using After Effects Pro, the Effects & Presets palette's menu includes an option to show only effects that support 16 bit-per-channel (bpc) images. For more about using 16 bpc footage items, see Chapter 4, "Compositions."

Applying Effects

Although effects are numerous and varied, you apply all of them in essentially the same way.

You can also save any combination of effects (as well as animation keyframes) as a preset. To learn how to save and apply a preset, see the section "Saving and Applying Effect Presets" later in this chapter.

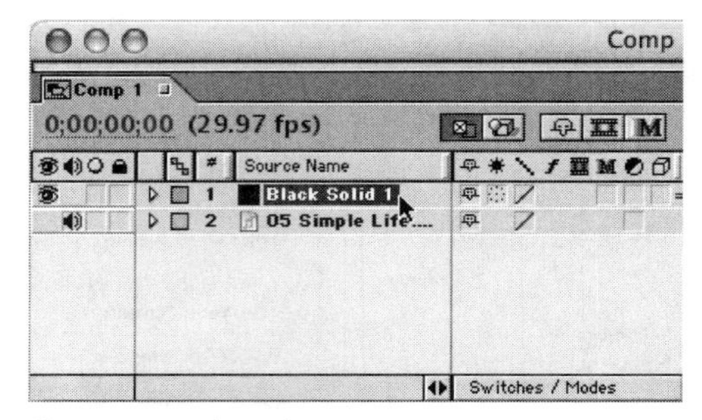

Figure 10.15 Select a layer.

To apply an effect:

1. Select a layer in a composition (**Figure 10.15**).
2. *Do any of the following:*
   - ▲ Double-click the effect or preset you want to apply in the Effects & Presets palette (**Figure 10.16**).
   - ▲ Choose Effect and then choose an effect category and an individual effect from the submenu (**Figure 10.17**).
   - ▲ Ctrl-click (Mac) or right-click (Windows) and hold the mouse button to access an Effects menu.
3. If an options dialog box appears, select options for the effect and click OK to close the dialog box.

   An Effect Controls window appears with the effect selected (**Figure 10.18**).
4. Using controls in the Effect Controls window or in the expanded layer outline of the Timeline window, adjust the property values for the effect, and animate them if you want (**Figure 10.19**).

   The applied effect appears in the composition (**Figure 10.20**). The quality and aspects (such as shading or shadows) of the effect depends on the preview options you specify; see Chapter 8, "Playback, Previews, and RAM," for more information.

Figure 10.16 In the Effects & Presets palette, double-click the effect or preset...

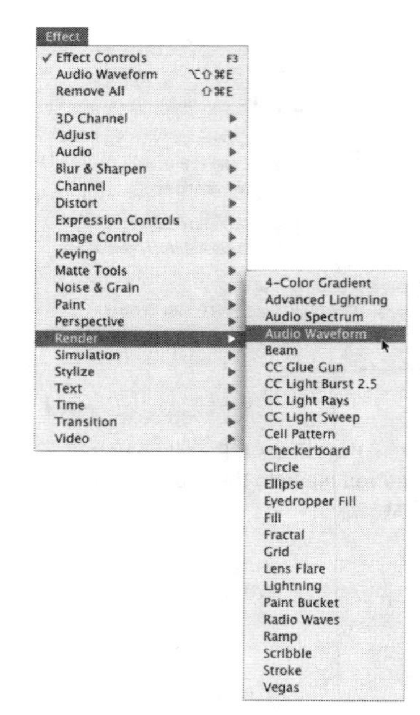

Figure 10.17 ...or choose an effect from the Effect menu.

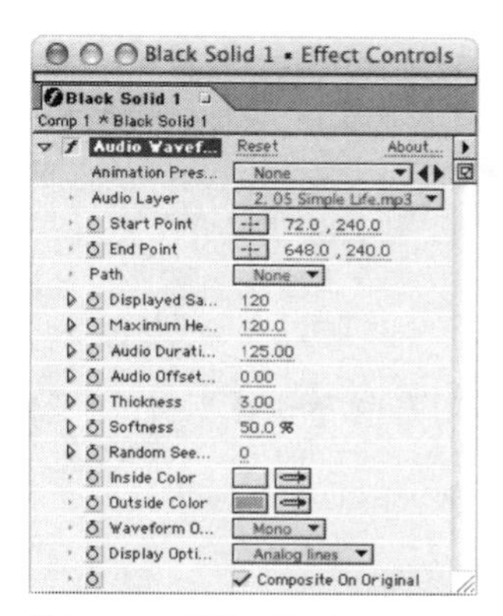

Figure 10.18 The effect appears selected in the Effect Controls window. You can adjust the settings here...

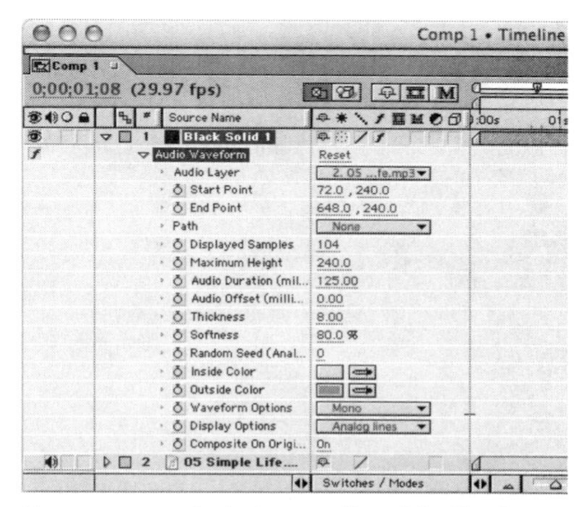

Figure 10.19 ...or in the layer outline of the Timeline window.

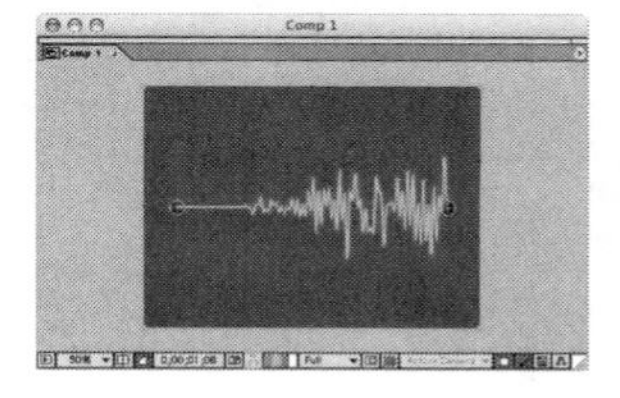

Figure 10.20 You can view and preview the effect in the Composition window.

To apply the most recent effect:

1. Select a layer in a composition.
2. *Do one of the following:*
   - ▲ Choose Effect and select the most recently used effect from the top of the menu (**Figure 10.21**).
   - ▲ Press Shift-Command-Option-E (Mac) or Shift-Ctrl-Alt-E (Windows).

   The effect is applied to the selected layer.

✔ Tips

- New users sometimes use the techniques described in the previous tasks to access an effect's controls; however, these methods only add another instance of an effect. If you want to adjust an effect, use the controls in the Timeline window or the Effect Controls window (as explained later in this chapter).
- Many effects are best applied to solid-black layers—particularly those that don't rely on a layer's underlying pixels, such as Render effects. This often permits you to manipulate an effect more independently. Other times, you may want to use the effect to interact with a solid color to create graphical elements.

Figure 10.21 Choose Effect and select the most recently applied effect from the menu.

Viewing Effect Property Controls

Once you add effects to a layer, you can view their property controls in the Timeline window or the Effect Controls window.

To view an effect in the Timeline window:

1. In the Timeline window, select a layer.
2. Press E.

   All effects applied to the layer appear in the layer outline (**Figure 10.22**).
3. To view property controls for the effect, click the triangle next to the name of the effect to expand the layer outline. You can also expand some property controls.

   The layer outline expands to reveal properties of the effect (**Figure 10.23**).

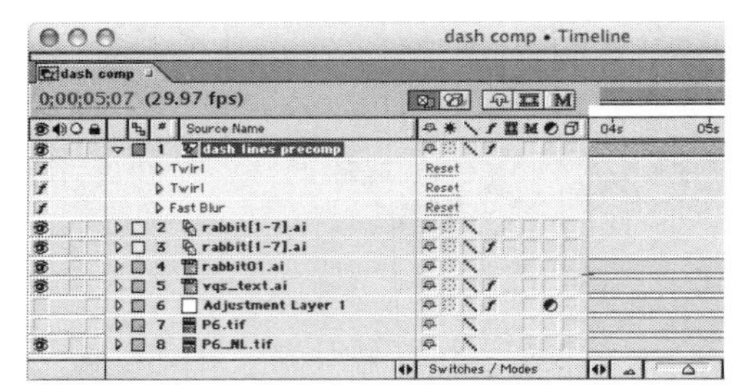

Figure 10.22 Select a layer and press E to reveal the effects applied to the layer in the layer outline.

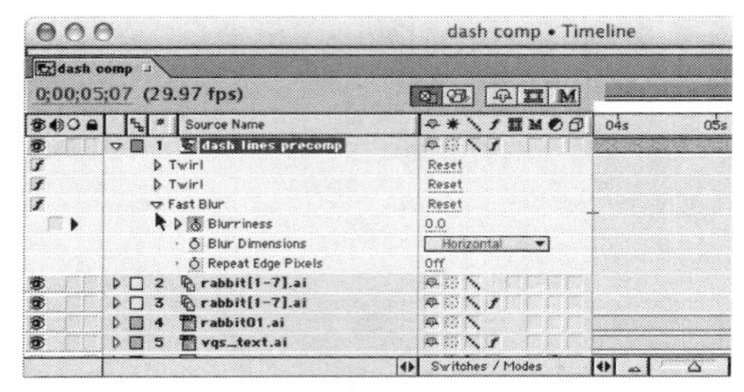

Figure 10.23 Click the triangle next to the effect name to expand the outline even more. Some effect property controls can also be expanded.

To view effects in the Effect Controls window:

1. Select a layer that contains one or more effects.
2. *Do either of the following:*
   - ▲ Press Shift-Command-T (Mac) or Shift-Ctrl-T (Windows).
   - ▲ Choose Effect > Effect Controls (**Figure 10.24**).

   The Effect Controls window opens. If it's already open, the selected layer's name tab appears in front and the effects it contains appear in the window; name tabs for other layers appear in the background (**Figure 10.25**).

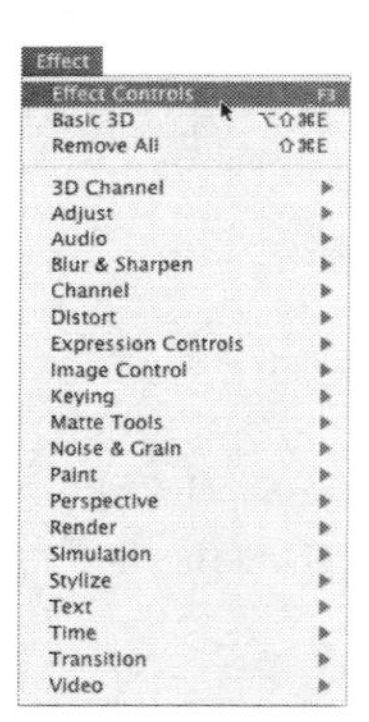

Figure 10.24 To open the Effect Controls window, double-click the effect in the layer outline, or select a layer and choose Effect > Effect Controls.

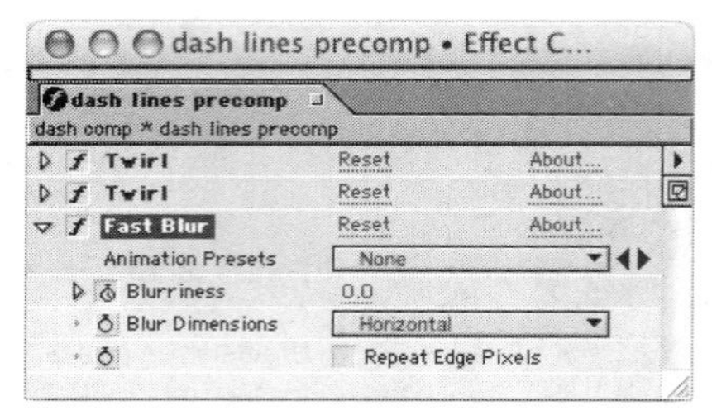

Figure 10.25 The Effect Controls window opens. If it's already open, the selected layer's effects are brought to the front of the window.

✔ Tip

- You can also open an Effect Controls window by double-clicking the name of an effect in the layer outline.

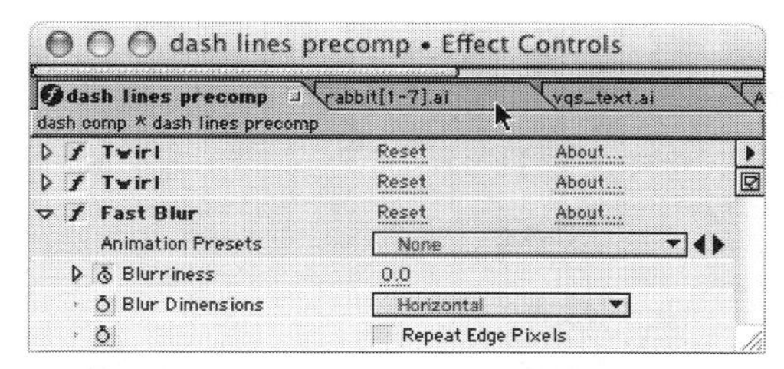

Figure 10.26 Like other windows in After Effects, the Effect Controls window uses tabbed displays. You can click the tab that corresponds to the layer you want to adjust...

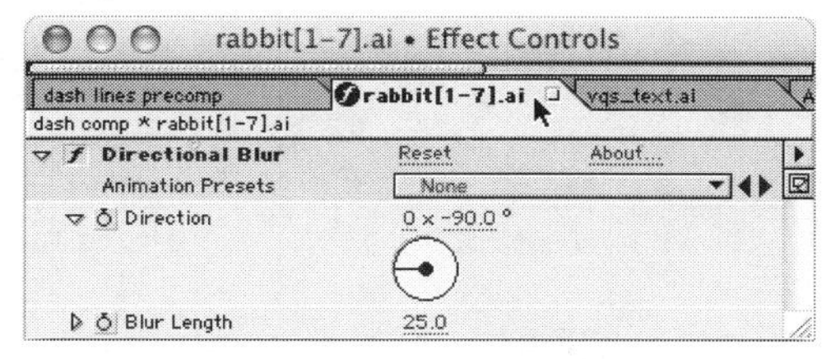

Figure 10.27 ...and its effect controls will be brought to the front of the window.

Using the Effect Controls Window

The Effect Controls window lists the effects for a layer and includes controls for adjusting each effect property. Tabs allow the window to contain the effects for more than one layer.

You can also save any combination of effects using controls in the Effect Controls window; see the section "Saving and Applying Effect Presets" later in this chapter.

To select a layer in the Effect Controls window:

◆ In the Effect Controls window, click the tab for the layer that contains the effects you want to view.

  The name tab appears in front, and the effect properties appear in the window (**Figures 10.26** and **10.27**).

To expand and collapse effects:

1. *Do either of the following:*
   - ▲ In the Effect Controls window, click the triangle next to the effect name to expand or collapse the property controls.
   - ▲ With the Effect Controls window selected, press the grave accent (`).

   This expands or collapses the effect's main heading but not individual effect properties (**Figures 10.28** and **10.29**).
2. To expand or collapse individual property controls, click the triangle next to the property name.

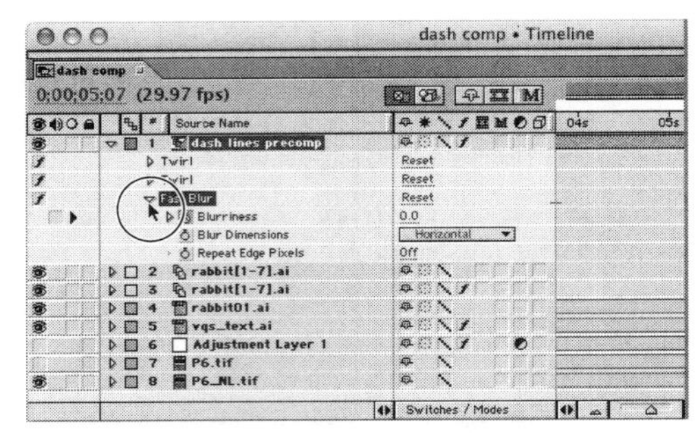

Figure 10.28 Click the triangle next to an effect's name or select the effect and press the grave accent (`) to expand...

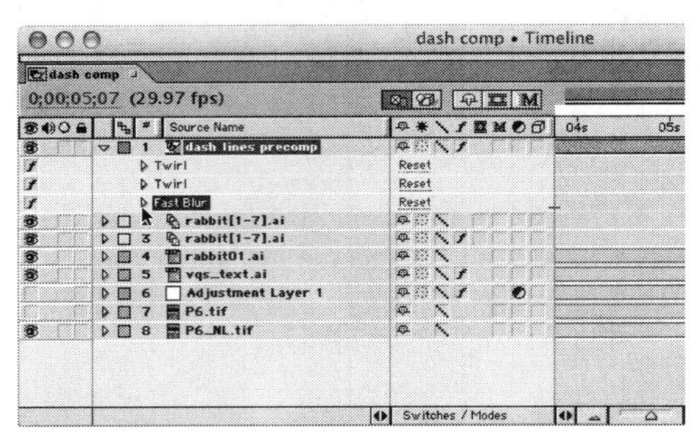

Figure 10.29 ...and collapse the effect property.

To select previous and next effects:

- With the Effect Controls window selected, *do one of the following:*
  - ▲ To select the next effect, press the down arrow.
  - ▲ To select the previous effect, press the up arrow.

✔ Tip

- Pressing the grave accent (`) expands items in the Effect Controls window only when the window is selected; when the Timeline window is selected, the same shortcut expands layers in the Timeline window's layer outline.

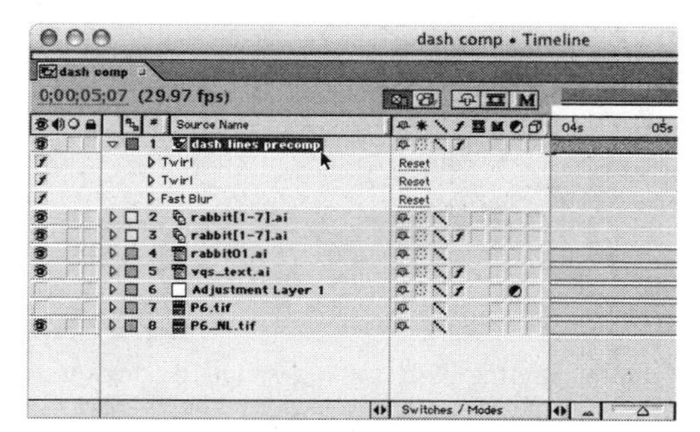

Figure 10.30 Select a layer...

Figure 10.31 ...and choose Effect > Remove All. Or use the keyboard shortcut...

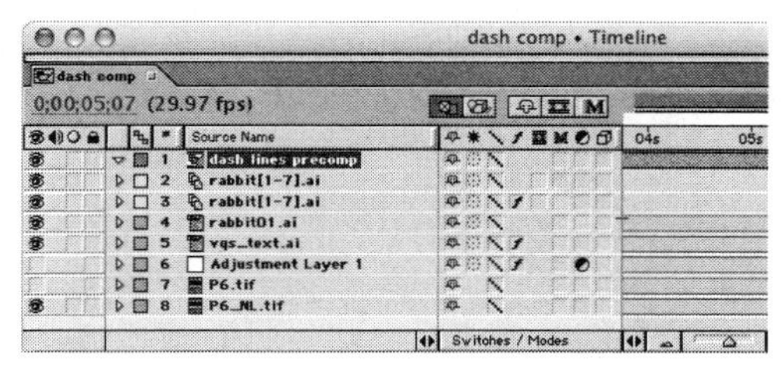

Figure 10.32 ...and the effects will be removed. (The expanded layer outline is shown for purposes of illustration.)

Removing and Resetting Effects

If you don't like an effect, remove it. If you need to restore the default settings, reset them.

To remove an effect:

1. In the Effect Controls window, select the name of an effect.
2. Press Delete (Mac) or Backspace (Windows).

   The effect is removed.

To remove all effects for a layer:

1. Select a layer containing one or more effects (**Figure 10.30**).
2. Choose Effect > Remove All, or press Shift-Command-E (Mac) or Shift-Ctrl-E (Windows) (**Figure 10.31**).

   All effects are removed from the layer (**Figure 10.32**).

To reset an effect to its default settings:

Do either of the following:

- In the Switches panel of the expanded Layer window, click Reset for the effect.
- For the effect in the Effect Controls window, click Reset (**Figure 10.33**).

  All the values for the effect are restored to the defaults.

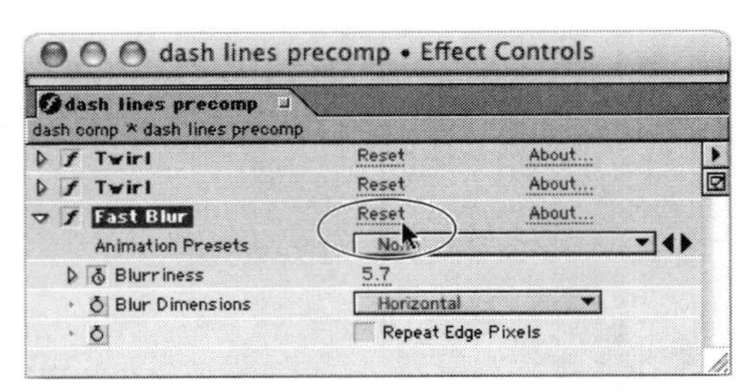

Figure 10.33 In the Effect Controls window, clicking Reset returns all of the effect's properties to their defaults.

✔ Tip

- In addition to a Reset button, each effect includes an About button that displays the name and version number of each effect. This is handy when you need to verify the version, or if you're working on an unfamiliar system. A handful of effects also include a button to access additional options not listed in the Effect Controls window. Depending on the effect, the button is labeled Options, Edit Text, or the like.

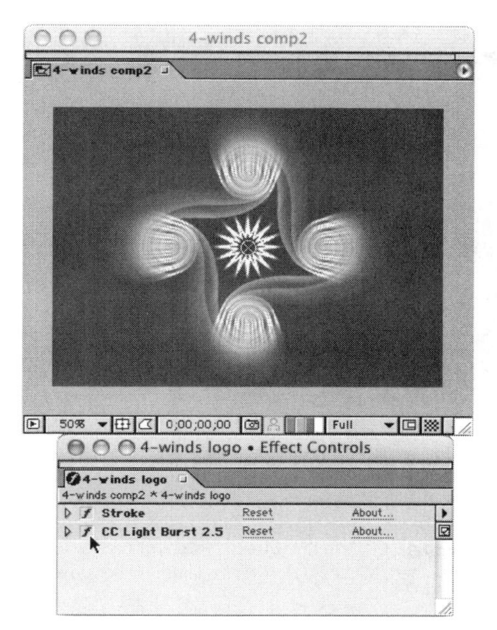

Figure 10.34 In the Effect Controls window, clicking the Effect icon next to the effect name...

Figure 10.35 ...toggles the icon off and disables the effect.

Disabling Effects Temporarily

You can turn off effects temporarily without removing them from the layer. Doing so is helpful when you want to see a single effect without other effects obscuring your view. Once you're satisfied with an effect's settings, you may want to disable it to speed up frame rendering.

To disable and enable individual effects:

- In the Timeline window or the Effect Controls window, click the Effect icon next to the effect's name.

  When the icon is visible, the effect is enabled; when the icon is hidden, the effect is disabled (**Figures 10.34** and **10.35**).

To disable and enable all effects in a layer:

- In the Switches/Modes panel of the Timeline window, click the Effect icon next to a layer.

  When the icon is visible, all effects for the layer are enabled; when the icon is hidden, all effects are disabled (**Figures 10.36** and **10.37**).

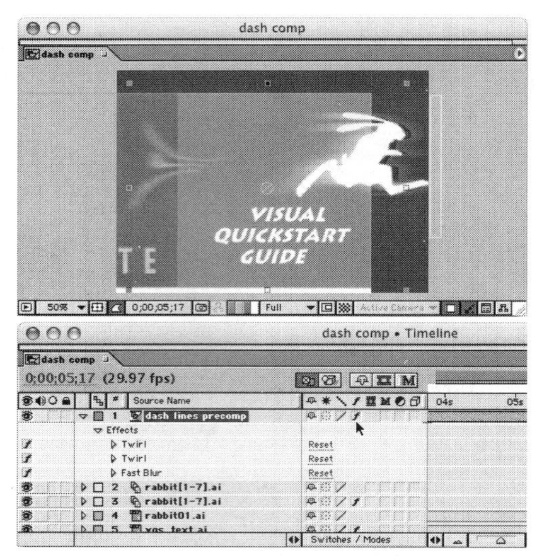

Figure 10.36 Clicking the Effect switch for a layer in the Switches/Modes panel of the Timeline window...

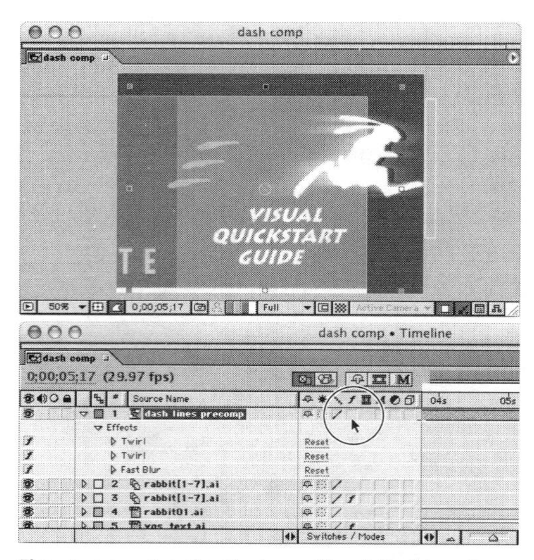

Figure 10.37 ...toggles the icon off and disables all effects contained by the layer.

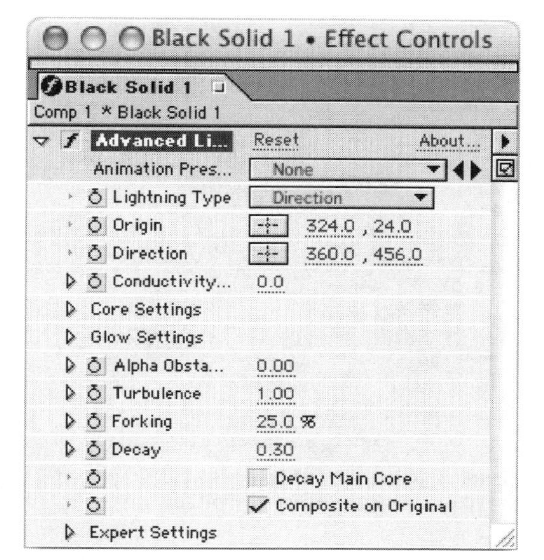

Figure 10.38 The Effect Controls window furnishes you with a convenient alternative to the effect property controls in the layer outline, especially when the effect includes special graphical controls.

Adjusting Effects in the Effect Controls Window

Although you can adjust effect properties in the layer outline just as you would any other layer property (using techniques covered in Chapter 7) the roomier Effect Controls window can accommodate larger, more graphical controls for several effect properties (**Figure 10.38**). The following sections describe how to use several common controls for adjusting color, angle, value, and effect point.

Of course, covering every possible graphical control is beyond the scope of this chapter. Other effects may offer a color range control (Hue/Saturation); a grid of control points (Mesh Warp); a histogram (Levels); or other graphs, such as those that represent an image's input/output levels (Curves) or an audio layer's frequency response (Parametric EQ). Third-party plug-ins may offer other exotic controls. Consult the documentation for each effect for detailed information on its individual controls.

Setting Color in the Effect Controls Window

The Effect Controls window allows you to choose colors by selecting a color swatch to open a color picker, or by selecting an eyedropper to sample a screen color.

To set the color using a color picker:

1. For an effect in the Effect Controls window, click the color swatch (**Figure 10.39**).

   A color picker appears (**Figure 10.40**).

2. Use the controls in the color picker to select a color.

   The particular controls differ, depending on your platform.

3. Click OK to close the color picker.

   The color you selected appears in the color swatch for the effect property.

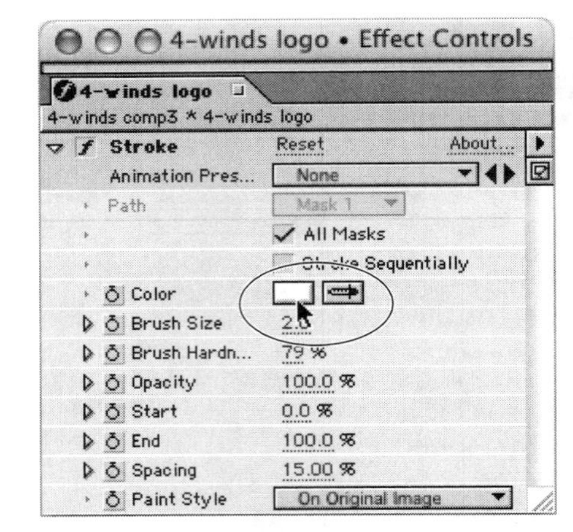

Figure 10.39 In the Effect Controls window, click the color swatch to open a color picker.

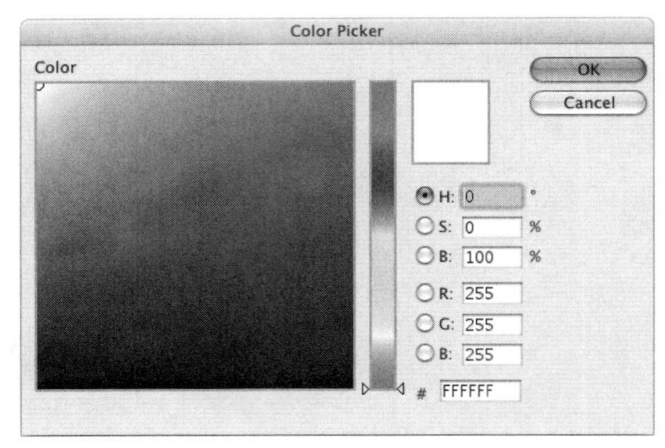

Figure 10.40 Choose a color using the color picker.

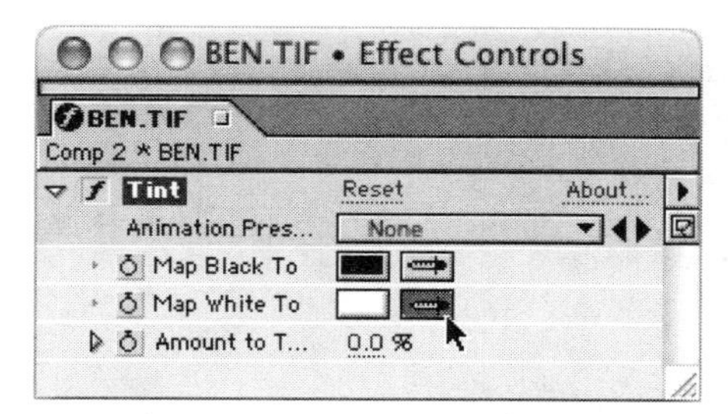

Figure 10.41 In the Effect Controls window, click the Eyedropper button.

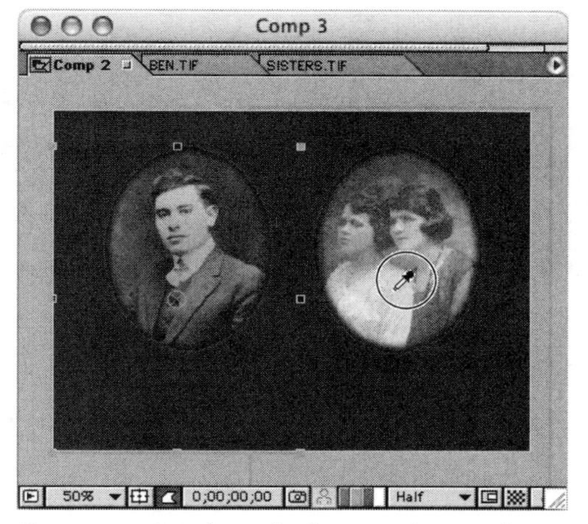

Figure 10.42 Sample a color from anywhere on the screen. In this example, colors from the second image are sampled to tint the first image.

To set the color using the Eyedropper tool:

1. In the Effect Controls window, click the Eyedropper button (**Figure 10.41**).
2. Position the cursor over a color onscreen.

   The mouse pointer appears as an Eyedropper icon (**Figure 10.42**).
3. Click a color to sample it.

   The color you sampled appears in the color swatch for the effect property.

✔ Tip

- By default, After Effects uses its own color picker for selecting colors. However, you can have After Effects use your system's color picker by selecting the appropriate option in the General panel of the Preferences dialog box.

Setting Values in the Effect Controls Window

You can set many effect properties numerically via scrubbable hot text (dragging on an underlined value) or by using a contextual menu to open a value dialog box (see Chapter 7). Alternatively, you can use a Value slider. The range of values represented by the slider doesn't necessarily represent the maximum value range for the effect property. If necessary, you can change the slider's range.

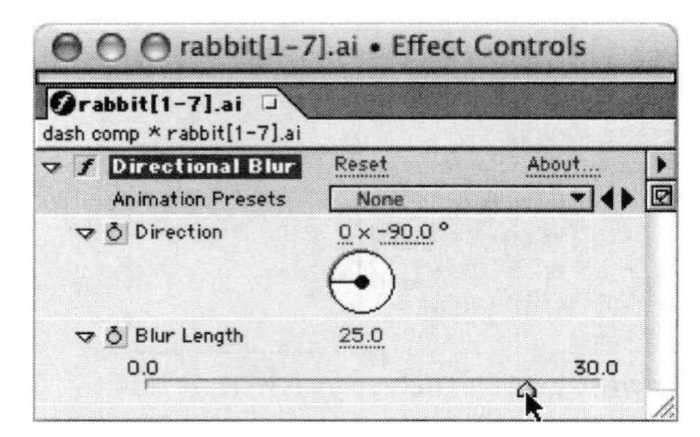

Figure 10.43 Drag a slider to change an effect property value.

To set values using a slider:

1. If necessary, click the triangle next to the name of the layer property to reveal a slider control.
2. Drag the slider left or right to change the value of the property (**Figure 10.43**).

   The current numeric value appears as an underlined number next to the effect property.

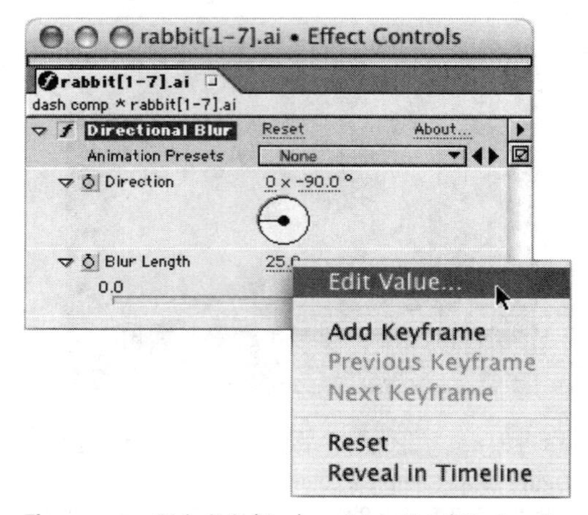

Figure 10.44 Ctrl-click (Mac) or right-click (Windows) the property value and choose Edit Value.

To change the range of the Value slider:

1. Ctrl-click (Mac) or right-click (Windows) the underlined value number next to the layer property and choose Edit Value (**Figure 10.44**).

   A Value dialog box appears. The maximum range possible for the values appears in the dialog box.
2. In the Slider Range fields of the property's Value dialog box, enter the lowest and highest values you want the slider to represent (**Figure 10.45**).
3. Click OK to close the dialog box.

   The slider range reflects the values you entered.

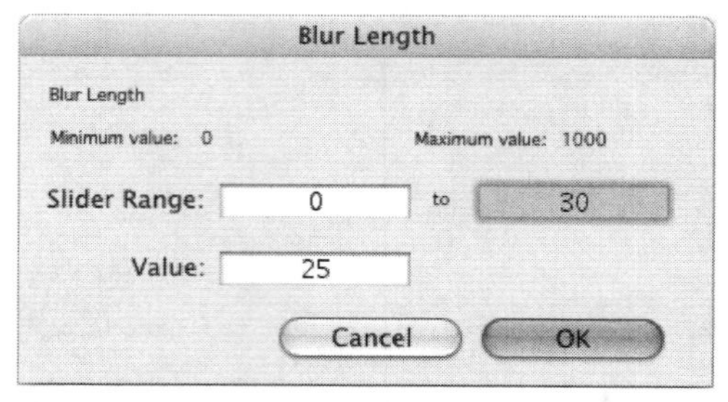

Figure 10.45 In the Value dialog box, enter a new range for the slider.

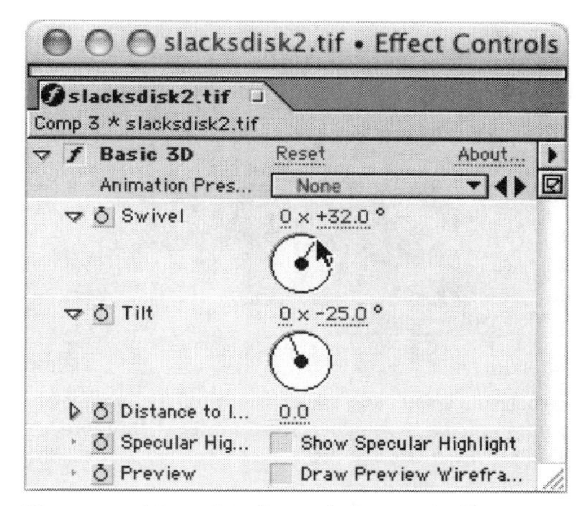

Figure 10.46 Dragging the angle line works like turning a knob. Drag it to change the angle value for an effect property.

Figure 10.47 In this example, adjusting the Basic 3D effect's Tilt and Swivel properties makes this flat scanned image of a CD look more three-dimensional.

Setting the Angle in the Effect Controls Window

In the Effect Controls window, you can enter the angle for an effect property numerically or by using an angle controller. Like slider controls, angle controllers allow you to continually adjust properties. Dragging the controller is a lot like turning a knob: The angle of the line gives you a visual indication of the angle of the effect property.

To set an angle:

1. For an effect in the Effect Controls window, click the triangle next to an angle property to reveal an angle controller.
2. In the angle controller, *do either of the following*:
   - ▲ Click inside the angle controller circle to move the angle line to that position.
   - ▲ Drag the angle line to a new position (**Figure 10.46**).

   The underlined numbers above the angle controller circle display the angle value. The layer reflects your adjustments (**Figure 10.47**).

✔ Tips

- To set angles greater than 360 degrees, drag the angle line more than one revolution.
- Once you start dragging, you may drag the cursor outside the angle controller to move it with greater precision.

Setting an Effect Point

An *effect point* represents the position of an effect on a layer: It can be the focus of a Lens Flare effect, the center point of a Reflection effect, or the starting point for Path Text. Some effects require more than one effect point, such as the start and end of a Stroke effect or the four corners of the Corner Pin effect.

You can set the effect point with the Effect Controls window's Effect Point button, or by manipulating it in the Composition or Layer window. Because effects are applied to a layer, the coordinates of an effect point refer to the layer, not the composition.

When you animate the effect point over time, you can view and manipulate its path in the Layer window just as you would adjust an anchor point path or motion path in the Composition window (**Figure 10.48**). (See Chapter 15, "Keyframe Interpolation," for more about adjusting the motion path.) In most ways, the effect point path works just like any other kind of motion path. Unlike a layer's position, however, the effect point's coordinates are unaffected by the layer's anchor point (see Chapter 7).

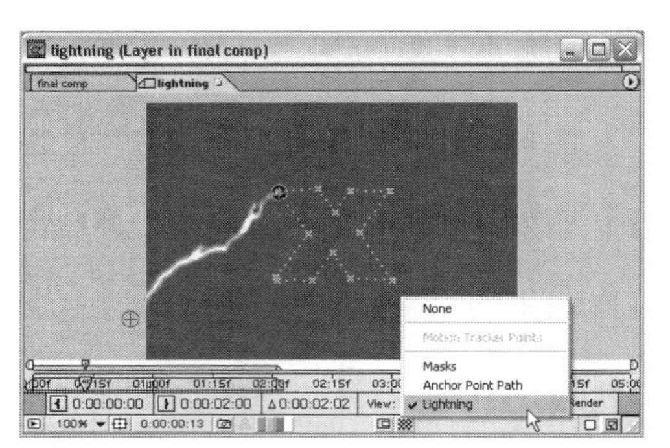

Figure 10.48 You can view and manipulate an effect point in the Layer window. See Chapter 15 for more about using motion paths.

To set an effect point with the Effect Point button:

1. In the Effect Controls window, click the Effect Point button for an effect property (**Figure 10.49**).

   Any effect property that uses layer coordinate values has an Effect Point button. When the button is active, the cursor becomes the Effect Point icon when positioned in a Composition or Layer window.

2. Position the cursor in a Composition or Layer window, and click to set the effect point (**Figure 10.50**).

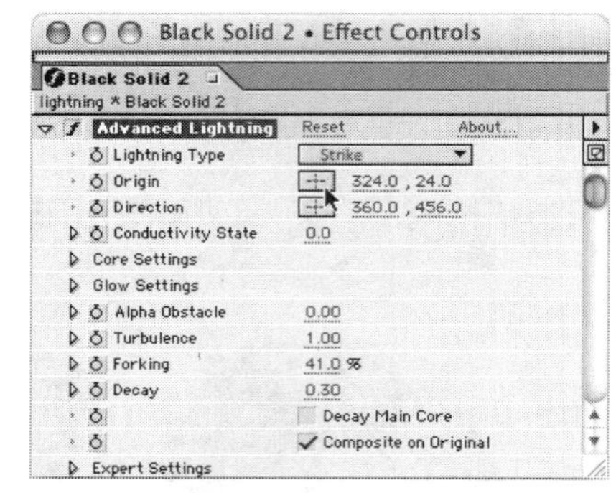

Figure 10.49 Click the effect Point button for an effect property.

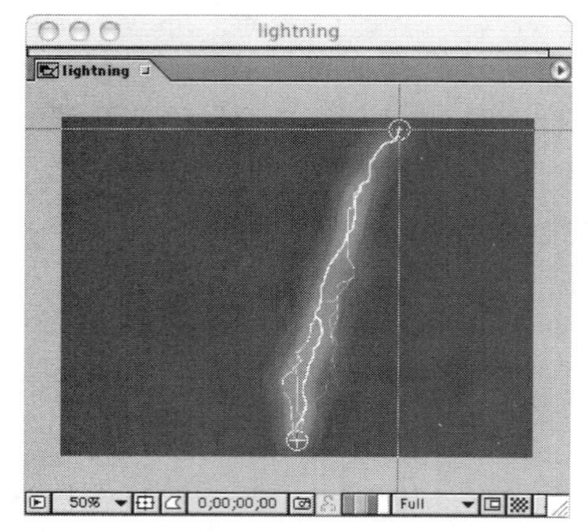

Figure 10.50 Position the cursor in a Layer or Comp window (shown here), and click to set the effect point.

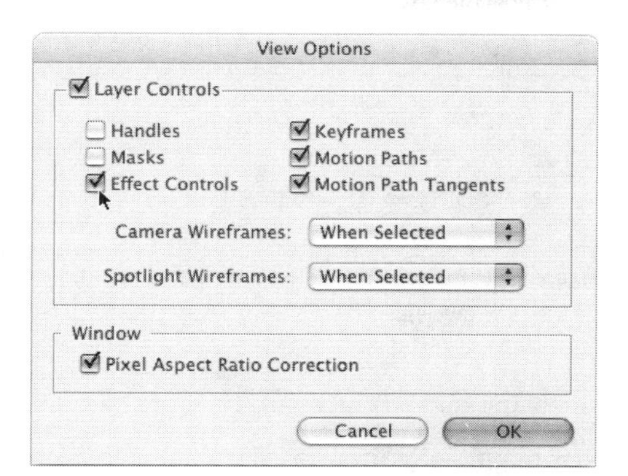

Figure 10.51 Make sure Effect Controls is checked in the Composition window's View Options dialog box...

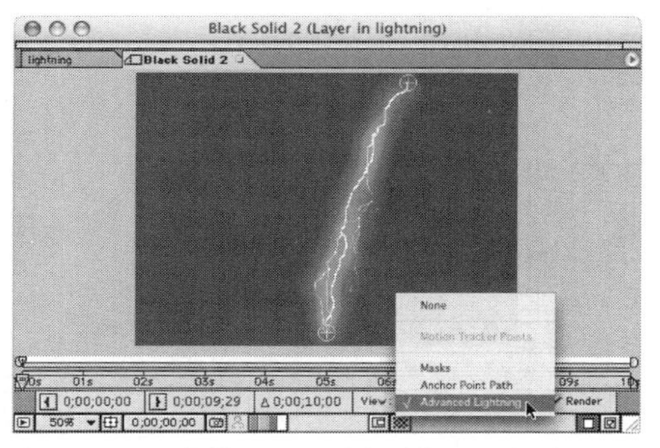

Figure 10.52 ...or the name of the effect is checked in the Layer window.

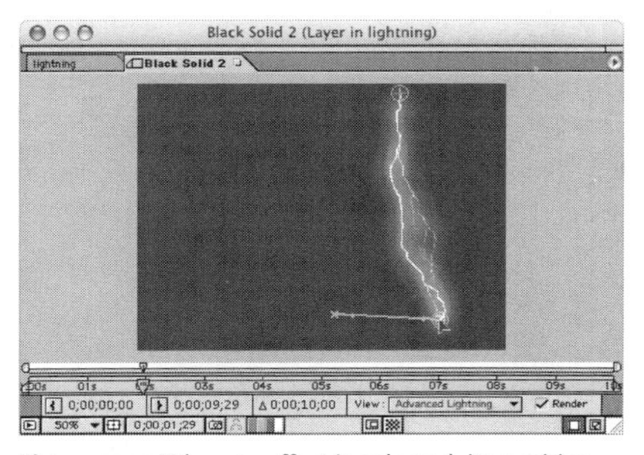

Figure 10.53 When an effect is selected, its position effect points appear in the Composition window and its motion path is visible in the Layer window (shown here). In this example, the effect points correspond to the ends of the lightning effect.

The coordinate values reflect the effect point you chose. Even if you clicked the Effect Point icon in the Composition window, the coordinate values correspond to the coordinate system of the layer that contains the effect.

To set the effect point by dragging in the Composition or Layer window:

1. To view the effect point in the Composition or Layer window, *do one of the following:*
   - ▲ In the Composition window's View Options dialog box, make sure Effect Controls is checked (**Figure 10.51**).
   - ▲ In the Layer window menu, make sure the name of the effect is checked (**Figure 10.52**).
2. In the Effect Controls window, click the name of the effect whose effect point value you want to change.

   In the Composition or Layer window, a crosshairs icon indicates the position of each effect point at the current time. The Layer window also shows the path of a selected effect point property (**Figure 10.53**).
3. In the Composition window or Layer window, drag the Effect Point icon to a new position (**Figure 10.54**).

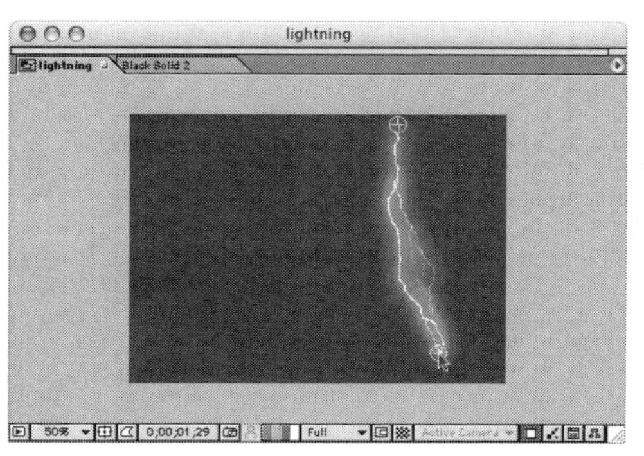

Figure 10.54 In the Composition window, drag the Effect Point icon to a new position.

Saving and Applying Effect Presets

Occasionally, you'll create a complex effect that you're particularly proud of or that you need to reuse frequently. You can save a combination of effect settings—including keyframes—as a *preset*.

You save preset effects as independent, cross-platform files, which use an `.ffx` extension. Because preset effects are independent files, you can store them separately from your project so that you can easily access them for other projects or share them with other After Effects artists. To further facilitate your work, After Effects makes it possible for you to access your saved presets via the Animation > Recent Animation Presets menu command.

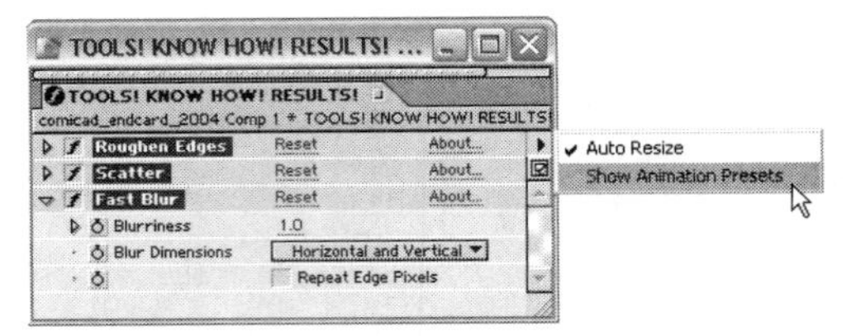

Figure 10.55 In the Effect Controls window's menu, choose Show Animation Presets.

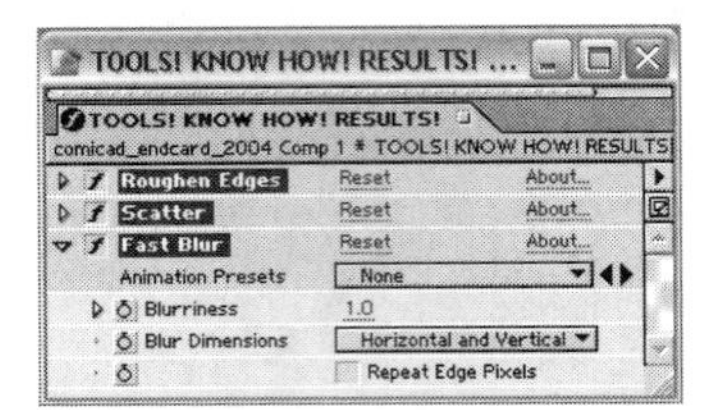

Figure 10.56 An Animation Presets pull-down menu appears.

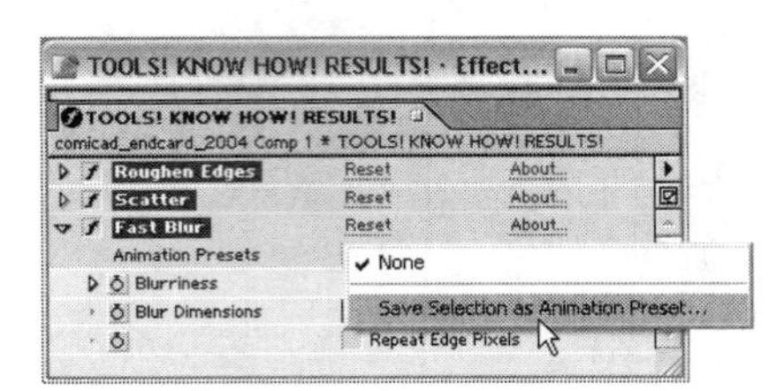

Figure 10.57 In the Effect Controls window, select one or more of the effects you applied to the layer, and choose Save Selection as Animation Preset in the Animation Presets pull-down menu...

To view presets in the Effect Controls window:

- In the Effect Controls window's menu, select Show Animation Presets (**Figure 10.55**).

  When the option is selected, a layer's effects listed in the Effect Controls window include an Animation Presets pull-down menu (**Figure 10.56**); otherwise the pull-down menu is hidden.

To save effects as a preset:

1. Apply one or more effects to a layer in the composition.

   If you want, animate them over time (using techniques explained in Chapter 7).

2. In the Effect Controls window, select one or more of the effects you applied to the layer.

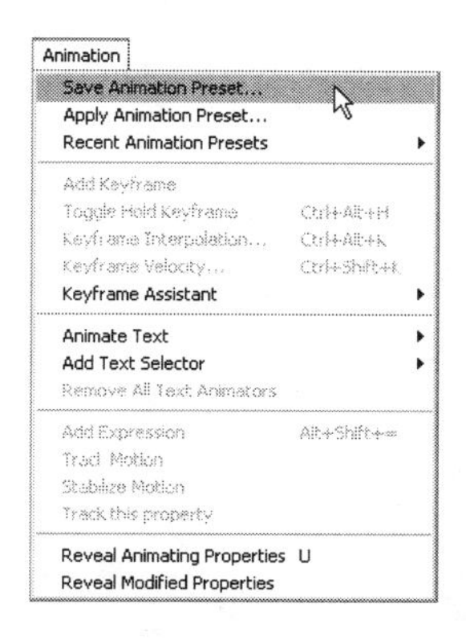

Figure 10.58 ...or choose Animation > Save Animation Preset.

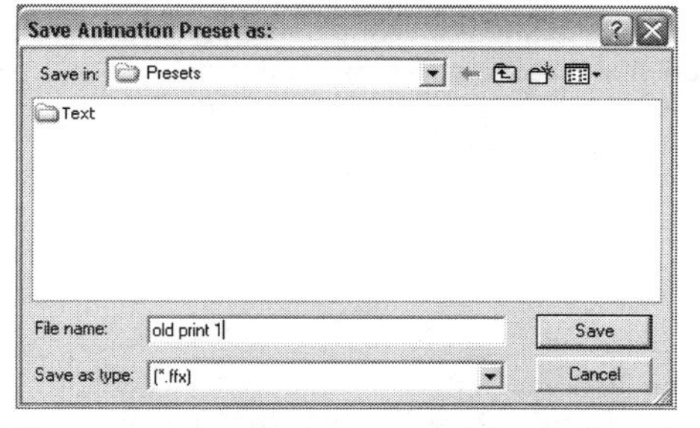

Figure 10.59 Specify the name and destination of the preset file in the "Save Animation Preset as" dialog box.

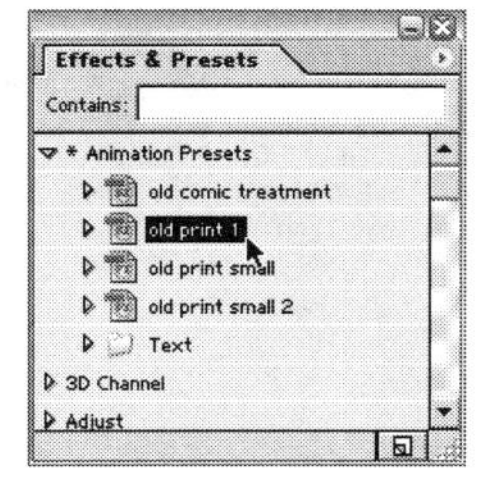

Figure 10.60 Select a layer, and apply a preset by using an option in the Animation menu or by double-clicking the preset in the Effects & Presets palette (shown here).

3. *Do either of the following:*
   - ▲ In any effect's Animation Preset pull-down menu, choose Save Selection as Animation Preset (**Figure 10.57**).
   - ▲ Choose Animation > Save Animation Preset (**Figure 10.58**).

   A "Save Animation Preset as" dialog box appears.
4. In the "Save Animation Preset as" dialog box, specify the name and destination of the preset file (**Figure 10.59**).

   The file uses the `.ffx` extension.
5. Click Save to save the settings and close the dialog box.

   The preset is added to the appropriate categories in the Effects & Presets palette.

To apply a preset effect:

1. Select the layers to which you want to apply a preset, and set the current time to where you want keyframes (if included in the preset) to begin.
2. *Do one of the following:*
   - ▲ In the Effects & Presets palette, double-click the name of the preset you want to apply to the selected layers (**Figure 10.60**).
   - ▲ Choose Animation > Apply Animation Preset.
   - ▲ Choose Animation > Apply Recent Preset, and select the name of a recently used preset.

   The preset is applied to the selected layers. Any animated properties' keyframes begin at the current time.

To apply an effect or preset by dragging:

1. In the Effects & Presets palette, locate and select the effect or preset you want to apply.
2. Drag the selected effect or preset to *any of the following places:*
   - ▲ The target layer's name in the Timeline window
   - ▲ The target layer's effect list heading in the Timeline window
   - ▲ Any position in the target layer's list of effects in the Timeline window (**Figure 10.61**)
   - ▲ The target layer's list of effects in the Effect Controls palette (**Figure 10.62**)
   - ▲ The target layer in the Comp window; the Info palette displays the name of the currently targeted layer as you drag over it (**Figure 10.63**)

   When you release the mouse, the effect is added to the layer.

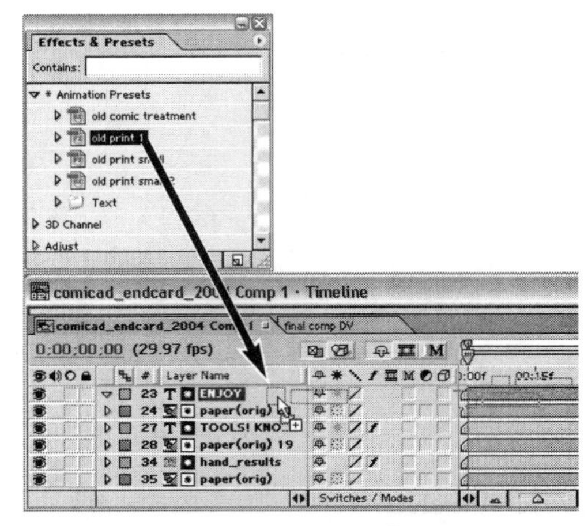

Figure 10.61 You can also drag an effect or presets icon to the target layer in the Timeline, dropping it on its name, effect property heading, or any position in its effect list.

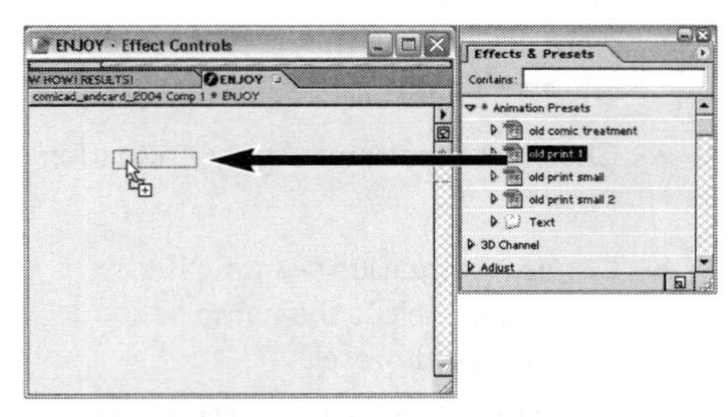

Figure 10.62 Alternatively, you can drag the effect to the layer's effect list in the Effect Controls palette...

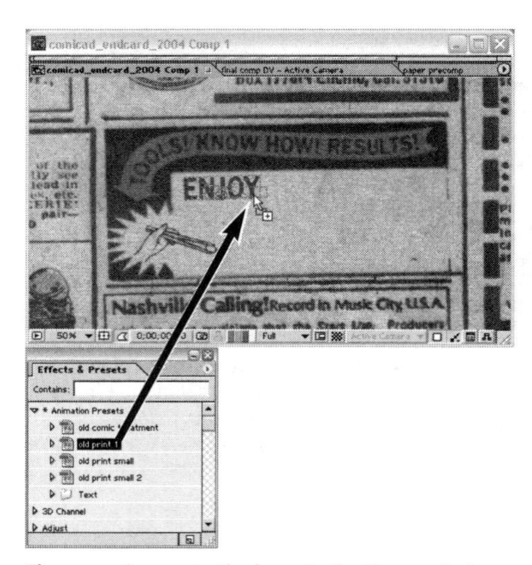

Figure 10.63 ... or to the layer in the Comp window (use the Info palette to verify you have targeted the proper layer).

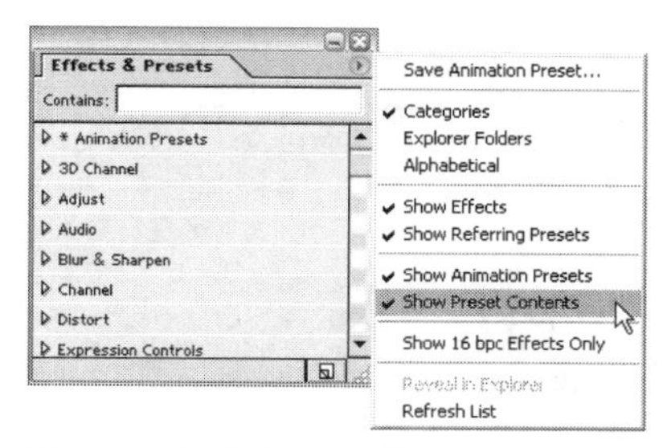

Figure 10.64 Make sure Show Preset Contents is checked.

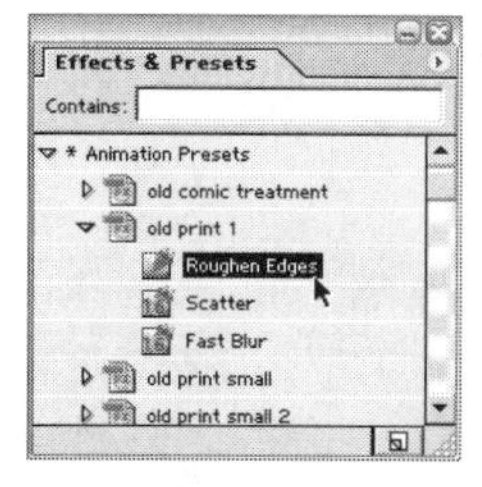

Figure 10.65 In the Effects & Presets palette, double-click an individual effect in a preset...

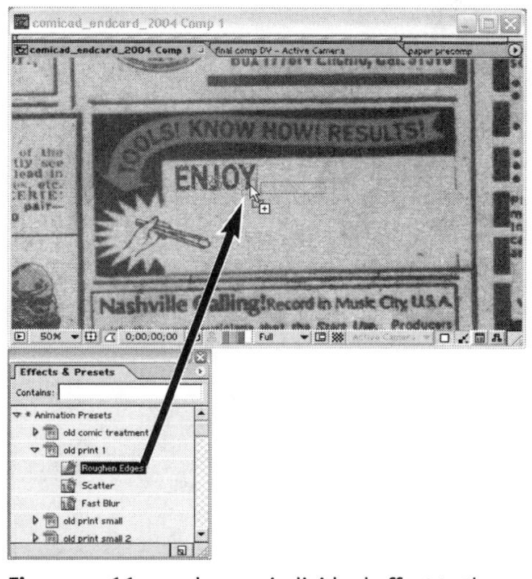

Figure 10.66 ... or drag an individual effect to the target layer.

To apply an animation preset's effect only:

1. In the Effects & Presets palette's menu, make sure Show Preset Contents is checked (**Figure 10.64**).

   In the Effects & Presets palette, each preset lists its constituent effects. Click the triangle next to the preset's name to see the effects it contains.

2. *Do either of the following:*

   - Select the target layer, and double-click the individual effect in the Effects & Presets palette (**Figure 10.65**).
   - Drag the effect from the Effects & Presets palette to the targeted layer (**Figure 10.66**).

   The individual effect is applied to the layer.

Copying and Pasting Effects

To save time and labor, you can copy effects from one layer into another.

To copy a layer's effects into another layer:

1. In the Effect Controls window, select one or more effects (**Figure 10.67**).
2. Select Edit > Copy, or press Command-C (Mac) or Ctrl-C (Windows).
3. In the Timeline window, select one or more layers (**Figure 10.68**).
4. Choose Edit > Paste, or press Command-V (Mac) or Ctrl-V (Windows).

   The selected layer contains the pasted effects; however, it doesn't contain the same keyframes (**Figure 10.69**).

✔ Tip

- You can also copy and paste keyframes from one property to another property that uses compatible values. For example, you could copy position keyframes to an Effect Point property. See Chapter 7 to review.

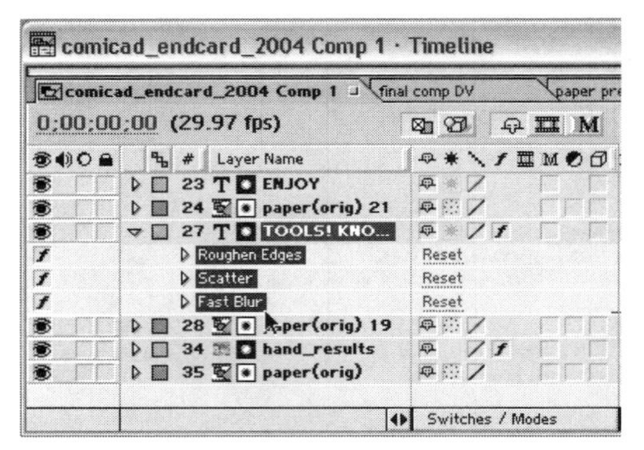

Figure 10.67 In the Effect Controls window, select one or more effects, and press Command-C (Mac) or Ctrl-C (Windows).

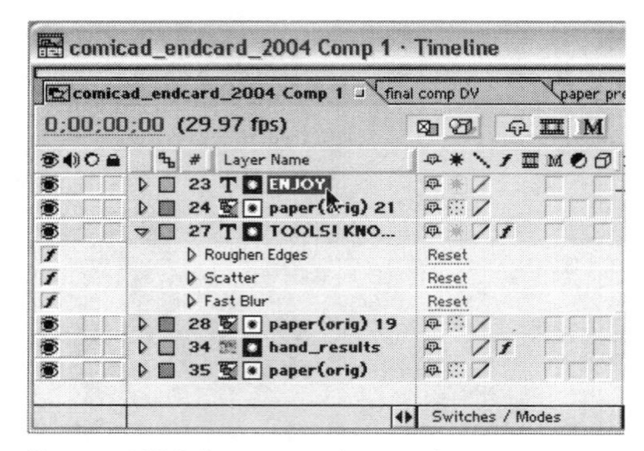

Figure 10.68 Select a target layer and press Command-V (Mac) or Ctrl-V (Windows).

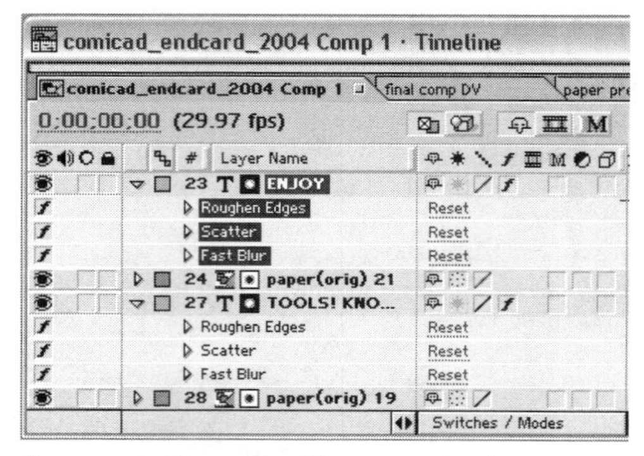

Figure 10.69 The selected layer contains the pasted effects, but it doesn't contain the same keyframes. (You can press E to view the selected layer's effects in the layer outline.)

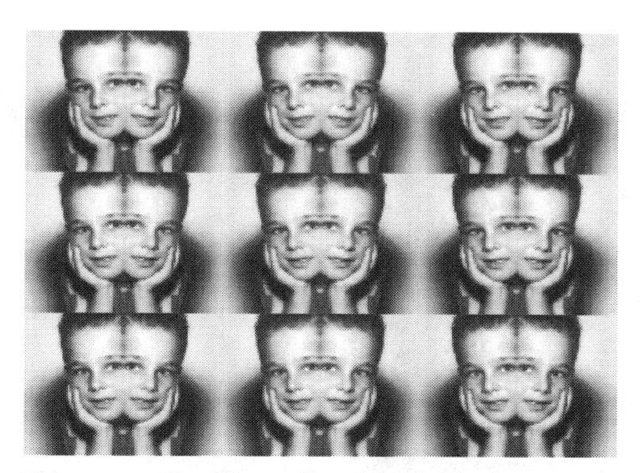

Figure 10.70 The Mirror effect followed by the Motion Tile effect results in this image...

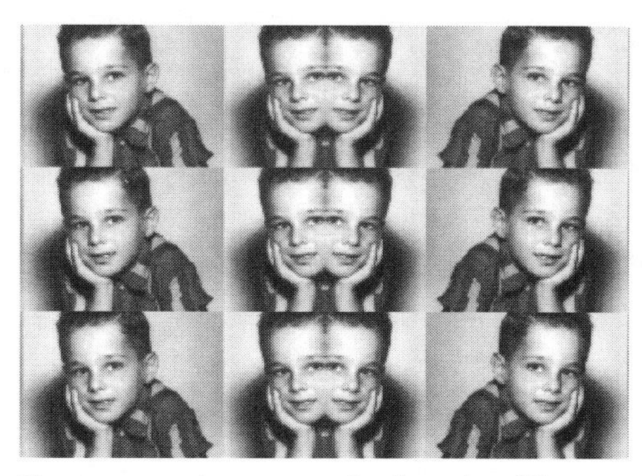

Figure 10.71 ...whereas reversing the order of the effects results in this image.

Applying Multiple Effects

The Effect Controls window lists effects in the order you add them, from top to bottom. Because each effect is applied to the result of the one above it, changing the order of effects can change the final appearance (or sound) of the layer (**Figures 10.70** and **10.71**). You can reorder effects in the Effect Controls window as well as directly in the layer outline of the Timeline window.

To reorder effects:

1. In the Effect Controls window or in the layer outline of the Timeline window, drag the name of an effect up or down to a new position in the effect stacking order.

   A dark horizontal line indicates the effect's new position when you release the mouse (**Figure 10.72**).

2. Release the mouse button to place the effect in its new position in the list (**Figure 10.73**).

   Changing the order of effects in the list changes the order in which they're applied to the layer.

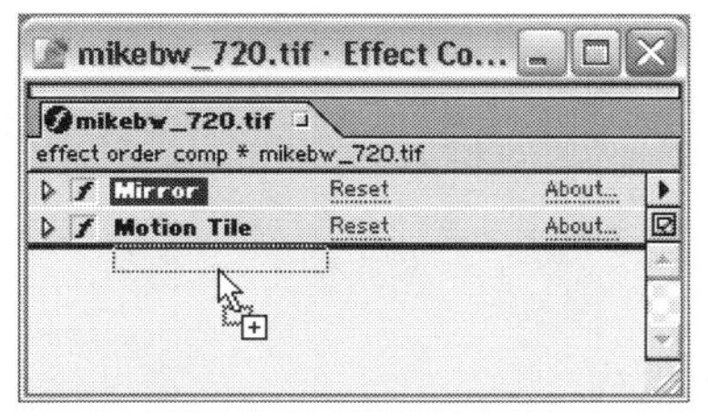

Figure 10.72 Drag the name of an effect up or down to a new position in the stacking order. A dark line indicates the effect's new position.

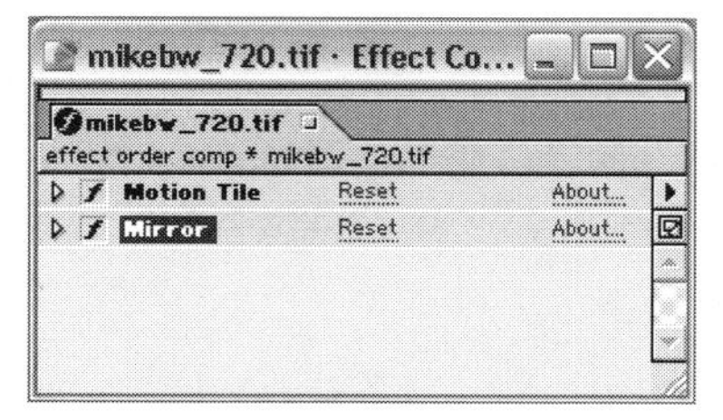

Figure 10.73 Release the mouse to place the effect in its new position in the list.

Applying Effects to an Adjustment Layer

As you'll recall from Chapter 5, "Layer Basics," the effects contained in an adjustment layer are applied to all the layers below it. You save time and effort by applying effects to a single layer rather than multiple layers. You can create an adjustment layer within After Effects; you can also convert a visual layer into an adjustment layer.

Although the concept of adjustment layers is simple enough, it's worth revisiting the topic to examine some of the possibilities it affords. In this section, you'll learn how you can limit the effects of an adjustment layer by using a mask or by employing a layer's existing alpha channel.

Although a mask ordinarily modifies a layer's alpha channel to define opaque and transparent areas of a layer's image, applying a mask to an adjustment layer—which by definition can't contain an image—allows the masked area of the effect to influence the lower layers (the areas outside the mask remain unaffected) (**Figure 10.74**).

You can also use the alpha channel of another layer in a similar manner, by converting the layer to an adjustment layer. As an adjustment layer, its image is ignored. However, any effects you add to the layer are restricted to the areas defined by its alpha channel.

Figure 10.74 Masking an adjustment layer restricts its effects. Here, the Blur and Brightness & Contrast filters affect only masked areas (defined by an elliptical mask that's inverted).

Figure 10.75 Clicking the Adjustment Layer switch converts a layer into an adjustment layer.

Figure 10.76 Here a solid containing the Invert effect has been converted into an adjustment layer. The solid isn't visible, but its effect alters the underlying layers, making the left side of the image look like a negative.

To convert a layer to an adjustment layer, and vice versa:

- In the Switches area of the Timeline window, click the Adjustment Layer switch for the layer you want to convert to make the icon appear or disappear.

  When the Adjustment Layer icon is visible, the layer functions as an adjustment layer—that is, its image disappears from the Composition window, and its effects are applied to lower layers (**Figures 10.75** and **10.76**).

  When the Adjustment Layer icon isn't visible, the layer functions as a standard layer, and its image appears in the composition. If the adjustment layer was created in After Effects, it becomes a solid layer. Any effects contained by the layer are applied only to that layer.

Understanding Compound Effects

Effects that require two layers to operate are called *compound effects*. Rather than appear within a separate category, compound effects are instead distributed among effects in various categories. Although some compound effects use the word *compound* in their names, you can identify others only by knowing their controls.

As with other effects, you apply compound effects to the layers you want to alter. Unlike other effects, however, compound effects rely on a second layer—an effect source or modifying layer—which acts as a kind of map for the effect. Typically, this takes the form of a grayscale image because many compound effects are based on the modifying layer's brightness levels. In a Compound Blur effect, for example, the brightness levels of the modifying layer determine the placement and intensity of the blurry areas of the target layer (see "Using the Compound Blur Effect" in Chapter 11). The modifying layer can be a still image, movie, or nested composition (**Figure 10.77**).

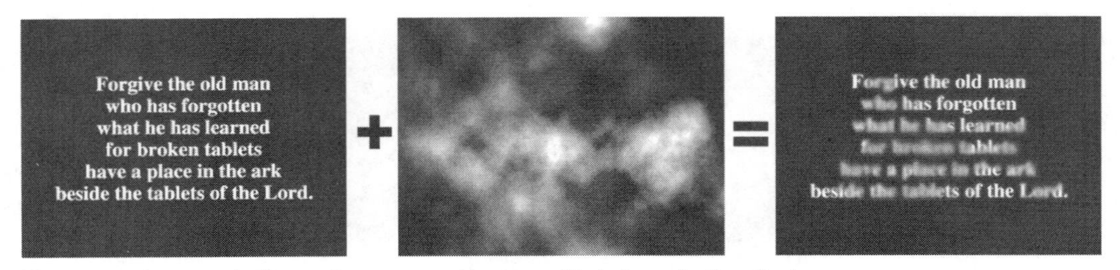

Figure 10.77 Compound effects rely on a second layer as a kind of map for the effect.

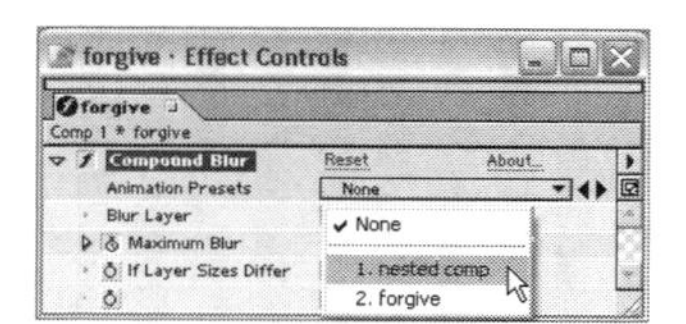

Figure 10.78 Compound effects contain a pull-down menu to specify the modifying layer, or effect source.

Using Compound Effects

Due to their peculiar nature, compound effects have certain unique features. This section summarizes those attributes; Chapter 11 describes the steps entailed in creating a few simple compound effects. More complex techniques are addressed in Chapter 17.

Specifying an effect source

In compound effects, you must use a pull-down menu to specify the modifying layer (**Figure 10.78**). Although the modifying layer must be included in the composition to appear in the list, you usually switch off its video in the Timeline window. This is necessary because the modifying layer appears in the composition only as an effect source, not a visible layer.

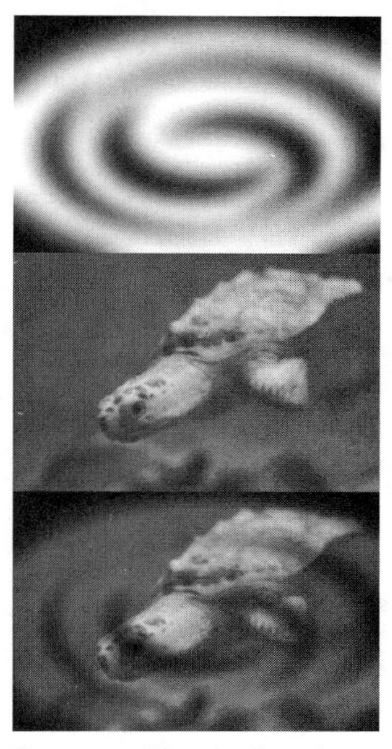

Figure 10.79 When the dimensions of the modifying layer match those of the layer it affects, the final result is more predictable. This example shows the effect source, target image, and result of the Gradient Wipe effect.

Resolving size differences between source and target layers

Because compound effects use the pixels of the modifying layer as a map, that layer's dimensions should match the layer it affects (**Figure 10.79**). This way, your results will be more predictable and easier to control. If the dimensions of the two layers don't match, compound effects offer several ways to compensate (**Figure 10.80**). Keep in mind, however, that although the following options can work to your advantage, they can also produce unwanted results:

continues on next page

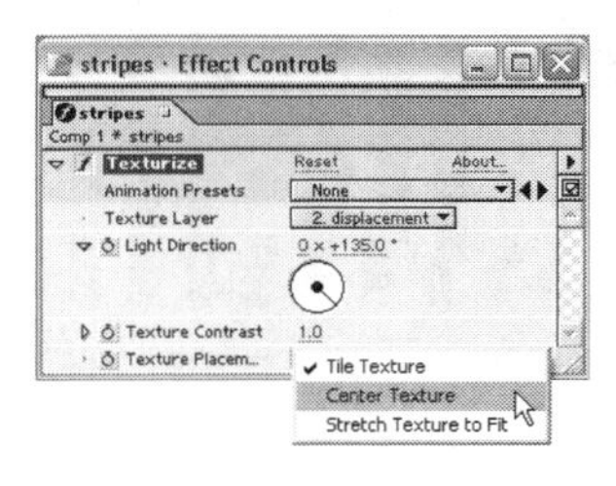

Figure 10.80 If the dimensions of the two layers don't match, compound effects offer ways to compensate for the difference.

Tile repeats the modifying layer to map the entire target layer. In some cases, the modifying layer won't tile evenly, cutting off some tiles. If images don't tile seamlessly, the edges may be evident in the effect.

Center positions the modifying layer in the center of the target layer. If the modifying layer is smaller, the effect may appear to be cut off; if it's larger, the extraneous portions won't be used in the effect.

Stretch to Fit scales the modifying layer to match the dimensions of the target layer. Sometimes, this can distort the modifying layer or make it difficult to position.

Using a nested composition as the effect source

It's important to understand that the three placement options described previously don't alter the modifying layer itself, only the way its pixels are mapped to the target layer. Conversely, scaling or positioning the modifying layer in the composition doesn't influence the compound effect. This is the case because the compound effect refers directly to the effect source, before any mask, effect, or transform property changes occur (**Figures 10.81**, **10.82**, and **10.83**).

Figure 10.81 Compound effects refer directly to the effect source—before any mask, effect, or transform property changes have occurred. Apply the Displacement Map effect to this layer...

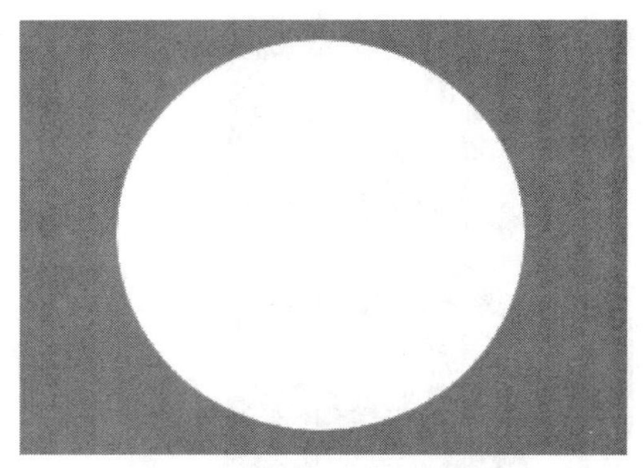

Figure 10.82 ...and use this layer as the effect source (the displacement map)...

Figure 10.83 ...and this is the result.

Figure 10.84 If a layer requires treatment before becoming an effect source, place it into another comp first. Here, the effect source is scaled and repositioned.

Figure 10.85 You must use the nested comp as the effect source to achieve the desired result.

If a layer needs to be scaled (or otherwise treated) before it becomes an effect source, place it into another composition first. The nested composition, in turn, can serve as the modifying layer for the compound effect. This way, you can make any necessary changes to the layer within a composition—before it becomes the effect source. And unlike the layer it contains, the dimensions of the composition can be set to match the compound effect's target layer. As a result, the nested composition—and the layer it contains—maps perfectly to the target layer of the compound effect (**Figures 10.84** and **10.85**).

If all this talk of nesting sounds complicated, don't worry: Chapter 17 revisits such topics as nesting and precomposing in greater detail.

Animating Effects

Apart from the fact that you can use the Effect Controls window to adjust values, animating effect properties is no different than animating any other properties. As you learned back in Chapter 7, once you activate the Stopwatch for a property, the procedure for creating keyframes is simple: Set the current time, set a property value, repeat.

Unlike transform and mask properties, however, each effect can contain numerous animated properties—a fact that can lead to an extremely long (and sometimes unwieldy) expanded layer outline or Effect Controls window. For this reason, you may want to take advantage of property features you overlooked in the past. Remember to use pop-up slider controls to avoid expanding the layer outline ad infinitum. You may also want to reacquaint yourself with the keyboard shortcuts for hiding properties from the layer outline (showing just the animated properties).

Better yet, learn how you can use the Effect Controls window to control the keyframing process. Now that the palette includes a Stopwatch icon, you can initiate the keyframing process right from the Effects Controls window. You can also use a contextual menu to set, remove, and navigate property keyframes.

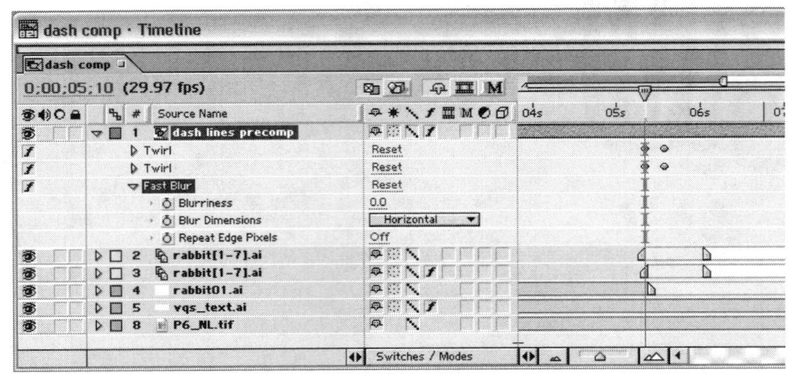

Figure 10.86 Set the current time to the frame at which you want to set an effect property keyframe.

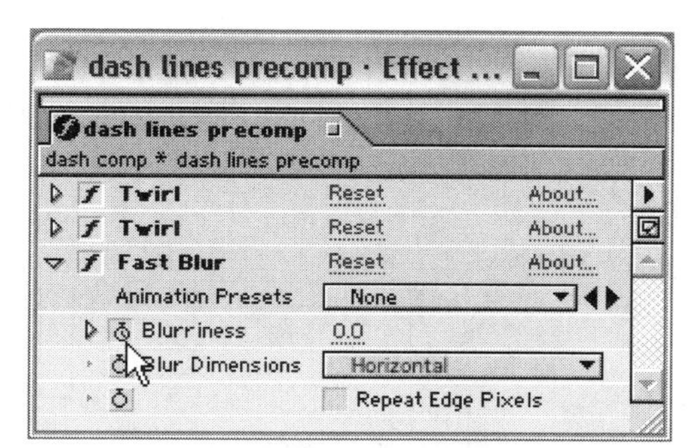

Figure 10.87 In the Effect Controls window or in the Timeline's layer outline (shown here), select the Stopwatch icon next to the effect property you want to keyframe.

To set keyframes from the Effect Controls window:

1. Select the layer containing the effect you want to keyframe, and reveal the effect in the Effect Controls window.
2. Set the current time to the frame at which you want to set an effect property keyframe (**Figure 10.86**).
3. In the Effect Controls window, select the Stopwatch icon next to the name of the property you want to animate (**Figure 10.87**).

   Doing so activates the keyframing process. In the Timeline window, a keyframe appears at the current time (**Figure 10.88**).
4. Adjust the value of the property in the Effect Controls window.
5. Set the current time to the point at which you want to set another keyframe.
6. Using the controls in the Effect Controls window, alter the property's values.

   In the Timeline, a new keyframe appears for the property at the current time.
7. Repeat steps 4 and 5 as needed.

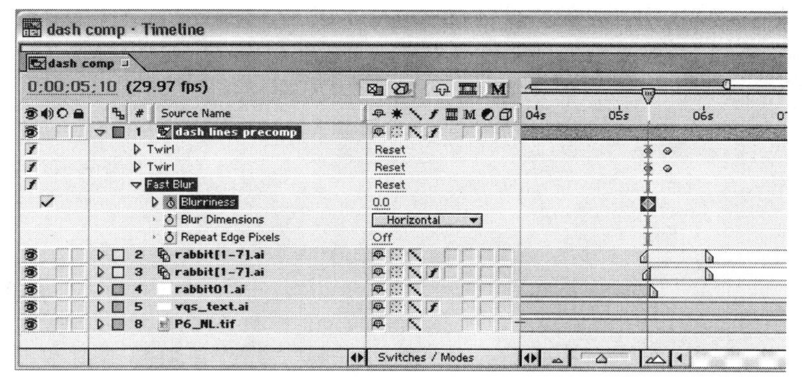

Figure 10.88 A keyframe appears at the current time. The layer outline shown here is expanded for the purpose of illustration; using the Effect Controls window lets you avoid using the layer outline.

To use a contextual menu to set and navigate keyframes:

1. In the Effect Controls window, Ctrl-click (Mac) or right-click (Windows) the name of an effect property to invoke a contextual menu (**Figure 10.89**).
2. In the contextual menu, *choose one of the following options:*

   Edit Value—Changes the property value at the current time numerically, or changes the range of a Value slider.

   Remove Keyframe—Available if the current time is cued to a keyframe. Removes the property's keyframe at the current time.

   Add Keyframe—Available if you *are not* cued to a keyframe. Adds a keyframe for the property at the current time. The keyframe uses interpolated values, unless and until you adjust the values.

   Previous Keyframe—Moves the current time to the previous keyframe (if one exists).

   Next Keyframe—Moves the current time to the next keyframe (if one exists).

   Reset—Resets the property to its default value for the current keyframe.

   Reveal in Timeline—Expands the layer outline to reveal the current keyframe in the Timeline window.

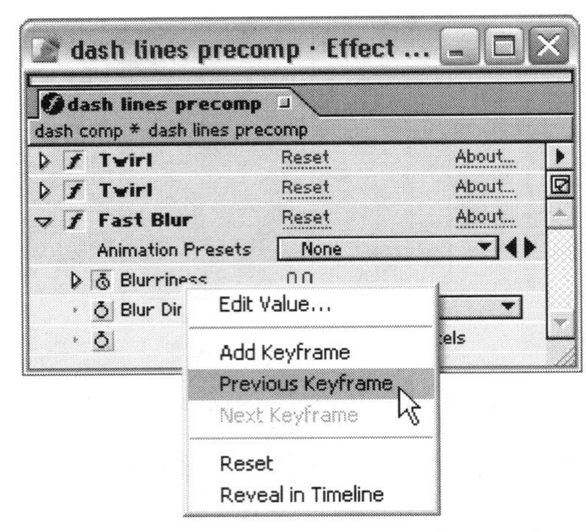

Figure 10.89 Ctrl-click (Mac) or right-click (Windows) the name of an effect property to invoke a contextual menu. In this figure, the current time isn't cued to a keyframe, so the Add Keyframe option is present. When the current time is cued to a keyframe, the Remove Keyframe option is available instead.

EFFECTS IN ACTION

This book can't hope to describe in detail each effect and how to apply it—much less the infinite iterations and combinations of these effects. Nor would it be useful to do so. Instead, this chapter briefly describes each effect category and then provides step-by-step instructions for using some prime examples of each. Focusing on standard effects—which, as you know, are available in both the Standard and the Professional versions—will also make the best use of limited space. Consequently, the chapter excludes examples from the 3D Channel and Matte Tools categories, which contain only Professional effects. And although the chapter lists Pro-only effects, it omits the effects users can download separately from the Adobe Web site as an incentive to register the software. When you download these plug-ins, they're installed in a separate folder within the After Effects Plug-Ins folder, but they appear in existing effects categories (albeit with the software developer's initials preceding the effect's name; for example, CC Radial Blur).

As you'll see, even the standard effects cover a vast range. Although this chapter can't provide ready-made recipes, it can encourage you to devise your own innovative applications for effects as well as inspire inventive combinations. For additional guidance, turn to After Effects' online documentation and to your own experiments.

3D Channel Effects

Effects in this category can use information saved in a number of 3D file formats, enabling you to composite scenes created in 3D software in After Effects.

Because 3D Channel effects are included in After Effects Pro only and appeal to a more select group of users, no examples are provided here.

3D Channel effects include:

- 3D Channel Extract (Pro only)
- Depth Matte (Pro only)
- Depth of Field (Pro only)
- Fog 3D (Pro only)
- ID Matte (Pro only)

Adjust Effects

Some readers will already be familiar with the effects in this category from working with Adobe Photoshop or similar image-editing software. The critical difference between these programs and After Effects is that After Effects' Adjust effects are nondestructive. As you learned in Chapter 3, "Managing Footage," nothing you do in After Effects actually alters the source files—something even Photoshop gurus may find liberating. You'll likely become accustomed to making many more adjustments to still images in After Effects and using Photoshop only for its unique advantages—retouching, cloning, selecting, and the like.

Adjust effects include the following:

- Auto Color
- Auto Contrast
- Auto Levels
- Brightness and Contrast
- Channel Mixer
- Color Balance
- Color Stabilizer (Pro only)
- Curves
- Hue/Saturation
- Levels
- Levels (Individual Controls)
- Photo Filter
- Posterize
- Threshold

Using the Levels Effect

Whether you're working in Photoshop or After Effects, you'll find Levels to be one of the most useful effects at your disposal. Although the online documentation provides an explanation of the effect, you may have a hard time deciphering the jargon and drawing out a useful method for working with Levels. The following explanation should help.

Reading the histogram

In the Levels effect's controls, you'll immediately notice a dark shape that resembles a silhouette of distant hills. This shape is a map, or graph, of all the pixels in the image, called a *histogram*. In the histogram, the darkest pixels appear on the left, and the brightest appear on the right. The height of the "mountains" represents the number of pixels at a given brightness level (**Figure 11.1**).

A high peak in the histogram indicates that a relatively large number of pixels share a brightness value. If the mountain range of your histogram spans the entire horizontal scale, that means your image contains a wide range of brightness values, from dark to light. A narrower range, in contrast, indicates that the image lacks a full range of values, which may make it a good candidate for level adjustments.

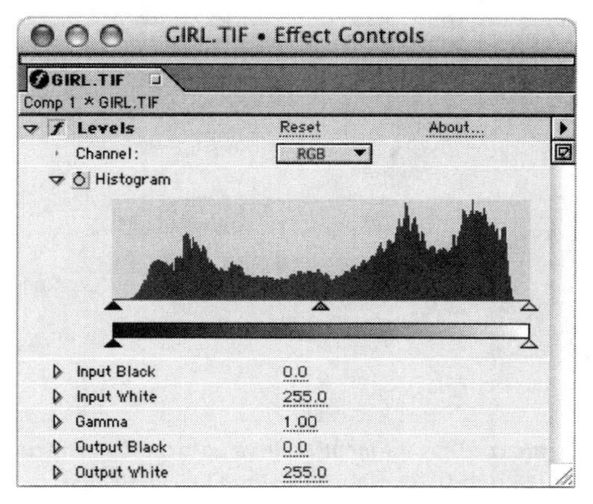

Figure 11.1 A histogram represents all of an image's pixels, arranged from darkest to lightest.

Redistributing values

The histogram represents the image, or *input levels*. Below the histogram, a bar with a gradient from black to white represents the *output levels*. The final levels of the image will depend on how you redistribute, or map, the input levels to the output levels.

Three triangles specify how the input levels are mapped. The left triangle controls Input Black, the right triangle controls Input White, and the center triangle represents Gamma. The output levels are controlled by the lower-left triangle (Output Black) and the lower-right triangle (Output White).

As you move Input Black to the right, more pixels are mapped to the Output Black value. As you move Input White to the left, more pixels are mapped to the Output White value. The midtones, as indicated by the Gamma triangle, move in relation to the other controls. To adjust midtones manually, you can drag the Gamma control.

By default, the Output Black value is 0, or completely black; the Output White value is 255, or completely white. Moving these controls changes the minimum and maximum brightness levels.

You can see and adjust the numeric values for all of the histogram controls in the lower section of the Effect Controls window.

To increase contrast using the Levels effect:

1. Select a layer.
2. Choose Effect > Adjust > Levels, or double-click Levels in the Effects & Presets palette (**Figure 11.2**).
   The Effect Controls window appears, with the layer's Levels effect selected. The Levels effect displays a histogram.
3. Adjust the black levels by *doing either of the following:*
   - ▲ In the Levels histogram, drag the Input Black triangle to the right (**Figure 11.3**).
   - ▲ Change the Input Black value numerically or by using the slider control. (To reveal the slider control, click the triangle next to Input Black.)

   All pixels below the Input Black value are mapped to black. The Gamma point adjusts automatically.
4. Adjust the white levels by *doing either of the following:*
   - ▲ In the Levels histogram, drag the Input White triangle to the left (**Figure 11.4**).
   - ▲ Change the Input White value numerically or by using the slider control. (To reveal the slider control, click the triangle next to Input White.)

   All pixels above the Input Black value are mapped to white. The Gamma point adjusts automatically.

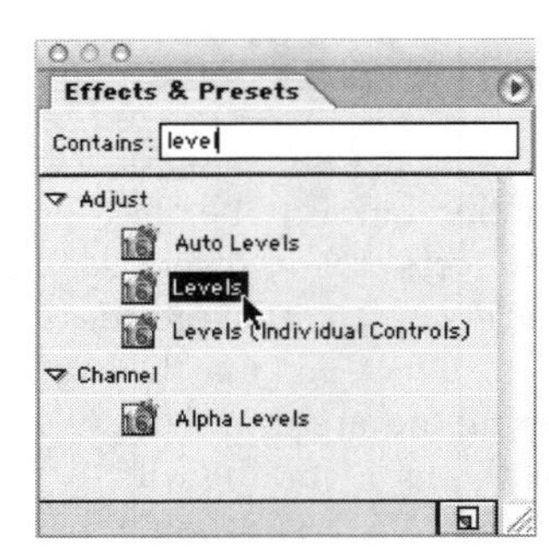

Figure 11.2 In the Effects & Presets palette, double-click Levels.

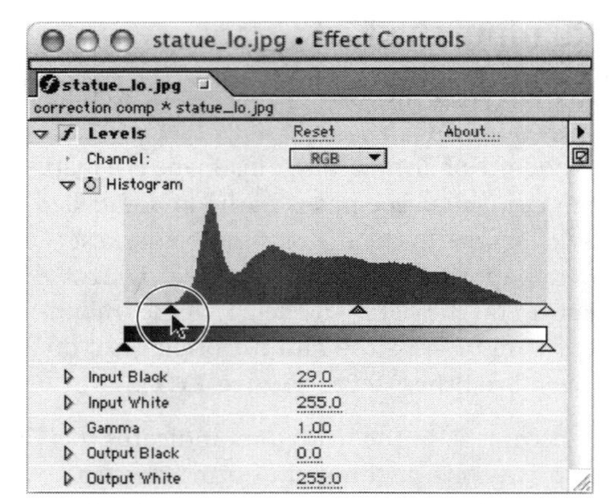

Figure 11.3 Drag the Input Black triangle to the right to map more pixels to the Output Black value (set to 0).

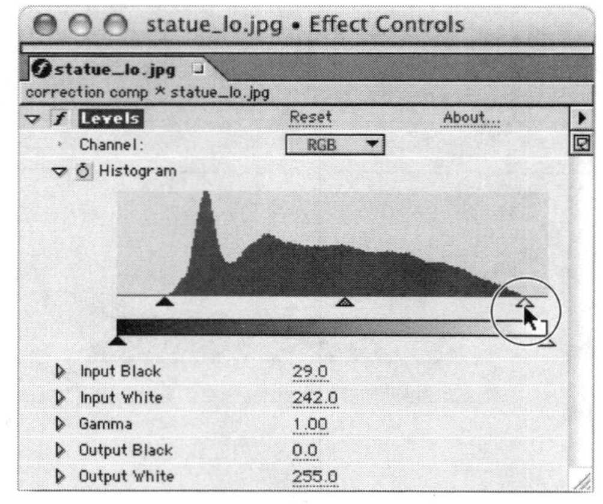

Figure 11.4 Drag the Input White value to the left to map more pixels to the Output White value (set to 255).

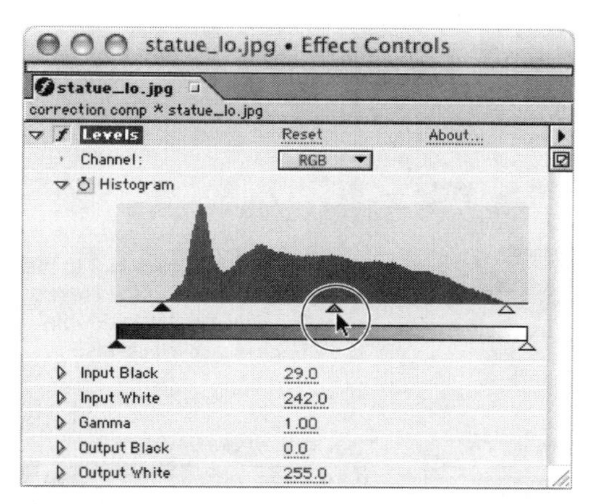

Figure 11.5 To adjust the midtones manually, drag the Gamma slider.

Figure 11.6 As you make adjustments, compare the contrast of the original image...

Figure 11.7 ...to the image you get with the new Levels settings.

5. To adjust the midtones manually, drag the Gamma slider (**Figure 11.5**).

   Dragging left maps more pixels toward the Input White value, brightening the image; dragging right darkens the image.

6. Monitor your progress in the Composition window (**Figures 11.6** and **11.7**).

TV to RGB

As you know, your computer's RGB color space measures brightness on a scale from 0 to 255. Video's native color space, on the other hand, has a more limited brightness range. If your video capture device doesn't attempt to compensate for this difference, your video's black level translates to 16, and its white level corresponds to 235. As a result, the video blacks can appear disappointingly gray on computer screens, and the whites rather dull.

You can use the Levels effect to scale video levels to the full range by setting the input levels to 16 and 235, and the output levels to 0 and 255. Before you do anything, though, check the histogram to confirm that this change is necessary. And, of course, learn about your capture equipment and video drivers to find out how they handle the translation. Also see the sidebar at the end of this chapter, "Illegal and Dangerous (or, Do You Know Where Your Levels Are?)"

To decrease the luminance range using the Levels effect:

1. Select a layer.
2. Choose Effect > Adjust > Levels, or double-click Levels in the Effects & Presets palette (**Figure 11.8**).
   The Effect Controls window appears, with the layer's Levels effect selected.
3. To adjust the Output Black level, *do either of the following:*
   - ▲ Drag the Output Black slider to the right (**Figure 11.9**).
   - ▲ Change the Output Black value numerically or by using the slider control.
4. To adjust the Output White level, *do either of the following:*
   - ▲ Drag the Output White slider to the left (**Figure 11.10**).
   - ▲ Change the Output White value numerically or by using the slider control.

✔ Tips

- Remember: You can toggle the effect between enabled and disabled to compare the image before and after your Levels adjustment.
- For an even greater degree of control, use Levels (Individual Controls) or the Curves effect. Conversely, you make a quick and automatic adjustment by applying Auto-Levels.

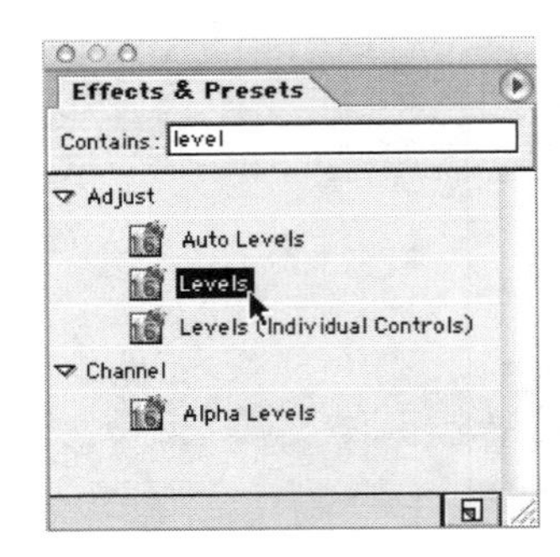

Figure 11.8 In the Effects & Presets palette, double-click Levels.

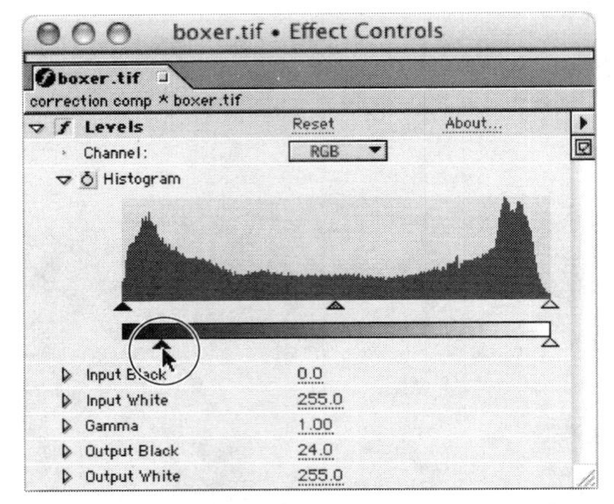

Figure 11.9 Drag the Output Black slider to the right.

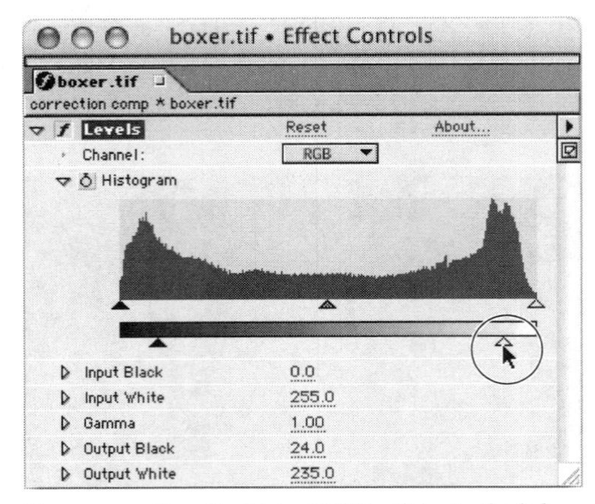

Figure 11.10 Drag the Output White slider to the left.

Audio Effects

After Effects includes several effects for processing audio layers. You'll usually use these to enhance certain aspects of the audio while deemphasizing unwanted sounds—a process commonly referred to as *audio sweetening*. Other times, you may want to deliberately distort the audio to create special effects.

Standard Audio effects include the following:

- Backwards
- Bass and Treble
- Delay
- Flange & Chorus (Pro only)
- High-Low Pass (Pro only)
- Modulator (Pro only)
- Parametric EQ (Pro only)
- Reverb (Pro only)
- Stereo Mixer

✔ Tip

- If you need more precise audio editing or a more extensive set of audio-processing tools, turn to a dedicated digital audio workstation (DAW) or nonlinear editing system (NLE) with good audio-editing features.

Stereo as Mono

Not all applications save stereo audio as a single file. Digidesign's popular audio editing system Pro Tools, for example, works with stereo audio as two mono tracks. In this case, you import both tracks and align them in a composition. Because even mono tracks have a left and right channel—albeit identical ones—you use the Stereo Mixer effect to send each audio layer to the appropriate track. Set the left level to zero for the layer corresponding to the right track; set the right level to zero for the layer corresponding to the left track. Once you've restored two discrete channels, you can adjust their pan and levels as usual.

Using the Stereo Mixer Effect

The Stereo Mixer effect is one of the more versatile of the standard Audio effects. As its name indicates, you can use the Stereo Mixer to control the levels and pan values of each of the left and right audio channels of an audio layer. The effect also provides a switch to invert the phase of the channels, so that sounds with the same frequency can't cancel each other out.

In addition to manipulating audio channels separately, you can also take advantage of other aspects of the Stereo Mixer effect. Because it uses percentage values rather than decibel values, many users find it easier to get predictable fades with the Stereo Mixer effect than with the Audio Levels control. Also, because Audio effect properties are always rendered before the Audio Level property, you can use the Stereo Mixer effect to adjust the levels before adding another effect. (See Chapter 17, "Complex Projects," for more about the order in which After Effects renders adjustments to layers in a comp.)

To use the Stereo Mixer effect:

1. Select an audio layer (**Figure 11.11**).
2. Choose Effect > Audio > Stereo Mixer, or double-click Stereo Mixer in the Effects & Presets palette (**Figure 11.12**).

   The Effect Controls window appears with the layer's Stereo Mixer effect selected (**Figure 11.13**).
3. Set a value for Left Pan.

   A value of –100 pans the left channel completely to the left; a value of 100 pans the left channel completely to the right.

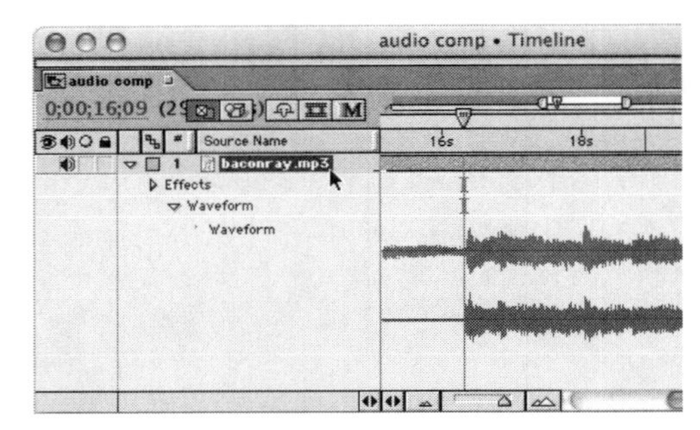

Figure 11.11 Select an audio layer.

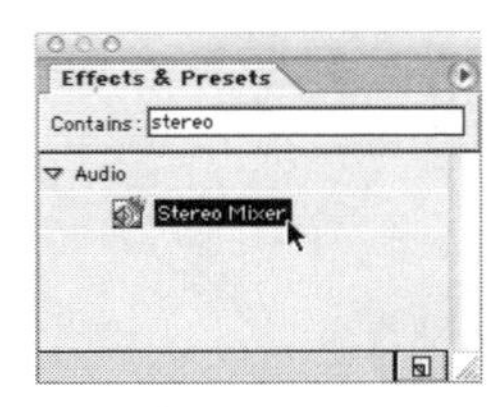

Figure 11.12 In the Effects & Presets palette, double-click Stereo Mixer.

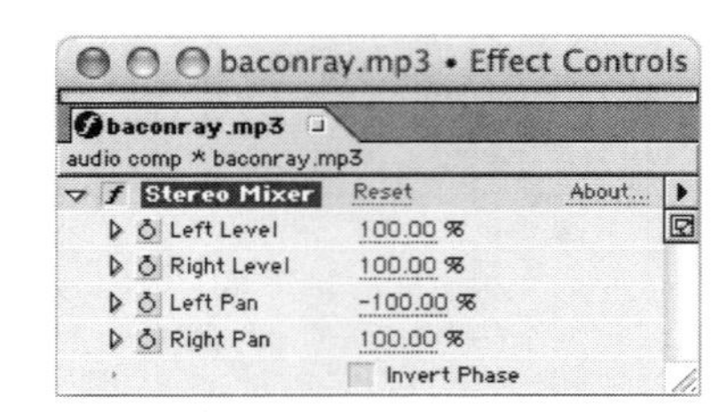

Figure 11.13 The Effect Controls window appears with the layer's Stereo Mixer effect selected.

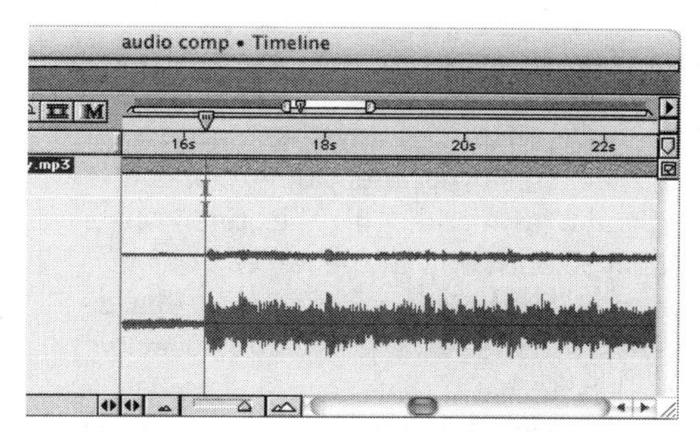

Figure 11.14 Panning the left channel to the right channel redistributes the audio. As this waveform shows, the volume in the left decreases, whereas the volume in the right increases.

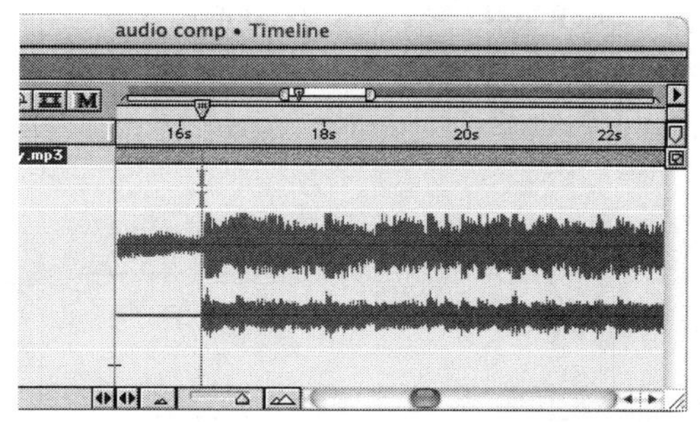

Figure 11.15 In addition to panning, the Stereo Mixer effect also lets you control the levels of each channel. This waveform shows that the levels for the left channel have been increased; the right channel remains untouched.

Figure 11.16 To invert the audio phase, click Invert Phase.

4. Set a value for Right Pan.

   As with the left channel, a value of –100 pans the right channel completely to the left; a value of 100 pans the right channel completely to the right.

5. Set a value for Left Level and another for Right Level.

   A value of 100 percent equals the normal, unprocessed level. Lower values (0 percent minimum) cut the level; higher values (400 percent maximum) boost the level.

   Stereo Mixer settings are reflected in the audio waveform display (**Figures 11.14** and **11.15**).

6. To invert the audio phase, click Invert Phase (**Figure 11.16**).

   See the sidebar "Phased-Out: What's a Phase, and Why Would You Want to Invert It?" for an explanation of phase.

Using the Stereo Mixer Effect

Phased-Out: What's a Phase, and Why Would You Want to Invert It?

Adding two waves of the same frequency results in a larger wave. You can create this effect yourself by panning one audio channel to another: The new waveform becomes larger and the sound peaks higher on the meters. This occurs because the waves are in *phase*—that is, they rise and fall synchronously. When added together, the waves reinforce one another (**Figure 11.17**). Conversely, when waves of the same frequency have opposite phases, they cancel each other out.

If you slept through physics class, you can conduct this experiment now: Duplicate an audio layer and apply the Stereo Mixer effect to one copy. In the Effect Controls window for the effect, click Invert Phase. When you preview the two audio tracks, you'll hear that they've cancelled each other out (**Figure 11.18**). This phenomenon can make an otherwise great-sounding stereo mix sound bad when played as a mono track. If your stereo mix suffers from this problem when delivered on mono systems, you can invert the phase of an audio layer to restore cancelled-out sounds.

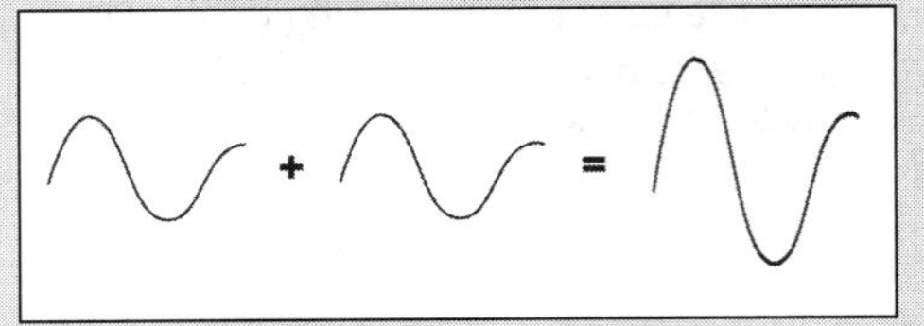

Figure 11.17 When added together, waves of the same frequency reinforce one another...

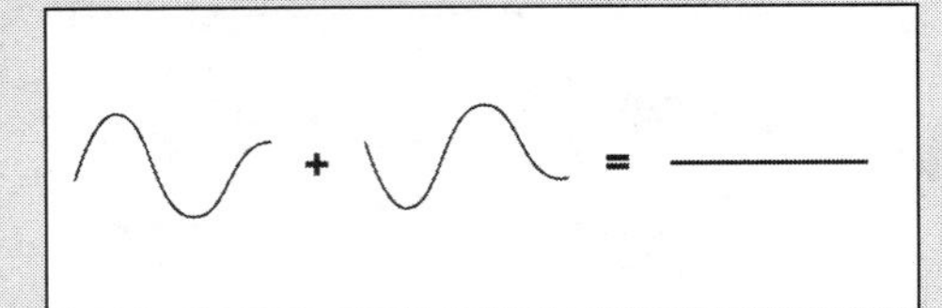

Figure 11.18 ...unless their phases are reversed; then, they cancel each other out.

Moving in Stereo

A *monophonic* (or mono) recording distributes the audio between the two channels evenly and plays back the same sounds through the left and right speakers. In a *stereophonic* (or stereo) recording, audio is mixed differently in the left channel and the right channel. When the audio is played through stereo speakers, the separate channels give the sound a sense of space and location. (Just as your two eyes help you discern distance, your ears help you determine the apparent location of sound.)

In After Effects, stereo and mono audio files appear as a single layer. Expanding the layer outline reveals a waveform for each of the left and right tracks—the left on top, the right below. In a mono track, each track's audio is identical. In a stereo track, each track's audio is unique.

Panning the tracks redistributes the audio between the left and right speakers (**Figures 11.19** and **11.20**). When you apply the Stereo Mixer effect, the default value is −100 for left pan and 100 for right pan. So, the Stereo Mixer effect retains the layer's left and right stereo tracks by default.

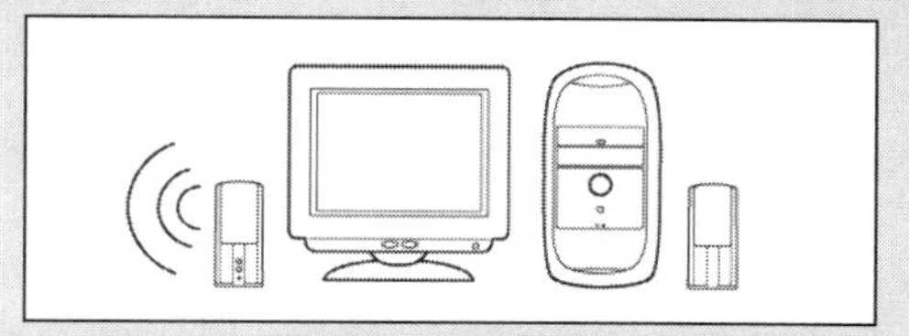

Figure 11.19 Panning audio left sends it to the left speaker.

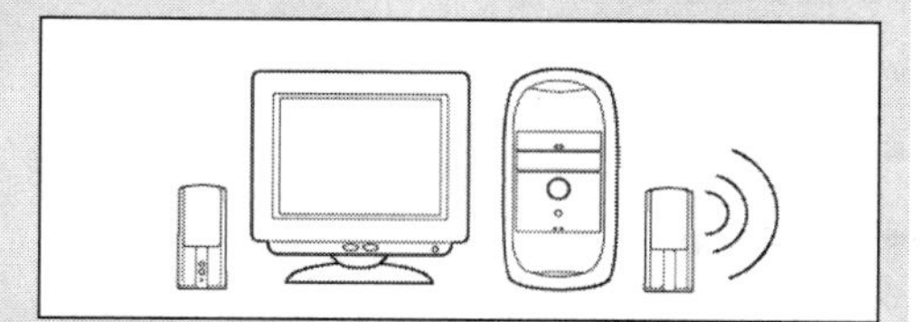

Figure 11.20 Panning audio right sends it to the right speaker.

Blur and Sharpen Effects

Even if you don't have any experience with image-editing software, you probably know that Blur effects cause an image to appear softer and out of focus, whereas Sharpen effects make an image appear crisper, with more defined edges.

Blur and Sharpen effects include the following:

- Box Blur
- Channel Blur
- Compound Blur
- Directional Blur
- Fast Blur
- Gaussian Blur
- Radial Blur
- Sharpen
- Unsharp Mask

✔ Tip

- As compared with printed images, video resolutions are low. To make matters worse, compression schemes add edge blockiness and other visual artifacts—features that sharpening can bring out, doing more harm than good. Thus, the message is clear: When you use a Sharpen effect, do so with care.

Unsharp Isn't Not Sharp (It's Sharper)

Despite its confusing name, Unsharp Mask is, in fact, a sharpening effect. And it doesn't require a mask. The name is derived from an old compositing technique used with stat cameras in commercial print shops.

Both the Sharpen and Unsharp Mask effects sharpen an image by adjusting the contrast between neighboring pixels. Unsharp Mask, however, provides independent control for adjusting the contrast at edges. Now that you know what it is, you may find yourself abandoning the plain, old Sharpen effect for Unsharp Mask.

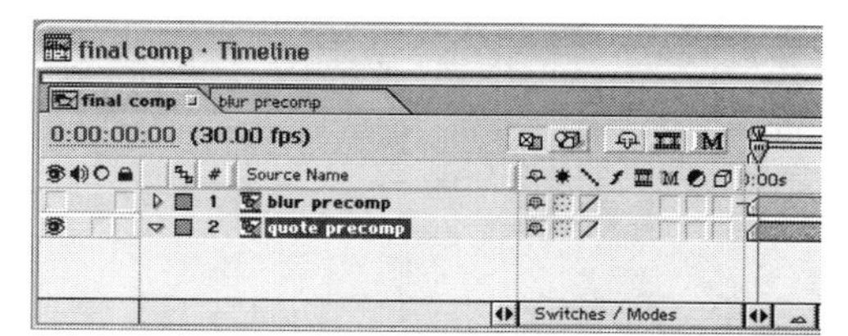

Figure 11.21 Arrange a target layer and an effect source (or blur layer) in a composition. Switch off the video for the blur layer by clicking the Eye icon.

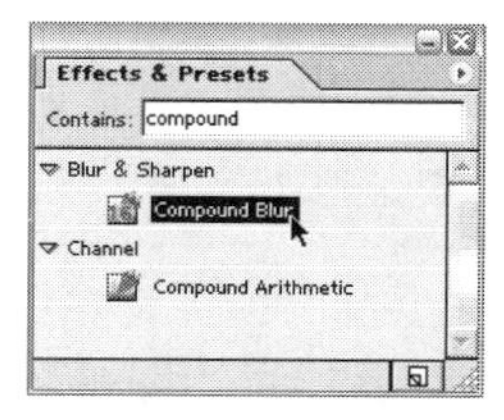

Figure 11.22 Select the target layer, and double-click Compound Blur in the Effects & Presets palette.

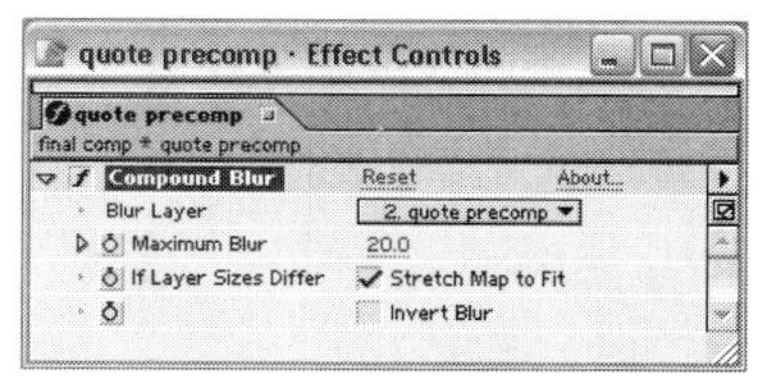

Figure 11.23 The Effect Controls window appears with the layer's Compound Blur effect selected.

Using the Compound Blur Effect

The Compound Blur effect is a little less straightforward than the other Blur and Sharpen effects, largely because it's a compound effect. (Compound effects are discussed in more detail in Chapter 10, "Effect Fundamentals.") Like all compound effects, Compound Blur requires a *target layer* (the layer you want to blur) and a *source layer* (which serves as the blur layer). The blur layer can be any grayscale image (bright areas cause more blur; dark areas cause less blur). For the most predictable results, the blur layer should have the same dimensions as the target layer.

To use the Compound Blur effect:

1. Place the two layers to be blurred in the composition.

   The target layer will serve as the visible, blurred layer; the source layer will define the areas to be blurred.

   Because brightness levels define the degree of blurriness, a grayscale image will suffice for the source layer.

2. In the Timeline window, click the Eye icon for the source layer to make it invisible (**Figure 11.21**).

   The Eye icon disappears, preventing the source layer image from appearing in the composition.

3. Select the target layer and choose Effect > Blur & Sharpen > Compound Blur, or double-click Compound Blur in the Effects & Presets palette (**Figure 11.22**).

   The Effect Controls window appears with the layer's Compound Blur effect selected (**Figure 11.23**).

continues on next page

4. In the Effect Controls window, choose the source layer from the Blur Layer pull-down menu (**Figure 11.24**).

5. Choose *any of the following options:*

   Maximum Blur sets the upper limit for the amount of blur caused by the brightest areas of the blur layer (the source layer) (**Figure 11.25**).

   Stretch Map to Fit resizes the source layer to match the size of the target layer.

   Invert Blur reverses the blurring effects of the bright and dark areas of the source layer.

   The source layer defines the amount of blur in the target layer. The brightness values of the source layer determine the areas and intensity of the effect in the target layer (**Figure 11.26**). Brighter areas result in more blur.

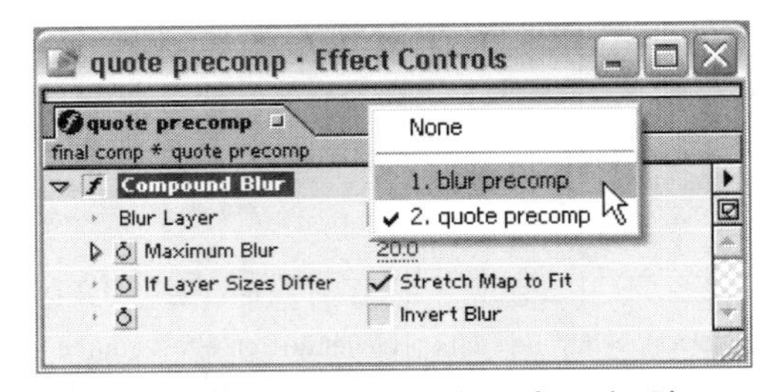

Figure 11.24 Choose the source layer from the Blur Layer pull-down menu.

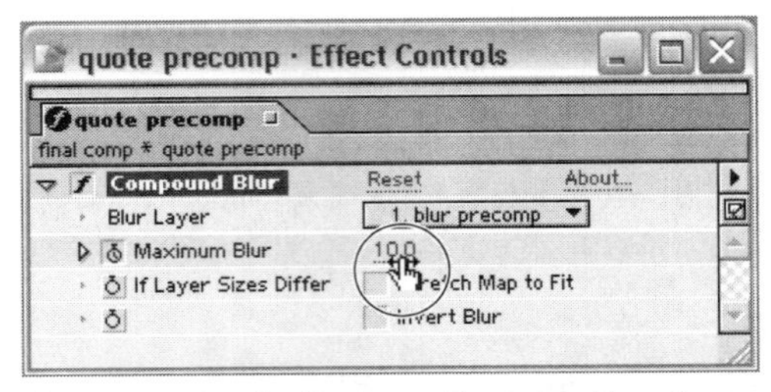

Figure 11.25 Set the Maximum Blur value. Here, the activated Stopwatch icon indicates the Maximum Blur value is being keyframed.

✔ Tips

- Before you add one of the Blur effects, you should be aware that the Motion Blur switch automatically adds a blur to moving objects (see Chapter 14, "More Layer Techniques").
- If you don't have any ready-to-use blur layer footage, why not create your own? You can use a combination of solids, masks, or effects to create a dynamic grayscale movie. If necessary, add one of the other Blur effects to soften it into a useable blur map.

Figure 11.26 The brightness values of the blur layer and the Maximum Blur value combine to determine the areas and intensity of the Compound Blur effect in the target layer. In this example, a moving blur layer obscures different parts of the text over time.

Channel Effects

Channel effects manipulate the individual channels of an image (R, G, B, and Alpha) or their resulting color values (hue, saturation, and luminance).

Channel effects include the following:

- 3D Glasses
- Alpha Levels (Pro only)
- Arithmetic
- Blend
- Calculations
- Channel Combiner
- Cineon Converter
- Compound Arithmetic
- Invert
- Minimax
- Remove Color Matting
- Set Channels
- Set Matte
- Shift Channels
- Solid Composite

Using the Blend Effect

Blend is a compound effect designed to combine two layers using one of five modes: crossfade, color only, tint, darken, and lighten. Blend can provide an alternative to using the cross-dissolve transition or layer modes to combine images. Used as a cross-dissolve, Blend achieves a slightly different look, especially in the way luminance values mix at the midpoint of the transition. Because transfer modes (covered in Chapter 14) can't be animated, the Blend effect also offers a way to animate the relative blending values over time.

When using the Blend effect, be mindful of the limitations imposed by all compound effects. If the effect source layer needs to be pretreated, use a nested composition. (See "Using Compound Effects" in Chapter 10, "Effects Fundamentals.")

To use the Blend effect:

1. Place the two layers to be blended in the same composition.

   One layer will contain the Blend effect; the other layer will serve as the effect source.

2. In the Timeline window, click the Eye icon for the effect source layer to make it invisible (**Figure 11.27**).

   The Eye icon disappears, and the layer's visibility is turned off.

3. Select the layer you want to blend, and choose Effect > Channel > Blend, or double-click Blend in the Effects & Presets palette (**Figure 11.28**).

   The layer's Blend effect appears selected in the Effect Controls window (**Figure 11.29**).

4. In the Effect Controls window, choose the effect source layer in the Blend With Layer pull-down menu (**Figure 11.30**).

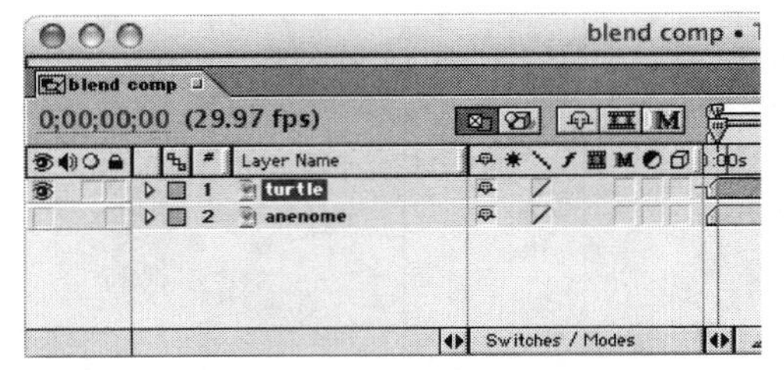

Figure 11.27 Arrange a target layer and an effect source (or blend layer) in a composition. Switch off the video for the blend layer.

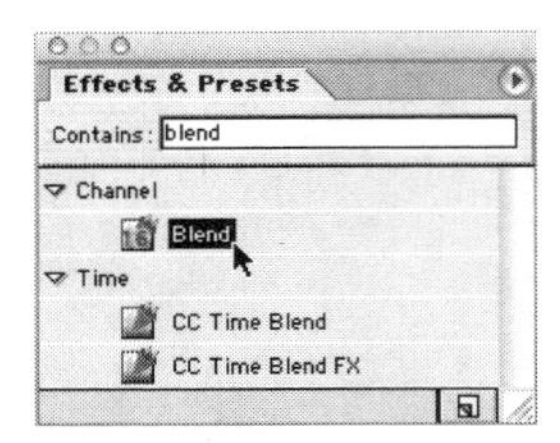

Figure 11.28 Select the layer you want to blend, and double-click Blend in the Effects & Presets palette.

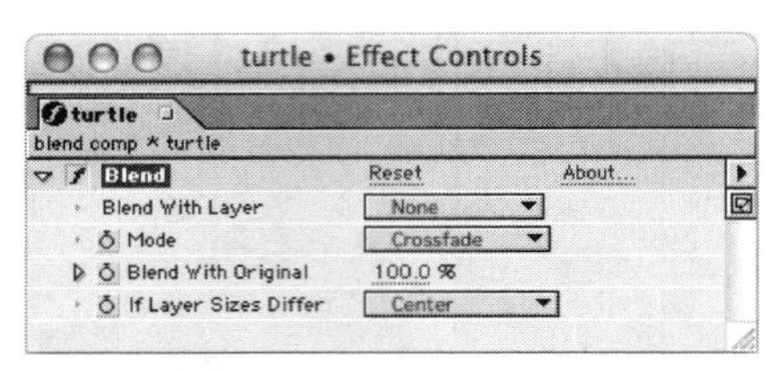

Figure 11.29 The layer's Blend effect appears selected in the Effect Controls window.

Figure 11.30 Choose the effect source layer in the Blend With Layer pull-down menu.

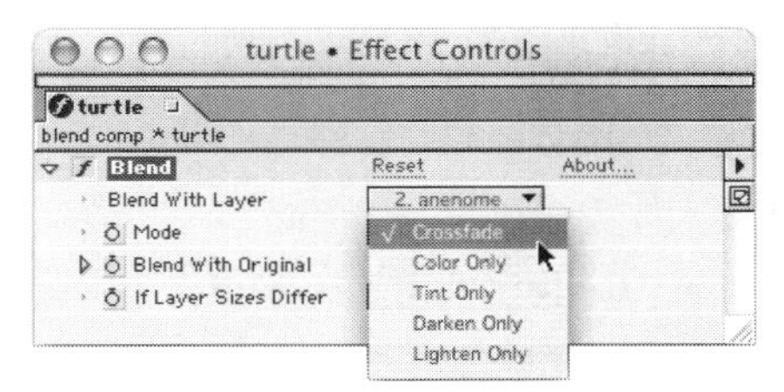

Figure 11.31 Choose a blending method from the Mode pull-down menu.

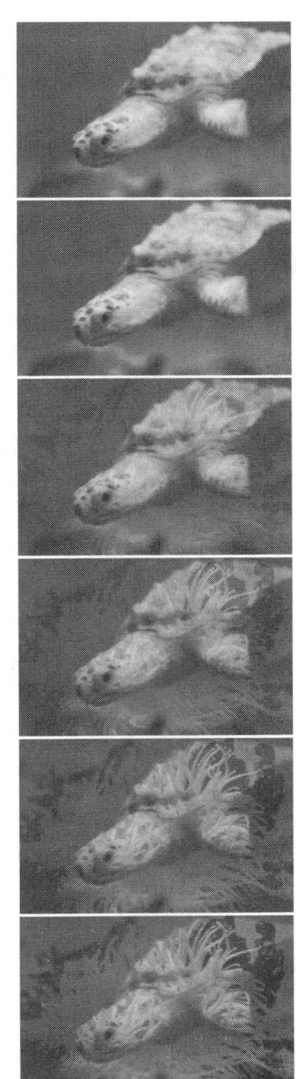

Figure 11.32 Animating the blend effect can result in a variation of a cross-dissolve or take advantage of the other mode options.

5. Specify how the layer combines with the blend layer by choosing a blending method from the Mode pull-down menu (**Figure 11.31**):

   Crossfade fades between the image and the blend layer.

   Color Only colorizes the image according to the colors of corresponding pixels in the blend layer.

   Tint Only tints only the colored pixels in the image according to the colors in the blend layer.

   Darken Only darkens pixels in the image that are lighter than the corresponding pixels in the blend layer.

   Lighten Only lightens pixels in the image that are darker than the corresponding pixels in the blend layer.

6. Set a value for Blend With Original.

   A value of 100 percent reveals only the layer containing the effect; a value of 0 percent reveals only the effect source layer.

7. If necessary, choose an option from the If Layer Size Differs pull-down menu:

   ▲ Center

   ▲ Stretch to Fit

8. Animate the effect using the techniques you learned in Chapter 7, "Properties and Keyframes."

   Animating the Blend effect can result in a variation of a cross-dissolve or take advantage of the other mode options (**Figure 11.32**).

Distort Effects

Effects in the Distort category are designed to shift pixels to deform images. Although more complex morphing effects are reserved for the After Effects Pro, the Standard package does include the Smear effect. As usual, don't let the category name limit the way you use these effects; often, a distortion may appear quite natural.

Note that the Distort category includes the Transform effect. The Transform effect allows you to apply transformations (position, rotation, anchor point) to a layer at the effect stage of rendering. See Chapter 17 for more about circumventing the rendering order to achieve certain results.

Distort effects include the following:

- Bezier Warp (Pro only)
- Bulge (Pro only)
- Corner Pin (Pro only)
- Displacement Map
- Liquify
- Magnify
- Mesh Warp (Pro only)
- Mirror
- Offset
- Optics Compensation (Pro only)
- Polar Coordinates
- Reshape (Pro only)
- Smear
- Spherize
- Transform
- Turbulent Displace
- Twirl
- Warp
- Wave Warp

Figure 11.33 Pixels of a layer image...

Figure 11.34 ...are shifted according to a displacement map layer...

Figure 11.35 ...resulting in the final image.

Using the Displacement Map Effect

In Chapter 10, "Effects Fundamentals," you learned how compound effects alter a layer by referring to another layer, which serves as a map for the effect. The Displacement Map effect shifts the pixels of the selected layer based on the pixel values of an effect source layer, appropriately called the *displacement map.*

Unlike the effect source of many compound effects, the displacement-map layer can be either a grayscale or color image. The color values used to displace pixels in the selected layer depend on the options you choose. As a rule, however, a pixel with a higher or lower value displaces pixels by the maximum amount, whereas a midrange value doesn't displace any pixels. Depending on the nature of the displacement map and the effect options you choose, the effect can make an image appear as though it's refracting through a glass prism or smearing like paint (**Figures 11.33**, **11.34**, and **11.35**).

To use the Displacement Map effect:

1. Arrange at least two layers in the composition (**Figure 11.36**):
   - ▲ A target layer, which will contain the effect
   - ▲ A displacement map layer, which will serve as the effect source

   Layers can be nested compositions.

continues on next page

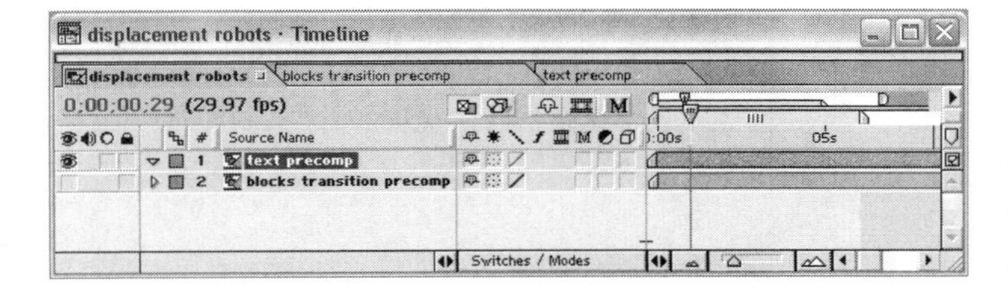

Figure 11.36 Arrange the layer that will contain the effect and the displacement map in the composition. Turn off the video switch for the displacement map so that its image won't appear in the output.

2. To prevent the displacement map from appearing in the composition output, deselect its Video switch.
3. Select the target layer and choose Effect > Distort > Displacement Map, or double-click Displacement Map in the Effects & Presets palette (**Figure 11.37**).

   The Displacement Map effect appears selected in the Effect Controls window.
4. In the Displacement Map Layer pull-down menu, select the displacement map layer (**Figure 11.38**).
5. Choose the pixel attributes used to calculate displacement in the Use For Horizontal Displacement and Use For Vertical Displacement pull-down menus (**Figure 11.39**).

   You can choose from any channel value (RGBA) or calculated color value (luminance, hue, and so on). Full displaces all pixels the maximum positive amount; Off displaces them the maximum negative amount. Half produces no displacement.
6. Set values for the maximum horizontal and maximum vertical displacement (**Figure 11.40**).

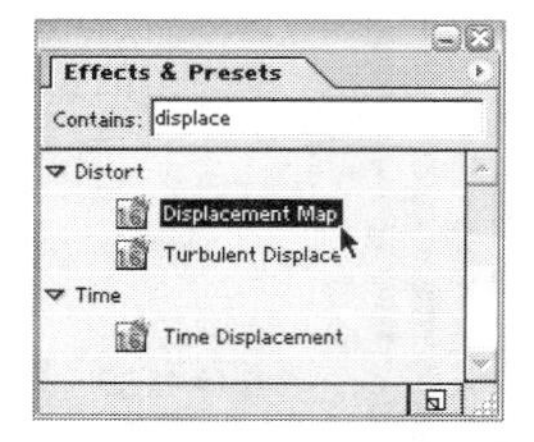

Figure 11.37 Select the target layer and double-click Displacement Map in the Effects & Presets palette.

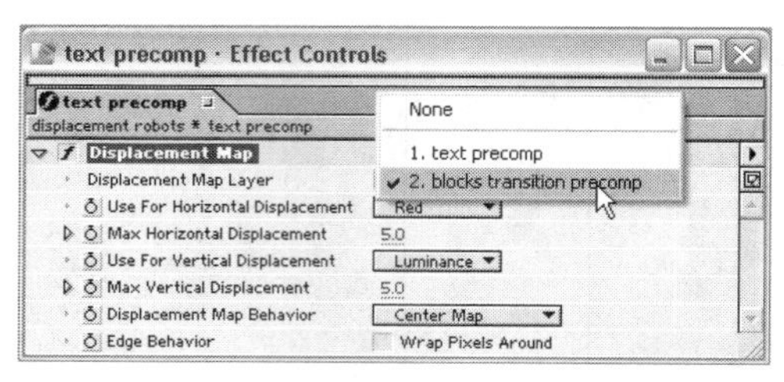

Figure 11.38 In the Displacement Map Layer pull-down menu, select the displacement map layer.

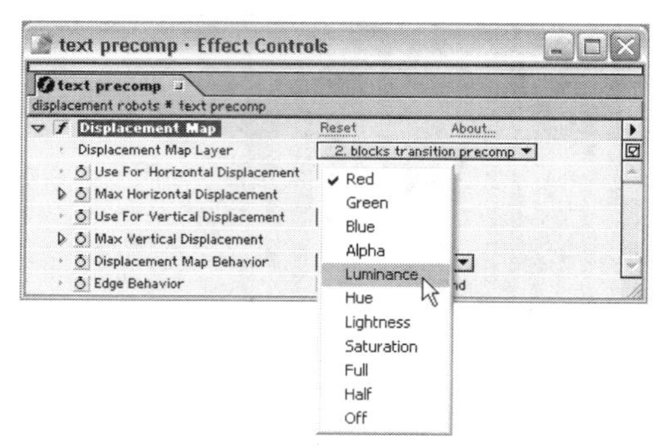

Figure 11.39 Choose the values used to calculate horizontal and vertical displacement.

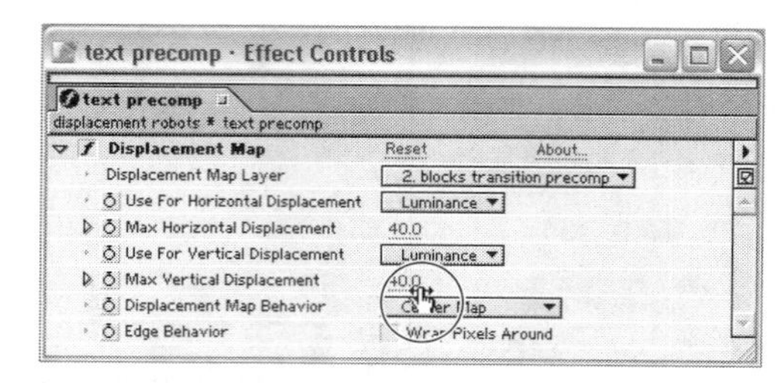

Figure 11.40 Set the maximum displacement.

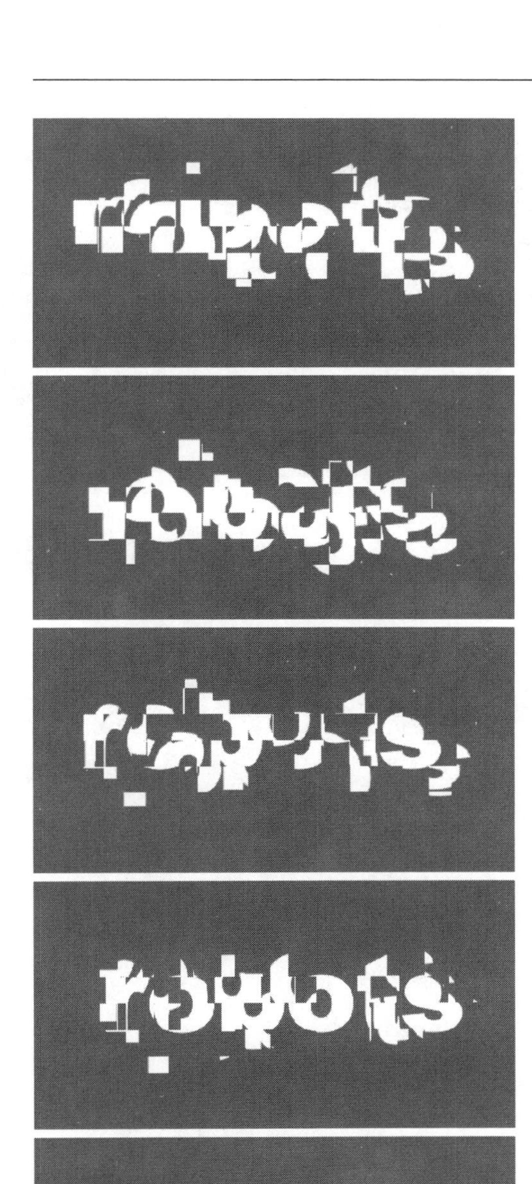

Figure 11.41 Pixels are displaced according to the displacement map layer and the options you chose. Here, the displacement map is a grid of boxes that gradually transitions into a field of gray (which doesn't displace the target text).

7. In the Displacement Map Behavior pull-down menu, choose how the pixels of the displacement-map layer are mapped to the layer containing the effect:
   - ▲ Center Map
   - ▲ Stretch to Fit
   - ▲ Tile Map
8. To repeat the pixels of the image to extend to the edges of the frame, select Wrap Pixels Around.

   The pixels of the image are shifted according to the displacement map (**Figure 11.41**).

✔ Tip

- The Displacement Map effect is subject to the same special considerations as other compound effects. See Chapter 10 for more information about using compound effects.

Image Control Effects

Most Image Control effects change the color or brightness values in a layer. Because these effects tend to be straightforward, this section simply offers a couple of tips. However, the Grow Bounds effect stands out from the other effects in this category and is covered in detail in the next section.

Image Control effects include the following:

- Change Color
- Change to Color
- Color Balance (HLS)
- Color Link
- Colorama
- Equalize
- Gamma/Pedestal/Gain
- Grow Bounds
- PS Arbitrary Map
- Tint

✔ Tips

- Tinting an image causes it to lose contrast. Try using the Levels effect to restore the contrast, or turn to the Hue/Saturation effect.
- Color Balance is a legacy effect, included to support projects created with older versions of After Effects that use the effect. Its function has been absorbed by the Hue/Saturation effect (in the Adjust category). Although it doesn't offer the control of the Hue/Saturation effect, Color Balance is a little easier to use.

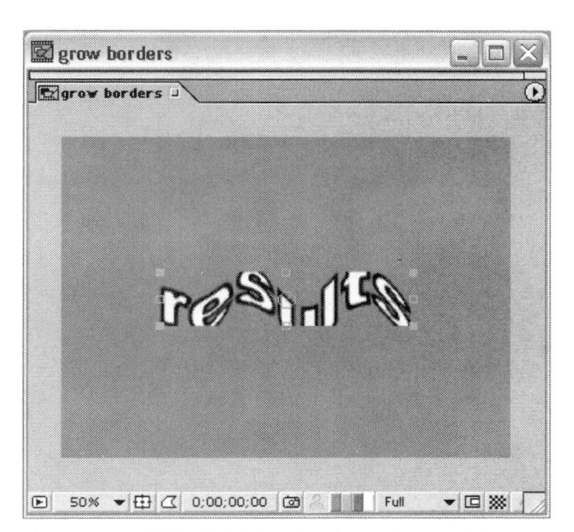

Figure 11.42 Select the layer that requires the Grow Bounds effect. This layer's boundaries cut off the image resulting from applying the Ripple effect.

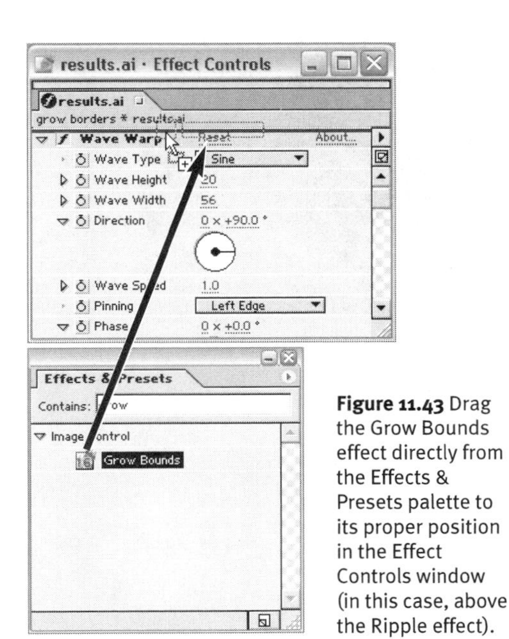

Figure 11.43 Drag the Grow Bounds effect directly from the Effects & Presets palette to its proper position in the Effect Controls window (in this case, above the Ripple effect).

Using the Grow Bounds Effect

The Grow Bounds effect differs from most other effects in the Image Control category. Rather than manipulate color values, Grow Bounds expands a layer's boundaries. This functionality can solve a particular problem you may encounter when working with effects.

Many effects (such as Distortion effects) move an image's pixels; others (Glow and Blur effects, for example) create new pixels from the image. At times, the layer's own boundaries cut off these effects, effectively cropping the final image. Applying the Grow Bounds effect expands a layer's dimensions to accommodate the new image. Using the Grow Bounds effect spares you from having to first precompose the layer in a comp with larger dimensions and then apply the distortion effect (for example) to the nested comp. (See Chapter 17 for more about precomposing and nesting.)

To use the Grow Bounds effect:

1. Select the layer containing an effect that causes the image to exceed the layer's boundaries (**Figure 11.42**).
2. Drag Grow Bounds from the Effects & Presets palette directly to the expanded layer outline or to the Effect Controls window, making sure you place the effect above the effect that causes the image to exceed the layer's boundaries (**Figure 11.43**).

   Alternatively, you can apply the effect using other methods (explained in Chapter 10) and reorder the effects in a separate step.

   The Grow Bounds effect appears selected in the layer's tab in the Effect Controls window.

continues on next page

3. In the layer's tab in the Effect Controls window, expand the Grow Bounds effect to reveal the Pixels property, and increase the value until the layer's edges no longer crop the image (**Figures 11.44** and **11.45**).

   Because Grow Bounds expands the usable dimensions of the layer, it can change the appearance of the subsequent effects.

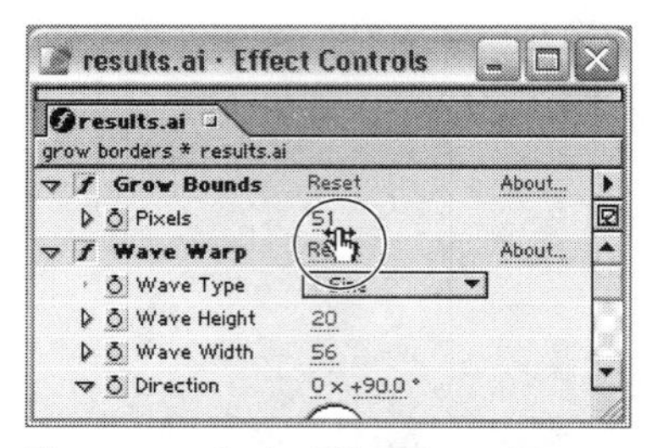

Figure 11.44 In the Effect Controls window, increase the Grow Bounds effect's Pixels property value...

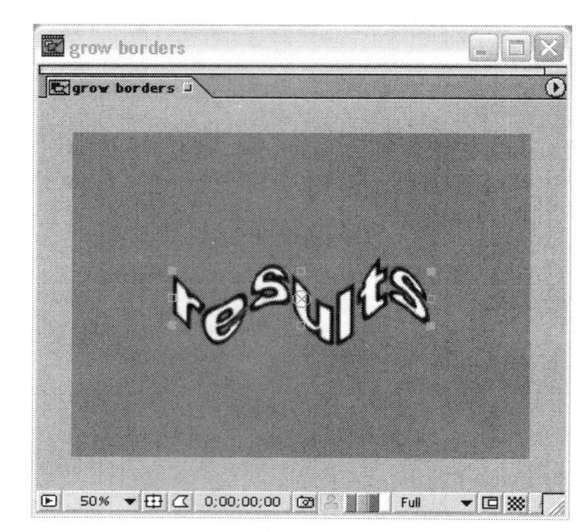

Figure 11.45 ...until the layer's boundaries include the full image.

Keying Effects

Keying effects make pixels transparent based on specified characteristics, typically luminance or chrominance values. The Keying effects included in the Standard version of After Effects are relatively simple to use, so they won't be covered here. They're also somewhat crude, compared to those found in the Professional version. For serious compositing with keys, you'll need After Effects Pro's superior suite of keying effects.

Keying effects include:

- Color Difference Key (Pro only)
- Color Key
- Color Range
- Difference Matte (Pro only)
- Extract (Pro only)
- Inner/Outer Key (Pro only)
- Linear Color Key (Pro only)
- Luma Key
- Spill Suppressor (Pro only)

✔ Tips

- If part of a composited subject contains the key color, you can prevent that part of the image from becoming transparent by using a *hold-out matte*. Masking the area in a duplicate layer and superimposing it over the original layer (containing the key) makes the area appear opaque.
- Keying effects can be much more effective when used in conjunction with Matte Tools, explained in the next section.

Matte Tools Effects

The Matte Tools category includes two effects available only in After Effects Professional. Both effects are used to "choke" a matte.

As you may know, the grayscale image that describes the opaque and transparent parts of a corresponding image is called a *matte*. *Choking* a matte is jargon for slightly contracting the matte's edges (although you can use the same effect to expand the matte). Because it's notoriously difficult to derive a good matte (or, in compositing parlance, *pull* a good matte) using keying techniques, keying effects can be greatly enhanced by applying a matte choker.

Matte Tools effects include:

- Matte Choker (Pro only)
- Simple Choker (Pro only)

Keying

The terms *key* and *keying* refer to their physical counterpart, the keyhole. Keying "cuts a hole" in an image, making the hole transparent. The hole is filled with another image—in the case of After Effects, the image created by lower layers. You typically key out, or remove, parts of an image based on luminance (brightness) or chrominance (color).

Chrominance-based keying effects are commonly used to combine a moving subject with a different background. The subject is shot against a colored background, usually a blue or green backdrop called a *bluescreen* or a *greenscreen*, respectively. Provided the subject doesn't contain the *key color*, a chrominance-based keying effect (or *key*) can remove the background while leaving the subject opaque.

Noise & Grain Effects

When you're acquiring an image, image artifacts such as noise and grain are usually unwelcome (and often inevitable). On the other hand, grain can be a characteristic quality of a particular film stock or shooting style. Whether you want to remove noise and grain to clean up an image, or introduce it to create an effect or match footage, you'll find what you're looking for in this category.

The standard noise effects are straightforward, so this section just offers a few tips. Although Fractal Noise and the grain effects are more complex, they're Pro-only and won't be covered here.

Noise & Grain effects include:

- Add Grain (Pro only)
- Dust & Scratches
- Fractal Noise (Pro only)
- Match Grain (Pro only)
- Median
- Noise
- Noise Alpha
- Noise HLS
- Noise HLS Auto
- Remove Grain (Pro only)

✔ Tips

- Users of previous versions will notice that the Noise & Grain category is new. It contains effects moved from other categories as well as the new suite of grain effects.
- Although a Median effect with a low Radius value may resemble a blur effect, it's quite different. The Median effect changes the value of each pixel to the median value of the surrounding pixels. You determine the sample size by setting the Radius property. For this reason, the Median effect can more effectively reduce a halftone pattern.
- Try applying the Unsharp Mask effect after the Median effect (or blur effects) to bring back detail in the edges.

Perspective Effects

Ever since After Effects introduced 3D compositing (in version 5), the Basic 3D and Drop Shadow effects may sit unused in the Perspective submenu. However, effects like Basic 3D and shadow effects provide a simpler alternative to using 3D lights and layers. And until After Effects can extrude layers, the Bevel effects provide a good way of giving objects the appearance of depth.

Perspective effects include:

- Basic 3D
- Bevel Alpha
- Bevel Edges
- Drop Shadow
- Radial Shadow

Using Bevel Alpha

Both Bevel Edges and Bevel Alpha give a layer a dimensional, lighted quality. Bevel Edges tends to create sharp-cornered bevels that are useful primarily for simple geometric shapes. Bevel Alpha's subtler effect is especially useful for giving dimension to text.

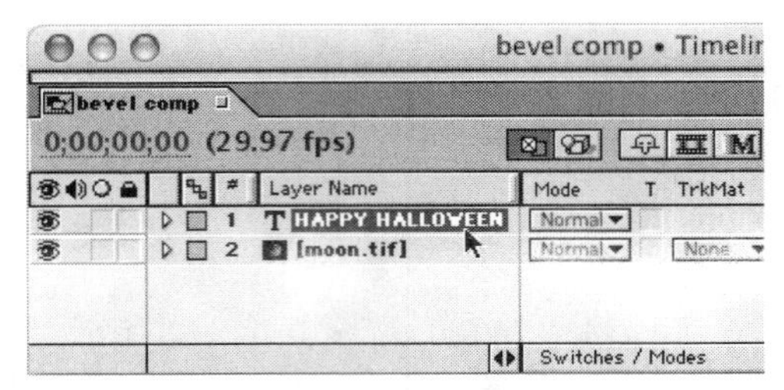

Figure 11.46 Select a layer containing an alpha channel.

To use the Bevel Alpha effect:

1. Select a layer containing an alpha channel (**Figure 11.46**).
2. Choose Effect > Perspective > Bevel Alpha, or double-click Bevel Alpha in the Effects & Presets palette (**Figure 11.47**).

   The layer's Bevel Alpha effect appears selected in the Effect Controls window (**Figure 11.48**).

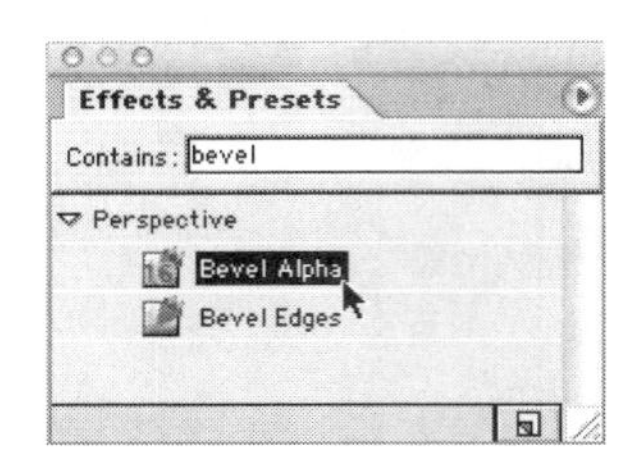

Figure 11.47 In the Effects & Presets palette, double-click the Bevel Alpha effect.

3. *Set the following properties* for the effect:

   Edge Thickness sets the width of the beveled edge, giving a sense of depth.

   Light Angle sets the implied direction of the light source, resulting in highlights and shadows.

   Light Color sets the color of the light on the beveled edge.

   Light Intensity sets the brightness of the light on the beveled edge.

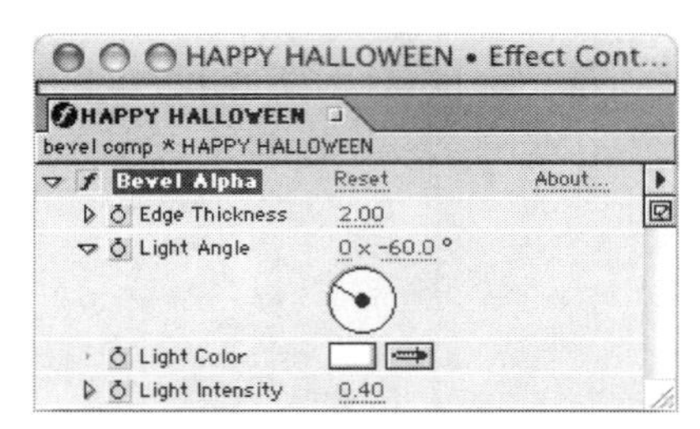

Figure 11.48 The layer's Bevel Alpha effect appears selected in the Effect Controls window.

4. If you want, animate the effect properties over time using the techniques you learned in Chapter 7.

   Beveled layers take on a dimensional character (**Figure 11.49**).

✔ Tips

- Although bevel effects give the appearance of three dimensions, they aren't true 3D effects. If you convert the beveled layer into a 3D layer, you'll see that it remains flat, with no third dimension or thickness. Turn to third-party plug-ins or dedicated 3D software to create true 3D elements.
- Whereas the Drop Shadow effect simulates an infinite light source, the newer Radial Shadow gives the appearance of a shadow cast by a point light source. Unlike the Drop Shadow effect, the Radial Shadow creates the shadow from the layer's alpha channel. For this reason, the edges of the layer may crop the shadow. If so, apply the Grow Bounds effect (described in the section "Image Control Effects," earlier in this chapter) or precomp the layer (as explained in Chapter 17).

Figure 11.49 Beveled layers take on a dimensional character.

Render Effects

Unlike effects that use existing pixels as the basis for image manipulation, effects in the Render category generate their own images.

Render effects include the following:

- 4-Color Gradient
- Advanced Lightning (Pro only)
- Audio Spectrum
- Audio Waveform
- Beam
- Cell Pattern
- Checkerboard
- Circle
- Ellipse
- Eyedropper Fill
- Fill
- Fractal
- Grid
- Lens Flare
- Lightning
- Paint Bucket
- Radio Waves
- Ramp
- Scribble
- Stroke
- Vegas

Using the Audio Waveform Effect

The Audio Waveform and Audio Spectrum effects are variations of compound effects. In these two effects, the layer containing the effect refers to an audio layer as the effect source. The result is interesting graphical elements based on audio elements. To clarify: As visual—not audio—effects, these must be applied to image layers.

You assign the audio layer just as you would the source for any other compound effect—abiding by similar restrictions. Namely, the effect refers directly to the audio layer, before any other audio effects are applied. If you need to pretreat the audio layer, you must do so in another composition. The nested composition can serve as the effect source. (See "Using Compound Effects" in Chapter 10.)

The Audio Waveform effect contains 14 dynamic properties. The following task summarizes the basic settings. Experiment with other settings to change the appearance and behavior of the waveform.

To use Audio Waveform:

1. Make sure two layers are included in the composition:

   ▲ An image layer that will contain the effect

   ▲ An audio layer that will serve as the effect source

   The audio layer's Audio switch doesn't have to be on for the effect to work.

2. Select an image layer (**Figure 11.50**).

   You must apply this effect to an image layer, not an audio layer. A black solid makes a good choice.

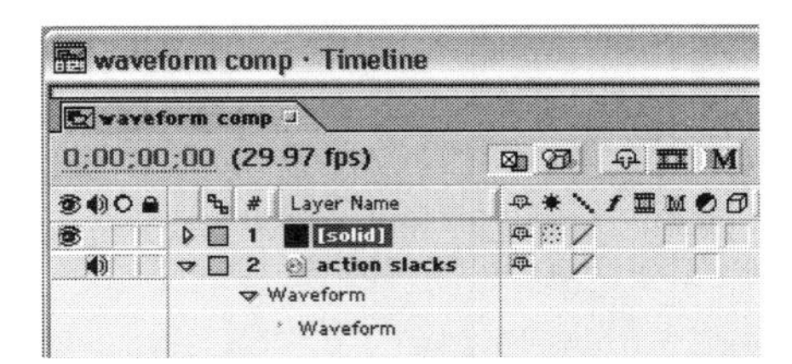

Figure 11.50 Select an image layer.

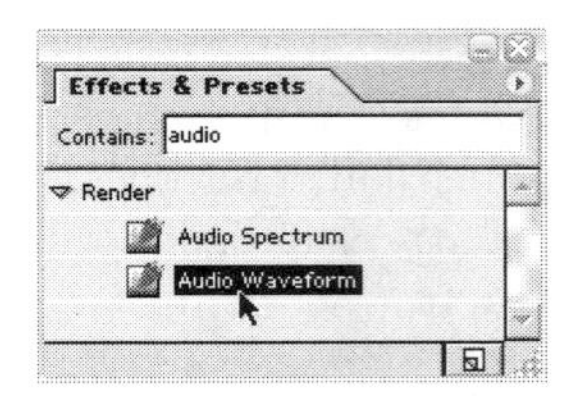

Figure 11.51 In the Effects & Presets palette, double-click Audio Waveform.

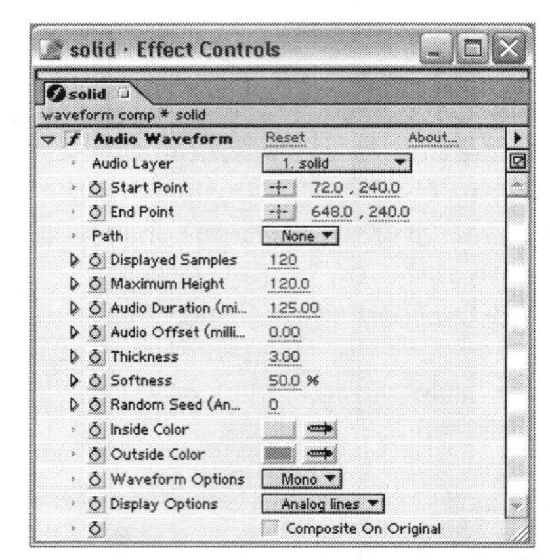

Figure 11.52 The Audio Waveform effect appears selected in the Effect Controls window.

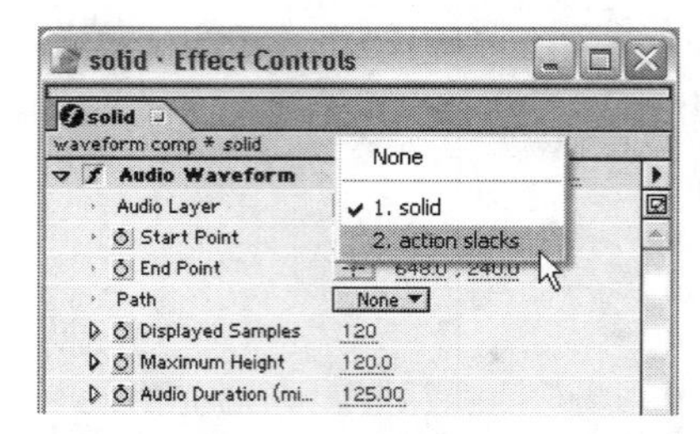

Figure 11.53 Choose an audio layer in the Audio Layer pull-down menu.

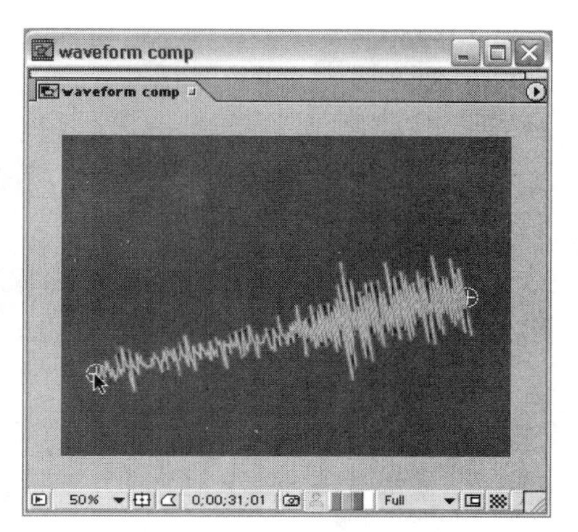

Figure 11.54 Drag the Start and End points in the Composition window.

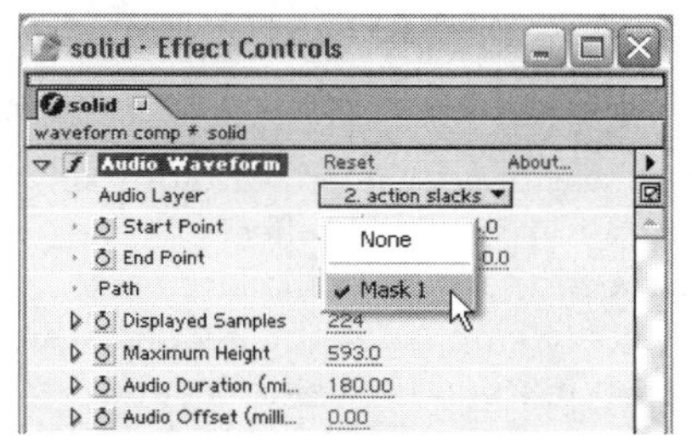

Figure 11.55 Choose a path from the Path pull-down menu.

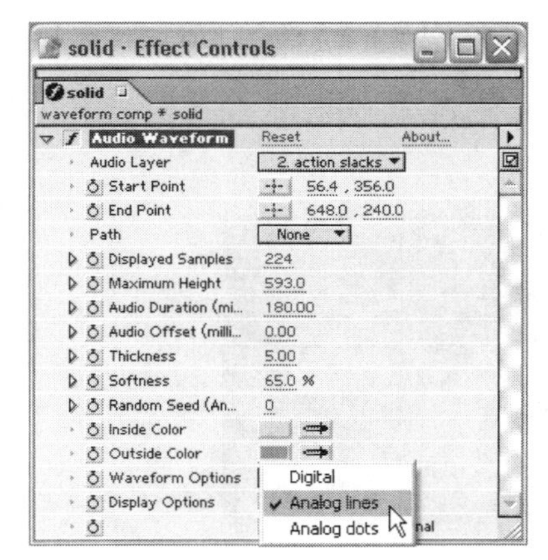

Figure 11.56 Choose an option from the Display Options pull-down menu.

3. Choose Effect > Render > Audio Waveform, or double-click Audio Waveform in the Effects & Presets palette (**Figure 11.51**).

   The Audio Waveform effect appears selected in the Effect Controls window (**Figure 11.52**). A line representing an inert audio waveform appears in the Composition window.

4. Choose an audio layer from the Audio Layer pull-down menu (**Figure 11.53**).

5. To set the path for the waveform display, *do any of the following:*

   - ▲ Set values for the Start and End points.
   - ▲ Click the Crosshairs button next to the Start or End point to set the points in the Composition window (**Figure 11.54**).
   - ▲ Choose a path from the Path pull-down menu (**Figure 11.55**).

   To set Start and End points, you must set the Path pull-down menu to None.

6. *Choose an option* from the Display Options pull-down menu (**Figure 11.56**):

   Digital represents the sound as a series of vertical lines.

   Analog lines represents the sound as a continuous, fluctuating line.

   Analog dots represents the sound as moving dots.

7. *Choose an option* from the Waveform Options pull-down menu:

   Mono uses both left and right channels to create the waveform.

   Left uses the audio in the left channel to create the waveform.

   Right uses the audio in the right channel to create the waveform.

   If the audio layer is monophonic, this option has no effect.

continues on next page

8. *Do one of the following:*
   - ▲ To composite the waveform on the layer containing the effect, click Composite On Original.
   - ▲ To make the layer transparent and reveal layers lower in the stacking order, leave the Composite On Original box unselected.
9. To adjust the appearance and behavior of the waveform, *set values for other properties*:

   Displayed Samples sets the number of audio samples to display.

   Maximum Height sets the maximum height in pixels.

   Audio Duration sets the duration (in milliseconds) used to create the waveform.

   Audio Offset sets the lag time before creating the waveform.

   Thickness sets the width of the lines in the waveform.

   Softness sets the softness of the lines in the waveform.

   Random Seed specifies the amount of randomness in the waveform pattern.

   Inside Color specifies the color of the inner area of the display.

   Outside Color specifies the color of the outer edge of the display.

   Even if properties remain static, the waveform responds to the audio effect source (**Figure 11.57**).

✔ Tips

- Don't let the effect's name prevent you from putting it to imaginative use. The waveform can also express itself as dots instead of a line (**Figure 11.58**); and it doesn't necessarily have to imply sound waves. Experiment with different settings and applications.
- Don't feel obligated to use the audible soundtrack as the source for Audio Spectrum and Audio Waveform effects. Use whatever audio yields a good effect as the effect source, and switch off its audio.
- Another way to get a good waveform or spectrum is to use audio effects to preprocess a copy of your audio layer. Use the effects to emphasize the frequencies that result in a good visual effect and deemphasize ones that don't. Make sure you precompose or nest the audio in another composition before you use it as the effect source. (See Chapter 17 for more about precomposing and nesting.)

Figure 11.57 The effect creates dynamic visuals from the audio modifying layer's audio track.

Figure 11.58 In this variation, the Analog Dots option is selected, and the waveform follows an elliptical mask.

Simulation Effects

Simulation effects mimic the behavior of natural phenomena, such as the refraction of light through water or a material shattered by a percussive force. These effects work best in conjunction with one another, or include extensive sets of properties. Space considerations allow for only a quick rundown of these effects here.

Simulation effects include the following:

- Card Dance
- Caustics
- Foam
- Particle Playground (Pro only)
- Shatter
- Wave World

Stylize Effects

The Stylize effect category encompasses a range of effects used to make images abstract or to impart a distinctive visual characteristic.

Stylize effects include the following:

- Brush Strokes
- Color Emboss
- Emboss
- Find Edges
- Glow (Pro only)
- Leave Color
- Mosaic
- Motion Tile
- Roughen Edges
- Scatter (Pro only)
- Strobe Light
- Texturize
- Write-On

✔ Tips

- Effect names can be misleading, limiting the way you think of them. Take some time to compare effects and see how they work.
- A number of third-party plug-ins simulate painterly effects. Corel's Painter is a full-fledged program dedicated to simulating realistic brush strokes and even outputting animations.

Using Texturize

The Texturize effect uses the pixels from one layer to give another layer a textured or embossed appearance. The luminance values of the effect source determine the relative intensity of the texture; you can modify the overall effect using the effect's property controls. Like all compound effects, Texturize utilizes the effect source directly, before layer modifications (masks, effects, and transform properties) are applied. If you need to adjust the texture layer, do so in a separate comp and then nest the comp for use as the effect source. (For a more detailed explanation of compound effects, see Chapter 10.)

Figure 11.59 Arrange the target layer and effect source in a comp, and set the effect source's video switch off.

Figure 11.60 Select the target layer, and double-click the Texturize effect in the Effects & Presets palette.

To use the Texturize effect:

1. Arrange the layer you want to texturize (the target layer) and the layer containing the texture (the effect source) in a composition. Set the texture layer video off (**Figure 11.59**).

   If the effect source requires modifications, precompose the layer and use the nested comp as the source.

2. Select the target layer and choose Effect > Stylize > Texturize, or double-click the Texturize effect in the Effects & Presets palette (**Figure 11.60**).

   The Texturize effect appears selected in the target layer's tab in the Effect Controls window.

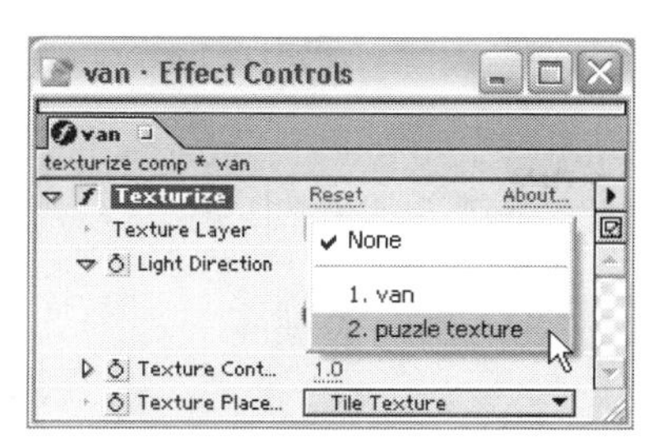

Figure 11.61 In Effect Controls window, choose the effect source layer in the Texturize Layer pull-down menu.

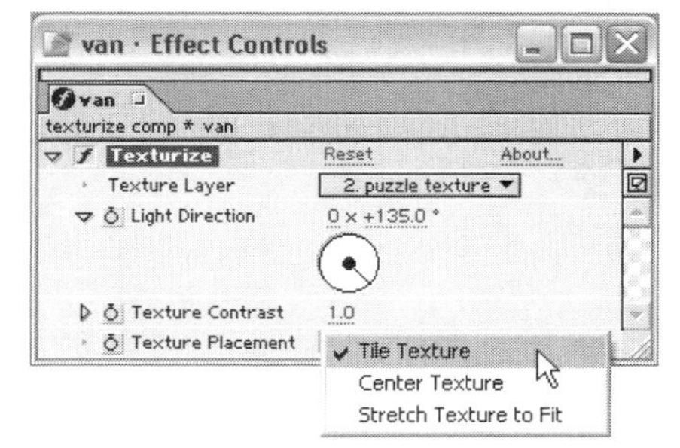

Figure 11.62 Specify how you want to map the effect source to the target layer in the Texture Placement pull-down menu. In this example, the sizes of the target and the effect source layers match, so Center Texture works fine.

3. In the Effect Controls window, choose the effect source layer in the Texturize Layer pull-down menu (**Figure 11.61**).

   The effect source's texture is mapped to the target layer.

4. In the Effect Controls window, *choose an option* for Texture Placement (**Figure 11.62**):

   Tile Texture

   Center Texture

   Stretch Texture to Fit

   For a complete explanation of these options, see the section "Using Compound Effects" in Chapter 10.

5. *Set other property values:*

   Light Direction—Sets the angle of the apparent light source cast on the texture

   Texture Contrast—Sets the opacity of the light and shadow created by the texture

   The Texturize effect modifies the target layer according to the settings you specified (**Figure 11.63**).

Figure 11.63 In the Comp window, you can see how the effect source gives the target layer a texturized appearance. In this case, it makes the layer look like a jigsaw puzzle.

Text Effects

With the introduction of direct text-creation and animation tools (covered in Chapter 12, "Creating and Animating Text"), you may wonder if you'll ever use the Text effects again. The Type tool comes with a complement of full-featured character and paragraph palettes. Moreover, the newer text animation controls far surpass the Text effects' relatively meager property controls. And, After Effects comes loaded with attractive text animation presets.

The Numbers effect contains unique property controls you may find useful in certain circumstances. For example, you can use the Numbers effect to quickly simulate a display of the date, time, or timecode.

But for most purposes, the newer text-creation and animation techniques are far more flexible than these Text effects. Instead of providing examples of text effects here, this book concentrates on explaining the newer and more powerful text-creation tools in Chapter 12.

Text effects include the following:

- Basic Text
- Numbers
- Path Text

Time Effects

The Time category contains four effects that manipulate the playback timing of a layer's frames.

Time effects include the following:

- Echo
- Posterize Time
- Time Difference
- Time Displacement (Pro only)

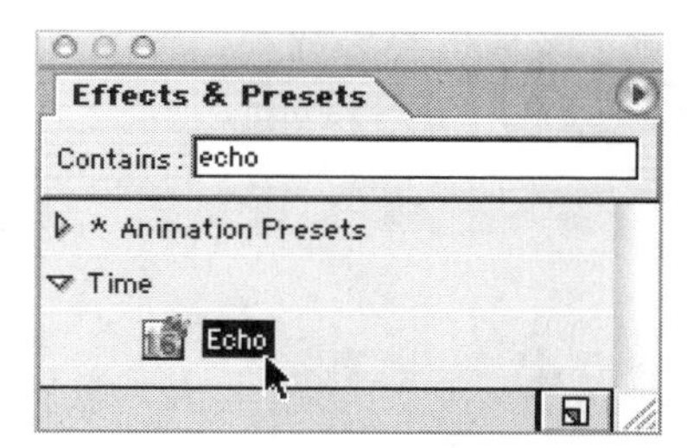

Figure 11.64 Select a layer, and double-click the Echo effect in the Effects & Presets palette.

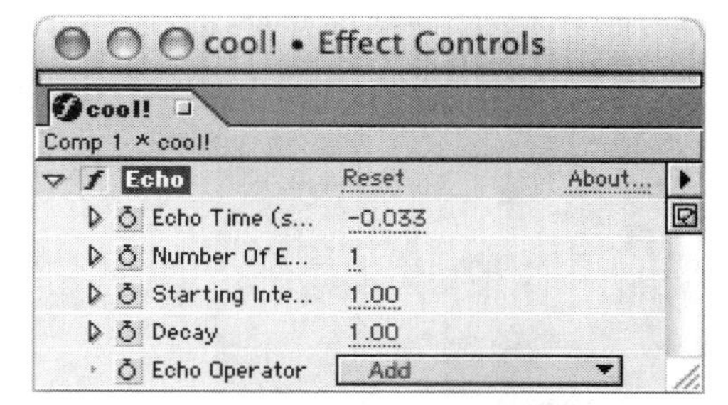

Figure 11.65 The Echo effect appears selected in the Effect Controls window.

Using the Echo Effect

The Echo effect displays frames from different times in a layer and combines them with the current frame.

Although the Echo effect doesn't refer to a separate modifying layer in the way a compound effect does, it works in a similar fashion. Echo cancels out other effects unless you precompose the layer before you apply the effect. And, of course, the Echo effect is only apparent where there's motion within a frame.

To use Echo:

1. Select a layer and choose Effect > Time > Echo, or double-click the Echo effect in the Effects & Presets palette (**Figure 11.64**).

   The Echo effect appears selected in the Effect Controls window (**Figure 11.65**).

2. *Set values for several properties:*

   Echo Time sets the number of frames between echo frames. Negative numbers specify frames previous to the current frame; positive values specify frames after the current frame.

   Number of Echoes sets the number of frames combined to create the echo.

   Starting Intensity sets the opacity of the first frame of the echo frames. A value of 1 indicates full intensity.

   Decay sets the factor by which the intensity changes for subsequent echo frames. A value of 1 produces no decay; a value of .5 decreases the intensity of each echo frame by half the intensity of the previous one.

continues on next page

3. *Choose a method* for combining echo frames from the Echo Operator menu (**Figure 11.66**):

   Add combines pixel values.

   Maximum uses the maximum pixel values.

   Minimum uses the minimum pixel values.

   Screen multiplies the inverse brightness values of the colors in all echo frames, so that colors are never darker than the layer image.

   Composite In Back uses the layer's alpha channel to composite echoes back to front.

   Composite In Front uses the layer's alpha channel to composite echoes front to back.

   Blend combines pixels evenly, in the same manner as the Blend effect and similar to a cross-dissolve.

4. Animate the effect using techniques you learned in Chapter 7.

5. Preview the effect using the techniques discussed in Chapter 8, "Playback, Previews, and RAM."

   Motion in the frame appears to trail, or smear (**Figure 11.67**).

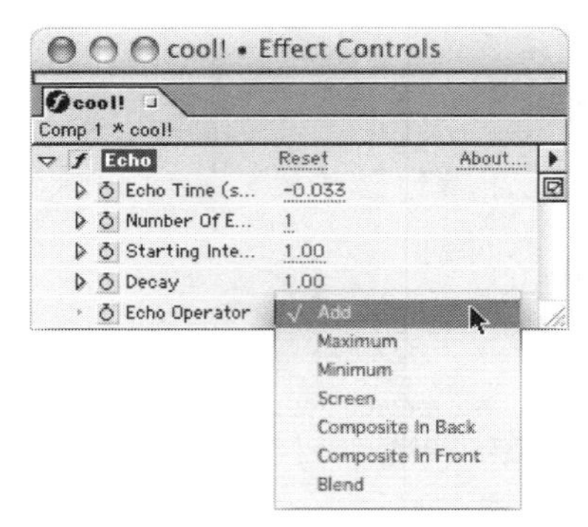

Figure 11.66 Choose a method for combining echo frames from the Echo Operator menu.

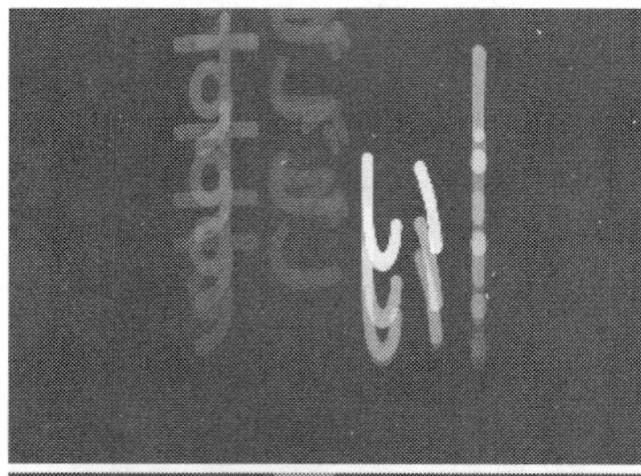

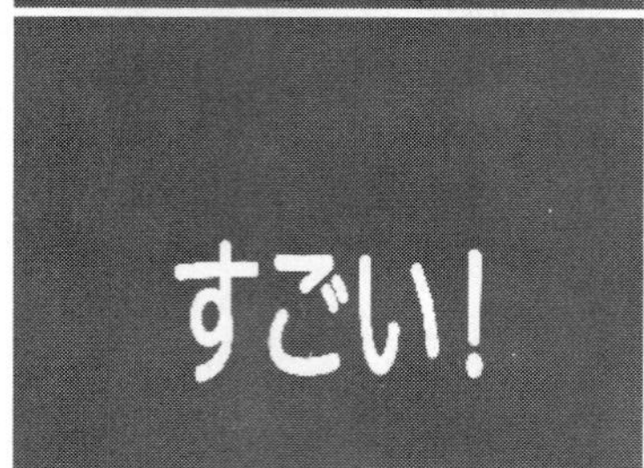

Figure 11.67 Motion in the frame appears to trail. The text animation preset Raining Characters In uses an Echo effect. Here, the preset has been modified to make the Echo effect more apparent.

Transition Effects

Transition effects create the kind of A-B roll transitions you frequently use in non-linear editing (or with a video switcher, for those of you familiar with more traditional video tools). In other words, they create progressively larger areas of transparency in one layer to gradually reveal the layers beneath.

As you discovered in Chapter 7 constructing transitions in After Effects isn't the same as doing so with traditional non-linear editing (NLE) software. You set up most transition effects by setting keyframes for the Transition Completion property—just as you'd create a crossfade by animating a layer's Opacity property. The notable exception is the Gradient Wipe effect. To use it, you must arrange the layers much more as you would in an NLE program. The Gradient Wipe effect is covered in detail in the following section.

Transition effects include the following:

- Block Dissolve
- Card Wipe
- Gradient Wipe
- Iris Wipe
- Linear Wipe
- Radial Wipe
- Venetian Blinds

✔ Tip

- As with any other type of effect, you don't have to use Transition effects exactly the way they were designed. For example, you can use transitions with solid colors to create patterns and other graphical elements. Prerender or precompose these sequences and use them as mattes or effect sources for compound effects.

Using the Gradient Wipe Effect

Although its name might lead you to believe that the Gradient Wipe effect resembles a plain-vanilla gradient or a tacky wipe transition, this effect is far more versatile than that.

As a compound effect, Gradient Wipe makes a layer gradually transparent, based on the luminance values of another layer (called a *gradient layer)*. The first areas to become transparent correspond with the darkest areas of the gradient layer; the last areas to become transparent correspond with the brightest areas. Of course, the gradient layer doesn't have to be a simple gradient; you can achieve an infinite variety of transitions by creating custom patterns to use as the effect source.

To create a simple transition using the Gradient Wipe effect:

1. Arrange three layers in the composition for a transition:

   ▲ Place the layer you want to transition *from* (Layer A) higher in the stacking order.

   ▲ Place the layer you want to transition *to* (Layer B) lower in the stacking order.

   ▲ Place the gradient layer between the other two layers.

   The layers should overlap so that the In point of the gradient layer aligns with the In point of Layer B, and the Out point of the gradient layer aligns with Layer A. The overlapping area will equal the duration of the transition (**Figure 11.68**).

2. Switch off the video for the gradient layer.

   This way, the gradient layer won't appear in the output image; it only serves as the effect source.

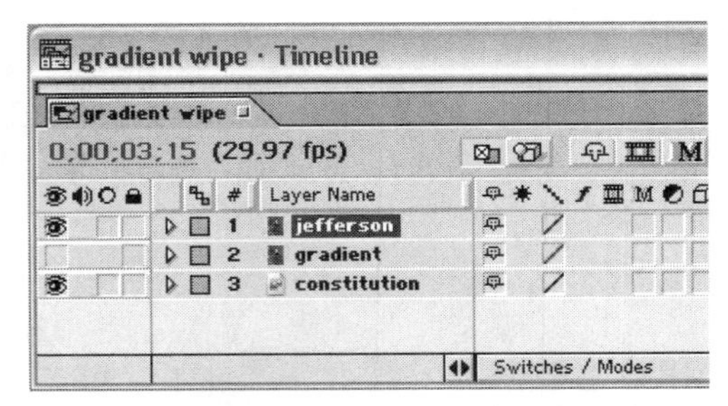

Figure 11.68 Arrange three layers in the composition for a gradient transition.

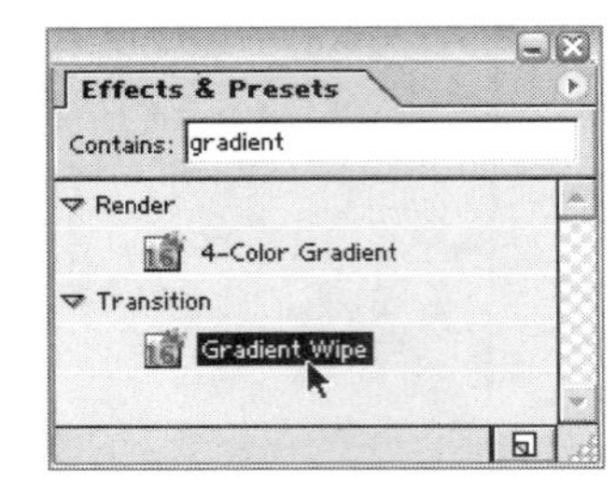

Figure 11.69 Select Layer A, and double-click the Gradient Wipe effect in the Effects & Presets palette.

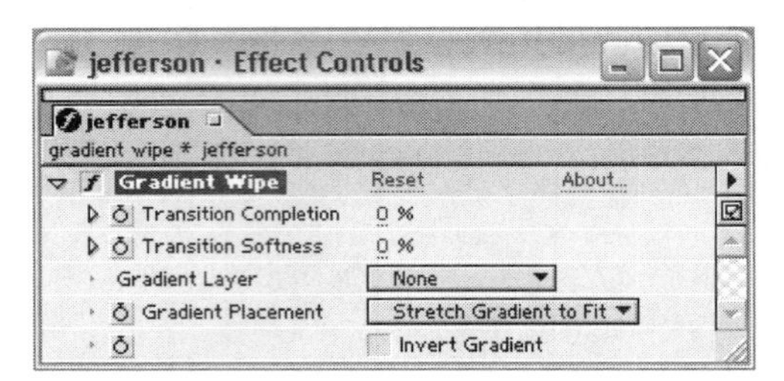

Figure 11.70 The Gradient Wipe effect appears selected in the Effect Controls window.

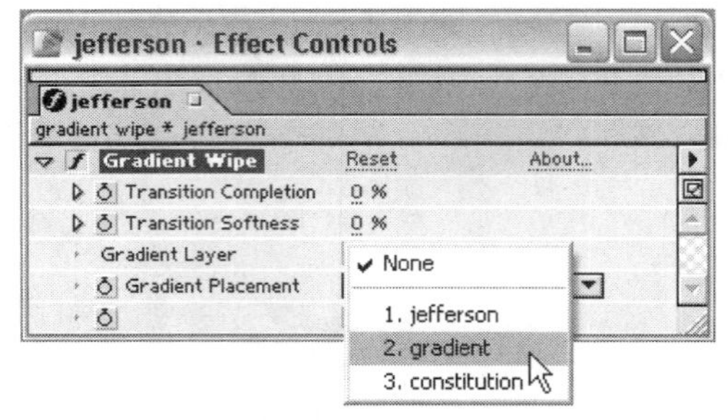

Figure 11.71 In the Gradient Layer pull-down menu, specify the gradient layer.

3. Select the layer you want to transition from (Layer A), and set the current time to the frame you want the Gradient Wipe transition to begin.

   This aligns with Layer A's In point.

4. Choose Effect > Transition > Gradient Wipe, or double-click the Gradient Wipe effect in the Effects & Presets palette (**Figure 11.69**).

   The Gradient Wipe effect appears selected in the Effect Controls window (**Figure 11.70**).

5. In the Gradient Layer pull-down menu, specify the gradient layer (**Figure 11.71**).

   If the size of the gradient differs from the layer containing the effect, *choose a placement option* in the Gradient Placement pull-down menu:

   ▲ Tile Gradient

   ▲ Center Gradient

   ▲ Stretch Gradient to Fit

6. To adjust the softness of the Gradient Wipe, set the Transition Softness value.

7. Set the Transition Completion slider to 0 percent, and click the Stopwatch icon to initiate the keyframing process and set the first keyframe for this property (**Figure 11.72**).

   A keyframe is set for the property at the current time.

8. Set the current time to the frame at which you want the gradient transition to end.

   In a typical transition, this aligns with the Out point of Layer A and the gradient layer (**Figure 11.73**).

continues on next page

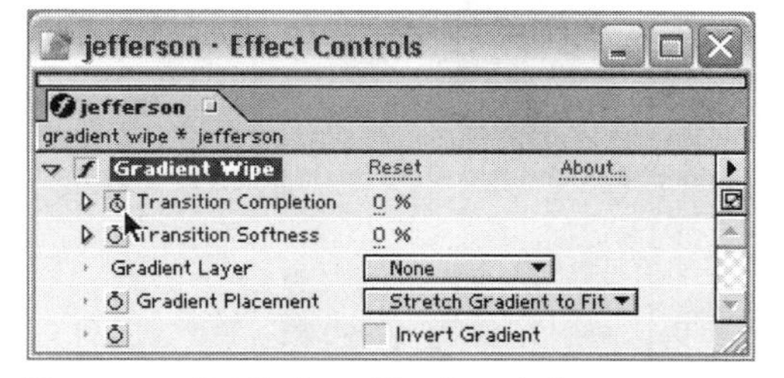

Figure 11.72 Set the Transition Completion property to 0 percent, and select the Stopwatch icon to initiate the keyframing process and set the first keyframe.

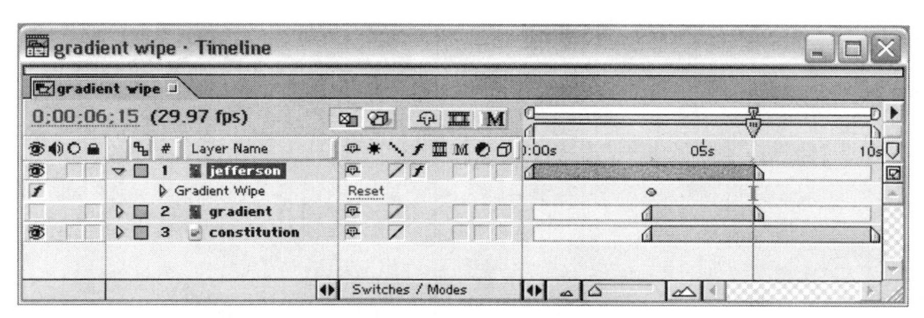

Figure 11.73 Set the current time to the frame at which you want the gradient transition to end. In a typical transition, this aligns with the Out point of Layer A.

9. In the Effect Controls window, set the Transition Completion property to 100 percent (**Figure 11.74**).

   Another keyframe is created for the property automatically (**Figure 11.75**).

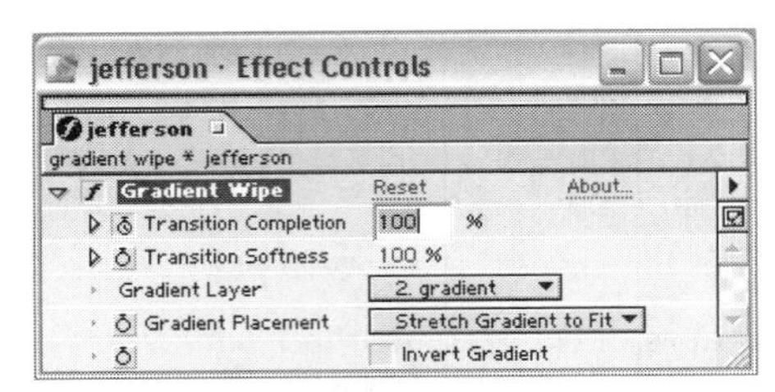

Figure 11.74 Set the Transition Completion property to 100 percent to create the second keyframe.

Video Effects

The Video category contains the following three effects, which are designed to handle issues surrounding video output:

- Broadcast Colors
- Reduce Interlace Flicker
- Timecode

Figure 11.75 The Gradient Wipe transition is as versatile as the number of gradients you create. In this example, the gradient layer lets the figure fade out last.

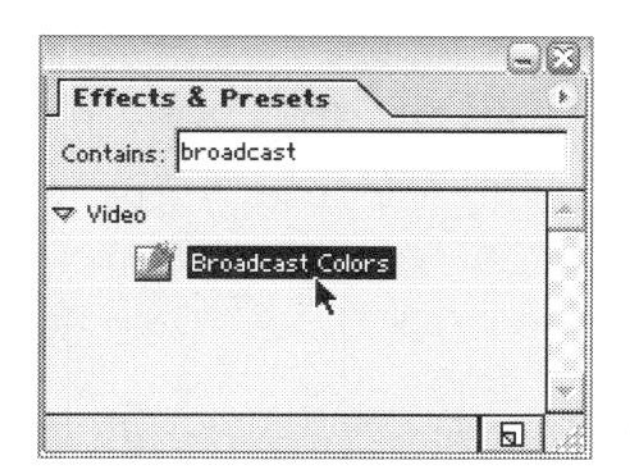

Figure 11.76 Select a layer (or adjustment layer), and double-click the Broadcast Colors effect in the Effects & Presets palette.

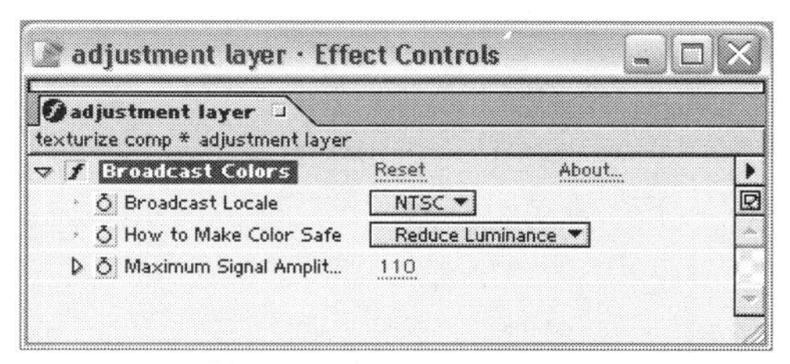

Figure 11.77 The Broadcast Colors effect appears selected in the Effect Controls window.

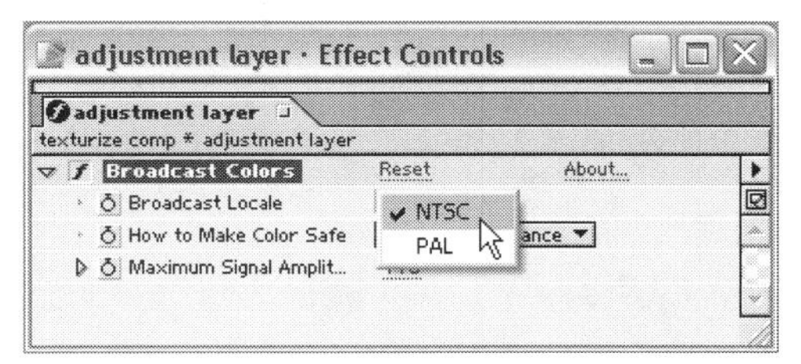

Figure 11.78 Choose a standard in the Broadcast Locale pull-down menu.

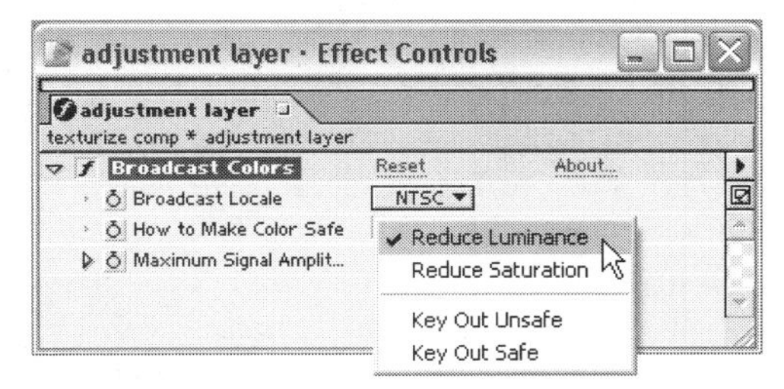

Figure 11.79 Choose a method to correct the levels in the How to Make Color Safe pull-down menu.

Using Broadcast Colors

You use the Broadcast Colors effect to change the brightness and saturation levels of images to ensure that they comply with video standards. See the sidebar "Illegal and Dangerous (or, Do You Know Where Your Levels Are?)" for some technical grounding.

To use the Broadcast Colors effect:

1. Select a layer.

   To apply the effect to multiple layers, use an adjustment layer.

2. Choose Effect > Video > Broadcast Colors, or double-click the Broadcast Colors effect in the Effects & Presets palette (**Figure 11.76**).

   The Broadcast Colors effect appears selected in the Effect Controls window (**Figure 11.77**).

3. *Choose a standard* from the Broadcast Locale pull-down menu (**Figure 11.78**):

   NTSC is the video standard used in North America and Japan.

   PAL is the video standard common in many countries outside North America.

4. *Choose a method* to correct the levels in the How to Make Color Safe pull-down menu (**Figure 11.79**):

   Reduce Luminance corrects unsafe levels by shifting luminance toward black.

   Reduce Saturation corrects unsafe levels by shifting colors toward a grayscale value of a similar brightness (the default setting).

   Key Out Unsafe identifies unsafe areas by making them transparent.

   Key Out Safe identifies unsafe areas by making all other areas transparent.

5. Set the Maximum Signal Amplitude.

   The maximum setting is 120; however, the default setting is a more cautious 110 IRE.

Waveform Monitor and Vectorscope Aren't Surf Reports

Video technicians use two instruments to objectively evaluate video levels: a waveform monitor and a vectorscope.

A *waveform monitor* accurately measures luminance in IRE (pronounced letter-by-letter), which is named after the Institute of Radio Engineers and measures the voltage of the video signal (some of which is interpreted as luminance). A good waveform monitor also displays parts of the video signal reserved for other information, like synch, which is also measured in IRE. A *vectorscope* measures chrominance, or the color components of the signal.

When video professionals look at a tape (like the one you output from After Effects, for example), they calibrate their equipment to faithfully reproduce the video signal. They do this by looking at a color-bar pattern through a waveform monitor and a vectorscope. Assuming the color bars match the levels of the other images on the tape, setting up the bars ensures that the luminance and chrominance are displayed and copied as you intended. (For you print folks, color bars are analogous to a color chip chart, or Pantone colors.)

If you don't want to spring for a professional waveform and vectorscope, good software versions are available. Check out the calibration tools from Echo Fire.

Illegal and Dangerous (or, Do You Know Where Your Levels Are?)

In video, luminance (brightness) values are measured in IRE. The luminance range for broadcast video is restricted so that black registers 15 IRE and white registers 100 IRE. When chrominance (color) is taken into account, the upward limit is 120 IRE. Any picture levels outside that range are considered illegal and don't meet broadcast specifications.

Video colors face similar restrictions. Because video's native color model has a much smaller gamut, or range, than your computer's RGB colors, your computer lets you produce much more saturated colors than video allows. Anything more saturated than video's safe colors will appear noisy or even bleed into areas where it doesn't belong.

In a video facility, technicians process the video signal to reign in unruly luminance and chrominance levels and keep them within the legal limits. On the other hand, your computer's video drivers or output card may introduce some discipline before your animation gets to tape by clipping the levels on output. The problem is similar to preparing images for printing in CMYK. Although you may be willing to let others solve the problem for you, the results can be at best unpredictable and at worst tragic.

Nip the problem in the bud by taking preventative steps. Learn how your equipment handles video levels on input and output. Avoid illegal levels and dangerous colors. And, if necessary, apply the Broadcast Colors effect.

12

Creating and Animating Text

With all its strengths in animation and compositing motion footage, you might expect After Effects to possess more limited text-creation tools, leaving serious typesetting to Photoshop or Illustrator. Not so. After Effects lets you create text with the same ease and flexibility as its software siblings.

True, in older versions of After Effects, creating text meant applying the Basic Text or Path Text effect to a layer. Those effects still exist; but since After Effects 6, you can create a text layer by typing with a type tool directly in a Comp window. Moreover, you can adjust the text using full-featured Character and Paragraph palettes. You can even convert a text layer imported from Photoshop into a text layer you can edit in After Effects. And as in Illustrator, you can convert text into outlines you can manipulate as mask paths.

Naturally, you can animate text layers as you would any other layer in a comp. But you can also animate *the text itself*. Text layers include unique properties that allow you to change the content of the text over time and, yes—like the old Path Text effect—animate the text along a mask path you specify. But more amazing, you can animate individual components of the text—a line, a word, a character—as though it were its own layer. It's like having a text-based animation system within the layer-based animation system. And although the text-animation paradigm employs a unique feature called *animator groups*—each consisting of the properties and parts of the text you want to affect—it also uses the familiar keyframing process you learned about in Chapter 7, "Properties and Keyframes." Animator groups let you create intricate animations using relatively simple controls. Or, if you prefer, you can just apply a "canned" text animation. After Effects includes an astonishingly varied, useful, and generous collection of preset animations you can apply to text with a click of the mouse. OK, *double-click*.

Creating Type

After Effects' Tools palette includes two tools for creating type: the Horizontal Type and Vertical Type tools. Both tools occupy the same location in the palette, but you can access them by pressing and holding one tool to expand the palette and reveal the other (**Figure 12.1**). As you've guessed, the tool you choose depends on whether you want the type to be oriented horizontally or vertically (**Figure 12.2**).

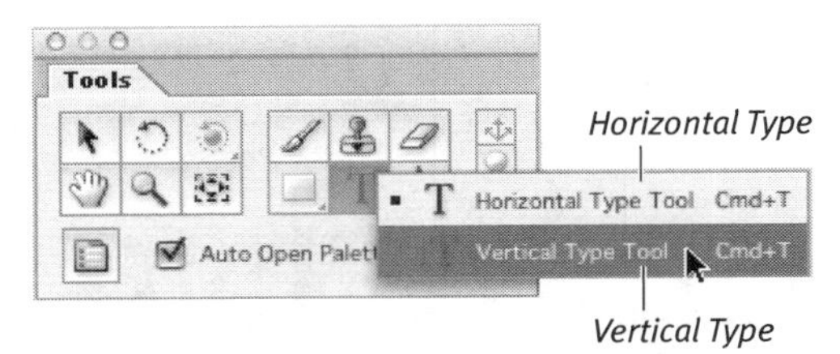

Figure 12.1 Press and hold either type tool to expand the palette and reveal the other.

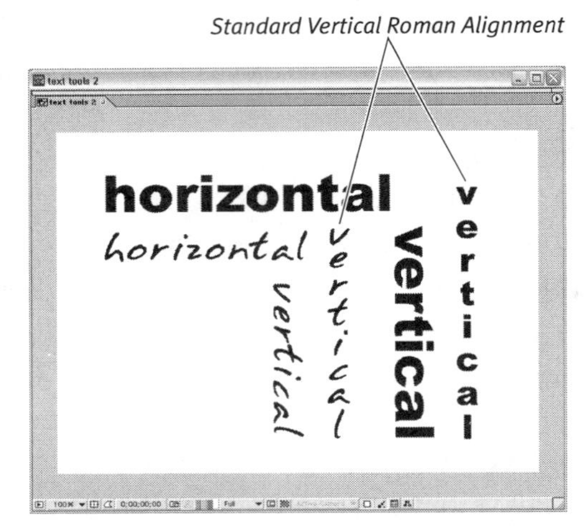

Figure 12.2 The Horizontal Type tool created the "horizontal" text; the Vertical Type tool created the "vertical" text. The way characters appear in a vertical line depends on whether you specify Standard Vertical Roman Alignment.

Point text and paragraph text

Apart from orientation, both tools allow you to create two kinds of text objects: *point text* and *paragraph text*. When you create point text, you use a type tool to set the insertion point and start typing. When you create paragraph text, on the other hand, you first define a *text box* that contains the text.

Initially, there seems to be little difference between the two methods (**Figure 12.3**). But a big practical distinction emerges when it's time to edit the text. With both kinds of text, changing the size of the text layer's bounding box transforms the text—that is, scales or stretches it. That's because the bounding box really consists of layer handles that work like any other layer's handles. But in contrast to point text, paragraph text also lets you resize its *text box*. Paragraph text *reflows* to fit in its text box, creating line breaks if necessary (**Figure 12.4**). This behavior is also known as *word wrap*.

So, as its name suggests, paragraph text is better suited for lengthier messages that may need to be reflowed to better fit the comp or that require paragraph-style layout adjustments, such as margins.

Figure 12.3 Although the point text on top doesn't look any different from the paragraph text on the bottom...

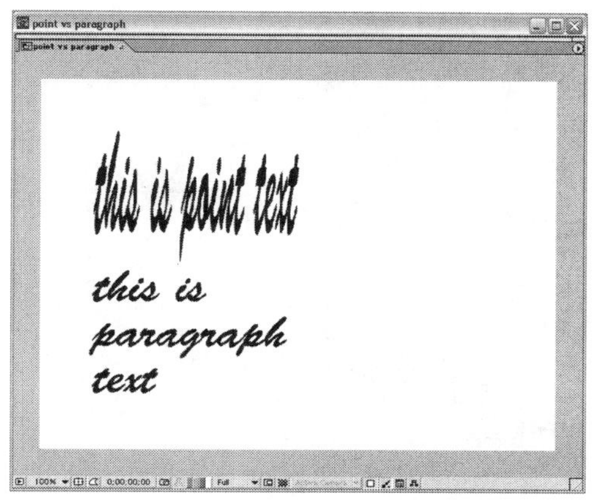

Figure 12.4...resizing the point text's bounding box (its normal layer handles) scales the type, whereas resizing the paragraph text's text box reflows the type.

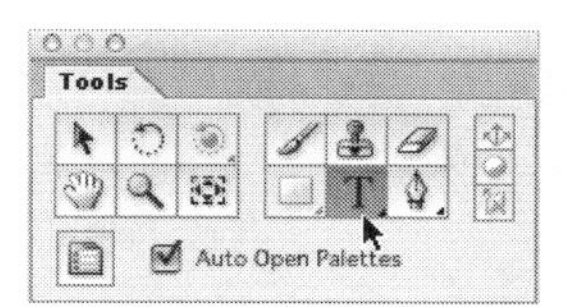

Figure 12.5 Choose the Vertical Type or Horizontal Type tool (shown here).

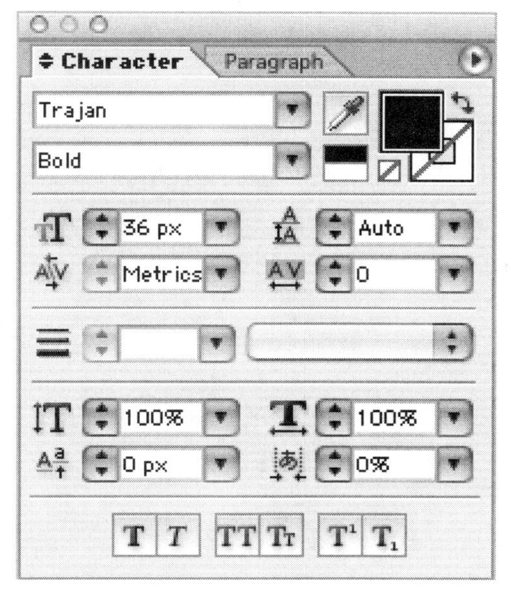

Figure 12.6 Specify how you want the text to look by choosing options in the Character and Paragraph palettes.

✔ Tips

- The four corner handles of a layer's bounding box appear as solid boxes, whereas all the corner handles of a text box appear hollow.
- The vertical orientation is particularly useful for Chinese, Japanese, and Korean text.

To create point text:

1. In the Tools palette, *choose either of the following tools:*

   ▲ **Horizontal Type** [T] —Creates horizontally oriented text (**Figure 12.5**)

   ▲ **Vertical Type** [↓T] —Creates vertically oriented text

   Both tools occupy the same location in the palette. To choose the hidden tool, press and hold the tool button to expand the palette, or use the keyboard shortcut Cmd-T (Mac) or Ctrl-T (Windows).

2. Specify character and paragraph options using controls in the appropriate palette (**Figure 12.6**).

   You can select and modify the text at any time. See sections later in this chapter for more information.

3. In the Composition window, position the mouse where you want the text to begin.

   As you position the mouse pointer, it appears as an I-beam icon [I]. The short horizontal line in the I-beam icon indicates the location of the text's baseline.

4. When the I-beam icon is where you want, click the mouse.

   A vertical line appears where you clicked, indicating the text's insertion point.

continues on next page

5. Type the text you want (**Figure 12.7**).

   Text appears at the insertion point, using the current character settings (font, size, fill color, and so on) and paragraph settings. The direction in which characters proceed from the insertion point depends on the current alignment or justification setting (see "Aligning and Justifying Paragraphs" later in this chapter).

6. When you're finished typing, choose the Selection tool.

   In the Comp window, bounding box handles indicate that the new text object is selected. In the Timeline window, a text layer appears, and its name matches what you typed (**Figure 12.8**).

Figure 12.7 Click to set the text's insertion point (indicated by a vertical line), and type the message you want.

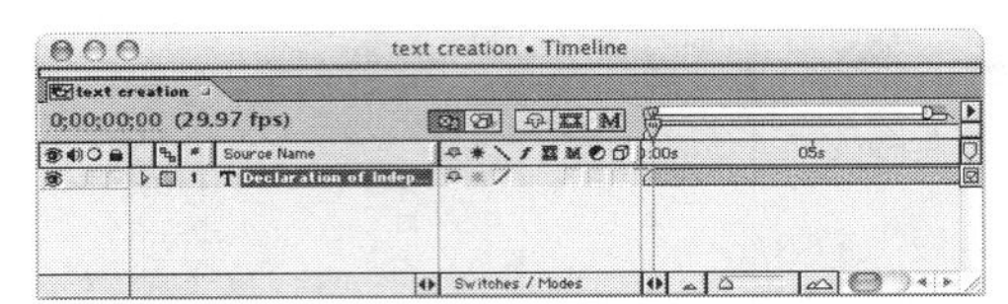

Figure 12.8 When you choose the Selection tool, the new text layer is selected in the Comp window. In the Timeline window, its layer name matches what you typed.

To create paragraph text:

1. In the Tools palette, *choose either of the following tools:*
   - ▲ **Horizontal Type** —Creates horizontally oriented text (**Figure 12.9**)
   - ▲ **Vertical Type** —Creates vertically oriented text

   Both tools occupy the same location in the palette. To choose the hidden tool, press and hold the tool button to expand the palette, or use the keyboard shortcut Cmd-T (Mac) or Ctrl-T (Windows).

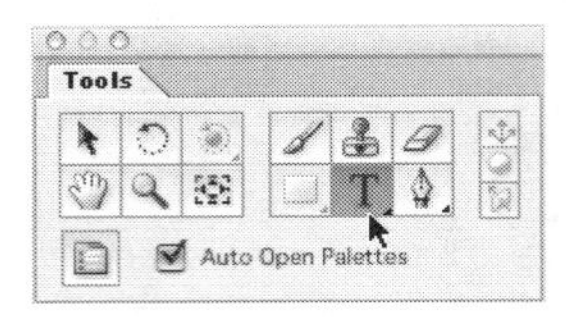

Figure 12.9 Choose the Vertical Type or Horizontal Type tool (shown here).

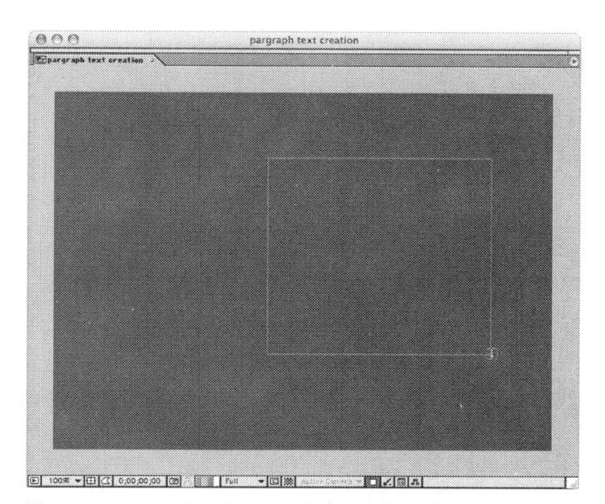

Figure 12.10 In the Comp window, drag the mouse diagonally to define the size of the text box.

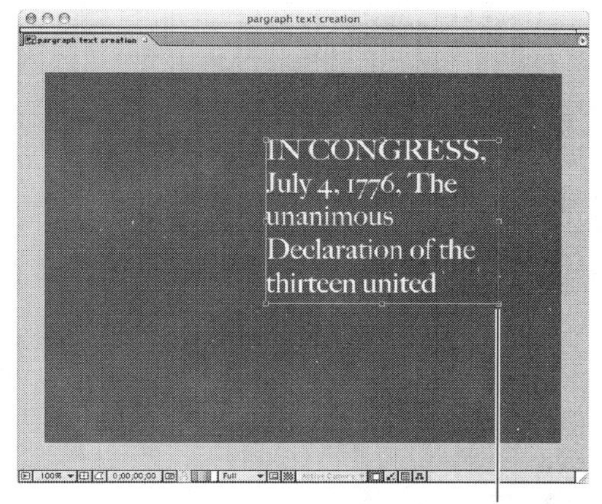

Figure 12.11 When text reaches the side border of the text box, it flows to the next line automatically. If you type more than the text box can contain vertically, the text box's bottom-right handle displays a plus sign (+).

2. In the Composition window, drag the mouse diagonally to define a text box (**Figure 12.10**).

   When you release the mouse, a text box appears with a vertical insertion point icon in the upper-left corner.

3. Type the text you want.

   When the text box you defined can't contain the text horizontally, the text continues on the next line (by means of a *soft return*). Text that exceeds the vertical limit of its text box remains hidden until you resize the text box. When text is hidden this way, the bottom-right handle of the text box includes a plus sign, or crosshairs ⊞ (**Figure 12.11**).

4. To resize the text box to include hidden text or reflow visible text, drag any of its eight handles.

   The text reflows to fit within the text box. When the text box is large enough to hold all the text, the bottom-right handle no longer displays a plus sign (**Figure 12.12**).

continues on next page

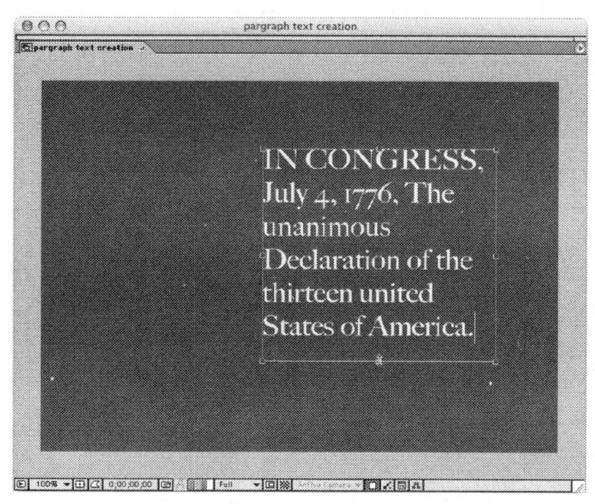

Figure 12.12 While in editing mode, you can drag the text box's handles to resize it and reveal hidden text.

5. When you're finished creating the message and resizing the text box, click the Selection tool.

   In the Timeline window, a text layer appears; its name matches what you typed. In the Comp window, bounding box handles indicate that the new text object is selected (**Figure 12.13**). Note that resizing the text layer's bounding box scales the text object. To change the size of the text box and reflow the text, you must enter text-editing mode (as explained in the following task, "To resize a text bounding box").

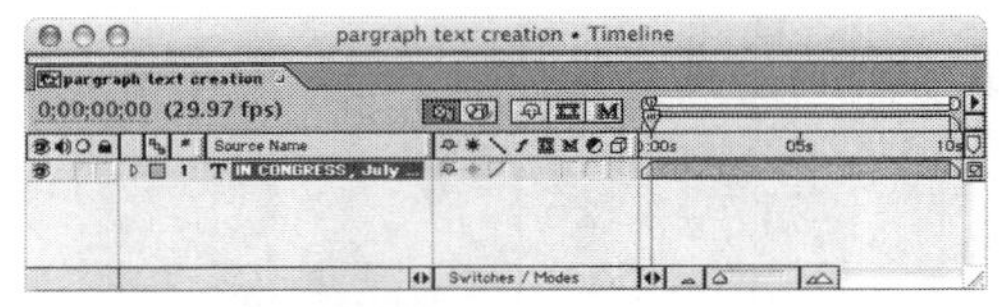

Figure 12.13 Choosing the Selection tool exits editing mode, and the text layer appears selected in the Comp window. In the Timeline window, the layer's name matches the text itself.

To resize a text bounding box:

1. *Do either of the following:*

   ▲ Select the Horizontal Type tool or Vertical Type tool, and click on paragraph text.

   ▲ Using the Selection tool, double-click on paragraph text (**Figure 12.14**).

   An insertion point cursor appears, indicating that you can edit the text. Text box handles also appear. Note that all the handles in a text box are hollow, whereas the four corners of regular layer handles (bounding box handles) are solid (**Figure 12.15**).

Figure 12.14 Clicking text with a type tool or double-clicking text with the Selection tool (shown here) activates text-editing mode. Layer handles are replaced by text box handles.

Figure 12.15 In text-editing mode, drag any of the text box handles to resize the box...

Figure 12.16...and reflow the text.

Figure 12.17 With a type tool, Ctrl-click (Mac) or right-click (Windows) the text layer, and choose the available option in the context menu.

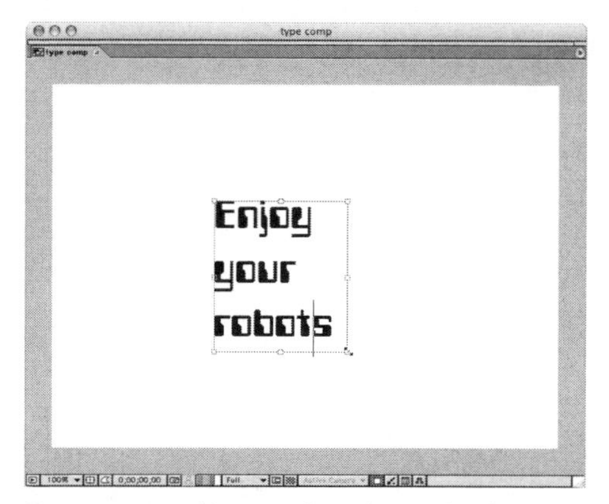

Figure 12.18 In this example, point text has been converted into paragraph text.

2. Drag any of the text box handles to resize the text box.

   The text contained in the box reflows to fit in the box horizontally (**Figure 12.16**). Text that doesn't fit in the text box vertically is hidden, and the text box's lower-right handle appears with a crosshair.

3. When you're finished editing the text box or text itself, make sure to choose the Selection tool to exit text-editing mode and select the text layer.

To convert point text to paragraph text, and vice versa:

1. Using the Selection tool, select the text layer you want to convert.

2. In the Character palette, select the Horizontal Type tool or Vertical Type tool.

3. With the type tool, Ctrl-click (Mac) or right-click (Windows) the text layer, and choose the appropriate option (**Figure 12.17**):

   ▲ **Convert to Paragraph Text**

   ▲ **Convert to Point Text**

   The text is converted (**Figure 12.18**). When you're converting paragraph text to point text, soft returns (line breaks caused when text reaches the edge of the text box) are converted into hard returns (line breaks caused by pressing Return [Mac] or Enter [Windows]).

To convert horizontal text to vertical text, and vice versa:

1. Using the Selection tool, select the text layer you want to convert.
2. In the Character palette, select the Horizontal Type tool or Vertical Type tool.
3. With the type tool, Ctrl-click (Mac) or right-click (Windows) the text layer, and choose the appropriate option (**Figure 12.19**):
   - ▲ **Horizontal**
   - ▲ **Vertical**

   The text is converted (**Figure 12.20**).

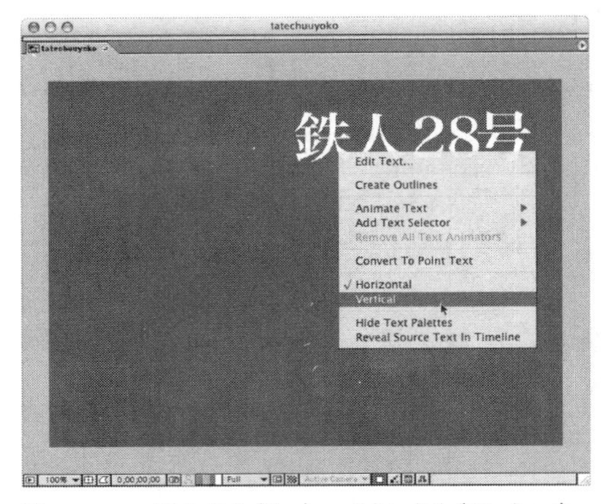

Figure 12.19 Ctrl-click (Mac) or right-click (Windows) the text, and choose the available option in the context menu. Here, horizontal text...

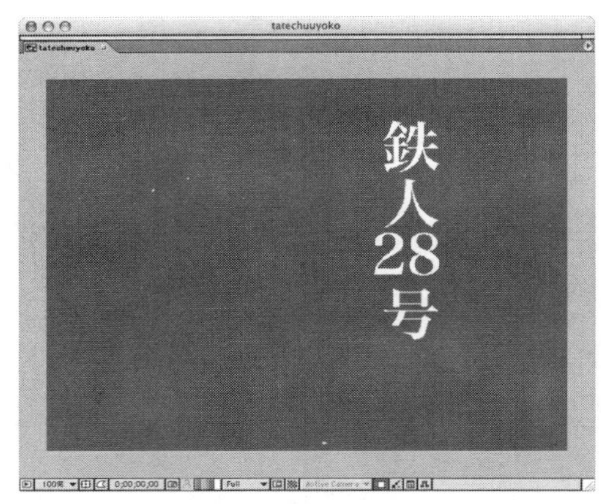

Figure 12.20...is converted into vertical text.

Figure 12.21 Select a range of vertical text. Here, Standard Vertical Roman Alignment is disabled, and characters appear sideways.

To change the alignment of vertically oriented text:

1. Select a range of characters in a vertical text layer (**Figure 12.21**).
2. In the Character palette, choose Standard Vertical Roman Alignment from the pull-down menu (**Figure 12.22**).

   When the option is selected, vertical text characters are upright; when the option is unselected, vertical text is sideways (**Figure 12.23**).

✔ Tip

- You can't convert a text layer from horizontal to vertical (or vice versa) when it's in text-editing mode.

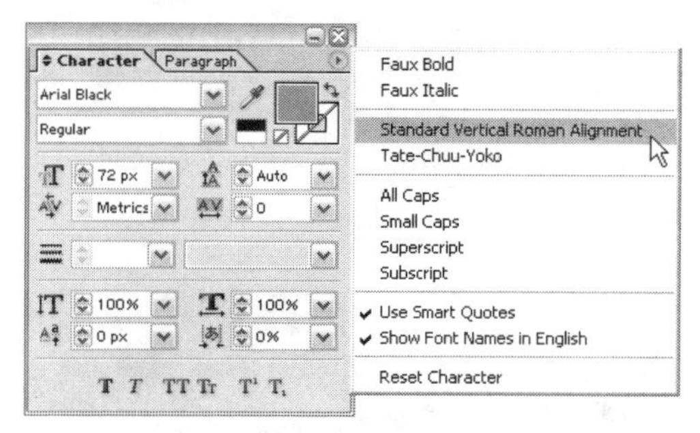

Figure 12.22 Choosing Standard Vertical Roman Alignment in the Character palette's pull-down menu...

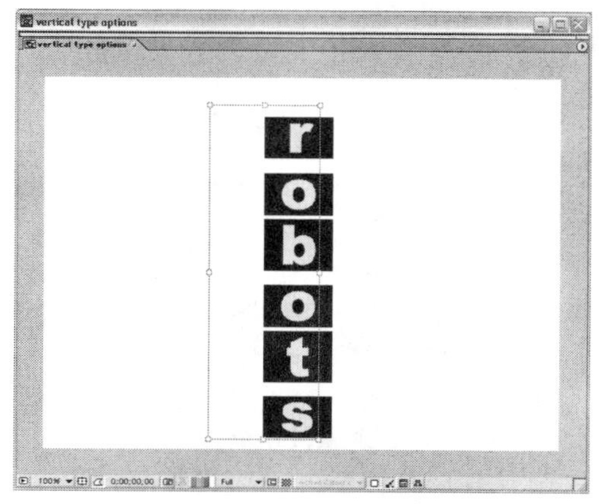

Figure 12.23...makes each character in the vertical line appear upright.

Editing Type

Making changes to type in After Effects is as easy and intuitive as in other Adobe applications, such as Illustrator or Photoshop. Just make sure to select the characters you want to modify first, and then use the Character and Paragraph palettes to make the adjustments.

It's worth noting that the methods discussed in the following sections change the content and attributes of the selected text. Of course, you can also modify the entire text layer, using the same methods you'd use to modify any other layer.

To select characters for editing:

1. To select all the characters in the text layer, double-click the layer in the Comp window with the Selection tool.

   All characters in the text layer appear highlighted (**Figure 12.24**).

2. With the characters highlighted, *do any of the following:*

   ▲ To set an insertion point between characters, click between the characters (**Figure 12.25**).

   ▲ To highlight a limited range of characters, click and drag to highlight the characters you want to adjust (**Figure 12.26**).

   If you set an insertion point, you can add or delete characters, or adjust the kerning. If you select a range of characters, you can change any of their attributes using controls in the Character and Paragraph palettes.

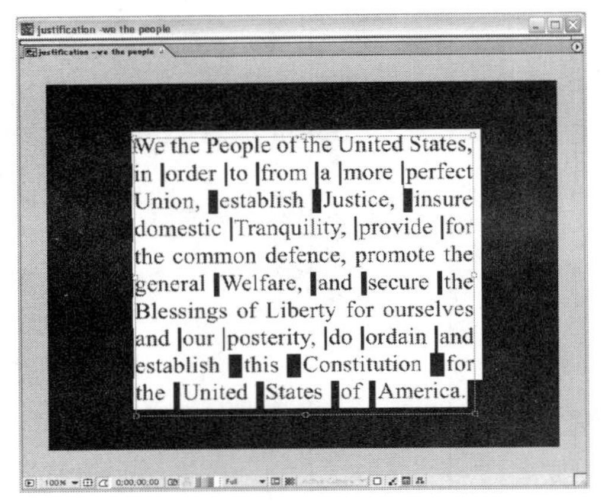

Figure 12.24 Double-clicking the text with the Selection tool activates editing mode. The text is highlighted (and for paragraph text, layer handles are replaced with text box handles).

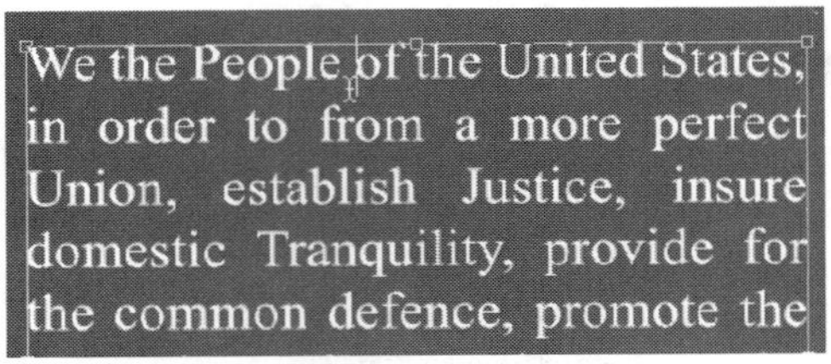

Figure 12.25 Click again to set an insertion point (indicated by a vertical line)...

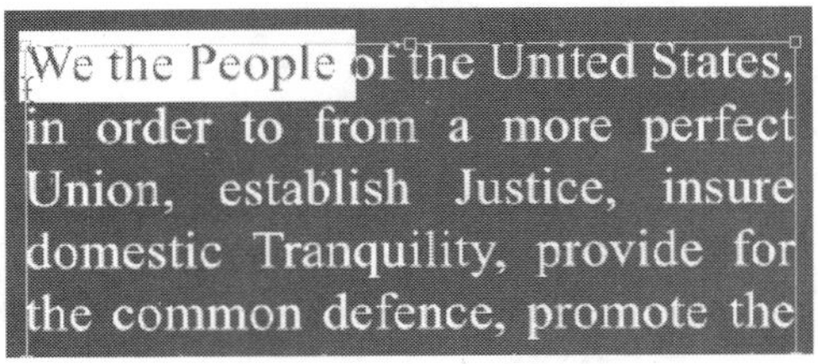

Figure 12.26...or click and drag to highlight a range of characters. Now you can edit the content or attributes of the selection.

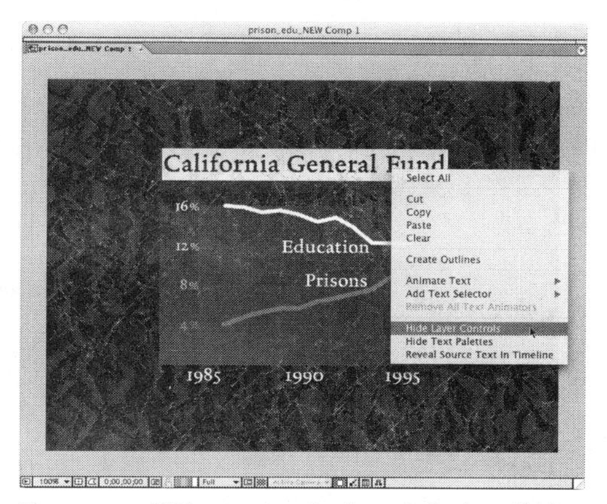

Figure 12.27 With a type tool selected, Option-clicking (Mac) or right-clicking (Windows) text and choosing Hide Layer Controls...

To show and hide layer controls:

- With a type tool selected, Option-click (Mac) or right-click (Windows) text, and choose the appropriate option (**Figure 12.27**):
  - **Hide Layer Controls**
  - **Show Layer Controls**

  The available option depends on the current status of the layer controls. Hiding layer controls prevents highlighted text from obscuring changes such as fill color and the like (**Figure 12.28**).

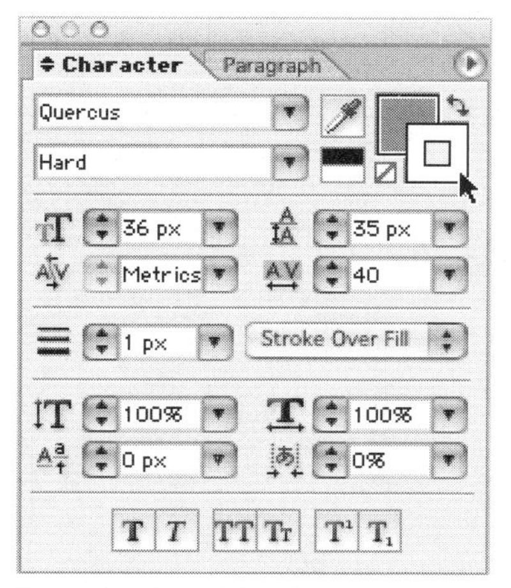

Figure 12.28...removes the highlight from the selection. Here, the text is selected, but the usual selection highlight is hidden so it's easier to see adjustments to fill and stroke.

To edit text imported from Photoshop:

1. Import a Photoshop file containing text.

   You can import a single layer as a footage item, or import a layered file as a comp. See Chapter 2, "Importing Footage into a Project."

2. If necessary, make the imported text a layer in a composition, and select the layer (**Figure 12.29**).

3. Choose Layer > Convert To Editable Text (**Figure 12.30**).

   The imported Photoshop text becomes an editable text layer (**Figure 12.31**).

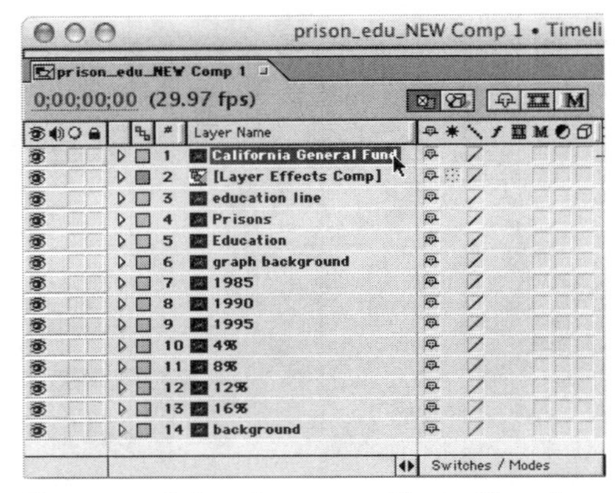

Figure 12.29 Select a layer created from a Photoshop text layer imported as a footage item.

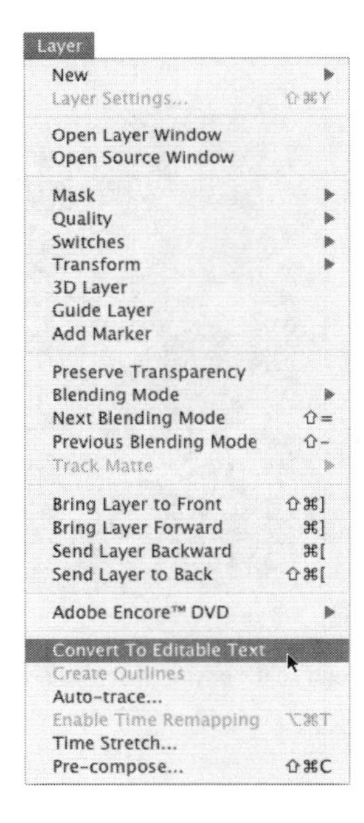

Figure 12.30 Choose Layer > Convert To Editable Text.

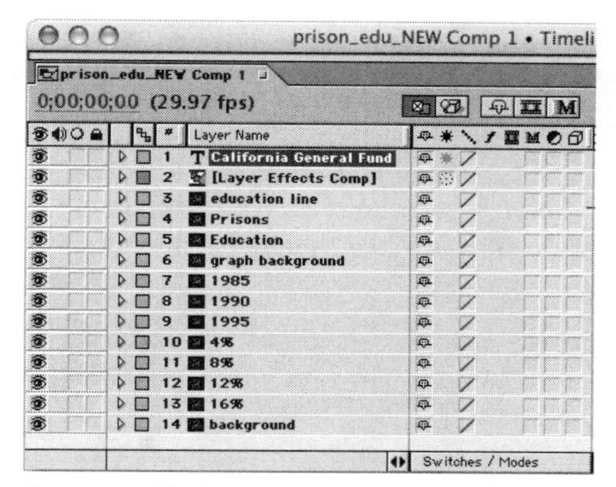

Figure 12.31 The imported Photoshop text becomes a text layer you can edit.

✔ Tips

- You can move the layer without deselecting a range of characters by pressing Cmd (Mac) or Ctrl (Windows) as you drag the text layer.
- Once you set the insertion point cursor, you can use the keyboard to move the insertion point cursor and highlight characters. Use the left and right arrow keys to move the cursor; press Shift-arrow to highlight one character at a time; or press Cmd-Shift-arrow (Mac) or Ctrl-Shift-arrow (Windows) to highlight a word at a time.
- To make changes to a source Photoshop file (or a file created with other Adobe programs), choose Edit > Edit Original.

Using the Character and Paragraph Palettes

After Effects includes two palettes for controlling aspects of type: the Character palette and the Paragraph palette. Both palettes are nearly identical to their counterparts in Photoshop and Illustrator. To make your workflow easier, you can set the palettes to open automatically whenever you select a type tool. Both palettes include intuitive buttons and pull-down menus for setting various format options. For options with numeric values, you can set a value in several convenient ways.

To open and close the Character and Paragraph palettes:

1. In the Tools palette, select either the Horizontal Type tool or Vertical Type tool.
   A Toggle Palettes button and the Auto Open Palettes option appear in the Tools palette. If Auto Open Palettes is selected, the Character and Paragraph palettes open automatically (see the next step).
2. In the Tools palette, *do either of the following* (**Figure 12.32**):
   - ▲ Select Auto Open Palettes.

   When the option is checked, selecting certain tools (such as type and paint tools) opens the related palettes automatically.
   - ▲ Click the Toggle Palettes button to toggle the Character and Paragraph palettes open and closed.

   Unless you separate their tabs, the Character and Paragraph palettes open in the same window by default (**Figure 12.33**).

✔ Tips

- As always, you can open or close any palette from the menu bar, by choosing Window > and selecting the name of the palette.
- When the Paintbrush, Clone, or Eraser tool is selected, the Auto Open Palettes option and Toggle Palettes button affect the Paint and Brush Tips palettes.

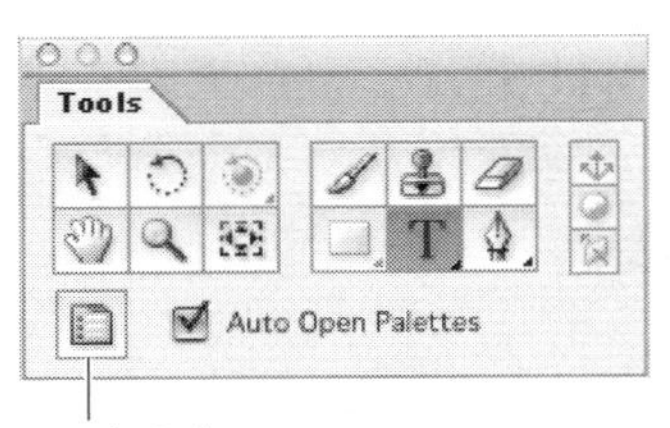

Figure 12.32 With Auto Open Palettes selected, the Character and Paragraph palettes open whenever you select a Type tool. Or, click the Toggle Palettes button to open and close the palettes manually.

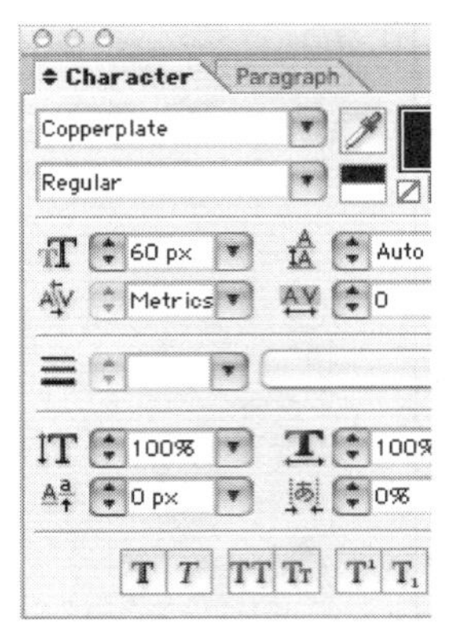

Figure 12.33 By default, the Character and Paragraph palettes open as tabbed palettes in the same window.

To set values in the Character and Paragraph palettes:

- In the Character or Paragraph palette, find the icon corresponding to the attribute you want to adjust, and *do any of the following:*
  - ▲ To change an attribute by scrubbing, drag the mouse pointer over the appropriate icon to the left (to decrease the value) or to the right (to increase the value) (**Figure 12.34**).
  - ▲ To change the value by increments, click the up or down arrow button next to the corresponding icon (**Figure 12.35**).

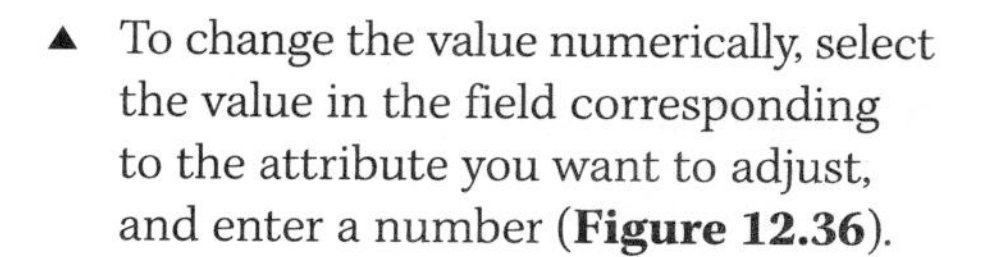

  - ▲ To change the value numerically, select the value in the field corresponding to the attribute you want to adjust, and enter a number (**Figure 12.36**).

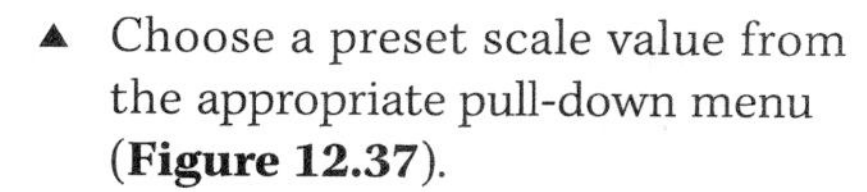

  - ▲ Choose a preset scale value from the appropriate pull-down menu (**Figure 12.37**).

Not all formatting options include the same set of controls. The units (pixels, percentages, and so on) and possible range of values depend on the formatting option you're adjusting. Certain formatting options use special buttons (alignment, justification) or controls (fill and stroke).

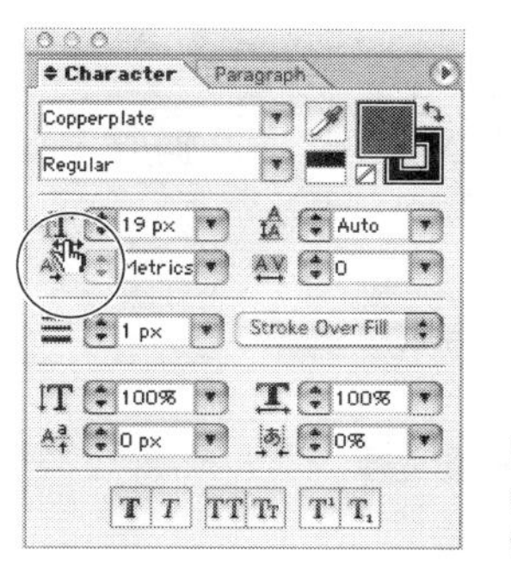

Figure 12.34 Scrub an icon to change its corresponding value...

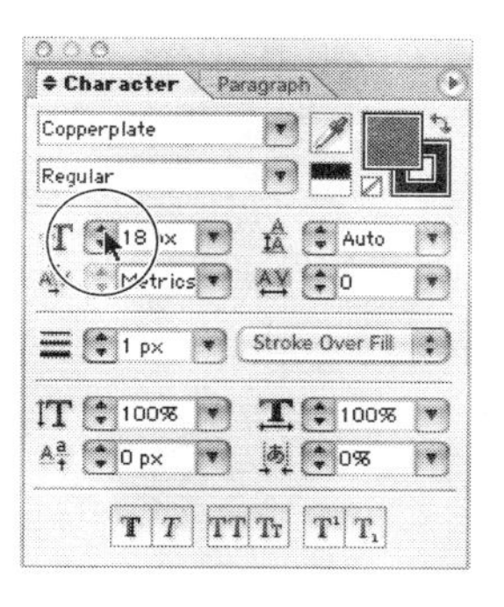

Figure 12.35 ...click its up or down arrow button...

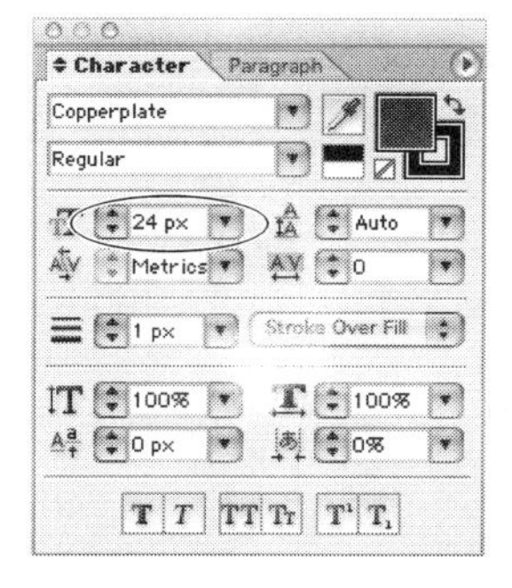

Figure 12.36 ...enter a value in its value field...

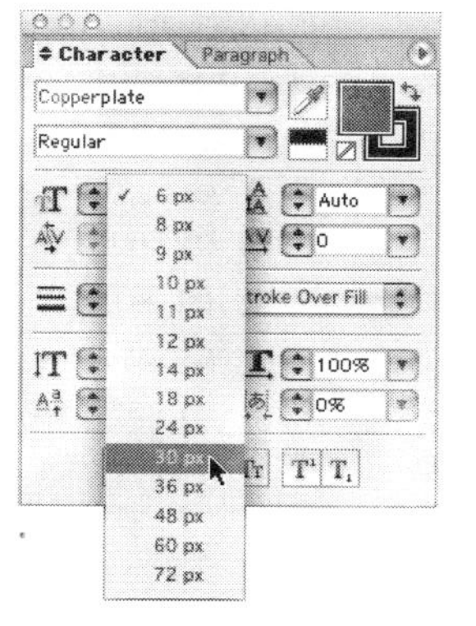

Figure 12.37 ...or choose a preset value from a pull-down menu (if available).

To reset a character or paragraph to its default settings:

1. In the text layer, select the characters or paragraphs you want to reset to their default formatting settings (**Figure 12.38**).
2. *Do either of the following:*
   - ▲ To reset selected characters, choose Reset Character from the Character palette's pull-down menu.
   - ▲ To reset selected paragraphs, choose Reset Paragraph from the Paragraph palette's pull-down menu.

   Both palettes contain a Reset option (**Figure 12.39**). The selection's formatting settings reset to its defaults (**Figure 12.40**).

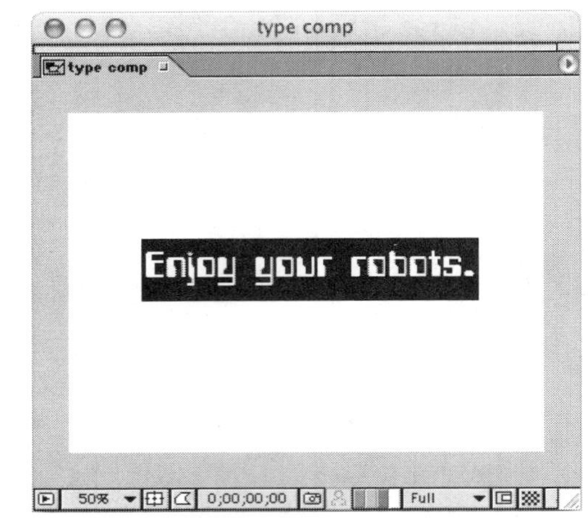

Figure 12.38 Select the characters you want to change to their default settings...

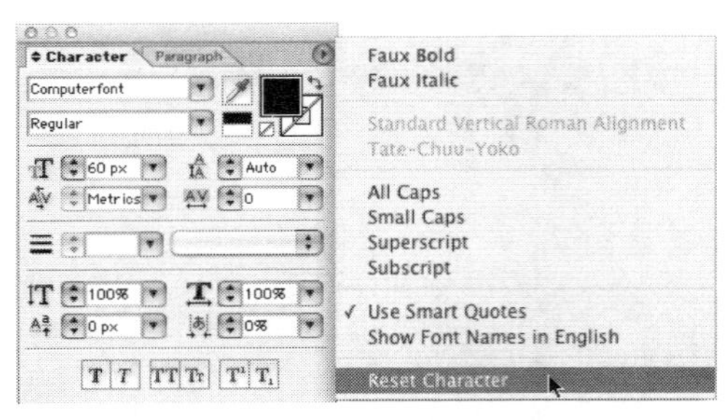

Figure 12.39...and choose Reset in the Paragraph palette or Character palette (shown here)...

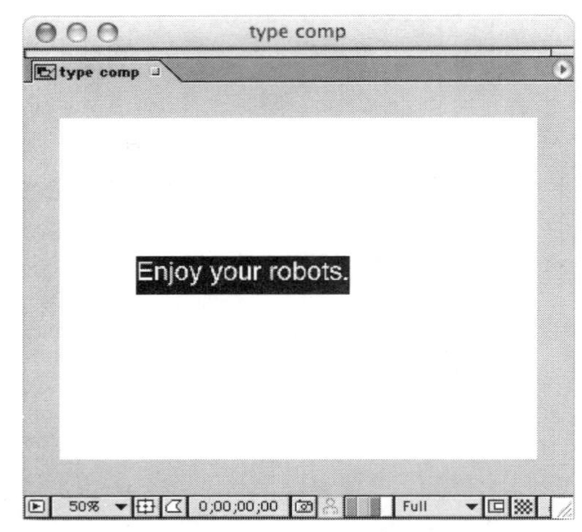

Figure 12.40...to reset the corresponding set of attributes.

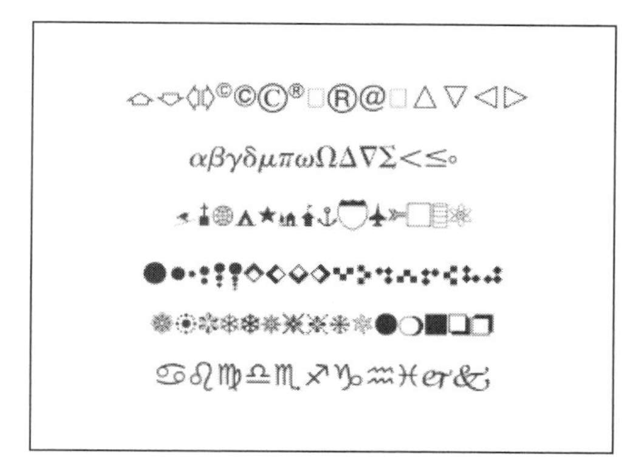

Figure 12.41 Don't forget that a host of specialized fonts—symbols, dingbats, ornaments, and so on—and foreign language fonts are at your disposal.

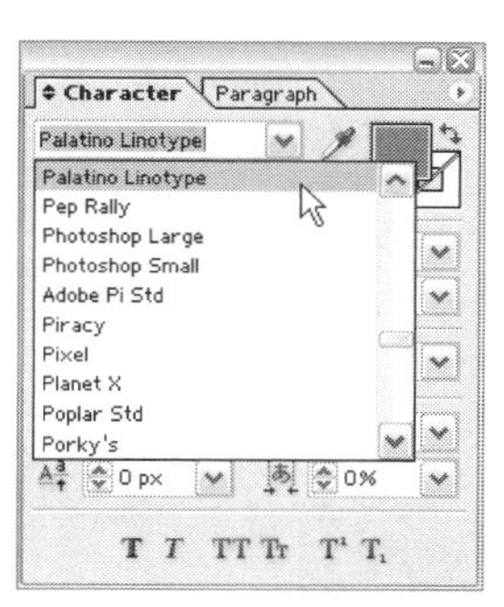

Figure 12.42 Choose the font you want from the Font pull-down menu.

Formatting Characters

You can set formatting options before you type, or you can apply formatting options to a range of selected characters. The Character palette includes a number of options found in other Adobe programs: font, style, fill and stroke, size, leading, tracking, kerning, scale, and baseline shift (and its exotic cousin, Tsume). You can also apply faux bold, faux italics, small caps, superscript, and subscript to fonts that don't include these forms. You can even use smart quotes in place of standard quotation marks.

Font and style

As you're probably aware, a *font* is a set of *typefaces*, or type designs; it determines the overall look of the text characters. Many fonts include a number of *styles*, or variations on the font: bold, italic, condensed, light, and so on.

Remember: Not all fonts resemble letters. By loading specialized fonts—often called symbols, dingbats, or ornaments—you can easily create useful graphic elements. These fonts are as versatile and scalable as any other elements, and you won't have to draw a thing (**Figure 12.41**).

And don't forget that many foreign-language fonts are also readily available. You can specify whether the font menu lists them in English or in their native language.

To set the font and style:

1. In the Character palette, choose a font from the Font pull-down menu (**Figure 12.42**).

   The font's default style option appears in the Style pull-down menu.

continues on next page

2. In the Style pull-down menu, specify the style you want (**Figure 12.43**).

   The options available in the list depend on the font you selected in step 1. The selected characters use the font you specified (**Figure 12.44**).

✔ Tips

- You can quickly choose a font name or style by typing the name in the appropriate field. As you type, After Effects specifies the font or style that most closely matches what you enter.
- If the font you're using doesn't include a bold or italic style option, you can apply a faux bold or faux italic style. See the section "Faux bold and faux italics" later in this chapter.
- For video output, avoid light text or text with fine features, like *serifs* (the little tapering corners of letters in so-called old-style typefaces, like this one). Interlacing causes fine horizontal lines to flicker, making some text difficult to read. See Chapter 2 for more about video interlacing.

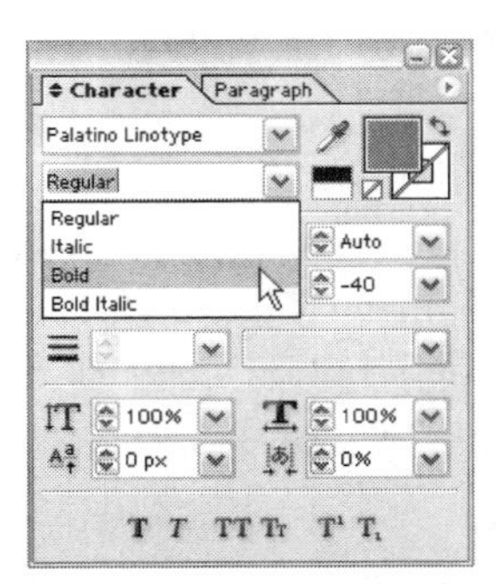

Figure 12.43 Choose a variation in the Style pull-down menu. Style options available in the pull-down menu depend on the font you select.

Fill and stroke

Each character has two possible color attributes: fill and stroke. Not surprisingly, the *fill color* is the color of the character: the color within its contours. The *stroke color* is the color of the character's contours: its outlines. Naturally, you can detect the stroke color only if the stroke has a thickness greater than zero. By default, applying a stroke color sets the stroke width to 1 pixel, but you can change the thickness and set whether the stroke is applied over or under the fill (see the task "To set stroke options" later in this chapter).

You can set the fill and stroke color by using controls in the Character palette. If you've used programs like Photoshop and Illustrator, you should already be familiar with these icons. If not, don't confuse the stroke color icon with the drop-shadow color or background color icons sometimes found in other, less-full-featured programs.

Figure 12.44 Selected and subsequent characters use the font and style you selected.

To set the fill and stroke color:

1. In the Character palette, click the icon for the color you want to set:

   ▲ **Fill Box**—Sets the fill color

   ▲ **Stroke Box**—Sets the stroke color

   The selected color's icon appears in front of the other icon.

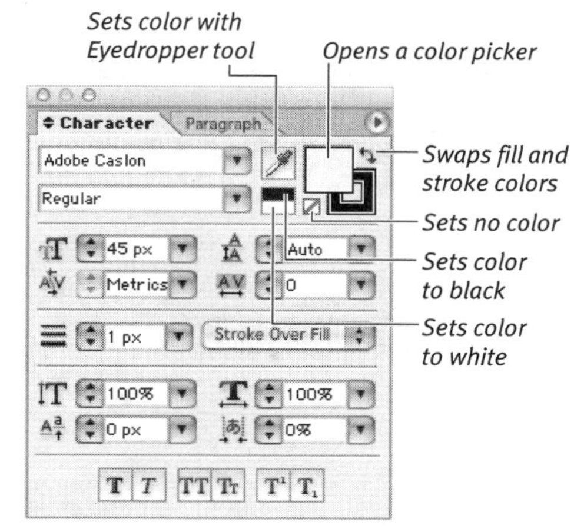

Figure 12.45 Click the Fill Box or Stroke Box to make it active; the active color's icon overlaps the other. Then set the active color by clicking the appropriate icon.

2. To set the active color, *do any of the following* (**Figure 12.45**):

   ▲ To sample a color from anywhere on the screen, click the Eyedropper icon, and then click the color.

   ▲ To set the color to black or white, click the appropriate color swatch under the Eyedropper icon.

   ▲ To set the color to transparent, click the No Fill/Stroke color icon.

   ▲ To set the color using a color picker, click the active color's icon.

   The active color box (fill or stroke) is set to the color you specify; the color is also applied to selected characters and to any subsequent characters you type.

To set the stroke width:

◆ In the Character palette, specify a value for Stroke Width (**Figure 12.46**).

  The stroke width you specified is applied to the selected characters (or to subsequent characters you type) (**Figure 12.47**). You can't set stroke options to characters with stroke color set to No Stroke.

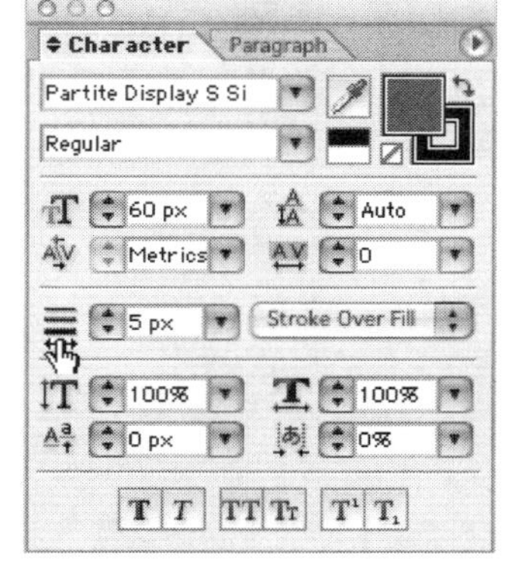

Figure 12.46 Set the Stroke Width, or thickness.

wafflepooldrunk

wafflepooldrunk

wafflepooldrunk

Figure 12.47 Here, words and characters use varying stroke widths.

FORMATTING CHARACTERS

To set stroke options:

- Select the characters you want to modify; and, in the Character palette, *select an option* from the Stroke pull-down menu (**Figure 12.48**):

  Fill Over Stroke applies the fill color over the stroke color, so that the fill covers half the thickness of the stroke.

  Stroke Over Fill applies the stroke color over the fill color, so that the entire thickness of the stroke is visible and covers part of the interior of the filled character.

  All Fills Over All Strokes affects the entire text layer.

  All Strokes Over All Fills affects the entire text layer.

  Selected and subsequent characters use the stroke options you specify (**Figure 12.49**).

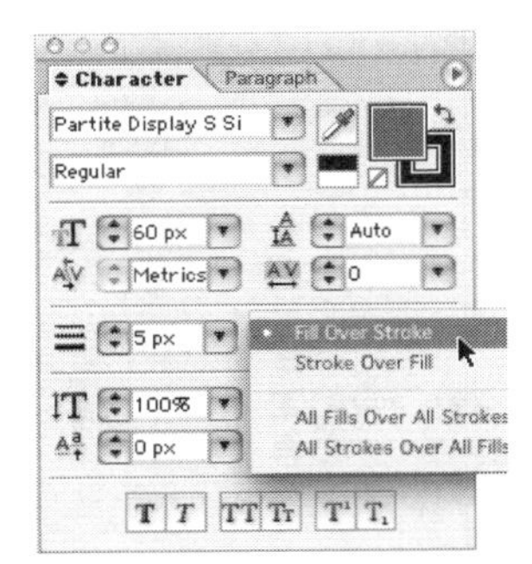

Figure 12.48 Specify how strokes are applied by choosing an option from the Stroke pull-down menu.

Figure 12.49 In this figure, you can see how applying the stroke over the fill (the upper text) contrasts with applying the fill over the stroke (the lower text).

Font size

The size determines—how else can you put it?—the size of a given font. In After Effects, font size is expressed in pixels (not points or picas, as in other programs). However, you should note that if you set two different fonts to the same size, one often appears larger than the other.

To set the font size:

- In the Character palette, specify a value for the font size (**Figure 12.50**).

  The font size you specified is applied to the selected characters (and to subsequent characters you type) (**Figure 12.51**).

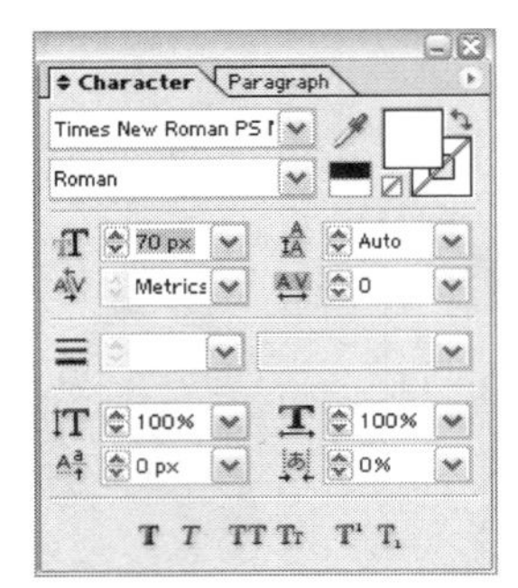

Figure 12.50 In After Effects, you specify the font size in pixels (not points or picas).

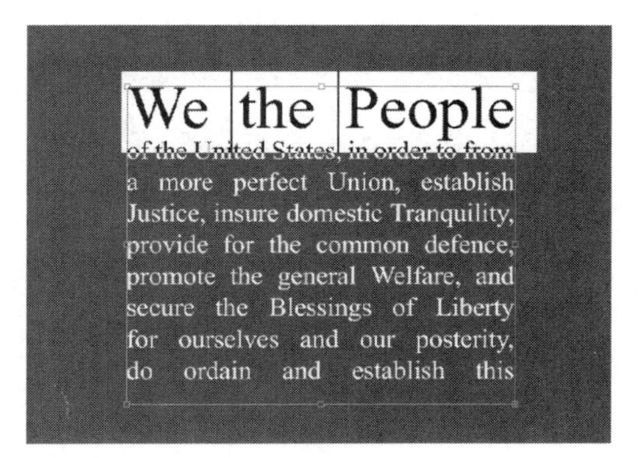

Figure 12.51 This text's font size is so large that the words can only be read once the text layer is animated to move through the screen.

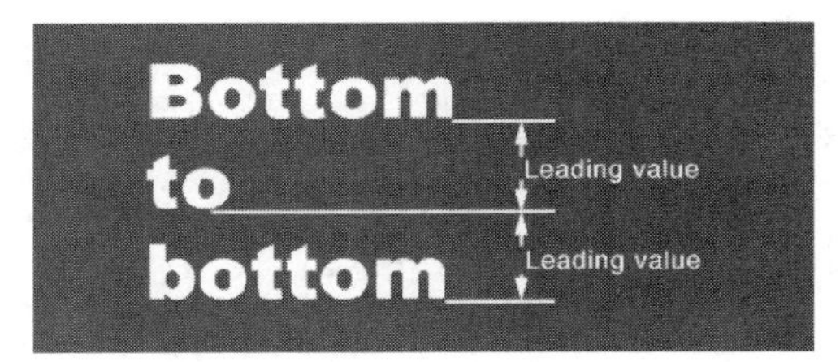

Figure 12.52 Bottom-to-bottom leading is measured from one baseline to the next.

Figure 12.53 Top-to-top leading is measured from the top of one line to the top of the next.

✔ **Tip**

- Dragging a text layer's handles scales the entire layer; it won't change the type size, per se, or even affect the horizontal or vertical scaling (explained later in this chapter). But because After Effects continuously rasterizes text layers, the text looks the same whether you resize the font size or the text layer itself.

Leading

Leading (which rhymes with *wedding)* defines the space between lines of text. The term *leading* refers to the strips of lead that typesetters of old placed between lines of metal type.

In After Effects, leading can be measured either from bottom to bottom or from top to top. The *bottom-to-bottom* method measures from the baseline (the invisible floor on which a line of text rests) of one line of text to the baseline of the next line (**Figure 12.52**). The *top-to-top* method, in contrast, measures leading from the top of one line to the top of the next (**Figure 12.53**). Consequently, the first line of text aligns with the top of the text box when you specify top-to-top measurement. (For more about baselines, see "Baseline shift" later in this chapter.)

continues on next page

Whatever method you use, increasing leading expands the space between lines, whereas a negative leading value reduces the space (**Figure 12.54**).

To adjust leading:

1. Select the lines of type you want to adjust.
2. In the Character palette, *do one of the following*:
   - ▲ Specify the value for leading (**Figure 12.55**).
   - ▲ To have After Effects calculate the leading, choose Auto from the pull-down menu.

   The leading you specified is applied to the selected characters (or to subsequent characters you type).

To specify how leading is measured:

◆ In the Paragraph palette's pull-down menu, select the leading measurement method you want (**Figure 12.56**):

Top-to-Top Leading measures between the tops of lines of type; this causes the first line of type to align with the top of the text box.

Bottom-to-Bottom Leading measures between the baselines of type; space is included between the top of the text box and the first line of type.

Leading is measured according to the method you specify.

✔ Tip

■ Leading is called Line Spacing in the controls for the Basic Text effect. Because the Path Text effect doesn't accept multiple lines of text, it doesn't include leading controls.

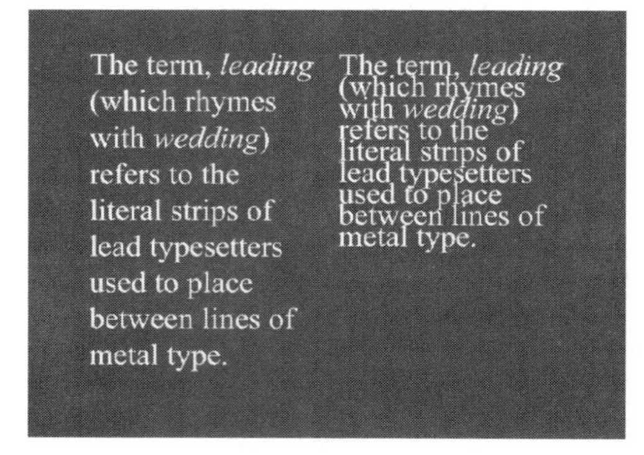

Figure 12.54 Leading can be loose (as in the text on the left) or so tight the text overlaps (as in the text on the right).

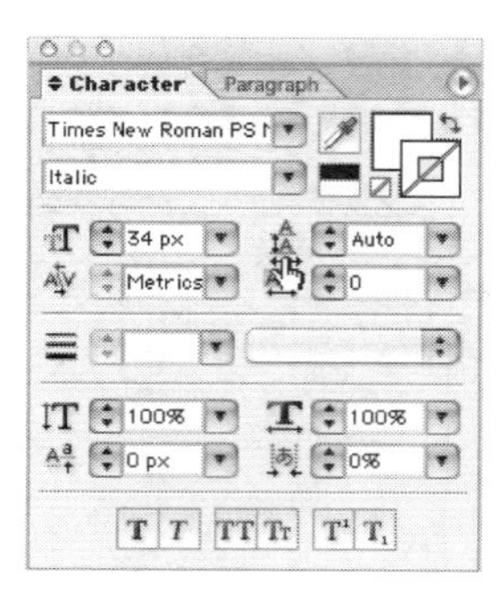

Figure 12.55 Set a value for leading, or choose Auto from the Leading pull-down menu.

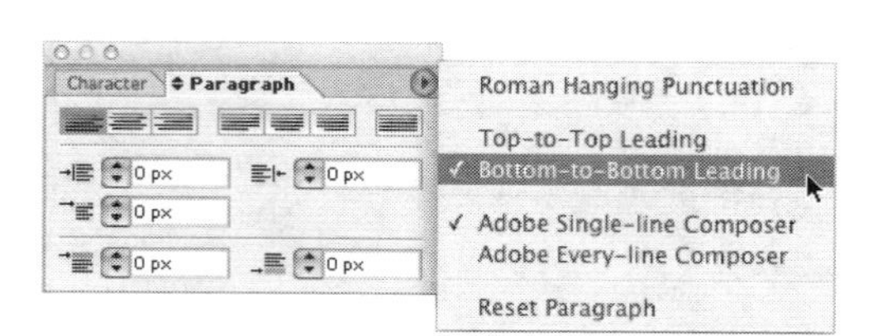

Figure 12.56 Specify how leading is measured in the Paragraph palette's pull-down menu.

Figure 12.57 You can adjust tracking to be tight (so tight that characters overlap) or loose.

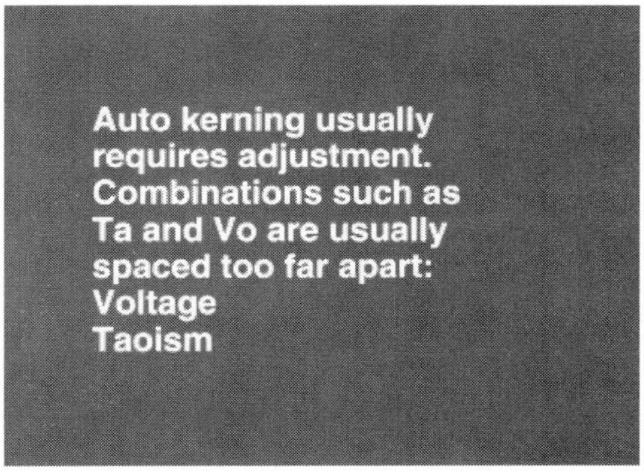

Figure 12.58 Automatic kerning is frequently imperfect, and sometimes it's awful.

Kerning and tracking

When you're working with text, you should understand the subtle but important differences between the typographic terms *tracking* and *kerning*.

Tracking refers to adjusting the overall space between letters in a range of text. High tracking values result in loose, generous letter spacing. Low or negative tracking values result in tight letter spacing or even overlapping letters (**Figure 12.57**).

Kerning describes the process of adjusting the value of *kern pairs*, spacing that the typeface's designer built into particular pairs of characters. This can be an important feature because automatic kerning is rarely perfect; sometimes it can be awful (**Figure 12.58**). As you kern, the space between letters is expressed in *em spaces*, a measurement based on the size of the type.

You can kern between a pair of characters or across a range of characters. The effects of tracking and kerning are cumulative. Typically, you should use tracking to adjust the overall spacing and then use kerning to fine-tune spaces between pairs of characters.

✔ Tips

- The Basic Text effect lets you control tracking but not kerning. The Path Text effect, in contrast, includes kerning controls.
- You can control how overlapping characters interact by setting a blending mode for individual characters. See the section "Blending Characters" later in this chapter. See "Using Blending Modes," in Chapter 14, "More Layer Techniques," for a detailed description of each mode.

To adjust kerning:

1. Set the insertion point cursor between two characters, or select a range of characters.
2. In the Character palette, *do one of the following:*
   - ▲ Specify the value for kerning (**Figure 12.59**).
   - ▲ To have After Effects calculate the kerning, *choose either of the following options* from the pull-down menu:

   Metrics uses the kern pair values built into the font's design.

   Optical sets the value according to the shape of adjacent characters.

   The kerning you specified is applied to the selected characters (or to subsequent characters you type).

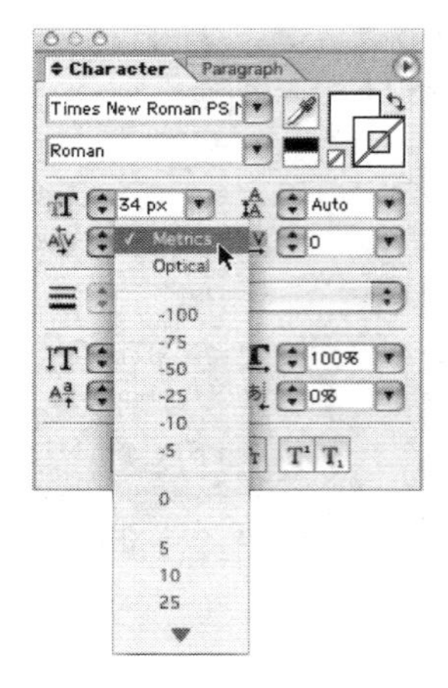

Figure 12.59 Specify a value for kerning, or have After Effects calculate it automatically using the Metrics or Optical method.

To adjust tracking:

1. Select the range of type you want to adjust.
2. In the Character palette, specify the value for tracking (**Figure 12.60**).

   The tracking value you specified is applied to the selected characters (or to subsequent characters you type).

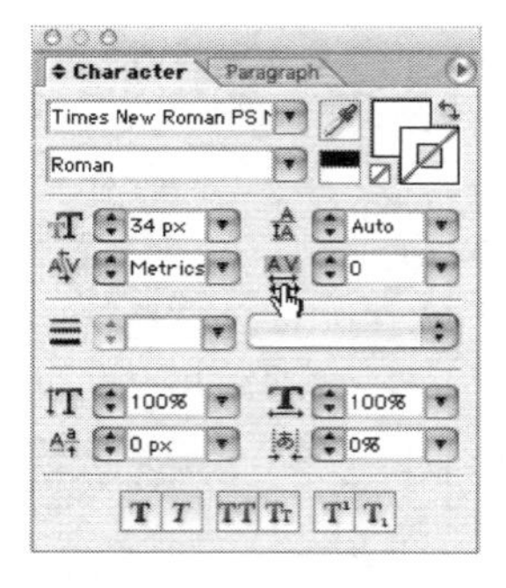

Figure 12.60 Set the tracking, or overall character spacing.

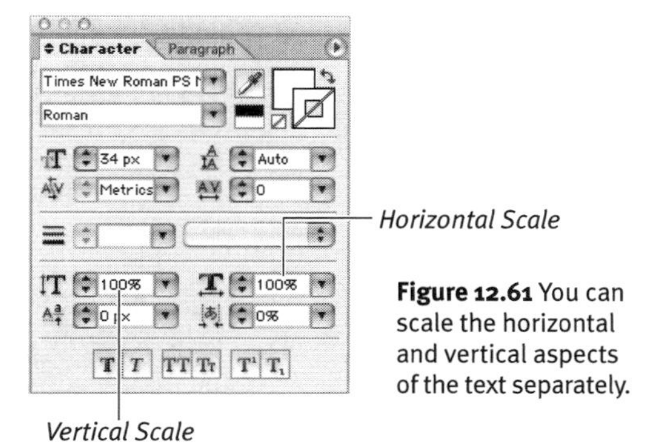

Figure 12.61 You can scale the horizontal and vertical aspects of the text separately.

Figure 12.62 In this example, you can contrast the original unmodified text with the same text scaled horizontally and vertically.

Vertical and horizontal scale

Using controls in the Character palette, you can scale the horizontal or vertical aspect of selected characters, effectively stretching or compressing them. If you scale all the text in the layer, the result is the same as using the text layer's Scale property. But with the Character palette, you don't have to scale *all* the characters; you can scale just the characters you want.

To adjust scale:

1. Select the range of type you want to adjust.
2. In the Character palette, specify the value for Horizontal Scale or Vertical Scale (**Figure 12.61**).

   The scale you specified is applied to the selected characters (or to subsequent characters you type) (**Figure 12.62**).

✔ Tip

- You can skew characters (among other things) using type animation controls, as explained in the sections on animating type later in this chapter.

Baseline shift

Horizontally oriented type "sits" on an invisible line, or *baseline*. Often, it's useful to shift the baseline up or down so that some characters are higher or lower relative to the other characters in the line. For example, shifting the baseline lets you create the mathematical notation for a fraction with typefaces that don't include fractions (and without resorting to using more than one text layer).

To adjust the baseline shift:

1. Select the range of type you want to adjust.
2. In the Character palette, specify a value for Baseline Shift (**Figure 12.63**).

   The baseline shift you specified is applied to the selected characters (or to subsequent characters you type) (**Figure 12.64**).

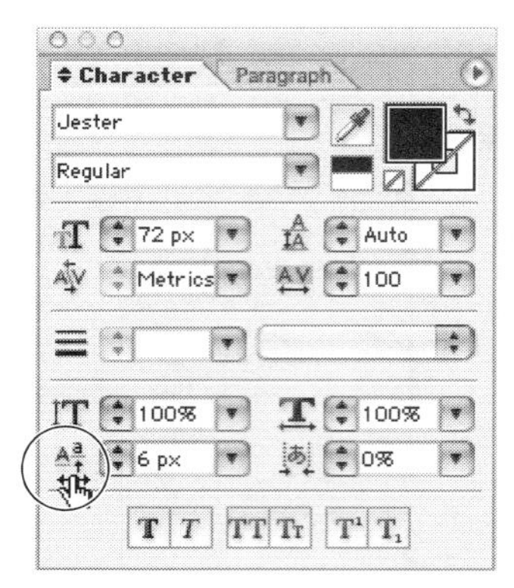

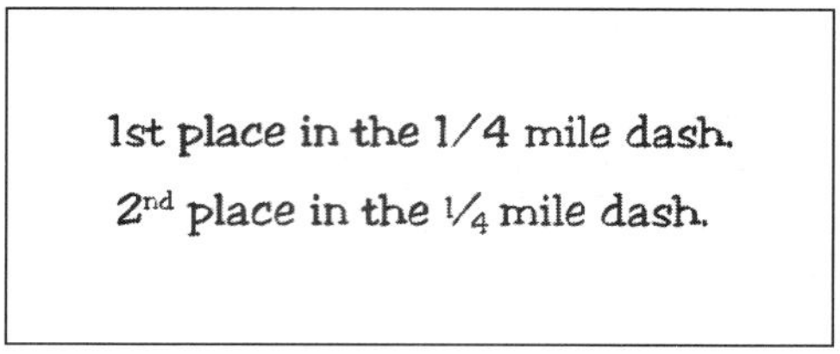

Figure 12.63 Specify a value for Baseline Shift.

1st place in the 1/4 mile dash.

2nd place in the $^{1}/_{4}$ mile dash.

Figure 12.64 Here, the baselines of characters have been shifted to create the fraction within the text. (The font size of the numerals has also been reduced.)

✔ Tips

- Note that there are separate controls for creating superscript and subscript characters; there's no need to fake these type forms by cleverly shifting the baseline or by inserting a separate text layer.
- Parts of a character that extend below the baseline—such as the bottom of a lowercase *J*—are called *descenders*. Take descenders into account when you're typesetting, especially for text positioned near the bottom of television's title-safe zone.
- The next button in the palette is for adjusting tsume. Because tsume adjusts spacing in Chinese, Japanese, and Korean fonts, it's covered in the section "Setting Options for Chinese, Japanese, and Korean Text" later in this chapter.

Character
Paragraph
Palatino
Roman
36 px
Auto
Metrics
0
100%
100%
0 px
0%
Faux Bold
Faux Italics

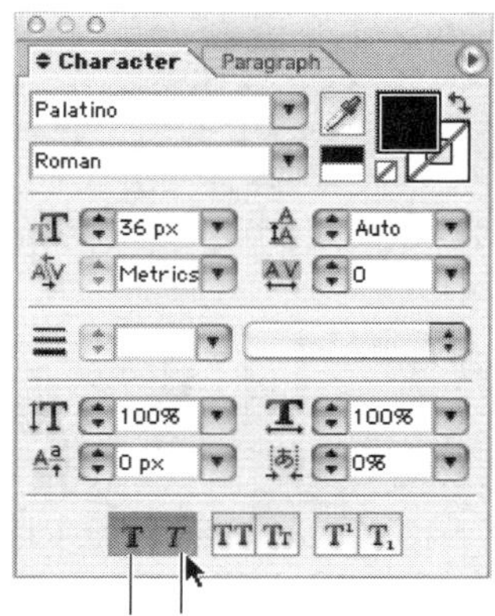

Figure 12.65 Click the Faux Bold or Faux Italics buttons to simulate these styles in fonts that don't include them by design.

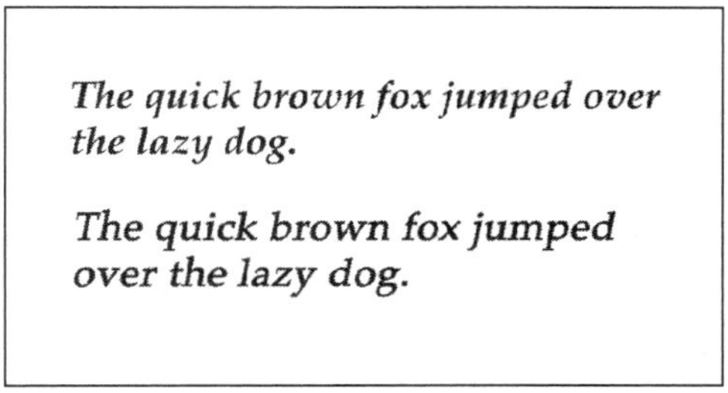

The quick brown fox jumped over the lazy dog.
The quick brown fox jumped over the lazy dog.

Figure 12.66 As you can see, a font that includes a bold and italic typeface (top) looks better than the result of faking those styles (bottom). But if you have no other option, faux bold and faux italics can do the trick.

Faux bold and faux italics

Although many fonts include boldface and italic styles (see "Font and Style" earlier in this chapter), others lack these options. In such cases you can create these typographic effects using the *faux bold* and *faux italic* options. Whereas legitimate bold and italic styles are carefully designed variations of the font, faux bold and faux italics are just that: *faux*, or fake. Using a method more akin to distortion than design, they simulate a bold and italic typeface. Even so, the effect can be convincing, if not ideal.

To specify faux bold and faux italics:

1. Select the range of type you want to adjust.
2. In the character palette, *do any of the following* (**Figure 12.65**):
   - ▲ Select the Faux Bold button **T** to make the selected type bold.
   - ▲ Select the Faux Italics button *T* to make the selected type italic.

   The selected characters (or subsequent characters you type) reflect your choices (**Figure 12.66**).

All caps and small caps

Some fonts include all-caps and small-caps typefaces. All caps is a variation designed to present the font in all capital letters, whereas a small-caps typeface uses a miniature version of capital letters in place of lowercase letters. If the font you're using doesn't include an all-caps or small-caps typeface, you can simulate it in much the same way you simulate a bold or italic font (see the previous section, "Faux bold and faux italics").

To convert lowercase to uppercase:

1. Select the range of type you want to adjust.
2. In the Character palette, select the All Caps button TT (**Figures 12.67** and **12.68**).
   The selected lowercase characters (and subsequent lowercase characters you type) are converted to uppercase (**Figure 12.69**).
   You can select characters converted to uppercase and deselect the All Caps option to make the characters lowercase again.

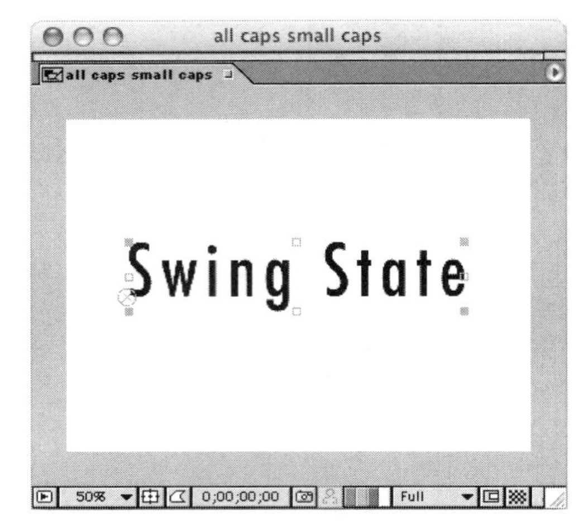

Figure 12.67 Selecting lowercase characters...

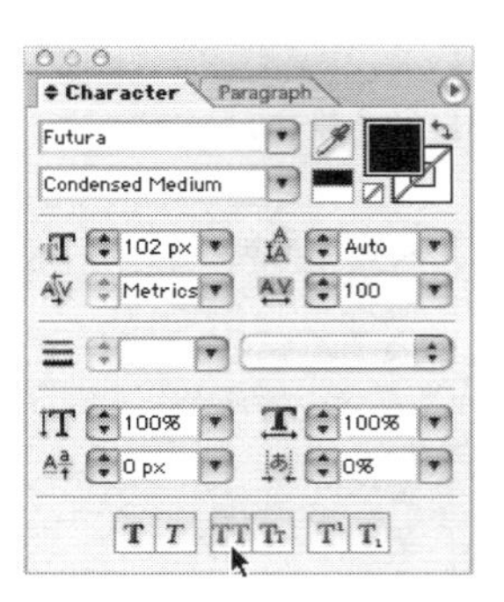

Figure 12.68...and clicking the All Caps button...

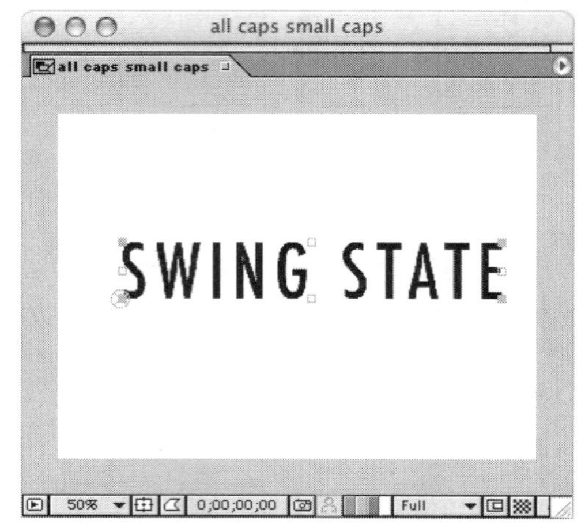

Figure 12.69...converts the characters to uppercase.

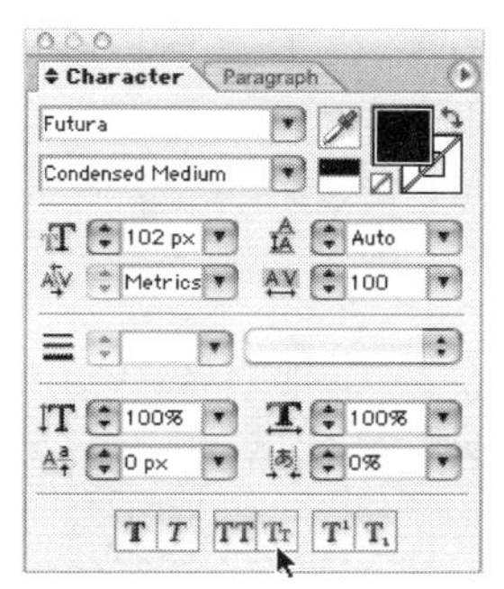

Figure 12.70 Selecting the Small Caps button instead...

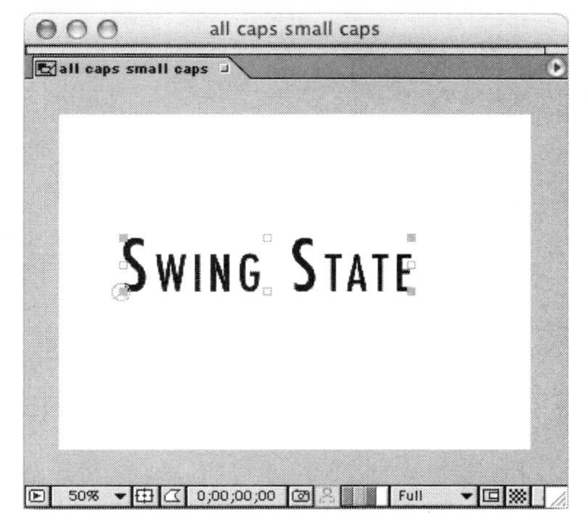

Figure 12.71...converts the selection to small caps.

To specify small caps:

1. Select the range of type you want to adjust.
2. In the Character palette, select the Small Caps button (**Figure 12.70**).

   The selected lowercase characters (or subsequent lowercase characters you type) are converted into small caps. Uppercase characters are unaffected (**Figure 12.71**).

   You can select characters converted to small caps and deselect the option to make the characters lowercase again.

Superscript and subscript

The last buttons in the Character palette let you specify characters as superscript and subscript. *Superscript* characters appear higher (and usually smaller) than the rest of a line of text, whereas *subscript* characters appear lower (and usually smaller) than the other characters. These forms are often associated with scientific notation. With proper typesetting, the 2 in the familiar equation $E=Mc^2$, is superscript; the 2 in the chemical notation for water, H_2O, is subscript. As with bold and italics, some characters are already superscripted. In most fonts, for example, the trademark symbol ™ (Option-2 on the Mac or Alt-0153 on Windows) is already superscripted. To superscript or subscript other characters, you can use the buttons in the Character palette.

To make text superscript or subscript:

1. Select the range of type you want to adjust.
2. In the character palette, do any of the following (**Figure 12.72**):
   - ▲ To make the selected type superscript, select the Superscript button T^1.
   - ▲ To make the selected type subscript, select the Subscript button T_1.

   The selected characters (and subsequent characters you type) reflect your choices (**Figure 12.73**).

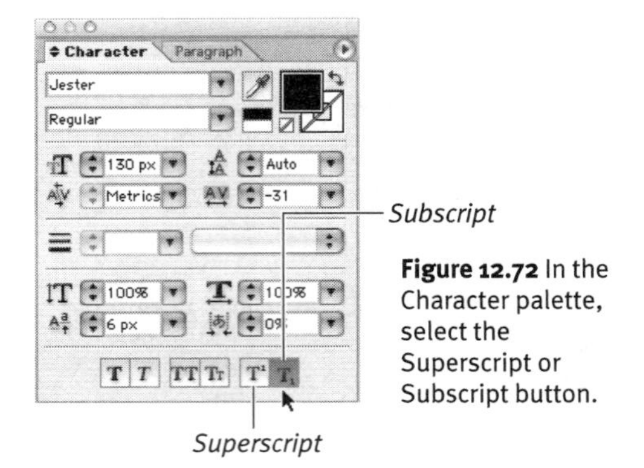

Figure 12.72 In the Character palette, select the Superscript or Subscript button.

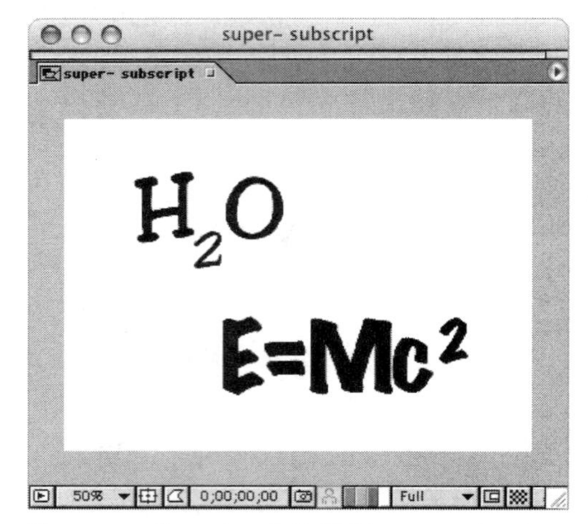

Figure 12.73 Here, the 2 in $E=Mc^2$ is superscripted; the 2 in H_2O is subscripted.

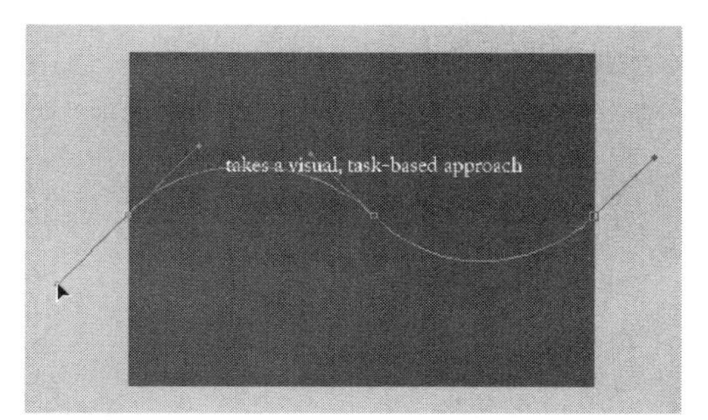

Figure 12.84 Create a text layer, and, with the layer selected, create a mask path.

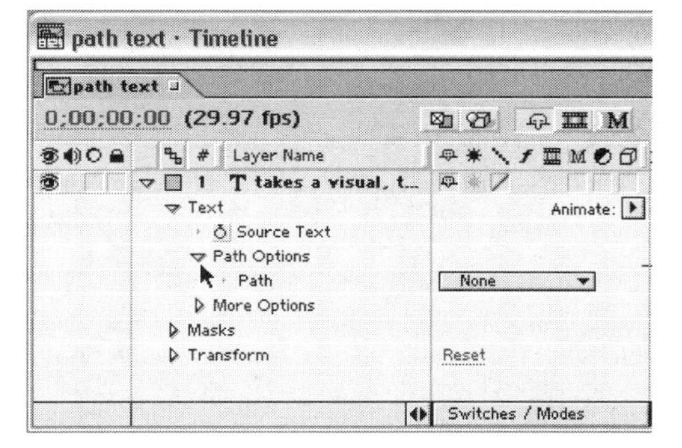

Figure 12.85 In the Timeline window, expand the text layer's property outline to reveal its Path Options property heading.

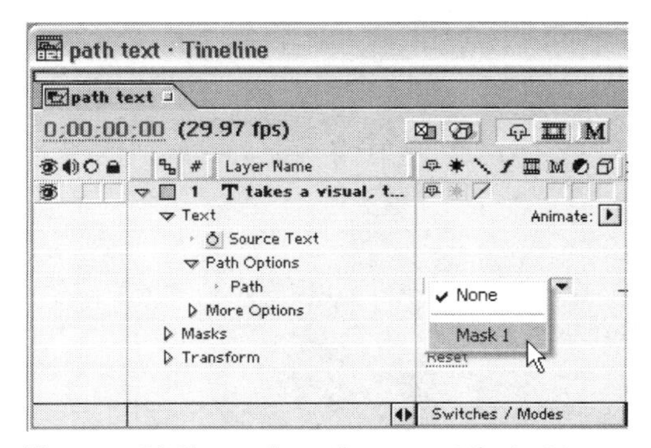

Figure 12.86 Choose the path you want the text to follow in the Path pull-down menu.

Making Text Follow a Path

You can make the type in any text layer follow a path you specify—without sacrificing any of the formatting or text animation options available to the text layer.

To create path text:

1. Create and format a text layer.

   You can use any of the techniques discussed earlier in this chapter.

2. With the text layer selected, create a mask path to serve as the baseline of the text (**Figure 12.84**).

   Use any of the techniques described in Chapter 9, "Mask Essentials." In the Timeline window, the mask you create appears in the text layer's property outline.

3. In the Timeline window, expand the text layer's property outline; then expand its Text property heading and Path Options property heading (**Figure 12.85**).

4. In the Path pull-down menu, choose the path you created in step 2 (**Figure 12.86**).

   The text uses the specified path as its baseline (**Figure 12.87**).

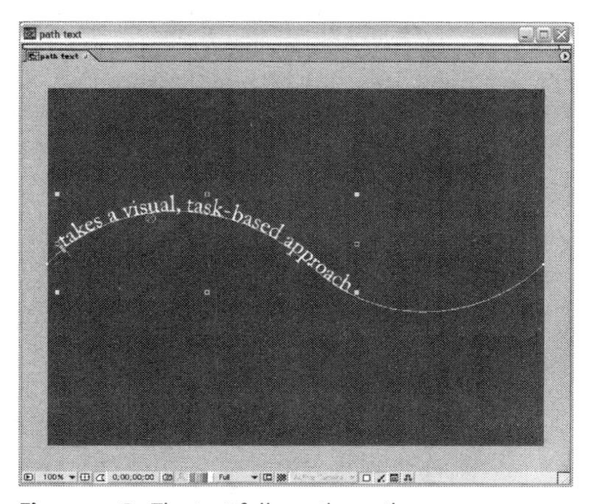

Figure 12.87 The text follows the path.

To animate path text:

1. Create path text as described in the previous task, "To create path text."
2. Set the current time to the frame where you want the animation to begin.
3. In the path text layer's property outline, set the First Margin value to specify the text's starting point on the path, and click the Stopwatch icon to set the initial keyframe (**Figure 12.88**).
4. Set the current time to the frame where you want the animation to end, and set the First Margin value to set the text's starting point on the path when the animation ends (**Figure 12.89**).

   When you preview the animation, the text moves along the path (**Figure 12.90**). Use the techniques covered in Chapter 7, "Properties and Keyframes," and Chapter 15, "Keyframe Interpolation," to refine the animation.

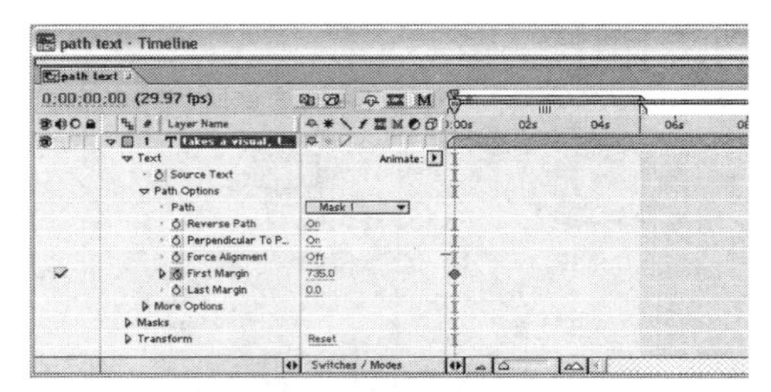

Figure 12.88 Set the current time to the frame where you want the animation to begin, and set a keyframe for the First Margin property value.

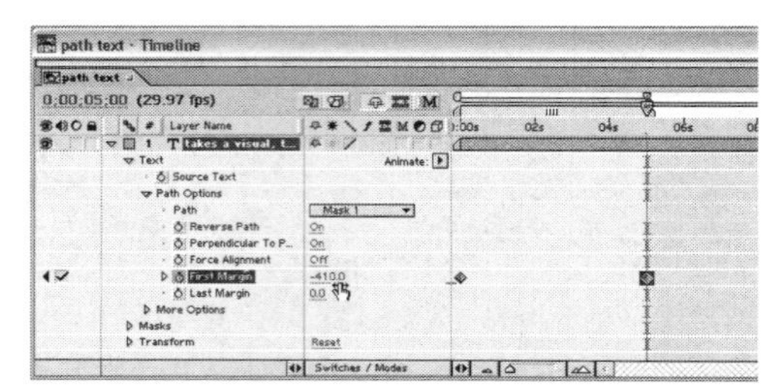

Figure 12.89 Set the current time to the frame where you want the animation to end, and change the First Margin property value to its final position along the path.

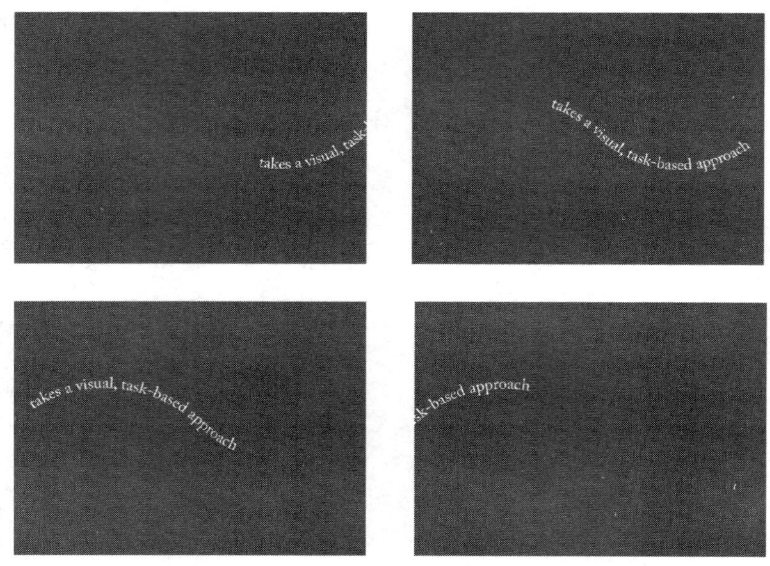

Figure 12.90 Animating the First Margin property moves the text along the path.

Formatting Paragraph Text

Whenever paragraph text reaches the edge of the text box, it flows into another line automatically—something often referred to as a *soft return*. A new *paragraph* occurs when you press Return (Mac) or Enter (Windows), also known as a *hard return*.

You can control each paragraph independently, using a Paragraph palette that's nearly indistinguishable from the one found in Illustrator and Photoshop. An intuitive set of controls lets you set alignment, justification, and indentation. You can also specify hanging punctuation and determine how After Effects creates automatic line breaks within each paragraph.

Aligning and justifying paragraphs

Aligning and justifying paragraph text in After Effects is as easy as in any good word-processing program.

As you probably know, *alignment* determines how the lines in a paragraph are positioned relative to the margins (the left and right sides of the text box). As usual, you can set whether the lines align flush with the left or right or are centered horizontally in the box.

Justification alters the spacing in each line of text so that all the lines are flush with both the right and left margins. (Think of the neat, justified columns you find in a newspaper.) Typically, the last line in a paragraph is shorter than the rest and doesn't easily lend itself to justification. After Effects lets you set whether the last line is aligned with the left side or right side of the text box or is centered horizontally. Or, you can justify all the lines, including the last line of the paragraph.

The following tasks illustrate alignment and justification for horizontal text. You can set alignment and justification options for vertically oriented paragraph text, as well; the icons on the buttons will change accordingly. For example, the Align Left button becomes the Align Top button.

To align paragraph text:

1. Select one or more paragraphs you want to format.
2. In the Paragraph palette, *select one of the following buttons* to set the selected paragraph's alignment (**Figure 12.91**):
   - ▲ **Align Left**
   - ▲ **Align Center**
   - ▲ **Align Right**

continues on next page

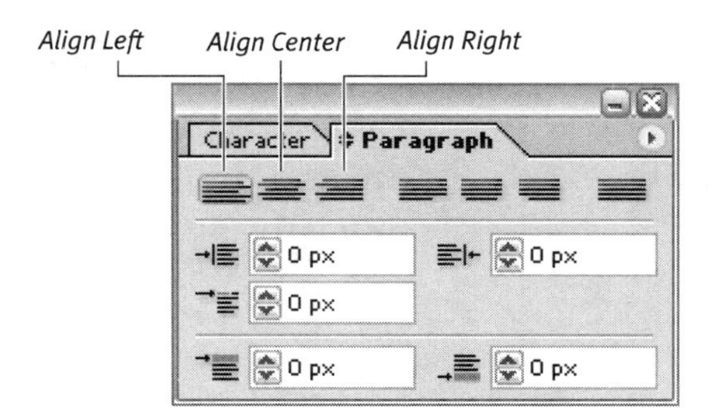

Figure 12.91 Select the button that corresponds with the paragraph alignment you want.

The paragraph aligns according to your choice (**Figure 12.92**).

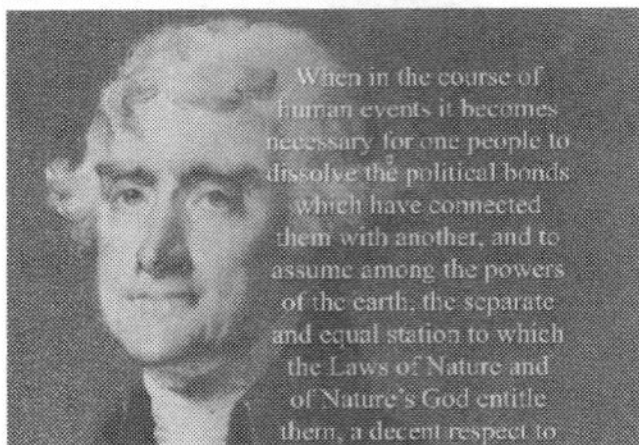

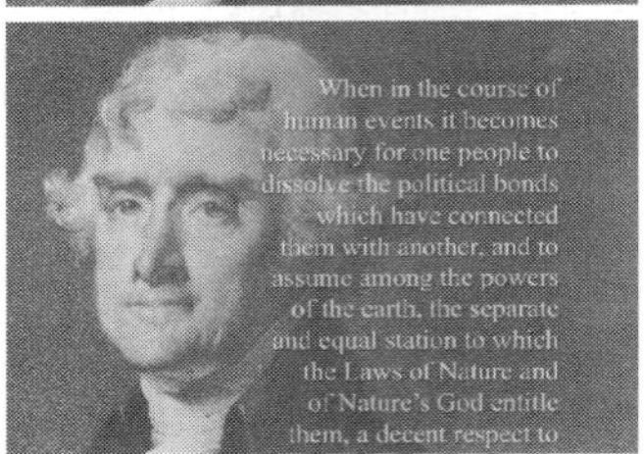

Figure 12.92 Compare the effect of the three alignment options in this composition.

To justify paragraph text:

1. Select one or more paragraphs you want to format.
2. In the Paragraph palette, select the button to set the selected paragraph's justification (**Figure 12.93**):
   - ▲ **Justify Last Left**
   - ▲ **Justify Last Center**
   - ▲ **Justify Last Right**
   - ▲ **Justify All**

   The paragraph is justified, and the last line uses the justification you specified (**Figure 12.94**).

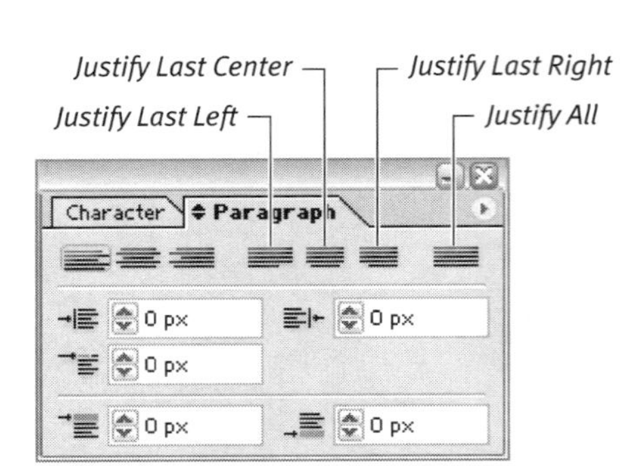

Figure 12.93 Justifying a paragraph eliminates ragged edges, with the possible exception of the last line in a paragraph. The four options format the last line differently.

We the People of the United States, in order to from a more perfect Union, establish Justice, insure domestic Tranquility, provide for the common defence, promote the general Welfare, and secure the Blessings of Liberty for ourselves and our posterity, do ordain and establish this Constitution for the United States of America.

We the People of the United States, in order to from a more perfect Union, establish Justice, insure domestic Tranquility, provide for the common defence, promote the general Welfare, and secure the Blessings of Liberty for ourselves and our posterity, do ordain and establish this Constitution for the United States of America.

Figure 12.94 Choosing Justify Last Left (the top paragraph) leaves the last line ragged. However, choosing Justify All (the bottom paragraph) can result in awkward spacing in the last line.

Indenting paragraphs

Indenting a line of text increases one or both of its margins, shifting it away from the margins defined by the sides of the text box. You can indent each paragraph's left and right margins, and indent the left margin of each paragraph's first line separately.

To indent paragraphs:

1. Select one or more paragraphs you want to format.
2. In the Paragraph palette, specify the selected paragraph's Left Indent or Right Indent or the indent of the first line (**Figure 12.95**).

   The indent you specified is applied to the selected paragraph (and subsequent paragraphs you create) (**Figure 12.96**).

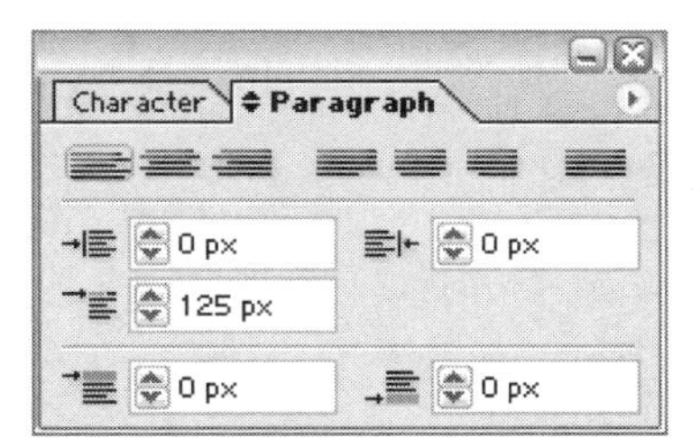

Figure 12.95 Specify a paragraph indent option.

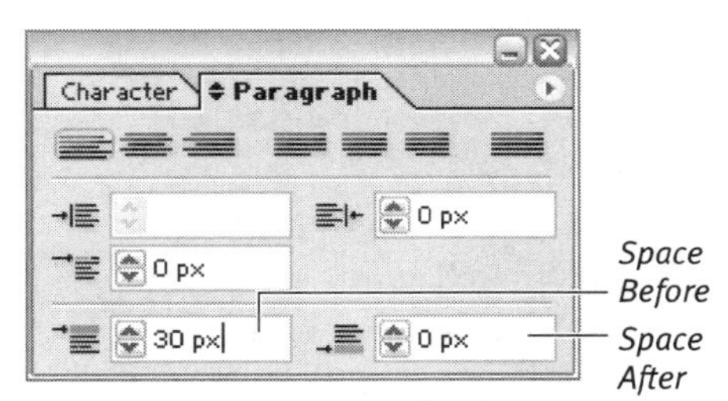

Figure 12.97 In the Paragraph palette, set the Space Before and Space After.

Spacing paragraphs

As you know, a hard return—pressing Return (Mac) or Enter (Windows)—creates a new line and paragraph. You can specify the space before or after new paragraphs, independent of the line spacing (or leading) within each paragraph.

To set paragraph spacing:

1. Select one or more paragraphs you want to format.
2. In the Paragraph palette, specify a value for the spacing before or spacing after (**Figure 12.97**).

   The spacing you specified is applied to the selected paragraph and subsequent paragraphs (**Figure 12.98**).

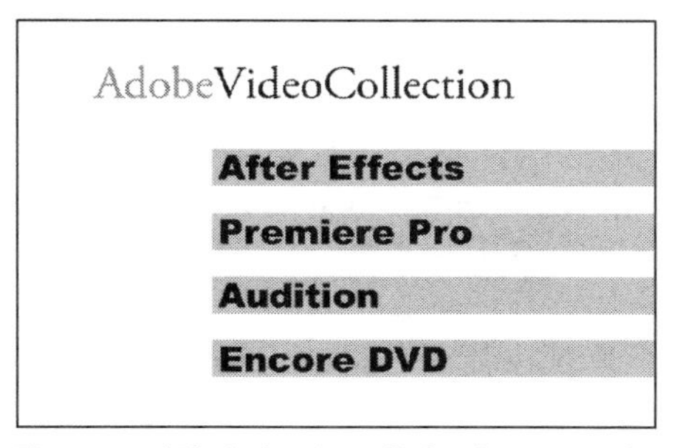

Figure 12.96 The indent is applied to the paragraph. This example shows a single text layer, but the list of software is indented 125 pixels.

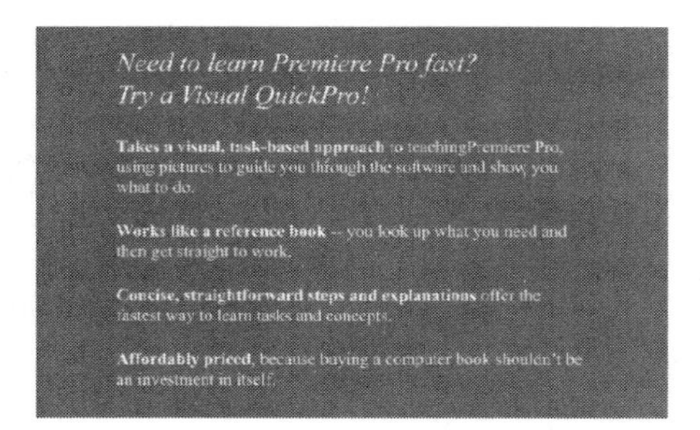

Figure 12.98 Here, a single text layer contains several paragraphs. The extra space between paragraphs was created by increasing the default Spacing After value.

Hanging punctuation

Generally, the alignment or justification option you apply to a paragraph applies to punctuation marks, as well. However, you can also specify that a paragraph use *hanging punctuation*. Hanging punctuation allows punctuation marks to appear outside the text box. For example, in a quotation with left alignment, the open quote "hangs" outside the left edge of text box, like a gargoyle perched on the side of a building (**Figure 12.99**).

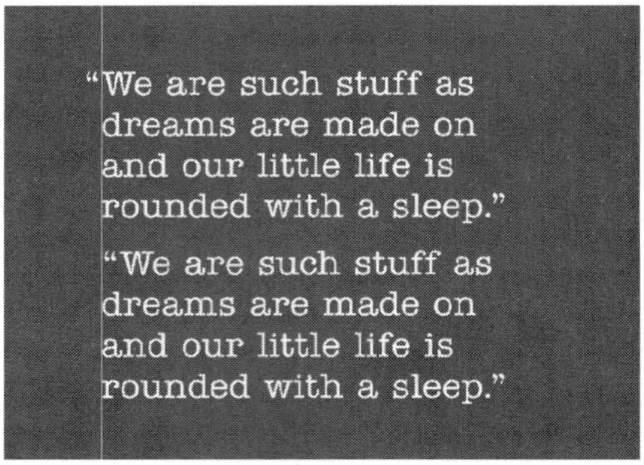

Figure 12.99 Hanging punctuation places punctuation marks outside the text box. In this example, guides clarify the difference between using and not using hanging punctuation.

To specify the hanging punctuation option:

1. Select one or more paragraphs you want to format.
2. In the Paragraph palette's pull-down menu, choose Roman Hanging Punctuation (**Figure 12.100**).

   When the option is selected, punctuation at the beginning or end of the paragraph appears outside the paragraph's margins; when the option is unselected, the punctuation marks appear within the margins.

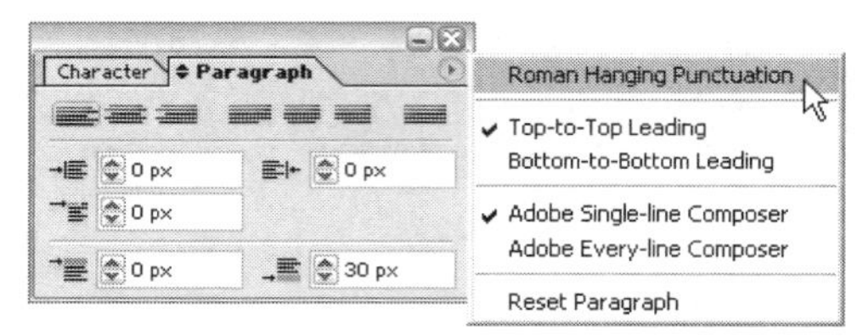

Figure 12.100 To enable hanging punctuation, select Roman Hanging Punctuation in the Paragraph palette's pull-down menu.

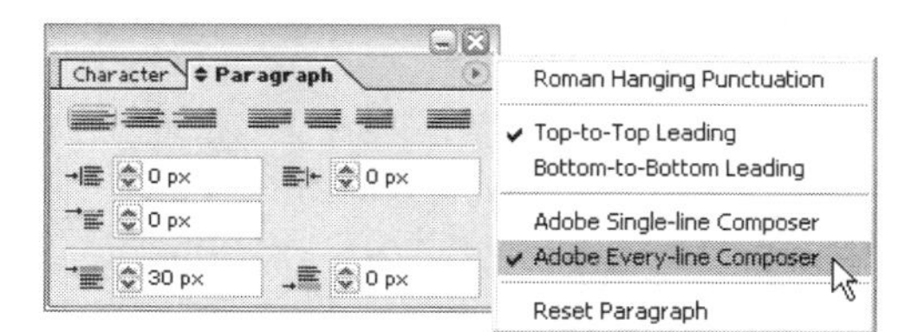

Figure 12.101 In the Paragraph palette's pull-down menu, choose the composer you want to use.

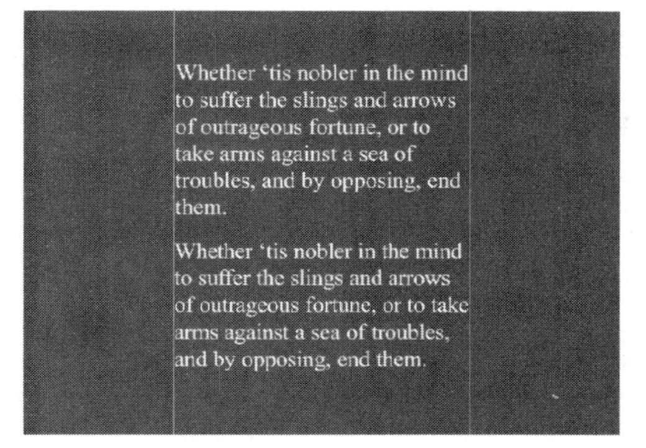

Figure 12.102 Depending on the paragraph, you may see a difference between choosing Single-line Composer (the paragraph on the top) and Every-line Composer (the paragraph on the bottom).

Specifying how After Effects calculates line breaks

To determine how a paragraph flows within its text box, After Effects considers the character and paragraph options you specified and chooses the best possible line breaks—the soft returns that end one line and begin another. After Effects *composes* (as it's called) the text by employing either of two methods:

Adobe Single Line Composer evaluates each line separately to determine where to place line breaks. This relatively simple method works well if you prefer to control line breaks manually.

Adobe Every Line Composer, in contrast, evaluates all the lines in a paragraph to determine the line breaks. By comparing the possible line breaks for a range of lines, After Effects reduces the occurrence of unattractive line breaks and hyphens and achieves more even spacing.

To specify line break options:

1. Select one or more paragraphs you want to format.
2. In the Paragraph palette's pull-down menu, choose the option you want (**Figure 12.101**):
   - ▲ **Adobe Single-line Composer**
   - ▲ **Adobe Every-line Composer**

   The selected paragraph uses the option you specify (**Figure 12.102**).

Animating Text

In most respects, text layers are just like other layers, and include the same layer properties you learned about in Chapter 7. But text layers have a number of unique Text properties, as well. This way, you can animate the layer, and the text within the layer. But unlike other layers, you can't open a text layer in a Layer window.

Standard layer properties

Text layers include the same Transform properties—Anchor Point, Position, Scale, Rotation, and Opacity—that you'll find in any layer (and learned about in Chapter 7). Text layers accept masks and effects, and like other layers, you can make a text layer 3D. But naturally, the standard layer property controls affect the *layer as a whole*; they can't alter the content of the text (what it says), or apply to characters individually (not without using masks, anyway).

Text properties

A special set of Text properties makes it possible to animate words or individual characters without complex keyframing, elaborate masking techniques, or resorting to using numerous text layers.

Source Text—lets you change the content of the text message over time. This way, a single text layer can convey a series of messages. Used in combination with Animator Groups and Selectors (described below), you can change the content more gradually. For example, you can make the letters in a word appear to "encode" themselves, cycling through other letters, and gradually "decode" themselves into another word.

Path Text—lets you make a line of text follow a path that you specify. You can animate the border to make the text appear to glide over the path. You can also specify other options, such as whether the type is perpendicular to the path.

Animator Groups—allow you to animate properties of any range of characters within the text. Each Animator Group you create can include any number or combination of properties, including both familiar Transform properties, and properties unique to text. You can specify the range of text affected by the Animator properties with one or more *Range Selectors*. Numerous other options let you fine-tune the animation.

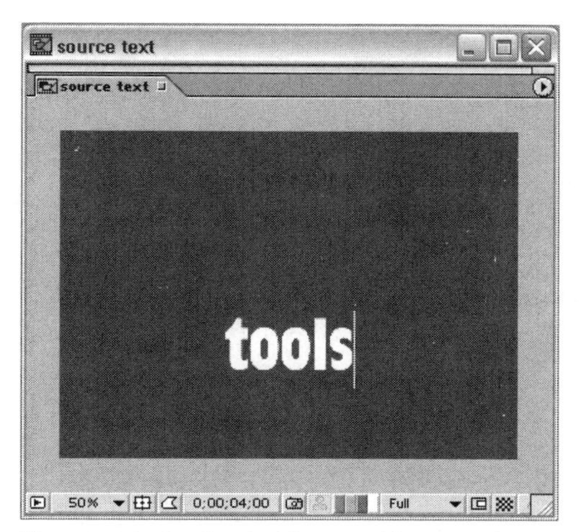

Figure 12.103 Create a text layer, and format and arrange it into its initial state (before animating it).

Animating Source Text

You can animate a text layer's *source text*, the actual content of the text message. Source text keyframes always use Hold interpolation. As you'll see in Chapter 17, "Complex Projects," Hold interpolation retains a keyframe value until the next keyframe value is reached. Therefore, the message instantly changes to the text you specify at each keyframe. This way, a single layer can contain multiple text messages; you won't have to create multiple layers.

Note that you can change the source text while animating other properties. For example, by creating an animator group and animating the Character Offset property, you can change the characters in a word—"encoding" or "decoding" it. Changing an encoded word's Source Text during the animation lets you make one word change into another.

To animate source text:

1. Create and format a text layer and arrange the layer in the comp (**Figure 12.103**).

   To create the text layer, use techniques described earlier in this chapter. To arrange the layer in the comp, use techniques covered in Chapter 5, "Layer Basics," and Chapter 6, "Layer Editing."
2. Set the current time to the frame where you want the message you created in step 1 to begin.

continues on next page

3. In the Timeline window, expand the text layer's property outline, and click the Stopwatch icon for the layer's Source Text property.

   An initial keyframe is created for the Source Text property (**Figure 12.104**). Source Text keyframes always use the Hold interpolation method (see Chapter 15, "Keyframe Interpolation").

4. Set the current time to the frame where you want a new message to appear.

5. Select the text, and type a new message (**Figure 12.105**).

   A new Hold keyframe appears at the current time for the layer's Source Text property (**Figure 12.106**).

6. Repeat steps 4 and 5, as needed.

   When you preview the animation, each message appears until the current time reaches the next Source Text keyframe.

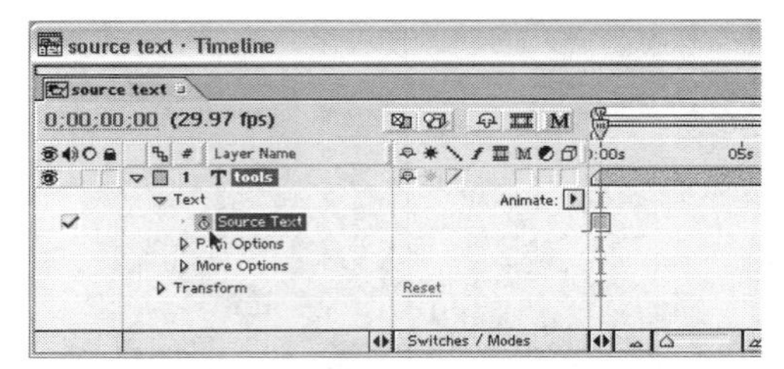

Figure 12.104 In the text layer's property outline, click the Source Text property's Stopwatch icon to create an initial keyframe.

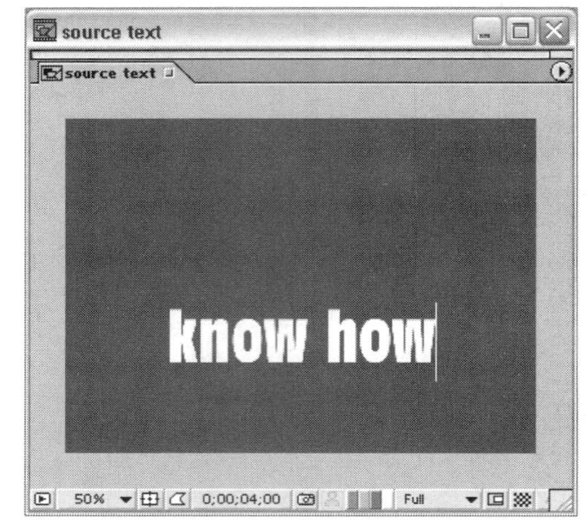

Figure 12.105 Set the current time to the frame where you want the message to change, and edit the text...

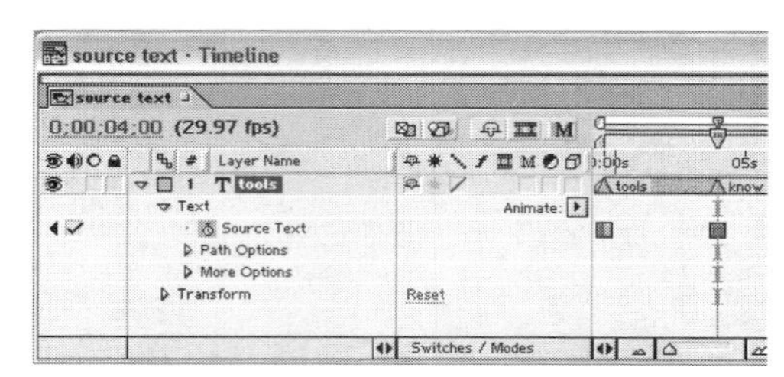

Figure 12.106...to create a new Hold keyframe for the Source Text property (seen here in the layer outline).

Using Text Animation Presets

As you learned in Chapter 10, "Effects Fundamentals," you can save any combination of effects and animation keyframes as a preset. Because they're listed in the Effects & Presets palette, presets are easy to apply; and because they're saved as separate files, they're easy to share.

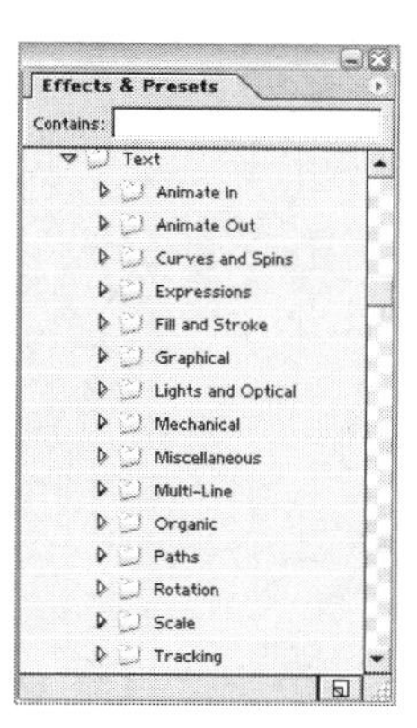

Figure 12.107 The Effects & Presets palette contains numerous preset text animations.

After Effects includes a generous and varied collection of text animation presets, conveniently sorted by category in the Effects & Presets palette (**Figure 12.107**). Chances are, you're just as likely to modify one of these excellent presets as you are to build a text animation from scratch.

As you learn about text animation, start by examining some of the presets. Once you see what text animation can do, dig into the sections on animator groups to find out what makes them tick and, ultimately, how to create your own.

To view a gallery of text animation presets:

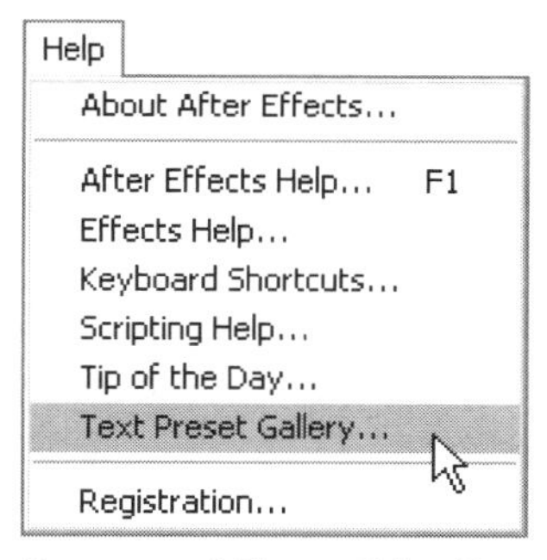

Figure 12.108 Choose Help > Text Preset Gallery.

1. Choose Help > Text Preset Gallery (**Figure 12.108**).

   The After Effects Help system opens in your browser, set to the page Gallery of Text Animation Presets.

2. To view text animation samples by category, click the appropriate link under Related Subtopics (**Figure 12.109**).

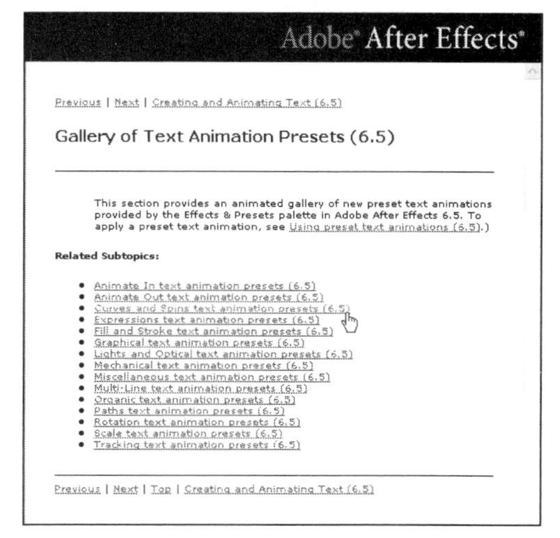

Figure 12.109 Click the category of text animations for which you want to see examples.

To apply a text animation preset:

1. Create and format a text layer, and select the layer (**Figure 12.110**).

   Make sure to select the entire text layer, not a range of characters. To animate part of a text layer, you can use range selectors (as explained later in this chapter).

2. In the Effects & Presets palette, double-click the text animation preset you want to apply to the selected text (**Figure 12.111**).

   The preset you specified is applied to the selected text (**Figure 12.112**). For more about using the Effects & Presets palette, see Chapter 10, "Effects Fundamentals."

3. If you want, modify the effect by changing the position or value of its keyframed text animation properties (as explained in Chapter 7). You can also add, delete, or modify the preset effect's Animator properties or Range Selector values (as explained later in this chapter).

Figure 12.110 Create and format a text layer.

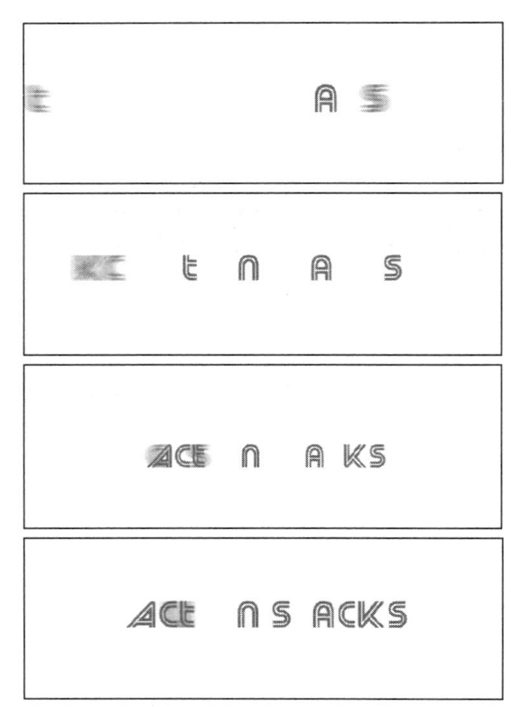

Figure 12.112 The preset is applied to the selected text layer.

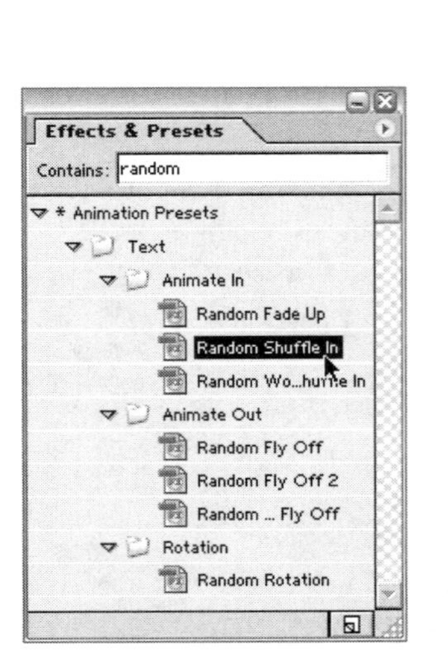

Figure 12.111 With the text layer selected, double-click the text preset you want in the Effects & Presets palette.

Using Text Animation Presets

Understanding Animator Groups

You animate type by adding one or more *animator groups* to a text layer. Animator groups appear in the layer outline under a text layer's Text property heading (**Figure 12.113**). You create an animator group by choosing a property you want to affect in the layer's Animator pull-down menu. You can add as many groups as you need to achieve the animation you want.

Each animator group consists of at least one *animator property* and one *selector*. You can add properties and selectors to a group by using its Add pull-down menu.

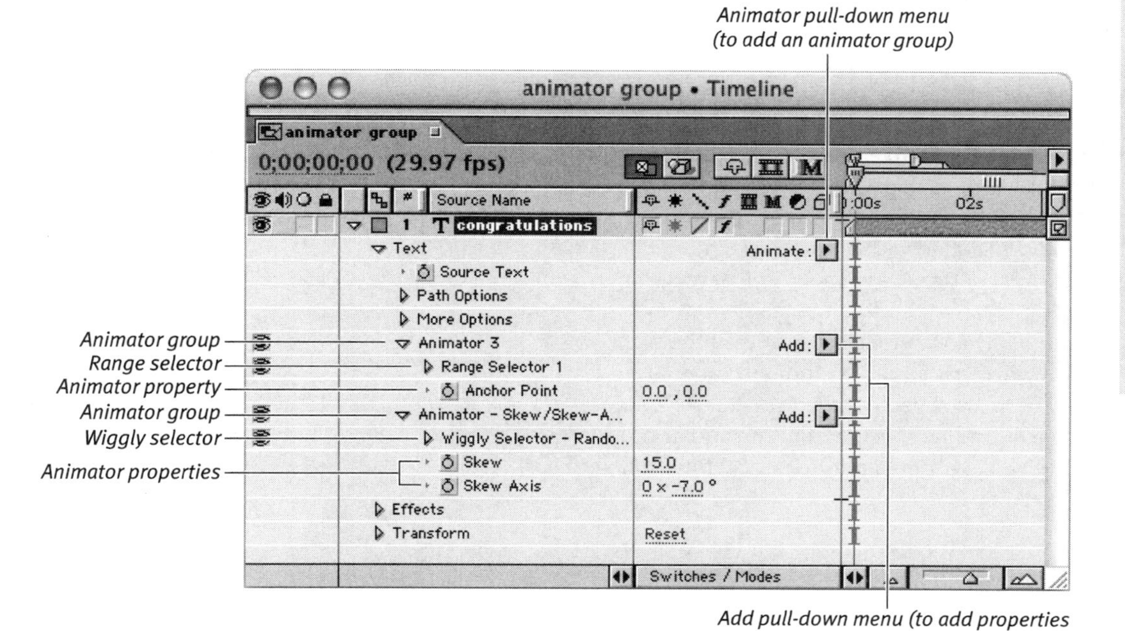

Figure 12.113 Animator groups appear in the layer outline.

Animator properties

Animator properties include familiar transform properties (such as position, rotation, and so on), properties unique to text (such as fill, stroke, tracking, and so on), and each character's value (the numerical code that determines which character is displayed). Each animator group can have any number and combination of properties, which can be set to any value. But unlike when you're animating layers, you probably won't animate the property values to create the animation. Instead, you'll animate the range of characters affected by the properties by keyframing a selector.

Range selectors

A *selector* lets you specify a *range*, or the part of the type that's affected by an animator group's properties. Thus, most animations are achieved by animating the range, not the properties. Selectors are comparable to layer masks in that they limit the areas affected by your adjustments. Just as you can add multiple masks to a layer, you can add multiple selectors to an animator group. Multiple selectors let you specify ranges that you couldn't define with a single selector (such as a discontinuous range of characters). In addition to a standard range selector, you can apply a wiggly selector to vary the selection, giving it a more random or organic feel. You can also specify an expression selector, which can link the selection to another property, or base it on a mathematical function.

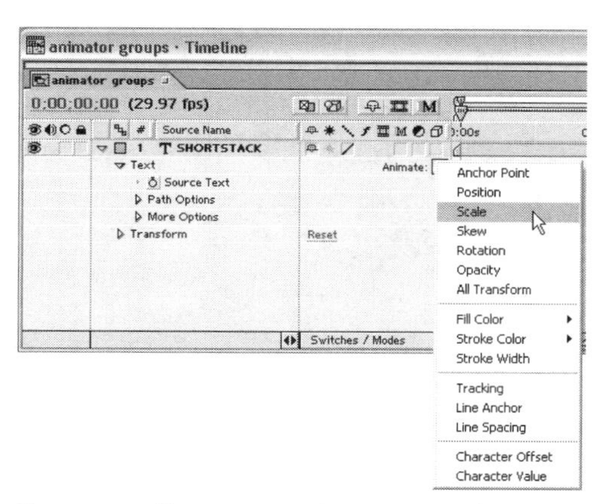

Figure 12.114 To create an animator group, choose a property in the Animate pull-down menu.

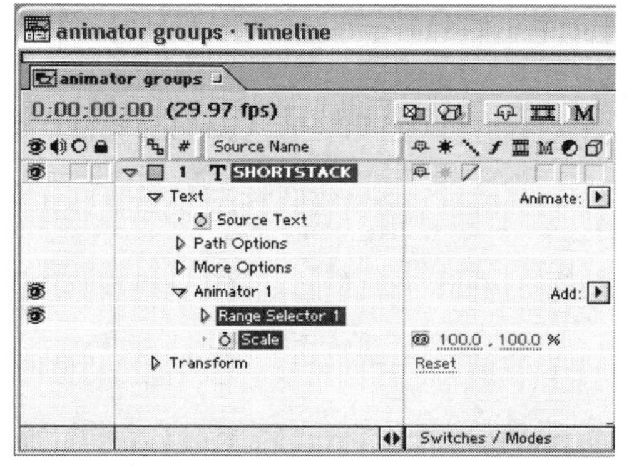

Figure 12.115 The new animator group includes the property you selected and a range selector.

Animating Type with Animator Groups

As you gleaned from the previous section, "Understanding Animator Groups," animator groups grant you a great deal of control over text animation and can include numerous components.

The following task provides an overview of the steps required to create a simple text animation. As you'll see, the basic steps include creating an animator group, specifying its property value and range, and then animating the range. For the sake of clarity, the task doesn't mention particular property and selector options; they're covered in detail in later sections. It also doesn't include steps to add animator groups or to add properties or selectors to existing groups. Follow this task to create a simple animation, and then explore later sections to add complexity to your text animations.

To animate type with animator groups:

1. Create and format a text layer.

   Use the techniques explained earlier in this chapter.

2. In the Timeline window, expand the text layer to reveal its Text property heading.

3. In the Switches or Modes panel of the Timeline window, choose the text property you want to animate from the Animate pull-down menu (**Figure 12.114**).

   An Animator property heading appears under the layer's Text property heading. The Animator property contains a Range Selector property heading and the property you specified (**Figure 12.115**).

continues on next page

4. Set the values for the property you specified in step 3.

   The values are applied to the entire text (**Figure 12.116**). You can limit the range of affected characters in step 4. Typically, you'll animate the range, not the property values (as explained in the next step).

5. Set the current time, and specify values for the range selector.

   You can set the range by dragging the Range Start and Range End icons in the Comp window (**Figure 12.117**), or by setting Start and End values in the property outline. For details, see "Specifying a Range" later in this chapter.

6. For the range properties you want to animate, click the Stopwatch icon to set the initial keyframe at the current time.

   You can set keyframes for any combination of the selector's Start, End, and Offset values (**Figure 12.118**).

7. Set the current time to another frame, and change the animated range property values to set another keyframe (**Figure 12.119**).

   For example, you can increase the range over time by animating the range's End property, or make the range travel through the characters by animating the Offset property.

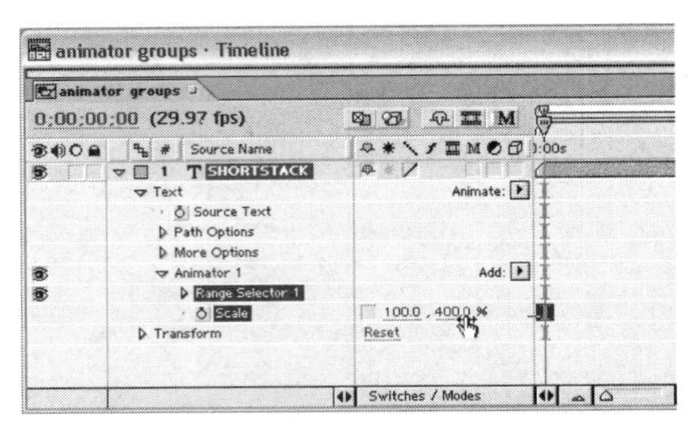

Figure 12.116 Set the property values. Here, the type's vertical scale has been increased. Until you limit the range, the property value affects all of the text.

Figure 12.117 Set the current time, and specify values for the range. In this example, the range's end has been moved next to its start, so the property doesn't affect any of the characters at the beginning of the animation.

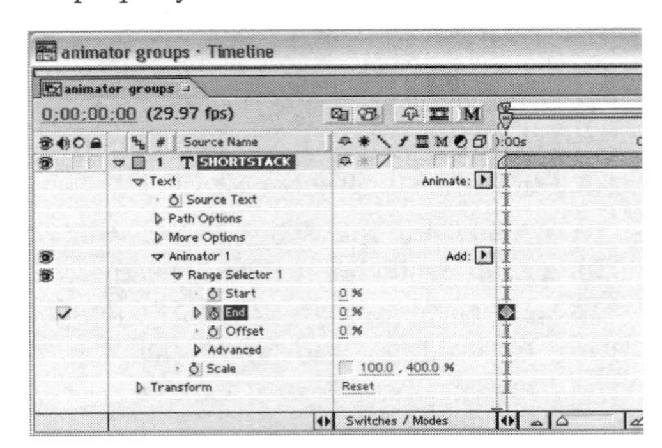

Figure 12.118 Click the Stopwatch icon to set the initial keyframe. Here, an initial keyframe is set for the end of the range.

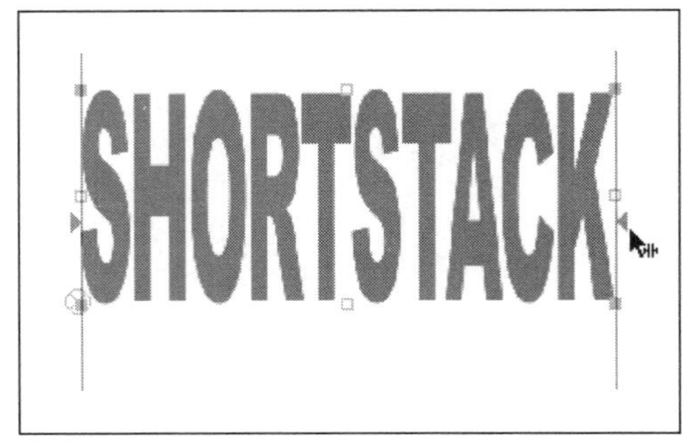

Figure 12.119 Set the current time to another frame, and change the range. Here, the current time is set 5 seconds later, and the end of the range has been moved from its original position (shown in Figure 12.117) so that all the characters are affected.

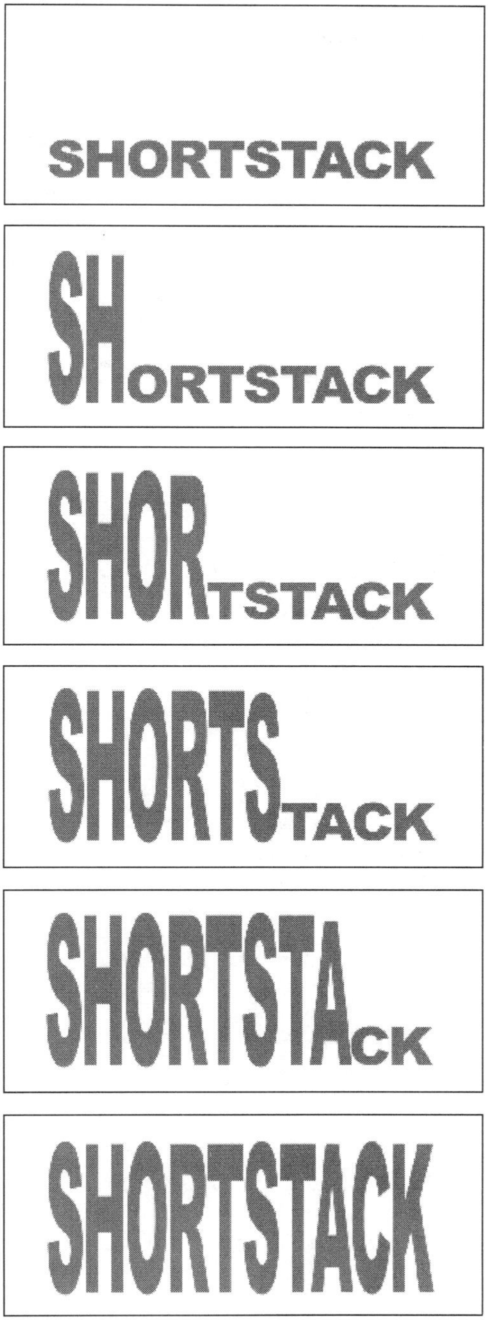

SHORTSTACK

SHORTSTACK

SHORTSTACK

SHORTSTACK

SHORTSTACK

SHORTSTACK

Figure 12.120 Previewing the animation shows how animating the range changes which parts of the text are affected by the animator property you set.

8. If necessary, repeat step 7 to create additional keyframes.
9. Preview the type animation using any of the techniques covered in Chapter 8, "Playback, Previews, and RAM."

   As the range animates, different parts of the text are affected by the properties in the animator group (**Figure 12.120**).

✔ Tip

- As with other elements in a project (comps, duplicate layers, expressions and so on), it's a good idea to give animator groups and range selectors unique names. This way, it's easier to distinguish them and to ascertain their purpose at a glance. Select the animator or range selector and press Return (Mac) or Enter (Windows), edit the name, and press Return (Mac) or Enter (Windows) when you're finished.

Creating Animator Groups

You can add any number of animator groups to a text layer, and each animator group can contain any combination of properties and range selectors. However, each group must contain at least one property and one selector.

To create an animator group:

1. If necessary, expand the text layer's property outline in the timeline window.
2. In the Switches/Modes panel of the Timeline, choose a property from the text layer's Animate pull-down menu (across from the layer's Text property) (**Figure 12.121**).

   An Animator property heading appears under the layer's Text property heading. The Animator property (called Animator 1 by default) contains a Range Selector property heading (called Range Selector 1 by default) and the property you specified (**Figure 12.122**).

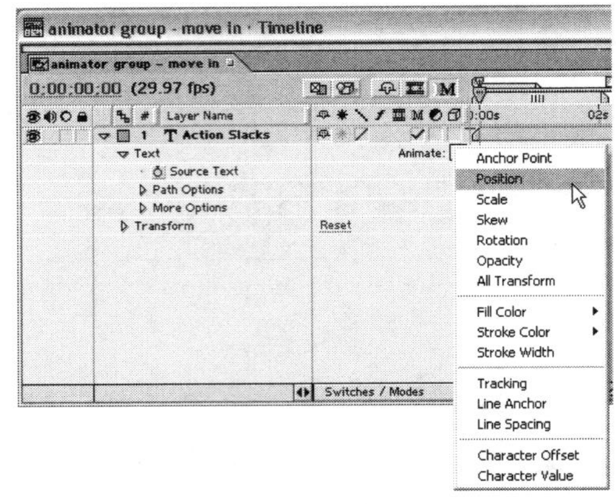

Figure 12.121 To create an animator group, choose a property from the Animate pull-down menu.

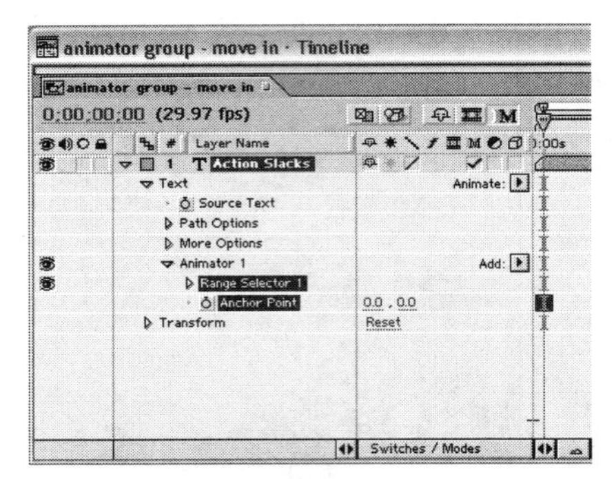

Figure 12.122 The animator group appears in the text layer's property outline; it contains the property and a default range selector.

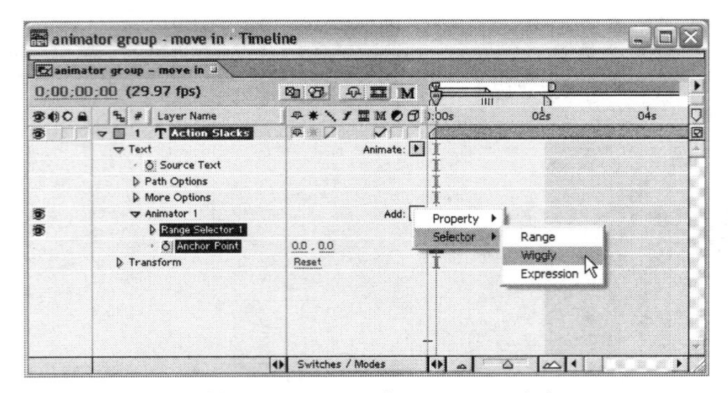

Figure 12.123 To add a property or selector to an existing animator group, select the appropriate option from the group's Add pull-down menu.

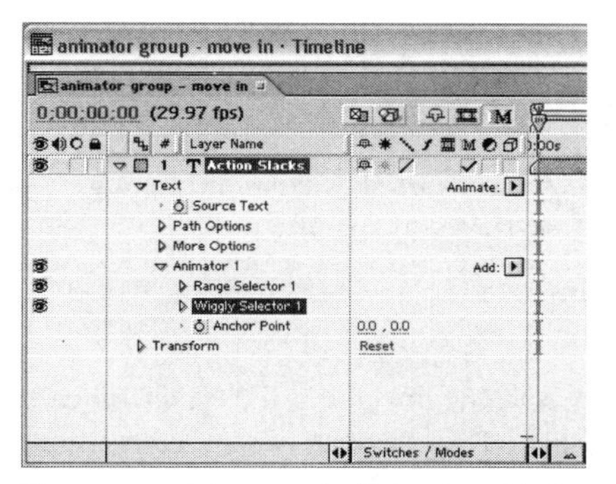

Figure 12.124 The group includes the added item. In this example, an additional selector has been added to the group.

To add to an animator group:

1. If necessary, expand the layer outline of a text layer containing at least one animator.
2. In the Switches or Modes panel, choose an option from the animator's Add pull-down menu (**Figure 12.123**):
   - ▲ **Property**—To add a property to the specified animator
   - ▲ **Selector**—To add a selector to the specified animator

   The property or selector is added to the animator (**Figure 12.124**).

To remove a group, property, or selector:

◆ In a text layer's property outline, select an animator group, animator property, or selector, and press Delete.

The selected item is removed from the layer.

✔ Tips

- As with other items in a project, it's a good idea to give animator groups unique, descriptive names. You can rename animator groups just like layers and other items: Select the name, press Return (Mac) or Enter (Windows), type the new name, and press Return (Mac) or Enter (Windows) again.
- Animator properties and selectors include a video switch just like layers. Turn a switch off to exclude the effects of the item.

Choosing Animator Group Properties

Each animator group can include any combination of animator properties, which you can specify when you create the group or add using the group's Add pull-down menu. You should already be familiar with transform properties (position, scale, and so on), which work with type much the same way they work with layers. (With type, however, you specify whether each character, word, or line possesses an anchor point.) You can also animate properties unique to text (fill, stroke, tracking, and so on), which you learned about earlier in this chapter. Finally, you can set each character's value—the numerical code that determines which character is displayed. The following list describes your choices of animator properties in detail.

Anchor Point sets the type's *anchor point:* the point at which all other transform properties are calculated. Whether all the text, each line, each word, or each character has an anchor point depends on the option you set for Anchor Point Grouping under the More Options property heading (within the Text property heading).

Position sets the type's placement in the comp, based on its anchor point. You can change the Position values either by using controls in the Timeline window or by using the Selection tool in the Comp window; when positioned over type, the Selection tool becomes a Move icon.

All Transform adds all transform properties (Anchor Point, Position, Scale, Rotation, and Opacity) to the animator group at once.

Skew sets the type's skew, or slant, along a skew axis that you specify.

Rotation sets the angle of the type, based on the anchor point you specified.

Opacity sets the opacity of the type. You can control fill and stroke opacity separately using the corresponding option (explained shortly).

Fill Color sets the color values of the fill (the color within the contours of the type) according to your choice in the submenu: RGB, Hue, Saturation, Brightness, or Opacity.

Stroke Color sets the color values of the stroke (the color of the type's outline) according to your choice in the submenu: RGB, Hue, Saturation, Brightness, or Opacity.

Stroke Width sets the thickness of the stroke.

Tracking sets the spacing between characters (see "Kerning and tracking" earlier in this chapter).

Line Anchor sets how tracking is aligned in each line of type—in other words, the point on which tracking calculations are based. To align tracking to the left edge of a line of type, set the value to 0 percent; to align tracking to the right edge, set the value to 100 percent.

Line Spacing sets the spacing between lines of type (see "Leading" earlier in this chapter).

Unicode

In After Effects, you can change a character from the one you typed initially to any other character by offsetting or specifying its Unicode value.

Developed by a group known as the Unicode Consortium, *Unicode* is a character-encoding scheme designed to supplant its more limited predecessor, ASCII. Whereas ASCII is an 8-bit standard capable of representing only 128 distinct characters, Unicode is a 16-bit scheme capable of representing 65,536 characters. The ambitious Unicode Consortium seeks to unify all character sets into a single table of characters encompassing all major world languages (including so-called dead languages) and symbols (such as signs that denote currency, and mathematical symbols). Unicode even includes space and encoding features to accommodate a language like Chinese—which represents ideas using a literally countless combination of ideographs.

Character Offset adds the value you specify to the characters' Unicode values, thereby replacing the characters with the characters corresponding to the new values. For example, specifying an offset value of 4 shifts the letters in the word *bet* four spaces alphabetically, so that the word becomes *fix*. (Of course, offsetting characters in a word doesn't usually result in another word.)

Character Value sets the characters' Unicode values, thereby replacing the characters with those corresponding to the new values. For example, setting the Character Value property to 63 replaces all characters in the range to question marks (?).

Character Range includes two options that specify whether to restrict the Character Value property. In the Character Range pull-down menu, choose Preserve Case and Digits to restrict characters to their character group—such as Roman, Katakana (a Japanese syllabary), symbols, and so on. Choose Full Unicode to permit unrestricted Character Values.

Choosing a Range Selector

When you create an animator group, it includes the property you specify along with a range selector. You can add three types of selectors to a group: range, wiggly, and expression. Each group can have any number or combination of selectors, but each animator group must have at least one selector.

When you use multiple selectors in a single animator group, you can specify how they interact by stipulating a mode, as explained in "Using Multiple Selectors and Selector Modes" later in this chapter.

Range

You can add range selectors to the same animator group to create more complex selections, in much the same way you can apply multiple masks to a layer to create complex masked areas. A range selector also includes a number of options to control how subsequent characters (or words, or lines of text) are added to the selection, the rate of change in a property value, and other aspects of the range.

Wiggly

A wiggly selector varies the range by the frequency and within limits you specify. Using a wiggly selector can make an animation seem more random or organic. You can use a wiggly selector by itself or to vary part of another selector.

Expression

Whereas the other selectors limit (range) and vary (wiggly) the range of text affected by the properties in the animator group, an expression selector controls the *amount* that properties are applied. It's called an expression selector because its Amount property's value is derived from a JavaScript-based formula known as an *expression*. As you'll learn in Chapter 17, "Complex Projects," an expression can link one property's values to any other value or specify the value using a kind of mathematical formula.

Whereas an expression selector controls only an animator group's Amount property in a text layer, standard expressions can be applied to any property in any layer. Otherwise, expression selectors work just like other expressions. For this reason, expression selectors are covered only briefly here, and a full explanation of expressions is reserved for Chapter 17.

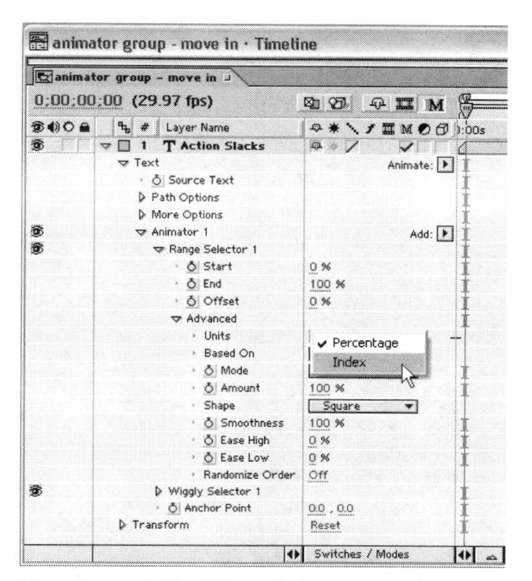

Figure 12.125 In the Units pull-down menu, choose whether range values are expressed as a percentage of the entire type or are expressed by indexing, or numbering, each unit.

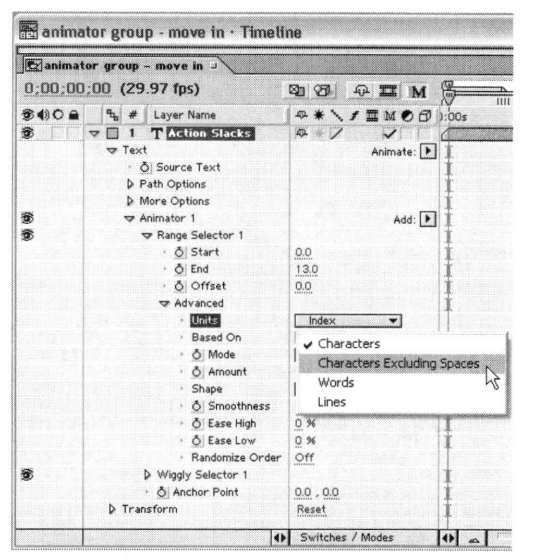

Figure 12.126 For Based On, choose the units on which the range is based.

Specifying a Range

You can set a range either by dragging its left and right borders in the Comp window or by using controls in the text layer's property outline. A range can be applied to different units of type: each character, word, or line. When you're specifying a range, these units are measured either in terms of a percentage of total units, or by the unit (1, 2, 3, and so on).

To specify how a range is measured:

1. In the layer outline of the Timeline window, expand the range selector you want to adjust, and expand its Advanced property heading.

2. To specify how start, end, and offset range values are expressed, choose an option in the Units pull-down menu (**Figure 12.125**):

   Percentage expresses values in percentages.

   Index expresses values according to a numerical indexing scheme, in which the first unit of text is assigned a value of 1, the next unit 2, and so on.

3. To specify the units on which a range is based (how the range is counted), choose an option in the Based On pull-down menu (**Figure 12.126**):

   Characters counts each character, including spaces, as a unit in the range.

   Characters Excluding Spaces counts each character as a unit in the range but excludes spaces.

   Words counts each word as a unit in the range.

   Lines counts each line (of a multiline text layer) as a unit in the range.

   The values for Start, End, and Offset are based on the option you specify.

To specify a range:

1. Expand the text layer animator group you want to adjust, and then expand the range selector you want to set.
2. To set the start of the range, *do either of the following:*
   - ▲ In the text layer's expanded outline, specify a value for Start.
   - ▲ With the text layer's animator group heading selected in the expanded outline, drag the Range Start icon in the Composition window (**Figure 12.127**).
3. To set the end of the range, *do either of the following:*
   - ▲ In the text layer's expanded outline, specify a value for End.
   - ▲ With the text layer's Animator property selected, drag the Range End icon in the Composition window (**Figure 12.128**).
4. To change both the Start and End values by the same amount, specify an Offset value in the text layer's expanded outline (**Figure 12.129**).

Figure 12.127 With the range selected in the property outline, you can drag the start of the range in the Comp window...

Figure 12.128...or drag the Range End icon to set the end of the range.

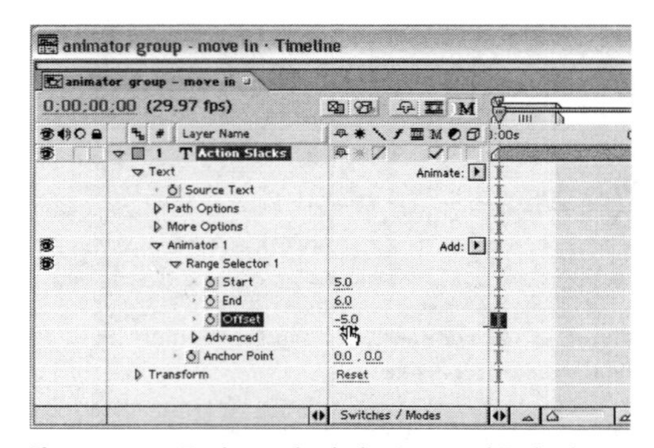

Figure 12.129 To change both the Start and End values by the same amount, change the Offset value in the property outline.

Understanding Range Selector Options

You can fine-tune the rate and manner in which the range includes units by specifying a number of options, listed under the Range Selector's Advanced category in the expanded property outline.

Shape

You define a range with distinct borders (for example, between characters in a word). However, you can think of those borders as having a *shape*. The shape you specify determines the rate at which units become included in the range (and, depending on the shape, excluded from the range, as well). In other words, the Shape option controls how soon units added to the range become fully included and achieve the maximum property value.

With some animator properties (such as Position and Scale), the literal shape associated with each option is evident visually. In each of the following examples, the animation is the same except for the selector's Shape option. The range increases character by character, from left to right, until it includes the entire word. Because the animation increases each character's height (the Y aspect of the Scale property), it's easy to see how the Shape option affects the range (**Figure 12.130**):

Square includes and excludes subsequent units (characters, words, and so on) in the range abruptly. You can fine-tune the transition time between units by adjusting the Smoothness value (described in the next section, "Other range options").

Ramp Up includes subsequent units in the range gradually, in a linear progression.

continues on next page

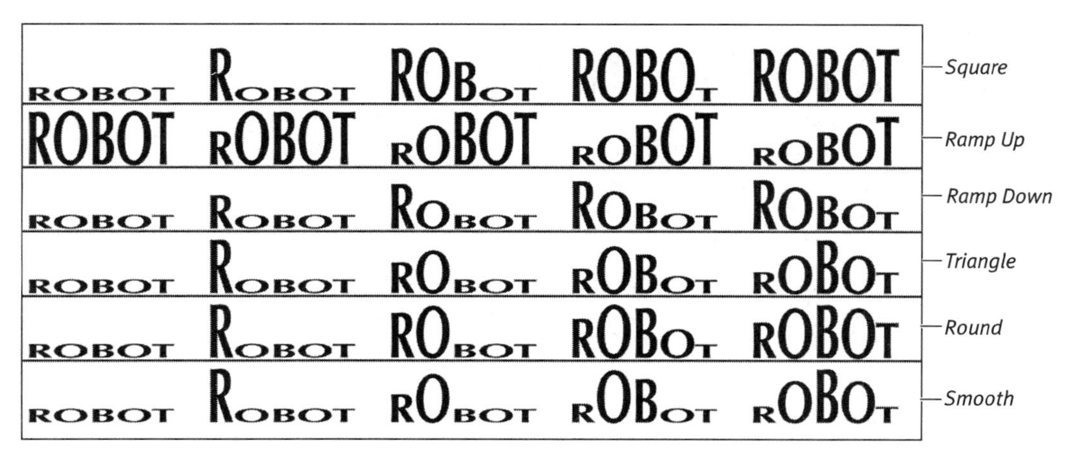

Figure 12.130 You can see how applying different Shape settings to the same animation affects the final result.

Ramp Down excludes subsequent units from the range gradually, in a linear progression.

Triangle includes subsequent units in the range gradually and then excludes preceding units gradually, using a linear progression.

Round includes subsequent units in the range gradually, using a curved, decelerating progression; and then excludes units gradually, using a curved, accelerating progression.

Smooth includes subsequent units in the range gradually, using a curved, accelerating progression; and then excludes units gradually, using a curved, decelerating progression.

Other range options

In the expanded property outline, a Range Selector's Advanced category includes other options that let you fine-tune the properties' rate of change or randomize the order of the range:

Smoothness adjusts the transition time between units (characters, and so on) when you specify the Square shape.

Ease High adjusts the animator property's rate of change as it approaches it maximum value, when the selection is in a fully included state. Setting the Ease High value to 100 percent eases the rate of change as it approaches its maximum, decelerating it; setting Ease High to −100 percent accelerates the rate of change as it approaches the maximum.

Ease Low adjusts the animator property's rate of change as it approaches it minimum value, when the selection is in a fully excluded state. Setting the Ease Low value to 100 percent eases the rate of change as it approaches its minimum, decelerating it; setting Ease Low to −100 percent accelerates the rate of change as it approaches the minimum.

Randomize Order, when turned on, randomizes the order in which the properties in the animator group are applied to the selection you specified with the range selector. For example, you can animate a range selector to gradually include all the letters in a word, from left to right; selecting Randomize Order applies the animator property to the characters in random order instead of sequential order.

Random Seed specifies the basis, or *seed*, on which a random order is generated. Therefore, duplicating a text animation also duplicates its selection order, even when the range is set to Randomize Order. To make the duplicate use a unique random order, change the Random Seed value.

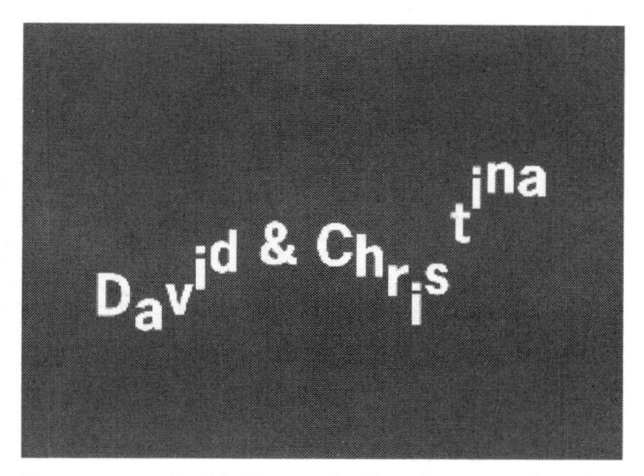

Figure 12.131 In this figure, the Text Bounce animation preset is applied to the text and affects the entire line...

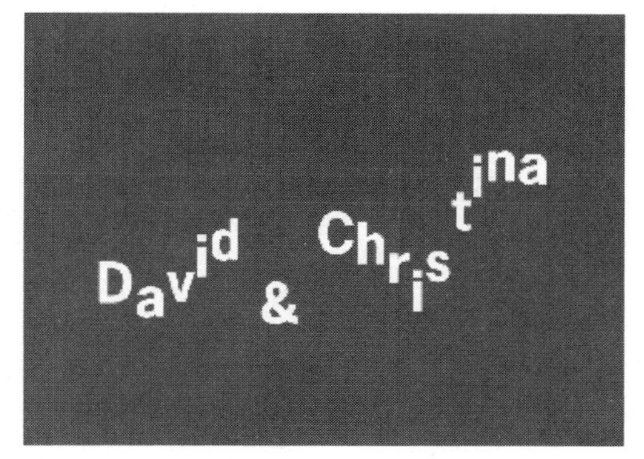

Figure 12.132...but adding a selector to single out the ampersand (&) and applying the Subtract mode excludes the character from the animation.

Using Multiple Selectors and Selector Modes

In an animator group's expanded outline, a range selector's Advanced category includes a Mode option. Selector modes are comparable to mask modes (covered in Chapter 9, "Mask Essentials"). Just as mask modes let you combine multiple masks to create shapes you couldn't achieve otherwise, *selector modes* let you combine multiple ranges. Selector modes dictate how one selector interacts with the selectors above it in the animator group's stacking order (**Figures 12.131** and **12.132**). As with layer masks, you don't need to change the mode if you're using only one selector in the group:

Add combines the range with the range defined by selectors higher in the animator group's stacking order. Properties are applied to the sum of the ranges.

Subtract subtracts the range from the range defined by the selectors higher in the animator group's stacking order. Properties are applied to the remaining area of the higher ranges.

Intersect includes only the area shared by the range and those above it in the stacking order. Properties are applied only where the range overlaps with the ranges above it in the stacking order.

Min applies the minimum value of properties where the range *doesn't* intersect with ranges above it.

Max applies the maximum value of properties where the range intersects with those above it.

Difference adds the range to those above it in the animator group's stacking order but excludes the area where the range and those above it in the stacking order overlap.

Specifying Wiggly Selector Options

A wiggly selector includes many of the options found in other selectors, plus a number of unique options to control variations in the selector. When you add a wiggly selector to an animator group, expand the selector's heading to reveal its options:

Min specifies the variation's lowest limit (the minimum value for the wiggler).

Max specifies the variation's highest limit (the maximum value for the wiggler).

Wiggles/Second sets the frequency of variation from the selected range (the number of variations per second).

Correlation sets the extent to which variations in the range match, or correlate, to units (characters, words, lines) in the range. Setting Correlation to 100 percent makes the units wiggle in unison; setting it to 0 percent makes the units wiggle independently.

Temporal Phase sets the starting value, or seed, of the temporal aspect (the timing of the variations). Adjust this value to vary animations that share other animator group

Spatial Phase sets the starting value, or seed, of the spatial aspect of the variations. Adjust this value to vary animations that share other animator group

Lock Dimensions wiggles, or varies, property dimensions—the X and Y dimensions, for example—by the same amount.

About Expression Selector Options

In Chapter 17, you'll learn that instead of keyframing a property, you can specify its values using an *expression*. For now, suffice it to say that an expression can link one property value to any other value. Expressions can also generate values based on a kind of mathematical formula.

An *expression selector* uses the same kind of scripting language to control the amount that animator properties are applied to a given range of text. When the Amount value is 0 percent, the property has no effect on the text within the range; when the value is 100 percent, the property is fully applied. An expression selector can be used by itself or in conjunction with other selectors. This way, an expression selector adds another variable—and another level of control—to an animator group.

As you'll discover in Chapter 17, you can create any sort of expression more quickly and easily using the handy pickwhip. Once you become more fluent in expression language (which is based on JavaScript), you can use the expression pull-down menu and even type in your own expressions.

13 Painting on a Layer

Although it appears as a single effect in the layer's property outline, the paint effect feels like an entirely separate set of features meriting a chapter of its own. In fact, the Tools palette includes several tools devoted to painting: the Brush tool, Eraser tool, and Clone Stamp tool. And the paint feature's numerous options require two specialized palettes: the Paint palette and Brush Tips palette. With the Brush and Eraser tools, you can simulate handwriting, create hand-drawn graphics, or alter a layer's alpha channel to create (or fix) a track matte. Or you can make more subtle adjustments to an image with each stroke by using blending modes. You can also use a Clone Stamp tool to retouch an image or to aid in tasks like wire removal.

Using your mouse—or better yet, a tablet and stylus—you can record strokes directly onto a layer in real time, change their characteristics, and play them back in a number of ways. The Brush Tips palette includes a varied set of preset brushes, and allows you to create and save your own variations—small or large, hard or soft-edged, round or elliptical. Because strokes are vector-based, you can scale them without adversely affecting resolution. And like all effects, brush strokes are nondestructive, which means that it doesn't alter your source files. In fact, even strokes you make with the Eraser tool are non-destructive.

Paint also deserves special attention because of its unique animation paradigm. Each stroke appears as its own layer-within-a-layer—that is, each stroke appears as a duration bar within the paint effect. This way, you can toggle strokes on and off, control how they're layered and how they interact with strokes lower in the stacking order, and precisely adjust when and how quickly they appear.

In this chapter, you'll learn this single effect's numerous options so you can explore its unlimited possibilities.

Using the Paint and Brush Tips palettes

After Effects includes two palettes for controlling paint: the Paint palette and Brush Tips palette. Both palettes are nearly identical to their counterparts in other Adobe Programs. To make your workflow easier, you can set the palettes to open automatically whenever you select the Brush, Clone, or Eraser tools.

To open and close the Paint and Brush Tips palettes:

1. In the Tools palette, *select any paint-related tool*:

   Brush tool

   Clone tool

   Eraser tool

   The Toggle Palettes button and the Auto Open Palettes option appear in the Tools palette. If Auto Open Palettes is already checked, the Paint and Brush Tips palettes also open automatically (see the next step).

2. In the Tools palette, *do any of the following* (**Figure 13.1**):

   ▲ Select Auto Open Palettes and choose a paint tool (the Brush, Eraser, or Clone Stamp tool). This automatically opens the tool's related palette.

   ▲ Click the Toggle Palettes button to toggle the Paint and Brush Tips palettes open and closed.

   Unless you separate their tabs, the Paint and Brush Tips palettes open in the same window by default (**Figure 13.2**).

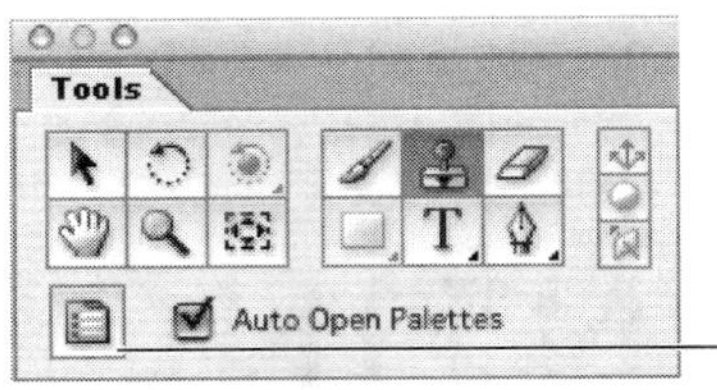

Figure 13.1 Select the Brush, Clone Stamp, or Eraser tools and then specify whether you want related palettes to open automatically. You can also toggle the palettes open or closed.

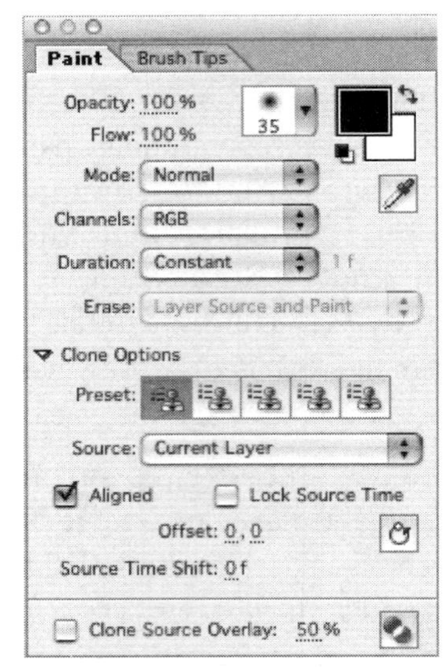

Figure 13.2 By default, the Paint and Brush Tips palettes open together in a single window.

✔ Tip

■ As always, you can open or close any palette from the menu bar, by choosing the name of the palette from the Window menu.

Figure 13.3 Opacity determines the paint's coverage strength; Flow determines the speed of coverage. Here, the words "Opacity," and "flow" are repeated, each time using a lower opacity or flow settings, respectively.

Specifying Paint Stroke Options

Before you start using the Brush and Eraser tools, take a moment to get a more detailed understanding of each option, starting with the options at the top of the Paint palette. These options not only allow you to control the character and color of each stroke, but also let you specify which of the layer's channels are affected by each stroke, and how long strokes appear.

Depending on the options you choose, you can make visible strokes, resembling those made by a loaded paintbrush or by an airbrush lightly applying each coat; or you can make strokes that affect the layer's alpha channel, effectively creating or modifying a matte. The strokes can appear for any length of time, or reenact the painting process. Later, you'll specify many of the same options to determine the effects of the Clone Stamp tool.

Generally, you set these options before you paint a stroke. However, you can change these and most other options by selecting the stroke under the Paint effect and adjusting its values in the property outline.

Opacity and Flow

Opacity and Flow settings determine the paint's coverage strength, and speed of coverage, respectively. Together, they can make paint seem opaque or semitransparent (**Figure 13.3**). When using the Eraser, the same options determine how effectively and quickly pixels are removed.

continues on next page

Opacity sets the maximum opacity of each stroke, from 0% to 100%; opacity is analogous to how well a real-world paint covers a surface. (A brush's Hardness setting also contributes to a stroke's opacity near its edges.)

Flow sets how quickly paint is applied with each stroke, from 0% to 100%. Lower Flow settings apply less of the paint color in a stroke, making the paint appear more transparent; low Flow values also result in greater spaces between brush tip marks when the brush's Spacing option is active (see "Customizing Brush Tips" later in this chapter).

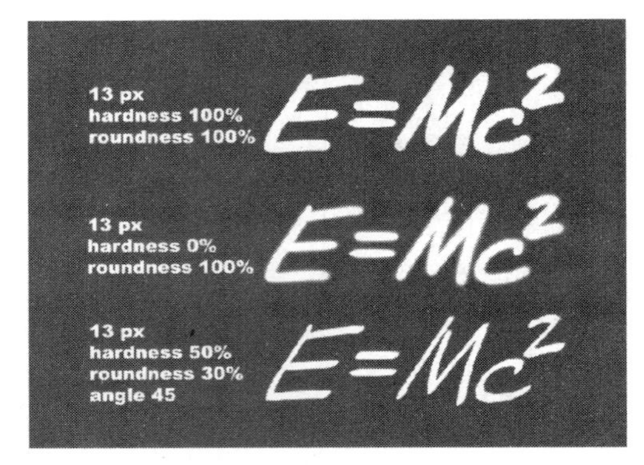

Figure 13.4 This figure shows strokes created by various brush tips.

Brush Tip

As you'd expect, the brush tip simulates the camel hair on the end of a brush (or the point of a pen, or the spray pattern of an airbrush). Brush tip settings define the character of strokes. The Paint palette displays the currently selected brush tip as an icon that represents its roundness, angle, and hardness settings; a number indicates the brush's size, in pixels (**Figure 13.4**). Clicking the arrow next to the current brush tip icon opens a Brush Tip Selector panel, from which you can select a preset brush tip (see "Using Brush Tips" later in this chapter) (**Figure 13.5**).

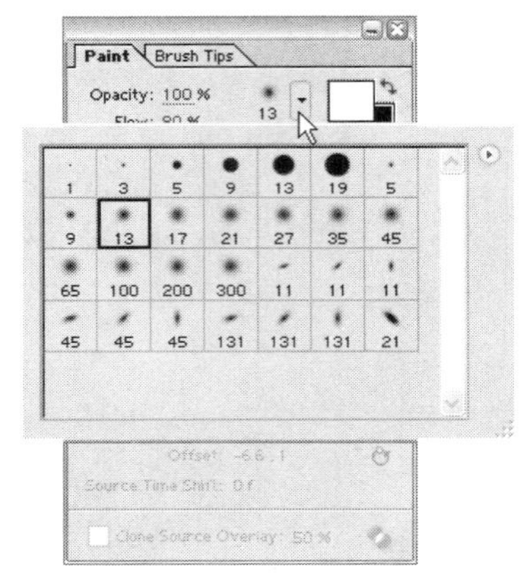

Figure 13.5 In the Paint palette, click the arrow next to the current brush tip icon to reveal the Brush Tips Selector.

Color

Like a real palette of paint, the Paint palette lets you choose the color you want to use. The upper left swatch sets the *foreground color*, which specifies the paint applied by the brush; the lower right swatch sets the *background color*, or secondary color. Clicking a swatch lets you choose a color from a color picker, or you can sample a color from the screen using a standard Eyedropper tool. Click the smaller icon to reset the foreground and background colors to black and white, respectively; click the Swap icon to switch the colors (**Figure 13.6**).

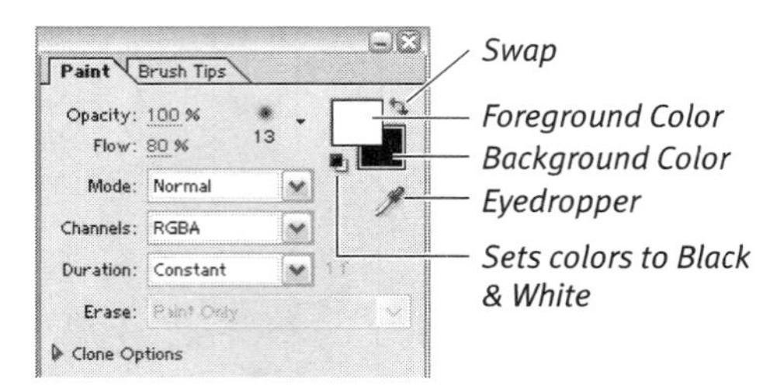

Figure 13.6 In the Paint palette, the upper left swatch sets the foreground color; the lower right swatch sets the background, or secondary color.

Figure 13.7 You can set how brushes interact with lower strokes or the underlying image with blending modes. Here, a soft, transparent brush uses a dodge mode to lighten shadows in this photo.

Figure 13.8 In this example, strokes are painted on the layer's alpha channel to reveal the parts of the layer's image (a tangerine) just as a mask or matte would do. Note that the Paint effect's Paint on Transparent option is on.

Mode

The Mode pull-down menu lets you specify how each stroke interacts with underlying pixels (**Figure 13.7**). The menu's blending mode options are explained in Chapter 14, "More Layer Techniques." However, the stroke blending mode menu doesn't include the Dissolve or Dancing Dissolve blending modes. Note that each stroke can use a blending mode, and the layer containing the paint effect (and all its strokes) can use a blending mode also.

Channels

The Channels pull-down menu specifies which of the layer's channels are affected by a stroke. You can affect the visible red, green, and blue channels (RGB), the alpha channel (which defines transparency), or all channels (RGBA). Painting on a layer's RGB channels creates visible strokes, while painting on its alpha channel affects its transparent areas. For example, you can animate strokes applied to a layer's alpha channel to reveal portions of the layer's image (**Figure 13.8**).

Duration

The Duration pull-down menu specifies how strokes are displayed over time. Duration options facilitate animating strokes the way you want—or if you prefer, keeping them static:

continues on next page

Constant displays all strokes from the current time to the end of the layer containing the stroke.

Write On reveals the stroke over time, from beginning to end, depending on the speed at which you paint it. You can change the speed of the effect by adjusting each stroke's End property; you can reverse or create a "write off" effect by adjusting the strokes' Start property (**Figure 13.9**).

Single Frame displays the stroke at the current frame only.

Custom displays the stroke for the number of frames you specify. Set the duration by adjusting the value that appears next to the Duration pull-down menu (**Figure 13.10**).

These options set each stroke's initial duration—and in the case of Write On, the stroke's initial End property's keyframes. After a stroke is created, you can't change the Duration setting in the property outline, per se; instead, you control when strokes are displayed by manipulating their duration bars, and by keyframing properties such as Start and End.

✔ Tips

- Remember, paint doesn't always have to act like paint. For example, by applying certain modes, you can subtly retouch an image. Use a lightening mode (like Dodge) to brighten unwanted shadows. If necessary, animate the layer to follow the area you want to affect.
- By painting on the layer's alpha channel, you can use the advantages of various brush tips and duration options to affect the layer's transparency in ways that might be more difficult to do using masks or other methods.

Figure 13.9 Strokes always start at the current time, but you can set how long they appear by setting a duration option. Here, the Write On option makes the strokes appear over time, to simulate handwriting.

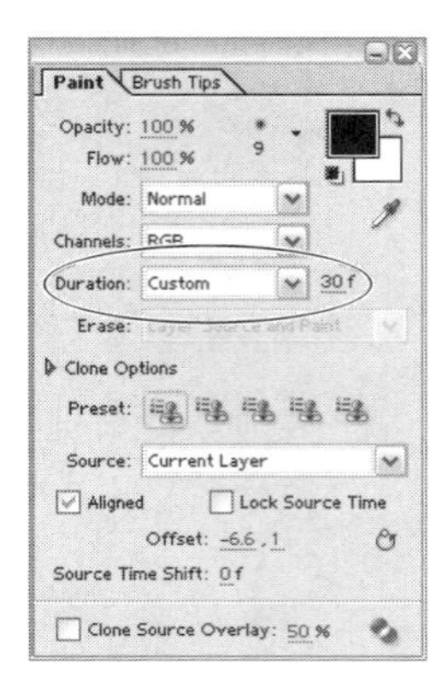

Figure 13.10 When you choose a Custom duration, specify the number of frames you want the stroke to appear.

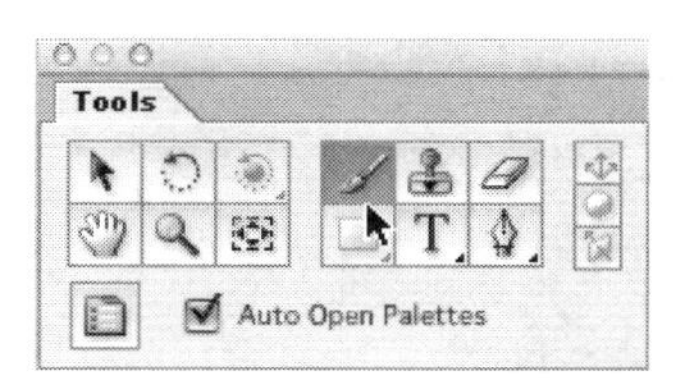

Figure 13.11 Select the Brush tool.

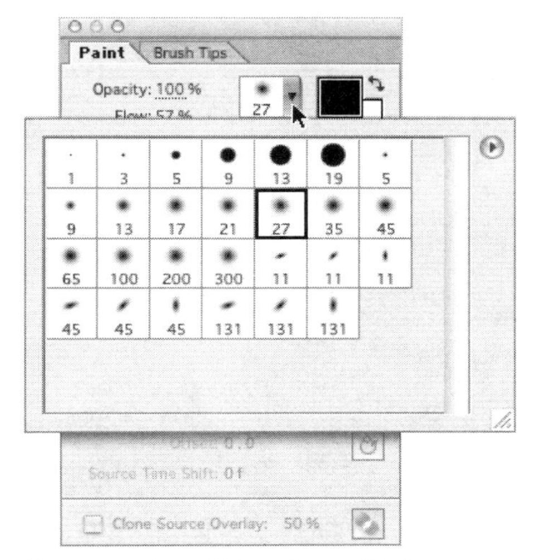

Figure 13.12 In the Paint palette, click the arrow next to the current brush tip to choose a brush from the Brush Tips Selector.

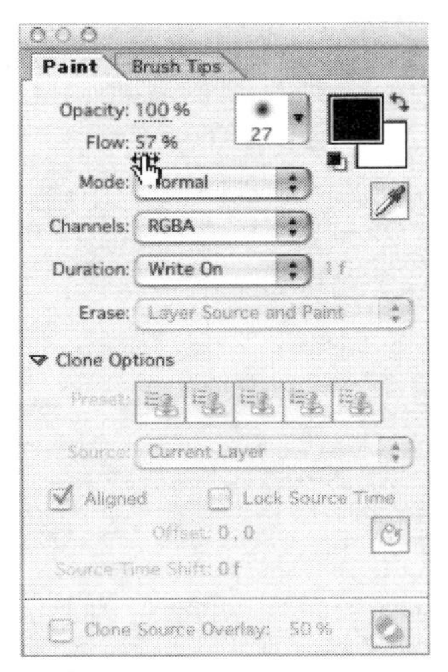

Figure 13.13 In the Paint palette, specify the brush's Opacity, Flow, and Color.

Painting with the Brush Tool

Generally speaking, painting in After Effects is as easy as grabbing a brush and painting on the layer. But at the same time, this straightforward task includes numerous options. Not only can you change the characteristics of the brush, but also which channels the strokes modify, and how long they appear on screen. (See the previous section, "Specifying Paint Stroke Options," for detailed descriptions of each menu option.)

To paint on a layer:

1. Open the layer you want to paint on in a Layer window.
2. In the Tools palette, select the Brush tool (**Figure 13.11**).

   If the Auto Open Palettes option is selected, the Paint and Brush Tips palettes open.
3. To choose a brush, *do either of the following*:
   - ▲ In the Paint palette, click the arrow next to the current brush tip and choose a preset brush from the Brush Tips selector (**Figure 13.12**).
   - ▲ In the Brush Tips palette, specify a custom brush
4. In the Paint palette, specify options for the brush attributes (**Figure 13.13**):

   Opacity sets the relative opacity of pixels in a stroke.

   Flow sets the speed, or relative number of pixels applied with each stroke.

   Foreground Color sets the brush's color.

   Background Color sets a secondary color.

   When using the Eraser tool, Opacity sets the strength of the eraser, and the Foreground Color has no effect.

continues on next page

5. To specify how brush strokes in the layer interact with the underlying image, choose a blending mode from the Mode pull-down menu (**Figure 13.14**).
6. To specify the layer channels affected by the strokes, choose an option from the Channels pull-down menu (**Figure 13.15**).
7. To specify how strokes appear over time, choose an option from the Duration pull-down menu (**Figure 13.16**).
8. Set the current time to the frame where you want the first stroke to begin.

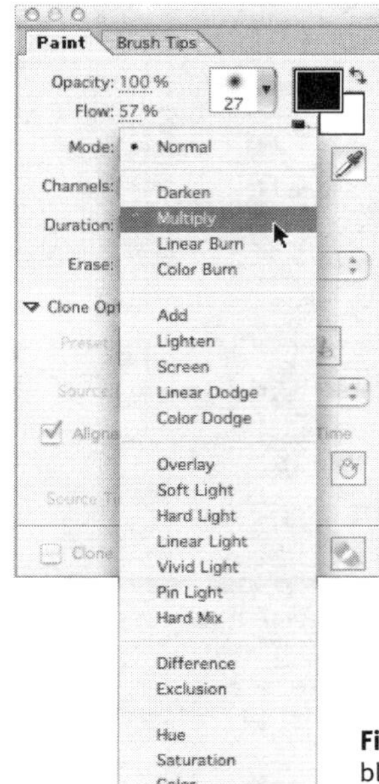

Figure 13.14 Choose a blending mode from the Mode pull-down menu. This example uses the Multiply mode.

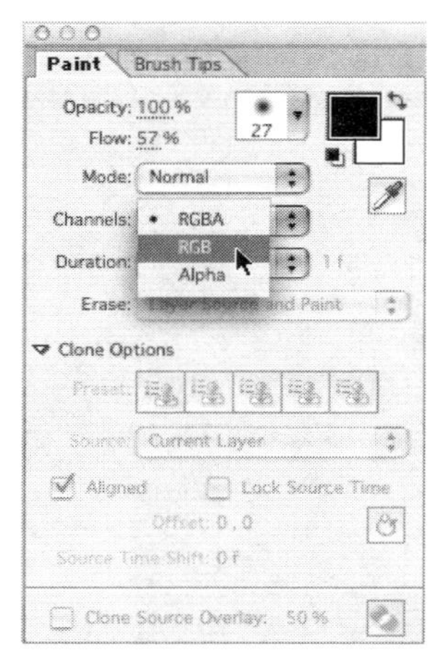

Figure 13.15 Specify the channels you want to paint on in the Channels pull-down menu. In this example, strokes are applied to the layer's RGB channels.

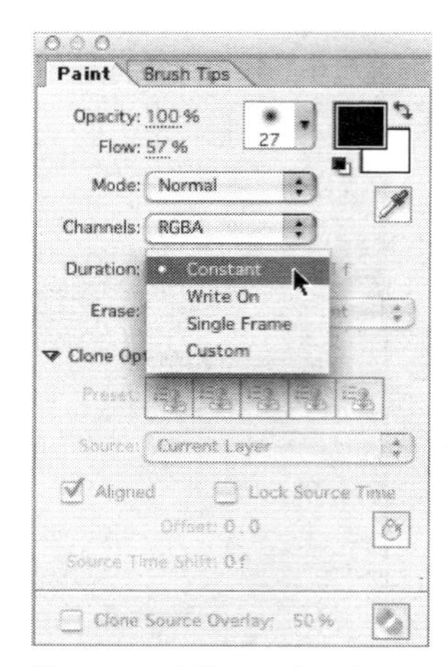

Figure 13.16 Choose how long you want the stroke to appear in the Duration pull-down menu. In this example, the strokes are set to appear from the current frame onward.

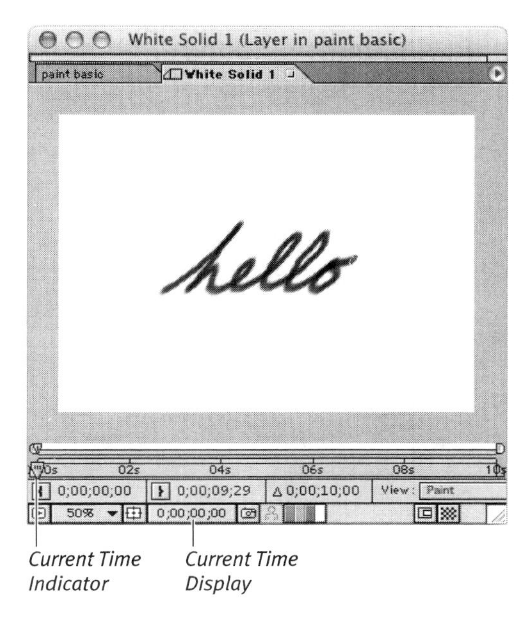

Figure 13.17 Drag the Brush in the Layer window to create a stroke that starts at the current time. You can't paint in the Comp window, but you can open a separate Comp window to see the results.

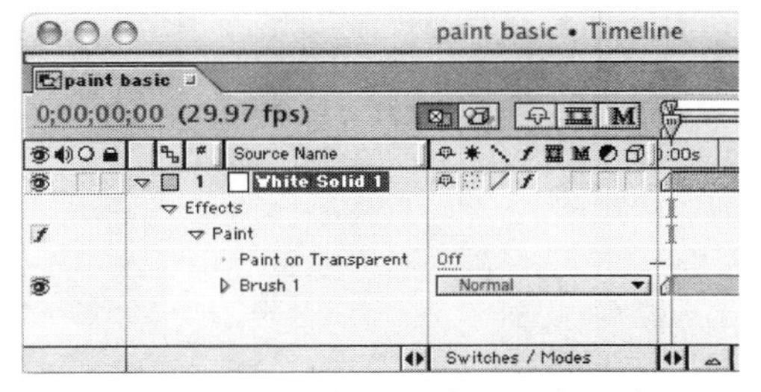

Figure 13.18 In the Timeline window, each stroke appears as an individual item.

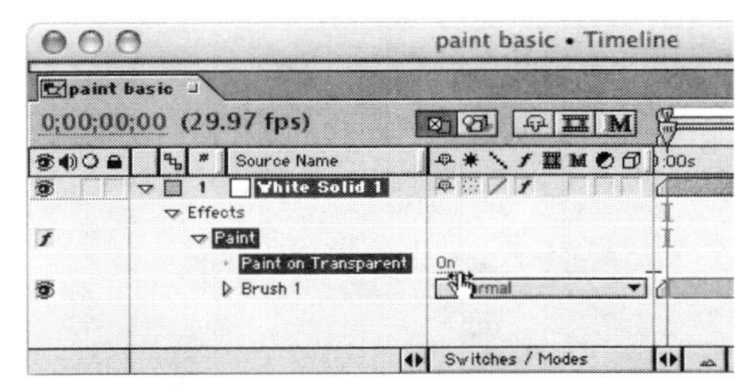

Figure 13.19 Under the Paint effect's property heading, set the Transparent option to On.

9. Using the Brush tool, drag in the Layer window to paint strokes on the layer (**Figure 13.17**).

   The mouse pointer appears as a circle that corresponds with the brush's size, angle, and roundness. Strokes use the options you specified. In the layer's property outline, the Paint effect appears. Expanding the Paint effect reveals that each stroke is listed separately and has a corresponding layer bar under the time ruler (**Figure 13.18**).

To make the painted layer transparent:

1. Select the layer containing the Paint effect.
2. In the layer's expanded property outline, expand the layer's Paint effect property heading.

   or

   Open the Effect Controls window to view the layer's Paint effect.
3. Under the Paint effect's property heading, set the Paint on Transparent option to On (**Figure 13.19**).

   The selected layer becomes transparent, leaving only the Paint effect visible.

✔ Tip

- The Paint effect discussed in this chapter must be applied to a layer in its Layer window. After Effects Professional also includes a Vector Paint effect that you can use to paint in the Comp window. However, it uses a different toolset and procedures.

Erasing Strokes

In practice, the Eraser tool does just what you'd expect: it removes pixels from a layer. You can specify whether it affects the target layer's pixels and paint strokes, paint only, or just the most recent paint stroke.

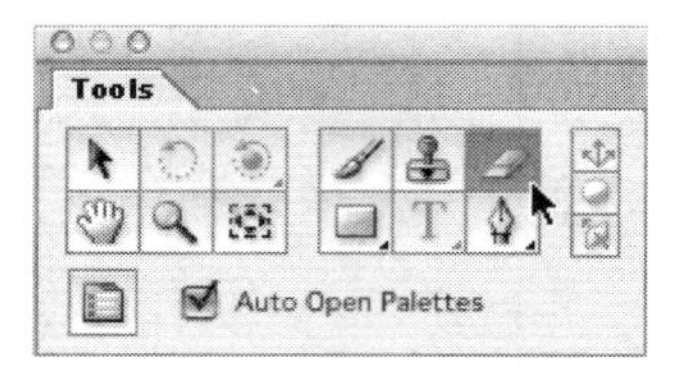

Figure 13.20 Select the Eraser tool.

But it might be more accurate to say that the Eraser *negates* pixels rather than removes them. A look in the Paint effect's property outline reveals that Eraser strokes appear in the stacking order along with Brush strokes. Like the other paint options, Eraser strokes are non-destructive; they don't permanently affect either the layer or paint strokes. Turn off an Eraser stroke's video (by clicking its Eye icon in the timeline) and its effects disappear.

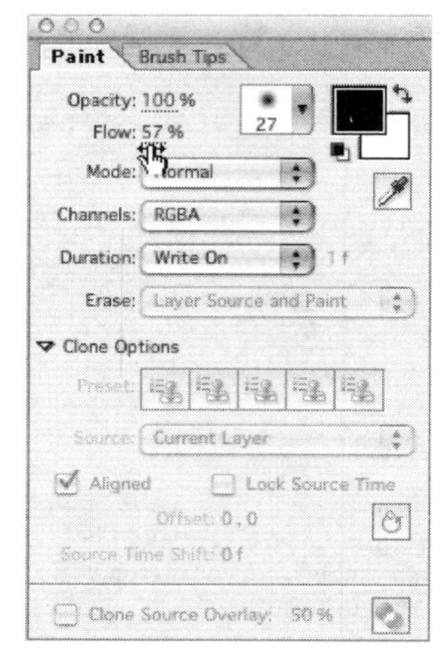

Figure 13.21 In the Paint palette, set the Opacity and Flow. These options help determine how completely pixels are removed with each stroke.

So in most respects, the Eraser works just like a Brush—except it's an "anti-brush." The Eraser tool uses the same brush tips as the Brush tool, but naturally, you can't apply a color to an Eraser. And whereas a brush's Opacity and Flow settings control the strength of the brush—how thick you lay on the painted pixels—the same settings control how thoroughly the Eraser removes pixels. Otherwise, settings are analogous to the Brush tool.

To use the Eraser tool:

1. In the Tools palette, select the Eraser tool (**Figure 13.20**).
2. In the Paint palette, specify values for Opacity and Flow (**Figure 13.21**).

   When using the Eraser, Opacity and Flow refer to the eraser's "strength."

To create a brush tip:

1. In the Brush Tips palette, specify the brush's attributes, including Diameter, Angle, Roundness, and so on.

   In the preview area of the Brush Tips palette, the brush's icon reflects your choices.

   See the section "Customizing Brush Tips," later in this chapter, for a detailed explanation of brush tip options.

2. Click the Save icon (**Figure 13.33**).

   A Choose Name dialog box appears with a descriptive name for the brush already entered.

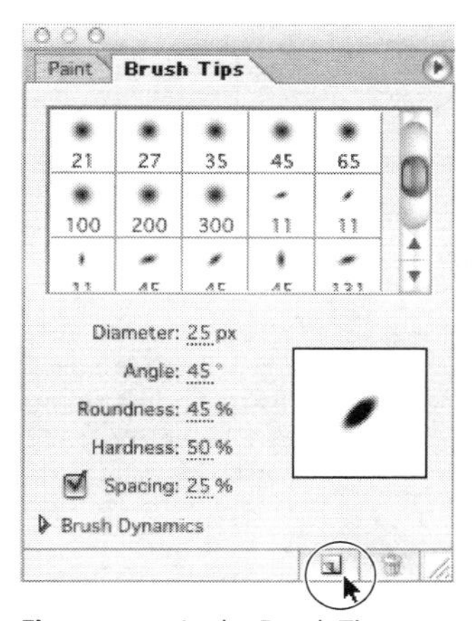

Figure 13.33 In the Brush Tips palette, set the brush's attributes and click the Save icon.

3. In the Choose Name dialog box, leave the suggested name or enter a custom name for the new brush and click OK (**Figure 13.34**).

   The brush tip appears selected among the other preset brush tips (**Figure 13.35**). The new brush tip uses the attributes of the brush that was selected most recently. How presets appear in the palette depends on the option you choose in the Brush Tips palette's pull-down menu.

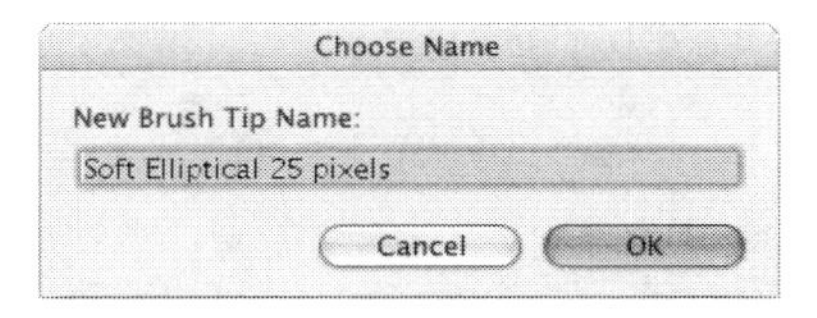

Figure 13.34 Name the new brush tip in the Choose Name dialog box.

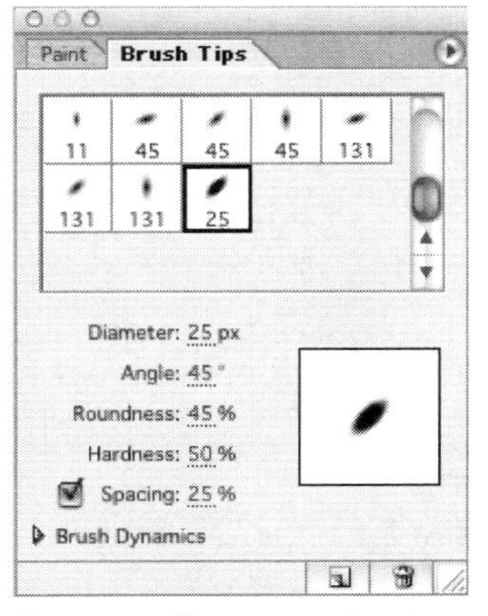

Figure 13.35 Your custom brush tip appears in the preset brush tips area (shown here) and in Brush Tips Selector of the Paint palette.

To rename a preset brush tip:

1. In the Brush Tips palette, double-click the brush tip you want to rename (**Figure 13.36**).

   A Choose Name dialog box appears.

2. In the Choose Name dialog box, type a new name for the brush tip and click OK (**Figure 13.37**).

To remove a preset brush tip:

1. In the Brush Tips palette, click the preset brush tip you want to remove and click the delete icon (**Figure 13.38**).

   After Effects prompts you to confirm your choice (**Figure 13.39**).

2. In the warning dialog box, click OK.

   The brush you selected is removed from the list of presets (**Figure 13.40**).

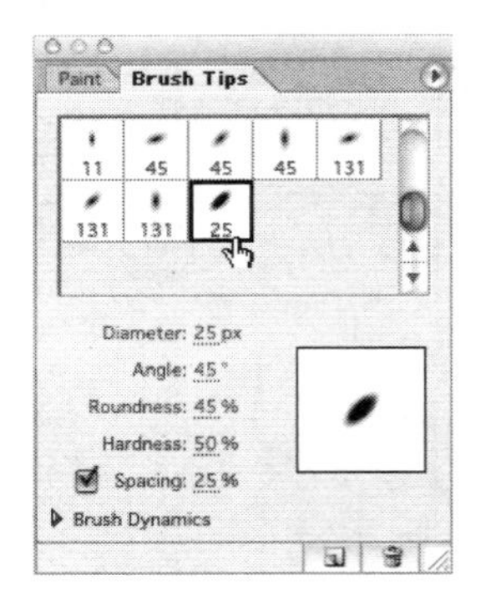

Figure 13.36 Double-click the brush tip you want to rename in the Brush Tips palette,

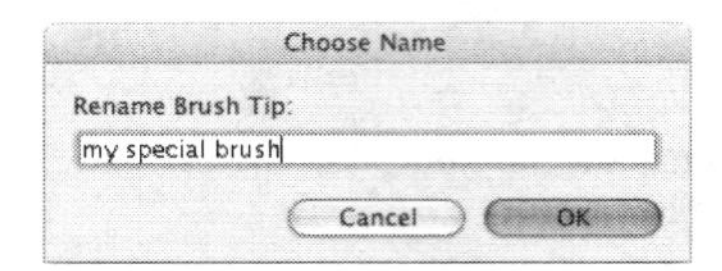

Figure 13.37 Enter a new name in the Choose Name dialog box and click OK.

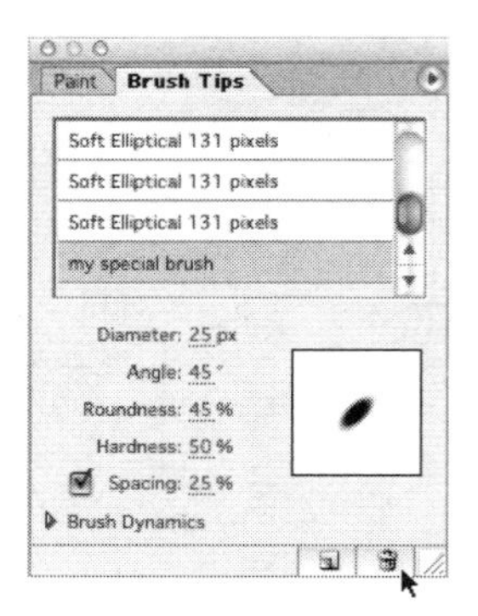

Figure 13.38 In the Brush Tips palette, click the brush tip you want to remove and click the trash icon.

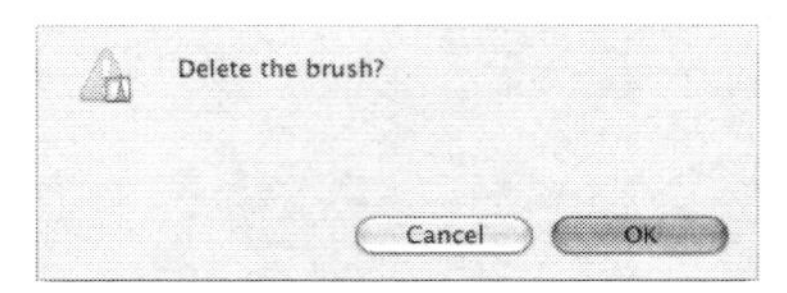

Figure 13.39 Confirm your choice by clicking OK.

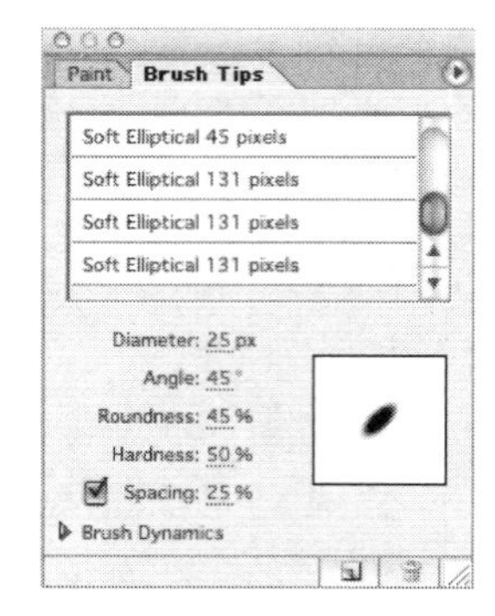

Figure 13.40 The selected brush is removed from the palette.

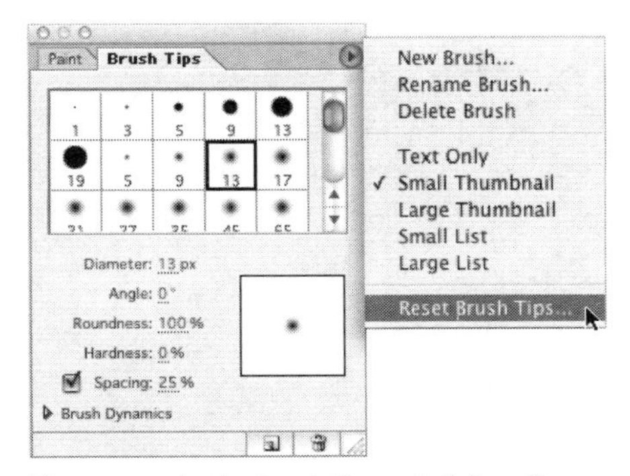

Figure 13.41 In the Brush Tips palette's pull-down menu, choose Reset Brush Tips.

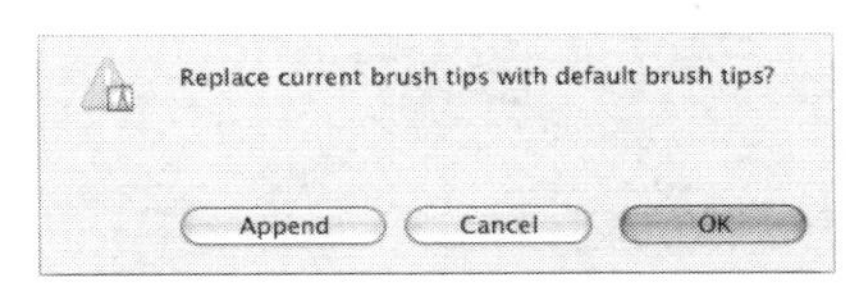

Figure 13.42 In the dialog box that appears, specify whether you want to Append the default brush tips to the current set. Otherwise, click OK to replace the current set with the default set.

To restore default brush tip presets:

1. In the Brush Tips palette's pull-down menu, choose Reset Brush Tips (**Figure 13.41**).

   A dialog box appears prompting you to replace or append the current set of preset brushes with the default set.

2. In the dialog box, *do either of the following* (**Figure 13.42**):

   ▲ To add the default brushes to the current set of presets, click Append.

   ▲ To replace the current set of preset brushes with the default set (removing any custom presets), click OK.

The default set of brushes either replaces or adds to the current set of presets, depending on your choice.

Customizing Brush Tips

Even though the Paint and Brush Tips palettes include a useful assortment of preset brush tips, chances are you'll want to create your own brush tips to suit a particular task. As you learned in the previous section, "Using Brush Tips," you can save each of your special brush tips as a preset, which appears in the preset selector area of the Paint and Brush Tips palettes. Controlling a brush's attributes gives you a great deal of control over the character of the strokes it produces. This section covers the brush tip options; the next section, "Using Brush Dynamics," explains how to vary these qualities with a pen and tablet.

In the Brush Tips palette, you can specify the following attributes for each brush (**Figure 13.43**):

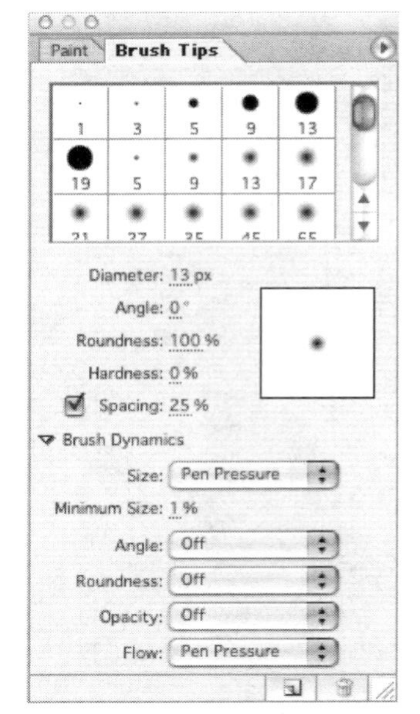

Figure 13.43 The Brush Tips palette includes several options so you can create custom brushes.

Diameter determines the size, measured in pixels, across the diameter of its widest axis (for elliptical brushes) (**Figure 13.44**).

Figure 13.44 The strokes in this figure use different diameters.

Angle specifies the amount, measured in degrees, from which the widest axis of an elliptical brush deviates from the horizontal.

Roundness refers to the width of a brush's shortest diameter, expressed as a percentage of its widest diameter (determined by the Diameter value): 100% creates a circular brush; 0% creates a linear brush; intermediate values create an elliptical brush (**Figure 13.45**).

Figure 13.45 The stroke on top was created using a perfectly round brush, while lower strokes used smaller Roundness settings and an Angle of 45 degrees. Otherwise, the strokes are identical.

Figure 13.46 These strokes are identical, except for their hardness settings.

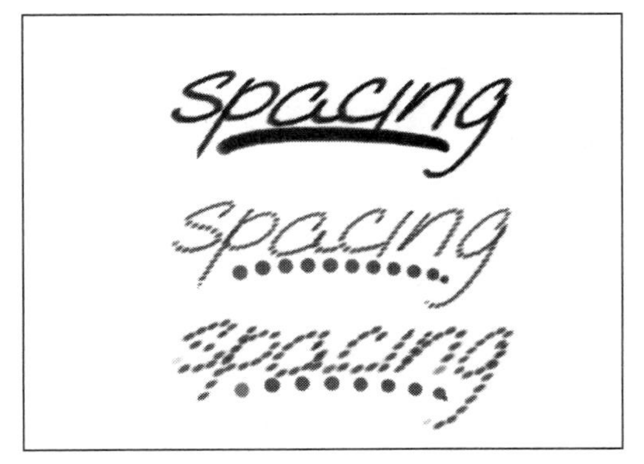

Figure 13.47 The three words, "spacing," are identical, except for their spacing values.

Hardness sets the relative opacity of the brush's stroke from its center to the edges, analogous to feathering the edge of the brush. At 100%, the brush is opaque from its center to its edges (though the edge is antialiased); at 0% the brush's edge has the maximum feather (though its center is opaque). Don't confuse hardness with the brush's overall Opacity, which you can set in the Paint palette (**Figure 13.46**).

Spacing indicates the distance between brush marks within a stroke, expressed as a percentage of the brush's diameter. Setting the spacing to a relatively low value allows the brush to create continuous stroke marks; setting spacing to a higher value makes the brush tip "make contact" with the layer intermittently, creating a stroke with gaps between brush marks. The speed with which you paint the stroke also affects the spacing. Moving the brush more quickly as you paint results in greater spacing between marks (**Figure 13.47**). You can set the Spacing to values over 100%.

Using Brush Dynamics

You don't have to be a traditionalist to know that painting with a computer program isn't quite as tactile as using actual brushes and canvas. But swapping your mouse for a tablet and stylus (such as those available from the computer peripheral manufacturer, Wacom) makes you feel a lot more like a painter. Just as important, using a stylus makes your strokes actually look more "painterly." That's because you can set the attributes of each stroke—its size, angle, roundness, opacity, and flow—to vary with the pressure you apply to the tablet or the tilt of the pen. If your *stylus* (sometimes referred to simply as a pen) has a little wheel control, you can use it to vary the brush also.

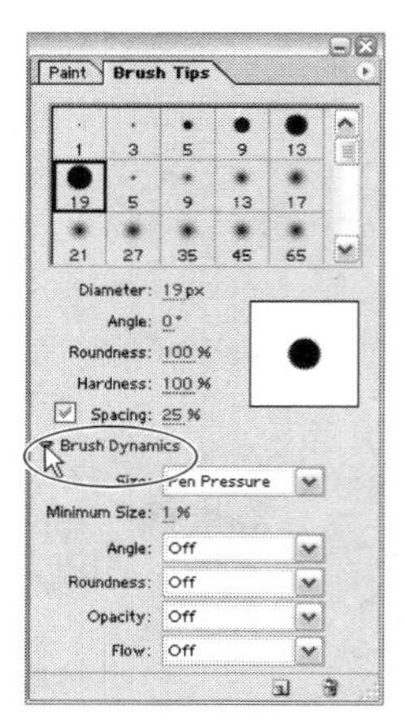

Figure 13.48 In the Brush Tips palette, expand the Brush Dynamics heading.

To set brush dynamics options:

1. In the Brush Tips palette, expand the Brush Dynamics heading (**Figure 13.48**).

   A number of options appear.

2. For each of the attributes listed in the Brush Dynamics area, choose an option from the pull-down menu (**Figure 13.49**).

   Off disables the dynamic option, and uses the static setting you specified elsewhere in the Brush Tips or Paint palettes.

   Pen Pressure varies the attribute according to the pressure of the pen on the tablet; pressing harder increases the value.

   Pen Tilt varies the attribute according to the angle of the pen in relation to the tablet. For example, tilting the pen away from the angle perpendicular to the tablet can decrease the brush's Roundness.

   Stylus Wheel varies the attribute when you scroll the pen's wheel control (a small roller on the side of the pen).

3. If you enabled Size, specify a Minimum Size (**Figure 13.50**).

   The brush's smallest possible diameter is limited by the value (1%-100%) you specify.

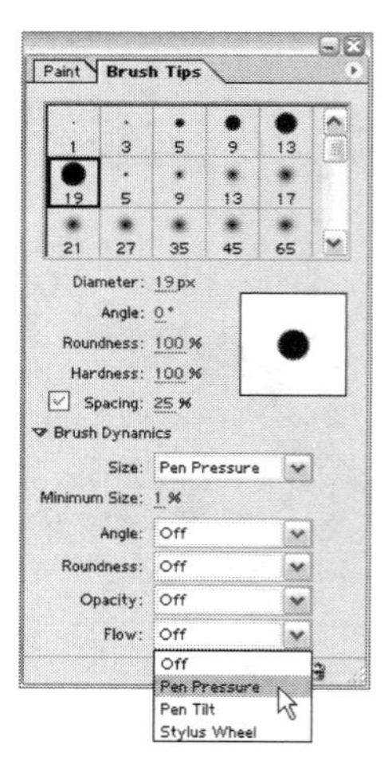

Figure 13.49 Specify which of the pen's characteristics affect each of the brush's attributes in the corresponding pull-down menu.

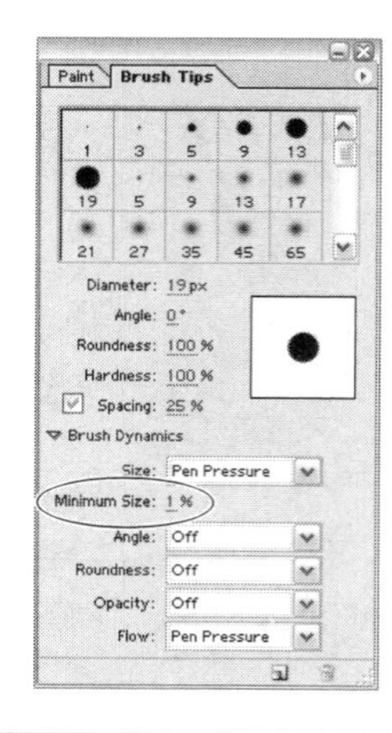

Figure 13.50 If you enabled Size, specify a Minimum Size.

Adjusting Strokes

As you learned in the chapter's introduction, paint is an effect. This means it appears in the layer's property outline under its Effects category. But in contrast to other effects, the Effect Controls window provides almost no controls for Paint. And whereas most effects include a single set of properties (however extensive they may be), the paint effect lists each stroke individually, and each stroke contains its own set of properties.

So the strokes are really layers within the layer containing the effect. Each stroke has its own duration bar, it's own video switch, and its own set of properties that can be keyframed (**Figure 13.51**). This way, you can precisely control when each stroke appears and for how long. And in the case of animated strokes, this paradigm lets you specify how quickly a stroke draws onto the screen.

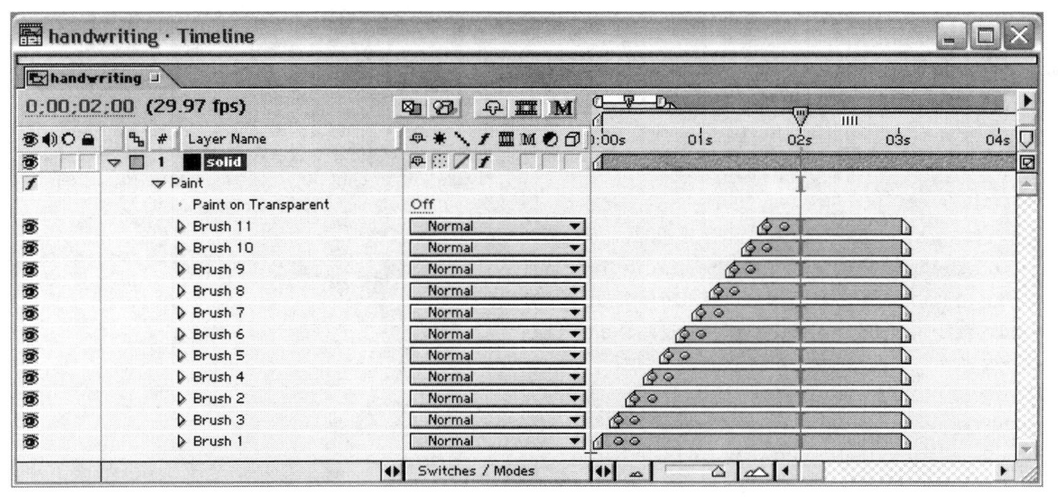

Figure 13.51 Each stroke has its own duration bar, it's own video switch, and its own set of properties that you can animate with keyframes.

Strokes in the Timeline

Setting the current frame determines a stroke's initial In point. Its duration depends on the Duration option you specified in the Paint palette: Constant, Write On, Single Frame, or Custom (see the section "Specifying Paint Stroke Options" earlier in this chapter). As with layers, the strokes' stacking order in the property outline determines the order in which strokes are applied, and their blending mode determines how they interact with strokes lower in the stack.

In general, you can manipulate strokes just as you would adjust layers: switch them on and off; change their stacking order; set their In and Out points and duration; and view, adjust, and keyframe their properties. However, the keyboard shortcuts you use with layers (cuing to or setting In and Out points, for example) don't work with strokes' duration bars.

In addition to all the properties that are unique to strokes, each stroke also includes its own set of Transform properties. You can use these to set each stroke's Anchor Point, Position, Scale, and Rotation. Remember, for strokes, Opacity is listed in the other Stroke Options property category (**Figure 13.52**).

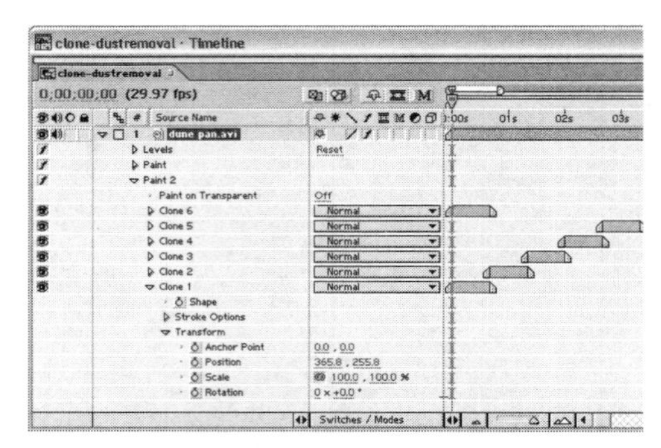

Figure 13.52 Each stroke includes Stroke Options and Transform properties.

Selecting strokes

Selecting a stroke in the layer's property outline makes it visible in its Layer window. A stroke appears as a thin line running though the center of the painted line, much like a selected mask path is visible in the center of a stroked path. An anchor point icon appears at the beginning of the stroke (**Figure 13.53**). When a stroke is selected, you can use the Selection tool [icon] to drag it to a new position within the layer. (You can always move the layer within the comp, but that moves the entire layer—its image, its paint and any other effects it contains.)

Figure 13.53 When a stroke is selected, it appears with a line through its center (assuming the paint is visible). An anchor point icon also appears at the beginning of each selected stroke.

Figure 13.54 To see and manipulate strokes in the Layer window, choose the Paint effect in the Layer window's View pull-down menu.

Figure 13.55 When the Layer contains more than one Paint effect, choose the one you want. Strokes of paint effects higher in the stacking order are visible, but you can only manipulate strokes in the selected effect.

However, strokes only appear in a Layer window when the Paint effect is selected in the Layer window's View pull-down menu. This occurs automatically when you apply paint, but can get confusing if you work on other tasks and return to the Layer window to find the paint effect is no longer selected—and no longer visible. The same holds true if the layer contains more than one paint effect; make sure the Layer window's View pull-down menu is set to the Paint effect you want.

Multiple Paint effects

Painting multiple strokes adds to the current Paint effect and a single layer can contain more than one Paint effect. This can be useful when you want to treat sets of strokes as separate groups. For example, you can disable all of one Paint effect's strokes by clicking its effect icon. However, the Layer window can only show the Paint effect you specify in the View pull-down menu. The strokes of any Paint effects higher in the stacking order are *visible*, but you can't tell whether they're selected; paint effects lower in the stacking order than the selected effect aren't even visible in the Layer window (**Figures 13.54** and **13.55**). You must choose a Paint effect in the View pull-down menu in order to view and drag its selected strokes in the Layer window.

You can duplicate or add a Paint effect as you would any other effect. When you add strokes to a Paint effect, make sure to select the effect you want to modify in the layer's View pull-down menu.

✔ Tip

- It can be useful to view the layer you're painting in a Layer window, and the composition that contains the layer in a separate Comp window.

Animating Strokes

The following tasks apply what you learned in this chapter to achieve a few common paint effects. The first employs the Duration option, Write On, to simulate natural writing. The next task explains how to adjust the timing of the strokes in the Timeline window. The last task shows how to animate a stroke by keyframing its Shape property, making it appear as though one stroke is transforming into another.

These tasks focus on employing different animation techniques, and don't cover other options (such as brush tips, channels, and modes) in any detail. To find out about those options, refer back to the appropriate sections earlier in the chapter.

To animate strokes using the Write-On option:

1. In the Tools palette, select a paint tool (**Figure 13.56**).
2. In the Paint palette, specify paint options, including Opacity, Flow, Color, Mode, and Channels.

   For a detailed explanation, see "Specifying Paint Stroke Options" earlier in this chapter.
3. In the Paint palette's Duration pull-down menu, choose Write On (**Figure 13.57**).
4. Set the current time to the frame where you want the first stroke to begin (**Figure 13.58**).

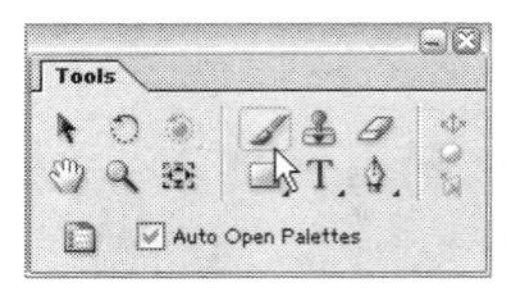

Figure 13.56 Paint tools include the Brush, Clone, or Eraser. In this example, the Brush tool is selected.

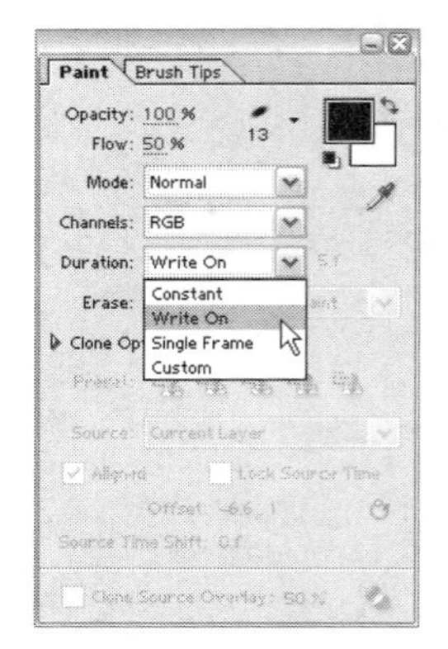

Figure 13.57 Choose Write On from the Paint palette's Duration pull-down menu.

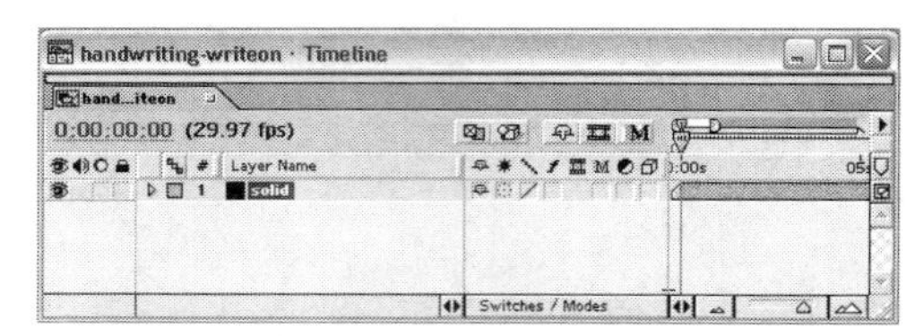

Figure 13.58 Set the current time to the frame where you want the first stroke to begin.

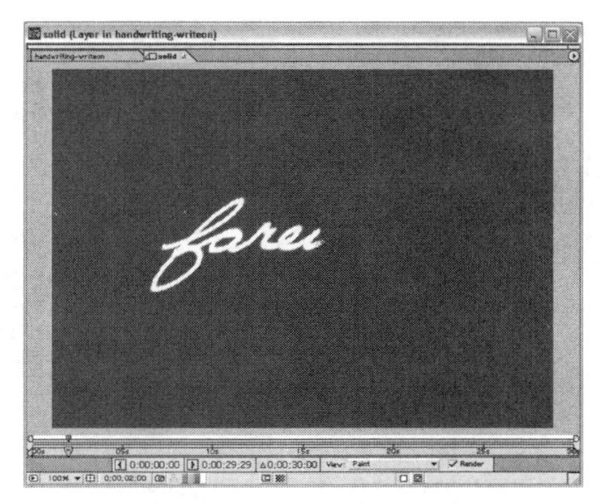

Figure 13.59 Drag in the layer's Layer window to draw or write in the layer. Lifting the mouse or pen ends the stroke, and because Write On is selected, the stroke disappears.

5. Using the Brush tool, drag in the Layer window to paint strokes on the layer (**Figure 13.59**).

   The speed at which you paint determines the duration and speed of the stroke animation. Lifting the mouse or pen to start a new stroke creates a separate brush layer in the Paint effect's property outline (**Figure 13.60**).

6. Preview the stroke animation in the Layer or Comp window.

   Strokes appear gradually, as you painted them (**Figure 13.61**).

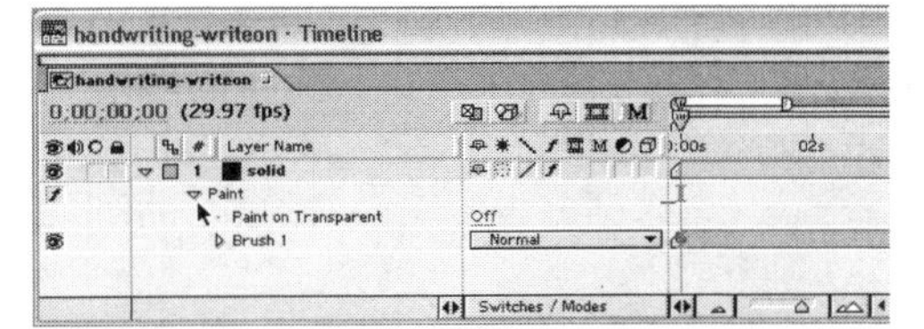

Figure 13.60 Each stroke appears in the layer's property outline, under its Paint effect. The Write On option animates the stroke's End property automatically.

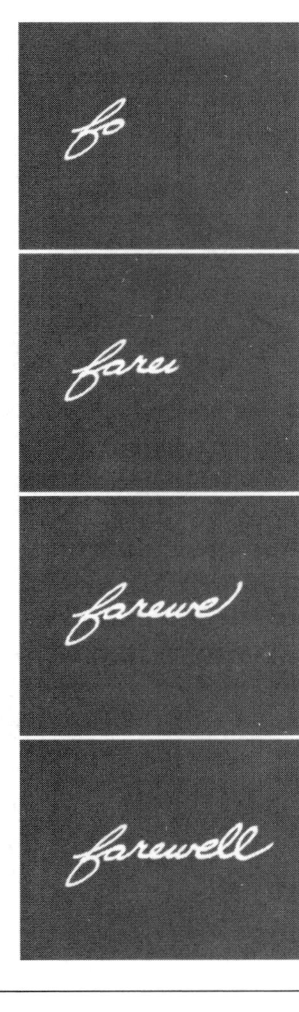

Figure 13.61 When you preview the animation, strokes appear in the same manner in which they were painted.

To adjust the speed of an animated stroke:

1. Animate a stroke using the Write On option, as described in the previous task.
2. Expand the property outline for the layer containing the stroke animation.
3. Expand the Stroke Option's property heading to reveal the End property (**Figure 13.62**).
4. In the time ruler, move the End property's keyframes to adjust the speed of the Write On effect (**Figure 13.63**).
5. Change the keyframe's interpolation option to adjust the rate of change between keyframes.

   See Chapter 7, "Properties and Keyframes," and Chapter 15, "Keyframe Interpolation," for more information.

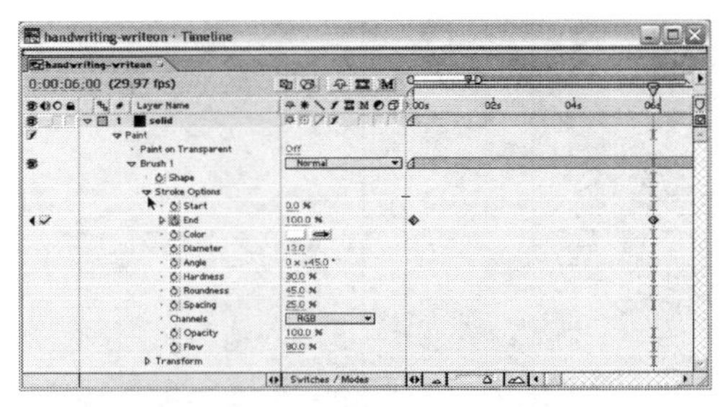

Figure 13.62 Expand a layer's property outline to reveal its Paint effect's End property.

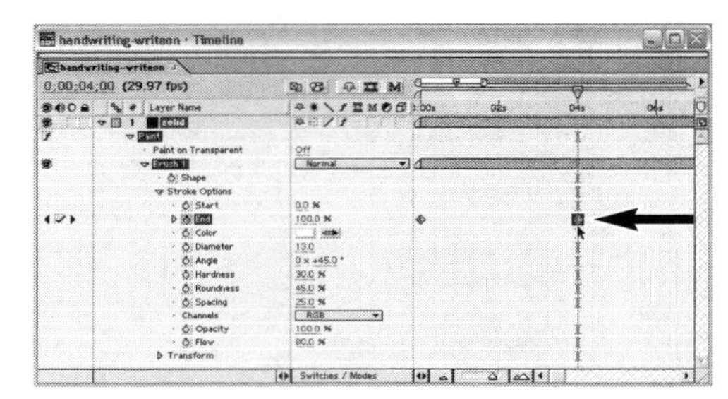

Figure 13.63 Move the End property's keyframes to change the speed of the Write On effect. Here, the last keyframe is moved closer to the first keyframe to make the writing appear more quickly.

✔ Tips

- Essentially, the Write On option animates the End property automatically. You can animate any stroke to create the same effect manually by animating the End property and duration of any stroke.
- The Write On option works effortlessly when animating a single stroke. However, lifting the mouse or pen creates multiple strokes that all begin at the current time. Therefore, multiple strokes will animate simultaneously, which doesn't simulate natural handwriting. To make each stroke animate sequentially, you'll have to change the in points (and possibly, the durations, too).

Figure 13.64 Set the current time and paint the stroke's initial shape.

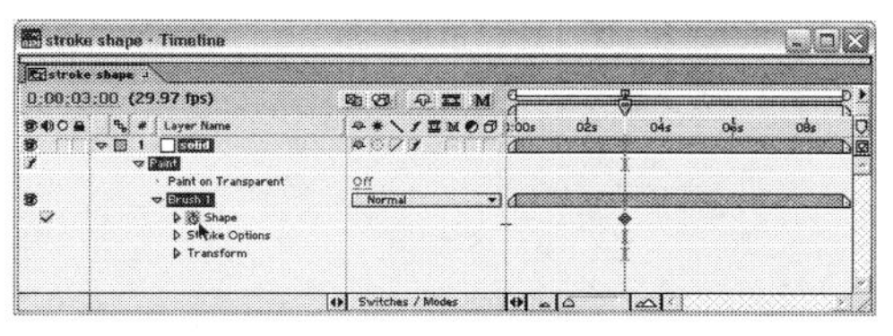

Figure 13.65 In the layer's property outline, expand the Paint effect and click the Shape property's Stopwatch icon to set the intial keyframe.

Figure 13.66 With the previous stroke selected, set the current time to the frame where you want the stroke to assume a new shape and paint that shape.

To animate a stroke by keyframing its Shape:

1. Set the time you want the stroke to begin, and using a paint tool and the techniques described earlier in this chapter, create a stroke in a layer (**Figure 13.64**).
2. In the Timeline window, expand the Layer's property outline to reveal the stroke you want to animate.
3. Set the current time to the frame where you want the stroke's shape to begin changing, and select the Shape property's Stopwatch icon.
   A Shape keyframe appears at the current time for the stroke (**Figure 13.65**).
4. Set the current time to the frame where you want to paint a new stroke.
5. With the first stroke selected, paint a new stroke (**Figure 13.66**).
   Instead of creating a new stroke layer, a new Shape keyframe appears in the selected stroke's property outline (**Figure 13.67**).

continues on next page

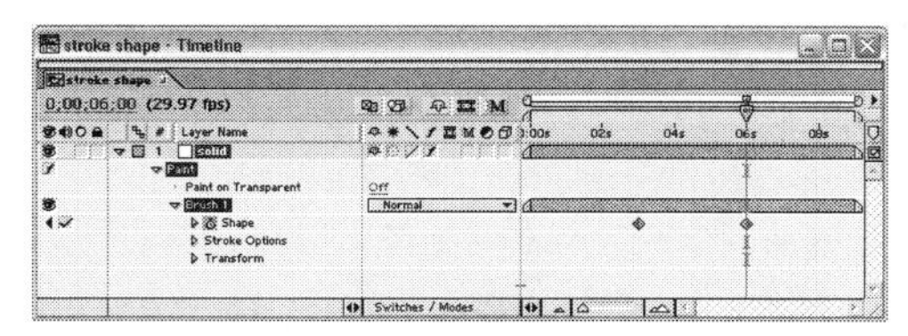

Figure 13.67 Instead of creating a new stroke, the same stroke gets a new Shape keyframe at the current time.

6. Repeat Step 5, as needed.
7. Preview the stroke animation.

   The stroke transforms from the shape defined by one keyframe to the shape defined by the next keyframe (**Figure 13.68**).

✔ Tip

- You can keyframe any stroke or paint option that includes a Stopwatch icon in the Paint effect's property outline or Effect Controls Window.

Figure 13.68 When you preview the animation, the stroke transforms from one shape into another. In this example, the line that crosses the "t" was created as a separate stroke using the Write On option.

Cloning

Like the Brush tool, the Clone Stamp tool adds pixels to a layer, using the paint brush options you specify (Duration, Brush Tip, and the like). But as the name implies, the Clone Stamp doesn't add pixels according to a specified color; instead, it copies, or *clones*, pixels from a layer's image. Photoshop veterans will instantly recognize the Clone Stamp tool, and appreciate its value in retouching an image. They'll also have a big head start on using the tool; it works nearly the same in After Effects—except non-destructively, and over time.

As when you use the other paint tools, you must first specify brush options for the Clone Stamp tool. But instead of specifying a color, you specify the layer, frame, and location of the pixels you want to copy to the target layer. Once you've set these options, you simply paint pixels from the source to the target.

For the sake of clarity, the following sections break down the cloning process into smaller tasks: setting the sample point, and then cloning. After that, you'll learn how to make cloning easier by superimposing the source image over the target image and saving clone options as convenient presets.

Setting the sample point for cloning

When cloning, pixels are copied, or *sampled*, from a particular layer, frame, and physical location in a source image. You can specify these three aspects of the clone source by using the Paint palette or by sampling manually. You can change the sample point at any time using either method, as needed.

You'll also need to understand the difference between setting a fixed sample point and one that maintains a consistent relationship with strokes in the target layer. In terms of space, you specify your choice with the Paint palette's Aligned option; in terms of time, you specify your choice with the Lock Source Time option.

The Aligned option

The starting point for a clone stroke in the target layer always corresponds to the sample point you set in the source image. The Paint palette displays the distance between the stroke's starting point in the target and the sample point in the source as the Offset value. (Naturally, when the target and source are different images, the distance is the difference in the corresponding points in each image's own coordinate system.)

continues on next page

However, the Aligned option determines which pixels are copied in subsequent strokes (**Figure 13.69**). By default, the Aligned option is selected and pixels are always copied from a point in the source that is a consistent distance (the Offset value) from the corresponding location of the Clone Stamp in the target image (**Figure 13.70**). In contrast, unchecking Aligned copies pixels using the initial sample as a fixed starting point (**Figure 13.71**).

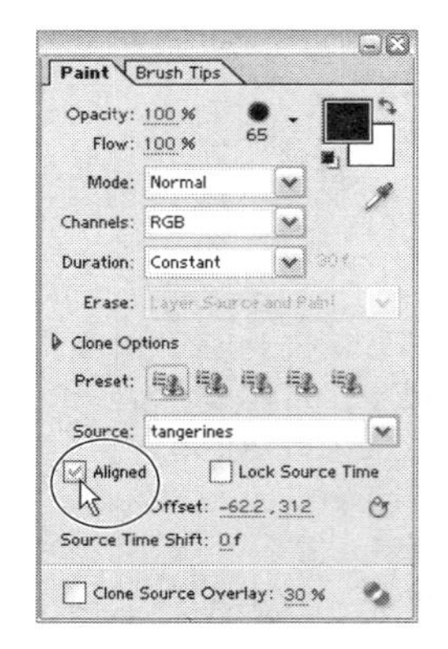

Figure 13.69 The Aligned option determines whether pixels are copied from a fixed point or offset from a corresponding location of the Clone Stamp.

The Lock Source Time option

The Lock Source Time option sets whether the Clone Stamp tool copies pixels from a fixed frame or maintains a time difference between the target frame and source frame (**Figure 13.72**). When Lock Source Time is selected, pixels are copied from a fixed frame which the Paint palette displays as the Source Time. If you change the target frame, the Source Time remains the same (unless you change it manually or sample from a different source frame). When Lock Source Time is unchecked, the Paint palette displays a Source Time Shift value. This way, After Effects maintains a time difference between the target frame and source frame (**Figure 13.73**).

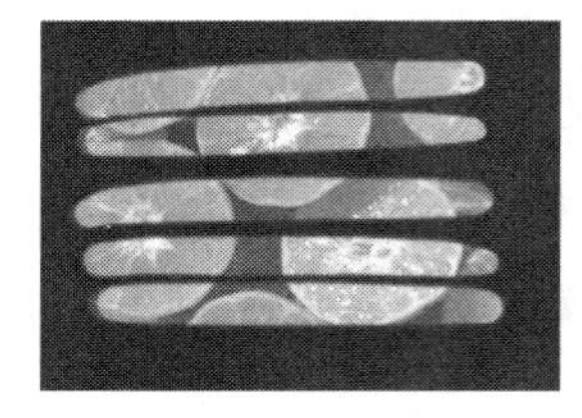

Figure 13.70 With Aligned checked, pixels are copied from a consistent distance from the corresponding location of the Clone Stamp.

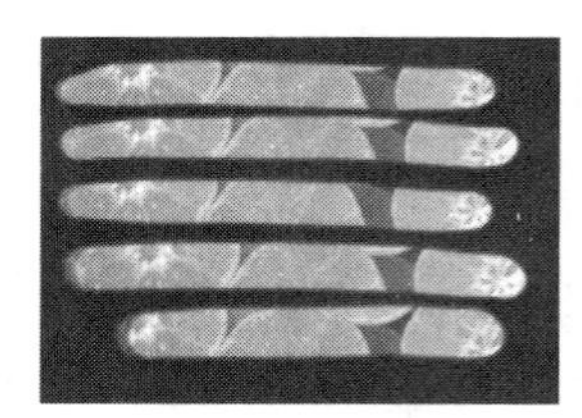

Figure 13.71 With Aligned unchecked, all strokes copy pixels from a fixed sample point in the source.

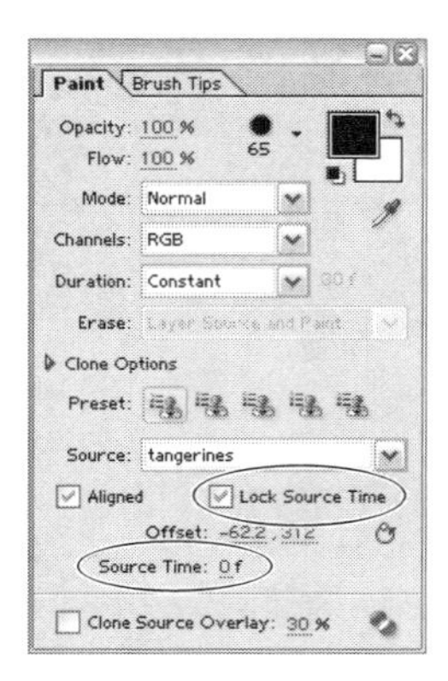

Figure 13.72 Checking Lock Source Time lets you specify a Source Time—a fixed frame from which to copy pixels.

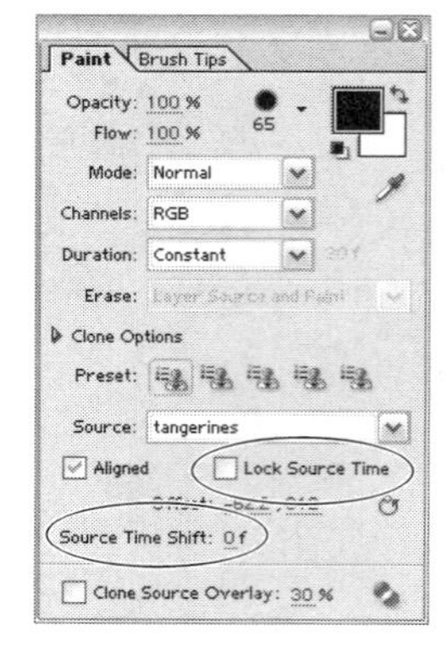

Figure 13.73 Unchecking Lock Source Time lets you specify a Source Time Shift—a consistent time difference between the target layer frame and source layer frame.

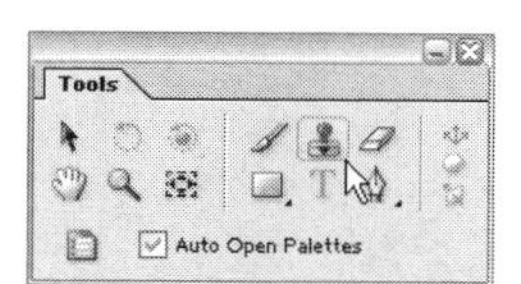

Figure 13.74 Select the Clone Stamp tool.

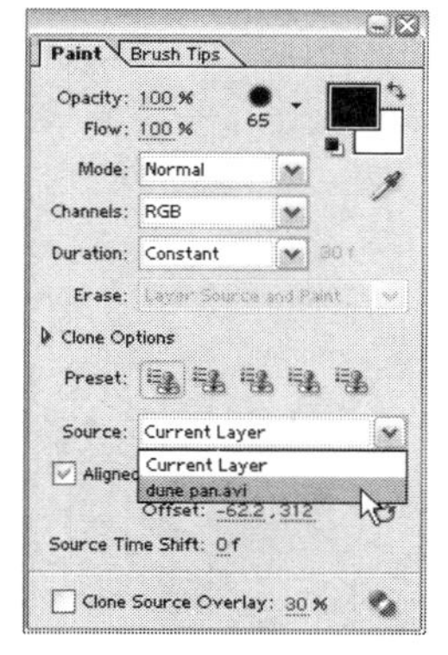

Figure 13.75 From the Paint palette's Source pull-down menu, specify the layer from which you want to clone.

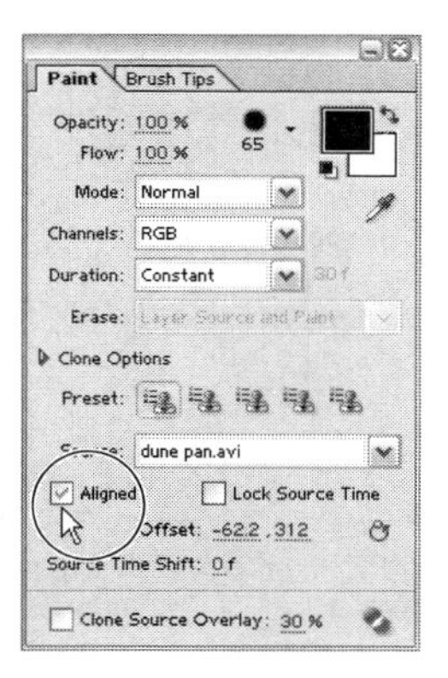

Figure 13.76 In the Paint palette, check Aligned if you want the sample point in the source to maintain a consistent relationship with each stroke in the target; uncheck Aligned to sample from the same point in the source layer with each stroke.

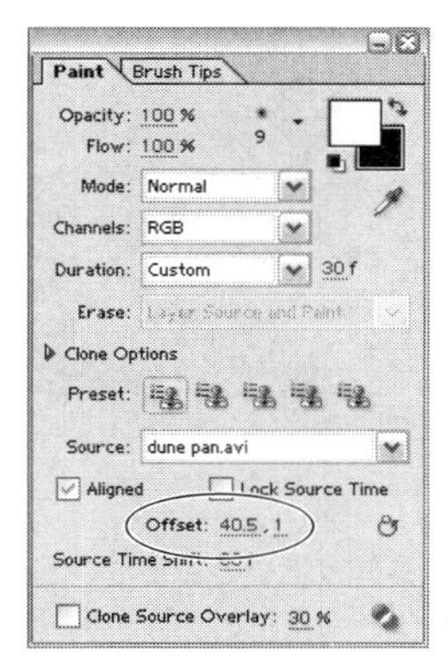

Figure 13.77 To specify an offset between the sample point in the source layer and the beginning of the stroke in the target layer, set X and Y values for Offset.

To set a clone source in the Paint palette:

1. If necessary, arrange the source and target layers in a composition.
2. Select the Clone Stamp tool (**Figure 13.74**).

   Clone Stamp options appear in the Paint palette.
3. In the Paint palette's Source pull-down menu, select the source layer from which the Clone Stamp tool will sample pixels (**Figure 13.75**).
4. *Do either of the following:*
   - ▲ To clone from a point offset from the corresponding point in the target layer, check Aligned (**Figure 13.76**):
   - ▲ To clone from the same starting point in the source layer with each new stroke, uncheck Aligned.
5. Specify the difference, or *offset*, between the starting point of the sample (in the source layer) and the stroke (in the target layer), by setting X and Y values for the Offset value.

   Offset values are expressed as the distance from the sample point to the stroke point in pixels, measured along the x and y axes (**Figure 13.77**).

continues on next page

6. *Do either of the following:*
   - ▲ To specify a specific source frame from which to sample, check Lock Source Time and specify a value for Source Time (**Figure 13.78**).
   - ▲ To specify a consistent time difference between the target frame and source frame, uncheck Lock Source Time and specify a value for Source Time Shift (**Figure 13.79**).

   Checking or unchecking Lock Source Time makes the corresponding time value appear in the Paint palette.

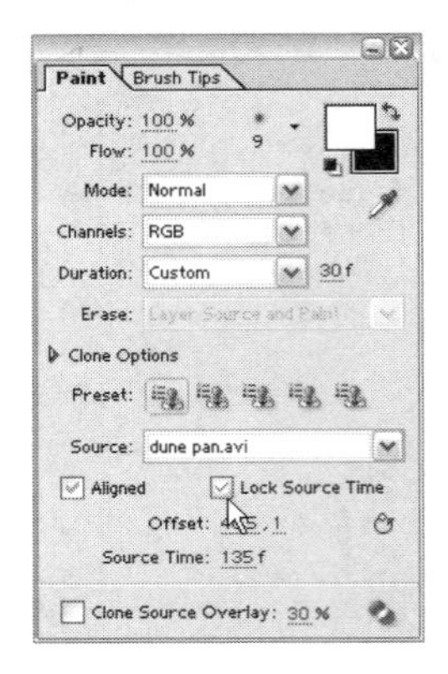

Figure 13.78 To sample from the same source frame regardless of the target frame, check Lock Source Time.

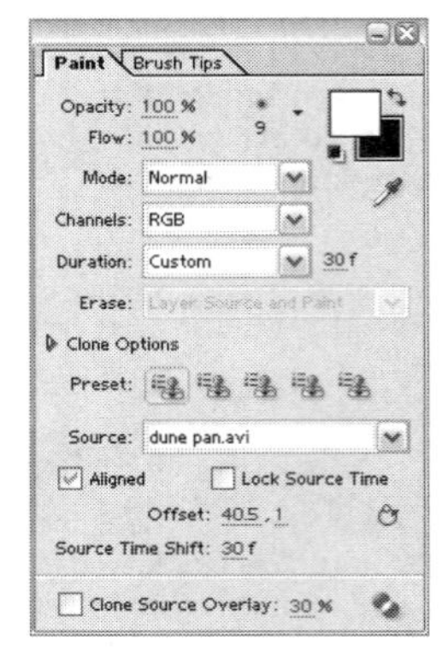

Figure 13.79 To maintain a consistent time difference between the source frame and the target frame, leave Lock Source Time unchecked and specify a value for Source Time Shift.

To set a clone source by clicking:

1. Follow steps 1-2 in the previous task, "To set a clone source in the Paint palette."
2. Specify options for the Aligned and Lock Source Time check boxes, as described in the previous task.
3. Set the current time to the frame from which you want to sample in the source layer, and Option-click (Mac) or Alt-click (Windows) the sample point in the source layer's Layer window (**Figure 13.80**).

   In the Paint palette, the source layer's name appears in the Source pull-down menu, and values appear for Offset. Values also appear for Source Time or Source Time Shift, depending on the options you chose above.

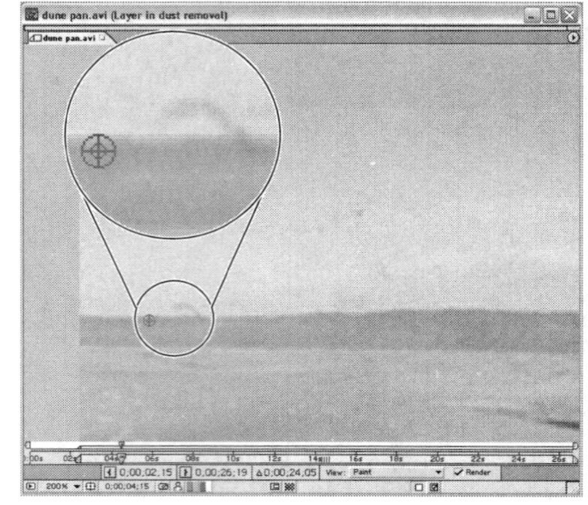

Figure 13.80 Option-click (Mac) or Alt-click (Windows) to set the sample point in the source image. Here, the sample is taken from a future frame in order to eliminate an obtrusive string of dust on the lens.

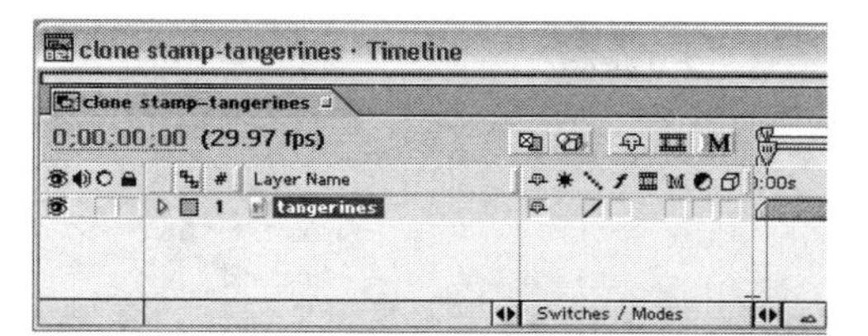

Figure 13.81 This example uses the same layer for the target and source.

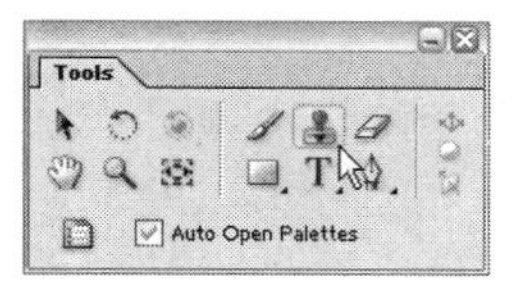

Figure 13.82 Choose the Clone Stamp tool.

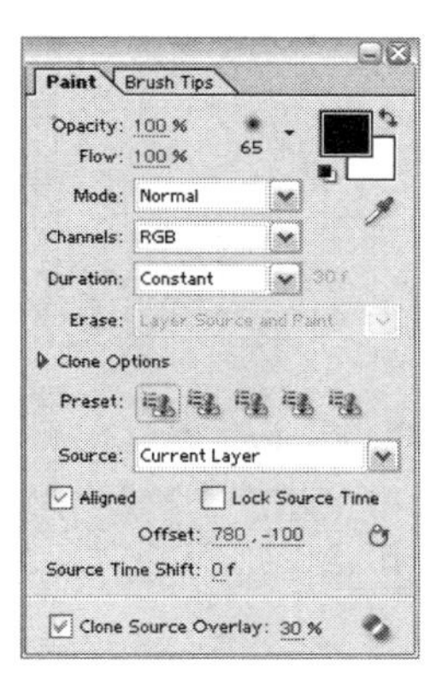

Figure 13.83 Specify paint options, such as Opacity, Flow, Mode and Duration.

Using the Clone Stamp Tool

Now that you understand how setting a sample point works, you can integrate that knowledge into the overall cloning process. Once you master this task, turn to later sections to learn about additional features, including overlaying the clone source's image over the target, and saving Clone Stamp settings.

To clone pixels:

1. Arrange the clone source and target layers in a Comp window and open the target layer in a separate Layer window (**Figure 13.81**).

   The Comp window must be selected for the source layer to appear in the pull-down menu in step 4.

2. In the Tools palette, choose the Clone Stamp tool (**Figure 13.82**).

3. In the Paint and Brush Tips palettes, specify a brush tip and paint options, such as Opacity, Flow, Mode, and Duration (**Figure 13.83**).

   See the "Specifying Paint Options" and "Using Brush Tips" sections earlier in this chapter.

continues on next page

4. Specify the sample source by *doing either of the following*:
   - ▲ Using the Clone Stamp tool, Option-click (Mac) or Alt-click (Windows) in the source Layer window at the frame and location you want to sample (**Figure 13.84**).
   - ▲ In the Paint palette, specify the settings you want for the Source, Aligned, Lock Source Time (including the Source Time or Source Time Shift), and Offset options. (See the section "Setting the sample point for cloning" earlier in this chapter.)
5. Set the current time to the frame from which you want to clone pixels onto the target layer.
6. Click or drag in the target layer's Layer window.

   Pixels from the source layer are painted onto the target layer, according to the options you specified (**Figure 13.85**). In the target layer's property outline, the Paint effect appears and includes each clone stroke you make (**Figure 13.86**).

✔ Tip

- ■ You can create a perfectly straight cloned stroke by clicking the stroke's starting point and Shift-clicking its ending point. This technique is great for cloning out linear elements such as wires or power lines.

Figure 13.84 Option-clicking (Mac) or Alt-clicking (Windows) changes the cursor into a crosshairs icon and sets the sample point (the layer, frame, and location of the source pixels).

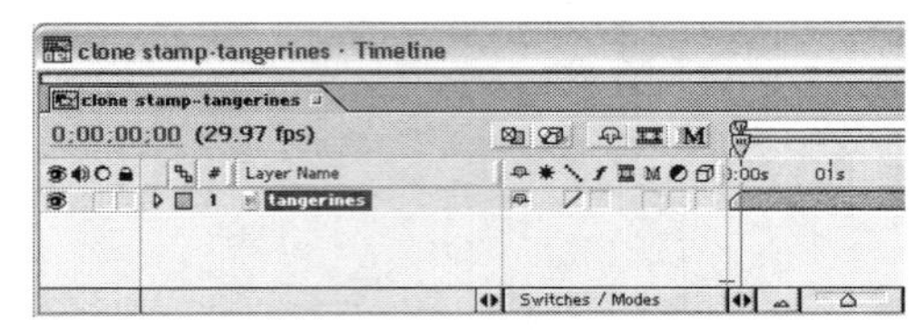

Figure 13.85 Click or drag in the target layer with the Clone Stamp tool to copy pixels from the source layer. Here, cloning eliminates a distracting seed from the tangerine image.

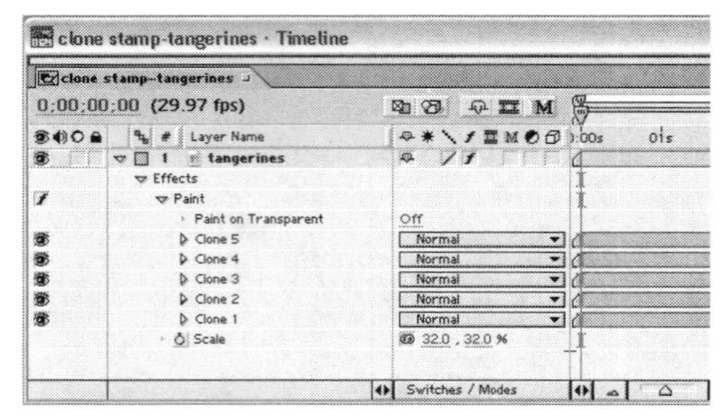

Figure 13.86 In the target layer's property outline, the Paint effect appears and includes each clone stroke you make.

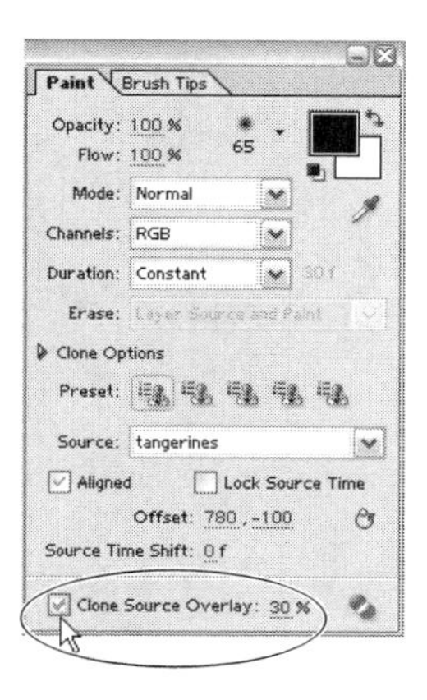

Figure 13.87 In the Paint palette, check Clone Source Overlay and specify the source layer's opacity.

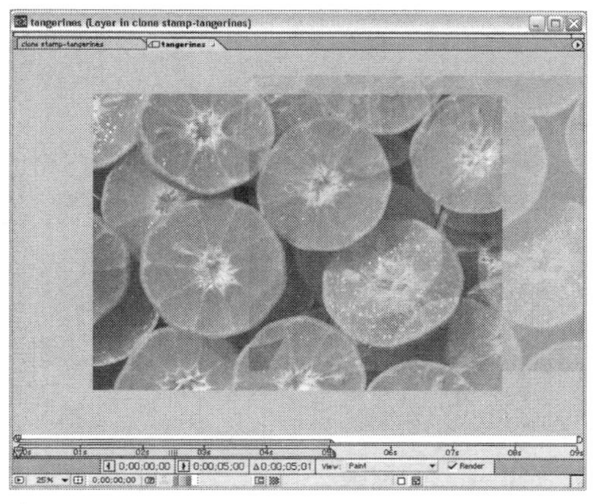

Figure 13.88 The overlay appears when the Clone Stamp tool is positioned over the target layer's image.

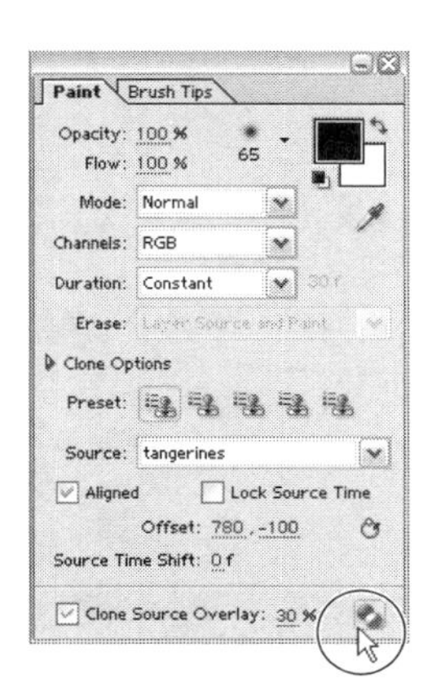

Figure 13.89 To see differences in the source and target layers more easily, click the Difference mode button in the Paint palette.

Overlaying the Clone Source

Although cloning can be painstaking, the most recent version of After Effects makes the process easier by letting you superimpose the source image over the target layer as you clone.

To superimpose the source over the target layer as you clone:

1. Prepare layers for cloning and set options for the Clone Stamp tool, as explained in the previous task, "To clone pixels."
2. In the Paint palette, check Clone Source Overlay and specify the source layer's opacity (**Figure 13.87**).

   The overlay appears when the Clone Stamp tool is positioned over the target layer's image (**Figure 13.88**).
3. To apply the Difference blending mode to the superimposed source layer image, click the Difference Mode button (**Figure 13.89**).

   The Difference blending mode can help you identify differences between similar source and target frames. See Chapter 14 for more about blending modes.

✔ Tip

- You can also toggle the overlay by pressing Option+Shift (Mac) or Alt+Shift (Windows) as you use the Clone Stamp tool.

Saving Clone Stamp Settings

Meticulous retouching can require that you switch Clone Stamp tool settings often. Luckily, the Paint Palette includes five Clone Stamp Preset buttons that you can use to store and quickly recall settings.

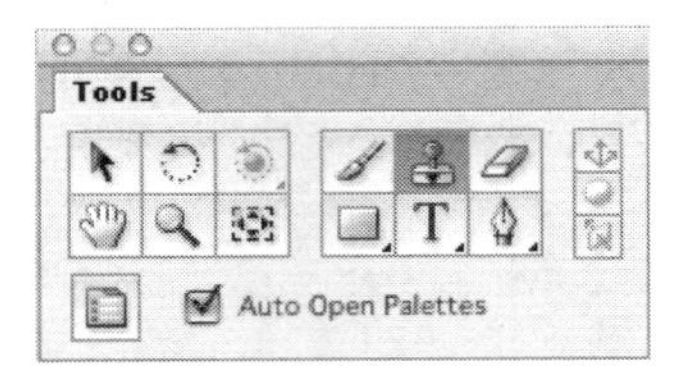

Figure 13.90 Select the Clone Stamp tool.

To save clone stamp settings:

1. In the Paint palette, select the Clone Stamp tool (**Figure 13.90**).
   The Clone Options become available.
2. In the Clone Options area of the Paint Palette, click a Clone Stamp Preset button.
3. Specify the options you want (as described in the previous sections) to associate with the selected preset button (**Figure 13.91**).
   The options you specify are associated with the selected preset button.

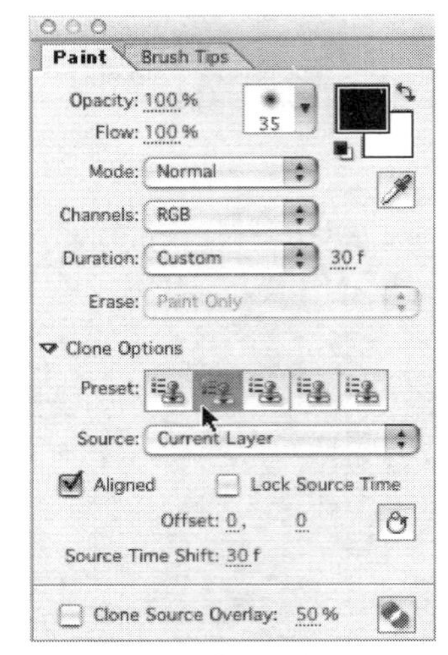

Figure 13.91 In the Paint palette, click a Clone Stamp Preset button and specify the settings you want associated with the button.

To use a clone stamp preset:

1. In the Paint palette, select the Clone Stamp tool.
2. *Do either of the following:*
   - ▲ Click the Clone Stamp button that corresponds to the preset you want to use.
   - ▲ Press the number keyboard shortcut that corresponds to the preset you want: 3=first preset; 4=second preset; 5=third preset; 6=fourth preset; 7=fifth preset.
3. Use the Clone Stamp tool, as explained in the previous tasks.

14 More Layer Techniques

This chapter tackles a handful of techniques. First, you'll learn about a pair of layer switches—Frame Blending and Motion Blur—that influence how After Effects deals with motion between frames. Then, you'll play with the comp's frame rate itself using Time Remapping. Armed with that knowledge, you'll be ready to take a closer look at the Switches panel's alter ego, the Modes panel. In the Modes panel, you'll discover a long list of ways to blend a layer with underlying layers, and you'll expand your repertoire of compositing tools. You'll also find out what the mysterious *T* option really stands for and, more importantly, how to use it. Finally, you'll complete your tour of the Modes panel by learning about yet another compositing option, Track Mattes.

Using Frame Blending

When the frame rate of motion footage is lower than that of the composition, movement within the frame can appear jerky—either because the footage's native frame rate is lower than that of the composition, or because you time-stretched the footage. Whatever the case, After Effects reconciles this difference by repeating frames of the source footage. For example, each frame of a 15-fps movie is displayed twice in a composition with a frame rate of 30 fps. However, because there aren't enough unique frames to represent full motion, the result can sometimes resemble a crude flip-book animation.

In these instances, you can smooth the motion by activating the Frame Blending switch. When frame blending is on, After Effects interpolates between original frames, blending them rather than simply repeating them (**Figures 14.1** and **14.2**).

Because frame blending can significantly slow previewing and rendering, you may want to apply it to layers but refrain from enabling it until you're ready to render the final animation.

Figure 14.1 Ordinarily, After Effects interpolates frames by repeating the original frames. Because this simple animation is interpreted as 15 frames per second, frames are repeated to compensate for a 30-fps composition.

Figure 14.2 When Frame Blending is applied and enabled, it blends the original frames to create interpolated frames.

To apply or remove frame blending in a layer:

1. If necessary, click the Switches/Modes button to make the layer switches appear.
2. Select the Frame Blending switch for a layer created from motion footage (**Figure 14.3**).

   As long as the layer's frame rate is lower than the composition's frame rate, interpolated frames are blended together.

To enable or disable frame blending for all layers in a composition:

Do either of the following:

- Click the Enable Frame Blending button at the top of the Timeline window (**Figure 14.4**).
- Select Enable Frame Blending in the Timeline pull-down menu.

  When the Frame Blending button is selected or the Enable Frame Blending item is checked, frame blending is enabled for all layers with frame blending applied.

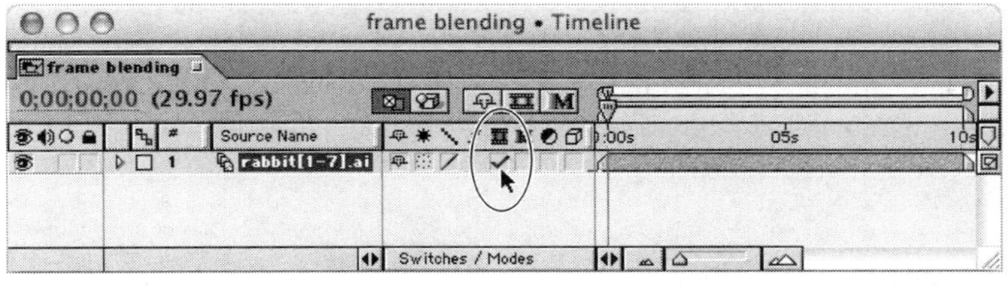

Figure 14.3 Select the Frame Blending switch for a layer created from motion footage.

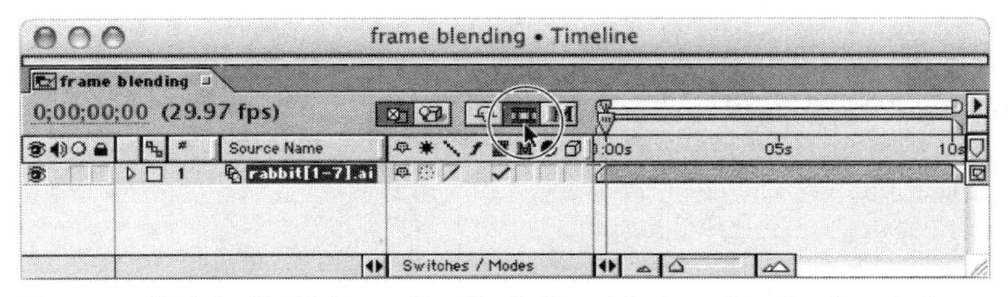

Figure 14.4 Click the Enable Frame Blending button at the top of the Timeline window.

Using Motion Blur

Ordinarily, an animated layer appears sharp and distinct as it moves through the frame of a composition (**Figure 14.5**). This can appear unnatural, however, because you're accustomed to seeing objects blur as they move. In the time it takes to perceive the object at a single position (or, in the case of a camera, to record it to a frame), that object has occupied a continuous range of positions, causing it to appear blurred.

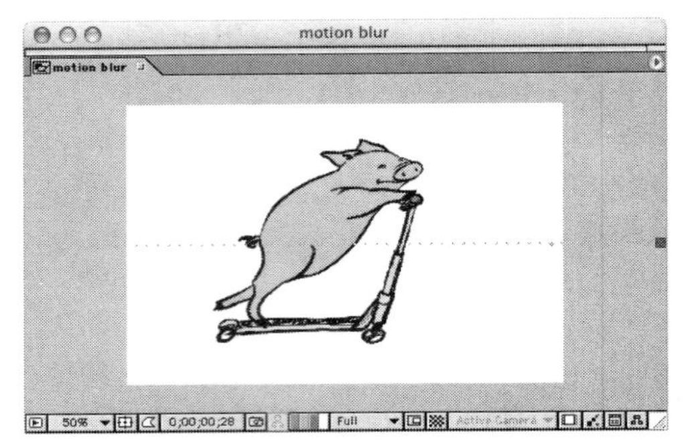

Figure 14.5 Ordinarily, an animated layer appears sharp and distinct as it moves through the frame of the composition.

To simulate this effect, you can activate the Motion Blur switch for an animated layer (**Figure 14.6**). To reduce the time it takes to preview your animation, you may want to apply motion blur to layers but wait to enable it until you're ready to render.

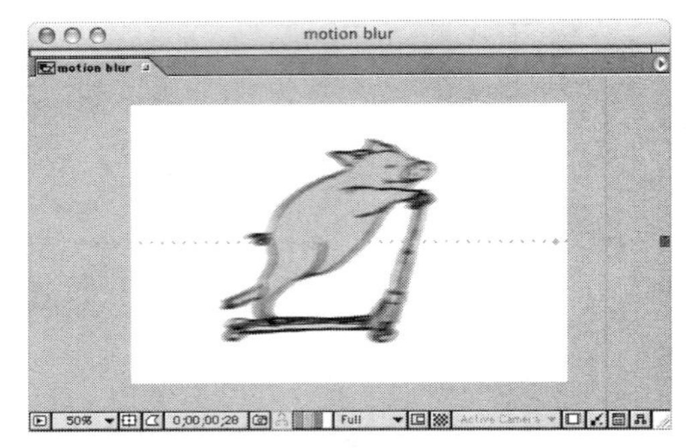

Figure 14.6 To simulate a more natural-looking, blurred motion, activate the Motion Blur switch for an animated layer.

Because motion blur simulates the blur captured by a camera, it uses similar controls. As with a film camera, a Shutter Angle control works with the frame rate to simulate exposure time and thus the amount of blur. For example, using a 180-degree shutter angle with a 30-fps composition simulates a one-fifteenth-second exposure (180 degrees = 50% × 360 degrees; 50% × 30 fps = 1/15 sec). Increasing the shutter angle increases the amount of blur.

To apply or remove motion blur:

1. If necessary, click the Switches/Modes button to make the layer switches appear.
2. Select the Motion Blur switch for a layer with animated motion (**Figure 14.7**).

   When the Motion Blur switch is checked, motion blur is applied to the layer. The Motion Blur button determines whether motion blur is enabled (see the next task for details).

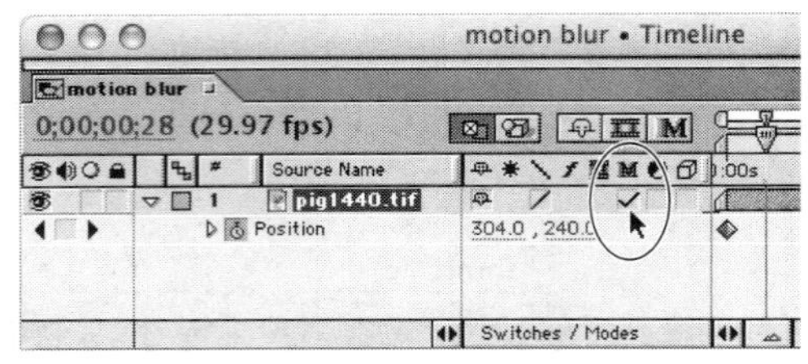

Figure 14.7 Select the Motion Blur switch for a layer with animated motion to apply motion blur.

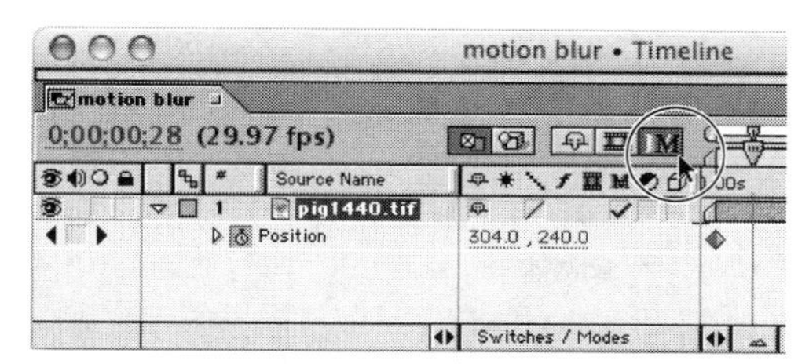

Figure 14.8 Click the Enable Motion Blur button at the top of the Timeline window to enable motion blur for the layers with motion blur applied to them.

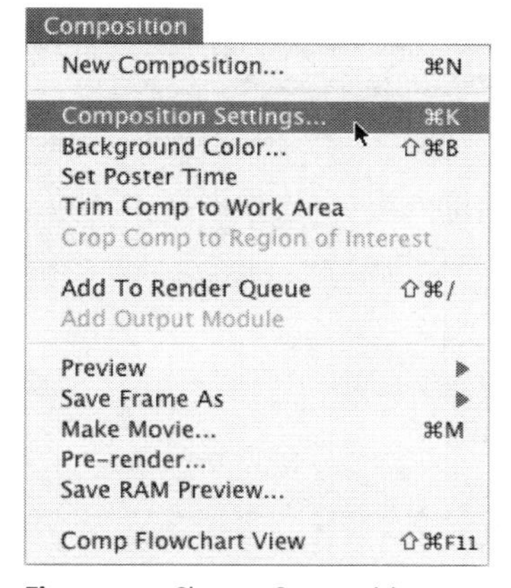

Figure 14.9 Choose Composition > Composition Settings.

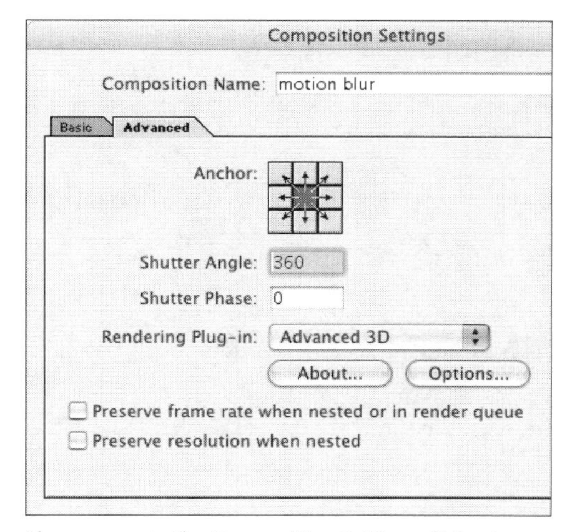

Figure 14.10 In the Composition Settings dialog box, enter a value for the shutter angle, in degrees.

To enable or disable motion blur for all layers in a composition:

Do either of the following:

- Click the Enable Motion Blur button at the top of the Timeline window (**Figure 14.8**).
- Select Enable Motion Blur in the Timeline pull-down menu.

  When the Motion Blur button is selected or the Enable Motion Blur item is checked, motion blur is enabled for all layers with motion blur applied.

To set the shutter angle for motion blur for previews:

1. Choose Composition > Composition Settings (**Figure 14.9**).

   The Composition Settings dialog box appears.

2. In the Advanced panel of the Composition dialog box, enter a value for the shutter angle, in degrees (**Figure 14.10**).

   You may enter a value between 0 and 360 degrees. The higher the value, the greater the amount of blur. The value you set is applied to playback and preview.

3. Click OK to close the Composition Settings dialog box.

✔ Tips

- When you render the final output, you can choose whether to enable motion blur and frame blending in the Render Queue window. This way, you don't have to return to your composition to check the setting. See Chapter 18, "Output."
- The Render Queue window also allows you to reset the shutter angle for motion blur before you render a movie.
- You can apply motion blur to a mask.

Understanding Time Remapping

Back in Chapter 6, "Layer Editing," you learned how to change the speed of a layer using the Time Stretch command (or by changing the layer's Stretch value in the In/Out panel in the Timeline window). Although it's useful, the Time Stretch command is limited to changing the layer's overall playback speed. To make the playback speed up, slow down, reverse, or come to a halt (or *freeze frame*), you need to use *time remapping*.

In a normal layer, there's a direct relationship between the layer's time and the frame you see and hear. In a time-remapped layer, the normal time controls show the layer's elapsed time but no longer dictate which frame is displayed (or heard) at that time. Instead, the Time Remap values determine the visible (or audible) frame at that time.

For example, when you first apply time remapping, keyframes appear at the layer's In and Out points, and the Time Remap values at those keyframes match the layer's original time values. Initially, there's no change in the layer's playback (**Figure 14.11**). However, changing the Time Remap value of the keyframe at the end of the clip (say, at 10 seconds) to a frame in the middle of the clip (5 seconds) redistributes, or *remaps*, the first 5 seconds of the layer over 10 seconds—slowing down the frame rate between keyframes (**Figure 14.12**).

Figure 14.11 Here, the Time Remap property values match the layer's original time values. The layer time is the top number; the remapped time is the lower number.

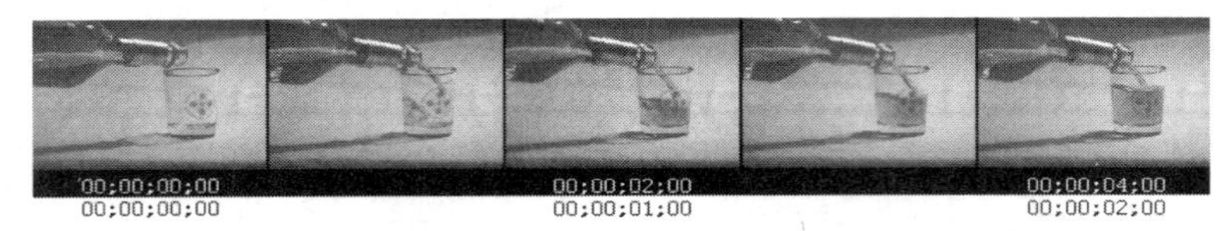

Figure 14.12 Here, the last Time Remap keyframe is still positioned at 04;00 into the clip, but its value has been changed to the frame at 02;00. The layer's frame rate slows between the keyframes.

This example achieves a result similar to that of the Time Stretch command. But consider that you can set additional time-remapped keyframes in the same layer and apply the temporal interpolation methods covered in Chapter 15, "Keyframe Interpolation."

Using the same layer as in the previous example, suppose you set a time-remap keyframe at 5 seconds into the clip and leave its value set to 5 seconds. The layer plays normally between the first and second keyframes (the first 5 seconds). But if you change the Time Remap value of the last keyframe—positioned 10 seconds into the clip—to 5 seconds (not the keyframe's position in time, just its value), then playback reverses between the second and third keyframes (**Figure 14.13**).

Time remapping can sound confusing, but it works just like keyframing other properties. But whereas most keyframes define a visible characteristic (like position) at a given frame, a time-remap keyframe specifies the *frame* you see (or hear) at a given point in the layer's time.

Figure 14.13 Here, the layer plays back normally between the first keyframe and a second keyframe, set halfway through the layer's duration. The Time Remap value of the last keyframe—positioned at 04;00—has been changed to 00;00, which reverses the playback.

Controlling Time Remap Values in the Layer Window

When you enable time remapping on a layer, the Layer window displays additional controls for changing the frame rate. In addition to the layer's ordinary time ruler, current time indicator (CTI), and current time display, a corresponding remap-time ruler, marker, and display also appear (**Figure 14.14**).

As is the case for any property value, you can set keyframes for the Time Remap property using controls in the Timeline window (**Figure 14.15**). As usual, use the check box in the property's keyframe navigator to set keyframes that use previously interpolated values. Expand the property to view a value graph; drag control points on the graph to change the value of the corresponding keyframe. This technique allows you to accelerate, decelerate, or reverse playback speed (see the task "To change playback speed over time," later in this chapter). For more about viewing and using a value graph and using interpolation methods (how After Effects calculates property values between keyframes), see Chapter 15.

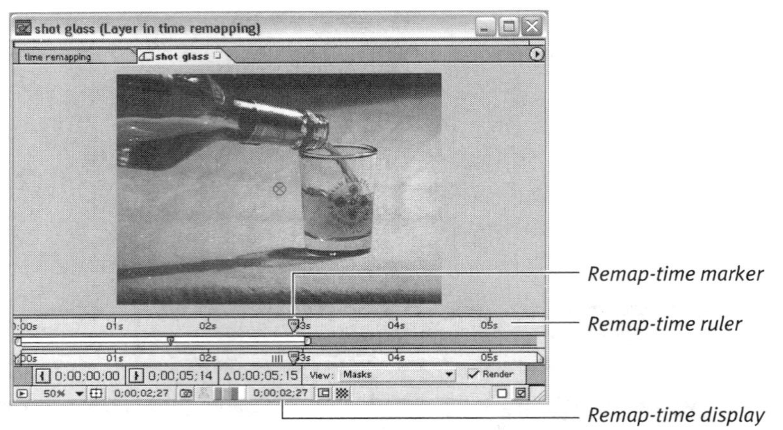

Figure 14.14 Enabling time remapping makes additional controls appear in the Layer window.

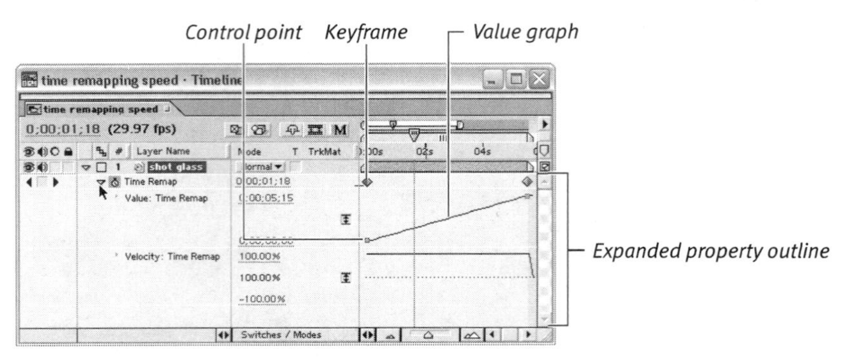

Figure 14.15 You also use controls in the Timeline window to control Time Remap values and set keyframes.

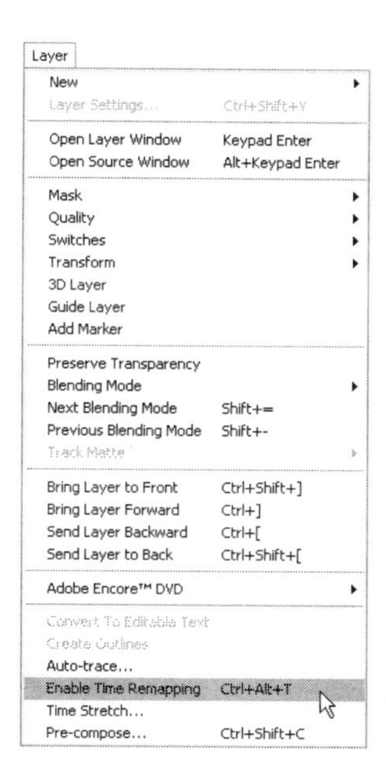

Figure 14.16 Select a layer and choose Layer > Enable Time Remapping.

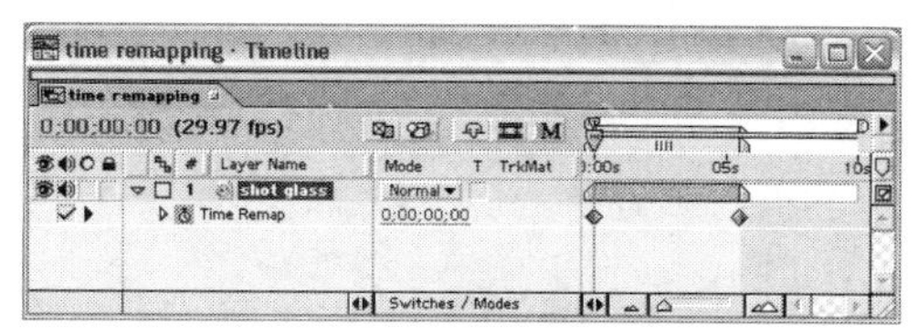

Figure 14.17 After Effects sets a time-remap keyframe at the layer's In and Out points automatically. However, the values match the layer's original values, and the layer's frame rate remains unchanged.

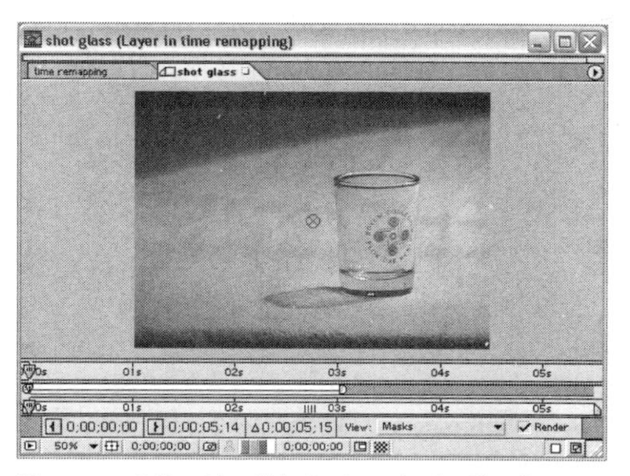

Figure 14.18 Double-click the layer in the Timeline window to view it in a Layer window and use the time-remapping controls.

Using Time Remapping

The tasks in this section explain how to enable time remapping for a layer and how to set keyframes to pause, reverse, or change the speed of playback. Turn to Chapter 15 for more about keyframe interpolation and how you can specify the way After Effects calculates property changes from one keyframe to the next.

To enable time remapping:

1. Select a layer, and choose Layer > Enable Time Remapping (**Figure 14.16**).

   In the Timeline window, the Time Remap property appears in the layer outline for the selected layer. After Effects creates keyframes at the beginning and ending of the layer automatically (**Figure 14.17**).

2. In the Timeline window, double-click the layer to view it in a Layer window.

   In addition to the standard controls, the Layer window includes time-remapping controls (**Figure 14.18**).

To create a freeze frame with time remapping:

1. Select a layer, and enable time remapping as explained in the previous task, "To enable time remapping."

   After Effects sets beginning and ending keyframes automatically.

2. Set the current time to the frame where you want the layer's playback to stop (**Figure 14.19**).

3. In the Timeline window, click the box in the keyframe navigator for the layer's Time Remap property.

   A keyframe appears at the current time, using the previously interpolated value. In this case, the Time Remap value matches the frame's original value (**Figure 14.20**).

4. With the new keyframe selected, choose Animation > Toggle Hold Keyframe (**Figure 14.21**).

   The new keyframe uses Hold interpolation, evidenced by its Hold keyframe icon (**Figure 14.22**). This holds the Time Remap value until the next keyframe is reached.

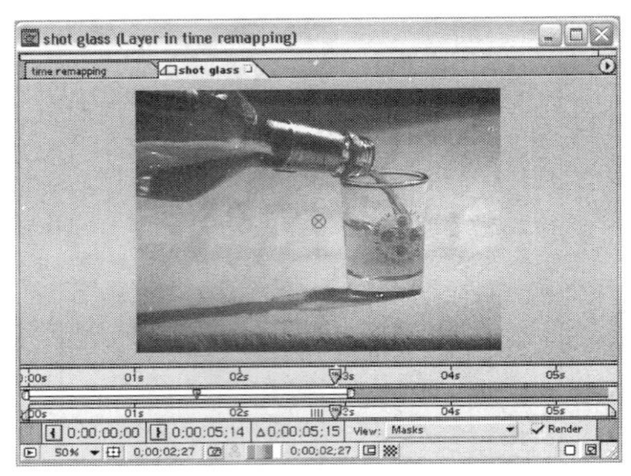

Figure 14.19 Set the current time to the frame where you want playback to stop. There's no need to change the remap time; it should match the current time.

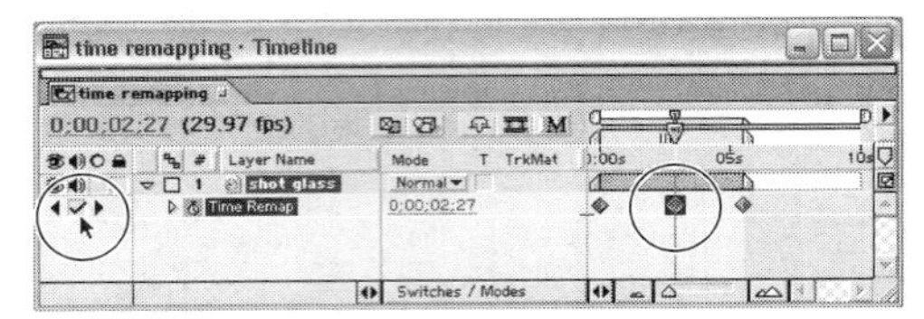

Figure 14.20 In the Timeline window, click the box in the Time Remap property's keyframe navigator to create a keyframe at the current frame.

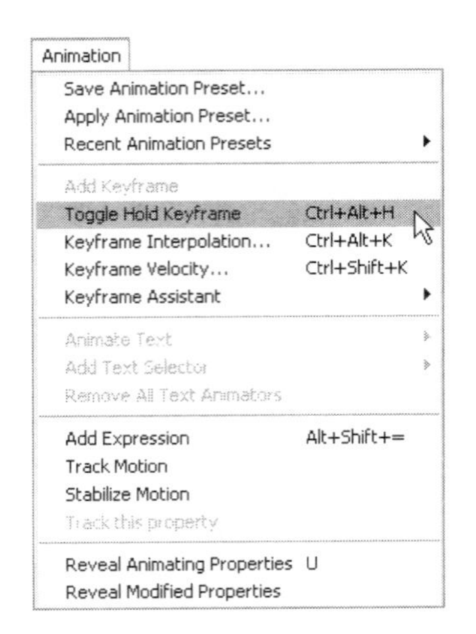

Figure 14.21 With the new keyframe selected, choose Animation > Toggle Hold Keyframe.

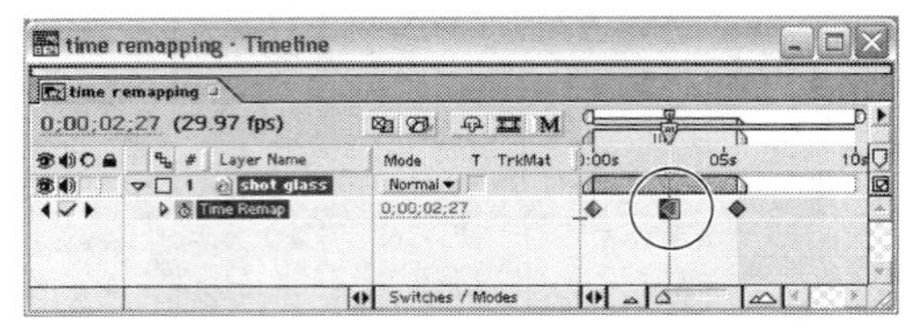

Figure 14.22 The keyframe icon changes to a Hold keyframe icon, indicating that the property value will remain at that value until the next keyframe is reached.

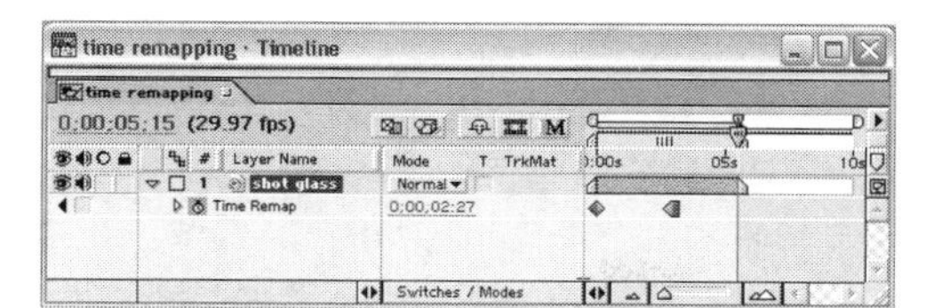

Figure 14.23 Select the last keyframe, and press Delete (Mac) or Backspace (Windows). The layer's playback now freezes at the Hold keyframe you created in steps 3 and 4.

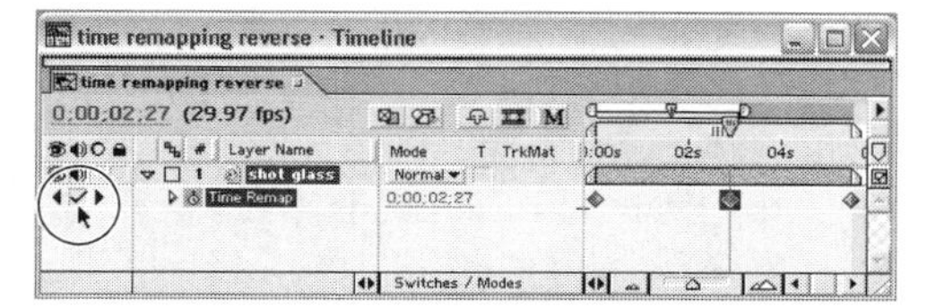

Figure 14.24 Set the current time to the point where you want the layer's playback to reverse, and click the box in the Time Remap property's keyframe navigator to set a keyframe.

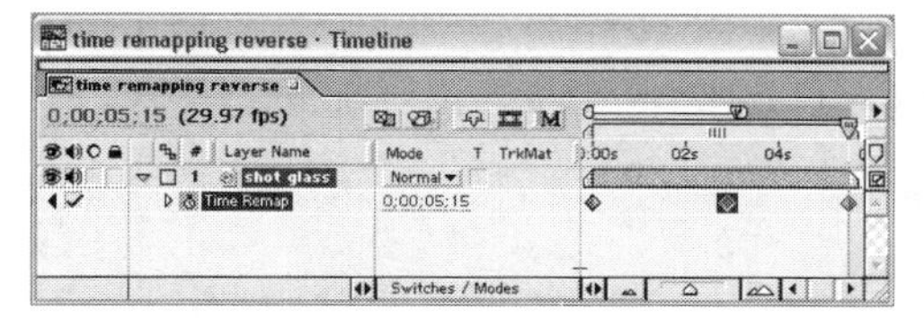

Figure 14.25 Set the current time to the point where you want the reversed playback to end. Here, the current time is set to the Out point (which changes the keyframe value that was set automatically when remapping was applied).

Figure 14.26 In the Layer window, drag the remap-time marker to a time earlier than the one you chose in step 3.

5. Select the last keyframe, and press Delete (Mac) or Backspace (Windows).

   The last keyframe is removed (**Figure 14.23**). The layer's frames play back at normal speed; then the layer freezes when it reaches the Hold keyframe.

6. View the remapped layer in the Layer or Comp window by dragging the CTI.

   You can't use RAM previews to see the layer play back using the remapped frame rate.

To reverse playback:

1. Select a layer and enable time remapping, as explained in the task "To enable time remapping" earlier in this section.

2. Set the current time to the frame where you want the layer's playback direction to reverse, and click the box in the Time Remap property's keyframe navigator.

   A keyframe appears at the current time, using the previously interpolated value. In this case, the keyframe's value matches the frame's original value (**Figure 14.24**).

3. Set the current frame later in time, to the point where you want the reversed playback to end (**Figure 14.25**).

4. In the Layer window, drag the remap-time indicator to an earlier frame (**Figure 14.26**).

   The layer's original frame value is mapped to the frame you specified with the remap-time indicator.

continues on next page

5. View the time-remapped layer in the Layer or Comp window by dragging the CTI.

   You can't use RAM previews to see the layer play back using the remapped frame rate. The layer's frames play back normally until the keyframe you set in step 2; the layer then plays in reverse until the keyframe you set in step 3. The remap frame you set in step 4 determines the actual frame played by the time the last keyframe is reached (**Figure 14.27**).

To change playback speed over time:

1. Select a layer, and enable time remapping as explained in the task "To enable time remapping" earlier in this section.
2. In the Timeline window, expand the selected layer's Time Remap property to reveal its property graph (**Figure 14.28**).
3. Set the current time to the frame where you want the speed change to begin, and click the box in the Time Remap property's keyframe navigator (**Figure 14.29**).

   A keyframe appears at the current time; its value matches the frame's original time value.
4. In the Time Remap property's value graph, drag the control point that corresponds to the keyframe you set in step 3 *in either of the following ways:*

Figure 14.27 The layer plays forward between the first and second keyframes and then plays in reverse between the second and last keyframes.

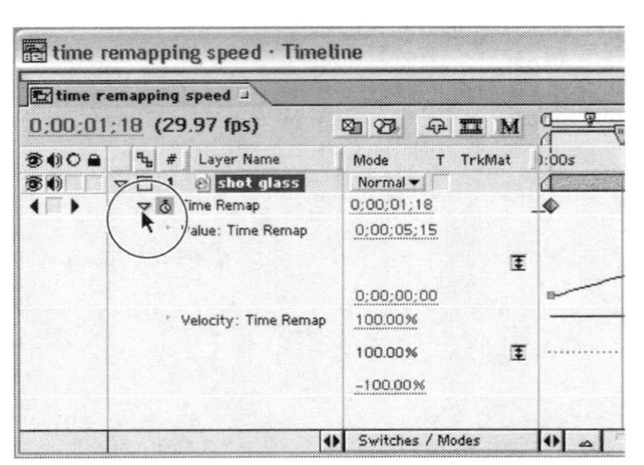

Figure 14.28 In the Timeline window, expand the layer's Time Remap property to reveal its value graph.

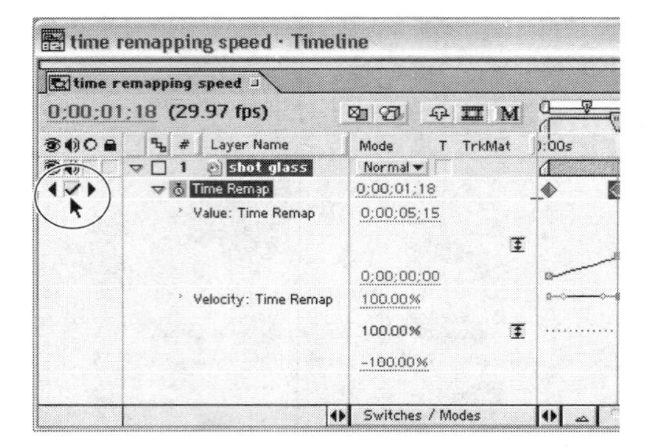

Figure 14.29 Set the current time when you want the speed to change to begin, and click the box in the keyframe navigator.

▲ To slow playback speed, drag the control point down (**Figure 14.30**).

▲ To increase playback speed, drag the control point up (**Figure 14.31**).

When the value is higher than the previous keyframe's value, the layer plays forward; when the value is lower, the layer plays in reverse. If the layer is already playing in reverse, drag the value graph's control point in the opposite direction.

5. Repeat steps 3 and 4 as needed.

   The layer's playback speed and direction change according to your choices.

6. View the remapped layer in the Layer or Comp window by dragging the CTI.

   You can't use RAM previews to see the layer play back using the remapped frame rate.

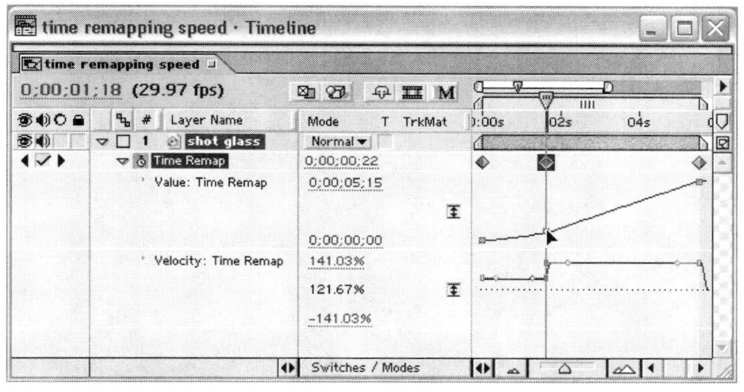

Figure 14.30 In the value graph, drag the control point corresponding to the keyframe. Decreasing the slope decreases speed; here, motion slows between the first and second keyframes.

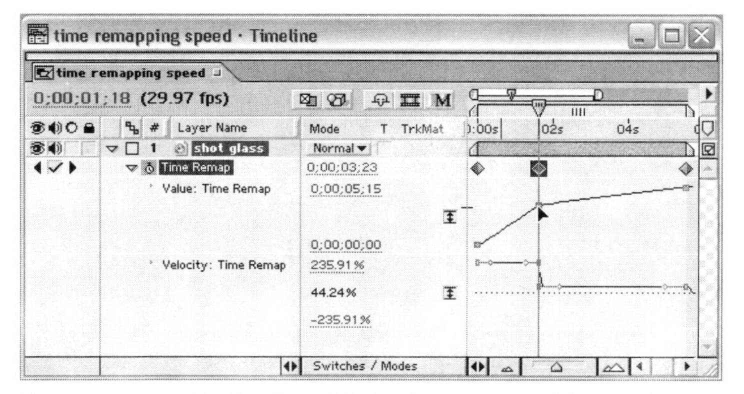

Figure 14.31 Increasing the slope of the line increases speed; here, motion between the first and second keyframe speeds up.

Using Blending Modes

In previous chapters, you learned that higher layers in the stacking order are superimposed on lower layers according to their alpha channel (which can also be modified with masks) or their Opacity property value. If you want to combine layers in more varied and subtle ways, you can use a variety of blending modes. By default, the blending mode is set to Normal. You can change the mode by selecting an option from the Mode menu in (you guessed it) the Modes panel of the Timeline window. When you do, the Video switch for the layer displays a darkened Eye icon (**Figure 14.32**).

A blending mode changes the value of a layer's pixels according to the values of the corresponding pixels in the underlying image. Depending on how the values interact, the result often appears as a blend of the two. You may recognize most of the blending modes from Photoshop; you'll find they work the same way here.

Although most layer modes only blend color values (RGB channels), some—such as the Stencil and Silhouette modes—affect transparency (alpha channel) information.

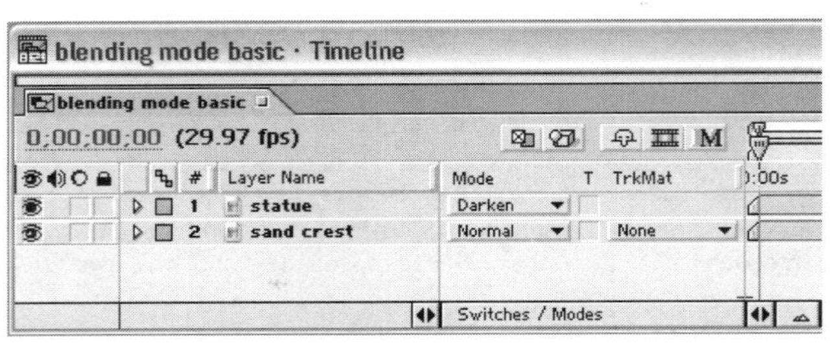

Figure 14.32 When you select a blending mode from the Mode pull-down menu, the Video switch displays a darkened Eye icon.

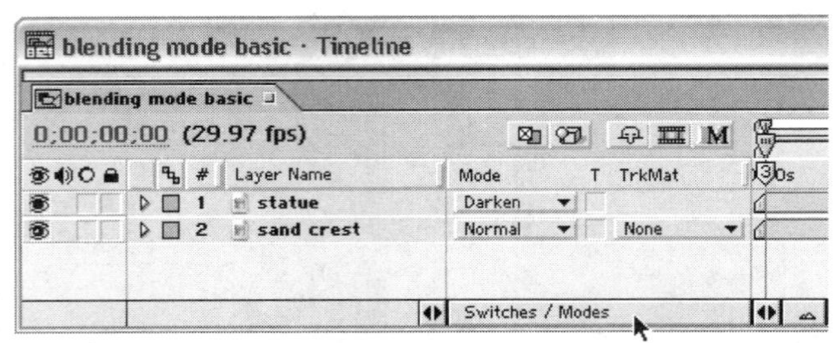

Figure 14.33 If necessary, click the Switches/Modes button to make the Modes menu appear.

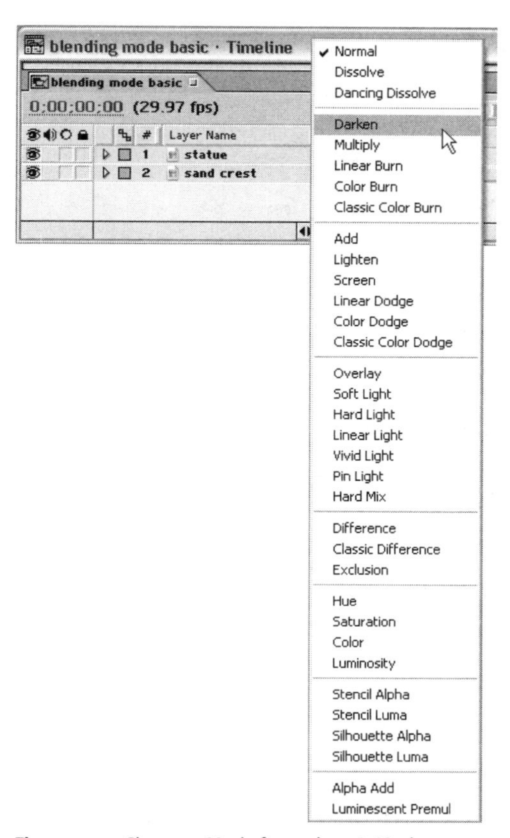

Figure 14.34 Choose a Mode from a layer's Modes menu.

To apply a layer mode:

1. If necessary, click the Switches/Modes button to make the Modes menu appear (**Figure 14.33**).
2. Choose a mode from a layer's Modes menu (**Figure 14.34**).

   The Video switch for the layer becomes a darkened eye. The mode you select affects how the layer combines with underlying layers. See the following section, "Blending Mode Types."

✔ Tips

- You can view the Switches and Modes panels simultaneously. Ctrl-click (Mac) or right-click (Windows) a panel to choose the Modes panel from the contextual menu.
- As you apply blending modes, bear in mind that After Effects renders the bottommost layer first and works its way up the stacking order. Because a blending mode determines how a layer interacts with the image beneath it, the resulting image becomes the underlying image for layer modes applied to the next higher layer in the stacking order, and so on. For more about render order, see Chapter 17, "Complex Projects."

Blending Mode Types

This section describes blending modes in the order they appear in the Modes pull-down menu. On the menu, they're grouped by category. However, you may also find it useful to contrast the images that use opposite blending modes; for example, contrast Darken to Lighten, Multiply with Screen, or a Burn mode to a Dodge mode.

The effect of any layer mode depends on various aspects of the image to which it's applied and of the underlying image. Certain types of modes are better suited to certain types of images, and vice versa. Note that most modes are based on the pixel values of visible channels, not on transparency information. However, Dissolve and Dancing Dissolve depend on a layer's transparency property. Transparency, Stencil and Silhouette, and Alpha Manipulation categories also affect alpha channels.

The following figures illustrate each blending mode using three images. The top-left image shows the layer before the blending mode is applied; the top-right image shows the underlying image; and the larger lower figure depicts the result of applying the blending mode to the top layer (the top-left image). Because these black-and-white figures can't fully represent the way modes affect the resulting color, some modes aren't illustrated here. You can always see the full-color results for yourself.

Transparency modes

Transparency modes alter the alpha channel of the layer to combine it with the underlying image.

Normal is the default layer mode. The layer combines with underlying layers according to its opacity setting.

Dissolve replaces pixels of the layer with underlying pixels, based on the layer's Opacity value. In contrast to Normal mode, pixels are either completely transparent or completely opaque. Thus, this mode ignores partial transparency, including feathered masks. At 100 percent opacity, this mode has no effect; a lower opacity value makes more of the pixels transparent. This mode was designed to emulate the Dissolve transition found in programs like Macromedia Director (**Figure 14.35**).

Dancing Dissolve works like the Dissolve mode except that the position of transparent pixels varies over time—even if the layer's opacity value remains the same.

Figure 14.35 Here, the text layer is set to Dissolve mode, and its opacity is set to 50 percent.

Figure 14.36 Different blending modes are applied to this nested comp. Images include white sand dunes (top left); a mountain and blue sky (top right); a red, white, and blue flag with a soft drop shadow; and a grayscale spanning from white to black in 10 steps.

Figure 14.37 This image of bright orange tangerines serves as the underlying image.

Brightness-reducing modes

These modes result in a darker overall image. In the following examples, a nested composition consisting of four images (**Figure 14.36**) is combined with an underlying image (**Figure 14.37**) using various blending modes.

Darken compares the color values of each channel of the layer with those of the underlying image and takes the darker of the two. Because the values of individual channels are compared, colors can shift drastically (**Figure 14.38**).

Multiply multiplies the color values of the layer with the color values of the underlying image and then divides the result by 255. The resulting value is darker than the two and never brighter than the original. When applied to a high-contrast black-and-white image, Multiply preserves the black areas and allows the underlying image to show through the white areas of the layer. Remember, though, that the alpha is not affected (**Figure 14.39**).

continues on next page

Figure 14.38 Darken.

Figure 14.39 Multiply.

Linear Burn darkens the layer by decreasing the brightness according to the color values of the underlying image. White areas in the layer remain unchanged (**Figure 14.40**).

Figure 14.40 Linear Burn.

Color Burn darkens the layer by increasing its contrast according to the color values of the underlying image. White areas in the layer remain unchanged (**Figure 14.41**). Color Burn is identical to the Color Burn mode in Adobe Photoshop.

Figure 14.41 Color Burn.

Classic Color Burn is the Color Burn mode in After Effects 5.0 and earlier. It uses the color values of the layer to darken the underlying image, which dominates the resulting image. White areas of the layer allow the underlying image to show through unaffected, whereas dark areas darken the underlying image

Brightness-enhancing modes

The following modes increase the brightness of the resulting image.

Add combines the brightness values of a layer with the underlying image to produce a brighter image overall. Pure-black areas in the layer reveal the underlying image unchanged; pure-white areas in the underlying image show through unchanged (**Figure 14.42**).

Figure 14.42 Add.

Lighten compares the color values of each channel of the layer with those of the underlying image and takes the lighter of the two. Because the values of individual channels are compared, colors can shift drastically (**Figure 14.43**).

Screen mode, as the opposite of Multiply mode, multiplies the inverse brightness values of the layer and underlying image and then divides the result by 255. The resulting value is brighter than the two and never

Figure 14.43 Lighten.

Figure 14.44 Screen.

darker than the original. This mode is particularly useful for compositing an image on a black background with the underlying image (**Figure 14.44**).

Linear Dodge lightens the layer by increasing the brightness according to the color values of the underlying image. Black areas in the layer remain unchanged (**Figure 14.45**). This mode is the opposite of Linear Burn.

Color Dodge is identical to the Color Burn mode in Adobe Photoshop. It lightens the layer by decreasing its contrast according to the color values of the underlying image. Black areas in the layer remain unchanged (**Figure 14.46**). This mode is the opposite of Color Burn.

Classic Color Dodge is identical to the Color Dodge mode in After Effects 5.0 and earlier. It uses a layer's color values—not just its brightness—to brighten the underlying image, which ends up dominating the resulting image. Black areas of the layer allow the underlying image to show through unaffected; white areas brighten the underlying image.

Figure 14.45 Linear Dodge.

Figure 14.46 Color Dodge.

Combination modes

The modes in this section apply different calculations (such as multiply and screen) depending on whether the underlying image's pixels are above or below a certain threshold value (such as 50 percent gray).

Overlay multiplies areas that are darker than 50 percent gray and screens areas that are brighter than 50 percent gray. This means that dark areas become darker and bright areas become brighter. Colors mix with the underlying colors, increasing saturation. Middle grays allow underlying pixels to show through unaffected. As a result, the underlying layer tends to be more visible (**Figure 14.47**). A favorite mode for creating attractive blends, Overlay can also be useful when applied to a solid color.

Soft Light lightens the layer when the underlying image is lighter than 50 percent gray and darkens the layer when the underlying image is darker than 50 percent gray. However, black pixels in the layer never result in pure black, and white pixels never result in pure white. The underlying image dominates the resulting image and has diminished contrast (**Figure 14.48**).

Hard Light multiplies the layer when the underlying pixels are darker than 50 percent gray and screens the layer when underlying pixels are lighter than 50 percent gray. As the name implies, the result is a harsher version of Soft Light, which means the layer comes through more strongly than the underlying image (**Figure 14.49**).

Figure 14.47 Overlay.

Figure 14.48 Soft Light.

Figure 14.49 Hard Light.

Figure 14.50 Linear Light.

Figure 14.51 Vivid Light.

Figure 14.52 Pin Light.

Linear Light applies a Linear Burn to the layer in areas where the underlying pixels are lighter than 50 percent gray; it applies a Linear Dodge to the layer in areas where the underlying pixels are darker than 50 percent gray (**Figure 14.50**). (Previous sections cover the Linear Burn and Linear Dodge modes.)

Vivid Light applies a Color Burn in areas where the underlying image is lighter than 50 percent gray; it applies a Color Dodge in areas where the underlying image is darker than 50 percent gray (**Figure 14.51**). (Previous sections cover the Color Burn and Color Dodge modes.)

Pin Light replaces colors in the layer with those of the underlying image, depending on the brightness of colors in the underlying image. Pixels in the layer are replaced where the underlying image is lighter than 50 percent gray and the pixels in the layer are darker than the corresponding pixels in the underlying image. Pixels are also replaced where the underlying image is darker than 50 percent gray and the pixels in the layer are darker than the corresponding pixels in the underlying image (**Figure 14.52**).

continues on next page

Dodge and Burn Modes

Dodge and *burn* are photography terms that Photoshop uses as well. *Dodging* refers to the technique of blocking light from a photographic print so that the white paper is protected from exposure, allowing the area to remain lighter. *Burning* refers to the technique of lengthening a photographic print's exposure to light in order to darken areas of the image.

Hard Mix replaces colors in the same manner as the Pin Light mode but also reduces the number of tonal levels in the result (as in a Posterize effect) (**Figure 14.53**).

Difference and exclusion modes

These blending modes are particularly useful in identifying differences between the layer and the underlying image that share pixel values.

Difference is identical to the Difference mode in Adobe Photoshop. It subtracts the layer's individual channel values from those of the underlying image and displays the absolute value. (In math, the *difference* is the result of subtraction; an *absolute value* is the number without regard to whether it's negative or positive.) Because the values of individual channels are compared, colors can shift drastically. White in the layer inverts the underlying color; black leaves the underlying color unchanged. When colors in the layer and underlying image match, the result is black (**Figures 14.54** and **14.55**). You can use Difference mode to create a *difference matte*. When a scene with a subject is combined with a clean scene (without the subject), only the difference appears in the resulting image.

Classic Difference is identical to the Difference mode in After Effects 5.0 and earlier. It subtracts the layer's channel values from those of the underlying image and displays the absolute value.

Figure 14.53 Hard Mix.

Figure 14.54 Difference.

Figure 14.55 It's easier to see the Difference mode here; wherever the white areas overlap, the pixels are replaced by black.

Figure 14.70 When composited without Preserve Underlying Transparency selected, the entire highlight is superimposed over the underlying image.

Figure 14.71 When Preserve Underlying Transparency is selected, the opaque areas of the highlight layer appear only in the opaque areas of the underlying image.

Preserving Underlying Transparency

To the right of the Mode menu is a layer switch in a column marked simply *T*. This innocuous-looking little T switch performs an important function: It preserves the underlying transparency. When you select this option, the opaque areas of a layer display only where they overlap with opaque areas in the underlying image (**Figures 14.70** and **14.71**).

The Preserve Underlying Transparency option is commonly used to make it appear as though light is being reflected from the surface of the underlying solid. You can use Preserve Underlying Transparency in conjunction with any layer mode or track matte. When you activate it, the Video switch becomes a darkened Eye icon.

To preserve underlying transparency:

1. If necessary, click the Switches/Modes button in the Timeline window to display the Modes panel.
2. For a layer you want to composite with the underlying image, click the box under the T heading (**Figure 14.72**).

   A check indicates Preserve Underlying Transparency is active; no check indicates it's inactive. When you activate the option, the Video switch becomes a darkened Eye icon.

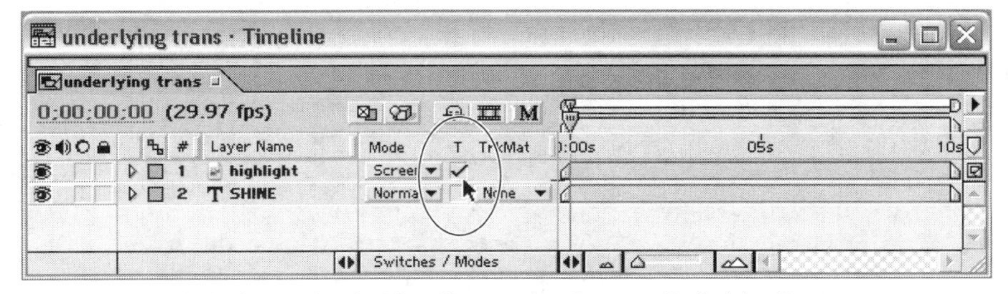

Figure 14.72 Click the box under the T heading to select Preserve Underlying Transparency.

Track Mattes

Thus far, you've learned to define transparent areas in a layer by using the Opacity property, alpha channels, masks, and certain layer modes and effects—all options that are part of the layer itself. Sometimes, however, you won't want to use the transparency provided by the image, or you may find that creating a mask is impractical. This is especially true if you want to use a moving image or one that lacks an alpha channel to define transparency. Whatever the case, you may want to use a separate image to define transparency. Any image used to define transparency in another image is called a *matte*. Because mattes use alpha-channel or luminance information to create transparency, they're usually grayscale images (or images converted into grayscale).

In After Effects, *track matte* refers to a method of defining transparency using an image layer, called the *fill*, and a separate matte layer. In the Timeline window, the matte must be directly above the fill in the stacking order. Because the matte is only included to define transparency, not to appear in the output, its Video switch is turned off. The track matte is assigned to the fill layer using the Track Matte pull-down menu in the Switches panel. Transparent areas reveal the underlying image, which consists of lower layers in the stacking order (**Figures 14.73** and **14.74**).

Types of track mattes

The Track Matte pull-down menu lists several track matte options (**Figure 14.75**). Each option specifies whether the matte's alpha or luminance information is used to define transparency in the fill layer. Ordinarily, white defines opaque areas, and black defines transparent areas. Inverted options reverse the opaque and transparent areas.

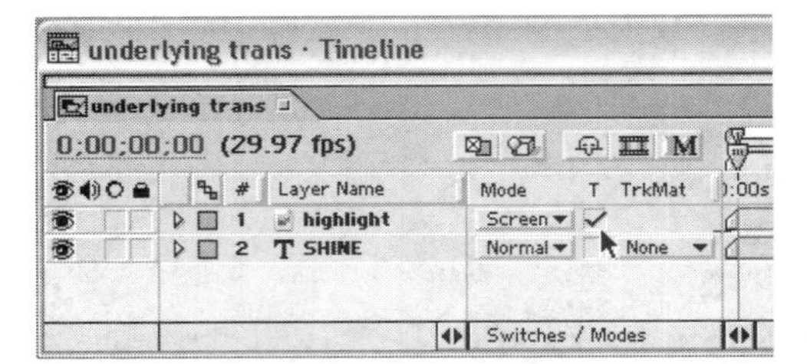

Figure 14.73 Arrange the matte, the fill, and the background layers in the timeline. Note the settings in the A/V panel and the Modes panel.

Figure 14.74 The matte, the fill, the background, and the final composite.

15 Keyframe Interpolation

In Chapter 7, "Properties and Keyframes," you learned to animate layer properties over time by setting keyframes. By defining only the most important, or *key*, frames, you assume the role of head animator. After Effects fills the role of assistant animator, providing all the in-between frames, or *tweens*, using what's known as an *interpolation method* to determine their values.

Fortunately, you can instruct your assistant to use a range of interpolation methods. Some methods create steady changes from one keyframe to the next; others vary the rate of change. Movement can take a direct path or a curved route; an action can glide in for a soft landing or blast off in a burst of speed.

Without a choice of interpolation methods, your loyal assistant's abilities would be severely limited. If animated values always proceeded directly and mechanically from one keyframe to another, all but the most basic animations would seem lifeless and robotic. To create a curved movement would require so many keyframes you'd begin to wonder why you had an assistant at all. Calculating acceleration or deceleration in speed would present an even thornier problem.

This chapter explains how you can assign various interpolation methods to keyframes to impart nuance and variation to your animations. You'll not only learn to decipher how After Effects depicts the ineffable qualities of motion, speed, and acceleration, but you'll also see how it harnesses them. In the process, you'll begin to realize that there's a big difference between animating something and bringing it to life.

Spatial and Temporal Interpolation

After Effects applies interpolation methods to two categories of information: spatial and temporal.

Spatial interpolation refers to how After Effects calculates changes in position—in other words, how a layer or its anchor point moves in the space of the composition. Does it proceed directly from one keyframe to the next, or does it take a curved route (**Figures 15.1** and **15.2**)?

Temporal interpolation refers to any property value's rate of change between keyframes. Does the value change at a constant rate from one keyframe to the next, or does it accelerate or decelerate (**Figures 15.3** and **15.4**)?

After Effects calculates both spatial and temporal interpolation using the same set of methods, or interpolation types. Controlling the interpolation between keyframes allows you to set fewer keyframes than you could otherwise—without sacrificing precise control over your animation.

Spatial interpolation and the motion path

Spatial interpolation is represented as a motion path (**Figure 15.5**). Changes in a layer's position value appear as a motion path in the Composition window; changes in a layer's anchor-point value appear in its Layer window. Effect point paths can also appear in a Layer window.

You can directly manipulate the motion path to control the movement precisely from one keyframe to the next. You'll find that editing motion paths works in much the same way as editing mask paths. Although a motion path provides a rough indication of speed, it doesn't provide you with accurate control over the speed or the temporal interpolation.

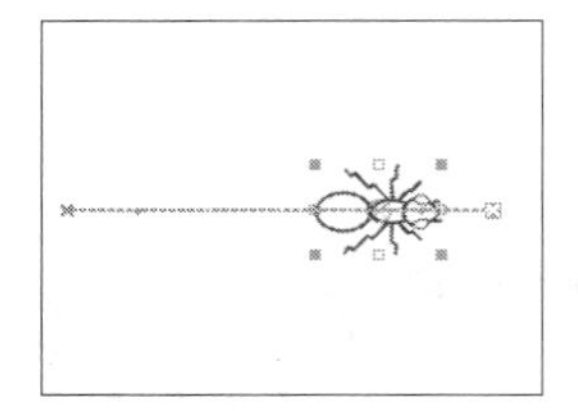

Figure 15.1 Spatial interpolation determines how After Effects calculates changes in position between keyframes. Movement may proceed directly...

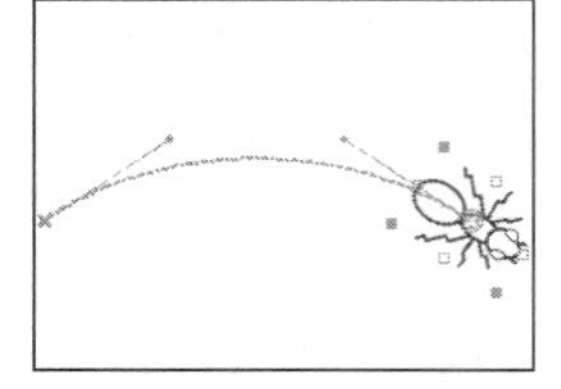

Figure 15.2 ...or take a more curved, indirect route.

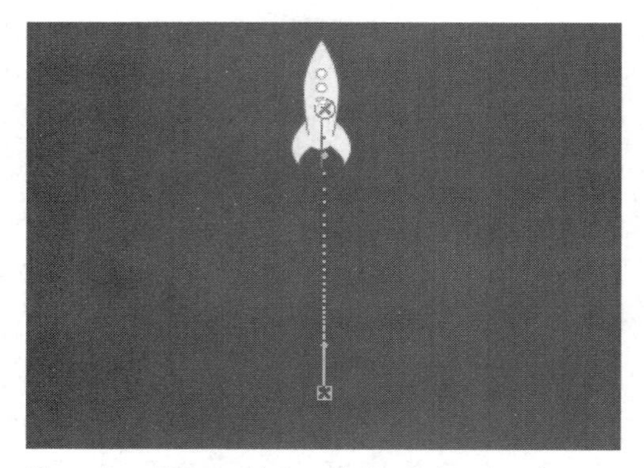

Figure 15.3 Temporal interpolation determines how After Effects calculates changes in speed or velocity. Temporal interpolation can create acceleration...

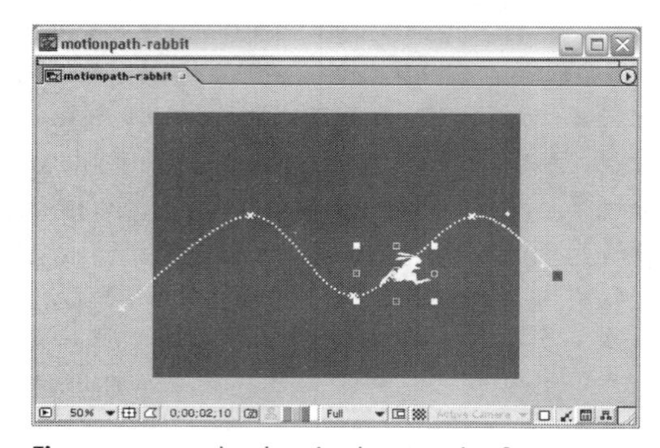

Figure 15.4 ...or deceleration between keyframes.

Temporal interpolation and the value, speed, and velocity graphs

Temporal interpolation is displayed in a speed graph (for spatial properties) or in a value graph and velocity graph (for other properties). When you expand a layer property, these graphs appear in the time graph of the Timeline window (**Figure 15.6**). You can directly manipulate these graphs to gain precise control over the speed and acceleration of a value from one keyframe to the next.

Although changing the curve of a graph is not unlike changing the curve of a motion path, it can be more difficult to interpret what the change means. Before you can take advantage of the control these graphs provide, you need to understand how each curve corresponds to rates of change from one keyframe to the next.

Keep reading to find out about the interpolation types and how they work spatially. Then move on to learn about the temporal effects of interpolation.

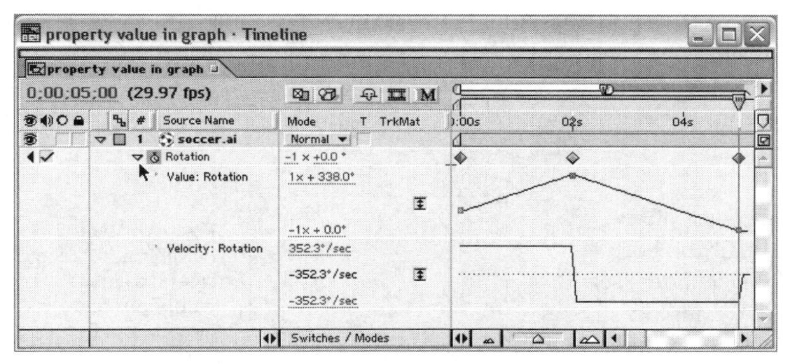

Figure 15.5 You can view and control spatial interpolation in the motion path.

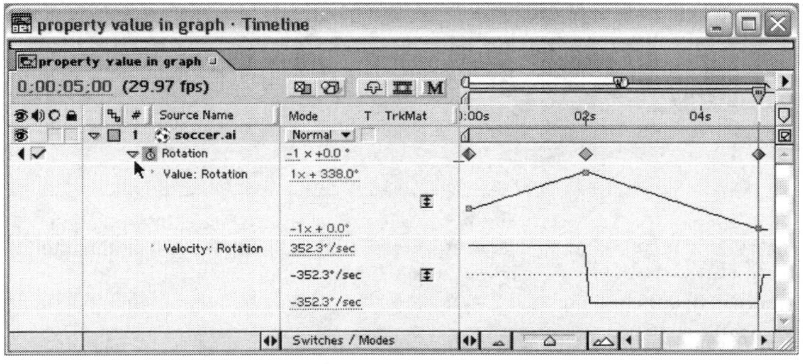

Figure 15.6 You can view and control temporal interpolation in a speed, value, or velocity graph.

Interpolation Types

With the exception of hold interpolation, After Effects uses the same methods to calculate both spatial and temporal interpolation.

No interpolation

No interpolation is applied to properties that have no keyframes and aren't animated. Static properties display an I-beam icon in the layer outline (rather than keyframes), and the Stopwatch icon isn't selected.

Linear

Linear interpolation dictates a constant rate of change from one keyframe to the next. Spatially, linear interpolation defines a straight path from one keyframe to the next; temporally, linear interpolation results in a constant speed between keyframes (**Figures 15.7** and **15.8**).

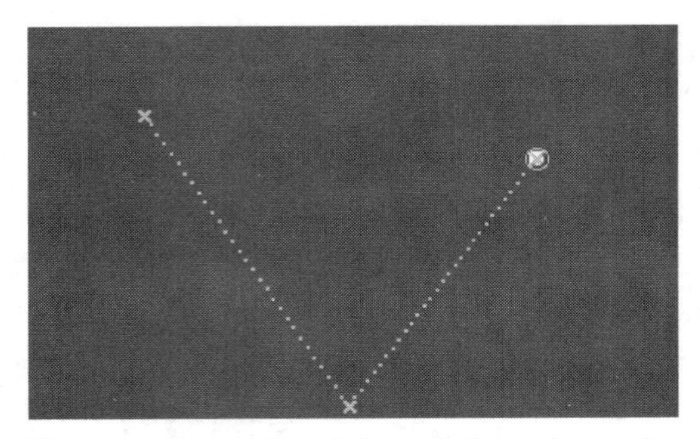

Figure 15.7 Linear interpolation calculates changes in a linear fashion. Spatially, linear interpolation defines a straight path.

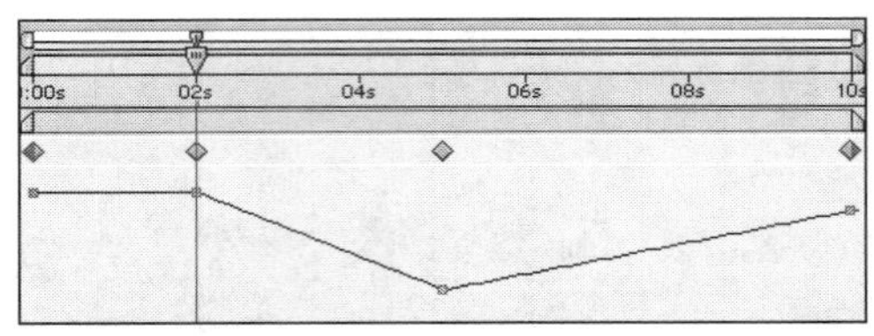

Figure 15.8 Temporally, linear interpolation results in a constant rate of change between keyframes.

Auto Bézier

Auto Bézier interpolation automatically reduces the rate of change equally on both sides of a keyframe. Spatially, a keyframe set to auto Bézier is comparable to a smooth point, with two equal direction lines extending from it. It results in a smooth, symmetrical curve in a motion path. Temporally, auto Bézier interpolation reduces the rate of change equally before and after a keyframe, creating a gradual deceleration that eases into and out of the keyframe (**Figures 15.9** and **15.10**).

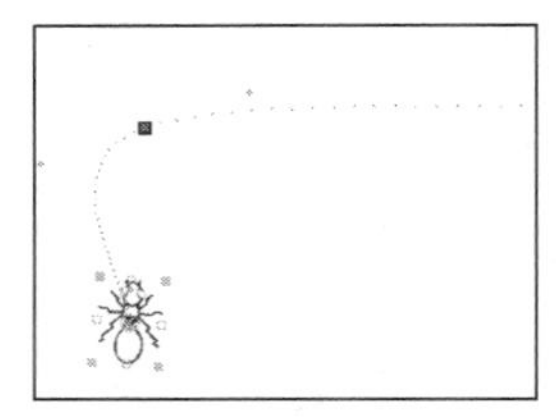

Figure 15.9 Auto Bézier interpolation creates a curved path, with equal incoming and outgoing interpolation.

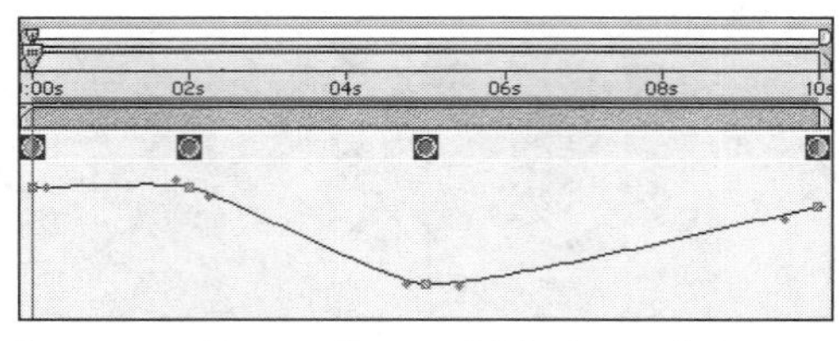

Figure 15.10 Temporally, auto Bézier interpolation reduces the rate of change equally before and after a keyframe.

Continuous Bézier

Like auto Bézier, continuous Bézier interpolation reduces the rate of change on both sides of a keyframe. However, continuous Bézier interpolation is set manually, so it doesn't affect the incoming and outgoing rates of change equally. In the motion path, continuous Bézier interpolation results in a smooth and continuous, but asymmetrical, curve. In the value graph, continuous Bézier interpolation manually and unequally reduces the rate of change before and after a keyframe (**Figures 15.11** and **15.12**).

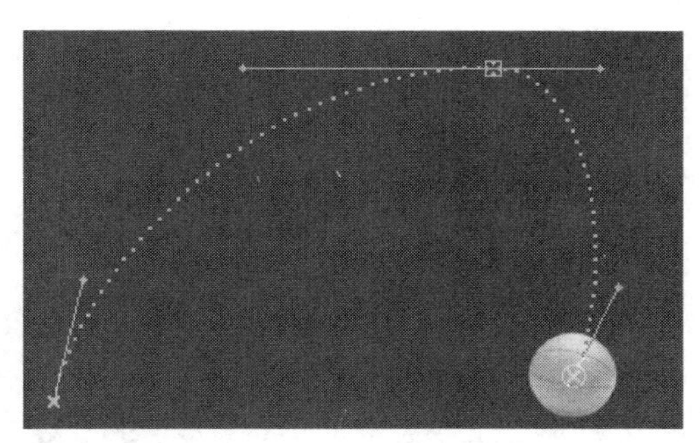

Figure 15.11 You manually set continuous Bézier interpolation to create an asymmetrically curved path.

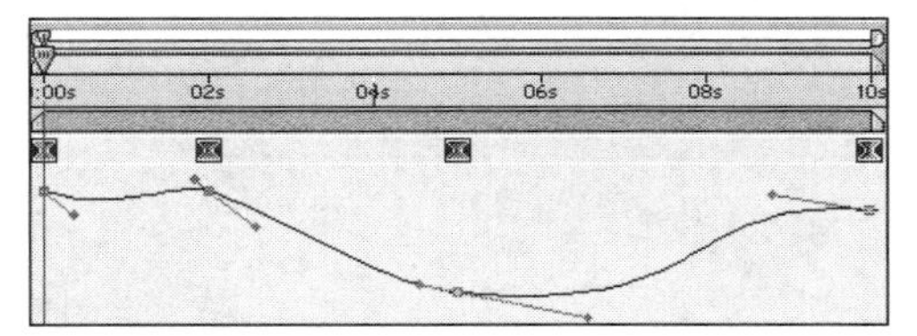

Figure 15.12 Continuous Bézier interpolation reduces the rate of change by different amounts on either side of a keyframe.

Bézier

Like continuous Bézier, you set Bézier interpolation manually. Bézier interpolation can either decrease or increase the rate of change on either or both sides of a keyframe. Spatially, Bézier keyframes are comparable to a corner point in a mask path. As in a corner point, the direction lines extending from the keyframe are unequal and discontinuous. In a motion path, Bézier interpolation creates a discontinuous curve, or *cusp*, at the keyframe. In the value graph, Bézier interpolation can reduce or increase the rate of change before and after a keyframe (**Figures 15.13** and **15.14**). For example, Bézier interpolation can be used to create a sharp acceleration at a keyframe (such as when a ball falls and bounces).

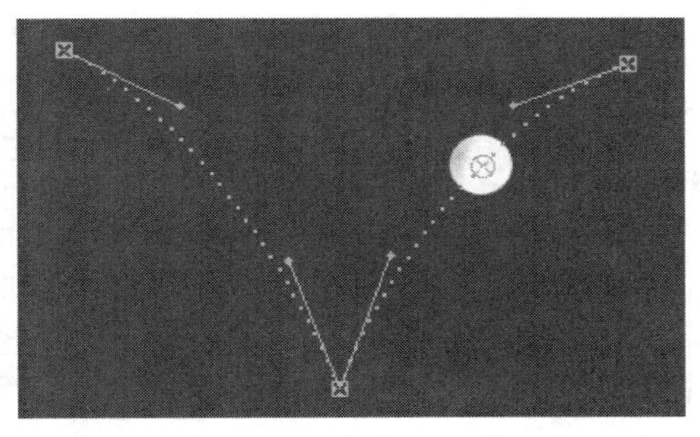

Figure 15.13 Bézier interpolation can allow the motion path to follow discontinuous curves.

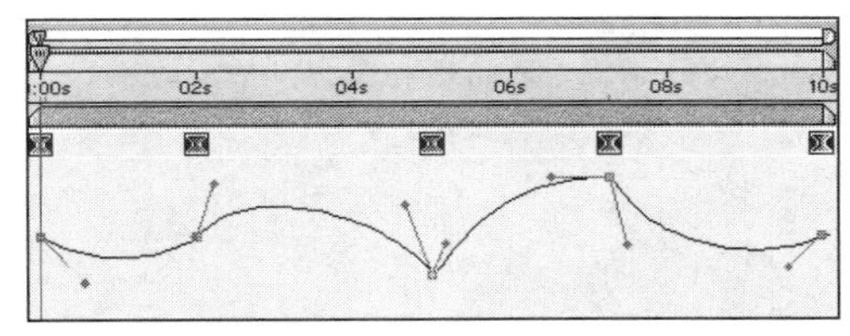

Figure 15.14 Temporally, Bézier interpolation can create quick acceleration and deceleration.

Qu'est-ce Que C'est Bézier? *Qui Est* Bézier?

In case your French is rusty, Bézier is pronounced *bez-ee-yay*, after the late Pierre Etienne Bézier, who developed the math behind his namesake curve in the 1970s for use in computer-aided design and manufacture. This same math became the basis for Adobe Postscript fonts, path-based drawing, and—yes—the interpolation methods used in computer animation. Bézier died in 1999. Merci, Monsieur Bézier.

Hold

Although you can observe its effects both spatially and temporally, hold interpolation is a strictly temporal type of interpolation, halting changes in a property's value at the keyframe. The value remains fixed until the current frame of the composition reaches the next keyframe, where the property is set to a new value instantly. For example, specifying hold keyframes for a layer's Position property can cause it to disappear suddenly and then reappear in different places. When hold interpolation is applied to position keyframes, no motion path connects the keyframes displayed in the Composition window (**Figures 15.15** and **15.16**).

Mixed incoming and outgoing interpolation

A keyframe can use different interpolation types for its incoming and outgoing interpolation. A keyframe's incoming and outgoing spatial interpolation can be a mix of linear and Bézier. A keyframe's temporal interpolation may use any combination of linear, Bézier, and hold for its incoming and outgoing interpolation (**Figure 15.17**).

Figure 15.15 Keyframes of spatial properties that use hold interpolation remain frozen in position until the next keyframe, where they suddenly reappear.

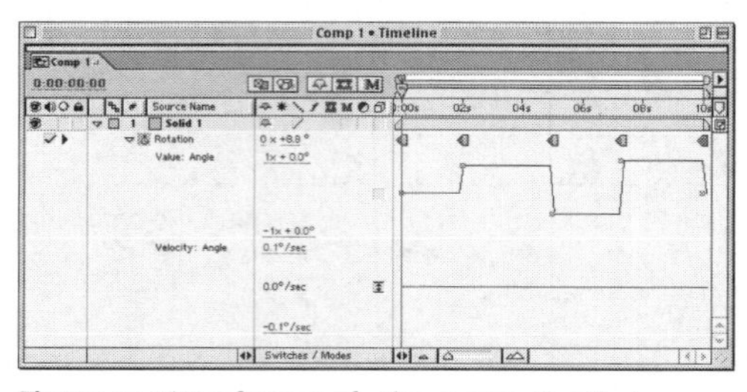

Figure 15.16 Keyframes of other properties that use hold interpolation also retain their current value until the next keyframe. The speed of a held property displays as 0.

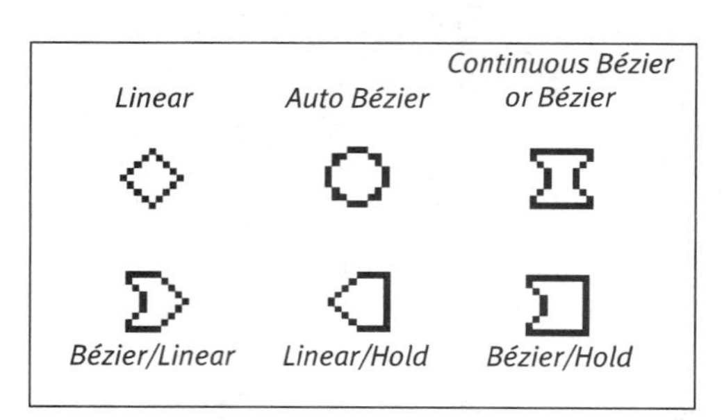

Figure 15.17 Keyframes indicate whether they use different incoming and outgoing interpolation.

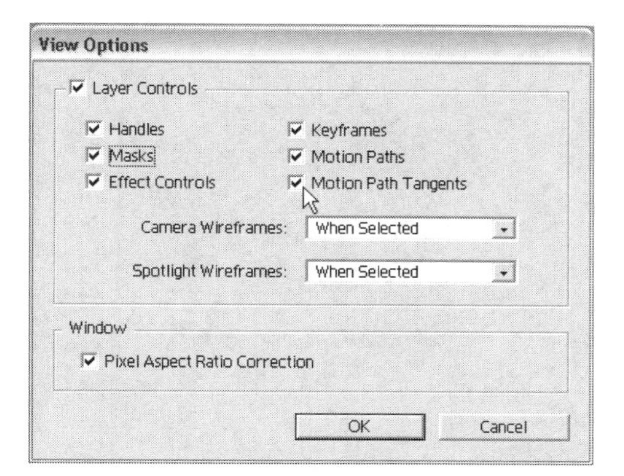

Figure 15.18 In the View Options dialog box, select the information you want to view.

Viewing Motion Paths and Spatial Interpolation

When animated, only three property types result in a motion path: layer position, effect point, and anchor point. To manipulate spatial interpolation, make sure you can view the proper controls in the Composition or Layer window. Position and effect-point paths appear in a Composition window; anchor-point paths appear in a Layer window. The following tasks describe how to use the pull-down menus in each window to view the information you need.

To show or hide motion-path information in the Composition window:

1. In the Composition window's pull-down menu, select View Options.

   A View Options dialog box appears.

2. Select the information you want to show (**Figure 15.18**). A check indicates that the information appears in the Composition window; no check indicates that it's hidden.

   Handles displays the layer frame with dots, or handles, around its perimeter. The handles are used to scale the layer.

   Masks displays layer masks (see Chapter 9, "Mask Essentials," for more about using masks.) A View Masks button provides a more convenient alternative to selecting this option.

   Effect Controls displays graphical controls, such as effect-point handles, that you can use to adjust certain effects.

continues on next page

Keyframes displays each keyframe of the selected layer's position as an *x*. Selecting a keyframe in either the Composition window or layer outline highlights the keyframe. The number of visible keyframes depends on how you set the motion-path preferences.

Motion Paths displays the course the selected layer will follow as a dotted line connecting keyframes. The spacing of the dots indicates the speed of motion.

Motion Path Tangents displays the tangents, or direction handles, extending from selected keyframes on the motion path. Tangents only extend from keyframes that use one of the three types of Bézier interpolation.

The View Options dialog box also includes options for viewing camera and spotlight wireframes. These options are explained in Chapter 16, "3D Layers." The Comp window displays the information you specified (**Figure 15.19**).

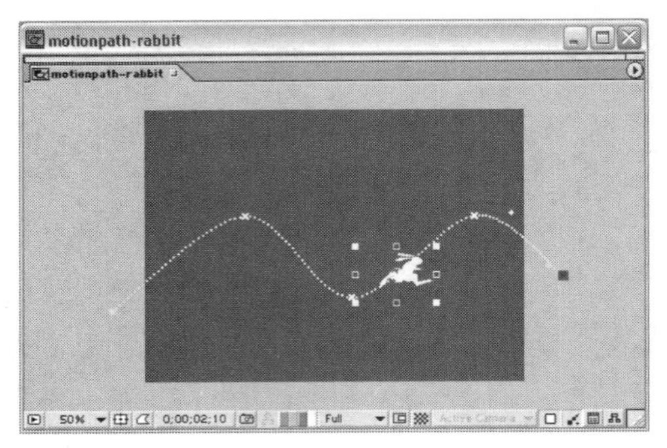

Figure 15.19 The Composition window can display motion-path information for a selected layer.

To view the anchor-point path in a Layer window:

- In the Layer window's View pull-down menu, select Anchor Point Path (**Figure 15.20**).

  Anchor Point Path becomes the visible option in the Layer window's View menu. In the image area of the Layer window, anchor point paths become visible, and mask paths are hidden (**Figure 15.21**).

Figure 15.20 In the Layer window's View pull-down menu, select Anchor Point Path to view the anchor point's motion path.

Figure 15.21 The anchor-point motion path appears in a Layer window.

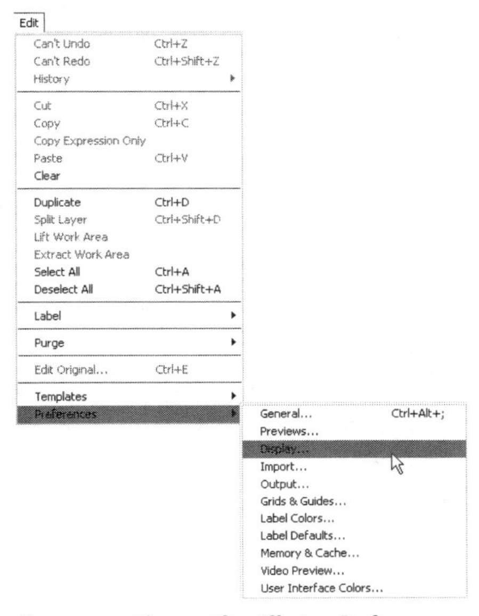

Figure 15.22 Choose After Effects > Preferences > Display (Mac) or Edit > Preferences > Display (Windows).

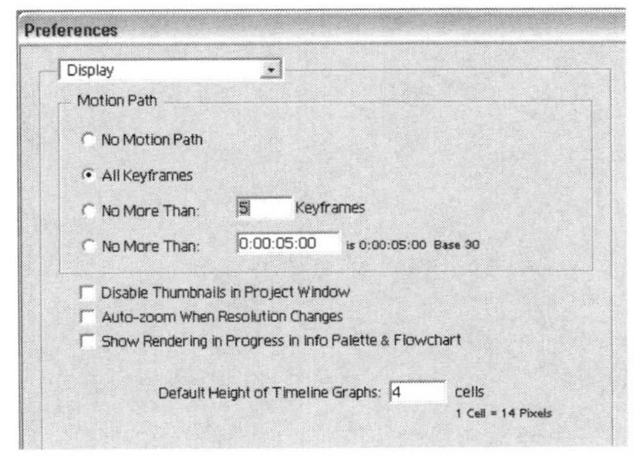

Figure 15.23 The Display panel of the Preferences dialog box appears.

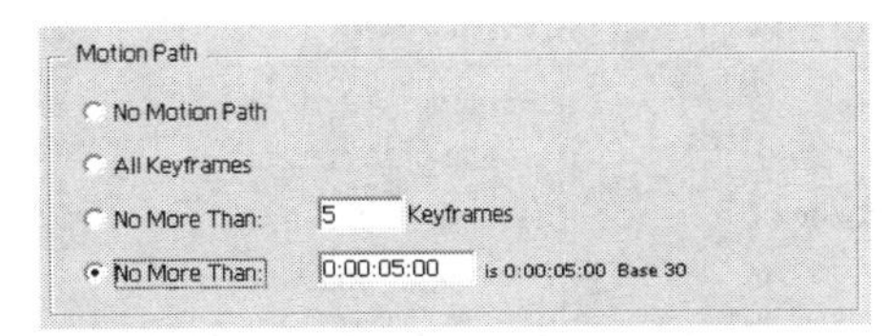

Figure 15.24 In the Motion Path section of the Preferences dialog box, choose an option.

To set motion-path preferences:

1. Choose After Effects > Preferences > Display (Mac) or Edit > Preferences > Display (Windows) (**Figure 15.22**).

   The Display panel of the Preferences dialog box appears (**Figure 15.23**).

2. In the Motion Path section of the Preferences dialog box, *choose one of the following* options (**Figure 15.24**):

   ▲ **No Motion Path** prevents keyframes and motion paths from displaying.

   ▲ **All Keyframes** displays all spatial keyframes for the selected layer.

   ▲ **No More Than [ ] Keyframes** allows you to enter the maximum number of keyframes displayed, starting from the current time.

   ▲ **No More Than [ ] time** allows you to limit the number of keyframes displayed to those within a specified amount of time, beginning at the current time.

3. Click OK to close the Preferences dialog box.

Comparing Motion Paths and Mask Paths

As suggested in Chapter 9, mask paths have a lot in common with motion paths. Although mask paths define shapes rather than movement, editing a motion path is nearly identical to changing the shape of a mask path. Comparing the terminology used to describe each kind of path helps reveal their similarities.

Table 15.1

Comparing path terminology

Mask path	Analogous motion path
Mask path control	Motion path control
Control point	Keyframe
Anchor point	Linear interpolation
Smooth point	Auto Bézier or continuous Bézier interpolation
Corner point	Bézier interpolation

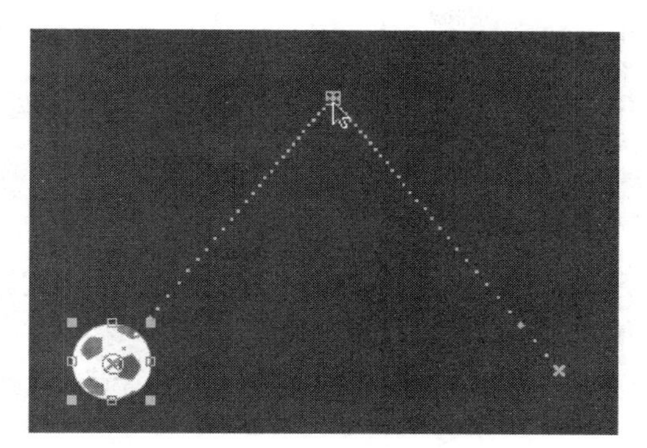

Figure 15.25 Select one or more keyframes in the motion path.

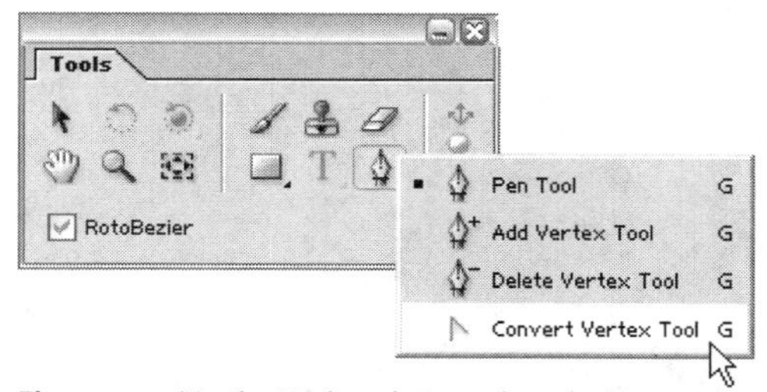

Figure 15.26 In the Tools palette, select the Pen tool or the Convert Vertex tool.

Specifying Spatial Interpolation in the Motion Path

In Chapter 7, you learned that you can change the spatial positioning of each keyframe by dragging it directly into a Composition or Layer window. This section focuses on using spatial interpolation to change the course of the motion path from one keyframe to the next.

Because you can apply your mastery of mask paths to editing motion paths, this section reviews the key points. As you become more comfortable with editing paths, learn how to toggle from the Selection tool to the Pen tool. Switching tools from the keyboard will save you many trips to the Tools palette.

Bear in mind that the motion path allows you to control movement, but it provides little control over timing. Generally, you should adjust the motion path first and then fine-tune the timing and temporal interpolation.

To convert a spatial interpolation from auto Bézier to linear, and vice versa:

1. Select a layer with an animated property to reveal its motion path in a Composition or Layer window.

   Position and effect-point paths appear in the Composition window; anchor-point paths appear in the Layer window.

2. Select one or more keyframes in the motion path (**Figure 15.25**).

3. In Tools, select the Pen tool or the Convert Vertex tool (**Figure 15.26**).

continues on next page

4. In the motion path, click a Keyframe icon to convert it.

   If you're using the Pen tool, it becomes the Convert Vertex tool when you position it over a keyframe (**Figure 15.27**). A keyframe using linear interpolation is converted to auto Bézier, with two equal control handles extending from the keyframe. Any Bézier-type keyframe is converted to linear, with no direction handles.

5. In the Tools palette, choose the Selection tool.

   Once you convert a keyframe, adjust it with the Selection tool. Just clicking it without changing tools will convert it back again.

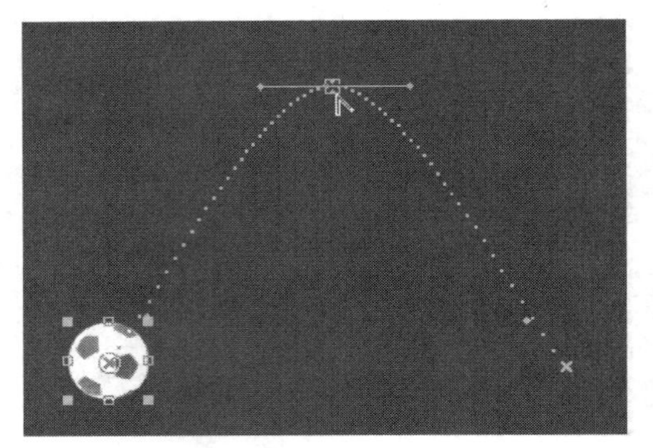

Figure 15.27 Clicking a keyframe with the Convert Vertex tool changes the keyframe from auto Bézier to linear, and vice versa.

To convert continuous Bézier to Bézier, and vice versa:

1. Select a layer with an animated property to reveal its motion path in a Composition or Layer window.

2. Select one or more keyframes in the motion path (**Figure 15.28**).

3. In Tools, select the Pen tool or the Convert Vertex tool as shown in Figure 15.26.

4. In the motion path, drag a direction handle (**Figure 15.29**).

   If you're using the Pen tool, it becomes the Convert Vertex tool when you position it over a direction handle. Dragging a direction handle of a Bézier keyframe converts it to continuous Bézier with two related direction handles; dragging a direction handle of a continuous Bézier keyframe splits the direction handles, converting it to Bézier.

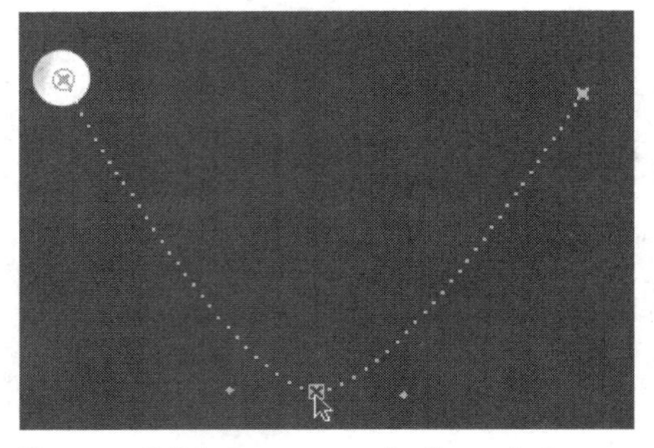

Figure 15.28 Select one or more keyframes in the motion path.

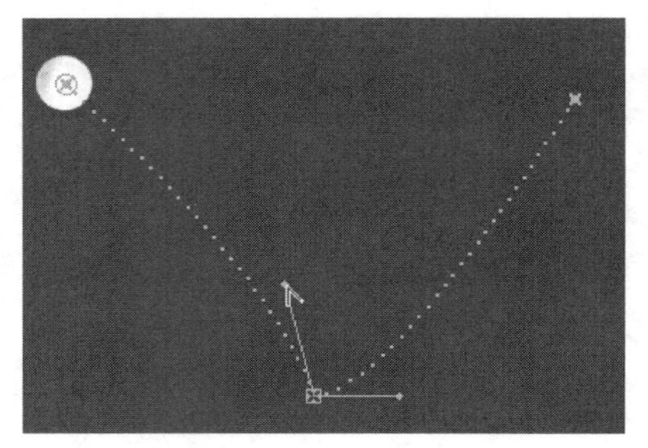

Figure 15.29 In the motion path, drag a direction handle with the Convert Vertex tool to change continuous Bézier to Bézier, and vice versa.

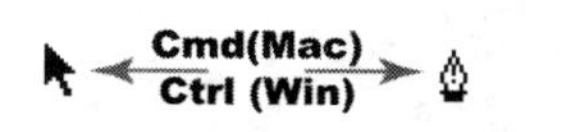

Figure 15.30 Press and hold the Command (Mac) or Ctrl (Windows) key to toggle between the Selection tool and the currently selected Pen tool.

5. In the Tools palette, choose the Selection tool.

   Once you convert a keyframe, adjust its direction handles with the Selection tool. Otherwise, you'll convert it back again.

To toggle between the Selection tool and the Pen tool:

1. Press and hold the Command (Mac) or Ctrl (Windows) key.

   If the Selection tool is selected, it changes to the Pen tool currently visible in the Tools palette. If one of the Pen tools is selected, it changes to the Selection tool (**Figure 15.30**).

2. Release the key to continue using the currently selected tool.

✔ Tips

- Most of the time, you'll want to use the Selection tool but keep the Pen tool visible in the Tools palette. Use the Selection tool to adjust the motion path; temporarily toggle to the Pen tool to add or convert keyframes.
- The Bézier rules you learned in Chapter 9 can help you create smooth curves for a motion path as well. For more details, see the Chapter 9 sidebar "Smooth and Shapely Curves."

Specifying the Default Spatial Interpolation

Ordinarily, motion-path keyframes use auto Bézier interpolation. If most of your spatial animation requires linear interpolation (or if you simply prefer it as your initial setting), you can change the default in the Preferences dialog box.

To set the default spatial interpolation:

1. Choose After Effects > Preferences > General (Mac) or Edit > Preferences > General (**Figure 15.31**).

   The General panel of the Preferences dialog box appears.

2. In the General Preferences dialog box, *do either of the following* (**Figure 15.32**):

   - ▲ Select Default Spatial Interpolation to Linear to make new motion paths use linear interpolation.
   - ▲ Unselect Default Spatial Interpolation to Linear to make new motion paths use auto Bézier interpolation.

3. Click OK to close the Preferences dialog box.

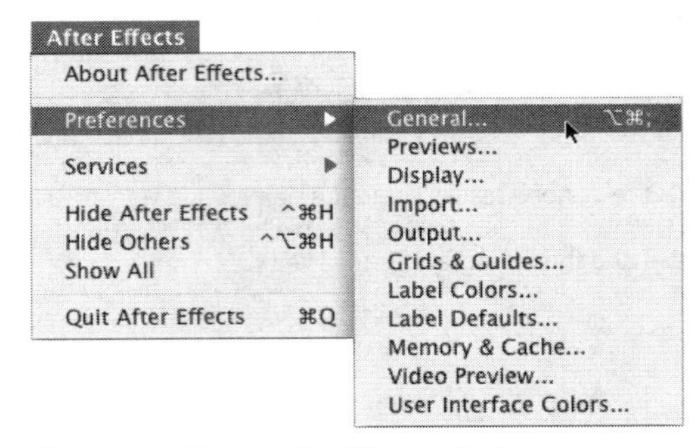

Figure 15.31 Choose After Effects > Preferences > General (Mac) or Edit > Preferences > General (Windows).

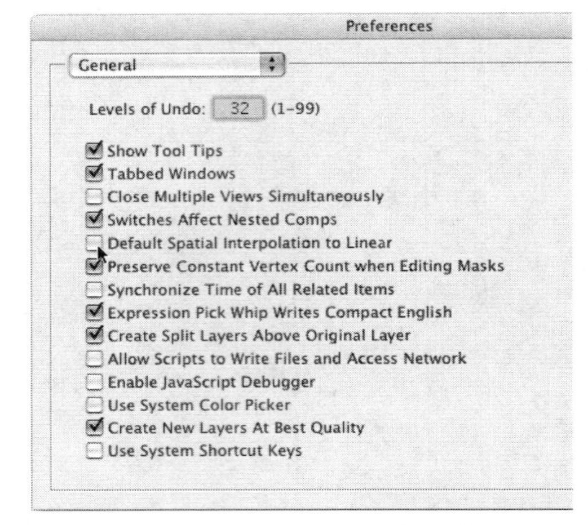

Figure 15.32 In the General panel of the Preferences dialog box, choose whether to use linear interpolation as the default.

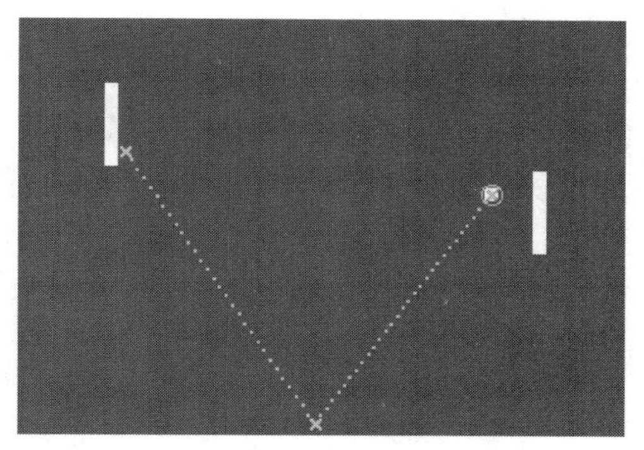

Figure 15.33 Use linear interpolation to create sharp-cornered, abrupt changes in direction.

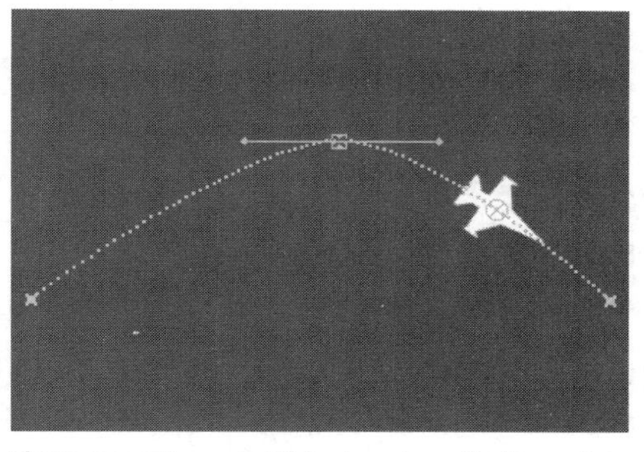

Figure 15.34 Use auto Bézier to automatically create perfectly even, continuous curves.

Mastering Spatial Interpolation

As you can see, editing a motion path is just like changing the shape of an open mask. The crucial difference, of course, is that a motion path defines movement. Try your hand at the following examples and see how the shape of the path corresponds to each interpolation method and how the interpolation method influences motion.

Once you master the motion through spatial interpolation, use temporal interpolation to fine-tune the rates of change for any property.

Linear interpolation

Use linear interpolation to create sharp-cornered, abrupt changes in direction. The ball in the old "pong" game ricocheting off a paddle would use linear interpolation (**Figure 15.33**).

Auto Bézier interpolation

Use auto Bézier to create perfectly even, continuous curves automatically. When an object turns, it rarely takes a sharp, linear change in direction. A satellite in an elliptical orbit, for example, takes even, round turns (**Figure 15.34**). (In addition, the satellite might auto-orient its rotation according to the direction of its movement. See "Orienting Rotation to a Motion Path Automatically" later in this chapter.)

Continuous Bézier interpolation

Use continuous Bézier interpolation to create a continuous but uneven curve. Viewed from the side, a basketball follows a continuously curved path; but as the ball loses momentum and gravity takes over, the curve becomes uneven. Dragging one handle of an auto Bézier keyframe changes it to continuous Bézier—it keeps the handles related and continuous but makes them unequal (**Figure 15.35**).

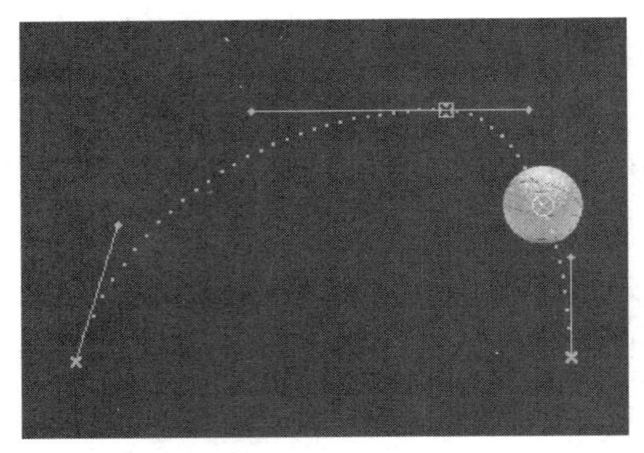

Figure 15.35 Use continuous Bézier to create a continuous but uneven curve.

Bézier interpolation

Use Bézier interpolation to create discontinuous curves, sometimes called *cusps*. Viewed from the side, a ball bounce looks a lot like the ricocheting pong ball, but its course is curved like that of the basketball. Because the relationship between the incoming and outgoing direction handles is broken, Bézier interpolation achieves the discontinuous curve of a ball's bouncing path (**Figure 15.36**).

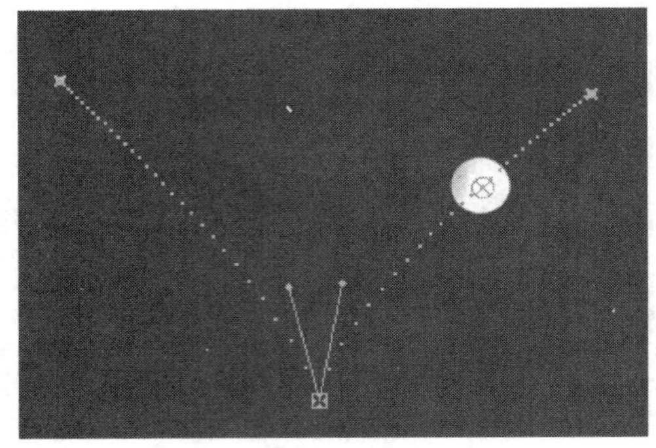

Figure 15.36 Use Bézier to create discontinuous curves.

✔ Tip

- Again, the motion path and the types of spatial interpolation it uses only affect motion. For truly convincing animation, you must also adjust speed (by controlling the time between keyframes) and acceleration (via temporal interpolation). In addition, consider other physical attributes associated with motion—for example, the blurred motion of fast-moving objects (see Chapter 14, "More Layer Techniques," for more about motion blur), or distortion and elasticity (say, the squashing effect when a ball strikes the ground).

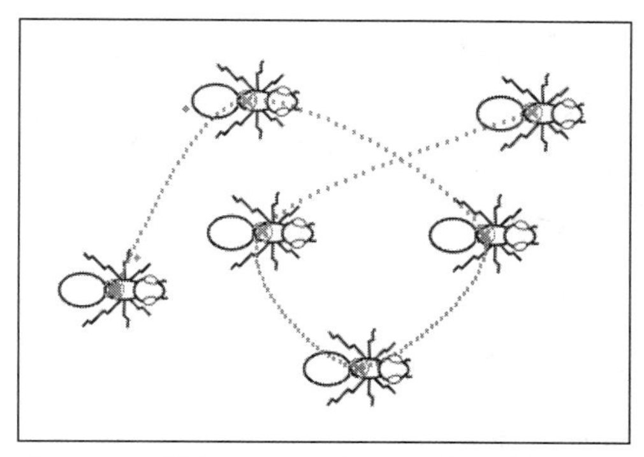

Figure 15.37 Without auto-orient rotation, objects remain upright as they follow the motion path (unless you add rotation). Notice that the ant remains parallel to the window frame.

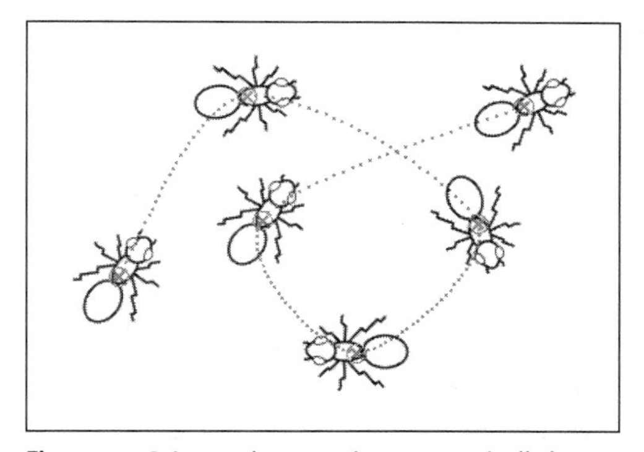

Figure 15.38 Auto-orient rotation automatically keeps a layer perpendicular to the motion path. The ant's position changes as it moves along the path.

Orienting Rotation to a Motion Path Automatically

As a layer follows a motion path, its rotation remains unaffected. In other words, the layer maintains its upright position as it follows the path: Picture, for example, someone riding up an escalator, or the cabins on a Ferris wheel; they remain upright although they follow a sloped or curved path (**Figure 15.37**). Frequently, you want the object to orient its rotation to remain perpendicular to the motion path: Now picture a roller coaster climbing a hill (**Figure 15.38**).

Fortunately, you don't have to painstakingly keyframe a layer's Rotation property to ensure that it remains oriented to the motion path; After Effects' Auto-Orient Rotation command does that for you. Technically, auto-orient rotation isn't a type of spatial interpolation; however, like an interpolation method, it dictates the behavior of a layer along a motion path—and in so doing saves you a lot of keyframing work.

To auto-orient rotation to the motion path:

1. Select a layer (**Figure 15.39**).
2. Choose Layer > Transform > Auto-Orient, or press Option-Command-O (Mac) or Alt-Control-O (Windows) (**Figure 15.40**).

   The Auto-Orientation dialog box appears.
3. In the Auto-Orientation dialog box, *choose either of the following:*
   - ▲ **Off**—Controls the layer's rotation manually
   - ▲ **Orient Along Path**—Makes the layer automatically orient its *X*-axis tangent to the motion path
4. Click OK to close the Auto-Orientation dialog box.

✔ Tips

- You can use the Path Text effect to make text follow a path while automatically remaining perpendicular to it. Text you create using the text-creation tools can also follow a path you specify.
- Chapter 16, "3D Layers," covers 3D compositing, including auto-orient options for 3D layers, cameras, and lights.

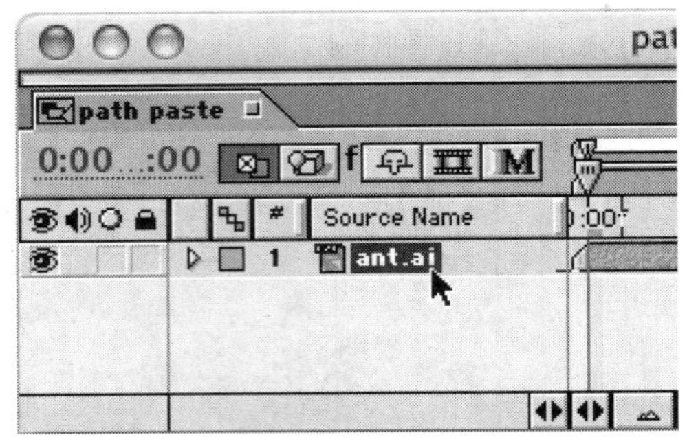

Figure 15.39 Select a layer.

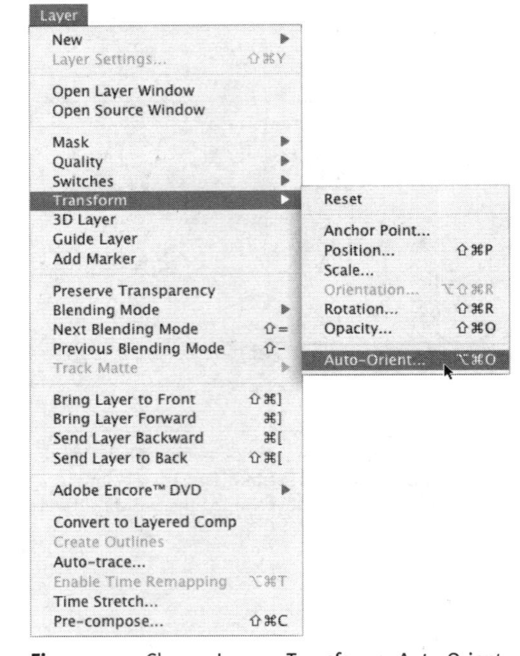

Figure 15.40 Choose Layer > Transform > Auto-Orient.

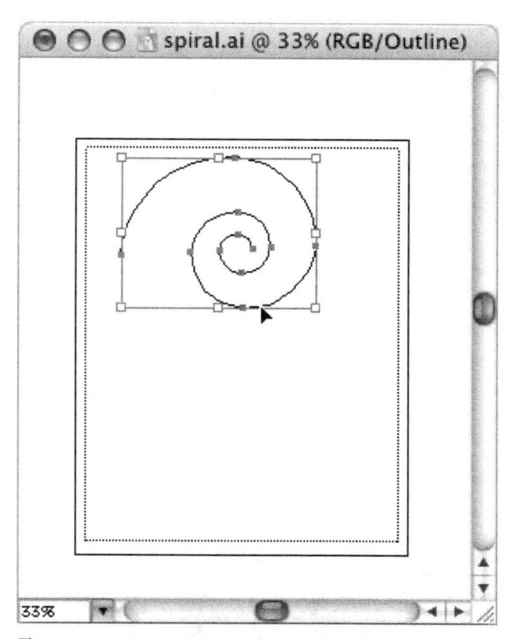

Figure 15.41 In a Layer window, select an open mask path. You can also copy a path from Photoshop or Illustrator (shown here).

Edit
Undo ⌘Z
Redo ⇧⌘Z
Cut ⌘X
Copy ⌘C
Paste ⌘V
Paste in Front ⌘F
Paste in Back ⌘B
Clear
Define Pattern...
Edit Original
Assign Profile...
Color Settings...
Keyboard Shortcuts... ⌥⇧⌘K

Figure 15.42 Choose Edit > Copy, or press Command-C (Mac) or Ctrl-C (Windows) (Illustrator's Copy command).

Converting Mask Paths into Motion Paths

An open mask path not only is analogous to a motion path, it can also be converted into one.

To paste a mask path as a motion path:

1. In a Layer window, select an open mask path (**Figure 15.41**).
2. Choose Edit > Copy, or press Command-C (Mac) or Ctrl-C (Windows) (**Figure 15.42**).
3. In the Timeline window, expand the layer outline to reveal the spatial property you want to paste the path into.

   You can use the Position, Effect Point, or Anchor Point property.
4. Select the property name.

   The property's keyframes are highlighted. If the property has no keyframes, the I-beam icon is highlighted.
5. Set the current time to the frame where you want the pasted keyframes to start (**Figure 15.43**).

continues on next page

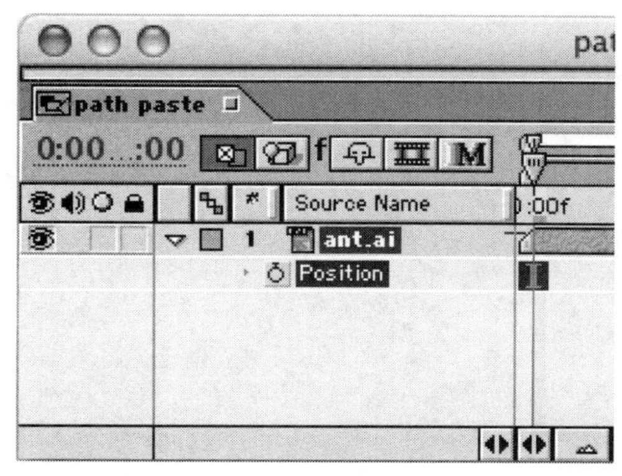

Figure 15.43 Select the property name, and set the current time to the frame where you want the pasted keyframes to start.

6. Choose Edit > Paste, or press Command-V (Mac) or Ctrl-V (Windows) (**Figure 15.44**).

   The keyframes appear in the property track, beginning at the current time and ending two seconds later (**Figure 15.45**).

7. Edit the motion path as you would any other (**Figure 15.46**).

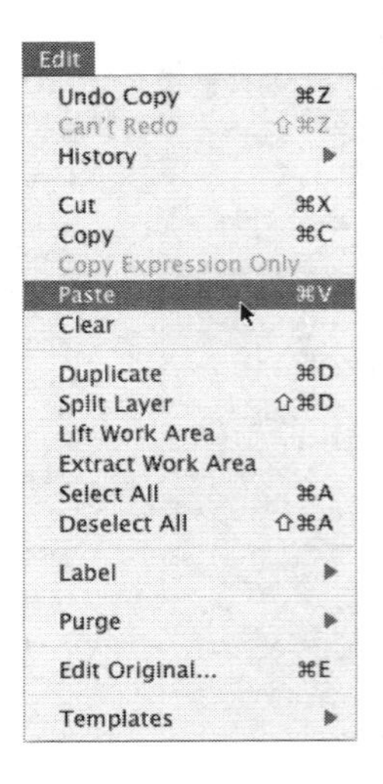

Figure 15.44 Choose Edit > Paste, or press Command-V (Mac) or Ctrl-V (Windows).

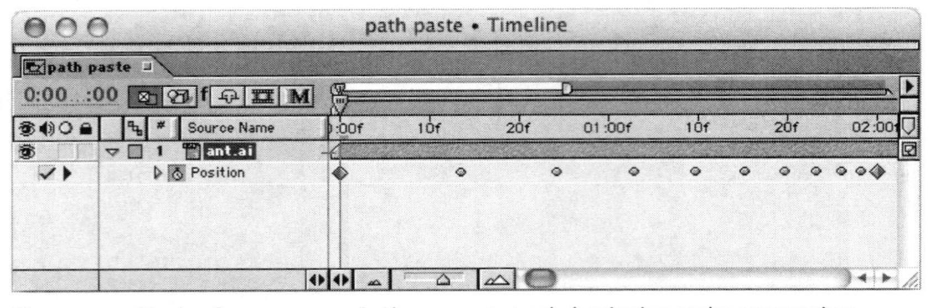

Figure 15.45 The keyframes appear in the property track, beginning at the current time.

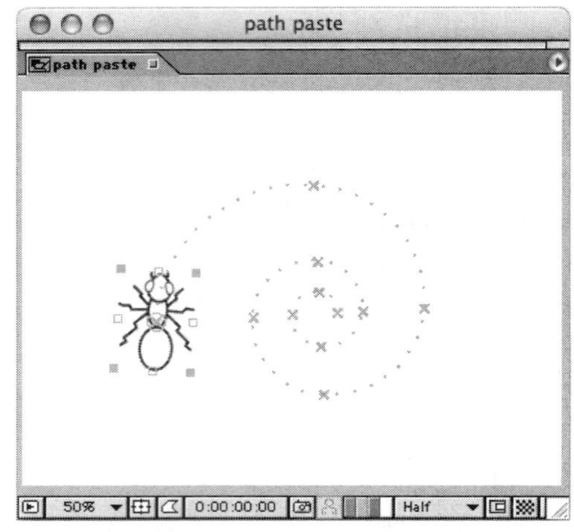

Figure 15.46 Edit the motion path as you would any other.

Using a Value, Speed, or Velocity Graph

To control the temporal interpolation manually, you must reveal a graph of the layer property. Most properties in the layer outline expand to reveal a value graph and a velocity graph. In contrast, spatial properties—Position, Effect Point, and Anchor Point—expand to reveal a speed graph.

Value graph

A *value graph* measures a (nonspatial) property's value vertically and its time horizontally (**Figure 15.47**). The units in which values are expressed depend on the type of property: Rotation is measured in rotations and degrees, Opacity in percentages, and so on. The slope of the line between keyframes represents the rate of change, in units/second. Straight lines indicate a constant rate; curved lines indicate a changing rate, or acceleration.

The Switches/Modes panel of the Timeline window displays other useful information about the value graph:

Highest Value displays the value of the keyframe with the greatest value.

Lowest Value displays the value of the keyframe with the least value.

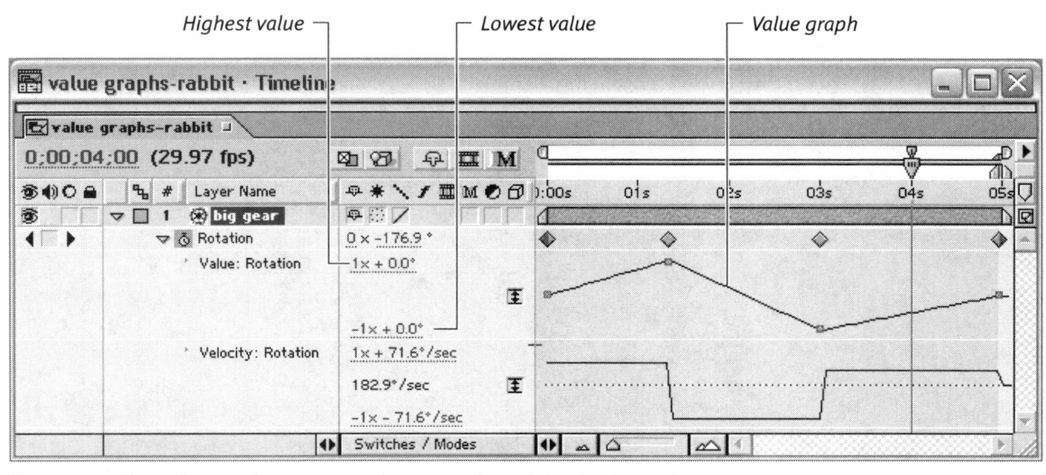

Figure 15.47 The value graph measures value vertically and time horizontally.

Speed and velocity graphs

A speed graph measures rates of change in pixels/sec (**Figure 15.48**). The units measured by a velocity graph depend on the property type: degrees of rotation/sec, percentage opacity/sec, and so on. Regardless of the specific property, the rate of change (units/sec) is measured vertically, and time (sec) is measured horizontally in both graphs. The slope of the graph represents acceleration (units/sec/sec), which is dictated by the temporal interpolation method.

You can adjust the curve by dragging the *ease handles*. Ease handles look and work a bit like direction handles, but they always extend horizontally from a keyframe. As you drag an ease handle, see how it influences curves in both the speed (or velocity) graph and the value graph. (Consult the section "Analyzing the graphs" to see how each graph represents value changes.)

The Switches/Modes panel of the Timeline window displays other useful information about the speed or velocity graph:

Highest Speed is the property value's highest rate of change at any frame.

Lowest Speed is the property value's lowest rate of change at any frame.

Current Speed is the property value's speed at the current frame.

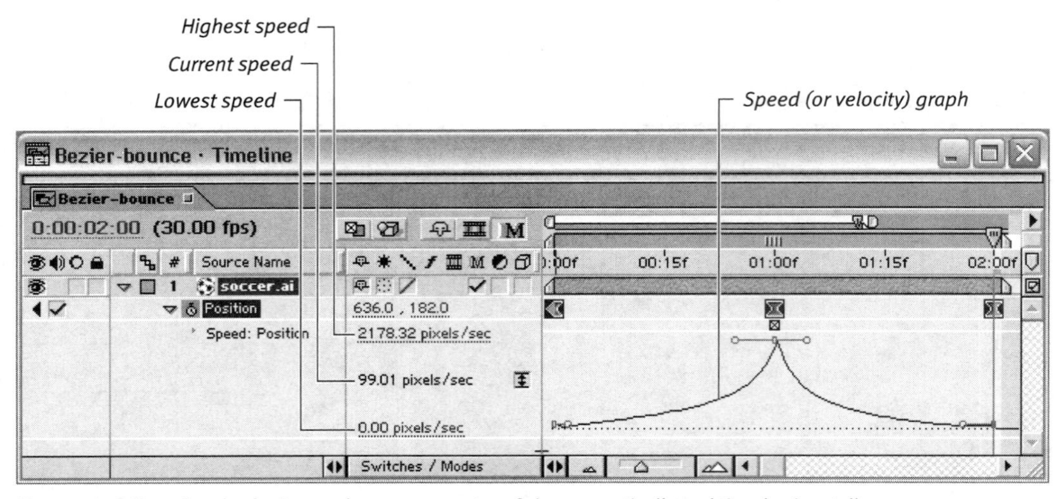

Figure 15.48 Speed and velocity graphs measure rates of change vertically and time horizontally.

Viewing Property Graphs

Because they can take up so much screen space, you'll keep property graphs hidden most of the time. Reveal a property graph whenever you want to analyze or adjust the property's interpolated values.

To view a property graph:

1. In the Timeline window, expand the layer outline to reveal the animated properties for which you want to view a value graph (**Figure 15.49**).
2. Click the triangle to the left of the property name in the layer outline (**Figure 15.50**).

   The triangle spins clockwise to reveal the graph for the property. If there's no triangle, this indicates that the property presently contains no keyframes.

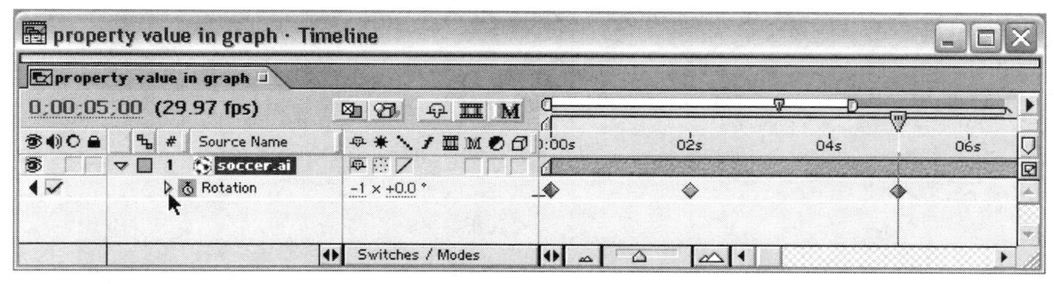

Figure 15.49 Expand the layer outline to reveal the anzimated properties that you want to view for a value graph.

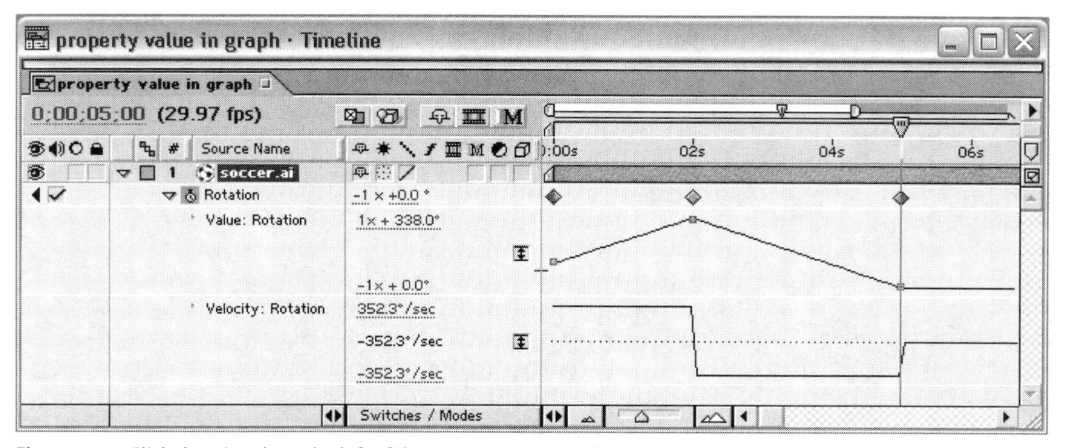

Figure 15.50 Click the triangle to the left of the property name in the layer outline to view the graph.

To change the boundaries of a property graph:

1. Click the triangle to the left of the property name in the layer outline to reveal a property graph.
2. Position the cursor over the bottom of the property's graph track in the Timeline window (**Figure 15.51**).
   The cursor changes into an icon with up and down arrows.
3. Drag the cursor up to reduce the height of the value graph, or drag it down to increase the height (**Figure 15.52**).

✔ Tip

- Here's a reminder of something you learned in Chapter 7: Press U to reveal all the animated properties of all the selected layers.

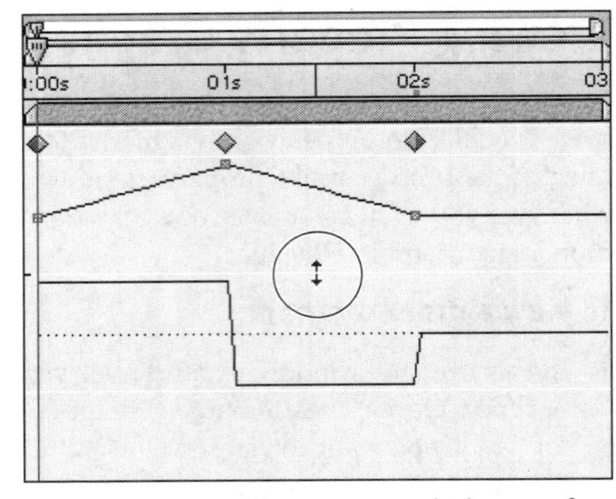

Figure 15.51 Position the cursor over the bottom of the property's graph track until the cursor changes to indicate vertical resizing.

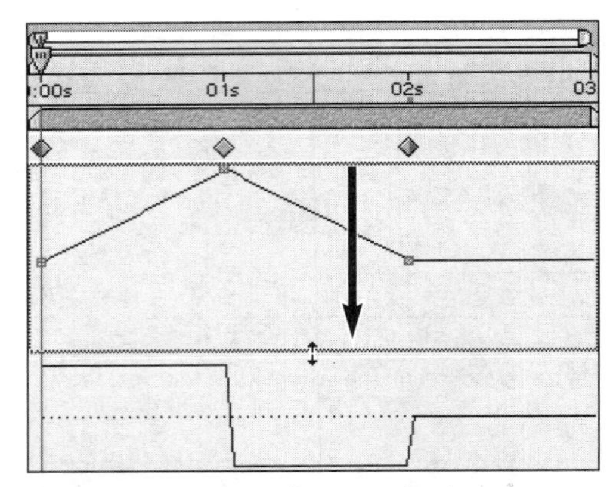

Figure 15.52 Drag up or down to resize the graph's border.

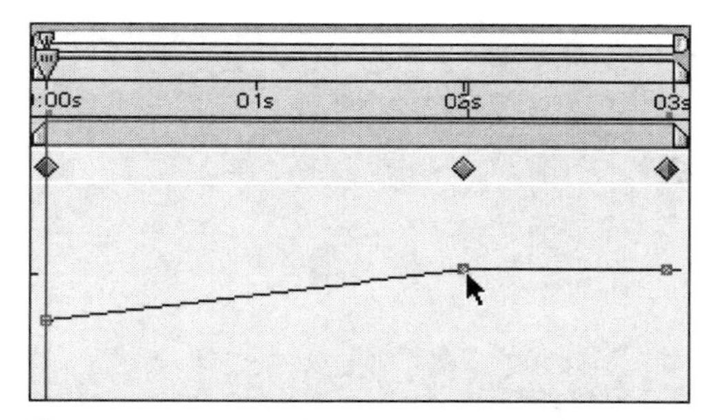

Figure 15.53 Increase the speed between keyframes...

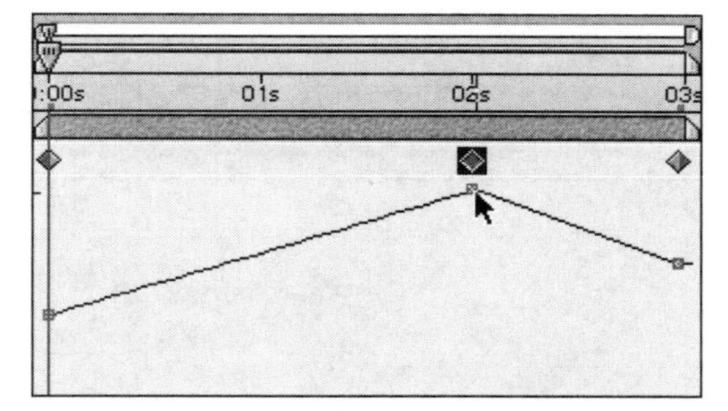

Figure 15.54 ...by increasing the difference in value...

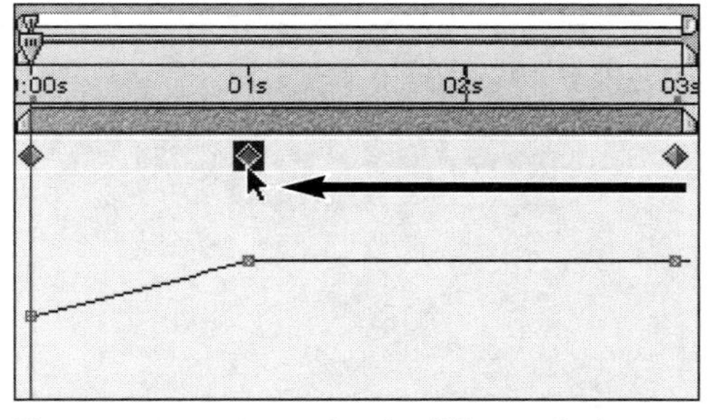

Figure 15.55 ...or decreasing the difference in time.

Speed, Velocity, and Acceleration

In After Effects, spatial properties expand to reveal a speed graph; other properties expand to reveal a value graph and a velocity graph. Before you use these graphs to control temporal interpolation, you must understand the concepts of speed, velocity, and acceleration.

Speed and velocity

Back in physics class, you learned the following:

$$\text{Speed} = \frac{\text{distance}}{\text{time}}$$

If physics class is but a distant memory, imagine a car's speedometer, which expresses speed in miles per hour. In After Effects, the units of measure are smaller—pixels/sec—but the concept is the same: A fast-moving object covers a greater distance in less time; a slow-moving object covers less distance in a greater amount time.

You can describe other properties in similar terms: a fast fade or quick rotation, for example. In After Effects, the rate of change of a nonspatial property is called *velocity*.

When you think about it, speed and velocity measure different properties in the same way: as a change in value/change in time. For this reason, speed and velocity are often discussed interchangeably, and the two graphs work the same way.

You can control the speed of an action by changing either the difference in value or the difference in time between keyframes (**Figures 15.53**, **15.54**, and **15.55**).

continues on next page

For example, if a fan blade appears to rotate too slowly, you can increase the number of rotations. Ten rotations in one second spin much faster than one rotation per second. Alternatively, you can decrease the time an action takes to make a corresponding change in value. For example, if a character crosses the screen too slowly, you can have the character traverse the same distance in less time. Crossing the screen in one second is faster than traveling the same distance in five seconds.

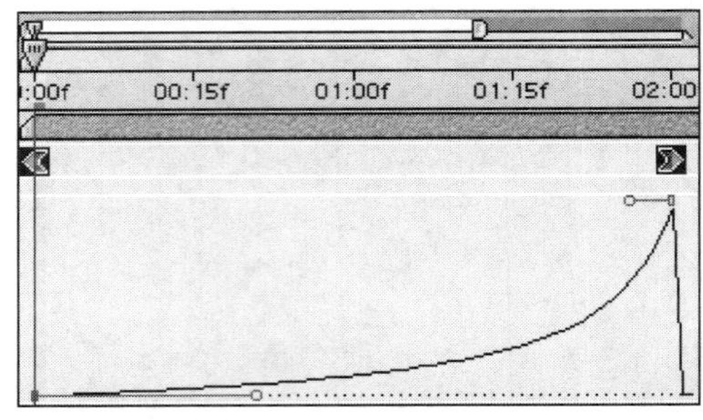

Figure 15.56 Temporal interpolation affects speed changes between keyframes to achieve acceleration...

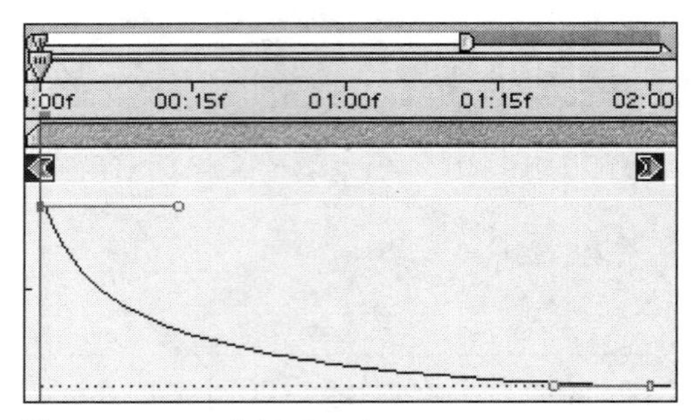

Figure 15.57 ...and deceleration.

Temporal interpolation and acceleration

Speed and velocity can remain constant, or they can vary from moment to moment. When speed changes over time, it's called *acceleration* or *deceleration*. In After Effects, you can control changes in speed with temporal interpolation (**Figures 15.56** and **15.57**).

It's important to understand that temporal interpolation doesn't affect speed directly. Temporal interpolation affects neither the values of the keyframes nor the amount of time between them. If it takes one second for an image to go from Point A to Point B, no type of temporal interpolation will change that fact. Instead, temporal interpolation determines how the speed changes in that second—at a constant speed (like the hands of a clock), accelerating from its starting point (like a rocket at liftoff), decelerating (like a docking boat), or (in the case of hold interpolation) suddenly appearing in the next position.

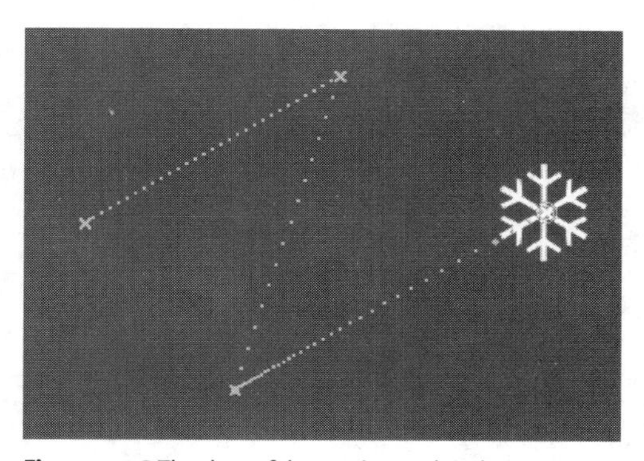

Figure 15.58 The dots of the motion path indicate speed.

Figure 15.59 Hold interpolation displays keyframes without a motion path.

Viewing Speed in the Motion Path

The speed of spatial properties is represented in both the speed graph and the motion path. In the motion path, the spacing between dots indicates speed. Closely spaced dots indicate slower speeds; more widely spaced dots indicate faster speeds. If the dot spacing changes between keyframes, this means the speed is changing—accelerating or decelerating (**Figure 15.58**). When hold temporal interpolation is applied to a spatial property, no motion path connects it with the adjacent keyframe (**Figure 15.59**). As you alter the speed or temporal interpolation of a spatial property, watch how the motion path also changes.

Changing Property Values in a Value Graph

In Chapter 7, you learned several methods of adjusting keyframe values. The following tasks describe how to change the values using a property's value graph. In a value graph, you can add keyframes and change their values but not their positions in time.

To change layer-property values in the value graph:

1. Expand the layer outline to view the value graph for a layer property (**Figure 15.60**).
2. In Tools, make sure the Selection tool is chosen.
3. In the value graph, drag a keyframe up to increase the value or down to decrease the value (**Figure 15.61**).

   You may drag the value beyond the current top or bottom of the graph. The value graph will resize to accommodate the range of values.

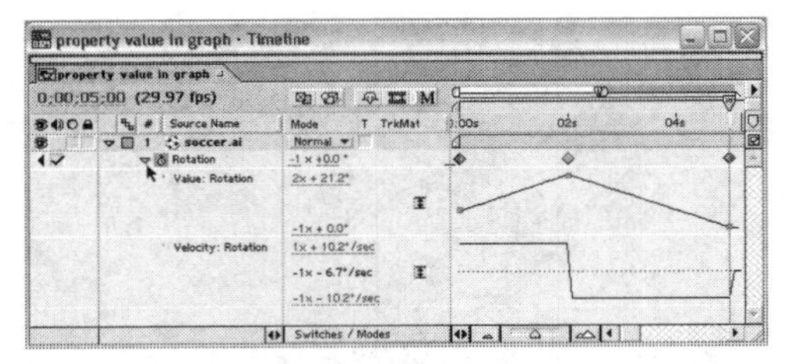

Figure 15.60 Expand the layer outline to view the value graph for a layer property.

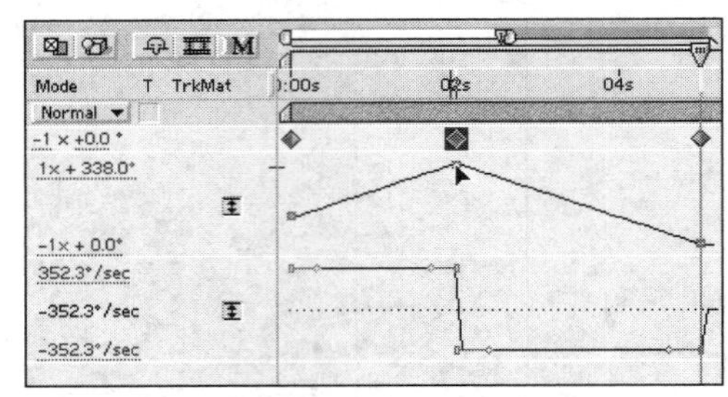

Figure 15.61 Drag a keyframe up to increase the value or down to decrease the value.

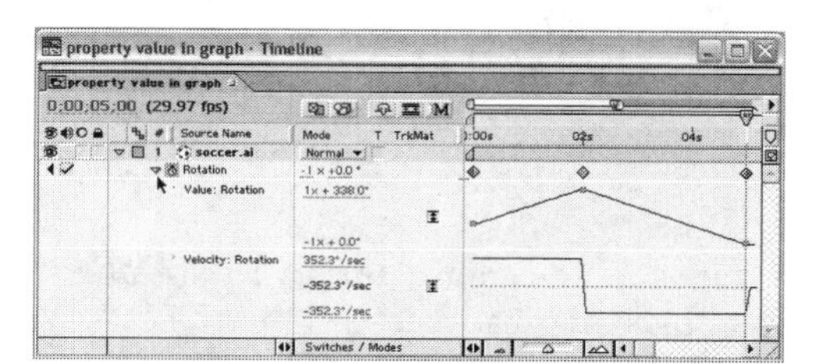

Figure 15.62 Expand the layer outline to view the value graph for a layer property.

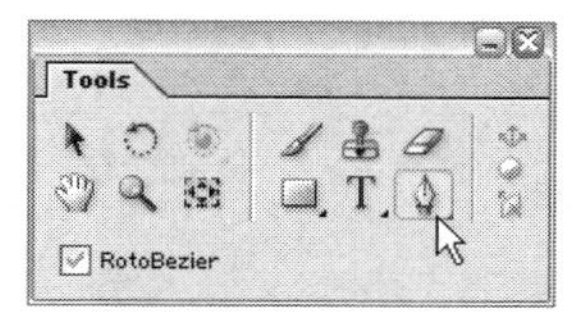

Figure 15.63 In the Tools palette, choose the Pen tool.

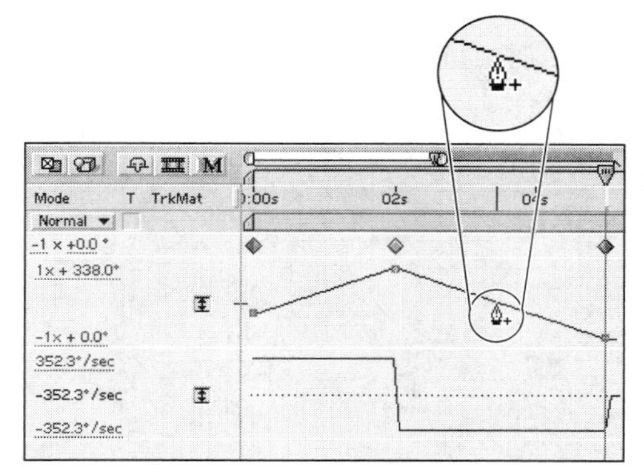

Figure 15.64 The Pen tool becomes the Add Vertex tool. Click the value graph to create a new keyframe.

To add keyframes to the value graph:

1. Expand the layer outline to view the value graph for a layer property (**Figure 15.62**).
2. In Tools, choose the Pen tool (**Figure 15.63**).
3. Position the Pen tool over the line in the value graph until the Pen tool appears as an Add Vertex tool (a Pen tool with a plus sign).
4. Click the value graph to create a new keyframe (**Figure 15.64**).

   A keyframe appears as a dot in the value graph and as a Keyframe icon in the property track. Initially, the keyframe uses the default interpolation type.
5. To stop adding keyframes, choose the Selection tool in the Tools palette.

✔ Tips

- If you use the Pen tool to add a keyframe to the value graph, dragging extends a direction handle.
- In the value graph, you can change only the value of the keyframe, not its position in time. To move the keyframe in time, you must drag the Keyframe icon above the value graph.

Recognizing Temporal Interpolation

After Effects represents temporal interpolation differently, depending on where you look. The Keyframe icons indicate the type of incoming and outgoing interpolation. Below the icons, graphs provide detailed information and control over temporal interpolation.

Analyzing the graphs

Compare the value and velocity graphs to see how each depicts the same temporal interpolation (**Figure 15.65**). You can manipulate the graphs directly to alter the rates of change between keyframes.

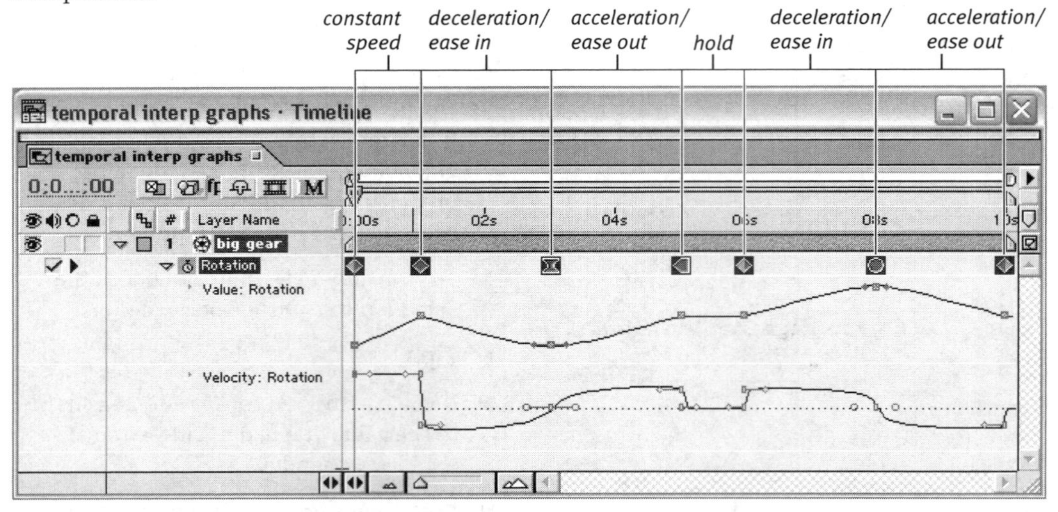

Figure 15.65 The value graph shows changes in value; the velocity and speed graphs show changes in speed. Examine how each graph shape corresponds with certain types of temporal interpolation.

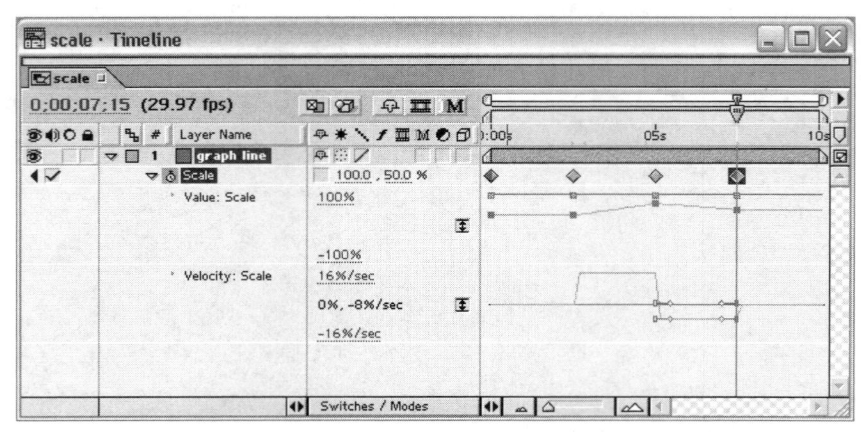

Figure 15.66 Scale, for example, consists of separate vertical and horizontal values. Such properties display two graphs, one for each value.

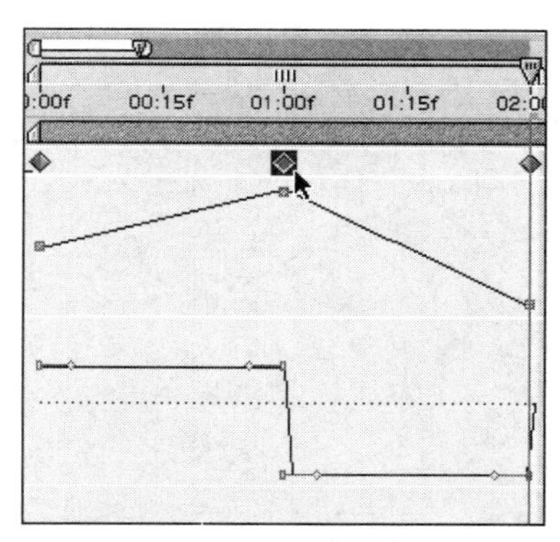

Figure 15.67 Command-click (Mac) or Ctrl-click (Windows) a Keyframe icon to toggle between linear interpolation (with a diamond-shaped icon)...

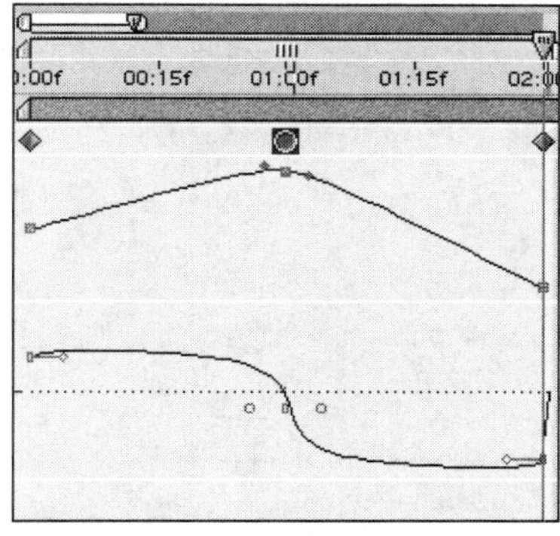

Figure 15.68 ...and auto Bézier interpolation (with a circular icon).

Adjusting Temporal Interpolation in the Value Graph

For nonspatial properties, you can adjust temporal interpolation in either a value graph or a velocity graph. Adjusting the rates of change in the value graph is much like creating Bézier curves in a motion path. In the value graph, the property value is measured vertically and time is measured horizontally.

Note that some properties have two aspects. A 2D layer's Scale property, for example, has separate vertical and horizontal values. If you adjust these aspects separately, the property displays two graphs, one for each value (**Figure 15.66**).

To toggle between linear and auto Bézier temporal interpolation:

1. Expand the layer outline to reveal an animated layer property.
2. In either the property's track in the time ruler or the value graph, Command-click (Mac) or Ctrl-click (Windows) a Keyframe icon to toggle between linear and auto Bézier interpolation (**Figure 15.67**).
3. The Keyframe icon changes from Bézier-type interpolation to linear, or from linear to auto Bézier (**Figure 15.68**).

Table 15.2

Recognizing temporal interpolation

Temporal interpolation	In the value graph	In the speed/velocity graph
No speed change	Horizontal line	Horizontal line
Constant speed	Straight line with any slope	Horizontal line
Sudden speed change	Sharp corner	Disconnected line/ease handles
Acceleration	Curve with steep slope	Upward-sloping curve
Deceleration	Curve with shallow slope	Downward-sloping curve
Holding	Horizontal line, unconnected	Horizontal line, where current speed = 0

To convert auto Bézier interpolation to continuous Bézier:

1. Expand the layer outline to reveal a value graph for a nonspatial property.
2. Select one or more auto Bézier keyframes in the motion path.
3. In the value graph, drag a direction handle (**Figure 15.69**).

   The Keyframe icon in the property track changes from auto Bézier to continuous Bézier. The direction handles become unequal but retain their continuous relationship.

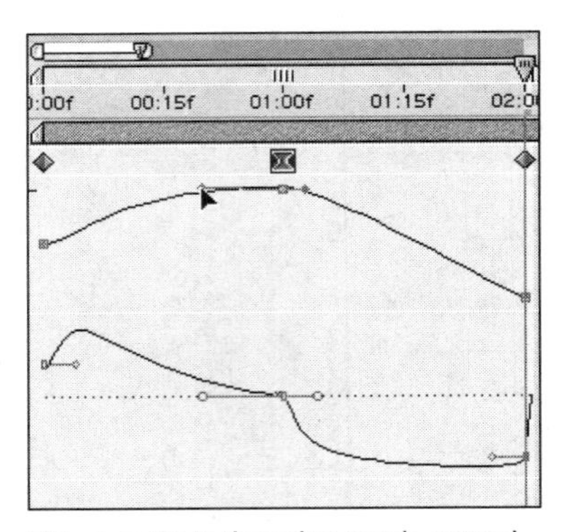

Figure 15.69 In the value graph, extend a direction line manually to use continuous Bézier interpolation.

To convert continuous Bézier to Bézier, and vice versa:

1. Expand the layer outline to reveal a value graph for a nonspatial property.
2. Select one or more keyframes in the motion path.
3. In the value graph, Command-drag (Mac) or Ctrl-drag (Windows) a direction handle (**Figure 15.70**).

   The Selection tool becomes the Convert Vertex tool when you position it over a direction handle. Dragging a direction handle of a Bézier keyframe converts it to continuous Bézier with two related direction handles; dragging a direction handle of a continuous Bézier keyframe splits the direction handles, converting it to Bézier (**Figure 15.71**).

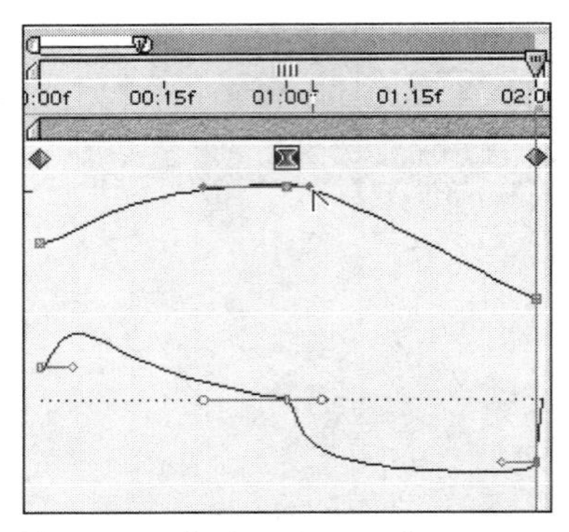

Figure 15.70 In the value graph, Command-drag (Mac) or Ctrl-drag (Windows) a direction handle.

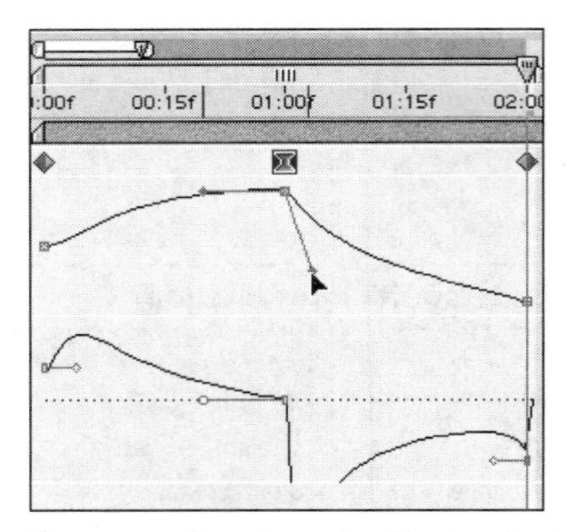

Figure 15.71 Dragging a direction handle of a continuous Bézier keyframe splits the direction handles, converting it to Bézier.

✔ Tip

- As usual, avoid converting a keyframe unintentionally: Invoke the Convert Vertex tool only when you want to convert a keyframe; otherwise, use the Selection tool.

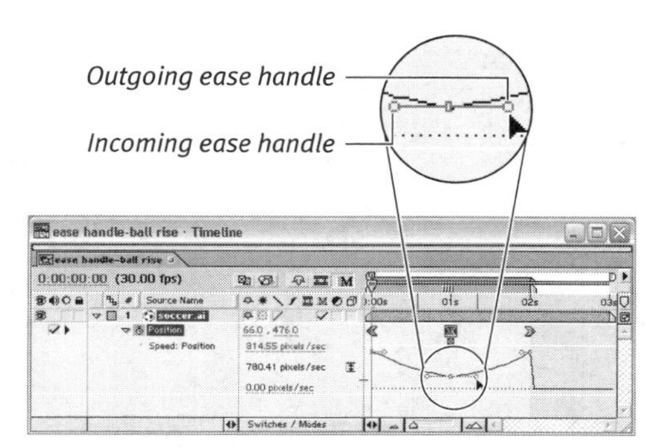

Figure 15.72 Ease handles behave much like direction handles.

Adjusting Temporal Interpolation in the Speed and Velocity Graphs

Speed and velocity graphs take some getting used to: Although curve-manipulation techniques are similar to other path-editing techniques in principle, they feel different in practice. Don't worry: With patience and experience, you'll get the hang of them.

In speed and velocity graphs, *ease handles* are comparable to the direction handles on a Bézier curve. Like direction handles, ease handles influence the shape of the curve. In this case, however, the curve charts a change in speed—acceleration and deceleration (**Figure 15.72**).

The vertical position of an ease handle corresponds to the property value's rate of change at the keyframe—its speed or velocity at that moment. Dragging the ease handle up increases the rate of change; dragging it down decreases the rate of change.

The incoming ease handle affects the curve to the left of a keyframe; the outgoing ease handle affects the curve to the right. Extending the incoming ease handle increases the rate of change from the previous keyframe, resulting in a more pronounced acceleration or deceleration. Retracting the handle decreases the rate of change, resulting in a more constant velocity from the previous keyframe to the one you're adjusting. Extending and retracting the outgoing ease handle has the same effect on the next keyframe.

You can move the incoming and outgoing ease handles in tandem (much like a smooth point or continuous Bézier) or separately (like a corner point or Bézier). Ease handles literally split, occupying different vertical positions on the graph.

To adjust the temporal interpolation:

1. Expand the layer outline to view the speed or velocity graph for an animated layer property.
2. Select the keyframes you want to adjust (**Figure 15.73**).
3. *Do any of the following* to the incoming or outgoing ease handles:
   - ▲ Drag an ease handle up to increase the incoming or outgoing speed at a keyframe (**Figure 15.74**).
   - ▲ Drag an ease handle down to decrease the incoming or outgoing speed at a keyframe.
   - ▲ Drag an incoming ease handle to the left to increase the influence of the previous keyframe's value (**Figure 15.75**).
   - ▲ Drag an outgoing ease handle to the right to increase the influence of the next keyframe's value.
   - ▲ Command-drag (Mac) or Control-drag (Windows) an ease handle to split the ease handles, allowing them to move independently of one another.

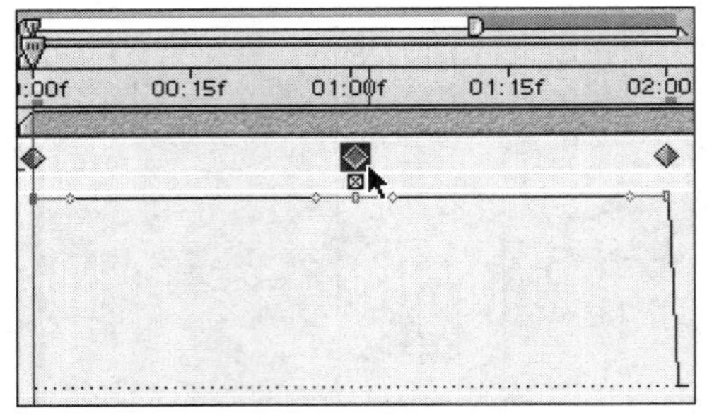

Figure 15.73 Select the keyframes you want to adjust.

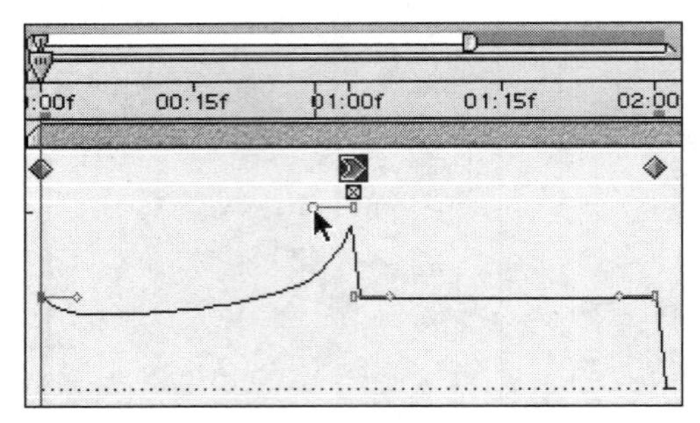

Figure 15.74 Drag an ease handle up to increase the incoming or outgoing speed at a keyframe.

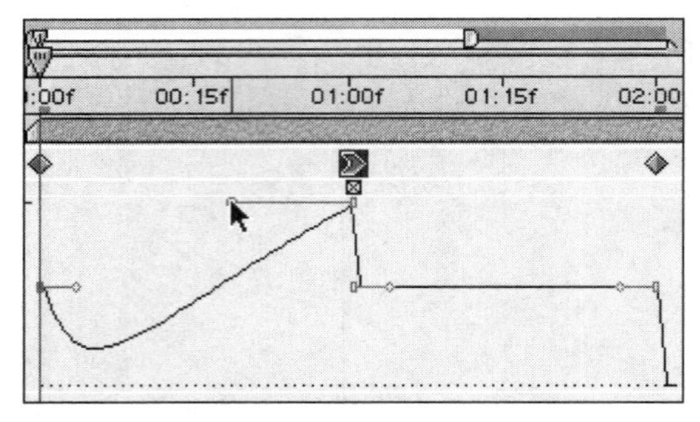

Figure 15.75 Drag an incoming ease handle to the left to increase the influence of the previous keyframe's value.

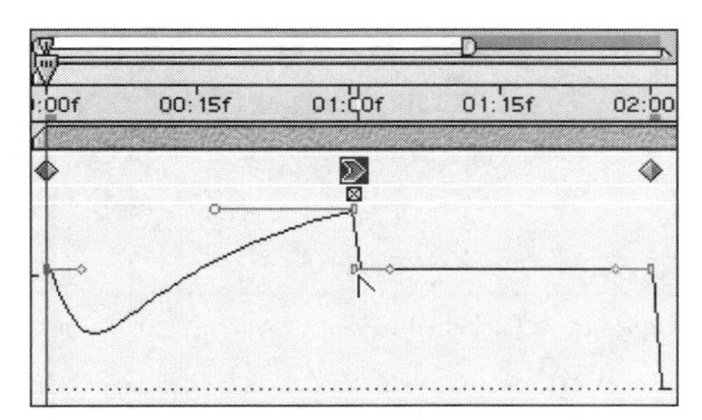

Figure 15.76 Command-click (Mac) or Ctrl-click (Windows) the center of an ease handle...

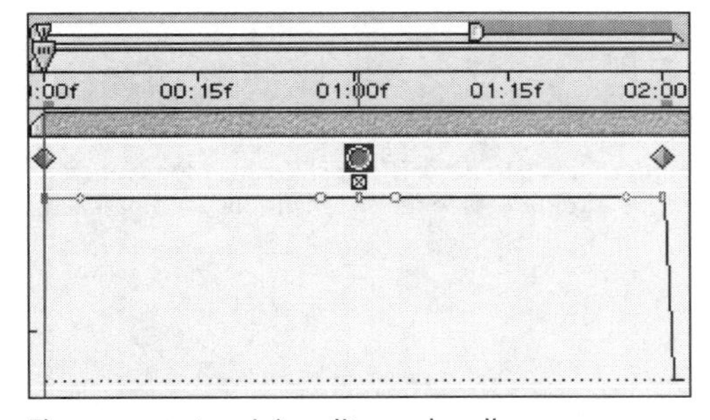

Figure 15.77...to rejoin split ease handles; or Command-drag (Mac) or Ctrl-drag (Windows) to split the ease handles again, allowing them to move independently of one another.

▲ Command-drag (Mac) or Control-drag (Windows) a split ease handle to rejoin the incoming and outgoing handles (**Figures 15.76** and **15.77**).

✔ Tip

■ Notice how splitting ease handles works in the same way as converting continuous Bézier direction handles to independent Bézier direction handles. Pressing Command (Mac) or Ctrl (Windows) temporarily invokes the Convert tool. Like direction handles, ease handles remain split until you reconvert them.

Resizing Property Graphs Automatically

When you're adjusting ease handles, it's possible to drag controls off the scale in the value or speed/velocity graph. You can make the graphs resize automatically by selecting a button in the Switches panel of the Timeline window.

To adjust the size of a property graph automatically:

- When a keyframe's controls are positioned outside the confines of its value or speed/velocity graph (**Figure 15.78**), click the box in the Switches panel to make the Resize icon appear (**Figure 15.79**).

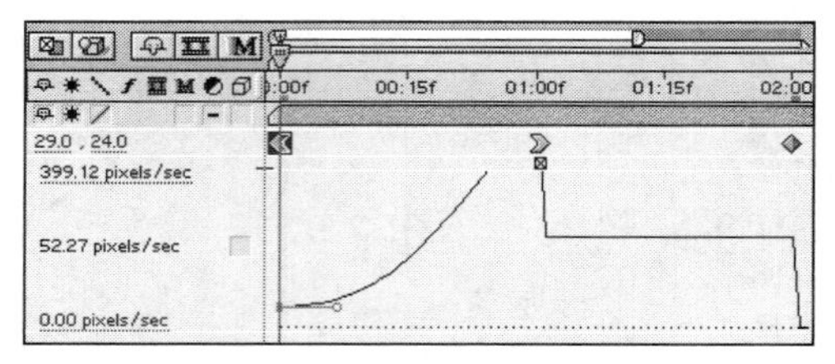

Figure 15.78 Click the box in the Switches panel...

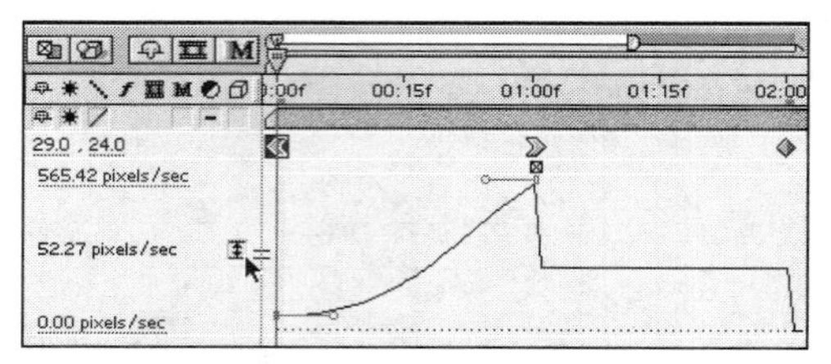

Figure 15.79 ...to make the Resize icon appear and cause After Effects to resize the graphs automatically.

Mastering Temporal Interpolation

Remember the examples of spatial interpolation methods earlier in this chapter? Now you can take the same examples and make their movement more convincing by adjusting their temporal interpolation. Experiment with the temporal interpolation of nonspatial properties until you're comfortable with value, speed, and velocity graphs.

Linear interpolation

A ball from a pong game ricocheting off a paddle could use linear temporal interpolation to maintain a constant speed through the keyframe (**Figure 15.80**). However, a billiard ball in a similar real-world situation would gradually lose speed.

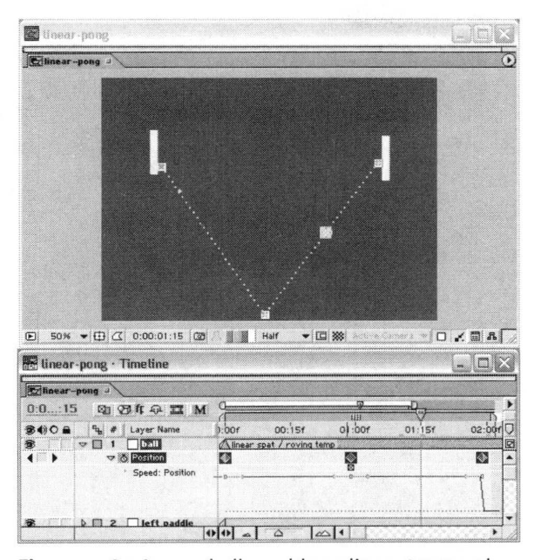

Figure 15.80 A pong ball would use linear temporal interpolation through a keyframe.

Auto Bézier interpolation

With linear interpolation, speed changes instantaneously; in the real world, however, this is rarely the case. Use auto Bézier interpolation to change speed more gradually (**Figure 15.81**). The effects of this type of interpolation are easiest to see when the value changes are great. You might try it with a nonspatial property, such as rotation, to see the difference more clearly.

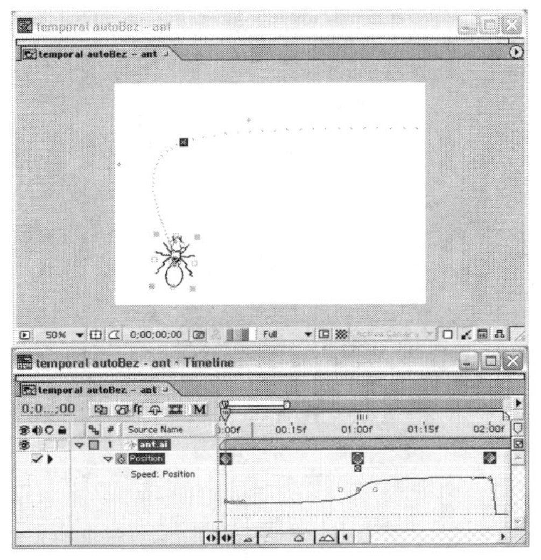

Figure 15.81 Auto Bézier interpolation automatically creates gradual speed changes.

Continuous Bézier interpolation

A flying ball moves fastest just after it's first propelled; it then loses speed at its apex and accelerates one more time as it falls to earth. Use continuous Bézier temporal interpolation to ease the ball's speed at its apex (**Figure 15.82**).

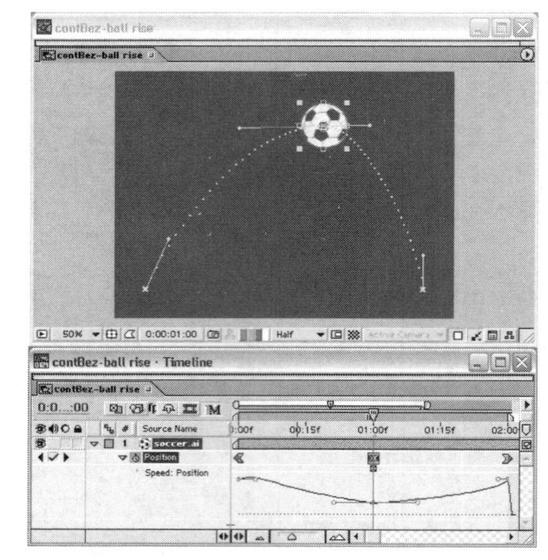

Figure 15.82 Use continuous Bézier interpolation to ease a ball's speed at its apex manually; it then accelerates again as it falls.

Bézier interpolation

A bouncing ball accelerates as it falls. After the bounce, gravity's pull begins to slow it down. You can use Bézier interpolation to create a sharp increase of speed at the bounce (**Figure 15.83**).

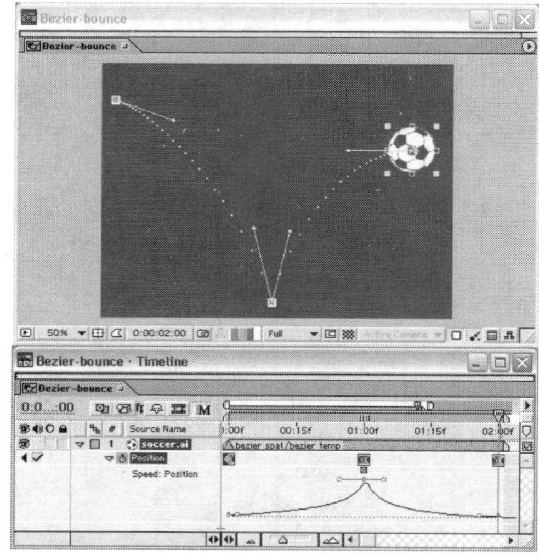

Figure 15.83 Use Bézier interpolation to accelerate a ball through the bounce.

✔ Tips

- Spatial and temporal interpolation methods for a given keyframe don't have to match (as they do in these examples).
- If you're using After Effects Professional, you can employ Motion Math scripts to automate the creation of keyframes that simulate naturalistic physics and relationships between layers. The gravity.mm script, for example, can calculate a bounce automatically.
- You can define relationships among properties by using After Effects' Expressions feature. See Chapter 17 for details.

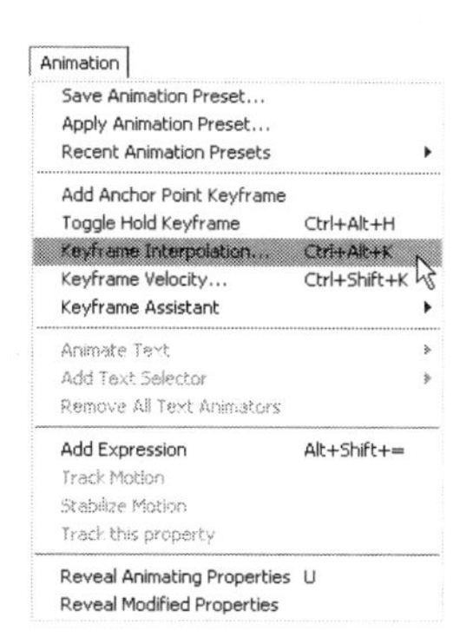

Figure 15.95 Choose Animation > Keyframe Interpolation.

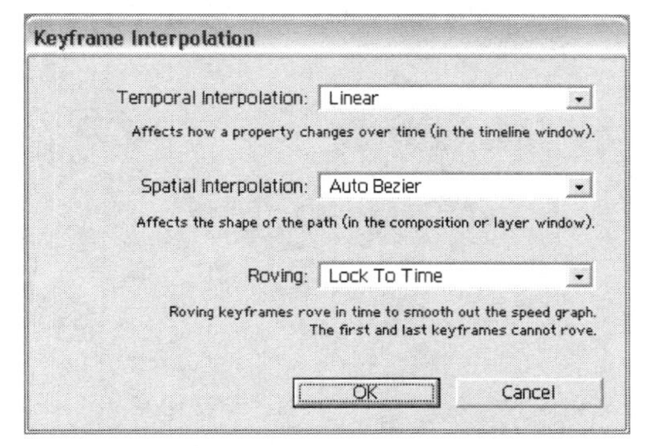

Figure 15.96 The Keyframe Interpolation dialog box appears.

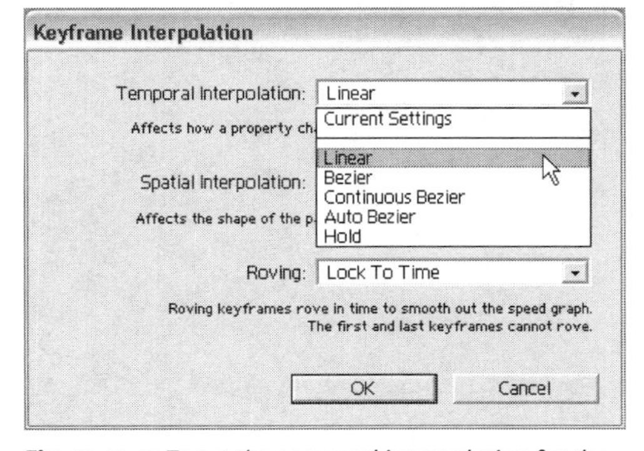

Figure 15.97 To set the temporal interpolation for the selected keyframes, select an option from the pull-down menu.

Changing Interpolation

You can also specify keyframe interpolation and roving keyframes using a dialog box. This is one way you can apply hold interpolation to a keyframe.

To change a keyframe's interpolation type using a dialog box:

1. Select one or more keyframes for a layer property.
2. Choose Animation > Keyframe Interpolation, or press Option-Command-K (Mac) or Alt-Ctrl-K (Windows) (**Figure 15.95**).

   The Keyframe Interpolation dialog box appears (**Figure 15.96**).
3. To set the temporal interpolation for the selected keyframes, select an option from the pull-down menu (**Figure 15.97**):

   Current Settings retains the temporal interpolation methods currently applied to the selected keyframes. Use this setting when you want to change other interpolation settings but preserve the temporal interpolation.

   Linear, **Bézier**, **Continuous Bézier**, **Auto Bézier**, and **Hold** apply the temporal interpolation method you choose to selected keyframes, using default values.

continues on next page

4. To set the spatial interpolation for the selected keyframes, select an option from the pull-down menu (**Figure 15.98**):

   Current Settings retains the spatial interpolation methods currently applied to the selected keyframes. Use this setting when you want to change other interpolation settings but preserve the spatial interpolation

   Linear, **Bézier**, **Continuous Bézier**, and **Auto Bézier** apply the spatial interpolation method you choose to selected keyframes, using default values.

5. For roving keyframes, choose an option for spatial layer properties (**Figure 15.99**):

   Current Settings retains the time-positioning method used by selected keyframes.

   Rove Across Time turns the selected keyframes into roving keyframes, which are repositioned in time automatically to reduce the rates of change between the nonroving keyframes before and after the selection.

   Lock To Time makes selected keyframes standard, time-specific keyframes.

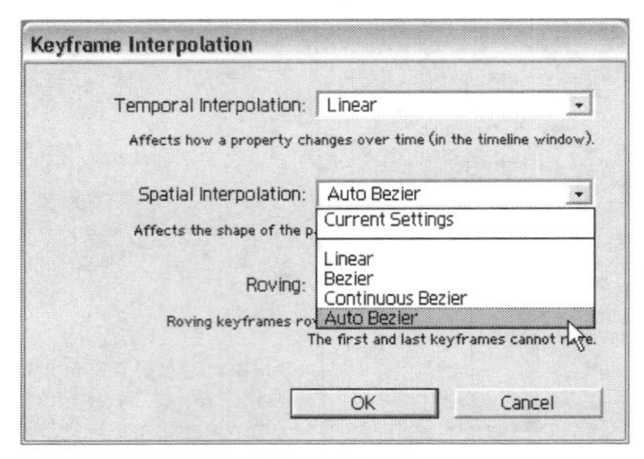

Figure 15.98 To set the spatial interpolation for the selected keyframes, select an option from the pull-down menu.

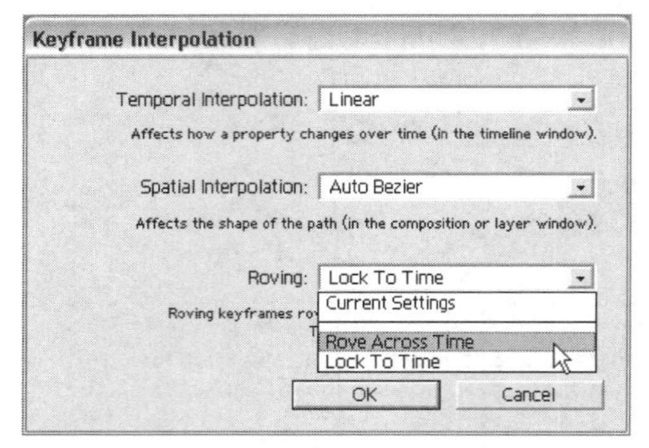

Figure 15.99 For roving keyframes, choose an option for spatial layer properties.

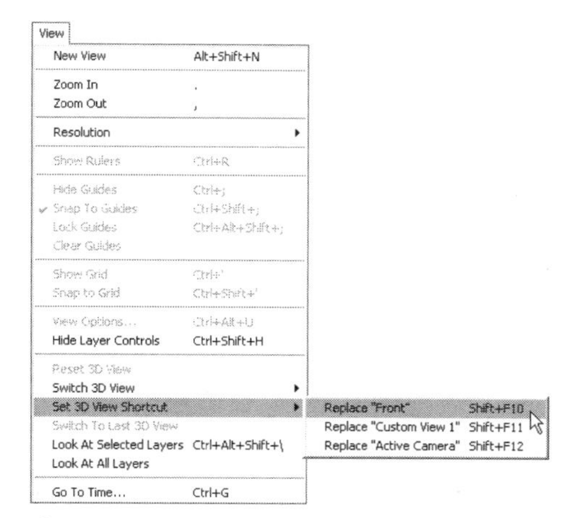

Figure 16.7 Choose View > Set 3D View Shortcut, and select the view you want to replace for the F10, F11, or F12 shortcut.

To set or replace 3D-view shortcuts:

1. In the 3D Views pull-down menu of the Composition window, select the view to which you want to assign a shortcut.
2. *Do either of the following:*
   - ▲ Choose View > Set 3D View Shortcut, and select the view you want to replace for the F10, F11, or F12 shortcut (**Figure 16.7**).
   - ▲ Press Shift-F10, Shift-F11, or Shift-F12.

   The view shortcut you selected is replaced by the current 3D view. Pressing the shortcut button selects the corresponding view.

To toggle among 3D views:

- ◆ Press F10, F11, or F12.

  The 3D view saved for the corresponding shortcut is selected in the Composition window.

✔ Tips

- As you progress through this chapter, view your 3D layers from different angles. After you grow accustomed to adjusting 3D layer properties, you'll learn how to adjust the views themselves using Camera tools. Finally, you'll create your own cameras and move them around the 3D composition. In other words, take it one step at a time.
- When you're working with 3D layers and cameras, it can be particularly useful to view the same comp or layer from different angles. To do so, choose Workspace > and select a preset workspace for one, two, or four comp views. You can also arrange and save a custom view.

Using Axis Modes

In the layer outline, the spatial transform properties (Position and Rotation properties) are expressed in terms of *X, Y,* and *Z* axes, which intersect at the center of your composition's 3D "world." When you transform a layer by dragging in the Composition window, however, you won't always want changes to occur according to these world axes.

Axis modes let you specify whether transformations you make in the Comp window are expressed in terms of the 3D object (Local Axis mode), the 3D world (World Axis mode), or the current view (View Axis mode). Choosing how the axes are aligned makes moving and rotating 3D objects in the Comp window a more flexible and intuitive process. The axis mode you employ doesn't affect transformations you make using the property controls in the layer outline; instead, these are expressed in terms of the world axis coordinate system.

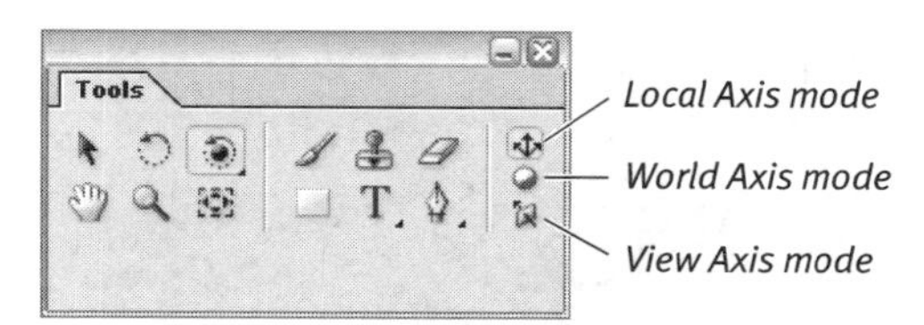

Figure 16.8 In Tools palette, select an axis mode.

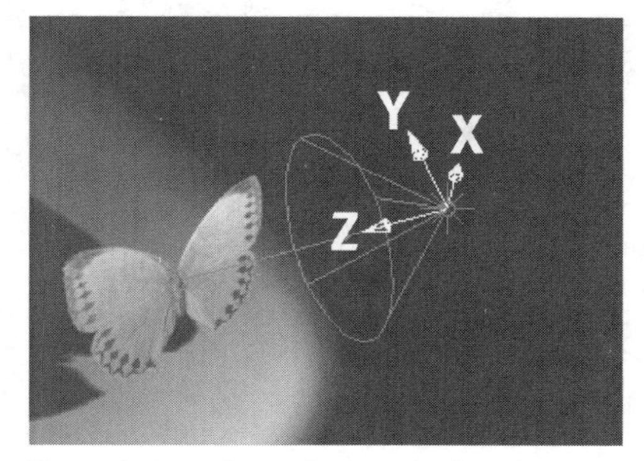

Figure 16.9 Here, the Local Axis mode aligns the axes to the selected object (a light). *X* is red, *Y* is green, and *Z* is blue. In Figures 16.9–16.11, the axes are highlighted and labeled to make them identifiable in a black and white image.

To change axis modes:

1. Select a 3D layer, camera, or light.
2. In the Tools palette, select an axis mode (**Figure 16.8**):

   Local Axis mode —Aligns the axes used for transformations to the selected 3D object (**Figure 16.9**).

   World Axis mode —Aligns the axes used for transformations to the 3D space of the composition **(Figure 16.10)**.

   View Axis mode —Aligns the axes used for transformations to the current view (**Figure 16.11**).

   The set of axes you select appears in the Composition window.
3. Transform the selected object in the Composition window by dragging it or by altering its transform properties in the layer outline.

   Transformations occur according to the axes you selected. However, the transformation property values in the layer outline continue to be expressed in absolute terms, according to the world axis coordinate system.

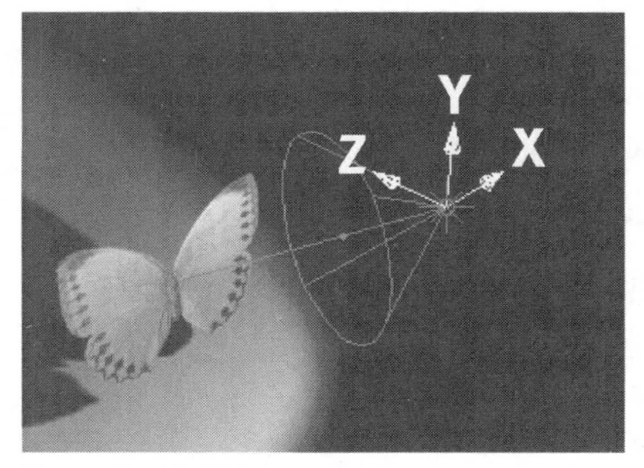

Figure 16.10 World Axis mode aligns the axes to the 3D world of the composition.

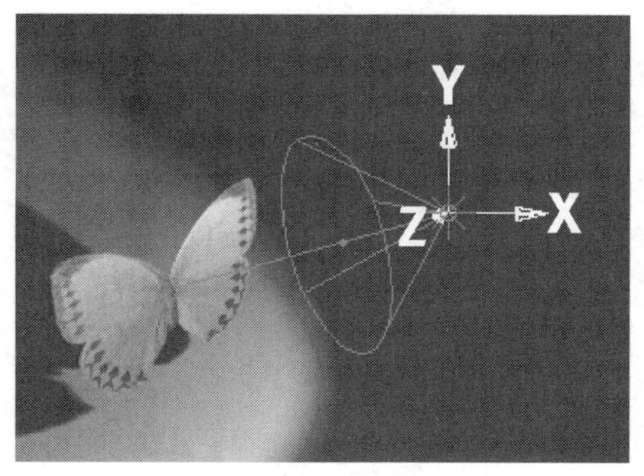

Figure 16.11 View Axis mode aligns the axes to the current 3D view.

Using 3D Position

For 3D layers, position is expressed as a three-dimensional property with values for *X*, *Y*, and *Z* coordinates along the world axes. As with 2D position, 3D position corresponds to a layer's anchor point.

Figure 16.12 In the Composition window, position the Selection tool over the axis along which you want to move the layer. The Selection tool icon should include the axis letter.

To move a 3D layer in the Comp window:

1. In the 3D View pull-down menu, select a view.
2. In Tools, select an axis mode.
3. Select a 3D layer, camera, or light.

   The selected layer's axes appear. The *X* axis is red; the *Y* axis is green; the *Z* axis is blue. The axes align according to the axis mode you specified.
4. In the Composition window, position the Selection tool over the axis along which you want to move the layer (**Figure 16.12**).

   The Selection tool icon includes the letter corresponding to the axis:

   [X] to move the layer along the *X* axis,
   [Y] to move the layer along the *Y* axis, or
   [Z] to move the layer along the *Z* axis.

Figure 16.13 Drag the layer along the selected axis.

5. Drag the layer along the selected axis (**Figure 16.13**).

   In the layer outline of the Timeline window, the layer's Position property reflects the changes in terms of the world axis coordinate system.

✔ Tips

- You can change the anchor point of a 3D layer just as you would a 2D layer—except that the anchor point for 3D layers includes a value for its *Z*-axis coordinate. You will only be able to adjust the *X* and *Y* values of an anchor point in a Layer window. To adjust an anchor point's position along the *Z* axis, use the property controls in the layer outline, or drag the anchor point in the Composition window using the Pan Behind tool. As you'll recall from Chapter 7, "Properties and Keyframes," the Pan Behind tool recalculates position as it transforms the anchor point, leaving the layer's relative position in the composition undisturbed.
- Lights and cameras can also have transform properties that define their point of interest. See "Using the Point of Interest" later in this chapter.

Using 3D Orientation and Rotation

Making a layer three-dimensional adds a *Z*-axis dimension not only to its Position property but also to its Rotation property. However, the properties that control the way a layer rotates along its axes fall into two categories: Orientation and Rotation (**Figure 16.14**). The property you choose to adjust depends on the task at hand.

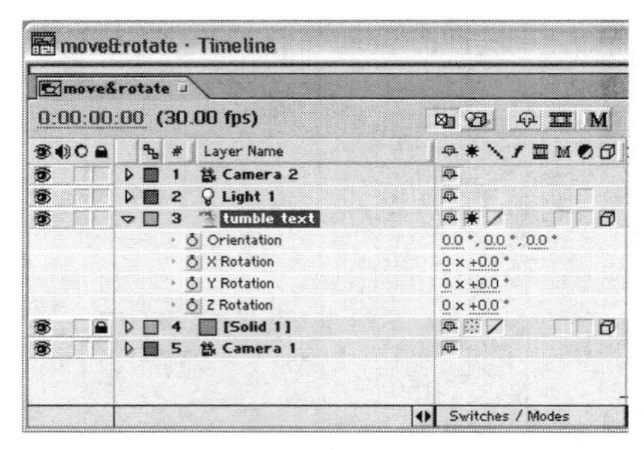

Figure 16.14 Three-dimensional layers, cameras, and lights can be rotated using a single Orientation property, or *X*, *Y*, and *Z* Rotation properties.

The Orientation property is expressed as a three-dimensional value: *x*, *y*, and *z* angles. In the Comp window, you adjust orientation with the standard Rotation tool.

You adjust rotation using three separate property values: X Rotation, Y Rotation, and Z Rotation. Unlike orientation, Rotation properties allow you to adjust the number of rotations in addition to the angle along each axis. You can adjust Rotation values in the Composition window by using a Rotation tool option.

Orientation vs. Rotation

When you're animating a layer's rotation in 3D, the Orientation property and the Rotation properties offer unique advantages and disadvantages. Choose the method best suited for the task at hand—and to avoid confusion, try not to use both methods simultaneously.

You may find that it's easier to achieve predictable results by animating the Orientation property rather than the Rotation properties, because interpolated Orientation values take the shortest path between one keyframe and the next. You can also smooth orientation using Bézier curves (just as you'd smooth a motion path for position). However, Orientation doesn't allow for multiple rotations along an axis. And although Orientation's speed graph allows you to ease motion, it doesn't display rates of change in rotations per second. Because of these limitations, some animators prefer to use Orientation to set rotational position—its angle or tilt in 3D space—and animate using the Rotation property.

Separate Rotation property values permit more keyframing options than Orientation does, but the results can be more difficult to control. Each Rotation property permits multiple rotations and can display a velocity graph that accurately measures the rotations per second at any frame.

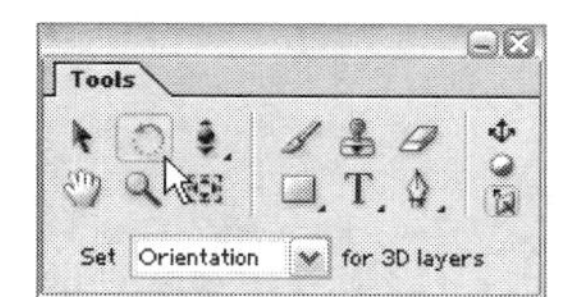

Figure 16.15 In the Tools palette, select the Rotation tool.

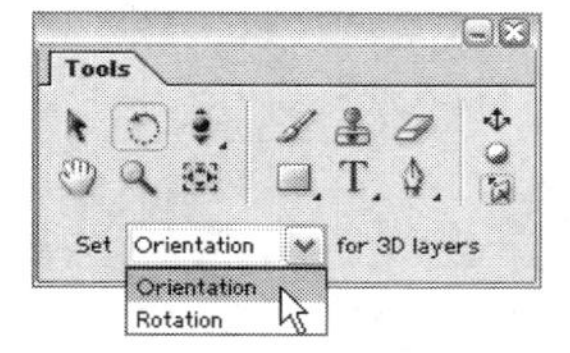

Figure 16.16 In the pull-down menu, choose Orientation.

To adjust the orientation in the Comp window:

1. In the 3D View pull-down menu, select a view.
2. In the Tools palette, select an axis mode.
3. Select a 3D layer, camera, or light.

   The selected layer's axes appear. The *X* axis is red; the *Y* axis is green; the *Z* axis is blue. The axes align according to the axis mode you specified.
4. In the Tools palette, select the Rotation tool (**Figure 16.15**).

   A pull-down menu containing rotation options appears in the Tools palette.
5. In the pull-down menu, choose Orientation (**Figure 16.16**).
6. In the Composition window, *do one of the following:*

   ▲ To adjust the orientation along all axes, drag the Rotation tool in any direction (**Figures 16.17** and **16.18**).

continues on next page

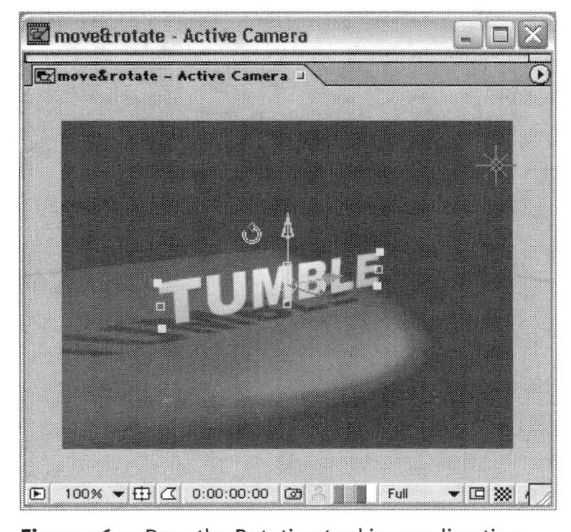

Figure 16.17 Drag the Rotation tool in any direction...

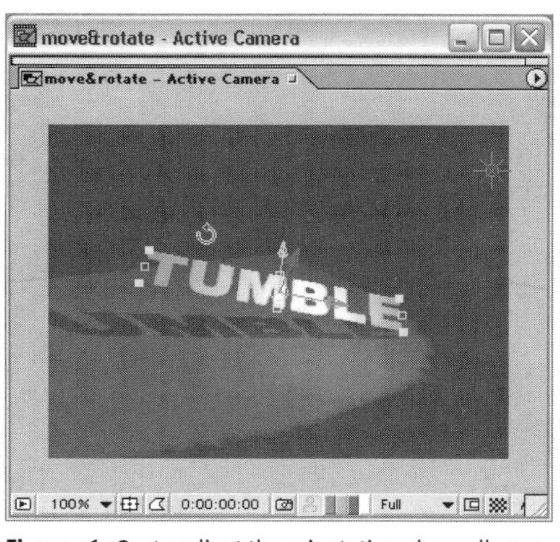

Figure 16.18 ...to adjust the orientation along all axes.

- To adjust the orientation along a single axis, position the Rotation tool over the axis you want to adjust so that the Rotation icon displays the letter corresponding to the axis, and then drag (**Figures 16.19** and **16.20**).

If the Orientation property's Stopwatch icon isn't activated, this will remain the Orientation value of the layer for the layer's duration. If the Stopwatch is activated, an orientation keyframe is created at this frame.

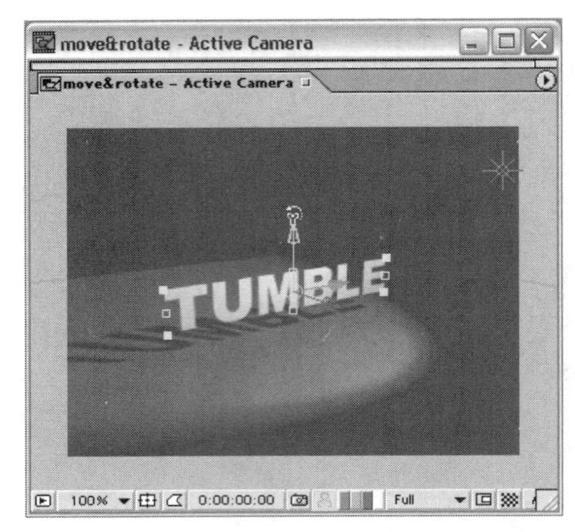

Figure 16.19 Position the Rotation tool over the axis you want to adjust so that the Rotation tool icon displays the axis letter...

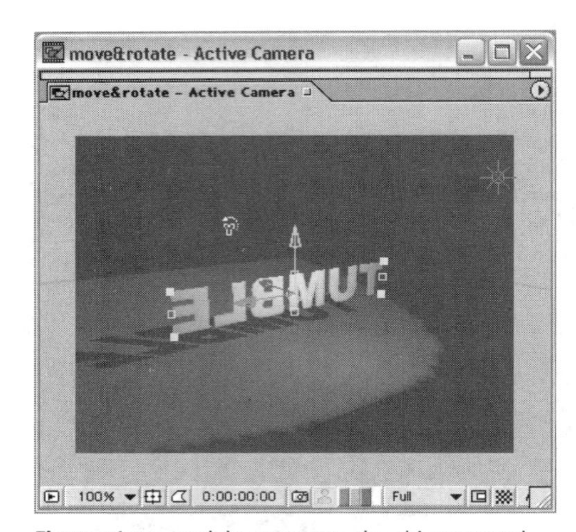

Figure 16.20 ...and drag to rotate the object around that axis.

To adjust 3D rotation in the Composition window:

1. In the 3D View pull-down menu, select a view.
2. In the Tools palette, select an axis mode.
3. Select a 3D layer, camera, or light.

   The selected layer's axes appear. The *X* axis is red; the *Y* axis is green; the *Z* axis is blue. The axes align according to the axis mode you specified.
4. In the Tools palette, select the Rotation tool (**Figure 16.21**).

   A pull-down menu containing rotation options appears in the Tools palette.

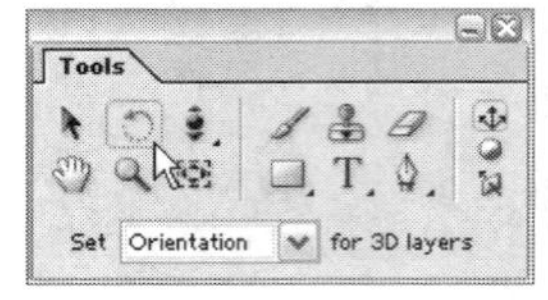

Figure 16.21 In the Tools palette, select the Rotation tool.

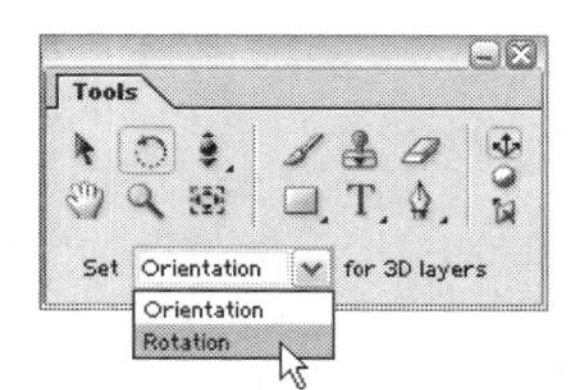

Figure 16.22 In the pull-down menu, choose Rotation.

Figure 16.23 Position the 3D Rotation tool over the axis around which you want to rotate the 3D object, and then drag.

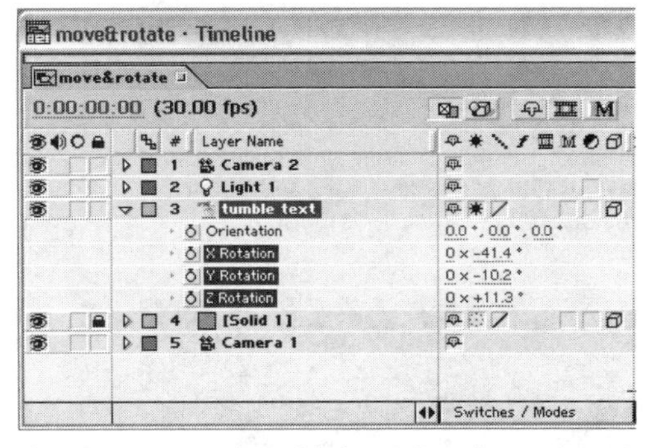

Figure 16.24 Dragging with the 3D Rotation tool adjusts the layer's 3D Rotation properties, not its Orientation properties.

5. In the pull-down menu, choose Rotation (**Figure 16.22**).
6. In the Composition window, position the 3D Rotation tool over the axis around which you want to rotate the 3D object (**Figure 16.23**).

   The 3D Rotation tool displays the letter corresponding to the axis.
7. Drag to rotate the 3D layer, camera, or light around the selected axis.

   If the Stopwatch icons for the Rotation properties aren't activated, the Rotation values are set for the layer's duration (**Figure 16.24**). If the Stopwatch icons are activated, rotation keyframes are created at this frame.

✔ Tip

- As usual, don't forget to switch back to the Selection tool after you've finished using the Rotation tool (or any other tool). Otherwise, you could easily make accidental changes to layers.

Auto-Orienting 3D Layers

Using the Auto-Orientation command, you can make a 3D layer automatically rotate along its motion path or toward the top camera layer (see "Using Cameras" later in this chapter)—which saves you the trouble of keyframing the Orientation property manually. Alternatively, you can leave Auto-Orientation off and adjust the layer's rotation independently of other factors.

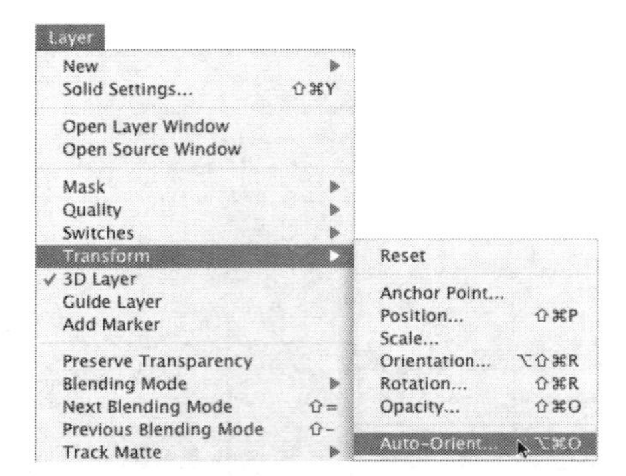

Figure 16.25 Choose Layer > Transform > Auto-Orient.

To specify an Auto-Orientation setting:

1. Select a 3D layer.
2. Choose Layer > Transform > Auto-Orient, or press Command-Option-O (Mac) or Ctrl-Alt-O (Windows) (**Figure 16.25**).

   The Auto-Orientation dialog box appears (**Figure 16.26**).

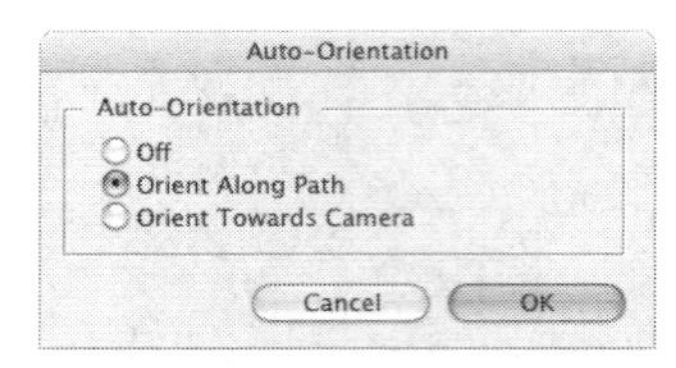

Figure 16.26 The Auto-Orientation dialog box appears.

3. In the Auto-Orientation dialog box, *select one of the following* options:

   Off—Turns off Auto-Orient and adjusts rotation independently.

   Orient Along Path—Makes the layer rotate so that its local *Z* axis points in the direction of the layer's motion path (**Figure 16.27**).

   Orient Towards Camera—Makes the layer rotate so that its local *Z* axis points in the direction of the top camera layer (**Figure 16.28**).

   For more information, see "Using Cameras" later in this chapter.

4. Click OK to close the dialog box.

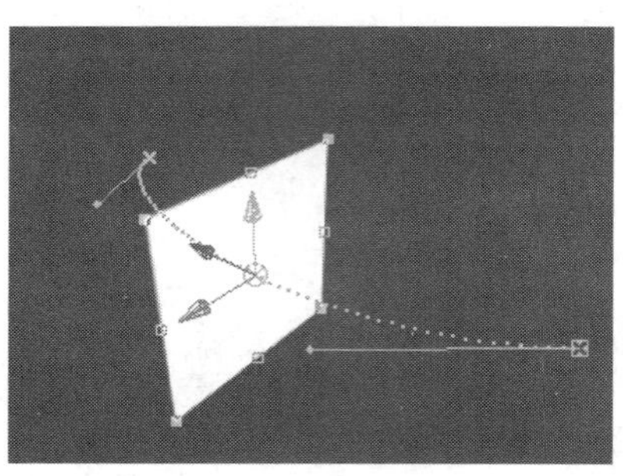

Figure 16.27 Orient Along Path makes the layer rotate so that its local *Z* axis points in the direction of the layer's motion.

✔ Tip

- You can also apply special Auto-Orientation options to cameras and lights. See "Using the Point of Interest" later in this chapter.

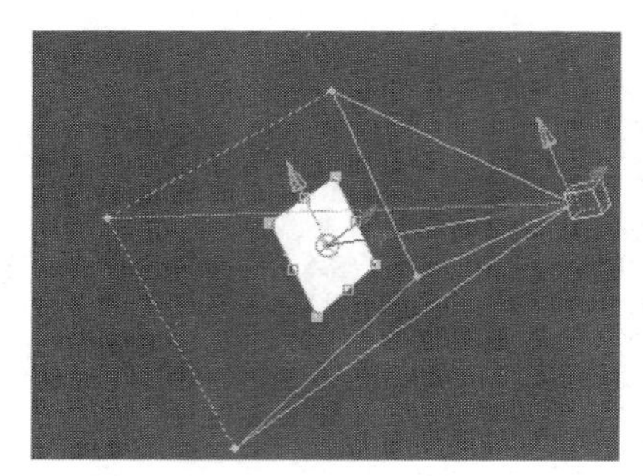

Figure 16.28 Orient Towards Camera makes the layer rotate so that its local *Z* axis points in the direction of the active camera.

Using 3D Material Options

Three-dimensional layers add a property category called Material Options that defines how 3D layers respond to lights in a comp. For more about lights, see "Using Lights" later in this chapter.

To set a 3D layer's Material Options:

1. Select a 3D layer.
2. Expand the layer outline to reveal the Material Options properties, or press AA (**Figure 16.29**).

   The layer's Material Options properties are revealed in the layer outline.
3. Set each Material Options property:

   Casts Shadows—Turn this option on to enable the layer to cast shadows on other layers within the range of the shadow. This property can't be keyframed.

   Light Transmission—Adjust this value to set the percentage of light that shines through a layer. A value of zero causes the layer to act as an opaque object and cast a black shadow. Increasing the value allows light to pass through the object and cast a colored shadow, much like a transparency or stained glass does.

   Accepts Shadows—Turn this option on to enable shadows cast from other layers to appear on the layer. This property can't be keyframed.

   Accepts Lights—Turn this option on to enable the layer to be illuminated by lights in the composition. This property can't be keyframed.

   Ambient—Adjust this value to set the amount of *ambient*, or nondirectional, reflectivity of the layer.

   Diffuse—Adjust this value to set the amount of *diffuse*, or omnidirectional, reflectivity of the layer.

continues on next page

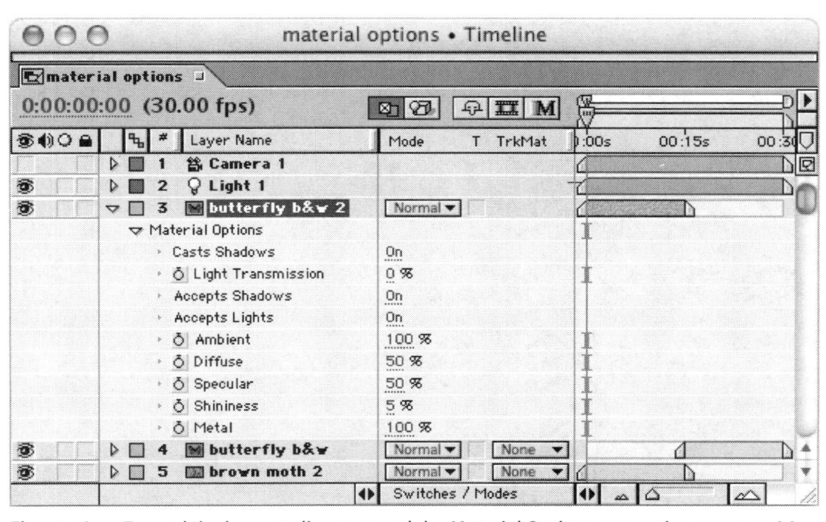

Figure 16.29 Expand the layer outline to reveal the Material Options properties, or press AA.

Specular—Adjust this value to set the amount of *specular*, or directional, reflectivity of the layer.

Shininess—Adjust this value to set the size of the layer's *specular highlight*, or shininess. This property is available only when the Specular property value is greater than 0 percent.

Metal—Adjust this value to specify the color of the specular highlight (as defined by the Specular and Shininess values). A value of 100 percent sets the color to match the layer, whereas a value of 0 percent sets the color to match the light source.

The layer in the Composition window reflects your choices (**Figures 16.30** and **16.31**).

Figure 16.30 In this example, both 3D layers use the default material options, with Casts Shadows turned on.

Figure 16.31 Here, the Casts Shadows and Accepts Shadows settings are off on the left layer, and the Diffuse property on the right layer has been increased from 50 percent to 100 percent.

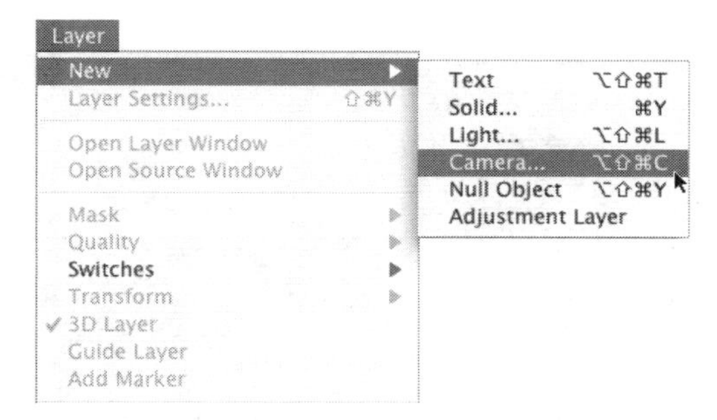

Figure 16.32 Choose Layer > New > Camera.

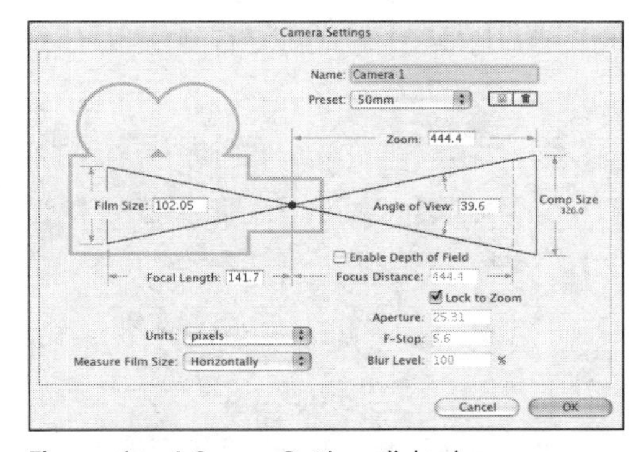

Figure 16.33 A Camera Settings dialog box appears.

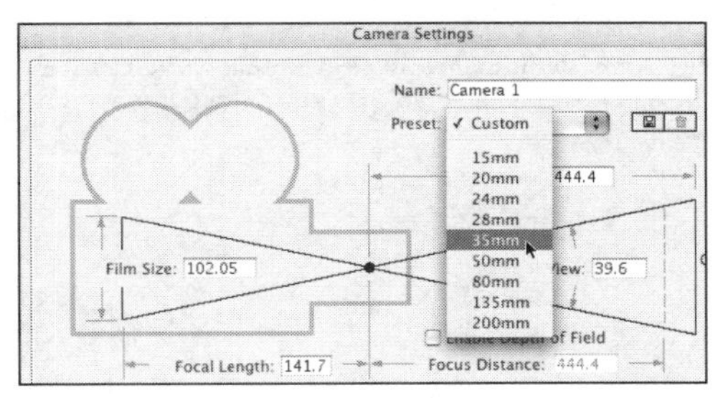

Figure 16.34 Select a preset camera from the Preset pull-down menu.

Using Cameras

You can view a composition from any angle by creating one or more 3D cameras. Cameras emulate the optical characteristics of real cameras. However, unlike real cameras, you can move these cameras through space unrestrained by tripods, gravity, or even union rules. This task summarizes how to create a new camera; the following sections explain each camera setting in detail.

To create a camera:

1. *Do either of the following:*
   - ▲ Choose Layer > New > Camera (**Figure 16.32**).
   - ▲ Press Shift-Option-Command-C (Mac) or Shift-Alt-Ctrl-C (Windows).

   A Camera Settings dialog box appears (**Figure 16.33**).
2. In the Camera Settings dialog box, *do one of the following:*
   - ▲ Select a preset camera from the Preset pull-down menu (**Figure 16.34**).

   Presets are designed to emulate a 35mm camera of the specified focal length. Although presets are named for particular focal lengths, they set various camera settings automatically.
   - ▲ Choose the custom camera options you want.

   See "Choosing Camera Settings" in the next section for a detailed description of each camera setting option.
3. To give the camera a custom name, enter one in the Name field of the Camera Settings dialog box.

   If you don't enter a name, After Effects uses the default naming scheme.

continues on next page

4. Click OK to close the Camera Settings dialog box.

   The new camera appears as the top layer in the composition, starting at the current time and using the default duration for still footage (**Figure 16.35**). The camera's default position depends on the camera settings you chose. Its default point of interest is at the center of the composition (see "Using the Point of Interest" later in this chapter). You can also switch the 3D view to see the camera's positioning in the Composition window (**Figure 16.36**). (See "Viewing 3D Layers in the Comp Window" earlier in this chapter.)

✔ Tips

- If you don't name cameras, After Effects applies default names—Camera 1, Camera 2, and so on. When you delete a camera, After Effects assigns the lowest available number to the next camera you create. To avoid confusion, always give your cameras custom names. Note that always naming cameras will help you avoid problems when using expressions.
- To revisit the camera settings, double-click the camera's name in the Timeline window's layer outline.

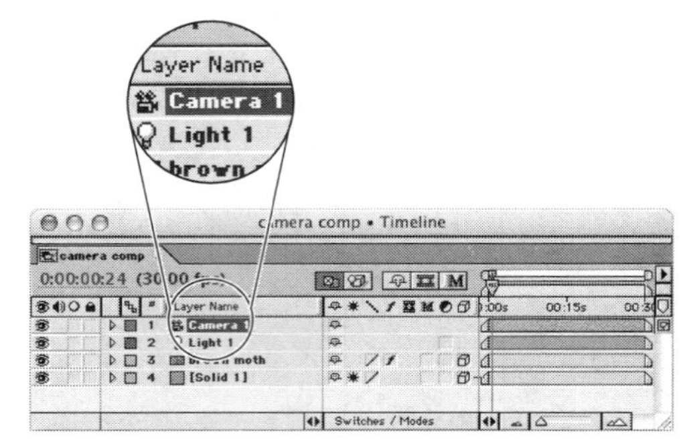

Figure 16.35 The new camera appears as the top layer in the composition, starting at the current time and using the default duration for still footage.

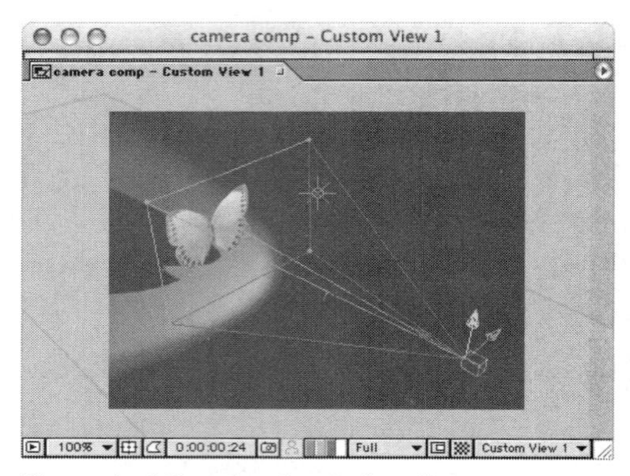

Figure 16.36 Changing the 3D view allows you to see the camera as a selectable object in the Composition window.

Choosing Camera Settings

When you create a camera, the Camera Settings dialog box prompts you to set various attributes for it—such as focal length and film size—that emulate physical cameras.

You can choose from a list of presets, designed to mimic a number of typical real-world cameras. Or, if you prefer, you can customize the settings. The dialog box provides a helpful illustration of the camera attributes (although it's not to scale, of course).

The following tasks divide an explanation of camera settings into two parts. The first explains the basic settings, which govern film size and most of the camera's optical attributes. The next task explains the Depth of Field settings, which can be activated to mimic the limited focus range of real-world cameras.

To choose basic camera settings:

1. *Do one of the following:*
   - ▲ To create a new camera, press Shift-Option-Command-C (Mac) or Shift-Alt-Ctrl-C (Windows).
   - ▲ To modify a camera in the composition, double-click the name of the camera you want to modify in the layer outline of the Timeline window.

   The Camera Settings dialog box appears (**Figure 16.37**).

continues on next page

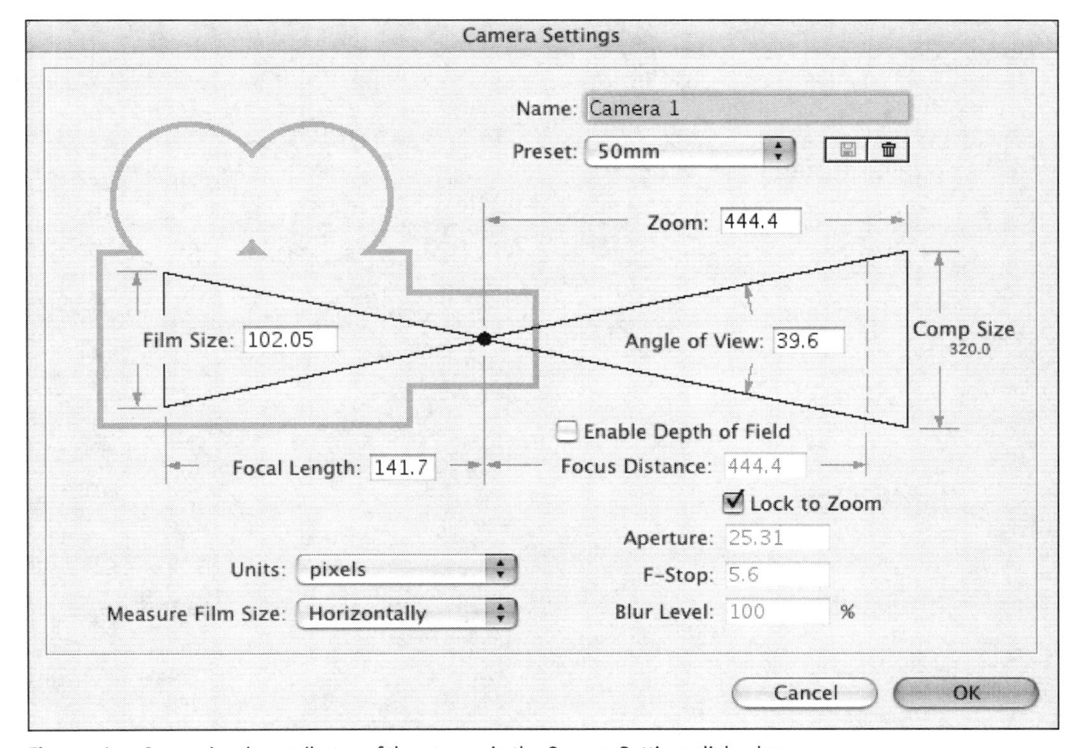

Figure 16.37 Customize the attributes of the camera in the Camera Settings dialog box.

2. In the Camera Settings dialog box, enter a name in the Name field.

   If you don't enter a name, After Effects will use the default naming scheme in which the first camera is called Camera 1 and additional cameras are numbered in ascending order. If you delete a camera that uses this naming scheme, however, new cameras are named using the lowest available number.

3. If you want to use predefined camera settings, select a preset from the Preset pull-down menu.

   Presets are designed to emulate a 35mm camera of the specified focal length. Although Presets are named for particular focal lengths, they set various camera settings automatically. You can also create a Custom camera by modifying individual settings manually.

4. In the same dialog box, choose the units by which measurements are expressed:

   Units—Sets whether the variables in the Camera Settings dialog box are expressed in pixels, inches, or millimeters (**Figure 16.38**).

   Measure Film Size—Measures film size horizontally, vertically, or diagonally (**Figure 16.39**).

   Typically, film size is measured horizontally. In other words, 35mm motion picture film measures 35mm across the image area. Measured vertically, the image is about 26.25mm.

5. Enter the following variables:

   Zoom—Sets the distance between the camera's focal point and the image plane.

   Angle of View—Sets the width of the scene included in the image. Angle of view is directly related to Focal Length, Film Size, and Zoom. Thus, adjusting this setting changes those variables, and vice versa.

   Film Size—Controls the size of the exposed area of the film being simulated. When you change Film Size, Zoom and Angle are adjusted automatically to maintain the width of the scene in the camera's view.

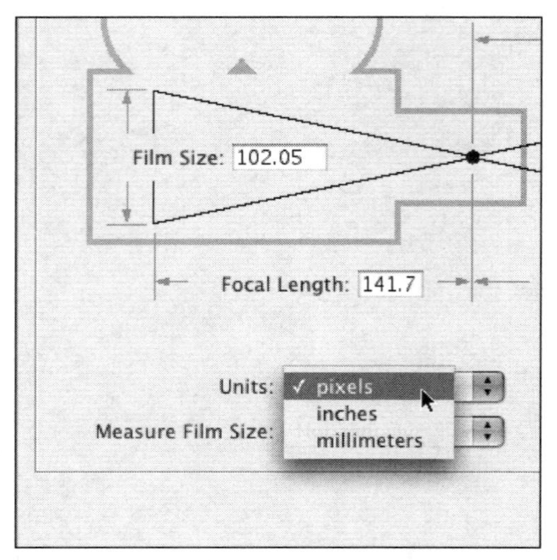

Figure 16.38 Select a unit of measure for the Camera Settings dialog box in the Units pull-down menu.

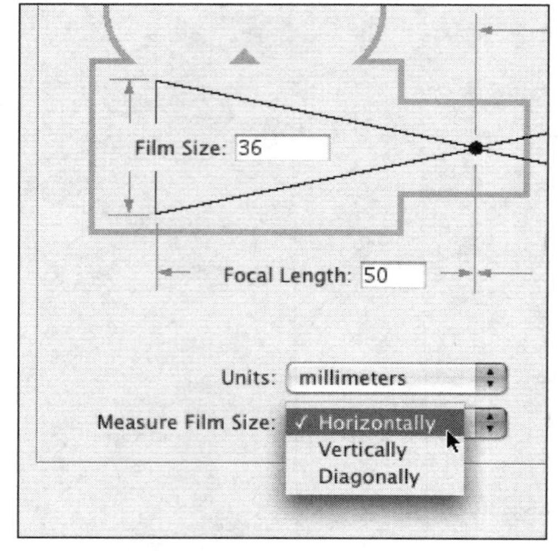

Figure 16.39 Select a unit of measure from the Measure Film Size pull-down menu.

Focal Length—Controls the distance between the focal point and the film plane of the camera. When you change Focal Length, the Zoom value changes automatically to maintain the scene's width in the camera's view.

6. Click OK to close the Camera Settings dialog box.

To select Depth of Field options:

1. In the Camera Settings dialog box, select Enable Depth of Field (**Figure 16.40**).

   Selecting this option activates variables that affect the range of distance when the image is in focus, including Focus Distance, Aperture, F-Stop, and Blur Level.

2. To keep Focus Distance and Zoom the same, select Lock to Zoom.

   Unselect this option to allow Focus Distance and Zoom to be adjusted independently.

3. In the same dialog box, set the following options:

   Focus Distance—Sets the distance from the camera's focal point to the focal plane (the plane of space that is in perfect focus) (**Figure 16.41**).

   If Lock to Zoom is selected, adjusting Focus Distance also adjusts Zoom.

   Aperture—Sets the size of the lens opening. Because the Aperture and F-Stop settings measure the same thing in different ways, adjusting one results in a corresponding change in the other. Aperture (or F-Stop) is directly related to depth of field (see the sidebar "Depth of Field—in Depth").

   F-Stop—Sets the aperture in terms of *f/stop*, a measurement system commonly used in photography. An f/stop is expressed as the ratio of the focal length to the aperture. On a real camera, increasing the f/stop by one full stop decreases the aperture to allow half the amount of light to expose the film; decreasing it by one stop doubles the amount of light. The term *stopping down* the lens refers to reducing aperture size.

   Blur Level—Controls the amount of blur that results when a layer is outside the camera's depth of field. A value of 100 percent creates the amount of blur appropriate to the other camera settings. Lower values reduce the blur.

continues on next page

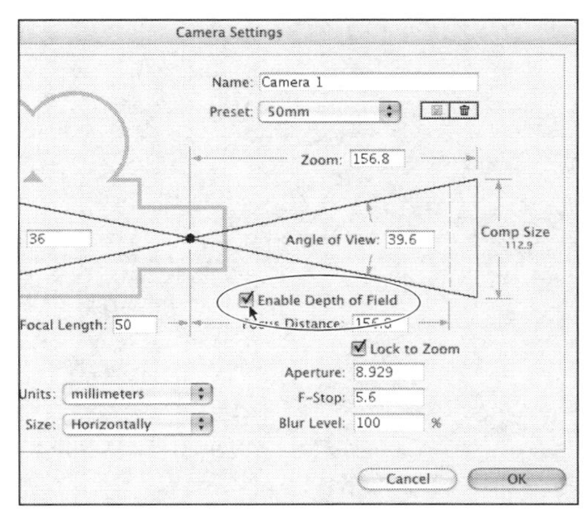

Figure 16.40 In the Camera Settings dialog box, select Enable Depth of Field.

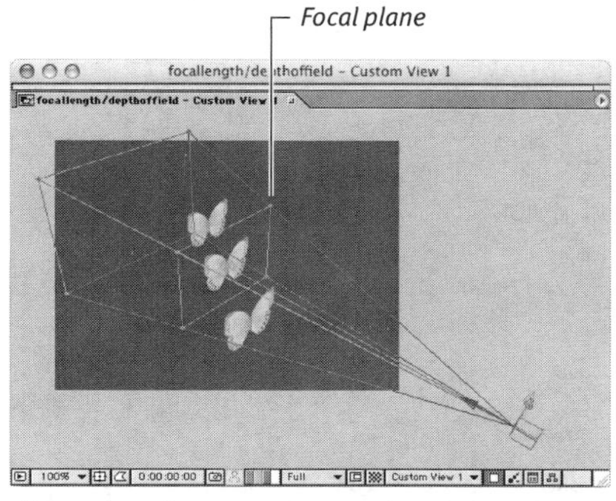

Figure 16.41 The Focus Distance value defines the distance from the camera to the focal plane. When Lock to Zoom isn't selected, you can see the focal plane represented in a selected camera's icon.

4. Click OK to close the Camera Settings dialog box.

   When viewed through the camera, objects outside the depth of field appear blurred (**Figure 16.42**).

✔ Tips

- After Effects uses the term *position,* which is synonymous with the camera's Position property. In the physical world, the camera's position is synonymous with its focal point. In a real camera, the focal point defines where the light in the lens converges into a single point before it goes on to expose the film at the film plane (**Figure 16.43**). Distances associated with a camera are measured from its focal point.
- The Camera Settings dialog box includes buttons to save and delete camera presets. They look like the buttons you use to save and delete composition presets.
- Photographers may wonder why the cameras in After Effects seem to have controls for everything but shutter speed and shutter angle. You'll find these controls in the Advanced panel of the Composition Settings dialog box. See Chapter 4, "Compositions," for more information.
- You can switch focus from one object in the scene to another, a technique cinematographers call *rack focus* or *pulling focus.* Make sure the Lock to Zoom camera setting is unselected, and animate the Focus Distance property.

Figure 16.42 Here, the focal plane intersects the center butterfly, and objects outside the depth of field appear blurry.

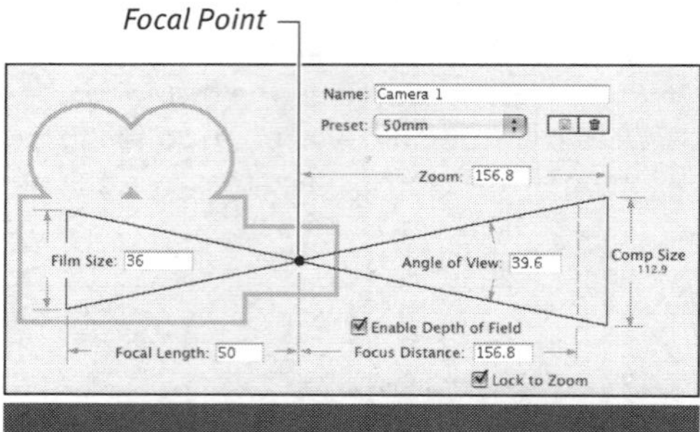

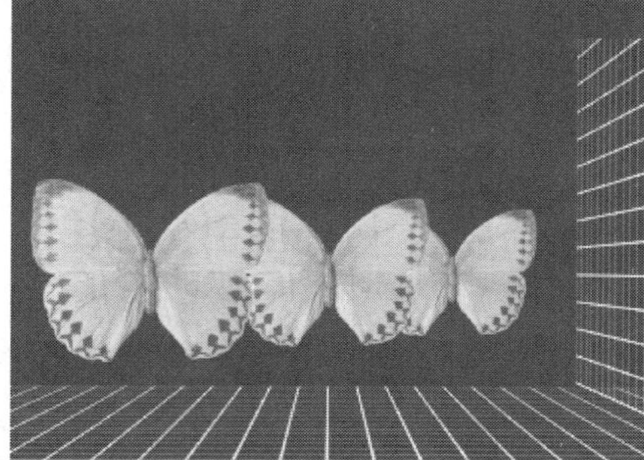

Figure 16.43 The camera's position corresponds to the focal point, which is illustrated in the Camera Settings dialog box but not labeled.

Choosing a Lens

For 35mm film, a 50mm focal length produces an image that closely resembles human sight. Assuming film size remains constant, other focal lengths introduce distortions in perspective and apparent distances. Lenses with shorter focal lengths are called *wide angle*, and lenses with longer focal lengths are referred to as *telephoto*. The differences between the image you capture using wide and telephoto lenses can be summarized as follows:

- A wide-angle lens captures a wider area of the scene than a longer lens placed at the same distance from the subject (**Figure 16.44**).
- A wide-angle lens makes the subject look smaller than when viewed through a telephoto lens placed at the same distance from the subject.
- A wide-angle lens exaggerates depth, so that the movement along the axis seems greater; a telephoto lens compresses depth, so that the same movement along the *Z* axis seems less (**Figure 16.45**).
- A change in angle through a wide-angle lens seems less pronounced than the same change in angle through a telephoto lens, when the subject appears at the same apparent size in the frame.

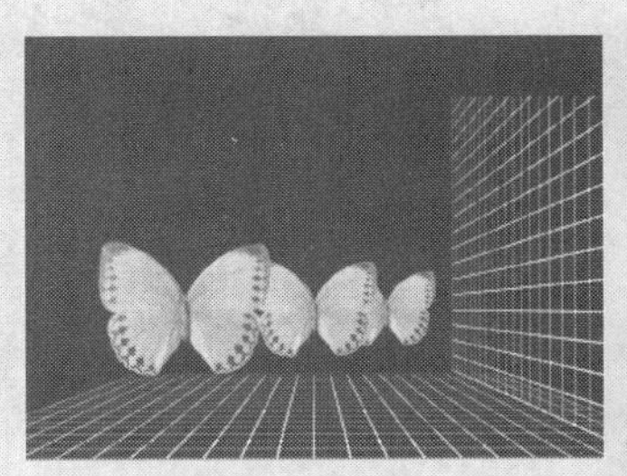
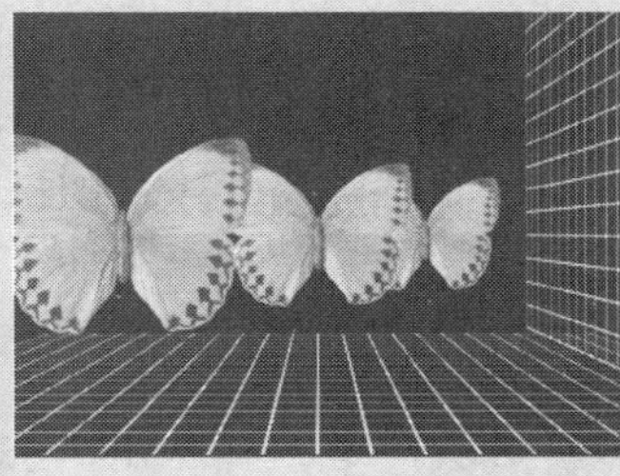
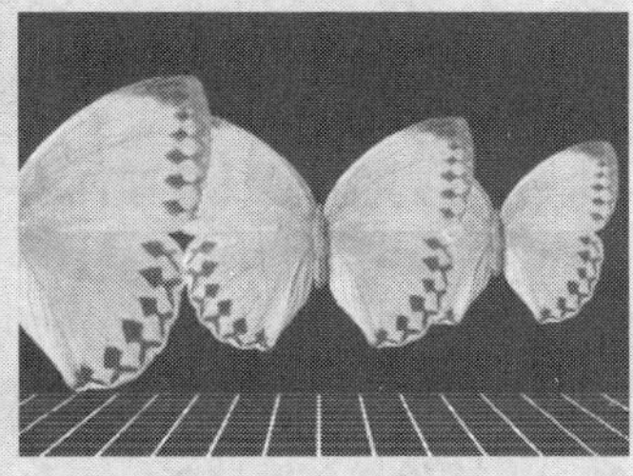

Figure 16.44 A wide-angle lens captures a wider area of the scene than a longer lens placed at the same distance from the subject. In each successive image the focal length increases, but the distance from the subject is fixed.

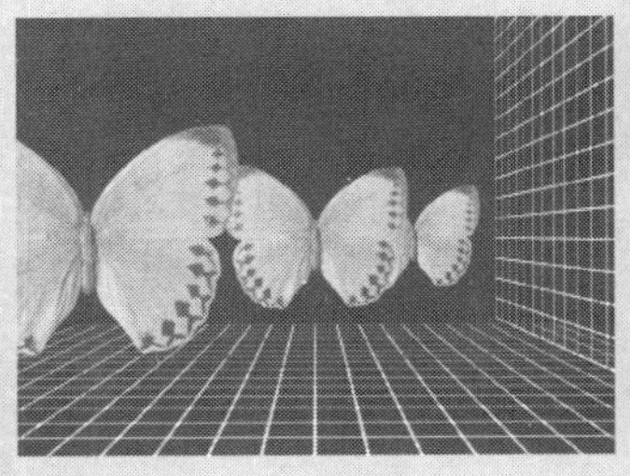
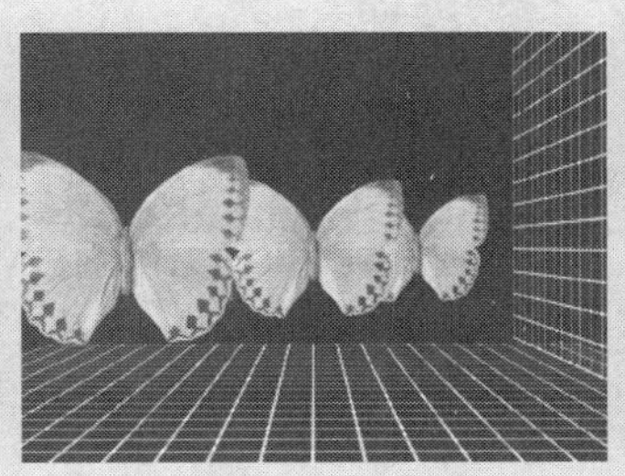
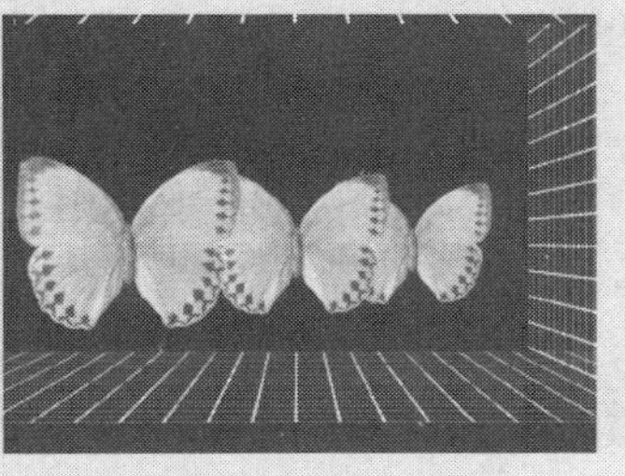

Figure 16.45 A wide-angle lens exaggerates depth, and a telephoto lens compresses depth. These three images show three cameras of different focal lengths. The camera's distance from the subject has been adjusted to maintain the subject's size in the frame.

Depth of Field—In Depth

If you're planning to use Depth of Field options in the Camera Settings dialog box, you should probably know something about how depth of field works in real camera optics:

- Depth of field decreases as you increase focal length and increases as you decrease focal length (**Figures 16.46** and **16.47**).
- Depth of field increases as you close the aperture (**Figures 16.48** and **16.49**).

continues on next page

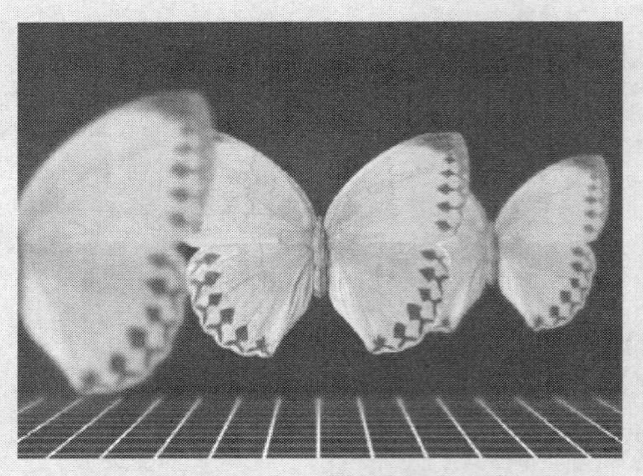

Figure 16.46 Depth of field decreases as you increase focal length...

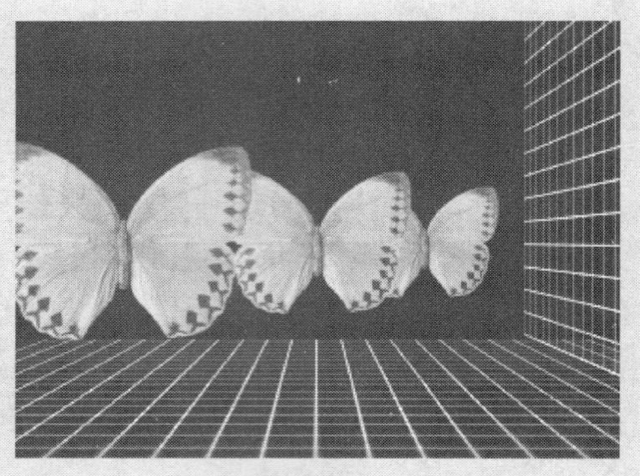

Figure 16.47 ...and increases as you decrease focal length.

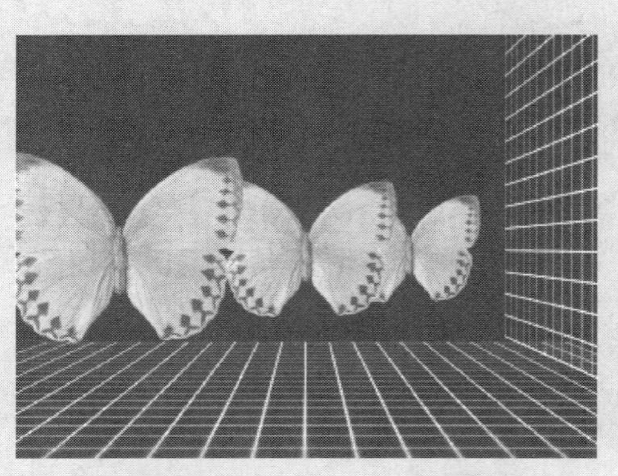

Figure 16.48 Depth of field increases as you close the aperture...

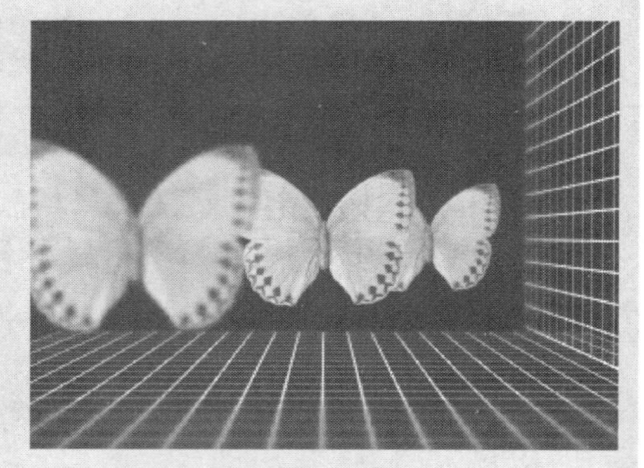

Figure 16.49 ...and decreases as you open the aperture.

Depth of Field—In Depth *(continued)*

- Depth of field increases as the distance to the subject increases; depth of field decreases as the distance to the subject decreases (**Figures 16.50** and **16.51**).
- There's less depth of field in front of the plane of focus than behind it (**Figure 16.52**).

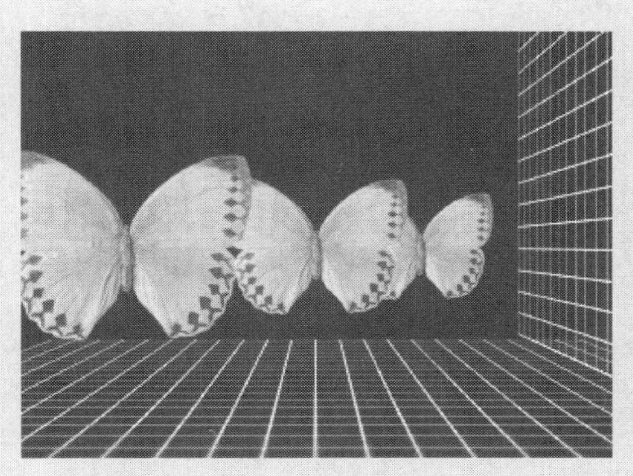

Figure 16.50 Depth of field increases as the distance from the subject increases.

Figure 16.51 Depth of field decreases as the distance from the subject decreases.

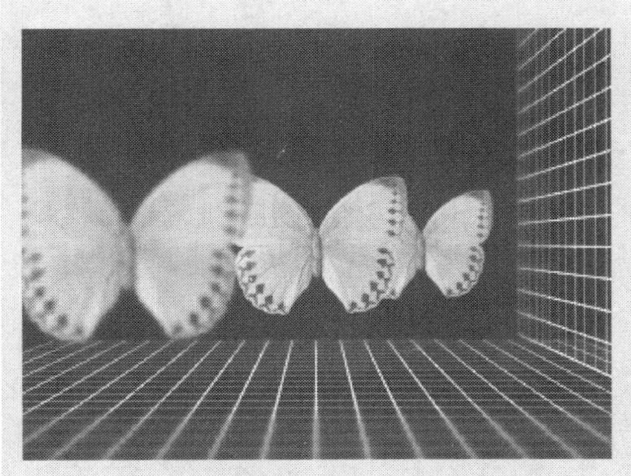

Figure 16.52 There's less depth of field in front of the plane of focus than behind it. In this example, the nearest and farthest butterflies are positioned the same distance from the focal plane, but the near one is much blurrier.

Using Lights

You can create any number of lights to illuminate a 3D scene, and you can select and control these lights much as you would in the real world. In After Effects, however, lights are only evident when they illuminate 3D layers that are set to accept lights. You can select a light to place it in the scene and then point it at a subject, but you'll never see a lighting instrument in the scene. Pointing a light into a camera won't cause a lens flare or overexposed image—in fact, you won't see anything at all. And you'll never blow a lamp or overload a circuit breaker.

As in the "Using Cameras" section, this section contains two tasks: The first summarizes how to create a light; the second describes light settings in more detail.

To create a light:

1. *Do either of the following:*
   - ▲ Choose Layer > New > Light (**Figure 16.53**).
   - ▲ Press Shift-Option-Command-L (Mac) or Shift-Alt-Ctrl-L (Windows).

   A Light Settings dialog box appears (**Figure 16.54**).
2. Enter the name for the light in the Name field.

   If you don't enter a name, After Effects uses the default naming scheme.
3. In the same dialog box, select the type of light you want from the pull-down menu (**Figure 16.55**):

   Parallel—Radiates directional light from an infinite distance. In this respect, a parallel light simulates sunlight (**Figure 16.56**).

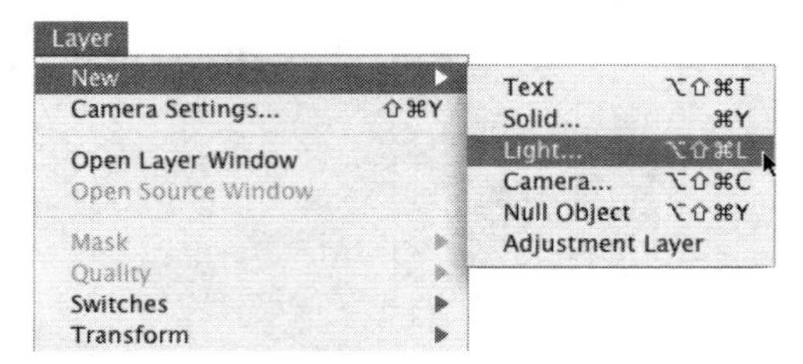

Figure 16.53 Choose Layer > New > Light.

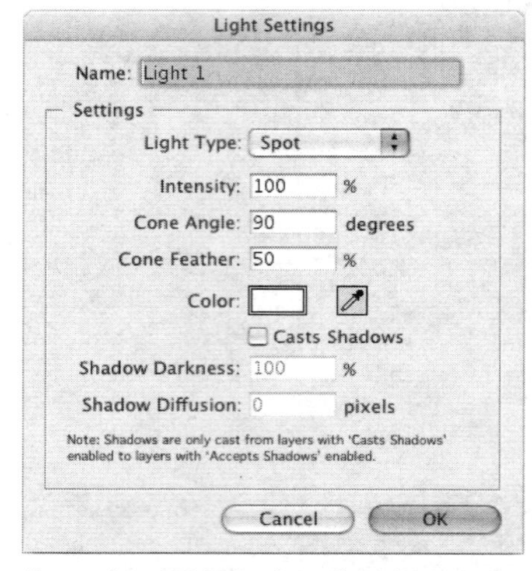

Figure 16.54 A Light Settings dialog box appears.

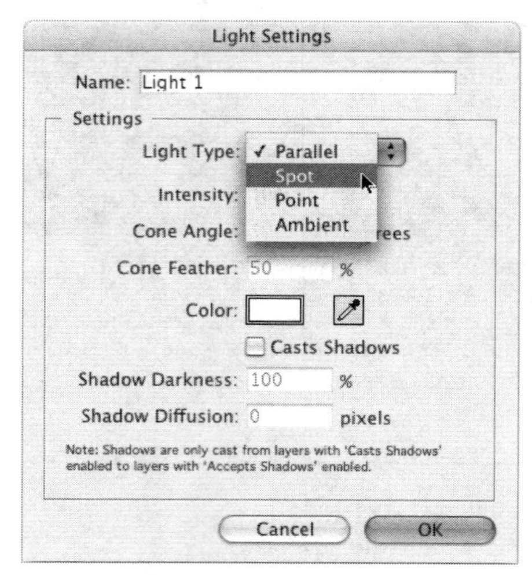

Figure 16.55 In the Light Settings dialog box, select the type of light you want from the pull-down menu.

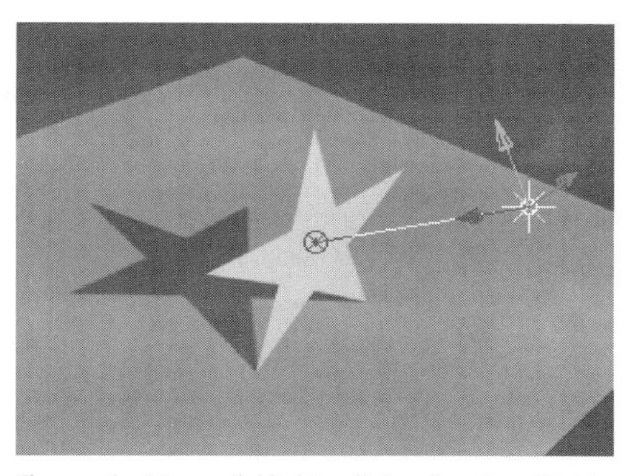

Figure 16.56 A parallel light radiates directional light from a source infinitely far away, much like sunlight.

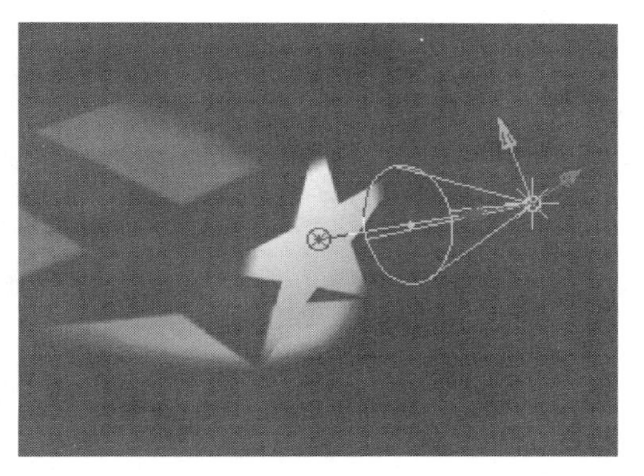

Figure 16.57 A spot light is constrained by a cone and appears much like the lights used in film and stage productions.

Spot—Radiates from a source positioned within an opaque cone, allowing the light to emit only through its open end. Adjusting the cone's angle changes the spread of the light. This type of light emulates those commonly used in film and stage productions (**Figure 16.57**).

Point—Emits omnidirectional light from its point of origin, comparable to a bare bulb or an unflickering signal flare (**Figure 16.58**).

Ambient—Doesn't emanate from a specific source but rather contributes to the overall illumination of the scene. Ambient light settings only include those for intensity and color (**Figure 16.59**).

The type of light you select determines which options are available in the Light Settings dialog box.

continues on next page

Figure 16.58 A point light emits an omnidirectional light, much like a bare bulb.

Figure 16.59 An ambient light contributes to the overall illumination of the 3D space. Here, an ambient light is set to 30 percent intensity.

4. Specify the light settings available for the type of light you selected.

   See the next section, "Choosing Light Settings," for more information.

5. Click OK to close the Light Settings dialog box.

   The new light appears as the top layer in the composition, starting at the current time and using the default duration for still footage (**Figure 16.60**). The light's default position depends on the type of light you select.

✔ Tips

- You can revisit the Light Settings dialog box at any time by double-clicking the name of the light in the layer outline of the Timeline window.
- If you need a lens flare or visible light beams, try an effect. After Effects includes a lens flare, and many third-party plug-in packages create light beams and other lighting effects.

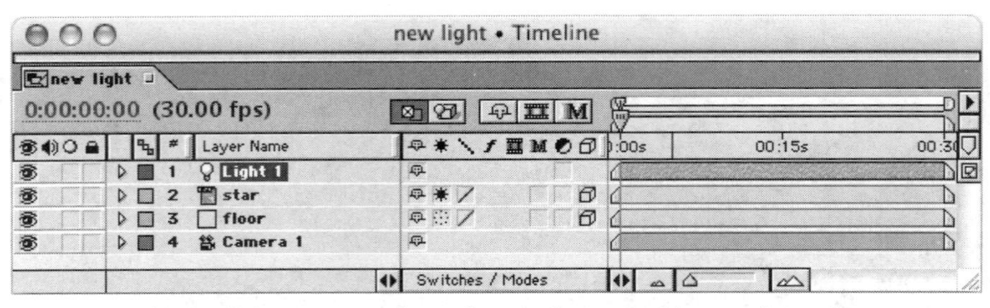

Figure 16.60 The new light appears as the top layer in the composition, starting at the current time and using the default duration for still footage.

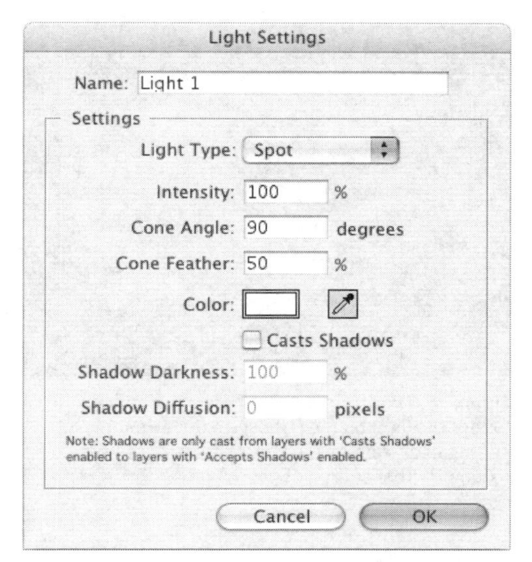

Figure 16.61 In the Light Settings dialog box, specify the settings available for the type of light you're using.

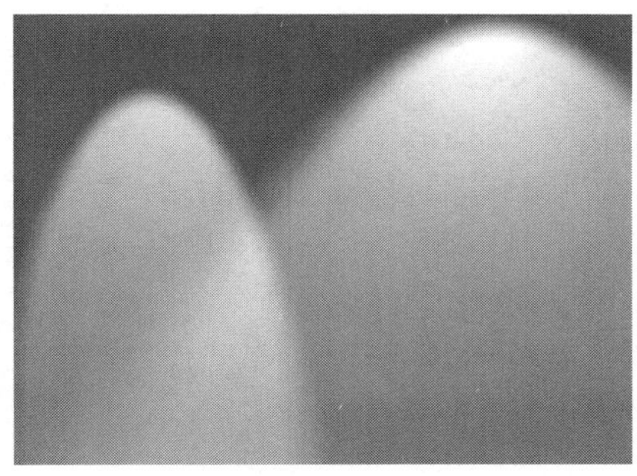

Figure 16.62 Both spot lights are the same intensity and distance from the layer. The light on the left uses a 45-degree cone angle; the light on the right uses a 90-degree cone angle.

Choosing Light Settings

The options available in the Light Settings dialog box depend on the type of light you're using. They control the character of the light and the shadows it casts.

To select light settings:

1. *Do one of the following:*
   - ▲ To create a new light, press Shift-Option-Command-L (Mac) or Shift-Alt-Ctrl-L (Windows).
   - ▲ To modify a light in the composition, double-click the name of the light you want to modify in the layer outline of the Timeline window.

   The Light Settings dialog box appears (**Figure 16.61**).

2. In the Light Settings dialog box, specify the following options:

   Intensity—Sets the brightness of light. Negative values create nonlight—that is, they subtract color from an already illuminated layer, in effect shining darkness onto a layer.

   Cone Angle—Sets the angle of the cone used to restrict a spot type of light. Wider cone angles emit a broader span of light; smaller angles restrict the light to a narrower area (**Figure 16.62**).

continues on next page

Cone Feather—Sets the softness of the edges of a spot type of light. Larger values create a softer light edge (**Figure 16.63**).

Color—Selects the light's color; comparable to placing a colored gel over a light. You can use the color swatch or eyedropper control.

Casts Shadows—When selected, makes the light cast shadows onto layers with the Accepts Shadows property selected. See "Using 3D Material Options" earlier in this chapter, for more information.

Shadow Darkness—Sets the darkness level of shadows cast by the light. This option is available only when the light's Casts Shadows option is enabled.

Shadow Diffusion—Sets the softness of shadows, based on the apparent distance between the light and the layers casting shadows made by the light. Larger values create softer shadows. This option is available only when the light's Casts Shadows option is enabled.

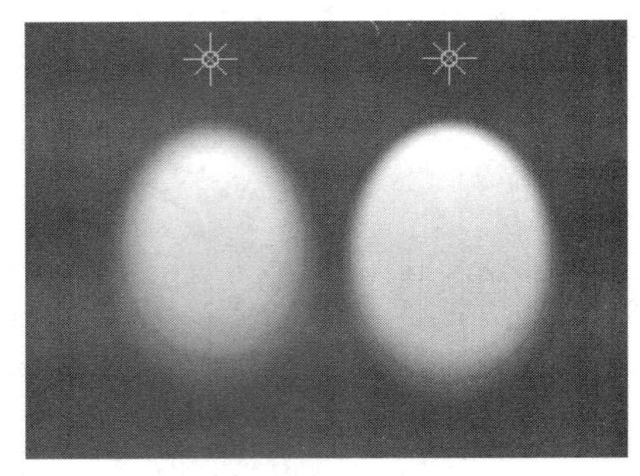

Figure 16.63 Both spot lights here are identical, except the light on the left uses a Cone Feather setting of 25 whereas the light on the right uses a Cone Feather setting of 50.

Using the Point of Interest

Point of Interest is a transform property unique to cameras and lights. Simply put, the Point of Interest property defines the point in space at which the camera or light is pointed. By default, a new camera's or light's point of interest is at the center of the composition (at the coordinates (0,0,0) in terms of the world axes). In the Composition window, the point of interest appears as a crosshair at the end of a line extending from a camera or light (**Figure 16.64**).

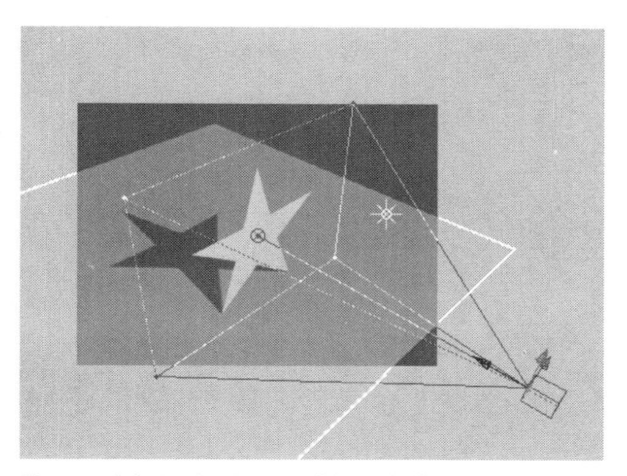

Figure 16.64 In the Composition window, the point of interest appears as a crosshair at the end of a line extending from a camera or light.

As you can see, a camera's or light's Point of Interest value is closely related to its other transform property values: A change in position or rotation can affect the point of interest, and vice versa.

Because of its relationship to other transform properties, the Point of Interest property is available only when you activate a 3D object's Auto-Orient option. When you animate the position of a light or camera, auto-orienting a layer saves you the effort of setting rotation keyframes manually.

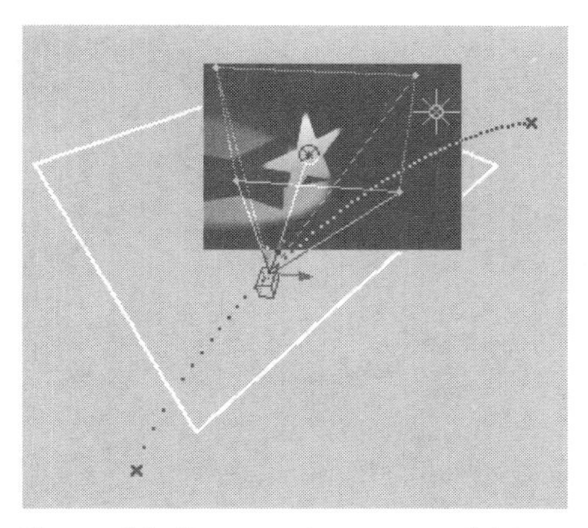

Figure 16.65 You can set a camera or light to automatically orient toward its point of interest as it moves.

By default, cameras and lights are set to orient toward the point of interest automatically. That is, moving a camera or light causes it to rotate so that it always points toward its point of interest. When applied to a camera, this setting may create a point of view similar to that of careless drivers who turn their head to see an accident as they drive by (**Figure 16.65**).

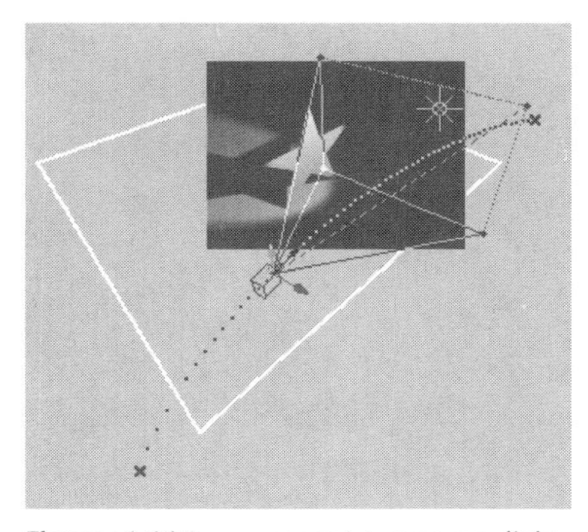

Figure 16.66 Or you can set a camera or light to automatically orient along its motion path.

You can also set each light or camera to auto-orient along its motion path. When applied to a camera, this setting might mimic the view from a roller coaster, automatically rotating the camera to point in a 3D tangent to the motion path (**Figure 16.66**).

continues on next page

Finally, you can turn off the Auto-Orient setting so that the light's or camera's orientation isn't automatically adjusted to maintain a relationship with its motion path or point of interest. When you set Auto-Orient to off, the light or camera loses its Point of Interest property.

To choose the Auto-Orient setting for cameras and lights:

1. Select the camera or light you want to adjust.
2. Choose Layer > Transform > Auto-Orient (**Figure 16.67**).

   An Auto-Orientation dialog box appears (**Figure 16.68**).
3. In the Auto-Orientation dialog box, *choose an option:*

   Off—Turns off Auto-Orient, so that the camera or light rotates independently of its motion path or point of interest. Selecting this option eliminates the camera's or light's Point of Interest property.

   Orient Along Path—Makes the camera or light rotate automatically so that it remains oriented to its motion path.

   Orient Towards Point of Interest—Makes the camera or light rotate automatically as you move it so that it remains oriented toward the point of interest.

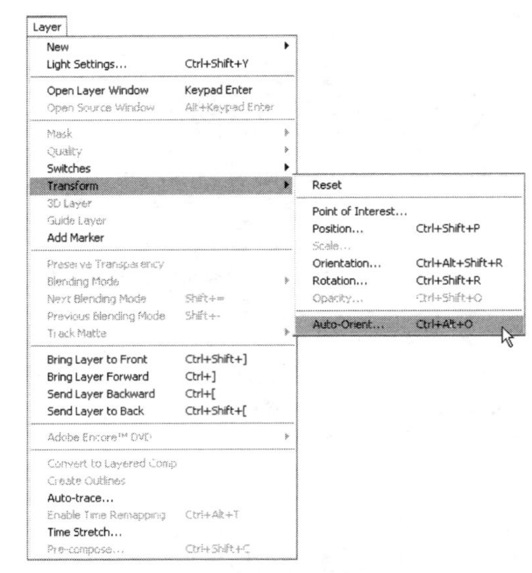

Figure 16.67 Choose Layer > Transform > Auto-Orient.

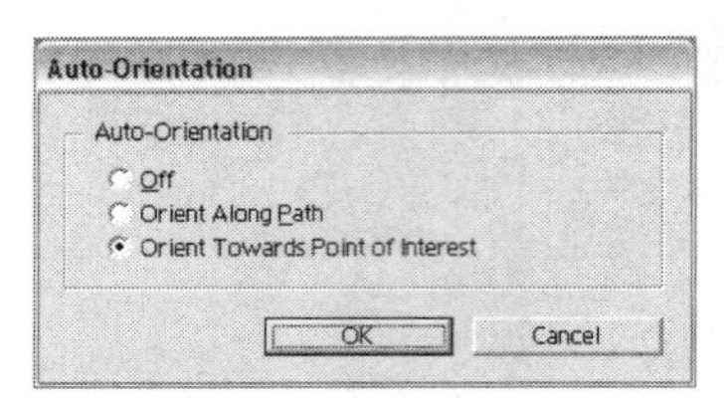

Figure 16.68 An Auto-Orientation dialog box appears.

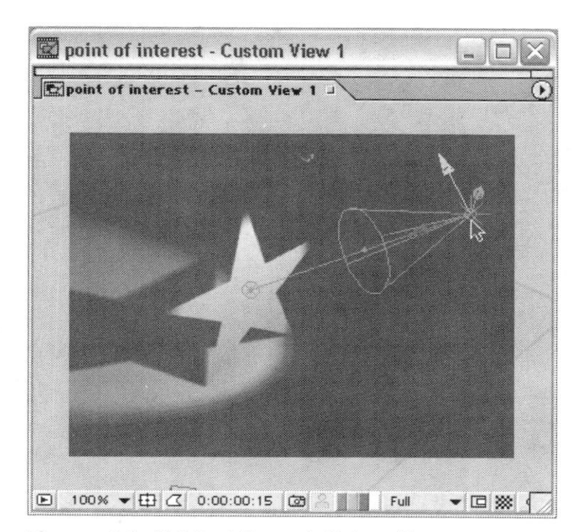

Figure 16.69 If Orient Towards Point of Interest is active...

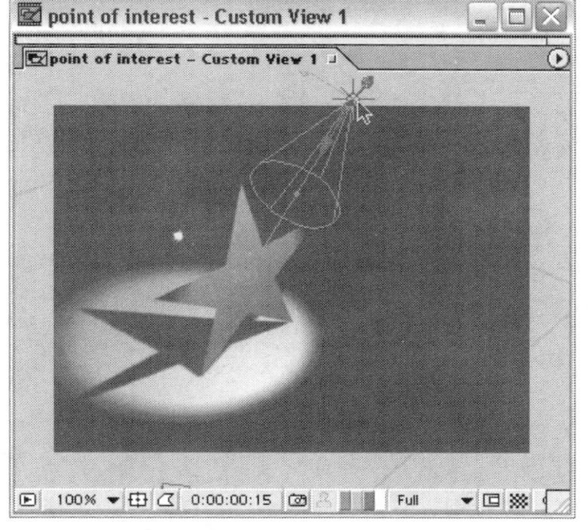

Figure 16.70 ...dragging the camera or light orients it automatically.

To move a light or camera without changing the point of interest:

1. Select a camera or light.
2. In the 3D View pull-down menu, select a view.

   You may also want to choose a different magnification setting in the Composition pull-down menu so that you can see the light or camera in the Composition window.
3. In the Tools palette, select an axis mode.

   The selected layer's axes appear. The *X* axis is red; the *Y* axis is green; the *Z* axis is blue. The axes align according to the axis mode you specified.
4. If necessary, make sure Auto-Orient is set to Orient Towards Point of Interest.

   This is the default setting.
5. *Do any of the following:*
   - ▲ In the Composition window, drag the camera or light (**Figure 16.69**).

   Make sure the Selection tool icon doesn't include an axis letter. If it does, you'll move the camera or light by an axis, and the point of interest will move in tandem with the camera or light.
   - ▲ In the Composition window, position the Selection tool over an axis (so that the cursor displays the letter corresponding to the axis), and Command-drag (Mac) or Ctrl-drag (Windows) (**Figure 16.70**).
   - ▲ In the layer outline, adjust the light's or camera's Position property.

   The selected camera's or light's position changes, but the camera rotates so that its point of interest remains stationary.

To move a camera or light and the point of interest:

1. Select a camera or light.
2. In the 3D View pull-down menu, select a view.

   You may also want to choose a different magnification setting in the Composition pull-down menu so that you can see the light or camera in the Composition window.
3. In the Tools palette, select an axis mode.

   The selected layer's axes appear. The *X* axis is red; the *Y* axis is green; the *Z* axis is blue. The axes align according to the axis mode you specified.
4. If necessary, make sure Auto-Orient is set to Orient Towards Point of Interest. This is the default setting.
5. In the Composition window, position the Selection tool over a camera's or light's axes.

   The Selection tool icon appears with a letter that corresponds to the axis (**Figure 16.71**).
6. Drag the camera or light along the selected axis (**Figure 16.72**).

   As you move the camera or light, its point of interest moves accordingly.

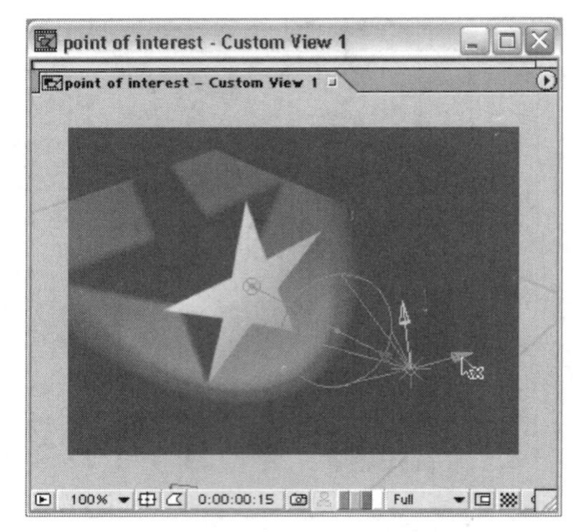

Figure 16.71 Command-dragging (Mac) or Ctrl-dragging (Windows) the camera or light by one of its axes also activates the Orient Towards Point of Interest command...

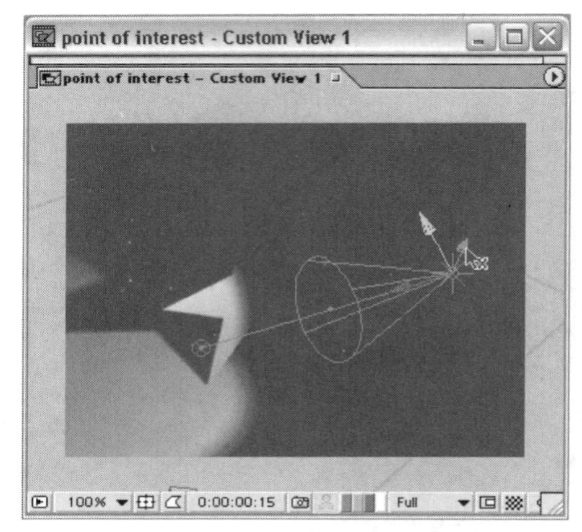

Figure 16.72 ...but dragging the camera or light by one of its axes doesn't allow it to auto-orient. Here, moving the light also moves its point of interest away from the star layer.

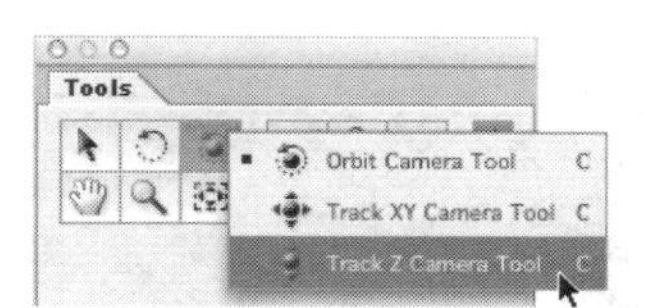

Figure 16.73 Select the Camera tool you want to use.

Figure 16.74 When Auto-Orient is set to Orient Towards Point of Interest, dragging with the Orbit Camera tool...

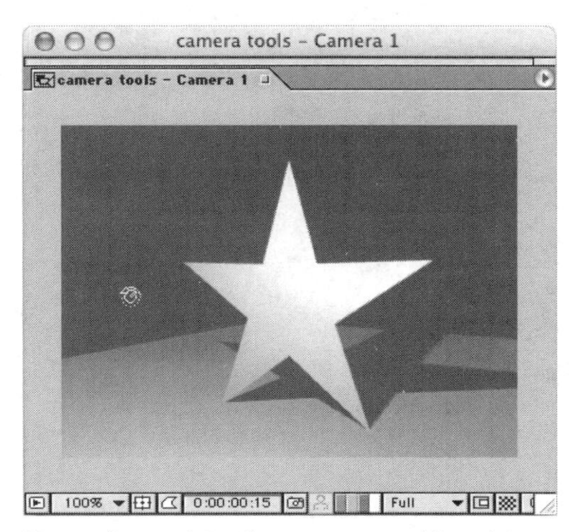

Figure 16.75 ...rotates the camera around its point of interest. Otherwise, the camera rotates around its position.

Using Camera Tools

Camera tools provide you with another way to easily adjust camera views. In contrast to dragging the camera from a separate camera view, Camera tools let you change a camera's Position property while viewing the composition from the camera's point of view. Although it's harder to see the camera's motion path, you get to see the movement from the camera's perspective. You can also use Camera tools to adjust one of the Custom 3D views (see "Viewing 3D Layers in the Comp Window" earlier in this chapter).

To adjust the view using Camera tools:

1. In the 3D View's pull-down menu of the Composition window, select a Camera or Custom view.

   Note that you can't adjust Orthogonal views (Front, Back, Left, Right, Top, Bottom) with Camera tools.

2. If necessary, set the camera's Auto-Orient option to determine how the Orbit Camera tool functions.

   See the next step to learn how Auto-Orient options affect the Orbit Camera tool.

3. In the Tools palette, select a Camera tool (**Figure 16.73**):

   Orbit Camera —Rotates the camera around its point of interest when Auto-Orient is set to Orient Towards Point of Interest. Otherwise, the camera rotates around its position (much like a camera panning on a tripod) (**Figures 16.74** and **16.75**).

continues on next page

Track XY Camera —Moves the camera along its *X* and *Y* axes (similar to a real-world camera tracking right or left, or craning up or down). Regardless of the Auto-Orient setting, the camera's rotation is unaffected (**Figure 16.76**).

Track Z Camera —Moves the camera along its *Z* axis (similar to a camera dollying in or out). Regardless of the Auto-Orient setting, the camera's rotation remains unaffected (**Figure 16.77**).

4. In the Composition window, drag the selected camera tool.

   The Custom view or camera position changes according to the Camera tool you use.

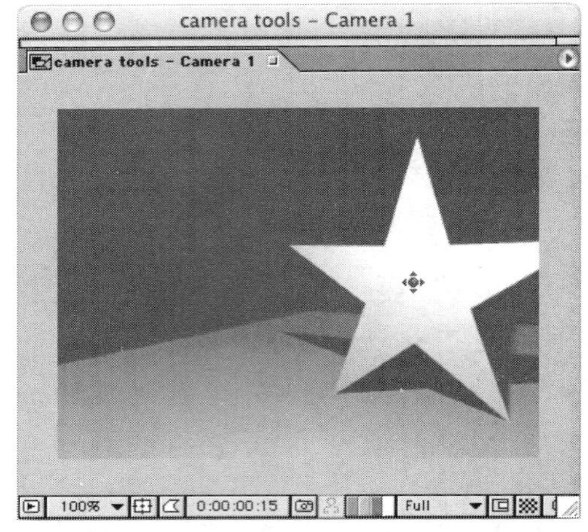

Figure 16.76 Dragging with the Track XY Camera tool lets you move the camera along its *X* and *Y* axes. Here, the camera is tracking left (from its position in Figure 16.75).

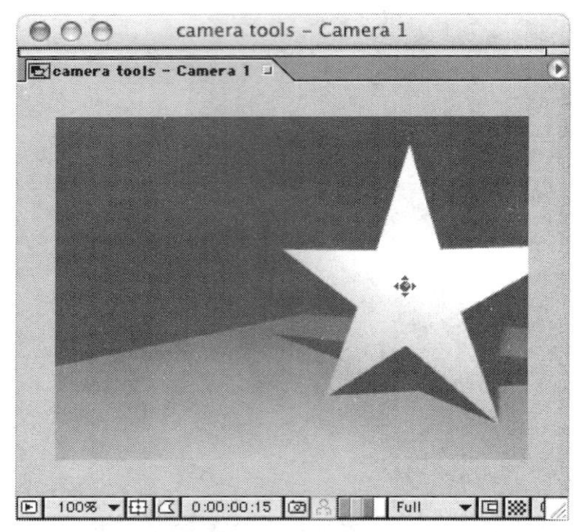

Figure 16.77 Dragging with the Track Z Camera tool lets you move the camera along its *Z* axis. Here, the camera is dollying back from its position in Figure 16.76.

Camera Moves

In film and video production, camera movement is described by the following terms:

Pan—To rotate the camera (typically, on a tripod) on its horizontal axis without moving its position; this causes the scene to scroll through the frame left or right, but the camera's view spans an arc, not a line.

Tilt—To rotate the camera on its vertical axis without moving its position; this causes the scene to scroll through the frame up or down, but the camera's view spans an arc, not a line.

Zoom—To change a camera's focal length (using a zoom lens, rather than a fixed lens) without moving the camera position; this causes the subject to appear larger (when zooming in) or smaller (when zooming out). Because zooming doesn't give the viewer a sense of moving through space, most filmmakers strongly favor a dolly shot.

Track—To move the camera's position left or right (perpendicular to the direction it's pointing). When tracking to keep a subject in the frame, the camera move is often called a *follow shot*.

Dolly—To move the camera closer to the subject (*dolly in*) or farther away from the subject (*dolly out*).

Crane—To move the camera up (*crane up*) or down (*crane down*), often with the assistance of a crane or a device with a hinged arm, called a *jib*.

Previewing 3D

Draft 3D disables lights and shadows as well as blur caused by camera depth-of-field settings. As you've made your way through this book, you've encountered several ways of reducing a composition's preview quality so that you can increase rendering speed. The increased processing demands of 3D compositing will make you appreciate this trade-off even more.

To enable or disable Draft 3D mode:

▲ In the Timeline window, click the Draft 3D mode button (**Figure 16.78**).

The image in the Composition window no longer previews 3D lights, shadows, or depth-of-field blur. Click the button again to deselect it and turn off Draft 3D (**Figures 16.79** and **16.80**).

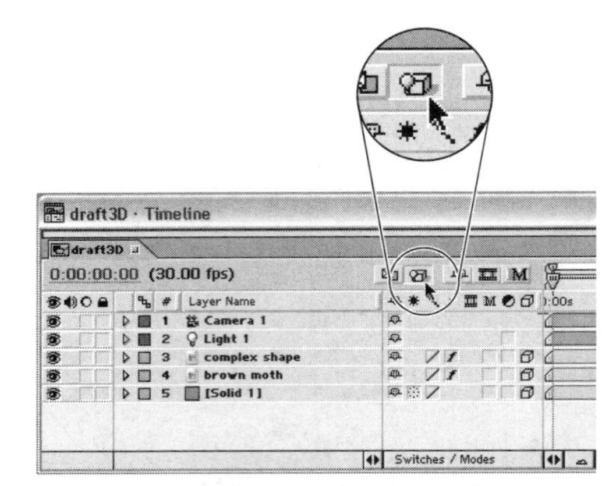

Figure 16.78 In the Timeline window, click the Draft 3D mode button.

Figure 16.79 When Draft 3D mode is off, the Composition window displays lights, shadows, and depth-of-field blur.

Figure 16.80 With Draft 3D mode on, the Composition window doesn't preview lights, shadows, or depth-of-field blur.

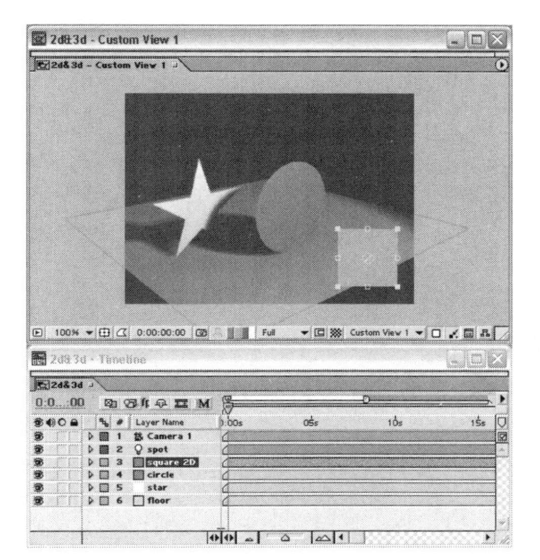

Figure 16.81 In this example, the stacking order prevents the 2D layer from splitting the 3D layers into separately rendered worlds.

Understanding 3D Layer Order

As you learned in Chapter 5, "Layer Basics," layers listed higher in the Timeline window's layer outline appear in front of other layers in the Composition window. After Effects always renders 2D layers in order, from the bottom of the layer stacking order to the top. (See "Rendering Order" in Chapter 17, "Complex Projects.")

However, the simple 2D stacking order becomes irrelevant in 3D compositing, where object layering is determined by objects' relative positions in 3D space according to the current 3D view.

For 3D layers, After Effects renders from the most distant layer (with the highest *Z*-coordinate value) to the closest (with the lowest *Z*-coordinate value).

Combining 2D and 3D

When a composition contains both 2D and 3D layers, the rendering order becomes even more complex, combining aspects of both 2D and 3D rendering. Once again, layers are rendered from the bottom of the stacking order to the top. However, 3D layers are rendered in independent sets, separated by 2D layers.

In other words, placing a 2D layer so that it doesn't separate the 3D layers in the Timeline's stacking order allows the 3D layers to interact geometrically. 3D layers appear in front of one another and interact with lights and shadows according to their position in 3D space (as well as according to light settings and material options). The 2D layers neither share the same space as 3D layers nor interact with lights or cameras (**Figure 16.81**).

continues on next page

In contrast, positioning a 2D layer between 3D layers in the stacking order splits the 3D layers into separate groups. Although the 3D layers share the same lights and cameras, they exist in identical but separate 3D "worlds" and are rendered independently of one another (**Figure 16.82**).

✔ Tip

- For more on working effectively with the rendering order, see "Rendering Order" in Chapter 17.

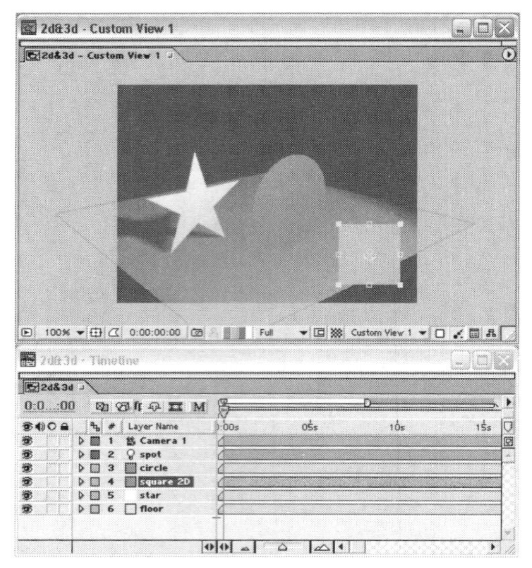

Figure 16.82 In this example, the 2D layer's position in the stacking order causes the 3D layers to be rendered separately. Notice how the star no longer casts or accepts shadows.

17

Complex Projects

As your projects become more ambitious, their structures will grow increasingly complex as well. A typical project contains not only layers created from individual footage items but also layers created from other compositions—called *nested compositions*. In this chapter, you'll find out how to employ nesting to group layers into a single element as well as to manipulate a project's hierarchy to create effects you couldn't otherwise achieve.

After Effects includes several other features that help you create complex projects without resorting to complicated procedures. The new Parenting feature, for example, makes it possible to create a hierarchical relationship between a "parent" layer and any number of "child" layers—thus allowing you to link or group layers so that they behave as a single system.

Using another powerful feature—Expressions—you can create relationships between layer properties (in the same layer, in different layers, even in layers contained within different compositions). This means that rather than keyframing multiple properties independently, you can link one property's values to another property's values using a JavaScript-based instruction, or *expression*. (Don't worry: This chapter also provides the JavaScript basics you'll need to feel confident about working with expressions.)

Finally, this chapter provides the lowdown on *render order*, After Effects' hierarchical scheme for rendering frames. You'll learn how render order influences your results, as well as how *you* can influence render order. You'll also find out how to inspect your work using the Flowchart view, as well as how to reduce render and preview time via a process called *prerendering*.

Nesting

In Chapter 4, "Compositions," you learned that a composition used as a layer in another composition is called a *nested composition*. Such compositions can serve various interconnected purposes.

Nesting enables you to treat several layers as a group (in much the same way that you group various elements in other graphics programs, such as Illustrator and Quark Express). When you're working with a nested composition, you can manipulate several layers as a unit rather than keyframe each individually (**Figures 17.1** and **17.2**).

Similarly, you can use a nested composition as often as you would any single layer—which means you need only build a multilayered animation once to use it several times in a composition. As you can see, nesting can spare you a lot of tedious copying and pasting as well as an unwieldy number of redundant layers (**Figure 17.3**).

Whether a nested composition is used multiple times in one composition or several, you can revise every instance in a single step; each nested composition reflects any changes you make to its source. To speed the revision process, it makes sense to use nested compositions for components you plan to reuse.

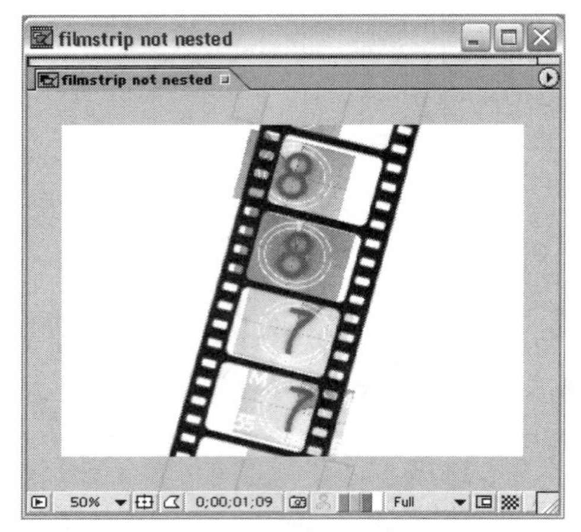

Figure 17.1 Doing something as simple as adjusting the rotation can be difficult if you need to apply it to a number of separate layers.

Figure 17.2 Nesting the composition containing those layers lets you treat them as a single element.

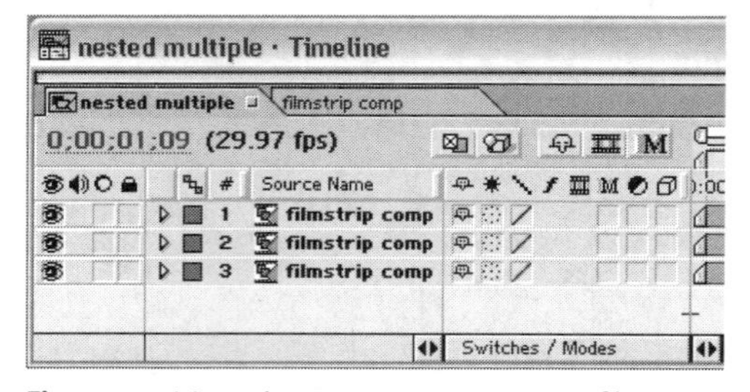

Figure 17.3 It's easier to repeat a sequence of layers as a nested composition. You can revise multiple copies in a single step by altering layers in the source composition.

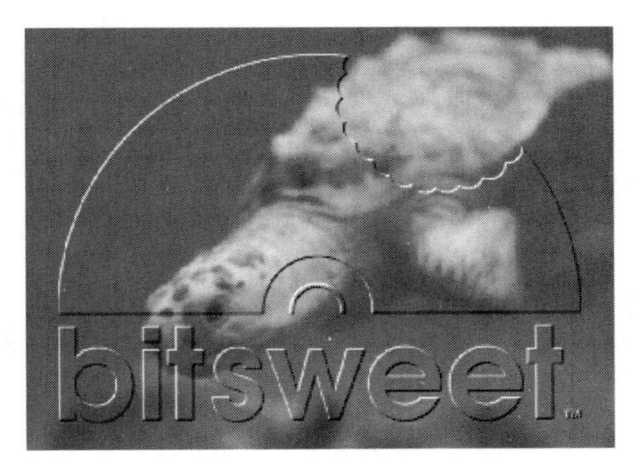

Figure 17.4 By using a nested composition, you can change render order and create effects you couldn't otherwise achieve—for example, compound effects like this one bypass transform adjustments like scale and position.

Figure 17.5 However, you can use a nested composition as the effect source. This way, transform properties are calculated in the nested composition before they're used as an effect source.

Nested compositions can also help you circumvent After Effects' default rendering order. The sequence in which properties are rendered often makes it difficult or impossible to achieve the desired effect. Although you can't break the rules, you can use nesting to work the system (**Figures 17.4** and **17.5**). To learn more about rendering order, move on to the next section, "Rendering Order."

To nest a composition:

1. Display the Composition window or Timeline window of the composition that will contain the nested composition.
2. Drag a composition you want to nest from the Project window to any of the following (**Figure 17.6**):
   - ▲ Composition window of the target composition
   - ▲ Timeline window of the target composition
   - ▲ Name or icon of the target composition in the Project window

   The composition becomes a layer in the target composition, beginning at the current time and having the same duration as the original composition.

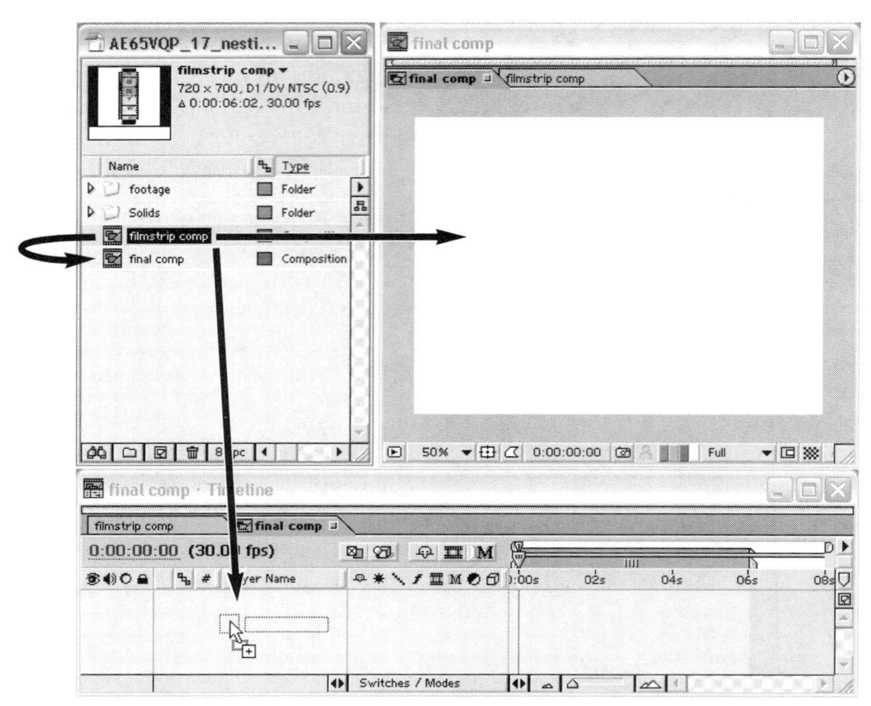

Figure 17.6 Drag a composition you want to nest from the Project window to the Composition window, the Timeline window, or the icon of the target composition.

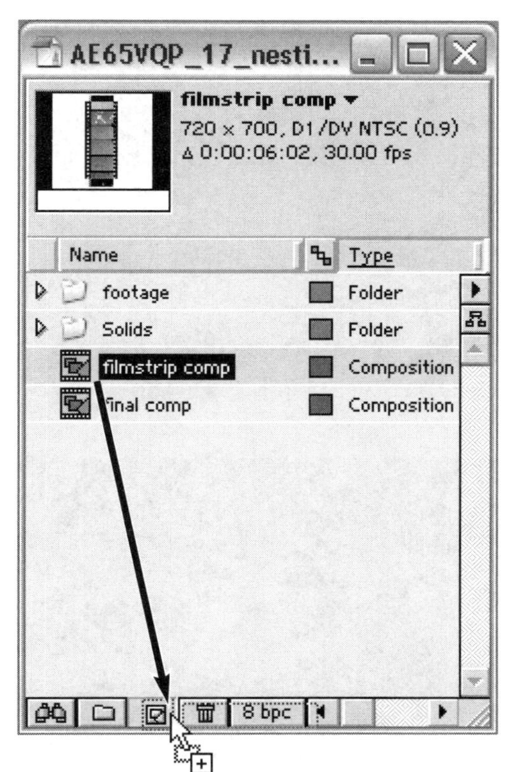

Figure 17.7 Dragging a composition to the Composition icon nests the composition in another composition that has the same settings.

To nest one composition in a new composition with the same settings:

- Drag a composition in the Project window to the Composition icon at the bottom of the Project window (**Figure 17.7**).

  The composition becomes a layer in a new composition that uses the same composition settings as the nested one.

✔ Tips

- Nesting will help you get around some of the compound-effect restrictions that you learned about in Chapter 10, "Effects Fundamentals."
- To find out how to turn selected layers into a nested composition retroactively, see "Precomposing" later in this chapter.
- Like nesting, the new Parenting feature can also link layers as a group or system. See "Using Parenting" later in this chapter.
- By creating relationships between layer properties, the new Expressions feature provides another method of working around After Effects' rendering order.

Rendering Order

When After Effects renders frames for playback or output, it calculates each attribute in a particular sequence referred to as the *rendering order.*

Having interpreted the source footage according to your specifications, After Effects processes each frame layer by layer. Starting with a composition's bottom layer, After Effects renders layer properties in the order they're listed in the layer outline: masks, effects, and transform. Then, the program processes layer modes and track mattes before combining the layer with the underlying layers. Rendering proceeds in this fashion for successively higher layers in the stacking order until the frame is complete (**Figures 17.8**, **17.9**, **17.10**, **17.11**, and **17.12**).

Figure 17.8 Starting with the bottom layer...

Figure 17.9 ...After Effects renders the masks first...

Figure 17.10 ...then applies effects in the order they appear in the Effect Controls window...

Figure 17.11 ...then calculates transform properties...

Figure 17.12 ...and finally calculates track mattes and modes before combining the layer with the underlying image.

For audio layers, rendering proceeds in the same sequence: effects followed by levels. If you were to change the audio speed, time remapping would be calculated first and time stretch would be calculated last.

Now that After Effects supports 3D compositing, rendering order can be determined by a layer's relative *Z*-coordinate values as well as by whether the composition contains a mix of 2D and 3D layers. See "Understanding 3D Layer Order" in Chapter 16, "3D Layers," for more information.

To identify most problems you're likely to encounter with an animation, you need to understand its render order and how to circumvent it.

Subverting the Render Order

If you were to strictly adhere to the render order, certain effects would be impossible to achieve. For example, you might want to use the Motion Tile effect to replicate a rotating object. However, rendering order dictates that the Motion Tile effect be rendered before the rotation, a transform property. Unfortunately, this causes the layer to rotate after tiling—*not* the effect you desire (**Figure 17.13**). To solve the problem, you must defy the rendering order so that the effects are calculated after transformations (**Figure 17.14**).

Although you can't alter the rendering order directly, you can do so indirectly. For example, you can subvert render order by using the Transform effect or an adjustment layer, or by nesting or precomposing. In some cases, you can use an expression to make continual adjustments to a property automatically, effectively defeating limitations imposed by the rendering order.

Transform effect

In many instances, you'll need a transform property to render before an effect property. Fortunately, all of the transform properties (as well as the Skew and Shutter Angle properties) are also available as Transform effects. By placing the Transform effect higher on the list in the Effect Controls window, you can render it before subsequent effects on the list (**Figure 17.15**).

Figure 17.13 Because After Effects calculates effects before transform properties, the layer is tiled before it rotates—which, in this case, isn't the result we want.

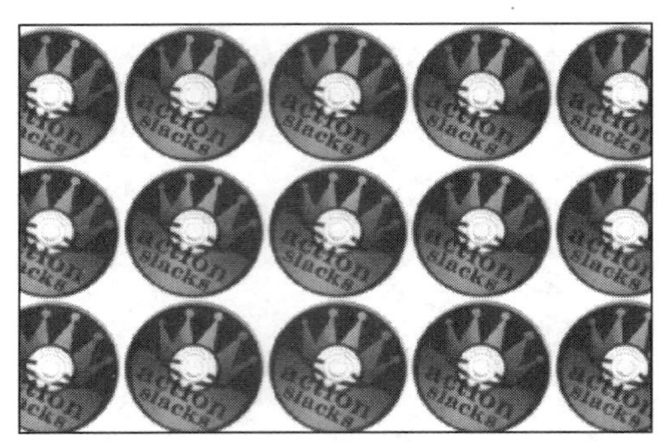

Figure 17.14 To create the desired effect, the effect must be calculated before the rotation.

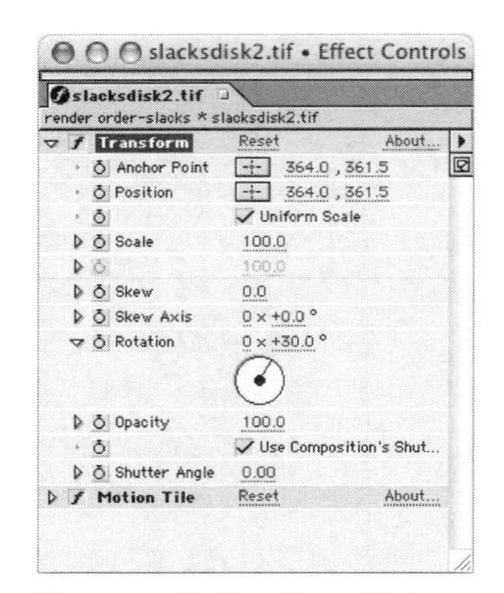

Figure 17.15 The Transform effect emulates the actual transform properties. To render it before other effects, you can place it higher in the list in the Effect Controls window.

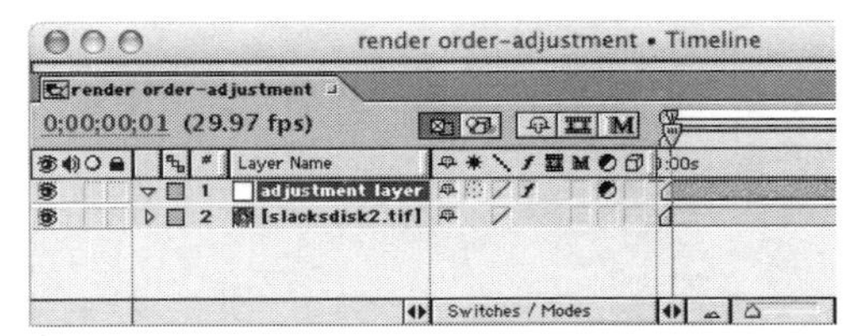

Figure 17.16 You can postpone the rendering of an effect by placing it in an adjustment layer higher in the layer stack.

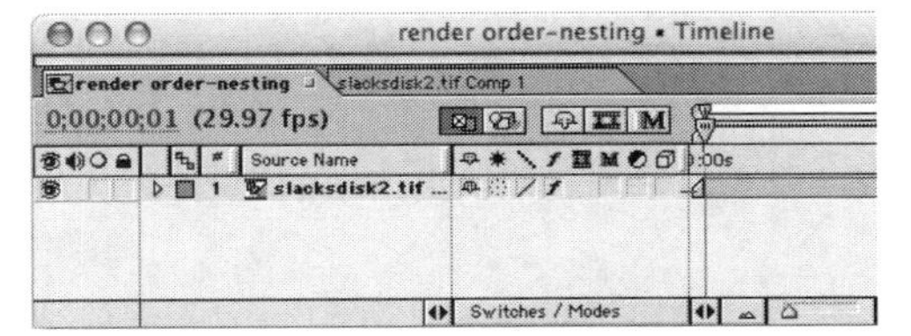

Figure 17.17 You can also use a nested composition to effectively change the render order. Before After Effects renders the nested composition as a layer, it must complete the rendering sequence within the nested composition.

Adjustment layer

Because the render order proceeds from the bottom of the layer stack, you can postpone rendering an effect by placing it in an adjustment layer. After Effects then calculates the properties in the lower layers before the adjustment layer affects them (**Figure 17.16**).

As you'll recall from Chapter 10, the effects contained in an adjustment layer are applied to all the underlying layers. To limit an adjustment layer's effects to just some of those lower layers, you must nest or precompose them with the adjustment layer.

Nesting or precomposing

Another way to effectively change the rendering order is to place layers in a nested composition. (*Precomposing* refers to another method of creating a nested composition—you might think of it as nesting retroactively—so it works the same way.)

As you'll recall, nesting describes the process of using a composition as a layer in another composition. Before After Effects can render the nested composition as a layer, however, it must complete the rendering sequence within the nested composition. In other words, the properties of the layers contained by the nested composition are calculated first. Then, the nested composition is treated like the other layers, and its properties are processed according to the render order (**Figure 17.17**).

Expressions

In some cases, an expression can compensate for the unwanted effects of the rendering order. For example, an expression can link an effect property to a transform property, so that the effect adjusts dynamically to compensate for the fact that it's calculated before the transformations.

Synchronizing Time

As you've no doubt noticed, windows related to the same composition display the same time. Naturally, windows related to different compositions aren't synchronized in this way. So what happens when a composition is nested?

You can set a preference that determines whether the times displayed in windows of nested composition are synchronized with related windows (**Figures 17.18** and **17.19**).

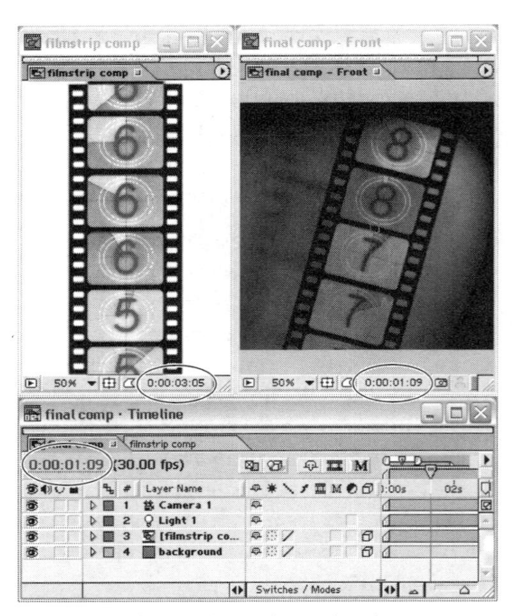

Figure 17.18 The time in windows related to a composition can update independently of the windows related to its nested compositions...

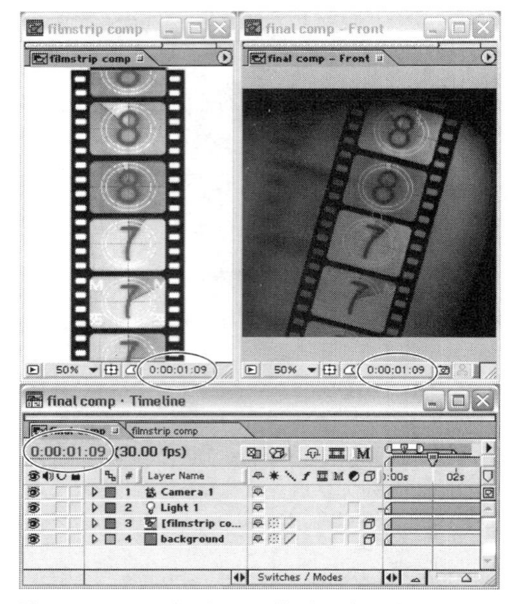

Figure 17.19...or the time in all related windows can be synchronized.

Figure 17.20 Choose Edit > Preferences > General.

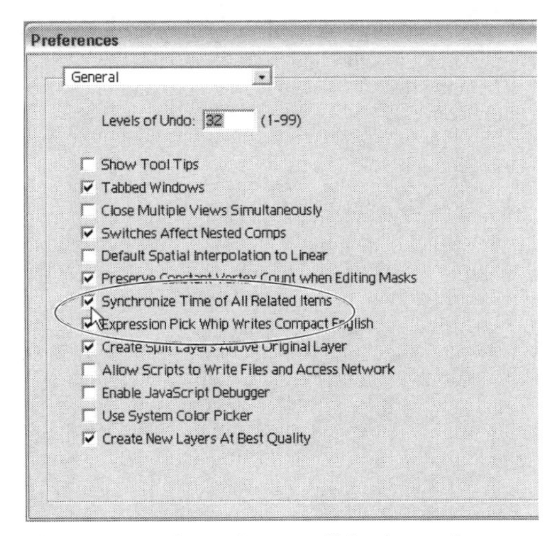

Figure 17.21 In the Preferences dialog box, select Synchronize Time of All Related Items.

To synchronize times of related items:

1. Choose Edit > Preferences > General (**Figure 17.20**).

   The General panel of the Preferences dialog box appears.

2. In the Preferences dialog box, select Synchronize Time of All Related Items (**Figure 17.21**).

Using the Flowchart View

The Flowchart view enables you to see the structure and hierarchy of the current composition or the entire project. In the Flowchart View window, you can view the relationship between project and/or composition elements in flowchart fashion (**Figure 17.22**). This can be particularly useful for evaluating your final composition, which typically contains nested compositions. It also provides a good way to familiarize yourself with an old project or one that someone else has produced.

You can customize the layout and level of detail of the flowchart. You can even open a composition directly from the Flowchart view. However, you can't use the Flowchart view to change the way your project is organized.

To display the Flowchart view:

Do one of the following:

- To view a flowchart for the current composition, click the Flowchart View button in the Composition window (**Figure 17.23**).
- To view a flowchart for the entire project, click the Flowchart View button in the Project window (**Figure 17.24**).

  A Flowchart window appears.

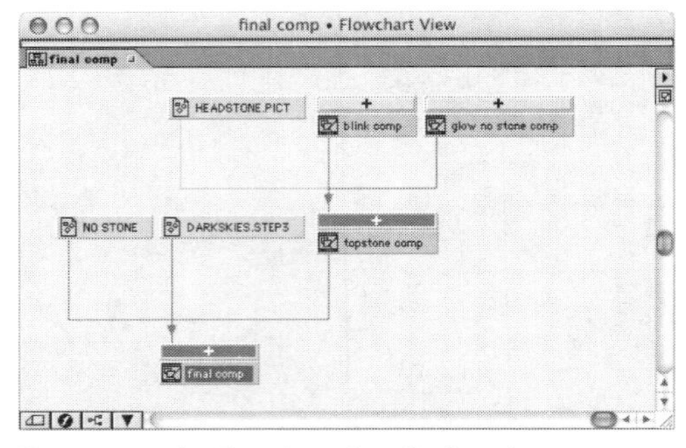

Figure 17.22 The Flowchart view displays the structure of a project or composition as a flowchart.

Figure 17.23 Click the Flowchart View button in the Composition window to view a flowchart of the composition...

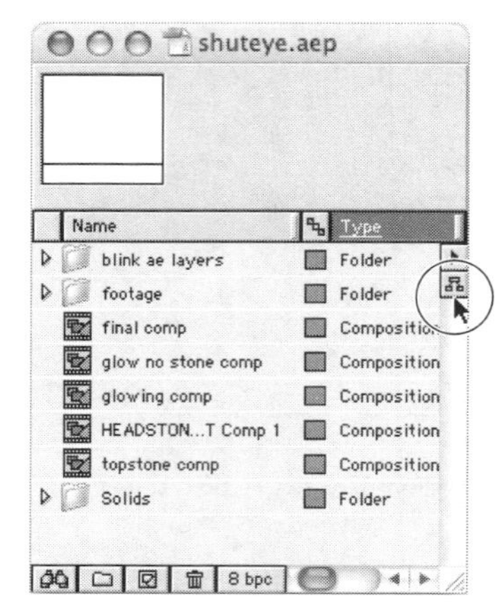

Figure 17.24 ...or click the Flowchart View button in the Project window to view a flowchart of the entire project.

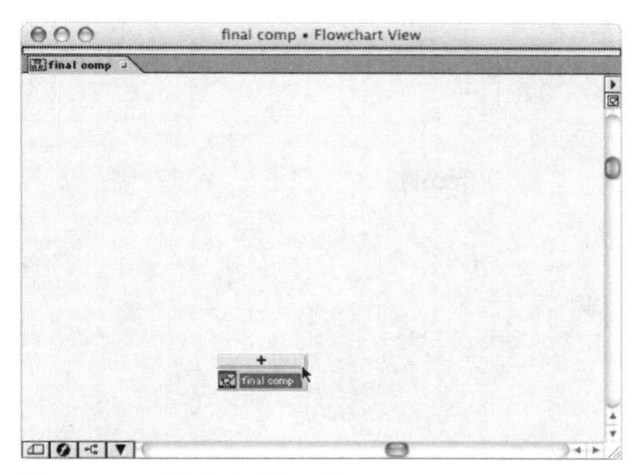

Figure 17.25 Click the Plus sign...

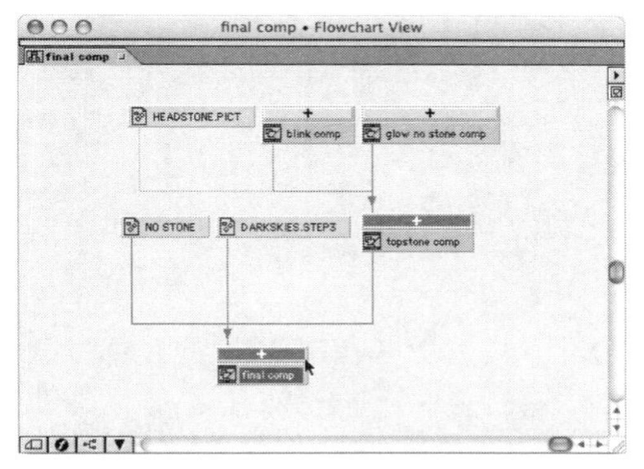

Figure 17.26 ...to expand a composition's flowchart. Click again to collapse it.

To customize the Flowchart view:

Do any of the following:

- To expand or collapse a composition in the flowchart, click the plus sign at the top of a composition item in the flowchart (**Figures 17.25** and **17.26**).
- To change the size of the Flowchart view, drag the corner of the window.
- To move items in the flowchart, drag them to a new position (**Figure 17.27**).
- To show or hide layers in the flowchart, click the Layer button (**Figure 17.28**).

continues on next page

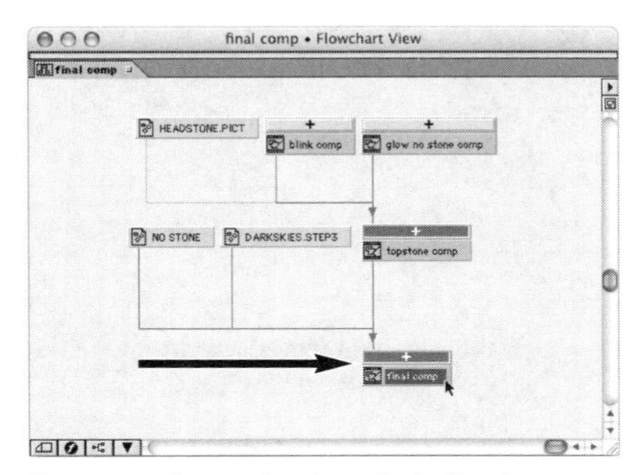

Figure 17.27 You can drag items in the flowchart to arrange them; however, you can't change their relationships.

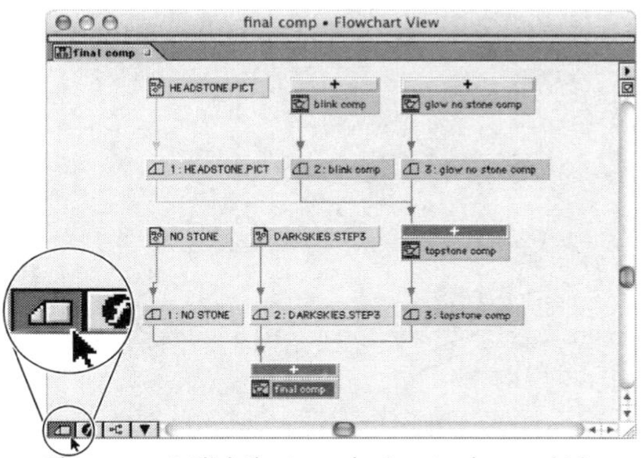

Figure 17.28 Click the Layer button to show or hide layers in the flowchart.

- To show or hide effects for layers, click the Effects button (**Figure 17.29**).
- To toggle between straight and angled lines in the flowchart, click the Line Format/Cleanup button (**Figure 17.30**).
- To clean up the flowchart, Option-click (Mac) or Alt-click (Windows) the Line Format/Cleanup button.
- To change the arrangement of the flowchart, choose an option from the Flow Direction pull-down menu (**Figure 17.31**):
  - ▲ Top to Bottom
  - ▲ Bottom to Top
  - ▲ Left to Right
  - ▲ Right to Left

  The direction of the flowchart changes according to your choice (**Figure 17.32**).

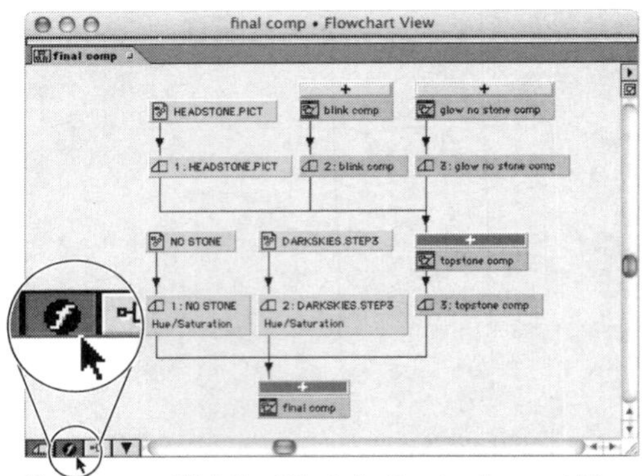

Figure 17.29 Click the Effects button to show or hide effect names with the layers.

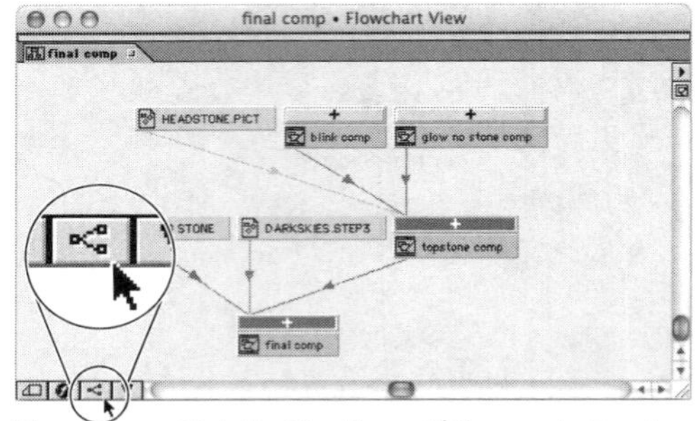

Figure 17.30 Click the Line Format/Cleanup button to toggle between straight and angled lines in the flowchart.

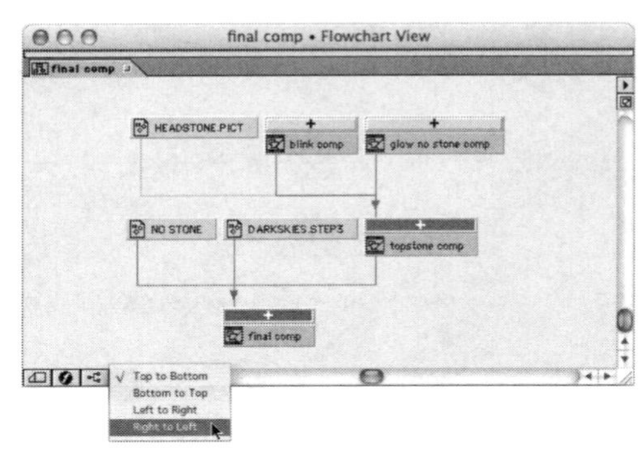

Figure 17.31 Choose an option from the Flow Direction pull-down menu.

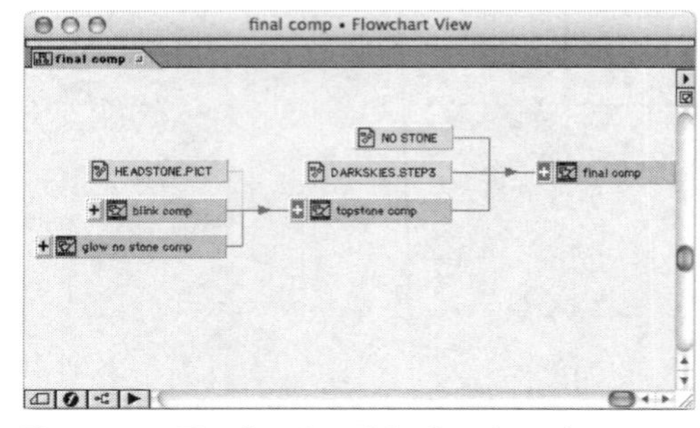

Figure 17.32 The direction of the flowchart changes according to your choice.

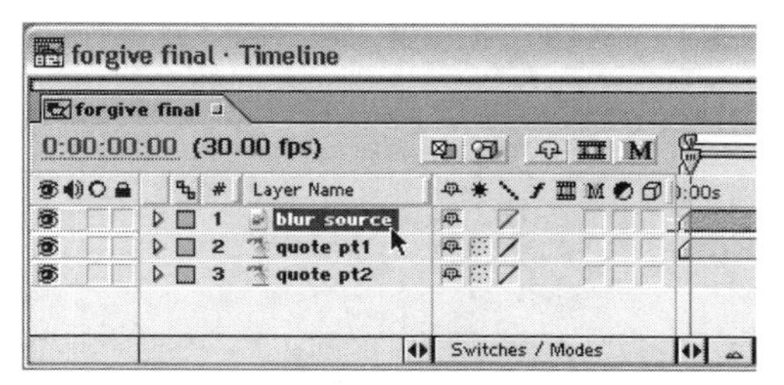

Figure 17.33 Precomposing allows you to select one or more layers...

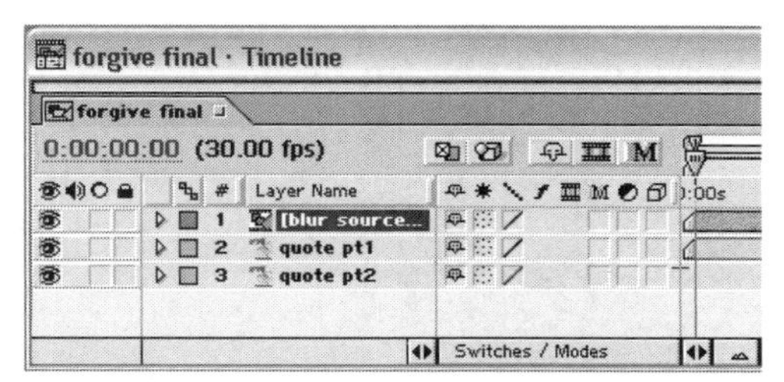

Figure 17.34 ...and place them into a nested composition.

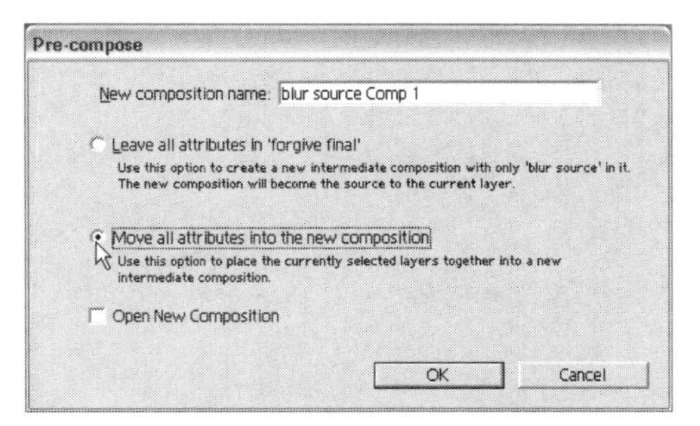

Figure 17.35 When you precompose one or more layers, After Effects prompts you with a dialog box of options.

Precomposing

As you've no doubt figured out by now, it can take a fair amount of planning to nest compositions and create hierarchies of elements. However, you can't always anticipate the need to nest. Often, you realize that layers should be contained in a nested composition only after they're part of the current composition. Fortunately, you can repackage layers of an existing composition into a nested composition by using a method called *precomposing*.

The Pre-compose command places one or more selected layers in a nested composition (or, if you prefer, a *precomp*)—thus accomplishing in a single step what could otherwise be a tedious reorganization process (**Figures 17.33** and **17.34**).

When you precompose more than one layer, their properties (masks, effects, transform) and associated keyframes are retained and moved into the nested composition. When you precompose a single layer, on the other hand, you may choose whether its properties and keyframes move with it or remain in the current composition (becoming properties of the nested composition). After Effects prompts you with a dialog box that lists your choices (**Figure 17.35**):

Leave all attributes in [current composition] moves a single layer into a nested composition. The nested composition has the size and duration of the layer, and it acquires the layer's properties and keyframes.

Move all attributes into the new composition moves one or more layers into a nested composition, which has the size and duration of the current composition. All properties and keyframes are retained by the layers and move with them into the nested composition.

Open new composition opens the newly created nested composition automatically. Leaving this option unselected creates a nested composition but leaves the current composition open.

To precompose one or more layers:

1. Select one or more layers in the Timeline window (**Figure 17.36**).
2. *Do either of the following:*
   - ▲ Choose Layer > Pre-compose (**Figure 17.37**).
   - ▲ Press Shift-Command-C (Mac) or Shift-Ctrl-C (Windows).

   A Pre-compose dialog box appears (**Figure 17.38**).
3. In the Pre-compose dialog box, *select an option:*
   - ▲ Leave all attributes in [current composition]
   - ▲ Move all attributes into the new composition

   If you're precomposing more than one layer, only the second option is available.

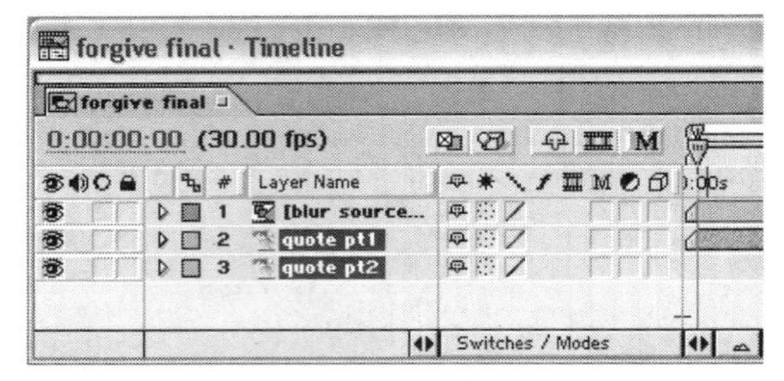

Figure 17.36 Select one or more layers in the Timeline window.

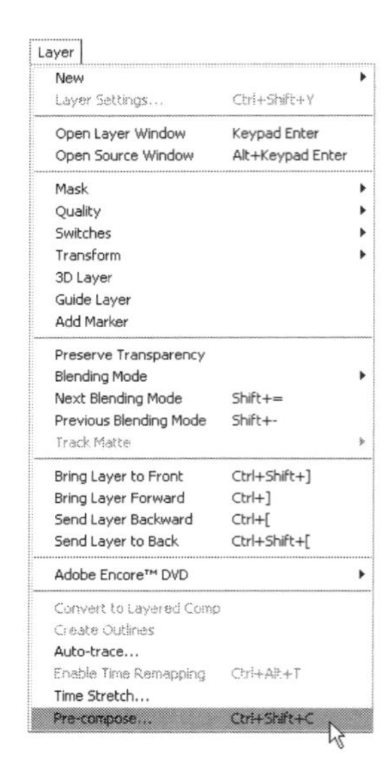

Figure 17.37 Choose Layer > Pre-compose.

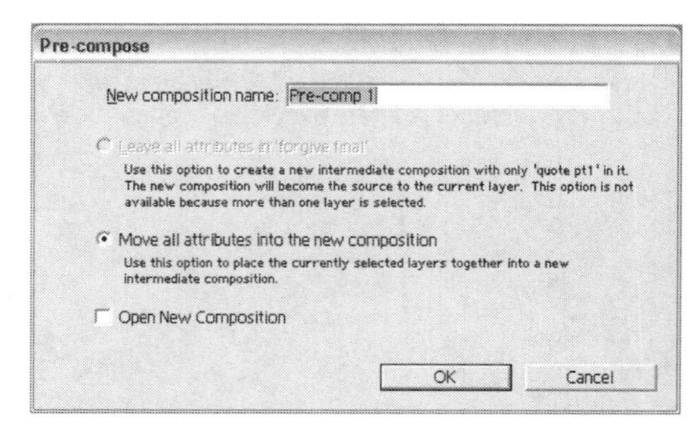

Figure 17.38 In the Pre-compose dialog box, select an option.

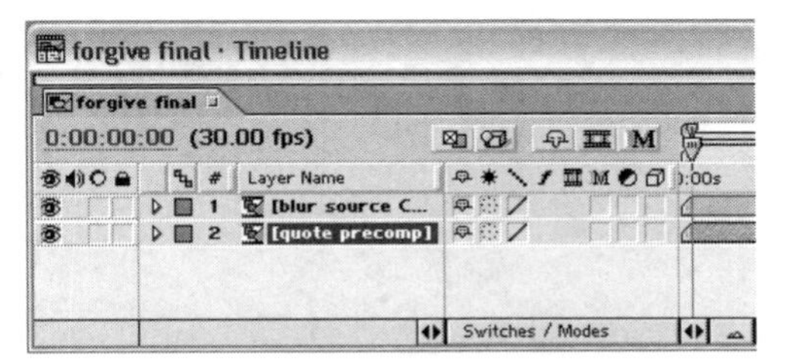

Figure 17.39 The selected layers are moved into another composition, which replaces them in the current composition.

4. To have After Effects open the nested composition automatically, select Open New Composition.

5. Click OK to close the Pre-compose dialog box.

   The selected layers are moved into another composition, which is nested in the current composition (**Figure 17.39**). The nested composition is also listed in the Project window.

✔ Tip

■ The term *precompose* has replaced what much older versions of After Effects referred to as *compify*.

Collapsing Transformations

Sometimes the render order in nested compositions can cause image resolution to degrade. This happens because transform properties, such as Scale, are calculated at every tier in the project hierarchy: first in the most deeply nested composition, then in the next, and so on. At each level, the image is rasterized—that is, its resolution is defined and then redefined in successive compositions.

Scaling down an image in a nested composition rasterizes the image at the smaller size and, consequently, at a lower resolution (**Figures 17.40** and **17.41**). Because the smaller image becomes the source for successive compositions, scaling it up again makes the reduced resolution more apparent (**Figure 17.42**).

This rescaling process is sometimes unavoidable, especially when a boss or client dictates revisions. In such circumstances, you can maintain image quality by *collapsing transformations.*

By collapsing transformations, you prevent After Effects from rasterizing the image in every successive composition, instead forcing it to calculate all the transform property changes and rasterize the image only once—in the composition with the Collapse Transformations switch selected. This way, the composition uses the resolution of the source image rather than that of intermediate versions (**Figure 17.43**).

Figure 17.40 When an image at one resolution...

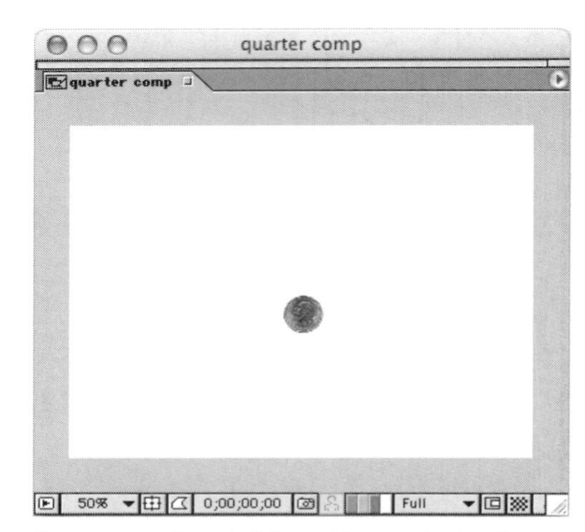

Figure 17.41 ...is scaled down, it's rasterized at the new size.

Figure 17.42 Scaling the image up again in a subsequent composition doesn't restore the original resolution.

Figure 17.43 By collapsing transformations, you can postpone rasterization until rendering reaches the nested composition in which the switch is selected.

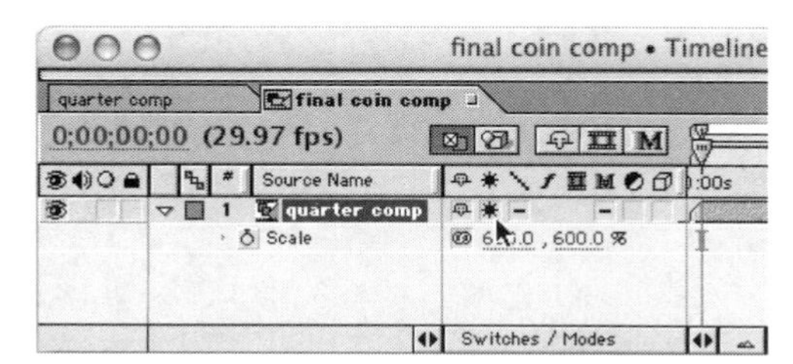

Figure 17.44 Click the Collapse Transformations switch for a nested composition.

One surprising result of the Collapse Transformations setting is that it ignores the frame size of nested compositions. This means layers that had been cropped by the border of a nested composition will appear uncropped in the collapsed composition. You can add a stencil mode or mask to a layer in a nested composition to reestablish the frame edge.

You should also realize that the Opacity settings for the nested compositions are retained and combine with the opacity of the layer that uses collapsed transformations.

To collapse transformations:

1. If necessary, click the Switches/Modes button in the Timeline window to display the Switches panel.
2. For a nested composition, select the Collapse Transformations switch (**Figure 17.44**).

   The same switch is used to continuously rasterize a layer created from path-based artwork

✔ Tips

- Collapse Transformations was called Collapse Geometrics in older versions of After Effects.
- When applied to a layer created from a path-based illustration (such as an Illustrator file), the Collapse Transformations switch functions as the Continuously Rasterize switch. See Chapter 2, "Importing Footage into a Project," for more information.
- Naturally, scaling a bitmapped image beyond 100 percent makes its pixels visible, regardless of the Collapse Transformations setting.

Recursive Switches

By default, controls for nested compositions operate recursively. That is, setting a switch for a nested composition also sets the switch for the layers nested within it. These switches include Collapse Transformations, Continuously Rasterize, and Quality. The composition's Resolution, Enable Motion Blur setting, and Enable Frame Blending setting also operate recursively.

In general, recursive switches can save you time and effort. Sometimes, however, recursive switches can produce undesired results. In a complex project, for example, you might enable Collapse Transformations for a nested composition. If the nested composition contained yet another composition, its Collapse Transformations switch would be enabled as well. As a result, you might unintentionally reveal parts of layers that had been cropped by the nested comp's frame edges. Similarly, recursive switches could prevent you from enabling Motion Blur selectively in a series of nested compositions. As a rule, use recursive switches. If using a switch has unintended consequences, disable recursive switches.

To enable or disable recursive switches:

1. Choose After Effects > Preferences > General (Mac) or Edit > Preferences > General (Windows) (**Figure 17.45**).

   The General panel of the Preferences dialog box appears.

2. In the Preferences dialog box, select Switches Affect Nested Comps (**Figure 17.46**).

   Select the check box to set recursive switches as the default; unselect it to set switches for nested compositions individually.

Figure 17.45 Choose After Effects > Preferences > General (Mac) or Edit > Preferences > General (Windows).

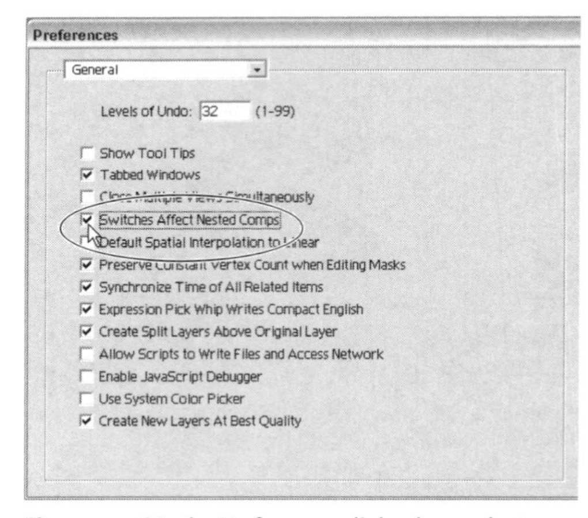

Figure 17.46 In the Preferences dialog box, select Switches Affect Nested Comps.

✔ Tip

- Previous versions of After Effects used the term *recursive switches*, but the current version avoids jargon and instead uses the phrase *Switches Affect Nested Comps*.

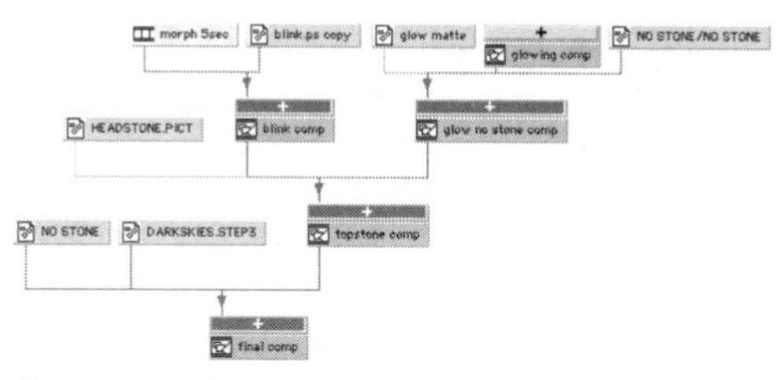

Figure 17.47 By prerendering, you avoid rendering every element of a nested composition...

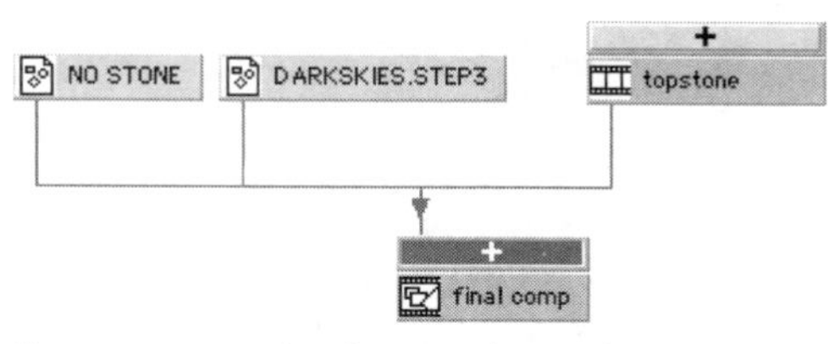

Figure 17.48 ...and replace it with a rendered version. (This flowchart illustrates the process; the actual Flowchart view will continue to show the nested composition.)

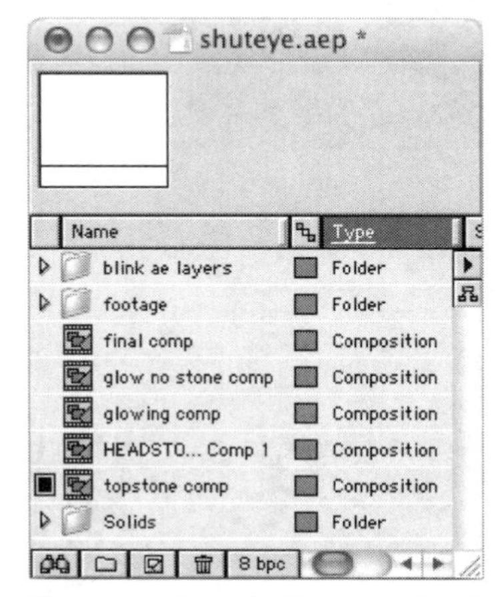

Figure 17.49 Because the prerendered movie is a proxy, you can always switch back to the nested composition.

Prerendering

It seems that if you're not occupied with making the project better, you're preoccupied with making it render faster. Prerendering is one strategy you can use to reduce rendering times.

Typically, you'll complete work on nested compositions long before the final composition is ready—which makes it all the more frustrating to wait for them to render (not to mention unnecessary).

In a process known as *prerendering*, you can render nested compositions and use the movie file as a proxy. Thereafter, render times are reduced because After Effects refers to the movie instead of calculating every element in the nested composition (**Figures 17.47** and **17.48**). If you decide you need to make changes, you can stop using the proxy and switch back to the source composition (**Figure 17.49**). Prerender the composition again to save the changes in the proxy. As you'll learn in Chapter 18, "Output," you can set a post-render action to prerender a comp and set the rendered file as a proxy in a single step.

To reduce render times for the final output, make sure that the Pre-render settings are compatible with the settings of your final file and that you've set the Render settings to Use Proxies.

To use prerendering, consult Chapter 18 as well as the "Proxies and Placeholders" section of Chapter 3, "Managing Footage."

Parenting Layers

Often, you need layers to act as a group or an integrated system. For example, you might want to connect the parts of a machine or simulate the orbits of a planetary system. You can do either of these things by establishing a relationship between one layer's transformation properties and the transformation properties of one or more other layers—a technique fittingly known as *parenting* (**Figures 17.50** and **17.51**).

Figure 17.50 Parenting establishes a relationship between one layer's transformation properties and that of one or more other layers. Using parenting, all the layers that make up the panels of this aperture move in unison.

Figure 17.51 In this example, parenting links all of the layers so that they move as a single paper airplane.

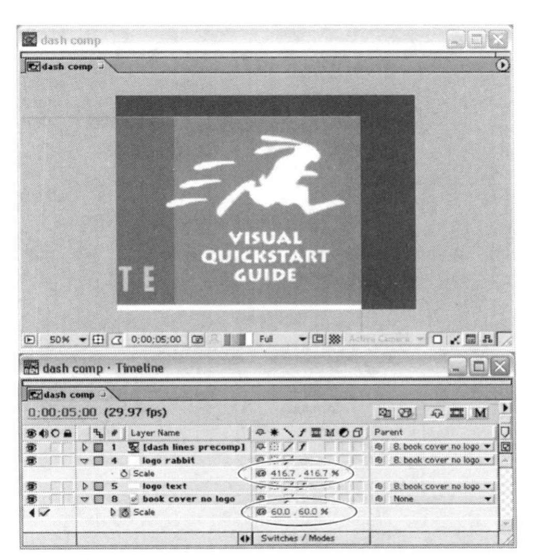

Figure 17.52 Although the child layer's (the rabbit logo's) and parent layer's (the book cover's) transform properties are linked...

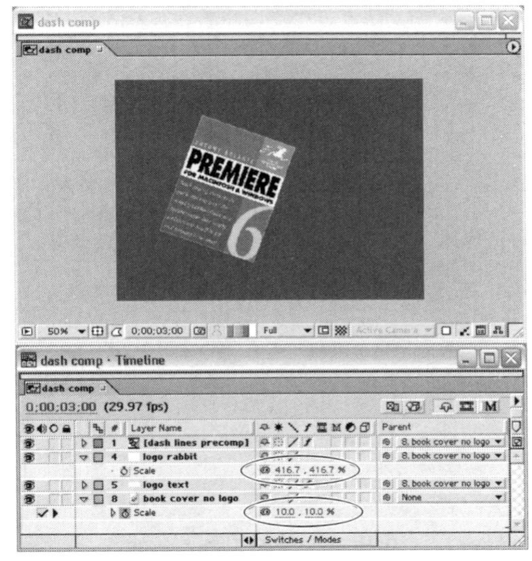

Figure 17.53 ...changing the parent's property value isn't reflected in the child layer's property value display.

Changing a parent layer's transformation property (with the exception of its Opacity property) provokes a corresponding change in its related child layers. For example, if you were to change a parent layer's position, the child layers' positions would change accordingly. Although you can animate child layers independently, the transformations will occur relative to the parent, not the composition. In the layer outline of the timeline, note that child layers' property values don't reflect the layer's actual appearance, which is a product of the parent's property values. For example, scaling the parent layer also scales the child layer—even though the child layer's Scale property continues to display the same value (**Figures 17.52** and **17.53**).

Jumping

When you assign (or remove) a parent-child relationship, you can specify whether the child layer *jumps*—that is, changes its transform properties relative to its parent layer. Ordinarily, assigning a parent-child relationship leaves the child layer's transform properties unchanged—until you make subsequent alterations to either the parent or child layers (**Figure 17.54**). In contrast, when you set the child layer to jump, its transformation properties are immediately altered relative to the parent layer (**Figure 17.55**). Conversely, you can make a child layer jump when you remove the parent-child relationship, so that its transform properties immediately shift relative to the composition.

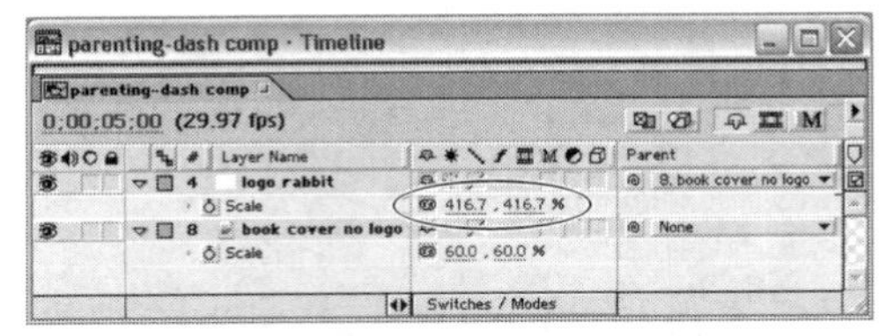

Figure 17.54 Ordinarily, assigning a parent-child relationship leaves the child-layer's relative transform properties unchanged in the Comp window, by changing its values.

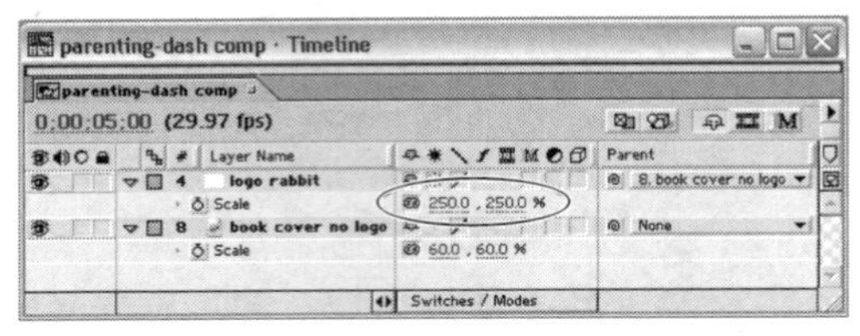

Figure 17.55 In contrast, when you have the child layer jump, its transformation properties are altered relative to the parent layer immediately.

To assign a parent-child relationship:

1. If necessary, reveal the Parenting panel in the Timeline window by choosing Panels > Parent in the Timeline pull-down menu.
2. For the child layer, *do either of the following:*
   - ▲ Choose the layer you want to assign as the parent in the Parent pull-down menu (**Figure 17.56**).
   - ▲ Drag the Pickwhip to the layer you want to designate as the parent (**Figure 17.57**).

   You can drag the Pickwhip anywhere in the layer's horizontal track in the layer outline to select it. The name of the parent layer appears in the Parenting pull-down menu for the child layer.

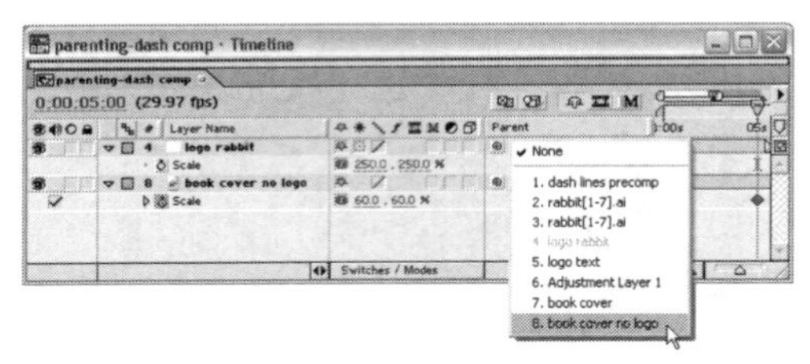

Figure 17.56 Choose the layer you want to assign as the parent in the Parent pull-down menu...

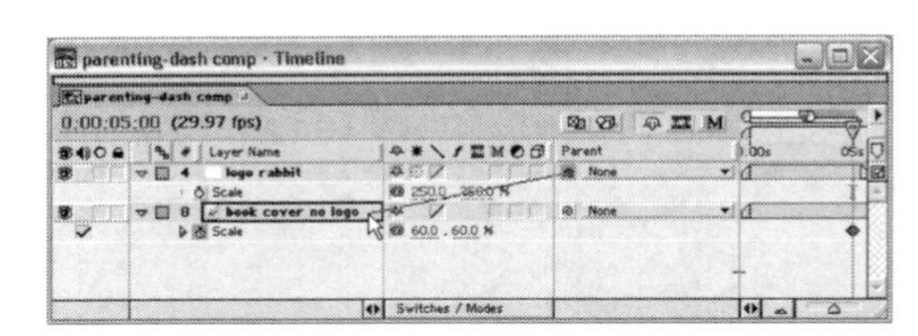

Figure 17.57 ...or drag the Parenting Pickwhip to anywhere in the parent layer's horizontal track in the Timeline window.

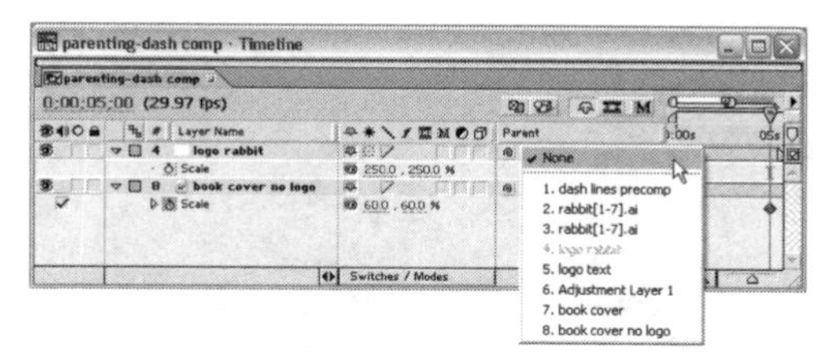

Figure 17.58 In the Parent pull-down menu for the child layer, choose None to cut the apron strings.

To remove a parent from a layer:

◆ In the Parent pull-down menu for the child layer, choose None (**Figure 17.58**).

The parent-child relationship is removed, and you can now transform the layer.

To make a child jump when assigning or removing a parent:

◆ Press Option (Mac) or Alt (Windows) when you select a layer name in the Parent pull-down menu, or select a layer with the Parent Pickwhip.

Using Null Objects

You can add invisible layers, called *null objects,* to a composition to create sophisticated animations that don't rely on the movement of visible layers. Because these layers aren't visible in previews or output, you can't apply effects to them. When selected, a null object appears in the Composition window as a framed outline. A null object's anchor point is positioned in its upper-left corner (**Figure 17.59**). Otherwise, null objects behave like other layers.

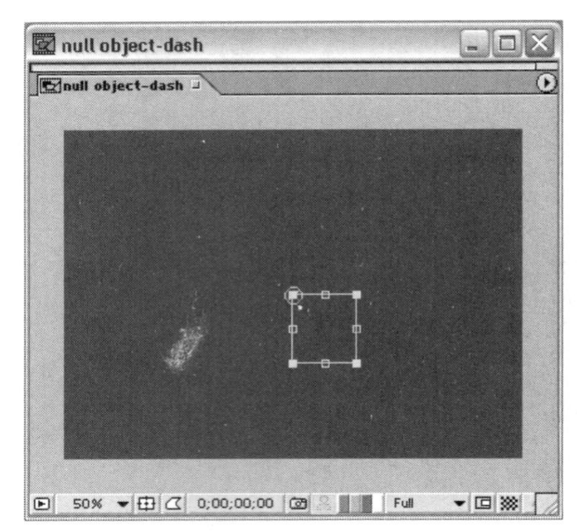

Figure 17.59 When selected, null objects appear in the Composition window as a framed outline. A null object's anchor point is positioned in its upper left corner.

To create a null object:

- Choose Layer > New > Null Object (**Figure 17.60**).

  A Null Object layer appears as the top layer in the Timeline, beginning at the current time and using the specified default duration for still images (**Figure 17.61**).

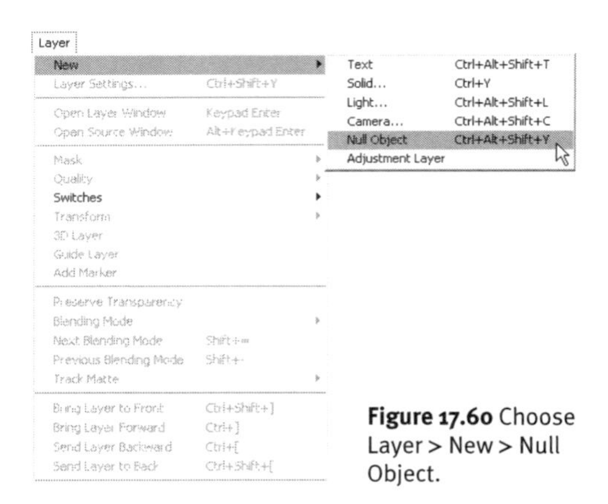

Figure 17.60 Choose Layer > New > Null Object.

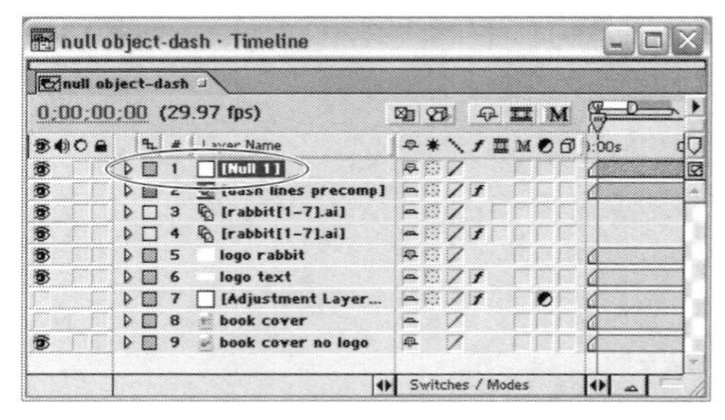

Figure 17.61 A Null Object layer appears as the top layer in the Timeline, beginning at the current time and using the specified default duration for still images.

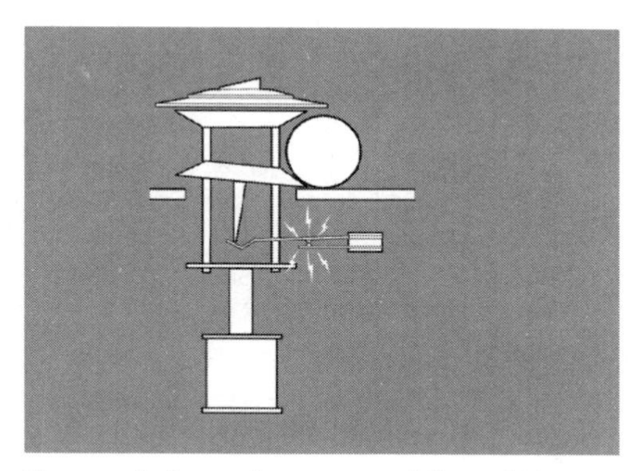

Figure 17.62 Expressions are especially useful in depicting the parts of a machine. Here, the position of the pinball can trigger the movement of parts of the bumper.

Using Expressions

Expressions define relationships between layer properties (in the same layer, in different layers, even in layers that reside in different compositions). Rather than keyframe properties independently, you can link the values of one property to another, using a JavaScript-based instruction, or *expression*. Expressions allow you to create sophisticated relationships between properties that you could otherwise produce only via painstaking keyframing (or by using the Production Bundle's Motion Math feature). Expressions can also use a mathematical formula to arrive at a property's values.

Expressions are especially useful for depicting the parts of a machine: wheels turning as a car moves, a small gear turning in response to a larger gear, or a meter increasing in height as a dial is turned (**Figure 17.62**). Because you can link all kinds of properties using simple or complex formulas, expressions afford endless possibilities. And because you can change the timing of the whole system by modifying a single element, you save time and effort as well.

Since expressions are based on JavaScript, experience with that language or a similar scripting language gives you a definite head start. However, even with no knowledge of JavaScript and only basic math skills, you can create useful expressions. Using the Pickwhip tool, you can generate a basic expression automatically. You can then modify your basic expression by appending a little simple arithmetic. When you're ready to write your own scripts, After Effects supplies the terms you need in a convenient pull-down menu.

To create an expression using the Expression Pickwhip:

1. Expand the layer outline to reveal the properties you want to link via an expression (**Figure 17.63**).
2. With the property selected, *do either of the following:*
   - ▲ Choose Animation > Add Expression (**Figure 17.64**).
   - ▲ Press Shift-Option-Equal sign (Mac) or Shift-Alt-Equal sign (Windows).

   An Equal Sign icon appears next to the property to indicate an expression is enabled. The property also expands to reveal buttons in the Switches panel of the timeline. Under the time ruler, the expression script appears selected (**Figure 17.65**).
3. In the Switches panel, click the Expression Pickwhip button, and drag the Pickwhip to the name of the property value to which you want to link the expression (**Figure 17.66**).

   The property's name becomes highlighted when the Pickwhip touches it. When you release the mouse, the expression script is entered in the script area under the time ruler (**Figure 17.67**).
4. Modify the script by doing *either of the following* (**Figure 17.68**):
   - ▲ Enter changes or additions to the script using standard JavaScript syntax.
   - ▲ Use the Expressions pull-down menu to select from a list of common scripting terms.

   If you make a mistake, After Effects will prompt you with a warning dialog box and advise you to correct the script.

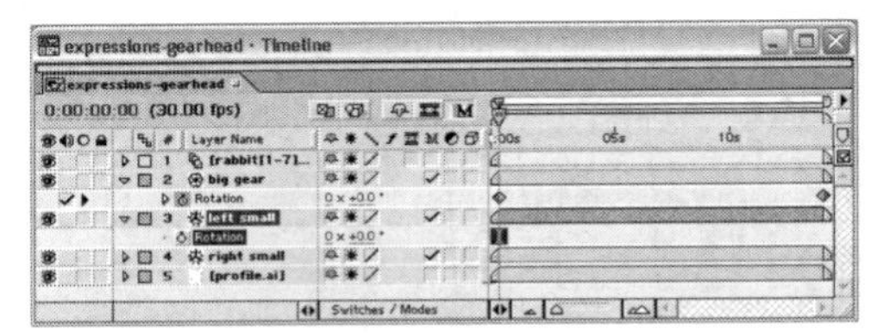

Figure 17.63 Expand the layer outline to reveal the properties you want to link using an expression.

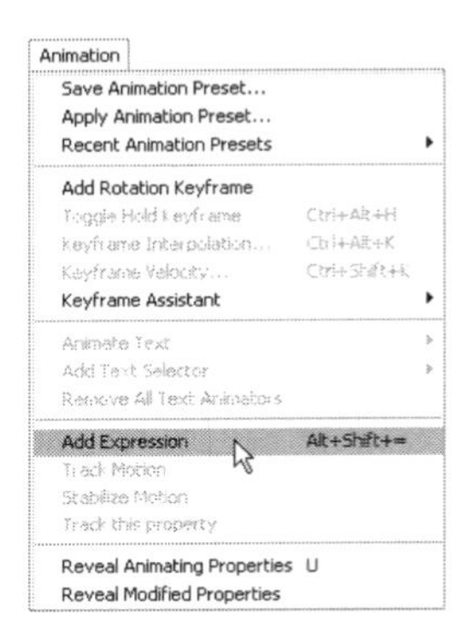

Figure 17.64 Choose Animation > Add Expression, or press Shift-Option-Equal sign (Mac) or Shift-Alt-Equal sign (Windows).

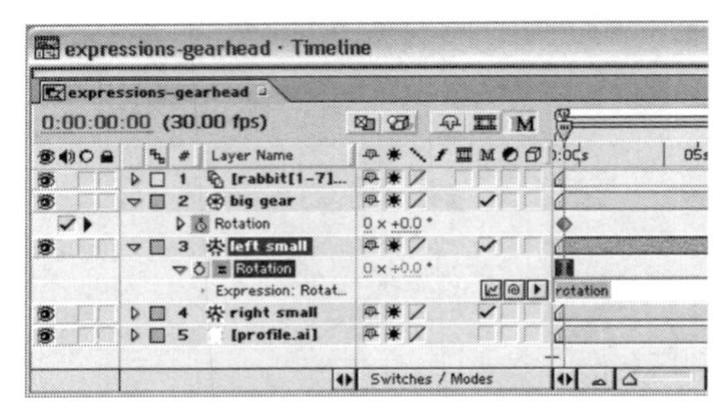

Figure 17.65 An Equal Sign icon appears next to the property, and the property expands to reveal buttons in the Switches panel. In the time ruler area, the expression script appears selected.

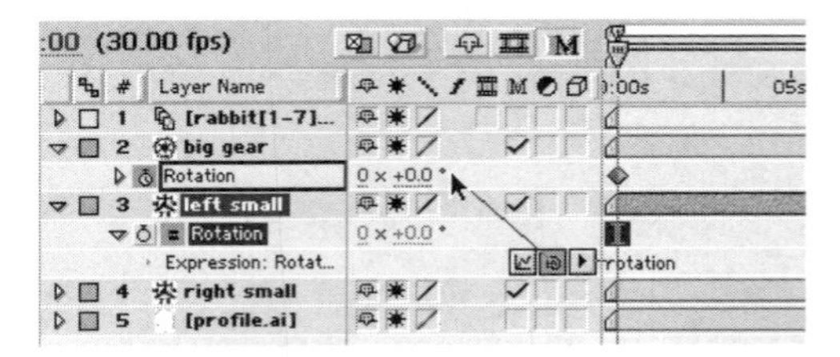

Figure 17.66 In the Switches panel, drag the Expression Pickwhip to the name of the property value to which you want to link the expression.

5. Keyframe the linked property—the one without the expression—using the methods you learned in Chapter 7, "Properties and Keyframes."

   The property using the expression changes automatically according to the relationship defined by the expression (**Figure 17.69**).

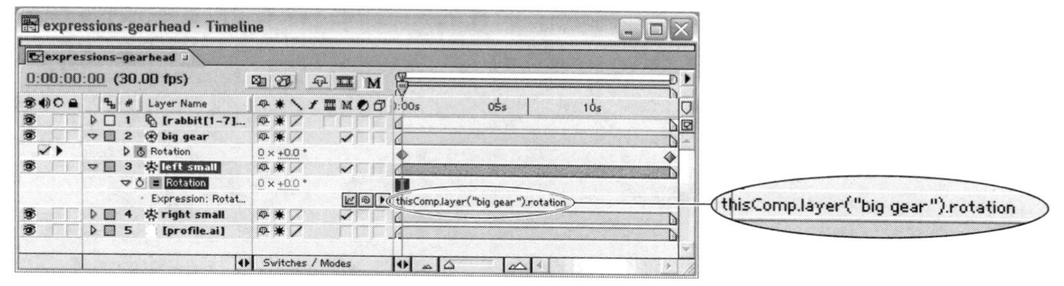

Figure 17.67 When you release the mouse, the expression script is entered in the script area under the time ruler.

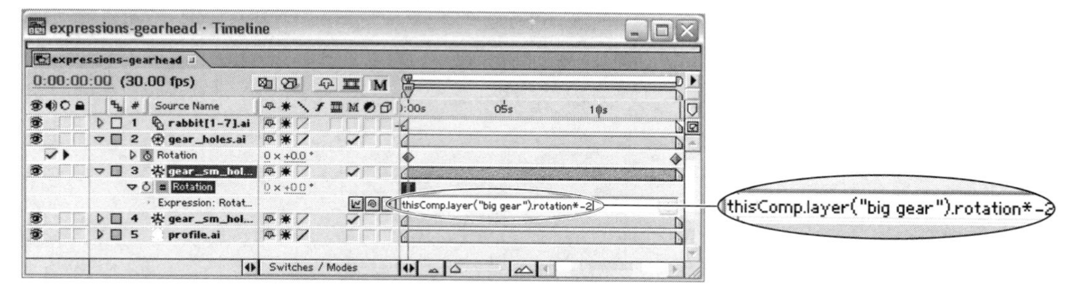

Figure 17.68 If necessary, modify the script manually. Here, "*-2" is added to the script to multiply the rotation value by negative two.

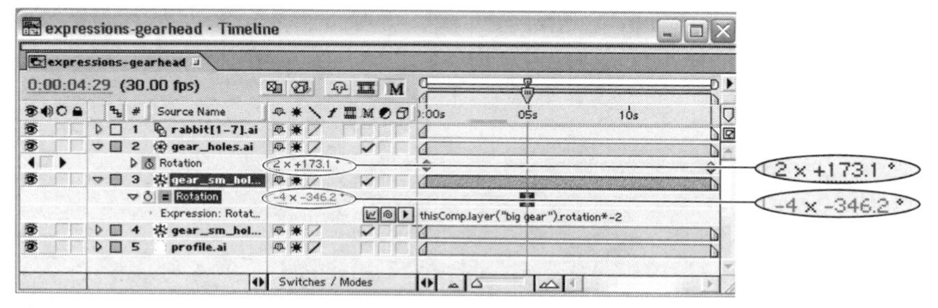

Figure 17.69 The property using the expression changes automatically, according to the relationship defined by the expression.

To disable and enable expressions:

- In the layer outline, click the Expression icon next to the property containing the expression to toggle it on and off.

  An Equal Sign icon indicates the expression is enabled; a crossed-out equal sign indicates the expression has been temporarily disabled (**Figure 17.70**).

Figure 17.70 An Equal Sign icon indicates that the expression is enabled; a crossed-out equal sign indicates that the expression is temporarily disabled.

✔ Tips

- Despite their similar names, JavaScript isn't related to Java.
- Although expressions usually define relationships between layer properties, you can modify a property using an expression alone—without linking it to another property. An expression used to create random values is one such example.
- You can save an expression by copying and pasting it into a text-editing program such as Simple Text (Mac) or Notepad (Windows). However, because expressions refer to layers and properties specific to the project, you may want to add comments to the expression to help you apply it to future projects. You may even want to save a version of the current project (and the necessary source files) to use for future reference.

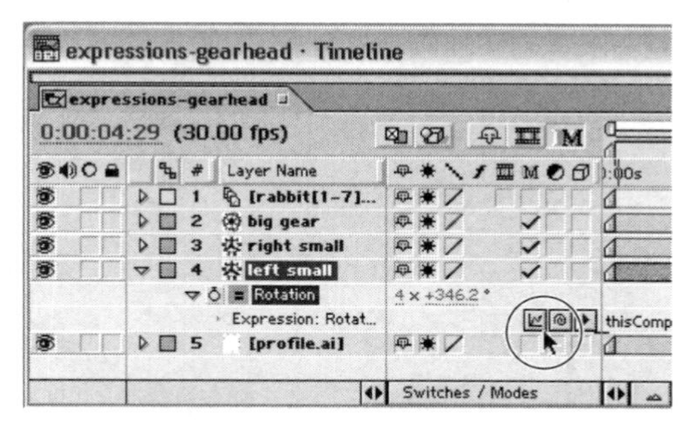

Figure 17.71 In the Switches panel, click the Graph Overlay icon.

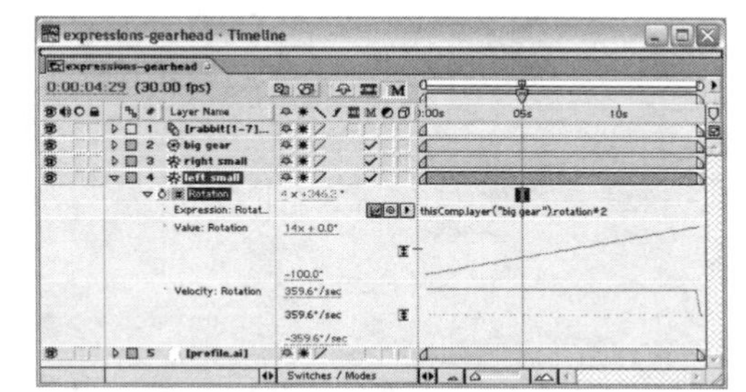

Figure 17.72 A black graph shows the property's value or speed/velocity before the expression is applied; a red graph shows the property's value or speed/velocity after the expression has been applied.

Viewing Expressions

Although expressions don't create keyframes, you can see how an expression modifies the property by revealing a property graph.

To view an expression graph:

1. Expand the layer outline to reveal the layer property containing the expression.
2. In the Switches panel, click the Graph Overlay icon (**Figure 17.71**).

   Graphs appear below the expression (**Figure 17.72**). A black graph shows the property's value or speed/velocity before the expression is applied; a red graph shows the property's value or speed/velocity after the expression has been applied. See Chapter 15, "Keyframe Interpolation," for more about reading property graphs.

✔ Tips

- To view expressions for all layers in the composition, select the layers and press EE.
- You can convert property values calculated by an expression into keyframed values by choosing Animation > Keyframe Assistant > Convert Expression to Keyframes.

Using the Expression Language Menu

When you start writing your own expressions, you'll discover that the language's vocabulary is extensive. Fortunately, you can plug in most of the terms you'll need automatically, by selecting them from a categorized list contained in a convenient pull-down menu.

To use the Expression pull-down menu:

1. Expand the layer outline to reveal the property you want to adjust with an expression.
2. With the property selected, *do either of the following:*
   - ▲ Choose Animation > Add Expression.
   - ▲ Press Shift-Option-Equal sign (Mac) or Shift-Alt-Equal sign (Windows).

   An Expression On icon appears next to the property, and a default expression appears under the time ruler. The default expression won't modify the property values. The property also expands to reveal buttons in the Switches panel of the timeline.
3. In the Switches panel of the timeline, click the Expressions pull-down menu.

   A categorized menu of expression-language terms appears (**Figure 17.73**).
4. In the pull-down menu, select the term you need.

   In the time ruler area of the timeline, the term appears in the expression text. A cursor appears at the end of the text, indicating the insertion point for additional expression terms (**Figure 17.74**).

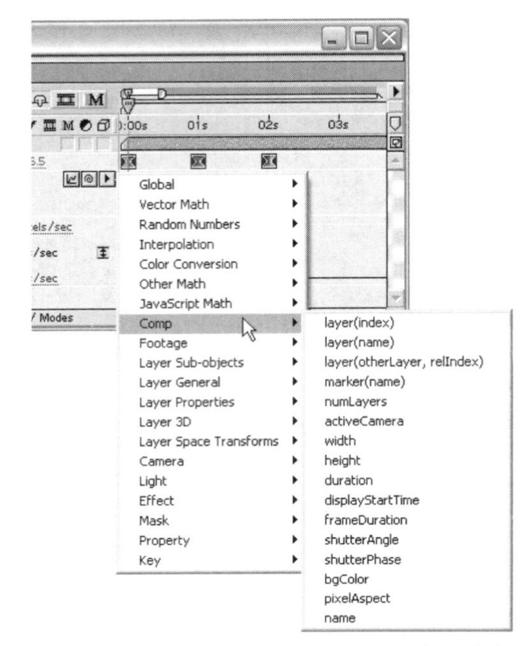

Figure 17.73 In the Switches panel of the timeline, click the Expressions pull-down menu to make a categorized menu of expression-language terms appear.

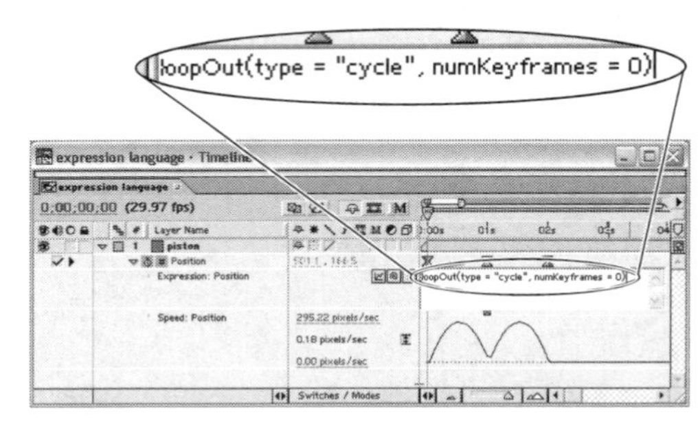

Figure 17.74 The term appears in the expression text. A cursor appears at the end of the text, indicating the insertion point for additional expression terms.

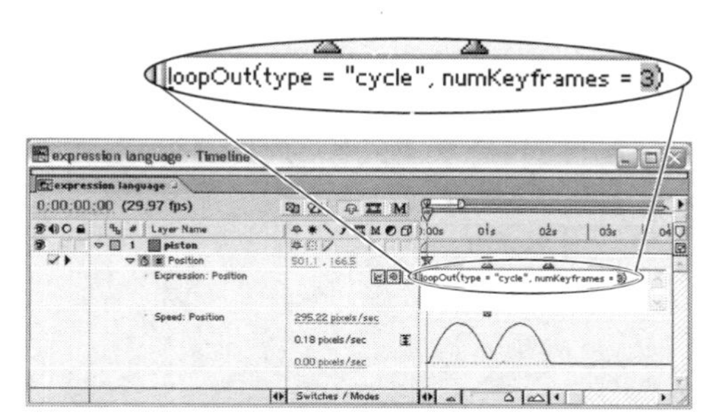

Figure 17.75 If necessary, enter expression language manually.

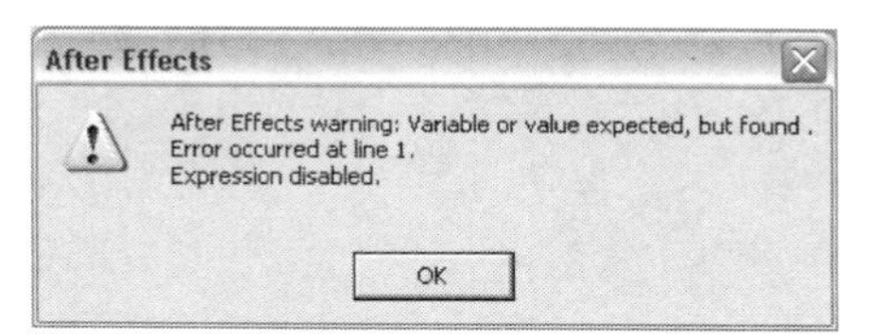

Figure 17.76 If you exit editing mode before the expression is complete or if the expression uses incorrect syntax, an error dialog box appears.

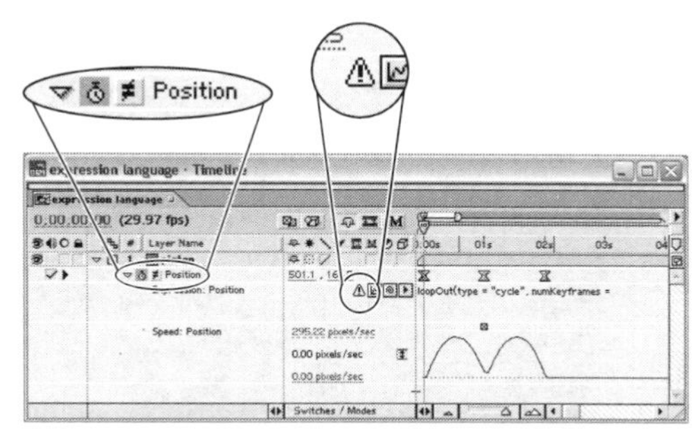

Figure 17.77 When you close the dialog box, a Warning icon appears in the Switches panel, and the expression is disabled automatically. Click the Warning icon to reopen the Warning dialog box.

5. If necessary, enter expression language manually (**Figure 17.75**).
6. Repeat steps 3 through 5 as needed.
7. Click anywhere outside the expression text field to get out of edit mode.

✔ Tip

- If you exit expression-editing mode before the expression is complete, or if the expression uses incorrect syntax, an error dialog box appears containing a description of the problem (**Figure 17.76**). When you close the dialog box, a Warning icon appears in the Switches panel, and the expression is disabled automatically (**Figure 17.77**). You must correct the expression language to enable it. Click the Warning icon to reopen the warning dialog box.

Writing Expressions

Once you've created a few simple expressions with the Pickwhip, you'll probably want to try writing some of your own—a process that can appear daunting if you don't have experience with JavaScript or scripting in general (especially since After Effects discourages your early attempts with warning dialog boxes about syntax errors, bad arguments, and the like).

Once you understand a few basic concepts, however, you should feel confident enough to experiment a bit. You'll also find it easier to decipher Adobe's Expressions guide (or an entire book on the subject of JavaScript) and to analyze other expressions.

JavaScript Rules

You'll notice that expressions use JavaScript objects (see the following section, "Expression syntax") that are unique to After Effects (and thus aren't applicable to scripting for the Web). Other than this difference in vocabulary, JavaScript syntax works the same. Expressions' mother tongue, JavaScript, follows several rules that you should know from the start.

- JavaScript is case sensitive, which means that words must use capitalization consistently if they are to be interpreted correctly. For example, an object called "tony" is different than one called "Tony."
- JavaScript ignores spaces, tabs, and line breaks—except in certain circumstances. For example, the object `comp("final comp")` uses a space in the string "final comp," which you need to include whenever you refer to that comp. Such spaces are part of the literal string: in this case, the name of the comp, which is in quotes. Also, the accidental placement of spaces in a number or string (alphanumeric) value will cause syntax errors. Otherwise, feel free to use spaces, tabs, or line breaks to make your scripts easier to read.
- JavaScript includes a number of reserved words, which you aren't allowed to use as part of a script. For a full list of these reserved words, consult a JavaScript manual.

Expression lexicon

As is the case with any language, an expression must follow rules if it is to make sense. Only certain terms are part of the scripting language's lexicon, and each statement must be constructed using a particular syntax.

Translating a simple expression

Consider the following example, which was created by dragging the Expression Pickwhip to a Rotation property:

```
this_comp.layer("panel1").rotation
```

This simple expression links a layer's property (in this case, Rotation) to the Rotation property of a layer called panel1. A plain-English translation would read something like the following: "To set Rotation values for this property, look in this composition, find the layer called panel1, and take its Rotation value." Adjusting panel1's Rotation property results in a corresponding change in the layer containing the expression.

Typically, you would modify the expression:

```
this_comp.layer("aper1").rotation+60
```

The `+60` adds 60 to the rotational value, which is measured in degrees. So setting panel1's Rotation value to 30 degrees would cause the layer containing the expression to rotate 90 degrees (30+60=90).

✔ Tip

- You may be familiar with JavaScript as it applies to Web design. Expressions are based on the same core JavaScript language but not particular JavaScript interpreters, which are browser-specific.

Expression syntax

By familiarizing yourself with a few basic terms, you'll be better able to decipher Adobe's Expressions reference or a JavaScript guide. Match the following terms with **Figures 17.78** and **17.79** to familiarize yourself with basic Expression/JavaScript terminology and syntax:

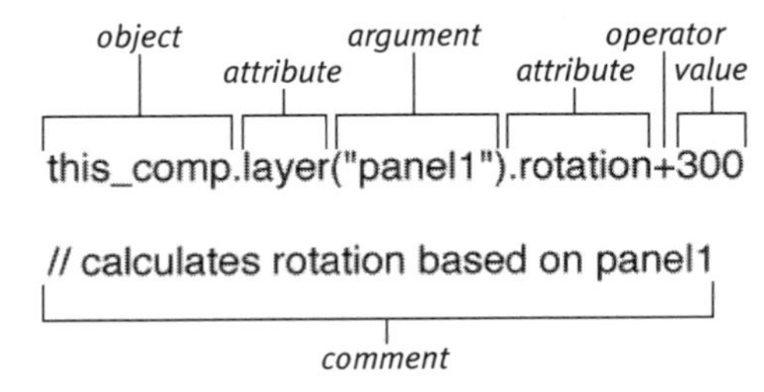

Figure 17.78 Familiarize yourself with some of the terms used to describe an expression. Here's a sample of a simple statement that uses the proper dot syntax.

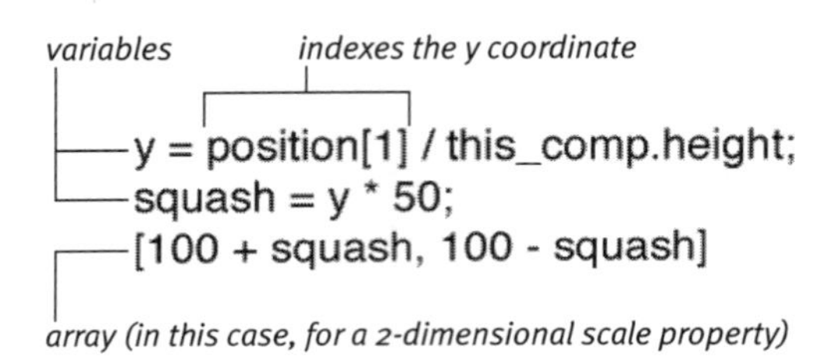

Figure 17.79 Here's another expression applied to a Scale property of a layer depicting a bouncing ball. It makes the ball "squash," or compress, according to its position. Note how the expression uses variables to define the layer's scale in terms of its *y* coordinate position.

Statement denotes a complete thought or command in JavaScript (as it does in any other language).

Dot syntax describes how each statement is constructed. Each part of the statement is separated by a dot, or period. Statements in the same expression are separated by semicolons (;).

Comments are included in scripts for your reference only; the program ignores them. Comments must appear between double slashes (//) and the end of the line:

```
// this is a comment.
```

Objects refer to any named data and are comparable to nouns in other languages. After Effects' expression language includes objects unique to the program, such as comps and layers.

Attributes are the named values of an object and can apply to more than one object. For example, `width` is an attribute in the following statement: `this_comp.width`. Attributes can also return, or result in, other objects. For example, the statement fragment `layer ("panel1")` retrieves the layer by name.

Methods are similar to attributes, but rather than retrieve data—such as layer names—they specify data. Methods are followed by parentheses, which (depending on the method) contain certain variables or values. For example, the method `random(100)` used in an expression for a layer's Opacity value would make the layer's opacity randomly fluctuate between 0 and 100 percent.

Values denote quantitative data, such as a number. However, a value can also be a string (alphanumeric data) or an array.

Array denotes a collection of data values referred to by a number. Arrays are said to have *dimensions*, which usually correspond to the aspects of a property value. For example, a Position property (in 2D space) has two dimensions: x and y coordinate values. A Scale property in 2D space can have one or two dimensions: an overall scale value or separate width and height values. In the Expressions Guide, an arrays' dimension appears within brackets: [ ].

Index denotes the numbering schemes used to refer to values in arrays or objects. Arrays are indexed starting from 0. For example, `position[0]` retrieves the position's x coordinate, and `position[1]` retrieves to the position's y coordinate. Objects like layers, masks, and effect parameters are indexed starting from 1. For example, `layer(1)` refers to the top layer in the comp. However, it's better to refer to such objects by name than by index.

Variables are names associated with a value and are said to *store* the value. For example, your expression can contain the statement `radius = 20` to assign the variable `radius` the value of 20. Later in the expression, you can use the variable as part of another statement. Variables and attributes are essentially the same, except that you can invent the name of a variable.

Operators are symbols used to perform a calculation, many of which you're familiar with from basic arithmetic. Operators that assign values, such as `x=y`, are known as *assignments*. Operators can also compare values, such as `x<y` (if x is less than y). Such operators are called *comparisons* and result in a value of true or false, or 1 and 0, respectively.

Arguments describe the type of data—such as a number, array, or string—required to specify an object. For example, the object `Comp(name)` requires a string, or alphanumeric data, in place of `name`. Therefore, the argument is a string. In this case, the actual name of the comp should be placed in the parentheses and—because it's a so-called literal string value—within quotes: `Comp("final comp")`. In contrast, the object `this_comp` doesn't require an argument. This type of global object is complete in and of itself—that is, you don't need to specify additional data.

Returns can be thought of as another way of saying, "results in this type of data." For example, the statement `this_comp.layer("panel1").rotation` returns a number—specifically, the Rotation property value of the layer called panel1.

✔ Tips

- Throughout this book, you've been advised to give your layers and comps descriptive names (rather than use the default names) and to refrain from changing them. The former habit helps you make clear expressions; the latter keeps your expressions from losing their links and becoming disabled.
- Although the term *property* is used in JavaScript, After Effects' Expressions reference substitutes the term *attribute* to avoid confusion with layer properties (which can be attributes in an expression).

18

OUTPUT

Finally.

The beginning of this book likened your project and compositions to a musical score. Now that you've written and rehearsed that score, it's time to put on the show!

In your case, that show is a movie file or image sequence of a rendered composition. You can create movies for computer presentation (via CD-ROM or the Web). Or—with the aid of additional equipment or a service bureau—you can transfer your animation to broadcast-video format, or even to film. On the other hand, your movie might serve as a prerendered element of a larger composition. Whatever the case, the rendering-process variables are the same.

Your particular output goals (and, unfortunately, your equipment's limitations) will help determine a wide range of output settings; this chapter will guide you through those myriad options. You'll also get a chance to apply what you've learned thus far about your output goals. (You have been reading those sidebars, haven't you?) Although this chapter can't cover every output specification, it can provide you with enough information so that you know which questions to ask to derive your own answers.

The Render Queue Window

You control the rendering process from the Render Queue window, listing the items you want to render and assigning their rendering settings (**Figure 18.1**). This section provides an overview of the Render Queue window; following sections explain each feature in more detail.

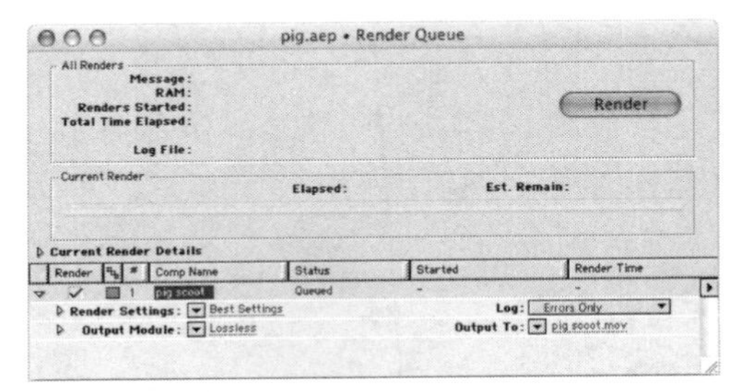

Figure 18.1 You control and monitor the rendering process from the Render Queue window.

Rendering progress

The top of the window contains buttons to start, stop, or pause the render. It also displays information about rendering progress. Clicking the triangle next to Current Render Details reveals detailed information about the current render (**Figure 18.2**). This information not only indicates the remaining rendering time and disk space, it also helps you identify the areas of the composition that render more slowly than others.

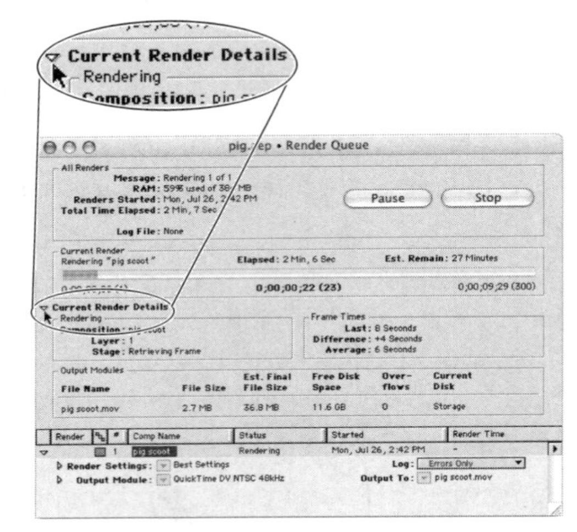

Figure 18.2 Clicking the triangle next to Current Render Details reveals detailed information about the current render.

Rendering settings

The lower portion of the Render Queue window is the "queue" portion of the window: This is where you list items in the order you want to render them. You can assign rendering settings to each item as well as render the same item with different settings.

By default, the triangle next to each item's name is set to reveal four types of information (**Figure 18.3**).

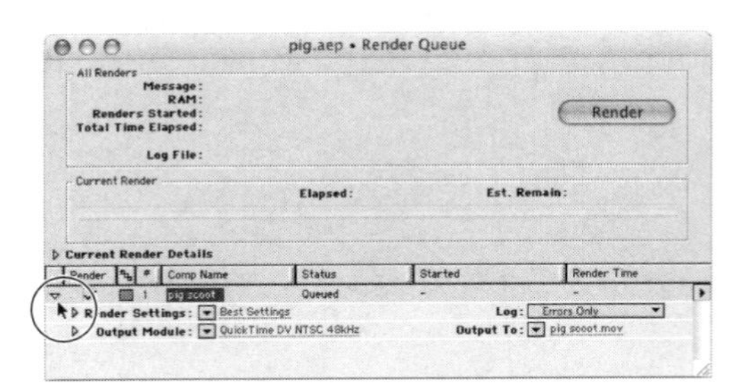

Figure 18.3 By default, the triangle next to the name of each item points down to reveal four categories of information.

On the left side, the settings you assign each item in the queue are grouped into two categories: Render Settings and Output Module. The first step, Render Settings, calculates each frame for output. Once the attributes of the frames have been rendered, the Output Module determines how they're saved to disk. Clicking the triangle next to each setting category reveals a summary of the setting (**Figure 18.4**). These settings are explained in detail later in this chapter.

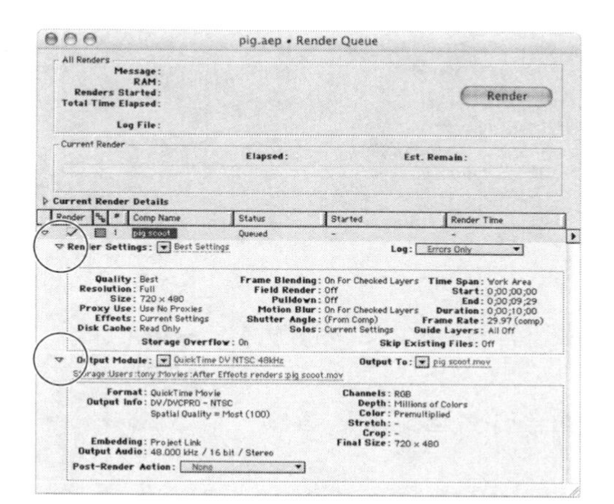

Figure 18.4 Clicking the arrow next to the Render Settings and Output Module options reveals a summary of each group of settings.

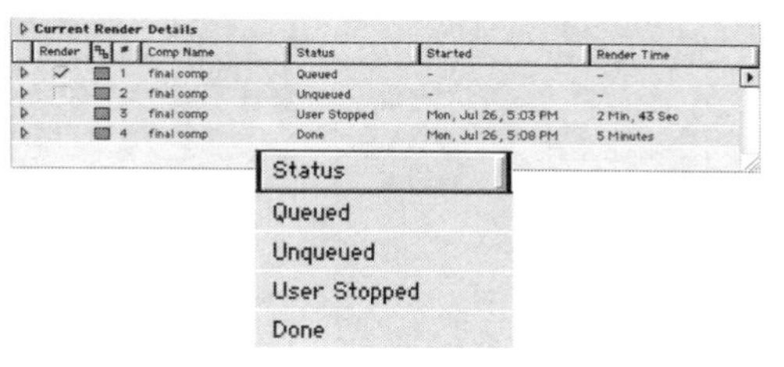

Figure 18.5 When the view of the items in the queue is collapsed, it's easier to see customizable columns of information, including the rendering status.

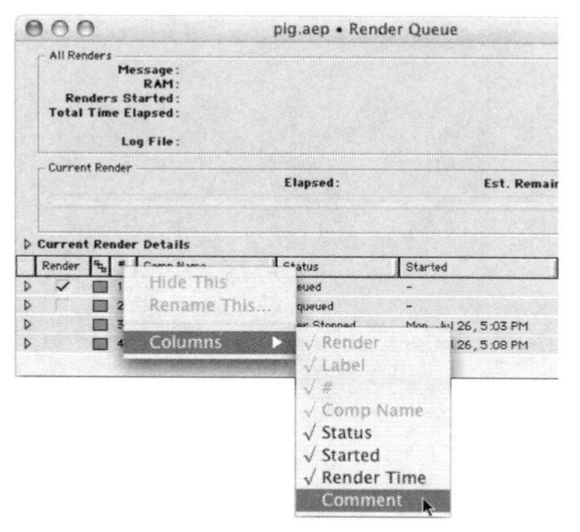

Figure 18.6 Ctrl-click (Mac) or right-click (Windows) to use a contextual menu to customize the panel headings.

On the right side, you can specify the type of record After Effects generates in the Log pull-down menu; you can also specify a name and destination for Output To.

Panel headings and Render Status

Clicking the triangle next to each item collapses the queue information, making several columns of information more apparent (**Figure 18.5**). Although most panel headings are self-explanatory, Render Status merits special attention because it indicates the current state of each item in the queue:

Queued indicates that the item is ready to be rendered.

Unqueued indicates that the item is listed but not ready for rendering, meaning you need to assign a name and destination to it, or you need to check the Render option.

Failed indicates that the render was unsuccessful. Check the render log generated by After Effects to determine the error.

User Stopped indicates that you stopped the rendering process.

Done indicates that the item has been rendered successfully.

After an item is rendered or stopped, it remains in the Render Queue window until you remove it. Although you can't change the status of rendered items, you can duplicate them as other items in the queue. You can then assign new settings to the new item and render it.

✔ Tip

- You can customize the panel headings of the Render Queue window just as you would the Project window panel headings. Ctrl-click (Mac) or right-click (Windows) to invoke a contextual menu (**Figure 18.6**).

Making a Movie

This section explains how to add a composition to the Render Queue window using the Make Movie command. Later sections focus on the Render Queue window and choosing specific settings.

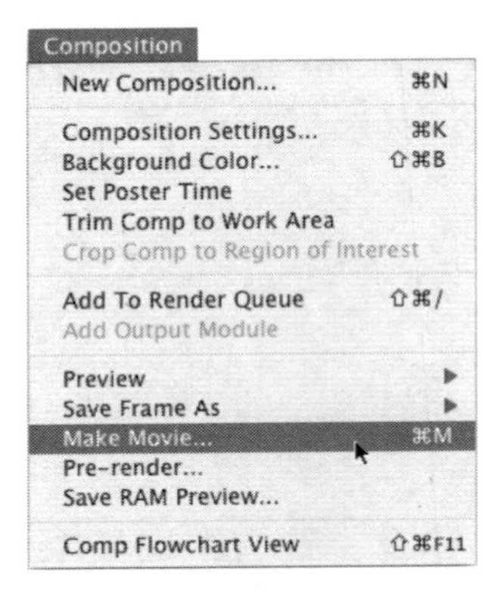

Figure 18.7 Choose Composition > Make Movie.

To make a movie from a composition:

1. Make sure to save your project.
2. Select a composition.

   Projects frequently contain several compositions; make sure you select the one you want to output.
3. Choose Composition > Make Movie, or press Command-M (Mac) or Ctrl-M (Windows) (**Figure 18.7**).

   A Save As dialog box appears (**Figure 18.8**).
4. In the Save As dialog box, specify a name and destination for the final movie.

   If you want to save the movie as a single file, make sure your chosen destination has sufficient storage space to contain it.
5. Click Save to close the Save As dialog box.

   The composition appears as an item in the Render Queue window (**Figure 18.9**).

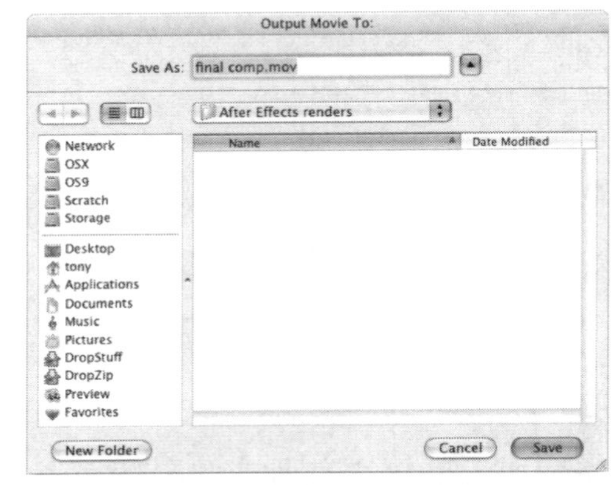

Figure 18.8 A Save As dialog box appears. Specify the name and destination for the rendered composition.

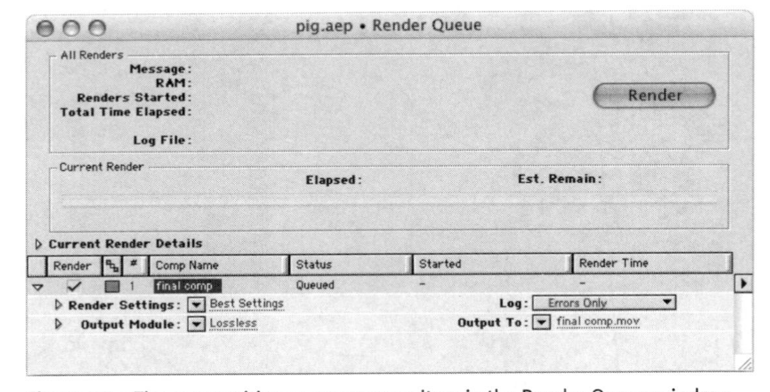

Figure 18.9 The composition appears as an item in the Render Queue window.

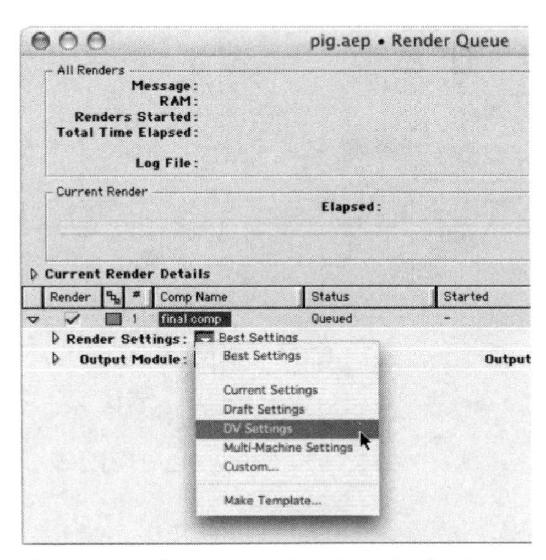

Figure 18.10 Choose a template from the Render Settings pull-down menu, or click the underlined name of the current settings to open a dialog box.

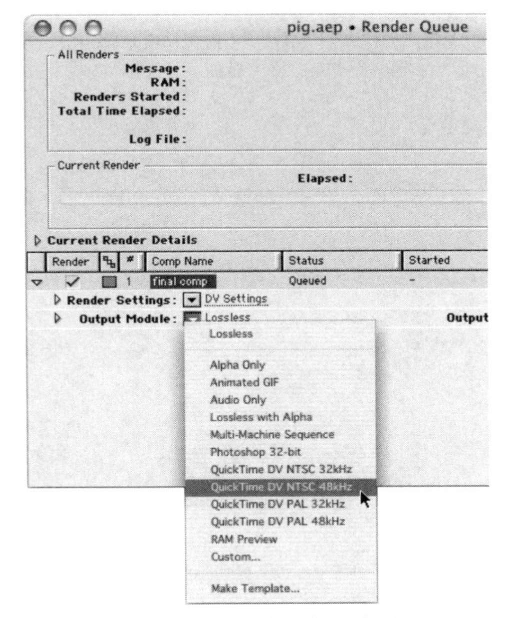

Figure 18.11 Choose a template from the Output Module pull-down menu, or click the underlined name of the current settings to open a dialog box.

6. In the Render Queue window, choose render settings by doing *one of the following:*
   - ▲ Choose a template from the Render Settings pull-down menu (**Figure 18.10**).
   - ▲ Click the name of the current render settings to open the Render Settings dialog box.
7. In the Render Queue window, choose output options by doing *one of the following:*
   - ▲ Choose a template from the Output Module pull-down menu (**Figure 18.11**).
   - ▲ Click the name of the current output options to open the Output Options dialog box.
8. In the Render Queue dialog box, choose an option from the Log pull-down menu (**Figure 18.12**):
   - ▲ Errors Only
   - ▲ Plus Settings
   - ▲ Plus Per Frame Info

continues on next page

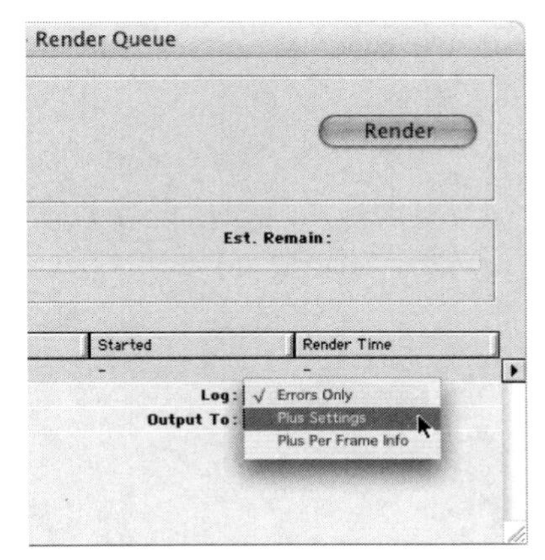

Figure 18.12 Select the type of log After Effects will generate in the Log pull-down menu.

9. Click the Render button near the top of the Render Queue window (**Figure 18.13**).

   After Effects begins to render the composition. A progress bar and rendering-time data indicate the elapsed render time as well as the estimated time remaining in the rendering process (**Figure 18.14**). After Effects sounds a chime when rendering is complete.

✔ Tips

- To reopen the Save As dialog box so that you can change the name or destination of the saved movie, click the name of the movie next to Output To (**Figure 18.15**).
- To speed up rendering, close or collapse the Composition window *before* you begin rendering. This way, After Effects doesn't need to update the Composition window as rendering progresses.

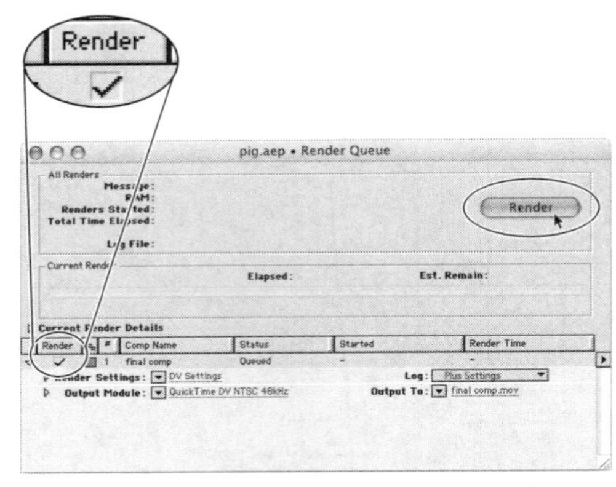

Figure 18.13 Make sure the Render column is checked for the item, and click Render.

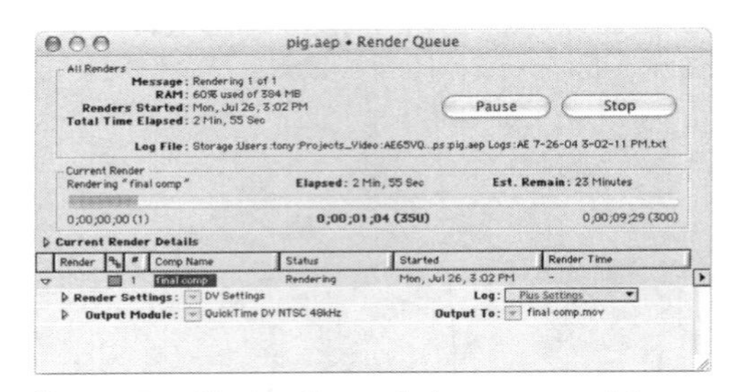

Figure 18.14 Monitor the rendering progress at the top of the Render Queue window.

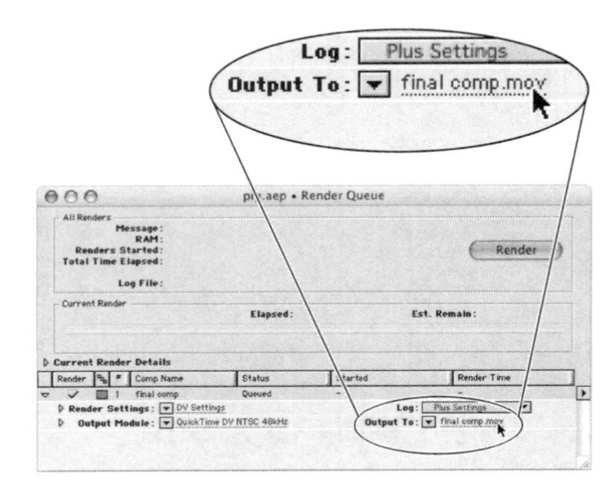

Figure 18.15 To change the name or destination of the saved movie, click the name of the movie next to Output To.

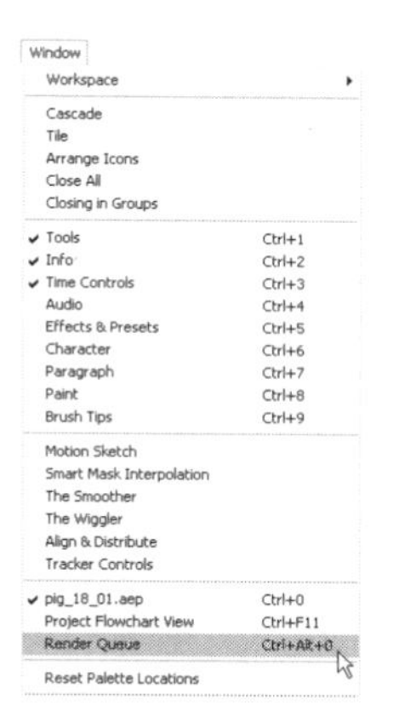

Figure 18.16 If the Render Queue window isn't open, choose Window > Render Queue.

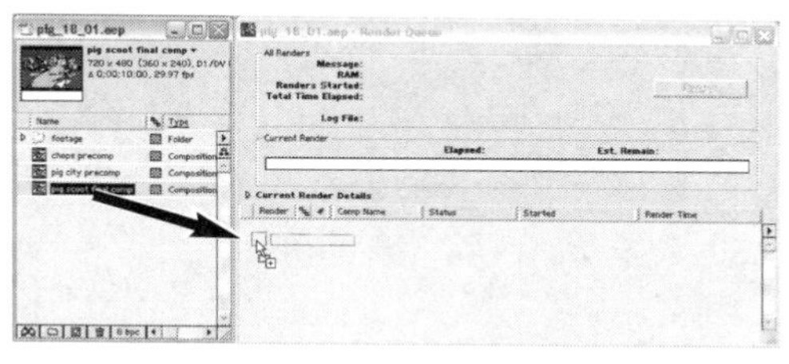

Figure 18.17 To add a composition to the queue, drag a Composition icon from the Project window to the Render Queue window.

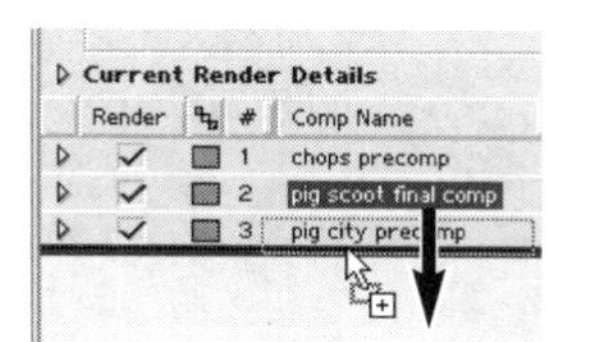

Figure 18.18 To change the order of the compositions in the queue, drag an item up or down.

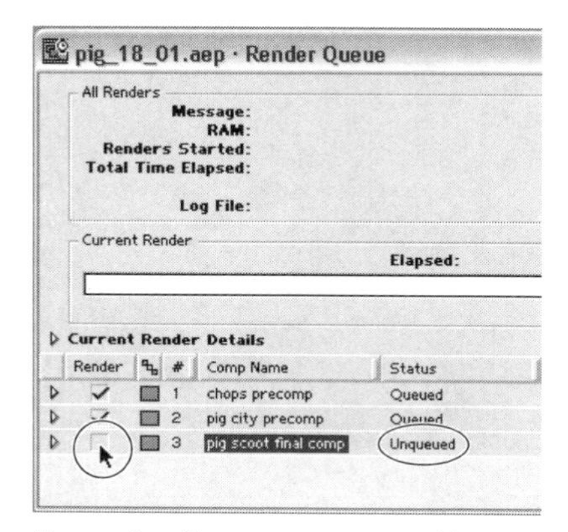

Figure 18.19 To unqueue a composition, click the Render option box to unselect it.

Using the Render Queue Window

Among other things, the Render Queue window is just that: a queue, or line, of compositions waiting to be rendered.

To manage items in the render queue:

1. If the Render Queue window isn't open, choose Window > Render Queue (**Figure 18.16**).

   A Render Queue window appears. Previously queued compositions are listed in the queue.

2. In the Render Queue window, *do any of the following:*

   ▲ To add a composition to the queue, drag a Composition icon from the Project window to the Render Queue window (**Figure 18.17**).

   ▲ To remove a composition from the queue, select a composition in the queue and press Delete.

   ▲ To change the order of the compositions in the queue, drag a composition up or down (**Figure 18.18**).

   A dark horizontal line indicates where the composition's new position in the queue will be when you release the mouse.

   ▲ To prevent a composition in the queue from rendering, click the Render option box to unselect it (**Figure 18.19**).

   The composition remains in the list, but its status changes to Unqueued; this means it won't render until you select the Render option box.

Pausing and Stopping Rendering

After you click the Render button, Pause and Stop buttons appear in its place. Pausing a render comes in handy if you need to access other programs, or if you didn't plan ahead and find you need to clear some drive space for the render. Stopping a render won't adversely affect a frame sequence—you can pick up where you left off—but it will disturb the integrity of a movie file, creating two movies instead of one.

To pause rendering:

1. After the composition has begun to render, click the Pause button in the Render Queue window (**Figure 18.20**).

   During the pause in rendering, you can use other applications or manage files on the desktop. You will not, however, be able to do anything in After Effects (not even close a window) except restart the render.

2. To resume rendering, click Continue.

   After Effects continues to render to the same file from where it left off.

To stop rendering:

- After the composition has begun rendering, click the Stop button in the Render Queue window (**Figure 18.21**).

  When rendering stops, the composition's status changes to User Stopped. A new item—with an Unqueued status—is added to the queue. If you render this item, it will render a new movie, starting with the next unrendered frame of the interrupted movie (**Figure 18.22**).

✔ Tip

- Pausing allows you to use other programs or the desktop, but not After Effects. If you want to collapse the Composition window, do it before you start rendering.

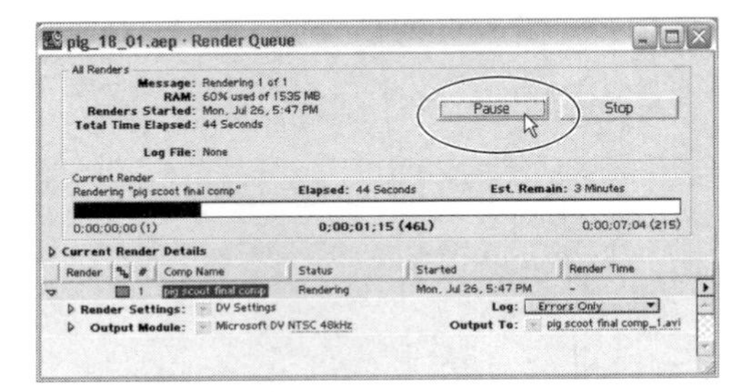

Figure 18.20 Click the Pause button in the Render Queue window to pause rendering and use the desktop or other programs.

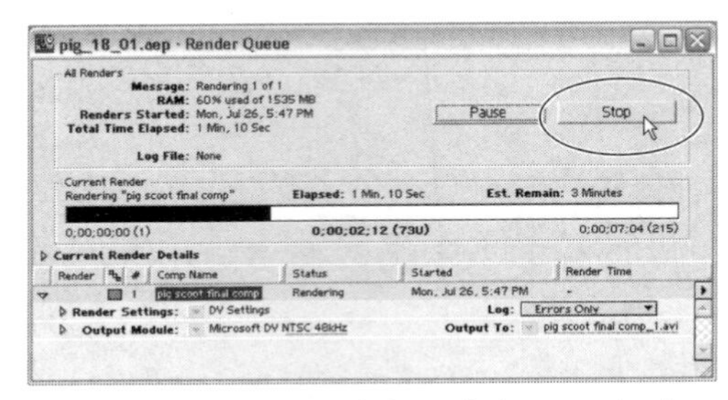

Figure 18.21 Click Stop to halt rendering completely.

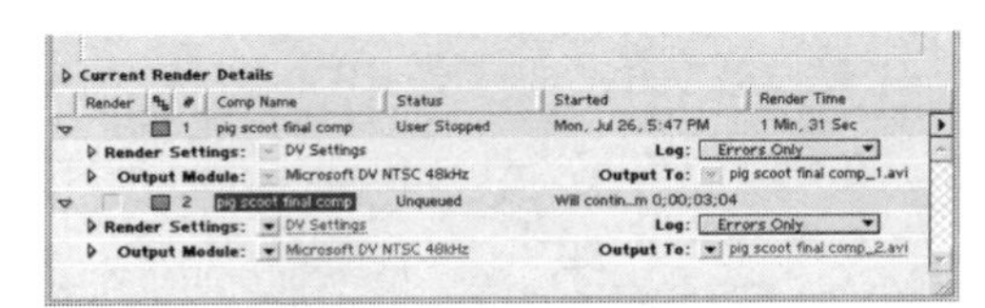

Figure 18.22 When you stop the rendering, the item's status changes to User Stopped, and a new item is added with the status Unqueued. This item will start rendering at the next unrendered frame.

Pausing and Stopping Rendering

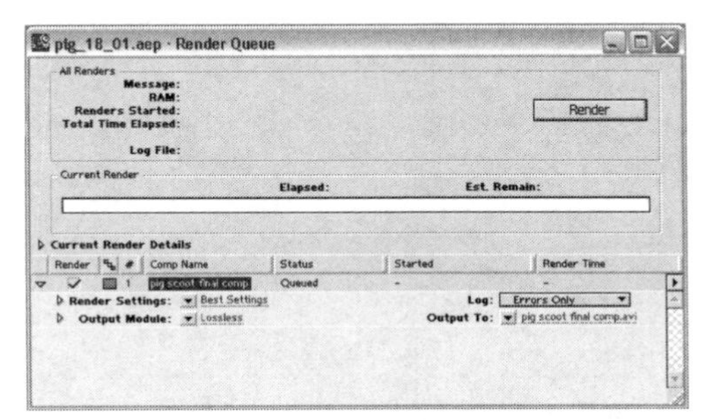

Figure 18.23 Select an item in the Render Queue window.

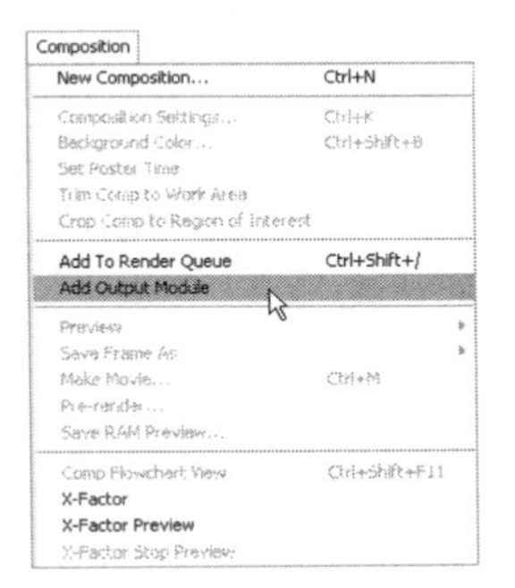

Figure 18.24 Choose Composition > Add Output Module.

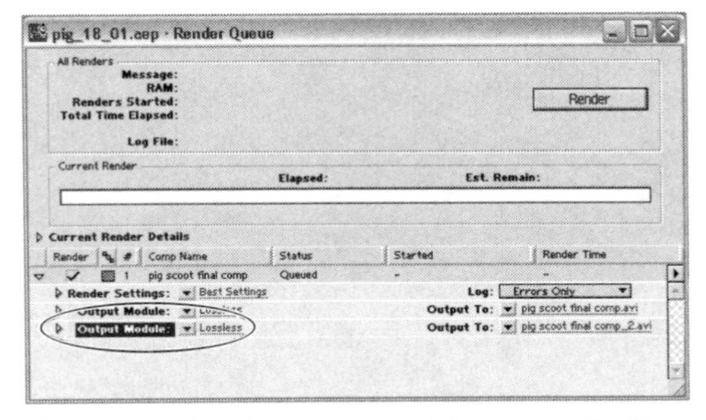

Figure 18.25 Another output module appears for the item in the queue.

Assigning Multiple Output Modules

You can assign more than one output module to a single item in the queue—a capability that allows you to easily create multiple versions of the same composition.

To assign additional output modules:

1. Select an item in the Render Queue window (**Figure 18.23**).
2. Choose Composition > Add Output Module (**Figure 18.24**).

   Another output module appears for the item in the queue (**Figure 18.25**).
3. Specify settings or a template for the output module and render the items in the queue (as explained earlier in this chapter in the section "Making a Movie").

Choosing Render Settings

Determining render settings is the first step in the rendering process. These settings dictate how each frame of a composition is calculated for the final output, in much the same way that composition settings calculate frames for playback in the Composition window.

Initially, the render settings are set to match the composition's current settings. Although in some cases these settings may meet your output goals, it's best to take a more active role in choosing render settings. By selecting each render setting (or by using a template of settings), you can ensure that each layer of your composition—including those in nested compositions—uses the settings you want before it's saved to disk.

To choose render settings manually:

1. In the render queue, click the underlined name of the render settings (**Figure 18.26**).

   A Render Settings dialog box appears (**Figure 18.27**).

2. In the Render Settings dialog box, make a selection *for each of the following options:*

   Quality sets the quality for all layers (**Figure 18.28**). (See "Quality Setting Switches" in Chapter 5, "Layer Basics.")

   Resolution sets the resolution for all layers in a composition. (See "Resolution" in Chapter 4, "Compositions.") Setting the resolution to Half, for example, renders every other pixel, resulting in an image with half the dimensions of the full-sized composition (**Figure 18.29**).

   Disk Cache specifies whether After Effects uses the current cache settings—the ones you specified in the Memory & Cache panel of the Preferences dialog box. Setting this option to Read Only specifies that no new frames are written to the cache during rendering (**Figure 18.30**).

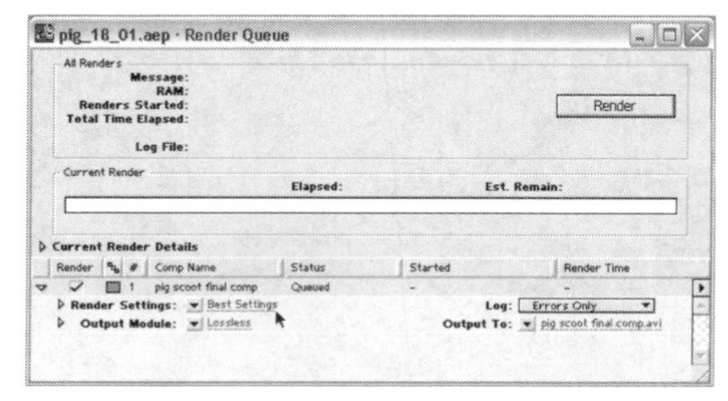

Figure 18.26 In the render queue, click the underlined name of the render settings.

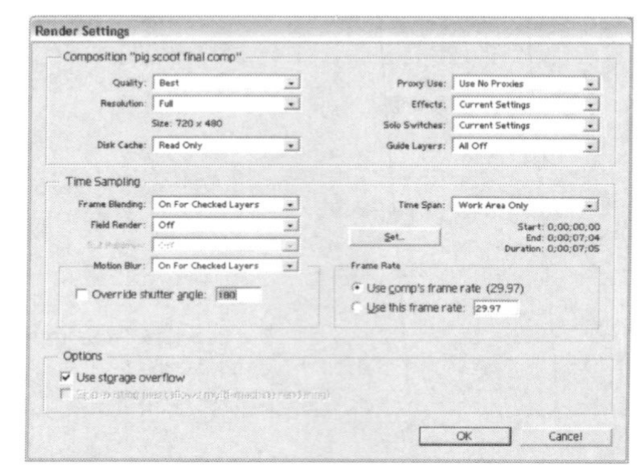

Figure 18.27 In the Render Settings dialog box, specify various settings for rendering the frames of the composition.

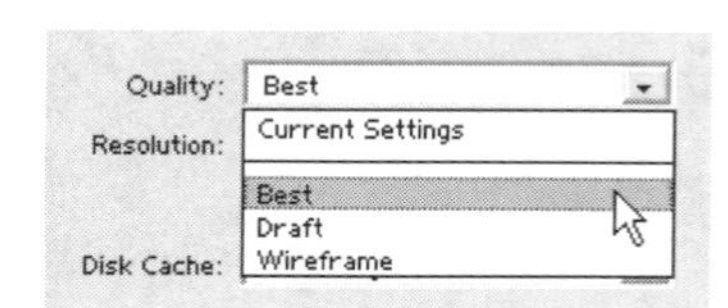

Figure 18.28 Set the Quality setting for all layers from the Quality pull-down menu.

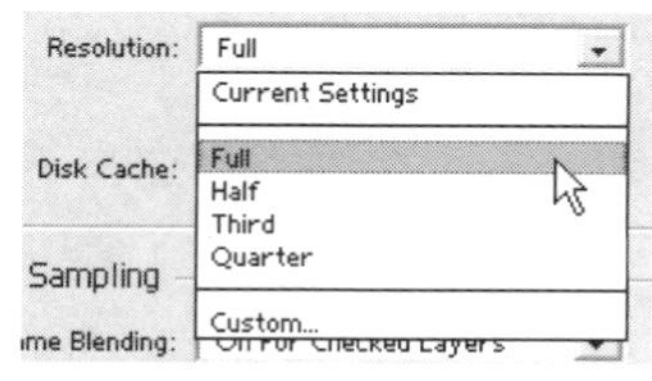

Figure 18.29 Set the resolution for all layers in the composition in the Resolution pull-down menu.

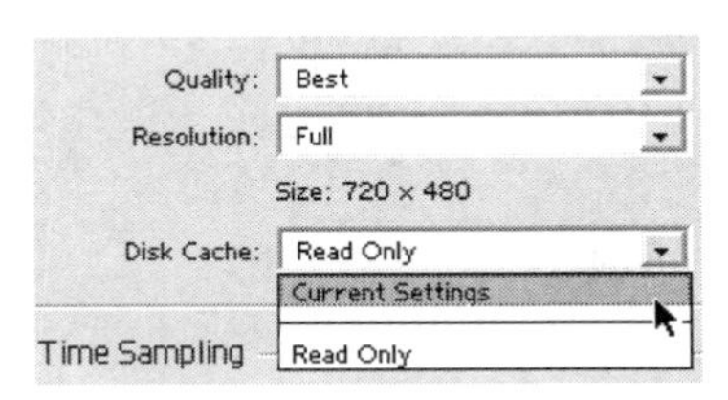

Figure 18.30 Specify an option for Disk Cache.

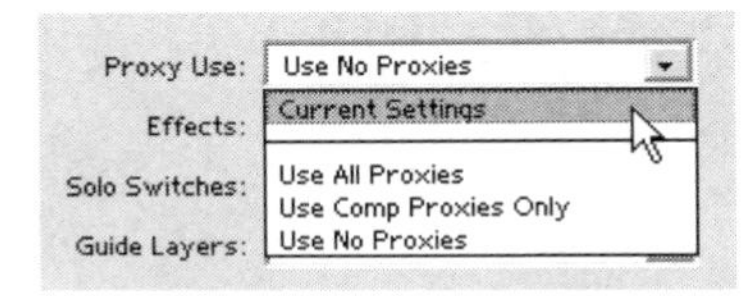

Figure 18.31 Specify whether proxies or source footage are used for output in the Proxy Use pull-down menu.

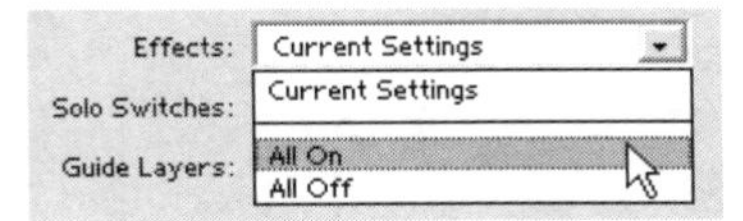

Figure 18.32 In the Effects menu, specify whether effects appear in the output.

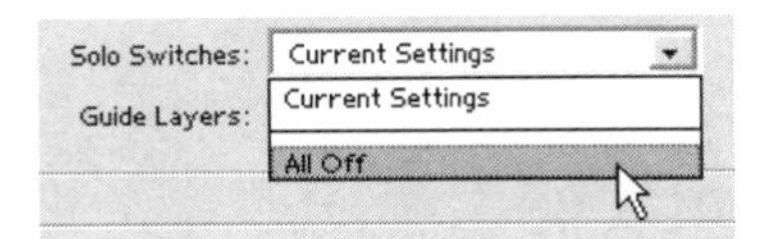

Figure 18.33 In the Solo Switches pull-down menu, specify whether to render layers with the Solo switch activated or to render layers without regard to their Solo switch.

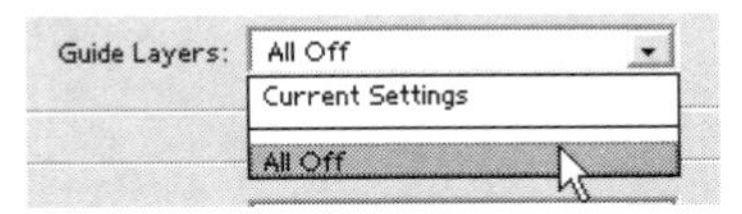

Figure 18.34 In the Guide Layers pull-down menu, specify whether to render guide layers or to turn guide layers off.

Proxy Use specifies whether proxies or source footage are used for output (**Figure 18.31**). (See "Proxies and Placeholders" in Chapter 3, "Managing Footage.")

Effects specifies whether effects appear in the output. (See "Disabling Effects Temporarily" in Chapter 10, "Effects Fundamentals.") Set Effects to All On to enable all effects, including ones you had disabled temporarily; set it to Current Settings to exclude effects you disabled deliberately (**Figure 18.32**).

Solo Switches specifies whether After Effects renders only layers with their Solo switch on (see "Switching Video and Audio On and Off" in Chapter 5) or turns all Solo switches off and renders all the layers in the comp (**Figure 18.33**).

Guide Layers specifies whether After Effects renders guide layers or deactivates all guide layers (**Figure 18.34**).

Frame Blending specifies whether frame blending is applied to layers with the Frame Blending switch enabled (regardless of a composition's Frame Blending setting) (**Figure 18.35**). (See "Using Frame Blending" in Chapter 14, "More Layer Techniques.")

continues on next page

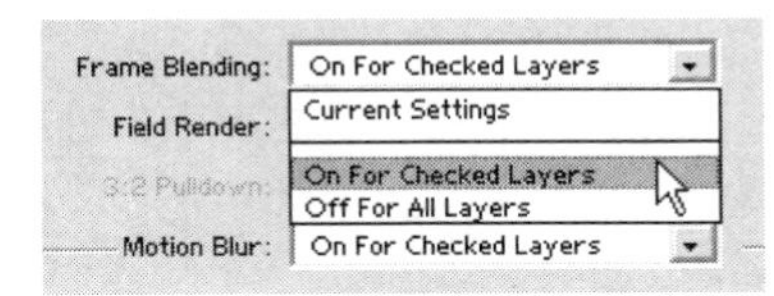

Figure 18.35 In the Frame Blending pull-down menu, specify whether frame blending is applied to layers with the Frame Blending switch enabled.

Field Render specifies whether to field-render the output movie and, if so, which field is dominant. (See the sidebar "Working the Fields: Interlaced Video and Field Order" in Chapter 2, "Importing Footage into a Project.") Set this option to Off unless the output is destined for video (**Figure 18.36**).

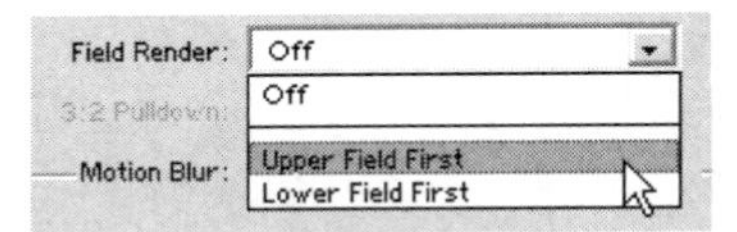

Figure 18.36 In the Field Render pull-down menu, choose whether to field-render the output.

3:2 Pulldown specifies whether to reintroduce pulldown to the footage and determines the phase of the pulldown. (See the sidebar "The Lowdown on Pulldown" in Chapter 2.) You only need to set the proper phase if the movie will be cut back into the original footage (**Figure 18.37**).

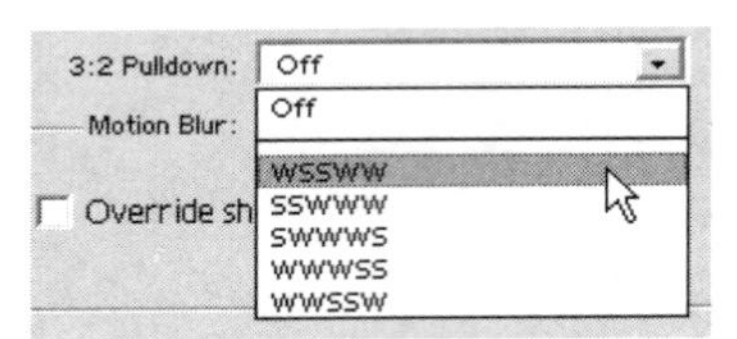

Figure 18.37 To reintroduce pulldown to the footage, choose an option from the 3:2 Pulldown menu.

Motion Blur specifies whether motion blur is applied to layers with the Motion Blur switch enabled, regardless of a composition's Motion Blur setting. Or, you can set this option to respect the composition's current Motion Blur setting. When you enable motion blur, it uses the settings you specified in the Composition settings (see "Using Motion Blur," in Chapter 14). Alternatively, you can select "Override shutter angle" and enter the shutter angle to be used instead. A setting of 360 degrees results in the maximum motion blur (**Figure 18.38**).

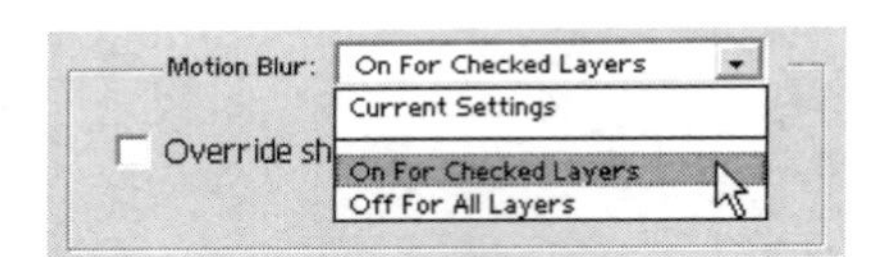

Figure 18.38 In the Motion Blur pull-down menu, specify whether motion blur is applied to layers with the Motion Blur switch enabled.

Time Span defines the part of the composition for output (**Figure 18.39**). Choosing Custom from the Time Span pull-down menu or clicking the Set button opens a Custom Time Span dialog box. (See "Setting the Work Area" in Chapter 8, "Playback, Previews, and RAM.")

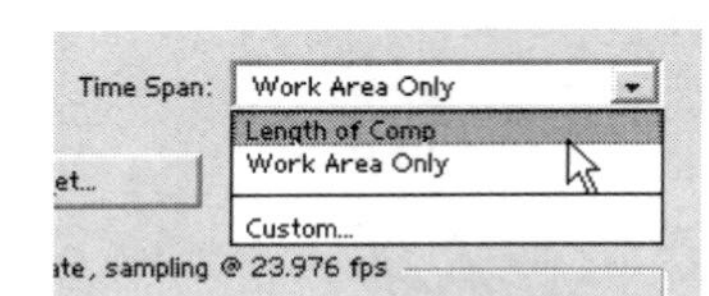

Figure 18.39 Define the part of the composition for output in the Time Span pull-down menu.

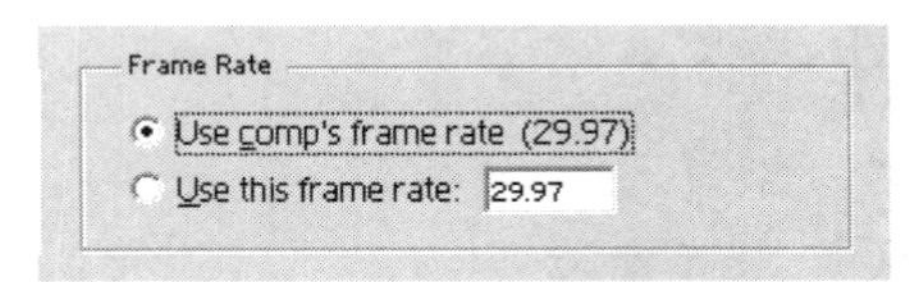

Figure 18.40 Select the frame rate of the composition, or enter a custom frame rate.

Figure 18.41 Select "Use storage overflow" to ensure that rendering continues to an overflow volume when the output file exceeds the capacity of the first storage volume.

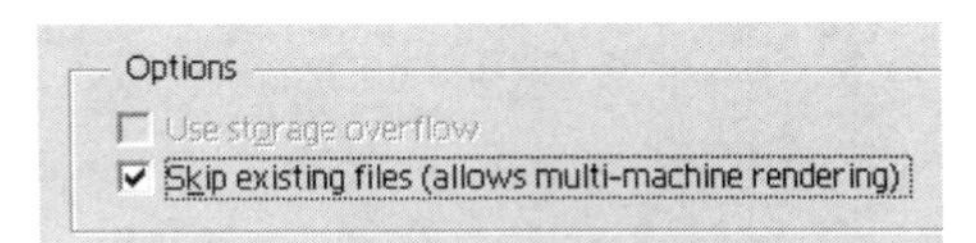

Figure 18.42 Select "Skip existing files" to enable After Effects to render or rerender frames of an existing frame sequence.

Frame Rate sets the frame rate used to render the composition. You may select the composition's frame rate or enter a custom frame rate. (See "Frame rate," in Chapter 4.) As you'll recall from Chapter 4, the Frame Rate setting doesn't affect playback speed, just smoothness (**Figure 18.40**).

"Use storage overflow" determines whether rendering continues to an overflow volume when the output file exceeds the capacity of the first storage volume (**Figure 18.41**). (See "Setting Overflow Volumes" later in this chapter.)

"Skip existing files" enables After Effects to render or rerender frames of an existing frame sequence. This option also allows multiple computers to render parts of the same image sequence to a Watch folder (**Figure 18.42**). (Consult your After Effects documentation for more about network rendering features.)

3. Click OK to close the Render Settings dialog box and return to the Render Queue window.

Choosing Output-Module Settings

Choosing output-module settings is the second step in the movie-making process. These settings determine how processed frames are saved.

To choose an output module manually:

1. In the render queue, click the underlined name of the output module (**Figure 18.43**).

   An Output Module Settings dialog box appears (**Figure 18.44**).

2. In the Output Module Settings dialog box, make a selection *for each of the following options:*

   Format determines the output's file format, and includes a variety of movie and still-image-sequence formats (**Figure 18.45**). Although your particular project and/or equipment will dictate your choice, QuickTime Movie and Video for Windows are common choices for motion files, and TIFF and PICT sequences are common choices for still-image formats.

   Embed determines whether After Effects embeds a project link into the output movie. When opening the output file in a program that supports project links—such as Adobe Premiere Pro—you can use the Edit Original command to reopen the source project and make any necessary changes to it. Select Project Link from the pull-down menu to create a link between the output file and the source project. Select Project Link and Copy to embed both a link to the original project and a copy of the project into the output file. If the original project isn't available when you use the Edit Original command, After Effects will allow you to open the embedded copy of the project (**Figure 18.46**).

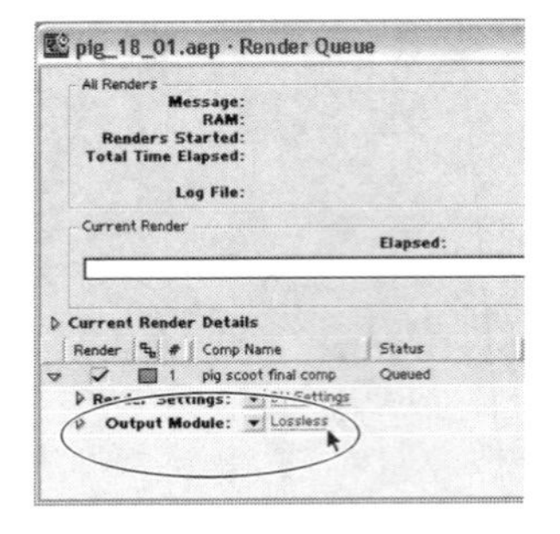

Figure 18.43 In the render queue, click the underlined name of the output module.

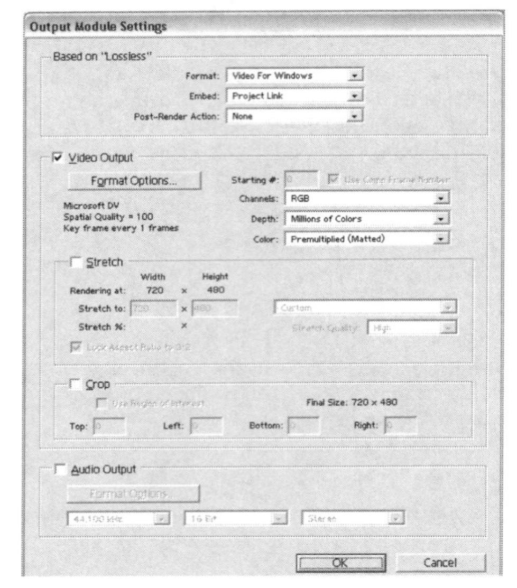

Figure 18.44 An Output Module Settings dialog box appears.

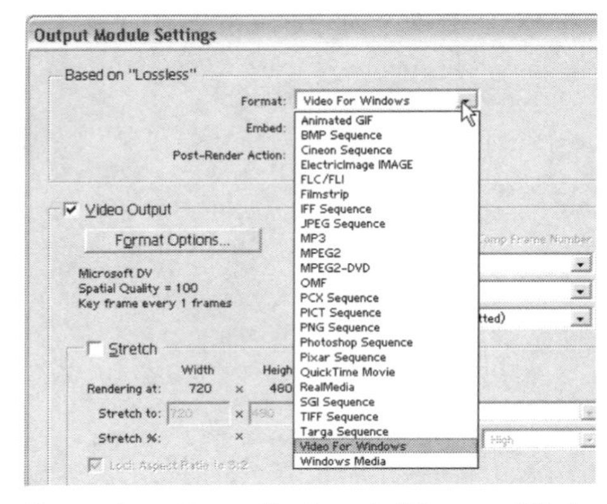

Figure 18.45 Choose the format of the saved file in the Format pull-down menu.

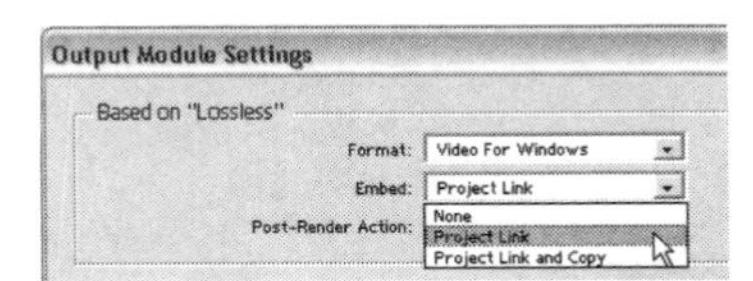

Figure 18.46 Embed determines whether After Effects embeds a project link into the output movie.

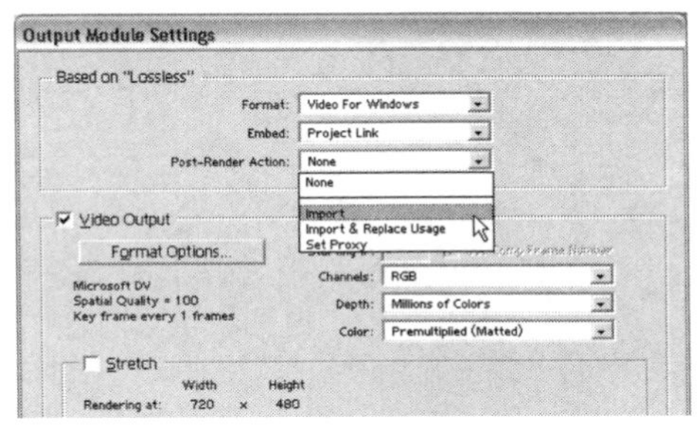

Figure 18.47 In the Post-Render Action pull-down menu, choose whether you want to use the rendered movie in the project. You can import the rendered movie, use it in place of its source footage, or set it as a proxy for its source footage.

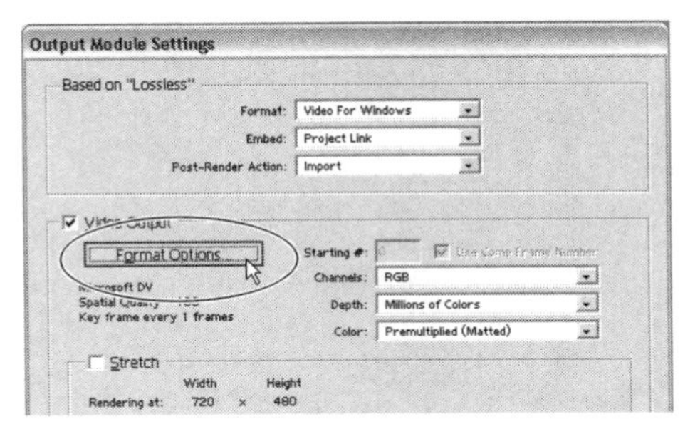

Figure 18.48 Click Format Options to open a dialog box containing format-specific settings.

Figure 18.49 When exporting a still image sequence, specify the starting number, or select Use Comp Frame Number.

Post-Render Action specifies whether After Effects utilizes the rendered movie in the project. You can instruct After Effects to import the movie, replace the source composition (including its nested instances) with the movie, or use the movie as a proxy in place of its source (**Figure 18.47**). This way, you can replace complex, processing-intensive elements with a single, easy-to-render footage item—thereby reducing render times. Using a post-render action is part of a strategy called *prerendering*; see "Prerendering" in Chapter 17, "Complex Projects."

Format Options opens a dialog box that includes options associated with particular formats (**Figure 18.48**). For example, if you chose QuickTime Movie as the format, the Format Options button would open a Compression Settings dialog box for QuickTime movies. (See "Movie Files and Compression" later in this chapter.)

Starting # lets you specify the starting frame number in the filenames when you're exporting an image sequence. Alternatively, you can select Use Comp Frame Number to match exported frame numbers to the frame numbering in the comp (the option is checked by default) (**Figure 18.49**).

continues on next page

Channels specifies the channels present in the output (**Figure 18.50**). Depending on the format, you can choose to export the RGB channels, the alpha channel, or RGB + Alpha. (See the sidebar "Alpha Bits" in Chapter 2, "Importing Footage into a Project.")

Depth specifies the color depth of the output. The available options depend on the format and channels you selected (**Figure 18.51**).

Color specifies how color channels factor in the alpha channel (if one is present), determining whether the output uses a straight alpha or is premultiplied with black (**Figure 18.52**). (See the sidebar "Alpha Bits" in Chapter 2.)

Stretch lets you specify the frame size of your output. By selecting this option, you can choose common frame sizes from a pull-down menu or enter custom dimensions.

You may also choose between a low- and high-quality resizing method in the Stretch Quality pull-down menu. Stretch resizes the image after it's been rendered (**Figure 18.53**).

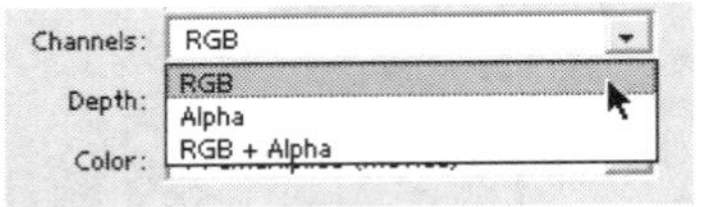

Figure 18.50 Specify the channels present in the output in the Channels pull-down menu.

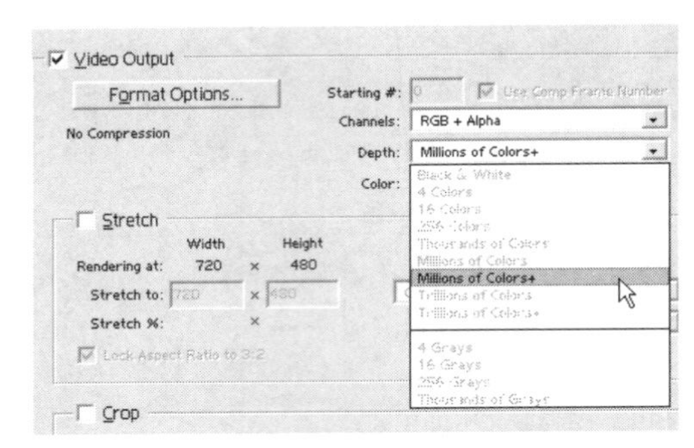

Figure 18.51 The options available in the Depth menu depend on the format and channels you selected.

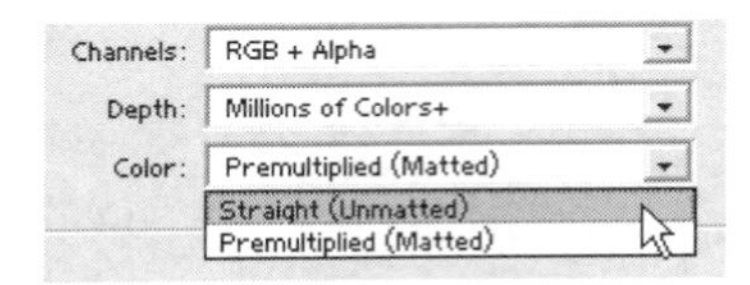

Figure 18.52 If you chose to output an alpha channel, use the Color pull-down menu to choose between straight alpha or premultiplied with black.

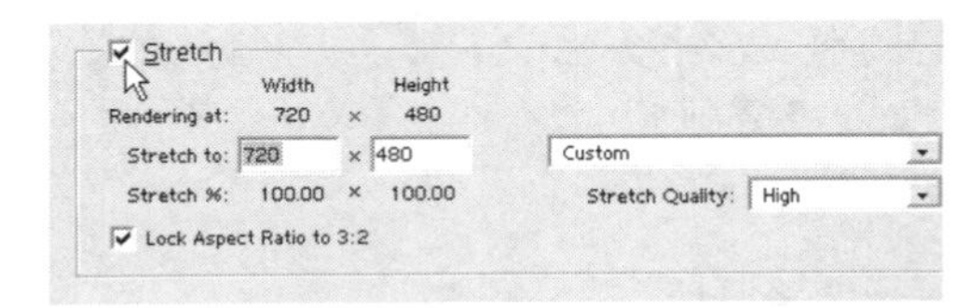

Figure 18.53 Select Stretch options to resize the image after it's been rendered.

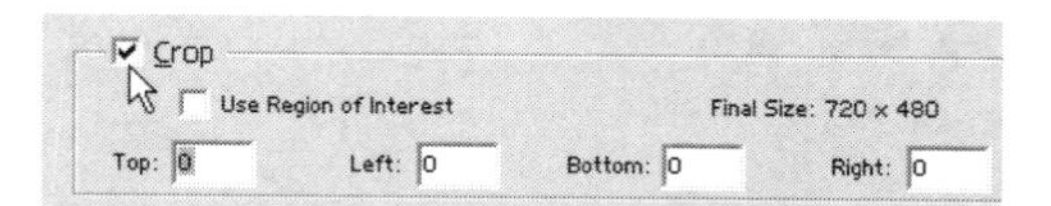

Figure 18.54 Select Crop options to add or remove pixels from the edges of the frame.

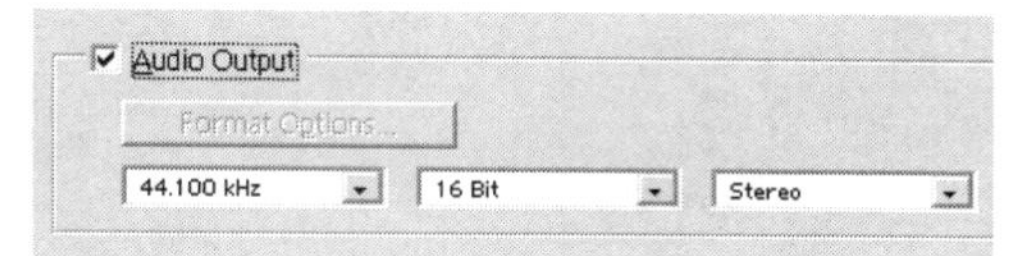

Figure 18.55 Specify the sample rate, bit depth, and whether the audio track is stereo or mono.

Crop lets you add or, more likely, remove pixels from the edges of the image frame (**Figure 18.54**). Cropping is useful for removing black edges from video footage. You can also use this option to reverse field dominance (see the sidebar "Reversing Field Order" in Chapter 2.)

Audio Output specifies the audio-track attributes (if any) of your output. Settings include sample rate, bit depth, and format (mono or stereo). (For more about audio, see the sidebars in Chapter 8.) Note that the Format Options button remains grayed out and doesn't permit you to apply audio compression (**Figure 18.55**). To compress the audio, you can use an option available under the Export command, or you can compress the final movie using a program such as QuickTime Pro or Media Cleaner Pro.

3. Click OK to close the Output Module dialog box and return to the Render Queue window.

Creating Templates

You should save your most commonly used settings as templates so that you can apply them by selecting templates in the Render Settings and Output Module pull-down menus in the Render Queue window. You can also make your most useful render settings and output-module templates your default settings. You can even save templates as stand-alone files that you can then move to other systems or share with other users.

To create a template:

1. *Do one of the following:*
   - ▲ To create a render settings template, choose Make Template in the Render Settings pull-down menu (**Figure 18.56**).
   - ▲ To create an output-module template, choose Make Template in the Output Module pull-down menu.

   Depending on your choice, a Render Settings Templates or Output Module Templates dialog box appears. An untitled template appears in the Settings Name field.
2. Click Edit in the Render Settings Templates or Output Module Templates dialog box (**Figure 18.57**).

   Depending on the type of template you're creating, the Render Settings dialog box or the Output Module dialog box appears (**Figure 18.58**).
3. Choose the render-settings or output-module options you want to save as a template.
4. When you've finished selecting settings, click OK to close the Render Settings or Output Module dialog box and return to the Render Settings Templates or Output Module Templates dialog box.

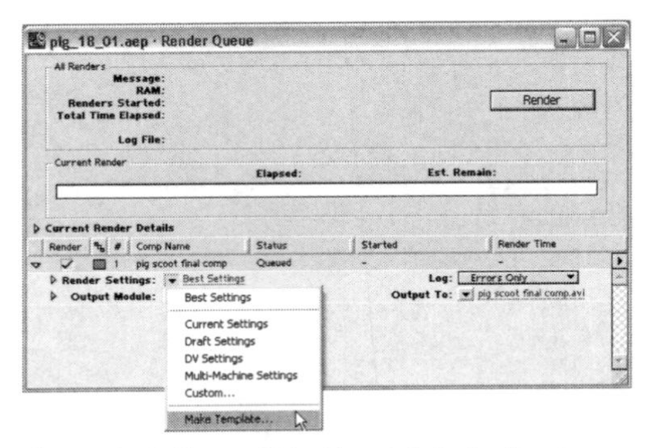

Figure 18.56 Choose Make Template in the Render Settings pull-down menu.

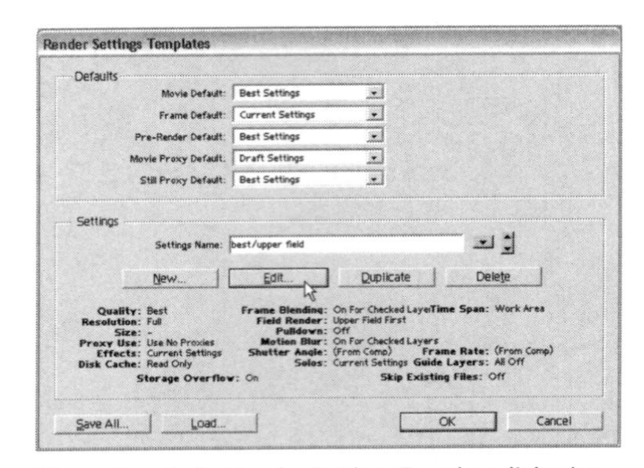

Figure 18.57 In the Render Settings Template dialog box, click Edit to specify settings for the untitled template.

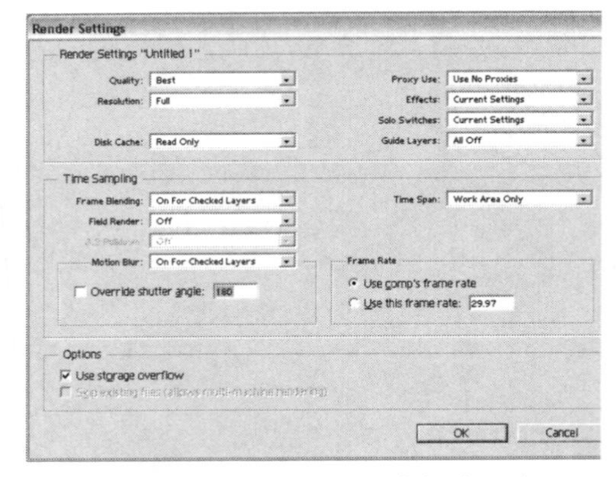

Figure 18.58 In the Render Settings dialog box, choose Render Settings options to save as a template, and click OK to return to the Render Settings Templates dialog box.

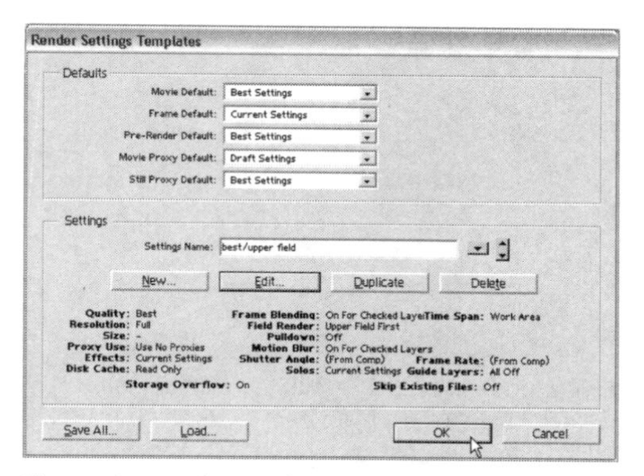

Figure 18.59 In the Render Settings Templates dialog box, enter a settings name for the new template, and click OK to close the dialog box.

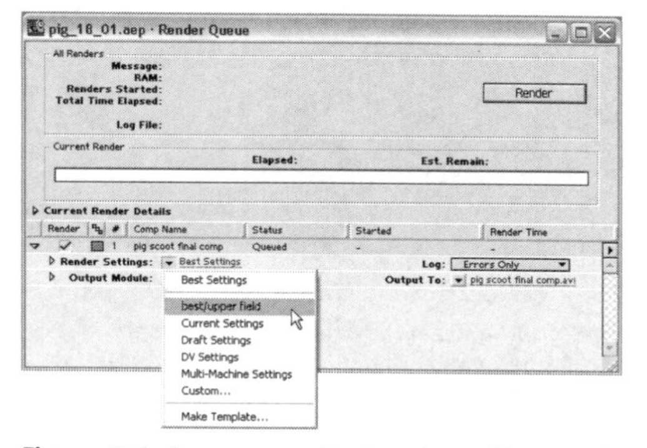

Figure 18.60 From now on, the template will appear in the Render Settings Templates pull-down menu in the Render Queue window.

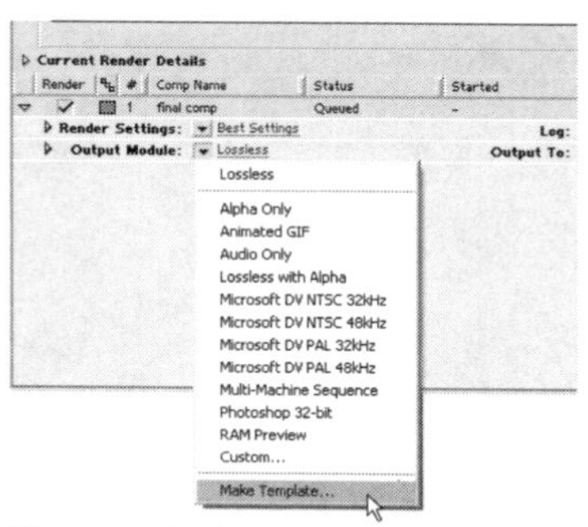

Figure 18.61 Choose Make Template in the Output Module pull-down menu.

5. In the Render Settings Templates or Output Module Templates dialog box, enter a settings name for the new template (**Figure 18.59**).
6. Click OK to close the dialog box and save the template.

   From now on, the template will appear in the appropriate pull-down menu in the Render Queue window (**Figure 18.60**).

To set a default template:

1. *Do one of the following:*
   - ▲ To set the default render settings template, choose Make Template in the Render Settings pull-down menu.
   - ▲ To set the default output module template, choose Make Template in the Output Module pull-down menu (**Figure 18.61**).

   Depending on your choice, the Output Module Templates dialog box or the Render Settings Templates dialog box appears (**Figure 18.62**).

continues on next page

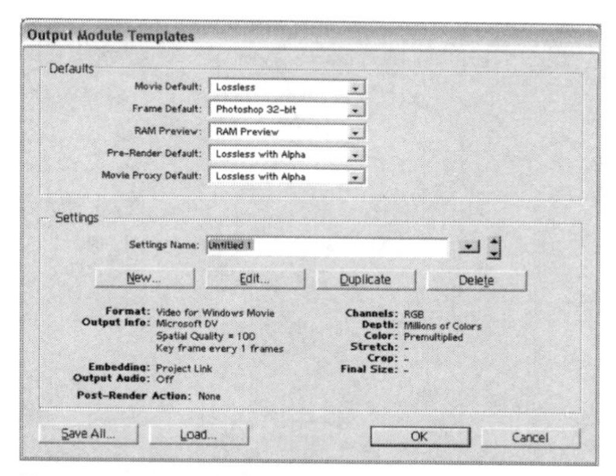

Figure 18.62 The Output Module Templates dialog box appears.

2. To set the default template for output movies, choose a template from the Movie Default pull-down menu (**Figure 18.63**).
3. To set the default template for output still frames, choose a template from the Frame Default pull-down menu (**Figure 18.64**).
4. To set the default template for RAM Previews, as well as the default template for Pre-Renders and Movie Proxies, choose an option from the appropriate pull-down menus.

   Pre-Render and Movie Proxy defaults affect movies created using Post-Render actions, explained in "Choosing Output-Module Settings" earlier in this chapter.
5. Click OK to close the dialog box.

   The selected templates become the default templates for the corresponding output types.

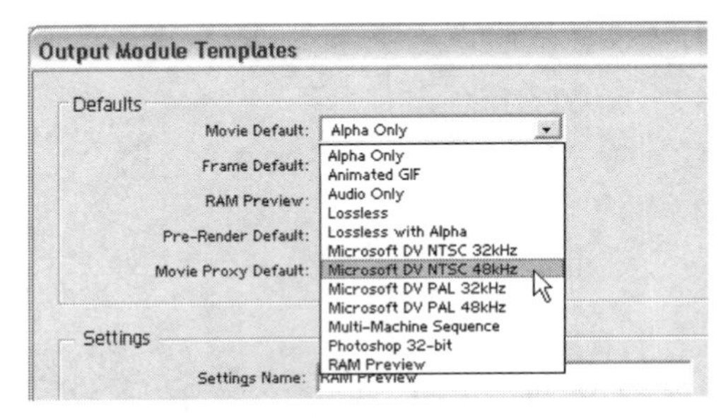

Figure 18.63 To set the default template for output movies, choose a template from the Movie Default pull-down menu.

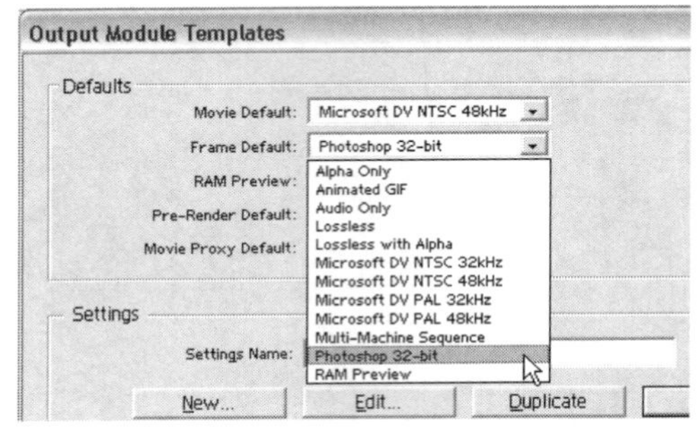

Figure 18.64 To set the default template for output still frames, choose a template from the Frame Default pull-down menu. Repeat the process for RAM previews, Pre-Render, and Movie Proxy.

To save templates as files:

1. In the Render Settings Templates or Output Module Templates dialog box, click Save All (**Figure 18.65**).

   A Save As dialog box appears.

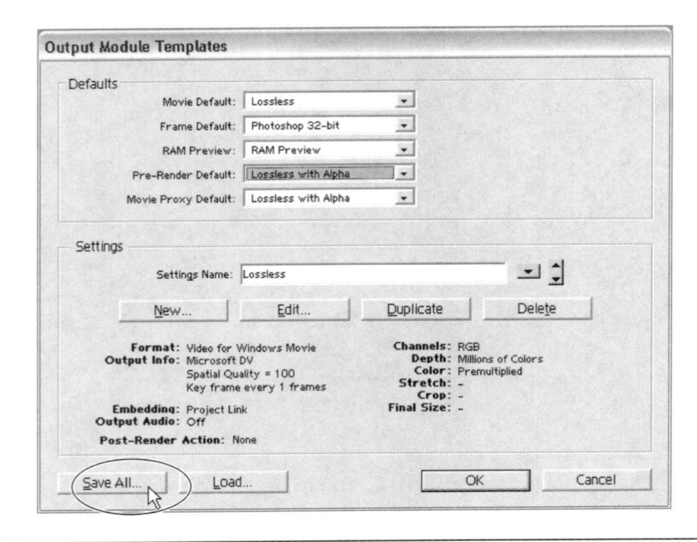

Figure 18.65 In the Render Settings Templates or Output Module Templates dialog box, click Save All.

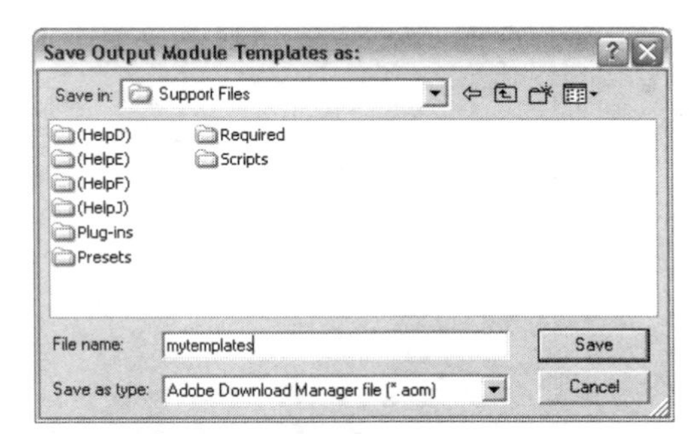

Figure 18.66 In the Save As dialog box, specify a name and destination for the saved template file.

2. In the Save As dialog box, specify a name and destination for the saved template file.

   The render settings template files use the `.ars` file extension. Output module template files use the `.aom` file extension (**Figure 18.66**).

3. Click Save to close the dialog box and save the file.

To load saved templates:

1. In the Render Settings Templates or Output Module Templates dialog box, click Load.

   An Open dialog box appears.

2. In the Open dialog box, locate a render-settings or output-module template file.

   The render-settings files use the `.ars` file extension; output-module template files use the `.aom` file extension.

3. Click OK to close the dialog box and load the settings.

   Depending on the type of file you loaded, the render-settings or output-module templates appear in their respective pull-down menus.

Saving Single Frames of a Composition

Frequently, you'll want to render just a single frame of a composition. For example, when an animation halts its motion, substituting a single still image for multiple static layers can lighten the rendering load. Or you may need a still for a storyboard or client review. After Effects allows you to save a single frame using the default frame settings or as a layered Photoshop file.

To save a composition frame as a still-image file:

1. Set the current time of the composition to the frame you want to export (**Figure 18.67**).
2. Choose Composition > Save Frame As > File (**Figure 18.68**).

   The composition appears selected in the Render Queue window (**Figure 18.69**).
3. To change the destination of the saved image, click the name of the file next to Output To.

   A Save As dialog box opens.
4. In the Save As dialog box, specify the destination and name of the saved frame (**Figure 18.70**).

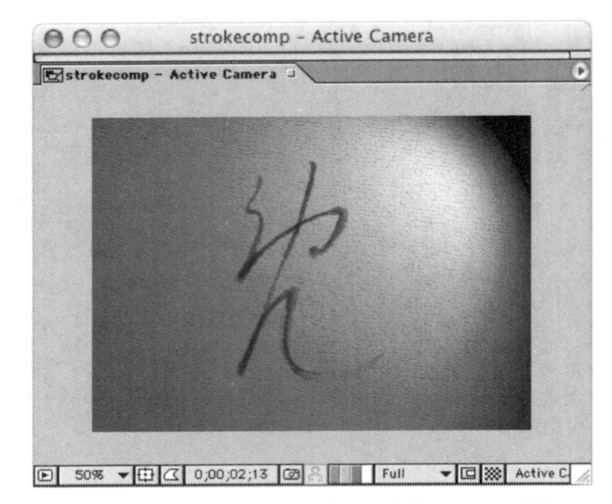

Figure 18.67 Set the current time of the composition to the frame you want to export.

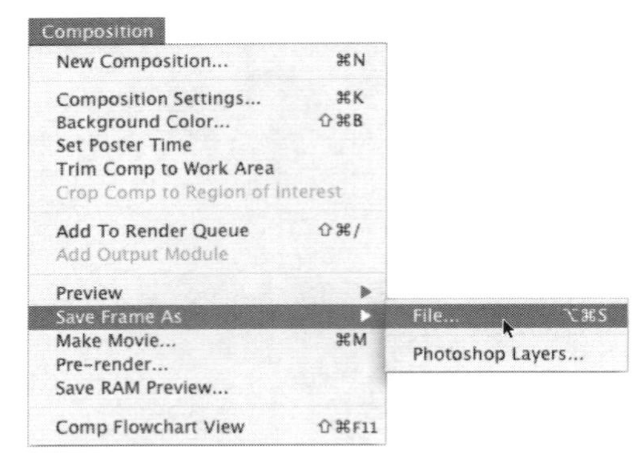

Figure 18.68 Choose Composition > Save Frame As > File.

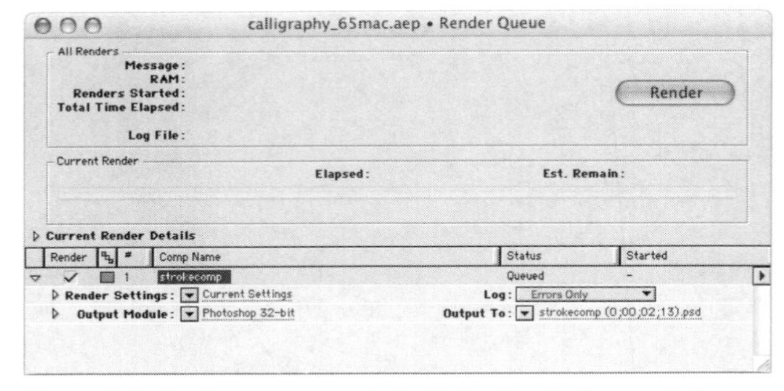

Figure 18.69 The item appears selected in the Render Queue window.

5. Click Save to close the Save As dialog box.
6. To change the default settings for frames, select render settings and output module settings, or choose templates.

   The previous sections explain how to select settings and save templates.
7. In the Render Queue window, click Render.

✔ Tips

- If you want to use the still frame in the project, make sure to specify a post-render action in the output module settings. See "Choosing Output-Module Settings" earlier in this chapter, and "Prerendering Complex Elements" in Chapter 17.
- You can export the current frame as a layered Photoshop file in a similar manner by choosing Composition > Save Frame As > Photoshop Layers.

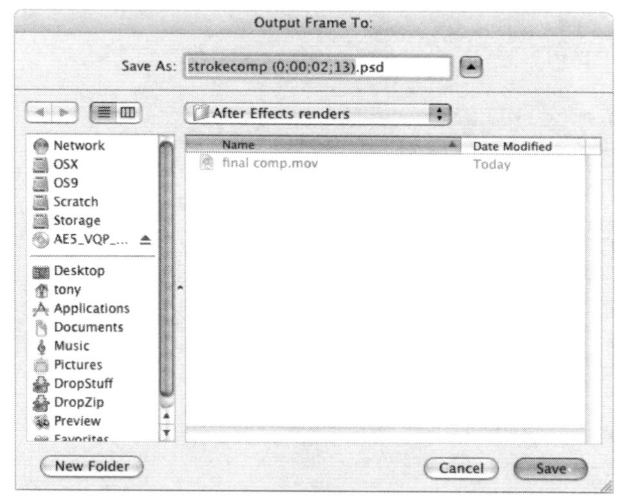

Figure 18.70 To change the destination of the saved file, click its name next to Output To, and in the Save As dialog box, specify the destination and name of the saved frame.

Exporting to SWF Format

Using After Effects' Export command, you can output your composition to a number of audio and video formats. This section, however, focuses on Macromedia's SWF format—a format that will be of particular interest to users creating animations for the Web.

For the uninitiated, SWF (often pronounced *swif)* stands for Shockwave Flash, the popular Flash Player format. Designed to deliver dynamic content over the Web's limited bandwidths, Flash animations include predominately vector-based graphics. Although they can include bitmapped images, such graphics significantly increase file size, thus limiting delivery speed.

The following tasks take you through the basic exporting process and provide a brief discussion of several export options for SWF files. However, some options require an understanding of the SWF format itself, HTML, or Web authoring—subjects that can't be addressed fully here.

For example, knowledge of HTML will help you determine whether you want to use the Include Object Names option to make names of objects in the composition appear in the exported file's source code. You'll also need to determine whether to include elements such as bitmapped images and motion blur, which can't be translated directly into SWF's native vector-based format. And only your familiarity with Internet bandwidth restrictions will help you design a composition appropriate for Web delivery. Consult your After Effects documentation to learn more about which features are supported for SWF export and other format-specific options.

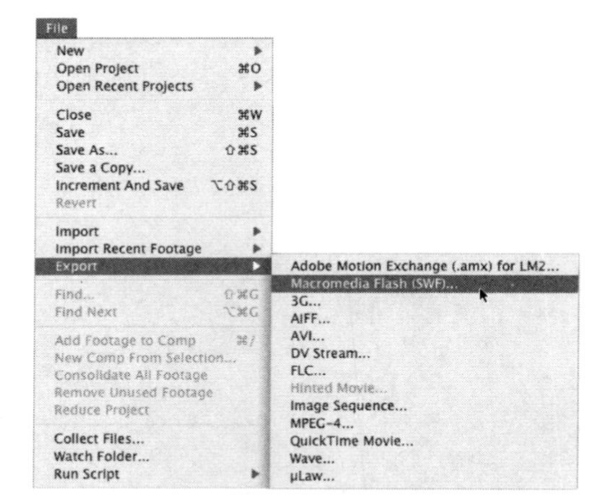

Figure 18.71 Choose File > Export > Macromedia Flash (SWF).

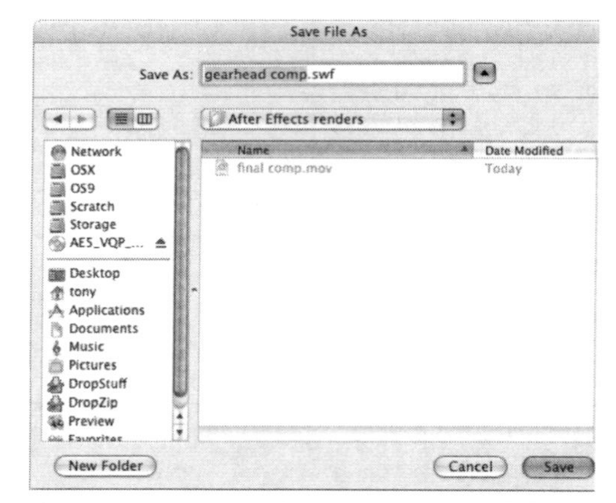

Figure 18.72 In the Save File As dialog box, specify the name and destination of the exported file and click OK (Mac) or Save (Windows).

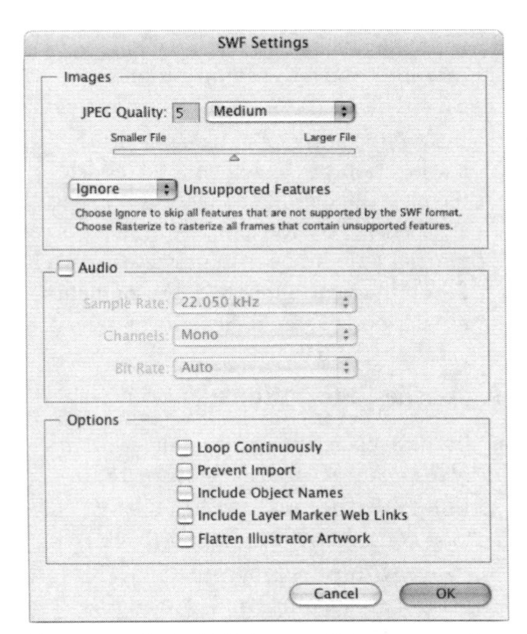

Figure 18.73 In the SWF Settings dialog box, specify JPEG Quality.

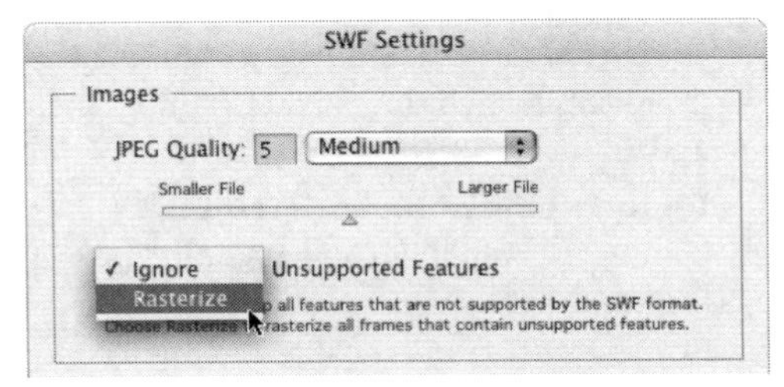

Figure 18.74 In the Unsupported Features pull-down menu, choose an option.

To export a composition to the SWF format:

1. Select the composition you want to export.
2. Choose File > Export > Macromedia Flash (SWF) (**Figure 18.71**).

   A Save File As dialog box appears.
3. In the Save File As dialog box, specify the name and destination of the exported file, and click OK (Mac) or Save (Windows) (**Figure 18.72**).

   A SWF Settings dialog box appears (**Figure 18.73**).
4. In the SWF Settings dialog box, specify JPEG image quality by *doing any of the following:*
   - ▲ Choose a quality setting from the JPEG Quality pull-down menu.
   - ▲ Enter a number from 0 to 10 in the JPEG Quality field, where 0 is the lowest possible quality.
   - ▲ Drag the JPEG Quality slider.
5. In the Unsupported Features pull-down menu, *choose either of the following options* (**Figure 18.74**):

   Ignore skips all features that aren't supported by the SWF format.

   Rasterize rasterizes all frames that contain unsupported features.

continues on next page

6. To export audio, click Audio and *specify the following options:*

   Sample Rate—Use this pull-down menu to choose from various sample rates. Higher sample rates produce better-quality sound but larger files.

   Channels—Use this pull-down menu to choose between exporting stereophonic and monophonic audio.

   Bit Rate—Use this pull-down menu to choose from various audio bit depths. Higher bit depths produce better-quality sound but larger files.

   See Chapter 8 for an explanation of audio sample rate, channels, and bit rates.

7. In the Options section of the SWF Settings dialog box, check the options you want.

   Specific options are explained in the following task.

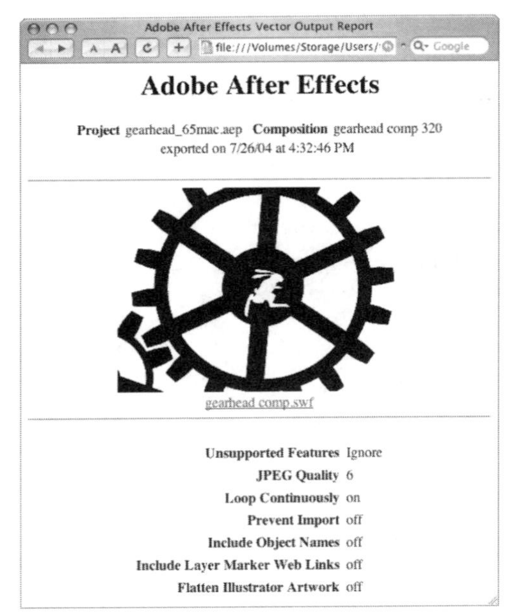

Figure 18.75 You can open the report file in a Web browser to preview the SWF file.

8. Click OK to close the SWF dialog box and export the composition as a SWF file.

   A SWF file and report file appear in the location you specified. The report file uses the naming convention `filenameR.htm`. You can open the report file in a Web browser to preview the SWF file and to view a report of the elements not supported by the SWF format (**Figure 18.75**).

To specify SWF options:

- In the SWF Settings dialog box, *select any of the following options* (**Figure 18.76**):

  Loop Continuously makes the SWF file loop continuously during playback.

  Prevent Import prevents the SWF file from being imported into editing programs.

  Include Object Names gives the SWF file's layers, masks, and effects the same names they have in After Effects. See your After Effects documentation for more about including object names in a SWF file.

  Include Layer Marker Web Links allows the Web links you specified in layer markers to be included in the SWF file. See your After Effects documentation for more about using Web links in layer markers and in SWF files.

  Flatten Illustrator Artwork flattens multilayer Illustrator artwork when exporting it to a SWF file.

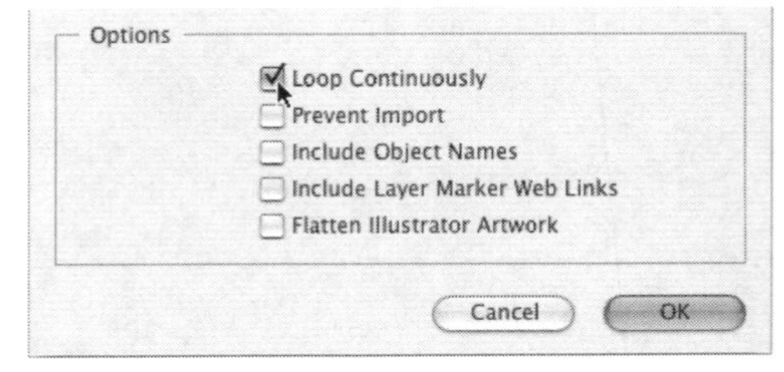

Figure 18.76 In the Options section of the SWF Settings dialog box, check the options you want.

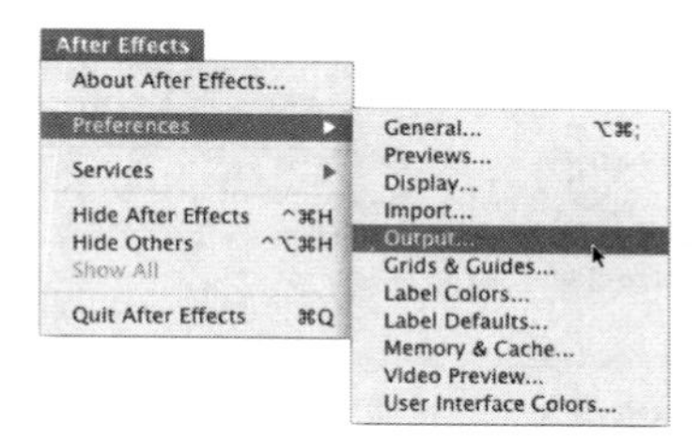

Figure 18.77 Choose After Effects > Preferences > Output (Mac) or Edit > Preferences > Output (Windows).

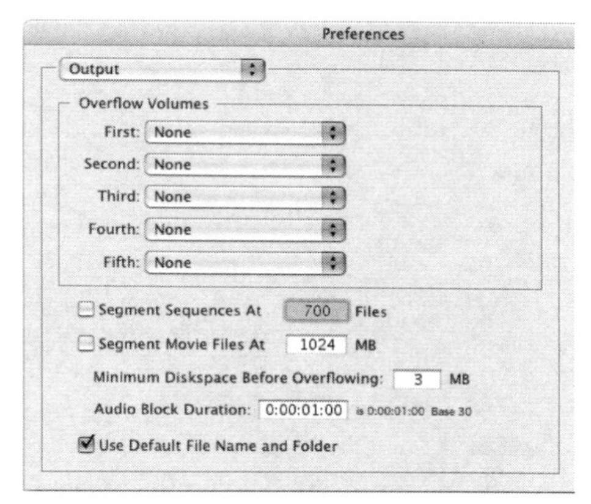

Figure 18.78 The Output panel of the Preferences dialog box opens.

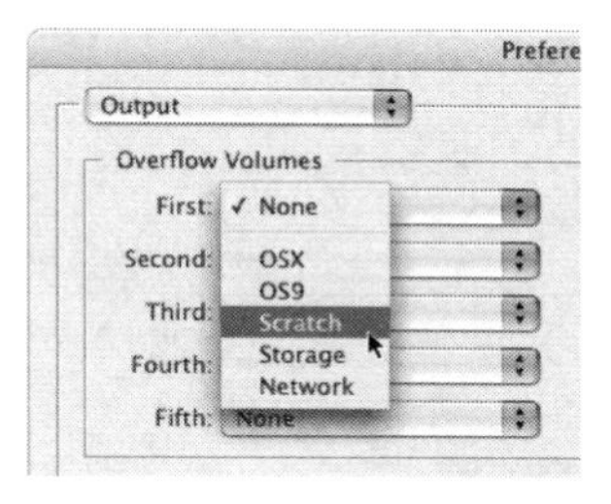

Figure 18.79 To specify overflow volumes, choose a storage volume from the Volume pull-down menus.

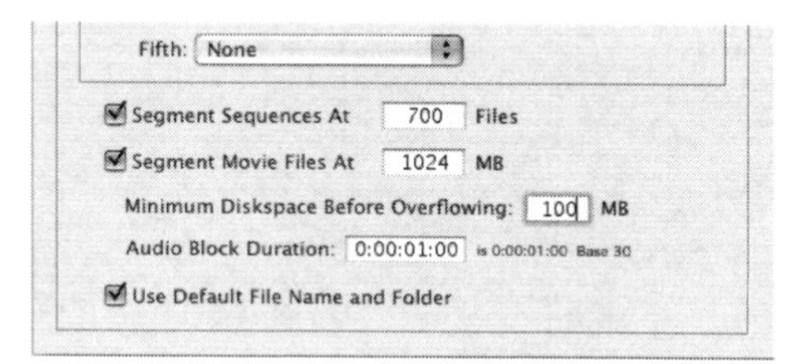

Figure 18.80 Specify the maximum number of files in Segment Sequences At; the maximum size of a file in Segment Movie Files At; and the Minimum Diskspace Before Overflowing.

Setting Overflow Volumes

As you're already well aware, movie files can consume enormous amounts of storage space. It's not unusual for a file or sequence to exceed either the file size limit imposed by the computer's operating system or the size of the storage volume. Fortunately, you can control overflow and thus avert errors and failed renders. When the rendered file or sequence reaches the limits you specify, it continues to render into a folder on the root level of an overflow volume.

To specify overflow volumes:

1. Choose After Effects > Preferences > Output (Mac) or Edit > Preferences > Output (Windows) (**Figure 18.77**).

   The Output panel of the Preferences dialog box opens (**Figure 18.78**).

2. To specify overflow volumes, choose a storage volume from the Volume pull-down menus in the Overflow Volumes section of the Preferences dialog box (**Figure 18.79**).

   A rendered file or sequence overflows into the first volume, then the second, and so on.

3. To set the maximum number of files that can be rendered to a single folder, click Segment Sequences At, and enter a maximum number (**Figure 18.80**).

4. To set the maximum size of a single rendered file, check Segment Movie Files At, and enter a maximum file size (in MB).

   Your operating system may have its own file size limit.

5. For Minimum Diskspace Before Overflowing, enter the minimum amount of storage space that must remain on the drive before rendering resumes on the next overflow volume.

6. Click OK to close the dialog box.

Movie Files and Compression

When you select QuickTime Movie or Video for Windows as the format, clicking the Format Options button opens a dialog box for choosing compression settings. To choose the settings most appropriate for your output goals, you need to know something about video compression in general as well particular compression schemes, or *codecs*.

Generally speaking, your playback equipment, image-quality goals, and data-rate limitations will dictate your compression choices. For example, if your movie file was destined for use with a nonlinear editing system, such as Avid or Media100, you would render it using the system's native codec. On the other hand, if you wanted to output an uncompressed file to maintain the highest image quality, you could deliver it to a postproduction facility to be transferred to tape or film (assuming your own hardware isn't able to play back such a large file in real time). Alternatively, you might need to present your movie on the Web—in which case choosing settings that produce a small file with a low data rate would be your top priority.

The following sections offer essential background information and guidance for choosing video compression settings in After Effects.

Compression in a Nutshell

Compression refers to techniques used to store large amounts of data in smaller packages. Without compression, digital video files are too large for most drives and processors to play back smoothly. In other words, an uncompressed file's *data rate*—the amount of data that must be processed in a given amount of time—is too high for most systems to deliver. To reduce the file size and data rates of digital video and audio, developers have devised various compression schemes, or *codecs*.

Compression schemes that reduce file size without discarding data are known as *lossless*. Storing data using lossless compression can be compared to writing a message in shorthand. When it's time to read the message, the data is decoded back into "longhand." Lossless compression reduces file size most when the image contains a lot of redundancy, such as large areas of a single color. Even then, the file sizes are relatively large because no data has been thrown out.

Lossy compression schemes discard data to reduce file size. Although such compression schemes are designed to discard data you're least likely to miss, the loss of quality is almost always noticeable. Usually, you can set the amount of compression to control the reduction in file size and quality.

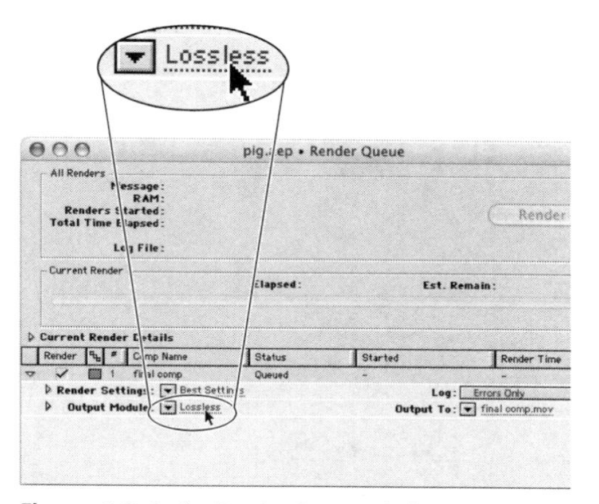

Figure 18.81 In the Render Queue window, click the underlined name of the output module.

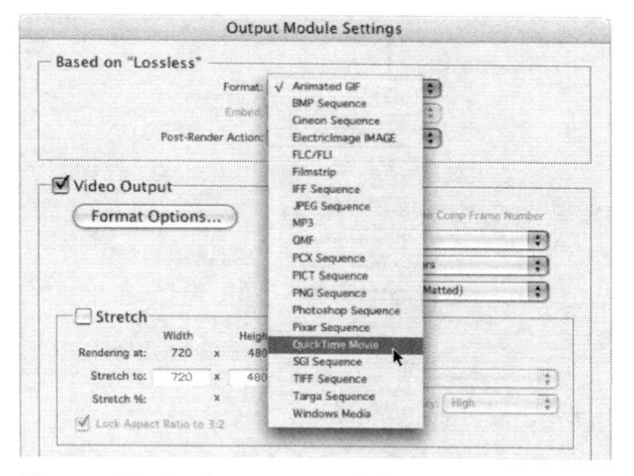

Figure 18.82 In the Format pull-down menu, choose QuickTime Movie.

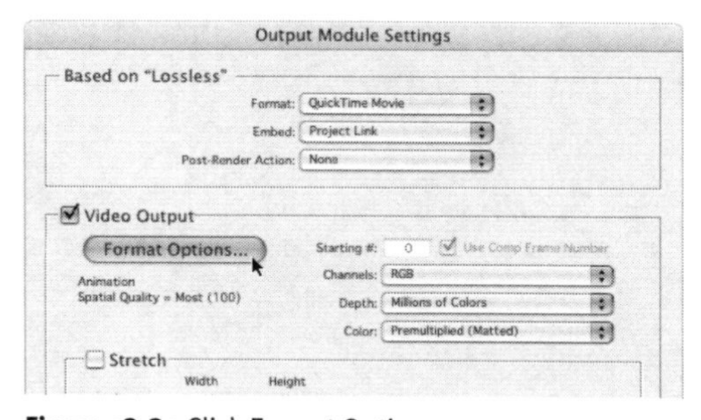

Figure 18.83 Click Format Options.

To set QuickTime compression settings:

1. In the Render Queue window, click the underlined name of the output module (**Figure 18.81**).

   The Output Module Settings dialog box opens.

2. In the Format pull-down menu of the Output Module Settings dialog box, choose QuickTime Movie (**Figure 18.82**).

3. In the Output Module Settings dialog box, click Format Options (**Figure 18.83**).

   A Compression Settings dialog box appears (**Figure 18.84**).

continues on next page

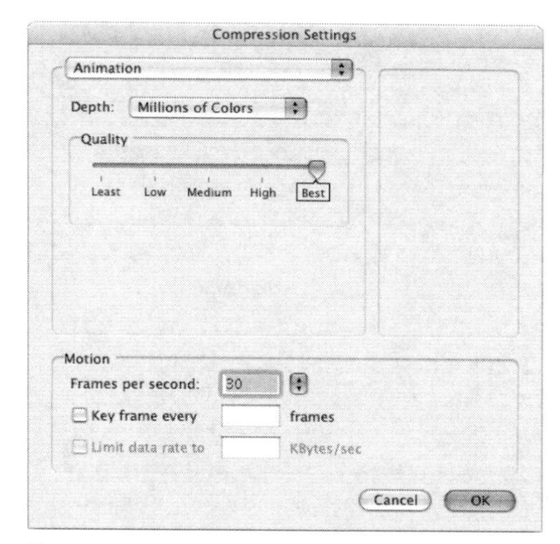

Figure 18.84 A Compression Settings dialog box appears.

4. In the Compression Settings dialog box, *do the following:*

   ▲ Choose a codec from the pull-down menu near the top of the dialog box (**Figure 18.85**).

   ▲ Choose a bit depth from the Depth pull-down menu (**Figure 18.86**).

   ▲ Adjust the Quality slider to set the amount of compression (**Figure 18.87**).

   ▲ Ignore the Frames Per Second option. (The frame rate you set in the Output Module settings overrides this setting.)

   ▲ Specify whether to use keyframes, and, if so, set their frequency.

   ▲ Specify whether to limit the maximum data rate, and, if so, enter the data rate in kilobytes/sec.

5. Click OK to close the dialog box.

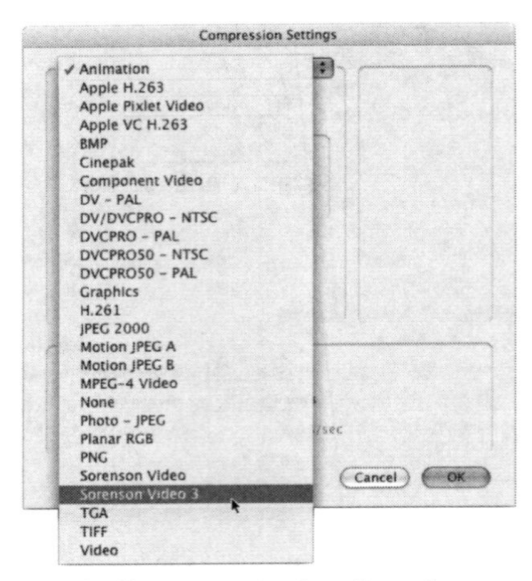

Figure 18.85 Choose a codec from the pull-down menu.

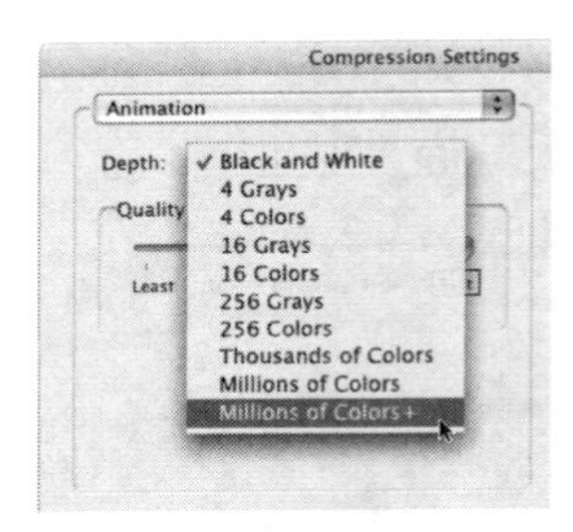

Figure 18.86 Choose a bit depth from the Depth pull-down menu.

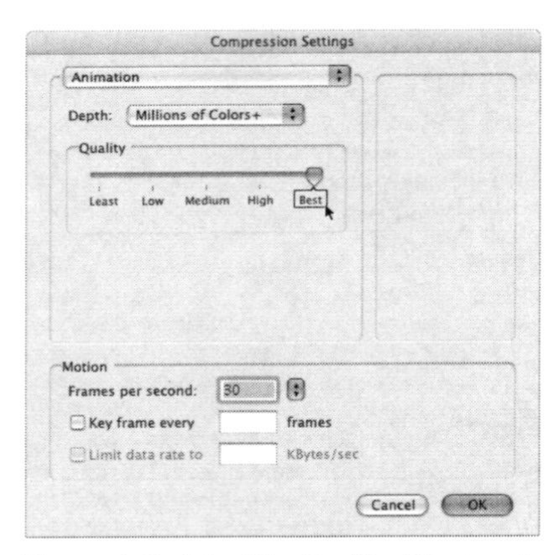

Figure 18.87 Adjust the Quality slider to set the amount of compression. If you want, specify the frequency of keyframes and limit the data rate.

Data Rates

A clip's file size relates directly to its *data rate*—the amount of information that the computer must process in a given amount of time to play back the clip smoothly. Most of the video and audio settings you choose influence the data rate of movies. In addition, many video codecs allow you to specify the maximum data rate for a movie file. You set a data rate according to the limitations of the target playback device and the specifications of the codec. In the Compression Settings dialog box, data rates are expressed in kilobytes/sec. Be aware that other programs may express data rates as kilobytes/frame or kilobits/sec.

To set Video for Windows compression settings:

1. In the Render Queue window, click the underlined name of the output module (**Figure 18.88**).

   The Output Module Settings dialog box opens.

2. In the Format pull-down menu, choose Video For Windows (**Figure 18.89**).

3. In the Render Queue window, click the Format Options button (**Figure 18.90**).

   A Video Compression dialog box appears (**Figure 18.91**).

4. In the Compression Settings dialog box, *do the following:*

   ▲ Choose a codec from the Compressor pull-down menu (**Figure 18.92**).

continues on next page

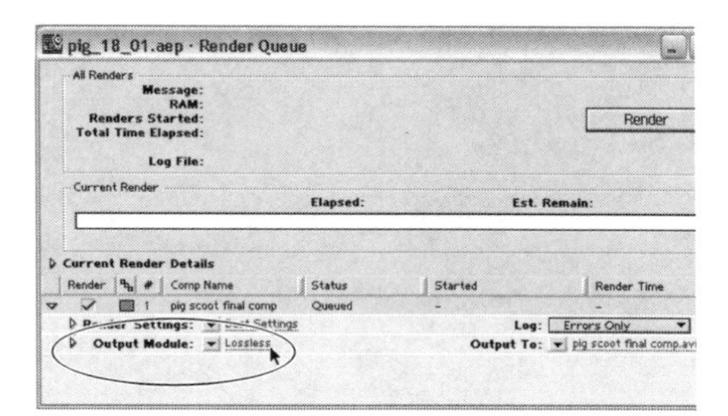

Figure 18.88 In the Render Queue window, click the underlined name of the output module.

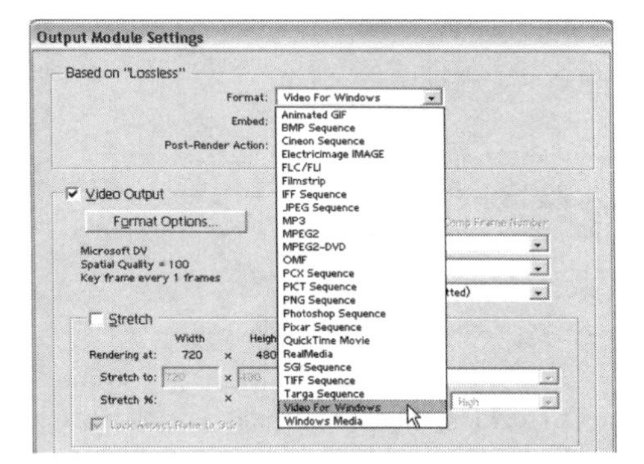

Figure 18.89 In the Format pull-down menu, choose Video For Windows.

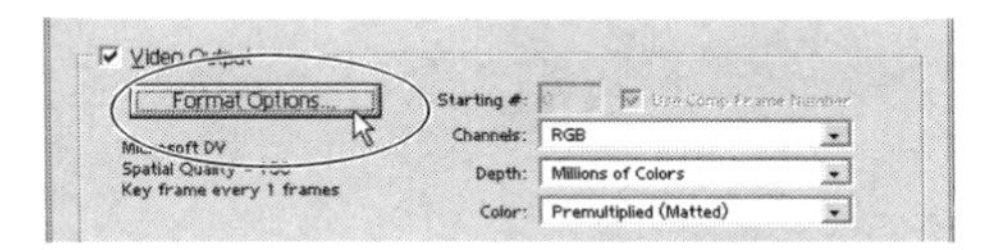

Figure 18.90 In the Render Queue window, click the Format Options button.

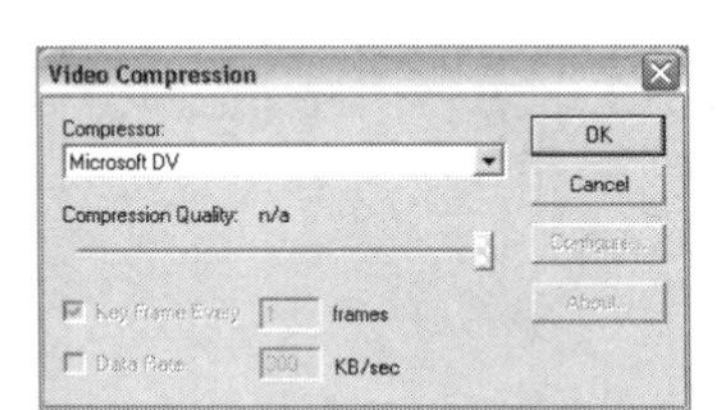

Figure 18.91 A Video Compression dialog box appears.

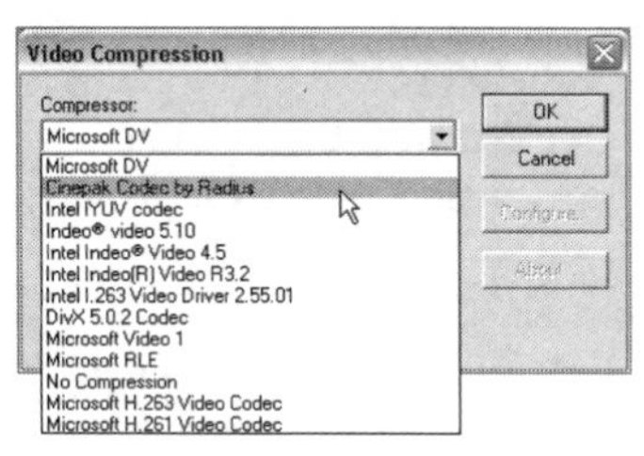

Figure 18.92 Choose a codec from the Compressor pull-down menu.

- Adjust the Quality slider to set the amount of compression (**Figure 18.93**).
- Specify whether to use keyframes, and, if so, set their frequency.
- Specify whether to limit the maximum data rate, and, if so, enter the data rate in kilobytes/ sec.

5. To access codec-specific options, click Configure (**Figure 18.94**).

   A codec-specific dialog box appears, in which you can select settings particular to the codec (**Figure 18.95**).

6. Click OK to close the Video Compression dialog box.

Keyframes

Many codecs—especially those designed for low data rates—use *keyframes* to optimize compression while maintaining the highest possible image quality. Keyframes are, in fact, essential to the compression technique called *frame differencing.*

In *frame differencing,* keyframes act as reference frames, against which subsequent frames are compared. Rather than describe each frame completely, frame differencing achieves more efficient compression by describing only the changes between keyframes.

Keyframes are most effective when the image differs greatly from the preceding frame. Some codecs allow you to set the frequency of keyframes, or they may insert keyframes automatically when the image changes significantly. A greater number of keyframes tends to make for better image quality but bigger files. Fewer keyframes usually results in smaller files but lower image quality.

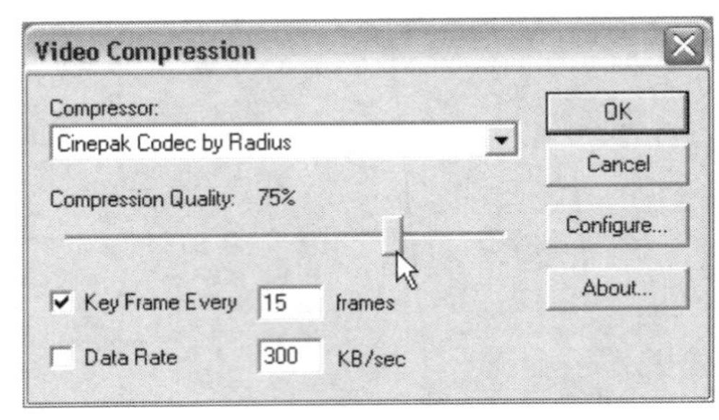

Figure 18.93 Adjust the Quality slider to set the amount of compression.

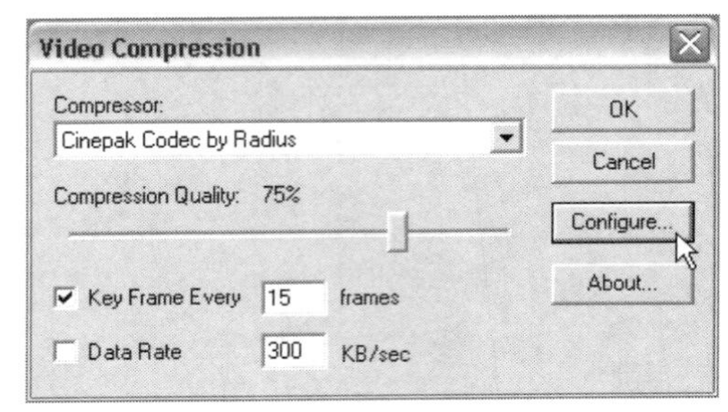

Figure 18.94 To access codec-specific options, click Configure.

Figure 18.95 When the Cinepak codec is selected, clicking the Configure button opens settings specific to Cinepak. Specifically, you can specify whether to compress to color or black and white.

QuickTime Video Codecs

The Compressor menu of the Compression Settings dialog box offers a long list of video codecs when you choose QuickTime as the format in the output module. The following are some of the most common choices:

Animation uses lossless compression at its 100 percent quality setting and supports an alpha channel when color depth is set to Millions of Colors +. Designed for images that contain large areas of flat color, such as cartoon animations, it can result in smaller file sizes than the None codec.

Cinepak compresses 24-bit video for data rates suitable for CD-ROM playback or Internet download, and it can be played back on older computers. Compression is slow.

DV-PAL and DV-NTSC compress video to the DV standard used by the MiniDV, DVCam, and DVCPro video formats.

Video supports Thousands of Colors. Designed for video content, it's good for fast, low-quality drafts.

Motion JPEG A and Motion JPEG B support video captured with some hardware capture cards.

None saves uncompressed images and supports an alpha channel when color depth is set to Millions of Colors +. It maintains the highest image quality but also results in the largest file sizes.

Sorenson Video yields high compression with high quality for data rates ideal for Internet download. However, it can be very slow to compress and only plays back on computers with relatively fast processors.

Codecs

Codec stands for *compression/decompression. Compression* refers to encoding a file and is synonymous with capture and rendering. *Decompression* refers to decoding a file and is associated with playback. *Codec* denotes a particular *compression scheme*—a method of compressing and decompressing a file.

There are software- and hardware-based codecs. QuickTime and Video for Windows include several software-based codecs; others are available as software plug-ins.

For most high-quality video capture and playback, however, you need a hardware-assisted codec. If your hardware capture card and its software are installed properly, the codec designed for the card appears in the Compressor menu in the Compression Settings dialog box.

Most capture cards also offer a software-only version of the codec. Although the software codec usually can't enable you to play back the clip smoothly, it does allow you to open and process the file on computers that don't have the necessary hardware.

Within each codec, you can generally control how much compression is applied by using a Quality slider, or you can define an upper limit for the data rate (see the sidebar "Data Rates" earlier in this chapter).

Video for Windows Codecs

Although Video for Windows is built into Windows 95, Microsoft no longer supports it; instead, it's being replaced by DirectShow/ActiveMovie. The `.avi` format is being replaced by `.asf` (Active Streaming Format).

When you choose Video for Windows as the format in the output module, the Compression Settings dialog box offers several video codecs, including the following options:

Cinepak compresses 24-bit video for data rates suitable for CD-ROM playback or Internet download, and for playback on older computers.

No Compression saves uncompressed images and supports an alpha channel when color depth is set to Millions of Colors +. It maintains the highest image quality but also results in the largest file sizes.

Intel Indeo is used for video distributed over the Internet for computers with fast (Pentium II or better) processors, and is designed to work with the Intel Audio Software codec.

Microsoft DV compresses video to the DV standard used by the MiniDV, DVCam, and DVCPro video formats.

Microsoft RLE is designed for images that contain large areas of flat 16-bit color (256 colors), such as cartoon animations. Lossless at its 100 percent quality setting, it's suitable for interim storage of title sequences and animations.

✔ Tip

- Rather than doing all the compression in After Effects, you may want to render a master version of your movie. A movie with relatively little compression and high quality makes a good source for creating other versions. Then you can turn to software dedicated to hard-core compression tasks, such as Media Cleaner Pro or Heuris MPEG Power Professional.

INDEX

Numbers

3:2 pulldown, 60, 61, 62, 127, 680
3D Channel effects, 374
3D layers, 206, 591–630
  auto-orienting, 604
  axis modes, 596–597
  cameras, 607–615
  combining with 2D layers, 629–630
  converting to 2D layers, 592
  designating, 592
  Draft mode, 628
  lights, 616–620
  Material Options, 605–606
  orienting, 600, 601–602
  Point of Interest, 621–624
  positioning, 598–599
  previewing, 628
  rendering, 132, 629–630
  rotating, 600, 602–603
  stacking order of, 629
  viewing, 593–595
3D plug-in, 132
8-bit channel mode, 27, 28
16-bit channel mode, 27, 28
16mm film standard, 25
24Pa pulldown, 60, 61, 63–64
32-bit images, 42
35mm film standard, 25
60-fps animation sequences, 58

A

acceleration
  hardware, 4
  temporal interpolation and, 572
action-safe zones, 102
adaptive resolution, 245, 255, 257
Add Vertex tool, 297, 311–312, 575
adjust effects, 374
Adjust Tension icon, 317
adjustment layers, 149–150
  applying effects to, 149, 364–365
  converting layers to, 365
  creating, 150
  render order and, 639
Adobe Illustrator. *See* Illustrator
Adobe Photoshop. *See* Photoshop
Adobe Premiere Pro. *See* Premiere Pro
Advanced 3D rendering plug-in, 132
Advanced Authoring Format (AAF) files, 6
advanced pulldown, 64
After Effects 6.5
  general description, 1
  integration with other Adobe programs, 2, 6
  interface features, 10–15
  minimum system requirements, 2
  new features, 5
  professional system additions, 4
  suggested system features, 3
  versions of, 7
  work flow overview, 9
After Effects Footage window, 92, 93, 96
After Effects Pro, 7
Align and Distribute palette, 14, 15
Aligned option, 507–508
aligning
  paragraphs, 453–454
  vertical text, 425
All Caps option, 444
Alpha Add mode, 540
Alpha Channel button, 110
alpha channels
  explained, 42–44
  importing files with, 40–44

paint strokes and, 483
premultiplied, 43, 44
saving files with, 43–44
setting interpretation for, 40–42
straight, 43
viewing, 110
Alpha Inverted Matte, 544
Alpha Matte, 543
alpha-manipulation modes, 540
Always Preview This View button, 278
ambient light, 617
anchor points, 211–213, 293, 298
3D layers, 599
converting, 313
repositioning, 212–213
text, 470
viewing paths for, 554
anchor positions, 129
angles
brush tip, 496
effect, 355
shutter, 130, 519
animated properties, 208, 209, 231–237
animated strokes, 502–506
keyframes and, 505–506
speed adjustments for, 504
Write On option, 502–503
animated text, 5, 417, 458–478
animator groups for, 458, 463–478
expression selectors and, 472, 478
path text as, 452, 458
presets for, 461–462
range selectors and, 464, 472–478
source text as, 458, 459–460
wiggly selectors and, 472, 478
animation
effects and, 370–372, 389
layer properties and, 231–237
motion blur for, 518–519
paint stroke, 502–506
text or type, 5, 417, 458–478
traveling mattes and, 539
animation presets, 242–244
applying, 243–244, 359, 361
saving, 242, 358–359
Animation video codec, 701
animator groups, 417, 458, 463–478
adding items to, 469
animating type with, 465–467
creating, 468
explained, 463–464
expression selectors for, 472, 478
properties for, 470
range selectors for, 472, 473–477
removing, 469
wiggly selectors for, 472, 478
animator properties, 463, 464, 470
Apply Interpretation command, 69
audio
bit depth, 270
exporting, 694
importing, 51, 56
layer markers and, 203
monophonic, 268, 379, 383
output options, 685
previewing, 263, 266–268
sample rates, 269
scrubbing, 262
setting properties for, 225–230
stereophonic, 268, 379, 383
sweetening, 379
toggling on and off, 162
Audio effects, 379–383
Audio Options dialog box, 228–229
Audio palette, 12, 13, 228–230
audio level settings, 229–230
resizing, 228
setting options in, 228–229
audio properties, 206, 225–230
audio waveform, 226–227
Audio Waveform effect, 402–404
auto Bézier interpolation, 550
converting to/from, 557–558, 578
spatial interpolation and, 561
temporal interpolation and, 583
toggling between linear interpolation and, 577
Auto Open Palettes option, 15, 430
Auto-Orientation dialog box, 564, 604, 622
auto-orienting
3D layers, 604, 622
rotation to motion paths, 563–564
A/V Features panel, Timeline window, 161
axis modes, 596–597

B

background
checkerboard, 133
solid-color, 145
background color, 133–134, 482
Background Color dialog box, 133–134
baseline shift, 442
Bevel Alpha effect, 400–401
Bevel Edges effect, 400
Bézier curves, 292–293
adjusting, 315
creating, 300–301

Bézier interpolation, 551
- converting to/from, 558–559, 578
- spatial interpolation and, 562
- temporal interpolation and, 584

bit depth
- audio, 270, 694
- color, 27–28

Bit Depth button, 28
Blend effect, 388–389
blending characters, 450
blending modes, 528–540
- alpha-manipulation, 540
- applying to layers, 529
- brightness, 531–533
- chrominance-based, 537–538
- combination, 534–536
- difference, 536
- dodge and burn, 532, 533, 535
- exclusion, 537
- explained, 528
- stencil and silhouette, 538–539
- transparency, 530
- types of, 530–540

bluescreen, 397
Blur effects, 384–386
bottom-to-bottom leading, 437, 438
brightness-enhancing modes, 532–533
brightness-reducing modes, 531–532
Broadcast Colors effect, 415
broadcast video, 36
brush dynamics, 498
brush tips, 482, 491–498
- brush dynamics, 498
- creating, 493
- customizing, 496–497
- removing, 494
- renaming, 494
- restoring, 495
- selecting, 491

Brush Tips palette, 14, 479, 493–498
- customizing brush tips, 496–497
- opening and closing, 480
- setting brush dynamics, 498
- working with brush tips, 493–496

Brush Tips Selector, 482, 491–492
- customizing, 492
- selecting brush tips in, 491

Brush tool, 485–487
burning technique, 535

C

cached data, 246, 281–283
Camera Settings dialog box, 607–615
Camera views, 593, 594
cameras, 607–615
- basic settings for, 609–611
- creating, 607–608
- depth of field options, 611–612, 614–615
- lenses for, 613
- Point of Interest and, 621–624
- terms describing movement of, 627
- tools for, 625–626

Caps Lock key, 261
Channel effects, 387
channels
- audio, 694
- output, 684
- paint stroke, 483
- viewing individual, 110
- *See also* alpha channels

chapter links, 199
character offset, 471
Character palette, 13, 419, 430–432
- opening and closing, 430
- resetting characters in, 432
- setting values in, 431

character range, 471
character value, 471
checkerboard background, 133
child layers, 653, 654–655
Choose Name dialog box, 119–120, 493
chrominance, 397, 416, 537
chrominance-based modes, 537–538
Cinepak video codec, 701, 702
CJK fonts, 448–449
Classic Color Burn mode, 532
Classic Color Dodge mode, 533
Classic Difference mode, 536
Clone Stamp tool, 507–514
- overlay feature, 513
- presets, 514
- saving settings in, 514
- setting options for, 507–508
- steps for using, 511–512

cloning, 507–514
- pixels, 511–512
- sample point setting for, 507
- source setting for, 509–510
- superimposing images and, 513

closed paths, 291, 318
closing
- folders, 83
- projects, 22
- tabbed windows, 18

codecs, 696, 700, 701–702
- QuickTime video, 701
- Video for Windows, 702

collapsing transformations, 648–649
Collect Files command, 86
color
  background, 133–134, 482
  bit depth, 27–28
  effect, 352–353
  fill and stroke, 434–436
  foreground, 482
  guideline, 107
  label, 80–81, 160
  light, 620
  mask, 322–323
  modes based on, 537–538
  output, 684
  paint, 482
  video, 416
Color Balance effect, 394
Color Burn mode, 532
Color Dodge mode, 532
Color mode, 537–538
color picker, 352
color value modes, 537–538
Comment heading panel, Project window, 78
comments, layer marker, 202
compifying. *See* precomposing
complex projects. *See* projects
Composition icon, 635
composition markers
  adding, 199–200
  moving, 200
  removing, 201
composition presets, 119–120, 122
Composition Settings dialog box, 116–117
  Advanced panel, 129–132, 519
  Basic panel, 116–128
  keyboard shortcut for opening, 118, 129
Composition window, 10, 135
  3D layers viewed in, 593–595
  annotated illustration, 135
  dragging footage into compositions in, 140, 141
  Fast Preview button, 255–256
  magnification options in, 98–99
  masks viewed in, 286, 288
  motion path information in, 553–554
  nesting compositions in, 152
  numerically cueing the time in, 138–139
  Pan Behind Tool used in, 327, 328
  repositioning layers in, 214–215
  rotating layers in, 218
  scaling layers in, 216–217
  selecting layers in, 154
  selecting masks or points in, 306–307
  setting effect points in, 357
  spatial controls in, 209–210
  stacking order of layers in, 156
  viewing area of, 121
compositions, 115–152
  adding footage to, 140–141
  adjustment layers in, 149–150
  anchor positions for, 129
  background color of, 133–134
  choosing settings for, 118
  creating, 116–117
  displaying information about, 72
  duration of, 128
  exporting to SWF format, 692–694
  frame rate of, 126–127
  frame size of, 121–122, 124
  importing layered files as, 48–49
  inserting layers in, 142–144
  making movies from, 672–674
  naming or renaming, 84, 117
  nested, 118, 131, 151–152, 369, 631, 632–636
  numerically cueing the time in, 138–139
  overlaying layers in, 142–144
  pixel aspect ratio of, 123
  precomposing layers in, 645–647
  presets for, 119–120, 122
  reducing memory requirements for, 275
  rendering plug-in for, 132
  resolution of, 124–125
  saving single frames of, 690–691
  selecting/deselecting layers in, 155
  shutter settings for, 130
  solid layers in, 145–148
  starting frame number for, 127
  time controls for, 137–139
Compound Blur effect, 385–386
compound effects, 366–369
compression, 696–702
  codecs for, 696, 700, 701–702
  explained, 696
  movie files and, 696–700
  QuickTime settings, 697–698, 701
  Video for Windows settings, 699–700, 702
Compression Settings dialog box, 697–698, 701, 702
Consolidate All Footage command, 86
contextual menus, 372
continuous Bézier interpolation, 550–551
  converting to/from, 558–559, 578
  spatial interpolation and, 562
  temporal interpolation and, 584
Continuously Rasterize switch, 168–169
contrast, 376–377
control points, 292
  adding, 311–312

converting, 313–314
deleting, 310
moving, 309–310
selecting, 306–307
Convert Vertex tool, 293, 297, 313–314, 316
converting
anchor points, 313
control points, 313–314
masks, 304
copying and pasting
effects, 362
keyframes, 239–240
mask paths, 565–566
corner points, 293, 299
converting, 314
cropping, 685
Cube icon, 592
cueing
current time to keyframes, 241
motion footage, 97
current time marker, 97
composition markers used with, 200
setting In or Out points with, 187
curves
adjusting, 315
creating, 300–301
cusp points, 299
Custom heading panel, Project window, 79
Custom views, 593
Cycle Mask Colors option, 323

D

Dancing Dissolve mode, 530
Darken mode, 531
data rate, 696, 698
deceleration, 572
Delete button, 120
Delete Vertex tool, 312
deleting
animator groups, 469
composition presets, 120
control points, 310
footage, 85
keyframes, 237
See also removing
Depth of Field options, 611–612, 614–615
deselecting
keyframes, 236
layers, 155
dialog boxes
setting property values in, 221–222
See also names of specific dialog boxes
Difference mode, 513, 536
direction lines, 292
DirectX technology, 3
disabling. *See* enabling and disabling
disk cache, 283, 678
Displacement Map effect, 391–393
Display panel, Preferences dialog box, 74, 555
displaying
grids, 100–101
guides, 106
heading panels, 77–78
In/Out panel, 185
layers, 161
Project window information, 72
RAM preview options, 274
rulers, 104
shy layers, 167
tabbed windows, 16
thumbnail images, 74
Time Controls palette, 137
video-safe zones, 100–101
See also hiding; viewing
Dissolve mode, 530
Distort effects, 390
dodging technique, 535
dongle, 7
double-byte fonts, 448–449
Draft 3D mode, 628
Draft Quality icon, 170
drawing mask shapes, 294
Drop Shadow effect, 401
drop-frame (DF) timecode, 25, 26
duplicate footage, 86
duplicating layers, 194
duration, 128, 186, 483–484
DV-PAL and DV-NTSC video codecs, 701
Dynamic Resolution button, 256

E

ease handles, 568, 579, 580–581
Echo effect, 409–410
edit marks, 180
editing layers, 171–203
changing playback speed, 197–198
duplicating layers, 194
In/Out panel for, 185–187
Layer window for, 178–179
markers used for, 199–203
moving layers in time, 184, 185–187
performing slip edits, 188
removing a range of frames, 192–193
sequencing and overlapping layers, 189–191
splitting layers, 195–196
terminology used for, 180

time graph for, 174–177
trimming layers, 180, 181–183
viewing layers, 172–173
editing text, 426–429
imported from Photoshop, 428–429
layer controls and, 427
selecting characters for, 426
Effect Controls window, 11, 16, 345–346
adjusting effects in, 351
angle controllers in, 355
applying effects in, 342
color options in, 352–353
effect presets in, 358–359
expanding/collapsing effects in, 346
keyframe options in, 371
reordering effects in, 363
resetting effects in, 348
selecting effects in, 346
setting values in, 354
viewing effects in, 344
Effect icon, 349–350
Effect Point button, 356–357
effect source, 367–369
effects, 206, 335–416
3D Channel, 374
Adjust, 374
adjustment layers and, 149, 364–365
angle settings for, 355
animating, 370–372
applying, 342–343, 360
Audio, 379–383
Audio Waveform, 402–404
Bevel Alpha, 400–401
Blend, 388–389
Blur, 384–386
Broadcast Colors, 415
categories of, 336
Channel, 387
colors for, 352–353
compound, 366–369
controls for adjusting, 5, 210, 351
copying and pasting, 362
disabling and enabling, 349–350
Displacement Map, 391–393
Distort, 390
Echo, 409–410
Gradient Wipe, 411, 412–414
Grow Bounds, 395–396
Image Control, 394–396
Keying, 397
Levels, 375–378
Matte Tools, 397
new types of, 5
Noise & Grain, 398
output render settings, 679
Paint, 479
Perspective, 399
preset, 358–361
property values for, 354
removing, 347
Render, 401
reordering, 363
resetting, 348
saving, 358–359
setting effect points, 356–357
Sharpen, 384
Simulation, 405
Stereo Mixer, 380–383
Stylize, 405
Text, 408
Texturize, 406–407
Time, 408
Transition, 411
Vector Paint, 5
Video, 414–415
viewing, 344
Effects & Presets palette, 13, 337–341
applying presets using, 244, 359
displaying all items in, 338
finding items in, 338
item inclusion options, 340
refreshing the list in, 341
revealing effects in the OS, 341
sorting the list in, 339
Elliptical Mask tool, 290, 294
em spaces, 439
embedded links, 682, 683
enabling and disabling
effects, 349–350
expressions, 660
frame blending, 517
motion blur, 519
recursive switches, 650
thumbnails, 74
time remapping, 523
End property, 504
EPS Options dialog box, 68
Equals Sign icon, 658, 660, 662
Eraser tool, 488–490
Every-line Composer, 457
Exclusion mode, 537
expanding masks, 329, 331
exporting
audio files, 694
compositions to SWF format, 692–694
expanded feature for, 6
single frames to Photoshop, 691
expression graph, 661

expression selectors, 472, 478
expressions, 631, 657–667
creating, 658–659
enabling and disabling, 660
enhanced features for, 5
error dialog box, 663
explained, 657
language menu, 662–663
layer names and, 159
rendering order and, 639
saving, 660
syntax, 666–667
translating, 665
viewing, 661
writing, 664–667
Expressions feature, 5, 631, 657–667
extract edit, 192
Eye icon, 161, 163, 488
Eyedropper tool, 353

F

Fast Preview options, 255–256
faux bold/italic type, 443
feathering, 329–330
Feet and Frames time display options, 25–26
field order, 52–55
cheat sheet for, 55
interpreting in video footage, 53
manually determining, 54–55
reversing, 54
field rendering, 680
files
format options, 682, 683
importing, 29–33, 40–44
project vs. source, 19
saving with alpha channels, 43–44
templates saved as, 688–689
file-type extensions, 73
fill color, 434–436
fill layer, 542
film
transferred to video, 60–64, 127
traveling mattes on, 539
Find dialog box, 75
finding items
in the Effects & Presets palette, 338
in the Project window, 75–76
Fit-to-Fill feature, 180
Flash Player format. *See* SWF format
flow options, 482
Flowchart view, 642–644
customizing, 643–644
displaying, 642
folders
creating in Project window, 82
importing, 33
organizing footage in, 82–83
renaming, 84
toggling open and closed, 83
fonts, 433
setting, 433–434
sizing, 436–437
footage
adding to compositions, 140–141
displaying information about, 72–74
duplicate, 86
EPS options, 68
file-type extensions and, 73
frame rate, 57–58
importing, 29–33
interpretation of, 40–42, 69–70
looping, 59
managing, 71
missing, 22
motion, 56
opening in original application, 94–95
pixel aspect ratio, 65–67
proxies and placeholders for, 87–91
removing from projects, 85–86
setting edit points for, 143
sorting, 77
unused, 85
viewing, 92–93
Footage window, 11, 71, 96
magnification options in, 98–99
opening movie files in, 93
viewing footage items in, 92
foreground color, 482
Format options, 682, 683
Frame Advance button, 54
frame blending, 516–517, 679
frame differencing, 700
frame number, start-frame, 127
frame rate
for compositions, 126–127
for footage, 57–58
for nested compositions, 131, 152
for rendering compositions, 681
for still-image sequences, 39
frames
removing a range of, 192–193
setting the size of, 121–122
Free Transform Points command, 319, 320
freeze frame, 520, 524–525
Full Quality icon, 170

G

General Preferences dialog box, 560, 641
geometrics. *See* transform properties
global properties, 208
Go To Time dialog box, 97, 138–139
gradient layers, 412
Gradient Wipe effect, 411, 412–414
Graph Overlay icon, 661
graphs
  expression, 661
  property, 569–570
  speed and velocity, 549, 568, 579–581
  time, 172, 174–177
  value, 549, 567, 574–575, 577–578
grayscale images, 545
greenscreen, 397
grid
  customizing, 103
  showing, 100–101
  transparency, 111
Grid & Guides panel, Preferences dialog box, 101, 103, 107
grouped palettes, 17
grouped windows, 16–18
  organizing, 17–18
  setting preferences for, 16–17
Grow Bounds effect, 395–396
guide layers, 150, 679
guides
  customizing, 107
  locking and unlocking, 106
  removing, 106
  repositioning, 106
  setting, 105
  showing and hiding, 106
  See also rulers

H

Hand tool, 99
handles, 154, 210, 292
hanging punctuation, 456
hard drive specifications, 3
Hard Light mode, 534
Hard Mix mode, 536
hard return, 453
hardware
  minimum requirements, 2
  professional additions, 4
  suggested features, 3
heading panels, 77–78
headings, 78
hiding
  guides, 106
  heading panels, 77–78
  In/Out panel, 185
  layers, 161
  masks, 288, 325
  RAM preview options, 274
  rulers, 104
  shy layers, 167
  thumbnail images, 74
  See also displaying
histogram, 375
hold interpolation, 552
hold-out matte, 397
horizontal text
  paragraph text as, 420
  point text as, 419
  scale controls for, 441
  vertical text conversions, 424
Horizontal Type tool, 418, 419, 420, 422, 424
Hue mode, 537
Hue/Saturation effect, 394

I

I-beam icon, 208
icons
  keyframe, 234–235
  Project window, 72
  window type, 16
  See also names of specific icons
Illustrator
  flattening artwork from, 694
  importing files from, 45–49
  using masks from, 321
image aspect ratio, 67
Image Control effects, 394–396
Import File dialog box, 30–31, 37, 47, 49, 50–51
Import Multiple Files dialog box, 30–31
Import panel, Preferences dialog box, 32, 34, 39
Import Project dialog box, 51
importing
  After Effects projects, 50
  audio, 51, 56
  default drag options for, 32
  expanded feature for, 6
  files, 29–33, 40–44
  folders, 33
  motion footage, 56
  Photoshop or Illustrator files, 45–49
  Premiere Pro projects, 50–51
  preventing, 694
  rendered movies, 683
  still images, 34–39

In and Out points, 180
aligning with current time marker, 187
keyboard shortcuts for, 183
setting, 143, 182–183
In panel, Timeline window, 185–187
Increment and Save command, 21
indenting paragraphs, 455
indices, keyframe, 234–235
Info palette, 12
insert edits, 142
inserting layers, 143–144
Intel Indeo video codec, 702
intelligent caching, 245
interactions, 247, 254
interface features, 10–15
palettes, 12–15
primary windows, 10–11
secondary windows, 11–12
interlaced video, 52
interpolation. *See* keyframe interpolation
Interpret Footage command, 29, 69, 127
Interpret Footage dialog box, 41
Alpha section, 42
EPS Options, 68
Fields and Pull-Down section, 53, 54, 61
Frame Rate section, 57–58
Loop setting, 59
More Options button, 68
Pixel Aspect Ratio setting, 65–66
interpretation of footage, 69–70
alpha channel settings, 40–42
fields in video footage, 53, 54
keyboard shortcuts for setting, 70
pixel aspect ratios, 65–66
reapplying to footage items, 69
removing 3:2 or 24Pa pulldown, 61
setting interpretation rules, 70
Interpretation Rules file, 70
inverting masks, 332
IRE values, 416

J

JavaScript, 657, 660, 664, 665, 666–667
JPEG image quality, 693
jumping, child layer, 654–655
justifying paragraphs, 453, 454

K

kerning, 439–440
key color, 397
keyboard shortcuts
for 3D views, 595
for interpretation settings, 70
for mask paths, 297
for nudging layer properties, 224
for opening Composition Settings dialog box, 118, 129
for playback and preview, 273
for setting In and Out points, 183
for setting the work area, 265
for time graph views, 177
for viewing layer properties, 208
for windows and palettes, 18
keyframe assistants, 586
Keyframe icons, 576
keyframe interpolation, 235, 547–590
auto-orient rotation option, 563–564
changing type of, 589–590
converting path types, 565–566
keyframe assistants, 586
methods of, 550–552
motion paths and, 548, 549, 553–559, 573
property graphs and, 569–570, 582
roving keyframes and, 587–588
spatial, 548, 549, 553–562, 573
speed and velocity graphs and, 549, 568, 571–572, 579–581
temporal, 548, 549, 567–585
value graphs and, 549, 567, 574–575, 577–578
Keyframe Interpolation dialog box, 589–590
Keyframe Velocity dialog box, 585
keyframes, 205, 210, 231–241
adding to value graphs, 575
animated strokes and, 505–506
compression using, 700
contextual menu for, 372
copying and pasting, 239–240
cueing the current time to, 241
deleting, 237
deselecting, 236
easing speed changes in, 586
effect property, 371
explained, 232
icons and indices, 234–235
interpolating, 235, 547–590
moving, 238
roving, 587–588
selecting, 236
setting for properties, 231–233
Keying effects, 206, 397

L

Label panel, Preferences dialog box, 80–81
labels, 80–81, 160
layer controls, 209–210, 427

Layer In/Out Time dialog box, 186
layer markers, 199
  adding, 201
  comments with, 202
  moving, 203
  removing, 203
  Web links in, 694
layer modes, 528–540
  applying, 529
  explained, 528
  types of, 530–540
  See also blending modes
layer outline, 207, 287
layer properties
  animating, 231–237
  changing values for, 574
  nudging, 224
  types of, 206
  viewing, 207–208
layer switches, 165–166
Layer Switches panel, Timeline window, 165–166
Layer window, 11, 178–179
  anchor point in, 212
  annotated illustration, 178
  layers viewed in, 173
  masks viewed in, 286, 288
  moving masks in, 326, 328
  opening, 178
  parts description, 179
  selecting masks or points in, 306–307
  setting effect points in, 357
  time remap values in, 522
  trimming layers in, 181, 182
  viewing anchor-point path in, 554
layered files
  importing as compositions, 48–49
  importing as single footage items, 46–47
layers, 115, 153–203, 515–545
  adjustment, 149–150, 364–365
  anchor point of, 211–213
  audio track for, 162
  blending modes for, 528–540
  changing playback speed of, 197–198, 526–527
  color labels for, 160
  combining 2D and 3D, 629–630
  converting to adjustment layers, 365
  copying effects between, 362
  creating in compositions, 140
  duplicating, 194
  editing, 171
  frame blending, 516–517
  freeze frame of, 524–525
  inserting, 142–144
  invisible, 656
  label colors for, 81
  locking and unlocking, 164
  markers used with, 199–203
  motion blur for, 518–519
  moving in time, 184, 185–187
  naming and renaming, 158–159
  nested compositions as, 152
  numbers for, 160
  opacity of, 219
  overlaying, 142–144
  painting on, 485–487
  parenting, 652–655
  positioning, 214–215
  precomposing, 645–647
  preserving underlying transparency of, 541
  properties of, 206
  quality settings for, 170
  rasterizing, 168–169
  removing effects from, 347
  rendering order of, 629–630
  reversing playback of, 198, 525–526
  rotating, 218
  scaling, 216–217
  selecting, 154–155, 345
  sequencing and overlapping, 189–191
  showing and hiding images for, 161
  shy, 167
  slip edits of, 188
  solid, 145–148
  soloing, 163
  splitting, 195–196
  stacking order of, 156–157
  switches for, 165–166
  text, 458
  time remapping, 520–527
  track mattes for, 542–545
  trimming, 180, 181–183
  video for, 162–163
  viewing, 161, 172–173
  See also 3D layers
leading, 437–438
lenses, camera, 613
Levels effect, 375–378
  decreasing luminance range, 378
  increasing contrast levels, 376–377
  reading the histogram, 375
  redistributing values, 375
lift edit, 192
Light Settings dialog box, 616–620
Lighten mode, 532
lights, 616–620
  creating, 616–618
  Point of Interest and, 621–624

selecting settings for, 619–620
types of, 616–617
line breaks, 457
line spacing, 438
Linear Burn mode, 532
Linear Dodge mode, 532
linear interpolation, 550
converting to/from, 557–558
spatial interpolation and, 561
temporal interpolation and, 583
toggling between auto Bézier interpolation and, 577
Linear Light mode, 535
links, embedded, 682, 683
Live Update feature, 254
Local Axis mode, 597
Lock icon, 164, 324
Lock Source Time option, 508
locking and unlocking
guides, 106
layers, 164
masks, 324–325
looping footage, 59, 694
lossless compression schemes, 696
lossy compression schemes, 696
Luma Inverted Matte, 544
Luma Matte, 544
luminance, 378, 397, 416
Luminescent Premul mode, 540
Luminosity mode, 538

M

Mac OS platform
minimum system requirements for, 2
running After Effects on, 8
setting RAM preferences on, 282
managing footage, 71–113
channels for, 110
cueing motion footage, 97
displaying information for, 72–74
finding items in projects, 75–76
folders used for, 82–83
grid display for, 100–101, 103
heading panel display options, 77–78
labels used in, 80–81
magnification options, 98–99
movie files, 93
naming the Comment heading panel, 78–79
opening footage in original application, 94–95
Project window and, 72–74
proxies and placeholders for, 87–91
removing footage from projects, 85–86
renaming folders or compositions, 84
resizing or reordering headings, 78
rulers and guides for, 104–107
snapshots for, 108–109
sorting footage items, 77
thumbnail display options, 74
video-safe zones, 100–102
viewing footage, 92–93
Marker dialog box, 202
markers, 199–203
adding, 199–200, 201
comments added to, 202
moving, 200, 203
removing, 201, 203
Mask Expansion property, 329
Mask Feather dialog box, 329
mask paths
converting into motion paths, 565–566
motion paths compared to, 556
masks, 206, 210, 285–334
Bézier curves and, 292–293, 300–301
building paths for, 295–297
colors assigned to, 322–323
control points in, 292, 306–307, 309–312
converting, 304
creation methods for, 290
drawing simple shapes for, 294
enhanced features for, 5
expanding or contracting, 331
feathering the edges of, 329–330
hiding and showing, 288, 325
Illustrator or Photoshop, 321
inverting, 332
locking and unlocking, 324–325
modes for working with, 333–334
moving, 309–310, 326–328
opacity of, 329, 330
panning layers behind, 328
reshaping, 305
RotoBezier, 292, 293, 302–303, 316–317
scaling and rotating, 319–320
segments in, 292
selecting, 306–308
targeting, 289
viewing, 286–288
Material Options properties, 605–606
Matte Tools effects, 397
matted alpha, 44
mattes, 542
hold-out, 397
track, 539, 542–545
Median effect, 398
memory
frame size and, 121
purging snapshots from, 109

reducing requirements for, 275
See also RAM
Memory & Cache panel, Preferences dialog box, 282, 283
Microsoft video codecs, 702
Microsoft Windows. *See* Windows platform
missing footage, 22
mixed interpolation, 552
modes
axis, 596–597
blending, 528–540
mask, 333–334
paint, 483
selector, 477
Modes panel, Timeline window, 165–166
monitors, 3, 4, 275
monophonic audio, 268, 379, 383
Motion Blur switch, 386, 518–519, 680
motion footage
cueing, 97
importing, 56
playing, 97
viewing a frame of, 97
Motion JPEG video codecs, 701
motion paths, 553–559
auto-orienting rotation to, 563–564
converting mask paths into, 565–566
displaying information on, 553–554
mask paths compared to, 556
setting preferences for, 555
smoothing motions in, 587–588
spatial interpolation in, 548, 549, 557–559
tangents for controlling, 210
viewing speed in, 573
Motion Sketch palette, 14, 233
Motion Tracker, 233
Move Anchor Point icon, 319
Move Guide icon, 105, 106
movie files
compressing, 696–702
making from compositions, 672–674
opening in Footage window, 93
saving RAM previews as, 279–280
moving
keyframes, 238
layers in time, 184, 185–187
markers, 200, 203
masks, 309–310, 326–328
Multiply mode, 531

N

naming and renaming
brush tips, 494
Comment heading panel, 78–79
compositions, 84, 117
folders, 84
layers, 158–159
navigator view, 176
nested compositions, 118, 151–152, 631, 632–636
background of, 133
creating, 634–635
effect source and, 368–369
layer markers and, 203
rendering order and, 633, 639
setting nesting options, 131
new features, 5–6
New Placeholder dialog box, 88
Noise & Grain effects, 398
non-drop frame (NDF) timecode, 25, 26
non-linear editing (NLE) programs, 4
NTSC video standard, 4, 415
nudging layer properties, 224
null objects, 656
Numbers effect, 408
numerical functions
cueing time in compositions, 138–139
moving layers in time, 186
setting property values, 221
temporal interpolation, 585

O

object names, 694
offline files, 87
offline footage, 22
offline quality, 88
opacity
layer, 219
mask, 329, 330
paint, 482
Open dialog box, 23, 243, 689
Open Media Framework (OMF) files, 6
open paths, 291, 318
OpenGL graphics card, 3, 5, 245, 258–260
3D rendering and, 132
explained, 258
Fast Preview options, 255, 256
setting preferences for, 259
specifying options for, 260
opening
folders, 83
footage in original application, 94–95
Layer windows, 178

movie files in Footage window, 93
projects, 23
optimizing performance, 3, 275
Orbit Camera tool, 625
orienting 3D layers, 600, 601–602
Orthogonal views, 593
Out panel, Timeline window, 185–187
Out points. *See* In and Out points
output, 669–702
assigning multiple output modules, 677
choosing output-module settings, 682–685
compression options, 696–702
exporting to SWF format, 692–694
making movies from compositions, 672–674
managing items in the render queue, 675
pausing and stopping rendering, 676
Render Queue window, 670–671, 675
saving single composition frames, 690–691
specifying overflow volumes, 695
templates created for, 686–689
Output Module Settings dialog box, 682–685, 697, 699
Output Module Templates dialog box, 686–689
output modules
assigning multiple modules, 677
choosing settings for, 682–685
Output panel, Preferences dialog box, 695
overflow volumes, 695
overlapping layers, 189, 191
overlay edits, 142
Overlay mode, 534
overlaying layers, 143–144
overscan, 102

P

Paint effects, 5, 479–514
adjusting strokes, 499–501
animating strokes, 502–506
brush tip options, 482, 491–498
cloning, 507–514
eraser options, 488–490
multiple, 501
painting on layers, 485–487
palettes for controlling, 480
stroke options, 481–484
Paint palette, 14, 479
Brush Tips Selector, 491–492
Clone Stamp settings, 507–510
Duration pull-down menu, 502
opening and closing, 480
options available in, 481–484
PAL video standard, 415
palettes, 12–15
docking, 17
grouped, 17
repositioning, 15
tabbed, 16–18
See also names of specific palettes
Pan Behind tool, 188, 211, 213, 327, 328, 599
panning, 380–381, 383
Paragraph palette, 13, 419
opening and closing, 430
resetting paragraphs in, 432
setting values in, 431
paragraph text, 418, 419, 453–457
aligning, 453–454
creating, 420–422
formatting, 453–457
hanging punctuation option, 456
indenting, 455
justifying, 453, 454
line break options, 457
point text conversions, 423
spacing, 455
parallel light, 616, 617
parent layers, 652–655
Parenting feature, 152, 631, 652–655
pasteboard, 121, 135
pasting. *See* copying and pasting
path text, 451–452, 458
animating, 452
creating, 451
paths, 210
building, 295–297
control points and segments, 292
hiding and showing, 288
keyboard shortcuts for, 297
motion, 548, 549, 553–559
open vs. closed, 291, 318
tools for creating, 290
Pen tool, 290, 291, 295–297, 298, 311
RotoBezier option, 302–303
Selection tool toggled with, 559
performance
enhancing, 5
hiding thumbnails for, 74
managing RAM for, 281–283
optimizing, 3, 275
Perspective effects, 399
phase, 62, 382
Photoshop
editing text imported from, 428–429
exporting single frames to, 691
importing files from, 45–49
using masks from, 321

Pickwhip tool, 654, 655, 657, 658–659, 665
Pin Light mode, 535
pixel aspect ratios (PARs), 65–67
  correcting, 112–113
  explained, 67
  interpreting, 65–66
  setting, 123
pixels, cloning, 511–512
placeholders, 87, 88–89
  creating, 88
  replacing with source footage, 89
playback, 247
  changing the speed of, 197–198, 526–527
  cueing footage for, 97
  keyboard shortcuts for, 273
  previews and, 247–248
  reversing, 198, 525–526
plug-ins
  3D rendering, 132
  third-party, 4
Plug-Ins folder, 335
point light, 617
Point of Interest, 621–624
  Auto-Orient setting and, 622
  lights and cameras oriented to, 623–624
point text, 418–419
  creating, 419–420
  paragraph text conversions, 423
positioning and repositioning
  2D layers, 214–215
  3D layers, 598–599
  anchor points, 212–213
  guides, 106
  palettes, 15
  subpixels, 214–215
post-render actions, 683
Pre-compose dialog box, 646–647
precomposing, 639, 645–647
Preferences command, 8
Preferences dialog box
  Display panel, 74, 555
  General panel, 16–17, 560, 641
  Grid & Guides panel, 101, 103, 107
  Import panel, 32, 34, 39, 40
  Label panel, 80–81
  Memory & Cache panel, 282, 283
  Output panel, 695
  Previews panel, 257, 259, 260, 267–268
  Video Preview panel, 249–250
Premiere Pro, importing projects from, 50–51
premultiplied alpha, 43, 44
prerendering process, 651, 683
Preserve Underlying Transparency option, 541
presets
  animation, 242–244, 461–462
  clone stamp, 514
  composition, 119–120, 122
  effect, 358–361
  text animation, 461–462
preshaped alpha, 44
previews, 245, 247, 263–280
  3D layer, 628
  audio, 263, 266–268
  fast, 255–256
  keyboard shortcuts for, 273
  playback and, 247–248
  RAM, 247, 273–280
  video, 249–250, 263
  wireframe, 263, 271–272
Previews panel, Preferences dialog box, 257, 259, 260, 267–268
processor speed, 3
Production Bundle, 7
Professional version of After Effects, 7
program link, 51
progressive scan, 52
project files, 19
Project Settings dialog box, 24, 27
Project window, 10, 20
  Bit Depth button, 28
  Comment heading panel, 78–79
  creating a folder in, 82
  Custom heading panel, 79
  displaying information in, 72–74
  dragging footage into compositions in, 140, 141
  finding items in, 75–76
  heading panel display options, 77–78
  imported files in, 31, 33, 48, 49
  nested compositions in, 152
  proxies in, 90–91
  renaming folders or compositions in, 84
  resizing or reordering headings in, 78
  sorting footage in, 77
  still-image sequences in, 38
  thumbnail display options, 74
  viewing footage in, 92–93
projects
  bit depth settings, 27–28
  closing, 22
  collapsing transformations in, 648–649
  complex, 631
  creating, 20
  expressions in, 657–667
  finding items in, 75–76
  Flowchart view of, 642–644

importing, 50–51
nested compositions in, 632–636
null objects in, 656
opening, 23
parenting layers in, 652–655
precomposing layers in, 645–647
prerendering, 651
recursive switches in, 650
removing footage from, 85–86
rendering order in, 636–639
saving, 21
synchronizing time in, 640–641
time display options, 24–26
properties, 205–244
anchor point, 211–213
animated, 208, 209, 231–237
audio, 206, 225–230
effect, 351, 354
global, 208
interpolation, 567–570, 574–575
keyboard shortcuts for, 224
keyframes and, 231–241
mask, 329–331
Material Options, 605–606
opacity, 219
optional controls for, 223
position, 214–215
rotation, 218
scale, 216–217
setting values for, 220–222
spatial controls, 209–210
text, 458
transform, 211–219
types of, 206
viewing, 207–208
property graphs, 569–570
resizing, 570, 582
viewing, 569
property track, 207
proxies, 88, 90–91
assigning to footage items, 90
render settings and, 679
stopping use of, 91
toggling between original footage and, 91
pulldown process, 60–64, 680
3:2 pulldown, 60, 61, 62, 127
24Pa pulldown, 60, 61, 63–64
purging
RAM cache, 281
snapshots, 109, 281

Q

quality settings, 170, 678
Quality switch, 170
QuickPro series, 2
QuickTime, 3
compression settings, 697–698
Footage window, 93
video codecs, 701
quotation marks, 447

R

Radial Shadow effect, 401
RAM
cached data in, 246, 281–283
calculating requirements for, 29
managing, 281–283
minimum requirements for, 2
optimizing, 275
purging data from, 281
setting preferences for, 282
suggested addition of, 3
See also memory
RAM previews, 245, 247, 273–280
creating, 277–278
playback and, 247–248
saving, 279–280
setting options for, 276
showing/hiding options for, 274
range selectors, 464, 472, 473–477
modes for, 477
options for, 475–476
specifying a range, 473–474
Range Start/End icons, 466, 474
rasterization, 68, 168–169, 648
Rectangular Mask tool, 290, 294
recursive switches, 650
refreshing windows, 261
region of interest, 245, 251
Remember Interpretation command, 69
removing
3:2 or 24Pa pulldown, 61
effects, 347
footage from projects, 85–86
guides, 106
markers, 201, 203
preset brush tips, 494
range of frames, 192–193
See also deleting
renaming. *See* naming and renaming
Render effects, 401
Render Queue window, 12, 131, 280, 670–671, 675
Render Settings dialog box, 678–681, 686

Render Settings Templates dialog box, 686–689
Render View window, 12
rendering
 3D layers, 132, 629–630
 assigning settings for, 670–671, 678–681
 information on status of, 671
 managing items in the render queue, 675
 monitoring progress of, 670
 pausing and stopping, 676
 templates created for, 686–689
rendering order, 636–639
 2D and 3D layers, 629–630
 nested compositions and, 633
 subverting, 638–639
rendering plug-in, 132
reordering
 effects, 363
 headings, 78
 layers, 157
Replace Footage dialog box, 89
repositioning. *See* positioning and repositioning
resampling, 214–215, 269
reshaping masks, 305
resizing. *See* sizing and resizing
resolution
 adaptive, 245, 255, 257
 frame size vs., 124
 imported files and, 29
 nested compositions and, 131, 152
 rasterization and, 169
 render settings and, 678
 setting for compositions, 125
reversing
 field order, 54
 layer playback, 198, 525–526
RGB channels, 43–44
RGB color space, 377
ripple delete, 192
ripple insert, 144
rotating
 2D layers, 218
 3D layers, 600, 602–603
 masks, 319–320
Rotation icon, 320
Rotation tool, 218, 601–603
rotational values, 218
RotoBezier masks, 292, 293
 adjusting tension of, 316–317
 creating, 302–303
roving keyframes, 587–588
rulers
 setting/resetting zero point of, 104–105
 showing or hiding, 104
 See also guides

S

safe zones, 100–102
 explained, 102
 setting default areas, 101
 showing, 100–101
sample rate, 269, 694
sampling, 507
Saturation mode, 537
Save As dialog box, 672, 688–689, 690
Save Project As dialog box, 21
saving
 animation presets, 242
 clone stamp settings, 514
 composition presets, 119–120
 expressions, 660
 files with alpha channels, 43–44
 preset effects, 358–359
 projects, 21
 RAM previews, 279–280
 single composition frames, 690
 templates, 688–689
Scale icon, 320
scaling
 layers, 216–217
 masks, 319–320
 text, 441
scan lines, 52
Scissors icon, 203
Screen mode, 532–533
scrubbable hot text, 220, 222
scrubbing audio, 262
searching. *See* finding items
segments, 292
selecting
 brush tips, 491–492
 effects, 346
 keyframes, 236
 layers, 154–155, 345
 masks, 306–308
 strokes, 500–501
Selection tool, 261, 306, 315
 Hand tool toggled with, 99
 Pen tool toggled with, 559
 text selection with, 426
selector modes, 477
selectors, 463, 464, 472–478
 expression, 472, 478
 range, 464, 472, 473–477
 wiggly, 472, 478
Sequence Layers dialog box, 190, 191
sequencing layers, 189–191
serifs, 434
Set In/Out buttons, 143

Set Proxy File dialog box, 90, 91
shadow options, 620
shapes
  Bézier curves, 292–293, 300–301
  closed and open, 291
  drawing for masks, 294
  keyframing, 505–506
  modifying, 305
  text animation, 475–476
  tools for creating, 290
Sharpen effects, 384
Shift-RAM preview, 273
Shockwave Flash format. *See* SWF format
shortcuts. *See* keyboard shortcuts
Show Last Snapshot button, 108, 109
showing. *See* displaying; viewing
shutter angle
  compositions, 130
  motion blur for previews, 519
shy layers, 167
silhouette modes, 539
Simulation effects, 405
Single-line Composer, 457
sizing and resizing
  Audio palette, 228
  audio waveform property track, 227
  fonts, 436–437
  frames, 121–122
  headings, 78
  property graphs, 570, 582
  text bounding box, 422–423
slide edits, 188
Slip Edit tool, 188
slip edits, 144, 188
Small Caps option, 444, 445
Smart Mask Interpolation palette, 14, 15
smart quotes, 447
smooth points, 293, 298, 299
  converting, 313–314
Smoother palette, 14, 15
SMPTE timecode, 26
Snap to Edges feature, 238
Snapshot button, 108
snapshots, 108–109, 281
Soft Light mode, 534
soft return, 453
Solid Footage Settings dialog box, 145–148
solid layers, 145–148
  changing settings for, 147–148
  creating, 145–146
soloing layers, 163, 679
Sorenson Video codec, 701
sorting footage items, 77
source files, 19
source footage
  replacing a placeholder with, 89
  setting edit points for, 143
source layers, 367–368, 385
source text, 458
  animating, 459–460
spacing paragraphs, 455
spatial controls, 209–210
spatial interpolation, 548, 553–562
  auto-orient rotation option, 563–564
  conversions in, 557–559
  default, 560
  mastering, 561–562
  methods of, 550–552
  motion paths and, 548, 549, 553–559
  speed and, 573
  See also temporal interpolation
Speaker icon, 162, 163
speed, 571–572
  animated stroke, 504
  automatically easing, 586
  changing for layer playback, 197–198, 526–527
  numerically adjusting, 585
  viewing in motion paths, 573
speed and velocity graphs, 549, 568, 571–572
  adjusting temporal interpolation in, 579–581
  ease handles in, 568, 579, 580–581
split-field frames, 62
splitting layers, 195–196
spot light, 617
stacking order, 156–157
  3D layers and, 629–630
  changing, 157
  split layers and, 196
standard pulldown, 63
Standard version of After Effects, 7
start-frame number, 127, 683
stencil modes, 538–539
Stereo Mixer effect, 230, 380–383
stereophonic audio, 268, 379, 383
still images
  importing sequences of, 37–39
  preparing for import, 35–36
  saving single frames as, 690–691
  setting default duration of, 34
still-image sequences, 37–39
  importing, 37–38
  setting default frame rate for, 39
Stopwatch icon, 208, 209, 232, 466, 505
storage overflow, 681, 695
straight alpha, 43
Stretch option, 197–198, 684

stroke options
  animated strokes, 502–506
  paint effects, 481–484, 499–506
  text effects, 434–436
styles
  guideline, 107
  project display, 24
  text, 433–434
Stylize effects, 405
subpixel positioning, 214–215
subscript text, 446
superscript text, 446
suppressing window updates, 261
SWF format, 692
  exporting compositions to, 693–694
  specifying options for, 694
SWF Settings dialog box, 693
switches
  layer, 165–166
  recursive, 650
Switches Affect Nested Comps option, 650
Switches panel, Timeline window, 165–166
syllabary, 448
synchronizing time, 640–641
syntax, expression, 666–667
system specifications
  minimum requirements, 2
  professional additions, 4
  suggested features, 3

T

T switch, 541
tabbed palettes, 17
tabbed windows, 16–18
  closing, 18
  organizing, 17–18
  setting preferences, 16–17
target layers, 367–368, 385
target masks, 289
tate-chuu-yoko, 449
telephoto lens, 613
templates, 686–689
  creating, 686–687
  default, 687–688
  loading, 689
  saving as files, 688–689
temporal interpolation, 548, 567–585
  acceleration and, 572
  adjusting, 577–578, 580, 585
  mastering, 583–584
  methods of, 550–552
  numerical adjustments of, 585
  property graphs and, 569–570, 582
  recognizing, 576, 577
  speed and velocity graphs and, 549, 568, 571–572, 579–581
  value graphs and, 549, 567, 574–575, 577–578
  See also spatial interpolation
text, 417–478
  animating, 5, 417, 452, 458–478
  baseline shift, 442
  blending characters, 450
  capital letter options, 444–445
  CJK fonts and, 448–449
  converting types of, 423–424
  creating, 418–425
  editing, 426–429
  faux bold/italic, 443
  fill and stroke, 434–436
  fonts, 433–434
  formatting, 433–447, 453–457
  horizontal, 419, 420, 424
  kerning and tracking, 439–440
  leading, 437–438
  line spacing, 438
  palettes for controlling, 430–432
  paragraph, 418, 419, 420–422, 423, 453–457
  path, 451–452
  point, 418, 419–420, 423
  scale controls, 441
  size of, 436–437
  smart quotes in, 447
  styles of, 433–434
  superscript/subscript, 446
  vertical, 419, 420, 424, 425
text animation presets, 461–462
text box, 418
  reflowing text in, 418, 421
  resizing, 419, 422–423
Text effects, 408
Texture Memory option, 260
Texturize effect, 406–407
third-party plug-ins, 4
three-dimensional layers. *See* 3D layers
three-point editing, 180
thumbnails, showing/hiding, 74
time
  cueing to keyframes, 241
  moving layers in, 184, 185–187
  numerically cueing in compositions, 138–139
  setting in the Timeline window, 138
  synchronizing, 640–641
  See also temporal interpolation
Time Controls palette, 12, 13, 97, 252–253
  annotated illustrations, 137, 252
  controls in, 139, 252
  displaying, 137

Frame Advance button, 54
RAM preview options, 274, 276
time display, 24–26
counting methods, 25, 26
display style options, 24
Feet and Frames display options, 25–26
Timecode Base display options, 25
Time effects, 408
time graph, 172, 174–177
annotated illustration, 174
keyboard shortcut, 177
parts description, 175
view options, 176–177
time marker, 136
time remapping, 520–527
controlling values for, 522
enabling, 523
explained, 520–521
freeze frame with, 524–525
playback speed changes with, 526
reverse playback with, 525–526
Time Span setting, 680
Time Stretch dialog box, 198
timecode, 26
Timeline window, 10, 16, 136
annotated illustration, 136
creating RAM previews in, 277–278
dragging footage into compositions in, 140, 141
In and Out panels of, 185–187
layer selection in, 154–155
mask selection in, 308
nested compositions in, 152
numerically cueing the time in, 138–139
paint stroke adjustments in, 500
setting the current time in, 138
stacking order of layers in, 157
time graph area of, 172, 174–177
trimming layers in, 181
viewing effects in, 344
Title-Action Safe button, 100
title-safe zones, 102
Toggle Palettes button, 430
Toggle Transparency Grid button, 111
tools, 12, 15
Camera, 625–626
mask path creation, 290
Professional version, 7
See also names of specific tools
Tools palette, 12, 15, 290, 480
top-to-top leading, 437, 438
tracing objects, 299
track mattes, 539, 542–545
creating, 544–545
types of, 542–544
Track XY Camera tool, 626
Track Z Camera tool, 626
Tracker Controls palette, 14–15
tracking, text, 439–440
Transfer Modes panel, Timeline window, 165–166
Transform effect, 390, 638
transform properties, 206, 211–219
anchor point, 211–213
opacity, 219
position, 214–215
rotation, 218
scale, 216–217
transformations, collapsing, 648–649
Transition effects, 206, 411–414
translating expressions, 665
transparency
blending modes for, 530
painted layer, 487
preserving underlying, 541
track mattes for defining, 542–545
viewing, 111
transparency grid, 111, 133, 179
Trash button, 85
traveling mattes, 539
trimming layers, 180, 181–183
tsume, 448
tweening, 232
type. *See* text
Type tool, 408
typefaces, 433

U

Unicode, 471
unlocking. *See* locking and unlocking
unmatted alpha, 44
unmultiplied RGB image, 43
Unsharp Mask effect, 384, 398
unused footage, 85
user interface, 6
User Interface Colors panel, 323

V

Value dialog box, 354
value graphs, 567
adding keyframes to, 575
adjusting temporal interpolation in, 577–578
changing property values in, 574–575

Value slider, 354
vector images, 169
Vector Paint effect, 5
vectorscope, 416
velocity, 571–572
numerically adjusting, 585
See also speed and velocity graphs
vertical text
changing alignment of, 425
horizontal text conversions, 424
paragraph text as, 420
point text as, 419
scale controls for, 441
Vertical Type tool, 418, 419, 420, 422, 424
video
color space adjustments, 377
compressing, 696–702
film transferred to, 60–64, 127
hiding/showing for layers, 162–163
instruments for evaluating, 416
interlaced, 52
interpreting fields in, 53, 54
previewing, 263
progressive scan, 52
QuickTime codecs for, 701
setting preferences for, 249–250
Video for Windows codecs for, 702
video capture/playback device, 4
Video Compression dialog box, 699–700
Video effects, 414–415
Video for Windows
compression settings, 699–700
Footage window, 93
video codecs, 702
video monitor, 4
Video Preview panel, Preferences dialog box, 249–250
video-safe zones, 100–102
View Axis mode, 597
View Options dialog box, 209–210, 553
viewing
3D layers, 593–595
audio waveforms, 226
channels, 110
effects, 344
expressions, 661
footage items, 92–93
frames of motion footage, 97
layers, 161, 172–173
masks, 286–288, 325
properties, 207–208
snapshots, 109
tabbed windows, 16
time graph, 176–177
video-safe zones, 100–101
See also displaying
Vivid Light mode, 535

W

Warning dialog box, 120
waveform monitor, 416
Web links, 199, 694
whole frames, 62
wide-angle lens, 613
Wiggler palette, 14, 15
wiggly selectors, 472, 478
windows
grouped, 16–18
icons indicating, 16
primary and secondary, 10–12
refreshing, 261
setting preferences for, 16–17
shortcuts for working with, 18
suppressing updates of, 261
tabbed, 16–18
See also names of specific windows
Windows platform
minimum system requirements for, 2
running After Effects on, 8
setting RAM preferences on, 282
Wireframe Interactions feature, 254
wireframe previews, 245, 255, 263, 271–272
word wrap, 418
work area, 245, 264–265
work area bar, 192, 264
work flow overview, 9
World Axis mode, 597
Write On option, 502–503, 504
writing expressions, 664–667

Z

zero point of rulers, 104–105